SIXTH EDITION

Corporate Finance

SIXTH EDITION

Corporate Finance

STEPHEN A. ROSS
Yale University

RANDOLPH W. WESTERFIELD
University of Southern California

JEFFREY JAFFE
Wharton School of Business
University of Pennsylvania

Boston   Burr Ridge, IL   Dubuque, IA   Madison, WI   New York   San Francisco   St. Louis
Bangkok   Bogotá   Caracas   Kuala Lumpur   Lisbon   London   Madrid   Mexico City
Milan   Montreal   New Delhi   Santiago   Seoul   Singapore   Sydney   Taipei   Toronto

To our family and friends with love and gratitude.

McGraw-Hill Higher Education
A Division of The **McGraw-Hill** *Companies*

CORPORATE FINANCE
Published by McGraw-Hill, an imprint of The McGraw-Hill Companies, Inc. 1221 Avenue of the Americas, New York, NY, 10020. Copyright © 2002, 1999, 1996, 1993, 1990, 1988 by The McGraw-Hill Companies, Inc. All rights reserved. No part of this publication may be reproduced or distributed in any form or by any means, or stored in a data base or retrieval system, without the prior written consent of The McGraw-Hill Companies, Inc., including, but not limited to, in any network or other electronic storage or transmission, or broadcast for distance learning.
Some ancillaries, including electronic and print components, may not be available to customers outside the United States.

This book is printed on acid-free paper.

domestic   2 3 4 5 6 7 8 9 0 DOW/DOW 0 9 8 7 6 5 4 3 2
international   2 3 4 5 6 7 8 9 0 DOW/DOW 0 9 8 7 6 5 4 3 2

ISBN   0-07-283137-5

Publisher: *John E Biernat*
Sponsoring editor: *Michele Janicek*
Developmental editor: *Erin Riley*
Executive marketing manager: *Rhonda Seelinger*
Senior project manager: *Jean Lou Hess*
Senior production supervisor: *Lori Koetters*
Media producer: *Melissa Kansa*
Senior designer: *Pam Verros*
Supplement producer: *Betty Hadala*
Cover photograph: *©David Muir/Masterfile*
Interior photograph: *©BeauRegard/Masterfile*
Typeface: *10/12 Times Roman*
Compositor: *Carlisle Communications, Ltd.*
Printer: *RR Donnelley*

Library of Congress Cataloging-in-Publication Data
Ross, Stephen A.
    Corporate finance / Stephen A. Ross, Randolph W. Westerfield, Jeffrey Jaffe.—6th ed.
        p. cm.—(The McGraw-Hill/Irwin series in finance, insurance, and real estate)
    Includes bibliographical references and index.
    ISBN 0-07-283137-5
    1. Corporations—Finance. I. Westerfield, Randolph. II. Jaffe, Jeffrey F., 1946– . III.
Title. IV. Series.
HG4026.R675 2001
658.15—dc21   2001030484

INTERNATIONAL EDITION ISBN 0-07-112420-9
Copyright © 2002. Exclusive rights by The McGraw-Hill Companies, Inc. for manufacture and export
This book cannot be re-exported from the country to which it is sold by McGraw-Hill.
The International Edition is not available in North America.

http://www.mhhe.com

About the Authors

Stephen A. Ross, *Sloan School of Management, Massachusetts Institute of Technology*
Stephen Ross is presently the Franco Modigliani Professor of Financial Economics at the Sloan School of Management, Massachusetts Institute of Technology. One of the most widely published authors in finance and economics, Professor Ross is recognized for his work in developing the Arbitrage Pricing Theory, as well as for having made substantial contributions to the discipline through his research in signaling, agency theory, option pricing, and the theory of the term structure of interest rates, among other topics. A past president of the American Finance Association, he currently serves as an associate editor of several academic and practitioner journals. He is a trustee of CalTech, and a director of the College Retirement Equity Fund (CREF), Freddie Mac, and Algorithmics, Inc. He is also the cochairman of Roll and Ross Asset Management Corporation.

Randolph W. Westerfield, *Marshall School of Business, University of Southern California*
Randolph W. Westerfield is Dean of the University of Southern California's Marshall School of Business and holder of the Robert R. Dockson Dean's Chair of Business Administration.

From 1988 to 1993, Professor Westerfield served as the chairman of the School's finance and business economics department and the Charles B. Thornton Professor of Finance. He came to USC from the Wharton School, University of Pennsylvania, where he was the chairman of the finance department and member of the finance faculty for 20 years. He is a member of the board of directors of the AACSB—the international association for management education, as well as Health Management Associates (HMA), and William Lyon Homes (WLH). His areas of expertise include corporate financial policy, investment management and analysis, mergers and acquisitions, and stock market price behavior.

Professor Westerfield has been consultant to a number of corporations, including AT&T, Mobil Oil, and Pacific Enterprises, as well as to the United Nations, the U.S. Departments of Justice and Labor, and the State of California.

Jeffrey F. Jaffe, *Wharton School of Business, University of Pennsylvania*   Jeffrey F. Jaffe has been a frequent contributor to finance and economic literature in such journals as the *Quarterly Economic Journal, The Journal of Finance, The Journal of Financial and Quantitative Analysis, The Journal of Financial Economics,* and *The Financial Analysts Journal.* His best known work concerns insider trading, where he showed both that corporate insiders earn abnormal profits from their trades and that regulation has little effect on these profits. He has also made contributions concerning initial public offerings, regulation of utilities, the behavior of marketmakers, the fluctuation of gold prices, the theoretical effect of inflation on the interest rate, the empirical effect of inflation on capital asset prices, the relationship between small capitalization stocks and the January effect, and the capital structure decision.

Preface

The teaching and the practicing of corporate finance are more challenging and exciting than ever before. The last decade has seen fundamental changes in financial markets and financial instruments. In the early years of the 21st century, we still see announcements in the financial press about such matters as takeovers, junk bonds, financial restructuring, initial public offerings, bankruptcy, and derivatives. In addition, there is the new recognition of "real" options (Chapters 21 and 22), private equity and venture capital (Chapter 19), and the disappearing dividend (Chapter 18). The world's financial markets are more integrated than ever before. Both the theory and practice of corporate finance have been moving ahead with uncommon speed, and our teaching must keep pace.

These developments place new burdens on the teaching of corporate finance. On one hand, the changing world of finance makes it more difficult to keep materials up to date. On the other hand, the teacher must distinguish the permanent from the temporary and avoid the temptation to follow fads. Our solution to this problem is to emphasize the modern fundamentals of the theory of finance and make the theory come to life with contemporary examples. Increasingly, many of these examples are outside the United States. All too often, the beginning student views corporate finance as a collection of unrelated topics that are unified largely because they are bound together between the covers of one book. As in the previous editions, our aim is to present corporate finance as the working of a small number of integrated and powerful institutions.

THE INTENDED AUDIENCE OF THIS BOOK

This book has been written for the introductory courses in corporate finance at the MBA level, and for the intermediate courses in many undergraduate programs. Some instructors will find our text appropriate for the introductory course at the undergraduate level as well.

We assume that most students either will have taken, or will be concurrently enrolled in, courses in accounting, statistics, and economics. This exposure will help students understand some of the more difficult material. However, the book is self-contained, and a prior knowledge of these areas is not essential. The only mathematics prerequisite is basic algebra.

NEW TO THE SIXTH EDITION

Following are the key revisions and updates to this edition:

- A complete update of all cost of capital discussions to emphasize its usefulness in capital budgeting, primarily in Chapters 12 and 17.

- A new appendix on performance evaluation and EVA in Chapter 12.
- A new section on liquidity and the cost of capital in Chapter 12.
- New evidence on efficient markets and CAPM in Chapter 13.
- New treatment on why firms choose different capital structures and dividend policies: the case of Qualcomm in Chapters 16 and 18.
- A redesign and rewrite of options and derivatives chapters into a new Part VI.
- Extension of options theory to mergers and acquisitions in Chapter 22.
- An expanded discussion of real options and their importance to capital budgeting in Chapter 23.
- New material on carveouts, spinoffs, and tracking stocks in Chapter 30.
- Many new end-of-chapter problems throughout all chapters.

ATTENTION TO PEDAGOGY

Executive Summary

Each chapter begins with a "roadmap" that describes the objectives of the chapter and how it connects with concepts already learned in previous chapters. Real company examples that will be discussed are highlighted in this section.

Case Study

There are 10 case studies that are highlighted in the Sixth Edition that present situations with real companies and how they rationalized the decisions they made to solve various problems. They provide extended examples of the material covered in the chapter. The cases are highlighted in the detailed Table of Contents.

In Their Own Words Boxes

Located throughout the Sixth Edition, this unique series consists of articles written by distinguished scholars or practitioners on key topics in the text.

Concept Questions

Included after each major section in a chapter, Concept Questions point to essential material and allow students to test their recall and comprehension before moving forward.

Key Terms

Students will note that important words are highlighted in boldface type the first time they appear. They are also listed at the end of the chapter, along with the page number on which they first appear, as well as in the glossary at the end of the book.

Demonstration Problems

We have provided worked-out examples throughout the text to give students a clear understanding of the logic and structure of the solution process. These examples are clearly called out in the text.

Highlighted Concepts

Throughout the text, important ideas are pulled out and presented in a copper box—signaling to students that this material is particularly relevant and critical for their understanding.

Numbered Equations

Key equations are numbered and listed on the back end sheets for easy reference.

The end of-chapter material reflects and builds on the concepts learned from the chapter and study features:

Summary and Conclusions

The numbered summary provides a quick review of key concepts in the chapter.

List of Key Terms

A list of the boldfaced key terms with page numbers is included for easy reference.

Suggested Readings

Each chapter is followed by a short, annotated list of books and articles to which interested students can refer for additional information.

Questions and Problems

Because solving problems is so critical to a student's learning, they have been revised, thoroughly reviewed, and accuracy-checked. The problem sets are graded for difficulty, moving from easier problems intended to build confidence and skill to more difficult problems designed to challenge the enthusiastic student. Problems have been grouped according to the concepts they test on. Additionally, we have tried to make the problems in the critical "concept" chapters, such as those on value, risk, and capital structure, especially challenging and interesting. We provide answers to selected problems in Appendix B at the end of the book.

Minicase

This end-of-chapter feature, located in Chapters 12 and 30, parallels the Case Study feature found in various chapters. These Minicases apply what is learned in a number of chapters to a real-world type of scenario. After presenting the facts, the student is given guidance in rationalizing a sound business decision.

SUPPLEMENTS PACKAGE

As with the text, developing supplements of extraordinary quality and utility was the primary objective. Each component in the supplement package underwent extensive review and revision.

FOR THE INSTRUCTOR

Instructor's Manual (0-07-233882-2)

Prepared by John Stansfield, University of Missouri, Columbia, this instructor's tool has been thoroughly revised and updated. Each chapter includes a list of transparencies/ PowerPoint slides, a brief chapter outline, an introduction, and an annotated outline. The annotated outline contains references to the transparencies/PowerPoint slides, additional explanations and examples, and teaching tips.

PowerPoint Presentation System (0-07-233883-0)

This presentation system was developed in conjunction with the Instructor's Manual by the same author, allowing for a complete and integrated teaching package. These slides contain useful outlines, summaries, and exhibits from the text. If you have PowerPoint installed on your PC, you have the ability to edit, print, or rearrange the complete transparency presentation to meet your specific needs.

Test Bank (0-07-233885-7)

The Test Bank, prepared by David Burnie, Western Michigan University, includes an average of 35 multiple-choice questions and problems per chapter, and 5 essay questions per chapter. Each question is labeled with the level of difficulty. About 30–40 percent of these problems are new or revised.

Computerized Testing Software (0-07-233881-4)

This software includes an easy-to-use menu system which allows quick access to all the powerful features available. The Keyword Search option lets you browse through the question bank for problems containing a specific word or phrase. Password protection is available for saved tests or for the entire database. Questions can be added, modified, or deleted. Available in Windows version.

Solutions Manual (0-07-233884-9)

The Solutions Manual, prepared by John A. Helmuth, University of Michigan, contains worked-out solutions for all of the problems, and has been thoroughly reviewed for accuracy. The Solutions Manual is also available to be purchased for your students.

Instructor CD-ROM (0-07-246238-8)

You can receive all of the supplements in an electronic format! The Instructor's Manual, PowerPoint, Test Bank, and Solutions Manual are all together on one convenient CD. The interface provides the instructor with a self-contained program that allows him or her to arrange the visual resources into his or her own presentation and add additional files as well.

Videos (0-07-250741-1)

These finance videos are 10-minute case studies on topics such as Financial Markets, Careers, Rightsizing, Capital Budgeting, EVA (Economic Value Added), Mergers and Acquisitions, and International Finance. Questions to accompany these videos can be found on the book's Online Learning Center.

FOR THE STUDENTS

Standard & Poor's Educational Version of Market Insight. If you purchased a new book, you will have received a *free* passcode card that will give you access to the same company and industry data that industry experts use. See *www.mhhe.com/edumarketinsight* for details on this exclusive partnership!

PowerWeb

If you purchased a new book, free access to PowerWeb—a dynamic supplement specific to your corporate finance course—is also available. Included are three levels of resource materials: articles from journals and magazines from the past year, weekly updates on current issues, and links to current news of the day. Also available is a series of study aids, such as quizzes, web links, and interactive exercises. See *www.dushkin.com/powerweb* for more details and access to this valuable resource.

Student Problem Manual (0-07-233880-6)

Written by Robert Hanson, Eastern Michigan University, the Student Problem Manual is a direct companion to the text. It is uniquely designed to involve the student in the learning process. Each chapter contains a Mission Statement, an average of 20 fill-in-the-blank Concept Test questions and answers, and an average of 15 problems and worked-out solutions. This product can be purchased separately or packaged with the text.

Online Learning Center

Visit the full web resource now available with the Sixth Edition at *www.mhhe.com/rwj*. The Information Center includes information on this new edition, and links for special offers.

The Instructor Center includes all of the teaching resources for the book, and the Student Center includes free online study materials—such as quizzes, study outlines, and spreadsheets—developed specifically for this edition. A feedback form is also available for your questions and comments.

ACKNOWLEDGMENTS

The plan for developing this edition began with a number of our colleagues who had an interest in the book and regularly teach the MBA introductory course. We integrated their comments and recommendations throughout the Sixth Edition. Contributors to this edition include:

R. Aggarwal, *John Carroll University*

Christopher Anderson, *University of Missouri–Columbia*

James J. Angel, *Georgetown University*

Kevin Bahr, *University of Wisconsin–Milwaukee*

Michael Barry, *Boston College*

William O. Brown, *Claremont McKenna College*

Bill Callahan, *Southern Methodist University*

Steven Carvell, *Cornell University*

Indudeep S. Chhachhi, *Western Kentucky University*

Jeffrey L. Coles, *Arizona State University*

Raymond Cox, *Central Michigan University*

John Crockett, *George Mason University*

Robert Duvic, *The University of Texas at Austin*

Steven Ferraro, *Pepperdine University*

Adlai Fisher, *New York University*

Yee-Tien Fu, *Stanford University*

Bruno Gerard, *University of Southern California*

Frank Ghannadian, *Mercer University–Atlanta*

John A. Helmuth, *University of Michigan–Dearborn*

Edith Hotchkiss, *Boston College*

Charles Hu, *Claremont McKenna College*

Raymond Jackson, *University of Massachusetts–Dartmouth*

Narayanan Jayaraman, *Georgia Institute of Technology*

Dolly King, *University of Wisconsin–Milwaukee*

Ronald Kudla, *The University of Akron*

Dilip Kumar Patro, *Rutgers University*

Youngsik Kwak, *Delaware State University*

Youngho Lee, *Howard University*

Yulong Ma, *Cal State—Long Beach*

Richard Miller, *Wesleyan University*

Naval Modani, *University of Central Florida*

Robert Nachtmann, *University of Pittsburgh*

Edward Nelling, *Georgia Tech*

Gregory Niehaus, *University of South Carolina*

Ingmar Nyman, *Hunter College*

Venky Panchapagesan, *Washington University–St. Louis*

Bulent Parker, *University of Wisconsin–Madison*

Christo Pirinsky, *Ohio State University*

Jeffrey Pontiff, *University of Washington*

N. Prabhala, *Yale University*

Mao Qiu, *University of Utah–Salt Lake City*

Latha Ramchand, *University of Houston*

Gabriel Ramirez, *Virginia Commonwealth University*

Stuart Rosenstein, *University of Colorado at Denver*

Bruce Rubin, *Old Dominion University*

Jaime Sabal, *New York University*

Andy Saporoschenko, *University of Akron*

William Sartoris, *Indiana University*

Faruk Selcuk, *University of Bridgeport*

Sudhir Singh, *Frostburg State University*

John S. Strong, *College of William and Mary*

Michael Sullivan, *University of Nevada–Las Vegas*

Andrew C. Thompson, *Virginia Polytechnic Institute*

Karin Thorburn, *Dartmouth College*

Satish Thosar, *University of Massachusetts–Dorchester*

Oscar Varela, *University of New Orleans*

Steven Venti, *Dartmouth College*

Susan White, *University of Texas–Austin*

Over the years, many others have contributed their time and expertise to the development and writing of this text. We extend our thanks once again for their assistance and countless insights:

James J. Angel, *Georgetown University*

Nasser Arshadi, *University of Missouri–St. Louis*

Robert Balik, *Western Michigan University*

John W. Ballantine, *Babson College*

Thomas Bankston, *Angelo State University*

Swati Bhatt, *Rutgers University*

Roger Bolton, *Williams College*

Gordon Bonner, *University of Delaware*

Brad Borber, *University of California–Davis*

Oswald Bowlin, *Texas Technical University*

Ronald Braswell, *Florida State University*

Kirt Butler, *Michigan State University*

Andreas Christofi, *Pennsylvania State University–Harrisburg*

James Cotter, *University of Iowa*

Jay Coughenour, *University of Massachusetts–Boston*

Arnold Cowan, *Iowa State University*

Mark Cross, *Louisiana Technical University*

Ron Crowe, *Jacksonville University*

William Damon, *Vanderbilt University*

Sudip Datta, *Bentley College*

Anand Desai, *University of Florida*

Miranda Lam Detzler, *University of Massachusetts–Boston*

David Distad, *University of California–Berkeley*

Dennis Draper, *University of Southern California*

Jean-Francois Dreyfus, *New York University*

Gene Drzycimski, *University of Wisconsin–Oshkosh*

Robert Eldridge, *Fairfield University*

Gary Emery, *University of Oklahoma*

Theodore Eytan, *City University of New York–Baruch College*

Don Fehrs, *University of Notre Dame*

Andrew Fields, *University of Delaware*

Paige Fields, *Texas A&M*

Michael Fishman, *Northwestern University*

Michael Goldstein, *University of Colorado*

Indra Guertler, *Babson College*

James Haltiner, *College of William and Mary*

Delvin Hawley, *University of Mississippi*

Hal Heaton, *Brigham Young University*

John Helmuth, *Rochester Institute of Technology*

Michael Hemler, *University of Notre Dame*

Stephen Heston, *Washington University*

Andrea Heuson, *University of Miami*

Hugh Hunter, *Eastern Washington University*

James Jackson, *Oklahoma State University*

Prem Jain, *Tulane University*

Brad Jordan, *University of Kentucky*

Jarl Kallberg, *New York University*

Jonathan Karpoff, *University of Washington*

Paul Keat, *American Graduate School of International Management*

Brian Kluger, *University of Cincinnati*

Narayana Kocherlakota, *University of Iowa*

Nelson Lacey, *University of Massachusetts*

Gene Lai, *University of Rhode Island*

Josef Lakonishok, *University of Illinois*

Dennis Lasser, *SUNY–Binghamton*

Paul Laux, *Case Western Reserve University*

Bong-Su Lee, *University of Minnesota*

James T. Lindley, *University of Southern Mississippi*

Dennis Logue, *Dartmouth College*

Michael Long, *Rutgers University*

Ileen Malitz, *Fairleigh Dickinson University*

Terry Maness, *Baylor University*

Surendra Mansinghka, *San Francisco State University*

Michael Mazzco, *Michigan State University*

Robert I. McDonald, *Northwestern University*

Hugh McLaughlin, *Bentley College*

Larry Merville, *University of Texas–Richardson*

Joe Messina, *San Francisco State University*

Roger Mesznik, *City College of New York–Baruch College*

Rick Meyer, *University of South Florida*

Richard Mull, *New Mexico State University*

Jim Musumeci, *Southern Illinois University–Carbondale*

Peder Nielsen, *Oregon State University*

Dennis Officer, *University of Kentucky*

Joseph Ogden, *State University of New York*

Ajay Patel, *University of Missouri–Columbia*

Glenn N. Pettengill, *Emporia State University*

Pegaret Pichler, *University of Maryland*

Franklin Potts, *Baylor University*

Annette Poulsen, *University of Georgia*

Latha Ramchand, *University of Houston*

Narendar Rao, *Northeastern Illinois University*

Steven Raymar, *Indiana University*

Stuart Rosenstein, *Southern Illinois University*

Patricia Ryan, *Drake University*

Anthony Sanders, *Ohio State University*

James Schallheim, *University of Utah*

Mary Jean Scheuer, *California State University at Northridge*

Lemma Senbet, *University of Maryland*

Kuldeep Shastri, *University of Pittsburgh*

Scott Smart, *Indiana University*

Jackie So, *Southern Illinois University*

John Stansfield, *Columbia College*

A. Charlene Sullivan, *Purdue University*

Timothy Sullivan, *Bentley College*

R. Bruce Swensen, *Adelphi University*

Ernest Swift, *Georgia State University*

Alex Tang, *Morgan State University*

Richard Taylor, *Arkansas State University*

Timothy Thompson, *Northwestern University*

Charles Trzcinka, *State University of New York–Buffalo*

Haluk Unal, *University of Maryland–College Park*

Avinash Verma, *Washington University*

Lankford Walker, *Eastern Illinois University*

Ralph Walkling, *Ohio State University*

F. Katherine Warne, *Southern Bell College*

Robert Whitelaw, *New York University*

Berry Wilson, *Georgetown University*

Thomas Zorn, *University of Nebraska–Lincoln*

Kent Zumwalt, *Colorado State University*

For their help on the Sixth Edition, we would like to thank Linda De Angelo, Dennis Draper, Kim Dietrich, Alan Shapiro, Harry De Angelo, Aris Protopapadakis, Anath Madhevan, and Suh-Pyng Ku, all of the Marshall School of Business at the University of Southern California. We also owe a debt of gratitude to Edward I. Altman, of New York University; Robert S. Hansen, of Virginia Tech; and Jay Ritter, of the University of Florida, who have provided several thoughtful comments and immeasurable help.

We would also like to thank Richard H. Cohen, University of Alaska, Anchorage, for his detailed proofing and helpful suggestions on the Solutions Manual.

Over the past three years, readers have provided assistance by detecting and reporting errors. Our goal is to offer the best textbook available on the subject, so this information was invaluable as we prepared the Sixth Edition. We want to ensure that all future editions are error-free and therefore we will offer $10 per arithmetic error to the first individual reporting it. Any arithmetic error resulting in subsequent errors will be counted double. All errors should be reported using the Feedback Form on the Corporate Finance Online Learning Center at *www.mhhe.com/rwj*.

In addition, Sandra Robinson and Wendy Wat have given significant assistance in preparing the manuscript.

Finally, we wish to thank our families and friends, Carol, Kate, Jon, Jan, Mark, and Lynne for their forbearance and help.

Stephen A. Ross
Randolph W. Westerfield
Jeffrey F. Jaffe

Brief Contents

Contents

Overview

To engage in business the financial managers of a firm must find answers to three kinds of important questions. First, what long-term investments should the firm take on? This is the capital budgeting decision. Second, how can cash be raised for the required investments? We call this the financing decision. Third, how will the firm manage its day-to-day cash and financial affairs? These decisions involve short-term finance and concern net working capital.

In Chapter 1 we discuss these important questions, briefly introducing the basic ideas of this book and describing the nature of the modern corporation and why it has emerged as the leading form of the business firm. Using the set-of-contracts perspective, the chapter discusses the goals of the modern corporation. Though the goals of shareholders and managers may not always be the same, conflicts usually will be resolved in favor of the shareholders. Finally, the chapter reviews some of the salient features of modern financial markets. This preliminary material will be familiar to students who have some background in accounting, finance, and economics.

Chapter 2 examines the basic accounting statements. It is review material for students with an accounting background. We describe the balance sheet and the income statement. The point of the chapter is to show the ways of converting data from accounting statements into cash flow. Understanding how to identify cash flow from accounting statements is especially important for later chapters on capital budgeting.

CHAPTER 1

Introduction to Corporate Finance

EXECUTIVE SUMMARY

The Video Product Company designs and manufactures very popular software for video game consoles. The company was started in 1999, and soon thereafter its game "Gadfly" appeared on the cover of *Billboard* magazine. Company sales in 2000 were over $20 million. Video Product's initial financing of $2 million came from Seed Ltd., a venture-capital firm, in exchange for a 15-percent equity stake in the company. Now the financial management of Video Product realizes that its initial financing was too small. In the long run Video Product would like to expand its design activity to the education and business areas. It would also like to significantly enhance its website for future Internet sales. However, at present the company has a short-run cash flow problem and cannot even buy $200,000 of materials to fill its holiday orders.

Video Product's experience illustrates the basic concerns of corporate finance:

1. What long-term investment strategy should a company take on?
2. How can cash be raised for the required investments?
3. How much short-term cash flow does a company need to pay its bills?

These are not the only questions of corporate finance. They are, however, among the most important questions and, taken in order, they provide a rough outline of our book.

One way that companies raise cash to finance their investment activities is by selling or "issuing" securities. The securities, sometimes called *financial instruments* or *claims,* may be roughly classified as *equity* or *debt,* loosely called *stocks* or *bonds.* The difference between equity and debt is a basic distinction in the modern theory of finance. All securities of a firm are claims that depend on or are contingent on the value of the firm.[1] In Section 1.2 we show how debt and equity securities depend on the firm's value, and we describe them as different contingent claims.

In Section 1.3 we discuss different organizational forms and the pros and cons of the decision to become a corporation.

In Section 1.4 we take a close look at the goals of the corporation and discuss why maximizing shareholder wealth is likely to be the primary goal of the corporation. Throughout the rest of the book, we assume that the firm's performance depends on the value it creates for its shareholders. Shareholders are better off when the value of their shares is increased by the firm's decisions.

A company raises cash by issuing securities to the financial markets. The market value of outstanding long-term corporate debt and equity securities traded in the U.S. financial markets is in excess of $25 trillion. In Section 1.5 we describe some of the basic features of the financial markets. Roughly speaking, there are two basic types of financial markets: the money markets and the capital markets. The last section of the chapter provides an outline of the rest of the book.

---

[1]We tend to use the words *firm, company,* and *business* interchangeably. However, there is a difference between a firm and a corporation. We discuss this difference in Section 1.3.

1.1 WHAT IS CORPORATE FINANCE?

Suppose you decide to start a firm to make tennis balls. To do this, you hire managers to buy raw materials, and you assemble a workforce that will produce and sell finished tennis balls. In the language of finance, you make an investment in assets such as inventory, machinery, land, and labor. The amount of cash you invest in assets must be matched by an equal amount of cash raised by financing. When you begin to sell tennis balls, your firm will generate cash. This is the basis of value creation. The purpose of the firm is to create value for you, the owner. The firm must generate more cash flow than it uses. The value is reflected in the framework of the simple balance-sheet model of the firm.

The Balance-Sheet Model of the Firm

Suppose we take a financial snapshot of the firm and its activities at a single point in time. Figure 1.1 shows a graphic conceptualization of the balance sheet, and it will help introduce you to corporate finance.

The assets of the firm are on the left-hand side of the balance sheet. These assets can be thought of as current and fixed. *Fixed assets* are those that will last a long time, such as buildings. Some fixed assets are tangible, such as machinery and equipment. Other fixed assets are intangible, such as patents, trademarks, and the quality of management. The other category of assets, *current assets,* comprises those that have short lives, such as inventory. The tennis balls that your firm has made but has not yet sold are part of its inventory. Unless you have overproduced, they will leave the firm shortly.

Before a company can invest in an asset, it must obtain financing, which means that it must raise the money to pay for the investment. The forms of financing are represented on the right-hand side of the balance sheet. A firm will issue (sell) pieces of paper called *debt*

■ FIGURE 1.1 **The Balance-Sheet Model of the Firm**

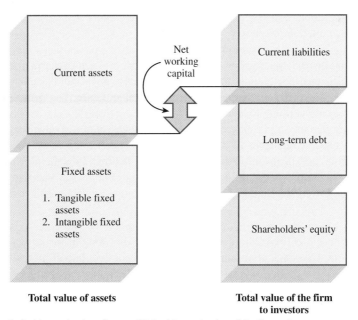

Left side, total value of assets. Right side, total value of the firm to investors, which determines how the value is distributed.

(loan agreements) or *equity shares* (stock certificates). Just as assets are classified as long-lived or short-lived, so too are liabilities. A short-term debt is called a *current liability*. Short-term debt represents loans and other obligations that must be repaid within one year. Long-term debt is debt that does not have to be repaid within one year. Shareholders' equity represents the difference between the value of the assets and the debt of the firm. In this sense it is a residual claim on the firm's assets.

From the balance-sheet model of the firm it is easy to see why finance can be thought of as the study of the following three questions:

1. In what long-lived assets should the firm invest? This question concerns the left-hand side of the balance sheet. Of course, the type and proportions of assets the firm needs tend to be set by the nature of the business. We use the terms **capital budgeting** and *capital expenditures* to describe the process of making and managing expenditures on long-lived assets.

2. How can the firm raise cash for required capital expenditures? This question concerns the right-hand side of the balance sheet. The answer to this involves the firm's **capital structure,** which represents the proportions of the firm's financing from current and long-term debt and equity.

3. How should short-term operating cash flows be managed? This question concerns the upper portion of the balance sheet. There is often a mismatch between the timing of cash inflows and cash outflows during operating activities. Furthermore, the amount and timing of operating cash flows are not known with certainty. The financial managers must attempt to manage the gaps in cash flow. From a balance-sheet perspective, short-term management of cash flow is associated with a firm's **net working capital.** Net working capital is defined as current assets minus current liabilities. From a financial perspective, the short-term cash flow problem comes from the mismatching of cash inflows and outflows. It is the subject of short-term finance.

Capital Structure

Financing arrangements determine how the value of the firm is sliced up. The persons or institutions that buy debt from the firm are called *creditors*.[2] The holders of equity shares are called *shareholders.*

Sometimes it is useful to think of the firm as a pie. Initially, the size of the pie will depend on how well the firm has made its investment decisions. After a firm has made its investment decisions, it determines the value of its assets (e.g., its buildings, land, and inventories).

The firm can then determine its capital structure. The firm might initially have raised the cash to invest in its assets by issuing more debt than equity; now it can consider changing that mix by issuing more equity and using the proceeds to buy back some of its debt. Financing decisions like this can be made independently of the original investment decisions. The decisions to issue debt and equity affect how the pie is sliced.

The pie we are thinking of is depicted in Figure 1.2. The size of the pie is the value of the firm in the financial markets. We can write the value of the firm, *V,* as

$$V = B + S$$

where B is the value of the debt and S is the value of the equity. The pie diagrams consider two ways of slicing the pie: 50 percent debt and 50 percent equity, and 25 percent

---

[2]We tend to use the words *creditors, debtholders,* and *bondholders* interchangeably. In later chapters we examine the differences among the kinds of creditors. In algebraic notation, we will usually refer to the firm's debt with the letter B (for bondholders).

■ FIGURE 1.2   Two Pie Models of the Firm

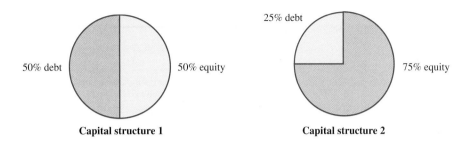

debt and 75 percent equity. The way the pie is sliced could affect its value. If so, the goal of the financial manager will be to choose the ratio of debt to equity that makes the value of the pie—that is, the value of the firm, V—as large as it can be.

The Financial Manager

In large firms the finance activity is usually associated with a top officer of the firm, such as the vice president and chief financial officer, and some lesser officers. Figure 1.3 depicts a general organizational structure emphasizing the finance activity within the firm. Reporting to the chief financial officer are the treasurer and the controller. The treasurer is responsible for handling cash flows, managing capital-expenditures decisions, and making financial plans. The controller handles the accounting function, which includes taxes, cost and financial accounting, and information systems.

We think that the most important job of a financial manager is to create value from the firm's capital budgeting, financing, and liquidity activities. How do financial managers create value?

1. The firm should try to buy assets that generate more cash than they cost.
2. The firm should sell bonds and stocks and other financial instruments that raise more cash than they cost.

Thus the firm must create more cash flow than it uses. The cash flows paid to bondholders and stockholders of the firm should be higher than the cash flows put into the firm by the bondholders and stockholders. To see how this is done, we can trace the cash flows from the firm to the financial markets and back again.

The interplay of the firm's finance with the financial markets is illustrated in Figure 1.4. The arrows in Figure 1.4 trace cash flow from the firm to the financial markets and back again. Suppose we begin with the firm's financing activities. To raise money the firm sells debt and equity shares to investors in the financial markets. This results in cash flows from the financial markets to the firm (A). This cash is invested in the investment activities of the firm (B) by the firm's management. The cash generated by the firm (C) is paid to shareholders and bondholders (F). The shareholders receive cash in the form of dividends; the bondholders who lent funds to the firm receive interest and, when the initial loan is repaid, principal. Not all of the firm's cash is paid out. Some is retained (E), and some is paid to the government as taxes (D).

Over time, if the cash paid to shareholders and bondholders (F) is greater than the cash raised in the financial markets (A), value will be created.

Identification of Cash Flows   Unfortunately, it is not all that easy to observe cash flows directly. Much of the information we obtain is in the form of accounting statements, and

■ FIGURE 1.3 **Hypothetical Organization Chart**

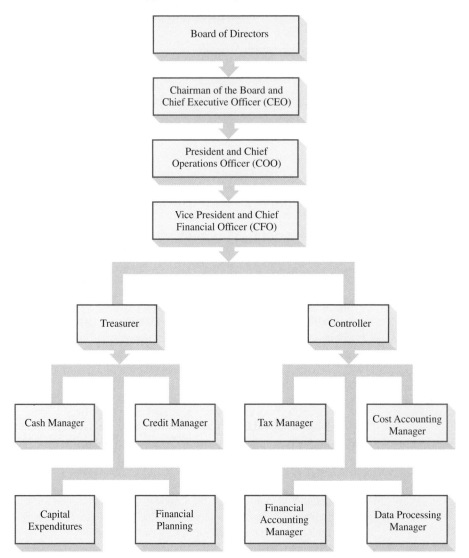

much of the work of financial analysis is to extract cash flow information from accounting statements. The following example illustrates how this is done.

EXAMPLE

The Midland Company refines and trades gold. At the end of the year it sold 2,500 ounces of gold for $1 million. The company had acquired the gold for $900,000 at the beginning of the year. The company paid cash for the gold when it was purchased. Unfortunately, it has yet to collect from the customer to whom the gold was sold. The following is a standard accounting of Midland's financial circumstances at year-end:

Skills Needed for the Chief Financial Officers of eFinance.com

Chief strategist: CFOs will need to use real-time financial information to make crucial decisions fast.

Chief dealmaker: CFOs must be adept at venture capital, mergers and acquisitions, and strategic partnerships.

Chief risk officer: Limiting risk will be even more important as markets become more global and hedging instruments become more complex.

Chief communicator: Gaining the confidence of Wall Street and the media will be essential.

Source: *Business Week,* August 28, 2000, p. 120.

THE MIDLAND COMPANY
Accounting View
Income Statement
Year Ended December 31

Sales	$1,000,000
−Costs	−900,000
Profit	$ 100,000

By generally accepted accounting principles (GAAP), the sale is recorded even though the customer has yet to pay. It is assumed that the customer will pay soon. From the accounting perspective, Midland seems to be profitable. However, the perspective of corporate finance is different. It focuses on cash flows:

THE MIDLAND COMPANY
Corporate Finance View
Income Statement
Year Ended December 31

Cash inflow	$ 0
Cash outflow	− 900,000
	−$900,000

The perspective of corporate finance is interested in whether cash flows are being created by the gold-trading operations of Midland. Value creation depends on cash flows. For Midland, value creation depends on whether and when it actually receives $1 million.

Timing of Cash Flows   The value of an investment made by the firm depends on the timing of cash flows. One of the most important assumptions of finance is that individuals prefer to receive cash flows earlier rather than later. One dollar received today is worth more than one dollar received next year. This time preference plays a role in stock and bond prices.

EXAMPLE

The Midland Company is attempting to choose between two proposals for new products. Both proposals will provide additional cash flows over a four-year period and will initially cost $10,000. The cash flows from the proposals are as follows:

■ FIGURE 1.4 **Cash Flows between the Firm and the Financial Markets**

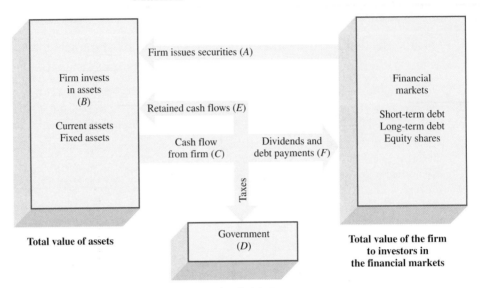

(A) Firm issues securities to raise cash (the financing decision).
(B) Firm invests in assets (capital budgeting).
(C) Firm's operations generate cash flow.
(D) Cash is paid to government as taxes.
(E) Retained cash flows are reinvested in firm.
(F) Cash is paid out to investors in the form of interest and dividends.

Year	New Product A	New Product B
1	$ 0	$ 4,000
2	0	4,000
3	0	4,000
4	20,000	4,000
Total	$20,000	$16,000

At first it appears that new product A would be best. However, the cash flows from proposal B come earlier than those of A. Without more information we cannot decide which set of cash flows would create the most value to the bondholders and shareholders. It depends on whether the value of getting cash from B up front outweighs the extra total cash from A. Bond and stock prices reflect this preference for earlier cash, and we will see how to use them to decide between A and B.

Risk of Cash Flows   The firm must consider risk. The amount and timing of cash flows are not usually known with certainty. Most investors have an aversion to risk.

EXAMPLE

The Midland Company is considering expanding operations overseas. It is evaluating Europe and Japan as possible sites. Europe is considered to be relatively safe, whereas operating in Japan is seen as very risky. In both cases the company would close down operations after one year.

After doing a complete financial analysis, Midland has come up with the following cash flows of the alternative plans for expansion under three equally likely scenarios—pessimistic, most likely, and optimistic:

	Pessimistic	Most Likely	Optimistic
Europe	$75,000	$100,000	$125,000
Japan	0	150,000	200,000

If we ignore the pessimistic scenario, perhaps Japan is the best alternative. When we take the pessimistic scenario into account, the choice is unclear. Japan appears to be riskier, but it also offers a higher expected level of cash flow. What is risk and how can it be defined? We must try to answer this important question. Corporate finance cannot avoid coping with risky alternatives, and much of our book is devoted to developing methods for evaluating risky opportunities.

CONCEPT QUESTIONS

- What are three basic questions of corporate finance?
- Describe capital structure.
- How is value created?
- List the three reasons why value creation is difficult.

1.2 CORPORATE SECURITIES AS CONTINGENT CLAIMS ON TOTAL FIRM VALUE

What is the essential difference between debt and equity? The answer can be found by thinking about what happens to the payoffs to debt and equity when the value of the firm changes.

The basic feature of a debt is that it is a promise by the borrowing firm to repay a fixed dollar amount by a certain date.

EXAMPLE

The Officer Corporation promises to pay $100 to the Brigham Insurance Company at the end of one year. This is a debt of the Officer Corporation. Holders of the debt will receive $100 if the value of the Officer Corporation's assets is equal to or more than $100 at the end of the year.

Formally, the debtholders have been promised an amount F at the end of the year. If the value of the firm, X, is equal to or greater than F at year-end, debtholders will get F. Of course, if the firm does not have enough to pay off the promised amount, the firm will be "broke." It may be forced to liquidate its assets for whatever they are worth, and the bondholders will receive X. Mathematically this means that the debtholders have a claim to X or F, whichever is smaller. Figure 1.5 illustrates the general nature of the payoff structure to debtholders.

Suppose at year-end the Officer Corporation's value is equal to $100. The firm has promised to pay the Brigham Insurance Company $100, so the debtholders will get $100.

Now suppose the Officer Corporation's value is $200 at year-end and the debtholders are promised $100. How much will the debtholders receive? It should be clear that they will receive the same amount as when the Officer Corporation was worth $100.

Suppose the firm's value is $75 at year-end and debtholders are promised $100. How much will the debtholders receive? In this case the debtholders will get $75.

■ FIGURE 1.5 **Debt and Equity as Contingent Claims**

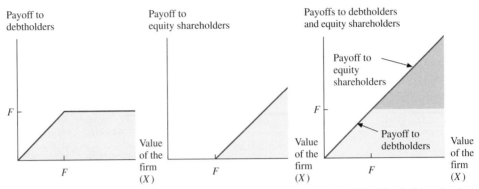

F is the promised payoff to debtholders. $X - F$ is the payoff to equity shareholders if $X - F > 0$. Otherwise the payoff is 0.

The stockholders' claim on firm value at the end of the period is the amount that remains after the debtholders are paid. Of course, stockholders get nothing if the firm's value is equal to or less than the amount promised to the debtholders.

EXAMPLE

The Officer Corporation will sell its assets for $200 at year-end. The firm has promised to pay the Brigham Insurance Company $100 at that time. The stockholders will get the residual value of $100.

Algebraically, the stockholders' claim is $X - F$ if $X > F$ and zero if $X \leq F$. This is depicted in Figure 1.5. The sum of the debtholders' claim and the stockholders' claim is always the value of the firm at the end of the period.

The debt and equity securities issued by a firm derive their value from the total value of the firm. In the words of finance theory, debt and equity securities are **contingent claims** on the total firm value.

When the value of the firm exceeds the amount promised to the debtholders, the shareholders obtain the residual of the firm's value over the amount promised the debtholders, and the debtholders obtain the amount promised. When the value of the firm is less than the amount promised the debtholders, the shareholders receive nothing and the debtholders get the value of the firm.

CONCEPT QUESTIONS

• What is a contingent claim?
• Describe equity and debt as contingent claims.

1.3 THE CORPORATE FIRM

The firm is a way of organizing the economic activity of many individuals, and there are many reasons why so much economic activity is carried out by firms and not by individuals. The theory of firms, however, does not tell us much about why most large firms are corporations rather than any of the other legal forms that firms can assume.

A basic problem of the firm is how to raise cash. The corporate form of business, that is, organizing the firm as a corporation, is the standard method for solving problems encountered in raising large amounts of cash. However, businesses can take other forms. In this section we consider the three basic legal forms of organizing firms, and we see how firms go about the task of raising large amounts of money under each form.

The Sole Proprietorship

A **sole proprietorship** is a business owned by one person. Suppose you decide to start a business to produce mousetraps. Going into business is simple: You announce to all who will listen, "Today I am going to build a better mousetrap."

Most large cities require that you obtain a business license. Afterward you can begin to hire as many people as you need and borrow whatever money you need. At year-end all the profits and the losses will be yours.

Here are some factors that are important in considering a sole proprietorship:

1. The sole proprietorship is the cheapest business to form. No formal charter is required, and few government regulations must be satisfied for most industries.
2. A sole proprietorship pays no corporate income taxes. All profits of the business are taxed as individual income.
3. The sole proprietorship has unlimited liability for business debts and obligations. No distinction is made between personal and business assets.
4. The life of the sole proprietorship is limited by the life of the sole proprietor.
5. Because the only money invested in the firm is the proprietor's, the equity money that can be raised by the sole proprietor is limited to the proprietor's personal wealth.

The Partnership

Any two or more persons can get together and form a **partnership.** Partnerships fall into two categories: (1) general partnerships and (2) limited partnerships.

In a *general partnership* all partners agree to provide some fraction of the work and cash and to share the profits and losses. Each partner is liable for the debts of the partnership. A partnership agreement specifies the nature of the arrangement. The partnership agreement may be an oral agreement or a formal document setting forth the understanding.

Limited partnerships permit the liability of some of the partners to be limited to the amount of cash each has contributed to the partnership. Limited partnerships usually require that (1) at least one partner be a general partner and (2) the limited partners do not participate in managing the business. Here are some things that are important when considering a partnership:

1. Partnerships are usually inexpensive and easy to form. Written documents are required in complicated arrangements, including general and limited partnerships. Business licenses and filing fees may be necessary.
2. General partners have unlimited liability for all debts. The liability of limited partners is usually limited to the contribution each has made to the partnership. If one general partner is unable to meet his or her commitment, the shortfall must be made up by the other general partners.
3. The general partnership is terminated when a general partner dies or withdraws (but this is not so for a limited partner). It is difficult for a partnership to transfer ownership without dissolving. Usually, all general partners must agree. However, limited partners may sell their interest in a business.

4. It is difficult for a partnership to raise large amounts of cash. Equity contributions are usually limited to a partner's ability and desire to contribute to the partnership. Many companies, such as Apple Computer, start life as a proprietorship or partnership, but at some point they choose to convert to corporate form.

5. Income from a partnership is taxed as personal income to the partners.

6. Management control resides with the general partners. Usually a majority vote is required on important matters, such as the amount of profit to be retained in the business.

It is very difficult for large business organizations to exist as sole proprietorships or partnerships. The main advantage is the cost of getting started. Afterward, the disadvantages, which may become severe, are (1) unlimited liability, (2) limited life of the enterprise, and (3) difficulty of transferring ownership. These three disadvantages lead to (4) the difficulty of raising cash.

The Corporation

Of the many forms of business enterprises, the **corporation** is by far the most important. It is a distinct legal entity. As such, a corporation can have a name and enjoy many of the legal powers of natural persons. For example, corporations can acquire and exchange property. Corporations can enter into contracts and may sue and be sued. For jurisdictional purposes, the corporation is a citizen of its state of incorporation. (It cannot vote, however.)

Starting a corporation is more complicated than starting a proprietorship or partnership. The incorporators must prepare articles of incorporation and a set of bylaws. The articles of incorporation must include the following:

1. Name of the corporation.

2. Intended life of the corporation (it may be forever).

3. Business purpose.

4. Number of shares of stock that the corporation is authorized to issue, with a statement of limitations and rights of different classes of shares.

5. Nature of the rights granted to shareholders.

6. Number of members of the initial board of directors.

The bylaws are the rules to be used by the corporation to regulate its own existence, and they concern its shareholders, directors, and officers. Bylaws range from the briefest possible statement of rules for the corporation's management to hundreds of pages of text.

In its simplest form, the corporation comprises three sets of distinct interests: the shareholders (the owners), the directors, and the corporation officers (the top management). Traditionally, the shareholders control the corporation's direction, policies, and activities. The shareholders elect a board of directors, who in turn selects top management. Members of top management serve as corporate officers and manage the operation of the corporation in the best interest of the shareholders. In closely held corporations with few shareholders there may be a large overlap among the shareholders, the directors, and the top management. However, in larger corporations the shareholders, directors, and the top management are likely to be distinct groups.

The potential separation of ownership from management gives the corporation several advantages over proprietorships and partnerships:

1. Because ownership in a corporation is represented by shares of stock, ownership can be readily transferred to new owners. Because the corporation exists independently of those who own its shares, there is no limit to the transferability of shares as there is in partnerships.

2. The corporation has unlimited life. Because the corporation is separate from its owners, the death or withdrawal of an owner does not affect its legal existence. The corporation can continue on after the original owners have withdrawn.

3. The shareholders' liability is limited to the amount invested in the ownership shares. For example, if a shareholder purchased $1,000 in shares of a corporation, the potential loss would be $1,000. In a partnership, a general partner with a $1,000 contribution could lose the $1,000 plus any other indebtedness of the partnership.

Limited liability, ease of ownership transfer, and perpetual succession are the major advantages of the corporation form of business organization. These give the corporation an enhanced ability to raise cash.

There is, however, one great disadvantage to incorporation. The federal government taxes corporate income. This tax is in addition to the personal income tax that shareholders pay on dividend income they receive. This is double taxation for shareholders when compared to taxation on proprietorships and partnerships.

CASE STUDY: *Making the Decision to Become a Corporation:*
The Case of PLM International, Inc.[3]

 In 1972, several entrepreneurs agreed to start a company they called PLM (Professional Lease Management, Inc.). Their idea was to sponsor, syndicate, and manage public and private limited partnerships with the purpose of acquiring and leasing transportation equipment. They created an operating subsidiary called FSI (Financial Services, Inc.) to be the general partner of each of the partnerships. PLM had limited success in its early years, but during the period 1981 to 1986 more than 27 public partnerships were formed. Each partnership was set up to acquire and lease transportation equipment, such as aircraft, tractors and trailers, cargo containers, and railcars, to transportation companies.

Until the Tax Reform Act of 1986, PLM enjoyed considerable success with its partnerships. It became one of the largest equipment-leasing firms in the United States. The partnerships appealed to high-tax-bracket individuals because unlike corporations, partnerships are not taxed. The partnerships were set up to be self-liquidating (i.e., all excess cash flow was to be distributed to the partners), and no reinvestment could take place. No ready market for the partnership units existed, and each partnership invested in a narrow class of transportation equipment. PLM's success depended on creating tax-sheltered cash flow from accelerated depreciation and investment tax credits. However, the 1986 Tax Reform Act had a devastating impact on tax-sheltered limited partnerships. The act substantially flattened personal tax rates, eliminated the investment tax credit, shortened depreciation schedules, and established an alternative minimum tax rate. The act caused PLM to think about different types of equipment-leasing organizational forms. What was needed was an organization form that could take advantage of potential growth and diversification opportunities and that wasn't based entirely upon tax sheltering.

In 1987 PLM, with the advice and assistance of the now-bankrupt Drexel Burnham Lambert investment banking firm, terminated its partnerships and converted consenting partnerships to a new umbrella corporation called PLM International. After much legal maneuvering, PLM International publicly announced that a majority of the partnerships had consented to the consolidation and incorporation. (A majority vote was needed for voluntary termination and some partnerships decided not to incorporate.) On February 2, 1988, PLM International's common stock began trading on the American Stock Exchange (AMEX) at about $8 per share. However, PLM International did not perform well, despite its conversion to a corporation. In April 2000, its stock was trading at only $5 per share.

---

[3]*The S–4 Registration Statement,* PLM International, Inc., filed with the Securities and Exchange Commission, Washington, D.C., August 1987, gives further details.

A COMPARISON OF PARTNERSHIP AND CORPORATIONS

	Corporation	Partnership
Liquidity and marketability	Shares can be exchanged without termination of the corporation. Common stock can be listed on stock exchange.	Units are subject to substantial restrictions on transferability. There is usually no established trading market for partnership units.
Voting rights	Usually each share of common stock entitles the holder to one vote per share on matters requiring a vote and on the election of the directors. Directors determine top management.	Some voting rights by limited partners. However, general partner has exclusive control and management of operations.
Taxation	Corporations have double taxation: Corporate income is taxable, and dividends to shareholders are also taxable.	Partnerships are not taxable. Partners pay taxes on distributed shares of partnership.
Reinvestment and dividend payout	Corporations have broad latitude on dividend payout decisions.	Partnerships are generally prohibited from reinvesting partnership cash flow. All net cash flow is distributed to partners.
Liability	Shareholders are not personally liable for obligations of the corporation.	Limited partners are not liable for obligations of partnerships. General partners may have unlimited liability.
Continuity of existence	Corporations have perpetual life.	Partnerships have limited life.

The decision to become a corporation is complicated, and there are several pros and cons. PLM International cited several basic reasons to support the consolidation and incorporation of its transportation-equipment–leasing activities.

- Enhanced access to equity and debt capital for future growth.
- The possibility of reinvestment for future profit opportunities.
- Better liquidity for investors through common stock listing on AMEX.

These are all good reasons for incorporating, and they provided potential benefits to the new shareholders of PLM International that may have outweighed the disadvantages of double taxation that came from incorporating. However, not all the PLM partnerships wanted to convert to the corporation. Sometimes it is not easy to determine whether a partnership or a corporation is the best organizational form. Corporate income is taxable at the personal and corporation levels. Because of this double taxation, firms having the most to gain from incorporation share the following characteristics:

- Low taxable income.
- Low marginal corporate tax rates.
- Low marginal personal tax rates among potential shareholders.

In addition, firms with high rates of reinvestment relative to current income are good candidates for the corporate form because corporations can more easily retain profits for reinvestment than partnerships. Also, it is easier for corporations to sell shares of stock on public stock markets to finance possible investment opportunities. ■ ■ ■ ■ ■

QUESTIONS

CONCEPT QUESTIONS
?
- Define a proprietorship, a partnership, and a corporation.
- What are the advantages of the corporate form of business organization?

1.4 GOALS OF THE CORPORATE FIRM

What is the primary goal of the corporation? The traditional answer is that managers in a corporation make decisions for the stockholders because the stockholders own and control the corporation. If so, the goal of the corporation is to add value for the stockholders. This goal is a little vague and so we will try to come up with a precise formulation. It is also impossible to give a definitive answer to this important question because the corporation is an artificial being, not a natural person. It exists in the "contemplation of the law."[4]

It is necessary to precisely identify who controls the corporation. We shall consider the **set-of-contracts viewpoint.** This viewpoint suggests the corporate firm will attempt to maximize the shareholders' wealth by taking actions that increase the current value per share of existing stock of the firm.

Agency Costs and the Set-of-Contracts Perspective

The set-of-contracts theory of the firm states that the firm can be viewed as a set of contracts.[5] One of the contract claims is a residual claim (equity) on the firm's assets and cash flows. The equity contract can be defined as a principal-agent relationship. The members of the management team are the agents, and the equity investors (shareholders) are the principals. It is assumed that the managers and the shareholders, if left alone, will each attempt to act in his or her own self-interest.

The shareholders, however, can discourage the managers from diverging from the shareholders' interests by devising appropriate incentives for managers and then monitoring their behavior. Doing so, unfortunately, is complicated and costly. The cost of resolving the conflicts of interest between managers and shareholders are special types of costs called *agency costs.* These costs are defined as the sum of (1) the monitoring costs of the shareholders and (2) the costs of implementing control devices. It can be expected that contracts will be devised that will provide the managers with appropriate incentives to maximize the shareholders' wealth. Thus, the set-of-contracts theory suggests that managers in the corporate firm will usually act in the best interest of shareholders. However, agency problems can never be perfectly solved and, as a consequence, shareholders may experience residual losses. *Residual losses* are the lost wealth of the shareholders due to divergent behavior of the managers.

Managerial Goals

Managerial goals may be different from those of shareholders. What goals will managers maximize if they are left to pursue their own rather than shareholders' goals?

Williamson proposes the notion of *expense preference.*[6] He argues that managers obtain value from certain kinds of expenses. In particular, company cars, office furniture, office location, and funds for discretionary investment have value to managers beyond that which comes from their productivity.

---

[4]These are the words of Chief Justice John Marshall from *The Trustees of Dartmouth College* v. *Woodward,* 4, Wheaton 636 (1819).

[5]M. C. Jensen and W. Meckling, "Theory of the Firm: Managerial Behavior, Agency Costs and Ownership Structure," *Journal of Financial Economics* 3 (1976).

[6]O. Williamson, "Managerial Discretion and Business Behavior," *American Economic Review* 53 (1963).

Donaldson conducted a series of interviews with the chief executives of several large companies.[7] He concluded that managers are influenced by two basic motivations:

1. *Survival.* Organizational survival means that management will always try to command sufficient resources to avoid the firm's going out of business.

2. *Independence and self-sufficiency.* This is the freedom to make decisions without encountering external parties or depending on outside financial markets. The Donaldson interviews suggested that managers do not like to issue new shares of stock. Instead, they like to be able to rely on internally generated cash flow.

These motivations lead to what Donaldson concludes is the basic financial objective of managers: the maximization of corporate wealth. Corporate wealth is that wealth over which management has effective control; it is closely associated with corporate growth and corporate size. Corporate wealth is not necessarily shareholder wealth. Corporate wealth tends to lead to increased growth by providing funds for growth and limiting the extent to which new equity is raised. Increased growth and size are not necessarily the same thing as increased shareholder wealth.

Separation of Ownership and Control

Some people argue that shareholders do not completely control the corporation. They argue that shareholder ownership is too diffuse and fragmented for effective control of management.[8] A striking feature of the modern large corporation is the diffusion of ownership among thousands of investors. For example, Table 1.1 shows that 3,700,000 persons and institutions own shares of AT&T stock.

One of the most important advantages of the corporate form of business organization is that it allows ownership of shares to be transferred. The resulting diffuse ownership, however,

■ TABLE 1.1 **Some of the World's Largest Industrial Corporations, 2000**

Company	Market Value* (in $ billions)	Shares Outstanding (in millions)	Number of Shareholders
Microsoft	$525.7	5209	92,130
General Electric	434.0	3714	534,000
Intel	400.1	3555	203,000
IBM	188.8	1875	616,000
AT&T	173.2	3194	3,700,000
Merck	138.7	2968	269,600
Pfizer	134.6	4138	105,000
Toyota	119.2	1875	100,000
Coca Cola	112.5	3464	366,000

Sources: *Value Line, Business Week,* and *Standard & Poor's Security Owners Stock Guide.*
*Market price multiplied by shares outstanding.

[7]G. Donaldson, *Managing Corporate Wealth: The Operations of a Comprehensive Financial Goals System* (New York: Praeger Publishers, 1984).

[8]Recent work by Gerald T. Garvey and Peter L. Swan, "The Economics of Corporate Governance: Beyond the Marshallian Firm," *Journal of Corporate Finance* 1 (1994), surveys literature on the stated assumption of shareholder maximization.

brings with it the separation of ownership and control of the large corporation. The possible separation of ownership and control raises an important question: Who controls the firm?

Do Shareholders Control Managerial Behavior?

The claim that managers can ignore the interests of shareholders is deduced from the fact that ownership in large corporations is widely dispersed. As a consequence, it is often claimed that individual shareholders cannot control management. There is some merit in this argument, but it is too simplistic.

When a conflict of interest exists between management and shareholders, who wins? Does management or the shareholders control the firm? There is no doubt that ownership in large corporations is diffuse when compared to the closely held corporation. However, several control devices used by shareholders bond management to the self-interest of shareholders:

1. Shareholders determine the membership of the board of directors by voting. Thus, shareholders control the directors, who in turn select the management team.
2. Contracts with management and arrangements for compensation, such as stock option plans, can be made so that management has an incentive to pursue the goal of the shareholders. Another device is called *performance shares*. These are shares of stock given to managers on the basis of performance as measured by earnings per share and similar criteria.
3. If the price of a firm's stock drops too low because of poor management, the firm may be acquired by another group of shareholders, by another firm, or by an individual. This is called a *takeover.* In a takeover, the top management of the acquired firm may find themselves out of a job. This puts pressure on the management to make decisions in the stockholders' interests. Fear of a takeover gives managers an incentive to take actions that will maximize stock prices.
4. Competition in the managerial labor market may force managers to perform in the best interest of stockholders. Otherwise they will be replaced. Firms willing to pay the most will lure good managers. These are likely to be firms that compensate managers based on the value they create.

The available evidence and theory are consistent with the ideas of shareholder control and shareholder value maximization. However, there can be no doubt that at times corporations pursue managerial goals at the expense of shareholders. There is also evidence that the diverse claims of customers, vendors, and employees must frequently be considered in the goals of the corporation.

CONCEPT QUESTIONS
- What are the two types of agency costs?
- How are managers bonded to shareholders?
- Can you recall some managerial goals?
- What is the set-of-contracts perspective?

1.5 FINANCIAL MARKETS

As indicated in Section 1.1, firms offer two basic types of securities to investors. *Debt securities* are contractual obligations to repay corporate borrowing. *Equity securities* are shares of common stock and preferred stock that represent noncontractual claims to the residual cash flow of the firm. Issues of debt and stock that are publicly sold by the firm are then traded on the financial markets.

The financial markets are composed of the **money markets** and the **capital markets.** Money markets are the markets for debt securities that will pay off in the short term (usually less than one year). Capital markets are the markets for long-term debt (with a maturity at over one year) and for equity shares.

The term *money market* applies to a group of loosely connected markets. They are dealer markets. Dealers are firms that make continuous quotations of prices for which they stand ready to buy and sell money-market instruments for their own inventory and at their own risk. Thus, the dealer is a principal in most transactions. This is different from a stockbroker acting as an agent for a customer in buying or selling common stock on most stock exchanges; an agent does not actually acquire the securities.

At the core of the money markets are the money-market banks (these are large banks in New York), more than 30 government securities dealers (some of which are the large banks), a dozen or so commercial-paper dealers, and a large number of money brokers. Money brokers specialize in finding short-term money for borrowers and placing money for lenders. The financial markets can be classified further as the *primary market* and the *secondary markets.*

The Primary Market: New Issues

The primary market is used when governments and corporations initially sell securities. Corporations engage in two types of primary-market sales of debt and equity: public offerings and private placements.

Most publicly offered corporate debt and equity come to the market underwritten by a syndicate of investment banking firms. The *underwriting* syndicate buys the new securities from the firm for the syndicate's own account and resells them at a higher price. Publicly issued debt and equity must be registered with the Securities and Exchange Commission. *Registration* requires the corporation to disclose all of the material information in a registration statement.

The legal, accounting, and other costs of preparing the registration statement are not negligible. In part to avoid these costs, privately placed debt and equity are sold on the basis of private negotiations to large financial institutions, such as insurance companies and mutual funds. Private placements are not registered with the Securities and Exchange Commission.

Secondary Markets

After debt and equity securities are originally sold, they are traded in the secondary markets. There are two kinds of secondary markets: the *auction markets* and the *dealer markets.*

The equity securities of most large U.S. firms trade in organized auction markets, such as the New York Stock Exchange, the American Stock Exchange, and regional exchanges, such as the Midwest Stock Exchange. The New York Stock Exchange (NYSE) is the most important auction exchange. It usually accounts for more than 85 percent of all shares traded in U.S. auction exchanges. Bond trading on auction exchanges is inconsequential.

Most debt securities are traded in dealer markets. The many bond dealers communicate with one another by telecommunications equipment—wires, computers, and telephones. Investors get in touch with dealers when they want to buy or sell, and can negotiate a deal. Some stocks are traded in the dealer markets. When they are, it is referred to as the *over-the-counter (OTC) market.*

In February 1971, the National Association of Securities Dealers made available to dealers and brokers in the OTC market an automated quotation system called the National Association of Securities Dealers Automated Quotation (NASDAQ) system. The market value of shares of OTC stocks in the NASDAQ system at the end of 1998 was about 25 percent of the market value of the shares on the NYSE.

Exchange Trading of Listed Stocks

Auction markets are different from dealer markets in two ways: First, trading in a given auction exchange takes place at a single site on the floor of the exchange. Second, transaction prices of shares traded on auction exchanges are communicated almost immediately to the public by computer and other devices.

The NYSE is one of the preeminent securities exchanges in the world. All transactions in stocks listed on the NYSE occur at a particular place on the floor of the exchange called a *post*. At the heart of the market is the specialist. Specialists are members of the NYSE who *make a market* in designated stocks. Specialists have an obligation to offer to buy and sell shares of their assigned NYSE stocks. It is believed that this makes the market liquid because the specialist assumes the role of a buyer for investors if they wish to sell and a seller if they wish to buy.

Listing

Firms that want their equity shares to be traded on the NYSE must apply for listing. To be listed initially on the NYSE a company is expected to satisfy certain minimum requirements. Some of these for U.S. companies are as follows:

1. Demonstrated earning power of either $2.5 million before taxes for the most recent year and $2 million before taxes for each of the preceding two years, *or* an aggregate for the last three years of $6.5 million together with a minimum in the most recent year of $4.5 million (all years must be profitable).
2. Net tangible assets equal to at least $40 million.
3. A market value for publicly held shares of $40 million.
4. A total of a least 1.1 million publicly held shares.
5. A total of at least 2,000 holders of 100 shares of stock or more.

The listing requirements for non–U.S. companies are somewhat more stringent. Table 1.2 gives the market value of NYSE-listed stocks and bonds.

■ TABLE 1.2 **Market Value of NYSE-Listed Securities**

End-of-Year	Number of Companies	Market Value ($ millions)
NYSE-listed stocks*		
1999	3025	12,296,057
1998	3114	10,864,472
1997	3047	9,413,109
1996	2907	7,300,351
NYSE-listed bonds†		
1999	416	2,401,605
1998	474	2,554,122
1997	533	2,625,357
1996	563	2,862,382

*Includes preferred stock and common stock.
†Includes government issues.
Source: Data from the *New York Stock Exchange Fact Book 1999*, published by the New York Stock Exchange. In the case of bonds, in some instances we report the face value.

CONCEPT QUESTIONS

?
- Distinguish between money markets and capital markets.
- What is listing?
- What is the difference between a primary market and a secondary market?

1.6 OUTLINE OF THE TEXT

Now that we've taken the quick tour through all of corporate finance, we can take a closer look at this book. The book is divided into eight parts. The long-term investment decision is covered first. Financing decisions and working capital are covered next. Finally a series of special topics are covered. Here are the eight parts:

Part I   Overview
Part II   Value and Capital Budgeting
Part III   Risk
Part IV   Capital Structure and Dividend Policy
Part V   Long-Term Financing
Part VI   Options, Futures, and Corporate Finance
Part VII   Financial Planning and Short-Term Finance
Part VIII   Special Topics

Part II describes how investment opportunities are valued in financial markets. This part contains basic theory. Because finance is a subject that builds understanding from the ground up, the material is very important. The most important concept in Part II is *net present value*. We develop the net present value rule into a tool for valuing investment alternatives. We discuss general formulas and apply them to a variety of different financial instruments.

Part III introduces basic measures of risk. The capital-asset pricing model (CAPM) and the arbitrage pricing theory (APT) are used to devise methods for incorporating risk in valuation. As part of this discussion, we describe the famous beta coefficient. Finally, we use the above pricing models to handle capital budgeting under risk.

Part IV examines two interrelated topics: capital structure and dividend policy. Capital structure is the extent to which the firm relies on debt. It cannot be separated from the amount of cash dividends the firm decides to pay out to its equity shareholders.

Part V concerns long-term financing. We describe the securities that corporations issue to raise cash, as well as the mechanics of offering securities for a public sale. Here we discuss call provisions, warrants, convertibles, and leasing.

Part VI discusses special contractual arrangements called Options.

Part VII is devoted to financial planning and short-term finance. The first chapter describes financial planning. Next we focus on managing the firm's current assets and current liabilities. We describe aspects of the firm's short-term financial management. Separate chapters on cash management and on credit management are included.

Part VIII covers two important special topics: mergers and international corporate finance.

KEY TERMS

Capital budgeting 4		Money markets 18	
Capital markets 18		Net working capital 4	
Capital structure 4		Partnership 11	
Contingent claims 10		Set-of-contracts viewpoint 15	
Corporation 12		Sole proprietorship 11	

SUGGESTED READINGS

Evidence is provided on the tax factor in choosing to incorporate in:
Mackie-Mason, J. K., and R. H. Gordon. "How Much Do Taxes Discourage Incorporation?"
   Journal of Finance (June 1997).

Do American managers pay too little attention to shareholders? This is the question posed in:
M. Miller. "Is American Corporate Governance Fatally Flawed?" *Journal of Applied Corporate
   Finance* (Winter 1994).

What are the patterns of corporate ownership around the world? This is the question posed by:
La Porta, R., F. Lopez-De-Silanes, and A. Shleifer. "Corporate Ownership Around the World."
   Journal of Finance 54 (1999).

Accounting Statements and Cash Flow

EXECUTIVE SUMMARY

Chapter 2 describes the basic accounting statements used for reporting corporate activity. The focus of the chapter is the practical details of cash flow. It will become obvious to you in the next several chapters that knowing how to determine cash flow helps the financial manager make better decisions. Students who have had accounting courses will not find the material new and can think of it as a review with an emphasis on finance. We will discuss cash flow further in later chapters.

2.1 THE BALANCE SHEET

The **balance sheet** is an accountant's snapshot of the firm's accounting value on a particular date, as though the firm stood momentarily still. The balance sheet has two sides: on the left are the *assets* and on the right are the *liabilities* and *stockholders' equity*. The balance sheet states what the firm owns and how it is financed. The accounting definition that underlies the balance sheet and describes the balance is

$$\text{Assets} \equiv \text{Liabilities} + \text{Stockholders' equity}$$

We have put a three-line equality in the balance equation to indicate that it must always hold, by definition. In fact, the stockholders' equity is *defined* to be the difference between the assets and the liabilities of the firm. In principle, equity is what the stockholders would have remaining after the firm discharged its obligations.

Table 2.1 gives the 20X2 and 20X1 balance sheet for the fictitious U.S. Composite Corporation. The assets in the balance sheet are listed in order by the length of time it normally would take an ongoing firm to convert them to cash. The asset side depends on the nature of the business and how management chooses to conduct it. Management must make decisions about cash versus marketable securities, credit versus cash sales, whether to make or buy commodities, whether to lease or purchase items, the types of business in which to engage, and so on. The liabilities and the stockholders' equity are listed in the order in which they must be paid.

The liabilities and stockholders' equity side reflects the types and proportions of financing, which depend on management's choice of capital structure, as between debt and equity and between current debt and long-term debt.

When analyzing a balance sheet, the financial manager should be aware of three concerns: accounting liquidity, debt versus equity, and value versus cost.

Accounting Liquidity

Accounting liquidity refers to the ease and quickness with which assets can be converted to cash. *Current assets* are the most liquid and include cash and those assets that will be turned into cash within a year from the date of the balance sheet. *Accounts receivable* are

■ TABLE 2.1   **The Balance Sheet of the U.S. Composite Corporation**

U.S. COMPOSITE CORPORATION
Balance Sheet
20X2 and 20X1
(in $ millions)

Assets	20X2	20X1	Liabilities (Debt) and Stockholders' Equity	20X2	20X1
Current assets:			Current liabilities:		
Cash and equivalents	$ 140	$ 107	Accounts payable	$ 213	$ 197
Accounts receivable	294	270	Notes payable	50	53
Inventories	269	280	Accrued expenses	223	205
Other	58	50	Total current liabilities	$ 486	$ 455
Total current assets	$ 761	$ 707			
			Long-term liabilities:		
Fixed assets:			Deferred taxes	$ 117	$ 104
Property, plant, and equipment	$1,423	$1,274	Long-term debt[1]	471	458
Less accumulated depreciation	(550)	(460)	Total long-term liabilities	$ 588	$ 562
Net property, plant, and equipment	873	814	Stockholders' equity:		
Intangible assets and others	245	221	Preferred stock	$ 39	$ 39
Total fixed assets	$1,118	$1,035	Common stock ($1 par value)	55	32
			Capital surplus	347	327
			Accumulated retained earnings	390	347
			Less treasury stock[2]	(26)	(20)
			Total equity	$ 805	$ 725
Total assets	$1,879	$1,742	Total liabilities and stockholders' equity[3]	$1,879	$1,742

Notes:

[1]Long-term debt rose by $471 million–$458 million = $13 million. This is the difference between $86 million new debt and $73 million in retirement of old debt.

[2]Treasury stock rose by $6 million. This reflects the repurchase of $6 million of U.S. Composite's company stock.

[3]U.S. Composite reports $43 million in new equity. The company issued 23 million shares at a price of $1.87. The par value of common stock increased by $23 million, and capital surplus increased by $20 million.

amounts not yet collected from customers for goods or services sold to them (after adjustment for potential bad debts). *Inventory* is composed of raw materials to be used in production, work in process, and finished goods. *Fixed assets* are the least liquid kind of assets. Tangible fixed assets include property, plant, and equipment. These assets do not convert to cash from normal business activity, and they are not usually used to pay expenses, such as payroll.

Some fixed assets are not tangible. Intangible assets have no physical existence but can be very valuable. Examples of intangible assets are the value of a trademark or the value of a patent. The more liquid a firm's assets, the less likely the firm is to experience problems meeting short-term obligations. Thus, the probability that a firm will avoid financial distress can be linked to the firm's liquidity. Unfortunately, liquid assets frequently have lower rates of return than fixed assets; for example, cash generates no investment income. To the extent a firm invests in liquid assets, it sacrifices an opportunity to invest in more profitable investment vehicles.

Debt versus Equity

Liabilities are obligations of the firm that require a payout of cash within a stipulated time period. Many liabilities involve contractual obligations to repay a stated amount and interest over a period. Thus, liabilities are debts and are frequently associated with nominally fixed cash burdens, called *debt service,* that put the firm in default of a contract if they are not paid. *Stockholders' equity* is a claim against the firm's assets that is residual and not fixed. In general terms, when the firm borrows, it gives the bondholders first claim on the firm's cash flow.[1] Bondholders can sue the firm if the firm defaults on its bond contracts. This may lead the firm to declare itself bankrupt. Stockholders' equity is the residual difference between assets and liabilities:

$$\text{Assets} - \text{Liabilities} \equiv \text{Stockholders' equity}$$

This is the stockholders' share in the firm stated in accounting terms. The accounting value of stockholders' equity increases when retained earnings are added. This occurs when the firm retains part of its earnings instead of paying them out as dividends.

Value versus Cost

The accounting value of a firm's assets is frequently referred to as the *carrying value* or the *book value* of the assets.[2] Under **generally accepted accounting principles (GAAP),** audited financial statements of firms in the United States carry the assets at cost.[3] Thus the terms *carrying value* and *book value* are unfortunate. They specifically say "value," when in fact the accounting numbers are based on cost. This misleads many readers of financial statements to think that the firm's assets are recorded at true market values. *Market value* is the price at which willing buyers and sellers trade the assets. It would be only a coincidence if accounting value and market value were the same. In fact, management's job is to create a value for the firm that is higher than its cost.

Many people use the balance sheet although the information each may wish to extract is not the same. A banker may look at a balance sheet for evidence of accounting liquidity and working capital. A supplier may also note the size of accounts payable and therefore the general promptness of payments. Many users of financial statements, including managers and investors, want to know the value of the firm, not its cost. This is not found on the balance sheet. In fact, many of the true resources of the firm do not appear on the balance sheet: good management, proprietary assets, favorable economic conditions, and so on.

CONCEPT QUESTIONS

- What is the balance-sheet equation?
- What three things should be kept in mind when looking at a balance sheet?

---

[1]Bondholders are investors in the firm's debt. They are creditors of the firm. In this discussion, the term *bondholder* means the same thing as *creditor.*

[2]Confusion often arises because many financial accounting terms have the same meaning. This presents a problem with jargon for the reader of financial statements. For example, the following terms usually refer to the same thing: assets minus liabilities, net worth, stockholders' equity, owner's equity, and equity capitalization.

[3]Formally, GAAP requires assets to be carried at the lower of cost or market value. In most instances cost is lower than market value.

2.2 THE INCOME STATEMENT

The **income statement** measures performance over a specific period of time, say, a year. The accounting definition of income is

$$\text{Revenue} - \text{Expenses} \equiv \text{Income}$$

If the balance sheet is like a snapshot, the income statement is like a video recording of what the people did between two snapshots. Table 2.2 gives the income statement for the U.S. Composite Corporation for 20X2.

The income statement usually includes several sections. The operations section reports the firm's revenues and expenses from principal operations. One number of particular importance is earnings before interest and taxes (EBIT), which summarizes earnings before taxes and financing costs. Among other things, the nonoperating section of the income statement includes all financing costs, such as interest expense. Usually a second section

■ TABLE 2.2   **The Income Statement of the U.S. Composite Corporation**

U.S. COMPOSITE CORPORATION **Income Statement** **20X2** **(in $ millions)**	
Total operating revenues	$2,262
Cost of goods sold	(1,655)
Selling, general, and administrative expenses	(327)
Depreciation	(90)
Operating income	$ 190
Other income	29
Earnings before interest and taxes (EBIT)	$ 219
Interest expense	(49)
Pretax income	$ 170
Taxes	(84)
Current: $ 71	
Deferred: $ 13	
Net income	$ 86
Retained earnings:	$ 43
Dividends:	$ 43

Notes:

1. There are 29 million shares outstanding. Earnings per share and dividends per share can be calculated as follows:

$$\text{Earnings per share} = \frac{\text{Net income}}{\text{Total shares outstanding}}$$
$$= \frac{\$86}{29}$$
$$= \$2.97 \text{ per share}$$

$$\text{Dividends per share} = \frac{\text{Dividends}}{\text{Total shares outstanding}}$$
$$= \frac{\$43}{29}$$
$$= \$1.48 \text{ per share}$$

reports as a separate item the amount of taxes levied on income. The last item on the income statement is the bottom line, or net income. Net income is frequently expressed per share of common stock, that is, earnings per share.

When analyzing an income statement, the financial manager should keep in mind GAAP, noncash items, time, and costs.

Generally Accepted Accounting Principles

Revenue is recognized on an income statement when the earnings process is virtually completed and an exchange of goods or services has occurred. Therefore, the unrealized appreciation in owning property will not be recognized as income. This provides a device for smoothing income by selling appreciated property at convenient times. For example, if the firm owns a tree farm that has doubled in value, then, in a year when its earnings from other businesses are down, it can raise overall earnings by selling some trees. The matching principle of GAAP dictates that revenues be matched with expenses. Thus, income is reported when it is earned, or accrued, even though no cash flow has necessarily occurred (for example, when goods are sold for credit, sales and profits are reported).

Noncash Items

The economic value of assets is intimately connected to their future incremental cash flows. However, cash flow does not appear on an income statement. There are several **noncash items** that are expenses against revenues, but that do not affect cash flow. The most important of these is *depreciation.* Depreciation reflects the accountant's estimate of the cost of equipment used up in the production process. For example, suppose an asset with a five-year life and no resale value is purchased for $1,000. According to accountants, the $1,000 cost must be expensed over the useful life of the asset. If straight-line depreciation is used, there will be five equal installments and $200 of depreciation expense will be incurred each year. From a finance perspective, the cost of the asset is the actual negative cash flow incurred when the asset is acquired (that is, $1,000, *not* the accountant's smoothed $200-per-year depreciation expense).

Another noncash expense is *deferred taxes.* Deferred taxes result from differences between accounting income and true taxable income.[4] Notice that the accounting tax shown on the income statement for the U.S. Composite Corporation is $84 million. It can be broken down as current taxes and deferred taxes. The current tax portion is actually sent to the tax authorities (for example, the Internal Revenue Service). The deferred tax portion is not. However, the theory is that if taxable income is less than accounting income in the current year, it will be more than accounting income later on. Consequently, the taxes that are not paid today will have to be paid in the future, and they represent a liability of the firm. This shows up on the balance sheet as deferred tax liability. From the cash flow perspective, though, deferred tax is not a cash outflow.

Time and Costs

It is often useful to think of all of future time as having two distinct parts, the *short run* and the *long run.* The short run is that period of time in which certain equipment, resources, and commitments of the firm are fixed; but the time is long enough for the firm to vary its output by using more labor and raw materials. The short run is not a precise period of time that will be the same for all industries. However, all firms making decisions in the short run have

---

[4]One situation in which taxable income may be lower than accounting income is when the firm uses accelerated depreciation expense procedures for the IRS but uses straight-line procedures allowed by GAAP for reporting purposes.

some fixed costs, that is, costs that will not change because of fixed commitments. In real business activity, examples of fixed costs are bond interest, overhead, and property taxes. Costs that are not fixed are variable. Variable costs change as the output of the firm changes; some examples are raw materials and wages for laborers on the production line.

In the long run, all costs are variable.[5] Financial accountants do not distinguish between variable costs and fixed costs. Instead, accounting costs usually fit into a classification that distinguishes product costs from period costs. Product costs are the total production costs incurred during a period—raw materials, direct labor, and manufacturing overhead—and are reported on the income statement as cost of goods sold. Both variable and fixed costs are included in product costs. Period costs are costs that are allocated to a time period; they are called *selling, general, and administrative expenses.* One period cost would be the company president's salary.

CONCEPT QUESTIONS

- What is the income statement equation?
- What are three things to keep in mind when looking at an income statement?
- What are noncash expenses?

2.3 NET WORKING CAPITAL

Net working capital is current assets minus current liabilities. Net working capital is positive when current assets are greater than current liabilities. This means the cash that will become available over the next 12 months will be greater than the cash that must be paid out. The net working capital of the U.S. Composite Corporation is $275 million in 20X2 and $252 million in 20X1:

	Current assets ($ millions)	−	Current liabilities ($ millions)	=	Net working capital ($ millions)
20X2	$761	−	$486	=	$275
20X1	707	−	455	=	252

In addition to investing in fixed assets (i.e., capital spending), a firm can invest in net working capital. This is called the *change in net working capital.* The **change in net working capital** in 20X2 is the difference between the net working capital in 20X2 and 20X1; that is, $275 million − $252 million = $23 million. The change in net working capital is usually positive in a growing firm.

CONCEPT QUESTIONS

- What is net working capital?
- What is the change in net working capital?

2.4 FINANCIAL CASH FLOW

Perhaps the most important item that can be extracted from financial statements is the actual **cash flow** of the firm. There is an official accounting statement called the *statement of cash flows.* This statement helps to explain the change in accounting cash and equivalents,

---

[5]When one famous economist was asked about the difference between the long run and the short run, he said, "In the long run we are all dead."

which for U.S. Composite is $33 million in 20X2. (See Appendix 2B.) Notice in Table 2.1 that Cash and equivalents increases from $107 million in 20X1 to $140 million in 20X2. However, we will look at cash flow from a different perspective, the perspective of finance. In finance the value of the firm is its ability to generate financial cash flow. (We will talk more about financial cash flow in Chapter 7.)

The first point we should mention is that cash flow is not the same as net working capital. For example, increasing inventory requires using cash. Because both inventories and cash are current assets, this does not affect net working capital. In this case, an increase in a particular net working capital account, such as inventory, is associated with decreasing cash flow.

Just as we established that the value of a firm's assets is always equal to the value of the liabilities and the value of the equity, the cash flows received from the firm's assets (that is, its operating activities), CF(A), must equal the cash flows to the firm's creditors, CF(B), and equity investors, CF(S):

$$CF(A) \equiv CF(B) + CF(S)$$

The first step in determining cash flows of the firm is to figure out the *cash flow from operations*. As can be seen in Table 2.3, operating cash flow is the cash flow generated by business activities, including sales of goods and services. Operating cash flow reflects tax payments, but not financing, capital spending, or changes in net working capital.

	In $ Millions
Earnings before interest and taxes	$219
Depreciation	90
Current taxes	(71)
Operating cash flow	$238

Another important component of cash flow involves *changes in fixed assets*. For example, when U.S. Composite sold its power systems subsidiary in 20X2 it generated $25 in cash flow. The net change in fixed assets equals sales of fixed assets minus the acquisition of fixed assets. The result is the cash flow used for capital spending:

Acquisition of fixed assets	$198	
Sales of fixed assets	(25)	
Capital spending	$173	(= $149 + $24 = increase in property, plant, and equipment + increase in intangible assets)

Cash flows are also used for making investments in net working capital. In the U.S. Composite Corporation in 20X2, *additions to net working capital* are

Additions to net working capital	$23

Total cash flows generated by the firm's assets are the sum of

Operating cash flow	$238
Capital spending	(173)
Additions to net working capital	(23)
Total cash flow of the firm	$42

■ TABLE 2.3 **Financial Cash Flow of the U.S. Composite Corporation**

U.S. COMPOSITE CORPORATION Financial Cash Flow 20X2 (in $ millions)	
Cash Flow of the Firm	

Operating cash flow
  (Earnings before interest and taxes
  plus depreciation minus taxes)
	$238

Capital spending
  (Acquisitions of fixed assets
  minus sales of fixed assets)
	(173)

Additions to net working capital	(23)
Total	$ 42
Cash Flow to Investors in the Firm	

Debt
  (Interest plus retirement of debt
  minus long-term debt financing)
	$ 36

Equity
  (Dividends plus repurchase of
  equity minus new equity financing)
	6

Total	$ 42

The total outgoing cash flow of the firm can be separated into cash flow paid to creditors and cash flow paid to stockholders. The cash flow paid to creditors represents a regrouping of the data in Table 2.3 and an explicit recording of interest expense. Creditors are paid an amount generally referred to as *debt service*. Debt service is interest payments plus repayments of principal (that is, retirement of debt).

An important source of cash flow is from selling new debt. U.S. Composite's long-term debt increased by $13 million (the difference between $86 million in new debt and $73 million in retirement of old debt.[6]) Thus, an increase in long-term debt is the net effect of new borrowing and repayment of maturing obligations plus interest expense.

Cash Flow Paid to Creditors (in $ millions)	
Interest	$49
Retirement of debt	73
Debt service	122
Proceeds from long-term debt sales	(86)
Total	$36

---

[6]New debt and the retirement of old debt are usually found in the "notes" to the balance sheet.

Cash flow of the firm also is paid to the stockholders. It is the net effect of paying dividends plus repurchasing outstanding shares of stock and issuing new shares of stock.

Cash Flow to Stockholders
(in $ millions)

Dividends	$43
Repurchase of stock	6
Cash to stockholders	49
Proceeds from new stock issue	(43)
Total	$ 6

Some important observations can be drawn from our discussion of cash flow:

1. Several types of cash flow are relevant to understanding the financial situation of the firm. **Operating cash flow,** defined as earnings before interest and depreciation minus taxes, measures the cash generated from operations not counting capital spending or working capital requirements. It should usually be positive; a firm is in trouble if operating cash flow is negative for a long time because the firm is not generating enough cash to pay operating costs. **Total cash flow of the firm** includes adjustments for capital spending and additions to net working capital. It will frequently be negative. When a firm is growing at a rapid rate, the spending on inventory and fixed assets can be higher than cash flow from sales.[7]

2. Net income is not cash flow. The net income of the U.S. Composite Corporation in 20X2 was $86 million, whereas cash flow was $42 million. The two numbers are not usually the same. In determining the economic and financial condition of a firm, cash flow is more revealing.

CONCEPT QUESTIONS
?

- How is cash flow different from changes in net working capital?
- What is the difference between operating cash flow and total cash flow of the firm?

2.5 SUMMARY AND CONCLUSIONS

Besides introducing you to corporate accounting, the purpose of this chapter has been to teach you how to determine cash flow from the accounting statements of a typical company.

1. Cash flow is generated by the firm and paid to creditors and shareholders. It can be classified as:
   a. Cash flow from operations.
   b. Cash flow from changes in fixed assets.
   c. Cash flow from changes in working capital.

---

[7]Sometimes financial analysts refer to a firm's **free cash flow.** Free cash flow is the cash flow in excess of that required to fund profitable capital projects. We call free cash flow the *total cash flow* of the firm.

2. Calculations of cash flow are not difficult, but they require care and particular attention to detail in properly accounting for noncash expenses such as depreciation and deferred taxes. It is especially important that you do not confuse cash flow with changes in net working capital and net income.

KEY TERMS

Balance sheet 22	Income statement 25
Cash flow 27	Noncash items 26
Change in net working capital 27	Operating cash flow 30
Free cash flow 30	Total cash flow of the firm 30
Generally accepted accounting principles (GAAP) 24	

SUGGESTED READING

There are many excellent textbooks on accounting. The one that we have found helpful is:
Kieso, D. E., and J. J. Weygandt. *Intermediate Accounting,* 7th ed. New York: John Wiley. 1992.

QUESTIONS AND PROBLEMS

The Balance Sheet

2.1 Prepare a December 31 balance sheet using the following data:

Cash	$ 4,000
Patents	82,000
Accounts payable	6,000
Accounts receivable	8,000
Taxes payable	2,000
Machinery	34,000
Bonds payable	7,000
Accumulated retained earnings	6,000
Capital surplus	19,000

The par value of the firm's common stock is $100.

2.2 The following table presents the long-term liabilities and stockholders' equity of Information Control Corp. of one year ago.

Long-term debt	$50,000,000
Preferred stock	30,000,000
Common stock	100,000,000
Retained earnings	20,000,000

During the past year, Information Control issued $10 million of new common stock. The firm generated $5 million of net income and paid $3 million of dividends. Construct today's balance sheet reflecting the changes that occurred at Information Control Corp. during the year.

The Income Statement

2.3 Prepare an income statement using the following data.

Sales	$500,000
Cost of goods sold	200,000
Administrative expenses	100,000
Interest expense	50,000

The firm's tax rate is 34 percent.

2.4 The Flying Lion Corporation reported the following data on the income statement of one of its divisions. Flying Lion Corporation has other profitable divisions.

	20X2	20X1
Net sales	$800,000	$500,000
Cost of goods sold	560,000	320,000
Operating expenses	75,000	56,000
Depreciation	300,000	200,000
Tax rate (%)	30	30

a. Prepare an income statement for each year.
b. Determine the operating cash flow during each year.

Financial Cash Flow

2.5 What are the differences between accounting profit and cash flow?

2.6 During 1998, the Senbet Discount Tire Company had gross sales of $1 million. The firm's cost of goods sold and selling expenses were $300,000 and $200,000, respectively. These figures do not include depreciation. Senbet also had notes payable of $1 million. These notes carried an interest rate of 10 percent. Depreciation was $100,000. Senbet's tax rate in 1998 was 35 percent.
a. What was Senbet's net operating income?
b. What were the firm's earnings before taxes?
c. What was Senbet's net income?
d. What was Senbet's operating cash flow?

2.7 The Stancil Corporation provided the following current information.

Proceeds from short-term borrowing	$ 6,000
Proceeds from long-term borrowing	20,000
Proceeds from the sale of common stock	1,000
Purchases of fixed assets	1,000
Purchases of inventories	4,000
Payment of dividends	22,000

Determine the cash flow for the Stancil Corporation.

2.8 Ritter Corporation's accountants prepared the following financial statements for year-end 20X2.

RITTER CORPORATION
Income Statement
20X2

Revenue	$400
Expenses	250
Depreciation	50
Net income	$100
Dividends	$ 50

RITTER CORPORATION
Balance Sheets
December 31

	20X2	20X1
Assets		
Current assets	$150	$100
Net fixed assets	200	100
Total assets	$350	$200
Liabilities and Equity		
Current liabilities	$ 75	$ 50
Long-term debt	75	0
Stockholders' equity	200	150
Total liabilities and equity	$350	$200

    a. Determine the change in net working capital in 20X2.
    b. Determine the cash flow during the year 20X2.

Appendix 2A Financial Statement Analysis

The objective of this appendix is to show how to rearrange information from financial statements into financial ratios that provide information about five areas of financial performance:

1. *Short-term solvency*—the ability of the firm to meet its short-run obligations.
2. *Activity*—the ability of the firm to control its investment in assets.
3. *Financial leverage*—the extent to which a firm relies on debt financing.
4. *Profitability*—the extent to which a firm is profitable.
5. *Value*—the value of the firm.

    Financial statements cannot provide the answers to the preceding five measures of performance. However, management must constantly evaluate how well the firm is doing, and financial statements provide useful information. The financial statements of the U.S. Composite Corporation, which appear in Tables 2.1, 2.2, and 2.3, provide the information for the examples that follow. (Monetary values are given in $ millions.)

Short-Term Solvency

Ratios of short-term solvency measure the ability of the firm to meet recurring financial obligations (that is, to pay its bills). To the extent a firm has sufficient cash flow, it will be able to avoid defaulting on its financial obligations and, thus, avoid experiencing financial distress. Accounting liquidity measures short-term solvency and is often associated with net working capital, the difference between current assets and current liabilities. Recall that current liabilities are debts that are due within one year from the date of the balance sheet. The basic source from which to pay these debts is current assets.

    The most widely used measures of accounting liquidity are the current ratio and the quick ratio.

Current Ratio   To find the current ratio, divide current assets by current liabilities. For the U.S. Composite Corporation, the figure for 20X2 is

$$\text{Current ratio} = \frac{\text{Total current assets}}{\text{Total current liabilities}} = \frac{761}{486} = 1.57$$

If a firm is having financial difficulty, it may not be able to pay its bills (accounts payable) on time or it may need to extend its bank credit (notes payable). As a consequence, current liabilities may rise faster than current assets and the current ratio may fall. This may be the first sign of financial trouble. Of course, a firm's current ratio should be calculated over several years for historical perspective, and it should be compared to the current ratios of other firms with similar operating activities.

Quick Ratio   The quick ratio is computed by subtracting inventories from current assets and dividing the difference (called *quick assets*) by current liabilities:

$$\text{Quick ratio} = \frac{\text{Quick assets}}{\text{Total current liabilities}} = \frac{492}{486} = 1.01$$

Quick assets are those current assets that are quickly convertible into cash. Inventories are the least liquid current assets. Many financial analysts believe it is important to determine a firm's ability to pay off current liabilities without relying on the sale of inventories.

Activity

Ratios of activity are constructed to measure how effectively the firm's assets are being managed. The level of a firm's investment in assets depends on many factors. For example, Toys 'Я Us might have a large stock of toys at the peak of the Christmas season; yet that same inventory in January would be undesirable. How can the appropriate level of investment in assets be measured? One logical starting point is to compare assets with sales for the year to arrive at turnover. The idea is to find out how effectively assets are used to generate sales.

Total Asset Turnover   The total asset turnover ratio is determined by dividing total operating revenues for the accounting period by the average of total assets. The total asset turnover ratio for the U.S. Composite Corporation for 20X2 is

$$\text{Total asset turnover}[8] = \frac{\text{Total operating revenues}}{\text{Total assets (average)}} = \frac{2{,}262}{1{,}810.5} = 1.25$$

$$\text{Average total assets} = \frac{1{,}879 + 1{,}742}{2} = 1{,}810.5$$

This ratio is intended to indicate how effectively a firm is using all of its assets. If the asset turnover ratio is high, the firm is presumably using its assets effectively in generating sales. If the ratio is low, the firm is not using its assets to their capacity and must either increase sales or dispose of some of the assets. One problem in interpreting this ratio is that it is maximized by using older assets because their accounting value is lower than newer assets. Also, firms with relatively small investments in fixed assets, such as retail and wholesale trade firms, tend to have high ratios of total asset turnover when compared with firms that require a large investment in fixed assets, such as manufacturing firms.

Receivables Turnover   The ratio of receivables turnover is calculated by dividing sales by average receivables during the accounting period. If the number of days in the year (365) is divided by the receivables turnover ratio, the average collection period can be determined. Net receivables are used for these calculations.[9] The receivables turnover ratio and average collection period for the U.S. Composite Corporation are

$$\text{Receivables turnover} = \frac{\text{Total operating revenues}}{\text{Receivables (average)}} = \frac{2{,}262}{282} = 8.02$$

$$\text{Average receivables} = \frac{294 + 270}{2} = 282$$

$$\text{Average collection period} = \frac{\text{Days in period}}{\text{Receivables turnover}} = \frac{365}{8.02} = 45.5 \text{ days}$$

The receivables turnover ratio and the average collection period provide some information on the success of the firm in managing its investment in accounts receivable. The actual value of these ratios reflects the firm's credit policy. If a firm has a liberal credit policy, the amount of its receivables will be higher than would otherwise be the case. One common rule of thumb that financial analysts use is that the average collection period of a firm should not exceed the time allowed for payment in the credit terms by more than 10 days.

---

[8]Notice that we use an average of total assets in our calculation of total asset turnover. Many financial analysts use the end of period total asset amount for simplicity.

[9]Net receivables are determined after an allowance for potential bad debts.

Inventory Turnover   The ratio of inventory turnover is calculated by dividing the cost of goods sold by average inventory. Because inventory is always stated in terms of historical cost, it must be divided by cost of goods sold instead of sales (sales include a margin for profit and are not commensurate with inventory). The number of days in the year divided by the ratio of inventory turnover yields the ratio of days in inventory. The ratio of days in inventory is the number of days it takes to get goods produced and sold; it is called ***shelf life*** for retail and wholesale trade firms. The inventory ratios for the U.S. Composite Corporation are

$$\text{Inventory turnover} = \frac{\text{Cost of goods sold}}{\text{Inventory (average)}} = \frac{1,655}{274.5} = 6.03$$

$$\text{Average inventory} = \frac{269 + 280}{2} = 274.5$$

$$\text{Days in inventory} = \frac{\text{Days in period}}{\text{Inventory turnover}} = \frac{365}{6.03} = 60.5 \text{ days}$$

The inventory ratios measure how quickly inventory is produced and sold. They are significantly affected by the production technology of goods being manufactured. It takes longer to produce a gas turbine engine than a loaf of bread. The ratios also are affected by the perishability of the finished goods. A large increase in the ratio of days in inventory could suggest an ominously high inventory of unsold finished goods or a change in the firm's product mix to goods with longer production periods.

The method of inventory valuation can materially affect the computed inventory ratios. Thus, financial analysts should be aware of the different inventory valuation methods and how they might affect the ratios.

Financial Leverage

Financial leverage is related to the extent to which a firm relies on debt financing rather than equity. Measures of financial leverage are tools in determining the probability that the firm will default on its debt contracts. The more debt a firm has, the more likely it is that the firm will become unable to fulfill its contractual obligations. In other words, too much debt can lead to a higher probability of insolvency and financial distress.

On the positive side, debt is an important form of financing, and provides a significant tax advantage because interest payments are tax deductible. If a firm uses debt, creditors and equity investors may have conflicts of interest. Creditors may want the firm to invest in less risky ventures than those the equity investors prefer.

Debt Ratio   The debt ratio is calculated by dividing total debt by total assets. We can also use several other ways to express the extent to which a firm uses debt, such as the debt-to-equity ratio and the equity multiplier (that is, total assets divided by equity). The debt ratios for the U.S. Composite Corporation for 20X2 are

$$\text{Debt ratio} = \frac{\text{Total debt}}{\text{Total assets}} = \frac{1,074}{1,879} = 0.57$$

$$\text{Debt-to-equity ratio} = \frac{\text{Total debt}}{\text{Total equity}} = \frac{1,074}{805} = 1.33$$

$$\text{Equity multiplier} = \frac{\text{Total assets}}{\text{Total equity}} = \frac{1,879}{805} = 2.33$$

Debt ratios provide information about protection of creditors from insolvency and the ability of firms to obtain additional financing for potentially attractive investment opportunities. However, debt is carried on the balance sheet simply as the unpaid balance. Consequently, no adjustment is made for the current level of interest rates (which may be higher or lower than when the debt was originally issued) or risk. Thus, the accounting value of debt may differ substantially from its market value. Some forms of debt may not appear on the balance sheet at all, such as pension liabilities or lease obligations.

Interest Coverage   The ratio of interest coverage is calculated by dividing earnings (before interest and taxes) by interest. This ratio emphasizes the ability of the firm to generate enough income to cover interest expense. This ratio for the U.S. Composite Corporation is

$$\text{Interest coverage} = \frac{\text{Earnings before interest and taxes}}{\text{Interest expense}} = \frac{219}{49} = 4.5$$

Interest expense is an obstacle that a firm must surmount if it is to avoid default. The ratio of interest coverage is directly connected to the ability of the firm to pay interest. However, it would probably make sense to add depreciation to income in computing this ratio and to include other financing expenses, such as payments of principal and lease payments.

A large debt burden is a problem only if the firm's cash flow is insufficient to make the required debt service payments. This is related to the uncertainty of future cash flows. Firms with predictable cash flows are frequently said to have more *debt capacity* than firms with high, uncertain cash flows. Therefore, it makes sense to compute the variability of the firm's cash flows. One possible way to do this is to calculate the standard deviation of cash flows relative to the average cash flow.

Profitability

One of the most difficult attributes of a firm to conceptualize and to measure is profitability. In a general sense, accounting profits are the difference between revenues and costs. Unfortunately, there is no completely unambiguous way to know when a firm is profitable. At best, a financial analyst can measure current or past accounting profitability. Many business opportunities, however, involve sacrificing current profits for future profits. For example, all new products require large start-up costs and, as a consequence, produce low initial profits. Thus, current profits can be a poor reflection of true future profitability. Another problem with accounting-based measures of profitability is that they ignore risk. It would be false to conclude that two firms with identical current profits were equally profitable if the risk of one was greater than the other.

The most important conceptual problem with accounting measures of profitability is they do not give us a benchmark for making comparisons. In general, a firm is profitable in the economic sense only if its profitability is greater than investors can achieve on their own in the capital markets.

Profit Margin   Profit margins are computed by dividing profits by total operating revenue and thus they express profits as a percentage of total operating revenue. The most important margin is the net profit margin. The net profit margin for the U.S. Composite Corporation is

$$\text{Net profit margin} = \frac{\text{Net income}}{\text{Total operating revenue}} = \frac{86}{2,262} = 0.038 \ (3.8\%)$$

$$\text{Gross profit margin} = \frac{\text{Earnings before interest and taxes}}{\text{Total operating revenues}} = \frac{219}{2,262} = 0.097 \ (9.7\%)$$

In general, profit margins reflect the firm's ability to produce a product or service at a low cost or a high price. Profit margins are not direct measures of profitability because they are based on total operating revenue, not on the investment made in assets by the firm or the equity investors. Trade firms tend to have low margins and service firms tend to have high margins.

Return on Assets   One common measure of managerial performance is the ratio of income to average total assets, both before tax and after tax. These ratios for the U.S. Composite Corporation for 20X2 are

$$\text{Net return on assets} = \frac{\text{Net income}}{\text{Average total assets}} = \frac{86}{1,810.5} = 0.0475 \ (4.75\%)$$

$$\text{Gross return on assets} = \frac{\text{Earnings before interest and taxes}}{\text{Average total assets}} = \frac{219}{1,810.5} = 0.121 \ (12.1\%)$$

One of the most interesting aspects of return on assets (ROA) is how some financial ratios can be linked together to compute ROA. One implication of this is usually referred to as the *DuPont system of financial control.* This system highlights the fact that ROA can be expressed in terms of the profit margin and asset turnover. The basic components of the system are as follows:

ROA =	Profit margin	$\times$	Asset turnover
ROA (net) =	$\dfrac{\text{Net income}}{\text{Total operating revenue}}$	$\times$	$\dfrac{\text{Total operating revenue}}{\text{Average total assets}}$
0.0475 =	0.038	$\times$	1.25
ROA (gross) =	$\dfrac{\text{Earnings before interest and taxes}}{\text{Total operating revenue}}$	$\times$	$\dfrac{\text{Total operating revenue}}{\text{Average total assets}}$
0.121 =	0.097	$\times$	1.25

Firms can increase ROA by increasing profit margins or asset turnover. Of course, competition limits their ability to do so simultaneously. Thus, firms tend to face a trade-off between turnover and margin. In retail trade, for example, mail-order outfits such as L. L. Bean have low margins and high turnover, whereas high-quality jewelry stores such as Tiffany's have high margins and low turnover.

It is often useful to describe financial strategies in terms of margins and turnover. Suppose a firm selling pneumatic equipment is thinking about providing customers with more liberal credit terms. This will probably decrease asset turnover (because receivables would increase more than sales). Thus, the margins will have to go up to keep ROA from falling.

Return on Equity   This ratio (ROE) is defined as net income (after interest and taxes) divided by average common stockholders' equity, which for the U.S. Composite Corporation is

$$\text{ROE} = \frac{\text{Net income}}{\text{Average stockholders' equity}} = \frac{86}{765} = 0.112 \ (11.27\%)$$

$$\text{Average stockholders' equity} = \frac{805 + 725}{2} = 765$$

The most important difference between ROA and ROE is due to financial leverage. To see this, consider the following breakdown of ROE:

ROE =	Profit margin	$\times$	Asset turnover	$\times$	Equity multiplier
=	$\dfrac{\text{Net income}}{\text{Total operating revenue}}$	$\times$	$\dfrac{\text{Total operating revenue}}{\text{Average total assets}}$	$\times$	$\dfrac{\text{Average total assets}}{\text{Average stockholders' equity}}$
0.112 =	0.038	$\times$	1.25	$\times$	2.36

From the preceding numbers, it would appear that financial leverage always magnifies ROE. Actually, this occurs only when ROA (gross) is greater than the interest rate on debt.

Payout Ratio   The payout ratio is the proportion of net income paid out in cash dividends. For the U.S. Composite Corporation

$$\text{Payout ratio} = \frac{\text{Cash dividends}}{\text{Net income}} = \frac{43}{86} = 0.5$$

The *retention ratio* for the U.S. Composite Corporation is

$$\text{Retention ratio} = \frac{\text{Retained earnings}}{\text{Net income}} = \frac{43}{86} = 0.5$$

$$\text{Retained earnings} = \text{Net income} - \text{Dividends}$$

The Sustainable Growth Rate

One ratio that is very helpful in financial analysis is called the sustainable growth rate. It is the maximum rate of growth a firm can maintain without increasing its financial leverage and using internal equity only. The precise value of sustainable growth can be calculated as

$$\text{Sustainable growth rate} = \text{ROE} \times \text{Retention ratio}$$

For the U.S. Composite Company, ROE is 11.2 percent. The retention ratio is 1/2, so we can calculate the sustainable growth rate as

$$\text{Sustainable growth rate} = 11.2 \times (1/2) = 5.6\%$$

The U.S. Composite Corporation can expand at a maximum rate of 5.6 percent per year with no external equity financing or without increasing financial leverage. (We discuss sustainable growth in Chapters 5 and 26.)

Market Value Ratios

We can learn many things from a close examination of balance sheets and income statements. However, one very important characteristic of a firm that cannot be found on an accounting statement is its market value.

Market Price   The market price of a share of common stock is the price that buyers and sellers establish when they trade the stock. The market value of the common equity of a firm is the market price of a share of common stock multiplied by the number of shares outstanding.

Sometimes the words "fair market value" are used to describe market prices. *Fair market value* is the amount at which common stock would change hands between a willing buyer and a willing seller, both having knowledge of the relevant facts. Thus, market prices give guesses about the true worth of the assets of a firm. In an efficient stock market, market prices reflect all relevant facts about firms, and thus market prices reveal the true value of the firm's underlying assets.

The market value of IBM is many times greater than that of Apple Computer. This may suggest nothing more than the fact that IBM is a bigger firm than Apple (hardly a surprising revelation). Financial analysts construct ratios to extract information that is independent of a firm's size.

Price-to-Earnings (P/E) Ratio   One way to calculate the P/E ratio is to divide the current market price by the earnings per share of common stock for the latest year. The P/E ratios of some of the largest firms in the United States and Japan are as follows:

P/E Ratios
2000

United States		Japan	
AT&T	24	Nippon Telegraph & Telephone	53
General Motors	8	Toyota Motor	44
Hewlett Packard	43	Sony	72

As can be seen, some firms have high P/E ratios (Sony, for example) and some firms have low ones (General Motors).

Dividend Yield   The dividend yield is calculated by annualizing the last observed dividend payment of a firm and dividing by the current market price:

$$\text{Dividend yield} = \frac{\text{Dividend per share}}{\text{Market price per share}}$$

The dividend yields for several large firms in the United States and Japan are:

Dividend Yield (%)
2000

United States		Japan	
AT&T	0.9	Nippon Telegraph & Telephone	0.4
General Motors	2.0	Toyota Motor	0.5
Hewlett Packard	0.6	Sony	0.3

Dividend yields are related to the market's perception of future growth prospects for firms. Firms with high growth prospects will generally have lower dividend yields.

Market-to-Book (M/B) Value and the **Q** ***ratio***   The market-to-book value ratio is calculated by dividing the market price per share by the book value per share.

The market-to-book ratios of several of the largest firms in the United States and Japan are:

Market-to-Book Ratios
2000

United States		Japan	
AT&T	1	Nippon Telegraph & Telephone	3.4
General Motors	2.4	Toyota Motor	2.8
Hewlett Packard	8	Sony	3.5

There is another ratio, called *Tobin's Q,* that is very much like the M/B ratio.[10] Tobin's Q ratio divides the market value of all of the firm's debt plus equity by the replacement value of the firm's assets. The Q ratios for several firms are:

		Q Ratio[11]
High Qs	Coca-Cola	4.2
	IBM	4.2
Low Qs	National Steel	0.53
	U.S. Steel	0.61

---

[10]Kee H. Chung and Stephen W. Pruitt, "A Simple Approximation of Tobin's Q," *Financial Management* Vol 23, No. 3 (Autumn 1994).

[11]E. B. Lindberg and S. Ross, "Tobin's Q and Industrial Organization," *Journal of Business* 54 (January 1981).

The *Q* ratio differs from the M/B ratio in that the *Q* ratio uses market value of the debt plus equity. It also uses the replacement value of all assets and not the historical cost value.

It should be obvious that if a firm has a *Q* ratio above 1 it has an incentive to invest that is probably greater than a firm with a *Q* ratio below 1. Firms with high *Q* ratios tend to be those firms with attractive investment opportunities or a significant competitive advantage.

Summary and Conclusions

Much research indicates that accounting statements provide important information about the value of the firm. Financial analysts and managers learn how to rearrange financial statements to squeeze out the maximum amount of information. In particular, analysts and managers use financial ratios to summarize the firm's liquidity, activity, financial leverage, and profitability. When possible, they also use market values. This appendix describes the most popular financial ratios. You should keep in mind the following points when trying to interpret financial statements:

1. Measures of profitability such as return on equity suffer from several potential deficiencies as indicators of performance. They do not take into account the risk or timing of cash flows.
2. Financial ratios are linked to one another. For example, return on equity is determined from the profit margins, the asset turnover ratio, and the financial leverage.

Appendix 2B Statement of Cash Flows

There is an official accounting statement called the statement of cash flows. This statement helps explain the change in accounting cash, which for U.S. Composite is $33 million in 20X2. It is very useful in understanding financial cash flow. Notice in Table 2.1 that cash increases from $107 million in 20X1 to $140 million in 20X2.

The first step in determining the change in cash is to figure out cash flow from operating activities. This is the cash flow that results from the firm's normal activities producing and selling goods and services. The second step is to make an adjustment for cash flow from investing activities. The final step is to make an adjustment for cash flow from financing activities. Financing activities are the net payments to creditors and owners (excluding interest expense) made during the year.

The three components of the statement of cash flows are determined below.

Cash Flow from Operating Activities

To calculate cash flow from operating activities we start with net income. Net income can be found on the income statement and is equal to 86. We now need to add back noncash expenses and adjust for changes in current assets and liabilities (other than cash). The result is cash flow from operating activities.

U.S. COMPOSITE CORPORATION
Cash Flow from Operating Activities
20X2
(in $ millions)

Net income	86
Depreciation	90
Deferred taxes	13
Change in assets and liabilities	
Accounts receivable	(24)
Inventories	11
Accounts payable	16
Accrued expense	18
Notes payable	(3)
Other	(8)
Cash flow from operating activities	199

Cash Flow from Investing Activities

Cash flow from investing activities involves changes in capital assets: acquisition of fixed assets and sales of fixed assets (i.e., net capital expenditures). The result for U.S. Composite is below.

U.S. COMPOSITE CORPORATION
Cash Flow from Investing Activities
20X2
(in $ millions)

Acquisition of fixed assets	(198)
Sales of fixed assets	25
Cash flow from investing activities	(173)

Cash Flow from Financing Activities

Cash flows to and from creditors and owners include changes in equity and debt.

U.S. COMPOSITE CORPORATION
Cash Flow from Financing Activities
20X2
(in $ millions)

Retirement of debt (includes notes)	$(73)
Proceeds from long-term debt sales	86
Dividends	(43)
Repurchase of stock	(6)
Proceeds from new stock issue	43
Cash flow from financing activities	$ 7

The statement of cash flows is the addition of cash flows from operations, cash flows from investing activities, and cash flows from financing activities, and is produced in Table 2.4. There is a close relationship between the official accounting statement called the statement of cash flows and the total cash flow of the firm used in finance. The difference between cash flow from financing activities and total cash flow of the firm (see Table 2.3) is interest expense.

■ TABLE 2A.4 **Statement of Consolidated Cash Flows of the U.S. Composite Corporation**

U.S. COMPOSITE CORPORATION
Statement of Cash Flows
20X2
(in $ millions)

Operations	
Net income	$ 86
Depreciation	90
Deferred taxes	13
Changes in assets and liabilities	
Accounts receivable	(24)
Inventories	11
Accounts payable	16
Accrued expenses	18
Notes payable	(3)
Other	(8)
Total cash flow from operations	$ 199
Investing activities	
Acquisition of fixed assets	$(198)
Sales of fixed assets	25
Total cash flow from investing activities	$(173)
Financing activities	
Retirement of debt (including notes)	$ (73)
Proceeds of long-term debt	86
Dividends	(43)
Repurchase of stock	(6)
Proceeds from new stock issues	43
Total cash flow from financing activities	$ 7
Change in cash (on the balance sheet)	$ 33

Appendix 2C U.S. FEDERAL TAX RATES

As of the printing date of this text, the following United States federal tax rules apply.

1. The top marginal rate for corporations is 39 percent (see Table 2.5). The highest marginal rate for individuals is 39.6 percent (see Table 2.6).

2. Short-term realized capital gains and ordinary income are taxed at the corporation's or individual's marginal rate.

3. For individuals, long-term capital gains (in excess of long-term and short-term capital losses) are taxed at a preferential rate. Generally, the top rate for long-term capital gains is 20 percent for capital assets held more than 18 months and 28 percent for capital assets held between one year and 18 months. For taxpayers in the 15 percent bracket, the rate is 15 percent for capital assets held between 12 and 18 months and 10 percent for assets held longer than 18 months.

■ TABLE 2A.5 **Corporation Income Tax Rates for 2000**

Corporations Taxable Income Over	Not Over	Tax Rate
$ 0	$ 50,000	15%
50,000	75,000	25
75,000	100,000	34
100,000	335,000	39
335,000	10,000,000	34
10,000,000	15,000,000	35
15,000,000	18,333,333	38
18,333,333	—	35

■ TABLE 2A.6 **Tax Rates for Married Individuals Filing Jointly and Surviving Spouses—2000**

Taxable Income				
Over	But Not Over	Pay	+ Percent on Excess	Of the Amount Over
$ 0	$ 41,200	$ 0	15%	$ 0
41,200	99,600	6,180.00	28	41,200
99,600	151,750	22,532.00	31	99,600
151,750	271,050	38,698.50	36	151,750
271,050	—	81,646.50	39.6	271,050

4. Dividends received by a U.S. corporation are 100 percent exempt from taxation if the dividend-paying corporation is fully owned by the other corporation. The exemption is 80 percent if the receiving corporation owns between 20 and 80 percent of the paying corporation. In all other cases, the exemption is 70 percent.

Alternative Minimum Tax (AMT)

Corporations and individuals must pay either their regularly calculated tax or an alternative minimum tax, whichever is higher. The alternative minimum tax is calculated with lower rates (either 26 or 28 percent for individuals or 20 percent for corporations) applied to a broader base of income. The broader base is determined by taking taxable income and adding back certain tax preference items, e.g., accelerated depreciation, which reduce regular taxable income. A corporation which had average gross receipts of less than $5 million for calendar years 1998 through 2000 is exempt from the alternative minimum tax as long as average gross receipts do not exceed $7.5 million.

Tax Operating Loss Carrybacks and Carryforwards

The federal tax law permits corporations to carry back net operating losses two years and to carry forward net operating losses for 20 years.

Value and Capital Budgeting

Firms and individuals invest in a large variety of assets. Some are real assets such as machinery and land, and some are financial assets such as stocks and bonds. The object of an investment is to maximize the value of the investment. In the simplest terms, this means to find assets that have more value to the firm than they cost. To do this we need a theory of value. We develop a theory of value in Part II.

Finance is the study of markets and instruments that deal with cash flows over time. In Chapter 3 we describe how financial markets allow us to determine the value of financial instruments. We study some stylized examples of money over time and show why financial markets and financial instruments are created. We introduce the basic principles of rational decision making. We apply these principles to a two-period investment. Here we introduce one of the most important ideas in finance: net present value (NPV). We show why net present value is useful and the conditions that make it applicable.

In Chapter 4 we extend the concept of net present value to more than one time period. The mathematics of compounding and discounting are presented. In Chapter 5 we apply net present value to bonds and stocks. This is a very important chapter because net present value can be used to determine the value of a wide variety of financial instruments.

Although we have made a strong case for using the NPV rule in Chapters 3 and 4, Chapter 6 presents four other rules: the payback rule, the accounting-rate-of-return rule, the internal rate of return (IRR), and the profitability index. Each of these alternatives has some redeeming features, but these qualities aren't sufficient to let any of the alternatives replace the NPV rule.

In Chapter 7 we analyze how to estimate the cash flows required for capital budgeting. We start the chapter with a discussion of the concept of incremental cash flows—the difference between the cash flows for the firm with and without the project. Chapter 8 focuses on assessing the reliability and reasonableness of estimates of NPV. The chapter introduces techniques for dealing with uncertain incremental cash flows in capital budgeting, including break-even analysis, decision trees, and sensitivity analysis.

CHAPTER 3

Financial Markets and Net Present Value: First Principles of Finance (Advanced)

EXECUTIVE SUMMARY

Finance refers to the process by which special markets deal with cash flows over time. These markets are called *financial markets*. Making investment and financing decisions requires an understanding of the basic economic principles of financial markets. This introductory chapter describes a financial market as one that makes it possible for individuals and corporations to borrow and lend. As a consequence, financial markets can be used by individuals to adjust their patterns of consumption over time and by corporations to adjust their patterns of investment spending over time. The main point of this chapter is that individuals and corporations can use the financial markets to help them make investment decisions. We introduce one of the most important ideas in finance: net present value.

3.1 THE FINANCIAL MARKET ECONOMY

Financial markets develop to facilitate borrowing and lending between individuals. Here we talk about how this happens. Suppose we describe the economic circumstances of two people, Tom and Leslie. Both Tom and Leslie have current income of $100,000. Tom is a very patient person, and some people call him a miser. He wants to consume only $50,000 of current income and save the rest. Leslie is a very impatient person, and some people call her extravagant. She wants to consume $150,000 this year. Tom and Leslie have different intertemporal consumption preferences.

Such preferences are personal matters and have more to do with psychology than with finance. However, it seems that Tom and Leslie could strike a deal: Tom could give up some of his income this year in exchange for future income that Leslie can promise to give him. Tom can *lend* $50,000 to Leslie, and Leslie can *borrow* $50,000 from Tom.

Suppose that they do strike this deal, with Tom giving up $50,000 this year in exchange for $55,000 next year. This is illustrated in Figure 3.1 with the basic cash flow time chart, a representation of the timing and amount of the cash flows. The cash flows that are received are represented by an arrow pointing up from the point on the time line at which the cash flow occurs. The cash flows paid out are represented by an arrow pointing down. In other words, for each dollar Tom trades away or lends, he gets a commitment to get it back as well as to receive 10 percent more.

In the language of finance, 10 percent is the annual rate of interest on the loan. When a dollar is lent out, the repayment of $1.10 can be thought of as being made up of two parts. First, the lender gets the dollar back; that is the *principal repayment*. Second, the lender receives an *interest payment,* which is $0.10 in this example.

■ FIGURE 3.1   Tom's and Leslie's Cash Flow

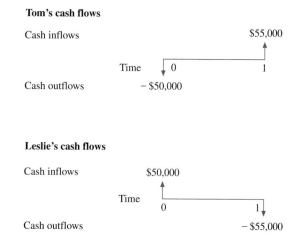

Now, not only have Tom and Leslie struck a deal, but as a by-product of their bargain they have created a financial instrument, the IOU. This piece of paper entitles whoever receives it to present it to Leslie in the next year and redeem it for $55,000. Financial instruments that entitle whoever possesses them to receive payment are called *bearer instruments* because whoever bears them can use them. Presumably there could be more such IOUs in the economy written by many different lenders and borrowers like Tom and Leslie.

The Anonymous Market

If the borrower does not care whom he has to pay back, and if the lender does not care whose IOUs he is holding, we could just as well drop Tom's and Leslie's names from their contract. All we need is a record book, in which we could record the fact that Tom has lent $50,000 and Leslie has borrowed $50,000 and that the terms of the loan, the interest rate, are 10 percent. Perhaps another person could keep the records for borrowers and lenders, for a fee, of course. In fact, and this is one of the virtues of such an arrangement, Tom and Leslie wouldn't even need to meet. Instead of needing to find and trade with each other, they could each trade with the record keeper. The record keeper could deal with thousands of such borrowers and lenders, none of whom would need to meet the other.

Institutions that perform this sort of market function, matching borrowers and lenders or traders, are called **financial intermediaries.** Stockbrokers and banks are examples of financial intermediaries in our modern world. A bank's depositors lend the bank money, and the bank makes loans from the funds it has on deposit. In essence, the bank is an intermediary between the depositors and the ultimate borrowers. To make the market work, we must be certain that the market clears. By *market clearing* we mean that the total amount that people like Tom wish to lend to the market should equal the total amount that people like Leslie wish to borrow.

Market Clearing

If the lenders wish to lend more than the borrowers want to borrow, then presumably the interest rate is too high. Because there would not be enough borrowing for all of the lenders at, say, 15 percent, there are really only two ways that the market could be made to clear. One is to ration the lenders. For example, if the lenders wish to lend $20 million when interest rates are at 15 percent and the borrowers wish to borrow only $8 million, the market could take, say, 8/20 of each dollar, or $0.40, from each of the lenders and distribute it to the borrowers. This is one possible scheme for making the market clear, but it is not one that would be sustainable in a free and competitive marketplace. Why not?

To answer this important question, let's go back to our lender, Tom. Tom sees that interest rates are 15 percent and, not surprisingly, rather than simply lending the $50,000 that he was willing to lend when rates were 10 percent, Tom decides that at the higher rates he would like to lend more, say $80,000. But since the lenders want to lend more money than the borrowers want to borrow, the record keepers tell Tom that they won't be able to take all of his $80,000; rather, they will take only 40 percent of it, or $32,000. With the interest rate at 15 percent, people are not willing to borrow enough to match up with all of the loans that are available at that rate.

Tom is not very pleased with that state of affairs, but he can do something to improve his situation. Suppose that he knows that Leslie is borrowing $20,000 in the market at the 15 percent interest rate. That means that Leslie must repay $20,000 on her loan next year plus the interest of 15 percent of $20,000 or 0.15 × $20,000 = $3,000. Suppose that Tom goes to Leslie and offers to lend her the $20,000 for 14 percent. Leslie is happy because she will save 1 percent on the deal and will need to pay back only $2,800 in interest next year. This is $200 less than if she had borrowed from the record keepers. Tom is happy too, because he has found a way to lend some of the money that the record keepers would not take. The net result of this transaction is that the record keepers have lost Leslie as a customer. Why should she borrow from them when Tom will lend her the money at a lower interest rate?

Tom and Leslie are not the only ones cutting side deals in the marketplace, and it is clear that the record keepers will not be able to maintain the 15 percent rate. The interest rate must fall if they are to stay in business.

Suppose, then, that the market clears at the rate of 10 percent. At this rate the amount of money that the lenders wish to lend is exactly equal to the amount that the borrowers desire. We refer to the interest rate that clears the market, 10 percent in our example, as the **equilibrium rate of interest.**

In this section we have shown that in the market for loans, bonds or IOUs are traded. These are *financial instruments.* The interest rate on these loans is set so that the total demand for such loans by borrowers equals the total supply of loans by lenders. At a higher interest rate, lenders wish to supply more loans than are demanded, and if the interest rate is lower than this equilibrium level, borrowers demand more loans than lenders are willing to supply.

CONCEPT QUESTIONS

- What is an interest rate?
- What are institutions that match borrowers and lenders called?
- What do we mean when we say a market clears? What is an equilibrium rate of interest?

3.2 MAKING CONSUMPTION CHOICES OVER TIME

Figure 3.2 illustrates the situation faced by a representative individual in the financial market. This person is assumed to have an income of $50,000 this year and an income of $60,000 next year. The market allows him not only to consume $50,000 worth of goods this year and $60,000 next year, but also to borrow and lend at the equilibrium interest rate.

The line *AB* in Figure 3.2 shows all of the consumption possibilities open to the person through borrowing or lending, and the shaded area contains all of the feasible choices. Let's look at this figure more closely to see exactly why points in the shaded area are available.

■ FIGURE 3.2 **Intertemporal Consumption Opportunities**

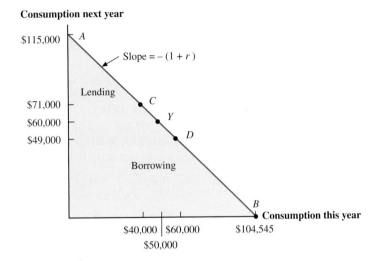

We will use the letter r to denote the interest rate—the equilibrium rate—in this market. The rate is risk-free because we assume that no default can take place. Look at point A on the vertical axis of Figure 3.2. Point A is a height of

$$A = \$60,000 + [\$50,000 \times (1 + r)]$$

For example, if the rate of interest is 10 percent, then point A would be

$$A = \$60,000 + [\$50,000 \times (1 + 0.1)]$$
$$= \$60,000 + \$55,000$$
$$= \$115,000$$

Point A is the maximum amount of wealth that this person can spend in the second year. He gets to point A by lending the full income that is available this year, $50,000, and consuming none of it. In the second year, then, he will have the second year's income of $60,000 plus the proceeds from the loan that he made in the first year, $55,000, for a total of $115,000.

Now let's take a look at point B. Point B is a distance of

$$B = \$50,000 + [\$60,000/(1 + r)]$$

along the horizontal axis. If the interest rate is 10 percent, point B will be

$$B = \$50,000 + [\$60,000/(1 + 0.1)]$$
$$= \$50,000 + \$54,545$$
$$= \$104,545$$

(We have rounded off to the nearest dollar.)

Why do we divide next year's income of $60,000 by $(1 + r)$, or 1.1 in the preceding computation? Point B represents the maximum amount available for this person to consume this year. To achieve that maximum he would borrow as much as possible and repay the loan from the income, $60,000, that he was going to receive next year. Because $60,000 will be available to repay the loan next year, we are asking how much he could borrow this year at an interest rate of r and still be able to repay the loan. The answer is

$$\$60,000/(1 + r)$$

because if he borrows this amount, he must repay it next year with interest. Thus, next year he must repay

$$[\$60,000/(1 + r)] \times (1 + r) = \$60,000$$

no matter what the interest rate, r, is. In our example we found that he could borrow $54,545 and, sure enough,

$$\$54,545 \times 1.1 = \$60,000$$

(after rounding off to the nearest dollar).

Furthermore, by borrowing and lending different amounts the person can achieve any point on the line *AB*. For example, point *C* is a point where he has chosen to lend $10,000 of today's income. This means that at point *C* he will have

$$\text{Consumption this year at point } C = \$50,000 - \$10,000 = \$40,000$$

and

$$\text{Consumption next year at point } C = \$60,000 + [\$10,000 \times (1 + r)] = \$71,000$$

when the interest rate is 10 percent.

Similarly, at point *D*, the individual has decided to borrow $10,000 and repay the loan next year. At point *D*, then,

$$\text{Consumption this year at point } D = \$50,000 + \$10,000 = \$60,000$$

and

$$\text{Consumption next year at point } D = \$60,000 - [\$10,000 \times (1 + r)] = \$49,000$$

at an interest rate of 10 percent.

In fact, this person can consume any point on the line *AB*. This line has a slope of $-(1 + r)$, which means that for each dollar that is added to the x coordinate along the line, $(1 + r)$ dollars are subtracted from the y coordinate. Moving along the line from point *A*, the initial point of $50,000 this year and $60,000 next year, toward point *B* gives the person more consumption today and less next year. In other words, moving toward point *B* is borrowing. Similarly, moving up toward point *A*, he is consuming less today and more next year and is lending. The line is a straight line because the individual has no effect on the interest rate. This is one of the assumptions of perfectly competitive financial markets.

Where will the person actually be? The answer to that question depends on the individual's tastes and personal situation, just as it did before there was a market. If the person is impatient, he might wish to borrow money at a point such as *D*, and if he is patient, he might wish to lend some of this year's income and enjoy more consumption next year at, for example, a point such as *C*.

Notice that whether we think of someone as patient or impatient depends on the interest rate he or she faces in the market. Suppose that our individual was impatient and chose to borrow $10,000 and move to point *D*. Now suppose that we raise the interest rate to 20 percent or even 50 percent. Suddenly our impatient person may become very patient and might prefer to lend some of this year's income to take advantage of the very high interest rate. The general result is depicted in Figure 3.3. We can see that lending at point *C'* yields much greater future income and consumption possibilities than before.[1]

---

[1] Those familiar with consumer theory might be aware of the surprising case where raising the interest rate actually makes people borrow more or lowering the rate makes them lend more. The latter case might occur, for example, if the decline in the interest rate made the lenders have so little consumption next year that they have no choice but to lend out even more than they were lending before just to subsist. Nothing we do depends on excluding such cases, but it is much easier to ignore them, and the resulting analysis fits the real markets more closely.

■ FIGURE 3.3   **The Effect of Different Interest Rates on Consumption Opportunities**

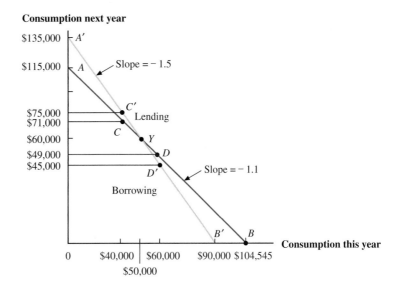

- How does an individual change his consumption across periods through borrowing and lending?
- How do interest rate changes affect one's degree of impatience?

3.3 THE COMPETITIVE MARKET

In the previous analysis we assumed the individual moves freely along the line *AB,* and we ignored—and assumed that the individual ignored—any effect his borrowing or lending decisions might have on the equilibrium interest rate itself. What would happen, though, if the total amount of loans outstanding in the market when the person was doing no borrowing or lending was $10 million, and if our person then decided to lend, say, $5 million? His lending would be half as much as the rest of the market put together, and it would not be unreasonable to think that the equilibrium interest rate would fall to induce more borrowers into the market to take his additional loans. In such a situation the person would have some power in the market to influence the equilibrium rate significantly, and he would take this power into consideration in making his decisions.

In the modern financial market, however, the total amount of borrowing and lending is not $10 million; rather, as we saw in Chapter 1, it is closer to $10 trillion. In such a huge market no one investor or even any single company can have a significant effect (although a government might). We assume, then, in all of our subsequent discussions and analyses that the financial market is competitive. By that we mean no individuals or firms think they have any effect whatsoever on the interest rates that they face no matter how much borrowing, lending, or investing they do. In the language of economics, individuals who respond to rates and prices by acting as though they have no influence on them are called *price takers,* and this assumption is sometimes called the *price-taking assumption.* It is the condition of **perfectly competitive financial markets** (or, more simply, *perfect markets*). The following conditions are likely to lead to this:

1. Trading is costless. Access to the financial markets is free.
2. Information about borrowing and lending opportunities is available.
3. There are many traders, and no single trader can have a significant impact on market prices.

How Many Interest Rates Are There in a Competitive Market?

An important point about this one-year market where no defaults can take place is that only one interest rate can be quoted in the market at any one time. Suppose that some competing record keepers decide to set up a rival market. To attract customers, their business plan is to offer lower interest rates, say, 9 percent. Their business plan is based on the hope that they will be able to attract borrowers away from the first market and soon have all of the business.

Their business plan will work, but it will do so beyond their wildest expectations. They will indeed attract the borrowers, all $11 million worth of them! But the matter doesn't stop there. By offering to borrow and lend at 9 percent when another market is offering 10 percent, they have created the proverbial money machine.

The world of finance is populated by sharp-eyed inhabitants who would not let this opportunity slip by them. Any one of these, whether a borrower or a lender, would go to the new market and borrow everything he could at the 9-percent rate. At the same time he was borrowing in the new market, he would also be striking a deal to lend in the old market at the 10-percent rate. If he could borrow $100 million at 9 percent and lend it at 10 percent, he would be able to net 1 percent, or $1 million, next year. He would repay the $109 million he owed to the new market from the $110 million he receives when the 10-percent loans he made in the original market are repaid, pocketing $1 million profit.

This process of striking a deal in one market and an offsetting deal in another market simultaneously and at more favorable terms is called *arbitrage,* and doing it is called arbitraging. Of course, someone must be paying for all this free money, and it must be the record keepers because the borrowers and the lenders are all making money. Our intrepid entrepreneurs will lose their proverbial shirts and go out of business. The moral of this is clear: As soon as different interest rates are offered for essentially the same risk-free loans, arbitrageurs will take advantage of the situation by borrowing at the low rate and lending at the high rate. The gap between the two rates will be closed quickly, and for all practical purposes there will be only one rate available in the market.

CONCEPT QUESTIONS

- What is the most important feature of a competitive financial market?
- What conditions are likely to lead to this?

3.4   THE BASIC PRINCIPLE

We have already shown how people use the financial markets to adjust their patterns of consumption over time to fit their particular preferences. By borrowing and lending, they can greatly expand their range of choices. They need only to have access to a market with an interest rate at which they can borrow and lend.

In the previous section we saw how these savings and consumption decisions depend on the interest rate. The financial markets also provide a benchmark against which proposed investments can be compared, and the interest rate is the basis for a test that any proposed investment must pass. The financial markets give the individual, the corporation, or even the government a standard of comparison for economic decisions. This benchmark is critical when investment decisions are being made.

The way we use the financial markets to aid us in making investment decisions is a direct consequence of our basic assumption that individuals can never be made worse off by increasing the range of choices open to them. People always can make use of the financial markets to adjust their savings and consumption by borrowing or lending. An investment project is worth undertaking only if it increases the range of choices in the financial markets. To do this the project must be at least as desirable as what is available in the financial markets.[2] If it were not as desirable as what the financial markets have to offer, people could simply use the financial markets instead of undertaking the investment. This point will govern us in all our investment decisions. It is the *first principle of investment decision making,* and it is the foundation on which all of our rules are built.

QUESTION

CONCEPT

?

• Describe the basic financial principle of investment decision making.

3.5 PRACTICING THE PRINCIPLE

Let us apply the basic principle of investment decision making to some concrete situations.

A Lending Example

Consider a person who is concerned only about this year and the next. She has an income of $100,000 this year and expects to make the same amount next year. The interest rate is 10 percent. This individual is thinking about investing in a piece of land that costs $70,000. She is certain that next year the land will be worth $75,000, a sure $5,000 gain. Should she undertake the investment? This situation is described in Figure 3.4 with the cash flow time chart.

A moment's thought should be all it takes to convince her that this is not an attractive business deal. By investing $70,000 in the land, she will have $75,000 available next year. Suppose, instead, that she puts the same $70,000 into a loan in the financial market. At the 10-percent rate of interest this $70,000 would grow to

$$(1 + 0.1) \times \$70,000 = \$77,000$$

next year.

It would be foolish to buy the land when the same $70,000 investment in the financial market would beat it by $2,000 (that is, $77,000 from the loan minus $75,000 from the land investment).

■ FIGURE 3.4 **Cash Flows for Investment in Land**

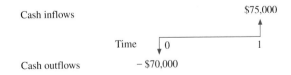

---

[2]You might wonder what to do if an investment is as desirable as an alternative in the financial markets. In principle, if there is a tie, it doesn't matter whether or not we take on the investment. In practice, we've never seen an exact tie.

■ FIGURE 3.5 **Consumption Opportunities with Borrowing and Lending**

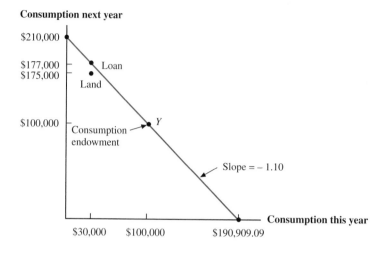

Figure 3.5 illustrates this situation. Notice that the $70,000 loan gives no less income today and $2,000 more next year. This example illustrates some amazing features of the financial markets. It is remarkable to consider all of the information that we did *not* use when arriving at the decision not to invest in the land. We did not need to know how much income the person has this year or next year. We also did not need to know whether the person preferred more income this year or next.

We did not need to know any of these other facts, and more important, the person making the decision did not need to know them either. She only needed to be able to compare the investment with a relevant alternative available in the financial market. When this investment fell short of that standard—by $2,000 in the previous example—regardless of what the individual wanted to do, she knew that she should not buy the land.

A Borrowing Example

Let us sweeten the deal a bit. Suppose that instead of being worth $75,000 next year the land would be worth $80,000. What should our investor do now? This case is a bit more difficult. After all, even if the land seems like a good deal, this person's income this year is $100,000. Does she really want to make a $70,000 investment this year? Won't that leave only $30,000 for consumption?

The answers to these questions are yes, the individual should buy the land; yes, she does want to make a $70,000 investment this year; and, most surprising of all, even though her income is $100,000, making the $70,000 investment will not leave her with $30,000 to consume this year! Now let us see how finance lets us get around the basic laws of arithmetic.

The financial markets are the key to solving our problem. First, the financial markets can be used as a standard of comparison against which any investment project must be measured. Second, they can be used as a tool to actually help the individual undertake investments. These twin features of the financial markets enable us to make the right investment decision.

Suppose that the person borrows the $70,000 initial investment that is needed to purchase the land. Next year she must repay this loan. Because the interest rate is 10 percent, she will owe the financial market $77,000 next year. This is depicted in Figure 3.6. Because the land will be worth $80,000 next year, she can sell it, pay off her debt of $77,000, and have $3,000 extra cash.

■ FIGURE 3.6   **Cash Flows of Borrowing to Purchase the Land**

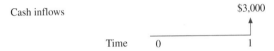

■ FIGURE 3.7   **Consumption Opportunities with Investment Opportunity and Borrowing and Lending**

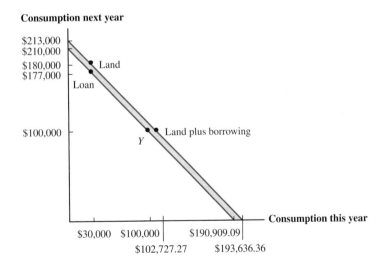

    If she wishes, this person can now consume an extra $3,000 worth of goods and services next year. This possibility is illustrated in Figure 3.7. In fact, even if she wants to do all of her consuming this year, she is still better off taking the investment. All she must do is take out a loan this year and repay it from the proceeds of the land next year and profit by $3,000.

    Furthermore, instead of borrowing just the $70,000 that she needed to purchase the land, she could have borrowed $72,727.27. She could have used $70,000 to buy the land and consumed the remaining $2,727.27.

We will call $2,727.27 the net present value of the transaction. Notice that it is equal to $3,000 × 1/1.1. How did we figure out that this was the exact amount that she could borrow? It was easy: If $72,727.27 is the amount that she borrows, then, because the interest rate is 10 percent, she must repay

$$\$72,727.27 \times (1 + 0.1) = \$80,000$$

next year, and that is exactly what the land will be worth. The line through the investment position in Figure 3.7 illustrates this borrowing possibility.

The amazing thing about both of these cases, one where the land is worth $75,000 next year and the other where it is worth $80,000 next year, is that we needed only to compare the investment with the financial markets to decide whether it was worth undertaking or not. This is one of the more important points in all of finance. It is true regardless of the consumption preferences of the individual. This is one of a number of **separation theorems** in finance. It states that the value of an investment to an individual is not dependent on consumption preferences. In our examples we showed that the person's decision to invest in land was not affected by consumption preferences. However, these preferences dictated whether she borrowed or lent.

QUESTIONS

- Describe how the financial markets can be used to evaluate investment alternatives.
- What is the separation theorem? Why is it important?

3.6 ILLUSTRATING THE INVESTMENT DECISION

Figure 3.2 describes the possibilities open to a person who has an income of $50,000 this year and $60,000 next year and faces a financial market in which the interest rate is 10 percent. But, at that moment, the person has no investment possibilities beyond the 10-percent borrowing and lending that is available in the financial market.

Suppose that we give this person the chance to undertake an investment project that will require a $30,000 outlay of cash this year and that will return $40,000 to the investor next year. Refer to Figure 3.2 and determine how you could include this new possibility in that figure and how you could use the figure to help you decide whether to undertake the investment.

Now look at Figure 3.8. In Figure 3.8 we have labeled the original point with $50,000 this year and $60,000 next year as point *A*. We have also added a new point *B*, with $20,000 available for consumption this year and $100,000 next year. The difference between point *A* and point *B* is that at point *A* the person is just where we started him off, and at point *B* the person has also decided to undertake the investment project. As a result of this decision the person at point *B* has

$$\$50,000 - \$30,000 = \$20,000$$

left for consumption this year, and

$$\$60,000 + \$40,000 = \$100,000$$

available next year. These are the coordinates of point *B*.

We must use our knowledge of the individual's borrowing and lending opportunities in order to decide whether to accept or reject the investment. This is illustrated in Figure 3.9. Figure 3.9 is similar to Figure 3.8, but in it we have drawn a line through point *A* that shows

■ FIGURE 3.8 **Consumption Choices with Investment but No Financial Markets**

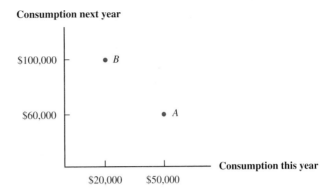

■ FIGURE 3.9 **Consumption Choices with Investment Opportunities and Financial Markets**

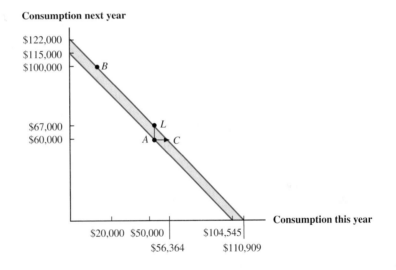

the possibilities open to the person if he stays at point *A* and does not take the investment. This line is exactly the same as the one in Figure 3.2. We have also drawn a parallel line through point *B* that shows the new possibilities that are available to the person if he undertakes the investment. The two lines are parallel because the slope of each is determined by the same interest rate, 10 percent. It does not matter whether the person takes the investment and goes to point *B* or does not and stays at point *A;* in the financial market, each dollar of lending is a dollar less available for consumption this year and moves him to the left by a dollar along the *x*-axis. Because the interest rate is 10 percent, the $1 loan repays $1.10 and it moves him up by $1.10 along the *y*-axis.

It is easy to see from Figure 3.9 that the investment has made the person better off. The line through point *B* is higher than the line through point *A*. Thus, no matter what pattern of consumption this person wanted this year and next, he could have more in each year if he undertook the investment.

For example, suppose that our individual wanted to consume everything this year. If he did not take the investment, the point where the line through point *A* intersected the *x*-axis would give the maximum amount of consumption he could enjoy this year. This point has $104,545 available this year. To recall how we found this figure, review the analysis of Figure 3.2. But in Figure 3.9 the line that goes through point *B* hits the *x*-axis at a higher point than the line that goes through point *A*. Along this line the person can have the $20,000 that is left after investing $30,000, plus all that he can borrow and repay with both next year's income and the proceeds from the investment. The total amount available to consume today is therefore

$$= \$50,000 - \$30,000 + (\$60,000 + \$40,000)/(1 + 0.1)$$
$$= \$20,000 + (\$100,000/1.1)$$
$$= \$110,909$$

The additional consumption available this year from undertaking the investment and using the financial market is the difference on the *x*-axis between the points where these two lines intersect:

$$\$110,909 - \$104,545 = \$6,364$$

This difference is an important measure of what the investment is worth to the person. It answers a variety of questions. For example, it is the answer to the question: How much money would we need to give the investor this year to make him just as well off as he is with the investment?

Because the line through point *B* is parallel to the line through point *A* but has been moved over by $6,364, we know that if we were to add this amount to the investor's current income this year at point *A* and take away the investment, he would wind up on the line through point *B* and with the same possibilities. If we do this, the person will have $56,364 this year and $60,000 next year, which is the situation of the point on the line through point *B* that lies to the right of point *A* in Figure 3.9. This is point *C*.

We could also ask a different question: How much money would we need to give the investor next year to make him just as well off as he is with the investment?

This is the same as asking how much higher the line through point *B* is than the line through point *A*. In other words, what is the difference in Figure 3.9 between the point where the line through *A* intercepts the *y*-axis and the point where the line through *B* intercepts the *y*-axis?

The point where the line through *A* intercepts the *y*-axis shows the maximum amount the person could consume next year if all of his current income were lent out and the proceeds of the loan were consumed along with next year's income.

As we showed in our analysis of Figure 3.2, this amount is $115,000. How does this compare with what the person can have next year if he takes the investment? By taking the investment we saw that he would be at point *B* where he has $20,000 left this year and would have $100,000 next year. By lending the $20,000 that is left this year and adding the proceeds of this loan to the $100,000, we find the line through *B* intercepts the *y*-axis at:

$$(\$20,000 \times 1.1) + \$100,000 = \$122,000$$

The difference between this amount and $115,000 is

$$\$122,000 - \$115,000 = \$7,000$$

which is the answer to the question of how much we would need to give the person next year to make him as well off as he is with the investment.

■ FIGURE 3.10 **Cash Flows for the Investment Project**

There is a simple relationship between these two numbers. If we multiply $6,364 by 1.1 we get $7,000! Consider why this must be so. The $6,364 is the amount of extra cash we must give the person this year to substitute for having the investment. In a financial market with a 10-percent rate of interest, however, $1 this year is worth exactly the same as $1.10 next year. Thus, $6,364 this year is the same as $6,364 × 1.1 next year. In other words, the person does not care whether he has the investment, $6,364, this year or $6,364 × 1.1 next year. But we already showed that the investor is equally willing to have the investment and to have $7,000 next year. This must mean that

$$\$6,364 \times 1.1 = \$7,000$$

You can also verify this relationship between these two variables by using Figure 3.9. Because the lines through A and B each have the same slope of -1.1, the difference of $7,000 between where they intersect on the x-axis must be in the ratio of 1.1 to 1.

Now we can show you how to evaluate the investment opportunity on a stand-alone basis. Here are the relevant facts: The individual must give up $30,000 this year to get $40,000 next year. These cash flows are illustrated in Figure 3.10.

The investment rule that follows from the previous analysis is the net present value (NPV) rule. Here we convert all consumption values to the present and add them up:

$$\begin{aligned}\text{Net present value} &= -\$30,000 + \$40,000 \times (1/1.1) \\ &= -\$30,000 + \$36,364 \\ &= \$6,364\end{aligned}$$

The future amount, $40,000, is called the *future value* (FV).

The net present value of an investment is a simple criterion for deciding whether or not to undertake an investment. NPV answers the question of how much cash an investor would need to have today as a substitute for making the investment. If the net present value is positive, the investment is worth taking on because doing so is essentially the same as receiving a cash payment equal to the net present value. If the net present value is negative, taking on the investment today is equivalent to giving up some cash today, and the investment should be rejected.

We use the term *net present value* to emphasize that we are already including the current cost of the investment in determining its value and not simply what it will return. For example, if the interest rate is 10 percent and an investment of $30,000 today will produce a total cash return of $40,000 in one year's time, the *present value* of the $40,000 by itself is

$$\$40,000/1.1 = \$36,364$$

but the *net present value* of the investment is $36,364 minus the original investment:

$$\text{Net present value} = \$36,364 - \$30,000 = \$6,364$$

The present value of a future cash flow is the value of that cash flow after considering the appropriate market interest rate. The net present value of an investment is the present value of the investment's future cash flows, minus the initial cost of the investment. We have just decided that our investment is a good opportunity. It has a positive net present value because it is worth more than it costs.

In general, the above can be stated in terms of the **net present value rule:**

An investment is worth making if it has a positive NPV. If an investment's NPV is negative, it should be rejected.

CONCEPT QUESTIONS

- Give the definitions of net present value, future value, and present value.
- What information does a person need to compute an investment's net present value?

3.7 CORPORATE INVESTMENT DECISION MAKING

Up to now, everything we have done has been from the perspective of the individual investor. How do corporations and firms make investment decisions? Aren't their decisions governed by a much more complicated set of rules and principles than the simple NPV rule that we have developed for individuals?

We return to questions of corporate decision making and corporate governance later in the book, but it is remarkable how well our central ideas and the NPV rule hold up even when applied to corporations.

Suppose that firms are just ways in which many investors can pool their resources to make large-scale business decisions. Suppose, for example, that you own 1 percent of some firm. Now suppose that this firm is considering whether or not to undertake some investment. If that investment passes the NPV rule, that is, if it has a positive NPV, then 1 percent of that NPV belongs to you. If the firm takes on this investment, the value of the whole firm will rise by the NPV and your investment in the firm will rise by 1 percent of the NPV of the investment. Similarly, the other shareholders in the firm will profit by having the firm take on the positive NPV project because the value of their shares in the firm will also increase. This means that the shareholders in the firm will be unanimous in wanting the firm to increase its value by taking on the positive NPV project. If you follow this line of reasoning, you will also be able to see why the shareholders would oppose the firm taking on any projects with a negative NPV because this would lower the value of their shares.

One difference between the firm and the individual is that the firm has no consumption endowment. In terms of our one-period consumption diagram, the firm starts at the origin. Figure 3.11 illustrates the situation of a firm with investment opportunity *B*. *B* is an investment that has a future value of $33,000 and will cost $25,000 now. If the interest rate is 10 percent, the NPV of *B* can be determined using the NPV rule. This is marked as point *C* in Figure 3.11. The cash flows of this investment are depicted in Figure 3.12.

$$\text{Net present value} =$$
$$-\$25,000 + [\$33,000 \times (1/1.1)] = \$5,000$$

One common objection to this line of reasoning is that people differ in their tastes and that they would not necessarily agree to take on or reject investments by the NPV rule. For instance, suppose that you and we each own some shares in a company. Further suppose that we are older than you and might be anxious to spend our money. Being younger, you might be more patient than we are and more willing to wait for a good long-term investment to pay off.

Because of the financial markets we all agree that the company should take on investments with positive NPVs and reject those with negative NPVs. If there were no financial markets, then, being impatient, we might want the company to do little or no investing so that we could have as much money as possible to consume now, and, being patient, you might prefer the company to make some investments. With financial markets, we are both satisfied by having the company follow the NPV rule.

■ FIGURE 3.11   Consumption Choices, the NPV Rule, and the Corporation

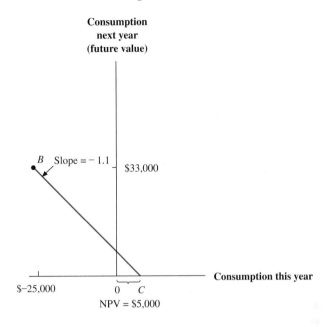

■ FIGURE 3.12   Corporate Investment Cash Flows

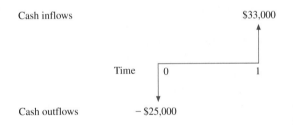

Suppose that the company takes on a positive NPV investment. Let us assume that this investment has a net payoff of $1 million next year. That means that the value of the company will increase by $1 million next year and, consequently, if you own 1 percent of the company's shares, the value of your shares will increase by 1 percent of $1 million, or $10,000, next year. Because you are patient, you might be prepared to wait for your $10,000 until next year. Being impatient, we do not want to wait, and with financial markets, we do not need to wait. We can simply borrow against the extra $10,000 we will have tomorrow and use the loan to consume more today.

In fact, if there is also a market for the firm's shares, we do not even need to borrow. After the company takes on a positive NPV investment, our shares in the company increase in value today. This is because owning the shares today entitles investors to their portion of the extra $1 million the company will have next year. This means that the shares would rise in value today by the present value of $1 million. Because you want to delay your consumption, you could wait until next year and sell your shares then to have extra consumption next year. Being impatient, we might sell our shares now and use the money to consume more today. If we owned 1 percent of the company's shares, we could sell our shares for an extra amount equal to the present value of $10,000.

In reality, shareholders in big companies do not vote on every investment decision, and the managers of big companies must have rules that they follow. We have seen that all shareholders in a company will be better off—no matter what their levels of patience or impatience—if these managers follow the NPV rule. This is a marvelous result because it makes it possible for many different owners to delegate decision-making powers to the managers. They need only tell the managers to follow the NPV rule, and if the managers do so, they will be doing exactly what the stockholders want them to do. Sometimes this form of the NPV rule is stated as having the managers maximize the value of the company. As we argued, the current value of the shares of the company will increase by the NPV of any investments that the company undertakes. This means that the managers of the company can make the shareholders as well off as possible by taking on all positive NPV projects and rejecting projects with negative NPVs.

Separating investment decision making from the owners is a basic requirement of the modern large firm. The separation theorem in financial markets says that all investors will want to accept or reject the same investment projects by using the NPV rule, regardless of their personal preferences. Investors can delegate the operations of the firm and require that managers use the NPV rule. Of course, much remains for us to discuss about this topic. For example, what insurance do stockholders have that managers will actually do what is best for them?

We discussed this possibility in Chapter 1, and we take up this interesting topic later in the book. For now, though, we no longer will consider our perspective to be that of the lone investor. Instead, thanks to the separation theorem, we will use the NPV rule for companies as well as for investors. Our justification of the NPV rule depends on the conditions necessary to derive the separation theorem. These conditions are the ones that result in competitive financial markets. The analysis we have presented has been restricted to risk-free cash flows in one time period. However, the separation theorem also can be derived for risky cash flows that extend beyond one period.

For the reader interested in studying further about the separation theorem, we include several suggested readings at the end of this chapter that build on the material we have presented.

• In terms of the net present value rule, what is the essential difference between the individual and the corporation?

3.8 Summary and Conclusions

Finance is a subject that builds understanding from the ground up. Whenever you come up against a new problem or issue in finance, you can always return to the basic principles of this chapter for guidance.

1. Financial markets exist because people want to adjust their consumption over time. They do this by borrowing and lending.

2. Financial markets provide the key test for investment decision making. Whether a particular investment decision should or should not be taken depends only on this test: If there is a superior alternative in the financial markets, the investment should be rejected; if not, the

investment is worth taking. The most important thing about this principle is that the investor need not use his preferences to decide whether the investment should be taken. Regardless of the individual's preference for consumption this year versus the next, regardless of how patient or impatient the individual is, making the proper investment decision depends only on comparing it with the alternatives in the financial markets.

3. The net present value of an investment helps us make the comparison between the investment and the financial market. If the NPV is positive, our rule tells us to undertake the investment. This illustrates the second major feature of the financial markets and investment. Not only does the NPV rule tell us which investments to accept and which to reject, the financial markets also provide us with the tools for actually acquiring the funds to make the investments. In short, we use the financial markets to decide both what to do and how to do it.

4. The NPV rule can be applied to corporations as well as to individuals. The separation theorem developed in this chapter conveys that all of the owners of the firm would agree that the firm should use the NPV rule even though each might differ in personal tastes for consumption and savings.

In the next chapter we learn more about the NPV rule by using it to examine a wide array of problems in finance.

KEY TERMS

Equilibrium rate of interest   48
Financial intermediaries   47
Net present value rule   60

Perfectly competitive financial market   51
Separation theorems   56

SUGGESTED READINGS

Two books that have good discussions of the consumption and savings decisions of individuals and the beginnings of financial markets are:
Fama, E. F., and M. H. Miller. *The Theory of Finance.* New York: Holt, Rinehart & Winston, 1971: Chapter 1.
Hirshleifer, J. *Investment, Interest and Capital.* Upper Saddle River, N.J.: Prentice Hall, 1970: Chapter 1.

The seminal work on the net present value rule is:
Fisher, I. G. *The Theory of Interest.* New York: Augustus M. Kelly, 1965. (This is a reprint of the 1930 edition.)

A rigorous treatment of the net present value rule along the lines of Irving Fisher can be found in:
Hirshleifer, J. "On the Theory of Optimal Investment Decision." *Journal of Political Economy* 66 (August 1958).

QUESTIONS AND PROBLEMS

Making Consumption Choices
3.1 Currently, Jim Morris makes $100,000. Next year his income will be $120,000. Jim is a big spender and he wants to consume $150,000 this year. The equilibrium interest rate is 10 percent. What will be Jim's consumption potential next year if he consumes $150,000 this year?

3.2 Rich Pettit is a miser. His current income is $50,000; next year he will earn $40,000. He plans to consume only $20,000 this year. The current interest rate is 12 percent. What will Rich's consumption potential be next year?

The Competitive Finance Market
3.3 What is the basic reason that financial markets develop?

Illustrating the Investment Decision

3.4 The following figure depicts the financial situation of Ms. J. Fawn. In period 0 her labor income and current consumption is $40; later, in period 1, her labor income and consumption will be $22. She has an opportunity to make the investment represented by point *D.* By borrowing and lending, she will be able to reach any point along the line *FDE.*

    a. What is the market rate of interest? (Hint: The new market interest rate line *EF* is parallel to *AH.*)

    b. What is the NPV of point *D?*

    c. If Ms. Fawn wishes to consume the same quantity in each period, how much should she consume in period 0?

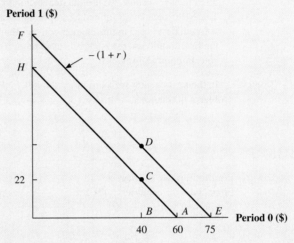

3.5 Harry Hernandez has $60,000 this year. He faces the investment opportunities represented by point *B* in the following figure. He wants to consume $20,000 this year and $67,500 next year. This pattern of consumption is represented by point *F.*

    a. What is the market interest rate?

    b. How much must Harry invest in financial assets and productive assets today if he follows an optimum strategy?

    c. What is the NPV of his investment in nonfinancial assets?

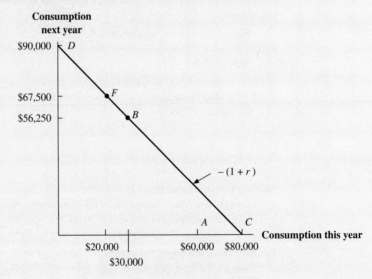

3.6 Suppose that the person in the land-investment example in the text wants to consume $60,000 this year.

    a. Detail a plan of investment and borrowing or lending that would permit her to consume $60,000 if the land investment is worth $75,000 next year.

    b. Detail a plan of investment and borrowing or lending that would permit her to consume $60,000 if the land investment is worth $80,000 next year.

    c. In which of these cases should she invest in the land?

    d. In each of these cases, how much will she be able to consume next year?

Corporate Investment Decision Making

3.7 *a.* Briefly explain why from the shareholders' perspective it is desirable for corporations to maximize NPV.

    b. What assumptions are necessary for this argument to be correct?

3.8 Consider a one-year world with perfect capital markets in which the interest rate is 10 percent. Suppose a firm has $12 million in cash. The firm invests $7 million today, and $5 million is paid to shareholders. The NPV of the firm's investment is $3 million. All shareholders are identical.

    a. How much cash will the firm receive next year from its investment?

    b. Suppose shareholders plan to spend $10 million today.

      (i) How can they do this?

      (ii) How much money will they have available to spend next year if they follow your plan?

3.9 To answer this question, refer to the following figure.

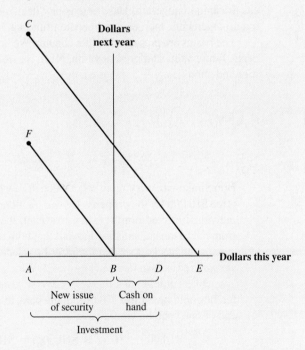

The Badvest Corporation is an all-equity firm with *BD* in cash on hand. It has an investment opportunity at point *C,* and it plans to invest *AD* in real assets today. Thus, the firm will need to raise *AB* by a new issue of equity.

    a. What is the present value of the investment?

    b. What is the rate of return on the old equity? Measure this rate of return from before the investment plans are announced to afterwards.

    c. What is the rate of return on the new equity?

CHAPTER 4

Net Present Value

·····

EXECUTIVE SUMMARY

We now examine one of the most important concepts in all of corporate finance, the relationship between $1 today and $1 in the future. Consider the following example: A firm is contemplating investing $1 million in a project that is expected to pay out $200,000 per year for nine years. Should the firm accept the project? One might say yes at first glance, since total inflows of $1.8 million (= $200,000 × 9) are greater than $1 million outflow. However, the $1 million is paid out *immediately,* whereas the $200,000 per year will be received in the future. Also, the immediate payment is known with certainty, whereas the later inflows can only be estimated. Thus, we need to know the relationship between a dollar today and a (possibly uncertain) dollar in the future before deciding on the project.

This relationship is called the *time-value-of-money concept.* It is important in such areas as capital budgeting, lease versus buy decisions, accounts receivable analysis, financing arrangements, mergers, and pension funding.

The basics are presented in this chapter. We begin by discussing two fundamental concepts, future value and present value. Next, we treat simplifying formulas such as perpetuities and annuities.

4.1 THE ONE-PERIOD CASE

EXAMPLE

Don Simkowitz is trying to sell a piece of raw land in Alaska. Yesterday, he was offered $10,000 for the property. He was about ready to accept the offer when another individual offered him $11,424. However, the second offer was to be paid a year from now. Don has satisfied himself that both buyers are honest and financially solvent, so he has no fear that the offer he selects will fall through. These two offers are pictured as cash flows in Figure 4.1. Which offer should Mr. Simkowitz choose?

Mike Tuttle, Don's financial advisor, points out that if Don takes the first offer, he could invest the $10,000 in the bank at an insured rate of 12 percent. At the end of one year, he would have

$$\underbrace{\$10,000}_{\substack{\text{Return of}\\\text{principal}}} + \underbrace{(0.12 \times \$10,000)}_{\text{Interest}} = \$10,000 \times 1.12 = \$11,200$$

Because this is less than the $11,424 Don could receive from the second offer, Mr. Tuttle recommends that he take the latter. This analysis uses the concept of **future value** or **compound value,** which is the value of a sum after investing over one or more periods. The compound or future value of $10,000 is $11,200.

■ FIGURE 4.1   **Cash Flow for Mr. Simkowitz's Sale**

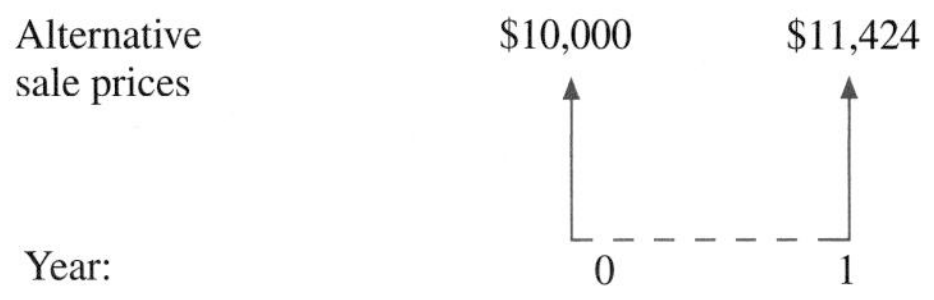

An alternative method employs the concept of **present value.** One can determine present value by asking the following question: How much money must Don put in the bank today so that he will have $11,424 next year? We can write this algebraically as

$$\text{PV} \times 1.12 = \$11,424 \tag{4.1}$$

We want to solve for present value (PV), the amount of money that yields $11,424 if invested at 12 percent today. Solving for PV, we have

$$\text{PV} = \frac{\$11,424}{1.12} = \$10,200$$

The formula for PV can be written as

Present Value of Investment:

$$\text{PV} = \frac{C_1}{1 + r}$$

where C_1 is cash flow at date 1 and r is the appropriate interest rate. r is the rate of return that Don Simkowitz requires on his land sale. It is sometimes referred to as the discount rate.

Present value analysis tells us that a payment of $11,424 to be received next year has a present value of $10,200 today. In other words, at a 12-percent interest rate, Mr. Simkowitz could not care less whether you gave him $10,200 today or $11,424 next year. If you gave him $10,200 today, he could put it in the bank and receive $11,424 next year.

Because the second offer has a present value of $10,200, whereas the first offer is for only $10,000, present value analysis also indicates that Mr. Simkowitz should take the second offer. In other words, both future value analysis and present value analysis lead to the same decision. As it turns out, present value analysis and future value analysis must always lead to the same decision.

As simple as this example is, it contains the basic principles that we will be working with over the next few chapters. We now use another example to develop the concept of net present value.

EXAMPLE ──

Louisa Dice, a financial analyst at Kaufman & Broad, a leading real estate firm, is thinking about recommending that Kaufman & Broad invest in a piece of land that costs $85,000. She is certain that next year the land will be worth $91,000, a sure $6,000 gain. Given that the guaranteed interest rate in the bank is 10 percent, should Kaufman & Broad undertake the investment in land? Ms. Dice's choice is described in Figure 4.2 with the cash flow time chart.

A moment's thought should be all it takes to convince her that this is not an attractive business deal. By investing $85,000 in the land, she will have $91,000 available next year. Suppose, instead, that Kaufman & Broad puts the same

■ FIGURE 4.2 Cash Flows for Land Investment

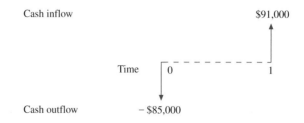

$85,000 into the bank. At the interest rate of 10 percent, this $85,000 would grow to

$$(1 + 0.10) \times \$85,000 = \$93,500$$

next year.

It would be foolish to buy the land when investing the same $85,000 in the financial market would produce an extra $2,500 (that is, $93,500 from the bank minus $91,000 from the land investment). This is a future-value calculation.

Alternatively, she could calculate the present value of the sale price next year as

$$\text{Present value} = \frac{\$91,000}{1.10} = \$82,727.27$$

Because the present value of next year's sales price is less than this year's purchase price of $85,000, present-value analysis also indicates that she should not recommend purchasing the property.

Frequently, businesspeople want to determine the exact *cost* or *benefit* of a decision. The decision to buy this year and sell next year can be evaluated as

Net Present Value of Investment:

$$-\$2,273 = \underset{\substack{\text{Cost of land} \\ \text{today}}}{-\$85,000} + \underset{\substack{\text{Present value of} \\ \text{next year's sales price}}}{\frac{\$91,000}{1.10}} \tag{4.2}$$

The formula for NPV can be written as

$$\text{NPV} = -\text{Cost} + \text{PV}$$

Equation (4.2) says that the value of the investment is −$2,273, after stating all the benefits and all the costs as of date 0. We say that −$2,273 is the **net present value** (NPV) of the investment. That is, NPV is the present value of future cash flows minus the present value of the cost of the investment. Because the net present value is negative, Louisa Dice should not recommend purchasing the land.

Both the Simkowitz and the Dice examples deal with perfect certainty. That is, Don Simkowitz knows with perfect certainty that he could sell his land for $11,424 next year. Similarly, Louisa Dice knows with perfect certainty that Kaufman & Broad could receive $91,000 for selling its land. Unfortunately, businesspeople frequently do not know future cash flows. This uncertainty is treated in the next example.

■ FIGURE 4.3 **Cash Flows for Investment in Painting**

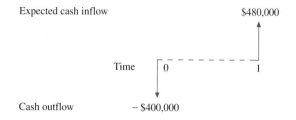

EXAMPLE

Professional Artworks, Inc., is a firm that speculates in modern paintings. The manager is thinking of buying an original Picasso for $400,000 with the intention of selling it at the end of one year. The manager *expects* that the painting will be worth $480,000 in one year. The relevant cash flows are depicted in Figure 4.3.

Of course, this is only an expectation—the painting could be worth more or less than $480,000. Suppose the guaranteed interest rate granted by banks is 10 percent. Should the firm purchase the piece of art?

Our first thought might be to discount at the interest rate, yielding

$$\frac{\$480,000}{1.10} = \$436,364$$

Because $436,364 is greater than $400,000, it looks at first glance as if the painting should be purchased. However, 10 percent is the return one can earn on a riskless investment. Because the painting is quite risky, a higher *discount rate* is called for. The manager chooses a rate of 25 percent to reflect this risk. In other words, he argues that a 25-percent expected return is fair compensation for an investment as risky as this painting.

The present value of the painting becomes

$$\frac{\$480,000}{1.25} = \$384,000$$

Thus, the manager believes that the painting is currently overpriced at $400,000 and does not make the purchase.

The preceding analysis is typical of decision making in today's corporations, though real-world examples are, of course, much more complex. Unfortunately, any example with risk poses a problem not faced by a riskless example. In an example with riskless cash flows, the appropriate interest rate can be determined by simply checking with a few banks.[1] The selection of the discount rate for a risky investment is quite a difficult task. We simply don't know at this point whether the discount rate on the painting should be 11 percent, 25 percent, 52 percent, or some other percentage.

---

[1] In Chapter 9, we discuss estimation of the riskless rate in more detail.

Because the choice of a discount rate is so difficult, we merely wanted to broach the subject here. The rest of the chapter will revert to examples under perfect certainty. We must wait until the specific material on risk and return is covered in later chapters before a risk-adjusted analysis can be presented.

QUESTIONS

- Define future value and present value.
- How does one use net present value when making an investment decision?

4.2 THE MULTIPERIOD CASE

The previous section presented the calculation of future value and present value for one period only. We will now perform the calculations for the multiperiod case.

Future Value and Compounding

Suppose an individual were to make a loan of $1. At the end of the first year, the borrower would owe the lender the principal amount of $1 plus the interest on the loan at the interest rate of r. For the specific case where the interest rate is, say, 9 percent, the borrower owes the lender

$$\$1 \times (1 + r) = \$1 \times 1.09 = \$1.09$$

At the end of the year, though, the lender has two choices. She can either take the $1.09—or, more generally, $(1 + r)$—out of the capital market, or she can leave it in and lend it again for a second year. The process of leaving the money in the capital market and lending it for another year is called **compounding.**

Suppose that the lender decides to compound her loan for another year. She does this by taking the proceeds from her first one-year loan, $1.09, and lending this amount for the next year. At the end of next year, then, the borrower will owe her

$$\$1 \times (1 + r) \times (1 + r) = \$1 \times (1 + r)^2 = 1 + 2r + r^2$$
$$\$1 \times (1.09) \times (1.09) = \$1 \times (1.09)^2 = \$1 + \$0.18 + 0.0081 = \$1.1881$$

This is the total she will receive two years from now by compounding the loan.

In other words, the capital market enables the investor, by providing a ready opportunity for lending, to transform $1 today into $1.1881 at the end of two years. At the end of three years, the cash will be $1 \times (1.09)^3 = \$1.2950$.

The most important point to notice is that the total amount that the lender receives is not just the $1 that she lent out plus two years' worth of interest on $1:

$$2 \times r = 2 \times \$0.09 = \$0.18$$

The lender also gets back an amount r^2, which is the interest in the second year on the interest that was earned in the first year. The term, $2 \times r$, represents **simple interest** over the two years, and the term, r^2, is referred to as the *interest on interest*. In our example this latter amount is exactly

$$r^2 = (\$0.09)^2 = \$0.0081$$

When cash is invested at **compound interest,** each interest payment is reinvested. With simple interest, the interest is not reinvested. Benjamin Franklin's statement, "Money makes money and the money that money makes makes more money," is a colorful way of explaining compound interest. The difference between compound interest and simple interest is illustrated

■ FIGURE 4.4 **Simple and Compound Interest**

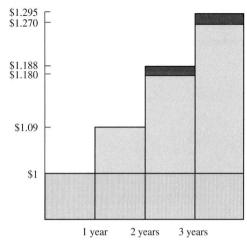

1 year   2 years   3 years

The dark-shaded area indicates the difference between
compound and simple interest. The difference is substantial
over a period of many years or decades.

in Figure 4.4. In this example the difference does not amount to much because the loan is for
$1. If the loan were for $1 million, the lender would receive $1,188,100 in two years' time. Of
this amount, $8,100 is interest on interest. The lesson is that those small numbers beyond the
decimal point can add up to big dollar amounts when the transactions are for big amounts. In
addition, the longer-lasting the loan, the more important interest on interest becomes.

The general formula for an investment over many periods can be written as

Future Value of an Investment:
$$FV = C_0 \times (1 + r)^T$$

where C_0 is the cash to be invested at date 0, r is the interest rate, and T is the number of
periods over which the cash is invested.

EXAMPLE

Suh-Pyng Ku has put $500 in a savings account at the First National Bank of Kent.
The account earns 7 percent, compounded annually. How much will Ms. Ku have
at the end of three years?

$$\$500 \times 1.07 \times 1.07 \times 1.07 = \$500 \times (1.07)^3 = \$612.52$$

Figure 4.5 illustrates the growth of Ms. Ku's account.

EXAMPLE

Jay Ritter invested $1,000 in the stock of the SDH Company. The company pays
a current dividend of $2, which is expected to grow by 20 percent per year for the
next two years. What will the dividend of the SDH Company be after two years?

$$\$2 \times (1.20)^2 = \$2.88$$

Figure 4.6 illustrates the increasing value of SDH's dividends.

■ FIGURE 4.5   **Suh-Pyng Ku's Savings Account**

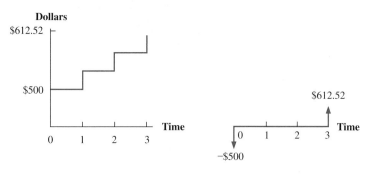

■ FIGURE 4.6   **The Growth of the SDH Dividends**

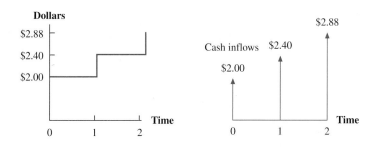

The two previous examples can be calculated in any one of three ways. The computations could be done by hand, by calculator, or with the help of a table. The appropriate table is Table A.3, which appears in the back of the text. This table presents *Future values of $1 at the end of t periods.* The table is used by locating the appropriate interest rate on the horizontal and the appropriate number of periods on the vertical.

For example, Suh-Pyng Ku would look at the following portion of Table A.3:

	Interest rate		
Period	6%	7%	8%
1	1.0600	1.0700	1.0800
2	1.1236	1.1449	1.1664
3	1.1910	1.2250	1.2597
4	1.2625	1.3108	1.3605

She could calculate the future value of her $500 as

$$\underset{\substack{\text{Initial}\\\text{investment}}}{\$500} \quad\times\quad \underset{\substack{\text{Future value}\\\text{of }\$1}}{1.2250} \quad=\quad \$612.50$$

In the example concerning Suh-Pyng Ku, we gave you both the initial investment and the interest rate and then asked you to calculate the future value. Alternatively, the interest rate could have been unknown, as shown in the following example.

■ FIGURE 4.7 **Cash Flows for Purchase of Carl Voigt's Car**

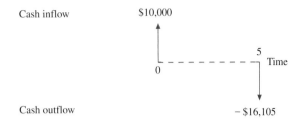

EXAMPLE

Carl Voigt, who recently won $10,000 in the lottery, wants to buy a car in five years. Carl estimates that the car will cost $16,105 at that time. His cash flows are displayed in Figure 4.7.

What interest rate must he earn to be able to afford the car?

The ratio of purchase price to initial cash is

$$\frac{\$16,105}{\$10,000} = 1.6105$$

Thus, he must earn an interest rate that allows $1 to become $1.6105 in five years. Table A.3 tells us that an interest rate of 10 percent will allow him to purchase the car.

One can express the problem algebraically as

$$\$10,000 \times (1 + r)^5 = \$16,105$$

where r is the interest rate needed to purchase the car. Because $16,105/$10,000 = 1.6105, we have

$$(1 + r)^5 = 1.6105$$

Either the table or any sophisticated hand calculator solves[2] for r.

The Power of Compounding: A Digression

Most people who have had any experience with compounding are impressed with its power over long periods of time. Take the stock market, for example. Ibbotson and Sinquefield have calculated what the stock market returned as a whole from 1926 through 1999.[3] They find that one dollar placed in these stocks at the beginning of 1926 would have been worth $2,845.63 at the end of 1999. This is 11.35 percent compounded annually for 74 years, i.e., $(1.1135)^{74} = \$2,845.63$. (*Note:* We are rounding 11.346 to 11.35.)

The example illustrates the great difference between compound and simple interest. At 11.35 percent, simple interest on $1 is 11.35 cents a year. Simple interest over 74 years is $8.40 (74 × $0.1135). That is, an individual withdrawing 11.35 cents every year would have withdrawn $8.40 (74 × $0.1135) over 74 years. This is quite a bit below the $2,845.63 that was obtained by reinvestment of all principal and interest.

---

[2]Conceptually, we are taking the fifth roots of both sides of the equation. That is,

$$r = \sqrt[5]{1.6105} - 1$$

[3]*Stocks, Bonds, Bills and Inflation* [SBBI]. 1999 Yearbook. Ibbotson Associates, Chicago, 2000.

The results are more impressive over even longer periods of time. A person with no experience in compounding might think that the value of $1 at the end of 148 years would be twice the value of $1 at the end of 74 years, if the yearly rate of return stayed the same. Actually the value of $1 at the end of 148 years would be the *square* of the value of $1 at the end of 74 years. That is, if the annual rate of return remained the same, a $1 investment in common stocks should be worth $8,097,610.1[$1 × (2845.63 × 2845.63)].

A few years ago an archaeologist unearthed a relic stating that Julius Caesar lent the Roman equivalent of one penny to someone. Since there was no record of the penny ever being repaid, the archaeologist wondered what the interest and principal would be if a descendant of Caesar tried to collect from a descendant of the borrower in the 20th century. The archaeologist felt that a rate of 6 percent might be appropriate. To his surprise, the principal and interest due after more than 2,000 years was far greater than the entire wealth on earth.

The power of compounding can explain why the parents of well-to-do families frequently bequeath wealth to their grandchildren rather than to their children. That is, they skip a generation. The parents would rather make the grandchildren very rich than make the children moderately rich. We have found that in these families the grandchildren have a more positive view of the power of compounding than do the children.

EXAMPLE

Some people have said that it was the best real estate deal in history. Peter Minuit, director–general of New Netherlands, the Dutch West India Company's Colony in North America, in 1626 allegedly bought Manhattan Island for 60 guilders worth of trinkets from native Americans. By 1667 the Dutch were forced to exchange it for Suriname with the British (perhaps the worst real estate deal ever). This sounds cheap but did the Dutch really get the better end of the deal? It is reported that 60 guilders was worth about $24 at the prevailing exchange rate. If the native Americans had sold the trinkets at a fair market value and invested the $24 at 5 percent (tax free), it would now, 375 years later, be worth more than $2.0 billion. Today, Manhattan is undoubtedly worth more than $2 billion, and so at a 5 percent rate of return, the native Americans got the worst of the deal. However, if invested at 10 percent, the amount of money they received would be worth about

$$\$24 \, (1 + r)^{\text{T}} = 1.1^{375} \cong \$72 \text{ quadrillion}$$

This is a lot of money. In fact, $72 quadrillion is more than all the real estate in the world is worth today. No one in the history of the world has ever been able to find an investment yielding 10% every year for 375 years.

Present Value and Discounting

We now know that an annual interest rate of 9 percent enables the investor to transform $1 today into $1.1881 two years from now. In addition, we would like to know:

How much would an investor need to lend today so that she could receive $1 two years from today?

Algebraically, we can write this as

$$\text{PV} \times (1.09)^2 = \$1$$

In the preceding equation, PV stands for present value, the amount of money we must lend today in order to receive $1 in two years' time.

■ FIGURE 4.8 **Compounding and Discounting**

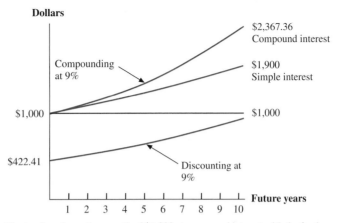

Dollars

$2,367.36
Compound interest

Compounding
at 9%

$1,900
Simple interest

$1,000

$1,000

$422.41

Discounting at
9%

Future years

1   2   3   4   5   6   7   8   9   10

The top line shows the growth of $1,000 at compound interest with the funds invested at 9 percent: $1,000 \times (1.09)^{10} = \$2,367.36$. Simple interest is shown on the next line. It is $1,000 + [10 \times (\$1,000 \times 0.09)] = \$1,900$. The bottom line shows the discounted value of $1,000 if the interest rate is 9 percent.

Solving for PV in this equation, we have

$$PV = \frac{\$1}{1.1881} = \$0.84$$

This process of calculating the present value of a future cash flow is called **discounting.** It is the opposite of compounding. The difference between compounding and discounting is illustrated in Figure 4.8.

To be certain that $0.84 is in fact the present value of $1 to be received in two years, we must check whether or not, if we loaned out $0.84 and rolled over the loan for two years, we would get exactly $1 back. If this were the case, the capital markets would be saying that $1 received in two years' time is equivalent to having $0.84 today. Checking the exact numbers, we get

$$\$0.84168 \times 1.09 \times 1.09 = \$1$$

In other words, when we have capital markets with a sure interest rate of 9 percent, we are indifferent between receiving $0.84 today or $1 in two years. We have no reason to treat these two choices differently from each other, because if we had $0.84 today and loaned it out for two years, it would return $1 to us at the end of that time. The value 0.84 $[1/(1.09)^2]$ is called the **present value factor.** It is the factor used to calculate the present value of a future cash flow.

In the multiperiod case, the formula for PV can be written as

Present Value of Investment

$$PV = \frac{C_T}{(1 + r)^T} \tag{4.3}$$

where C_T is cash flow at date T and r is the appropriate interest rate.

EXAMPLE

Bernard Dumas will receive $10,000 three years from now. Bernard can earn 8 percent on his investments, and so the **appropriate discount rate** is 8 percent. What is the present value of his future cash flow?

■ Figure 4.9 Discounting Bernard Dumas' Opportunity

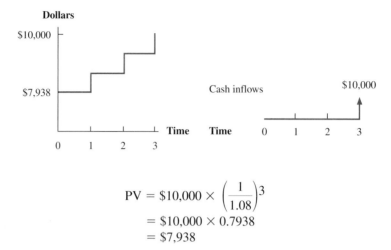

$$PV = \$10,000 \times \left(\frac{1}{1.08}\right)^3$$
$$= \$10,000 \times 0.7938$$
$$= \$7,938$$

Figure 4.9 illustrates the application of the present value factor to Bernard's investment.

When his investments grow at an 8 percent rate of interest, Bernard Dumas is equally inclined toward receiving $7,938 now and receiving $10,000 in three years' time. After all, he could convert the $7,938 he receives today into $10,000 in three years by lending it at an interest rate of 8 percent.

Bernard Dumas could have reached his present value calculation in one of three ways. The computation could have been done by hand, by calculator, or with the help of Table A.1, which appears in the back of the text. This table presents *present value of $1 to be received after t periods.* The table is used by locating the appropriate interest rate on the horizontal and the appropriate number of periods on the vertical. For example, Bernard Dumas would look at the following portion of Table A.1:

	Interest rate		
Period	7%	8%	9%
1	0.9346	0.9259	0.9174
2	0.8734	0.8573	0.8417
3	0.8163	0.7938	0.7722
4	0.7629	0.7350	0.7084

The appropriate present value factor is 0.7938.

In the preceding example, we gave both the interest rate and the future cash flow. Alternatively, the interest rate could have been unknown.

EXAMPLE

A customer of the Chaffkin Corp. wants to buy a tugboat today. Rather than paying immediately, he will pay $50,000 in three years. It will cost the Chaffkin Corp. $38,610 to build the tugboat immediately. The relevant cash flows to Chaffkin Corp. are displayed in Figure 4.10. By charging what interest rate would the Chaffkin Corp. neither gain nor lose on the sale?

■ FIGURE 4.10 **Cash Flows for Tugboat**

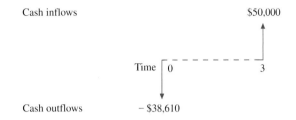

The ratio of construction cost to sale price is

$$\frac{\$38{,}610}{\$50{,}000} = 0.7722$$

We must determine the interest rate that allows \$1 to be received in three years to have a present value of \$0.7722. Table A.1 tells us that 9 percent is that interest rate.[4]

Frequently, an investor or a business will receive more than one cash flow. The present value of the set of cash flows is simply the sum of the present values of the individual cash flows. This is illustrated in the following example.

EXAMPLE

Dennis Draper has won the Kentucky state lottery and will receive the following set of cash flows over the next two years:

Year	Cash Flow
1	\$2,000
2	\$5,000

Mr. Draper can currently earn 6 percent in his passbook savings account, and so, the appropriate discount rate is 6 percent. The present value of the cash flows is

Year	Cash Flow × Present Value Factor	= Present Value

Year	Cash Flow × Present Value Factor = Present Value
1	$\$2{,}000 \times \dfrac{1}{1.06} = 0.943 = \$1{,}887$
2	$\$5{,}000 \times \left(\dfrac{1}{1.06}\right)^{2} = 0.890 = \$4{,}450$
	Total \$6,337

In other words, Mr. Draper is equally inclined toward receiving \$6,337 today and receiving \$2,000 and \$5,000 over the next two years.

---

[4]Algebraically, we are solving for r in the equation

$$\frac{\$50{,}000}{(1 + r)^{3}} = \$38{,}610$$

or, equivalently,

$$\frac{\$1}{(1 + r)^{3}} = \$0.7722$$

EXAMPLE

Finance.com has an opportunity to invest in a new high-speed computer that costs $50,000. The computer will generate cash flows (from cost savings) of $25,000 one year from now, $20,000 two years from now, and $15,000 three years from now. The computer will be worthless after three years, and no additional cash flows will occur. Finance.com has determined that the appropriate discount rate is 7 percent for this investment. Should Finance.com make this investment in a new high-speed computer? What is the present value of the investment?

The cash flows and present value factors of the proposed computer are as follows.

	Cash Flows	Present Value Factor
Year 0	−$50,000	$1 = 1$
1	$25,000	$\dfrac{1}{1.07} = 0.9346$
2	$20,000	$\left(\dfrac{1}{1.07}\right)^2 = 0.8734$
3	$15,000	$\left(\dfrac{1}{1.07}\right)^3 = 0.8163$

The present values of the cash flows are:

$$\text{Cash flows} \times \text{Present value factor} = \text{Present value}$$

Year 0	−$50,000 × 1	= −$50,000
1	$25,000 × 0.9346	= $23,365
2	$20,000 × 0.8734	= $17,468
3	$15,000 × 0.8163	= $12,244.5
	Total:	$ 3,077.5

Finance.com should invest in a new high-speed computer because the present value of its future cash flows is greater than its cost. The NPV is $3,077.5.

The Algebraic Formula

To derive an algebraic formula for net present value of a cash flow, recall that the PV of receiving a cash flow one year from now is

$$PV = C_1/(1 + r)$$

and the PV of receiving a cash flow two years from now is

$$PV = C_2/(1 + r)^2$$

We can write the NPV of a T-period project as

$$NPV = -C_0 + \frac{C_1}{1 + r} + \frac{C_2}{(1 + r)^2} + \ldots + \frac{C_T}{(1 + r)^T} = -C_0 + \sum_{i=1}^{T} \frac{C_i}{(1 + r)^i}$$

The initial flow, $-C_0$, is assumed to be negative because it represents an investment. The Σ is shorthand for the sum of the series.

CONCEPT QUESTIONS
?
• What is the difference between simple interest and compound interest?
• What is the formula for the net present value of a project?

4.3 COMPOUNDING PERIODS

So far we have assumed that compounding and discounting occur yearly. Sometimes compounding may occur more frequently than just once a year. For example, imagine that a bank pays a 10-percent interest rate "compounded semiannually." This means that a $1,000 deposit in the bank would be worth $1,000 × 1.05 = $1,050 after six months, and $1,050 × 1.05 = $1,102.50 at the end of the year.

The end-of-the-year wealth can be written as[5]

$$\$1,000\left(1 + \frac{0.10}{2}\right)^2 = \$1,000 \times (1.05)^2 = \$1,102.50$$

Of course, a $1,000 deposit would be worth $1,100 ($1,000 × 1.10) with yearly compounding. Note that the future value at the end of one year is greater with semiannual compounding than with yearly compounding. With yearly compounding, the original $1,000 remains the investment base for the full year. The original $1,000 is the investment base only for the first six months with semiannual compounding. The base over the second six months is $1,050. Hence, one gets *interest on interest* with semiannual compounding.

Because $1,000 × 1.1025 = $1,102.50, 10 percent compounded semiannually is the same as 10.25 percent compounded annually. In other words, a rational investor could not care less whether she is quoted a rate of 10 percent compounded semiannually, or a rate of 10.25 percent compounded annually.

Quarterly compounding at 10 percent yields wealth at the end of one year of

$$\$1,000\left(1 + \frac{0.10}{4}\right)^4 = \$1,103.81$$

More generally, compounding an investment m times a year provides end-of-year wealth of

$$C_0\left(1 + \frac{r}{m}\right)^m \tag{4.4}$$

where C_0 is one's initial investment and r is the **stated annual interest rate.** The stated annual interest rate is the annual interest rate without consideration of compounding. Banks and other financial institutions may use other names for the stated annual interest rate. **Annual percentage rate** is perhaps the most common synonym.

EXAMPLE

What is the end-of-year wealth if Jane Christine receives a stated annual interest rate of 24 percent compounded monthly on a $1 investment?

Using (4.4), her wealth is

$$\$1\left(1 + \frac{0.24}{12}\right)^{12} = \$1 \times (1.02)^{12}$$
$$= \$1.2682$$

---

[5]In addition to using a calculator, one can still use Table A.3 when the compounding period is less than a year. Here, one sets the interest rate at 5 percent and the number of periods at two.

The annual rate of return is 26.82 percent. This annual rate of return is either called the **effective annual interest rate** or the **effective annual yield.** Due to compounding, the effective annual interest rate is greater than the stated annual interest rate of 24 percent. Algebraically, we can rewrite the effective annual interest rate as

Effective Annual Interest Rate:

$$\left(1 + \frac{r}{m}\right)^m - 1 \tag{4.5}$$

Students are often bothered by the subtraction of 1 in (4.5). Note that end-of-year wealth is composed of both the interest earned over the year and the original principal. We remove the original principal by subtracting one in (4.5).

EXAMPLE

If the stated annual rate of interest, 8 percent, is compounded quarterly, what is the effective annual rate of interest?

Using (4.5), we have

$$\left(1 + \frac{r}{m}\right)^m - 1 = \left(1 + \frac{0.08}{4}\right)^4 - 1 = 0.0824 = 8.24\%$$

Referring back to our original example where $C_0 = \$1,000$ and $r = 10\%$, we can generate the following table:

C_0	Compounding Frequency (m)	C_1	Effective Annual Interest Rate = $\left(1 + \dfrac{r}{m}\right)^m - 1$
\$1,000	Yearly ($m = 1$)	\$1,100.00	0.10
1,000	Semiannually ($m = 2$)	1,102.50	0.1025
1,000	Quarterly ($m = 4$)	1,103.81	0.10381
1,000	Daily ($m = 365$)	1,105.16	0.10516

Distinction between Stated Annual Interest Rate and Effective Annual Interest Rate

The distinction between the stated annual interest rate (SAIR) and the effective annual interest rate (EAIR) is frequently quite troubling to students. One can reduce the confusion by noting that the SAIR becomes meaningful only if the compounding interval is given. For example, for an SAIR of 10 percent, the future value at the end of one year with semiannual compounding is $[1 + (.10/2)]^2 = 1.1025$. The future value with quarterly compounding is $[1 + (.10/4)]^4 = 1.1038$. If the SAIR is 10 percent but no compounding interval is given, one cannot calculate future value. In other words, one does not know whether to compound semiannually, quarterly, or over some other interval.

By contrast, the EAIR is meaningful *without* a compounding interval. For example, an EAIR of 10.25 percent means that a \$1 investment will be worth \$1.1025 in one year. One can think of this as an SAIR of 10 percent with semiannual compounding or an SAIR of 10.25 percent with annual compounding, or some other possibility.

Compounding over Many Years

Formula (4.4) applies for an investment over one year. For an investment over one or more (*T*) years, the formula becomes

Future Value with Compounding:

$$FV = C_0\left(1 + \frac{r}{m}\right)^{mT}$$

(4.6)

EXAMPLE

Harry DeAngelo is investing $5,000 at a stated annual interest rate of 12 percent per year, compounded quarterly, for five years. What is his wealth at the end of five years?

Using formula (4.6), his wealth is

$$\$5,000 \times \left(1 + \frac{0.12}{4}\right)^{4 \times 5} = \$5,000 \times (1.03)^{20} = \$5,000 \times 1.8061 = \$9,030.50$$

Continuous Compounding (Advanced)

The previous discussion shows that one can compound much more frequently than once a year. One could compound semiannually, quarterly, monthly, daily, hourly, each minute, or even more often. The limiting case would be to compound every infinitesimal instant, which is commonly called **continuous compounding.** Surprisingly, banks and other financial institutions frequently quote continuously compounded rates, which is why we study them.

Though the idea of compounding this rapidly may boggle the mind, a simple formula is involved. With continuous compounding, the value at the end of *T* years is expressed as

$$C_0 \times e^{rT}$$

(4.7)

where C_0 is the initial investment, *r* is the stated annual interest rate, and *T* is the number of years over which the investment runs. The number *e* is a constant and is approximately equal to 2.718. It is not an unknown like C_0, *r*, and *T*.

EXAMPLE

Linda DeFond invested $1,000 at a continuously compounded rate of 10 percent for one year. What is the value of her wealth at the end of one year?

From formula (4.7) we have

$$\$1,000 \times e^{0.10} = \$1,000 \times 1.1052 = \$1,105.20$$

This number can easily be read from our Table A.5. One merely sets *r*, the value on the horizontal dimension, to 10% and *T*, the value on the vertical dimension, to 1. For this problem, the relevant portion of the table is

Period (T)	Continuously compounded rate (r)		
	9%	10%	11%
1	1.0942	1.1052	1.1163
2	1.1972	1.2214	1.2461
3	1.3100	1.3499	1.3910

Note that a continuously compounded rate of 10 percent is equivalent to an annually compounded rate of 10.52 percent. In other words, Linda DeFond could not care less whether her bank quoted a continuously compounded rate of 10 percent or a 10.52-percent rate, compounded annually.

EXAMPLE

Linda DeFond's brother, Mark, invested $1,000 at a continuously compounded rate of 10 percent for two years.

The appropriate formula here is

$$\$1,000 \times e^{0.10 \times 2} = \$1,000 \times e^{0.20} = \$1,221.40$$

Using the portion of the table of continuously compounded rates reproduced above, we find the value to be 1.2214.

Figure 4.11 illustrates the relationship among annual, semiannual, and continuous compounding. Semiannual compounding gives rise to both a smoother curve and a higher ending value than does annual compounding. Continuous compounding has both the smoothest curve and the highest ending value of all.

EXAMPLE

The Michigan state lottery is going to pay you $1,000 at the end of four years. If the annual continuously compounded rate of interest is 8 percent, what is the present value of this payment?

$$\$1,000 \times \frac{1}{e^{0.08 \times 4}} = \$1,000 \times \frac{1}{1.3771} = \$726.16$$

QUESTIONS

CONCEPT

?

- What is a stated annual interest rate?
- What is an effective annual interest rate?
- What is the relationship between the stated annual interest rate and the effective annual interest rate?
- Define continuous compounding.

■ **FIGURE 4.11   Annual, Semiannual, and Continuous Compounding**

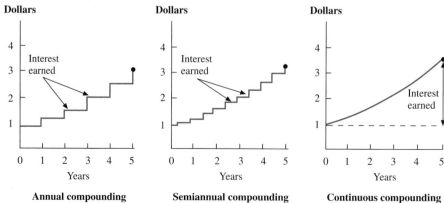

Annual compounding   Semiannual compounding   Continuous compounding

4.4 SIMPLIFICATIONS

The first part of this chapter has examined the concepts of future value and present value. Although these concepts allow one to answer a host of problems concerning the time value of money, the human effort involved can frequently be excessive. For example, consider a bank calculating the present value on a 20-year monthly mortgage. Because this mortgage has 240 (20 $\times$ 12) payments, a lot of time is needed to perform a conceptually simple task.

Because many basic finance problems are potentially so time-consuming, we search out simplifications in this section. We provide simplifying formulas for four classes of cash flow streams:

- Perpetuity
- Growing perpetuity
- Annuity
- Growing annuity

Perpetuity

A **perpetuity** is a constant stream of cash flows without end. If you are thinking that perpetuities have no relevance to reality, it will surprise you that there is a well-known case of an unending cash flow stream: the British bonds called *consols.* An investor purchasing a consol is entitled to receive yearly interest from the British government forever.

How can the price of a consol be determined? Consider a consol that pays a coupon of C dollars each year and will do so forever. Simply applying the PV formula gives us

$$\text{PV} = \frac{C}{1+r} + \frac{C}{(1+r)^2} + \frac{C}{(1+r)^3} + \dots$$

where the dots at the end of the formula stand for the infinite string of terms that continues the formula. Series like the preceding one are called *geometric series.* It is well known that even though they have an infinite number of terms, the whole series has a finite sum because each term is only a fraction of the preceding term. Before turning to our calculus books, though, it is worth going back to our original principles to see if a bit of financial intuition can help us find the PV.

The present value of the consol is the present value of all of its future coupons. In other words, it is an amount of money that, if an investor had it today, would enable him to achieve the same pattern of expenditures that the consol and its coupons would. Suppose that an investor wanted to spend exactly C dollars each year. If he had the consol, he could do this. How much money must he have today to spend the same amount? Clearly he would need exactly enough so that the interest on the money would be C dollars per year. If he had any more, he could spend more than C dollars each year. If he had any less, he would eventually run out of money spending C dollars per year.

The amount that will give the investor C dollars each year, and therefore the present value of the consol, is simply

$$\text{PV} = \frac{C}{r} \tag{4.8}$$

To confirm that this is the right answer, notice that if we lend the amount C/r, the interest it earns each year will be

$$\text{Interest} = \frac{C}{r} \times r = C$$

which is exactly the consol payment.[6] To sum up, we have shown that for a consol

Formula for Present Value of Perpetuity:

$$PV = \frac{C}{1 + r} + \frac{C}{(1 + r)^2} + \frac{C}{(1 + r)^3} + \ldots$$

$$= \frac{C}{r}$$

It is comforting to know how easily we can use a bit of financial intuition to solve this mathematical problem.

EXAMPLE

Consider a perpetuity paying $100 a year. If the relevant interest rate is 8 percent, what is the value of the consol?

Using formula (4.8), we have

$$PV = \frac{\$100}{0.08} = \$1,250$$

Now suppose that interest rates fall to 6 percent. Using (4.8), the value of the perpetuity is

$$PV = \frac{\$100}{0.06} = \$1,666.67$$

Note that the value of the perpetuity rises with a drop in the interest rate. Conversely, the value of the perpetuity falls with a rise in the interest rate.

Growing Perpetuity

Imagine an apartment building where cash flows to the landlord after expenses will be $100,000 next year. These cash flows are expected to rise at 5 percent per year. If one assumes that this rise will continue indefinitely, the cash flow stream is termed a **growing perpetuity.** The relevant interest rate is 11 percent. Therefore, the appropriate discount rate is 11 percent and the present value of the cash flows can be represented as

$$PV = \frac{\$100,000}{1.11} + \frac{\$100,000(1.05)}{(1.11)^2} + \frac{\$100,000(1.05)^2}{(1.11)^3} + \ldots + \frac{\$100,000(1.05)^{N-1}}{(1.11)^N} + \ldots$$

---

[6]We can prove this by looking at the PV equation:

$$PV = C/(1 + r) + C/(1 + r)^2 + \ldots$$

Let $C/(1 + r) = a$ and $1/(1 + r) = x$. We now have

$$PV = a(1 + x + x^2 + \ldots) \qquad (1)$$

Next we can multiply by x:

$$xPV = ax + ax^2 + \ldots \qquad (2)$$

Subtracting (2) from (1) gives

$$PV(1 - x) = a$$

Now we substitute for a and x and rearrange:

$$PV = C/r$$

Algebraically, we can write the formula as

$$PV = \frac{C}{1 + r} + \frac{C \times (1 + g)}{(1 + r)^2} + \frac{C \times (1 + g)^2}{(1 + r)^3} + \dots + \frac{C \times (1 + g)^{N-1}}{(1 + r)^N} + \dots (4.9)$$

where C is the cash flow to be received one period hence, g is the rate of growth per period, expressed as a percentage, and r is the appropriate discount rate.

Fortunately, formula (4.9) reduces to the following simplification:[7]

Formula for Present Value of Growing Perpetuity:

$$PV = \frac{C}{r - g} \tag{4.10}$$

From formula (4.10), the present value of the cash flows from the apartment building is

$$\frac{\$100,000}{0.11 - 0.05} = \$1,666,667$$

There are three important points concerning the growing perpetuity formula:

1. *The Numerator.* The numerator in (4.10) is the cash flow one period hence, not at date 0. Consider the following example:

EXAMPLE

Rothstein Corporation is *just about* to pay a dividend of $3.00 per share. Investors anticipate that the annual dividend will rise by 6 percent a year forever. The applicable interest rate is 11 percent. What is the price of the stock today?

The numerator in formula (4.10) is the cash flow to be received next period. Since the growth rate is 6 percent, the dividend next year is $3.18 ($3.00 × 1.06). The price of the stock today is

$$\$66.60 = \underset{\substack{\text{Imminent} \\ \text{dividend}}}{\$3.00} + \underset{\substack{\text{Present value of all} \\ \text{dividends beginning} \\ \text{a year from now}}}{\frac{\$3.18}{0.11 - 0.06}}$$

The price of $66.60 includes both the dividend to be received immediately and the present value of all dividends beginning a year from now. Formula (4.10) only makes it possible to calculate the present value of all dividends beginning a year from now. Be sure you understand this example; test questions on this subject always seem to trip up a few of our students.

---

[7]PV is the sum of an infinite geometric series:

$$PV = a(1 + x + x^2 + \cdots)$$

where $a = C/(1 + r)$ and $x = (1 + g)/(1 + r)$. Previously we showed that the sum of an infinite geometric series is $a/(1 - x)$. Using this result and substituting for a and x, we find

$$PV = C/(r - g)$$

Note that this geometric series converges to a finite sum only when x is less than 1. This implies that the growth rate, g, must be less than the interest rate, r.

2. *The Interest Rate and the Growth Rate.* The interest rate *r* must be greater than the growth rate *g* for the growing perpetuity formula to work. Consider the case in which the growth rate approaches the interest rate in magnitude. Then the denominator in the growing perpetuity formula gets infinitesimally small and the present value grows infinitely large. The present value is in fact undefined when *r* is less than *g*.

3. *The Timing Assumption.* Cash generally flows into and out of real-world firms both randomly and nearly continuously. However, formula (4.10) assumes that cash flows are received and disbursed at regular and discrete points in time. In the example of the apartment, we assumed that the net cash flows of $100,000 only occurred once a year. In reality, rent checks are commonly received every month. Payments for maintenance and other expenses may occur anytime within the year.

The growing perpetuity formula of (4.10) can be applied only by assuming a regular and discrete pattern of cash flow. Although this assumption is sensible because the formula saves so much time, the user should never forget that it is an *assumption.* This point will be mentioned again in the chapters ahead.

A few words should be said about terminology. Authors of financial textbooks generally use one of two conventions to refer to time. A minority of financial writers treat cash flows as being received on exact *dates,* for example date 0, date 1, and so forth. Under this convention, date 0 represents the present time. However, because a year is an interval, not a specific moment in time, the great majority of authors refer to cash flows that occur at the end of a year (or alternatively, the end of a *period*). Under this *end-of-the-year* convention, the end of year 0 is the present, the end of year 1 occurs one period hence, and so on. (The beginning of year 0 has already passed and is not generally referred to.)[8]

The interchangeability of the two conventions can be seen from the following chart:

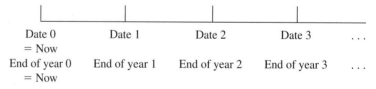

Date 0	Date 1	Date 2	Date 3	. . .
= Now				
End of year 0	End of year 1	End of year 2	End of year 3	. . .
= Now				

We strongly believe that the *dates convention* reduces ambiguity. However, we use both conventions because you are likely to see the *end-of-year convention* in later courses. In fact, both conventions may appear in the same example for the sake of practice.

Annuity

An **annuity** is a level stream of regular payments that lasts for a fixed number of periods. Not surprisingly, annuities are among the most common kinds of financial instruments. The pensions that people receive when they retire are often in the form of an annuity. Leases and mortgages are also often annuities.

To figure out the present value of an annuity we need to evaluate the following equation:

$$\frac{C}{1 + r} + \frac{C}{(1 + r)^2} + \frac{C}{(1 + r)^3} + \ldots + \frac{C}{(1 + r)^T}$$

The present value of only receiving the coupons for *T* periods must be less than the present value of a consol, but how much less? To answer this we have to look at consols a bit more closely.

---

[8]Sometimes financial writers merely speak of a cash flow in year *x*. Although this terminology is ambiguous, such writers generally mean the *end of year x*.

Consider the following time chart:

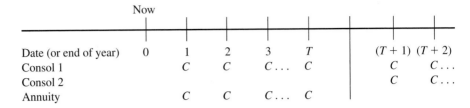

Date (or end of year)	0	1	2	3	T	(T + 1)	(T + 2)
Consol 1		C	C	C ...	C	C	C ...
Consol 2						C	C ...
Annuity		C	C	C ...	C		

Consol 1 is a normal consol with its first payment at date 1. The first payment of consol 2 occurs at date $T + 1$.

The present value of having a cash flow of C at each of T dates is equal to the present value of consol 1 minus the present value of consol 2. The present value of consol 1 is given by

$$\text{PV} = \frac{C}{r} \tag{4.11}$$

Consol 2 is just a consol with its first payment at date $T + 1$. From the perpetuity formula, this consol will be worth C/r at date T.[9] However, we do not want the value at date T. We want the value now; in other words, the present value at date 0. We must discount C/r back by T periods. Therefore, the present value of consol 2 is

$$\text{PV} = \frac{C}{r}\left[\frac{1}{(1 + r)^T}\right] \tag{4.12}$$

The present value of having cash flows for T years is the present value of a consol with its first payment at date 1 minus the present value of a consol with its first payment at date $T + 1$. Thus, the present value of an annuity is formula (4.11) minus formula (4.12). This can be written as

$$\frac{C}{r} - \frac{C}{r}\left[\frac{1}{(1 + r)^T}\right]$$

This simplifies to

Formula for Present Value of Annuity:[10, 11]

$$\text{PV} = C\left[\frac{1}{r} - \frac{1}{r(1 + r)^T}\right] \tag{4.13}$$

EXAMPLE

Mark Young has just won the state lottery, paying $50,000 a year for 20 years. He is to receive his first payment a year from now. The state advertises this as the Million Dollar Lottery because $1,000,000 = $50,000 \times 20$. If the interest rate is 8 percent, what is the true value of the lottery?

---

[9]Students frequently think that C/r is the present value at date $T + 1$ because the consol's first payment is at date $T + 1$. However, the formula values the annuity as of one period prior to the first payment.

[10]This can also be written as

$$C[1 - 1/(1 + r)^T]/r$$

[11]We can also provide a formula for the future value of an annuity.

$$\text{FV} = C\left[\frac{(1 + r)^T}{r} - \frac{1}{r}\right]$$

Formula (4.13) yields

$$\text{Present value of Million Dollar Lottery} = \$50,000 \times \left[\frac{1}{0.08} - \frac{1}{0.08(1.08)^{20}}\right]$$

$$\begin{array}{ccc} \text{Periodic payment} & & \text{Annuity factor} \\ = \$50,000 & \times & 9.8181 \\ = \$490,905 & & \end{array}$$

Rather than being overjoyed at winning, Mr. Young sues the state for misrepresentation and fraud. His legal brief states that he was promised $1 million but received only $490,905.[12]

The term we use to compute the value of the stream of level payments, *C*, for *T* years is called an **annuity factor.** The annuity factor in the current example is 9.8181. Because the annuity factor is used so often in PV calculations, we have included it in Table A.2 in the back of this book. The table gives the values of these factors for a range of interest rates, *r*, and maturity dates, *T*.

The annuity factor as expressed in the brackets of (4.13) is a complex formula. For simplification, we may from time to time refer to the annuity factor as

$$A_r^T \tag{4.14}$$

That is, expression (4.14) stands for the present value of $1 a year for *T* years at an interest rate of *r*.

Our experience is that annuity formulas are not hard, but tricky, for the beginning student. We present four tricks below.

Trick 1: A Delayed Annuity   One of the tricks in working with annuities or perpetuities is getting the timing exactly right. This is particularly true when an annuity or perpetuity begins at a date many periods in the future. We have found that even the brightest beginning student can make errors here. Consider the following example.

EXAMPLE

Danielle Caravello will receive a four-year annuity of $500 per year, beginning at date 6. If the interest rate is 10 percent, what is the present value of her annuity? This situation can be graphed as:

---

[12]To solve this problem on a common type HP19B II financial calculator, you should do the following:

a. Press "FIN" and "TVM."
b. Enter the payment 50,000 and press "PMT."
c. Enter the interest rate 8 and press "I % YR."
d. Enter the number of periods 20 and press "N."
e. Finally, press "PV" to solve.

Notice your answer is $490,907.370372. The calculator uses 11 digits for the annuity factor and the answer, whereas the example uses only 4 digits in the annuity factor and rounds the final answer to the nearest dollar. That is why the answer in the text example differs from the one using the calculator. In practice, the answer using the calculator is the best because it is more precise.

The analysis involves two steps:

1. Calculate the present value of the annuity using (4.13). This is

Present Value of Annuity at Date 5:

$$\$500\left[\frac{1}{0.10} - \frac{1}{0.10(1.10)^4}\right] = \$500 \times A_{0.10}^4$$

$$= \$500 \times 3.1699$$

$$= \$1,584.95$$

Note that $\$1,584.95$ represents the present value at *date 5*.

Students frequently think that $\$1,584.95$ is the present value at date 6, because the annuity begins at date 6. However, our formula values the annuity as of one period prior to the first payment. This can be seen in the most typical case where the first payment occurs at date 1. The formula values the annuity as of date 0 here.

2. Discount the present value of the annuity back to date 0. That is

Present Value at Date 0:

$$\frac{\$1,584.95}{(1.10)^5} = \$984.13$$

Again, it is worthwhile mentioning that, because the annuity formula brings Danielle's annuity back to date 5, the second calculation must discount over the remaining 5 periods. The two-step procedure is graphed in Figure 4.12.

Trick 2: Annuity in Advance   The annuity formula of (4.13) assumes that the first annuity payment begins a full period hence. This type of annuity is frequently called an *annuity in arrears*. What happens if the annuity begins today, in other words, at date 0?

EXAMPLE

In a previous example, Mark Young received $\$50,000$ a year for 20 years from the state lottery. In that example, he was to receive the first payment a year from the winning date. Let us now assume that the first payment occurs immediately. The total number of payments remains 20.

Under this new assumption, we have a 19-date annuity with the first payment occurring at date 1—plus an extra payment at date 0. The present value is

$$\underset{\text{Payment at date 0}}{\$50,000} + \underset{\text{19-year annuity}}{\$50,000 \times A_{0.08}^{19}}$$

$$= \$50,000 + (\$50,000 \times 9.6036)$$

$$= \$530,180$$

■ FIGURE 4.12   **Discounting Danielle Caravello's Annuity**

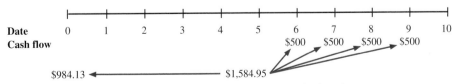

Step one: Discount the four payments back to date 5 by using the annuity formula.
Step two: Discount the present value at date 5 ($\$1,584.95$) back to present value at date 0.

$530,180, the present value in this example, is greater than $490,905, the present value in the earlier lottery example. This is to be expected because the annuity of the current example begins earlier. An annuity with an immediate initial payment is called an *annuity in advance*. Always remember that formula (4.13), as well as Table A.2, in this book refers to an *annuity in arrears*.

Trick 3: The Infrequent Annuity   The following example treats an annuity with payments occurring less frequently than once a year.

EXAMPLE

Ms. Ann Chen receives an annuity of $450, payable once every two years. The annuity stretches out over 20 years. The first payment occurs at date 2, that is, two years from today. The annual interest rate is 6 percent.

The trick is to determine the interest rate over a two-year period. The interest rate over two years is

$$(1.06 \times 1.06) - 1 = 12.36\%$$

That is, $100 invested over two years will yield $112.36.

What we want is the present value of a $450 annuity over 10 periods, with an interest rate of 12.36 percent per period. This is

$$\$450\left[\frac{1}{0.1236} - \frac{1}{0.1236 \times (1.1236)^{10}}\right] = \$450 \times A^{10}_{0.1236} = \$2,505.57$$

Trick 4: Equating Present Value of Two Annuities   The following example equates the present value of inflows with the present value of outflows.

EXAMPLE

Harold and Helen Nash are saving for the college education of their newborn daughter, Susan. The Nashes estimate that college expenses will run $30,000 per year when their daughter reaches college in 18 years. The annual interest rate over the next few decades will be 14 percent. How much money must they deposit in the bank each year so that their daughter will be completely supported through four years of college?

To simplify the calculations, we assume that Susan is born today. Her parents will make the first of her four annual tuition payments on her 18th birthday. They will make equal bank deposits on each of her first 17 birthdays, but no deposit at date 0. This is illustrated as

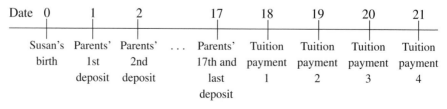

Mr. and Ms. Nash will be making deposits to the bank over the next 17 years. They will be withdrawing $30,000 per year over the following four years. We can be sure they will be able to withdraw fully $30,000 per year if the present value of the deposits is equal to the present value of the four $30,000 withdrawals.

This calculation requires three steps. The first two determine the present value of the withdrawals. The final step determines yearly deposits that will have a present value equal to that of the withdrawals.

1. We calculate the present value of the four years at college using the annuity formula.

$$\$30,000 \times \left[\frac{1}{0.14} - \frac{1}{0.14 \times (1.14)^4} \right] = \$30,000 \times A_{0.14}^4$$
$$= \$30,000 \times 2.9137 = \$87,411$$

We assume that Susan enters college on her 18th birthday. Given our discussion in Trick 1 $87,411 represents the present value at date 17.

2. We calculate the present value of the college education at date 0 as

$$\frac{\$87,411}{(1.14)^{17}} = \$9,422.91$$

3. Assuming that Helen and Harold Nash make deposits to the bank at the end of each of the 17 years, we calculate the annual deposit that will yield a present value of all deposits of $9,422.91. This is calculated as

$$C \times A_{0.14}^{17} = \$9,422.91$$

Because $A_{0.14}^{17} = 6.3729$,

$$C = \frac{\$9,422.91}{6.3729} = \$1,478.59$$

Thus, deposits of $1,478.59 made at the end of each of the first 17 years and invested at 14 percent will provide enough money to make tuition payments of $30,000 over the following four years.

An alternative method would be to (1) calculate the present value of the tuition payments at Susan's 18th birthday and (2) calculate annual deposits such that the future value of the deposits at her 18th birthday equals the present value of the tuition payments at that date. Although this technique can also provide the right answer, we have found that it is more likely to lead to errors. Therefore, we only equate present values in our presentation.

Growing Annuity

Cash flows in business are very likely to grow over time, due either to real growth or to inflation. The growing perpetuity, which assumes an infinite number of cash flows, provides one formula to handle this growth. We now consider a **growing annuity,** which is a *finite* number of growing cash flows. Because perpetuities of any kind are rare, a formula for a growing annuity would be useful indeed. The formula is[13]

Formula for Present Value of Growing Annuity:

$$PV = C\left[\frac{1}{r-g} - \frac{1}{r-g} \times \left(\frac{1+g}{1+r}\right)^T\right] \tag{4.15}$$

where, as before, C is the payment to occur at the end of the first period, r is the interest rate, g is the rate of growth per period, expressed as a percentage, and T is the number of periods for the annuity.

EXAMPLE

Stuart Gabriel, a second-year MBA student, has just been offered a job at $80,000 a year. He anticipates his salary increasing by 9 percent a year until his retirement in 40 years. Given an interest rate of 20 percent, what is the present value of his lifetime salary?

We simplify by assuming he will be paid his $80,000 salary exactly one year from now, and that his salary will continue to be paid in annual installments. The appropriate discount rate is 20 percent. From (4.15), the calculation is

$$
\begin{array}{l}
\text{Present value}\\
\quad\text{of Stuart's} = \$80,000 \times \left[\frac{1}{0.20 - 0.09} - \frac{1}{0.20 - 0.09}\left(\frac{1.09}{1.20}\right)^{40}\right] = \$711,731\\
\text{lifetime salary}
\end{array}
$$

Though the growing annuity is quite useful, it is more tedious than the other simplifying formulas. Whereas most sophisticated calculators have special programs for perpetuity, growing perpetuity, and annuity, there is no special program for growing annuity. Hence, one must calculate all the terms in formula (4.15) directly.

EXAMPLE

In a previous example, Harold and Helen Nash planned to make 17 identical payments in order to fund the college education of their daughter, Susan. Alternatively, imagine that they planned to increase their payments at 4 percent per year. What would their first payment be?

---

[13]This can be proved as follows. A growing annuity can be viewed as the difference between two growing perpetuities. Consider a growing perpetuity A, where the first payment of C occurs at date 1. Next, consider growing perpetuity B, where the first payment of $C(1 + g)^T$ is made at date $T + 1$. Both perpetuities grow at rate g. The growing annuity over T periods is the difference between annuity A and annuity B. This can be represented as:

Date	0	1	2	3	$\cdots$	T	$T+1$	$T+2$	$T+3$
Perpetuity A	C	$C \times (1+g)$	$C \times (1+g)^2$	$\cdots$	$C \times (1+g)^{T-1}$	$C \times (1+g)^T$	$C \times (1+g)^{T+1}$	$C \times (1+g)^{T+2}\cdots$
Perpetuity B						$C \times (1+g)^T$	$C \times (1+g)^{T+1}$	$C \times (1+g)^{T+2}\cdots$
Annuity	C	$C \times (1+g)$	$C \times (1+g)^2$	$\cdots$	$C \times (1+g)^{T-1}$			

The value of perpetuity A is

$$\frac{C}{r-g}$$

The value of perpetuity B is

$$\frac{C \times (1+g)^T}{r-g} \times \frac{1}{(1+r)^T}$$

The difference between the two perpetuities is given by (4.15).

The first two steps of the previous Nash family example showed that the present value of the college costs was $9,422.91. These two steps would be the same here. However, the third step must be altered. Now we must ask, How much should their first payment be so that, if payments increase by 4 percent per year, the present value of all payments will be $9,422.91?

We set the growing-annuity formula equal to $9,422.91 and solve for C.

$$C\left[\frac{1}{r-g} - \frac{1}{r-g}\left(\frac{1+g}{1+r}\right)^T\right] = C\left[\frac{1}{0.14-0.04} - \frac{1}{0.14-0.04}\left(\frac{1.04}{1.14}\right)^{17}\right]$$
$$= \$9,422.91$$

Here, $C = \$1,192.78$. Thus, the deposit on their daughter's first birthday is $1,192.78, the deposit on the second birthday is $1,240.49 ($1.04 \times \$1,192.78$), and so on.

CONCEPT QUESTIONS

- What are the formulas for perpetuity, growing perpetuity, annuity, and growing annuity?
- What are three important points concerning the growing-perpetuity formula?
- What are four tricks concerning annuities?

CASE STUDY: *Making the Decision to Convert Lottery Prize Winnings: The Case of the Singer Asset Finance Company*

■ ■ ■ ■ ■

In 1987, Rosalind Setchfield won more than $1.3 million in the Arizona state lottery. The winnings were to be paid in 20 yearly installments of $65,276.79. Six years later, in 1995, Mrs. Setchfield received a phone call from a salesman for the Singer Asset Finance Company of West Palm Beach, Florida. The Singer company offered to give her $140,000 immediately for one-half of the next nine lottery checks (i.e., $140,000 now for $32,638.39 × 9 = $293,745.51 over nine years). Singer is a prize broker with many employees whose main job is to track down million-dollar-lottery prize-winners like Mrs. Setchfield. Singer knows that many people are eager to trade all or part of their promised winnings for a discounted lump sum immediately. Singer is part of a growing $700 million prize-broker business. Singer and Woodbridge Sterling Capital currently account for about 80 percent of the market for lottery prize conversions. Prize brokers like Singer resell their rights to receive future payouts (called structured payouts) to institutional investors such as SunAmerica, Inc., or the John Hancock Mutual Life Insurance Co. In the case of Mrs. Setchfield, the investor was the Enhance Financial Service Group, a New York municipal bond reinsurer. Singer had arranged to sell its stake in Mrs. Setchfield's lottery prize to Enhance for $196,000 and would make a quick $56,000 profit if she accepted the offer. Mrs. Setchfield accepted Singer's offer and the deal was made.

How was Singer able to structure a deal that resulted in a $56,000 profit? The answer is that individuals and institutions have different intertemporal consumption preferences. Mrs. Setchfield's family had experienced some financial difficulties and was in need of some immediate cash. She didn't want to wait nine years for her prize winnings. On the other hand, the Enhance Group had some excess cash and was very willing to make a $196,000 investment in order to receive the rights to obtain half of Mrs. Setchfield's prize winnings, or $32,638.39 a year for nine years. The discount rate the Enhance Group applied to the future payouts was about 8.96 percent (i.e., the discount rate that equates the present value of $196,000 with Singer's right to receive their equal payments of $32,638.39).

The discount rate that Mrs. Setchfield used was 18.1 percent, reflecting her aversion to deferred cash flows.

Source: Vanessa Williams, "How Major Players Turn Lottery Jackpots into Guaranteed Bet," *The Wall Street Journal*, September 23, 1997. ■ ■ ■ ■ ■

4.5 WHAT IS A FIRM WORTH?

Suppose you are in the business of trying to determine the value of small companies. (You are a business appraiser.) How can you determine what a firm is worth? One way to think about the question of how much a firm is worth is to calculate the present value of its future cash flows.

Let us consider the example of a firm that is expected to generate net cash flows (cash inflows minus cash outflows) of $5,000 in the first year and $2,000 for each of the next five years. The firm can be sold for $10,000 seven years from now. The owners of the firm would like to be able to make 10 percent on their investment in the firm.

The value of the firm is found by multiplying the net cash flows by the appropriate present-value factor. The value of the firm is simply the sum of the present values of the individual net cash flows.

The present value of the net cash flows is given next.

The Present Value of the Firm

End of Year	Net Cash Flow of the Firm	Present Value Factor (10%)	Present Value of Net Cash Flows
1	$ 5,000	.90909	$ 4,545.45
2	2,000	.82645	1,652.90
3	2,000	.75131	1,502.62
4	2,000	.68301	1,366.02
5	2,000	.62092	1,241.84
6	2,000	.56447	1,128.94
7	10,000	.51315	5,131.58
		Present value of firm	$16,569.35

We can also use the simplifying formula for an annuity to give us

$$\frac{\$5,000}{1.1} + \frac{(2,000 \times A_{0.10}^5)}{1.1} + \frac{10,000}{(1.1)^7} = \$16,569.35$$

Suppose you have the opportunity to acquire the firm for $12,000. Should you acquire the firm? The answer is yes because the NPV is positive.

$$\text{NPV} = \text{PV} - \text{Cost}$$
$$\$4,569.35 = \$16,569.35 - \$12,000$$

The incremental value (NPV) of acquiring the firm is $4,569.35.

EXAMPLE

The Trojan Pizza Company is contemplating investing $1 million in four new outlets in Los Angeles. Andrew Lo, the firm's Chief Financial Officer (CFO), has estimated that the investments will pay out cash flows of $200,000 per year for nine years and nothing thereafter. (The cash flows will occur at the end of each year and there will be no cash flow after year 9.) Mr. Lo has determined that the relevant discount rate for this investment is 15 percent. This is the rate of return that the firm can earn at comparable projects. Should the Trojan Pizza Company make the investments in the new outlets?

The decision can be evaluated as:

$$\text{NPV} = -\$1,000,000 + \frac{\$200,000}{1.15} + \frac{\$200,000}{(1.15)^2} + \ldots + \frac{\$200,000}{(1.15)^9}$$

$$= -\$1,000,000 + \$200,000 \times A_{0.15}^9$$

$$= -\$1,000,000 + \$954,316.78$$

$$= -\$45,683.22$$

The present value of the four new outlets is only \$954,316.78. The outlets are worth less than they cost. The Trojan Pizza Company should not make the investment because the NPV is −\$45,683.22. If the Trojan Pizza Company requires a 15 percent rate of return, the new outlets are not a good investment.

4.6 SUMMARY AND CONCLUSIONS

1. Two basic concepts, *future value* and *present value,* were introduced in the beginning of this chapter. With a 10-percent interest rate, an investor with \$1 today can generate a future value of \$1.10 in a year, \$1.21 [\$1 × (1.10)^2] in two years, and so on. Conversely, present-value analysis places a current value on a later cash flow. With the same 10-percent interest rate, a dollar to be received in one year has a present value of \$0.909 (\$1/1.10) in year 0. A dollar to be received in two years has a present value of \$0.826 [\$1/(1.10)^2].

2. One commonly expresses the interest rate as, say, 12 percent per year. However, one can speak of the interest rate as 3 percent per quarter. Although the stated annual interest rate remains 12 percent (3 percent × 4), the effective annual interest rate is 12.55 percent [(1.03)^4 − 1]. In other words, the compounding process increases the future value of an investment. The limiting case is continuous compounding, where funds are assumed to be reinvested every infinitesimal instant.

3. A basic quantitative technique for financial decision making is net present value analysis. The net present value formula for an investment that generates cash flows (C_i) in future periods is

$$\text{NPV} = -C_0 + \frac{C_1}{(1+r)} + \frac{C_2}{(1+r)^2} + \ldots + \frac{C_N}{(1+r)^N} = -C_0 + \sum_{i=1}^{N} \frac{C_i}{(1+r)^i}$$

The formula assumes that the cash flow at date 0 is the initial investment (a cash outflow).

4. Frequently, the actual calculation of present value is long and tedious. The computation of the present value of a long-term mortgage with monthly payments is a good example of this. We presented four simplifying formulas:

$$\textbf{Perpetuity: PV} = \frac{C}{r}$$

$$\textbf{Growing perpetuity: PV} = \frac{C}{r-g}$$

$$\textbf{Annuity: PV} = C\left[\frac{1}{r} - \frac{1}{r \times (1+r)^T}\right]$$

$$\textbf{Growing annuity: PV} = C\left[\frac{1}{r-g} - \frac{1}{r-g} \times \left(\frac{1+g}{1+r}\right)^T\right]$$

5. We stressed a few practical considerations in the application of these formulas:

a. The numerator in each of the formulas, *C*, is the cash flow to be received *one full period hence*.
b. Cash flows are generally irregular in practice. To avoid unwieldy problems, assumptions to create more regular cash flows are made both in this textbook and in the real world.
c. A number of present value problems involve annuities (or perpetuities) beginning a few periods hence. Students should practice combining the annuity (or perpetuity) formula with the discounting formula to solve these problems.
d. Annuities and perpetuities may have periods of every two or every *n* years, rather than once a year. The annuity and perpetuity formulas can easily handle such circumstances.
e. One frequently encounters problems where the present value of one annuity must be equated with the present value of another annuity.

KEY TERMS

Annuity 86	Effective annual yield 80
Annuity factor 88	Future value 66
Annual percentage rate 79	Growing annuity 91
Appropriate discount rate 75	Growing perpetuity 84
Compounding 70	Net present value 68
Compound interest 70	Perpetuity 83
Compound value 66	Present value 67
Continuous compounding 81	Present value factor 75
Discounting 75	Simple interest 70
Effective annual interest rate 80	Stated annual interest rate 79

SUGGESTED READINGS

To learn how to perform the mathematics of present value, we encourage you to see the handbooks that come with the Hewlett-Packard HP 19BII calculator.

We also recommend:
White, M. *Financial Analysis with a Calculator.* 3rd ed. Burr Ridge, Ill.: Irwin/McGraw-Hill, 1998.

QUESTIONS AND PROBLEMS[14]

Annual Compounding

4.1 Compute the future value of $1,000 compounded annually for
   a. 10 years at 5 percent.
   b. 10 years at 7 percent.
   c. 20 years at 5 percent.
   d. Why is the interest earned in part *c* not twice the amount earned in part *a?*

4.2 Calculate the present value of the following cash flows discounted at 10 percent.
   a. $1,000 received seven years from today.
   b. $2,000 received one year from today.
   c. $500 received eight years from today.

4.3 Would you rather receive $1,000 today or $2,000 in 10 years if the discount rate is 8 percent?

---

[14]The following conventions are used in the questions and problems for this chapter.

If more frequent compounding than once a year is indicated, the problem will either state: (1) both a stated annual interest rate and a compounding period, or (2) an effective annual interest rate.

If annual compounding is indicated, the problem will provide an annual interest rate. Since the stated annual interest rate and the effective annual interest rate are the same here, we use the simpler annual interest rate.

4.4   The government has issued a bond that will pay $1,000 in 25 years. The bond will pay no interim coupon payments. What is the present value of the bond if the discount rate is 10 percent?

4.5   A firm has an estimated pension liability of $1.5 million due 27 years from today. If the firm can invest in a risk-free security that has a stated annual interest rate of 8 percent, how much must the firm invest today to be able to make the $1.5 million payment?

4.6   You have won the Florida state lottery. Lottery officials offer you the choice of the following alternative payouts:

Alternative 1: $10,000 one year from now.

Alternative 2: $20,000 five years from now.

Which alternative should you choose if the discount rate is:
a. 0 percent?
b. 10 percent?
c. 20 percent?
d. What discount rate makes the two alternatives equally attractive to you?

4.7   You are selling your house. The Smiths have offered you $115,000. They will pay you immediately. The Joneses have offered you $150,000, but they cannot pay you until three years from today. The interest rate is 10 percent. Which offer should you choose?

4.8   Suppose you bought a bond that will pay $1,000 in 20 years. No intermediate coupon payments will be made. If the appropriate discount rate for the bond is 8 percent,
a. what is the current price of the bond?
b. what will the price be 10 years from today?
c. what will the price be 15 years from today?

4.9   Suppose you deposit $1,000 in an account at the end of each of the next four years. If the account earns 12 percent, how much will be in the account at the end of seven years?

4.10 Ann Woodhouse is considering the purchase of a house. She expects that she will own the house for 10 years and then sell it for $5 million. What is the most she would be willing to pay for the house if the appropriate discount rate is 12 percent?

4.11 You have the opportunity to make an investment that costs $900,000. If you make this investment now, you will receive $120,000 one year from today, $250,000 and $800,000 two and three years from today, respectively. The appropriate discount rate for this investment is 12 percent.
a. Should you make the investment?
b. What is the net present value (NPV) of this opportunity?
c. If the discount rate is 11 percent, should you invest? Compute the NPV to support your answer.

4.12 You have the opportunity to invest in a machine that will cost $340,000. The machine will generate cash flows of $100,000 at the end of each year and require maintenance costs of $10,000 at the beginning of each year. If the economic life of the machine is five years and the relevant discount rate is 10 percent, should you buy the machine? What if the relevant discount rate is 9 percent?

4.13 Today a firm signed a contract to sell a capital asset for $90,000. The firm will receive payment five years from today. The asset costs $60,000 to produce.
a. If the appropriate discount rate is 10 percent, is the firm making a profit on this item?
b. At what appropriate discount rate will the firm break even?

4.14 Your aunt owns an auto dealership. She promised to give you $3,000 in trade-in value for your car when you graduate one year from now, while your roommate offered you $3,500 for the car now. The prevailing interest rate is 12 percent. If the future value of benefit from owning the car for one year is expected to be $1,000, should you accept your aunt's offer?

Compounding Periods

4.15 What is the future value three years hence of $1,000 invested in an account with a stated annual interest rate of 8 percent,
      a. compounded annually?
      b. compounded semiannually?
      c. compounded monthly?
      d. compounded continuously?
      e. Why does the future value increase as the compounding period shortens?

4.16 Compute the future value of $1,000 continuously compounded for
      a. 5 years at a stated annual interest rate of 12 percent.
      b. 3 years at a stated annual interest rate of 10 percent.
      c. 10 years at a stated annual interest rate of 5 percent.
      d. 8 years at a stated annual interest rate of 7 percent.

4.17 Calculate the present value of $5,000 in 12 years at a stated annual interest rate of 10 percent, compounded quarterly.

4.18 Bank America offers a stated annual interest rate of 4.1 percent, compounded quarterly, while Bank USA offers a stated annual interest rate of 4.05 percent, compounded monthly. In which bank should you deposit your money?

Perpetuities and Growing Perpetuities

4.19 The market interest rate is 15 percent. What is the price of a consol bond that pays $120 annually?

4.20 A prestigious investment bank designed a new security that pays a quarterly dividend of $10 permanently. What is the price of the security if the stated annual interest rate is 12 percent, compounded quarterly?

4.21 World Transportation, Inc., is expected to initiate its quarterly dividend of $1 five years from today and the dividend is expected to remain constant permanently. What is the price of World Transportation stock if the stated annual interest rate is 15 percent, compounded quarterly?

4.22 Assuming an interest rate of 10 percent, calculate the present value of the following streams of yearly payments:
      a. $1,000 per year forever, with the first payment one year from today.
      b. $500 per year forever, with the first payment two years from today.
      c. $2,420 per year forever, with the first payment three years from today.

4.23 Given an interest rate of 10 percent per year, what is the value at date $t = 5$ (i.e., the end of year 5) of a perpetual stream of $120 annual payments starting at date $t = 9$?

4.24 Harris, Inc., paid a $3 dividend yesterday. If the firm raises its dividend at 5 percent every year and the appropriate discount rate is 12 percent, what is the price of Harris stock?

4.25 In its most recent corporate report, Williams, Inc., apologized to its stockholders for not paying a dividend. The report states that management will pay a $1 dividend next year. That dividend will grow at 4 percent every year thereafter. If the discount rate is 10 percent, how much are you willing to pay for a share of Williams, Inc.?

4.26 Mark Weinstein has been working on an advanced technology in laser eye surgery. The technology is expected to be available to the medical industry two years from today and will generate annual income of $200,000 growing at 5 percent perpetually. What is the present value of the technology if the discount rate is 10 percent?

Annuities and Growing Annuities

4.27 IDEC Pharmaceuticals is considering a drug project that costs $100,000 today and is expected to generate end-of-year annual cash flow of $50,000 forever. At what discount rate would IDEC be indifferent between accepting or rejecting the project?

4.28 Should you buy an asset that will generate income of $1,200 per year for eight years? The price of the asset is $6,200 and the annual interest rate is 10 percent.

4.29 What is the present value of end-of-year cash flows of $2,000 per year, with the first cash flow received three years from today and the last one 22 years from today? Use a discount rate of 8 percent.

4.30 What is the value of a 15-year annuity that pays $500 a year? The annuity's first payment is at the end of year 6 and the annual interest rate is 12 percent for years 1 through 5 and 15 percent thereafter.

4.31 You are offered the opportunity to buy a note for $12,800. The note is certain to pay $2,000 at the end of each of the next 10 years. If you buy the note, what rate of interest will you receive?

4.32 You need $25,000 five years from now. You budget to make equal payments at the end of every year into an account that pays an annual interest rate of 7 percent.
 a. What are your annual payments?
 b. Your rich uncle died and left you $20,000. How much of it must you put into the same account as a lump sum today to meet your goal?

4.33 Nancy Ferris bought a building for $120,000. She paid 15 percent down and agreed to pay the balance in 20 equal annual installments. What are the equal installments if the annual interest rate is 10 percent?

4.34 Jack Ferguson has signed a three-year contract to work for a computer software company. He expects to receive a base salary of $5,000 a month and a bonus of $10,000 at year-end. All payments are made at the end of periods. What is the present value of the contract if the stated annual interest rate, compounded monthly, is 12 percent?

4.35 Peter Green bought a $15,000 Honda Civic with 20 percent down and financed the rest with a four-year loan at 8 percent stated annual interest rate, compounded monthly. What is his monthly payment if he starts the payment one month after the purchase?

4.36 You have recently won the super jackpot in the Illinois state lottery. On reading the fine print, you discover that you have the following two options:
 a. You receive $160,000 at the beginning of each year for 31 years. The income would be taxed at a rate of 28 percent. Taxes are withheld when the checks are issued.
 b. You receive $1,750,000 now, but you do not have access to the full amount immediately. The $1,750,000 would be taxed at 28 percent. You are able to take $446,000 of the after-tax amount now. The remaining $814,000 will be placed in a 30-year annuity account that pays $101,055 on a before-tax basis at the end of each year.

Using a discount rate of 10 percent, which option should you select?

4.37 On September 1, 1998, Susan Chao bought a motorcycle for $10,000. She paid $1,000 down and financed the balance with a five-year loan at a stated annual interest rate of 9.6 percent, compounded monthly. She started the monthly payment exactly one month after the purchase, i.e., October, 1998. In the middle of October, 2000, she got a new job and decided to pay off the loan. If the bank charges her 1 percent prepayment penalty based on the loan balance, how much should she pay the bank on November 1, 2000?

4.38 Assume that the cost of a college education will be $20,000 per year when your child enters college 12 years from now. You currently have $10,000 to invest. What rate of interest must your investment earn to pay the cost of a four-year college education for your child? For simplicity, assume the entire cost of the college education must be paid when your child enters college.

4.39 You are saving for the college education of your two children. They are two years apart in age; one will begin college in 15 years, the other will begin in 17 years. You estimate your children's college expenses to be $21,000 per year per child. The annual interest rate is 15 percent. How much money must you deposit in an account each year to fund your children's education? You will begin payments one year from today. You will make your last deposit when your oldest child enters college.

4.40 A well-known insurance company offers a policy known as the "Estate Creator Six Pay." Typically the policy is bought by a parent or grandparent for a child at the child's birth.

The details of the policy are as follows: The purchaser (say, the parent) makes the following six payments to the insurance company.

First birthday	$750	Fourth birthday	$800
Second birthday	$750	Fifth birthday	$800
Third birthday	$750	Sixth birthday	$800

No more payments are made after the child's sixth birthday. When the child reaches age 65, he or she receives $250,000. If the relevant interest rate is 6 percent for the first six years and 7 percent for all subsequent years, is the policy worth buying?

4.41 Your company is considering leasing a $120,000 piece of equipment for the next 10 years. Your company can buy the equipment outright or lease it. The annual lease payments of $15,000 are due at the beginning of each year. The lease includes an option for your company to buy the equipment for $25,000 at the end of the leasing period (i.e., 10 years). Should your company accept the lease offer if the appropriate discount rate is 8 percent a year?

4.42 You are saving for your retirement. You have decided that one year from today you will deposit 2 percent of your annual salary in an account which will earn 8 percent per year. Your salary last year was $50,000, and it will increase at 4 percent per year throughout your career. How much money will you have for your retirement, which will begin in 40 years?

4.43 You must decide whether or not to purchase new capital equipment. The cost of the machine is $5,000. It will produce the following cash flows. The appropriate discount rate is 10 percent.

Year	Cash Flow
1	$ 700
2	900
3	1,000
4	1,000
5	1,000
6	1,000
7	1,250
8	1,375

Should you purchase the equipment?

4.44 When Marilyn Monroe died, ex-husband Joe DiMaggio vowed to place fresh flowers on her grave every Sunday as long as he lived. A bunch of fresh flowers that the former baseball player thought appropriate for the star cost about $5 when she died in 1962. Based on actuarial tables, "Joltin' Joe" could expect to live for 30 years after the actress died. Assume that the stated annual interest rate, compounded weekly, is 10.4 percent. Also, assume that the rate of inflation is 3.9 percent per year, when expressed as a stated annual inflation rate, compounded weekly. Assuming that each year has exactly 52 weeks, what is the present value of this commitment?

4.45 Your younger brother has come to you for advice. He is about to enter college and has two options open to him. His first option is to study engineering. If he does this, his undergraduate degree would cost him $12,000 a year for four years. Having obtained this, he would need to gain two years of practical experience: in the first year he would earn $20,000, in the second year he would earn $25,000. He would then need to obtain his master's degree, which will cost $15,000 a year for two years. After that he will be fully qualified and can earn $40,000 per year for 25 years.

His other alternative is to study accounting. If he does this, he would pay $13,000 a year for four years and then he would earn $31,000 per year for 30 years.

The effort involved in the two careers is the same, so he is only interested in the earnings the jobs provide. All earnings and costs are paid at the end of the year. What advice would you give him if the market interest rate is 5 percent? A day later he comes back and says he took your advice, but in fact, the market interest rate was 6 percent. Has your brother made the right choice?

4.46 In January 1984, Richard "Goose" Gossage signed a contract to play for the San Diego Padres that guaranteed him a minimum of $9,955,000. The guaranteed payments were $875,000 for 1984, $650,000 for 1985, $800,000 in 1986, $1 million in 1987, $1 million in 1988, and $300,000 in 1989. In addition, the contract called for $5,330,000 in deferred money payable at the rate of $240,000 per year from 1990 through 2006 and then $125,000 a year from 2007 through 2016. If the effective annual rate of interest is 9 percent and all payments are made on July 1 of each year, what would the present value of these guaranteed payments be on January 1, 1984? Assume an interest rate of 4.4 percent per six months. If he were to receive an equal annual salary at the end of each of the five years from 1984 through 1988, what would his equivalent annual salary be? Ignore taxes throughout this problem.

4.47 Ms. Adams has received a job offer from a large investment bank as an assistant to the vice president. Her base salary will be $35,000. She will receive her first annual salary payment one year from the day she begins to work. In addition, she will get an immediate $10,000 bonus for joining the company. Her salary will grow at 4 percent each year. Each year she will receive a bonus equal to 10 percent of her salary. Ms. Adams is expected to work for 25 years. What is the present value of the offer if the discount rate is 12 percent?

4.48 Justin Leonard has just arranged to purchase a $400,000 vacation home in the Bahamas with a 20% down payment. The mortgage has an 8% annual percentage rate (APR) and calls for equal monthly payments over the next 30 years. His first payment will be due one month from now. However, the mortgage has an 8-year balloon payment, meaning that the loan must be paid off then. There were no other transaction costs or finance charges. How big will Justin's balloon payment be in 8 years?

4.49 You want to lease a set of golf clubs from Pings Ltd. for $4,000. The lease contract is in the form of 24 months of equal payments at a 12% annual percentage rate (APR). Suppose payments are due in the beginning of the month and your first payment is due immediately. What will your monthly lease payment be?

4.50 A 10-year annuity pays $900 per year, with payments made at the end of each year. The first $900 will be paid 5 years from now. If the APR is 8% and interest is compounded quarterly, what is the present value of this annuity?

What Is a Firm Worth?

4.51 Southern California Publishing Company is trying to decide whether or not to revise its popular textbook, *Financial Psychoanalysis Made Simple.* They have estimated that the revision will cost $40,000. Cash flows from increased sales will be $10,000 the first year. These cash flows will increase by 7 percent per year. The book will go out of print five years from now. Assume the initial cost is paid now and all revenues are received at the end of each year. If the company requires a 10 percent return for such an investment, should it undertake the revision?

4.52 Ernie Els wants to save money to meet two objectives. First, he would like to be able to retire 30 years from now with a retirement income of $300,000 per year for 20 years beginning at the end of the 31 years from now. Second, he would like to purchase a cabin in the mountains 10 years from now at an estimated cost of $350,000. He can afford to save only $40,000 per year for the first 10 years. He expects to earn 7 percent per year from investments. Assuming he saves the same amount each year, what must Ernie save annually from years 11 to 30 to meet his objectives?

CHAPTER 5

How to Value Bonds and Stocks

Executive Summary

The previous chapter discussed the mathematics of compounding, discounting, and present value. We also showed how to value a firm. We now use the mathematics of compounding and discounting to determine the present values of financial obligations of the firm, beginning with a discussion of how bonds are valued. Since the future cash flows of bonds are known, application of net-present-value techniques is fairly straightforward. The uncertainty of future cash flows makes the pricing of stocks according to NPV more difficult.

5.1 Definition and Example of a Bond

A *bond* is a certificate showing that a borrower owes a specified sum. In order to repay the money, the borrower has agreed to make interest and principal payments on designated dates. For example, imagine that Kreuger Enterprises just issued 100,000 bonds for $1,000 each, where the bonds have a coupon rate of 5 percent and a maturity of two years. Interest on the bonds is to be paid yearly. This means that:

1. $100 million (100,000 × $1,000) has been borrowed by the firm.
2. The firm must pay interest of $5 million (5% × $100 million) at the end of one year.
3. The firm must pay both $5 million of interest and $100 million of principal at the end of two years.

We now consider how to value a few different types of bonds.

5.2 How to Value Bonds

Pure Discount Bonds

The **pure discount bond** is perhaps the simplest kind of bond. It promises a single payment, say $1, at a fixed future date. If the payment is one year from now, it is called a *one-year discount bond;* if it is two years from now, it is called a *two-year discount bond,* and so on. The date when the issuer of the bond makes the last payment is called the **maturity date** of the bond, or just its *maturity* for short. The bond is said to mature or *expire* on the date of its final payment. The payment at maturity ($1 in this example) is termed the bond's **face value.**

Pure discount bonds are often called *zero-coupon bonds* or zeros to emphasize the fact that the holder receives no cash payments until maturity. We will use the terms *zero, bullet,* and *discount* interchangeably to refer to bonds that pay no coupons.

■ FIGURE 5.1   **Different Types of Bonds: *C*, Coupon Paid Every 6 Months; *F*, Face Value at Year 4 (maturity for pure discount and coupon bonds)**

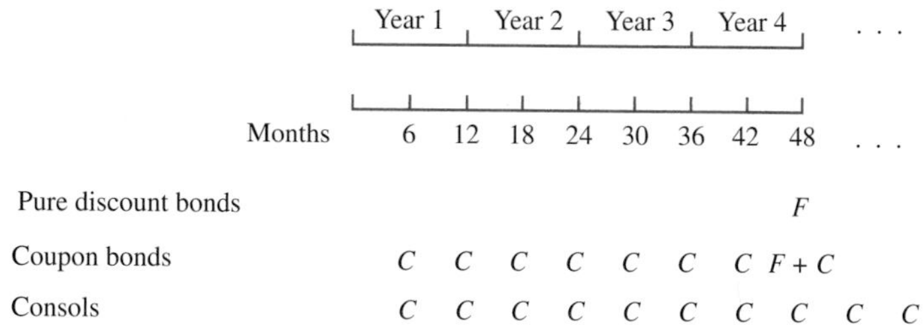

	Year 1	Year 2	Year 3	Year 4	. . .

Months	6	12	18	24	30	36	42	48	. . .
Pure discount bonds								*F*	
Coupon bonds	*C*	*C*	*C*	*C*	*C*	*C*	*C*	*F* + *C*	
Consols	*C*	*C*	*C*	*C*	*C*	*C*	*C*	*C*	*C*	*C*

The first row of Figure 5.1 shows the pattern of cash flows from a four-year pure discount bond. Note that the face value, *F*, is paid when the bond expires in the 48th month. There are no payments of either interest or principal prior to this date.

In the previous chapter, we indicated that one discounts a future cash flow to determine its present value. The present value of a pure discount bond can easily be determined by the techniques of the previous chapter. For short, we sometimes speak of the *value* of a bond instead of its present value.

Consider a pure discount bond that pays a face value of *F* in *T* years, where the interest rate is *r* in each of the *T* years. (We also refer to this rate as the *market interest rate.*) Because the face value is the only cash flow that the bond pays, the present value of this face amount is

Value of a Pure Discount Bond:
$$\text{PV} = \frac{F}{(1 + r)^T}$$

The present value formula can produce some surprising results. Suppose that the interest rate is 10 percent. Consider a bond with a face value of $1 million that matures in 20 years. Applying the formula to this bond, its PV is given by

$$\text{PV} = \frac{\$1 \text{ million}}{(1.1)^{20}}$$
$$= \$148,644$$

or only about 15 percent of the face value.

Level-Coupon Bonds

Many bonds, however, are not of the simple, pure discount variety. Typical bonds issued by either governments or corporations offer cash payments not just at maturity, but also at regular times in between. For example, payments on U.S. government issues and American corporate bonds are made every six months until the bond matures. These payments are called the **coupons** of the bond. The middle row of Figure 5.1 illustrates the case of a four-year, *level-coupon bond:* The coupon, *C,* is paid every six months and is the same throughout the life of the bond.

Note that the face value of the bond, *F,* is paid at maturity (end of year 4). *F* is sometimes called the *principal* or the *denomination*. Bonds issued in the United States typically have face values of $1,000, though this can vary with the type of bond.

As we mentioned before, the value of a bond is simply the present value of its cash flows. Therefore, the value of a level-coupon bond is merely the present value of its stream of coupon payments plus the present value of its repayment of principal. Because a level-coupon bond is just an annuity of C each period, together with a payment at maturity of $1,000, the value of a level-coupon bond is

Value of a Level-Coupon Bond:

$$PV = \frac{C}{1 + r} + \frac{C}{(1 + r)^2} + \ldots + \frac{C}{(1 + r)^T} + \frac{\$1,000}{(1 + r)^T}$$

where C is the coupon and the face value, F, is $1,000. The value of the bond can be rewritten as

Value of a Level-Coupon Bond:

$$PV = C \times A_r^T + \frac{\$1,000}{(1 + r)^T}$$

As mentioned in the previous chapter, A_r^T is the present value of an annuity of $1 per period for T periods at an interest rate per period of r.

EXAMPLE

Suppose it is November 2000 and we are considering a government bond. We see in *The Wall Street Journal* some *13s* of November 2004. This is jargon that means the annual coupon rate is 13 percent.[1] The face value is $1,000, implying that the yearly coupon is $130 (13% × $1,000). Interest is paid each May and November, implying that the coupon every six months is $65 ($130/2). The face value will be paid out in November 2004, four years from now. By this we mean that the purchaser obtains claims to the following cash flows:

5/01	11/01	5/02	11/02	5/03	11/03	5/04	11/04
$65	$65	$65	$65	$65	$65	$65	$65 + $1,000

If the stated annual interest rate in the market is 10 percent per year, what is the present value of the bond?

Our work on compounding in the previous chapter showed that the interest rate over any six-month interval is one half of the stated annual interest rate. In the current example, this semiannual rate is 5 percent (10%/2). Since the coupon payment in each six-month period is $65, and there are eight of these six-month periods from November 2000 to November 2004, the present value of the bond is

$$
\begin{aligned}
PV &= \frac{\$65}{(1.05)} + \frac{\$65}{(1.05)^2} + \ldots + \frac{\$65}{(1.05)^8} + \frac{\$1,000}{(1.05)^8} \\
&= \$65 \times A_{0.05}^8 + \$1,000/(1.05)^8 \\
&= (\$65 \times 6.463) + (\$1,000 \times 0.677) \\
&= \$420.095 + \$677 \\
&= \$1,097.095
\end{aligned}
$$

Traders will generally quote the bond as 109.7095,[2] indicating that it is selling at 109.7095 percent of the face value of $1,000.

---

[1]The coupon rate is specific to the bond. The coupon rate indicates what cash flow should appear in the numerator of the NPV equation. The coupon rate does *not* appear in the denominator of the NPV equation.

[2]Bond prices are actually quoted in 32nds of a dollar, so a quote this precise would not be given.

At this point, it is worthwhile to relate the above example of bond-pricing to the discussion of compounding in the previous chapter. At that time we distinguished between the stated annual interest rate and the effective annual interest rate. In particular, we pointed out that the effective annual interest rate is

$$(1 + r/m)^m - 1$$

where r is the stated annual interest rate and m is the number of compounding intervals. Since $r = 10\%$ and $m = 2$ (because the bond makes semiannual payments), the effective annual interest rate is

$$[1 + (0.10/2)]^2 - 1 = (1.05)^2 - 1 = 10.25\%$$

In other words, because the bond is paying interest twice a year, the bondholder earns a 10.25-percent return when compounding is considered.[3]

One final note concerning level-coupon bonds: Although the preceding example concerns government bonds, corporate bonds are identical in form. For example, DuPont Corporation has an 8½-percent bond maturing in 2006. This means that DuPont will make semiannual payments of $42.50 (8½%/2 × $1,000) between now and 2006 for each face value of $1,000.

Consols

Not all bonds have a final maturity date. As we mentioned in the previous chapter, consols are bonds that never stop paying a coupon, have no final maturity date, and therefore never mature. Thus, a consol is a perpetuity. In the 18th century the Bank of England issued such bonds, called "English consols." These were bonds that the Bank of England guaranteed would pay the holder a cash flow forever! Through wars and depressions, the Bank of England continued to honor this commitment, and you can still buy such bonds in London today. The U.S. government also once sold consols to raise money to build the Panama Canal. Even though these U.S. bonds were supposed to last forever and to pay their coupons forever, don't go looking for any. There is a special clause in the bond contract that gives the government the right to buy them back from the holders, and that is what the government has done. Clauses like that are *call provisions*, and we study them later.

An important example of a consol, though, is called *preferred stock*. Preferred stock is stock that is issued by corporations and that provides the holder a fixed dividend in perpetuity. If there were never any question that the firm would actually pay the dividend on the preferred stock, such stock would in fact be a consol.

These instruments can be valued by the perpetuity formula of the previous chapter. For example, if the marketwide interest rate is 10 percent, a consol with a yearly interest payment of $50 is valued at

$$\frac{\$50}{0.10} = \$500$$

QUESTIONS

CONCEPT

?

- Define pure discount bonds, level-coupon bonds, and consols.
- Contrast the stated interest rate and the effective annual interest rate for bonds paying semiannual interest.

---

[3]For an excellent discussion of how to value semiannual payments, see J. T. Lindley, B. P. Helms, and M. Haddad, "A Measurement of the Errors in Intra-Period Compounding and Bond Valuation," *The Financial Review* 22 (February 1987). We benefited from several conversations with the authors of this article.

5.3 Bond Concepts

We complete our discussion on bonds by considering two concepts concerning them. First, we examine the relationship between interest rates and bond prices. Second, we define the concept of yield to maturity.

Interest Rates and Bond Prices

The above discussion on level-coupon bonds allows us to relate bond prices to interest rates. Consider the following example.

Example

The interest rate is 10 percent. A two-year bond with a 10-percent coupon pays interest of $100 ($1,000 × 10%). For simplicity, we assume that the interest is paid annually. The bond is priced at its face value of $1,000:

$$\$1,000 = \frac{\$100}{1.10} + \frac{\$1,000 + \$100}{(1.10)^2}$$

If the interest rate unexpectedly rises to 12 percent, the bond sells at

$$\$966.20 = \frac{\$100}{1.12} + \frac{\$1,000 + \$100}{(1.12)^2}$$

Because $966.20 is below $1,000, the bond is said to sell at a **discount.** This is a sensible result. Now that the interest rate is 12 percent, a newly issued bond with a 12-percent coupon rate will sell at $1,000. This newly issued bond will have coupon payments of $120 (0.12 × $1,000). Because our bond has interest payments of only $100, investors will pay less than $1,000 for it.

If interest rates fell to 8 percent, the bond would sell at

$$\$1,035.67 = \frac{\$100}{1.08} + \frac{\$1,000 + \$100}{(1.08)^2}$$

Because $1,035.67 is above $1,000, the bond is said to sell at a **premium.**

Thus, we find that bond prices fall with a rise in interest rates and rise with a fall in interest rates. Furthermore, the general principle is that a level-coupon bond sells in the following ways.

1. At the face value of $1,000 if the coupon rate is equal to the marketwide interest rate.
2. At a discount if the coupon rate is below the marketwide interest rate.
3. At a premium if the coupon rate is above the marketwide interest rate.

Yield to Maturity

Let's now consider the previous example *in reverse.* If our bond is selling at $1,035.67, what return is a bondholder receiving? This can be answered by considering the following equation:

$$\$1,035.67 = \frac{\$100}{1 + y} + \frac{\$1,000 + \$100}{(1 + y)^2}$$

THE PRESENT VALUE FORMULAS FOR BONDS

Pure Discount Bonds

$$PV = \frac{F}{(1 + r)^T}$$

Level-Coupon Bonds

$$PV = C\left[\frac{1}{r} - \frac{1}{r \times (1 + r)^T}\right] + \frac{F}{(1 + r)^T} = C \times A_r^T + \frac{F}{(1 + r)^T}$$

where F is typically $1,000 for a level-coupon bond.

Consols

$$PV = \frac{C}{r}$$

The unknown, y, is the discount rate that equates the price of the bond with the discounted value of the coupons and face value. Our earlier work implies that $y = 8\%$. Thus, traders state that the bond is yielding an 8-percent return. Bond traders also state that the bond has a **yield to maturity** of 8 percent. The yield to maturity is frequently called the bond's yield for short. So we would say the bond with its 10-percent coupon is priced to yield 8 percent at $1,035.67.

Bond Market Reporting

Almost all corporate bonds are traded by institutional investors and are traded on the over-the-counter market (OTC for short). There is a corporate bond market associated with the New York Stock Exchange. This bond market is mostly a retail market for individual investors for smaller trades. It represents a very small fraction of total corporate bond trading.

Table 5.1 reproduces some bond data that can be found in *The Wall Street Journal* on any particular day. At the bottom of the list you will find AT&T and an entry AT&T 8⅛/22. This entry represents AT&T bonds that mature in the year 2022 and have a coupon rate of 8⅛. The coupon rate means 8⅛ percent of the par value (or face value) of $1,000. Therefore, the annual coupon for AT&T bonds is $81.25.

Under the heading "Close," you will find the last price for the AT&T bonds at the close of this particular day. The price is quoted as a percentage of the par value. So the last price for the AT&T bonds on this particular day was 100 percent of $1,000 or $1,000.00. This bond is trading at a price less than its par value, and so it is trading at a "discount." The last column is "Net Chg." AT&T bonds traded up from the day before by ⅜ of 1 percent. The AT&T bonds have a current yield of 8.1 percent. The current yield is simply the current coupon divided by the current price, or 81.25 divided by 1,000, equal to 8.1 percent (rounded to one decimal place).

You should know from our discussion of bond yields that the current yield is not the same thing as the bonds' yield to maturity. The yield to maturity is not usually reported on a daily basis by the financial press. The "Vol" column is the daily volume of 97. This is the number of bonds that were traded on the New York Stock Exchange on this particular day.

■ TABLE 5.1 **Bond Market Reporting**

Bonds	Cur Yld.	Vol.	Close	Net Chg.	
AMF 10⅞ 06	25.3	10	43		...
AMR 9s16	8.8	25	102	−	⅜
ATT 5⅛ 01	5.2	30	98½	+	5/16
ATT 7⅛ 02	7.1	55	100⅛	−	⅛
ATT 6½ 02	6.6	50	99	+	⅞
ATT 6¾ 04	6.9	52	97¾	+	⅜
ATT 5⅝ 04	6.0	138	94⅜		...
ATT 7½ 06	7.4	60	100¾	−	½
ATT 7¾ 07	7.6	83	101½	+	½
ATT 6s09	6.7	40	89	+	⅝
ATT 8⅛ 22	8.1	97	100	+	⅜

CONCEPT QUESTIONS
?
- What is the relationship between interest rates and bond prices?
- How does one calculate the yield to maturity on a bond?

5.4 THE PRESENT VALUE OF COMMON STOCKS

Dividends versus Capital Gains

Our goal in this section is to value common stocks. We learned in the previous chapter that an asset's value is determined by the present value of its future cash flows. A stock provides two kinds of cash flows. First, most stocks pay dividends on a regular basis. Second, the stockholder receives the sale price when she sells the stock. Thus, in order to value common stocks, we need to answer an interesting question: Is the value of a stock equal to

1. The discounted present value of the sum of next period's dividend plus next period's stock price, or
2. The discounted present value of all future dividends?

This is the kind of question that students would love to see on a multiple-choice exam, because both (1) and (2) are right.

To see that (1) and (2) are the same, let's start with an individual who will buy the stock and hold it for one year. In other words, she has a one-year *holding period*. In addition, she is willing to pay P_0 for the stock today. That is, she calculates

$$P_0 = \frac{\text{Div}_1}{1 + r} + \frac{P_1}{1 + r} \tag{5.1}$$

Div_1 is the dividend paid at year's end and P_1 is the price at year's end. P_0 is the PV of the common-stock investment. The term in the denominator, r, is the discount rate of the stock. It will be equal to the interest rate in the case where the stock is riskless. It is likely to be greater than the interest rate in the case where the stock is risky.

That seems easy enough, but where does P_1 come from? P_1 is not pulled out of thin air. Rather, there must be a buyer at the end of year 1 who is willing to purchase the stock for P_1. This buyer determines price by

$$P_1 = \frac{\text{Div}_2}{1 + r} + \frac{P_2}{1 + r} \qquad (5.2)$$

Substituting the value of P_1 from (5.2) into equation (5.1) yields

$$P_0 = \frac{1}{1 + r}\left[\text{Div}_1 + \left(\frac{\text{Div}_2 + P_2}{1 + r}\right)\right]$$

$$= \frac{\text{Div}_1}{1 + r} + \frac{\text{Div}_2}{(1 + r)^2} + \frac{P_2}{(1 + r)^2} \qquad (5.3)$$

We can ask a similar question for formula (5.3): Where does P_2 come from? An investor at the end of year 2 is willing to pay P_2 because of the dividend and stock price at year 3. This process can be repeated *ad nauseam*.[4] At the end, we are left with

$$P_0 = \frac{\text{Div}_1}{1 + r} + \frac{\text{Div}_2}{(1 + r)^2} + \frac{\text{Div}_3}{(1 + r)^3} + \ldots = \sum_{t=1}^{\infty}\frac{\text{Div}_t}{(1 + r)^t} \qquad (5.4)$$

Thus the value of a firm's common stock to the investor is equal to the present value of all of the expected future dividends.

This is a very useful result. A common objection to applying present value analysis to stocks is that investors are too shortsighted to care about the long-run stream of dividends. These critics argue that an investor will generally not look past his or her time horizon. Thus, prices in a market dominated by short-term investors will reflect only near-term dividends. However, our discussion shows that a long-run dividend-discount model holds even when investors have short-term time horizons. Although an investor may want to cash out early, she must find another investor who is willing to buy. The price this second investor pays is dependent on dividends *after* his date of purchase.

Valuation of Different Types of Stocks

The above discussion shows that the value of the firm is the present value of its future dividends. How do we apply this idea in practice? Equation (5.4) represents a very general model and is applicable regardless of whether the level of expected dividends is growing, fluctuating, or constant. The general model can be simplified if the firm's dividends are expected to follow some basic patterns: (1) zero growth, (2) constant growth, and (3) differential growth. These cases are illustrated in Figure 5.2.

Case 1 (Zero Growth)   The value of a stock with a constant dividend is given by

$$P_0 = \frac{\text{Div}_1}{1 + r} + \frac{\text{Div}_2}{(1 + r)^2} + \ldots = \frac{\text{Div}}{r}$$

Here it is assumed that $\text{Div}_1 = \text{Div}_2 = \ldots = \text{Div}$. This is just an application of the perpetuity formula of the previous chapter.

Case 2 (Constant Growth)   Dividends grow at rate g, as follows:

End of Year	1	2	3	4	...
Dividend	Div	Div$(1 + g)$	Div$(1 + g)^2$	Div$(1 + g)^3$	

Note that Div is the dividend at the end of the *first* period.

---

[4]This procedure reminds us of the physicist lecturing on the origins of the universe. He was approached by an elderly gentleman in the audience who disagreed with the lecture. The attendee said that the universe rests on the back of a huge turtle. When the physicist asked what the turtle rested on, the gentleman said another turtle. Anticipating the physicist's objections, the attendee said, "Don't tire yourself out, young fellow. It's turtles all the way down."

■ FIGURE 5.2 **Zero-Growth, Constant-Growth, and Differential-Growth Patterns**

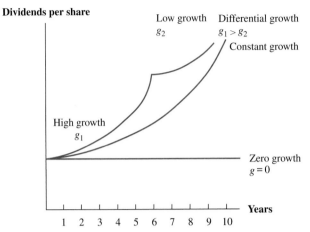

Dividend-growth models

Zero growth: $P_0 = \dfrac{Div}{r}$

Constant growth: $P_0 = \dfrac{Div}{r - g}$

Differential growth: $P_0 = \displaystyle\sum_{t=1}^{T} \dfrac{Div\,(1 + g_1)^t}{(1 + r)^t} + \dfrac{\dfrac{Div_{T+1}}{r - g_2}}{(1 + r)^T}$

<hr>

EXAMPLE

Hampshire Products will pay a dividend of $4 per share a year from now. Financial analysts believe that dividends will rise at 6 percent per year for the foreseeable future. What is the dividend per share at the end of each of the first five years?

End of Year	1	2	3	4	5
Dividend	$4.00	$4 \times (1.06) = $4.24	$4 \times (1.06)^2 = $4.4944	$4 \times (1.06)^3 = $4.7641	$4 \times (1.06)^4 = $5.0499

The value of a common stock with dividends growing at a constant rate is

$$P_0 = \frac{Div}{1 + r} + \frac{Div\,(1 + g)}{(1 + r)^2} + \frac{Div\,(1 + g)^2}{(1 + r)^3} + \frac{Div(1 + g)^3}{(1 + r)^4} + \dots$$

$$= \frac{Div}{r - g}$$

where *g* is the growth rate. Div is the dividend on the stock at the end of the first period. This is the formula for the present value of a growing perpetuity, which we derived in the previous chapter.

<hr>

EXAMPLE

Suppose an investor is considering the purchase of a share of the Utah Mining Company. The stock will pay a $3 dividend a year from today. This dividend is expected to grow at 10 percent per year ($g = 10\%$) for the foreseeable future. The investor thinks that the required return (r) on this stock is 15 percent, given her assessment of Utah Mining's risk. (We also refer to r as the discount rate of the stock.) What is the value of a share of Utah Mining Company's stock?

Using the constant growth formula of case 2, we assess the value to be $60:

$$\$60 = \frac{\$3}{0.15 - 0.10}$$

P_0 is quite dependent on the value of g. If g had been estimated to be 12½ percent, the value of the share would have been

$$\$120 = \frac{\$3}{0.15 - 0.125}$$

The stock price doubles (from $60 to $120) when g only increases 25 percent (from 10 percent to 12.5 percent). Because of P_0's dependency on g, one must maintain a healthy sense of skepticism when using this constant growth of dividends model.

Furthermore, note that P_0 is equal to infinity when the growth rate, g, equals the discount rate, r. Because stock prices do not grow infinitely, an estimate of g greater than r implies an error in estimation. More will be said of this point later.

Case 3 (Differential Growth)   In this case, an algebraic formula would be too unwieldy. Instead, we present examples.

EXAMPLE

Consider the stock of Elixir Drug Company, which has a new back-rub ointment and is enjoying rapid growth. The dividend for a share of stock a year from today will be $1.15. During the next four years, the dividend will grow at 15 percent per year ($g_1 = 15\%$). After that, growth (g_2) will be equal to 10 percent per year. Can you calculate the present value of the stock if the required return (r) is 15 percent?

Figure 5.3 displays the growth in the dividends. We need to apply a two-step process to discount these dividends. We first calculate the net present value of the dividends growing at 15 percent per annum. That is, we first calculate the present value of the dividends at the end of each of the first five years. Second, we calculate the present value of the dividends beginning at the end of year 6.

Calculate Present Value of First Five Dividends   The present value of dividend payments in years 1 through 5 is as follows:

Future Year	Growth Rate (g_1)	Expected Dividend	Present Value
1	0.15	$1.15	$1
2	0.15	1.3225	1
3	0.15	1.5209	1
4	0.15	1.7490	1
5	0.15	2.0114	1
Years 1–5	The present value of dividends = $5		

The growing-annuity formula of the previous chapter could normally be used in this step. However, note that dividends grow at 15 percent, which is also the discount rate. Since $g = r$, the growing-annuity formula cannot be used in this example.

■ FIGURE 5.3   Growth in Dividends for Elixir Drug Company

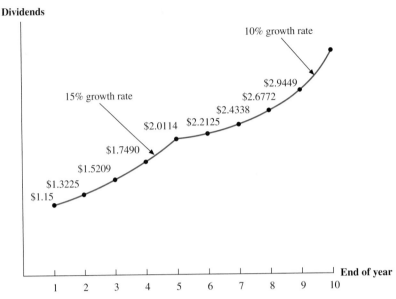

Calculate Present Value of Dividends Beginning at End of Year 6   This is the procedure for deferred perpetuities and deferred annuities that we mentioned in the previous chapter. The dividends beginning at the end of year 6 are

End of Year	6	7	8	9
Dividend	$\text{Div}_5 \times (1 + g_2)$	$\text{Div}_5 \times (1 + g_2)^2$	$\text{Div}_5 \times (1 + g_2)^3$	$\text{Div}_5 \times (1 + g_2)^4$
	$\$2.0114 \times 1.10$	$2.0114 \times (1.10)^2$	$2.0114 \times (1.10)^3$	$2.0114 \times (1.10)^4$
	$= \$2.2125$	$= \$2.4338$	$= \$2.6772$	$= \$2.9449$

As stated in the previous chapter, the growing-perpetuity formula calculates present value as of one year prior to the first payment. Because the payment begins at the end of year 6, the present value formula calculates present value as of the end of year 5.

The price at the end of year 5 is given by

$$P_5 = \frac{\text{Div}_6}{r - g_2} = \frac{\$2.2125}{0.15 - 0.10}$$
$$= \$44.25$$

The present value of P_5 at the end of year 0 is

$$\frac{P_5}{(1 + r)^5} = \frac{\$44.25}{(1.15)^5} = \$22$$

The present value of *all* dividends as of the end of year 0 is $27 ($22 + $5).

5.5 ESTIMATES OF PARAMETERS IN THE DIVIDEND-DISCOUNT MODEL

The value of the firm is a function of its growth rate, *g*, and its discount rate, *r*. How does one estimate these variables?

Where Does g Come From?

The previous discussion on stocks assumed that dividends grow at the rate *g*. We now want to estimate this rate of growth. Consider a business whose earnings next year are expected to be the same as earnings this year unless a *net investment* is made. This situation is likely to occur, because net investment is equal to gross, or total, investment less depreciation. A net investment of zero occurs when *total investment* equals depreciation. If total investment is equal to depreciation, the firm's physical plant is maintained, consistent with no growth in earnings.

Net investment will be positive only if some earnings are not paid out as dividends, that is, only if some earnings are retained.[5] This leads to the following equation:

$$\underbrace{\begin{array}{c}\text{Earnings}\\\text{next}\\\text{year}\end{array} = \begin{array}{c}\text{Earnings}\\\text{this}\\\text{year}\end{array} + \begin{array}{c}\text{Retained}\\\text{earnings}\\\text{this year}\end{array} \times \begin{array}{c}\text{Return on}\\\text{retained}\\\text{earnings}\end{array}}_{\text{Increase in earnings}} \qquad (5.5)$$

The increase in earnings is a function of both the *retained earnings* and the *return on the retained earnings.*

We now divide both sides of (5.5) by earnings this year, yielding

$$\frac{\text{Earnings next year}}{\text{Earnings this year}} =$$

$$\frac{\text{Earnings this year}}{\text{Earnings this year}} + \left(\frac{\text{Retained earnings this year}}{\text{Earnings this year}}\right) \times \text{Return on retained earnings} \qquad (5.6)$$

The left-hand side of (5.6) is simply one plus the growth rate in earnings, which we write as $1 + g$.[6] The ratio of retained earnings to earnings is called the **retention ratio.** Thus, we can write

$$1 + g = 1 + \text{Retention ratio} \times \text{Return on retained earnings} \qquad (5.7)$$

It is difficult for a financial analyst to determine the return to be expected on currently retained earnings, because the details on forthcoming projects are not generally public information. However, it is frequently assumed that the projects selected in the current year have an anticipated return equal to returns from projects in other years. Here, we can estimate the anticipated return on current retained earnings by the historical **return on equity,** or ROE. After all, ROE is simply the return on the firm's entire equity, which is the return on the cumulation of all the firm's past projects.[7]

From (5.7), we have a simple way to estimate growth:

Formula for Firm's Growth Rate:

$$g = \text{Retention ratio} \times \text{Return on retained earnings} \qquad (5.8)$$

---

[5]We ignore the possibility of the issuance of stocks or bonds in order to raise capital. These possibilities are considered in later chapters.

[6]Previously *g* referred to growth in dividends. However, the growth in earnings is equal to the growth rate in dividends in this context, because as we will presently see, the ratio of dividends to earnings is held constant.

[7]Students frequently wonder whether return on equity (ROE) or return on assets (ROA) should be used here. ROA and ROE are identical in our model because debt financing is ignored. However, most real-world firms have debt. Because debt is treated in later chapters, we are not yet able to treat this issue in depth now. Suffice it to say that ROE is the appropriate rate, because both ROE for the firm as a whole and the return to equityholders from a future project are calculated after interest has been deducted.

EXAMPLE

Pagemaster Enterprises just reported earnings of $2 million. It plans to retain 40 percent of its earnings. The historical return on equity (ROE) has been 0.16, a figure that is expected to continue into the future. How much will earnings grow over the coming year?

We first perform the calculation without reference to equation (5.8). Then we use (5.8) as a check.

Calculation without Reference to Equation (5.8)   The firm will retain $800,000 (40% × $2 million). Assuming that historical ROE is an appropriate estimate for future returns, the anticipated increase in earnings is

$$\$800,000 \times 0.16 = \$128,000$$

The percentage growth in earnings is

$$\frac{\text{Change in earnings}}{\text{Total earnings}} = \frac{\$128,000}{\$2 \text{ million}} = 0.064$$

This implies that earnings in one year will be $2,128,000 ($2,000,000 × 1.064).

Check Using Equation (5.8)   We use g = Retention ratio × ROE. We have

$$g = 0.4 \times 0.16 = 0.064$$

Where Does r Come From?

In this section, we want to estimate r, the rate used to discount the cash flows of a particular stock. There are two methods developed by academics. We present one method below but must defer the second until we give it extensive treatment in later chapters.

The first method begins with the concept that the value of a growing perpetuity is

$$P_0 = \frac{\text{Div}}{r - g}$$

Solving for r, we have

$$r = \frac{\text{Div}}{P_0} + g \tag{5.9}$$

As stated earlier, Div refers to the dividend to be received one year hence.

Thus, the discount rate can be broken into two parts. The ratio, Div/P_0, places the dividend return on a percentage basis, frequently called the *dividend yield.* The second term, g, is the growth rate of dividends.

Because information on both dividends and stock price is publicly available, the first term on the right-hand side of equation (5.9) can be easily calculated. The second term on the right-hand side, g, can be estimated from (5.8).

EXAMPLE

Pagemaster Enterprises, the company examined in the previous example, has 1,000,000 shares of stock outstanding. The stock is selling at $10. What is the required return on the stock?

Because the retention ratio is 40 percent, the **payout ratio** is 60 percent (1 − Retention ratio). The payout ratio is the ratio of dividends/earnings. Because earnings a year from now will be $2,128,000 ($2,000,000 × 1.064), dividends will be $1,276,800

(0.60 × $2,128,000). Dividends per share will be $1.28 ($1,276,800/1,000,000). Given our previous result that $g = 0.064$, we calculate r from (5.9) as follows:

$$0.192 = \frac{\$1.28}{\$10.00} + 0.064$$

A Healthy Sense of Skepticism

It is important to emphasize that our approach merely *estimates g;* our approach does not *determine g* precisely. We mentioned earlier that our estimate of g is based on a number of assumptions. For example, we assume that the return on reinvestment of future retained earnings is equal to the firm's past ROE. We assume that the future retention ratio is equal to the past retention ratio. Our estimate for g will be off if these assumptions prove to be wrong.

Unfortunately, the determination of r is highly dependent on g. For example, if g is estimated to be 0, r equals 12.8 percent ($1.28/$10.00). If g is estimated to be 12 percent, r equals 24.8 percent ($1.28/$10.00 + 12%). Thus, one should view estimates of r with a healthy sense of skepticism.

Because of the preceding, some financial economists generally argue that the estimation error for r or a single security is too large to be practical. Therefore, they suggest calculating the average r for an entire industry. This r would then be used to discount the dividends of a particular stock in the same industry.

One should be particularly skeptical of two polar cases when estimating r for individual securities. First, consider a firm currently paying no dividend. The stock price will be above zero because investors believe that the firm may initiate a dividend at some point or the firm may be acquired at some point. However, when a firm goes from no dividends to a positive number of dividends, the implied growth rate is *infinite*. Thus, equation (5.9) must be used with extreme caution here, if at all—a point we emphasize later in this chapter.

Second, we mentioned earlier that the value of the firm is infinite when g is equal to r. Because prices for stocks do not grow infinitely, an analyst whose estimate of g for a particular firm is equal to or above r must have made a mistake. Most likely, the analyst's high estimate for g is correct for the next few years. However, firms simply cannot maintain an abnormally high growth rate *forever*. The analyst's error was to use a short-run estimate of g in a model requiring a perpetual growth rate.

5.6 GROWTH OPPORTUNITIES

We previously spoke of the growth rate of dividends. We now want to address the related concept of growth opportunities. Imagine a company with a level stream of earnings per share in perpetuity. The company pays all of these earnings out to stockholders as dividends. Hence,

$$\text{EPS} = \text{Div}$$

where EPS is *earnings per share* and Div is dividends per share. A company of this type is frequently called a *cash cow.*

From the perpetuity formula of the previous chapter, the value of a share of stock is:

Value of a Share of Stock when Firm Acts as a Cash Cow:

$$\frac{\text{EPS}}{r} = \frac{\text{Div}}{r}$$

where r is the discount rate on the firm's stock.

This policy of paying out all earnings as dividends may not be the optimal one. Many firms have *growth* opportunities, that is, opportunities to invest in profitable projects. Because these projects can represent a significant fraction of the firm's value, it would be foolish to forgo them in order to pay out all earnings as dividends.

Although firms frequently think in terms of a *set* of growth opportunities, let's focus on only one opportunity, that is, the opportunity to invest in a single project. Suppose the firm retains the entire dividend at date 1 in order to invest in a particular capital budgeting project. The net present value *per share* of the project as of date 0 is *NPVGO,* which stands for the *net present value (per share) of the growth opportunity.*

What is the price of a share of stock at date 0 if the firm decides to take on the project at date 1? Because the per share value of the project is added to the original stock price, the stock price must now be:

Stock Price after Firm Commits to New Project:

$$\frac{EPS}{r} + NPVGO \tag{5.10}$$

Thus, equation (5.10) indicates that the price of a share of stock can be viewed as the sum of two different items. The first term (EPS/r) is the value of the firm if it rested on its laurels, that is, if it simply distributed all earnings to the stockholders. The second term is the *additional* value if the firm retains earnings in order to fund new projects.

EXAMPLE

Sarro Shipping, Inc., expects to earn $1 million per year in perpetuity if it undertakes no new investment opportunities. There are 100,000 shares of stock outstanding, so earnings per share equal $10 ($1,000,000/100,000). The firm will have an opportunity at date 1 to spend $1,000,000 in a new marketing campaign. The new campaign will increase earnings in every subsequent period by $210,000 (or $2.10 per share). This is a 21-percent return per year on the project. The firm's discount rate is 10 percent. What is the value per share before and after deciding to accept the marketing campaign?

The value of a share of Sarro Shipping before the campaign is

Value of a Share of Sarro when Firm Acts as a Cash Cow:

$$\frac{EPS}{r} = \frac{\$10}{0.1} = \$100$$

The value of the marketing campaign as of date 1 is:

Value of Marketing Campaign at Date 1:

$$-\$1,000,000 + \frac{\$210,000}{0.1} = \$1,100,000 \tag{5.11}$$

Because the investment is made at date 1 and the first cash inflow occurs at date 2, equation (5.11) represents the value of the marketing campaign as of date 1. We determine the value at date 0 by discounting back one period as follows:

Value of Marketing Campaign at Date 0:

$$\frac{\$1,100,000}{1.1} = \$1,000,000$$

Thus, NPVGO per share is $10 ($1,000,000/100,000).

The price per share is

$$EPS/r + NPVGO = \$100 + \$10 = \$110$$

The calculation can also be made on a straight net-present-value basis. Because all the earnings at date 1 are spent on the marketing effort, no dividends are paid to stockholders at that date. Dividends in all subsequent periods are $1,210,000 ($1,000,000 + $210,000). In this case, $1,000,000 is the annual dividend when Sarro is a cash cow. The additional contribution to the dividend from the marketing effort is $210,000. Dividends per share are $12.10 ($1,210,000/100,000). Because these dividends start at date 2, the price per share at date 1 is $121 ($12.10/0.1). The price per share at date 0 is $110 ($121/1.1).

Note that value is created in this example because the project earned a 21-percent rate of return when the discount rate was only 10 percent. No value would have been created had the project earned a 10-percent rate of return. The NPVGO would have been zero, and value would have been negative had the project earned a percentage return below 10 percent. The NPVGO would be negative in that case.

Two conditions must be met in order to increase value.

1. Earnings must be retained so that projects can be funded.[8]
2. The projects must have positive net present value.

Surprisingly, a number of companies seem to invest in projects known to have *negative* net present values. For example, Jensen has pointed out that, in the late 1970s, oil companies and tobacco companies were flush with cash.[9] Due to declining markets in both industries, high dividends and low investment would have been the rational action. Unfortunately, a number of companies in both industries reinvested heavily in what were widely perceived to be negative-NPVGO projects. A study by McConnell and Muscarella documents this perception.[10] They find that, during the 1970s, the stock prices of oil companies generally decreased on the days that announcements of increases in exploration and development were made.

Given that NPV analysis (such as that presented in the previous chapter) is common knowledge in business, why would managers choose projects with negative NPVs? One conjecture is that some managers enjoy controlling a large company. Because paying dividends in lieu of reinvesting earnings reduces the size of the firm, some managers find it emotionally difficult to pay high dividends.

Growth in Earnings and Dividends versus Growth Opportunities

As mentioned earlier, a firm's value increases when it invests in growth opportunities with positive NPVGOs. A firm's value falls when it selects opportunities with negative NPVGOs. However, dividends grow whether projects with positive NPVs or negative NPVs are selected. This surprising result can be explained by the following example.

Example

Lane Supermarkets, a new firm, will earn $100,000 a year in perpetuity if it pays out all its earnings as dividends. However, the firm plans to invest 20 percent of its earnings in projects that earn 10 percent per year. The discount rate is 18 percent. An earlier formula tells us that the growth rate of dividends is

$$g = \text{Retention ratio} \times \text{Return on retained earnings} = 0.2 \times 0.10 = 2\%$$

---

[8]Later in the text we speak of issuing stock or debt in order to fund projects.

[9]M. C. Jensen, "Agency Costs of Free Cash Flows, Corporate Finance and Takeovers," *American Economic Review* (May 1986).

[10]J. J. McConnell and C. J. Muscarella, "Corporate Capital Expenditure Decisions and the Market Value of the Firm," *Journal of Financial Economics* 14 (1985).

For example, in this first year of the new policy, dividends are $80,000 [(1 − 0.2) × $100,000]. Dividends next year are $81,600 ($80,000 × 1.02). Dividends the following year are $83,232 [$80,000 × (1.02)²] and so on. Because dividends represent a fixed percentage of earnings, earnings must grow at 2 percent a year as well.

However, note that the policy reduces value because the rate of return on the projects of 10 percent is less than the discount rate of 18 percent. That is, the firm would have had a higher value at date 0 if it had a policy of paying all its earnings out as dividends. Thus, a policy of investing in projects with negative NPVs rather than paying out earnings as dividends will lead to growth in dividends and earnings, but will reduce value.

Dividends or Earnings: Which to Discount?

As mentioned earlier, this chapter applied the growing-perpetuity formula to the valuation of stocks. In our application, we discounted dividends, not earnings. This is sensible since investors select a stock for what they can get out of it. They only get two things out of a stock: dividends and the ultimate sales price, which is determined by what future investors expect to receive in dividends.

The calculated stock price would be too high were earnings to be discounted instead of dividends. As we saw in our estimation of a firm's growth rate, only a portion of earnings goes to the stockholders as dividends. The remainder is retained to generate future dividends. In our model, retained earnings are equal to the firm's investment. To discount earnings instead of dividends would be to ignore the investment that a firm must make today in order to generate future returns.

The No-Dividend Firm

Students frequently ask the following questions: If the dividend-discount model is correct, why aren't no-dividend stocks selling at zero? This is a good question and gets at the goals of the firm. A firm with many growth opportunities is faced with a dilemma. The firm can pay out dividends now, or it can forgo dividends now so that it can make investments that will generate even greater dividends in the future.[11] This is often a painful choice, because a strategy of dividend deferment may be optimal yet unpopular among certain stockholders.

Many firms choose to pay no dividends—and these firms sell at positive prices.[12] Rational shareholders believe that they will either receive dividends at some point or they will receive something just as good. That is, the firm will be acquired in a merger, with the stockholders receiving either cash or shares of stock at that time.

Of course, the actual application of the dividend-discount model is difficult for firms of this type. Clearly, the model for constant growth of dividends does not apply. Though the differential growth model can work in theory, the difficulties of estimating the date of first dividend, the growth rate of dividends after that date, and the ultimate merger price make application of the model quite difficult in reality.

Empirical evidence suggests that firms with high growth rates are likely to pay lower dividends, a result consistent with the above analysis. For example, consider McDonald's Corporation. The company started in the 1950s and grew rapidly for many years. It paid its first dividend in 1975, though it was a billion-dollar company (in both sales and market

---

[11]A third alternative is to issue stock so that the firm has enough cash both to pay dividends and to invest. This possibility is explored in a later chapter.

[12]For example, most Internet firms, such as Amazon.com, Earthlink, Inc., and Ebay, Inc., pay no dividends.

value of stockholder's equity) prior to that date. Why did it wait so long to pay a dividend? It waited because it had so many positive growth opportunities, that is, additional locations for new hamburger outlets, to take advantage of.

Utilities are an interesting contrast because, as a group, they have few growth opportunities. Because of this, they pay out a large fraction of their earnings in dividends. For example, Consolidated Edison, Sempra Energy, and Kansas City Power and Light have had payout ratios of over 70 percent in many recent years.

5.7 THE DIVIDEND-GROWTH MODEL AND THE NPVGO MODEL (ADVANCED)

This chapter has revealed that the price of a share of stock is the sum of its price as a cash cow plus the per-share value of its growth opportunities. The Sarro Shipping example illustrated this formula using only one growth opportunity. We also used the growing-perpetuity formula to price a stock with a steady growth in dividends. When the formula is applied to stocks, it is typically called the *dividend-growth model.* A steady growth in dividends results from a continual investment in growth opportunities, not just investment in a single opportunity. Therefore, it is worthwhile to compare the dividend-growth model with the *NPVGO model* when growth occurs through continual investing.

EXAMPLE

Cumberland Book Publishers has EPS of $10 at the end of the first year, a dividend-payout ratio of 40 percent, a discount rate of 16 percent, and a return on its retained earnings of 20 percent. Because the firm retains some of its earnings each year, it is selecting growth opportunities each year. This is different from Sarro Shipping, which had a growth opportunity in only one year. We wish to calculate the price per share using both the dividend-growth model and the NPVGO model.

The Dividend-Growth Model

The dividends at date 1 are $0.40 \times \$10 = \$4$ per share. The retention ratio is 0.60 $(1 - 0.40)$, implying a growth rate in dividends of 0.12 (0.60×0.20).

From the dividend-growth model, the price of a share of stock is

$$\frac{\text{Div}}{r - g} = \frac{\$4}{0.16 - 0.12} = \$100$$

The NPVGO Model

Using the NPVGO model, it is more difficult to value a firm with growth opportunities each year (like Cumberland) than a firm with growth opportunities in only one year (like Sarro). In order to value according to the NPVGO model, we need to calculate on a per-share basis (1) the net present value of a single growth opportunity, (2) the net present value of all growth opportunities, and (3) the stock price if the firm acts as a cash cow, that is, the value of the firm without these growth opportunities. The value of the firm is the sum of (2) + (3).

1. Value per Share of a Single Growth Opportunity   Out of the earnings per share of $10 at date 1, the firm retains $6 (0.6 $\times$ $10) at that date. The firm earns $1.20 ($6 $\times$ 0.20) per year in perpetuity on that $6 investment. The NPV from the investment is

Per-Share NPV Generated from Investment at Date 1:

$$-\$6 + \frac{\$1.20}{0.16} = \$1.50 \tag{5.12}$$

That is, the firm invests $6 in order to reap $1.20 per year on the investment. The earnings are discounted at 0.16, implying a value per share from the project of $1.50. Because the investment occurs at date 1 and the first cash flow occurs at date 2, $1.50 is the value of the investment at *date 1*. In other words, the NPV from the date 1 investment has *not* yet been brought back to date 0.

2. Value per Share of All Opportunities   As pointed out earlier, the growth rate of earnings and dividends is 12 percent. Because retained earnings are a fixed percentage of total earnings, retained earnings must also grow at 12 percent a year. That is, retained earnings at date 2 are $6.72 ($6 $\times$ 1.12), retained earnings at date 3 are $7.5264 [$6 $\times$ $(1.12)^2$], and so on.

Let's analyze the retained earnings at date 2 in more detail. Because projects will always earn 20 percent per year, the firm earns $1.344 ($6.72 $\times$ 0.20) in each future year on the $6.72 investment at date 2.

The NPV from the investment is

NPV per Share Generated from Investment at Date 2:

$$-\$6.72 + \frac{\$1.344}{0.16} = \$1.68 \tag{5.13}$$

$1.68 is the NPV as of date 2 of the investment made at date 2. The NPV from the date 2 investment has *not* yet been brought back to date 0.

Now consider the retained earnings at date 3 in more detail. The firm earns $1.5053 ($7.5264 $\times$ 0.20) per year on the investment of $7.5264 at date 3.

The NPV from the investment is

NPV per Share Generated from Investment at Date 3:

$$-\$7.5264 + \frac{\$1.5053}{0.16} = \$1.882 \tag{5.14}$$

From equations (5.12), (5.13), and (5.14), the NPV per share of all of the growth opportunities, discounted back to date 0, is

$$\frac{\$1.50}{1.16} + \frac{\$1.68}{(1.16)^2} + \frac{\$1.882}{(1.16)^3} + \ldots \tag{5.15}$$

Because it has an infinite number of terms, this expression looks quite difficult to compute. However, there is an easy simplification. Note that retained earnings are growing at 12 percent per year. Because all projects earn the same rate of return per year, the NPVs in (5.12), (5.13), and (5.14) are also growing at 12 percent per year. Hence, we can write equation (5.15) as

$$\frac{\$1.50}{1.16} + \frac{\$1.50 \times 1.12}{(1.16)^2} + \frac{\$1.50 \times (1.12)^2}{(1.16)^3} + \ldots$$

This is a growth perpetuity whose value is

$$\text{NPVGO} = \$\frac{1.50}{0.16 - 0.12} = \$37.50$$

Because the first NPV of $1.50 occurs at date 1, the NPVGO is $37.50 as of date 0. In other words, the firm's policy of investing in new projects from retained earnings has an NPV of $37.50.

3. Value per Share if Firm Is a Cash Cow   We now assume that the firm pays out all of its earnings as dividends. The dividends would be $10 per year in this case. Since there would be no growth, the value per share would be evaluated by the perpetuity formula:

$$\frac{\text{Div}}{r} = \frac{\$10}{0.16} = \$62.50$$

Summation

Formula (5.10) states that value per share is the value of a cash cow plus the value of the growth opportunities. This is

$$\$100 = \$62.50 + \$37.50$$

Hence, value is the same whether calculated by a discounted-dividend approach or a growth-opportunities approach. The share prices from the two approaches must be equal, because the approaches are different yet equivalent methods of applying concepts of present value.

5.8 PRICE-EARNINGS RATIO

We argued earlier that one should not discount earnings in order to determine price per share. Nevertheless, financial analysts frequently relate earnings and price per share, as made evident by their heavy reliance on the price-earnings (or P/E) ratio.

Our previous discussion stated that

$$\text{Price per share} = \frac{\text{EPS}}{r} + \text{NPVGO}$$

Dividing by EPS yields

$$\frac{\text{Price per share}}{\text{EPS}} = \frac{1}{r} + \frac{\text{NPVGO}}{\text{EPS}}$$

The left-hand side is the formula for the price-earnings ratio. The equation shows that the P/E ratio is related to the net present value of growth opportunities. As an example, consider two firms, each having just reported earnings per share of $1. However, one firm has many valuable growth opportunities while the other firm has no growth opportunities at all. The firm with growth opportunities should sell at a higher price, because an investor is buying both current income of $1 and growth opportunities. Suppose that the firm with growth opportunities sells for $16 and the other firm sells for $8. The $1 earnings per share number appears in the denominator of the P/E ratio for both firms. Thus, the P/E ratio is 16 for the firm with growth opportunities, but only 8 for the firm without the opportunities.

This explanation seems to hold fairly well in the real world. Electronic and other high-tech stocks generally sell at very high P/E ratios (or *multiples,* as they are often called) because they are perceived to have high growth rates. In fact, some technology stocks sell at high prices even though the companies have never earned a profit. The P/E ratios of these companies are infinite. Conversely, railroads, utilities, and steel companies sell at lower multiples because of the prospects of lower growth.

■ TABLE 5.2 **International P/E Ratios**

Country Composite	1994	1997	2000
United States	24	21	30
Japan	101	44	38
Germany	35	31	31
Britain	18	18	20
France	29	25	27
Canada	45	25	21
Sweden	52	17	20
Italy	29	22	28

Source: Abstracted from "The Global 1000," *Business Week,* July 11, 1994, July 7, 1997, and *Forbes,* July 24, 2000.

Of course, the market is merely pricing *perceptions* of the future, not the future itself. We will argue later in the text that the stock market generally has realistic perceptions of a firm's prospects. However, this is not always true. In the late 1960s, many electronics firms were selling at multiples of 200 times earnings. The high perceived growth rates did not materialize, causing great declines in stock prices during the early 1970s. In earlier decades, fortunes were made in stocks like IBM and Xerox because the high growth rates were not anticipated by investors.

One of the most puzzling phenomena to American investors has been the high P/E ratios in the Japanese stock market. The average P/E ratio for the Tokyo Stock Exchange has varied between 40 and 100 in recent years, while the average American stock had a multiple of around 25 during this time. Our formula indicates that Japanese companies have been perceived to have great growth opportunities. However, American commentators have frequently suggested that investors in the Japanese markets have been overestimating these growth prospects.[13] This enigma (at least to American investors) can only be resolved with the passage of time. Some selected country average P/E ratios appear in Table 5.2. You can see Japan's P/E ratio has trended down.

There are two additional factors explaining the P/E ratio. The first is the discount rate, *r.* The above formula shows that the P/E ratio is *negatively* related to the firm's discount rate. We have already suggested that the discount rate is positively related to the stock's risk or variability. Thus, the P/E ratio is negatively related to the stock's risk. To see that this is a sensible result, consider two firms, *A* and *B,* behaving as cash cows. The stock market *expects* both firms to have annual earnings of $1 per share forever. However, the earnings of firm *A* are known with certainty while the earnings of firm *B* are quite variable. A rational stockholder is likely to pay more for a share of firm *A* because of the absence of risk. If a share of firm *A* sells at a higher price and both firms have the same EPS, the P/E ratio of firm *A* must be higher.

The second additional factor concerns the firm's choice of accounting methods. Under current accounting rules, companies are given a fair amount of leeway. For example, consider inventory accounting where either FIFO or LIFO may be used. In an inflationary environment, *FIFO (first in–first out)* accounting understates the true cost of inventory and hence inflates reported earnings. Inventory is valued according to more recent costs under *LIFO* (*last in–first out*), implying that reported earnings are lower here than they would be under

---

[13]It has been suggested that Japanese companies use more conservative accounting practices, thereby creating higher P/E ratios. This point, which will shortly be examined for firms in general, appears to explain only a small part of Japan's high multiples.

FIFO. Thus, LIFO inventory accounting is a more *conservative* method than FIFO. Similar accounting leeway exists for construction costs (*completed-contracts* versus *percentage-of-completion methods*) and depreciation (*accelerated depreciation* versus *straight-line depreciation*).

As an example, consider two identical firms, *C* and *D*. Firm *C* uses LIFO and reports earnings of $2 per share. Firm *D* uses the less conservative accounting assumptions of FIFO and reports earnings of $3 per share. The market knows that both firms are identical and prices both at $18 per share. This price-earnings ratio is 9 ($18/$2) for firm *C* and 6 ($18/$3) for firm *D*. Thus, the firm with the more conservative principles has the higher P/E ratio.

This last example depends on the assumption that the market sees through differences in accounting treatments. A significant portion of the academic community believes that the market sees through virtually all accounting differences. These academics are adherents of the hypothesis of *efficient capital markets,* a theory that we explore in great detail later in the text. Though many financial people might be more moderate in their beliefs regarding this issue, the consensus view is certainly that many of the accounting differences are seen through. Thus, the proposition that firms with conservative accountants have high P/E ratios is widely accepted.

This discussion argued that the P/E ratio is a function of three different factors. A company's ratio or multiple is likely to be high if (1) it has many growth opportunities, (2) it has low risk, and (3) it is accounted for in a conservative manner. While each of the three factors is important, it is our opinion that the first factor is much more so. Thus, our discussion of growth is quite relevant in understanding price-earnings multiples.

 • What are the three factors determining a firm's P/E ratio?

5.9 STOCK MARKET REPORTING

The Wall Street Journal, the *New York Times,* or your own local newspaper provides useful information on a large number of stocks in several stock exchanges. Table 5.3 reproduces what has been reported on a particular day for several stocks listed on the New York Stock Exchange. In Table 5.3, you can easily find the line for General Electric (i.e., "GenElec"). Reading left to right, the first two numbers are the high and low share prices over the last 52 weeks. For example, the highest price that General Electric traded for at the end of any particular day over the last 52 weeks was $60^{50}. This is read as 60 and the decimal .50. The stock symbol for General Electric is GE. Its annual dividend is $0.55. Most dividend-paying companies such as General Electric pay dividends on a quarterly basis. So the annual dividend is actually the last quarterly dividend of .138 multiplied by 4 (i.e., .138 × 4 = $0.55).

Some firms like GenenTech do not pay dividends. The Div column for GenenTech is blank. The "Yld" column stands for dividend yield. General Electric's dividend yield is the current annual dividend, $0.55, divided by the current closing daily price, which is $56^{63} (you can find the closing price for this particular day in the next to last column). Note that $0.55/56^{63} ≅ 1.0 percent. The next column is labeled PE, which is the symbol for the price-earnings ratio. The price-earnings ratio is the closing price divided by the current earnings per share (based upon the latest quarterly earnings per share multiplied by 4). General Electric's price-earnings ratio is 51. If we were financial analysts or investment bankers, we would say General Electric "sells for 51 times earnings." The next column is the volume of

■ TABLE 5.3 Stock Market Reporting of NYSE-Listed Securities

52 Weeks											
Hi	Lo	Stock	Sym	Div	Yld %	PE	Vol 100s	Hi	Lo	Close	Net Chg
53^{75}	19^{06}	Gap Inc	GPS	.09	.5	15	65172	20^{50}	19	19^{25}	− 1^{75}
22^{25}	9^{56}	GartnerGp	IT		...	22	2331	10^{94}	10^{31}	10^{94}	...
84	43	Gateway	GTW		...	31	23354	47^{40}	42^{15}	44^{62}	− 1^{29}
245	66^{88}	Genentech	DNA		...	dd	21468	159	147	149	− 4^{31}
15^{44}	2^{50}	GenDatacm	GDC		...	dd	456	4^{25}	4	4^{06}	− 0^{25}
64^{94}	36^{25}	GenDynam	GD	1.04	1.6	17	23318	64^{81}	63^{44}	64^{56}	+ 1
60^{50}	38^{21}	GenElec	GE	.55	1.0	51	183051	57^{69}	55^{31}	56^{63}	− 1^{44}
43^{94}	29^{38}	GenMills	GIS	1.10	2.9	18	5054	37^{94}	37^{31}	37^{69}	+ 0^{13}
94^{63}	56^{94}	GenMotor	GM	2.00	3.4	7	22653	61^{13}	58^{38}	58^{63}	− 1^{06}

shares traded on this particular day (in hundreds). For General Electric, 18,305,100 shares traded. This was a heavy trading day for General Electric. The last columns are the High, the Low, and the Last (Close) share prices on this day. The "Net Chg" tells us that the General Electric closing price of 56^{63} was lower than its closing price on the previous day by 1^{44}. In other words, the price of General Electric dropped from 58^{07} to 56^{63}, in one day.

From Table 5.3:

- What is the closing price of Gateways?
- What is the PE of Gateways?
- What is the annual dividend of General Motors?

5.10 SUMMARY AND CONCLUSIONS

In this chapter we use general present-value formulas from the previous chapter to price bonds and stock.

1. Pure discount bonds and perpetuities can be viewed as the polar cases of bonds. The value of a pure discount bond (also called a zero-coupon bond, or simply a zero) is

$$PV = \frac{F}{(1 + r)^T}$$

The value of a perpetuity (also called a *consol*) is

$$PV = \frac{C}{r}$$

2. Level-payment bonds can be viewed as an intermediate case. The coupon payments form an annuity and the principal repayment is a lump sum. The value of this type of bond is simply the sum of the values of its two parts.
3. The yield to maturity on a bond is that single rate that discounts the payments on the bond to its purchase price.
4. A stock can be valued by discounting its dividends. We mention three types of situations:
   a. The case of zero growth of dividends.
   b. The case of constant growth of dividends.
   c. The case of differential growth.
5. An estimate of the growth rate of a stock is needed for formulas (*4b*) or (*4c*) above. A useful estimate of the growth rate is

$$g = \text{Retention ratio} \times \text{Return on retained earnings}$$

6. It is worthwhile to view a share of stock as the sum of its worth, if the company behaves like a cash cow (the company does no investing), and the value per share of its growth opportunities. We write the value of a share as

$$\frac{\text{EPS}}{r} + \text{NPVGO}$$

We show that, in theory, share price must be the same whether the dividend-growth model or the above formula is used.
7. From accounting, we know that earnings are divided into two parts: dividends and retained earnings. Most firms continually retain earnings in order to create future dividends. One should not discount earnings to obtain price per share since part of earnings must be reinvested. Only dividends reach the stockholders and only they should be discounted to obtain share price.
8. We suggest that a firm's price-earnings ratio is a function of three factors:
   a. The per-share amount of the firm's valuable growth opportunities.
   b. The risk of the stock.
   c. The type of accounting method used by the firm.

KEY TERMS

Coupons 103	Premium 106
Discount 106	Pure discount bond 102
Face value 102	Retention ratio 113
Maturity date 102	Return on equity 113
Payout ratio 114	Yield to maturity 107

SUGGESTED READINGS

The best place to look for additional information is in investment textbooks. A good one is:
Bodie, Z., A. Kane, and A. Marcus. *Investments.* 5th ed. Burr Ridge, Ill.: Irwin/McGraw-Hill, 2002.

QUESTIONS AND PROBLEMS

How to Value Bonds

5.1 What is the present value of a 10-year, pure discount bond that pays $1,000 at maturity and is priced to yield the following rates?
   a. 5 percent

     b. 10 percent

     c. 15 percent

5.2 Microhard has issued a bond with the following characteristics:

Principal: $1,000
Term to maturity: 20 years
Coupon rate: 8 percent
Semiannual payments

Calculate the price of the Microhard bond if the stated annual interest rate is:

     a. 8 percent

     b. 10 percent

     c. 6 percent

5.3 Consider a bond with a face value of $1,000. The coupon is paid semiannually and the market interest rate (effective annual interest rate) is 12 percent. How much would you pay for the bond if

     a. the coupon rate is 8 percent and the remaining time to maturity is 20 years?

     b. the coupon rate is 10 percent and the remaining time to maturity is 15 years?

5.4 Pettit Trucking has issued an 8-percent, 20-year bond that pays interest semiannually. If the market prices the bond to yield an effective annual rate of 10 percent, what is the price of the bond?

5.5 A bond is sold at $923.14 (below its par value of $1,000). The bond has 15 years to maturity and investors require a 10-percent yield on the bond. What is the coupon rate for the bond if the coupon is paid semiannually?

5.6 You have just purchased a newly issued $1,000 five-year Vanguard Company bond at par. This five-year bond pays $60 in interest semiannually. You are also considering the purchase of another Vanguard Company bond that returns $30 in semiannual interest payments and has six years remaining before it matures. This bond has a face value of $1,000.

     a. What is effective annual return on the five-year bond?

     b. Assume that the rate you calculated in part (*a*) is the correct rate for the bond with six years remaining before it matures. What should you be willing to pay for that bond?

     c. How will your answer to part (*b*) change if the five-year bond pays $40 in semiannual interest?

Bond Concepts

5.7 Consider two bonds, bond *A* and bond *B,* with equal rates of 10 percent and the same face values of $1,000. The coupons are paid annually for both bonds. Bond *A* has 20 years to maturity while bond *B* has 10 years to maturity.

     a. What are the prices of the two bonds if the relevant market interest rate is 10 percent?

     b. If the market interest rate increases to 12 percent, what will be the prices of the two bonds?

     c. If the market interest rate decreases to 8 percent, what will be the prices of the two bonds?

5.8 *a.* If the market interest rate (the required rate of return that investors demand) unexpectedly increases, what effect would you expect this increase to have on the prices of long-term bonds? Why?

     b. What would be the effect of the rise in the interest rate on the general level of stock prices? Why?

5.9 Consider a bond that pays an $80 coupon annually and has a face value of $1,000. Calculate the yield to maturity if the bond has

     a. 20 years remaining to maturity and it is sold at $1,200.

     b. 10 years remaining to maturity and it is sold at $950.

5.10 The Sue Fleming Corporation has two different bonds currently outstanding. Bond *A* has a face value of $40,000 and matures in 20 years. The bond makes no payments for the first six years and then pays $2,000 semiannually for the subsequent eight years, and finally pays $2,500 semiannually for the last six years. Bond *B* also has a face value of $40,000 and a maturity of 20 years; it makes no coupon payments over the life of the bond. If the required rate of return is 12 percent compounded semiannually, what is the current price of Bond *A?* of Bond *B?*

The Present Value of Common Stocks

5.11 Use the following February 11, 2000, WSJ quotation for AT&T Corp. Which of the following statements is false?

   a. The closing price of the bond with the shortest time to maturity was $1,000.

   b. The annual coupon for the bond maturing in year 2016 is $90.00.

   c. The price on the day before this quotation (i.e., February 9) for the ATT bond maturing in year 2022 was $1.075 per bond contract.

   d. The current yield on the ATT bond maturing in year 2002 was 7.125%

   e. The ATT bond maturing in year 2002 has a yield to maturity less than 7.125%.

Bonds	Cur Yld	Vol	Close	Net Chg
ATT 9s 16	?	10	117	+ 1/4
ATT 5 1/8 01	?	5	100	+ 3/4
ATT 7 1/8 02	?	193	104 1/8	+ 1/4
ATT 8 1/8 22	?	39	107 3/8	− 1/8

5.12 Following are selected quotations for New York Exchange Bonds from the Wall Street Journal. Which of the following statements about Wilson's bond is false?

   a. The bond maturing in year 2000 has a yield to maturity greater than 6⅜%.

   b. The closing price of the bond with the shortest time to maturity on the day before this quotation was $1,003.25.

   c. This annual coupon for the bond maturing in year 2013 is $75.00.

   d. The current yield on the Wilson's bond with the longest time to maturity was 7.29%.

   e. None of the above.

Quotations as of 4 P.M. Eastern Time
Friday, April 23, 1999

Bonds	Current Yield	Vol	Close	Net
WILSON 6 3/8 99	?	76	100 3/8	− 1/8
WILSON 6 3/8 00	?	9	98	1/2
WILSON 7 1/4 02	?	39	103 5/8	1/8
WILSON 7 1/2 13	?	225	102 7/8	− 1/8

5.13 A common stock pays a current dividend of $2. The dividend is expected to grow at an 8-percent annual rate for the next three years; then it will grow at 4 percent in perpetuity. The appropriate discount rate is 12 percent. What is the price of this stock?

5.14 Use the following February 12, 1998, WSJ quotation for Merck & Co. to answer the next question.

52 Weeks					Yld		Vol				Net
Hi	Lo	Stock	Sym	Div	%	PE	100s	Hi	Lo	Close	Chg
120.	80.19	Merck	MRK	1.80	?	30	195111	115.9	114.5	115	−1.25

Which of the following statements is false?

   a. The dividend yield was about 1.6%.

   b. The 52 weeks' trading range was $39.81.

   c. The closing price per share on February 10, 1998, was $113.75.

   d. The closing price per share on February 11, 1998, was $115.

   e. The earnings per share were about $3.83.

5.15 Use the following stock quote.

52 Weeks					Yld	Vol				Net
Hi	Lo	Stock	Sym	Div	%	PE	100s	Hi	Lo	Close	Chg
126.25	72.50	Citigroup	CCI	1.30	1.32	16	20925	98.4	97.8	98.13	−.13

The expected growth rate in Citigroup's dividends is 7% a year. Suppose you use the discounted dividend model to price Citigroup's shares. The constant growth dividend model would suggest that the required return on the Citigroup's stock is what?

5.16 You own $100,000 worth of Smart Money stock. At the end of the first year you receive a dividend of $2 per share; at the end of year 2 you receive a $4 dividend. At the end of year 3 you sell the stock for $50 per share. Only ordinary (dividend) income is taxed at the rate of 28 percent. Taxes are paid at the time dividends are received. The required rate of return is 15 percent. How many shares of stock do you own?

5.17 Consider the stock of Davidson Company that will pay an annual dividend of $2 in the coming year. The dividend is expected to grow at a constant rate of 5 percent permanently. The market requires a 12-percent return on the company.
   a. What is the current price of a share of the stock?
   b. What will the stock price be 10 years from today?

5.18 Easy Type, Inc., is one of a myriad of companies selling word processor programs. Their newest program will cost $5 million to develop. First-year net cash flows will be $2 million. As a result of competition, profits will fall by 2 percent each year thereafter. All cash inflows will occur at year-end. If the market discount rate is 14 percent, what is the value of this new program?

5.19 Whizzkids, Inc., is experiencing a period of rapid growth. Earnings and dividends per share are expected to grow at a rate of 18 percent during the next two years, 15 percent in the third year, and at a constant rate of 6 percent thereafter. Whizzkids' last dividend, which has just been paid, was $1.15. If the required rate of return on the stock is 12 percent, what is the price of a share of the stock today?

5.20 Allen, Inc., is expected to pay an equal amount of dividends at the end of the first two years. Thereafter, the dividend will grow at a constant rate of 4 percent indefinitely. The stock is currently traded at $30. What is the expected dividend per share for the next year if the required rate of return is 12 percent?

5.21 Calamity Mining Company's reserves of ore are being depleted, and its costs of recovering a declining quantity of ore are rising each year. As a result, the company's earnings are declining at the rate of 10 percent per year. If the dividend per share that is about to be paid is $5 and the required rate of return is 14 percent, what is the value of the firm's stock?

5.22 The Highest Potential, Inc., will pay a quarterly dividend per share of $1 at the end of each of the next 12 quarters. Subsequently, the dividend will grow at a quarterly rate of 0.5 percent indefinitely. The appropriate rate of return on the stock is 10 percent. What is the current stock price?

Estimates of Parameters in the Dividend-Discount Model

5.23 The newspaper reported last week that Bradley Enterprises earned $20 million. The report also stated that the firm's return on equity remains on its historical trend of 14 percent. Bradley retains 60 percent of its earnings. What is the firm's growth rate of earnings? What will next year's earnings be?

5.24 Von Neumann Enterprises has just reported earnings of $10 million, and it plans to retain 75 percent of its earnings. The company has 1.25 million shares of common stock outstanding. The stock is selling at $30. The historical return on equity (ROE) of 12 percent is expected to continue in the future. What is the required rate of return on the stock?

Growth Opportunities

5.25 Rite Bite Enterprises sells toothpicks. Gross revenues last year were $3 million, and total costs were $1.5 million. Rite Bite has 1 million shares of common stock outstanding. Gross revenues and costs are expected to grow at 5 percent per year. Rite Bite pays no income taxes, and all earnings are paid out as dividends.

    a. If the appropriate discount rate is 15 percent and all cash flows are received at year's end, what is the price per share of Rite Bite stock?

    b. The president of Rite Bite decided to begin a program to produce toothbrushes. The project requires an immediate outlay of $15 million. In one year, another outlay of $5 million will be needed. The year after that, net cash inflows will be $6 million. This profit level will be maintained in perpetuity. What effect will undertaking this project have on the price per share of the stock?

5.26 California Electronics, Inc., expects to earn $100 million per year in perpetuity if it does not undertake any new projects. The firm has an opportunity that requires an investment of $15 million today and $5 million in one year. The new investment will begin to generate additional annual earnings of $10 million two years from today in perpetuity. The firm has 20 million shares of common stock outstanding, and the required rate of return on the stock is 15 percent.

    a. What is the price of a share of the stock if the firm does not undertake the new project?

    b. What is the value of the growth opportunities resulting from the new project?

    c. What is the price of a share of the stock if the firm undertakes the new project?

5.27 Suppose Smithfield Foods, Inc., has just paid a dividend of $1.40 per share. Sales and profits for Smithfield Foods are expected to grow at a rate of 5% per year. Its dividend is expected to grow by the same rate. If the required return is 10%, what is the value of a share of Smithfield Foods?

5.28 In order to buy back its own shares, Pennzoil Co. has decided to suspend its dividends for the next two years. It will resume its annual cash dividend of $2.00 a share 3 years from now. This level of dividends will be maintained for one more year. Thereafter, Pennzoil is expected to increase its cash dividend payments by an annual growth rate of 6% per year forever. The required rate of return on Pennzoil's stock is 16%. According to the discounted dividend model, what should Pennzoil's current share price be?

5.29 Four years ago, Ultramar Diamond Inc. paid a dividend of $0.80 per share. This year Ultramar paid a dividend of $1.66 per share. It is expected that the company will pay dividends growing at the same rate for the next 5 years. Thereafter, the growth rate will level at 8% per year. The required return on this stock is 18%. According to the discounted dividend model, what would Ultramar's cash dividend be in 7 years?

    a. $2.86

    b. $3.06

    c. $3.68

    d. $4.30

    e. $4.82

5.30 The Webster Co. has just paid a dividend of $5.25 per share. The company will increase its dividend by 15 percent next year and will then reduce its dividend growth by 3 percent each year until it reaches the industry average of 5 percent growth, after which the company will keep a constant growth, forever. The required rate of return for the Webster Co. is 14 percent. What will a share of stock sell for?

Price-Earnings Ratio

5.31 Consider Pacific Energy Company and U.S. Bluechips, Inc., both of which reported recent earnings of $800,000 and have 500,000 shares of common stock outstanding. Assume both firms have the same required rate of return of 15 percent a year.

    a. Pacific Energy Company has a new project that will generate cash flows of $100,000 each year in perpetuity. Calculate the P/E ratio of the company.

   b. U.S. Bluechips has a new project that will increase earnings by $200,000 in the coming year. The increased earnings will grow at 10 percent a year in perpetuity. Calculate the P/E ratio of the firm.

5.32 (Challenge Question) Lewin Skis Inc. (today) expects to earn $4.00 per share for each of the future operating periods (beginning at time 1) if the firm makes no new investments (and returns the earnings as dividends to the shareholders). However, Clint Williams, President and CEO, has discovered an opportunity to retain (and invest) 25% of the earnings beginning three years from today (starting at time 3). This opportunity to invest will continue (for each period) indefinitely. He expects to earn 40% (per year) on this new equity investment (ROE of 40), the return beginning one year after each investment is made. The firm's equity discount rate is 14% throughout.

   a. What is the price per share (now at time 0) of Lewin Skis Inc. stock *without* making the new investment?

   b. If the new investment is expected to be made, per the preceding information, what would the value of the stock (per share) be now (at time 0)?

   c. What is the expected capital gain yield for the second period, assuming the proposed investment is made? What is the expected capital gain yield for the second period if the proposed investment is *not* made?

   d. What is the expected dividend yield for the second period if the new investment is made? What is the expected dividend yield for the second period if the new investment is *not* made?

Appendix 5A THE TERM STRUCTURE OF INTEREST RATES, SPOT RATES, AND YIELD TO MATURITY

In the main body of this chapter, we have assumed that the interest rate is constant over all future periods. In reality, interest rates vary through time. This occurs primarily because inflation rates are expected to differ through time.

To illustrate, we consider two zero-coupon bonds. Bond A is a one-year bond and bond B is a two-year bond. Both have face values of $1,000. The one-year interest rate, r_1, is 8 percent. The two-year interest rate, r_2, is 10 percent. These two rates of interest are examples of *spot rates*. Perhaps this inequality in interest rates occurs because inflation is expected to be higher over the second year than over the first year. The two bonds are depicted in the following time chart.

We can easily calculate the present value for bond A and bond B as

$$PV_A = \$925.93 = \frac{\$1,000}{1.08}$$

$$PV_B = \$826.45 = \frac{\$1,000}{(1.10)^2}$$

Of course, if PV_A and PV_B were observable and the spot rates were not, we could determine the spot rates using the PV formula, because

$$PV_A = \$925.93 = \frac{\$1,000}{(1 + r_1)} \rightarrow r_1 = 8\%$$

and

$$PV_B = \$826.45 = \frac{\$1,000}{(1 + r_2)^2} \rightarrow r_2 = 10\%$$

Now we can see how the prices of more complicated bonds are determined. Try to do the next example. It illustrates the difference between spot rates and yields to maturity.

EXAMPLE

Given the spot rates, r_1 equals 8 percent and r_2 equals 10 percent, what should a 5-percent coupon, two-year bond cost? The cash flows C_1 and C_2 are illustrated in the following time chart.

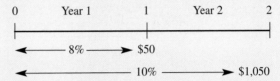

The bond can be viewed as a portfolio of zero-coupon bonds with one- and two-year maturities. Therefore,

$$PV = \frac{\$50}{1 + 0.08} + \frac{\$1,050}{(1 + 0.10)^2} = \$914.06 \qquad (A.1)$$

We now want to calculate a single rate for the bond. We do this by solving for y in the following equation:

$$\$914.06 = \frac{\$50}{1 + y} + \frac{\$1,050}{(1 + y)^2} \qquad (A.2)$$

In (A.2), y equals 9.95 percent. As mentioned in the chapter, we call y the *yield to maturity* on the bond. Solving for y for a multiyear bond is generally done by means of trial and error.[14] While this can take much time with paper and pencil, it is virtually instantaneous on a hand-held calculator.

It is worthwhile to contrast equation (A.1) and equation (A.2). In (A.1), we use the marketwide spot rates to determine the price of the bond. Once we get the bond price, we use (A.2) to calculate its yield to maturity. Because equation (A.1) employs two spot rates whereas only one appears in (A.2), we can think of yield to maturity as some sort of average of the two spot rates.[15]

Using the above spot rates, the yield to maturity of a two-year coupon bond whose coupon rate is 12 percent and PV equals $1,036.73 can be determined by

$$\$1,036.73 = \frac{\$120}{1 + r} + \frac{\$1,120}{(1 + r)^2} \rightarrow r = 9.89\%$$

As these calculations show, two bonds with the same maturity will usually have different yields to maturity if the coupons differ.

---

[14]The quadratic formula may be used to solve for y for a two-year bond. However, formulas generally do not apply for longer-term bonds.

[15]Yield to maturity is not a simple average of r_1 and r_2. Rather, financial economists speak of it as a time-weighted average of r_1 and r_2.

■ FIGURE 5A.1   **The Term Structure of Interest Rates**

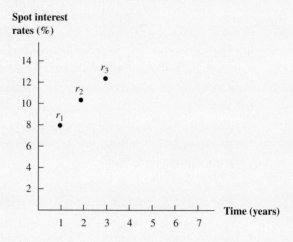

Spot interest rates (%)

Graphing the Term Structure   The *term structure* describes the relationship of spot rates with different maturities. Figure 5A.1 graphs a particular term structure. In Figure 5A.1 the spot rates are increasing with longer maturities, that is, $r_3 > r_2 > r_1$. Graphing the term structure is easy if we can observe spot rates. Unfortunately, this can be done only if there are enough zero-coupon government bonds.

A given term structure, such as that in Figure 5A.1, exists for only a moment in time, say, 10:00 A.M., July 30, 1990. Interest rates are likely to change in the next minute, so that a different (though quite similar) term structure would exist at 10:01 A.M.

QUESTION

CONCEPT

?

• What is the difference between a spot interest rate and the yield to maturity?

Explanations of the Term Structure

Figure 5A.1 showed one of many possible relationships between the spot rate and maturity. We now want to explore the relationship in more detail. We begin by defining a new term, the forward rate. Next, we relate this forward rate to future interest rates. Finally, we consider alternative theories of the term structure.

Definition of Forward Rate   Earlier in this appendix, we developed a two-year example where the spot rate over the first year is 8 percent and the spot rate over the two years is 10 percent. Here, an individual investing \$1 in a two-year zero-coupon bond would have $\$1 \times (1.10)^2$ in two years.

In order to pursue our discussion, it is worthwhile to rewrite[16]

$$\$1 \times (1.10)^2 = \$1 \times 1.08 \times 1.1204 \qquad\qquad (A.3)$$

---

[16]12.04 percent is equal to

$$\frac{(1.10)^2}{1.08} - 1$$

when rounding is performed after four digits.

■ FIGURE 5A.2   Breakdown of a Two-Year Spot Rate into a One-Year Spot Rate and Forward Rate over the Second Year

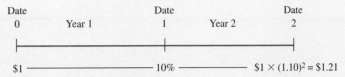

With a two-year spot rate of 10 percent, investor in two-year bond receives $1.21 at date 2.

This is the same return *as if* investor received the spot rate of 8 percent over the first year and 12.04-percent return over the second year.

$1 ——— 8% ——— $1.08 ——12.04% ——$1 × 1.08 × 1.1204 = $1.21

Because both the one-year spot rate and the two-year spot rate are known at date 0, the forward rate over the second year can be calculated at date 0.

Equation (A.3) tells us something important about the relationship between one- and two-year rates. When an individual invests in a two-year zero-coupon bond yielding 10 percent, his wealth at the end of two years is the same as if he received an 8-percent return over the first year and a 12.04-percent return over the second year. This hypothetical rate over the second year, 12.04 percent, is called the *forward rate*. Thus, we can think of an investor with a two-year zero-coupon bond as getting the one-year spot rate of 8 percent and *locking in* 12.04 percent over the second year. This relationship is presented in Figure 5A.2.

More generally, if we are given spot rates, r_1 and r_2, we can always determine the forward rate, f_2, such that:

$$(1 + r_2)^2 = (1 + r_1) \times (1 + f_2) \tag{A.4}$$

We solve for f_2, yielding:

$$f_2 = \frac{(1 + r_2)^2}{1 + r_1} - 1 \tag{A.5}$$

EXAMPLE

If the one-year spot rate is 7 percent and the two-year spot rate is 12 percent, what is f_2?

We plug in equation (A.5), yielding

$$f_2 = \frac{(1.12)^2}{1.07} - 1 = 17.23\%$$

Consider an individual investing in a two-year zero-coupon bond yielding 12 percent. We say it is as if he receives 7 percent over the first year and simultaneously locks in 17.23 percent over the second year. Note that both the one-year spot rate and the two-year spot rate are known at date 0. Because the forward rate is calculated from the one-year and two-year spot rates, it can be calculated at date 0 as well.

Forward rates can be calculated over later years as well. The general formula is

$$f_n = \frac{(1 + r_n)^n}{(1 + r_{n-1})^{n-1}} - 1 \tag{A.6}$$

where f_n is the forward rate over the *n*th year, r_n is the *n*-year spot rate, and r_{n-1} is the spot rate for $n - 1$ years.

EXAMPLE

Assume the following set of rates:

Year	Spot Rate
1	5%
2	6
3	7
4	6

What are the forward rates over each of the four years?

The forward rate over the first year is, *by definition,* equal to the one-year spot rate. Thus, we do not generally speak of the forward rate over the first year. The forward rates over the later years are

$$f_2 = \frac{(1.06)^2}{1.05} - 1 = 7.01\%$$

$$f_3 = \frac{(1.07)^3}{(1.06)^2} - 1 = 9.03\%$$

$$f_4 = \frac{(1.06)^4}{(1.07)^3} - 1 = 3.06\%$$

An individual investing $1 in the two-year zero-coupon bond receives $1.1236 [$1 \times (1.06)^2$] at date 2. He can be viewed as receiving the one-year spot rate of 5 percent over the first year and receiving the forward rate of 7.01 percent over the second year. An individual investing $1 in a three-year zero-coupon bond receives $1.2250 [$1 \times (1.07)^3$] at date 3. She can be viewed as receiving the two-year spot rate of 6 percent over the first two years and receiving the forward rate of 9.03 percent over the third year. An individual investing $1 in a four-year zero-coupon bond receives $1.2625 [$1 \times (1.06)^4$] at date 4. He can be viewed as receiving the three-year spot rate of 7 percent over the first three years and receiving the forward rate of 3.06 percent over the fourth year.

Note that all of the four spot rates in this problem are known at date 0. Because the forward rates are calculated from the spot rates, they can be determined at date 0 as well.

The material in this appendix is likely to be difficult for a student exposed to term structure for the first time. It helps to state what the student should know at this point. Given equations (A.5) and (A.6), a student should be able to calculate a set of forward rates given a set of spot rates. This can simply be viewed as a mechanical computation. In addition to the calculations, a student should understand the intuition of Figure 5A.2.

We now turn to the relationship between the forward rate and the expected spot rates in the future.

Estimating the Price of a Bond at a Future Date   In the example from the body of this chapter, we considered zero-coupon bonds paying $1,000 at maturity and selling at a discount prior to maturity. We now wish to change the example slightly. Now, each bond initially sells at par so that payment at maturity is above $1,000.[17] Keeping the spot rates at 8 percent and 10 percent, we have

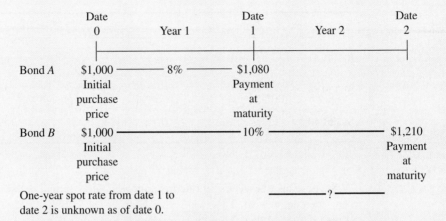

One-year spot rate from date 1 to   ——————?——————
date 2 is unknown as of date 0.

The payments at maturity are $1,080 and $1,210 for the one- and two-year zero-coupon bonds, respectively. The initial purchase price of $1,000 for each bond is determined as

$$\$1,000 = \frac{\$1,080}{1.08}$$

$$\$1,000 = \frac{\$1,210}{(1.10)^2}$$

We refer to the one-year bond as bond *A* and the two-year bond as bond *B*.

There will be a different one-year spot rate when date 1 arrives. This will be the spot rate from date 1 to date 2. We can also call it the spot rate over year 2. This spot rate is not known as of date 0. For example, should the rate of inflation rise between date 0 and date 1, the spot rate over year 2 would likely be high. Should the rate of inflation fall between date 0 and date 1, the spot rate over year 2 would likely be low.

Now that we have determined the price of each bond at date 0, we want to determine what the price of each bond will be at date 1. The price of the one-year bond (bond *A*) must be $1,080 at date 1, because the payment at maturity is made then. The hard part is determining what the price of the two-year bond (bond *B*) will be at that time.

Suppose we find that, on date 1, the one-year spot rate from date 1 to date 2 is 6 percent. We state that this is the one-year spot rate *over* year 2. This means that I can invest $1,000 at date 1 and receive $1,060 ($1,000 × 1.06) at date 2. Because one year has already passed for bond *B,* the bond has only one year left. Because bond *B* pays $1,210 at date 2, its value at date 1 is

$$\$1,141.51 = \frac{\$1,210}{1.06} \tag{A.7}$$

Note that no one *knew* ahead of time the price that bond *B* would sell for on date 1, because no one knew that the one-year spot rate over year 2 would be 6 percent.

---

[17]This change in assumptions simplifies our presentation but does not alter any of our conclusions.

■ TABLE 5A.1   **Price of Bond *B* at Date 1 as a Function of Spot Rate over Year 2**

Price of Bond B at Date 1	Spot Rate over Year 2
$\$1,141.51 = \dfrac{\$1,210}{1.06}$	6%
$\$1,130.84 = \dfrac{\$1,210}{1.07}$	7%
$\$1,061.40 = \dfrac{\$1,210}{1.14}$	14%

Suppose the one-year spot rate beginning at date 1 turned out not to be 6 percent, but to be 7 percent instead. This means that I can invest $1,000 at date 1 and receive $1,070 ($1,000 × 1.07) at date 2. In this case, the value of bond *B* at date 1 would be

$$\$1,130.84 = \frac{\$1,210}{1.07} \tag{A.8}$$

Finally, suppose that the one-year spot rate at date 1 turned out to be neither 6 percent nor 7 percent, but 14 percent instead. This means that I can invest $1,000 at date 1 and receive $1,140 ($1,000 × 1.14) at date 2. In this case, the value of bond *B* at date 1 would be

$$\$1,061.40 = \frac{\$1,210}{1.14}$$

The above possible bond prices are represented in Table 5A.1. The price that bond *B* will sell for on date 1 is not known before date 1 since the one-year spot rate prevailing over year 2 is not known until date 1.

It is important to reemphasize that, although the forward rate is known at date 0, the one-year spot rate beginning at date 1 is *unknown* ahead of time. Thus, the price of bond *B* at date 1 is unknown ahead of time. Prior to date 1, we can speak only of the amount that bond *B* is *expected* to sell for on date 1. We write this as[18]

The Amount that Bond *B* Is Expected to Sell for on Date 1:

$$\frac{\$1,210}{1 + \text{Spot rate expected over year 2}} \tag{A.9}$$

It is worthwhile making two points now. First, because each individual is different, the expected value of bond *B* differs across individuals. Later we will speak of a consensus expected value across investors. Second, equation (A.9) represents one's forecast of the price that the bond will be selling for on date 1. The forecast is made ahead of time, that is, on date 0.

---

[18]Technically, equation (A.9) is only an approximation due to *Jensen's inequality*. That is, expected values of

$$\frac{\$1,210}{1 + \text{Spot rate}} > \frac{\$1,210}{1 + \text{Spot rate expected over year 2}}$$

However, we ignore this very minor issue in the rest of the analysis.

The Relationship between Forward Rate over Second Year and Spot Rate Expected over Second Year

Given a forecast of bond B's price, an investor can choose one of two strategies at date 0:

I. Buy a one-year bond. Proceeds at date 1 would be

$$\$1,080 = \$1,000 \times 1.08 \tag{A.10}$$

II. Buy a two-year bond but sell at date 1. *Expected* proceeds would be

$$\frac{\$1,000 \times (1.10)^2}{1 + \text{Spot rate expected over year 2}} \tag{A.11}$$

Given our discussion of forward rates, we can rewrite (A.11) as

$$\frac{\$1,000 \times 1.08 \times 1.1204}{1 + \text{Spot rate expected over year 2}} \tag{A.12}$$

(Remember that 12.04 percent was the forward rate over year 2; i.e., $f_2 = 12.04\%$.)

Under what condition will the return from strategy I equal the expected return from strategy II? In other words, under what condition will formula (A.10) equal formula (A.12)?

The two strategies will yield the same expected return only when

$$12.04\% = \text{Spot rate expected over year 2} \tag{A.13}$$

In other words, if the forward rate equals the expected spot rate, one would expect to earn the same return over the first year whether one

1. invested in a one-year bond, or
2. invested in a two-year bond but sold after one year.

The Expectations Hypothesis

Equation (A.13) seems fairly reasonable. That is, it is reasonable that investors would set interest rates in such a way that the forward rate would equal the spot rate expected by the marketplace a year from now.[19] For example, imagine that individuals in the marketplace do not concern themselves with risk. If the forward rate, f_2, is less than the spot rate expected over year 2, individuals desiring to invest for one year would always buy a one-year bond. That is, our work above shows that an individual investing in a two-year bond but planning to sell at the end of one year would expect to earn less than if he simply bought a one-year bond.

Equation (A.13) was stated for the specific case where the forward rate was 12.04 percent. We can generalize this to:

Expectations Hypothesis:
$$f_2 = \text{Spot rate expected over year 2} \tag{A.14}$$

Equation (A.14) says that the forward rate over the second year is set to the spot rate that people expect to prevail over the second year. This is called the *expectations hypothesis*. It states that investors will set interest rates such that the forward rate over the second year is equal to the one-year spot rate expected over the second year.

---

[19]Of course, each individual will have different expectations, so (A.13) cannot hold for all individuals. However, financial economists generally speak of a *consensus* expectation. This is the expectation of the market as a whole.

Liquidity-Preference Hypothesis

At this point, many students think that equation (A.14) *must* hold. However, note that we developed (A.14) by assuming that investors were risk-neutral. Suppose, alternatively, that investors are adverse to risk.

Which strategy would appear more risky for an individual who wants to invest for one year?

I. Invest in a one-year bond.

II. Invest in a two-year bond but sell at the end of one year.

Strategy (I) has no risk because the investor knows that the rate of return must be r_1. Conversely, strategy (II) has much risk; the final return is dependent on what happens to interest rates.

Because strategy (II) has more risk than strategy (I), no risk-averse investor will choose strategy (II) if both strategies have the same expected return. Risk-averse investors can have no preference for one strategy over the other only when the expected return on strategy (II) is *above* the return on strategy (I). Because the two strategies have the same expected return when f_2 equals the spot rate expected over year 2, strategy (II) can only have a higher rate of return when

Liquidity-Preference Hypothesis:

$$f_2 > \text{Spot rate expected over year 2} \qquad (A.15)$$

That is, in order to induce investors to hold the riskier two-year bonds, the market sets the forward rate over the second year to be above the spot rate expected over the second year. Equation (A.15) is called the *liquidity-preference* hypothesis.

We developed the entire discussion by assuming that individuals are planning to invest over one year. We pointed out that for these types of individuals, a two-year bond has extra risk because it must be sold prematurely. What about those individuals who want to invest for two years? (We call these people investors with a two-year *time horizon.*)

They could choose one of the following strategies:

III. Buy a two-year zero-coupon bond.

IV. Buy a one-year bond. When the bond matures, immediately buy another one-year bond.

Strategy (III) has no risk for an investor with a two-year time horizon, because the proceeds to be received at date 2 are known as of date 0. However, strategy (IV) has risk since the spot rate over year 2 is unknown at date 0. It can be shown that risk-averse investors will prefer neither strategy (III) nor strategy (IV) over the other when

$$f_2 < \text{Spot rate expected over year 2} \qquad (A.16)$$

Note that the assumption of risk aversion gives contrary predictions. Relationship (A.15) holds for a market dominated by investors with a one-year time horizon. Relationship (A.16) holds for a market dominated by investors with a two-year time horizon. Financial economists have generally argued that the time horizon of the typical investor is generally much shorter than the maturity of typical bonds in the marketplace. Thus, economists view (A.15) as the best depiction of equilibrium in the bond market with *risk-averse* investors.

However, do we have a market of risk-neutral or risk-averse investors? In other words, can the expectations hypothesis of equation (A.14) or the liquidity-preference hypothesis of equation (A.15) be expected to hold? As we will learn later in this book, economists view investors as being risk-averse for the most part. Yet economists are never satisfied with a casual examination of a theory's assumptions. To them, empirical evidence of a theory's predictions must be the final arbiter.

There has been a great deal of empirical evidence on the term structure of interest rates. Unfortunately (perhaps fortunately for some students), we will not be able to present the evidence in any detail. Suffice it to say that, in our opinion, the evidence supports the liquidity-preference hypothesis over the expectations hypothesis. One simple result might give students the flavor of this research. Consider an individual choosing between one of the following two strategies:

  I. Invest in a 1-year bond.

II′. Invest in a 20-year bond but sell at the end of 1 year.

     (Strategy (II′) is identical to strategy (II), except that a 20-year bond is substituted for a 2-year bond.)

     The expectations hypothesis states that the expected returns on both strategies are identical. The liquidity-preference hypothesis states that the expected return on strategy (II′) should be above the expected return on strategy (I). Though no one knows what returns are actually expected over a particular time period, actual returns from the past may allow us to infer expectations. The results from January 1926 to December 1999 are illuminating. The average yearly return on strategy (I) is 3.8 percent and 5.5 percent on strategy (II′) over this time period.[20, 21] This evidence is generally considered to be consistent with the liquidity-preference hypothesis and inconsistent with the expectations hypothesis.

CONCEPT QUESTIONS

- Define the forward rate.
- What is the relationship between the one-year spot rate, the two-year spot rate, and the forward rate over the second year?
- What is the expectations hypothesis?
- What is the liquidity-preference hypothesis?

QUESTIONS AND PROBLEMS

A.1 The appropriate discount rate for cash flows received one year from today is 10 percent. The appropriate annual discount rate for cash flows received two years from today is 11 percent.
    a. What is the price of a two-year bond that pays an annual coupon of 6 percent?
    b. What is the yield to maturity of this bond?

A.2 The one-year spot rate equals 10 percent and the two-year spot rate equals 8 percent. What should a 5-percent coupon two-year bond cost?

A.3 If the one-year spot rate is 9 percent and the two-year spot rate is 10 percent, what is the forward rate?

A.4 Assume the following spot rates:

Maturity	Spot Rates (%)
1	5
2	7
3	10

What are the forward rates over each of the three years?

---

[20]Taken from *Stocks, Bonds, Bills and Inflation 2000 Yearbook* (Chicago: Ibbotson Associates, Inc.). Ibbotson Associates annually updates work by Roger G. Ibbotson and Rex A. Sinquefield.

[21]It is important to note that strategy (II′) does not involve buying a 20-year bond and holding it to maturity. Rather, it consists of buying a 20-year bond and selling it 1 year later, that is, when it has become a 19-year bond. This round-trip transaction occurs 74 times in the 74-year sample from January 1926 to December 1999.

CHAPTER 6

Some Alternative Investment Rules

EXECUTIVE SUMMARY

C hapter 4 examined the relationship between $1 today and $1 in the future. For example, a corporate project generating a set of cash flows can be valued by discounting these flows, an approach called the *net-present-value* (NPV) approach. While we believe that the NPV approach is the best one for evaluating capital budgeting projects, our treatment would be incomplete if we ignored alternative methods. This chapter examines these alternative methods. We first consider the NPV approach as a benchmark. Next we examine three alternatives—payback, accounting rates of return, and internal rate of return.

6.1 WHY USE NET PRESENT VALUE?

Before examining competitors of the NPV approach, we should ask: Why consider using NPV in the first place? Answering this question will put the rest of this chapter in a proper perspective. There are actually a number of arguments justifying the use of NPV, and you may have already seen the detailed one of Chapter 3. We now present one of the simplest justifications through an example.

EXAMPLE

The Alpha Corporation is considering investing in a riskless project costing $100. The project pays $107 at date 1 and has no other cash flows. The managers of the firm might contemplate one of two strategies:

1. Use $100 of corporate cash to invest in the project. The $107 will be paid as a dividend in one period.
2. Forgo the project and pay the $100 of corporate cash as a dividend today.

If strategy 2 is employed, the stockholder might deposit the dividend in the bank for one period. Because the project is riskless and lasts for one period, the stockholder would prefer strategy 1 if the bank interest rate was below 7 percent. In other words, the stockholder would prefer strategy 1 if strategy 2 produced less than $107 by the end of the year.

The comparison can easily be handled by NPV analysis. If the interest rate is 6 percent, the NPV of the project is

$$\$0.94 = -\$100 + \frac{\$107}{1.06}$$

Because the NPV is positive, the project should be accepted. Of course, a bank interest rate above 7 percent would cause the project's NPV to be negative, implying that the project should be rejected.

Thus, our basic point is:

Accepting positive NPV projects benefits the stockholders.

Although we used the simplest possible example, the results could easily be applied to more plausible situations. If the project lasted for many periods, we would calculate the NPV of the project by discounting all the cash flows. If the project were risky, we could determine the expected return on a stock whose risk is comparable to that of the project. This expected return would serve as the discount rate.

Having shown that NPV is a sensible approach, how can we tell whether alternative approaches are as good as NPV? The key to NPV is its three attributes:

1. ***NPV Uses Cash Flows*** Cash flows from a project can be used for other corporate purposes (e.g., dividend payments, other capital-budgeting projects, or payments of corporate interest). By contrast, earnings are an artificial construct. While earnings are useful to accountants, they should not be used in capital budgeting because they do not represent cash.
2. ***NPV Uses All the Cash Flows of the Project*** Other approaches ignore cash flows beyond a particular date; beware of these approaches.
3. ***NPV Discounts the Cash Flows Properly*** Other approaches may ignore the time value of money when handling cash flows. Beware of these approaches as well.

6.2 THE PAYBACK PERIOD RULE

Defining the Rule

One of the most popular alternatives to NPV is the **payback period rule.** Here is how the payback period rule works.

Consider a project with an initial investment of $-\$50,000$. Cash flows are $30,000, $20,000, and $10,000 in the first three years, respectively. These flows are illustrated in Figure 6.1. A useful way of writing down investments like the preceding is with the notation:

$$(-\$50,000, \$30,000, \$20,000, \$10,000)$$

The minus sign in front of the $50,000 reminds us that this is a cash outflow for the investor, and the commas between the different numbers indicate that they are received—or if they are cash outflows, that they are paid out—at different times. In this example we are assuming that the cash flows occur one year apart, with the first one occurring the moment we decide to take on the investment.

■ FIGURE 6.1 **Cash Flows of an Investment Project**

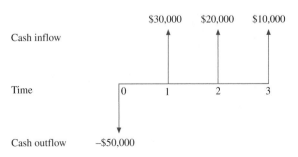

The firm receives cash flows of $30,000 and $20,000 in the first two years, which add up to the $50,000 original investment. This means that the firm has recovered its investment within two years. In this case two years is the *payback period* of the investment.

The payback period rule for making investment decisions is simple. A particular cut-off time, say two years, is selected. All investment projects that have payback periods of two years or less are accepted and all of those that pay off in more than two years—if at all—are rejected.

Problems with the Payback Method

There are at least three problems with the payback method. To illustrate the first two problems, we consider the three projects in Table 6.1. All three projects have the same three-year payback period, so they should all be equally attractive—right?

Actually, they are not equally attractive, as can be seen by a comparison of different *pairs* of projects.

Problem 1: Timing of Cash Flows within the Payback Period   Let us compare project *A* with project *B*. In years 1 through 3, the cash flows of project *A* rise from $20 to $50 while the cash flows of project *B* fall from $50 to $20. Because the large cash flow of $50 comes earlier with project *B,* its net present value must be higher. Nevertheless, we saw above that the payback periods of the two projects are identical. Thus, a problem with the payback period is that it does not consider the timing of the cash flows within the payback period. This shows that the payback method is inferior to NPV because, as we pointed out earlier, the NPV approach *discounts the cash flows properly.*

Problem 2: Payments after the Payback Period   Now consider projects *B* and *C,* which have identical cash flows within the payback period. However, project *C* is clearly preferred because it has the cash flow of $60,000 in the fourth year. Thus, another problem with the payback method is that it ignores all cash flows occurring after the payback period. This flaw is not present with the NPV approach because, as we pointed out earlier, the NPV approach *uses all the cash flows of the project.* The payback method forces managers to have an artificially short-term orientation, which may lead to decisions not in the shareholders' best interests.

Problem 3: Arbitrary Standard for Payback Period   We do not need to refer to Table 6.1 when considering a third problem with the payback approach. When a firm uses the NPV approach, it can go to the capital market to get the discount rate. There is no comparable guide for choosing the payback period, so the choice is arbitrary to some extent.

■ TABLE 6.1   **Expected Cash Flows for Projects *A* through *C* ($)**

Year	A	B	C
0	−100	−100	−100
1	20	50	50
2	30	30	30
3	50	20	20
4	60	60	60,000
Payback period (years)	3	3	3

Managerial Perspective

The payback rule is often used by large and sophisticated companies when making relatively small decisions. The decision to build a small warehouse, for example, or to pay for a tune-up for a truck is the sort of decision that is often made by lower-level management. Typically a manager might reason that a tune-up would cost, say, $200, and if it saved $120 each year in reduced fuel costs, it would pay for itself in less than two years. On such a basis the decision would be made.

Although the treasurer of the company might not have made the decision in the same way, the company endorses such decision making. Why would upper management condone or even encourage such retrograde activity in its employees? One answer would be that it is easy to make decisions using the payback rule. Multiply the tune-up decision into 50 such decisions a month, and the appeal of this simple rule becomes clearer.

Perhaps most important though, the payback rule also has some desirable features for managerial control. Just as important as the investment decision itself is the company's ability to evaluate the manager's decision-making ability. Under the NPV rule, a long time may pass before one decides whether or not a decision was correct. With the payback rule we know in two years whether the manager's assessment of the cash flows was correct.

It has also been suggested that firms with very good investment opportunities but no available cash may justifiably use the payback method. For example, the payback method could be used by small, privately held firms with good growth prospects but limited access to the capital markets. Quick cash recovery may enhance the reinvestment possibilities for such firms.

Notwithstanding all of the preceding rationale, it is not surprising to discover that as the decision grows in importance, which is to say when firms look at bigger projects, the NPV becomes the order of the day. When questions of controlling and evaluating the manager become less important than making the right investment decision, the payback period is used less frequently. For the big-ticket decisions, such as whether or not to buy a machine, build a factory, or acquire a company, the payback rule is seldom used.

Summary of the Payback Period Rule

To summarize, the payback period is not the same as the NPV rule and is therefore conceptually wrong. With its arbitrary cutoff date and its blindness to cash flows after that date, it can lead to some flagrantly foolish decisions if it is used too literally. Nevertheless, because it is so simple, companies often use it as a screen for making the myriad of minor investment decisions they continually face.

Although this means that you should be wary of trying to change rules like the payback period when you encounter them in companies, you should probably be careful not to fall into the sloppy financial thinking they represent. After this course you would do your company a disservice if you ever used the payback period instead of the NPV when you had a choice.

CONCEPT QUESTIONS
- List the problems of the payback period rule.
- What are some advantages?

6.3 THE DISCOUNTED PAYBACK PERIOD RULE

Aware of the pitfalls of the payback approach, some decision makers use a variant called the **discounted payback period rule.** Under this approach, we first discount the cash flows. Then we ask how long it takes for the discounted cash flows to equal the initial investment.

For example, suppose that the discount rate is 10 percent and the cash flows on a project are given by

$$(-\$100, \$50, \$50, \$20)$$

This investment has a payback period of two years, because the investment is paid back in that time.

To compute the project's discounted payback period, we first discount each of the cash flows at the 10-percent rate. In discounted terms, then, the cash flows look like

$$[-\$100, \$50/1.1, \$50/(1.1)^2, \$20/(1.1)^3] = (-\$100, \$45.45, \$41.32, \$15.03)$$

The discounted payback period of the original investment is simply the payback period for these discounted cash flows. The payback period for the discounted cash flows is slightly less than three years since the discounted cash flows over the three years are $101.80 ($45.45 + $41.32 + $15.03). As long as the cash flows are positive, the discounted payback period will never be smaller than the payback period, because discounting will lower the cash flows.

At first glance the discounted payback may seem like an attractive alternative, but on closer inspection we see that it has some of the same major flaws as the payback. Like payback, discounted payback first requires us to make a somewhat magical choice of an arbitrary cutoff period, and then it ignores all of the cash flows after that date.

If we have already gone to the trouble of discounting the cash flows, any small appeal to simplicity or to managerial control that payback may have, has been lost. We might just as well add up the discounted cash flows and use the NPV to make the decision. Although discounted payback looks a bit like the NPV, it is just a poor compromise between the payback method and the NPV.

6.4 THE AVERAGE ACCOUNTING RETURN

Defining the Rule

Another attractive and fatally flawed approach to making financial decisions is the **average accounting return.** The average accounting return is the average project earnings after taxes and depreciation, divided by the average book value of the investment during its life. In spite of its flaws, the average accounting return method is worth examining because it is used frequently in the real world.

EXAMPLE

Consider a company that is evaluating whether or not to buy a store in a newly built mall. The purchase price is $500,000. We will assume that the store has an estimated life of five years and will need to be completely scrapped or rebuilt at the end of that time. The projected yearly sales and expense figures are shown in Table 6.2.

It is worth looking carefully at this table. In fact, the first step in any project assessment is a careful look at the projected cash flows. When the store starts up, it is estimated that first-year sales will be $433,333 and that, after expenses, the before-tax cash flow will be $233,333. After the first year, sales are expected to rise and expenses are expected to fall, resulting in a before-tax cash flow of $300,000. After that, competition from other stores and the loss in novelty will drop before-tax cash flow to $166,667, $100,000, and $33,333, respectively, in the next three years.

■ TABLE 6.2   Projected Yearly Revenue and Costs for Average Accounting Return

	Year 1	Year 2	Year 3	Year 4	Year 5
Revenue	$433,333	$450,000	$266,667	$200,000	$133,333
Expenses	200,000	150,000	100,000	100,000	100,000
Before-tax cash flow	233,333	300,000	166,667	100,000	33,333
Depreciation	100,000	100,000	100,000	100,000	100,000
Earnings before taxes	133,333	200,000	66,667	0	−66,667
Taxes ($T_c = 0.25$)*	33,333	50,000	16,667	0	−16,667
Net income	$100,000	$150,000	$ 50,000	$ 0	−$ 50,000

$$\text{Average net income} = \frac{(\$100,000 + 150,000 + 50,000 + 0 - 50,000)}{5} = \$50,000$$

$$\text{Average investment} = \frac{\$500,000 + 0}{2} = \$250,000$$

$$\text{AAR} = \frac{\$50,000}{\$250,000} = 20\%$$

*Corporate tax rate $= T_c$. The tax rebate in year 5 of $-\$16,667$ occurs if the rest of the firm is profitable. Here, the loss in the project reduces taxes of entire firm.

To compute the average accounting return (AAR) on the project, we divide the average net income by the average amount invested. This can be done in three steps.

Step One: Determining Average Net Income   The net income in any year is the net cash flow minus depreciation and taxes. Depreciation is *not* a cash outflow.[1] Rather, it is a charge reflecting the fact that the investment in the store becomes less valuable every year.

We assume the project has a useful life of five years, at which time it will be worthless. Because the initial investment is $500,000 and because it will be worthless in five years, we will assume that it loses value at the rate of $100,000 each year. This steady loss in value of $100,000 is called *straight-line depreciation*. We subtract both depreciation and taxes from before-tax cash flow to derive the net income, as shown in Table 6.2. The net income over the five years is $100,000 in the first year, $150,000 in year 2, $50,000 in year 3, zero in year 4, and −$50,000 in the last year. The average net income over the life of the project is therefore

Average Net Income:

$$[\$100,000 + \$150,000 + \$50,000 + \$0 + (-\$50,000)]/5 = \$50,000$$

Step Two: Determining Average Investment   We stated earlier that, due to depreciation, the investment in the store becomes less valuable every year. Because depreciation is $100,000 per year, the value at the end of year zero is $500,000, the value at the end of year 1 is $400,000 and so on. What is the average value of the investment over the life of the investment?

The mechanical calculation is

Average Investment:

$$(\$500,000 + \$400,000 + \$300,000 + \$200,000 + \$100,000 + \$0)/6 = \$250,000 \quad (6.1)$$

---

[1]Depreciation will be treated in more detail in the next chapter.

We divide by 6 and not 5, because $500,000 is what the investment is worth at the beginning of the five years and $0 is what it is worth at the beginning of the sixth year. In other words, there are six terms in the parenthesis of equation (6.1).

Step Three: Determining AAR   The average return is simply

$$\text{AAR} = \frac{\$50,000}{\$250,000} = 20\%$$

If the firm had a targeted accounting rate of return greater than 20 percent, the project would be rejected, and if its targeted return were less than 20 percent, it would be accepted.

Analyzing the Average Accounting Return Method

By now you should be able to see what is wrong with the AAR method of making investment decisions.

The most important flaw in the AAR method is that it does not use the right raw materials. It uses the net income figures and the book value of the investment (from the accountant's books) to figure out whether to take the investment. Conversely, the NPV rule *uses cash flows.*

Second, AAR takes no account of timing. In the previous example, the AAR would have been the same if the $100,000 net income in the first year had occurred in the last year. However, delaying an inflow for five years would have made the investment less attractive under the NPV rule as well as by the common sense of the time value of money. That is, the NPV approach *discounts properly.*

Third, just as the payback period requires an arbitrary choice of a cutoff date, the AAR method offers no guidance on what the right targeted rate of return should be. It could be the discount rate in the market. But then again, because the AAR method is not the same as the present value method, it is not obvious that this would be the right choice.

Like the payback method, the AAR (and variations of it) is frequently used as a "backup" to discounted cash flow methods. Perhaps this is so because it is easy to calculate and uses accounting numbers readily available from the firm's accounting system.

QUESTIONS
CONCEPT

?

- What are the three steps in calculating AAR?
- What are some flaws with the AAR approach?

6.5 THE INTERNAL RATE OF RETURN

Now we come to the most important alternative to the NPV approach, the internal rate of return, universally known as the IRR. The IRR is about as close as you can get to the NPV without actually being the NPV. The basic rationale behind the IRR is that it tries to find a single number that summarizes the merits of a project. That number does not depend on the interest rate that prevails in the capital market. That is why it is called the internal rate of return; the number is internal or intrinsic to the project and does not depend on anything except the cash flows of the project.

For example, consider the simple project $(-\$100, \$110)$ in Figure 6.2. For a given rate, the net present value of this project can be described as

$$\text{NPV} = -\$100 + \frac{\$110}{1 + r} \tag{6.2}$$

■ FIGURE 6.2 Cash Flows for a Simple Project

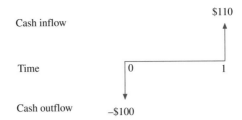

where r is the discount rate.

What must the discount rate be to make the NPV of the project equal to zero?

We begin by using an arbitrary discount rate of 0.08, which yields

$$\$1.85 = -\$100 + \frac{\$110}{1.08} \qquad (6.3)$$

Since the NPV in equation (6.3) is positive, we now try a higher discount rate, say, 0.12. This yields

$$-\$1.79 = -\$100 + \frac{\$110}{1.12} \qquad (6.4)$$

Since the NPV in equation (6.4) is negative, we lower the discount rate to, say, 0.10. This yields

$$0 = -\$100 + \frac{\$110}{1.10} \qquad (6.5)$$

This trial-and-error procedure tells us that the NPV of the project is zero when r equals 10 percent.[2] Thus, we say that 10 percent is the project's **internal rate of return** (IRR). In general, the IRR is the rate that causes the NPV of the project to be zero. The implication of this exercise is very simple. The firm should be equally willing to accept or reject the project if the discount rate is 10 percent. The firm should accept the project if the discount rate is below 10 percent. The firm should reject the project if the discount rate is above 10 percent.

The general investment rule is clear:

Accept the project if IRR is greater than the discount rate. Reject the project if IRR is less than the discount rate.

We refer to this as the **basic IRR rule.** Now we can try the more complicated example in Figure 6.3.

As we did in equations (6.3) to (6.5), we use trial and error to calculate the internal rate of return. We try 20 percent and 30 percent, yielding

Discount Rate	NPV
20%	$10.65
30	−18.39

---

[2]Of course, we could have directly solved for r in equation (6.2) after setting NPV equal to zero. However, with a long series of cash flows, one cannot generally directly solve for r. Instead, one is forced to use a trial-and-error method similar to that in (6.3), (6.4), and (6.5).

■ FIGURE 6.3   **Cash Flows for a More Complex Project**

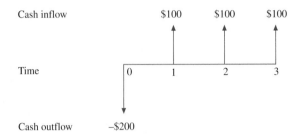

■ FIGURE 6.4   **Net Present Value (NPV) and Discount Rates for a More Complex Project**

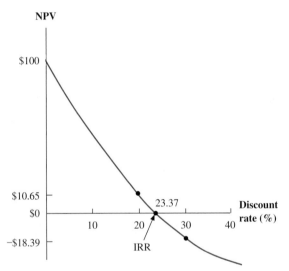

The NPV is positive for discount rates below the IRR and negative for discount rates above the IRR.

After much more trial and error, we find that the NPV of the project is zero when the discount rate is 23.37 percent. Thus, the IRR is 23.37 percent. With a 20-percent discount rate the NPV is positive and we would accept it. However, if the discount rate were 30 percent, we would reject it.

Algebraically, IRR is the unknown in the following equation:[3]

$$0 = -\$200 + \frac{\$100}{1 + IRR} + \frac{\$100}{(1 + IRR)^2} + \frac{\$100}{(1 + IRR)^3}$$

Figure 6.4 illustrates what it means to find the IRR for a project. The figure plots the NPV as a function of the discount rate. The curve crosses the horizontal axis at the IRR of 23.37 percent because this is where the NPV equals zero.

---

[3]One can derive the IRR directly for a problem with an initial outflow and either one or two subsequent inflows. In the case of two subsequent inflows, the quadratic formula is needed. In general, however, only trial and error will work for an outflow and three or more subsequent inflows. Hand calculators calculate IRR by trial and error, though at lightning speed.

It should also be clear that the NPV is positive for discount rates below the IRR and negative for discount rates above the IRR. This means that if we accept projects like this one when the discount rate is less than the IRR, we will be accepting positive NPV projects. Thus, the IRR rule will coincide exactly with the NPV rule.

If this were all there were to it, the IRR rule would always coincide with the NPV rule. This would be a wonderful discovery because it would mean that just by computing the IRR for a project we would be able to tell where it ranks among all of the projects we are considering. For example, if the IRR rule really works, a project with an IRR of 20 percent will always be at least as good as one with an IRR of 15 percent.

But the world of finance is not so kind. Unfortunately, the IRR rule and the NPV rule are the same only for examples like the ones above. Several problems with the IRR approach occur in more complicated situations.

CONCEPT QUESTION
?

• How does one calculate the IRR of a project?

6.6 PROBLEMS WITH THE IRR APPROACH

Definition of Independent and Mutually Exclusive Projects

An **independent project** is one whose acceptance or rejection is independent of the acceptance or rejection of other projects. For example, imagine that McDonald's is considering putting a hamburger outlet on a remote island. Acceptance or rejection of this unit is likely to be unrelated to the acceptance or rejection of any other restaurant in their system. The remoteness of the outlet in question insures that it will not pull sales away from other outlets.

Now consider the other extreme, **mutually exclusive investments.** What does it mean for two projects, *A* and *B,* to be mutually exclusive? You can accept *A* or you can accept *B* or you can reject both of them, but you cannot accept both of them. For example, *A* might be a decision to build an apartment house on a corner lot that you own, and *B* might be a decision to build a movie theater on the same lot.

We now present two general problems with the IRR approach that affect both independent and mutually exclusive projects. Next, we deal with two problems affecting mutually exclusive projects only.

Two General Problems Affecting Both Independent and Mutually Exclusive Projects

We begin our discussion with project *A,* which has the following cash flows:

$$(-\$100, \$130)$$

The IRR for project *A* is 30 percent. Table 6.3 provides other relevant information on the project. The relationship between NPV and the discount rate is shown for this project in Figure 6.5. As you can see, the NPV declines as the discount rate rises.

Problem 1: Investing or Financing?   Now consider project *B,* with cash flows of

$$(\$100, -\$130)$$

■ TABLE 6.3 **The Internal Rate of Return and Net Present Value**

	Project A			Project B			Project C		
Dates:	0	1	2	0	1	2	0	1	2
Cash flows	−$100	$130		$100	−$130		−$100	$230	−$132
IRR		30%			30%		10%	and	20%
NPV @ 10%		$18.2			−$18.2			0	
Accept if market rate		<30%			>30%		>10%	but	<20%
Financing or investing		Investing			Financing			Mixture	

These cash flows are exactly the reverse of the flows for project *A.* In project *B,* the firm receives funds first and then pays out funds later. While unusual, projects of this type do exist. For example, consider a corporation conducting a seminar where the participants pay in advance. Because large expenses are frequently incurred at the seminar date, cash inflows precede cash outflows.

Consider our trial-and-error method to calculate IRR:

$$- \$4 = + \$100 - \frac{\$130}{1.25}$$

$$\$0 = + \$100 - \frac{\$130}{1.30}$$

$$\$3.70 = + \$100 - \frac{\$130}{1.35}$$

As with project *A,* the internal rate of return is 30 percent. However, notice that the net present value is *negative* when the discount rate is *below* 30 percent. Conversely, the net present value is positive when the discount rate is above 30 percent. The decision rule is exactly the opposite of our previous result. For this type of a project, the rule is

Accept the project when IRR is less than the discount rate. Reject the project when IRR is greater than the discount rate.

This unusual decision rule follows from the graph of project *B* in Figure 6.5. The curve is upward sloping, implying that NPV is *positively* related to the discount rate.

The graph makes intuitive sense. Suppose that the firm wants to obtain $100 immediately. It can either (1) conduct project *B* or (2) borrow $100 from a bank. Thus, the project is actually a substitute for borrowing. In fact, because the IRR is 30 percent, taking on project *B* is tantamount to borrowing at 30 percent. If the firm can borrow from a bank at, say, only 25 percent, it should reject the project. However, if a firm can only borrow from a bank at, say, 35 percent, it should accept the project. Thus, project *B* will be accepted if and only if the discount rate is *above* the IRR.[4]

This should be contrasted with project *A.* If the firm has $100 of cash to invest, it can either (1) conduct project *A* or (2) lend $100 to the bank. The project is actually a substitute for lending. In fact, because the IRR is 30 percent, taking on project *A* is tantamount to lending at 30 percent. The firm should accept project *A* if the lending rate is below 30 percent. Conversely, the firm should reject project *A* if the lending rate is above 30 percent.

---

[4]This paragraph implicitly assumes that the cash flows of the project are risk-free. In this way, we can treat the borrowing rate as the discount rate for a firm needing $100. With risky cash flows, another discount rate would be chosen. However, the intuition behind the decision to accept when IRR is less than the discount rate would still apply.

■ FIGURE 6.5 **Net Present Value and Discount Rates for Projects *A*, *B*, and *C***

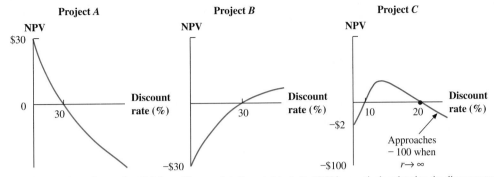

Project *A* has a cash outflow at date 0 followed by a cash inflow at date 1. Its NPV is negatively related to the discount rate.
Project *B* has a cash inflow at date 0 followed by a cash outflow at date 1. Its NPV is positively related to the discount rate.
Project *C* has two changes of sign in its cash flows. It has an outflow at date 0, an inflow at date 1, and an outflow at date 2.
Projects with more than one change of sign can have multiple rates of return.

Because the firm initially pays out money with project *A* but initially receives money with project *B*, we refer to project *A* as an investing-type project and project *B* as a financing-type project. Investing-type projects are the norm. Because the IRR rule is reversed for a financing-type project, we view this type of project as a problem—unless it is understood properly.

Problem 2: Multiple Rates of Return   Suppose the cash flows from a project are

$$(-\$100, \$230, -\$132)$$

Because this project has a negative cash flow, a positive cash flow, and another negative cash flow, we say that the project's cash flows exhibit two changes of signs, or "flip-flops." While this pattern of cash flows might look a bit strange at first, many projects require outflows of cash after receiving some inflows. An example would be a strip-mining project. The first stage in such a project is the initial investment in excavating the mine. Profits from operating the mine are received in the second stage. The third stage involves a further investment to reclaim the land and satisfy the requirements of environmental-protection legislation. Cash flows are negative at this stage.

Projects financed by lease arrangements also produce negative cash flows followed by positive ones. We study leasing carefully in a later chapter, but for now we will give you a hint. Using leases for financing can sometimes bring substantial tax advantages. These advantages are often sufficient to make an otherwise bad investment have positive cash flows following an initial outlay. But after a while the tax advantages decline or run out. The cash flows turn negative when this occurs.

It is easy to verify that this project has not one but two IRRs, 10 percent and 20 percent.[5] In a case like this, the IRR does not make any sense. What IRR are we to use, 10 percent or 20 percent? Because there is no good reason to use one over the other, IRR simply cannot be used here.

---

[5]The calculations are

$$-\$100 + \frac{\$230}{1.1} - \frac{\$132}{(1.1)^2}$$
$$0 = -\$100 + \$209.09 - \$109.09$$

and

$$-\$100 + \frac{\$230}{1.2} - \frac{\$132}{(1.2)^2}$$
$$0 = -\$100 + \$191.67 - \$91.67$$

Thus, we have multiple rates of return.

Of course, we should not feel too worried about multiple rates of return. After all, we can always fall back on NPV. Figure 6.5 plots the NPV for this project *C* as a function of the different discount rates. As it shows, the NPV is zero at both 10 percent and 20 percent. Furthermore, the NPV is positive for discount rates between 10 percent and 20 percent and negative outside of this range.

This example generates multiple internal rates of return because both an inflow and an outflow occur after the initial investment. In general, these flip-flops or changes in sign produce multiple IRRs. In theory, a cash flow stream with *M* changes in sign can have up to *M* positive internal rates of return.[6] As we pointed out, projects whose cash flows change sign repeatedly can occur in the real world.

Are We Ever Safe from the Multiple-IRR Problem?   If the first cash flow for a project is negative—because it is the initial investment—and if all of the remaining flows are positive, there can be only a single, unique IRR, no matter how many periods the project lasts. This is easy to understand by using the concept of the time value of money. For example, it is easy to verify that project *A* in Table 6.3 has an IRR of 30 percent, because using a 30-percent discount rate gives

$$\text{NPV} = -\$100 + \$130/(1.3)$$
$$= 0$$

How do we know that this is the only IRR? Suppose that we were to try a discount rate greater than 30 percent. In computing the NPV, changing the discount rate does not change the value of the initial cash flow of −$100 because that cash flow is not discounted. But raising the discount rate can only lower the present value of the future cash flows. In other words, because the NPV is zero at 30 percent, any increase in the rate will push the NPV into the negative range. Similarly, if we try a discount rate of less than 30 percent, the overall NPV of the project will be positive. Though this example has only one positive flow, the above reasoning still implies a single, unique IRR if there are many inflows (but no outflows) after the initial investment.

If the initial cash flow is positive—and if all of the remaining flows are negative—there can only be a single, unique IRR. This result follows from reasoning similar to that above. Both these cases have only one change of sign or flip-flop in the cash flows. Thus, we are safe from multiple IRRs whenever there is only one sign change in the cash flows.

---

[6]Those of you who are steeped in algebra might have recognized that finding the IRR is like finding the root of a polynomial equation. For a project with cash flows of $(C_0, \ldots, C_T)$, the formula for computing the IRR requires us to find the interest rate, *r*, that makes

$$\text{NPV} = C_0 + C_1/(1 + r) + \ldots + C_T/(1 + r)^T = 0$$

If we let the symbol *x* stand for the discount factor,

$$x = 1/(1 + r)$$

then the formula for the IRR becomes

$$\text{NPV} = C_0 + C_1 x + C_2 x^2 + \ldots + C_T x^T = 0$$

Finding the IRR, then, is the same as finding the roots of this polynomial equation. If a particular value *x** is a root of the equation, then, because

$$x = 1/(1 + r)$$

it follows that there is an associated IRR:

$$r^* = (1/x^*) - 1$$

From the theory of polynomials, it is well known that an *n*th-order polynomial has *n* roots. Each such root that is positive and less than 1 can have a sensible IRR associated with it. Applying Descartes's rules of signs gives the result that a stream of *n* cash flows can have up to *M* positive IRRs, where *M* is the number of changes of sign for the cash flows.

General Rules   The following chart summarizes our rules:[7]

Flows	Number of IRRs	IRR Criterion	NPV Criterion
First cash flow is negative and all remaining cash flows are positive.	1	Accept if IRR $> r$ Reject if IRR $< r$	Accept if NPV > 0 Reject if NPV < 0
First cash flow is positive and all remaining cash flows are negative.	1	Accept if IRR $< r$ Reject if IRR $> r$	Accept if NPV > 0 Reject if NPV < 0
Some cash flows after first are positive and some cash flows after first are negative.	May be more than 1	No valid IRR	Accept if NPV > 0 Reject if NPV < 0

Note that the NPV criterion is the same for each of the three cases. In other words, NPV analysis is always appropriate. Conversely, the IRR can be used only in certain cases. When it comes to NPV, the preacher's words, "You just can't lose with the stuff I use," clearly apply.

Problems Specific to Mutually Exclusive Projects

As mentioned earlier, two or more projects are mutually exclusive if the firm can, at most, accept only one of them. We now present two problems dealing with the application of the IRR approach to mutually exclusive projects. These two problems are quite similar, though logically distinct.

The Scale Problem   A professor we know motivates class discussions on this topic with the statement: "Students, I am prepared to let one of you choose between two mutually exclusive 'business' propositions. Opportunity 1—You give me $1 now and I'll give you $1.50 back at the end of the class period. Opportunity 2—You give me $10 and I'll give you $11 back at the end of the class period. You can only choose one of the two opportunities. And you cannot choose either opportunity more than once. I'll pick the first volunteer."

Which would you choose? The correct answer is opportunity 2.[8] To see this, look at the following chart:

	Cash Flow at Beginning of Class	Cash Flow at End of Class (90 minutes later)	NPV[9]	IRR
Opportunity 1	−$1	+$1.50	$0.50	50%
Opportunity 2	−10	+11.00	1.00	10

As we have stressed earlier in the text, one should choose the opportunity with the highest NPV. This is opportunity 2 in the example. Or, as one of the professor's students explained it: "I'm bigger than the professor, so I know I'll get my money back. And I have $10 in my pocket right now so I can choose either opportunity. At the end of the class,

---

[7]IRR stands for internal rate of return, NPV stands for net present value, and *r* stands for discount rate.

[8]The professor uses real money here. Though many students have done poorly on the professor's exams over the years, no student ever chose opportunity 1. The professor claims that his students are "money players."

[9]We assume a zero rate of interest because his class lasted only 90 minutes. It just seemed like a lot longer.

I'll be able to play two rounds of my favorite electronic game with opportunity 2 and still have my original investment, safe and sound.[10] The profit on opportunity 1 buys only one round."

We believe that this business proposition illustrates a defect with the internal rate of return criterion. The basic IRR rule says take opportunity 1, because the IRR is 50 percent. The IRR is only 10 percent for opportunity 2.

Where does IRR go wrong? The problem with IRR is that it ignores issues of scale. While opportunity 1 has a greater IRR, the investment is much smaller. In other words, the high percentage return on opportunity 1 is more than offset by the ability to earn at least a decent return[11] on a much bigger investment under opportunity 2.

Since IRR seems to be misguided here, can we adjust or correct it? We illustrate how in the next example.

EXAMPLE

Stanley Jaffe and Sherry Lansing have just purchased the rights to *Corporate Finance: The Motion Picture*. They will produce this major motion picture on either a small budget or a big budget. The estimated cash flows are

	Cash Flow at Date 0	Cash Flow at Date 1	NPV @ 25%	IRR
Small budget	−$10 million	$40 million	$22 million	300%
Large budget	−25 million	65 million	27 million	160

Because of high risk, a 25-percent discount rate is considered appropriate. Sherry wants to adopt the large budget because the NPV is higher. Stanley wants to adopt the small budget because the IRR is higher. Who is right?

For the reasons espoused in the classroom example above, NPV is correct. Hence, Sherry is right. However, Stanley is very stubborn where IRR is concerned. How can Sherry justify the large budget to Stanley using the IRR approach?

This is where incremental IRR comes in. She calculates the incremental cash flows from choosing the large budget instead of the small budget as

	Cash Flow at Date 0 (in $ millions)	Cash Flow at Date 1 (in $ millions)
Incremental cash flows from choosing large budget instead of small budget	−25 − (−10) = −15	65 − 40 = 25

This chart shows that the incremental cash flows are −$15 million at date 0 and $25 million at date 1. Sherry calculates incremental IRR as

Formula for Calculating the Incremental IRR:

$$0 = -\$15 \text{ million} + \frac{\$25 \text{ million}}{1 + \text{IRR}}$$

---

[10]At press time for this text, electronic games cost $0.50 apiece.

[11]A 10-percent return is more than decent over a 90-minute interval!

IRR equals 66.67 percent in this equation. Sherry says that the **incremental IRR** is 66.67 percent. Incremental IRR is the IRR on the incremental investment from choosing the large project instead of the small project.

In addition, we can calculate the NPV of the incremental cash flows:

NPV of Incremental Cash Flows:

$$- \$15 \text{ million } + \frac{\$25 \text{ million}}{1.25} = \$5 \text{ million}$$

We know the small-budget picture would be acceptable as an independent project since its NPV is positive. We want to know whether it is beneficial to invest an additional $15 million in order to make the large-budget picture instead of the small-budget picture. In other words, is it beneficial to invest an additional $15 million in order to receive an additional $25 million next year? First, the above calculations show the NPV on the incremental investment to be positive. Second, the incremental IRR of 66.67 percent is higher than the discount rate of 25 percent. For both reasons, the incremental investment can be justified. The second reason is what Stanley needed to hear to be convinced. Hence, the large-budget movie should be made.

In review, we can handle this example (or any mutually exclusive example) in one of three ways:

1. *Compare the NPVs of the two choices.* The NPV of the large-budget picture is greater than the NPV of the small-budget picture, that is, $27 million is greater than $22 million.

2. *Compare the incremental NPV from making the large-budget picture instead of the small-budget picture.* Because the incremental NPV equals $5 million, we choose the large-budget picture.

3. *Compare the incremental IRR to the discount rate.* Because the incremental IRR is 66.67 percent and the discount rate is 25 percent, we take the large-budget picture.

All three approaches always give the same decision. However, we must not compare the IRRs of the two pictures. If we did we would make the wrong choice, that is, we would accept the small-budget picture.

One final note here. Students often ask which project should be subtracted from the other in calculating incremental flows. Notice that we are subtracting the smaller project's cash flows from the bigger project's cash flows. This leaves an *outflow* at date 0. We then use the basic IRR rule on the incremental flows.[12]

The Timing Problem   Next we illustrate another, but very similar, problem with using the IRR approach to evaluate mutually exclusive projects.

EXAMPLE

Suppose that the Kaufold Corporation has two alternative uses for a warehouse. It can store toxic waste containers (investment *A*) or electronic equipment (investment *B*). The cash flows are as follows:

| | | | | | NPV | | | |
Year:	0	1	2	3	@0%	@10%	@15%	IRR
Investment *A*	−$10,000	$10,000	$1,000	$ 1,000	$2,000	$669	$ 109	16.04%
Investment *B*	−10,000	1,000	1,000	12,000	4,000	751	−484	12.94

---

[12]Alternatively, we could have subtracted the larger project's cash flows from the smaller project's cash flows. This would have left an *inflow* at date 0, making it necessary to use the IRR rule for financing situations. This would work but we find it more confusing.

We find that the NPV of investment *B* is higher with low discount rates, and the NPV of investment *A* is higher with high discount rates. This is not surprising if you look closely at the cash flow patterns. The cash flows of *A* occur early, whereas the cash flows of *B* occur later. If we assume a high discount rate, we favor investment *A* because we are implicitly assuming that the early cash flow (for example, $10,000 in year 1) can be reinvested at that rate. Because most of investment *B*'s cash flows occur in year 3, *B*'s value is relatively high with low discount rates.

The patterns of cash flow for both projects appear in Figure 6.6. Project *A* has an NPV of $2,000 at a discount rate of zero. This is calculated by simply adding up the cash flows without discounting them. Project *B* has an NPV of $4,000 at the zero rate. However, the NPV of project *B* declines more rapidly as the discount rate increases than does the NPV of project *A*. As we mentioned above, this occurs because the cash flows of *B* occur later. Both projects have the same NPV at a discount rate of 10.55 percent. The IRR for a project is the rate at which the NPV equals zero. Because the NPV of *B* declines more rapidly, *B* actually has a lower IRR.

As with the movie example presented above, we can select the better project with one of three different methods:

1. *Compare NPVs of the Two Projects.* Figure 6.6 aids our decision. If the discount rate is below 10.55 percent, one should choose project *B* because *B* has a higher NPV. If the rate is above 10.55 percent, one should choose project *A* because *A* has a higher NPV.

2. *Compare Incremental IRR to Discount Rate.* The above method employed NPV. Another way of determining that *B* is a better project is to subtract the cash flows of *A* from the cash flows of *B* and then to calculate the IRR. This is the incremental IRR approach we spoke of earlier.

   The incremental cash flows are

						NPV of Incremental Cash Flows		
Year:	0	1	2	3	Incremental IRR	@0%	@10%	@15%
B − A	0	−$9,000	0	$11,000	10.55%	$2,000	$83	−$593

   This chart shows that the incremental IRR is 10.55 percent. In other words, the NPV on the incremental investment is zero when the discount rate is 10.55 percent. Thus, if the relevant discount rate is below 10.55 percent, project *B* is preferred to project *A*. If the relevant discount rate is above 10.55 percent, project *A* is preferred to project *B*.[13]

3. *Calculate NPV on Incremental Cash Flows.* Finally, one could calculate the NPV on the incremental cash flows. The chart that appears with the previous method displays these NPVs. We find that the incremental NPV is positive when the discount rate is either 0 percent or 10 percent. The incremental NPV is negative if the discount rate is 15 percent. If the NPV is positive on the incremental flows, one should choose *B*. If the NPV is negative, one should choose *A*.

---

[13]In this example, we first showed that the NPVs of the two projects are equal when the discount rate is 10.55 percent. We next showed that the incremental IRR is also 10.55 percent. This is not a coincidence; this equality must *always* hold. The incremental IRR is the rate that causes the incremental cash flows to have zero NPV. The incremental cash flows have zero NPV when the two projects have the same NPV.

■ FIGURE 6.6   Net Present Value and the Internal Rate of Return for Mutually Exclusive Projects

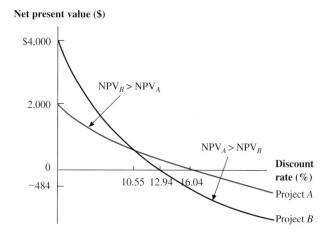

In summary, the same decision is reached whether one (*a*) compares the NPVs of the two projects, (*b*) compares the incremental IRR to the relevant discount rate, or (*c*) examines the NPV of the incremental cash flows. However, as mentioned earlier, one should not compare the IRR of project *A* with the IRR of project *B*.

We suggested earlier that one should subtract the cash flows of the smaller project from the cash flows of the bigger project. What do we do here since the two projects have the same initial investment? Our suggestion in this case is to perform the subtraction so that the first nonzero cash flow is negative. In the Kaufold Corporation example, we achieved this by subtracting *A* from *B*. In this way, we can still use the basic IRR rule for evaluating cash flows.

The preceding examples illustrate problems with the IRR approach in evaluating mutually exclusive projects. Both the professor-student example and the motion-picture example illustrate the problem that arises when mutually exclusive projects have different initial investments. The Kaufold Corp. example illustrates the problem that arises when mutually exclusive projects have different cash flow timing. When working with mutually exclusive projects, it is not necessary to determine whether it is the scale problem or the timing problem that exists. Very likely both occur in any real-world situation. Instead, the practitioner should simply use either an incremental IRR or an NPV approach.

Redeeming Qualities of the IRR

The IRR probably survives because it fills a need that the NPV does not. People seem to want a rule that summarizes the information about a project in a single rate of return. This single rate provides people with a simple way of discussing projects. For example, one manager in a firm might say to another, "Remodeling the north wing has a 20-percent IRR."

To their credit, however, companies that employ the IRR approach seem to understand its deficiencies. For example, companies frequently restrict managerial projections of cash flows to be negative at the beginning and strictly positive later. Perhaps, then, the ability of the IRR approach to capture a complex investment project in a single number and the ease of communicating that number explain the survival of the IRR.

A Test

To test your knowledge, consider the following two statements:

1. You must know the discount rate to compute the NPV of a project but you compute the IRR without referring to the discount rate.
2. Hence, the IRR rule is easier to apply than the NPV rule because you don't use the discount rate when applying IRR.

The first statement is true. The discount rate is needed to *compute* NPV. The IRR is *computed* by solving for the rate where the NPV is zero. No mention is made of the discount rate in the mere computation. However, the second statement is false. In order to *apply* IRR, you must compare the internal rate of return with the discount rate. Thus, the discount rate is needed for making a decision under either the NPV or IRR approach.

QUESTIONS
CONCEPT
?

- What is the difference between independent projects and mutually exclusive projects?
- What are two problems with the IRR approach that apply to both independent and mutually exclusive projects?
- What are two additional problems applying only to mutually exclusive projects?

6.7 THE PROFITABILITY INDEX

Another method that is used to evaluate projects is called the **profitability index.** It is the ratio of the present value of the future expected cash flows *after* initial investment divided by the amount of the initial investment. The profitability index can be represented as

$$\text{Profitability index (PI)} = \frac{\text{PV of cash flows } \textit{subsequent} \text{ to initial investment}}{\text{Initial investment}}$$

EXAMPLE

Hiram Finnegan, Inc., applies a 12-percent discount rate to two investment opportunities.

	Cash Flows ($000,000)			PV @12% of Cash Flows Subsequent to Initial Investment ($000,000)	Profit- ability Index	NPV @ 12% ($000,000)
Project	C_0	C_1	C_2			
1	−20	70	10	70.5	3.53	50.5
2	−10	15	40	45.3	4.53	35.3

For example, the profitability index is calculated for project 1 as follows. The present value of the cash flows *after* the initial investment are

$$\$70.5 = \frac{\$70}{1.12} + \frac{\$10}{(1.12)^2} \tag{6.6}$$

The profitability index is calculated by dividing the result of equation (6.6) by the initial investment of $20. This yields

$$3.53 = \frac{\$70.5}{\$20}$$

We consider three possibilities:

1. *Independent Projects.* We first assume that we have two independent projects. According to the NPV criterion, both projects should be accepted since NPV is positive in each case. The NPV is positive whenever the profitability index (PI) is greater than one. Thus, the PI *decision rule* is

   Accept an independent project if PI > 1.
   Reject if PI < 1.

2. *Mutually Exclusive Projects.* Let us assume that you can now only accept one project. NPV analysis says accept project 1 because this project has the bigger NPV. Because project 2 has the higher PI, the profitability index leads to the wrong selection.

   The problem with the profitability index for mutually exclusive projects is the same as the scale problem with the IRR that we mentioned earlier. Project 2 is smaller than project 1. Because the PI is a ratio, this index misses the fact that project 1 has a larger investment than project 2 has. Thus, like IRR, PI ignores differences of scale for mutually exclusive projects.

   However, like IRR, the flaw with the PI approach can be corrected using incremental analysis. We write the incremental cash flows after subtracting project 2 from project 1 as follows:

Project	Cash Flows ($000,000)			PV @12% of Cash Flows Subsequent to Initial Investment ($000,000)	Profit- ability Index	NPV @ 12% ($000,000)
	C_0	C_1	C_2			
1 − 2	−10	55	−30	25.2	2.52	15.2

   Because the profitability index on the incremental cash flows is greater than 1.0, we should choose the bigger project, that is, project 1. This is the same decision we get with the NPV approach.

3. *Capital Rationing.* The two cases above implicitly assumed that the firm could always attract enough capital to make any profitable investments. Now we consider the case when a firm does not have enough capital to fund all positive NPV projects. This is the case of **capital rationing.**

Imagine that the firm has a third project, as well as the first two. Project 3 has the following cash flows:

Project	Cash Flows ($000,000)			PV @12% of Cash Flows Subsequent to Initial Investment ($000,000)	Profit- ability Index	NPV @ 12% ($000,000)
	C_0	C_1	C_2			
3	−10	−5	60	43.4	4.34	33.4

Further, imagine that (*a*) the projects of Hiram Finnegan, Inc., are independent, but (*b*) the firm has only $20 million to invest. Because project 1 has an initial investment of $20 million, the firm cannot select both this project and another one. Conversely, because projects 2 and 3 have initial investments of $10 million each, both these projects can be chosen. In other words, the cash constraint forces the firm to choose either project 1 or projects 2 and 3.

What should the firm do? Individually, projects 2 and 3 have lower NPVs than project 1 has. However, when the NPVs of projects 2 and 3 are added together, they are higher than the NPV of project 1. Thus, common sense dictates that projects 2 and 3 shall be accepted.

What does our conclusion have to say about the NPV rule or the PI rule? In the case of limited funds, we cannot rank projects according to their NPVs. Instead, we should rank them according to the ratio of present value to initial investment. This is the PI rule. Both project 2 and project 3 have higher PI ratios than does project 1. Thus, they should be ranked ahead of project 1 when capital is rationed.

The usefulness of the profitability index under capital rationing can be explained in military terms. The Pentagon speaks highly of a weapon with a lot of "bang for the buck." In capital budgeting, the profitability index measures the bang (the dollar return) for the buck invested. Hence, it is useful for capital rationing.

It should be noted that the profitability index does not work if funds are also limited beyond the initial time period. For example, if heavy cash outflows elsewhere in the firm were to occur at date 1, project 3 might need to be rejected. In other words, the profitability index cannot handle capital rationing over multiple time periods.

CONCEPT QUESTIONS

- How does one calculate a project's profitability index?
- How is the profitability index applied to independent projects, mutually exclusive projects, and situations of capital rationing?

6.8 THE PRACTICE OF CAPITAL BUDGETING

Not all firms use capital budgeting procedures based on discounted cash flows. Some firms use the payback method, and others use the accounting-rate-of-return method. Most studies find that the most frequently used capital budgeting technique for large corporations is either the internal rate of return (IRR) or the net present value (NPV) or a combination of both.[14] Table 6.4 summarizes the results of a survey of large U.S. multinational firms and shows that over 80 percent of the responding firms use either NPV or IRR. Payback is rarely used as a primary method but it is the most frequently used secondary method.[15] A recent survey of capital budgeting techniques used by a very large sample of U.S. and Canadian firms is summarized in Table 6.5. Graham and Harvey find about 75 percent of all firms use the NPV and IRR in capital budgeting. They report large-dividend-paying firms with high leverage are more likely to use the NPV and IRR than small firms with low debt ratios that pay no dividends.[16]

Graham and Harvey find that the payback period is used by more than one-half of all firms. The payback criterion is more frequently used by small firms and by CEOs without an MBA.

---

[14]This conclusion is consistent with the results of L. Schall and G. Sundem, "Capital Budgeting Methods and Risk: A Further Analysis," *Financial Management* (Spring 1980). However, they report a tendency for firms to use less sophisticated capital budgeting methods in highly uncertain environments.

[15]This result is similar to that of L. Schall, G. Sundem, and W. R. Gerjsbeek, Jr., "Survey and Analysis of Capital Budgeting Methods," *Journal of Finance* (March 1978). They found that 86 percent of their respondents used discounted cash flow, but only 16 percent used it exclusively.

[16]John R. Graham and Campbell R. Harvey, "The Theory and Practice of Corporate Finance: Evidence from the Field," *Journal of Financial Economics* (forthcoming).

IN THEIR OWN WORDS

"Kitchen Confidential": Adventures in the Culinary Underbelly by Anthony Bourdain (Bloomsbury Press, 2000)

To want to own a restaurant can be a strange and terrible affliction. What causes such a destructive urge in so many otherwise sensible people? Why would anyone who has worked hard, saved money, often been successful in other fields, want to pump their hard-earned cash down a hole that statistically, at least, will almost surely prove dry? Why venture into an industry with enormous fixed expenses (rent, electricity, gas, water, linen, maintenance, insurance, license fees, trash removal, etc.), with a notoriously transient and unstable workforce and highly perishable inventory of assets? The chances of ever seeing a return on your investment are about one in five. What insidious spongi-form bacteria so riddles the brains of men and women that they stand there on the tracks, watching the lights of the oncoming locomotive, knowing full well it will eventually run them over? After all these years in the business, I still don't know.

■ TABLE 6.4   **Percentage of Large Multinational Responding Firms Using Different Types of Capital Budgeting Methods***

	Primary Technique	Secondary Technique
Average accounting return (AAR)	10.7%	14.6%
Payback period (PP)	5.0	37.6
Internal rate of return (IRR)	65.3	14.6
Net present value (NPV)	16.5	30.0
Other	2.5	3.2
	100 %	100 %

*The number of responding firms is 121.
Source: M. T. Stanley and S. B. Block, "A Survey of Multinational Capital Budgeting," *The Finance Review* (March 1984), pp. 36–51.

■ TABLE 6.5   **Percent of CFOs Who Always or Almost Always Use a Given Technique**

	% Always or Almost Always
Internal rate of return (IRR)	75.6%
Net present value (NPV)	74.9
Payback period	56.7
Discounted payback period	29.5
Accounting rate of return	30.3
Profitability index	11.9

Source: John R. Graham and Campbell R. Harvey, "The Theory and Practice of Corporate Finance: Evidence from the Field," *Journal of Financial Economics* (forthcoming). Based on a survey of 392 CFOs.

Noncash flow factors may occasionally play a role in capital budgeting decisions. The easy answer, of course, is ego. The classic example is the retired dentist who was always told he threw a great dinner party. "You should open a restaurant," his friends tell him. And our dentist believes them. He wants to get in the business—not to make money, no really, but to swan about the dining room signing dinner checks, like Rick in *Casablanca*. (See our In Their Own Words box.)

The use of quantitative techniques in capital budgeting varies with the industry. As one would imagine, firms that are better able to precisely estimate cash flows are more likely to use NPV. For example, estimation of cash flow in certain aspects of the oil business is quite feasible. Because of this, energy-related firms were among the first to use NPV analysis. Conversely, the cash flows in the motion-picture business are very hard to project. The grosses of the great hits like *Rocky, Star Wars, ET,* and *Fatal Attraction* were far, far greater than anyone imagined. The big failures like *Heaven's Gate* and *Howard the Duck* were unexpected as well. Because of this, NPV analysis is frowned upon in the movie business.

How does Hollywood perform capital budgeting? The information that a studio uses to accept or reject a movie idea comes from the *pitch*. An independent movie producer schedules an extremely brief meeting with a studio to pitch his or her idea for a movie. Consider the following four paragraphs of quotes concerning the pitch from the thoroughly delightful book *Reel Power*.[17]

"They [studio executives] don't want to know too much," says Ron Simpson. "They want to know concept . . . . They want to know what the three-liner is, because they want it to suggest the ad campaign. They want a title . . . . They don't want to hear any esoterica. And if the meeting lasts more than five minutes, they're probably not going to do the project."

"A guy comes in and says this is my idea: '*Jaws* on a spaceship,' " says writer Clay Frohman (*Under Fire*). "And they say, 'Brilliant, fantastic.' Becomes *Alien*. That is *Jaws* on a spaceship, ultimately . . . . And that's it. That's all they want to hear. Their attitude is 'Don't confuse us with the details of the story.' "

". . . Some high-concept stories are more appealing to the studios than others. The ideas liked best are sufficiently original that the audience will not feel it has already seen the movie, yet similar enough to past hits to reassure executives wary of anything too far-out. Thus, the frequently used shorthand: It's *Flashdance* in the country (*Footloose*) or *High Noon* in outer space (*Outland*)."

". . . One gambit not to use during a pitch," says executive Barbara Boyle, "is to talk about big box-office grosses your story is sure to make. Executives know as well as anyone that it's impossible to predict how much money a movie will make, and declarations to the contrary are considered pure malarkey."

---

[17]Mark Litwak, *Reel Power: The Struggle for Influence and Success in the New Hollywood* (New York: William Morrow and Company, Inc., 1986), pp. 73, 74, and 77.

6.9 SUMMARY AND CONCLUSIONS

1. In this chapter we cover different investment decision rules. We evaluate the most popular alternatives to the NPV: the payback period, the accounting rate of return, the internal rate of return, and the profitability index. In doing so, we learn more about the NPV.

2. While we find that the alternatives have some redeeming qualities, when all is said and done, they are not the NPV rule; for those of us in finance, that makes them decidedly second-rate.

3. Of the competitors to NPV, IRR must be ranked above either payback or accounting rate of return. In fact, IRR always reaches the same decision as NPV in the normal case where the initial outflows of an independent investment project are only followed by a series of inflows.

4. We classified the flaws of IRR into two types. First, we considered the general case applying to both independent and mutually exclusive projects. There appeared to be two problems here:
   a. Some projects have cash inflows followed by one or more outflows. The IRR rule is inverted here:
      One should accept when the IRR is *below* the discount rate.
   b. Some projects have a number of changes of sign in their cash flows. Here, there are likely to be multiple internal rates of return. The practitioner must use NPV here.

   Clearly, (*b*) is a bigger problem than (*a*). A new IRR criterion is called for with (*a*). No IRR criterion at all will work under (*b*).

5. Next, we considered the specific problems with the NPV for mutually exclusive projects. We showed that, either due to differences in size or in timing, the project with the highest IRR need not have the highest NPV. Hence, the IRR rule should not be applied. (Of course, NPV can still be applied.)

   However, we then calculated incremental cash flows. For ease of calculation, we suggested subtracting the cash flows of the smaller project from the cash flows of the larger project. In that way, the incremental initial cash flow is negative.

   One can correctly pick the better of two mutually exclusive projects in three other ways:
   a. Choose the project with the highest NPV.
   b. If the incremental IRR is greater than the discount rate, choose the bigger project.
   c. If the incremental NPV is positive, choose the bigger project.

6. We describe capital rationing as a case where funds are limited to a fixed dollar amount. With capital rationing the profitability index is a useful method of adjusting the NPV.

KEY TERMS

Average accounting return   144
Basic IRR rule   147
Capital rationing   159
Discounted payback period rule   143
Incremental IRR   155

Independent project   149
Internal rate of return   147
Mutually exclusive investments   149
Payback period rule   141
Profitability index   158

Suggested Readings

For a discussion of what capital budgeting techniques are used by large firms, see:
Schall, L., and G. Sundem. "Capital Budgeting Methods and Risk: A Further Analysis."
   Financial Management (Spring 1980).

Marc Ross presents an in-depth look at the capital budgeting procedures of 12 firms in the process industry:
Ross, Marc. "Capital Budgeting Practices of Twelve Large Manufacturers." *Financial Management* (Winter 1986).

Questions and Problems

The Payback Period Rule

6.1 Fuji Software, Inc., has the following projects.

Year	Project A	Project B
0	−$7,500	−$5,000
1	4,000	2,500
2	3,500	1,200
3	1,500	3,000

   a. Suppose Fuji's cutoff payback period is two years. Which of these two projects should be chosen?
   b. Suppose Fuji uses the NPV rule to rank these two projects. If the appropriate discount rate is 15 percent, which project should be chosen?

6.2 Suppose Peach Paving Company invests $1 million today on a new construction project. The project will generate annual cash flows of $150,000 in perpetuity. The appropriate annual discount rate for the project is 10 percent.
   a. What is the payback period for the project? If the Peach Paving Company desires to have a 10-year payback period, should the project be adopted?
   b. What is the discounted payback period for the project?
   c. What is the NPV of the project?

The Average Accounting Return

6.3 The annual, end-of-year, book-investment accounts for the machine whose purchase your firm is considering are shown below.

	Purchase Date	Year 1	Year 2	Year 3	Year 4
Gross investment	$16,000	$16,000	$16,000	$16,000	$16,000
Less: accumulated depreciation	0	4,000	8,000	12,000	16,000
Net investment	$16,000	$12,000	$ 8,000	$ 4,000	$ 0

   If your firm purchases this machine, you can expect it to generate, on average, $4,500 per year in additional net income.
   a. What is the average accounting return for this machine?
   b. What three flaws are inherent in this decision rule?

6.4 Western Printing Co. has an opportunity to purchase a $2 million new printing machine. It has an economic life of five years and will be worthless after that time. This new investment is expected to generate an annual net income of $100,000 one year from today and the income stream will grow at 7 percent per year subsequently. The company adopts a straight-line depreciation method (i.e., equal amounts of depreciation in each year). What is the average accounting return of the investment? Supposing Western Printing's AAR cutoff is 20 percent, should the machine be purchased?

6.5 Nokia Group has invested $8,000 in a high-tech project. This cost is depreciated on an accelerated basis that yields $4,000, $2,500, $1,500 of depreciation, respectively, during its three-year economic life. The project is expected to produce income before tax of $2,000 each year during its economic life. If the tax rate is 25%, what is the project's average accounting return (AAR)?

   a. 44.44%

   b. 50.23%

   c. 66.67%

   d. 70.00%

   e. 82.21%

The Internal Rate of Return

6.6 Compute the internal rate of return on projects with the following cash flows.

Cash Flows ($)

Year	Project A	Project B
0	−3,000	−6,000
1	2,500	5,000
2	1,000	2,000

6.7 CPC, Inc., has a project with the following cash flows.

Year	Cash Flows ($)
0	−8,000
1	4,000
2	3,000
3	2,000

   a. Compute the internal rate of return on the project.

   b. Suppose the appropriate discount rate is 8 percent. Should the project be adopted by CPC?

6.8 Compute the internal rate of return for the cash flows of the following two projects.

Cash Flows ($)

Time	A	B
0	−2,000	−1,500
1	2,000	500
2	8,000	1,000
3	−8,000	1,500

6.9 Suppose you are offered $5,000 today and obligated to make scheduled payments as follows:

Year	Cash Flows ($)
0	5,000
1	−2,500
2	−2,000
3	−1,000
4	−1,000

   a. What is the IRRs of this offer?

   b. If the appropriate discount rate is 10 percent, should you accept this offer?

   c. If the appropriate discount rate is 20 percent, should you accept this offer?

    d. What is the corresponding NPV of the project if the appropriate discount rates are 10 percent and 20 percent, respectively? Are the choices under the NPV rule consistent with those of the IRR rule?

6.10 As the Chief Financial Officer of the Orient Express, you are offered the following two mutually exclusive projects.

Year	Project A	Project B
0	−$5,000	−$100,000
1	3,500	65,000
2	3,500	65,000

    a. What are the IRRs of these two projects?
    b. If you are told only the IRRs of the projects, which would you choose?
    c. What did you ignore when you made your choice in part (*b*)?
    d. How can the problem be remedied?
    e. Compute the incremental IRR for the projects.
    f. Based on your answer to part (*e*), which project should you choose?
    g. Suppose you have determined that the appropriate discount rate for these projects is 15 percent. According to the NPV rule, which of these two projects should be adopted?

6.11 Consider two streams of cash flows, *A* and *B*. Cash flow *A* consists of $5,000 starting three years from today and growing at 4 percent in perpetuity. Cash flow *B* consists of −$6,000 starting two years from today and continuing in perpetuity. Assume the appropriate discount rate is 12 percent.
    a. What is the present value of each stream?
    b. What is the IRR of a project *C*, which is a combination of projects *A* and *B*; that is, *C* = *A* + *B*?
    c. If it is assumed that the discount rate is always positive, what is the rule related to IRR for assessing project *C* that would correspond to the NPV rule?

6.12 Project *A* involves an investment of $1 million, and project *B* involves an investment of $2 million. Both projects have a unique internal rate of return of 20 percent. Is the following statement true or false? Explain your answer.

    For any discount rate between 0 percent and 20 percent, inclusive, project *B* has an NPV twice as great as that of project *A*.

The Profitability Index
6.13 Suppose the following two mutually exclusive investment opportunities are available to the DeAngelo Firm. The appropriate discount rate is 10 percent.

Year	Project Alpha	Project Beta
0	−$500	−$2,000
1	−300	−300
2	700	1,800
3	600	1,700

    a. What is the NPV of project alpha and project beta?
    b. Which project would you recommend for the DeAngelo Firm?

6.14 The firm for which you work must choose between the following two mutually exclusive projects. The appropriate discount rate for the projects is 10 percent.

	C_0	C_1	C_2	Profitability Index	NPV
A	−$1,000	$1,000	$500	1.32	$322
B	−500	500	400	1.57	285

The firm chose to undertake *A*. At a luncheon for shareholders, the manager of a pension fund that owns a substantial amount of the firm's stock asks you why the firm chose project *A* instead of project *B* when *B* is more profitable.

How would you justify your firm's action? Are there any circumstances under which the pension fund manager's argument could be correct?

6.15 The treasurer of Davids, Inc., has projected the cash flows of projects *A, B,* and *C* as follows. Suppose the relevant discount rate is 12 percent a year.

Year	Project A	Project B	Project C
0	−$100,000	−$200,000	−$100,000
1	70,000	130,000	75,000
2	70,000	130,000	60,000

a. Compute the profitability indices for each of the three projects.
b. Compute the NPVs for each of the three projects.
c. Suppose these three projects are independent. Which projects should Davids accept based on the profitability index rule?
d. Suppose these three projects are mutually exclusive. Which project should Davids accept based on the profitability index rule?
e. Suppose Davids' budget for these projects is $300,000. The projects are not divisible. Which projects should Davids accept?

6.16 Bill plans to open a self-serve grooming center in a storefront. The grooming equipment will cost $160,000. Bill expects the after-tax cash inflows to be $40,000 annually for seven years, after which he plans to scrap the equipment and retire to the beaches of Jamaica. Assume the required return is 15%. What is the project's PI? Should it be accepted?

Comparison of Investment Rules

6.17 Define each of the following investment rules. In your definition state the criteria for accepting or rejecting an investment under each rule.
a. Payback period
b. Average accounting return
c. Internal rate of return
d. Profitability index
e. Net present value

6.18 Consider the following cash flows of two mutually exclusive projects for *Chinese Daily News*.

Year	New Sunday Early Edition	New Saturday Late Edition
0	−$1,200	−$2,100
1	600	1,000
2	550	900
3	450	800

a. Based on the payback period rule, which project should be chosen?
b. Suppose there is no corporate tax and the cash flows above are income before the depreciation. The firm uses a straight-line depreciation method (i.e., equal amounts of depreciation in each year). What is the average accounting return for each of these two projects?
c. Which project has a greater IRR?
d. Based on the incremental IRR rule, which project should be chosen?

6.19 Consider the following cash flows on two mutually exclusive projects that require an annual return of 15 percent. Working in the financial planning department for the Bahamas Recreation Corp., you are trying to compare different investment criteria to arrive at a sensible choice of these two projects.

Year	Deepwater Fishing	New Submarine Ride
0	−$600,000	−$1,800,000
1	270,000	1,000,000
2	350,000	700,000
3	300,000	900,000

   a. Based on the discounted payback period rule, which project should be chosen?
   b. If your decision rule is to accept the project with a greater IRR, which project should you choose?
   c. Since you are fully aware of the IRR rule's scale problem, you calculate the incremental IRR for the cash flows. Based on your computation, which project should you choose?
   d. To be prudent, you compute the NPV for both projects. Which project should you choose? Is it consistent with the incremental IRR rule?

6.20 The Utah Mining Corporation is set to open a gold mine near Provo, Utah. According to the treasurer, Steven Sample, "This is a golden opportunity." The mine will cost $600,000 to open. It will generate a cash inflow of $100,000 during the first year and the cash flows are projected to grow at 8 percent per year for 10 years. After 10 years the mine will be abandoned. Abandonment costs will be $50,000.
   a. What is the IRR for the gold mine?
   b. The Utah Mining Corporation requires a 10 percent return on such undertakings. Should the mine be opened?

CHAPTER 7

Net Present Value and Capital Budgeting

EXECUTIVE SUMMARY

In late 1990, the Boeing Company announced its intention to build the Boeing 777, a commercial airplane that would be able to carry up to 390 passengers and fly 7,600 miles. This was expected to be an enormous undertaking. Analysts believed the up-front investment and research and development expenditures necessary to manufacture the Boeing 777 would be as much as $8 billion. Delivery of the first planes was expected to take place in 1995 and to continue for at least 35 years. Was the Boeing 777 a good project for Boeing? In 1990, was the NPV for the Boeing 777 positive? This chapter attempts to show you how Boeing and other firms should go about trying to answer these important questions. The Boeing 777 is an example of capital budgeting decision making at the Boeing Company.

Previous chapters discussed the basics of capital budgeting and the net present value approach. We now want to move beyond these basics into the real-world application of these techniques. We want to show you how to use discounted cash flow (DCF) analysis and net present value (NPV) in capital budgeting decision making.

In this chapter, we show how to identify the relevant cash flows of a project, including initial investment outlays, requirements for working capital, and operating cash flows. We look at the effects of depreciation and taxes. We examine the impact of inflation on interest rates and on a project's discount rate, and we show why inflation must be handled consistently in NPV analysis.

7.1 INCREMENTAL CASH FLOWS

Cash Flows—Not Accounting Income

You may not have thought about it, but there is a big difference between corporate finance courses and financial accounting courses. Techniques in corporate finance generally use cash flows, whereas financial accounting generally stresses income or earnings numbers. Certainly, our text has followed this tradition since our net present value techniques discounted cash flows, not earnings. When considering a single project, we discounted the cash flows that the firm receives from the project. When valuing the firm as a whole, we discounted dividends—not earnings—because dividends are the cash flows that an investor receives.

There are many differences between earnings and cash flows. In fact, much of a standard financial accounting course delineates these differences. Because we have no desire to duplicate such course material, we merely discuss one example of the differences. Consider a firm buying a building for $100,000 today. The entire $100,000 is an immediate cash outflow. However, assuming straight-line depreciation over 20 years, only $5,000 ($100,000/20) is considered an accounting expense in the current year. Current earnings are thereby reduced only by $5,000. The remaining $95,000 is expensed over the following 19 years.

Because the seller of the property demands immediate payment, the cost at date 0 of the project to the firm is $100,000. Thus, the full $100,000 figure should be viewed as an immediate outflow for capital budgeting purposes. This is not merely our opinion but the unanimous verdict of both academics and practitioners.

In addition, it is not enough to use cash flows. In calculating the NPV of a project, only cash flows that are *incremental* to the project should be used. These cash flows are the changes in the firm's cash flows that occur as a direct consequence of accepting the project. That is, we are interested in the difference between the cash flows of the firm with the project and the cash flows of the firm without the project.

The use of incremental cash flows sounds easy enough, but pitfalls abound in the real world. In this section we describe how to avoid some of the pitfalls of determining incremental cash flows.

Sunk Costs

A **sunk cost** is a cost that has already occurred. Because sunk costs are in the past, they cannot be changed by the decision to accept or reject the project. Just as we "let bygones be bygones," we should ignore such costs. Sunk costs are not incremental cash outflows.

EXAMPLE

The General Milk Company is currently evaluating the NPV of establishing a line of chocolate milk. As part of the evaluation the company had paid a consulting firm $100,000 to perform a test-marketing analysis. This expenditure was made last year. Is this cost relevant for the capital budgeting decision now confronting the management of General Milk Company?

The answer is no. The $100,000 is not recoverable, so the $100,000 expenditure is a sunk cost, or spilled milk. Of course, the decision to spend $100,000 for a marketing analysis was a capital budgeting decision itself and was perfectly relevant *before* it was sunk. Our point is that once the company incurred the expense, the cost became irrelevant for any future decision.

Opportunity Costs

Your firm may have an asset that it is considering selling, leasing, or employing elsewhere in the business. If the asset is used in a new project, potential revenues from alternative uses are lost. These lost revenues can meaningfully be viewed as costs. They are called **opportunity costs** because, by taking the project, the firm forgoes other opportunities for using the assets.

EXAMPLE

Suppose the Weinstein Trading Company has an empty warehouse in Philadelphia that can be used to store a new line of electronic pinball machines. The company hopes to market the machines to affluent northeastern consumers. Should the cost of the warehouse and land be included in the costs associated with introducing a new line of electronic pinball machines?

The answer is yes. The use of a warehouse is not free; it has an opportunity cost. The cost is the cash that could be raised by the company if the decision to market the electronic pinball machines were rejected and the warehouse and land were put to some other use (or sold). If so, the NPV of the alternative uses becomes an opportunity cost of the decision to sell electronic pinball machines.

Side Effects

Another difficulty in determining incremental cash flows comes from the side effects of the proposed project on other parts of the firm. The most important side effect is **erosion.** Erosion is the cash flow transferred to a new project from customers and sales of other products of the firm.

EXAMPLE

Suppose the Innovative Motors Corporation (IMC) is determining the NPV of a new convertible sports car. Some of the customers who would purchase the car are owners of IMC's compact sedan. Are all sales and profits from the new convertible sports car incremental?

The answer is no because some of the cash flow represents transfers from other elements of IMC's product line. This is erosion, which must be included in the NPV calculation. Without taking erosion into account, IMC might erroneously calculate the NPV of the sports car to be, say, $100 million. If IMC's managers recognized that half the customers are transfers from the sedan and that lost sedan sales have an NPV of −$150 million, they would see that the true NPV is −$50 million ($100 million − $150 million).

CONCEPT QUESTIONS

- What are the three difficulties in determining incremental cash flows?
- Define sunk costs, opportunity costs, and side effects.

7.2 THE BALDWIN COMPANY: AN EXAMPLE

We next consider the example of a proposed investment in machinery and related items. Our example involves the Baldwin Company and colored bowling balls.

The Baldwin Company, originally established in 1965 to make footballs, is now a leading producer of tennis balls, baseballs, footballs, and golf balls. In 1973 the company introduced "High Flite," its first line of high-performance golf balls. The Baldwin management has sought opportunities in whatever businesses seem to have some potential for cash flow. In 1999 W. C. Meadows, vice president of the Baldwin Company, identified another segment of the sports ball market that looked promising and that he felt was not adequately served by larger manufacturers. That market was for brightly colored bowling balls, and he believed a large number of bowlers valued appearance and style above performance. He also believed that it would be difficult for competitors to take advantage of the opportunity because of Baldwin's cost advantages and because of its ability to use its highly developed marketing skills.

As a result, in late 2000 the Baldwin Company decided to evaluate the marketing potential of brightly colored bowling balls. Baldwin sent a questionnaire to consumers in three markets: Philadelphia, Los Angeles, and New Haven. The results of the three questionnaires were much better than expected and supported the conclusion that the brightly colored bowling ball could achieve a 10- to 15-percent share of the market. Of course, some people at Baldwin complained about the cost of the test marketing, which was $250,000. However, Meadows argued that it was a sunk cost and should not be included in project evaluation.

In any case, the Baldwin Company is now considering investing in a machine to produce bowling balls. The bowling balls would be produced in a building owned by the firm and located near Los Angeles. This building, which is vacant, and the land can be sold to net $150,000 after taxes. The adjusted basis of this property, the original purchase price of the property less depreciation, is zero.[1]

Working with his staff, Meadows is preparing an analysis of the proposed new product. He summarizes his assumptions as follows: The cost of the bowling ball machine is $100,000. The machine has an estimated market value at the end of five years of $30,000. Production by year during the five-year life of the machine is expected to be as follows: 5,000 units, 8,000 units, 12,000 units, 10,000 units, and 6,000 units. The price of bowling balls in the first year will be $20. The bowling ball market is highly competitive, so Meadows believes that the price of bowling balls will increase at only 2 percent per year, as compared to the anticipated general inflation rate of 5 percent. Conversely, the plastic used to produce bowling balls is rapidly becoming more expensive. Because of this, production cash outflows are expected to grow at 10 percent per year. First-year production costs will be $10 per unit. Meadows has determined, based upon Baldwin's taxable income, that the appropriate incremental corporate tax rate in the bowling ball project is 34 percent.

Net working capital is defined as the difference between current assets and current liabilities. Baldwin finds that it must maintain an investment in working capital. Like any manufacturing firm, it will purchase raw materials before production and sale, giving rise to an investment in inventory. It will maintain cash as a buffer against unforeseen expenditures. Its credit sales will generate accounts receivable. Management believes that the investment in the different items of working capital totals $10,000 in year 0, rises somewhat in the early years of the project, and falls to $0 by the project's end. In other words, the investment in working capital is completely recovered by the end of the project's life.

Projections based on these assumptions and Meadows's analysis appear in Tables 7.1 through 7.4. In these tables all cash flows are assumed to occur at the *end* of the year. Because of the large amount of data in these tables, it is important to see how the tables are related. Table 7.1 shows the basic data for both investment and income. Supplementary schedules on operations and depreciation, as presented in Tables 7.2 and 7.3, help explain where the numbers in Table 7.1 come from. Our goal is to obtain projections of cash flow. The data in Table 7.1 are all that are needed to calculate the relevant cash flows, as shown in Table 7.4.

An Analysis of the Project

Investments   The investment outlays required for the project are summarized in the top segment of Table 7.1. They consist of three parts:

1. *The Bowling Ball Machine.* The purchase requires a cash outflow of $100,000 at year 0. The firm realizes a cash inflow when the machine is sold in year 5. These cash flows are shown in line 1 of Table 7.1. As indicated in the footnote to the table, taxes are incurred when the asset is sold.

2. *The Opportunity Cost of Not Selling the Warehouse.* If Baldwin accepts the bowling-ball project, it will use a warehouse and land that could otherwise be sold. The estimated sales price of the warehouse and land is therefore included as an opportunity cost, as

---

[1]We use the term *adjusted basis* rather than *book value* because we are concerned with the firm's tax books, not its accounting books. This point is treated later in the chapter in the section entitled "Which Set of Books?" The current market value of the building and land is $227,272.73. We will assume the corporate tax rate is 34 percent, the basis is zero, and the after-tax net is $227,272.73 × (1 − 0.34) = $150,000.

**■ TABLE 7.1   The Worksheet for Cash Flows of the Baldwin Company (in $ thousands)
(All cash flows occur at the *end* of the year.)**

	Year 0	Year 1	Year 2	Year 3	Year 4	Year 5
Investments:						
(1) Bowling ball machine	−$100.00					$21.76*
(2) Accumulated depreciation		$20.00	$52.00	$71.20	$82.72	94.24
(3) Adjusted basis of machine after depreciation (end-of-year)		+80.00	48.00	28.80	17.28	5.76
(4) Opportunity cost (warehouse)	−150.00					150.00
(5) Net working capital (end-of-year)	10.00	10.00	16.32	24.97	21.22	0
(6) Change in net working capital	−10.00		−6.32	−8.65	3.75	21.22
(7) Total cash flow of investment [(1) + (4) + (6)]	−260.00		−6.32	−8.65	3.75	192.98
Income:						
(8) Sales revenues		$100.00	$163.20	$249.72	$212.20	$129.90
(9) Operating costs		50.00	88.00	145.20	133.10	87.84
(10) Depreciation		20.00	32.00	19.20	11.52	11.52
(11) Income before taxes [(8) − (9) − (10)]		30.00	43.20	85.32	67.58	30.54
(12) Tax at 34 percent		10.20	14.69	29.01	22.98	10.38
(13) Net income		19.80	28.51	56.31	44.60	20.16

*We assume that the ending market value of the capital investment at year 5 is $30 (in thousands). Capital gain is the difference between ending market value and adjusted basis of the machine. The adjusted basis is the original purchase price of the machine less depreciation. The capital gain is $24.24 ($30 − $5.76). We will assume the incremental corporate tax rate for Baldwin on this project is 34 percent. Capital gains are now taxed at the ordinary income rate, so the capital gains tax here is $8.24 [0.34 × ($30 − $5.76)]. The after-tax capital gain is $30 − [0.34 × ($30 − $5.76)] = $21.76.

■ TABLE 7.2   Operating Revenues and Costs of the Baldwin Company

(1)	(2)	(3)	(4)	(5)	(6)
			Sales	Cost	Operating
Year	Production	Price	Revenues	per Unit	Costs
1	5,000	$20.00	$100,000	$10.00	$ 50,000
2	8,000	20.40	163,200	11.00	88,000
3	12,000	20.81	249,720	12.10	145,200
4	10,000	21.22	212,200	13.31	133,100
5	6,000	21.65	129,900	14.64	87,840

Prices rise at 2% a year.
Unit costs rise at 10% a year.

presented in line 4. Opportunity costs are treated as cash flows for purposes of capital budgeting. However, the expenditures of $250,000 for test marketing are not included. The tests occurred in the past and should be viewed as a sunk cost.

3. *The Investment in Working Capital.* Required working capital appears in line 5. Working capital rises over the early years of the project as expansion occurs. However, all working capital is assumed to be recovered at the end, a common assumption in capital

■ TABLE 7.3 **Depreciation for the Baldwin Company**

Year	Recovery Period Class		
	3 Years	5 Years	7 Years
1	$ 33,340	$ 20,000	$ 14,280
2	44,440	32,000	24,490
3	14,810	19,200	17,490
4	7,410	11,520	12,500
5		11,520	8,920
6		5,760	8,920
7			8,920
8			4,480
Total	$100,000	$100,000	$100,000

These schedules are based on the IRS publication *Depreciation*. Details on depreciation are presented in the appendix. Three-year depreciation actually carries over four years because the IRS assumes you purchase in midyear.

■ TABLE 7.4 **Incremental Cash Flows for the Baldwin Company (in $ thousands)**

	Year 0	Year 1	Year 2	Year 3	Year 4	Year 5
(1) Sales revenue [line 8, Table 7.1]		$100.00	$163.20	$249.72	$212.20	$129.90
(2) Operating costs [line 9, Table 7.1]		−50.00	−88.00	−145.20	−133.10	−87.84
(3) Taxes [line 12, Table 7.1]		−10.20	−14.69	−29.01	−22.98	−10.38
(4) Cash flow from operations [(1) − (2) − (3)]		39.80	60.51	75.51	56.12	31.68
(5) Total cash flow of investment [line 7, Table 7.1]	−$260.00		−6.32	−8.65	3.75	192.98
(6) Total cash flow of project [(4) + (5)]	−260.00	39.80	54.19	66.86	59.87	224.66

NPV @   4%   123.641
            10%   51.588
            15%   5.472
            20%   −31.351

budgeting. In other words, all inventory is sold by the end, the cash balance maintained as a buffer is liquidated, and all accounts receivable are collected. Increases in working capital in the early years must be funded by cash generated elsewhere in the firm. Hence, these increases are viewed as cash *outflows*. Conversely, decreases in working capital in the later years are viewed as cash inflows. All of these cash flows are presented in line 6. A more complete discussion of working capital is provided later in this section. The total cash flow from the above three investments is shown in line 7.

Income and Taxes   Next, the determination of income is presented in the bottom segment of Table 7.1. While we are ultimately interested in cash flow—not income—we need the income calculation in order to determine taxes. Lines 8 and 9 of Table 7.1 show sales revenues and operating costs, respectively. The projections in these lines are based on the sales revenues and operating costs computed in columns 4 and 6 of Table 7.2. The estimates of revenues and costs follow from assumptions made by the corporate planning staff at Baldwin. In other words, the estimates critically depend on the fact that product prices are projected to increase at 2 percent per year and costs are projected to increase at 10 percent per year.

Depreciation of the $100,000 capital investment is based on the amount allowed by the 1986 Tax Reform Act.[2] Depreciation schedules under the act for three-year, five-year, and seven-year recovery periods are presented in Table 7.3. The IRS ruled that Baldwin is to depreciate its capital investment over five years, so the middle column of the table applies to this case. Depreciation from this middle column is reproduced in line 10 of Table 7.1. Income before taxes is calculated in line 11 of Table 7.1. Taxes are provided in line 12 of this table, and net income is calculated in line 13.

Cash Flow   Cash flow is finally determined in Table 7.4. We begin by reproducing lines 8, 9, and 12 in Table 7.1 as lines 1, 2, and 3 in Table 7.4. Cash flow from operations, which is sales minus both operating costs and taxes, is provided in line 4 of Table 7.4. Total investment cash flow, taken from line 7 of Table 7.1, appears as line 5 of Table 7.4. Cash flow from operations plus total cash flow of the investment equals total cash flow of the project, which is displayed as line 6 of Table 7.4. The bottom of the table presents the NPV of these cash flows for different discount rates.

Net Present Value   It is possible to calculate the NPV of the Baldwin bowling ball project from these cash flows. As can be seen at the bottom of Table 7.4, the NPV is $51,588 if 10 percent is the appropriate discount rate and −$31,351 if 20 percent is the appropriate discount rate. If the discount rate is 15.67 percent, the project will have a zero NPV. In other words, the project's internal rate of return is 15.67 percent. If the discount rate of the Baldwin bowling ball project is above 15.67 percent, it should not be accepted because its NPV would be negative.

Which Set of Books?

It should be noted that the firm's management generally keeps two sets of books, one for the IRS (called the *tax books*) and another for its annual report (called the *stockholders' books*). The tax books follow the rules of the IRS. The stockholders' books follow the rules of the *Financial Accounting Standards Board* (FASB), the governing body in accounting. The two sets of rules differ widely in certain areas. For example, income on municipal bonds is ignored for tax purposes while being treated as income by the FASB. The differences almost always benefit the firm, because the rules permit income on the stockholders' books to be higher than income on the tax books. That is, management can look profitable to the stockholders without needing to pay taxes on all of the reported profit. In fact, there are plenty of large companies that consistently report positive earnings to the stockholders while reporting losses to the IRS.

We present a synopsis of the IRS rules on depreciation in the appendix. The rules on depreciation for the stockholders' books differ, as they do in many other accounting areas. Which of the two sets of rules on depreciation do we want in order to create the previous tables for Baldwin? Clearly, we are interested in the IRS rules. Our purpose is to determine net cash flow, and tax payments are a cash outflow. The FASB regulations determine the calculation of accounting income, not cash flow.

---

[2]Depreciation rules are discussed in detail in the appendix to this chapter.

A Note on Net Working Capital

The investment in net working capital is an important part of any capital budgeting analysis. While we explicitly considered net working capital in lines 5 and 6 of Table 7.1, students may be wondering where the numbers in these lines came from. An investment in net working capital arises whenever (1) raw materials and other inventory are purchased prior to the sale of finished goods, (2) cash is kept in the project as a buffer against unexpected expenditures, and (3) credit sales are made, generating accounts receivable rather than cash. (The investment in net working capital is offset to the extent that purchases are made on credit, that is, when an accounts payable is created.) This investment in net working capital represents a cash outflow, because cash generated elsewhere in the firm is tied up in the project.

To see how the investment in net working capital is built from its component parts, we focus on year 1. We see in Table 7.1 that Baldwin's managers predict sales in year 1 to be $100,000 and operating costs to be $50,000. If both the sales and costs were cash transactions, the firm would receive $50,000 ($100,000 − $50,000).

However, the managers:

1. Forecast that $9,000 of the sales will be on credit, implying that cash receipts in year 1 will be only $91,000 ($100,000 − $9,000). The accounts receivable of $9,000 will be collected in year 2.

2. Believe that they can defer payment on $3,000 of the $50,000 of costs, implying that cash disbursements will be only $47,000 ($50,000 − $3,000). Of course, Baldwin will pay off the $3,000 of accounts payable in year 2.

3. Decide that inventory of $2,500 should be left on hand at year 1 to avoid *stockouts* (that is, running out of inventory) and other contingencies.

4. Decide that cash of $1,500 should be earmarked for the project at year 1 to avoid running out of cash.

Thus, net working capital in year 1 is

$$\underset{\substack{\text{Accounts} \\ \text{receivable}}}{\$9,000} \quad - \quad \underset{\substack{\text{Accounts} \\ \text{payable}}}{\$3,000} \quad + \quad \underset{\text{Inventory}}{\$2,500} \quad + \quad \underset{\text{Cash}}{\$1,500} \quad = \quad \underset{\substack{\text{Net working} \\ \text{capital}}}{\$10,000}$$

Because $10,000 of cash generated elsewhere in the firm must be used to offset this requirement for net working capital, Baldwin's managers correctly view the investment in net working capital as a cash outflow of the project. As the project grows over time, needs for net working capital increase. *Changes* in net working capital from year to year represent further cash flows, as indicated by the negative numbers for the first few years of line 6 of Table 7.1. However, in the declining years of the project, net working capital is reduced—ultimately to zero. That is, accounts receivable are finally collected, the project's cash buffer is returned to the rest of the corporation, and all remaining inventory is sold off. This frees up cash in the later years, as indicated by positive numbers in years 4 and 5 on line 6.

Typically, corporate worksheets (such as Table 7.1) treat net working capital as a whole. The individual components of working capital (receivables, inventory, etc.) do not generally appear in the worksheets. However, the reader should remember that the working capital numbers in the worksheets are not pulled out of thin air. Rather, they result from a meticulous forecast of the components, just as we illustrated for year 1.

Interest Expense

It may have bothered you that interest expense was ignored in the Baldwin example. After all, many projects are at least partially financed with debt, particularly a bowling ball machine that is likely to increase the debt capacity of the firm. As it turns out, our approach of assuming no debt financing is rather standard in the real world. Firms typically calculate a project's cash flows under the assumption that the project is financed only with equity. Any adjustments for debt financing are reflected in the discount rate, not the cash flows. The treatment of debt in capital budgeting will be covered in depth later in the text. Suffice it to say at this time that the full ramifications of debt financing are well beyond our current discussion.

QUESTIONS
• What are the items leading to cash flow in any year?
• Why did we determine income when NPV analysis discounts cash flows, not income?
• Why is working capital viewed as a cash outflow?

EXAMPLE

In late 1990, when the Boeing Company announced its intention to build a new passenger airplane called the Boeing 777, it anticipated it could sell several thousand planes over a 35-year period. Table 7.5 describes one set of possible (and hypothetical) cash flows of the Boeing 777. Although Boeing incurred several hundred million dollars of research and development prior to 1991, we ignore these costs because they are sunk costs. Notice also that we have subtracted depreciation from sales revenue for tax purposes but added it back for total cash flow.

It is possible to calculate the NPV of the Boeing 777 from these cash flows. If the discount rate is 10 percent, the NPV is positive whereas if the appropriate discount rate is 30 percent, the NPV is negative. The break-even discount rate is 19 percent. (Recall we also call the break-even discount rate the IRR.)

In May 2000, Boeing had delivered 282 777s—somewhat less than the deliveries hypothesized in Table 7.5.

7.3 INFLATION AND CAPITAL BUDGETING

Inflation is an important fact of economic life, and it must be considered in capital budgeting. We begin our examination of inflation by considering the relationship between interest rates and inflation.

Interest Rates and Inflation

Suppose that the one-year interest rate that the bank pays is 10 percent. This means that an individual who deposits $1,000 at date 0 will get $1,100 ($1,000 × 1.10) in one year. While 10 percent may seem like a handsome return, one can only put it in perspective after examining the rate of inflation.

Suppose that the rate of inflation is 6 percent over the year and it affects all goods equally. For example, a restaurant that charges $1.00 for a hamburger at date 0 charges $1.06 for the same hamburger at the end of the year. You can use your $1,000 to buy 1,000

■ TABLE 7.5 Incremental Cash Flows: Boeing 777

Year	Number of Planes Delivered	Sales Revenue	Operating Costs	Depreciation	Income before Taxes	Taxes	Change in NWC	Capital Expenditure	Investment	Depreciation Add-back	Total Cash Flow
1991			$ 865.00	$ 40.00	$ (905.00)	$ (307.70)		$400.00	$ 400.00	$ 40.00	$ (957.30)
1992			1,340.00	96.00	(1,436.00)	(488.24)		600.00	600.00	96.00	(1,451.76)
1993			1,240.00	116.40	(1,356.40)	(461.18)		300.00	300.00	116.40	(1,078.82)
1994			840.00	124.76	(964.76)	(328.02)		200.00	200.00	124.76	(711.98)
1995	14	$ 1,847.55	1,976.69	112.28	(241.42)	(82.08)	$ 181.06	1.85	182.91	112.28	(229.97)
1996	145	19,418.96	17,865.45	101.06	1,452.45	493.83	1,722.00	19.42	1,741.42	101.06	681.74
1997	140	19,244.23	16,550.04	90.95	2,603.24	885.10	(17.12)	19.42	2.30	90.95	1,806.79
1998	111	15,737.95	13,377.26	82.72	2,277.97	774.51	(343.62)	15.74	(327.88)	82.72	1,914.06
1999	107	16,257.35	13,656.17	77.75	2,523.43	857.97	50.90	16.26	67.16	77.75	1,676.05
2000	102	15,333.42	12,726.74	75.63	2,531.05	860.56	90.54	15.33	105.87	75.63	1,640.25
2001	92	14,289.29	11,860.11	75.00	2,354.18	800.42	(102.33)	14.29	(88.04)	75.00	1,716.80
2002	92	14,717.97	12,068.74	75.00	2,574.23	875.24	42.01	14.72	56.73	75.00	1,717.26
2003	105	17,233.97	14,131.85	99.46	3,002.66	1,020.90	246.57	244.64	491.21	99.46	1,590.01
2004	89	15,066.42	12,354.47	121.48	2,590.47	880.76	(212.42)	244.64	32.22	121.48	1,798.97
2005	111	19,468.56	17,911.07	116.83	1,440.66	489.82	431.41	19.47	450.88	116.83	616.79
2006	130	23,307.53	20,510.63	112.65	2,684.25	912.65	376.22	23.31	399.53	112.65	1,484.73
2007	118	21,911.40	18,843.81	100.20	2,967.39	1,008.91	(136.82)	21.91	(114.91)	100.20	2,173.59
2008	94	17,944.00	15,252.40	129.20	2,562.40	871.22	(388.81)	567.22	178.41	129.20	1,641.97
2009	123	24,103.23	22,174.98	96.99	1,831.26	622.63	603.60	24.10	627.70	96.99	677.92
2010	125	25,316.97	22,278.94	76.84	2,961.19	1,006.80	118.95	25.32	144.27	76.84	1,886.96
2011	125	26,076.48	22,425.77	65.81	3,584.90	1,218.87	74.43	26.08	100.51	65.81	2,331.33
2012	98	21,133.07	17,963.10	61.68	3,108.29	1,056.82	(484.45)	21.13	(463.32)	61.68	2,576.47
2013	84	18,550.25	15,582.21	57.96	2,910.08	989.43	(253.12)	18.55	(234.57)	57.96	2,213.18
2014	89	20,321.64	16,866.97	54.61	3,400.06	1,156.02	173.60	20.32	193.92	54.61	2,104.73
2015	89	20,931.29	17,372.97	52.83	3,505.49	1,191.87	59.75	20.93	80.68	52.83	2,285.77
2016	89	21,559.23	17,894.16	52.83	3,612.24	1,228.16	61.54	21.56	83.10	52.83	2,353.81
2017	89	22,206.00	18,430.98	52.83	3,722.19	1,265.54	63.38	22.21	85.59	52.83	2,423.89
2018	89	22,872.18	18,983.92	52.83	3,835.43	1,304.05	65.29	22.87	88.16	52.83	2,496.05
2019	89	23,558.35	19,553.43	47.52	3,957.40	1,345.52	67.24	23.56	90.80	47.52	2,568.60
2020	89	24,265.10	20,140.03	35.28	4,089.79	1,390.53	69.26	24.27	93.53	35.28	2,641.01
2021	89	24,993.05	20,744.23	28.36	4,220.46	1,434.96	71.34	24.99	96.33	28.36	2,717.53
2022	89	25,742.85	21,366.56	28.36	4,347.93	1,478.30	73.48	25.74	99.22	28.36	2,798.77
2023	89	26,515.13	22,007.56	28.36	4,479.21	1,522.93	75.68	26.52	102.20	28.36	2,882.44
2024	89	$27,310.58	$22,667.78	$ 16.05	$4,626.75	$1,573.10	$ 77.95	$ 27.31	$ 105.26	$ 16.05	$ 2,964.45

Notes:

Tax rate is 34 percent of taxable income.

Total cash flow can be determined by adding across the rows. Recall that total cash flow is equal to Sales revenue − Operating costs − Taxes − Investment.

Source: Robert Brumer, *Case Studies in Finance* (Burr Ridge, Ill.: Times Mirror/Irwin, 1997).

■ FIGURE 7.1 Calculation of Real Rate of Interest

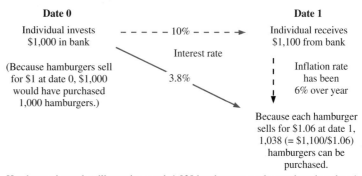

Hamburger is used as illustrative good. 1,038 hamburgers can be purchased on date 1 instead of 1,000 hamburgers at date 0. Real interest rate = 1,038/1,000 − 1 = 3.8%.

hamburgers at date 0. Alternatively, if you put all of your money in the bank, you can buy 1,038 ($1,100/$1.06) hamburgers at date 1. Thus, you are only able to increase your hamburger consumption by 3.8 percent by lending to the bank. Since the prices of all goods rise at this 6-percent rate, lending lets you increase your consumption of any single good or any combination of goods by only 3.8 percent. Thus, 3.8 percent is what you are *really* earning through your savings account, after adjusting for inflation. Economists refer to the 3.8-percent number as the **real interest rate.** Economists refer to the 10-percent rate as the **nominal interest rate** or simply the *interest rate.* This discussion is illustrated in Figure 7.1.

We have used an example with a specific nominal interest rate and a specific inflation rate. In general, the formula between real and nominal cash flows can be written as

$$1 + \text{Nominal interest rate} = (1 + \text{Real interest rate}) \times (1 + \text{Inflation rate})$$

Rearranging terms, we have

$$\text{Real interest rate} = \frac{1 + \text{Nominal interest rate}}{1 + \text{Inflation rate}} - 1 \qquad (7.1)$$

The formula indicates that the real interest rate in our example is 3.8 percent (1.10/1.06 − 1).

The above formula determines the real interest rate precisely. The following formula is an approximation:

$$\text{Real interest rate} \cong \text{Nominal interest rate} - \text{Inflation rate} \qquad (7.2)$$

The symbol $\cong$ indicates that the equation is approximately true. This latter formula calculates the real rate in our example as:

$$4\% = 10\% - 6\%$$

The student should be aware that, while equation (7.2) may seem more intuitive than equation (7.1), (7.2) is only an approximation.

This approximation is reasonably accurate for low rates of interest and inflation. In our example, the difference between the approximate calculation and the exact one is only .2 percent (4 percent − 3.8 percent). Unfortunately, the approximation becomes poor when rates are higher.

EXAMPLE

The little-known monarchy of Gerberovia recently had a nominal interest rate of 300 percent and an inflation rate of 280 percent. According to equation (7.2), the real interest rate is:

$$300\% - 280\% = 20\% \qquad \text{(Approximate formula)}$$

However, according to equation (7.1), this rate is:

$$\frac{1 + 300\%}{1 + 280\%} - 1 = 5.26\% \qquad \text{(Exact formula)}$$

The recent real and nominal interest rates for the United States are illustrated in Figure 7.2. The figure suggests that the nominal rate of interest exhibits more variability from year to year than does the real rate, a finding that seems to hold over most time periods.

Cash Flow and Inflation

The above analysis defines two types of interest rates, nominal rates and real rates, and relates them through equation (7.1). Capital budgeting requires data on cash flows as well as on interest rates. Like interest rates, cash flows can be expressed in either nominal or real terms.

A cash flow is expressed in nominal terms if the actual dollars to be received (or paid out) are given. A cash flow is expressed in real terms if the current or date 0 purchasing power of the cash flow is given. Like most definitions, these definitions are best explained by examples.

■ **FIGURE 7.2   Nominal and Real Interest Rates and Inflation for the United States**

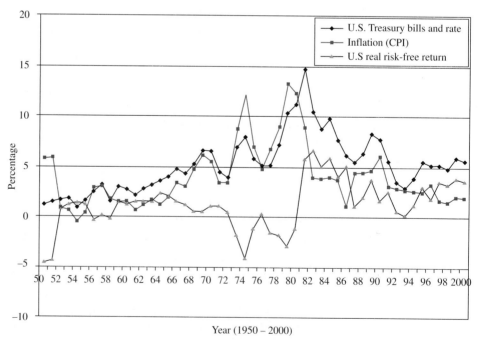

Nominal interest rates are based on three-month Treasury bills (or equivalent). The measure of inflation used is the Consumer Price Index. Real rates are calculated according to equation (7.1).

EXAMPLE

Burrows Publishing has just purchased the rights to the next book of famed romantic novelist Barbara Musk. Still unwritten, the book should be available to the public in four years. Currently, romantic novels sell for $10.00 in softcover. The publishers believe that inflation will be 6 percent a year over the next four years. Since romantic novels are so popular, the publishers anticipate that the prices of romantic novels will rise about 2 percent per year more than the inflation rate over the next four years. Not wanting to overprice, Burrows Publishing plans to sell the novel at $13.60 [$(1.08)^4 \times \$10.00$] four years from now. The firm anticipates selling 100,000 copies.

The expected cash flow in the fourth year of $1.36 million ($13.60 × 100,000) is a **nominal cash flow.** That is because the firm expects to receive $1.36 million at that time. In other words, a nominal cash flow reflects the actual dollars to be received in the future.

We determine the purchasing power of $1.36 million in four years as

$$\$1.08 \text{ million} = \frac{\$1.36 \text{ million}}{(1.06)^4}$$

The figure $1.08 million is a **real cash flow** since it is expressed in terms of date 0 purchasing power. Extending our hamburger example, the $1.36 million to be received in four years will only buy 1.08 million hamburgers because the price of a hamburger will rise from $1 to $1.26 [$\$1 \times (1.06)^4$] over the period.

EXAMPLE

EOBII Publishers, a competitor of Burrows, recently bought a printing press for $2,000,000 to be depreciated by the straight-line method over five years. This implies yearly depreciation of $400,000 ($2,000,000/5). Is this $400,000 figure a real or nominal quantity?

Depreciation is a *nominal* quantity because $400,000 is the actual tax deduction over each of the next four years. Depreciation becomes a real quantity if it is adjusted for purchasing power. Hence, $316,837 ($\$400,000/(1.06)^4$) is depreciation in the fourth year, expressed as a real quantity.

Discounting: Nominal or Real?

Our previous discussion showed that interest rates can be expressed in either nominal or real terms. Similarly, cash flows can be expressed in either nominal or real terms. Given these choices, how should one express interest rates and cash flows when performing capital budgeting?

Financial practitioners correctly stress the need to maintain *consistency* between cash flows and discount rates. That is,

Nominal cash flows must be discounted at the *nominal* rate.
Real cash flows must be discounted at the *real* rate.

EXAMPLE

Shields Electric forecasts the following nominal cash flows on a particular project:

Date:	0	1	2
Cash flow	−$1,000	$600	$650

The nominal interest rate is 14 percent, and the inflation rate is forecast to be 5 percent. What is the value of the project?

Using Nominal Quantities   The NPV can be calculated as

$$\$26.47 = -\$1,000 + \frac{\$600}{1.14} + \frac{\$650}{(1.14)^2}$$

The project should be accepted.

Using Real Quantities   The real cash flows are

Date:	0	1	2
Cash flow	−$1,000	$571.43 $\left(\frac{\$600}{1.05}\right)$	$589.57 $\left(\frac{\$650}{(1.05)^2}\right)$

The real interest rate is 8.57143 percent $(1.14/1.05 - 1)$.
   The NPV can be calculated as

$$\$26.47 = -\$1,000 + \frac{\$571.43}{1.0857143} + \frac{\$589.57}{(1.0857143)^2}$$

The NPV is the same when cash flows are expressed in real quantities. It must always be the case that the NPV is the same under the two different approaches.
   Because both approaches always yield the same result, which one should be used? Students will be happy to hear the following rule: Use the approach that is simpler. Since the Shields Electric case begins with nominal cash flows, nominal quantities produce a simpler calculation here.

EXAMPLE

Altshuler, Inc., used the following data for a capital budgeting project:

Year	0	1	2
Capital expenditure	$1,210		
Revenues (in real terms)		$1,900	$2,000
Cash expenses (in real terms)		950	1,000
Depreciation (straight line)		605	605

The president, David Altshuler, estimates inflation to be 10 percent per year over the next two years. In addition, he believes that the cash flows of the project should be discounted at the nominal rate of 15.5 percent. His firm's tax rate is 40 percent.

Mr. Altshuler forecasts all cash flows in *nominal* terms. Thus, he generates the following spreadsheet:

Year	0	1	2
Capital expenditure	−$1,210		
Revenues		$2,090 (= 1,900 × 1.10)	$2,420 (= 2,000 × (1.10)²)
−Expenses		−1,045 (= 950 × 1.10)	−1,210 (= 1,000 × (1.10)²)
−Depreciation		−605 (= 1,210/2)	−605
Taxable income		440	605
−Taxes (40%)		−176	−242
Income after taxes		264	363
+Depreciation		+605	+605
Cash flow		$ 869	$ 968

$$NPV = -\$1,210 + \frac{\$869}{1.155} + \frac{\$968}{(1.155)^2} = \$268$$

Mr. Altshuler's sidekick, Stuart Weiss, prefers working in real terms. He first calculates the real rate to be 5 percent (= 1.155/1.10 − 1). Next, he generates the following spreadsheet in *real* quantities:

Year	0	1	2
Capital expenditure	−$1,210		
Revenues		$1,900	$2,000
−Expenses		−950	−1,000
−Depreciation		−550 (= 605/1.1)	−500 (= 605/1.1)²)
Taxable income		400	500
−Taxes (40%)		−160	−200
Income after taxes		240	300
+Depreciation		+550	+500
Cash flow		$ 790	$ 800

$$NPV = -\$1,210 + \frac{\$790}{1.05} + \frac{\$800}{(1.05)^2} = \$268$$

In explaining his calculations to Mr. Altshuler, Mr. Weiss points out:

1. Since the capital expenditure occurs at date 0 (today), its nominal value and its real value are equal.
2. Since yearly depreciation of $605 is a nominal quantity, one converts it to a real quantity by discounting at the inflation rate of 10 percent.
3. It is no coincidence that both Mr. Altshuler and Mr. Weiss arrive at the same NPV number. Both methods must always give the same NPV.

QUESTIONS

?

- What is the difference between the nominal and the real interest rate?
- What is the difference between nominal and real cash flows?

7.4 Investments of Unequal Lives: The Equivalent Annual Cost Method

Suppose a firm must choose between two machines of unequal lives. Both machines can do the same job, but they have different operating costs and will last for different time periods. A simple application of the NPV rule suggests that we should take the machine whose costs have the lower present value. This could lead to the wrong decision, though, because the lower-cost machine may need to be replaced before the other one. If we are choosing between two mutually exclusive projects that have different lives, the projects must be evaluated on an equal-life basis. In other words, we must devise a method that takes into account all future replacement decisions. We first discuss the classic *replacement-chain* problem. Next, a more difficult replacement decision is examined.

Replacement Chain

Example

Downtown Athletic Club must choose between two mechanical tennis ball throwers. Machine *A* costs less than machine *B* but will not last as long. The cash outflows from the two machines are:

		Date			
Machine	0	1	2	3	4
A	$500	$120	$120	$120	
B	600	100	100	100	$100

Machine *A* costs $500 and lasts three years. There will be maintenance expenses of $120 to be paid at the end of each of the three years. Machine *B* costs $600 and lasts four years. There will be maintenance expenses of $100 to be paid at the end of each of the four years. We place all costs in *real* terms, an assumption greatly simplifying the analysis. Revenues per year are assumed to be the same, regardless of machine, so they are ignored in the analysis. Note that all numbers in the above chart are *outflows*.

To get a handle on the decision, we take the present value of the costs of each of the two machines:

$$\text{Machine } A: \$798.42 = \$500 + \frac{\$120}{1.1} + \frac{\$120}{(1.1)^2} + \frac{\$120}{(1.1)^3} \qquad (7.3)$$

$$\text{Machine } B: \$916.99 = \$600 + \frac{\$100}{1.1} + \frac{\$100}{(1.1)^2} + \frac{\$100}{(1.1)^3} + \frac{\$100}{(1.1)^4}$$

Machine *B* has a higher present value of outflows. A naive approach would be to select machine *A* because of the lower outflows. However, machine *B* has a longer life so perhaps its cost per year is actually lower. How might one properly adjust for the difference in useful life when comparing the two machines? We present two methods.

1. *Matching Cycles.* Suppose that we run the example for 12 years. Machine *A* would have four complete cycles in this case and machine *B* would have three, so a comparison would be appropriate. Consider machine *A*'s second cycle. The replacement of machine *A*

occurs at date 3. Thus, another $500 must be paid at date 3 with the yearly maintenance cost of $120 payable at dates 4, 5, and 6. Another cycle begins at date 6 and a final cycle begins at date 9. Our present value analysis of (7.3) tells us that the payments in the first cycle are equivalent to a payment of $798.42 at date 0. Similarly, the payments from the second cycle are equivalent to a payment of $798.42 at date 3. Carrying this out for all four cycles, the present value of all costs from machine *A* over 12 years is

Present Value of Costs of Machine *A* over 12 Years:

$$\$2{,}188 = \$798.42 + \frac{\$798.42}{(1.10)^3} + \frac{\$798.42}{(1.10)^6} + \frac{\$798.42}{(1.10)^9} \tag{7.4}$$

Now consider machine *B*'s second cycle. The replacement of machine *B* occurs at date 4. Thus, another $600 must be paid at this time, with yearly maintenance costs of $100 payable at dates 5, 6, 7, and 8. A third cycle completes the 12 years. Following our calculations for machine *A*, the present value of all costs from machine *B* over 12 years is

Present Value of Costs of Machine *B* over 12 Years:

$$\$1{,}971 = \$916.99 + \frac{\$916.99}{(1.10)^4} + \frac{\$916.99}{(1.10)^8}$$

Because both machines have complete cycles over the 12 years, a comparison of 12-year costs is appropriate. The present value of machine *B*'s costs is lower than the present value of machine *A*'s costs over the 12 years, implying that machine *B* should be chosen.

While the above approach is straightforward, it has one drawback: Sometimes the number of cycles is high, demanding an excessive amount of calculating time. For example, if machine *C* lasts for seven years and machine *D* lasts for 11 years, these two machines must be compared over a period of 77 (7 × 11) years. And if machines *C*, *D*, and *E* are compared, where machine *E* has a four-year cycle, a complete set of cycles occurs over 308 (7 × 11 × 4) years. Therefore, we offer the following alternative approach.

2. *Equivalent Annual Cost.* Equation (7.3) showed that payments of ($500, $120, $120, $120) are equivalent to a single payment of $798.42 at date 0. We now wish to equate the single payment of $798.42 at date 0 with a three-year annuity. Using techniques of previous chapters, we have

$$\$798.42 = C \times A^3_{0.10}$$

$A^3_{0.10}$ is an annuity of $1 a year for three years, discounted at 10 percent. *C* is the unknown—the annuity payment per year that causes the present value of all payments to equal $798.42. Because $A^3_{0.10}$ equals 2.4869, *C* equals $321.05 ($798.42/2.4869). Thus, a payment stream of ($500, $120, $120, $120) is equivalent to annuity payments of $321.05 made at the *end* of each year for three years. Of course, this calculation assumes only one cycle of machine *A*. Use of machine *A* over many cycles is equivalent to annual payments of $321.05 for an indefinite period into the future. We refer to $321.05 as the *equivalent annual cost* of machine *A*.

Now let us turn to machine *B*. We calculate its equivalent annual cost from

$$\$916.99 = C \times A^4_{0.10}$$

Because $A^4_{0.10}$ equals 3.1699, *C* equals $916.99/3.1699, or $289.28.

The following chart facilitates a comparison of machine *A* with machine *B*.

Date	0	1	2	3	4	5	...
Machine *A*		$321.05	$321.05	$321.05	$321.05	$321.05	...
Machine *B*		289.28	289.28	289.28	289.28	289.28	...

Repeated cycles of machine *A* give rise to yearly payments of $321.05 for an indefinite period into the future. Repeated cycles of machine *B* give rise to yearly payments of $289.28 for an indefinite period into the future. Clearly, machine *B* is preferred to machine *A*.

So far, we have presented two approaches: matching cycles and equivalent annual costs. Machine *B* was preferred under both methods. The two approaches are simply different ways of presenting the same information so that, for problems of this type, the same machine *must* be preferred under both approaches. In other words, use whichever method is easier for you since the decision will always be the same.

Assumptions in Replacement Chains   Strictly speaking, the two approaches make sense only if the time horizon is a multiple of 12 years. However, if the time horizon is long, but not known precisely, these approaches should still be satisfactory in practice.

The problem comes in if the time horizon is short. Suppose that the Downtown Athletic Club knows that a new machine will come on the market at date 5. The machine will be incredibly cheap and virtually maintenance-free, implying that it will replace either machine *A* or machine *B* immediately. Furthermore, its cheapness implies no salvage value for either *A* or *B*.

The relevant cash flows for *A* and *B* are

Date	0	1	2	3	4	5
Machine *A*	$500	$120	$120	$120 + $500	$120	$120
Machine *B*	600	100	100	100	100 + 600	100

Note the double cost of machine *A* at date 3. This occurs because machine *A* must be replaced at that time. However, maintenance costs still continue, because machine *A* remains in service until the day of its replacement. Similarly, there is a double cost of machine *B* at date 4.

Present values are

Present Value of Costs of Machine *A*:

$$\$1{,}331 = \$500 + \frac{\$120}{1.10} + \frac{\$120}{(1.10)^2} + \frac{\$620}{(1.10)^3} + \frac{\$120}{(1.10)^4} + \frac{\$120}{(1.10)^5}$$

Present Value of Costs of Machine *B*:

$$\$1{,}389 = \$600 + \frac{\$100}{1.10} + \frac{\$100}{(1.10)^2} + \frac{\$100}{(1.10)^3} + \frac{\$700}{(1.10)^4} + \frac{\$100}{(1.10)^5}$$

Thus, machine *B* is more costly. Why is machine *B* more costly here when it is less costly under strict replacement-chain assumptions? Machine *B* is hurt more than machine *A* by the termination at date 5 because *B*'s second cycle ends at date 8 while *A*'s second cycle ends at date 6.[3]

One final remark: Our analysis of replacement chains applies only if one anticipates replacement. The analysis would be different if no replacement were possible. This would occur if the only company that manufactured tennis ball throwers just went out of business and no new producers are expected to enter the field. In this case, machine *B* would generate revenues in the fourth year whereas machine *A* would not. In that case, simple net present value analysis for mutually exclusive projects including both revenues and costs would be appropriate.

---

[3]This reminds us of the famous *New Yorker* joke where two businessmen-types are conversing in heaven. One turns to the other and says, "The thing that gets me is that I still had 40,000 miles left on my radial tires."

The General Decision to Replace (Advanced)

The previous analysis concerned the choice between machine A and machine B, both of which were new acquisitions. More typically, firms must decide when to replace an existing machine with a new one. The analysis is actually quite straightforward. First, one calculates the *equivalent annual cost* (EAC) for the new equipment. Second, one calculates the yearly cost for the old equipment. This cost likely rises over time because the machine's maintenance expense should increase with age. Replacement should occur right before the cost of the old equipment exceeds the EAC on the new equipment. As with much else in finance, an example clarifies this criterion better than further explanation.

EXAMPLE

Consider the situation of BIKE. BIKE is contemplating whether to replace an existing machine or to spend money overhauling it. BIKE currently pays no taxes. The replacement machine costs $9,000 now and requires maintenance of $1,000 at the end of every year for eight years. At the end of eight years it would have a salvage value of $2,000 and would be sold. The existing machine requires increasing amounts of maintenance each year, and its salvage value falls each year, as shown:

Year	Maintenance	Salvage
Present	$ 0	$4,000
1	1,000	2,500
2	2,000	1,500
3	3,000	1,000
4	4,000	0

The existing machine can be sold for $4,000 now. If it is sold in one year, the resale price will be $2,500, and $1,000 must be spent on maintenance during the year to keep it running. For ease of calculation, we assume that this maintenance fee is paid at the end of the year. The machine will last for four more years before it falls apart. If BIKE faces an opportunity cost of capital of 15 percent, when should it replace the machine?

Equivalent Annual Cost of New Machine   The present value of the cost of the new replacement machine is as follows:

$$PV_{costs} = \$9,000 + \$1,000 \times A_{0.15}^8 - \frac{\$2,000}{(1.15)^8}$$

$$= \$9,000 + \$1,000 \times (4.4873) - \$2,000 \times (0.3269)$$

$$= \$12,833$$

Notice that the $2,000 salvage value is an inflow. It is treated as a *negative* number in the above equation because it *offsets* the cost of the machine.

The EAC of a new replacement machine equals

$$PV/\text{8-year annuity factor at } 15\% = \frac{PV}{A_{0.15}^8} = \frac{\$12,833}{4.4873} = \$2,860$$

Cost of Old Machine   If the new machine is purchased immediately, the existing machine can be sold for $4,000 today. Thus, a cost of keeping the existing machine for one more year is that BIKE must forgo receiving the $4,000 today. This $4,000 is an opportunity cost. The total cost of keeping the existing machine one more year includes the following:

1. The opportunity cost of not selling it now ($4,000).
2. Additional maintenance ($1,000).
3. Salvage value ($2,500).

Thus, the PV of the costs of keeping the machine one more year and selling it equals

$$\$4{,}000 + \frac{\$1{,}000}{1.15} - \frac{\$2{,}500}{1.15} = \$2{,}696$$

While we normally express cash flows in terms of present value, the analysis to come is made easier if we express the cash flow in terms of its future value one year from now. This future value is

$$\$2{,}696 \times 1.15 = \$3{,}100$$

In other words, the equivalent cost of keeping the machine for one year is $3,100 at the end of the year.

Making the Comparison   If we replace the machine immediately, we can view our annual expense as $2,860, beginning at the end of the year. This annual expense occurs forever, if we replace the new machine every eight years.
   This cash flow stream can be written as

	Year 1	Year 2	Year 3	Year 4	...
Expenses from replacing machine immediately	$2,860	$2,860	$2,860	$2,860	...

If we replace the old machine in one year, our expense from using the old machine for that final year can be viewed as $3,100, payable at the end of the year. After replacement, we can view our annual expense as $2,860, beginning at the end of two years. This annual expense occurs forever, if we replace the new machine every eight years. This cash flow stream can be written as

	Year 1	Year 2	Year 3	Year 4	...
Expenses from using old machine for one year and then replacing it	$3,100	$2,860	$2,860	$2,860	...

BIKE should replace the old machine immediately in order to minimize the expense at year 1.
   One caveat is in order. Perhaps the old machine's maintenance is high in the first year but drops after that. A decision to replace immediately might be premature in that case. Therefore, we need to check the cost of the old machine in future years.
   The cost of keeping the existing machine a second year is

$$\text{PV of costs at time 1} = \$2{,}500 + \frac{\$2{,}000}{1.15} - \frac{\$1{,}500}{1.15} = \$2{,}935$$

which has future value of $3,375 ($2,935 × 1.15).
   The costs of keeping the existing machine for years 3 and 4 are also greater than the EAC of buying a new machine. Thus, BIKE's decision to replace the old machine immediately still is valid.

• What is the equivalent annual cost method of capital budgeting?
• Can you list the assumptions that we must make to use EAC?

7.5 SUMMARY AND CONCLUSIONS

This chapter discusses a number of practical applications of capital budgeting.

1. Capital budgeting must be placed on an incremental basis. This means that sunk costs must be ignored, while both opportunity costs and side effects must be considered.
2. In the Baldwin case, we computed NPV using the following two steps:
   a. Calculate the net cash flow from all sources for each period.
   b. Calculate the NPV using the cash flows calculated above.
3. Inflation must be handled consistently. One approach is to express both cash flows and the discount rate in nominal terms. The other approach is to express both cash flow and the discount rate in real terms. Because either approach yields the same NPV calculation, the simpler method should be used. The simpler method will generally depend on the type of capital budgeting problem.
4. When a firm must choose between two machines of unequal lives, the firm can apply either the matching cycle approach or the equivalent annual cost approach. Since both approaches are different ways of presenting the same information, the same machine must be preferred under both approaches.

KEY TERMS

Erosion	171	Opportunity cost	170
Net working capital	172	Real cash flow	181
Nominal cash flow	181	Real interest rate	179
Nominal interest rate	179	Sunk cost	170

SUGGESTED READING

An excellent in-depth examination of the capital budgeting decision is contained in:
Copeland, T., T. Koller, and J. Murrin. *Valuation: Measuring and Managing the Value of Companies,* 2nd ed. The McKinsey Company, 1994.

QUESTIONS AND PROBLEMS

NPV and Capital Budgeting
7.1 Which of the following cash flows should be treated as incremental cash flows when computing the NPV of an investment?
   a. The reduction in the sales of the company's other products.
   b. The expenditure on plant and equipment.

c. The cost of research and development undertaken in connection with the product during the past three years.

d. The annual depreciation expense.

e. Dividend payments.

f. The resale value of plant and equipment at the end of the project's life.

g. Salary and medical costs for production employees on leave.

7.2 Your company currently produces and sells steel-shaft golf clubs. The Board of Directors wants you to look at introducing a new line of titanium bubble woods with graphite shaft. Which of the following costs are *not* relevant?

   I. Land you already own that will be used for the project and has a market value of $700,000.

   II. $300,000 drop in sales of steel-shaft clubs if titanium woods with graphite shaft are introduced.

   III. $200,000 spent on Research and Development last year on graphite shafts.

     a. I only

     b. II only

     c. III only

     d. I and III only

     e. II and III only

7.3 The Best Manufacturing Company is considering a new investment. Financial projections for the investment are tabulated below. (Cash flows are in $ thousands and the corporate tax rate is 34 percent.)

	Year 0	Year 1	Year 2	Year 3	Year 4
Sales revenue		7,000	7,000	7,000	7,000
Operating costs		2,000	2,000	2,000	2,000
Investment	10,000				
Depreciation		2,500	2,500	2,500	2,500
Net working capital (end of year)	200	250	300	200	0

a. Compute the incremental net income of the investment.

b. Compute the incremental cash flows of the investment.

c. Suppose the appropriate discount rate is 12 percent. What is the NPV of the project?

7.4 According to the February 7, 1983, issue of *The Sporting News,* the Kansas City Royals' designated hitter, Hal McRae, signed a three-year contract in January 1983 with the following provisions:

- $400,000 signing bonus.
- $250,000 salary per year for three years.
- 10 years of deferred payments of $125,000 per year (these payments begin in year 4).
- Several bonus provisions that total as much as $75,000 per year for the three years of the contract.

Assume that McRae has a 60-percent probability of receiving the bonuses each year, and that he signed the contract on January 1, 1983. (Hint: Use the expected bonuses as incremental cash flows.) Assume an effective annual interest rate of 12.36 percent, and ignore taxes. McRae's salary and bonus are paid at the end of the year. What was the present value of this contract in January when McRae signed it?

7.5 Benson Enterprises, Inc., is evaluating alternative uses for a three-story manufacturing and warehousing building that it has purchased for $225,000. The company could continue to rent the building to the present occupants for $12,000 per year. The present occupants have indicated an interest in staying in the building for at least another 15 years. Alternatively, the company could modify the existing structure to use for its own manufacturing and warehousing needs. Benson's production engineer feels the building could be adapted to handle one of two new product lines. The cost and revenue data for the two product alternatives follow.

	Product A	Product B
Initial cash outlay for building modifications	$ 36,000	$ 54,000
Initial cash outlay for equipment	144,000	162,000
Annual pretax cash revenues (generated for 15 years)	105,000	127,500
Annual pretax cash expenditures (generated for 15 years)	60,000	75,000

The building will be used for only 15 years for either product *A* or product *B*. After 15 years, the building will be too small for efficient production of either product line. At that time, Benson plans to rent the building to firms similar to the current occupants. To rent the building again, Benson will need to restore the building to its present layout. The estimated cash cost of restoring the building if product *A* has been undertaken is $3,750; if product *B* has been produced, the cash cost will be $28,125. These cash costs can be deducted for tax purposes in the year the expenditures occur.

Benson will depreciate the original building shell (purchased for $225,000) over a 30-year life to zero, regardless of which alternative it chooses. The building modifications and equipment purchases for either product are estimated to have a 15-year life; also, they can and will be depreciated on a straight-line basis. The firm's tax rate is 34 percent, and its required rate of return on such investments is 12 percent.

For simplicity, assume all cash flows for a given year occur at the end of the year. The initial outlays for modifications and equipment will occur at $t = 0$, and the restoration outlays will occur at the end of year 15. Also, Benson has other profitable ongoing operations that are sufficient to cover any losses.

Which use of the building would you recommend to management?

7.6 Samsung International has rice fields in California that are expected to produce average annual profits of $800,000 in real terms forever. Samsung has no depreciable assets and is an all-equity firm with 200,000 shares outstanding. The appropriate discount rate for its stock is 12 percent. Samsung has an investment opportunity with a gross present value of $1 million. The investment requires a $400,000 outlay now. Samsung has no other investment opportunities. Assume that all cash flows are received at the end of each year. What is the price per share of Samsung?

7.7 Dickinson Brothers, Inc., is considering investing in a machine to produce computer keyboards. The price of the machine will be $400,000 and its economic life five years. The machine will be fully depreciated by the straight-line method. The machine will produce 10,000 units of keyboards each year. The price of the keyboard will be $40 in the first year, and it will increase at 5 percent per year. The production cost per unit of the keyboard will be $20 in the first year, and it will increase at 10 percent per year. The corporate tax rate for the company is 34 percent. If the appropriate discount rate is 15 percent, what is the NPV of the investment?

7.8 Scott Investors, Inc., is considering the purchase of a $500,000 computer that has an economic life of five years. The computer will be depreciated based on the system enacted by the Tax Reform Act of 1986. (See Table 7.3 for the depreciation schedules.) The market value of the computer will be $100,000 in five years. The use of the computer will save five office employees whose annual salaries are $120,000. It also contributes to lower net working capital by $100,000 when they buy the computer. The net working capital will be recovered at the end of the period. The corporate tax rate is 34 percent. Is it worthwhile to buy the computer if the appropriate discount rate is 12 percent?

7.9 The Gap is considering buying an on-line cash register software from IBM so that it can effectively deal with its retail sales. The software package costs $750,000 and will be depreciated down to zero using the straight-line method over its five-year economic life. The marketing department predicts that sales will be $600,000 per year for the next three years, after which the market will cease to exist. Cost of goods sold and operating expenses are predicted to be 25 percent of sales. After three years the software can be sold for $40,000. The Gap also needs to add net working capital of $25,000 immediately. This additional net working capital will be recovered in full at the end of the project life. The corporate tax rate for Gap is 35 percent and the required rate of return on it is 17 percent. What is the NPV of the new software?

7.10 Etonic Inc. is considering an investment of $250,000 in an asset with an economic life of five years. The firm estimates that the nominal annual cash revenues and expenses will be $200,000 and $50,000, respectively. Both revenues and expenses are expected to grow at 3 percent per year as that of the expected annual inflation. Etonic will use straight-line method to depreciate its asset to zero over the economic life. The salvage value of the asset is estimated to be $30,000 in nominal terms at the end of five years. The one-time NWC investment of $10,000 is required immediately. Further, the nominal discount rate for all cash flows is 15 percent. All corporate cash flows are subject to a 35 percent tax rate. All cash flows, except the initial investment and the NWC, occur at the end of the year. What is the project's total nominal cash flow from assets in year 5?

7.11 Commercial Real Estate, Inc., is considering the purchase of a $4 million building to lease. The economic life of the building will be 20 years. Assume that the building will be fully depreciated by the straight-line method and its market value in 20 years will be zero. The company expects that annual lease payments will increase at 3 percent per year. The appropriate discount rate for cash flows of lease payments is 13 percent, while the discount rate for depreciation is 9 percent. The corporate tax rate is 34 percent. What is the least Commercial Real Estate should ask for the first-year lease? Assume that the annual lease payment starts right after the signature of the lease contract.

7.12 Royal Dutch Petroleum is considering going into a new project, which is typical for the firm. A capital tool required for the project costs $2 million. The marketing department predicts that sales will be $1.2 million per year for the next four years, after which the market will cease to exist. The tool, a five-year class capital tool, will be depreciated down to zero using the straight-line method. Cost of goods sold and operating expenses are predicted to be 25 percent of sales. After four years the tool can be sold for $150,000. Royal Dutch also needs to add net working capital of $100,000 immediately. This additional capital will be received in full at the end of the project life. The tax rate for Royal Dutch is 35 percent. The required rate of return on Royal Dutch is 16.55 percent.

Capital Budgeting with Inflation

7.13 Consider the following cash flows on two mutually exclusive projects.

Year	Project A	Project B
0	−$40,000	−$50,000
1	20,000	10,000
2	15,000	20,000
3	15,000	40,000

Cash flows of project *A* are expressed in real terms while those of project *B* are expressed in nominal terms. The appropriate nominal discount rate is 15 percent, and the inflation is 4 percent. Which project should you choose?

7.14 Sanders Enterprises, Inc., has been considering the purchase of a new manufacturing facility for $120,000. The facility is to be depreciated on a seven-year basis. It is expected to have no value after seven years. Operating revenues from the facility are expected to be $50,000 in the first year. The revenues are expected to increase at the inflation rate of 5 percent. Production costs in the first year are $20,000, and they are expected to increase at 7 percent per year. The real discount rate for risky cash flows is 14 percent, while the nominal riskless interest rate is 10 percent. The corporate tax rate is 34 percent. Should the company accept the suggestion?

7.15 Phillips Industries runs a small manufacturing operation. For this year, it expects to have real net cash flows of $120,000. Phillips is an ongoing operation, but it expects competitive pressures to erode its (inflation-adjusted) net cash flows at 6 percent per year. The appropriate real discount rate for Phillips is 11 percent. All net cash flows are received at year-end. What is the present value of the net cash flows from Phillips's operations?

7.16 Harry Gultekin, a small restaurant owner/manager, is contemplating the purchase of a larger restaurant from its owner who is retiring. Gultekin would finance the purchase by selling his existing small restaurant, taking a second mortgage on his house, selling the stocks and bonds that he owns, and, if necessary, taking out a bank loan. Because Gultekin would have almost all of his wealth in the restaurant, he wants a careful analysis of how much he should be willing to pay for the business. The present owner of the larger restaurant has supplied the following information about the restaurant from the past five years.

Year	Gross Revenue	Profit
−5	$875,000	$ 62,000
−4	883,000	28,000
−3	828,000	4,400
−2	931,000	96,000
Last	998,000	103,000

As with many small businesses, the larger restaurant is structured as a Subchapter S corporation. This structure gives the owner the advantage of limited liability, but the pretax profits flow directly through to the owner, without any corporate tax deducted. The preceding figures have not been adjusted for changes in the price level. There is general agreement that the average profits for the past five years are representative of what can be expected in the future, after adjusting for inflation.

Gultekin is of the opinion that he could earn at least $3,000 in current dollars per month as a hired manager. Gultekin feels he should subtract this amount from profits when analyzing the venture. Furthermore, he is aware of statistics showing that for restaurants of this size, approximately 6 percent of owners go out of business each year.

Gultekin has done some preliminary work to value the business. His analysis is as follows:

Year	Profits	Price-Level Factor	Profits (current dollars)	Imputed Managerial Wage	Net Profits
−5	$ 62,000	1.28	$ 79,400	$36,000	$ 43,400
−4	28,000	1.18	33,000	36,000	−3,000
−3	4,400	1.09	4,800	36,000	−31,200
−2	96,000	1.04	99,800	36,000	63,800
Last	103,000	1.00	103,000	36,000	67,000

The average profits for the past five years, expressed in current dollars, are $28,000. Using this average profit figure, Gultekin produced the following figures. These figures are in current dollars.

Year	Expected Profits if Business Continues	Probability of Cont.*	Risk-Adjusted Profits	Real Discount Factor 2%	Present Value
Next	$28,000	1.000	$28,000	0.980	$27,400
+2	28,000	0.940	26,300	0.961	25,300
+3	28,000	0.884	24,700	0.942	23,300
+4	28,000	0.831	23,300	0.924	21,500
.	.	.	.	.	.
.	.	.	.	.	.
.	.	.	.	.	.

*Probability of the business continuing. The probability of failing in any year is 6 percent. That probability compounds over the years.

Based on these calculations, Gultekin has calculated that the value of the restaurant is $350,000.

a. Assume that there is indeed a 6 percent per year probability of going out of business. Do you agree with Gultekin's assessment of the restaurant? In your answer, consider his treatment of inflation, his deduction of the managerial wage of $3,000 per month, and the manner in which he assessed risk.

b. What present value would you place on the revenue stream; in other words, how much would you advise Gultekin that he should be willing to pay for the restaurant?

7.17 The Biological Insect Control Corporation (BICC) has hired you as a consultant to evaluate the NPV of their proposed toad ranch. BICC plans to breed toads and sell them as ecologically desirable insect-control mechanisms. They anticipate that the business will continue in perpetuity. Following negligible start-up costs, BICC will incur the following nominal cash flows at the end of the year.

Revenues	$150,000
Labor costs	80,000
Other costs	40,000

The company will lease machinery from a firm for $20,000 per year. (The lease payment starts at the end of year 1.) The payments of the lease are fixed in nominal terms. Sales will increase at 5 percent per year in real terms. Labor costs will increase at 3 percent per year in real terms. Other costs will decrease at 1 percent per year in real terms. The rate of inflation is expected to be 6 percent per year. The real rate of discount for revenues and costs is 10 percent. The lease payments are risk-free; therefore, they must be discounted at the risk-free rate. The real risk-free rate is 7 percent. There are no taxes. All cash flows occur at year-end. What is the NPV of BICC's proposed toad ranch today?

7.18 Sony International has an investment opportunity to produce a new stereo color TV. The required investment on January 1 of this year is $32 million. The firm will depreciate the investment to zero using the straight-line method. The firm is in the 34-percent tax bracket. The price of the product on January 1 will be $400 per unit. That price will stay constant in real terms. Labor costs will be $15 per hour on January 1. They will increase at 2 percent per year in real terms. Energy costs will be $5 per physical unit on January 1; they will increase at 3 percent per year in real terms. The inflation rate is 5 percent. Revenues are received and costs are paid at year-end.

	Year 1	Year 2	Year 3	Year 4
Physical production, in units	100,000	200,000	200,000	150,000
Labor input, in hours	2,000,000	2,000,000	2,000,000	2,000,000
Energy input, physical units	200,000	200,000	200,000	200,000

The riskless nominal discount rate is 4 percent. The real discount rate for costs and revenues is 8 percent. Calculate the NPV of this project.

7.19 Sparkling Water, Inc., sells 2 million bottles of drinking water each year. Each bottle sells at $2.5 in real terms and costs per bottle are $0.7 in real terms. Sales income and costs occur at year-end. Sales income is expected to rise at a real rate of 7 percent annually, while real costs are expected to rise at 5 percent annually. The relevant, real discount rate is 10 percent. The corporate tax rate is 34 percent. What is Sparkling worth today?

7.20 International Buckeyes is building a factory that can make 1 million buckeyes a year for five years. The factory costs $6 million. In year 1, each buckeye will sell for $3.15 in nominal terms. The price will rise 5 percent each year in real terms. During the first year variable costs will be $0.2625 per buckeye in nominal terms and will rise by 2 percent each year in real terms. International Buckeyes will depreciate the value of the factory to zero over the five years by use of the straight-line method. International Buckeyes expects to be able to sell the factory for $638,140.78 at the end of year 5 (or $500,000 in real terms). The nominal discount rate for risky cash flows is 20 percent. The nominal discount rate for riskless cash flows is 11 percent. The rate of inflation is 5 percent. Cash flows, except the initial investment, occur at the end of the year. The corporate tax rate is 34 percent; capital gains are also taxed at 34 percent. What is the net present value of this project?

7.21 Majestic Mining Company (MMC) is negotiating for the purchase of a new piece of equipment for their current operations. MMC wants to know the maximum price that it should be willing to pay for the equipment. That is, how high must the price be for the equipment to have an NPV of zero? You are given the following facts:

a. The new equipment would replace existing equipment that has a current market value of $20,000.

b. The new equipment would not affect revenues, but before-tax operating costs would be reduced by $10,000 per year for eight years. These savings in cost would occur at year-end.

c. The old equipment is now five years old. It is expected to last for another eight years, and it is expected to have no resale value at the end of those eight years. It was purchased for $40,000 and is being depreciated to zero on a straight-line basis over 10 years.

d. The new equipment will be depreciated to zero using straight-line depreciation over five years. MMC expects to be able to sell the equipment for $5,000 at the end of eight years. The proceeds from this sale would be subject to taxes at the ordinary corporate income tax rate of 34 percent.

e. MMC has profitable ongoing operations.

f. The appropriate discount rate is 8 percent.

7.22 After extensive medical and marketing research, Pill, Inc., believes it can penetrate the pain reliever market. It can follow one of two strategies. The first is to manufacture a medication aimed at relieving headache pain. The second strategy is to make a pill designed to relieve headache and arthritis pain. Both products would be introduced at a price of $4 per package in real terms. The broader remedy would probably sell 10 million packages a year. This is twice the sales rate for the headache-only medication. Cash costs of production in the first year are expected to be $1.50 per package in real terms for the headache-only brand. Production costs are expected to be $1.70 in real terms for the more general pill. All prices and costs are expected to rise at the general inflation rate of 5 percent.

Either strategy would require further investment in plant. The headache-only pill could be produced using equipment that would cost $10.2 million, last three years, and have no resale value. The machinery required to produce the broader remedy would cost $12 million and last three years. At this time the firm would be able to sell it for $1 million (in real terms). The production machinery would need to be replaced every three years, at constant real costs.

Suppose that for both projects the firm will use straight-line depreciation. The firm faces a corporate tax rate of 34 percent. The firm believes the appropriate real discount rate is 13 percent. Capital gains are taxed at the ordinary corporate tax rate of 34 percent. Which pain reliever should the firm produce?

7.23 A machine that lasts four years has the following net cash outflows. $12,000 is the cost of purchasing the machine, and $6,000 is the annual year-end operating cost. At the end of four years, the machine is sold for $2,000; thus, the cash flow at year 4, C_4, is only $4,000.

C_0	C_1	C_2	C_3	C_4
$12,000	$6,000	$6,000	$6,000	$4,000

The cost of capital is 6 percent. What is the present value of the costs of operating a series of such machines in perpetuity?

7.24 A machine costs $60,000 and requires $5,000 maintenance for each year of its three-year life. After three years, this machine will be replaced. Assume a tax rate of 34 percent and a discount rate of 14 percent. If the machine is depreciated with a three-year straight-line without a salvage value, what is the equivalent annual cost (EAC)?

7.25 United Healthcare, Inc. needs a new admitting system, which costs $60,000 and requires $2,000 in maintenance for each year of its five-year life. The system will be depreciated straight-line down to zero without salvage value at the end of five years. Assume a tax rate of 35 percent and an annual discount rate of 18 percent. What is the equivalent annual cost of this admitting system?

7.26 Aviara Golf Academy is evaluating different golf practice equipment. The "easy as pie" equipment costs $45,000, has a three-year life, and costs $5,000 per year to operate. The relevant discount rate is 12 percent. Assume that the straight-line depreciation down to zero is used. Furthermore, it has a salvage value of $10,000. The relevant tax rate is 34 percent. What is the EAC of this equipment?

Replacement with Unequal Lives

7.27 Office Automation, Inc., is obliged to choose between two copiers, XX40 or RH45. XX40 costs less than RH45, but its economic life is shorter. The costs and maintenance expenses of these two copiers are given as follows. These cash flows are expressed in real terms.

Copier	Year 0	Year 1	Year 2	Year 3	Year 4	Year 5
XX40	$700	$100	$100	$100		
RH45	900	110	110	110	$110	$110

The inflation rate is 5 percent and the nominal discount rate is 14 percent. Assume that revenues are the same regardless of the copier, and that whichever copier the company chooses, it will buy the model forever. Which copier should the company choose? Ignore taxes and depreciation.

7.28 Fiber Glasses must choose between two kinds of facilities. Facility I costs $2.1 million and its economic life is seven years. The maintenance costs for facility I are $60,000 per year. Facility II costs $2.8 million and it lasts 10 years. The annual maintenance costs for facility II are $100,000 per year. Both facilities are fully depreciated by the straight-line method. The facilities will have no values after their economic lives. The corporate tax rate is 34 percent. Revenues from the facilities are the same. The company is assumed to earn a sufficient amount of revenues to generate tax shields from depreciation. If the appropriate discount rate is 10 percent, which facility should Fiber Glasses choose?

7.29 Pilot Plus Pens is considering when to replace its old machine. The replacement costs $3 million now and requires maintenance costs of $500,000 at the end of each year during the economic life of five years. At the end of five years the new machine would have a salvage value of $500,000. It will be fully depreciated by the straight-line method. The corporate tax rate is 34 percent and the appropriate discount rate is 12 percent. Maintenance cost, salvage value, depreciation, and book value of the existing machine are given as follows.

Year	Maintenance	Salvage	Depreciation	Book Value (end of year)
0	$ 400,000	$2,000,000	$200,000	$1,000,000
1	1,500,000	1,200,000	200,000	800,000
2	1,500,000	800,000	200,000	600,000
3	2,000,000	600,000	200,000	400,000
4	2,000,000	400,000	200,000	200,000

The company is assumed to earn a sufficient amount of revenues to generate tax shields from depreciation. When should the company replace the machine?

7.30 Gold Star Industries is in need of computers. They have narrowed the choices to the SAL 5000 and the DET 1000. They would need 10 SALs. Each SAL costs $3,750 and requires $500 of maintenance each year. At the end of the computer's eight-year life Gold Star expects to be able to sell each one for $500. On the other hand, Gold Star could buy eight DETs. DETs cost $5,250 each and each machine requires $700 of maintenance every year.

They last for six years and have a resale value of $600 for each one. Whichever model Gold Star chooses, it will buy that model forever. Ignore tax effects, and assume that maintenance costs occur at year-end. Which model should they buy if the appropriate discount rate is 11 percent?

7.31 BYO University is faced with the decision of which word processor to purchase for its typing pool. It can buy 10 Bang word processors which cost $8,000 each and have estimated annual, year-end maintenance costs of $2,000 per machine. The Bang word processors will be replaced at the end of year 4 and have no value at that time. Alternatively, BYO could buy 11 IOU word processors to accomplish the same work. The IOU word processors would need to be replaced after three years. They cost only $5,000 each, but annual, year-end maintenance costs will be $2,500 per machine. A reasonable forecast is that each IOU word processor will have a resale value of $500 at the end of three years.

The university's opportunity cost of funds for this type of investment is 14 percent. Because the university is a nonprofit institution, it does not pay taxes. It is anticipated that whichever manufacturer is chosen now will be the supplier of future machines. Would you recommend purchasing 10 Bang word processors or 11 IOU machines?

7.32 Station WJXT is considering the replacement of its old, fully depreciated sound mixer. Two new models are available. Mixer *X* has a cost of $400,000, a five-year expected life, and after-tax cash flow savings of $120,000 per year. Mixer *Y* has a cost of $600,000, an eight-year life, and after-tax cash flow savings of $130,000 per year. No new technological developments are expected. The cost of capital is 11 percent. Should WJXT replace the old mixer with *X* or *Y*?

7.33 Kaul Construction must choose between two pieces of equipment. Tamper *A* costs $600,000 and it will last five years. This tamper will require $110,000 of maintenance each year. Tamper *B* costs $750,000, but it will last seven years. Maintenance costs for Tamper *B* are $90,000 per year. Kaul incurs all maintenance costs at the end of the year. The appropriate discount rate for Kaul Construction is 12 percent.
a. Which machine should Kaul purchase?
b. What assumptions are you making in your analysis for part (*a*)?

7.34 Philben Pharmaceutics must decide when to replace its autoclave. Philben's current autoclave will require increasing amounts of maintenance each year. The resale value of the equipment falls every year. The following table presents this data.

Year	Maintenance Costs	Resale Value
Today	$ 0	$900
1	200	850
2	275	775
3	325	700
4	450	600
5	500	500

Philben can purchase a new autoclave for $3,000. The new equipment will have an economic life of six years. At the end of each of those years, the equipment will require $20 of maintenance. Philben expects to be able to sell the machine for $1,200 at the end of six years. Assume that Philben will pay no taxes. The appropriate discount rate for this decision is 10 percent. When should Philben replace its current machine?

7.35 (Challenge) A firm considers an investment of $28,000,000 (purchase price) in new equipment to replace old equipment that has a book value of $12,000,000 (market value of $20,000,000). If the firm replaces the old equipment with the new equipment, it expects to save $17,500,000 in pretax cash flow (net savings) savings the first year and an additional 12 percent (more than the previous year) per year for each of the following three years (total of four years). The old equipment has a four-year remaining life, being written off on a straight-line depreciation basis with no expected salvage value. The new equipment will be depreciated under the MACRS system (which uses a double-declining balance approach, the half-year convention in year 1, and the option to switch to straight-line when it is beneficial) using a three-year life. In addition, it is assumed that replacement of the old equipment with the new equipment would require an increase in working capital of $5,000,000, which would not be recovered until the end of the four-year investment. If the relevant tax rates is 40 percent, find:

a. The net investment (time 0 cash flow).

b. The after-tax cash flow for each period.

c. The internal rate of return, the net present value, and the profitability index.

CASE STUDY: *Goodweek Tires, Inc.*

■■■■■ After extensive research and development, Goodweek Tires, Inc., has recently developed a new tire, the SuperTread, and must decide whether to make the investment necessary to produce and market the SuperTread. The tire would be ideal for drivers doing a large amount of wet weather and off-road driving in addition to its normal freeway usage. The research and development costs so far total about $10 million. The SuperTread would be put on the market beginning this year and Goodweek expects it to stay on the market for a total of four years. Test marketing costing $5 million shows that there is a significant market for a SuperTread-type tire.

As a financial analyst at Goodweek Tires, you are asked by your CFO, Mr. Adam Smith, to evaluate the SuperTread project and provide a recommendation on whether to go ahead with the investment. You are informed that all previous investments in the SuperTread are sunk costs and only future cash flows should be considered. Except for the initial investment which will occur immediately, assume all cash flows will occur at year-end.

Goodweek must initially invest $120 million in production equipment to make the SuperTread. The equipment is expected to have a seven-year useful life. This equipment can be sold for $51,428,571 at the end of four years. Goodweek intends to sell the SuperTread to two distinct markets:

1. *The Original Equipment Manufacturer (OEM) Market* The OEM market consists primarily of the large automobile companies (e.g., General Motors) who buy tires for new cars. In the OEM market, the SuperTread is expected to sell for $36 per tire. The variable cost to produce each tire is $18.
2. *The Replacement Market* The replacement market consists of all tires purchased after the automobile has left the factory. This market allows higher margins and Goodweek expects to sell the SuperTread for $59 per tire there. Variable costs are the same as in the OEM market.

Goodweek Tires intends to raise prices at 1 percent *above* the inflation rate. Variable costs will also increase 1 percent *above* the inflation rate. In addition, the SuperTread project will incur $25 million in marketing and general administration costs the first year (this figure is expected to increase at the inflation rate in the subsequent years).

Goodweek's corporate tax rate is 40 percent. Annual inflation is expected to remain constant at 3.25 percent. The company uses a 15.9 percent discount rate to evaluate new product decisions.

The tire market

Automotive industry analysts expect automobile manufacturers to produce 2 million new cars this year and production to grow at 2.5 percent per year thereafter. Each new car needs four tires (the spare tires are undersized and are in a different category). Goodweek Tires expects the SuperTread to capture 11 percent of the OEM market.

Industry analysts estimate that the replacement tire market size will be 14 million tires this year and that it will grow at 2 percent annually. Goodweek expects the SuperTread to capture an 8 percent market share.

You decide to use the MACRS depreciation schedule (seven-year property class). You also decide to consider net working capital (NWC) requirements in this scenario. The immediate initial working capital requirement is $11 million, and thereafter the net working capital requirements will be 15 percent of sales. What will be the NPV, payback period, discounted payback period, AAR, IRR, and PI on this project? ■ ■ ■ ■ ■

Appendix 7A DEPRECIATION

The Baldwin case made some assumptions about depreciation. Where did these assumptions come from? Assets are currently depreciated for tax purposes according to the provisions of the 1986 Tax Reform Act. There are seven classes of depreciable property.

- The three-year class includes certain specialized short-lived property. Tractor units and racehorses over two years old are among the very few items fitting into this class.
- The five-year class includes (a) cars and trucks; (b) computers and peripheral equipment, as well as calculators, copiers, and typewriters; and (c) specific items used for research purposes.
- The seven-year class includes office furniture, equipment, books, and single-purpose agricultural structures. It is also a catch-all category, because any asset not designated to be in another class is included here.
- The 10-year class includes vessels, barges, tugs, and similar equipment related to water transportation.
- The 15-year class encompasses a variety of specialized items. Included are equipment of telephone distribution plants and similar equipment used for voice and data communications, and sewage treatment plants.
- The 20-year class includes farm buildings, sewer pipe, and other very long-lived equipment.
- Real property that is depreciable is separated into two classes: residential and nonresidential. The cost of residential property is recovered over 27½ years and nonresidential property over 31½ years.

Items in the three-, five-, and seven-year classes are depreciated using the 200-percent declining-balance method, with a switch to straight-line depreciation at a point specified in the Tax Reform Act. Items in the 15- and 20-year classes are depreciated using the 150-percent declining-balance method, with a switch to straight-line depreciation at a specified point. All real estate is depreciated on a straight-line basis.

All calculations of depreciation include a half-year convention, which treats all property as if it were placed in service at midyear. To be consistent, the IRS allows half a year of depreciation for the year in which property is disposed of or retired. The effect of this is to spread the deductions for property over one year more than the name of its class, for example, six tax years for five-year property.

CHAPTER 8

Strategy and Analysis in Using Net Present Value

EXECUTIVE SUMMARY

The previous chapter discussed how to identify the incremental cash flows involved in capital budgeting decisions. In this chapter we look more closely at what it is about a project that produces a positive net present value (NPV). The process of asking about the sources of positive NPV in capital budgeting is often referred to as *corporate strategy analysis*. We talk about corporate strategy analysis in the first part of the chapter. Next, we consider several analytical tools that help managers deal with the effects of uncertainty on incremental cash flows. The concepts of decision trees, scenario analysis, and break-even analysis are discussed.

8.1 CORPORATE STRATEGY AND POSITIVE NPV

The intuition behind discounted cash flow analysis is that a project must generate a higher rate of return than the one that can be earned in the capital markets. Only if this is true will a project's NPV be positive. A significant part of corporate strategy analysis is seeking investment opportunities that can produce positive NPV.

Simple "number crunching" in a discounted cash flow analysis can sometimes erroneously lead to a positive NPV calculation. In calculating discounted cash flows, it is always useful to ask: What is it about this project that produces a positive NPV? or Where does the positive NPV in capital budgeting come from? In other words, we must be able to point to the specific sources of positive increments to present value in doing discounted cash flow analysis. In general, it is sensible to assume that positive NPV projects are hard to find and that most project proposals are "guilty until proven innocent."

Here are some ways that firms create positive NPV:

1. Be the first to introduce a new product.
2. Further develop a core competency to produce goods or services at lower cost than competitors.
3. Create a barrier that makes it difficult for other firms to compete effectively.
4. Introduce variations on existing products to take advantage of unsatisfied demand.
5. Create product differentiation by aggressive advertising and marketing networks.
6. Use innovation in organizational processes to do all of the above.

This is undoubtedly a partial list of potential sources of positive NPV. However, it is important to keep in mind the fact that positive NPV projects are probably not common. Our basic economic intuition should tell us that it will be harder to find positive NPV projects in a competitive industry than a noncompetitive industry.

Now we ask another question: How can someone find out whether a firm is obtaining positive NPV from its operating and investment activities? First we talk about how share

HOW TO CREATE POSITIVE NPV

Type of Action	Examples
Introduce new product	Apple Corp. introduction of the first personal computer in 1976
Develop core technology	Honda's mastery of small-motor technology to efficiently produce automobiles, motorcycles, and lawn mowers
Create barrier to entry	Qualcomm patents on proprietary technology in CDMA wireless communication
Introduce variations on existing products	Chrysler's introduction of the minivan
Create product differentiation	Coca-Cola's use of advertising: "It's the real thing"
Utilize organizational innovation	Motorola's use of "Japanese management practice," including "just in time" inventory procurement, consensus decision making, and performance-based incentive systems
Exploit new technology	Yahoo! Inc.'s use of banner advertisements on the web and the digital distribution of new services

prices are related to long-term and short-term decision making. Next we explain how managers can find clues in share price behavior on whether they are making good decisions.

Corporate Strategy and the Stock Market

There should be a connection between the stock market and capital budgeting. If a firm invests in a project that is worth more than its cost, the project will produce positive NPV, and the firm's stock price should go up. However, the popular financial press frequently suggests that the best way for a firm to increase its share price is to report high short-term earnings (even if by doing so it "cooks the books"). As a consequence, it is often said that U.S. firms tend to reduce capital expenditures and research and development in order to increase short-term profits and stock prices.[1] Moreover, it is claimed that U.S. firms that have valid long-term goals and undertake long-term capital budgeting at the expense of short-term profits are hurt by shortsighted stock market reactions. Sometimes institutional investors are blamed for this state of affairs. By contrast, Japanese firms are said to have a long-term perspective and make the necessary investments in research and development to provide a competitive edge against U.S. firms.

Of course, these claims rest, in part, on the assumption that the U.S. stock market systematically overvalues short-term earnings and undervalues long-term earnings. The available evidence suggests the contrary. McConnell and Muscarella looked closely at the effect of corporate investment on the market value of equity.[2] They found that, for most industrial

---

[1] See Judith H. Dobrznyski, "More than Ever, It's Management for the Short Term," *Business Week* (November 24, 1986), p. 92. In this article Andrew Sigler, CEO of Champion International, is quoted as saying that U.S. managers are under great pressure to avoid long-term investments and to produce short-term earnings.

[2] John J. McConnell and Chris J. Muscarella, "Corporate Capital Expenditure Decisions and the Market Value of the Firm," *Journal of Financial Economics* (September 1985), pp. 399–422.

firms, announcements of increases in planned capital spending were associated with significant increases in the market value of the common stock and that announcements of decreases in capital spending had the opposite effect. The McConnell and Muscarella research suggests that the stock market does pay close attention to corporate capital spending and it reacts positively to firms making long-term investments.

In another highly regarded study, Woolridge studied the stock market reaction to the strategic capital spending programs of several hundred U.S. firms.[3] He looked at firms announcing joint ventures, research and development spending, new-product strategies, and capital spending for expansion and modernization. He found a strong positive stock reaction to these types of announcements. This finding provides significant support for the notion that the stock market encourages managers to make long-term strategic investment decisions in order to maximize shareholders' value. It strongly opposes the viewpoint that markets and managers are myopic.

CASE STUDY: *How Firms Can Learn about NPV from the Stock Market:*
The AT&T Decision to Acquire NCR and to Change Its CEO

■ ■ ■ ■ ■   Basic economic common sense tells us that the market value of a firm's outstanding shares reflects the stock market's assessment of future cash flows from the firm's investing activities. Therefore, it is not surprising that the stock market usually reacts positively to the proposed capital budgeting programs of U.S. firms. However, this is not always the case. Sometimes the stock market provides negative clues to a new project's NPV.

Consider AT&T's repeated attempts to penetrate the computer-manufacturing industry. On December 6, 1990, AT&T made a $90 per share or $6.12 billion cash offer for all of NCR Corporation's common stock. From December 4, 1990, to December 11, 1990, AT&T's stock dropped from $30⅜ per share to $29½, representing a loss of about $1 billion to the shareholders of AT&T. Five months later, when these firms finally agreed to a deal, AT&T's stock dropped again.

Why did AT&T buy NCR, a large computer manufacturer? Why did the stock market reaction suggest that the acquisition was a negative NPV investment for AT&T? AT&T was apparently convinced that the telecommunications and computer industries were becoming one industry. AT&T's basic idea was that telephone switches are big computers and success in computers means success in telephones. The message from the stock market is that AT&T could be wrong. That is, making computers is basically a manufacturing business and telephone communications is basically a service business. The core competency[4] of making computers (efficient manufacturing) is different from that of providing telecommunications for business (service support and software). Of course, even if AT&T had acquired NCR for the "right" reasons, it is possible that it paid too much. The negative stock market reaction suggests that AT&T shareholders believed that NCR was worth less than its cost to AT&T. On September 20, 1995, when AT&T announced its intention to spin off NCR (as well as Lucent), its stock price increased by about 11 percent.

On the other hand, when it was announced, on November 5, 1992, that AT&T was negotiating the purchase of one-third of McCaw Cellular Communications with the option to obtain voting control,

---

[3]J. Randall Woolridge, "Competitive Decline: Is a Myopic Stock Market to Blame?" *Journal of Applied Corporate Finance* (Spring 1988), pp. 26–36. Another interesting study has been conducted by Su Han Chan, John Martin, and John Kensinger, "Corporate Research and Development Expenditures and Share Value," *Journal of Financial Economics* 26 (1990), pp. 255–76. They report that the share-price responses to announcements of increased research and development are significantly positive, even when the firm's earnings were decreasing.

[4]Gregg Jarrell, ("For a Higher Share Price, Focus Your Business," *The Wall Street Journal,* September 13, 1991) reports that an increase in "focus" by a firm is typically associated with increases in its share price. Those companies that reduced their number of business lines from 1979 to 1988 had better stock market performance than other firms.

AT&T's stock price jumped from $42⅝ to $44⅜, representing a gain in market value close to $2 billion. Two years later, the Federal Communications Commission approved the acquisition of all of McCaw by AT&T, and AT&T's stock price was holding at over $55 per share. The positive stock market reaction suggests that the shareholders of AT&T believe that AT&T's acquisition of McCaw is a positive NPV decision. AT&T could use McCaw's cellular telephone network to bypass local telephone companies for completing long distance telephone calls, eliminating the access fees normally paid to them. Perhaps because of AT&T's spotty acquisition record, its stock price rose 13.5 percent when on October 17, 1997, it was learned that Robert Allen would step down and Michael Armstrong would become the new CEO. On June 24, 1998, when it was disclosed that AT&T appeared close to a deal to acquire TCI for $30 billion, AT&T's stock jumped 4 percent. The market believed that by buying TCI, which owned a large portfolio of cable lines, AT&T might be able to bypass the local phone monopolies of the "baby bells." TCI would offer AT&T a detour around the "last mile" and ultimately be part of AT&T's broadband strategy. AT&T's market share of long-distance business continues to fall and there have been reports of pressure by the credit rating agencies for it to reduce its $62 billion of debt and $3 billion of interest costs.

AT&T's stock price fell by more than 60 percent during the year 2000, a year that included AT&T's announced breakup into three companies: wireless, broadband, and business services. The stock market appeared to be very skeptical of AT&T's ability to carry out its long term strategy.

At the end of the year, it was reported that AT&T was expected to reduce its dividend by about 60 percent from its current level. This would be the first time in the company's more than 100-year history that it had cut its dividend. Upon the report of a dividend cut, AT&T's stock price increased.

Overall, the evidence suggests that firms can use the stock market to help potentially short-sighted managers make positive net present value decisions. Unfortunately only a few firms use the market as effectively as they could to help them make capital budgeting decisions. ■ ■ ■ ■ ■

CONCEPT QUESTIONS

?

- What are the ways a firm can create positive NPV projects?
- How can managers use the market to help them screen out negative NPV projects?

8.2 DECISION TREES

We have considered potential sources of value in NPV analysis. Moreover, we pointed out that there is a connection between the stock market and a firm's capital budgeting decisions. A savvy CEO can learn from the stock market. Now our interest is in coming up with estimates of NPV for a proposed project. A fundamental problem in NPV analysis is dealing with uncertain future outcomes. Furthermore, there is usually a sequence of decisions in NPV project analysis. This section introduces the device of **decision trees** for identifying the sequential decisions in NPV analysis.

Imagine you are the treasurer of the Solar Electronics Corporation (SEC), and the engineering group has recently developed the technology for solar-powered jet engines. The jet engine is to be used with 150-passenger commercial airplanes. The marketing staff has proposed that SEC develop some prototypes and conduct test marketing of the engine. A corporate planning group, including representatives from production, marketing, and engineering, has recommended that the firm go ahead with the test and development phase. They estimate that this preliminary phase will take a year and will cost $100 million. Furthermore, the group believes there is a 75-percent chance that the reproduction and marketing tests will prove successful.

Based on its experience in the industry, the company has a fairly accurate idea of how much the development and testing expenditures will cost. Sales of jet engines, however, are subject to (1) uncertainty about the demand for air travel in the future, (2) uncertainty about

■ TABLE 8.1   **Cash Flow Forecasts for Solar Electronics Corporation's Jet Engine Base Case (millions)***

Investment	Year 1	Year 2
Revenues		$6,000
Variable costs		(3,000)
Fixed costs		(1,791)
Depreciation		(300)
Pretax profit		909
Tax ($T_c = 0.34$)		(309)
Net profit		$ 600
Cash flow		$ 900
Initial investment costs	−$1,500	

*Assumptions: (1) Investment is depreciated in years 2 through 6 using the straight-line method; (2) tax rate is 34 percent; (3) the company receives no tax benefits on initial development costs.

future oil prices, (3) uncertainty about SEC's market share for engines for 150-passenger planes, and (4) uncertainty about the demand for 150-passenger planes relative to other sizes. Future oil prices will have a substantial impact on when airlines replace their existing fleets of Boeing 727 jets, because the 727s are much less fuel efficient compared with the new jets that will be produced over the next five years.

If the initial marketing tests are *successful,* SEC can acquire some land, build several new plants, and go ahead with full-scale production. This investment phase will cost $1,500 million. Production will occur over the next five years. The preliminary cash flow projection appears in Table 8.1. Should SEC decide to go ahead with investment and production on the jet engine, the NPV at a discount rate of 15 percent (in millions) is

$$\text{NPV} = -\$1,500 + \sum_{t=1}^{5} \frac{\$900}{(1.15)^t}$$

$$= -\$1,500 + \$900 \times A_{0.15}^5$$

$$= \$1,517$$

Note that the NPV is calculated as of date 1, the date at which the investment of $1,500 million is made. Later we bring this number back to date 0.

If the initial marketing tests are *unsuccessful,* SEC's $1,500 million investment has an NPV of −$3,611 million. (You will see how to calculate this number in the section.) This figure is also calculated as of date 1.

Figure 8.1 displays the problem concerning the jet engine as a decision tree. If SEC decides to conduct test marketing, there is a 75-percent probability that the test marketing will be successful. If the tests are successful, the firm faces a second decision: whether to invest $1,500 million in a project that yields $1,517 million NPV or to stop. If the tests are unsuccessful, the firm faces a different decision: whether to invest $1,500 million in a project that yields −$3,611 million NPV or to stop.

■ FIGURE 8.1 **Decision Tree ($ millions) for SEC**

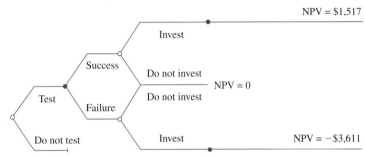

Open circles represent decision points; closed circles represent receipt of information.

As can be seen from Figure 8.1, SEC has the following two decisions to make:

1. Whether to test and develop the solar-powered jet engine.
2. Whether to invest for full-scale production following the results of the test.

One makes decisions in reverse order with decision trees. Thus, we analyze the second-stage investment of $1,500 million first. If the tests are successful, it is obvious that SEC should invest, because $1,517 million is greater than zero. Just as obviously, if the tests are unsuccessful, SEC should not invest.

Now we move back to the first stage, where the decision boils down to a simple question: Should SEC invest $100 million now to obtain a 75-percent chance of $1,517 million one year later? The expected payoff evaluated at date 1 (in millions) is

$$
\begin{aligned}
\text{Expected payoff} &= \left(\begin{array}{ccc} \text{Probability} & & \text{Payoff} \\ \text{of} & \times & \text{if} \\ \text{success} & & \text{successful} \end{array} \right) + \left(\begin{array}{ccc} \text{Probability} & & \text{Payoff} \\ \text{of} & \times & \text{if} \\ \text{failure} & & \text{failure} \end{array} \right) \\
&= \quad (0.75 \quad \times \quad \$1,517) \quad + \quad (0.25 \quad \times \quad \$0) \\
&= \$1,138
\end{aligned}
$$

The NPV of testing computed at date 0 (in millions) is

$$
\begin{aligned}
\text{NPV} &= -\$100 + \frac{\$1,138}{1.15} \\
&= \$890
\end{aligned}
$$

Thus, the firm should test the market for solar-powered jet engines.

Warning 1   We have used a discount rate of 15 percent for both the testing and the investment decisions. Perhaps a higher discount rate should have been used for the initial test-marketing decision, which is likely to be riskier than the investment decision.

Warning 2   It was assumed that after making the initial investment to produce solar engines and then being confronted with a low demand, SEC could lose money. This worst-case scenario leads to an NPV of −$3,611 million. This is an unlikely eventuality. Instead, it is more plausible to assume that SEC would try to sell its initial investment—patents, land, buildings, machinery, and prototypes—for $1,000 million. For example, faced with low demand, suppose SEC could scrap the initial investment. In this case, it would lose $500 million of the original investment. This is much better than if it produced the solar-powered jet engines and generated a negative NPV of $3,611 million. It is hard for decision trees to capture all of the managerial options in changing environments.

QUESTIONS
CONCEPT
?

- What is a decision tree?
- What are two potential problems in using decision trees?

8.3 SENSITIVITY ANALYSIS, SCENARIO ANALYSIS, AND BREAK-EVEN ANALYSIS

One thrust of this book is that NPV analysis is a superior capital budgeting technique. In fact, because the NPV approach uses cash flows rather than profits, uses all the cash flows, and discounts the cash flows properly, it is hard to find any theoretical fault with it. However, in our conversations with practical businesspeople, we hear the phrase "a false sense of security" frequently. These people point out that the documentation for capital budgeting proposals is often quite impressive. Cash flows are projected down to the last thousand dollars (or even the last dollar) for each year (or even each month). Opportunity costs and side effects are handled quite properly. Sunk costs are ignored—also quite properly. When a high net present value appears at the bottom, one's temptation is to say yes immediately. Nevertheless, the projected cash flow often goes unmet in practice, and the firm ends up with a money loser.

Sensitivity Analysis and Scenario Analysis

How can the firm get the net-present-value technique to live up to its potential? One approach is **sensitivity analysis** (a.k.a. *what-if analysis* and *bop* analysis[5]). This approach examines how sensitive a particular NPV calculation is to changes in underlying assumptions. We illustrate the technique with Solar Electronics' solar-powered jet engine from the previous section. As pointed out earlier, the cash flow forecasts for this project appear in Table 8.1. We begin by considering the assumptions underlying revenues, costs, and after-tax cash flows shown in the table.

Revenues   Sales projections for the proposed jet engine have been estimated by the marketing department as

$$\frac{\text{Number of jet}}{\text{engines sold}} = \text{Market Share} \times \frac{\text{Size of jet}}{\text{engine market}}$$

$$3,000 = 0.30 \times 10,000$$

$$\text{Sales revenues} = \frac{\text{Number of jet}}{\text{engines sold}} \times \frac{\text{Price per}}{\text{engine}}$$

$$\$6,000 \text{ million} = 3,000 \times \$2 \text{ million}$$

---

[5]Bop stands for best, optimistic, pessimistic.

Thus, it turns out that the revenue estimates depend on three assumptions.

1. Market share.
2. Size of jet engine market.
3. Price per engine.

Costs   Financial analysts frequently divide costs into two types: variable costs and fixed costs. **Variable costs** change as the output changes, and they are zero when production is zero. Costs of direct labor and raw materials are usually variable. It is common to assume that variable costs are proportional to production. A typical variable cost is one that is constant per unit of output. For example, if direct labor is variable and one unit of final output requires $10 of direct labor, then 100 units of final output should require $1,000 of direct labor.

Fixed costs are not dependent on the amount of goods or services produced during the period. Fixed costs are usually measured as costs per unit of time, such as rent per month or salaries per year. Naturally, fixed costs are not fixed forever. They are only fixed over a predetermined time period.

Variable costs per unit produced have been estimated by the engineering department at $1 million. Fixed costs are $1,791 million per year. The cost breakdowns are

$$
\begin{array}{ccccc}
\text{Variable} \\ \text{cost} & = & \begin{array}{c}\text{Variable cost} \\ \text{per unit}\end{array} & \times & \begin{array}{c}\text{Number of jet} \\ \text{engines sold}\end{array} \\
\$3{,}000 \text{ million} & = & \$1 \text{ million} & \times & 3{,}000 \\
\text{Total cost before taxes} & = & \text{Variable cost} & + & \text{Fixed cost} \\
\$4{,}791 \text{ million} & = & \$3{,}000 \text{ million} & + & \$1{,}791 \text{ million}
\end{array}
$$

The above estimates for market size, market share, price, variable cost, and fixed cost, as well as the estimate of initial investment, are presented in the middle column of Table 8.2. These figures represent the firm's expectations or best estimates of the different parameters. For purposes of comparison, the firm's analysts prepared both optimistic and pessimistic forecasts for the different variables. These are also provided in the table.

Standard sensitivity analysis calls for an NPV calculation for all three possibilities of a single variable, along with the expected forecast for all other variables. This procedure is illustrated in Table 8.3. For example, consider the NPV calculation of $8,154 million provided in the upper right-hand corner of this table. This occurs when the optimistic forecast of 20,000 units per year is used for market size. However, the expected forecasts from Table 8.2 are employed for all other variables when the $8,154 million figure is generated. Note that

■ **TABLE 8.2   Different Estimates for Solar Electronics' Solar Plane**

Variable	Pessimistic	Expected or Best	Optimistic
Market size (per year)	5,000	10,000	20,000
Market share	20%	30%	50%
Price	$1.9 million	$2 million	$2.2 million
Variable cost (per plane)	$1.2 million	$1 million	$0.8 million
Fixed cost (per year)	$1,891 million	$1,791 million	$1,741 million
Investment	$1,900 million	$1,500 million	$1,000 million

■ TABLE 8.3 **NPV Calculations as of Date 1 (in $ millions) for the Solar Plane Using Sensitivity Analysis**

	Pessimistic	Expected or Best	Optimistic
Market size	−$1,802*	$1,517	$8,154
Market share	−696*	1,517	5,942
Price	853	1,517	2,844
Variable cost	189	1,517	2,844
Fixed cost	1,295	1,517	1,628
Investment	1,208	1,517	1,903

Under sensitivity analysis, one input is varied while all other inputs are assumed to meet their expectation. For example, an NPV of −$1,802 occurs when the pessimistic forecast of 5,000 is used for market size. However, the expected forecasts from Table 8.2 are used for all other variables when −$1,802 is generated.

*We assume that the other divisions of the firm are profitable, implying that a loss on this project can offset income elsewhere in the firm. The firm reports a loss to the IRS in these two cases. Thus, the loss on the project generates a tax rebate to the firm.

the same number of $1,517 million appears in each row of the middle column of Table 8.3. This occurs because the expected forecast is used for the variable that was singled out, as well as for all other variables.

A table such as Table 8.3 can be used for a number of purposes. First, taken as a whole, the table can indicate whether NPV analysis should be trusted. In other words, it reduces the false sense of security we spoke of earlier. Suppose that NPV is positive when the expected forecast for each variable is used. However, further suppose that every number in the pessimistic column is wildly negative and every number in the optimistic column is wildly positive. Even a single error in this forecast greatly alters the estimate, making one leery of the net present value approach. A conservative manager might well scrap the entire NPV analysis in this case. Fortunately, this does not seem to be the case in Table 8.3, because all but two of the numbers are positive. Managers viewing the table will likely consider NPV analysis to be useful for the solar-powered jet engine.

Second, sensitivity analysis shows where more information is needed. For example, error in the investment appears to be relatively unimportant because even under the pessimistic scenario, the NPV of $1,208 million is still highly positive. By contrast, the pessimistic forecast for market share leads to a negative NPV of −$696 million, and a pessimistic forecast for market size leads to a substantially negative NPV of −$1,802 million. Because the effect of incorrect estimates on revenues is so much greater than the effect of incorrect estimates on costs, more information on the factors determining revenues might be needed.

Unfortunately, sensitivity analysis suffers from some drawbacks. For example, sensitivity analysis may unwittingly *increase* the false sense of security among managers. Suppose all pessimistic forecasts yield positive NPVs. A manager might feel that there is no way the project can lose money. Of course, the forecasters may simply have an optimistic view of a pessimistic forecast. To combat this, some companies do not treat optimistic and pessimistic forecasts subjectively. Rather, their pessimistic forecasts are al-

■ TABLE 8.4   **Cash Flow Forecast (in $ millions) under the Scenario of a Plane Crash***

	Year 1	Years 2–6
Revenues		$2,800
Variable costs		−1,400
Fixed costs		−1,791
Depreciation		−300
Pretax profit		−691
Tax ($T_c = 0.34$)[†]		235
Net profit		−456
Cash flow		−156
Initial investment cost	−$1,500	

*Assumptions are

Market size	7,000 (70 percent of expectation)
Market share	20% (2/3 of expectation)

Forecasts for all other variables are the expected forecasts as given in Table 8.2.

[†]Tax loss offsets income elsewhere in firm.

ways, say, 20 percent less than expected. Unfortunately, the cure in this case may be worse than the disease, because a deviation of a fixed percentage ignores the fact that some variables are easier to forecast than others.

In addition, sensitivity analysis treats each variable in isolation when, in reality, the different variables are likely to be related. For example, if ineffective management allows costs to get out of control, it is likely that variable costs, fixed costs, and investment will all rise above expectation at the same time. If the market is not receptive to a solar plane, both market share and price should decline together.

Managers frequently perform **scenario analysis,** a variant of sensitivity analysis, to minimize this problem. Simply put, this approach examines a number of different likely scenarios, where each scenario involves a confluence of factors. As a simple example, consider the effect of a few airline crashes. These crashes are likely to reduce flying in total, thereby limiting the demand for any new engines. Furthermore, even if the crashes did not involve solar-powered aircraft, the public could become more averse to any innovative and controversial technologies. Hence, SEC's market share might fall as well. Perhaps the cash flow calculations would look like those in Table 8.4 under the scenario of a plane crash. Given the calculations in the table, the NPV (in millions) would be

$$-\$2,023 = -\$1,500 - \$156 \times A_{0.15}^5$$

A series of scenarios like this might illuminate issues concerning the project better than a standard application of sensitivity analysis would.

Break-Even Analysis

Our discussion of sensitivity analysis and scenario analysis suggests that there are many ways to examine variability in forecasts. We now present another approach, **break-even analysis.** As its name implies, this approach determines the sales needed to break even. The approach is a useful complement to sensitivity analysis, because it also sheds light on the severity of incorrect forecasts. We calculate the break-even point in terms of both accounting profit and present value.

Accounting Profit   Net profit under four different sales forecasts is

Unit Sales	Net Profit (in $ millions)
0	−$1,380
1,000	−720
3,000	600
10,000	5,220

A more complete presentation of costs and revenues appears in Table 8.5.

We plot the revenues, costs, and profits under the different assumptions about sales in Figure 8.2. The revenue and cost curves cross at 2,091 jet engines. This is the break-even point, in other words, the point where the project generates no profits or losses. As long as sales are above 2,091 jet engines, the project will make a profit.

This break-even point can be calculated very easily. Because the sales price is $2 million per engine and the variable cost is $1 million per engine,[6] the after-tax difference per engine is

$$(\text{Sales price} - \text{Variable cost}) \times (1 - T_c) = (\$2 \text{ million} - \$1 \text{ million})$$
$$\times (1 - 0.34) = \$0.66 \text{ million}$$

where T_c is the corporate tax rate of 34 percent. This after-tax difference is called the **contribution margin** because it is the amount that each additional engine contributes to after-tax profit.

Fixed costs are $1,791 million and depreciation is $300 million, implying that the after-tax sum of these costs is

$$(\text{Fixed costs} + \text{Depreciation}) \times (1 - T_c) = (\$1,791 \text{ million} + \$300 \text{ million})$$
$$\times (1 - 0.34) = \$1,380 \text{ million}$$

■ TABLE 8.5   **Revenues and Costs of Project under Different Sales Assumptions (in $ millions, except unit sales)**

Year 1	Years 2–6								
Initial Investment	Annual Unit Sales	Revenues	Variable Costs	Fixed Costs	Depreciation	Taxes* ($T_c = 0.34$)	Net Profits	Operating Cash Flows	NPV (evaluated date 1)
$1,500	0	$ 0	$ 0	−$1,791	−$300	$ 711	−$1,380	−$1,080	−$ 5,120
1,500	1,000	2,000	−1,000	−1,791	−300	371	−720	−420	−2,908
1,500	3,000	6,000	−3,000	−1,791	−300	−309	600	900	1,517
1,500	10,000	20,000	−10,000	−1,791	−300	−2,689	5,220	5,520	17,004

*Loss is incurred in the first two rows. For tax purposes, this loss offsets income elsewhere in the firm.

---

[6]Though the previous section considered both optimistic and pessimistic forecasts for sales price and variable cost, break-even analysis only works with the expected or best estimates of these variables.

■ FIGURE 8.2   Break-Even Point Using Accounting Numbers

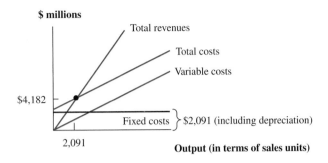

That is, the firm incurs costs of $1,380 million, regardless of the number of sales. Because each engine contributes $0.66 million, sales must reach the following level to offset the above costs:

Accounting Profit Break-Even Point:

$$\frac{(\text{Fixed costs} + \text{Depreciation}) \times (1 - T_c)}{(\text{Sales price} - \text{Variable costs}) \times (1 - T_c)} = \frac{\$1,380 \text{ million}}{\$0.66 \text{ million}} = 2,091$$

Thus, 2,091 engines is the break-even point required for an accounting profit.

Present Value   As we stated many times in the text, we are more interested in present value than we are in net profits. Therefore, we must calculate the present value of the cash flows. Given a discount rate of 15 percent, we have

Unit Sales	NPV ($ millions)
0	−5,120
1,000	−2,908
3,000	1,517
10,000	17,004

These NPV calculations are reproduced in the last column of Table 8.5. We can see that the NPV is negative if SEC produces 1,000 jet engines and positive if it produces 3,000 jet engines. Obviously, the zero NPV point occurs between 1,000 and 3,000 jet engines.

The present value break-even point can be calculated very easily. The firm originally invested $1,500 million. This initial investment can be expressed as a five-year equivalent annual cost (EAC), determined by dividing the initial investment by the appropriate five-year annuity factor:

$$\text{EAC} = \frac{\text{Initial investment}}{\text{5-year annuity factor at 15\%}}$$

$$= \frac{\text{Initial investment}}{A_{0.15}^5}$$

$$= \frac{\$1,500 \text{ million}}{3.3522} = \$447.5 \text{ million}$$

Note that the EAC of $447.5 million is greater than the yearly depreciation of $300 million. This must occur since the calculation of EAC implicitly assumes that the $1,500 million investment could have been invested at 15 percent.

After-tax costs, regardless of output, can be viewed as

$$\frac{\$1,528}{\text{million}} = \frac{\$447.5}{\text{million}} + \frac{\$1,791}{\text{million}} \times \quad 0.66 \quad - \frac{\$300}{\text{million}} \times 0.34$$

$$= \text{EAC} + \begin{matrix}\text{Fixed}\\\text{costs}\end{matrix} \times (1 - T_c) - \begin{matrix}\text{Depreci-}\\\text{ation}\end{matrix} \times T_c$$

That is, in addition to the initial investment's equivalent annual cost of $447.5 million, the firm pays fixed costs each year and receives a depreciation tax shield each year. The depreciation tax shield is written as a negative number because it offsets the costs in the equation. Because each plane contributes $0.66 million to after-tax profit, it will take the following sales to offset the above costs:

Present Value Break-Even Point:

$$\frac{\text{EAC} + \text{Fixed costs} \times (1 - T_c) - \text{Depreciation} \times T_c}{(\text{Sales price} - \text{Variable costs}) \times (1 - T_c)} = \frac{\$1,528 \text{ million}}{\$0.66 \text{ million}} = 2,315$$

Thus, 2,315 planes is the break-even point from the perspective of present value.

Why is the accounting break-even point different from the financial break-even point? When we use accounting profit as the basis for the break-even calculation, we subtract depreciation. Depreciation for the solar-jet-engines project is $300 million. If 2,091 solar jet engines are sold, SEC will generate sufficient revenues to cover the $300 million depreciation expense plus other costs. Unfortunately, at this level of sales SEC will not cover the economic opportunity costs of the $1,500 million laid out for the investment. If we take into account that the $1,500 million could have been invested at 15 percent, the true annual cost of the investment is $447.5 million and not $300 million. Depreciation understates the true costs of recovering the initial investment. Thus, companies that break even on an accounting basis are really losing money. They are losing the opportunity cost of the initial investment.

QUESTIONS
?

CONCEPT

- What is a sensitivity analysis?
- Why is it important to perform a sensitivity analysis?
- What is a break-even analysis?
- Describe how sensitivity analysis interacts with break-even analysis.

8.4 OPTIONS

The analysis we have presented so far is static. In fact, standard NPV analysis is somewhat static. Because corporations make decisions in a dynamic environment, they have options that should be considered in project valuation.

The Option to Expand

One of the most important options is the option to expand when economic prospects are good. The option to expand has value. Expansion pays off if demand is high. Recall the Solar Electronics Corporation (SEC) in Section 8.2. SEC's expenditure on the test-marketing program buys an option to produce new jet engines. This turned out to be a very valuable option. SEC had the option to produce new jet engines depending on the results of the test marketing.

There are many real-world examples. In 1977 Saab was the first car maker to introduce turbo-charged automobile engines in its gasoline model. Sales of the Saab 900 almost doubled after the introduction. In response to this high demand, Saab has increased its capacity and entered into joint ventures with other car makers to increase production. Now many automobile manufacturers use turbo chargers.

The Option to Abandon

The option to close a facility also has value. The SEC would not have been obligated to produce jet engines if the test-marketing results had been negative. Instead, SEC had the option to abandon the jet engine project if the results had been bad.

Take the case of General Motors (GM). On December 19, 1991, GM announced plans to close 21 factories and cut 74,000 jobs by the end of 1995. It said that it also intended to sell non-auto assets. Faced with low demand for its automobiles, GM decided to scrap the investment it had made in automobile manufacturing capacity, and it will likely lose much of its original investment in the 21 factories. However, this outcome is much better than would have occurred if GM continued to operate these factories in a declining auto market. On the day the factory closing was announced, GM's stock was marginally down by $0.125 (from $27.875 to $27.75). The stock market reaction was a signal that GM had waited too long to close its factories and that the declining demand GM was encountering was greater than expected. However, the market was relieved that GM had finally abandoned money-losing factories.

There is a special graveyard for abandoned products in the market for handheld computers. In October 1991, Momenta International Corporation introduced one of the very first handheld computers, a five-pound pen-based computer. Ten months later the company went bankrupt. Eo, a company backed by AT&T, demonstrated a new personal communicator in November 1992. The project was terminated in 1994. In January 1994, Motorola began shipping its Envoy, a wireless communicator. The computer was discontinued two years later. The point of our examples of failed handheld computer products is that a firm will frequently exercise its option of abandoning a project rather than keeping a money-losing product on the market in hopes that economic conditions will improve.

Discounted Cash Flows and Options

Conventional NPV analysis discounts a project's cash flows estimated for a certain project life. The decision is whether to accept the project or reject it. In practice, managers can expand or contract the scope of a project at various moments over its life. In theory, all such managerial options should be included in the project's value.

The market value of the project (M) will be the sum of the NPV of the project without options to expand or contract and the value of the managerial options (Opt):

$$M = \text{NPV} + \text{Opt}$$

EXAMPLE

Imagine two ways of producing Frisbees. Method A uses a conventional machine that has an active secondary market. Method B uses highly specialized machine tools for which there is no secondary market. Method B has no salvage value, but is more efficient. Method A has a salvage value, but is inefficient.

If production of Frisbees goes on until the machines used in methods A and B are used up, the NPV of B will be greater than that of A. However, if there is some possibility that production of Frisbees will be stopped before the end of the useful life of the Frisbee-making machines, method A may well be better. Method A's higher value in the secondary market increases its NPV relative to B's. There is a valuable embedded option to abandoning Method A.

An Example

Suppose we are analyzing a new product that will sell an expected 10 units a year in perpetuity at $10 net cash flow. In other words, we expect that cash flows will be $100 per year. At the end of the first year we will learn more about the economic viability of the new product. Specifically, we will know if the project will be a success or a failure. If the product is a success, unit sales will be revised to 20 and if the product is a failure, unit sales will be 0. Success and failure are equally likely. The discount rate is 10 percent and the initial investment outlay is $1,050. The dismantled equipment originally purchased for the project can be sold for scrap in one year for $500.

A standard discount cash flow analysis of the new product is very straightforward. The expected cash flows are $100 per year and the discount rate is 10 percent. The NPV of the product is:

$$\$100/.10 - \$1,050 = -\$50$$

So we shouldn't launch the new product. Correct? No! In one year we can sell out for $500 and we can learn more about the success or failure of our new product. If it is a success, we can continue to sell the product. But if it is a failure, we can abandon the product. The option to abandon in one year is valuable.

In one year if the cash flows are revised to $0, the PV of the project will be $0 and we will abandon the product for $500. The NPV will be $500. On the other hand, if we learn that we can sell 20 of the products, the PV of future cash flows will be $200/.10 = $2,000. The PV exceeds the abandonment value of $500. So we will continue to sell the product.

To sum up, we now have a new product that costs $1,050 today. In one year we expect a cash flow of $100. After one year the new product will be worth either $500 (if we abandon the product) or $2,000 (if we continue to sell the product). These outcomes are equally likely so we expect the project to be worth $500 + $2,000/2 = $1,250. The bottom line is that in one year we expect to have $100 in cash plus a project worth $1,250. At a 10-percent discount the project is worth $1,227.27 so the NPV is $1,227.27 − $1,050 = $177.27.

We should launch the new product! Notice the NPV of our new product has increased from −$50 to $177.27 or, by $227.27. How did this happen? The original analysis implicitly assumed we would launch the new product even though it was a failure. Actually, when we took a closer look, we saw that we were $500 better off if we abandoned the product. There was a 50-percent probability of this happening. So the expected cash flow from abandonment is $250. The PV of this amount is $250/1.1 = $227.27. The value of the option to abandon after one year is $227.27.

Robichek and Van Horne and Dye and Long were among the first to recognize the abandonment value in project analysis.[7] More recently, Myers and Majd constructed a model of abandonment based on an American put option with varying dividend yields and an uncertain exercise price.[8] They present a numerical procedure for calculating abandonment value in problems similar to that of the Frisbee-making machine.

---

[7]A. Robichek and J. Van Horne, "Abandonment Value and Capital Budgeting," *Journal of Finance* (December 1967); and E. Dye and H. Long, "Abandonment Value and Capital Budgeting: Comment," *Journal of Finance* (March 1969).

[8]S. C. Myers and S. Majd, "Calculating Abandonment Value Using Option Pricing Theory." Unpublished manuscript (June 1985).

Brennan and Schwartz use a gold mine to illustrate the value of managerial operations.[9] They show that the value of a gold mine will depend on management's ability to shut it down if the price of gold falls below a certain point, and the ability to reopen it subsequently if conditions are right. They show that valuation approaches that ignore these managerial options are likely to substantially underestimate the value of the project.

There are both qualitative and quantitative approaches to adjusting for option value in capital budgeting decisions. Most firms use qualitative approaches, such as subjective judgment. However, quantitative approaches are gaining acceptance. We talk about the quantitative approaches in Chapters 21 and 22.

8.5 Summary and Conclusions

This chapter discusses a number of practical applications of capital budgeting.

1. In Chapter 7, we observed how the net present value rule in capital budgeting is used. In Chapter 8, we ask about the sources of positive net present value and we explain what managers can do to create positive net present value.

2. Though NPV is the best capital budgeting approach conceptually, it has been criticized in practice for providing managers with a false sense of security. Sensitivity analysis shows NPV under varying assumptions, giving managers a better feel for the project's risks. Unfortunately, sensitivity analysis modifies only one variable at a time, while many variables are likely to vary together in the real world. Scenario analysis considers the joint movement of the different factors under different scenarios (e.g., war breaking out or oil prices skyrocketing). Finally, managers want to know how bad forecasts must be before a project loses money. Break-even analysis calculates the sales figure at which the project breaks even. Though break-even analysis is frequently performed on an accounting profit basis, we suggest that a net present value basis is more appropriate.

3. We talk about hidden options in doing discounted cash flow analysis of capital budgeting. We discuss the option to expand and the option to abandon.

Key Terms

Break-even analysis 209	Scenario analysis 209
Contribution margin 210	Sensitivity analysis 206
Decision trees 203	Variable costs 207
Fixed costs 207	

---

[9]M. J. Brennan and E. S. Schwartz, "A New Approach to Evaluating Natural Resource Investments," *Midland Corporate Finance Journal* 3 (Spring 1985).

Suggested Reading

The classic article on break-even analysis is:

Reinhart, U. E. "Breakeven Analysis for Lockheed's Tristar: An Application of Financial Theory." *Journal of Finance* (September 1977).

Questions and Problems

Decision Trees

8.1 Sony Electronics, Inc., has developed a new type of VCR. If the firm directly goes to the market with the product, there is only a 50 percent chance of success. On the other hand, if the firm conducts test marketing of the VCR, it will take a year and will cost $2 million. Through the test marketing, however, the firm is able to improve the product and increase the probability of success to 75 percent. If the new product proves successful, the present value (at the time when the firm starts selling it) of the payoff is $20 million, while if it turns out to be a failure, the present value of the payoff is $5 million. Should the firm conduct test marketing or go directly to the market? The appropriate discount rate is 15 percent.

8.2 The marketing manager for a growing consumer products firm is considering launching a new product. To determine consumers' interest in such a product, the manager can conduct a focus group that will cost $120,000 and has a 70 percent chance of correctly predicting the success of the product, or hire a consulting firm that will research the market at a cost of $400,000. The consulting firm boasts a correct assessment record of 90 percent. Of course going directly to the market with no prior testing will be the correct move 50 percent of the time. If the firm launches the product, and it is a success, the payoff will be $1.2 million. Which action will result in the highest expected payoff for the firm?

8.3 Tandem Bicycles is noticing a decline in sales due to the increase of lower-priced import products from the Far East. The CFO is considering a number of strategies to maintain its market share. The options she sees are the following:

- Price the products more aggressively, resulting in a $1.3 million decline in cash flows. The likelihood that Tandem will lose no cash flows to the imports is 55 percent; there is a 45 percent probability that they will lose only $550,000 in cash flows to the imports.
- Hire a lobbyist to convince the regulators that there should be important tariffs placed upon overseas manufacturers of bicycles. This will cost Tandem $800,000 and will have a 75 percent success rate, that is, no loss in cash flows to the importers. If the lobbyists do not succeed, Tandem Bicycles will lose $2 million in cash flows.

As the assistant to the CFO, which strategy would you recommend to your boss?

Accounting Break-Even Analysis

8.4 Samuelson Inc. has invested in a facility to produce calculators. The price of the machine is $600,000 and its economic life is five years. The machine is fully depreciated by the straight-line method and will produce 20,000 units of calculators in the first year. The variable production cost per unit of the calculator is $15, while fixed costs are $900,000. The corporate tax rate for the company is 30 percent. What should the sales price per unit of the calculator be for the firm to have a zero profit?

8.5 What is the minimum number of units that a distributor of big-screen TVs must sell in a given period to break even?

$$
\begin{aligned}
\text{Sales price} &= \$1,500 \\
\text{Variable costs} &= \$1,100 \\
\text{Fixed costs} &= \$120,000 \\
\text{Depreciation} &= \$20,000 \\
\text{Tax rate} &= 35\%
\end{aligned}
$$

8.6 You are considering investing in a fledgling company that cultivates abalone for sale to local restaurants. The proprietor says he'll return all profits to you after covering operating costs and his salary. How many abalone must be harvested and sold in the first year of operations for you to get any payback? (Assume no depreciation.)

$$
\begin{aligned}
\text{Price per adult abalone} &= \$2.00 \\
\text{Variable costs} &= \$0.72 \\
\text{Fixed costs} &= \$300,000 \\
\text{Salaries} &= \$40,000 \\
\text{Tax rate} &= 35\%
\end{aligned}
$$

How much profit will be returned to you if he sells 300,000 abalone?

Present Value Break-Even Analysis

8.7 Using the information in the problem above, what is the present value break-even point if the discount rate is 15 percent, initial investment is $140,000, and the life of the project is seven years? Assume a straight-line depreciation method with a zero salvage value.

8.8 Kids & Toys Inc. has purchased a $200,000 machine to produce toy cars. The machine will be fully depreciated by the straight-line method for its economic life of five years and will be worthless after its life. The firm expects that the sales price of the toy is $25 while its variable cost is $5. The firm should also pay $350,000 as fixed costs each year. The corporate tax rate for the company is 25 percent, and the appropriate discount rate is 12 percent. What is the present value break-even point?

8.9 The Cornchopper Company is considering the purchase of a new harvester. The company is currently involved in deliberations with the manufacturer and the parties have not come to settlement regarding the final purchase price. The management of Cornchopper has hired you to determine the break-even purchase price of the harvester. This price is that which will make the NPV of the project zero. Base your analysis on the following facts:

- The new harvester is not expected to affect revenues, but operating expenses will be reduced by $10,000 per year for 10 years.
- The old harvester is now 5 years old, with 10 years of its scheduled life remaining. It was purchased for $45,000. It has been depreciated on a straight-line basis.
- The old harvester has a current market value of $20,000.
- The new harvester will be depreciated on a straight-line basis over its 10-year life.
- The corporate tax rate is 34 percent.
- The firm's required rate of return is 15 percent.
- All cash flows occur at year-end. However, the initial investment, the proceeds from selling the old harvester, and any tax effects will occur immediately. Capital gains and losses are taxed at the corporate rate of 34 percent when they are realized.
- The expected market value of both harvesters at the end of their economic lives is zero.

Scenario Analysis

8.10 Ms. Thompson, as the CFO of a clock maker, is considering an investment of a $420,000 machine that has a seven-year life and no salvage value. The machine is depreciated by a straight-line method with a zero salvage over the seven years. The appropriate discount rate for cash flows of the project is 13 percent, and the corporate tax rate of the company is 35 percent. Calculate the NPV of the project in the following scenario. What is your conclusion about the project?

	Pessimistic	Expected	Optimistic
Unit sales	23,000	25,000	27,000
Price	$ 38	$ 40	$ 42
Variable costs	$ 21	$ 20	$ 19
Fixed costs	$320,000	$300,000	$280,000

8.11 You are the financial analyst for a manufacturer of tennis rackets that has identified a graphite-like material that it is considering using in its rackets. Given the following information about the results of launching a new racket, will you undertake the project? (Assumptions: Tax rate = 40%, Effective discount rate = 13%, Depreciation = $300,000 per year, and production will occur over the next five years only.)

	Pessimistic	Expected	Optimistic
Market size	110,000	120,000	130,000
Market share	22%	25%	27%
Price	$ 115	$ 120	$ 125
Variable costs	$ 72	$ 70	$ 68
Fixed costs	$ 850,000	$ 800,000	$ 750,000
Investment	$1,500,000	$1,500,000	$1,500,000

8.12 What would happen to the analysis done above if your competitor introduces a graphite composite that is even lighter than your product? What factors would this likely affect? Do an NPV analysis assuming market size increases (due to more awareness of graphite-based rackets) to the level predicted by the optimistic scenario but your market share decreases to the pessimistic level (due to competitive forces). What does this tell you about the relative importance of market size versus market share?

The Option to Abandon

8.13 You have been hired as a financial analyst to do a feasibility study of a new video game for Passivision. Marketing research suggests Passivision can sell 12,000 units per year at $62.50 net cash flow per unit for the next 10 years. Total annual operating cash flow is forecasted to be $62.50 × 12,000 = $750,000. The relevant discount rate is 10 percent. The required initial investment is $10 million.
   a. What is the base case NPV?
   b. After one year, the video game project can be abandoned for $200,000. After one year, expected cash flows will be revised upward to $1.5 million or to $0 with equal probability. What is the option value of abandonment? What is the revised NPV?

8.14 Allied Products is thinking about a new product launch. The vice president of marketing suggests that Allied Products can sell 2 million units per year at $100 net cash flow per unit for the next 10 years. Allied Products uses a 20-percent discount rate for new product launches and the required initial investment is $100 million.
   a. What is the base case NPV?
   b. After the first year, the project can be dismantled and sold for scrap for $50 million. If expected cash flows can be revised based on the first year's experience, when would it make sense to abandon the project? (Hint: At what level of expected cash flows does it make sense to abandon the project?)

Risk

■■■■■

T HIS part of the book examines the relationship between expected return and risk for portfolios and individual assets. When capital markets are in equilibrium, they determine a trade-off between expected return and risk. The returns that shareholders can expect to obtain in the capital markets are the ones they will require from firms when the firms evaluate risky investment projects. The shareholders' required return is the firm's cost of equity capital.

Chapter 9 examines the modern history of the U.S. capital markets. A central fact emerges: The return on risky assets has been higher on average than the return on risk-free assets. This fact supports the perspective for our examination of risk and return. In Chapter 9 we introduce several key intuitions of modern finance and show how they can be useful in determining a firm's cost of capital.

Chapters 10 and 11 contain more advanced discussions of risk and expected return. The chapters are self-contained and build on the material in Chapter 9.

Chapter 10 shows what determines the relationship between return and risk for portfolios. The model of risk and expected return used in the chapter is called the *capital-asset-pricing model* (CAPM).

Chapter 11 examines risk and return from another perspective: the arbitrage pricing theory (APT). This approach yields insights that one cannot get from the CAPM. The key concept is that the total risk of individual stocks can be divided into two parts: systematic and unsystematic. The fundamental principle of diversification is that, for highly diversified portfolios, unsystematic risk disappears; only systematic risk survives.

The section on risk finishes with a discussion in Chapter 12 on estimating a firm's cost of equity capital and some of the problems that are encountered in doing so.

PART III

CHAPTER 9

Capital Market Theory: An Overview

EXECUTIVE SUMMARY

We learned in Chapter 4 that riskless cash flows should be discounted at the riskless rate of interest. Because most capital-budgeting projects involve risky flows, a different discount rate must be used. The next four chapters are devoted to determining the discount rate for risky projects.

Past experience indicates that students find the upcoming material among the most difficult in the entire textbook. Because of this, we always teach the material by presenting the results and conclusions first. By seeing where we are going ahead of time, it is easier to absorb the material when we get there. A synopsis of the four chapters follows:

1. Because our ultimate goal is to discount risky cash flows, we must first find a way to measure risk. In the current chapter we measure the variability of an asset by the variance or standard deviation of its returns. If an individual holds only *one* asset, its variance or standard deviation would be the appropriate measure of risk.

2. While Chapter 9 considers one type of asset in isolation, Chapter 10 examines a portfolio of many assets. In this case, we are interested in the *contribution* of the security to the risk of the entire portfolio. Because much of an individual security's variance is dispersed in a large diversified portfolio, neither the security's variance nor its standard deviation can be viewed as the security's contribution to the risk of a large portfolio. Rather, this contribution is best measured by the security's beta (β). As an example, consider a stock whose returns are high when the returns on a large, diversified portfolio are low—and vice versa. This stock has a negative beta. In other words, it acts as a hedge, implying that the stock actually tends to reduce the risk of the portfolio. However, the stock could have a high variance, implying high risk for an investor holding only this security.

3. Investors will only hold a risky security if its expected return is high enough to compensate for its risk. Given the above, the expected return on a security should be positively related to the security's beta. In fact, the relationship between risk and expected return can be expressed more precisely by the following equation:

$$\begin{array}{c}\text{Expected return} \\ \text{on a security}\end{array} = \begin{array}{c}\text{Risk-free} \\ \text{rate}\end{array} + \text{Beta} \times \left(\begin{array}{c}\text{Expected return on} \\ \text{market portfolio}\end{array} - \begin{array}{c}\text{Risk-free} \\ \text{rate}\end{array} \right)$$

Because the term in parentheses on the right-hand side is positive, this equation says that the expected return on a security is a positive function of its beta. This equation is frequently referred to as the *capital-asset-pricing model* (CAPM).

4. We derive the relationship between risk and return in a different manner in Chapter 11. However, many of the conclusions are quite similar. This chapter is based on the *arbitrage pricing theory* (APT).

5. The theoretical ideas in Chapters 9, 10, and 11 are intellectually challenging. Fortunately, Chapter 12, which applies the above theory to the selection of discount rates, is much simpler. In a world where (*a*) a project has the same risk as the firm, and (*b*) the firm has no

debt, the expected return on the stock should serve as the project's discount rate. This expected return is taken from the capital-asset-pricing model, as presented above.

Because we have a long road ahead of us, the maxim that any journey begins with a single step applies here. We start with the perhaps mundane calculation of a security's return.

9.1 RETURNS

Dollar Returns

Suppose the Video Concept Company has several thousand shares of stock outstanding and you are a shareholder. Further suppose that you purchased some of the shares of stock in the company at the beginning of the year; it is now year-end and you want to figure out how well you have done on your investment. The return you get on an investment in stocks, like that in bonds or any other investment, comes in two forms.

First, over the year most companies pay dividends to shareholders. As the owner of stock in the Video Concept Company, you are a part owner of the company. If the company is profitable, it generally will distribute some of its profits to the shareholders. Therefore, as the owner of shares of stock, you will receive some cash, called a *dividend,* during the year.[1] This cash is the *income component* of your return. In addition to the dividends, the other part of your return is the *capital gain*—or, if it is negative, the *capital loss* (negative capital gain)—on the investment.

For example, suppose we are considering the cash flows of the investment in Figure 9.1 and you purchased 100 shares of stock at the beginning of the year at a price of $37 per share. Your total investment, then, would be

$$C_0 = \$37 \times 100 = \$3,700$$

Suppose that over the year the stock paid a dividend of $1.85 per share. During the year, then, you would have received income of

$$\text{Div} = \$1.85 \times 100 = \$185$$

Suppose, lastly, that at the end of the year the market price of the stock is $40.33 per share. Because the stock increased in price, you have a capital gain of

$$\text{Gain} = (\$40.33 - \$37) \times 100 = \$333$$

■ FIGURE 9.1 **Dollar Returns**

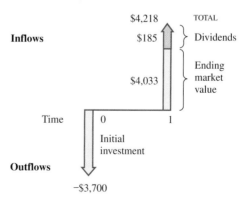

---

[1] In fact, companies often continue to pay dividends even when they have lost money during the year.

The capital gain, like the dividend, is part of the return that shareholders require to maintain their investment in the Video Concept Company. Of course, if the price of Video Concept stock had dropped in value to, say, $34.78, you would have recorded a capital loss of

$$\text{Loss} = (\$34.78 - \$37) \times 100 = -\$222$$

The *total dollar return* on your investment is the sum of the dividend income and the capital gain or loss on the investment:

$$\text{Total dollar return} = \text{Dividend income} + \text{Capital gain (or loss)}$$

(From now on we will refer to *capital losses* as *negative capital gains* and not distinguish them.) In our first example, then, the total dollar return is given by

$$\text{Total dollar return} = \$185 + \$333 = \$518$$

Notice that if you sold the stock at the end of the year, your total amount of cash would be the initial investment plus the total dollar return. In the preceding example, then, you would have

$$\text{Total cash if stock is sold} = \text{Initial investment} + \text{Total dollar return}$$
$$= \$3,700 + \$518$$
$$= \$4,218$$

As a check, notice that this is the same as the proceeds from the sale of stock plus the dividends:

$$\text{Proceeds from stock sale} + \text{Dividends}$$
$$= \$40.33 \times 100 + \$185$$
$$= \$4,033 + \$185$$
$$= \$4,218$$

Suppose, however, that you hold your Video Concept stock and don't sell it at year-end. Should you still consider the capital gain as part of your return? Does this violate our previous present value rule that only cash matters?

The answer to the first question is a strong yes, and the answer to the second question is an equally strong no. The capital gain is every bit as much a part of your return as is the dividend, and you should certainly count it as part of your total return. That you have decided to hold onto the stock and not sell or *realize* the gain or the loss in no way changes the fact that, if you want to, you could get the cash value of the stock.[2]

Percentage Returns

It is more convenient to summarize the information about returns in percentage terms than in dollars, because the percentages apply to any amount invested. The question we want to answer is: How much return do we get for each dollar invested? To find this out, let t stand for the year we are looking at, let P_t be the price of the stock at the beginning of the year, and let Div_{t+1} be the dividend paid on the stock during the year. Consider the cash flows in Figure 9.2.

---

[2]After all, you could always sell the stock at year-end and immediately buy it back. As we previously computed, the total dollar return on the investment would be $518 before you bought the stock back. The total amount of cash you would have at year-end would be this $518 plus your initial investment of $3,700. You would not lose this return when you bought back 100 shares of stock. In fact, you would be in exactly the same position as if you had not sold the stock (assuming, of course, that there are no tax consequences and no brokerage commissions from selling the stock).

■ FIGURE 9.2 **Percentage Returns**

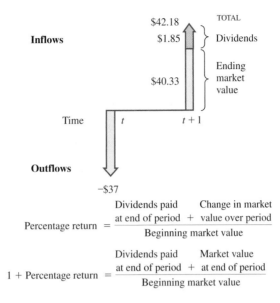

$$\text{Percentage return} = \frac{\begin{array}{c}\text{Dividends paid}\\\text{at end of period}\end{array} + \begin{array}{c}\text{Change in market}\\\text{value over period}\end{array}}{\text{Beginning market value}}$$

$$1 + \text{Percentage return} = \frac{\begin{array}{c}\text{Dividends paid}\\\text{at end of period}\end{array} + \begin{array}{c}\text{Market value}\\\text{at end of period}\end{array}}{\text{Beginning market value}}$$

In our example, the price at the beginning of the year was $37 per share and the dividend paid during the year on each share was $1.85. Hence the percentage of income return,[3] sometimes called the *dividend yield,* is

$$\text{Dividend yield} = \text{Div}_{t+1}/P_t = \$1.85/\$37 = 0.05 = 5\%$$

Capital gain is the change in the price of the stock divided by the initial price. Letting P_{t+1} be the price of the stock at year-end, the capital gain can be computed

$$\begin{aligned}\text{Capital gain} &= (P_{t+1} - P_t)/P_t = (\$40.33 - \$37)/\$37 \\ &= \$3.33/\$37 \\ &= 0.09 \\ &= 9\%\end{aligned}$$

Combining these two results, we find that the *total return* on the investment in Video Concept stock over the year, which we will label R_{t+1}, was

$$\begin{aligned}R_{t+1} &= \frac{\text{Div}_{t+1}}{P_t} + \frac{(P_{t+1} - P_t)}{P_t} \\ &= 5\% + 9\% \\ &= \$14\%\end{aligned}$$

From now on we will refer to returns in percentage terms.

EXAMPLE

Suppose a stock begins the year with a price of $25 per share and ends with a price of $35 per share. During the year it paid a $2 dividend per share. What are its dividend yield, its capital gain, and its total return for the year? We can imagine the cash flows in Figure 9.3.

---

[3]We will use 0.05 and 5 percent interchangeably. Keep in mind that, although $(0.05)^2 = 0.0025$, $(5^2)\% = 25\%$. Thus, it is important to keep track of parentheses so that decimal points land where they belong.

■ FIGURE 9.3   Cash Flow—An Investment Example

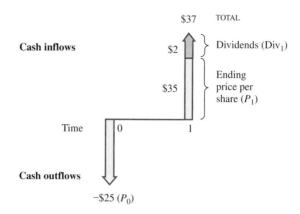

$$R_1 = \frac{\text{Div}_1}{P_0} + \frac{P_1 - P_0}{P_0}$$

$$= \frac{\$2}{\$25} + \frac{\$35 - \$25}{\$25} = \frac{\$12}{\$25}$$

$$= 8\% + 40\% = 48\%$$

Thus, the stock's dividend yield, its capital gain yield, and its total return are 8 percent, 40 percent, and 48 percent, respectively.

Suppose you had $5,000 invested. The total dollar return you would have received on an investment in the stock is $5,000 × 0.48 = $2,400. If you know the total dollar return on the stock, you do not need to know how many shares you would have had to purchase to figure out how much money you would have made on the $5,000 investment. You just use the total dollar return.[4]

QUESTIONS

- What are the two parts of total return?
- Why are unrealized capital gains or losses included in the calculation of returns?
- What is the difference between a dollar return and a percentage return?

---

[4]Consider the stock in the previous example. We have ignored the question of when during the year you receive the dividend. Does it make a difference? To explore this question, suppose first that the dividend is paid at the very beginning of the year, and you receive it the moment after you have purchased the stock. Suppose, too, that interest rates are 10 percent, and that immediately after receiving the dividend you loan it out. What will be your total return, including the loan proceeds, at the end of the year?

Alternatively, instead of loaning out the dividend you could have reinvested it and purchased more of the stock. If that is what you do with the dividend, what will your total return be? (Warning: This does not go on forever, and when you buy more stock with the cash from the dividend on your first purchase, you are too late to get yet another dividend on the new stock.)

Finally, suppose the dividend is paid at year-end. What answer would you get for the total return?

As you can see, by ignoring the question of when the dividend is paid when we calculate the return, we are implicitly assuming that it is received at the end of the year and cannot be reinvested during the year. The right way to figure out the return on a stock is to determine exactly when the dividend is received and to include the return that comes from reinvesting the dividend in the stock. This gives a pure stock return without confounding the issue by requiring knowledge of the interest rate during the year.

9.2 HOLDING-PERIOD RETURNS

A famous set of studies dealing with rates of return on common stocks, bonds, and Treasury bills was conducted by Roger Ibbotson and Rex Sinquefield.[5] They present year-by-year historical rates of return for the following five important types of financial instruments in the United States:

1. *Large-Company Common Stocks.* The common-stock portfolio is based on the Standard & Poor's (S&P) composite index. At present, the S&P composite includes 500 of the largest (in terms of market value) stocks in the United States.

2. *Small-Company Common Stocks.* This is a portfolio composed of the bottom fifth of stocks traded on the New York Stock Exchange in which stocks are ranked by market value (i.e., the price of the stock multiplied by the number of shares outstanding).

3. *Long-Term Corporate Bonds.* This is a portfolio of high-quality corporate bonds with a 20-year maturity.

4. *Long-Term U.S. Government Bonds.* This is a portfolio of U.S. government bonds with a maturity of 20 years.

5. *U.S. Treasury Bills.* This is a portfolio of Treasury bills of three-month maturity.

None of the returns are adjusted for taxes or transactions costs. In addition to the year-by-year returns on financial instruments, the year-to-year change in the consumer price index is computed. This is a basic measure of inflation. Year-by-year real returns can be calculated by subtracting annual inflation.

Before looking closely at the different portfolio returns, we graphically present the returns and risks available from U.S. capital markets in the 74-year period from 1926 to 1999. Figure 9.4 shows the growth of $1 invested at the beginning of 1926. Notice that the vertical axis is logarithmic, so that equal distances measure the same number of percentage changes. The figure shows that if $1 were invested in common stocks and all dividends were reinvested, the dollar would have grown to $2,845.63 by the end of 1999. The biggest growth was in the small-stock portfolio. If $1 were invested in small stocks in 1926, the investment would have grown to $6,640.79. However, when you look carefully at Figure 9.4, you can see great variability in the returns on small stocks, especially in the earlier part of the period. A dollar in long-term government bonds was very stable as compared with a dollar in common stocks. Figures 9.5 to 9.8 plot each year-to-year percentage return as a vertical bar drawn from the horizontal axis for common stocks, for small-company stocks, for long-term bonds and Treasury bills, and for inflation, respectively.

Figure 9.4 gives the growth of a dollar investment in the stock market from 1926 through 1999. In other words, it shows what the worth of the investment would have been if the dollar had been left in the stock market and if each year the dividends from the previous year had been reinvested in more stock. If R_t is the return in year t (expressed in decimals), the value you would have at the end of year T is the product of 1 plus the return in each of the years:

$$(1 + R_1) \times (1 + R_2) \times \ldots \times (1 + R_t) \times \ldots \times (1 + R_T)$$

---

[5]The most recent update of this work is *Stocks, Bonds, Bills and Inflation: 2000 Yearbook™* (Chicago: Ibbotson Associates). All rights reserved.

■ FIGURE 9.4   **A $1 Investment in Different Types of Portfolios,**
1926–1999 (Year-end 1925 = $1.00)

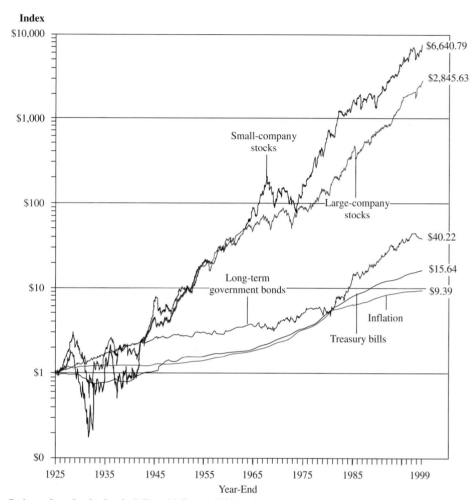

■ FIGURE 9.5   **Year-by-Year Total Returns on Common Stocks**

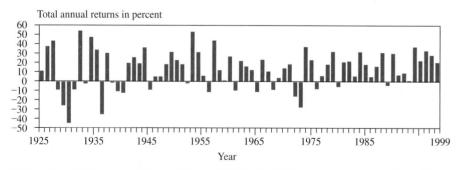

■ FIGURE 9.6 **Year-by-Year Total Returns on Small-Company Stocks**

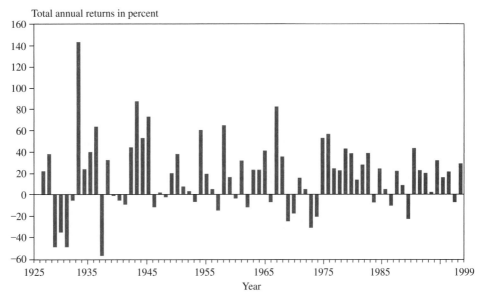

For example, if the returns were 11 percent, −5 percent, and 9 percent in a three-year period, an investment of $1 at the beginning of the period would be worth

$$(1 + R_1) \times (1 + R_2) \times (1 + R_3) = (\$1 + 0.11) \times (\$1 - 0.05) \times (\$1 + 0.09)$$
$$= \$1.11 \times \$0.95 \times \$1.09$$
$$= \$1.15$$

at the end of the three years. Notice that 0.15 or 15 percent is the total return and that it includes the return from reinvesting the first-year dividends in the stock market for two more years and reinvesting the second-year dividends for the final year. The 15 percent is called a three-year **holding-period return.** Table 9.1 gives the annual returns each year from 1926 to 1999. From this table you can determine holding-period returns for any combination of years.

CONCEPT QUESTIONS

?

- What is the largest one-period return in the 74-year history of common stocks we have displayed, and when did it occur? What is the smallest return, and when did it occur?
- In how many years did the common-stock return exceed 30 percent, and in how many years was it below 20 percent?
- For common stocks, what is the longest period of time without a single losing year? What is the longest streak of losing years?
- What is the longest period of time such that if you had invested at the beginning of the period, you would still not have had a positive return on your common-stock investment by the end?

■ FIGURE 9.7 **Year-by-Year Total Returns on Bonds and Bills**

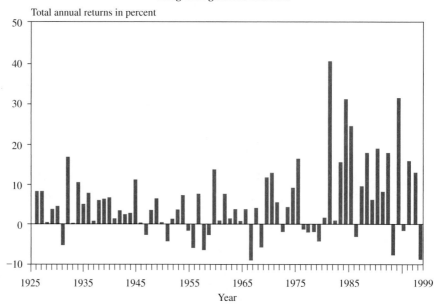

Long-term government bonds

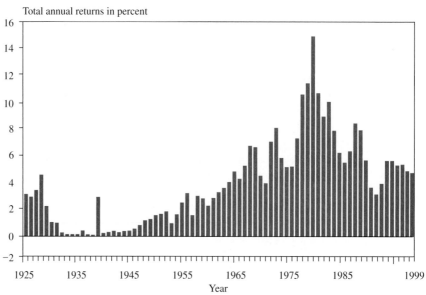

Treasury bills

Redrawn from *Stocks, Bonds, Bills and Inflation: 2000 Yearbook,*™ annual updates work by Roger G. Ibbotson and Rex A. Sinquefield (Chicago: Ibbotson Associates). All rights reserved.

■ FIGURE 9.8 **Year-by-Year Inflation**

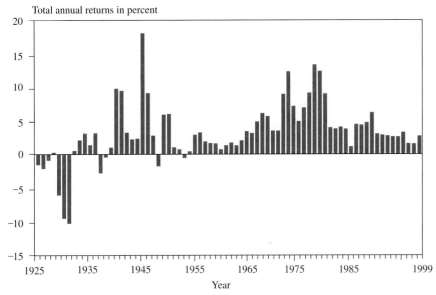

■ TABLE 9.1 **Year-by-Year Total Returns, 1926–1999**

Year	Large-Company Stocks	Long-Term Government Bonds	Long-Term Corporate Bonds	U.S. Treasury Bills	Inflation
1926	13.70%	6.40%	7.00%	4.40%	−1.10%
1927	35.80%	4.51%	6.54%	4.21%	−2.33%
1928	45.14%	0.18%	3.42%	4.87%	−1.14%
1929	−8.88%	5.66%	4.33%	6.05%	0.63%
1930	−25.22%	4.16%	6.34%	3.72%	−6.45%
1931	−43.75%	0.41%	−2.45%	2.63%	−9.23%
1932	−8.38%	5.61%	12.23%	2.95%	−10.29%
1933	53.11%	5.92%	5.24%	1.66%	0.68%
1934	−2.41%	5.95%	9.75%	1.04%	1.63%
1935	46.94%	3.22%	6.89%	0.29%	2.94%
1936	32.35%	1.73%	6.22%	0.15%	1.43%
1937	−35.68%	4.63%	2.50%	0.44%	2.81%
1938	32.29%	4.74%	4.36%	0.07%	−2.74%
1939	−1.54%	2.26%	4.28%	0.00%	0.00%
1940	−10.54%	4.25%	4.49%	0.00%	0.77%
1941	−12.14%	1.56%	1.78%	0.07%	9.90%
1942	20.98%	1.82%	3.14%	0.36%	9.01%
1943	25.52%	2.00%	3.35%	0.36%	2.97%
1944	19.46%	2.28%	3.12%	0.36%	2.26%
1945	36.35%	5.23%	3.51%	0.36%	2.31%
1946	−8.48%	0.54%	2.52%	0.43%	18.09%
1947	4.96%	−0.93%	0.46%	0.57%	8.83%

(continued)

Year	Large-Company Stocks	Long-Term Government Bonds	Long-Term Corporate Bonds	U.S. Treasury Bills	Inflation
1948	4.95%	2.62%	3.72%	0.99%	2.98%
1949	17.74%	4.53%	4.32%	1.12%	−2.08%
1950	30.04%	−0.92%	1.91%	1.25%	5.99%
1951	23.88%	−0.14%	−0.24%	1.51%	5.94%
1952	18.44%	2.42%	3.45%	1.76%	0.81%
1953	−1.11%	2.32%	2.05%	1.93%	0.74%
1954	52.44%	3.07%	4.65%	0.98%	−0.73%
1955	31.65%	−0.69%	1.07%	1.68%	0.34%
1956	6.90%	−1.61%	−1.78%	2.66%	3.01%
1957	−10.53%	6.75%	4.48%	3.34%	2.92%
1958	43.73%	−1.61%	0.85%	1.79%	1.76%
1959	12.02%	−1.89%	0.15%	3.35%	1.67%
1960	0.45%	11.04%	6.71%	3.13%	1.40%
1961	26.90%	2.24%	3.69%	2.32%	0.66%
1962	−8.79%	6.03%	6.20%	2.80%	1.31%
1963	22.72%	1.42%	3.17%	3.20%	1.65%
1964	16.43%	3.89%	3.97%	3.56%	0.98%
1965	12.37%	1.05%	2.10%	4.02%	1.95%
1966	−10.10%	4.81%	−0.26%	4.90%	3.43%
1967	24.04%	−2.36%	−1.17%	4.49%	3.05%
1968	11.03%	1.66%	4.17%	5.42%	4.70%
1969	−8.47%	−4.82%	−2.46%	6.81%	6.20%
1970	4.00%	18.15%	11.18%	6.68%	5.56%
1971	14.35%	11.39%	9.70%	4.51%	3.28%
1972	19.00%	2.51%	8.32%	4.04%	3.40%
1973	−14.85%	3.50%	2.99%	6.98%	8.72%
1974	−26.58%	3.82%	0.22%	8.09%	16.20%
1975	37.42%	5.63%	11.04%	6.04%	3.40%
1976	23.76%	15.20%	14.57%	5.16%	4.84%
1977	−7.38%	0.55%	5.50%	5.26%	6.71%
1978	6.54%	−0.99%	1.84%	7.23%	9.02%
1979	18.59%	0.50%	−1.55%	10.32%	13.30%
1980	32.61%	−0.63%	−4.99%	12.04%	12.51%
1981	−4.97%	2.62%	8.98%	15.21%	8.92%
1982	21.67%	43.98%	34.90%	11.28%	3.85%
1983	22.57%	2.03%	7.30%	8.89%	3.78%
1984	6.19%	15.96%	17.10%	10.04%	3.96%
1985	31.85%	30.34%	29.37%	7.70%	3.79%
1986	18.68%	22.86%	21.26%	6.18%	1.10%
1987	5.22%	−3.24%	−1.82%	5.87%	4.44%
1988	16.58%	6.86%	13.78%	6.73%	4.42%
1989	31.75%	18.64%	15.30%	8.48%	4.65%
1990	−3.13%	7.26%	8.60%	7.85%	6.10%
1991	30.53%	18.52%	15.63%	5.71%	3.06%
1992	7.62%	8.52%	10.88%	3.57%	2.89%
1993	10.07%	13.45%	14.68%	3.08%	2.75%
1994	1.27%	−7.31%	−2.42%	4.15%	2.68%
1995	37.80%	24.86%	22.03%	5.64%	2.53%
1996	22.74%	1.63%	3.87%	5.12%	3.32%
1997	33.43%	10.89%	11.11%	5.22%	1.70%
1998	28.13%	13.44%	11.44%	5.06%	1.61%
1999	21.03%	−7.12%	−2.30%	4.85%	2.69%

■ FIGURE 9.9   **Histogram of Returns on Common Stocks, 1926–1999**

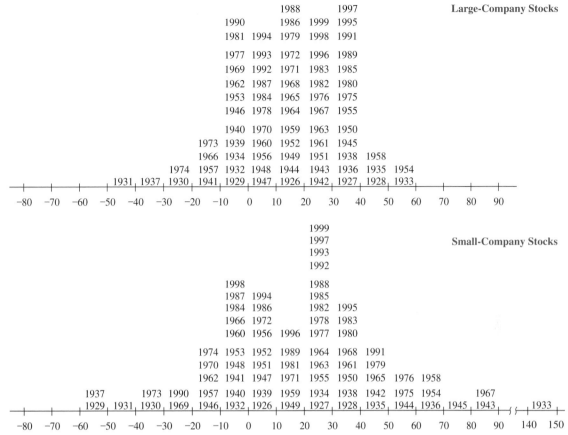

9.3 RETURN STATISTICS

The history of capital-market returns is too complicated to be handled in its undigested form. To use the history we must first find some manageable ways of describing it, dramatically condensing the detailed data into a few simple statements.

This is where two important numbers summarizing the history come in. The first and most natural number is some single measure that best describes the past annual returns on the stock market. In other words, what is our best estimate of the return that an investor could have realized in a particular year over the 1926-to-1999 period? This is the *average return.*

Figure 9.9 plots the histogram of the yearly stock market returns given in Table 9.1. This plot is the **frequency distribution** of the numbers. The height of the graph gives the number of sample observations in the range on the horizontal axis.

Given a frequency distribution like that in Figure 9.9, we can calculate the **average** or **mean** of the distribution. To compute the arithmetic average of the distribution, we add up all of the values and divide by the total (T) number (74 in our case because we have 74 years of data). The bar over the R is used to represent the mean, and the formula is the ordinary formula for the average:

$$\text{Mean} = \bar{R} = \frac{(R_1 + \ldots + R_T)}{T}$$

The arithmetic mean of the 74 annual returns from 1926 to 1999 is 13.3 percent.

EXAMPLE

The returns on common stock from 1926 to 1929 are 0.1370, 0.3580, 0.4514, and −0.0888, respectively. (These numbers are taken from Table 9.1.) The average, or mean, return over these four years is

$$\bar{R} = \frac{0.1370 + 0.3580 + 0.4514 - 0.0888}{4} = 0.2144$$

9.4 AVERAGE STOCK RETURNS AND RISK-FREE RETURNS

Now that we have computed the average return on the stock market, it seems sensible to compare it with the returns on other securities. The most obvious comparison is with the low-variability returns in the government-bond market. These are free of most of the volatility we see in the stock market.

The government borrows money by issuing bonds, which the investing public holds. As we discussed in an earlier chapter, these bonds come in many forms, and the ones we will look at here are called *Treasury bills,* or *T-bills.* Once a week the government sells some bills at an auction. A typical bill is a pure discount bond that will mature in a year or less. Because the government can raise taxes to pay for the debt it incurs—a trick that many of us would like to be able to perform—this debt is virtually free of the risk of default. Thus we will call this the *risk-free return* over a short time (one year or less).[6]

An interesting comparison, then, is between the virtually risk-free return on T-bills and the very risky return on common stocks. This difference between risky returns and risk-free returns is often called the *excess return on the risky asset.* It is called *excess* because it is the additional return resulting from the riskiness of common stocks and is interpreted as a **risk premium.**

Table 9.2 shows the average stock return, bond return, T-bill return, and inflation rate for the period from 1926 through 1999. From this we can derive excess returns. The average excess return from common stocks for the entire period was 9.5 percent (13.3% − 3.8%).

One of the most significant observations of stock market data is this long-run excess of the stock return over the risk-free return. An investor for this period was rewarded for investment in the stock market with an extra or excess return over what would have been achieved by simply investing in T-bills.

Why was there such a reward? Does it mean that it never pays to invest in T-bills and that someone who invested in them instead of in the stock market needs a course in finance? A complete answer to these questions lies at the heart of modern finance, and Chapter 10 is devoted entirely to this. However, part of the answer can be found in the variability of the

---

[6]A Treasury bill with a 90-day maturity is risk-free only during that particular time period.

TABLE 9.2 **Total Annual Returns, 1926–1999**

Series	Arithmetic mean	Risk premium (relative to U.S. Treasury bills)	Standard deviation	Distribution
Large-company stocks	13.3%	9.5%	20.1%	
Small-company stocks	17.6	13.8	33.6	*
Long-term corporate bonds	5.9	2.1	8.7	
Long-term government bonds	5.5	1.7	9.3	
Intermediate-term government bonds	5.4	1.6	5.8	
U.S. Treasury bills	3.8		3.2	
Inflation	3.2		4.5	

−90%   0%   90%

*The 1933 small-company stock total return was 142.9 percent.

Modified from *Stocks, Bonds, Bills and Inflation: 2000 Yearbook,*™ annual updates work by Roger G. Ibbotson and Rex. A. Sinquefield (Chicago: Ibbotson Associates). All rights reserved.

various types of investments. We see in Table 9.1 many years when an investment in T-bills achieved higher returns than an investment in common stocks. Also, we note that the returns from an investment in common stocks are frequently negative whereas an investment in T-bills never produces a negative return. So, we now turn our attention to measuring the variability of returns and an introductory discussion of risk.

Now we look more closely at Table 9.2. We see that the standard deviation of T-bills is substantially less than that of common stocks. This suggests that the risk of T-bills is less than that of common stocks. Because the answer turns on the riskiness of investments in common stock, we now turn our attention to measuring this risk.

CONCEPT QUESTIONS ?
• What is the major observation about capital markets that we will seek to explain?
• What does the observation tell us about investors for the period from 1926 through 1999?

9.5 RISK STATISTICS

The second number that we use to characterize the distribution of returns is a measure of the risk in returns. There is no universally agreed-upon definition of risk. One way to think about the risk of returns on common stock is in terms of how spread out the frequency distribution in Figure 9.9 is.[7] The spread, or dispersion, of a distribution is a measure of how much a particular return can deviate from the mean return. If the distribution is very spread out, the returns that will occur are very uncertain. By contrast, a distribution whose returns are all within a few percentage points of each other is tight, and the returns are less uncertain. The measures of risk we will discuss are variance and standard deviation.

Variance

The **variance** and its square root, the **standard deviation,** are the most common measures of variability or dispersion. We will use Var and σ^2 to denote the variance and SD and σ to represent the standard deviation. σ is, of course, the Greek letter sigma.

EXAMPLE

The returns on common stocks from 1926 to 1929 are (in decimals) 0.1370, 0.3580, 0.4514, and −0.0888, respectively. The variance of this sample is computed as

$$\text{Var} = \frac{1}{T-1}\ (R_1 - \overline{R})^2 + (R_2 - \overline{R})^2 + (R_3 - \overline{R})^2 + (R_4 - \overline{R})^2$$

$$0.0582 = \tfrac{1}{3}[(0.1370 - 0.2144)^2 + (0.3580 - 0.2144)^2 +$$
$$(0.4514 - 0.2144)^2 + (-0.0888 - 0.2144)^2]$$

$$\text{SD} = \sqrt{0.0582} = 0.2413 \quad (\text{i.e., } 24.13\%)$$

This formula tells us just what to do: Take the T individual returns ($R_1, R_2, \ldots$) and subtract the average return $\overline{R}$, square the result, and add them up. Finally, this total must be divided by the number of returns less one ($T - 1$). The standard deviation is always just the square root of the variance.

Using the actual stock returns in Table 9.1 for the 74-year period from 1926 through 1999 in the above formula, the resulting standard deviation of stock returns is 20.1 percent. The standard deviation is the standard statistical measure of the spread of a sample, and it will be the measure we use most of the time. Its interpretation is facilitated by a discussion of the normal distribution.

Normal Distribution and Its Implications for Standard Deviation

A large enough sample drawn from a **normal distribution** looks like the bell-shaped curve drawn in Figure 9.10. As you can see, this distribution is *symmetric* about its mean, not *skewed,* and it has a much cleaner shape than the actual distribution of yearly returns drawn

---

[7]Several condensed frequency distributions are also in the extreme right column of Table 9.2.

■ FIGURE 9.10   **The Normal Distribution**

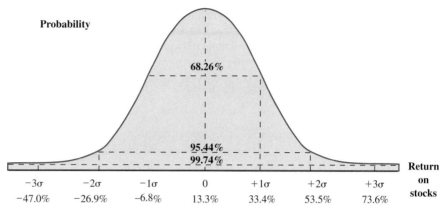

In the case of a normal distribution, there is a 68.26-percent probability that a return will be within one standard deviation of the mean. In this example, there is a 68.26-percent probability that a yearly return will be between −6.8 percent and 33.4 percent.

There is a 95.44-percent probability that a return will be within two standard deviations of the mean. In this example, there is a 95.44-percent probability that a yearly return will be between −26.9 percent and 53.5 percent.

Finally, there is a 99.74-percent probability that a return will be within three standard deviations of the mean. In this example, there is a 99.74-percent probability that a yearly return will be between −47.0 percent and 73.6 percent.

in Figure 9.9.[8] Of course, if we had been able to observe stock market returns for 1,000 years, we might have filled in a lot of the jumps and jerks in Figure 9.9 and had a smoother curve.

In classical statistics the normal distribution plays a central role, and the standard deviation is the usual way to represent the spread of a normal distribution. For the normal distribution, the probability of having a return that is above or below the mean by a certain amount depends only on the standard deviation. For example, the probability of having a return that is within one standard deviation of the mean of the distribution is approximately 0.68 or 2/3, and the probability of having a return that is within two standard deviations of the mean is approximately 0.95.

The 20.1-percent standard deviation we found for stock returns from 1926 through 1999 can now be interpreted in the following way: If stock returns are roughly normally distributed, the probability that a yearly return will fall within 20.1 percent of the mean of 13.3 percent will be approximately 2/3. That is, about 2/3 of the yearly returns will be between −6.8 percent and +33.4 percent. (Note that −6.8% = 13.3% − 20.1% and 33.4% = 13.3% + 20.1%.) The probability that the return in any year will fall within two standard deviations is about 0.95. That is, about 95 percent of yearly returns will be between −26.9 percent and 53.5 percent.

The distribution in Figure 9.10 is a theoretical distribution, sometimes called the *population distribution* or *true distribution*. There is no assurance that the actual distribution of observations in a given sample will produce a histogram that looks exactly like the theoretical distribution. We can see how messy the actual frequency function of historical observations

---

[8]Some people define risk as the possibility of obtaining a return below the average. Some measures of risk, such as *semivariance,* use only the negative deviations from the average return. However, for symmetric distributions, such as the normal distribution, this method of measuring downside risk is equivalent to measuring risk with deviations from the mean on both sides.

is by observing Figure 9.9. If we were to keep on generating observations for a long enough period of time, however, the aberrations in the sample would disappear, and the actual historical distribution would start to look like the underlying theoretical distribution.

This points out that sampling error exists in any individual sample. In other words, the distribution of the sample only approximates the true distribution: we always measure the truth with some error. For example, we do not know what the true expected return was for common stocks in the 74-year history. However, we are sure that our 13.3 percent realized return is very close to it.

CONCEPT QUESTIONS
- What is the definition of sample estimates of variance and standard deviation?
- How does the normal distribution help us interpret standard deviation?

9.6 SUMMARY AND CONCLUSIONS

1. This chapter presents returns for a number of different asset classes. The general conclusion is that stocks have outperformed bonds over most of the 20th century, though stocks have also exhibited more risk.

2. The statistical measures in this chapter are necessary building blocks for the material of the next three chapters. In particular, standard deviation and variance measure the variability of the return on an individual security and on portfolios of securities. In the next chapter, we will argue that standard deviation and variance are appropriate measures of the risk of an individual security if an investor's portfolio is composed of that security only.

KEY TERMS

Average (mean)   231
Capital gain   223
Frequency distribution   231
Holding-period return   227

Normal distribution   234
Risk premium   232
Standard deviation   234
Variance   234

SUGGESTED READINGS

An important record of the performance of financial instruments in the U.S. capital markets can be found in:
Ibbotson, Roger G., and Rex A. Sinquefield. *Stocks, Bonds, Bills and Inflation: 2000 Yearbook.*™ Chicago: Ibbotson Associates.

What is the equity risk premium? This is the question addressed by:
Cornell, Bradford. *The Equity Risk Premium: The Long Term Future of the Stock Market.* New York: John Wiley, 1999 and Shiller, Robert S. *Irrational Exuberance.* Princeton, N.J.: Princeton University Press, 2000.

For a look at market risk premiums worldwide, see:
Jorion, P., and W. N. Goetzmann, "Global Stock Markets in the Twentieth Century." *Journal of Finance* 54 (1999).

QUESTIONS AND PROBLEMS

Returns

9.1 Last year, you bought 500 shares of Twedt El Dee stock at $37 per share. You have received total dividends of $1,000 during the year. Currently, Twedt El Dee stock sells for $38.
   a. How much did you earn in capital gains?
   b. What was your total dollar return?
   c. What was your percentage return?
   d. Must you sell the Twedt El Dee stock to include the capital gains in your return? Explain.

9.2 Mr. Alexander Bell invested $10,400 in 200 shares of First Industries stock a year ago and has received total dividends of $600 during the period. He sold the stock today at $54.25.
   a. What was his total dollar return?
   b. What was his capital gain?
   c. What was his percentage return?
   d. What was the stock's dividend yield?

9.3 Suppose a stock had an initial price of $42 per share. During the year, the stock paid a dividend of $2.40 per share. At the end of the year, the price is $31 per share. What is the percentage return on this stock?

9.4 Lydian Stock currently sells for $52 per share. You intend to buy the stock today and hold it for two years. During those two years, you expect to receive dividends at the year-ends that total $5.50 per share. Finally, you expect to sell the Lydian stock for $54.75 per share. What is your expected holding-period return on Lydian stock?

9.5 Use the information from Ibbotson and Sinquefield provided in the text to compute the nominal and real annual returns from 1926 to 1997 for each of the following items.
   a. Common stock
   b. Long-term corporate bonds
   c. Long-term government bonds
   d. U.S. Treasury bills

9.6 Suppose the current interest rate on U.S. Treasury bills is 6.2 percent. Ibbotson and Sinquefield found the average return on Treasury bills from 1926 through 1997 to be 3.8 percent. The average return on common stock during the same period was 13.0 percent. Given this information, what is the current expected return on common stocks?

9.7 Two stocks, Koke and Pepsee, had the same prices two years ago. During the last two years, Koke's stock price had first increased by 10 percent and then dropped by 10 percent, while Pepsee's stock price had first dropped by 10 percent and then increased by 10 percent. Do these two stocks have the same prices today? Explain.

9.8 S&P 500 index returns of common stocks for the period 1981–1985 are as follows. Calculate the five-year holding-period return.

	1981	1982	1983	1984	1985
S&P 500 index return (%)	−4.91	21.41	22.51	6.27	32.16

9.9 *The Wall Street Journal* announced yesterday that the current rate for one-year Treasury bills is 4.36 percent, while an Ibbotson and Sinquefield study shows that the average return on Treasury bills for the period 1926–1997 is 3.8 percent. During the same period the average return on long-term corporate bonds is 6.1 percent. What is the risk premium of the long-term corporate bonds? What is the expected return on the market of long-term corporate bonds?

Average Returns, Expected Returns, and Variance

9.10 During the past seven years, the returns on a portfolio of long-term corporate bonds were the following:

Year	Long-Term Corporate Bonds
−7	−2.6%
−6	−1.0
−5	43.8
−4	4.7
−3	16.4
−2	30.1
Last	19.9

a. Calculate the average return for long-term corporate bonds over this period.
b. Calculate the variance and the standard deviation of the returns for long-term corporate bonds during this period.

9.11 The following are the returns during the past seven years on a market portfolio of common stocks and on Treasury bills.

Year	Common Stocks	Treasury Bills
−7	32.4%	11.2%
−6	−4.9	14.7
−5	21.4	10.5
−4	22.5	8.8
−3	6.3	9.9
−2	32.2	7.7
Last	18.5	6.2

The realized risk premium is the return on the common stocks less the return on the Treasury bills.
a. Calculate the realized risk premium of common stocks over T-bills in each year.
b. Calculate the average risk premium of common stocks over T-bills during the period.
c. Is it possible that this observed risk premium can be negative? Explain.

9.12 The probability that the economy will experience moderate growth next year is 0.6. The probability of a recession is 0.2, and the probability of a rapid expansion is also 0.2. If the economy falls into a recession, you can expect to receive a return on your portfolio of 5 percent. With moderate growth your return will be 8 percent. If there is a rapid expansion, your portfolio will return 15 percent.
a. What is your expected return?
b. What is the standard deviation of that return?

9.13 The probability that the economy will experience moderate growth next year is 0.4. The probability of a recession is 0.3, and the probability of a rapid expansion is also 0.3. If the economy falls into a recession, you can expect to receive a return on your portfolio of 2 percent. With moderate growth your return will be 5 percent. If there is a rapid expansion, your portfolio will return 10 percent.
a. What is your expected return?
b. What is the standard deviation of that return?

9.14 The returns on the market and on Trebli stock are shown below for the five possible states of the economy that might prevail next year.

Economic Condition	Probability	Market Return	Trebli Return
Rapid expansion	0.12	0.23	0.12
Moderate expansion	0.40	0.18	0.09
No growth	0.25	0.15	0.05
Moderate contraction	0.15	0.09	0.01
Serious contraction	0.08	0.03	−0.02

    a. What is the expected return on the market?
    b. What is the expected return on Trebli stock?

9.15 Four equally likely states of the economy may prevail next year. Below are the returns on the stocks of *P* and *Q* companies under each of the possible states.

State	P Stock	Q Stock
1	0.04	0.05
2	0.06	0.07
3	0.09	0.10
4	0.04	0.14

    a. What is the expected return on each stock?
    b. What is the variance of the returns of each stock?

9.16 The returns on the small-company stocks and on the S&P composite index of common stocks from 1935 through 1939 are tabulated below.

Year	Small-Company Stocks	Market Index of Common Stocks
1935	47.7%	40.2%
1936	33.9	64.8
1937	−35.0	−58.0
1938	31.0	32.8
1939	− 0.5	0.4

    a. Calculate the average return for the small-company stocks and the market index of common stocks.
    b. Calculate the variance and standard deviation of returns for the small-company stocks and the market index of common stocks.

9.17 The following data are the returns for 1980 through 1986 on five types of capital-market instruments: common stocks, small-capitalization stocks, long-term corporate bonds, long-term U.S. government bonds, and U.S. Treasury bills.

Year	Common Stock	Small Stocks	Long-Term Corporate Bonds	Long-Term Government Bonds	U.S. Treasury Bills
1980	0.3242	0.3988	−0.0262	−0.0395	0.1124
1981	−0.0491	0.1388	−0.0096	0.0185	0.1471
1982	0.2141	0.2801	0.4379	0.4035	0.1054
1983	0.2251	0.3967	0.0470	0.0068	0.0880
1984	0.0627	−0.0667	0.1639	0.1543	0.0985
1985	0.3216	0.2466	0.3090	0.3097	0.0772
1986	0.1847	0.0685	0.1985	0.2444	0.0616

Calculate the average return and variance for each type of security.

Return and Risk Statistics

9.18 Ibbotson and Sinquefield have reported the returns on small-company stocks and U.S. Treasury bills for the period 1986–1991 as follows.

Year	Small-Company Stocks	U.S. Treasury Bills
1986	6.85%	6.16%
1987	−9.30	5.47
1988	22.87	6.35
1989	10.18	8.37
1990	−21.56	7.81
1991	44.63	5.60

  a. Calculate the average returns on small-company stocks and U.S. Treasury bills.
  b. Calculate the variances and standard deviations of the returns on small-company stocks and U.S. Treasury bills.
  c. Compare the returns and risks of these two types of securities.

9.19 Suppose International Trading Company's stock returns follow a normal distribution with a mean of 17.5 percent and a standard deviation of 8.5 percent. What is the range of returns in which about 95 percent of International Trading's stock returns are located?

9.20 The returns on the market of common stocks and on Treasury bills are contingent on the economy as follows.

Economic Condition	Probability	Market Return	Treasury Bills
Recession	0.25	−8.2%	3.5%
Normal	0.50	12.3	3.5
Boom	0.25	25.8	3.5

  a. Calculate the expected returns on the market and Treasury bills.
  b. Calculate the expected risk premium.

Appendix 9A THE HISTORICAL MARKET RISK PREMIUM: THE VERY LONG RUN

The data in Chapter 9 indicate that the returns on common stock have historically been much higher than the returns on short-term government securities. This phenomenon has bothered economists, since it is difficult to justify why large numbers of rational investors purchase the lower yielding bills and bonds.

In 1985 Mehra and Prescott published a very influential paper that showed that the historical returns for common stocks are far too high when compared to the rates of return on short-term government securities.[9] They point out that the difference in returns (frequently called the *market risk premium for equity*) implies a very high degree of risk aversion on the part of investors. Since the publication of the Mehra and Prescott research, financial economists have tried to explain the so-called equity risk premium puzzle. The high historical equity risk premium is especially intriguing compared to the very low historical rate of return on Treasury securities. This seems to imply behavior that has not actually hap-

---

[9] Rajnish Mehra and Edward C. Prescott, "The Equity Premium: A Puzzle," *Journal of Monetary Economics* 15 (1985), pp. 145–61.

■ TABLE 9A.1

	1802–1870	1871–1925	1926–1999	Overall 1802–1999
Common Stock	6.8	8.5	13.3	9.7
Treasury bills	5.4	4.1	3.8	4.4
Risk premium	1.4	4.4	9.5	5.3

pened. For example, if people have been very risk-averse and historical borrowing rates have been low, it suggests that persons should have been willing to borrow in periods of economic uncertainty and downturn to avoid the possibility of a reduced standard of living. However, we do not observe increased borrowing during recessions.

The equity risk premium puzzle of Mehra and Prescott has been generally viewed as an unexplained paradox. However, recently, Jeremy Seigel has shown that the historical risk premium may be substantially lower than previously realized (see Table 9A.1). He shows that, while the risk premium averaged 9.5 percent from 1926 to 1999, it averaged only 1.4 percent from 1802 to 1870, and 4.4 percent from 1871 to 1925.[10] It is puzzling that the trend has been rising over the last 200 years. It has been especially high since 1926. However, the key point is that historically the risk premium has been lower than in more recent times and we should be somewhat cautious about assumptions we make concerning the current risk premium.

---

[10]Jeremy J. Seigel, *Stocks for the Long Run,* 2nd ed. (New York City: McGraw-Hill, 1998).

CHAPTER 10

Return and Risk: The Capital-Asset-Pricing Model (CAPM)

····

EXECUTIVE SUMMARY

The previous chapter achieved two purposes. First, we acquainted you with the history of U.S. capital markets. Second, we presented statistics such as expected return, variance, and standard deviation. Our ultimate goal in the next three chapters is to determine the appropriate discount rate for capital budgeting projects. Because the discount rate on a project is a function of its risk, the discussion in the previous chapter on standard deviation is a necessary first step. However, we shall see that standard deviation is not the final word on risk.

Our next step is to investigate the relationship between the risk and the return of individual securities when these securities are part of a large portfolio. This task is taken up in Chapter 10. The actual treatment of the appropriate discount rate for capital budgeting is reserved for Chapter 12.

The crux of the current chapter can be summarized as follows: An individual who holds one security should use expected return as the measure of the security's return. Standard deviation or variance is the proper measure of the security's risk. An individual who holds a diversified portfolio cares about the *contribution* of each security to the expected return and the risk of the portfolio. It turns out that a security's expected return is the appropriate measure of the security's contribution to the expected return on the portfolio. However, neither the security's variance nor the security's standard deviation is an appropriate measure of a security's contribution to the risk of a portfolio. The contribution of a security to the risk of a portfolio is best measured by beta.

10.1 INDIVIDUAL SECURITIES

In the first part of Chapter 10 we will examine the characteristics of individual securities. In particular, we will discuss:

1. *Expected Return.* This is the return that an individual expects a stock to earn over the next period. Of course, because this is only an expectation, the actual return may be either higher or lower. An individual's expectation may simply be the average return per period a security has earned in the past. Alternatively, it may be based on a detailed analysis of a firm's prospects, on some computer-based model, or on special (or inside) information.

2. *Variance and Standard Deviation.* There are many ways to assess the volatility of a security's return. One of the most common is variance, which is a measure of the squared deviations of a security's return from its expected return. Standard deviation is the square root of the variance.

3. *Covariance and Correlation.* Returns on individual securities are related to one another. Covariance is a statistic measuring the interrelationship between two securities. Alternatively,

this relationship can be restated in terms of the correlation between the two securities. Covariance and correlation are building blocks to an understanding of the beta coefficient.

10.2 EXPECTED RETURN, VARIANCE, AND COVARIANCE

Expected Return and Variance

Suppose financial analysts believe that there are four equally likely states of the economy: depression, recession, normal, and boom times. The returns on the Supertech Company are expected to follow the economy closely, while the returns on the Slowpoke Company are not. The return predictions are as follows:

	Supertech Returns R_{At}	Slowpoke Returns R_{Bt}
Depression	-20%	5%
Recession	10	20
Normal	30	-12
Boom	50	9

Variance can be calculated in four steps. An additional step is needed to calculate standard deviation. (The calculations are presented in Table 10.1.) The steps are:

1. Calculate the expected return:

Supertech:

$$\frac{-0.20 + 0.10 + 0.30 + 0.50}{4} = 0.175 = 17.5\% = \overline{R}_A$$

Slowpoke:

$$\frac{0.05 + 0.20 - 0.12 + 0.09}{4} = 0.055 = 5.5\% = \overline{R}_B$$

2. For each company, calculate the deviation of each possible return from the company's expected return given previously. This is presented in the third column of Table 10.1.

3. The deviations we have calculated are indications of the dispersion of returns. However, because some are positive and some are negative, it is difficult to work with them in this form. For example, if we were to simply add up all the deviations for a single company, we would get zero as the sum.

    To make the deviations more meaningful, we multiply each one by itself. Now all the numbers are positive, implying that their sum must be positive as well. The squared deviations are presented in the last column of Table 10.1.

4. For each company, calculate the average squared deviation, which is the variance:[1]

Supertech:

$$\frac{0.140625 + 0.005625 + 0.015625 + 0.105625}{4} = 0.066875$$

---

[1]In this example, the four states give rise to four *possible* outcomes for each stock. Had we used past data, the outcomes would have actually occurred. In that case, statisticians argue that the correct divisor is $N - 1$, where N is the number of observations. Thus the denominator would be 3 $(= (4 - 1))$ in the case of past data, not 4. Note that the example in Section 9.5 involved past data and we used a divisor of $N - 1$. While this difference causes grief to both students and textbook writers, it is a minor point in practice. In the real world, samples are generally so large that using N or $N - 1$ in the denominator has virtually no effect on the calculation of variance.

■ TABLE 10.1   Calculating Variance and Standard Deviation

(1) State of Economy	(2) Rate of Return	(3) Deviation from Expected Return	(4) Squared Value of Deviation
	Supertech*	**(Expected return = 0.175)**	
	R_{At}	$(R_{At} - \bar{R}_A)$	$(R_{At} - \bar{R}_A)^2$
Depression	−0.20	−0.375	0.140625
		(= −0.20 − 0.175)	[= (−0.375)²]
Recession	0.10	−0.075	0.005625
Normal	0.30	0.125	0.015625
Boom	0.50	0.325	0.105625
			0.267500
	Slowpoke†	**(Expected return = 0.055)**	
	R_{Bt}	$(R_{Bt} - \bar{R}_B)$	$(R_{Bt} - \bar{R}_B)^2$
Depression	0.05	−0.005	0.000025
		(= 0.05 − 0.055)	[= (−0.005)²]
Recession	0.20	0.145	0.021025
Normal	−0.12	−0.175	0.030625
Boom	0.09	0.035	0.001225
			0.052900

$$* \bar{R}_A = \frac{-0.20 + 0.10 + 0.30 + 0.50}{4} = 0.175 = 17.5\%$$

$$\text{Var}(R_A) = \sigma_A^2 = \frac{0.2675}{4} = 0.066875$$

$$\text{SD}(R_A) = \sigma_A = \sqrt{0.066875} = 0.2586 = 25.86\%$$

$$† \bar{R}_B = \frac{0.05 + 0.20 - 0.12 + 0.09}{4} = 0.055 = 5.5\%$$

$$\text{Var}(R_B) = \sigma_B^2 = \frac{0.0529}{4} = 0.013225$$

$$\text{SD}(R_B) = \sigma_B = \sqrt{0.013225} = 0.1150 = 11.50\%$$

Slowpoke:

$$\frac{0.000025 + 0.021025 + 0.030625 + 0.001225}{4} = 0.013225$$

Thus, the variance of Supertech is 0.066875, and the variance of Slowpoke is 0.013225.

5. Calculate standard deviation by taking the square root of the variance:

Supertech:

$$\sqrt{0.066875} = 0.2586 = 25.86\%$$

Slowpoke:

$$\sqrt{0.013225} = 0.1150 = 11.50\%$$

Algebraically, the formula for variance can be expressed as

$$\text{Var}(R) = \text{Expected value of } (R - \bar{R})^2$$

where $\bar{R}$ is the security's expected return and R is the actual return.

A look at the four-step calculation for variance makes it clear why it is a measure of the spread of the sample of returns. For each observation, one squares the difference between the actual return and the expected return. One then takes an average of these squared differences. Squaring the differences makes them all positive. If we used the differences between each return and the expected return and then averaged these differences, we would get zero because the returns that were above the mean would cancel the ones below.

However, because the variance is still expressed in squared terms, it is difficult to interpret. Standard deviation has a much simpler interpretation, which was provided in Section 9.5. Standard deviation is simply the square root of the variance. The general formula for the standard deviation is

$$SD(R) = \sqrt{Var(R)}$$

Covariance and Correlation

Variance and standard deviation measure the variability of individual stocks. We now wish to measure the relationship between the return on one stock and the return on another. Enter **covariance** and **correlation.**

Covariance and correlation measure how two random variables are related. We explain these terms by extending the Supertech and Slowpoke example presented earlier in this chapter.

EXAMPLE

We have already determined the expected returns and standard deviations for both Supertech and Slowpoke. (The expected returns are 0.175 and 0.055 for Supertech and Slowpoke, respectively. The standard deviations are 0.2586 and 0.1150, respectively.) In addition, we calculated the deviation of each possible return from the expected return for each firm. Using these data, covariance can be calculated in two steps. An extra step is needed to calculate correlation.

1. For each state of the economy, multiply Supertech's deviation from its expected return and Slowpoke's deviation from its expected return together. For example, Supertech's rate of return in a depression is −0.20, which is −0.375 (−0.20 − 0.175) from its expected return. Slowpoke's rate of return in a depression is 0.05, which is −0.005 (0.05 − 0.055) from its expected return. Multiplying the two deviations together yields 0.001875 [(−0.375) × (−0.005)]. The actual calculations are given in the last column of Table 10.2. This procedure can be written algebraically as

$$(R_{At} - \overline{R}_A) \times (R_{Bt} - \overline{R}_B) \tag{10.1}$$

where R_{At} and R_{Bt} are the returns on Supertech and Slowpoke in state t. $\overline{R}_A$ and $\overline{R}_B$ are the expected returns on the two securities.

2. Calculate the average value of the four states in the last column. This average is the covariance. That is,[2]

$$\sigma_{AB} = Cov(R_A, R_B) = \frac{-0.0195}{4} = -0.004875$$

---

[2]As with variance, we divided by N (4 in this example) because the four states give rise to four *possible* outcomes. However, had we used past data, the correct divisor would be $N − 1$ (3 in this example).

■ TABLE 10.2 Calculating Covariance and Correlation

State of Economy	Rate of Return of Supertech R_{At}	Deviation from Expected Return $(R_{At} - \bar{R}_A)$	Rate of Return of Slowpoke R_{Bt}	Deviation from Expected Return $(R_{Bt} - \bar{R}_B)$	Product of Deviations $(R_{At} - \bar{R}_A) \times (R_{Bt} - \bar{R}_B)$
		(Expected return = 0.175)		(Expected return = 0.055)	
Depression	−0.20	−0.375 (= −0.20 − 0.175)	0.05	−0.005 (= 0.05 − 0.055)	0.001875 (= −0.375 × −0.005)
Recession	0.10	−0.075	0.20	0.145	−0.010875 (= −0.075 × 0.145)
Normal	0.30	0.125	−0.12	−0.175	−0.021875 (= 0.125 × −0.175)
Boom	0.50	0.325	0.09	0.035	0.011375 (= 0.325 × 0.035)
	0.70		0.22		−0.0195

$$\sigma_{AB} = \mathrm{Cov}(R_A, R_B) = \frac{-0.0195}{4} = -0.004875$$

$$\rho_{AB} = \mathrm{Corr}(R_A, R_B) = \frac{\mathrm{Cov}(R_A, R_B)}{SD(R_A) \times SD(R_B)} = \frac{-0.004875}{0.2586 \times 0.1150} = -0.1639$$

Note that we represent the covariance between Supertech and Slowpoke as either $\mathrm{Cov}(R_A, R_B)$ or σ_{AB}. Equation (10.1) illustrates the intuition of covariance. Suppose Supertech's return is generally above its average when Slowpoke's return is above its average, and Supertech's return is generally below its average when Slowpoke's return is below its average. This is indicative of a positive dependency or a positive relationship between the two returns. Note that the term in equation (10.1) will be *positive* in any state where both returns are *above* their averages. In addition, (10.1) will still be *positive* in any state where both terms are *below* their averages. Thus, a positive relationship between the two returns will give rise to a positive value for covariance.

Conversely, suppose Supertech's return is generally above its average when Slowpoke's return is below its average, and Supertech's return is generally below its average when Slowpoke's return is above its average. This is indicative of a negative dependency or a negative relationship between the two returns. Note that the term in equation (10.1) will be *negative* in any state where one return is above its average and the other return is below its average. Thus, a negative relationship between the two returns will give rise to a negative value for covariance.

Finally, suppose there is no relation between the two returns. In this case, knowing whether the return on Supertech is above or below its expected return tells us nothing about the return on Slowpoke. In the covariance formula, then, there will be no tendency for the deviations to be positive or negative together. On average, they will tend to offset each other and cancel out, making the covariance zero.

Of course, even if the two returns are unrelated to each other, the covariance formula will not equal zero exactly in any actual history. This is due to sampling error; randomness alone will make the calculation positive or negative. But for a historical sample that is long enough, if the two returns are not related to each other, we should expect the covariance to come close to zero.

The covariance formula seems to capture what we are looking for. If the two returns are positively related to each other, they will have a positive covariance, and if they are negatively related to each other, the covariance will be negative. Last, and very important, if they are unrelated, the covariance should be zero.

The formula for covariance can be written algebraically as

$$\sigma_{AB} = \text{Cov}(R_A, R_B) = \text{Expected value of } [(R_A - \overline{R}_A) \times (R_B - \overline{R}_B)]$$

where $\overline{R}_A$ and $\overline{R}_B$ are the expected returns for the two securities, and R_A and R_B are the actual returns. The ordering of the two variables is unimportant. That is, the covariance of A with B is equal to the covariance of B with A. This can be stated more formally as $\text{Cov}(R_A, R_B) = \text{Cov}(R_B, R_A)$ or $\sigma_{AB} = \sigma_{BA}$.

The covariance we calculated is -0.004875. A negative number like this implies that the return on one stock is likely to be above its average when the return on the other stock is below its average, and vice versa. However, the size of the number is difficult to interpret. Like the variance figure, the covariance is in squared deviation units. Until we can put it in perspective, we don't know what to make of it.

We solve the problem by computing the correlation:

3. To calculate the correlation, divide the covariance by the standard deviations of both of the two securities. For our example, we have:

$$\rho_{AB} = \text{Corr}(R_A, R_B) = \frac{\text{Cov}(R_A, R_B)}{\sigma_A \times \sigma_B} = \frac{-0.004875}{0.2586 \times 0.1150} = -0.1639 \qquad (10.2)$$

where σ_A and σ_B are the standard deviations of Supertech and Slowpoke, respectively. Note that we represent the correlation between Supertech and Slowpoke either as $\text{Corr}(R_A, R_B)$ or ρ_{AB}. As with covariance, the ordering of the two variables is unimportant. That is, the correlation of A with B is equal to the correlation of B with A. More formally, $\text{Corr}(R_A, R_B) = \text{Corr}(R_B, R_A)$ or $\rho_{AB} = \rho_{BA}$.

Because the standard deviation is always positive, the sign of the correlation between two variables must be the same as that of the covariance between the two variables. If the correlation is positive, we say that the variables are *positively correlated;* if it is negative, we say that they are *negatively correlated;* and if it is zero, we say that they are *uncorrelated.* Furthermore, it can be proved that the correlation is always between $+1$ and -1. This is due to the standardizing procedure of dividing by the two standard deviations.

We can compare the correlation between different *pairs* of securities. For example, it turns out that the correlation between General Motors and Ford is much higher than the correlation between General Motors and IBM. Hence, we can state that the first pair of securities is more interrelated than the second pair.

Figure 10.1 shows the three benchmark cases for two assets, A and B. The figure shows two assets with return correlations of $+1$, -1, and 0. This implies perfect positive correlation, perfect negative correlation, and no correlation, respectively. The graphs in the figure plot the separate returns on the two securities through time.

10.3 The Return and Risk for Portfolios

Suppose that an investor has estimates of the expected returns and standard deviations on individual securities and the correlations between securities. How then does the investor choose the best combination or **portfolio** of securities to hold? Obviously, the investor would like a portfolio with a high expected return and a low standard deviation of return. It is therefore worthwhile to consider:

■ FIGURE 10.1   **Examples of Different Correlation Coefficients—the Graphs in the Figure Plot the Separate Returns on the Two Securities through Time**

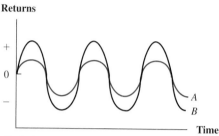

Perfect positive correlation
$Corr(R_A, R_B) = 1$

Both the return on security *A* and the return on security *B* are higher than average at the same time. Both the return on security *A* and the return on security *B* are lower than average at the same time.

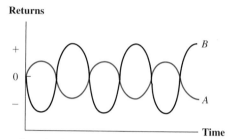

Perfect negative correlation
$Corr(R_A, R_B) = -1$

Security *A* has a higher-than-average return when security *B* has a lower-than-average return, and vice versa.

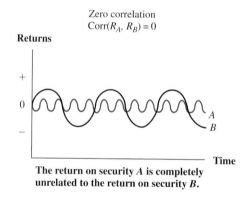

Zero correlation
$Corr(R_A, R_B) = 0$

The return on security *A* is completely unrelated to the return on security *B*.

1. The relationship between the expected return on individual securities and the expected return on a portfolio made up of these securities.
2. The relationship between the standard deviations of individual securities, the correlations between these securities, and the standard deviation of a portfolio made up of these securities.

The Example of Supertech and Slowpoke

In order to analyze the above two relationships, we will use the same example of Supertech and Slowpoke that was presented previously. The relevant calculations are as follows.

The Expected Return on a Portfolio

The formula for expected return on a portfolio is very simple:

The expected return on a portfolio is simply a weighted average of the expected returns on the individual securities.

RELEVANT DATA FROM EXAMPLE OF SUPERTECH AND SLOWPOKE

Item	Symbol	Value
Expected return on Supertech	$\overline{R}_{Super}$	0.175 = 17.5%
Expected return on Slowpoke	$\overline{R}_{Slow}$	0.055 = 5.5%
Variance of Supertech	σ^2_{Super}	0.066875
Variance of Slowpoke	σ^2_{Slow}	0.013225
Standard deviation of Supertech	σ_{Super}	0.2586 = 25.86%
Standard deviation of Slowpoke	σ_{Slow}	0.1150 = 11.50%
Covariance between Supertech and Slowpoke	$\sigma_{Super, Slow}$	−0.004875
Correlation between Supertech and Slowpoke	$\rho_{Super, Slow}$	−0.1639

EXAMPLE

Consider Supertech and Slowpoke. From the preceding box, we find that the expected returns on these two securities are 17.5 percent and 5.5 percent, respectively.

The expected return on a portfolio of these two securities alone can be written as

$$\text{Expected return on portfolio} = X_{Super}(17.5\%) + X_{Slow}(5.5\%) = \overline{R}_P$$

where X_{Super} is the percentage of the portfolio in Supertech and X_{Slow} is the percentage of the portfolio in Slowpoke. If the investor with $100 invests $60 in Supertech and $40 in Slowpoke, the expected return on the portfolio can be written as

$$\text{Expected return on portfolio} = 0.6 \times 17.5\% + 0.4 \times 5.5\% = 12.7\%$$

Algebraically, we can write

$$\text{Expected return on portfolio} = X_A\overline{R}_A + X_B\overline{R}_B = \overline{R}_P \qquad (10.3)$$

where X_A and X_B are the proportions of the total portfolio in the assets A and B, respectively. (Because our investor can only invest in two securities, $X_A + X_B$ must equal 1 or 100 percent.) $\overline{R}_A$ and $\overline{R}_B$ are the expected returns on the two securities.

Now consider two stocks, each with an expected return of 10 percent. The expected return on a portfolio composed of these two stocks must be 10 percent, regardless of the proportions of the two stocks held. This result may seem obvious at this point, but it will become important later. The result implies that you do not reduce or *dissipate* your expected return by investing in a number of securities. Rather, the expected return on your portfolio is simply a weighted average of the expected returns on the individual assets in the portfolio.

Variance and Standard Deviation of a Portfolio

The Variance   The formula for the variance of a portfolio composed of two securities, A and B, is

The Variance of the Portfolio:

$$\text{Var(portfolio)} = X_A^2\,\sigma_A^2 + 2X_AX_B\sigma_{A,B} + X_B^2\,\sigma_B^2$$

Note that there are three terms on the right-hand side of the equation. The first term involves the variance of $A(\sigma_A^2)$, the second term involves the covariance between the two securities $(\sigma_{A,B})$, and the third term involves the variance of $B(\sigma_B^2)$. (As stated earlier in this chapter, $\sigma_{A,B} = \sigma_{B,A}$. That is, the ordering of the variables is not relevant when expressing the covariance between two securities.)

The formula indicates an important point. The variance of a portfolio depends on both the variances of the individual securities and the covariance between the two securities. The variance of a security measures the variability of an individual security's return. Covariance measures the relationship between the two securities. For given variances of the individual securities, a positive relationship or covariance between the two securities increases the variance of the entire portfolio. A negative relationship or covariance between the two securities decreases the variance of the entire portfolio. This important result seems to square with common sense. If one of your securities tends to go up when the other goes down, or vice versa, your two securities are offsetting each other. You are achieving what we call a *hedge* in finance, and the risk of your entire portfolio will be low. However, if both your securities rise and fall together, you are not hedging at all. Hence, the risk of your entire portfolio will be higher.

The variance formula for our two securities, Super and Slow, is

$$\text{Var(portfolio)} = X_{\text{Super}}^2 \sigma_{\text{Super}}^2 + 2X_{\text{Super}}X_{\text{Slow}}\sigma_{\text{Super, Slow}} + X_{\text{Slow}}^2 \sigma_{\text{Slow}}^2 \qquad (10.4)$$

Given our earlier assumption that an individual with \$100 invests \$60 in Supertech and \$40 in Slowpoke, $X_{\text{Super}} = 0.6$ and $X_{\text{Slow}} = 0.4$. Using this assumption and the relevant data from the box above, the variance of the portfolio is

$$0.023851 = 0.36 \times 0.066875 + 2 \times [0.6 \times 0.4 \times (-0.004875)]$$
$$+ 0.16 \times 0.013225 \qquad (10.4')$$

The Matrix Approach   Alternatively, equation (10.4) can be expressed in the following matrix format:

	Supertech	*Slowpoke*
Supertech	$X_{\text{Super}}^2 \sigma_{\text{Super}}^2$ $0.024075 = 0.36 \times 0.066875$	$X_{\text{Super}}X_{\text{Slow}}\sigma_{\text{Super, Slow}}$ $-0.00117 = 0.6 \times 0.4 \times (-0.004875)$
Slowpoke	$X_{\text{Super}}X_{\text{Slow}}\sigma_{\text{Super, Slow}}$ $-0.00117 = 0.6 \times 0.4 \times (-0.004875)$	$X_{\text{Slow}}^2 \sigma_{\text{Slow}}^2$ $0.002116 = 0.16 \times 0.013225$

There are four boxes in the matrix. We can add the terms in the boxes to obtain equation (10.4), the variance of a portfolio composed of the two securities. The term in the upper left-hand corner involves the variance of Supertech. The term in the lower right-hand corner involves the variance of Slowpoke. The other two boxes contain the term involving the covariance. These two boxes are identical, indicating why the covariance term is multiplied by 2 in equation (10.4).

At this point, students often find the box approach to be more confusing than equation (10.4). However, the box approach is easily generalized to more than two securities, a task we perform later in this chapter.

Standard Deviation of a Portfolio   Given (10.4'), we can now determine the standard deviation of the portfolio's return. This is

$$\sigma_P = \text{SD(portfolio)} = \sqrt{\text{Var(portfolio)}} = \sqrt{0.023851} \qquad (10.5)$$
$$= 0.1544 = 15.44\%$$

The interpretation of the standard deviation of the portfolio is the same as the interpretation of the standard deviation of an individual security. The expected return on our portfolio is 12.7 percent. A return of -2.74 percent ($12.7\% - 15.44\%$) is one standard deviation below the mean and a return of 28.14 percent ($12.7\% + 15.44\%$) is one standard deviation above the mean. If the return on the portfolio is normally distributed, a return between -2.74 percent and $+28.14$ percent occurs about 68 percent of the time.[3]

The Diversification Effect   It is instructive to compare the standard deviation of the portfolio with the standard deviation of the individual securities. The weighted average of the standard deviations of the individual securities is

$$\text{Weighted average of standard deviations} = X_{\text{Super}}\sigma_{\text{Super}} + X_{\text{Slow}}\sigma_{\text{Slow}} \tag{10.6}$$
$$0.2012 = 0.6 \times 0.2586 + 0.4 \times 0.115$$

One of the most important results in this chapter concerns the difference between equations (10.5) and (10.6). In our example, the standard deviation of the portfolio is *less* than a weighted average of the standard deviations of the individual securities.

We pointed out earlier that the expected return on the portfolio is a weighted average of the expected returns on the individual securities. Thus, we get a different type of result for the standard deviation of a portfolio than we do for the expected return on a portfolio.

It is generally argued that our result for the standard deviation of a portfolio is due to diversification. For example, Supertech and Slowpoke are slightly negatively correlated ($\rho = -0.1639$). Supertech's return is likely to be a little below average if Slowpoke's return is above average. Similarly, Supertech's return is likely to be a little above average if Slowpoke's return is below average. Thus, the standard deviation of a portfolio composed of the two securities is less than a weighted average of the standard deviations of the two securities.

The above example has negative correlation. Clearly, there will be less benefit from diversification if the two securities exhibit positive correlation. How high must the positive correlation be before all diversification benefits vanish?

To answer this question, let us rewrite (10.4) in terms of correlation rather than covariance. The covariance can be rewritten as[4]

$$\sigma_{\text{Super, Slow}} = \rho_{\text{Super, Slow}}\sigma_{\text{Super}}\sigma_{\text{Slow}} \tag{10.7}$$

The formula states that the covariance between any two securities is simply the correlation between the two securities multiplied by the standard deviations of each. In other words, covariance incorporates both (1) the correlation between the two assets and (2) the variability of each of the two securities as measured by standard deviation.

From our calculations earlier in this chapter we know that the correlation between the two securities is -0.1639. Given the variances used in equation (10.4'), the standard deviations are 0.2586 and 0.115 for Supertech and Slowpoke, respectively. Thus, the variance of a portfolio can be expressed as

Variance of the portfolio's return

$$= X_{\text{Super}}^2\,\sigma_{\text{Super}}^2 + 2X_{\text{Super}}X_{\text{Slow}}\rho_{\text{Super, Slow}}\sigma_{\text{Super}}\sigma_{\text{Slow}} + X_{\text{Slow}}^2\,\sigma_{\text{Slow}}^2 \tag{10.8}$$
$$0.023851 = 0.36 \times 0.066875 + 2 \times 0.6 \times 0.4 \times (-0.1639)$$
$$\times\, 0.2586 \times 0.115 + 0.16 \times 0.013225$$

---

[3]There are only four equally probable returns for Supertech and Slowpoke, so neither security possesses a normal distribution. Thus, probabilities would be slightly different in our example.

[4]As with covariance, the ordering of the two securities is not relevant when expressing the correlation between the two securities. That is, $\rho_{\text{Super,Slow}} = \rho_{\text{Slow,Super}}$.

The middle term on the right-hand side is now written in terms of correlation, ρ, not covariance.

Suppose $\rho_{Super, Slow} = 1$, the highest possible value for correlation. Assume all the other parameters in the example are the same. The variance of the portfolio is

$$\begin{array}{l}\text{Variance of the}\\\text{portfolio's return}\end{array} = 0.040466 = 0.36 \times 0.066875 + 2 \times (0.6 \times 0.4 \times 1 \times 0.2586 \\ \times 0.115) + 0.16 \times 0.013225$$

The standard deviation is

$$\text{Standard variation of portfolio's return} = \sqrt{0.040466} = 0.2012 = 20.12\% \quad (10.9)$$

Note that equations (10.9) and (10.6) are equal. That is, the standard deviation of a portfolio's return is equal to the weighted average of the standard deviations of the individual returns when $\rho = 1$. Inspection of (10.8) indicates that the variance and hence the standard deviation of the portfolio must fall as the correlation drops below 1. This leads to:

> As long as $\rho < 1$, the standard deviation of a portfolio of two securities is *less* than the weighted average of the standard deviations of the individual securities.

In other words, the diversification effect applies as long as there is less than perfect correlation (as long as $\rho < 1$). Thus, our Supertech-Slowpoke example is a case of overkill. We illustrated diversification by an example with negative correlation. We could have illustrated diversification by an example with positive correlation—as long as it was not *perfect* positive correlation.

An Extension to Many Assets   The preceding insight can be extended to the case of many assets. That is, as long as correlations between pairs of securities are less than 1, the standard deviation of a portfolio of many assets is less than the weighted average of the standard deviations of the individual securities.

Now consider Table 10.3, which shows the standard deviation of the Standard & Poor's 500 Index and the standard deviations of some of the individual securities listed in the index over a recent 10-year period. Note that all of the individual securities in the table have higher standard deviations than that of the index. In general, the standard deviations of most of the individual securities in an index will be above the standard deviation of the index itself, though a few of the securities could have lower standard deviations than that of the index.

CONCEPT QUESTIONS

- What are the formulas for the expected return, variance, and standard deviation of a portfolio of two assets?
- What is the diversification effect?
- What are the highest and lowest possible values for the correlation coefficient?

10.4 THE EFFICIENT SET FOR TWO ASSETS

Our results on expected returns and standard deviations are graphed in Figure 10.2. In the figure, there is a dot labeled Slowpoke and a dot labeled Supertech. Each dot represents both the expected return and the standard deviation for an individual security. As can be seen, Supertech has both a higher expected return and a higher standard deviation.

■ TABLE 10.3   **Standard Deviations for Standard & Poor's 500 Index and for Selected Stocks in the Index**

Asset	Standard Deviation
S&P 500 Index	13.33%
Bell Atlantic	28.60
Ford Motor Co.	31.39
Walt Disney Co.	41.05
General Electric	29.54
IBM	32.18
McDonald's Corp.	32.38
Sears, Roebuck & Co.	29.76
Toys "R" Us Inc.	32.23
Amazon.com	59.21

As long as the correlations between pairs of securities are less than 1, the standard deviation of an index is less than the weighted average of the standard deviations of the individual securities within the index.

■ FIGURE 10.2   **Expected Returns and Standard Deviations for Supertech, Slowpoke, and a Portfolio Composed of 60 Percent in Supertech and 40 Percent in Slowpoke**

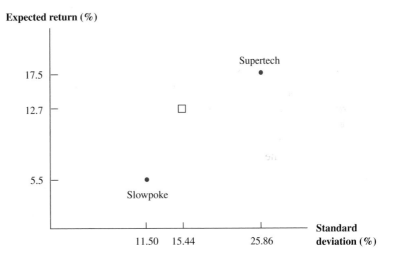

The box or "☐" in the graph represents a portfolio with 60 percent invested in Supertech and 40 percent invested in Slowpoke. You will recall that we have previously calculated both the expected return and the standard deviation for this portfolio.

The choice of 60 percent in Supertech and 40 percent in Slowpoke is just one of an infinite number of portfolios that can be created. The set of portfolios is sketched by the curved line in Figure 10.3.

■ FIGURE 10.3   **Set of Portfolios Composed of Holdings in Supertech and Slowpoke (correlation between the two securities is −0.1639)**

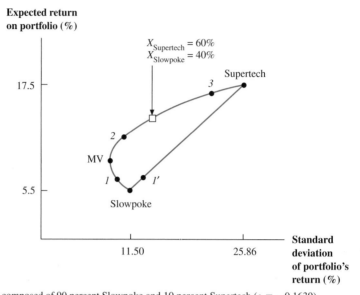

Portfolio *1* is composed of 90 percent Slowpoke and 10 percent Supertech ($\rho = -0.1639$).
Portfolio *2* is composed of 50 percent Slowpoke and 50 percent Supertech ($\rho = -0.1639$).
Portfolio *3* is composed of 10 percent Slowpoke and 90 percent Supertech ($\rho = -0.1639$).
Portfolio *1′* is composed of 90 percent Slowpoke and 10 percent Supertech ($\rho = 1$).
Point MV denotes the mimimum variance portfolio. This is the portfolio with the lowest possible variance. By definition, the same portfolio must also have the lowest possible standard deviation.

Consider portfolio *1*. This is a portfolio composed of 90 percent Slowpoke and 10 percent Supertech. Because it is weighted so heavily toward Slowpoke, it appears close to the Slowpoke point on the graph. Portfolio *2* is higher on the curve because it is composed of 50 percent Slowpoke and 50 percent Supertech. Portfolio *3* is close to the Supertech point on the graph because it is composed of 90 percent Supertech and 10 percent Slowpoke.

There are a few important points concerning this graph.

1. We argued that the diversification effect occurs whenever the correlation between the two securities is below 1. The correlation between Supertech and Slowpoke is −0.1639. The diversification effect can be illustrated by comparison with the straight line between the Supertech point and the Slowpoke point. The straight line represents points that would have been generated had the correlation coefficient between the two securities been 1. The diversification effect is illustrated in the figure since the curved line is always to the left of the straight line. Consider point *1′*. This represents a portfolio composed of 90 percent in Slowpoke and 10 percent in Supertech *if* the correlation between the two were exactly 1. We argue that there is no diversification effect if $\rho = 1$. However, the diversification effect applies to the curved line, because point *1* has the same expected return as point *1′* but has a lower standard deviation. (Points *2′* and *3′* are omitted to reduce the clutter of Figure 10.3.)

Though the straight line and the curved line are both represented in Figure 10.3, they do not simultaneously exist in the same world. *Either* $\rho = -0.1639$ and the curve exists *or* $\rho = 1$ and the straight line exists. In other words, though an investor can choose between different points on the curve if $\rho = -0.1639$, she cannot choose between points on the curve and points on the straight line.

2. The point MV represents the minimum variance portfolio. This is the portfolio with the lowest possible variance. By definition, this portfolio must also have the lowest possible standard deviation. (The term *minimum variance portfolio* is standard in the literature, and we will use that term. Perhaps minimum standard deviation would actually be better, because standard deviation, not variance, is measured on the horizontal axis of Figure 10.3.)

3. An individual contemplating an investment in a portfolio of Slowpoke and Supertech faces an **opportunity set** or **feasible set** represented by the curved line in Figure 10.3. That is, he can achieve any point on the curve by selecting the appropriate mix between the two securities. He cannot achieve any point above the curve because he cannot increase the return on the individual securities, decrease the standard deviations of the securities, or decrease the correlation between the two securities. Neither can he achieve points below the curve because he cannot lower the returns on the individual securities, increase the standard deviations of the securities, or increase the correlation. (Of course, he would not want to achieve points below the curve, even if he were able to do so.)

Were he relatively tolerant of risk, he might choose portfolio *3*. (In fact, he could even choose the end point by investing all his money in Supertech.) An investor with less tolerance for risk might choose portfolio *2*. An investor wanting as little risk as possible would choose MV, the portfolio with minimum variance or minimum standard deviation.

4. Note that the curve is backward bending between the Slowpoke point and MV. This indicates that, for a portion of the feasible set, standard deviation actually decreases as one increases expected return. Students frequently ask, "How can an increase in the proportion of the risky security, Supertech, lead to a reduction in the risk of the portfolio?"

This surprising finding is due to the diversification effect. The returns on the two securities are negatively correlated with each other. One security tends to go up when the other goes down and vice versa. Thus, an addition of a small amount of Supertech acts as a hedge to a portfolio composed only of Slowpoke. The risk of the portfolio is reduced, implying backward bending. Actually, backward bending always occurs if $\rho \leq 0$. It may or may not occur when $\rho > 0$. Of course, the curve bends backward only for a portion of its length. As one continues to increase the percentage of Supertech in the portfolio, the high standard deviation of this security eventually causes the standard deviation of the entire portfolio to rise.

5. No investor would want to hold a portfolio with an expected return below that of the minimum variance portfolio. For example, no investor would choose portfolio *1*. This portfolio has less expected return but more standard deviation than the minimum variance portfolio has. We say that portfolios such as portfolio *1* are *dominated* by the minimum variance portfolio. Though the entire curve from Slowpoke to Supertech is called the *feasible set,* investors only consider the curve from MV to Supertech. Hence, the curve from MV to Supertech is called the **efficient set** or the **efficient frontier.**

Figure 10.3 represents the opportunity set where $\rho = -0.1639$. It is worthwhile to examine Figure 10.4, which shows different curves for different correlations. As can be seen, the lower the correlation, the more bend there is in the curve. This indicates that the diversification effect rises as ρ declines. The greatest bend occurs in the limiting case where $\rho = -1$. This is perfect negative correlation. While this extreme case where $\rho = -1$ seems to fascinate students, it has little practical importance. Most pairs of securities exhibit positive correlation. Strong negative correlation, let alone perfect negative correlation, are unlikely occurrences indeed.[5]

---

[5]A major exception occurs with derivative securities. For example, the correlation between a stock and a put on the stock is generally strongly negative. Puts will be treated later in the text.

■ FIGURE 10.4   **Opportunity Sets Composed of Holdings in Supertech and Slowpoke**

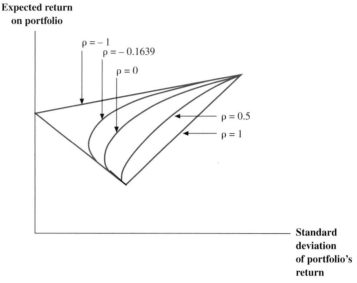

Each curve represents a different correlation. The lower the correlation, the more bend in the curve.

Note that there is only one correlation between a pair of securities. We stated earlier that the correlation between Slowpoke and Supertech is −0.1639. Thus, the curve in Figure 10.4 representing this correlation is the correct one, and the other curves should be viewed as merely hypothetical.

The graphs we examined are not mere intellectual curiosities. Rather, efficient sets can easily be calculated in the real world. As mentioned earlier, data on returns, standard deviations, and correlations are generally taken from past observations, though subjective notions can be used to determine the values of these parameters as well. Once the parameters have been determined, any one of a whole host of software packages can be purchased to generate an efficient set. However, the choice of the preferred portfolio within the efficient set is up to you. As with other important decisions like what job to choose, what house or car to buy, and how much time to allocate to this course, there is no computer program to choose the preferred portfolio.

An efficient set can be generated where the two individual assets are portfolios themselves. For example, the two assets in Figure 10.5 are a diversified portfolio of American stocks and a diversified portfolio of foreign stocks. Expected returns, standard deviations, and the correlation coefficient were calculated over the recent past. No subjectivity entered the analysis. The U.S. stock portfolio with a standard deviation of about 0.173 is less risky than the foreign stock portfolio, which has a standard deviation of about 0.222. However, combining a small percentage of the foreign stock portfolio with the U.S. portfolio actually reduces risk, as can be seen by the backward-bending nature of the curve. In other words, the diversification benefits from combining two different portfolios more than offset the introduction of a riskier set of stocks into one's holdings. The minimum variance portfolio occurs with about 80 percent of one's funds in American stocks and about 20 percent in foreign stocks. Addition of foreign securities beyond this point increases the risk of one's entire portfolio.

■ FIGURE 10.5   **Return/Risk Trade-off for World Stocks: Portfolio of U.S. and Foreign Stocks**

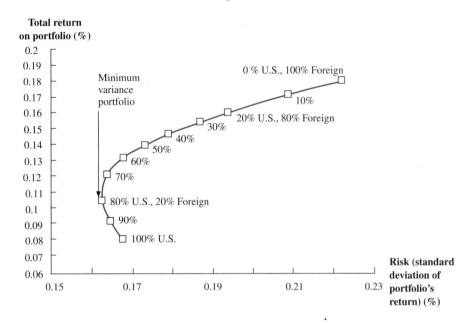

The backward-bending curve in Figure 10.5 is important information that has not bypassed American money managers. In recent years, pension-fund and mutual-fund managers in the United States have sought out investment opportunities overseas. Another point worth pondering concerns the potential pitfalls of using only past data to estimate future returns. The stock markets of many foreign countries have had phenomenal growth in the past 25 years. Thus, a graph like Figure 10.5 makes a large investment in these foreign markets seem attractive. However, because abnormally high returns cannot be sustained forever, some subjectivity must be used when forecasting future expected returns.

CONCEPT QUESTION

- What is the relationship between the shape of the efficient set for two assets and the correlation between the two assets?

10.5 THE EFFICIENT SET FOR MANY SECURITIES

The previous discussion concerned two securities. We found that a simple curve sketched out all the possible portfolios. Because investors generally hold more than two securities, we should look at the same graph when more than two securities are held. The shaded area in Figure 10.6 represents the opportunity set or feasible set when many securities are considered. The shaded area represents all the possible combinations of expected return and standard deviation for a portfolio. For example, in a universe of 100 securities, point 1 might represent a portfolio of, say, 40 securities. Point 2 might represent a portfolio of 80 securities. Point 3 might represent a different set of 80 securities, or the same 80 securities held in different proportions, or something else. Obviously, the combinations are virtually endless. However, note

■ FIGURE 10.6   **The Feasible Set of Portfolios Constructed from Many Securities**

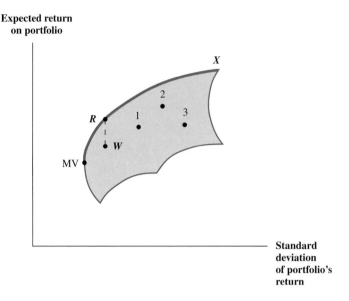

that all possible combinations fit into a confined region. No security or combination of securities can fall outside of the shaded region. That is, no one can choose a portfolio with an expected return above that given by the shaded region. Furthermore, no one can choose a portfolio with a standard deviation below that given in the shady area. Perhaps more surprisingly, no one can choose an expected return below that given in the curve. In other words, the capital markets actually prevent a self-destructive person from taking on a guaranteed loss.[6]

So far, Figure 10.6 is different from the earlier graphs. When only two securities are involved, all the combinations lie on a single curve. Conversely, with many securities the combinations cover an entire area. However, notice that an individual will want to be somewhere on the upper edge between MV and X. The upper edge, which we indicate in Figure 10.6 by a thick curve, is called the *efficient set.* Any point below the efficient set would receive less expected return and the same standard deviation as a point on the efficient set. For example, consider R on the efficient set and W directly below it. If W contains the risk you desire, you should choose R instead in order to receive a higher expected return.

In the final analysis, Figure 10.6 is quite similar to Figure 10.3. The efficient set in Figure 10.3 runs from MV to Supertech. It contains various combinations of the securities Supertech and Slowpoke. The efficient set in Figure 10.6 runs from MV to X. It contains various combinations of many securities. The fact that a whole shaded area appears in Figure 10.6 but not in Figure 10.3 is just not an important difference; no investor would choose any point below the efficient set in Figure 10.6 anyway.

We mentioned before that an efficient set for two securities can be traced out easily in the real world. The task becomes more difficult when additional securities are included because the number of observations grows. For example, using subjective analysis to estimate expected returns and standard deviations for, say, 100 or 500 securities may very well become overwhelming, and the difficulties with correlations may be greater still. There are almost 5,000 correlations between pairs of securities from a universe of 100 securities.

---

[6]Of course, someone dead set on parting with his money can do so. For example, he can trade frequently without purpose, so that commissions more than offset the positive expected returns on the portfolio.

■ TABLE 10.4 **Matrix Used to Calculate the Variance of a Portfolio**

Stock	1	2	3	...	N
1	$X_1^2\sigma_1^2$	$X_1X_2\mathrm{Cov}(R_1,R_2)$	$X_1X_3\mathrm{Cov}(R_1,R_3)$		$X_1X_N\mathrm{Cov}(R_1,R_N)$
2	$X_2X_1\mathrm{Cov}(R_2,R_1)$	$X_2^2\sigma_2^2$	$X_2X_3\mathrm{Cov}(R_2,R_3)$		$X_2X_N\mathrm{Cov}(R_2,R_N)$
3	$X_3X_1\mathrm{Cov}(R_3,R_1)$	$X_3X_2\mathrm{Cov}(R_3,R_2)$	$X_3^2\sigma_3^2$		$X_3X_N\mathrm{Cov}(R_3,R_N)$
.					
.					
.					
N	$X_NX_1\mathrm{Cov}(R_N,R_1)$	$X_NX_2\mathrm{Cov}(R_N,R_2)$	$X_NX_3\mathrm{Cov}(R_N,R_3)$		$X_N^2\sigma_N^2$

The variance of the portfolio is the sum of the terms in all the boxes.
σ_i is the standard deviation of stock *i*.
$\mathrm{Cov}(R_i, R_j)$ is the covariance between stock *i* and stock *j*.
Terms involving the standard deviation of a single security appear on the diagonal. Terms involving covariance between two securities appear off the diagonal.

Though much of the mathematics of efficient-set computation had been derived in the 1950s,[7] the high cost of computer time restricted application of the principles. In recent years, the cost has been drastically reduced. A number of software packages allow the calculation of an efficient set for portfolios of moderate size. By all accounts these packages sell quite briskly, so that our discussion above would appear to be important in practice.

Variance and Standard Deviation in a Portfolio of Many Assets

We earlier calculated the formulas for variance and standard deviation in the two-asset case. Because we considered a portfolio of many assets in Figure 10.6, it is worthwhile to calculate the formulas for variance and standard deviation in the many-asset case. The formula for the variance of a portfolio of many assets can be viewed as an extension of the formula for the variance of two assets.

To develop the formula, we employ the same type of matrix that we used in the two-asset case. This matrix is displayed in Table 10.4. Assuming that there are N assets, we write the numbers 1 through N on the horizontal axis and 1 through N on the vertical axis. This creates a matrix of $N \times N = N^2$ boxes. The variance of the portfolio is the sum of the terms in all the boxes.

Consider, for example, the box in the second row and the third column. The term in the box is $X_2X_3 \mathrm{Cov}(R_2, R_3)$. X_2 and X_3 are the percentages of the entire portfolio that are invested in the second asset and the third asset, respectively. For example, if an individual with a portfolio of $1,000 invests $100 in the second asset, $X_2 = 10\%$ ($100/$1,000). $\mathrm{Cov}(R_3, R_2)$ is the covariance between the returns on the third asset and the returns on the second asset. Next, note the box in the third row and the second column. The term in this box is $X_3X_2 \mathrm{Cov}(R_3, R_2)$. Because $\mathrm{Cov}(R_3, R_2) = \mathrm{Cov}(R_2, R_3)$, both boxes have the same value. The second security and the third security make up one pair of stocks. In fact, every pair of stocks appears twice in the table, once in the lower left-hand side and once in the upper right-hand side.

---

[7]The classic treatise is Harry Markowitz, *Portfolio Selection* (New York: John Wiley & Sons, 1959). Markowitz won the Nobel Prize in economics in 1990 for his work on modern portfolio theory.

■ TABLE 10.5   Number of Variance and Covariance Terms as a Function of the Number of Stocks in the Portfolio

Number of Stocks in Portfolio	Total Number of Terms	Number of Variance Terms (number of terms on diagonal)	Number of Covariance Terms (number of terms off diagonal)
1	1	1	0
2	4	2	2
3	9	3	6
10	100	10	90
100	10,000	100	9,900
.	.	.	.
.	.	.	.
.	.	.	.
N	N^2	N	$N^2 - N$

In a large portfolio, the number of terms involving covariance between two securities is much greater than the number of terms involving variance of a single security.

Now consider boxes on the diagonal. For example, the term in the first box on the diagonal is $X_1^2 \sigma_1^2$. Here, σ_1^2 is the variance of the return on the first security.

Thus, the diagonal terms in the matrix contain the variances of the different stocks. The off-diagonal terms contain the covariances. Table 10.5 relates the numbers of diagonal and off-diagonal elements to the size of the matrix. The number of diagonal terms (number of variance terms) is always the same as the number of stocks in the portfolio. The number of off-diagonal terms (number of covariance terms) rises much faster than the number of diagonal terms. For example, a portfolio of 100 stocks has 9,900 covariance terms. Since the variance of a portfolio's returns is the sum of all the boxes, we have:

The variance of the return on a portfolio with many securities is more dependent on the covariances between the individual securities than on the variances of the individual securities.

CONCEPT QUESTIONS

- What is the formula for the variance of a portfolio for many assets?
- How can the formula be expressed in terms of a box or matrix?

10.6 DIVERSIFICATION: AN EXAMPLE

The preceding point can be illustrated by altering the matrix in Table 10.4 slightly. Suppose that we make the following three assumptions:

1. All securities possess the same variance, which we write as $\overline{\text{var}}$. In other words, $\sigma_i^2 = \overline{\text{var}}$ for every security.
2. All covariances in Table 10.4 are the same. We represent this uniform covariance as $\overline{\text{cov}}$. In other words, $\text{Cov}(R_i, R_j) = \overline{\text{cov}}$ for every pair of securities. It can easily be shown that $\overline{\text{var}} > \overline{\text{cov}}$.

■ TABLE 10.6 **Matrix Used to Calculate the Variance of a Portfolio When (a) All Securities Possess the Same Variance, Which We Represent as $\overline{var}$; (b) All Pairs of Securities Possess the Same Covariance, Which We Represent as $\overline{cov}$; (c) All Securities Are Held in the Same Proportion, Which Is 1/N**

Stock	1	2	3	...	N
1	$(1/N^2)\overline{var}$	$(1/N^2)\overline{cov}$	$(1/N^2)\overline{cov}$		$(1/N^2)\overline{cov}$
2	$(1/N^2)\overline{cov}$	$(1/N^2)\overline{var}$	$(1/N^2)\overline{cov}$		$(1/N^2)\overline{cov}$
3	$(1/N^2)\overline{cov}$	$(1/N^2)\overline{cov}$	$(1/N^2)\overline{var}$		$(1/N^2)\overline{cov}$
.					
.					
.					
N	$(1/N^2)\overline{cov}$	$(1/N^2)\overline{cov}$	$(1/N^2)\overline{cov}$		$(1/N^2)\overline{var}$

3. All securities are equally weighted in the portfolio. Because there are N assets, the weight of each asset in the portfolio is $1/N$. In other words, $X_i = 1/N$ for each security i.

Table 10.6 is the matrix of variances and covariances under these three simplifying assumptions. Note that all of the diagonal terms are identical. Similarly, all of the off-diagonal terms are identical. As with Table 10.4, the variance of the portfolio is the sum of the terms in the boxes in Table 10.6. We know that there are N diagonal terms involving variance. Similarly, there are $N \times (N - 1)$ off-diagonal terms involving covariance. Summing across all the boxes in Table 10.6 we can express the variances of the portfolio as

$$\text{Variance of portfolio} = \underset{\substack{\text{Number of}\\\text{diagonal}\\\text{terms}}}{N} \times \underset{\substack{\text{Each}\\\text{diagonal}\\\text{term}}}{\left(\frac{1}{N^2}\right)\overline{var}} + \underset{\substack{\text{Number of}\\\text{off-diagonal}\\\text{terms}}}{N(N-1)} \times \underset{\substack{\text{Each}\\\text{off-diagonal}\\\text{term}}}{\left(\frac{1}{N^2}\right)\overline{cov}} \quad (10.10)$$

$$= \left(\frac{1}{N}\right)\overline{var} + \left(\frac{N^2 - N}{N^2}\right)\overline{cov}$$

$$= \left(\frac{1}{N}\right)\overline{var} + \left(1 - \frac{1}{N}\right)\overline{cov}$$

Equation (10.10) expresses the variance of our special portfolio as a weighted sum of the average security variance and the average covariance.[8]

---

[8]Equation (10.10) is actually a weighted *average* of the variance and covariance terms because the weights, $1/N$ and $1 - 1/N$, sum to 1.

Now, let's increase the number of securities in the portfolio without limit. The variance of the portfolio becomes

$$\text{Variance of portfolio (when } N \to \infty) = \overline{\text{cov}} \qquad (10.11)$$

This occurs because (1) the weight on the variance term, $1/N$, goes to 0 as N goes to infinity, and (2) the weight on the covariance term, $1 - 1/N$, goes to 1 as N goes to infinity.

Formula (10.11) provides an interesting and important result. In our special portfolio, the variances of the individual securities completely vanish as the number of securities becomes large. However, the covariance terms remain. In fact, the variance of the portfolio becomes the average covariance, $\overline{\text{cov}}$. One often hears that one should diversify. In other words, you should not put all your eggs in one basket. The effect of diversification on the risk of a portfolio can be illustrated in this example. The variances of the individual securities are diversified away, but the covariance terms cannot be diversified away.

The fact that part, but not all, of one's risk can be diversified away should be explored. Consider Mr. Smith, who brings $1,000 to the roulette table at a casino. It would be very risky if he put all his money on one spin of the wheel. For example, imagine that he put the full $1,000 on red at the table. If the wheel showed red, he would get $2,000, but if the wheel showed black, he would lose everything. Suppose, instead, he divided his money over 1,000 different spins by betting $1 at a time on red. Probability theory tells us that he could count on winning about 50 percent of the time. This means that he could count on pretty nearly getting all his original $1,000 back.[9] In other words, risk is essentially eliminated with 1,000 different spins.

Now, let's contrast this with our stock market example, which we illustrate in Figure 10.7. The variance of the portfolio with only one security is, of course, $\overline{\text{var}}$ because the variance of a portfolio with one security is the variance of the security. The variance of the portfolio drops as more securities are added, which is evidence of the diversification effect. However, unlike Mr. Smith's roulette example, the portfolio's variance can never drop to zero. Rather it reaches a floor of $\overline{\text{cov}}$, which is the covariance of each pair of securities.[10]

Because the variance of the portfolio asymptotically approaches $\overline{\text{cov}}$, each additional security continues to reduce risk. Thus, if there were neither commissions nor other transactions costs, it could be argued that one can never achieve too much diversification. However, there is a cost to diversification in the real world. Commissions per dollar invested fall as one makes larger purchases in a single stock. Unfortunately, one must buy fewer shares of each security when buying more and more different securities. Comparing the costs and benefits of diversification, Meir Statman argues that a portfolio of about 30 stocks is needed to achieve optimal diversification.[11]

We mentioned earlier that $\overline{\text{var}}$ must be greater than $\overline{\text{cov}}$. Thus, the variance of a security's return can be broken down in the following way:

$$
\begin{array}{ccc}
\text{Total risk of} & & \text{Unsystematic or} \\
\text{individual security} & = \text{Portfolio risk} \;+\; & \text{diversifiable risk} \\
(\overline{\text{var}}) & (\overline{\text{cov}}) & (\overline{\text{var}} - \overline{\text{cov}})
\end{array}
$$

Total risk, which is $\overline{\text{var}}$ in our example, is the risk that one bears by holding onto one security only. *Portfolio risk* is the risk that one still bears after achieving full diversification,

---

[9]This example ignores the casino's cut.

[10]Though it is harder to show, this risk reduction effect also applies to the general case where variances and covariances are *not* equal.

[11]Meir Statman, "How Many Stocks Make a Diversified Portfolio?" *Journal of Financial and Quantitative Analysis* (September 1987).

■ FIGURE 10.7   **Relationship between the Variance of a Portfolio's Return and the Number of Securities in the Portfolio***

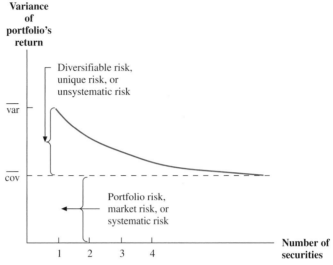

*This graph assumes
    a. All securities have constant variance, var.
    b. All securities have constant covariance, cov.
    c. All securities are equally weighted in portfolio.
The variance of a portfolio drops as more securities are added to the portfolio. However, it does not drop to zero. Rather, $\overline{\text{cov}}$ serves as the floor.

which is $\overline{\text{cov}}$ in our example. Portfolio risk is often called **systematic** or **market risk** as well. **Diversifiable, unique,** or **unsystematic risk** is that risk that can be diversified away in a large portfolio, which must be $(\overline{\text{var}} - \overline{\text{cov}})$ by definition.

To an individual who selects a diversified portfolio, the total risk of an individual security is not important. When considering adding a security to a diversified portfolio, the individual cares about only that portion of the risk of a security that cannot be diversified away. This risk can alternatively be viewed as the *contribution* of a security to the risk of an entire portfolio. We will talk later about the case where securities make different contributions to the risk of the entire portfolio.

Risk and the Sensible Investor

Having gone to all this trouble to show that unsystematic risk disappears in a well-diversified portfolio, how do we know that investors even want such portfolios? Suppose they like risk and don't want it to disappear?

We must admit that, theoretically at least, this is possible, but we will argue that it does not describe what we think of as the typical investor. Our typical investor is **risk averse.** Risk-averse behavior can be defined in many ways, but we prefer the following example: A fair gamble is one with zero expected return; a risk-averse investor would prefer to avoid fair gambles.

Why do investors choose well-diversified portfolios? Our answer is that they are risk averse, and risk-averse people avoid unnecessary risk, such as the unsystematic risk on a stock. If you do not think this is much of an answer, consider whether you would take on such a risk. For example, suppose you had worked all summer and had saved $5,000, which you intended to use for your college expenses. Now, suppose someone came up to you and offered to flip a coin for the money: heads, you would double your money, and tails, you would lose it all.

Would you take such a bet? Perhaps you would, but most people would not. Leaving aside any moral question that might surround gambling and recognizing that some people would take such a bet, it's our view that the average investor would not.

To induce the typical risk-averse investor to take a fair gamble, you must sweeten the pot. For example, you might need to raise the odds of winning from 50–50 to 70–30 or higher. The risk-averse investor can be induced to take fair gambles only if they are sweetened so that they become unfair to the investor's advantage.

CONCEPT QUESTIONS

?

- What are the two components of the total risk of a security?
- Why doesn't diversification eliminate all risk?

10.7 RISKLESS BORROWING AND LENDING

Figure 10.6 assumes that all the securities on the efficient set are risky. Alternatively, an investor could combine a risky investment with an investment in a riskless or *risk-free* security, such as an investment in United States Treasury bills. This is illustrated in the following example.

EXAMPLE

Ms. Bagwell is considering investing in the common stock of Merville Enterprises. In addition, Ms. Bagwell will either borrow or lend at the risk-free rate. The relevant parameters are

	Common Stock of Merville	Risk-Free Asset
Expected return	14%	10%
Standard deviation	0.20	0

Suppose Ms. Bagwell chooses to invest a total of $1,000, $350 of which is to be invested in Merville Enterprises and $650 placed in the risk-free asset. The expected return on her total investment is simply a weighted average of the two returns:

$$\text{Expected return on portfolio composed of one riskless and one risky asset} = 0.114 = (0.35 \times 0.14) + (0.65 \times 0.10) \quad (10.12)$$

Because the expected return on the portfolio is a weighted average of the expected return on the risky asset (Merville Enterprises) and the risk-free return, the calculation is analogous to the way we treated two risky assets. In other words, equation (10.3) applies here.

Using equation (10.4), the formula for the variance of the portfolio can be written as

$$X_{\text{Merville}}^2 \, \sigma_{\text{Merville}}^2 \;+\; 2X_{\text{Merville}}X_{\text{Risk-free}}\sigma_{\text{Merville, Risk-free}} \;+\; X_{\text{Risk-free}}^2 \, \sigma_{\text{Risk-free}}^2$$

■ TABLE 10.6 **Matrix Used to Calculate the Variance of a Portfolio When (a) All Securities Possess the Same Variance, Which We Represent as $\overline{\text{var}}$; (b) All Pairs of Securities Possess the Same Covariance, Which We Represent as $\overline{\text{cov}}$; (c) All Securities Are Held in the Same Proportion, Which Is 1/N**

Stock	1	2	3	...	N
1	$(1/N^2)\overline{\text{var}}$	$(1/N^2)\overline{\text{cov}}$	$(1/N^2)\overline{\text{cov}}$		$(1/N^2)\overline{\text{cov}}$
2	$(1/N^2)\overline{\text{cov}}$	$(1/N^2)\overline{\text{var}}$	$(1/N^2)\overline{\text{cov}}$		$(1/N^2)\overline{\text{cov}}$
3	$(1/N^2)\overline{\text{cov}}$	$(1/N^2)\overline{\text{cov}}$	$(1/N^2)\overline{\text{var}}$		$(1/N^2)\overline{\text{cov}}$
.					
.					
.					
N	$(1/N^2)\overline{\text{cov}}$	$(1/N^2)\overline{\text{cov}}$	$(1/N^2)\overline{\text{cov}}$		$(1/N^2)\overline{\text{var}}$

3. All securities are equally weighted in the portfolio. Because there are N assets, the weight of each asset in the portfolio is $1/N$. In other words, $X_i = 1/N$ for each security i.

Table 10.6 is the matrix of variances and covariances under these three simplifying assumptions. Note that all of the diagonal terms are identical. Similarly, all of the off-diagonal terms are identical. As with Table 10.4, the variance of the portfolio is the sum of the terms in the boxes in Table 10.6. We know that there are N diagonal terms involving variance. Similarly, there are $N \times (N - 1)$ off-diagonal terms involving covariance. Summing across all the boxes in Table 10.6 we can express the variances of the portfolio as

$$\text{Variance of portfolio} = \underset{\substack{\text{Number of}\\ \text{diagonal}\\ \text{terms}}}{N} \times \underset{\substack{\text{Each}\\ \text{diagonal}\\ \text{term}}}{\left(\frac{1}{N^2}\right)\overline{\text{var}}} + \underset{\substack{\text{Number of}\\ \text{off-diagonal}\\ \text{terms}}}{N(N-1)} \times \underset{\substack{\text{Each}\\ \text{off-diagonal}\\ \text{term}}}{\left(\frac{1}{N^2}\right)\overline{\text{cov}}} \quad (10.10)$$

$$= \left(\frac{1}{N}\right)\overline{\text{var}} + \left(\frac{N^2 - N}{N^2}\right)\overline{\text{cov}}$$

$$= \left(\frac{1}{N}\right)\overline{\text{var}} + \left(1 - \frac{1}{N}\right)\overline{\text{cov}}$$

Equation (10.10) expresses the variance of our special portfolio as a weighted sum of the average security variance and the average covariance.[8]

---

[8]Equation (10.10) is actually a weighted *average* of the variance and covariance terms because the weights, $1/N$ and $1 - 1/N$, sum to 1.

Now, let's increase the number of securities in the portfolio without limit. The variance of the portfolio becomes

$$\text{Variance of portfolio (when } N \rightarrow \infty) = \overline{\text{cov}} \tag{10.11}$$

This occurs because (1) the weight on the variance term, $1/N$, goes to 0 as N goes to infinity, and (2) the weight on the covariance term, $1 - 1/N$, goes to 1 as N goes to infinity.

Formula (10.11) provides an interesting and important result. In our special portfolio, the variances of the individual securities completely vanish as the number of securities becomes large. However, the covariance terms remain. In fact, the variance of the portfolio becomes the average covariance, $\overline{\text{cov}}$. One often hears that one should diversify. In other words, you should not put all your eggs in one basket. The effect of diversification on the risk of a portfolio can be illustrated in this example. The variances of the individual securities are diversified away, but the covariance terms cannot be diversified away.

The fact that part, but not all, of one's risk can be diversified away should be explored. Consider Mr. Smith, who brings $1,000 to the roulette table at a casino. It would be very risky if he put all his money on one spin of the wheel. For example, imagine that he put the full $1,000 on red at the table. If the wheel showed red, he would get $2,000, but if the wheel showed black, he would lose everything. Suppose, instead, he divided his money over 1,000 different spins by betting $1 at a time on red. Probability theory tells us that he could count on winning about 50 percent of the time. This means that he could count on pretty nearly getting all his original $1,000 back.[9] In other words, risk is essentially eliminated with 1,000 different spins.

Now, let's contrast this with our stock market example, which we illustrate in Figure 10.7. The variance of the portfolio with only one security is, of course, $\overline{\text{var}}$ because the variance of a portfolio with one security is the variance of the security. The variance of the portfolio drops as more securities are added, which is evidence of the diversification effect. However, unlike Mr. Smith's roulette example, the portfolio's variance can never drop to zero. Rather it reaches a floor of $\overline{\text{cov}}$, which is the covariance of each pair of securities.[10]

Because the variance of the portfolio asymptotically approaches $\overline{\text{cov}}$, each additional security continues to reduce risk. Thus, if there were neither commissions nor other transactions costs, it could be argued that one can never achieve too much diversification. However, there is a cost to diversification in the real world. Commissions per dollar invested fall as one makes larger purchases in a single stock. Unfortunately, one must buy fewer shares of each security when buying more and more different securities. Comparing the costs and benefits of diversification, Meir Statman argues that a portfolio of about 30 stocks is needed to achieve optimal diversification.[11]

We mentioned earlier that $\overline{\text{var}}$ must be greater than $\overline{\text{cov}}$. Thus, the variance of a security's return can be broken down in the following way:

$$\begin{array}{ccc} \text{Total risk of} & & \text{Unsystematic or} \\ \text{individual security} = \text{Portfolio risk} + \text{diversifiable risk} \\ (\overline{\text{var}}) & (\overline{\text{cov}}) & (\overline{\text{var}} - \overline{\text{cov}}) \end{array}$$

Total risk, which is $\overline{\text{var}}$ in our example, is the risk that one bears by holding onto one security only. *Portfolio risk* is the risk that one still bears after achieving full diversification,

---

[9]This example ignores the casino's cut.

[10]Though it is harder to show, this risk reduction effect also applies to the general case where variances and covariances are *not* equal.

[11]Meir Statman, "How Many Stocks Make a Diversified Portfolio?" *Journal of Financial and Quantitative Analysis* (September 1987).

■ FIGURE 10.8 **Relationship between Expected Return and Risk for a Portfolio of One Risky Asset and One Riskless Asset**

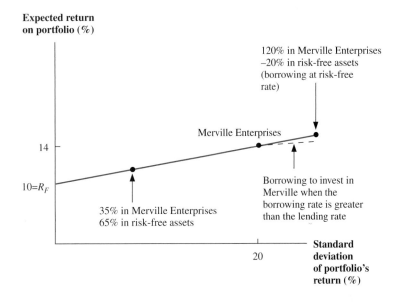

However, by definition, the risk-free asset has no variability. Thus, both $\sigma_{\text{Merville, Risk-free}}$ and $\sigma^2_{\text{Risk-free}}$ are equal to zero, reducing the above expression to

Variance of portfolio composed
of one riskless and one risky asset =   (10.13)
$$X^2_{\text{Merville}} \, \sigma^2_{\text{Merville}} = (0.35)^2 \times (0.20)^2 = 0.0049$$

The standard deviation of the portfolio is

Standard deviation of portfolio composed
    of one riskless and one risky asset =   (10.14)
$$X_{\text{Merville}}\sigma_{\text{Merville}} = 0.35 \times 0.20 = 0.07$$

The relationship between risk and expected return for one risky and one risk-less asset can be seen in Figure 10.8. Ms. Bagwell's split of 35–65 percent between the two assets is represented on a *straight* line between the risk-free rate and a pure investment in Merville Enterprises. Note that, unlike the case of two risky assets, the opportunity set is straight, not curved.

Suppose that, alternatively, Ms. Bagwell borrows $200 at the risk-free rate. Combining this with her original sum of $1,000, she invests a total of $1,200 in Merville. Her expected return would be

Expected return on portfolio
    formed by borrowing   = 14.8% = 1.20 × 0.14 + (−0.2 × 0.10)
    to invest in risky asset

Here, she invests 120 percent of her original investment of $1,000 by borrowing 20 percent of her original investment. Note that the return of 14.8 percent is greater than the 14-percent expected return on Merville Enterprises. This occurs because she is borrowing at 10 percent to invest in a security with an expected return greater than 10 percent.

The standard deviation is

Standard deviation of portfolio formed
by borrowing to invest in risky asset $= 0.24 = 1.20 \times 0.2$

The standard deviation of 0.24 is greater than 0.20, the standard deviation of the Merville investment, because borrowing increases the variability of the investment. This investment also appears in Figure 10.8.

So far, we have assumed that Ms. Bagwell is able to borrow at the same rate at which she can lend.[12] Now let us consider the case where the borrowing rate is above the lending rate. The dotted line in Figure 10.8 illustrates the opportunity set for borrowing opportunities in this case. The dotted line is below the solid line because a higher borrowing rate lowers the expected return on the investment.

The Optimal Portfolio

The previous section concerned a portfolio formed between one riskless asset and one risky asset. In reality, an investor is likely to combine an investment in the riskless asset with a *portfolio* of risky assets. This is illustrated in Figure 10.9.

Consider point *Q,* representing a portfolio of securities. Point *Q* is in the interior of the feasible set of risky securities. Let us assume the point represents a portfolio of 30 percent in AT&T, 45 percent in General Motors (GM), and 25 percent in IBM. Individuals com-

■ FIGURE 10.9   **Relationship between Expected Return and Standard Deviation for an Investment in a Combination of Risky Securities and the Riskless Asset**

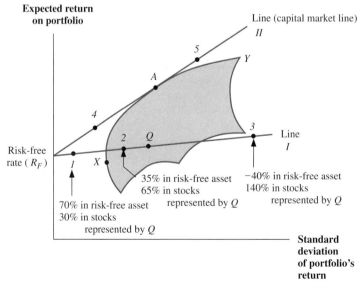

Portfolio *Q* is composed of 30 percent AT&T, 45 percent GM, 25 percent IBM.

---

[12]Surprisingly, this appears to be a decent approximation because a large number of investors are able to borrow from a stockbroker (called *going on margin*) when purchasing stocks. The borrowing rate here is very near the riskless rate of interest, particularly for large investors. More will be said about this in a later chapter.

bining investments in Q with investments in the riskless asset would achieve points along the straight line from R_F to Q. We refer to this as line I. For example, point I on the line represents a portfolio of 70 percent in the riskless asset and 30 percent in stocks represented by Q. An investor with $100 choosing point I as his portfolio would put $70 in the risk-free asset and $30 in Q. This can be restated as $70 in the riskless asset, $9 (0.3 × $30) in AT&T, $13.50 (0.45 × $30) in GM, and $7.50 (0.25 × $30) in IBM. Point 2 also represents a portfolio of the risk-free asset and Q, with more (65%) being invested in Q.

Point 3 is obtained by borrowing to invest in Q. For example, an investor with $100 of his own would borrow $40 from the bank or broker in order to invest $140 in Q. This can be stated as borrowing $40 and contributing $100 of one's money in order to invest $42 (0.3 × $140) in AT&T, $63 (0.45 × $140) in GM, and $35 (0.25 × $140) in IBM.

The above investments can be summarized as:

	Point Q	Point 1 (lending $70)	Point 3 (borrowing $40)
AT&T	$ 30	$ 9	$ 42
GM	45	13.50	63
IBM	25	7.50	35
Risk-free	0	70.00	−40
Total investment	$100	$100	$100

Though any investor can obtain any point on line I, no point on the line is optimal. To see this, consider line II, a line running from R_F through A. Point A represents a portfolio of risky securities. Line II represents portfolios formed by combinations of the risk-free asset and the securities in A. Points between R_F and A are portfolios in which some money is invested in the riskless asset and the rest is placed in A. Points past A are achieved by borrowing at the riskless rate to buy more of A than one could with one's original funds alone.

As drawn, line II is tangent to the efficient set of risky securities. Whatever point an individual can obtain on line I, he can obtain a point with the same standard deviation and a higher expected return on line II. In fact, because line II is tangent to the efficient set of risky assets, it provides the investor with the best possible opportunities. In other words, line II can be viewed as the efficient set of *all* assets, both risky and riskless. An investor with a fair degree of risk aversion might choose a point between R_F and A, perhaps point 4. An individual with less risk aversion might choose a point closer to A or even beyond A. For example, point 5 corresponds to an individual borrowing money to increase his investment in A.

The graph illustrates an important point. With riskless borrowing and lending, the portfolio of *risky* assets held by any investor would always be point A. Regardless of the investor's tolerance for risk, he would never choose any other point on the efficient set of risky assets (represented by curve *XAY*) nor any point in the interior of the feasible region. Rather, he would combine the securities of A with the riskless assets if he had high aversion to risk. He would borrow the riskless asset to invest more funds in A had he low aversion to risk.

This result establishes what financial economists call the **separation principle.** That is, the investor's investment decision consists of two separate steps:

1. After estimating (a) the expected returns and variances of individual securities, and (b) the covariances between pairs of securities, the investor calculates the efficient set of risky assets, represented by curve *XAY* in Figure 10.9. He then determines point A, the tangency between the risk-free rate and the efficient set of risky assets (curve *XAY*). Point A represents the portfolio of risky assets that the investor will hold. This point is determined solely from his estimates of returns, variances, and covariances. No personal characteristics, such as degree of risk aversion, are needed in this step.

2. The investor must now determine how he will combine point *A,* his portfolio of risky assets, with the riskless asset. He might invest some of his funds in the riskless asset and some in portfolio *A.* He would end up at a point on the line between R_F and *A* in this case. Alternatively, he might borrow at the risk-free rate and contribute some of his own funds as well, investing the sum in portfolio *A.* He would end up at a point on line *II* beyond *A.* His position in the riskless asset, that is, his choice of where on the line he wants to be, is determined by his internal characteristics, such as his ability to tolerate risk.

CONCEPT QUESTIONS
?

- What is the formula for the standard deviation of a portfolio composed of one riskless and one risky asset?
- How does one determine the optimal portfolio among the efficient set of risky assets?

10.8 MARKET EQUILIBRIUM

Definition of the Market-Equilibrium Portfolio

The above analysis concerns one investor. His estimates of the expected returns and variances for individual securities and the covariances between pairs of securities are his and his alone. Other investors would obviously have different estimates of the above variables. However, the estimates might not vary much because all investors would be forming expectations from the same data on past price movements and other publicly available information.

Financial economists often imagine a world where all investors possess the *same* estimates on expected returns, variances, and covariances. Though this can never be literally true, it can be thought of as a useful simplifying assumption in a world where investors have access to similar sources of information. This assumption is called **homogeneous expectations.**[13]

If all investors had homogeneous expectations, Figure 10.9 would be the same for all individuals. That is, all investors would sketch out the same efficient set of risky assets because they would be working with the same inputs. This efficient set of risky assets is represented by the curve *XAY.* Because the same risk-free rate would apply to everyone, all investors would view point *A* as the portfolio of risky assets to be held.

This point *A* takes on great importance because all investors would purchase the risky securities that it represents. Those investors with a high degree of risk aversion might combine *A* with an investment in the riskless asset, achieving point *4,* for example. Others with low aversion to risk might borrow to achieve, say, point *5.* Because this is a very important conclusion, we restate it:

In a world with homogeneous expectations, all investors would hold the portfolio of risky assets represented by point A.

If all investors choose the same portfolio of risky assets, it is possible to determine what that portfolio is. Common sense tells us that it is a market-value-weighted portfolio of all existing securities. It is the **market portfolio.**

In practice, financial economists use a broad-based index such as the Standard & Poor's (S&P) 500 as a proxy for the market portfolio. Of course all investors do not hold the same portfolio in practice. However, we know that a large number of investors hold di-

---

[13]The assumption of homogeneous expectations states that all investors have the same beliefs concerning returns, variances, and covariances. It does not say that all investors have the same aversion to risk.

versified portfolios, particularly when mutual funds or pension funds are included. A broad-based index is a good proxy for the highly diversified portfolios of many investors.

Definition of Risk When Investors Hold the Market Portfolio

The previous section states that many investors hold diversified portfolios similar to broad-based indices. This result allows us to be more precise about the risk of a security in the context of a diversified portfolio.

Researchers have shown that the best measure of the risk of a security in a large portfolio is the *beta* of the security. We illustrate beta by an example.

EXAMPLE

Consider the following possible returns on both the stock of Jelco, Inc., and on the market:

State	Type of Economy	Return on Market (percent)	Return on Jelco, Inc. (percent)
I	Bull	15	25
II	Bull	15	15
III	Bear	−5	−5
IV	Bear	−5	−15

Though the return on the market has only two possible outcomes (15% and −5%), the return on Jelco has four possible outcomes. It is helpful to consider the expected return on a security for a given return on the market. Assuming each state is equally likely, we have

Type of Economy	Return on Market (percent)	Expected Return on Jelco, Inc. (percent)
Bull	15%	$20\% = 25\% \times \frac{1}{2} + 15\% \times \frac{1}{2}$
Bear	−5%	$-10\% = -5\% \times \frac{1}{2} + (-15\%) \times \frac{1}{2}$

Jelco, Inc., responds to market movements because its expected return is greater in bullish states than in bearish states. We now calculate exactly how responsive the security is to market movements. The market's return in a bullish economy is 20 percent [15% − (−5%)] greater than the market's return in a bearish economy. However, the expected return on Jelco in a bullish economy is 30 percent [20% − (−10%)] greater than its expected return in a bearish state. Thus, Jelco, Inc., has a responsiveness coefficient of 1.5 (30%/20%).

This relationship appears in Figure 10.10. The returns for both Jelco and the market in each state are plotted as four points. In addition, we plot the expected return on the security for each of the two possible returns on the market. These two points, each of which we designate by an X, are joined by a line called the **characteristic line** of the security. The slope of the line is 1.5, the number calculated in the previous paragraph. This responsiveness coefficient of 1.5 is the **beta** of Jelco.

The interpretation of beta from Figure 10.10 is intuitive. The graph tells us that the returns of Jelco are magnified 1.5 times over those of the market. When the market does well, Jelco's stock is expected to do even better. When the market does poorly, Jelco's stock is expected to do even worse. Now imagine an individual with

■ FIGURE 10.10 Performance of Jelco, Inc., and the Market Portfolio

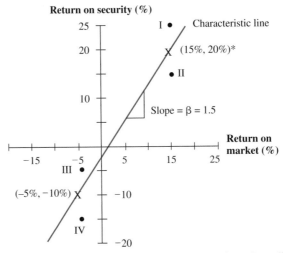

The two points marked X represent the expected return on Jelco for each possible outcome of the market portfolio. The expected return on Jelco is positively related to the return on the market. Because the slope is 1.5, we say that Jelco's beta is 1.5. Beta measures the responsiveness of the security's return to movement in the market.
*(20%, 15%) refers to the point where the return on the security is 20 percent and the return on the market is 15 percent.

a portfolio near that of the market who is considering the addition of Jelco to his portfolio. Because of Jelco's *magnification factor* of 1.5, he will view this stock as contributing much to the risk of the portfolio. (We will show shortly that the beta of the average security in the market is 1.) Jelco contributes more to the risk of a large, diversified portfolio than does an average security because Jelco is more responsive to movements in the market.

Further insight can be gleaned by examining securities with negative betas. One should view these securities as either hedges or insurance policies. The security is expected to do well when the market does poorly and vice versa. Because of this, adding a negative-beta security to a large, diversified portfolio actually reduces the risk of the portfolio.[14]

Table 10.7 presents empirical estimates of betas for individual securities. As can be seen, some securities are more responsive to the market than others. For example, Oracle has a beta of 1.63. This means that, for every 1 percent movement in the market,[15] Oracle is expected to move 1.63 percent in the same direction. Conversely, Green Mountain Power has a beta of only 0.26. This means that, for every 1 percent movement in the market, Green Mountain is expected to move 0.26 percent in the same direction.

We can summarize our discussion of beta by saying:

Beta measures the responsiveness of a security to movements in the market portfolio.

---

[14]Unfortunately, empirical evidence shows that virtually no stocks have negative betas.

[15]In Table 10.7, we use the Standard & Poor's 500 Index as the proxy for the market portfolio.

■ TABLE 10.7 **Estimates of Beta for Selected Individual Stocks**

Stock	Beta
High-beta stocks	
Oracle, Inc.	1.63
Inprise Corporation	1.58
Citicorp	2.29
Average-beta stocks	
Du Pont	1.08
Kimberly-Clark Corp.	0.80
Ford Motor Co.	0.96
Low-beta stocks	
Green Mountain Power	0.26
Homestake Mining	0.22
Bell Atlantic	0.37

The beta is defined as $\text{Cov}(R_i, R_M)/\text{Var}(R_M)$, where $\text{Cov}(R_i, R_M)$ is the covariance of the return on an individual stock, R_i, and the return on the market, R_M. $\text{Var}(R_M)$ is the variance of the return on the market, R_M.

The Formula for Beta

Our discussion so far has stressed the intuition behind beta. The actual definition of beta is

$$\beta_i = \frac{\text{Cov}(R_i, R_M)}{\sigma^2(R_M)} \tag{10.15}$$

where $\text{Cov}(R_i, R_M)$ is the covariance between the return on asset i and the return on the market portfolio and $\sigma^2(R_M)$ is the variance of the market.

One useful property is that the average beta across all securities, when weighted by the proportion of each security's market value to that of the market portfolio, is 1. That is,

$$\sum_{i=1}^{N} X_i \beta_i = 1 \tag{10.16}$$

where X_i is the proportion of security i's market value to that of the entire market and N is the number of securities in the market.

Equation (10.16) is intuitive, once you think about it. If you weight all securities by their market values, the resulting portfolio is the market. By definition, the beta of the market portfolio is 1. That is, for every 1 percent movement in the market, the market must move 1 percent—*by definition.*

A Test

We have put these questions on past corporate finance examinations:

1. What sort of investor rationally views the variance (or standard deviation) of an individual security's return as the security's proper measure of risk?
2. What sort of investor rationally views the beta of a security as the security's proper measure of risk?

A good answer might be something like the following:

> A rational, risk-averse investor views the variance (or standard deviation) of her portfolio's return as the proper measure of the risk of her portfolio. If for some reason or another the

investor can hold only one security, the variance of that security's return becomes the variance of the portfolio's return. Hence, the variance of the security's return is the security's proper measure of risk.

If an individual holds a diversified portfolio, she still views the variance (or standard deviation) of her portfolio's return as the proper measure of the risk of her portfolio. However, she is no longer interested in the variance of each individual security's return. Rather, she is interested in the contribution of an individual security to the variance of the portfolio.

Under the assumption of homogeneous expectations, all individuals hold the market portfolio. Thus, we measure risk as the contribution of an individual security to the variance of the market portfolio. This contribution, when standardized properly, is the beta of the security. While very few investors hold the market portfolio exactly, many hold reasonably diversified portfolios. These portfolios are close enough to the market portfolio so that the beta of a security is likely to be a reasonable measure of its risk.

CONCEPT QUESTIONS
- If all investors have homogeneous expectations, what portfolio of risky assets do they hold?
- What is the formula for beta?
- Why is beta the appropriate measure of risk for a single security in a large portfolio?

10.9 RELATIONSHIP BETWEEN RISK AND EXPECTED RETURN (CAPM)

It is commonplace to argue that the expected return on an asset should be positively related to its risk. That is, individuals will hold a risky asset only if its expected return compensates for its risk. In this section, we first estimate the expected return on the stock market as a whole. Next, we estimate expected returns on individual securities.

Expected Return on Market

Financial economists frequently argue that the expected return on the market can be represented as:

$$\overline{R}_M = R_F + \text{Risk premium}$$

In words, the expected return on the market is the sum of the risk-free rate plus some compensation for the risk inherent in the market portfolio. Note that the equation refers to the *expected* return on the market, not the actual return in a particular month or year. Because stocks have risk, the actual return on the market over a particular period can, of course, be below R_F, or can even be negative.

Since investors want compensation for risk, the risk premium is presumably positive. But exactly how positive is it? It is generally argued that the best estimate for the risk premium in the future is the average risk premium in the past. As reported in Chapter 9, Ibbotson and Sinquefield found that the expected return on common stocks was 13.3 percent over 1926–1999. The average risk-free rate over the same time interval was 3.8 percent. Thus, the average difference between the two was 9.5 percent (13.3% − 3.8%).

■ FIGURE 10.11   **Relationship between Expected Return on an Individual Security and Beta of the Security**

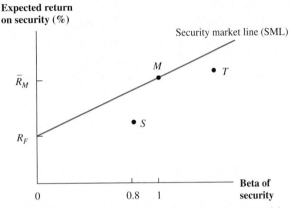

The Security Market Line (SML) is the graphical depiction of the capital-asset-pricing model (CAPM).
The expected return on a stock with a beta of 0 is equal to the risk-free rate.
The expected return on a stock with a beta of 1 is equal to the expected return on the market.

Financial economists find this to be a useful estimate of the difference to occur in the future. We will use it frequently in this text.[16]

For example, if the risk-free rate, generally estimated by the yield on a one-year Treasury bill, is 4 percent, the expected return on the market is

$$13.5\% = 4\% + 9.5\%$$

Expected Return on Individual Security

Now that we have estimated the expected return on the market as a whole, what is the expected return on an individual security? We have argued that the beta of a security is the appropriate measure of risk in a large, diversified portfolio. Since most investors are diversified, the expected return on a security should be positively related to its beta. This is illustrated in Figure 10.11.

Actually, financial economists can be more precise about the relationship between expected return and beta. They posit that, under plausible conditions, the relationship between expected return and beta can be represented by the following equation.[17]

Capital-Asset-Pricing Model:

$$\overline{R} = R_F + \beta \times (\overline{R}_M - R_F) \tag{10.17}$$

Expected return on a security	=	Risk-free rate	+	Beta of the security	×	Difference between expected return on market and risk-free rate

---

[16]This is not the only way to estimate the market-risk premium. In fact, there are several useful ways to estimate the market-risk premium. For example, refer to Table 9.2 and note the average return on common stocks (13.3%) and long-term government bonds (5.5%). One could argue that the long-term government bond return is the best measure of the long-term historical risk-free rate. If so, a good estimate of the historical market risk premium would be 13.3% − 5.5% = 8.8%. With this empirical version of the CAPM, one would use the current long-term government bond return to estimate the current risk-free rate.

[17]This relationship was first proposed independently by John Lintner and William F. Sharpe.

This formula, which is called the **capital-asset-pricing model** (or CAPM for short), implies that the expected return on a security is linearly related to its beta. Since the average return on the market has been higher than the average risk-free rate over long periods of time, $\overline{R}_M - R_F$ is presumably positive. Thus, the formula implies that the expected return on a security is *positively* related to its beta. The formula can be illustrated by assuming a few special cases:

- *Assume that* β = 0. Here $\overline{R} = R_F$, that is, the expected return on the security is equal to the risk-free rate. Because a security with zero beta has no relevant risk, its expected return should equal the risk-free rate.
- *Assume that* β = 1. Equation (10.17) reduces to $\overline{R} = \overline{R}_M$. That is, the expected return on the security is equal to the expected return on the market. This makes sense since the beta of the market portfolio is also 1.

Formula (10.17) can be represented graphically by the upward-sloping line in Figure 10.11. Note that the line begins at R_F and rises to $\overline{R}_M$ when beta is 1. This line is frequently called the **security market line** (SML).

As with any line, the SML has both a slope and an intercept. R_F, the risk-free rate, is the intercept. Because the beta of a security is the horizontal axis, $R_M - R_F$ is the slope. The line will be upward-sloping as long as the expected return on the market is greater than the risk-free rate. Because the market portfolio is a risky asset, theory suggests that its expected return is above the risk-free rate. In addition, the empirical evidence of the previous chapter showed that the average return per year on the market portfolio over the past 74 years was 9.5 percent above the risk-free rate.

EXAMPLE

The stock of Aardvark Enterprises has a beta of 1.5 and that of Zebra Enterprises has a beta of 0.7. The risk-free rate is 7 percent, and the difference between the expected return on the market and the risk-free rate is 9.5 percent. The expected returns on the two securities are:

Expected Return for Aardvark:

$$21.25\% = 7\% + 1.5 \times 9.5\% \tag{10.18}$$

Expected Return for Zebra:

$$13.65\% = 7\% + 0.7 \times 9.5\%$$

Three additional points concerning the CAPM should be mentioned:

1. *Linearity.* The intuition behind an upwardly sloping curve is clear. Because beta is the appropriate measure of risk, high-beta securities should have an expected return above that of low-beta securities. However, both Figure 10.11 and equation (10.17) show something more than an upwardly sloping curve; the relationship between expected return and beta corresponds to a *straight* line.

It is easy to show that the line of Figure 10.11 is straight. To see this, consider security *S* with, say, a beta of 0.8. This security is represented by a point below the security market line in the figure. Any investor could duplicate the beta of security *S* by buying a portfolio with 20 percent in the risk-free asset and 80 percent in a security with a beta of 1. However, the homemade portfolio would itself lie on the SML. In other words, the portfolio dominates security *S* because the portfolio has a higher expected return and the same beta.

Now consider security *T* with, say, a beta greater than 1. This security is also below the SML in Figure 10.11. Any investor could duplicate the beta of security *T* by borrowing to invest in a security with a beta of 1. This portfolio must also lie on the SML, thereby dominating security *T*.

Because no one would hold either *S* or *T*, their stock prices would drop. This price adjustment would raise the expected returns on the two securities. The price adjustment would continue until the two securities lay on the security market line. The preceding example considered two overpriced stocks and a straight SML. Securities lying above the SML are *underpriced*. Their prices must rise until their expected returns lie on the line. If the SML is itself curved, many stocks would be mispriced. In equilibrium, all securities would be held only when prices changed so that the SML became straight. In other words, linearity would be achieved.

2. *Portfolios as well as securities.* Our discussion of the CAPM considered individual securities. Does the relationship in Figure 10.11 and equation (10.17) hold for portfolios as well?

Yes. To see this, consider a portfolio formed by investing equally in our two securities, Aardvark and Zebra. The expected return on the portfolio is

Expected Return on Portfolio:

$$17.45\% = 0.5 \times 21.25\% + 0.5 \times 13.65\% \tag{10.19}$$

The beta of the portfolio is simply a weighted average of the betas of the two securities. Thus we have

Beta of Portfolio:

$$1.1 = 0.5 \times 1.5 + 0.5 \times 0.7$$

Under the CAPM, the expected return on the portfolio is

$$17.45\% = 7\% + 1.1 \times 9.5\% \tag{10.20}$$

Because the expected return in (10.19) is the same as the expected return in (10.20), the example shows that the CAPM holds for portfolios as well as for individual securities.

3. *A potential confusion.* Students often confuse the SML in Figure 10.11 with line *II* in Figure 10.9. Actually, the lines are quite different. Line *II* traces the efficient set of portfolios formed from both risky assets and the riskless asset. Each point on the line represents an entire portfolio. Point *A* is a portfolio composed entirely of risky assets. Every other point on the line represents a portfolio of the securities in *A* combined with the riskless asset. The axes on Figure 10.9 are the expected return on a *portfolio* and the standard deviation of a *portfolio*. Individual securities do not lie along line *II*.

The SML in Figure 10.11 relates expected return to beta. Figure 10.11 differs from Figure 10.9 in at least two ways. First, beta appears in the horizontal axis of Figure 10.11, but standard deviation appears in the horizontal axis of Figure 10.9. Second, the SML in Figure 10.11 holds both for all individual securities and for all possible portfolios, whereas line *II* in Figure 10.9 holds only for efficient portfolios.

We stated earlier that, under homogeneous expectations, point *A* in Figure 10.9 becomes the market portfolio. In this situation, line *II* is referred to as the **capital market line** (CML).

CONCEPT QUESTIONS
?
- Why is the SML a straight line?
- What is the capital-asset-pricing model?
- What are the differences between the capital market line and the security market line?

10.10 SUMMARY AND CONCLUSIONS

This chapter sets forth the fundamentals of modern portfolio theory. Our basic points are these:

1. This chapter shows us how to calculate the expected return and variance for individual securities, and the covariance and correlation for pairs of securities. Given these statistics, the expected return and variance for a portfolio of two securities A and B can be written as

$$\text{Expected return on portfolio} = X_A \overline{R}_A + X_B \overline{R}_B$$
$$\text{Var(portfolio)} = X_A^2 \sigma_A^2 + 2X_A X_B \sigma_{AB} + X_B^2 \sigma_B^2$$

2. In our notation, X stands for the proportion of a security in one's portfolio. By varying X, one can trace out the efficient set of portfolios. We graphed the efficient set for the two-asset case as a curve, pointing out that the degree of curvature or bend in the graph reflects the diversification effect: The lower the correlation between the two securities, the greater the bend. The same general shape of the efficient set holds in a world of many assets.

3. Just as the formula for variance in the two-asset case is computed from a 2×2 matrix, the variance formula is computed from an $N×N$ matrix in the N-asset case. We show that, with a large number of assets, there are many more covariance terms than variance terms in the matrix. In fact, the variance terms are effectively diversified away in a large portfolio but the covariance terms are not. Thus, a diversified portfolio can only eliminate some, but not all, of the risk of the individual securities.

4. The efficient set of risky assets can be combined with riskless borrowing and lending. In this case, a rational investor will always choose to hold the portfolio of risky securities represented by point A in Figure 10.9. Then he can either borrow or lend at the riskless rate to achieve any desired point on line II in the figure.

5. The contribution of a security to the risk of a large, well-diversified portfolio is proportional to the covariance of the security's return with the market's return. This contribution, when standardized, is called the beta. The beta of a security can also be interpreted as the responsiveness of a security's return to that of the market.

6. The CAPM states that

$$\overline{R} = R_F + \beta(\overline{R}_M - R_F)$$

In other words, the expected return on a security is positively (and linearly) related to the security's beta.

KEY TERMS

Beta   269
Capital-asset-pricing model   274
Capital market line   275
Characteristic line   269
Correlation   245
Covariance   245
Diversifiable (unique)
   (unsystematic) risk   263
Efficient set (efficient frontier)   255

Homogeneous expectations   268
Market portfolio   268
Opportunity (feasible) set   255
Portfolio   247
Risk averse   263
Security market line   274
Separation principle   267
Systematic (market) risk   263

Suggested Readings

The capital-asset-pricing model was originally published in these two classic articles:

Lintner, J. "Security Prices, Risk and Maximal Gains from Diversification." *Journal of Finance* (December 1965).

Sharpe, W. F. "Capital Asset Prices: A Theory of Market Equilibrium under Conditions of Risk." *Journal of Finance* (September 1964). (William F. Sharpe won the Nobel Prize in Economics in 1990 for his development of CAPM.)

The seminal influence of Harry Markowitz is described in:

Markowitz, H. "Travels along the Efficient Frontier." *Dow Jones Asset Management* (May/June 1997).

Questions and Problems

Expected Return, Variance, and Covariance

10.1 Ms. Sharp thinks that the distribution of rates of return on Q-mart stock is as follows.

State of Economy	Probability of State Occurring	Q-mart Stock Return (%)
Depression	0.10	−4.5%
Recession	0.20	4.4
Normal	0.50	12.0
Boom	0.20	20.7

a. What is the expected return for the stock?

b. What is the standard deviation of returns for the stock?

10.2 Suppose you have invested only in two stocks, *A* and *B*. You expect that returns on the stocks depend on the following three states of economy, which are equally likely to happen.

State of Economy	Return on Stock A (%)	Return on Stock B (%)
Bear	6.3%	−3.7%
Normal	10.5	6.4
Bull	15.6	25.3

a. Calculate the expected return of each stock.

b. Calculate the standard deviation of returns of each stock.

c. Calculate the covariance and correlation between the two stocks.

10.3 Mr. Henry can invest in Highbull stock or Slowbear stock. His projection of the returns on these two stocks is as follows:

State of Economy	Probability of State Occurring	Return on Highbull Stock (%)	Return on Slowbear Stock (%)
Recession	0.25	−2.0%	5.0%
Normal	0.60	9.2	6.2
Boom	0.15	15.4	7.4

a. Calculate the expected return of each stock.

b. Calculate the standard deviation of return of each stock.

c. Calculate the covariance and correlation between the two stocks.

Portfolios

10.4 A portfolio consists of 120 shares of Atlas stock, which sells for $50 per share, and 150 shares of Babcock stock, which sells for $20 per share. What are the weights of the two stocks in this portfolio?

10.5 Security F has an expected return of 12 percent and a standard deviation of 9 percent per year. Security G has an expected return of 18 percent and a standard deviation of 25 percent per year.
   a. What is the expected return on a portfolio composed of 30 percent of security F and 70 percent of security G?
   b. If the correlation coefficient between the returns of F and G is 0.2, what is the standard deviation of the portfolio?

10.6 Suppose the expected returns and standard deviations of stocks A and B are $\bar{R}_A = 0.15$, $\bar{R}_B = 0.25$, $\sigma_A = 0.1$, and $\sigma_B = 0.2$, respectively.
   a. Calculate the expected return and standard deviation of a portfolio that is composed of 40 percent A and 60 percent B when the correlation coefficient between the stocks is 0.5.
   b. Calculate the standard deviation of a portfolio that is composed of 40 percent A and 60 percent B when the correlation coefficient between the stocks is -0.5.
   c. How does the correlation coefficient affect the standard deviation of the portfolio?

10.7 Suppose Janet Smith holds 100 shares of Macrosoft stock and 300 shares of Intelligence stock. Macrosoft stock is currently sold at $80 per share, while Intelligence stock is sold at $40. The expected return of Macrosoft stock is 15 percent, while that of Intelligence stock is 20 percent. The standard deviation of Macrosoft is 8 percent, while that of Intelligence is 20 percent. The correlation coefficient between the stocks is 0.38.
   a. Calculate the expected return and standard deviation of her portfolio.
   b. Today she sold 200 shares of Intelligence stock to pay the tuition. Calculate the expected return and standard deviation of her new portfolio.

10.8 Consider the possible rates of return that you might obtain over the next year. You can invest in stock U or stock V.

State of Economy	Probability of State Occurring	Stock U Return if State Occurs (%)	Stock V Return if State Occurs (%)
Recession	0.2	7%	-5%
Normal	0.5	7	10
Boom	0.3	7	25

   a. Determine the expected return, variance, and the standard deviation for stock U and stock V.
   b. Determine the covariance and correlation between the returns of stock U and stock V.
   c. Determine the expected return and standard deviation of an equally weighted portfolio of stock U and stock V.

10.9 Suppose there are only two stocks in the world: stock A and stock B. The expected returns of these two stocks are 10 percent and 20 percent, while the standard deviations of the stocks are 5 percent and 15 percent, respectively. The correlation coefficient of the two stocks is zero.
   a. Calculate the expected return and standard deviation of a portfolio that is composed of 30 percent A and 70 percent B.
   b. Calculate the expected return and standard deviation of a portfolio that is composed of 90 percent A and 10 percent B.
   c. Suppose you are risk averse. Would you hold 100 percent stock A? How about 100 percent stock B?

10.10 If a portfolio has a positive weight for each asset, can the expected return on the portfolio be greater than the return on the asset in the portfolio that has the highest return? Can the expected return on the portfolio be less that the return on the asset in the portfolio with the lowest return? Explain.

10.11 Miss Maple is considering two securities, A and B, and the relevant information is given below:

State of Economy	Probability	Return on Security A (%)	Return on Security B (%)
Bear	0.4	3.0%	6.5%
Bull	0.6	15.0	6.5

a. Calculate the expected returns and standard deviations of the two securities.
b. Suppose Miss Maple invested $2,500 in security A and $3,500 in security B. Calculate the expected return and standard deviation of her portfolio.
c. Suppose Miss Maple borrowed from her friend 40 shares of security B, which is currently sold at $50, and sold all shares of the security. (She promised her friend to pay back in a year with the same number of shares of security B.) Then she bought security A with the proceeds obtained in the sales of security B shares and the cash of $6,000 she owned. Calculate the expected return and standard deviation of the portfolio.

10.12 A broker has advised you not to invest in oil industry stocks because, in her opinion, they are far too risky. She has shown you evidence of how wildly the prices of oil stocks have fluctuated in the recent past. She demonstrated that the standard deviation of oil stocks is very high relative to most stocks. Do you think the broker's advice is sound for a risk-averse investor like you? Why or why not?

10.13 There are three securities in the market. The following chart shows their possible payoffs.

State	Probability of Outcome	Return on Security 1	Return on Security 2	Return on Security 3
1	0.10	0.25	0.25	0.10
2	0.40	0.20	0.15	0.15
3	0.40	0.15	0.20	0.20
4	0.10	0.10	0.10	0.25

a. What are the expected return and standard deviation of each security?
b. What are the covariances and correlations between the pairs of securities?
c. What are the expected return and standard deviation of a portfolio with half of its funds invested in security *1* and half in security *2?*
d. What are the expected return and standard deviation of a portfolio with half of its funds invested in security *1* and half in security *3?*
e. What are the expected return and standard deviation of a portfolio with half of its funds invested in security *2* and half in security *3?*
f. What do your answers in parts (a), (c), (d), and (e) imply about diversification?

10.14 Suppose that there are two stocks, A and B. Suppose that their returns are independent. Stock A has a 40-percent chance of having a return of 15 percent and 60-percent chance of a return of 10 percent. Stock B has a one-half chance of a 35-percent return and a one-half chance of a −5-percent return.
a. Write the list of all of the possible outcomes and their probabilities.
b. What is the expected return on a portfolio with 50 percent invested in stock A and 50 percent invested in stock B?

10.15 Assume there are N securities in the market. The expected return of every security is 10 percent. All securities also have the same variance of 0.0144. The covariance between any pair of securities is 0.0064.

    a. What are the expected return and variance of an equally weighted portfolio containing all *N* securities? Note: The weight of each security in the portfolio is 1/*N*.

    b. What will happen to the variance as *N* gets larger?

    c. What security characteristics are most important in the determination of the variance of a well-diversified portfolio?

10.16 Is the following statement true or false? Explain.

    The most important characteristic in determining the variance of a well-diversified portfolio is the variance of the individual stocks.

10.17 Briefly explain why the covariance of a security with the rest of a portfolio is a more appropriate measure of risk than the security's variance.

10.18 Comment on the following quotation from a leading investment analyst.

    Stocks that move perfectly with the market have a beta of 1. Betas get higher as volatility goes up and lower as it goes down. Thus, Southern Co., a utility whose shares have traded close to $12 for most of the past three years, has a low beta. At the other extreme, there's Texas Instruments, which has been as high as $150 and as low as its current $75.

10.19 Assume that there are two stocks with the following characteristics. The covariance between the returns on the stocks is 0.001.

	Expected Return	Standard Deviation
A	0.05	0.1
B	0.10	0.2

    a. What is the expected return on the minimum variance portfolio? (Hint: Find the portfolio weights X_A and X_B such that the portfolio variance is minimized. Remember that the sum of the weights must equal 1.)

    b. If $Cov(R_A, R_B) = -0.02$, what are the minimum variance weights?

    c. What is the portfolio variance when $Cov(R_A, R_B) = -0.02$?

10.20 Assume a world with homogeneous expectations (i.e., everybody agrees on expected returns and standard deviations). In this world the market portfolio has an expected return of 12 percent and a standard deviation of 10 percent. The risk-free asset has an expected return of 5 percent.

    a. What should the expected return of the portfolio be if it has a standard deviation of 7 percent?

    b. What should the standard deviation of the portfolio be if it has an expected return of 20 percent?

10.21 Consider the following information on the returns on the market and Fuji stock.

Type of Economy	Expected Return on Market (%)	Expected Return on Fuji (%)
Bear	2.5%	3.4%
Bull	16.3	12.8

    a. Calculate the beta of Fuji. What is the responsiveness of Fuji's return to movements of the market?

    b. Suppose the estimate of expected return on the market is −4.0 percent when the type of economy is Bear. Using your answer in part (*a*), what should the expected return on Fuji be in this case?

10.22 William Shakespeare's character Polonius in *Hamlet* says, "Neither a borrower nor a lender be." Under the assumptions of the CAPM, what would be the composition of Polonius's portfolio?

10.23 Securities *A, B,* and *C* have the following characteristics.

Security	E(R)%	Beta
A	10%	0.7
B	14	1.2
C	20	1.8

    a. What is the expected return on a portfolio with equal weights?

    b. What is the beta of a portfolio with equal weights?

    c. Are the three securities priced in equilibrium?

The CAPM

10.24 The Alpha firm makes pneumatic equipment. Its beta is 1.2. The market risk premium is 8.5 percent, and the current risk-free rate is 6 percent. What is the expected return for the Alpha firm?

10.25 Suppose the beta for the Ross Corporation is 0.80. The risk-free rate is 6 percent, and the market risk premium is 8.5 percent. What is the expected return for the Ross Corporation?

10.26 The risk-free rate is 8 percent. The beta for the Jordan Company is 1.5, and the expected return of the market is 15 percent. What is the expected return for the Jordan Company?

10.27 Suppose the market risk premium is 7.5 percent and the risk-free rate is 3.7 percent. The expected return of TriStar Textiles is 14.2 percent. What is the beta for TriStar Textiles?

10.28 Consider the following two stocks:

	Beta	Expected Return
Murck Pharmaceutical	1.4	25%
Pizer Drug Corp.	0.7	14%

Assume the CAPM holds. Based upon the CAPM, what is the return on the market? What is the risk-free rate?

10.29 Suppose you observe the following situation:

		Return if a State Occurs	
State of Economy	Probability of State	Stock A	Stock B
Bust	.25	−.10	−.30
Normal	.50	.10	.05
Boom	.25	.20	.40

    a. Calculate the expected return of each stock.

    b. Assuming the CAPM is true and stock *A*'s beta is greater than stock *B*'s beta by .25, what is the risk premium?

10.30 *a.* Draw the security market line for the case where the market-risk premium is 5 percent and the risk-free rate is 7 percent.

    b. Suppose that an asset has a beta of −1 and an expected return of 4 percent. Plot it on the graph you drew in part (*a*). Is the security properly priced? If not, explain what will happen in this market.

    c. Suppose that an asset has a beta of 3 and an expected return of 20 percent. Plot it on the graph you drew in part (*a*). Is the security properly priced? If not, explain what will happen in this market.

10.31 A stock has a beta of 1.8. A security analyst who specializes in studying this stock expects its return to be 18 percent. Suppose the risk-free rate is 5 percent and the market-risk premium is 8 percent. Is the analyst pessimistic or optimistic about this stock relative to the market's expectations?

10.32 Suppose the expected return on the market is 13.8 percent and the risk-free rate is 6.4 percent. Solomon Inc. stock has a beta of 1.2.

a. What is the expected return on the Solomon stock?

b. If the risk-free rate decreases to 3.5 percent, what is the expected return on the Solomon stock?

10.33 The expected return on a portfolio that combines the risk-free asset and the asset at the point of tangency to the efficient set is 25 percent. The expected return was calculated under the following assumptions:

The risk-free rate is 5 percent.

The expected return on the market portfolio of risky assets is 20 percent.

The standard deviation of the efficient portfolio is 4 percent.

In this environment, what expected rate of return would a security earn if it had a 0.5 correlation with the market and a standard deviation of 2 percent?

10.34 Suppose the current risk-free rate is 7.6 percent. Potpourri Inc. stock has a beta of 1.7 and an expected return of 16.7 percent. (Assume the CAPM is true.)

a. What is the risk premium on the market?

b. Magnolia Industries stock has a beta of 0.8. What is the expected return on the Magnolia stock?

c. Suppose you have invested $10,000 in both Potpourri and Magnolia, and the beta of the portfolio is 1.07. How much did you invest in each stock? What is the expected return on the portfolio?

10.35 Suppose the risk-free rate is 6.3 percent and the market portfolio has an expected rate of return of 14.8 percent. The market portfolio has a variance of 0.0121. Portfolio *Z* has a correlation coefficient with the market of 0.45 and a variance of 0.0169. According to the CAPM, what is the expected rate of return on portfolio *Z?*

10.36 The following data have been developed for the Durham Company.

$$\text{Variance of market returns} = 0.04326$$
$$\text{Covariance of the returns on Durham and the market} = 0.0635$$

Suppose the market risk premium is 9.4 percent and the expected return on Treasury bills is 4.9 percent.

a. Write the equation of the security market line.

b. What is the required return of Durham Company?

10.37 Johnson Paint stock has an expected return of 19 percent with a beta of 1.7, while Williamson Tire stock has an expected return of 14 percent with a beta of 1.2. Assume the CAPM is true. What is the expected return on the market? What is the risk-free rate?

10.38 Is the following statement true or false? Explain.

A risky security cannot have an expected return that is less than the risk-free rate because no risk-averse investor would be willing to hold this asset in equilibrium.

10.39 Suppose you have invested $30,000 in the following four stocks.

Security	Amount Invested	Beta
Stock *A*	$ 5,000	0.75
Stock *B*	10,000	1.10
Stock *C*	8,000	1.36
Stock *D*	7,000	1.88

The risk-free rate is 4 percent and the expected return on the market portfolio is 15 percent. Based on the CAPM, what is the expected return on the above portfolio?

10.40 You have been provided the following data on the securities of three firms and the market:

Security	$\overline{R}_i$	σ_i	ρ_{iM}	β_i
Firm A	0.13	0.12	(i)	0.90
Firm B	0.16	(ii)	0.40	1.10
Firm C	0.25	0.24	0.75	(iii)
The market	0.15	0.10	(iv)	(v)
The risk-free asset	0.05	(vi)	(vii)	$(viii)$

$\overline{R}_i$ = Average return of security i.

σ_i = Standard deviation of the return of i.

ρ_{iM} = Correlation coefficient of return on asset i with the market portfolio.

β_i = Beta coefficient of security i.

Assume the CAPM holds true.

a. Fill in the missing values in the table.

b. Provide an evaluation of the investment performance of the three firms.

c. What is your investment recommendation? Why?

10.41 There are two stocks in the market, stock A and stock B. The price of stock A today is $50. The price of stock A next year will be $40 if the economy is in a recession, $55 if the economy is normal, and $60 if the economy is expanding. The attendant probabilities of recession, normal times, and expansion are 0.1, 0.8, and 0.1, respectively. Stock A pays no dividend.

Assume the CAPM is true. Other information about the market includes:

$\text{SD}(R_M)$ = Standard deviation of the market portfolio
    = 0.10

$\text{SD}(R_B)$ = Standard deviation of stock B's return
    = 0.12

$\overline{R}_B$ = Expected return on stock B
    = 0.09

$\text{Corr}(R_A,R_M)$ = The correlation of stock A and the market
    = 0.8

$\text{Corr}(R_B,R_M)$ = The correlation of stock B and the market
    = 0.2

$\text{Corr}(R_A,R_B)$ = The correlation of stock A and stock B
    = 0.6

a. If you are a typical, risk-averse investor, which stock would you prefer? Why?

b. What are the expected return and standard deviation of a portfolio consisting of 70 percent of stock A and 30 percent of stock B?

c. What is the beta of the portfolio in part (b)?

Appendix 10A IS BETA DEAD?

The capital-asset-pricing model represents one of the most important advances in financial economics. It is clearly useful for investment purposes, since it shows how the expected return on an asset is related to its beta. In addition, we will show in Chapter 12 that it is useful in corporate finance, since the discount rate on a project is a function of the project's beta. However, one must never forget that, as with any other model, the CAPM is not revealed truth but, rather, a construct to be empirically tested.

The first empirical tests of the CAPM occurred over 20 years ago and were quite supportive. Using data from the 1930s to the 1960s, researchers showed that the average return on a portfolio of stocks was positively related to the beta of the portfolio,[18] a finding consistent with the CAPM. Though some evidence in these studies was less consistent with the CAPM,[19] financial economists were quick to embrace the CAPM following these empirical papers.

While a large body of empirical work developed in the following decades, often with varying results, the CAPM was not seriously called into question until the 1990s. Two papers by Fama and French[20] (yes, the same Fama whose joint paper in 1973 with James MacBeth supported the CAPM) present evidence inconsistent with the model. Their work has received a great deal of attention, both in academic circles and in the popular press, with newspaper articles displaying headlines such as "Beta Is Dead!" These papers make two related points. First, they conclude that the relationship between average return and beta is weak over the period from 1941 to 1990 and virtually nonexistent from 1963 to 1990. Second, they argue that the average return on a security is negatively related to both the firm's price-to-earnings (P/E) ratio and the firm's market value-to-book value (M/B) ratio. These contentions, if confirmed by other research, would be quite damaging to the CAPM. After all, the CAPM states that the expected returns on stocks should be related *only* to beta, and not to other factors such as P/E and M/B.

However, a number of researchers have criticized the Fama-French papers. While we avoid an in-depth discussion of the fine points of the debate, we mention a few issues. First, although Fama and French cannot reject the hypothesis that average returns are unrelated to beta, one can also not reject the hypothesis that average returns are related to beta exactly as specified by the CAPM. In other words, while 50 years of data seem like a lot, they may simply not be enough to test the CAPM properly. Second, the result with P/E and M/B may be due to a statistical fallacy called a hindsight bias.[21] Third, P/E and M/B are merely two of an infinite number of possible factors. Thus, the relationship between average return and both P/E and M/B may be spurious, being nothing more than the result of data mining. Fourth, average returns are positively related to beta over the period from 1927 to the present. There appears to be no compelling reason for emphasizing a shorter period than this one. Fifth, average returns are actually positively related to beta over shorter periods when annual data, rather than monthly data, are used to estimate beta.[22] There appears to be no compelling reason for preferring either monthly data over annual data or vice versa. Thus, we believe that, while the results of Fama and French are quite intriguing, they cannot be viewed as the final word.

---

[18]Perhaps the two most well-known papers were Fischer Black, Michael C. Jensen, and Myron S. Scholes, "The Capital Asset Pricing Model: Some Empirical Tests," in M. Jensen, ed., *Studies in the Theory of Capital Markets* (New York: Praeger, 1972), and Eugene F. Fama and James MacBeth, "Risk, Return and Equilibrium: Some Empirical Tests," *Journal of Political Economy* 8 (1973), pp. 607–36.

[19]For example, the studies suggest that the average return on a zero-beta portfolio is above the risk-free rate, a finding inconsistent with the CAPM.

[20]Eugene F. Fama and Kenneth R. French, "The Cross-Section of Expected Stock Returns," *Journal of Finance* 47 (1992), pp. 427–66, and E. F. Fama and K. R. French, "Common Risk Factors in the Returns on Stocks and Bonds," *Journal of Financial Economics* 17 (1993), pp. 3–56.

[21]For example, see William J. Breen and Robert A. Koraczyk, "On Selection Biases in Book-to-Market Based Tests of Asset Pricing Models," unpublished paper. Northwestern University, November 1993; and S. P. Kothari, Jay Shanken, and Richard G. Sloan, "Another Look at the Cross-Section of Expected Stock Returns," *Journal of Finance* (March 1995).

[22]Points 4 and 5 are addressed in the Kothari, Shanken, and Sloan paper.

CHAPTER 11

An Alternative View of Risk and Return: The Arbitrage Pricing Theory

EXECUTIVE SUMMARY

T he previous two chapters mentioned the obvious fact that returns on securities are variable. This variability is measured by variance and by standard deviation. Next, we mentioned the somewhat less obvious fact that the returns on securities are interdependent. We measured the degree of interdependence between a pair of securities by covariance and by correlation. This interdependence led to a number of interesting results. First, we showed that diversification in stocks can eliminate some, but not all, risk. By contrast, we showed that diversification in a casino can eliminate all risk. Second, the interdependence of returns led to the capital-asset-pricing model (CAPM). This model posits a positive (and linear) relationship between the beta of a security and its expected return.

The CAPM was developed in the early 1960s.[1] An alternative to the CAPM, called the *arbitrage pricing theory* (APT), has been developed more recently.[2] For our purposes, the differences between the two models stem from the APT's treatment of interrelationship among the returns on securities.[3] The APT assumes that returns on securities are generated by a number of industrywide and marketwide factors. Correlation between a pair of securities occurs when these two securities are affected by the same factor or factors. By contrast, though the CAPM allows correlation among securities, it does not specify the underlying factors causing the correlation.

Both the APT and the CAPM imply a positive relationship between expected return and risk. In our (perhaps biased) opinion, the APT allows this relationship to be developed in a particularly intuitive manner. In addition, the APT views risk more generally than just the standardized covariance or beta of a security with the market portfolio. Therefore, we offer this approach as an alternative to the CAPM.

---

[1] In particular, see Jack Treynor, "Toward a Theory of the Market Value of Risky Assets," unpublished manuscript (1961); William F. Sharpe, "Capital Asset Prices: A Theory of Market Equilibrium under Conditions of Risk," *Journal of Finance* (September 1964); and John Lintner, "The Valuation of Risky Assets and the Selection of Risky Investments in Stock Portfolios and Capital Budgets," *Review of Economics and Statistics* (February 1965).

[2] See Stephen A. Ross, "The Arbitrage Theory of Capital Asset Pricing," *Journal of Economic Theory* (December 1976).

[3] This is by no means the only difference in the assumptions of the two models. For example, the CAPM usually assumes either that the returns on assets are normally distributed or that investors have quadratic utility functions. The APT does not require either assumption. While this and other differences are quite important in research, they are not relevant to the material presented in our text.

11.1 FACTOR MODELS: ANNOUNCEMENTS, SURPRISES, AND EXPECTED RETURNS

We learned in the previous chapter how to construct portfolios and how to evaluate their returns. We now step back and examine the returns on individual securities more closely. By doing this we will find that the portfolios inherit and alter the properties of the securities they comprise.

To be concrete, let us consider the return on the stock of a company called Flyers. What will determine this stock's return in, say, the coming month?

The return on any stock traded in a financial market consists of two parts. First, the *normal* or *expected return* from the stock is the part of the return that shareholders in the market predict or expect. It depends on all of the information shareholders have that bears on the stock, and it uses all of our understanding of what will influence the stock in the next month.

The second part is the *uncertain* or *risky return* on the stock. This is the portion that comes from information that will be revealed within the month. The list of such information is endless, but here are some examples:

- News about Flyers' research.
- Government figures released on the gross national product (GNP).
- Results of the latest arms-control talks.
- Discovery that a rival's product has been tampered with.
- News that Flyers' sales figures are higher than expected.
- A sudden drop in interest rates.
- The unexpected retirement of Flyers' founder and president.

A way to write the return on Flyers' stock in the coming month, then, is

$$R = \bar{R} + U$$

where R is the actual total return in the month, $\bar{R}$ is the expected part of the return, and U stands for the unexpected part of the return.

Some care must be exercised in studying the effect of these or other news items on the return. For example, the government might give us GNP or unemployment figures for this month, but how much of that is new information for shareholders? Surely at the beginning of the month shareholders will have some idea or forecast of what the monthly GNP will be. To the extent to which the shareholders had forecast the government's announcement, that forecast should be factored into the expected part of the return as of the beginning of the month, $\bar{R}$. On the other hand, insofar as the announcement by the government is a surprise and to the extent to which it influences the return on the stock, it will be part of U, the unanticipated part of the return.

As an example, suppose shareholders in the market had forecast that the GNP increase this month would be 0.5 percent. If GNP influences our company's stock, this forecast will be part of the information shareholders use to form the expectation, $\bar{R}$, of the monthly return. If the actual announcement this month is exactly 0.5 percent, the same as the forecast, then the shareholders learned nothing new, and the announcement is not news. It is like hearing a rumor about a friend when you knew it all along. Another way of saying this is that shareholders had already discounted the announcement. This use of the word *discount* is different from that in computing present value, but the spirit is similar. When we discount a dollar in the future, we say that it is worth less to us because of the time value of money. When we discount an announcement or a news item in the future, we mean that it has less impact on the market because the market already knew much of it.

On the other hand, suppose the government announced that the actual GNP increase during the year was 1.5 percent. Now shareholders have learned something—that the increase is one percentage point higher than they had forecast. This difference between the actual result and the forecast, one percentage point in this example, is sometimes called the *innovation* or *surprise.*

Any announcement can be broken into two parts, the anticipated or expected part and the surprise or innovation:

$$\text{Announcement} = \text{Expected part} + \text{Surprise}$$

The expected part of any announcement is part of the information the market uses to form the expectation, $\overline{R}$, of the return on the stock. The surprise is the news that influences the unanticipated return on the stock, U.

To give another example, if shareholders knew in January that the president of a firm was going to resign, the official announcement in February will be fully expected and will be discounted by the market. Because the announcement was expected before February, its influence on the stock will have taken place before February. The announcement itself in February will contain no surprise and the stock's price should not change at all at the announcement in February.

When we speak of news, then, we refer to the surprise part of any announcement and not the portion that the market has expected and therefore has already discounted.

CONCEPT QUESTIONS

- What are the two basic parts of a return?
- Under what conditions will some news have no effect on common stock prices?

11.2 RISK: SYSTEMATIC AND UNSYSTEMATIC

The unanticipated part of the return—that portion resulting from surprises—is the true risk of any investment. After all, if we got what we had expected, there would be no risk and no uncertainty.

There are important differences, though, among various sources of risk. Look at our previous list of news stories. Some of these stories are directed specifically at Flyers, and some are more general. Which of the news items are of specific importance to Flyers?

Announcements about interest rates or GNP are clearly important for nearly all companies, whereas the news about Flyers' president, its research, its sales, or the affairs of a rival company are of specific interest to Flyers. We will divide these two types of announcements and the resulting risk, then, into two components: a systematic portion, called *systematic risk,* and the remainder, which we call *specific* or *unsystematic risk.* The following definitions describe the difference:

- A *systematic risk* is any risk that affects a large number of assets, each to a greater or lesser degree.
- An *unsystematic risk* is a risk that specifically affects a single asset or a small group of assets.[4]

Uncertainty about general economic conditions, such as GNP, interest rates, or inflation, is an example of systematic risk. These conditions affect nearly all stocks to some degree.

---

[4]In the previous chapter, we briefly mentioned that unsystematic risk is risk that can be diversified away in a large portfolio. This result will also follow from the present analysis.

An unanticipated or surprise increase in inflation affects wages and the costs of the supplies that companies buy, the value of the assets that companies own, and the prices at which companies sell their products. These forces to which all companies are susceptible are the essence of systematic risk.

In contrast, the announcement of a small oil strike by a company may very well affect that company alone or a few other companies. Certainly, it is unlikely to have an effect on the world oil market. To stress that such information is unsystematic and affects only some specific companies, we sometimes call it an *idiosyncratic risk*.

The distinction between a systematic risk and an unsystematic risk is never as exact as we make it out to be. Even the most narrow and peculiar bit of news about a company ripples through the economy. It reminds us of the tale of the war that was lost because one horse lost a shoe; even a minor event may have an impact on the world. But this degree of hair-splitting should not trouble us much. To paraphrase a Supreme Court Justice's comment when speaking of pornography, we may not be able to define a systematic risk and an unsystematic risk exactly, but we know them when we see them.

This permits us to break down the risk of Flyers' stock into its two components: the systematic and the unsystematic. As is traditional, we will use the Greek epsilon, ϵ, to represent the unsystematic risk and write

$$R = \bar{R} + U$$
$$= \bar{R} + m + \epsilon$$

where we have used the letter m to stand for the systematic risk. Sometimes systematic risk is referred to as *market risk*. This emphasizes the fact that m influences all assets in the market to some extent.

The important point about the way we have broken the total risk, U, into its two components, m and ϵ, is that ϵ, because it is specific to the company, is unrelated to the specific risk of most other companies. For example, the unsystematic risk on Flyers' stock, ϵ_F, is unrelated to the unsystematic risk of Xerox's stock, ϵ_X. The risk that Flyers' stock will go up or down because of a discovery by its research team—or its failure to discover something—probably is unrelated to any of the specific uncertainties that affect Xerox stock.

Using the terms of the previous chapter, this means that the unsystematic risk of Flyers' stock and Xerox's stock are unrelated to each other, or uncorrelated. In the symbols of statistics,

$$\text{Corr}(\epsilon_F, \epsilon_X) = 0$$

QUESTIONS
• Describe the difference between systematic risk and unsystematic risk.
• Why is unsystematic risk sometimes referred to as *idiosyncratic risk?*

11.3 SYSTEMATIC RISK AND BETAS

The fact that the unsystematic parts of the returns on two companies are unrelated to each other does not mean that the systematic portions are unrelated. On the contrary, because both companies are influenced by the same systematic risks, individual companies' systematic risks and therefore their total returns will be related.

For example, a surprise about inflation will influence almost all companies to some extent. How sensitive is Flyers' stock return to unanticipated changes in inflation? If Flyers' stock tends to go up on news that inflation is exceeding expectations, we would say that it is positively related to inflation. If the stock goes down when inflation exceeds expectations and up when inflation falls short of expectations, it is negatively related. In the unusual case where a stock's return is uncorrelated with inflation surprises, inflation has no effect on it.

We capture the influence of a systematic risk like inflation on a stock by using the **beta coefficient.** The beta coefficient, β, tells us the response of the stock's return to a systematic risk. In the previous chapter, beta measured the responsiveness of a security's return to a specific risk factor, the return on the market portfolio. We used this type of responsiveness to develop the capital-asset-pricing model. Because we now consider many types of systematic risks, our current work can be viewed as a generalization of our work in the previous chapter.

If a company's stock is positively related to the risk of inflation, that stock has a positive inflation beta. If it is negatively related to inflation, its inflation beta is negative, and if it is uncorrelated with inflation, its inflation beta is zero.

It's not hard to imagine some stocks with positive inflation betas and other stocks with negative inflation betas. The stock of a company owning gold mines will probably have a positive inflation beta because an unanticipated rise in inflation is usually associated with an increase in gold prices. On the other hand, an automobile company facing stiff foreign competition might find that an increase in inflation means that the wages it pays are higher, but that it cannot raise its prices to cover the increase. This profit squeeze, as the company's expenses rise faster than its revenues, would give its stock a negative inflation beta.

Some companies that have few assets and that act as brokers—buying items in competitive markets and reselling them in other markets—might be relatively unaffected by inflation, because their costs and their revenues would rise and fall together. Their stock would have an inflation beta of zero.

Some structure is useful at this point. Suppose we have identified three systematic risks on which we want to focus. We may believe that these three are sufficient to describe the systematic risks that influence stock returns. Three likely candidates are inflation, GNP, and interest rates. Thus, every stock will have a beta associated with each of these systematic risks: an inflation beta, a GNP beta, and an interest-rate beta. We can write the return on the stock, then, in the following form:

$$R = \overline{R} + U$$
$$= \overline{R} + m + \epsilon$$
$$= \overline{R} + \beta_I F_I + \beta_{GNP} F_{GNP} + \beta_r F_r + \epsilon$$

where we have used the symbol β_I to denote the stock's inflation beta, β_{GNP} for its GNP beta, and β_r to stand for its interest-rate beta. In the equation, F stands for a surprise, whether it be in inflation, GNP, or interest rates.

Let us go through an example to see how the surprises and the expected return add up to produce the total return, R, on a given stock. To make it more familiar, suppose that the return is over a horizon of a year and not just a month. Suppose that at the beginning of the year, inflation is forecast to be 5 percent for the year, GNP is forecast to increase by 2 percent, and interest rates are expected not to change. Suppose the stock we are looking at has the following betas:

$$\beta_I = 2$$
$$\beta_{GNP} = 1$$
$$\beta_r = -1.8$$

The magnitude of the beta describes how great an impact a systematic risk has on a stock's returns. A beta of +1 indicates that the stock's return rises and falls one for one with the systematic factor. This means, in our example, that because the stock has a GNP beta of 1, it experiences a 1-percent increase in return for every 1-percent surprise increase in GNP. If its GNP beta were −2, it would fall by 2 percent when there was an unanticipated increase of 1 percent in GNP, and it would rise by 2 percent if GNP experienced a surprise 1-percent decline.

Finally, let us suppose that during the year the following occurs: Inflation rises by 7 percent, GNP rises by only 1 percent, and interest rates fall by 2 percent. Last, suppose we learn some good news about the company, perhaps that it is succeeding quickly with some new business strategy, and that this unanticipated development contributes 5 percent to its return. In other words,

$$\epsilon = 5\%$$

Let us assemble all of this information to find what return the stock had during the year.

First, we must determine what news or surprises took place in the systematic factors. From our information we know that

$$\text{Expected inflation} = 5\%$$
$$\text{Expected GNP change} = 2\%$$

and

$$\text{Expected change in interest rates} = 0\%$$

This means that the market had discounted these changes, and the surprises will be the difference between what actually takes place and these expectations:

$$
\begin{aligned}
F_I &= \text{Surprise in inflation} \\
&= \text{Actual inflation} - \text{Expected inflation} \\
&= 7\% - 5\% \\
&= 2\%
\end{aligned}
$$

Similarly,

$$
\begin{aligned}
F_{\text{GNP}} &= \text{Surprise in GNP} \\
&= \text{Actual GNP} - \text{Expected GNP} \\
&= 1\% - 2\% \\
&= -1\%
\end{aligned}
$$

and

$$
\begin{aligned}
F_r &= \text{Surprise in change in interest rates} \\
&= \text{Actual change} - \text{Expected change} \\
&= -2\% - 0\% \\
&= -2\%
\end{aligned}
$$

The total effect of the systematic risks on the stock return, then, is

$$
\begin{aligned}
m &= \text{Systematic risk portion of return} \\
&= \beta_I F_I + \beta_{\text{GNP}} F_{\text{GNP}} + \beta_r F_r \\
&= [2 \times 2\%] + [1 \times (-1\%)] + [(-1.8) \times (-2\%)] \\
&= 6.6\%
\end{aligned}
$$

Combining this with the unsystematic risk portion, the total risky portion of the return on the stock is

$$m + \epsilon = 6.6\% + 5\% = 11.6\%$$

Last, if the expected return on the stock for the year was, say, 4 percent, the total return from all three components will be

$$
\begin{aligned}
R &= \bar{R} + m + \epsilon \\
&= 4\% + 6.6\% + 5\% \\
&= 15.6\%
\end{aligned}
$$

The model we have been looking at is called a **factor model,** and the systematic sources of risk, designated *F,* are called the *factors.* To be perfectly formal, a *k-factor model* is a model where each stock's return is generated by

$$R = \overline{R} + \beta_1 F_1 + \beta_2 F_2 + \ldots + \beta_k F_k + \epsilon$$

where ϵ is specific to a particular stock and uncorrelated with the ϵ term for other stocks. In our preceding example we had a three-factor model. We used inflation, GNP, and the change in interest rates as examples of systematic sources of risk, or factors. Researchers have not settled on what is the correct set of factors. Like so many other questions, this might be one of those matters that is never laid to rest.

In practice, researchers frequently use a one-factor model for returns. They do not use all of the sorts of economic factors we used previously as examples; instead, they use an index of stock market returns—like the S&P 500, or even a more broadly based index with more stocks in it—as the single factor. Using the single-factor model we can write returns as

$$R = \overline{R} + \beta(R_{S\&P500} - \overline{R}_{S\&P500}) + \epsilon$$

Where there is only one factor (the returns on the S&P 500–portfolio index), we do not need to put a subscript on the beta. In this form (with minor modifications) the factor model is called a **market model.** This term is employed because the index that is used for the factor is an index of returns on the whole (stock) market. The market model is written as

$$R = \overline{R} + \beta(R_M - \overline{R}_M) + \epsilon$$

where R_M is the return on the market portfolio.[5] The single β is called the *beta coefficient.*

CONCEPT QUESTIONS

?

- What is an inflation beta? A GNP beta? An interest-rate beta?
- What is the difference between a k-factor model and the market model?
- Define the beta coefficient.

11.4 PORTFOLIOS AND FACTOR MODELS

Now let us see what happens to portfolios of stocks when each of the stocks follows a one-factor model. For purposes of discussion, we will take the coming one-month period and examine returns. We could have used a day or a year or any other time period. If the period represents the time between decisions, however, we would rather it be short than long, and a month is a reasonable time frame to use.

We will create portfolios from a list of N stocks, and we will use a one-factor model to capture the systematic risk. The ith stock in the list will therefore have returns

$$R_i = \overline{R}_i + \beta_i F + \epsilon_i \tag{11.1}$$

where we have subscripted the variables to indicate that they relate to the ith stock. Notice that the factor F is not subscripted. The factor that represents systematic risk could be a surprise in GNP, or we could use the market model and let the difference between the S&P 500 return and what we expect that return to be, $R_{S\&P500} - \overline{R}_{S\&P500}$, be the factor. In either case, the factor applies to all of the stocks.

---

[5]Alternatively, the market model could be written as

$$R = \alpha + \beta R_M + \epsilon$$

Here alpha (α) is an intercept term equal $\overline{R} - \beta\overline{R}_M$.

■ FIGURE 11.1 **The One-Factor Model**

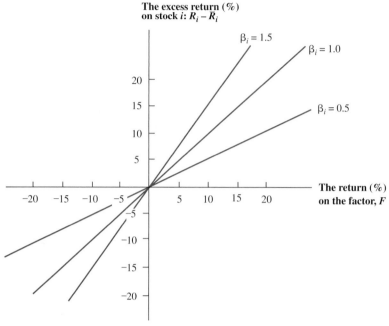

Each line represents a different security, where each security has a different beta.

The β_i is subscripted because it represents the unique way the factor influences the *i*th stock. To recapitulate our discussion of factor models, if β_i is zero, the returns on the *i*th stock are

$$R_i = \overline{R}_i + \epsilon_i$$

In words, the *i*th stock's returns are unaffected by the factor, *F*, if β_i is zero. If β_i is positive, positive changes in the factor raise the *i*th stock's returns, and declines lower them. Conversely, if β_i is negative, its returns and the factor move in opposite directions.

Figure 11.1 illustrates the relationship between a stock's excess returns, $R_i - \overline{R}_i$, and the factor *F* for different betas, where $\beta_i > 0$. The lines in Figure 11.1 plot equation (11.1) on the assumption that there has been no unsystematic risk. That is, $\epsilon_i = 0$. Because we are assuming positive betas, the lines slope upward, indicating that the return on the stock rises with *F*. Notice that if the factor is zero ($F = 0$), the line passes through zero on the *y*-axis.

Now let us see what happens when we create stock portfolios where each stock follows a one-factor model. Let X_i be the proportion of security *i* in the portfolio. That is, if an individual with a portfolio of $100 wants $20 in General Motors, we say $X_{GM} = 20\%$. Because the *X*s represent the proportions of wealth we are investing in each of the stocks, we know that they must add up to 100 percent or 1. That is,

$$X_1 + X_2 + X_3 + \ldots + X_N = 1$$

We know that the portfolio return is the weighted average of the returns on the individual assets in the portfolio. Algebraically, this can be written as:

$$R_P = X_1R_1 + X_2R_2 + X_3R_3 + \ldots + X_NR_N \tag{11.2}$$

We saw from equation (11.1) that each asset, in turn, is determined by both the factor F and the unsystematic risk of ϵ_i. Thus, by substituting equation (11.1) for each R_i in equation (11.2), we have

$$R_P = X_1(\overline{R}_1 + \beta_1 F + \epsilon_1) \qquad\qquad + X_2(\overline{R}_2 + \beta_2 F + \epsilon_2) \qquad (11.3)$$
$$\text{(Return on stock } 1) \qquad\qquad\qquad \text{(Return on stock } 2)$$

$$+ X_3(\overline{R}_3 + \beta_3 F + \epsilon_3) + \ldots + X_N(\overline{R}_N + \beta_N F + \epsilon_N)$$
$$\text{(Return on stock } 3) \qquad\qquad\qquad \text{(Return on stock } N)$$

Equation (11.3) shows us that the return on a portfolio is determined by three sets of parameters:

1. The expected return on each individual security, $\overline{R}_i$.
2. The beta of each security multiplied by the factor F.
3. The unsystematic risk of each individual security, ϵ_i.

We express equation (11.3) in terms of these three sets of parameters as

Weighted Average of Expected Returns:

$$R_P = X_1\overline{R}_1 + X_2\overline{R}_2 + X_3\overline{R}_3 + \ldots + X_N\overline{R}_N \qquad (11.4)$$

(Weighted Average of Betas)*F:*

$$+ (X_1\beta_1 + X_2\beta_2 + X_3\beta_3 + \ldots + X_N\beta_N)F$$

Weighted Average of Unsystematic Risks:

$$+ X_1\epsilon_1 + X_2\epsilon_2 + X_3\epsilon_3 + \ldots + X_N\epsilon_N$$

This rather imposing equation is actually straightforward. The first row is the weighted average of each security's expected return. The items in the parentheses of the second row represent the weighted average of each security's beta. This weighted average is, in turn, multiplied by the factor F. The third row represents a weighted average of the unsystematic risks of the individual securities.

Where does uncertainty appear in equation (11.4)? There is no uncertainty in the first row because only the expected value of each security's return appears there. Uncertainty in the second row is reflected by only one item, F. That is, while we know that the expected value of F is zero, we do not know what its value will be over a particular time period. Uncertainty in the third row is reflected by each unsystematic risk, ϵ_i.

Portfolios and Diversification

In the previous sections of this chapter, we expressed the return on a single security in terms of our factor model. Portfolios were treated next. Because investors generally hold diversified portfolios, we now want to know what equation (11.4) looks like in a *large* or diversified portfolio.[6]

As it turns out, something unusual occurs to equation (11.4); the third row actually *disappears* in a large portfolio. To see this, consider a gambler who divides $1,000 by betting on red over many spins of the roulette wheel. For example, he may participate in 1,000 spins, betting $1 at a time. Though we do not know ahead of time whether a particular spin will yield red or black, we can be confident that red will win about 50 percent of the time. Ignoring the house take, the investor can be expected to end up with just about his original $1,000.

---

[6]Technically, we can think of a large portfolio as one where an investor keeps increasing the number of securities without limit. In practice, *effective* diversification would occur if at least a few dozen securities were held.

Though we are concerned with stocks, not roulette wheels, the same principle applies. Each security has its own unsystematic risk, where the surprise for one stock is unrelated to the surprise of another stock. By investing a small amount in each security, the weighted average of the unsystematic risks will be very close to zero in a large portfolio.[7]

Although the third row completely vanishes in a large portfolio, nothing unusual occurs in either row 1 or row 2. Row 1 remains a weighted average of the expected returns on the individual securities as securities are added to the portfolio. Because there is no uncertainty at all in the first row, there is no way for diversification to cause this row to vanish. The terms inside the parentheses of the second row remain a weighted average of the betas. They do not vanish, either, when securities are added. Because the factor F is unaffected when securities are added to the portfolios, the second row does not vanish.

Why does the third row vanish while the second row does not, though both rows reflect uncertainty? The key is that there are many unsystematic risks in row 3. Because these risks are independent of each other, the effect of diversification becomes stronger as we add more assets to the portfolio. The resulting portfolio becomes less and less risky, and the return becomes more certain. However, the systematic risk, F, affects all securities because it is outside the parentheses in row 2. Since one cannot avoid this factor by investing in many securities, diversification does not occur in this row.

EXAMPLE

The preceding material can be further explained by the following example. We keep our one-factor model here but make three specific assumptions:

1. All securities have the same expected return of 10 percent. This assumption implies that the first row of equation (11.4) must also equal 10 percent because this row is a weighted average of the expected returns of the individual securities.

2. All securities have a beta of 1. The sum of the terms inside the parentheses in the second row of (11.4) must equal 1 because these terms are a weighted average of the individual betas. Since the terms inside the parentheses are multiplied by F, the value of the second row is $1 \times F = F$.

3. In this example, we focus on the behavior of one individual, Walter V. Bagehot. Mr. Bagehot decides to hold an equally weighted portfolio. That is, the proportion of each security in his portfolio is 1/N.

We can express the return on Mr. Bagehot's portfolio as

Return on Walter V. Bagehot's Portfolio:

$$R_P = 10\% + F + (\frac{1}{N}\epsilon_1 + \frac{1}{N}\epsilon_2 + \frac{1}{N}\epsilon_3 + \ldots + \frac{1}{N}\epsilon_N) \qquad (11.4')$$

From   From   From row 3 of (11.4)
row 1   row 2
of (11.4) of (11.4)

---

[7]More precisely, we say that the weighted average of the unsystematic risk approaches zero as the number of equally weighted securities in a portfolio approaches infinity.

■ FIGURE 11.2   **Diversification and the Portfolio Risk for an Equally Weighted Portfolio**

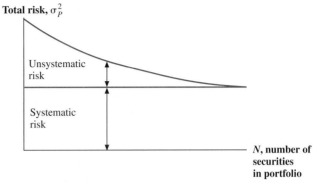

Total risk decreases as the number of securities in the portfolio rises. This drop occurs only in the unsystematic-risk component. Systematic risk is unaffected by diversification.

We mentioned before that, as N increases without limit, row 3 of (11.4) becomes equal to zero.[8] Thus, the return to Walter Bagehot's portfolio when the number of securities is very large is

$$R_P = 10\% + F \qquad (11.4'')$$

The key to diversification is exhibited in (11.4″). The unsystematic risk of row 3 vanishes, while the systematic risk of row 2 remains.

This is illustrated in Figure 11.2. Systematic risk, captured by variation in the factor F, is not reduced through diversification. Conversely, unsystematic risk diminishes as securities are added, vanishing as the number of securities becomes infinite. Our result is analogous to the diversification example of the previous chapter. In that chapter, we said that undiversifiable or systematic risk arises from positive covariances between securities. In this chapter, we say that systematic risk arises from a common factor F. Because a common factor causes positive covariances, the arguments of the two chapters are parallel.

QUESTIONS

- How can the return on a portfolio be expressed in terms of a factor model?
- What risk is diversified away in a large portfolio?

11.5 BETAS AND EXPECTED RETURNS

The Linear Relationship

We have argued many times that the expected return on a security compensates for its risk. In the previous chapter we showed that market beta (the standardized covariance of the security's returns with those of the market) was the appropriate measure of risk under the assumptions

---

[8]Our presentation on this point has been nonrigorous. The student interested in more rigor should note that the variance of row 3 is

$$\frac{1}{N^2}\sigma_\epsilon^2 + \frac{1}{N^2}\sigma_\epsilon^2 + \frac{1}{N^2}\sigma_\epsilon^2 + \ldots + \frac{1}{N^2}\sigma_\epsilon^2 = \frac{1}{N^2}N\sigma_\epsilon^2$$

where σ_ϵ^2 is the variance of each ϵ. This can be rewritten as σ_ϵ^2/N, which tends to 0 as N goes to infinity.

■ FIGURE 11.3 **A Graph of Beta and Expected Return for Individual Stocks under the One-Factor Model**

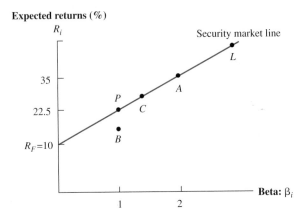

of homogeneous expectations and riskless borrowing and lending. The capital-asset-pricing model, which posited these assumptions, implied that the expected return on a security was positively (and linearly) related to its beta. We will find a similar relationship between risk and return in the one-factor model of this chapter.

We begin by noting that the relevant risk in large and well-diversified portfolios is all systematic because unsystematic risk is diversified away. An implication is that, when a well-diversified shareholder considers changing her holdings of a particular stock, she can ignore the security's unsystematic risk.

Notice that we are not claiming that stocks, like portfolios, have no unsystematic risk. Nor are we saying that the unsystematic risk of a stock will not affect its returns. Stocks do have unsystematic risk, and their actual returns do depend on the unsystematic risk. Because this risk washes out in a well-diversified portfolio, however, shareholders can ignore this unsystematic risk when they consider whether or not to add a stock to their portfolio. Therefore, if shareholders are ignoring the unsystematic risk, only the systematic risk of a stock can be related to its *expected* return.

This relationship is illustrated in the security market line of Figure 11.3. Points *P, C, A,* and *L* all lie on the line emanating from the risk-free rate of 10 percent. The points representing each of these four assets can be created by combinations of the risk-free rate and any of the other three assets. For example, since *A* has a beta of 2.0 and *P* has a beta of 1.0, a portfolio of 50 percent in asset *A* and 50 percent in the riskless rate has the same beta as asset *P.* The risk-free rate is 10 percent and the expected return on security *A* is 35 percent, implying that the combination's return of 22.5 percent [(10% + 35%)/2] is identical to security *P*'s expected return. Because security *P* has both the same beta and the same expected return as a combination of the riskless asset and security *A,* an individual is equally inclined to add a small amount of security *P* and to add a small amount of this combination to her portfolio. However, the unsystematic risk of security *P* need not be equal to the unsystematic risk of the combination of security *A* and the risk-free rate because unsystematic risk is diversified away in a large portfolio.

Of course, the potential combinations of points on the security market line are endless. One can duplicate *P* by combinations of the risk-free rate and either *C* or *L* (or both of them). One can duplicate *C* (or *A* or *L*) by borrowing at the risk-free rate to invest in *P.* The infinite number of points on the security market line that are not labeled can be used as well.

Now consider security *B*. Because its expected return is below the line, no investor would hold it. Instead, the investor would prefer security *P*, a combination of security *A* and the riskless asset, or some other combination. Thus, security *B*'s price is too high. Its price will fall in a competitive market, forcing its expected return back up to the line in equilibrium.

The preceding discussion allows us to provide an equation for the security market line of Figure 11.3. We know that a line can be described algebraically from two points. It is perhaps easiest to focus on the risk-free rate and asset *P*, since the risk-free rate has a beta of 0 and *P* has a beta of 1.

Because we know that the return on any zero-beta asset is R_F and the expected return on asset *P* is $\bar{R}_P$, it can easily be shown that

$$\bar{R} = R_F + \beta(\bar{R}_P - R_F) \tag{11.5}$$

In equation (11.5), $\bar{R}$ can be thought of as the expected return on any security or portfolio lying on the security market line. β is the beta of that security or portfolio.

The Market Portfolio and the Single Factor

In the CAPM, the beta of a security measures the security's responsiveness to movements in the market portfolio. In the one-factor model of the APT, the beta of a security measures its responsiveness to the factor. We now relate the market portfolio to the single factor.

A large, diversified portfolio has no unsystematic risk because the unsystematic risks of the individual securities are diversified away. Assuming enough securities so that the market portfolio is fully diversified and assuming that no security has a disproportionate market share, this portfolio is fully diversified and contains no unsystematic risk.[9] In other words, the market portfolio is perfectly correlated with the single factor, implying that the market portfolio is really a scaled-up or scaled-down version of the factor. After scaling properly, we can treat the market portfolio as the factor itself.

The market portfolio, like every security or portfolio, lies on the security market line. When the market portfolio is the factor, the beta of the market portfolio is 1 by definition. This is shown in Figure 11.4. (We deleted the securities and the specific expected returns from Figure 11.3 for clarity: the two graphs are otherwise identical.) With the market portfolio as the factor, equation (11.5) becomes

$$\bar{R} = R_F + \beta(\bar{R}_M - R_F)$$

where $\bar{R}_M$ is the expected return on the market. This equation shows that the expected return on any asset, $\bar{R}$, is linearly related to the security's beta. The equation is identical to that of the CAPM, which we developed in the previous chapter.

CONCEPT QUESTION

• What is the relationship between the one-factor model and the CAPM?

---

[9]This assumption is plausible in the real world. For example, even the market value of General Electric is only 3 percent to 4 percent of the market value of the S&P 500 Index.

■ FIGURE 11.4 **A Graph of Beta and Expected Return for Individual Stocks under the One-Factor Model**

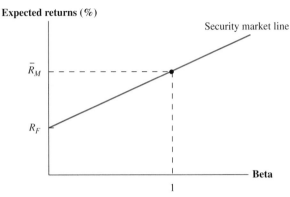

The factor is scaled so that it is identical to the market portfolio. The beta of the market portfolio is 1.

11.6 THE CAPITAL-ASSET-PRICING MODEL AND THE ARBITRAGE PRICING THEORY

The CAPM and the APT are alternative models of risk and return. It is worthwhile to consider the differences between the two models, both in terms of pedagogy and in terms of application.

Differences in Pedagogy

We feel that the CAPM has at least one strong advantage from the student's point of view. The derivation of the CAPM necessarily brings the reader through a discussion of efficient sets. This treatment—beginning with the case of two risky assets, moving to the case of many risky assets, and finishing when a riskless asset is added to the many risky ones—is of great intuitive value. This sort of presentation is not as easily accomplished with the APT.

However, the APT has an offsetting advantage. The model adds factors until the unsystematic risk of any security is uncorrelated with the unsystematic risk of every other security. Under this formulation, it is easily shown that (1) unsystematic risk steadily falls (and ultimately vanishes) as the number of securities in the portfolio increases but (2) the systematic risks do not decrease. This result was also shown in the CAPM, though the intuition was cloudier because the unsystematic risks could be correlated across securities.

Differences in Application

One advantage of the APT is that it can handle multiple factors while the CAPM ignores them. Although the bulk of our presentation in this chapter focused on the one-factor model, a multifactor model is probably more reflective of reality. That is, one must abstract from many marketwide and industrywide factors before the unsystematic risk of one security becomes uncorrelated with the unsystematic risks of other securities. Under this multifactor version of the APT, the relationship between risk and return can be expressed as:

$$\overline{R} = R_F + (\overline{R}_1 - R_F)\beta_1 + (\overline{R}_2 - R_F)\beta_2 + (\overline{R}_3 - R_F)\beta_3 + \ldots + (\overline{R}_K - R_F)\beta_K \quad (11.6)$$

In this equation, β_1 stands for the security's beta with respect to the first factor, β_2 stands for the security's beta with respect to the second factor, and so on. For example, if the first factor is GNP, β_1 is the security's GNP beta. The term $\overline{R}_1$ is the expected return on a security (or portfolio) whose beta with respect to the first factor is 1 and whose beta with respect to all other factors is zero. Because the market compensates for risk, $(\overline{R}_1 - R_F)$ will be positive in the normal case.[10] (An analogous interpretation can be given to $\overline{R}_2$, $\overline{R}_3$, and so on.)

The equation states that the security's expected return is related to the security's factor betas. The intuition in equation (11.6) is straightforward. Each factor represents risk that cannot be diversified away. The higher a security's beta with regard to a particular factor is, the higher is the risk that the security bears. In a rational world, the expected return on the security should compensate for this risk. The above equation states that the expected return is a summation of the risk-free rate plus the compensation for each type of risk that the security bears.

As an example, consider a study where the factors were monthly growth in industrial production (IP), change in expected inflation (ΔEI), unanticipated inflation (UI), unanticipated change in the risk premium between risky bonds and default-free bonds (URP), and unanticipated change in the difference between the return on long-term government bonds and the return on short-term government bonds (UBR).[11] Using the period 1958–1984, the empirical results of the study indicated that the expected monthly return on any stock, $\overline{R}_S$, can be described as

$$\overline{R}_S = 0.0041 + 0.0136\beta_{IP} - 0.0001\beta_{\Delta EI} - 0.0006\beta_{UI} + 0.0072\beta_{URP} - 0.0052\beta_{UBR}$$

Suppose a particular stock had the following betas: $\beta_{IP} = 1.1$, $\beta_{\Delta EI} = 2$, $\beta_{UI} = 3$, $\beta_{URP} = 0.1$, $\beta_{UBR} = 1.6$. The expected monthly return on that security would be

$$\begin{aligned}\overline{R}_S = 0.0041 &+ 0.0136 \times 1.1 - 0.0001 \times 2 \\ &- 0.0006 \times 3 + 0.0072 \times 0.1 - 0.0052 \times 1.6 = 0.0095\end{aligned}$$

Assuming that a firm is unlevered and that one of the firm's projects has risk equivalent to that of the firm, this value of 0.0095 (i.e., .95%) can be used as the monthly discount rate for the project. (Because annual data are often supplied for capital budgeting purposes, the annual rate of $0.120 [(1.0095)^{12} - 1]$ might be used instead.)

Because many factors appear on the right-hand side of equation (11.5), the APT formulation has the potential to measure expected returns more accurately than does the CAPM. However, as we mentioned earlier, one cannot easily determine which are the appropriate factors. The factors in the above study were included for reasons of both common sense and convenience. They were not derived from theory.

By contrast, the use of the market index in the CAPM formulation is implied by the theory of the previous chapter. We suggested in earlier chapters that the S&P 500 Index mirrors stock market movements quite well. Using the Ibbotson-Sinquefield results showing that the yearly return on the S&P 500 Index was, on average, 9.2 percent greater than the risk-free rate, the last chapter easily calculated expected returns on different securities from the CAPM.[12]

---

[10] Actually, $(\overline{R}_i - R_F)$ could be negative in the case where factor i is perceived as a hedge of some sort.

[11] N. Chen, R. Roll, and S. Ross, "Economic Forces and the Stock Market," *Journal of Business* (July 1986).

[12] Though many researchers assume that surrogates for the market portfolio are easily found, Richard Roll, "A Critique of the Asset Pricing Theory's Tests," *Journal of Financial Economics* (March 1977), argues that the absence of a universally acceptable proxy for the market portfolio seriously impairs application of the theory. After all, the market must include real estate, racehorses, and other assets that are not in the stock market.

11.7 EMPIRICAL APPROACHES TO ASSET PRICING

Empirical Models

The CAPM and the APT by no means exhaust the models and techniques used in practice to measure the expected return on risky assets. Both the CAPM and the APT are *risk-based models.* They each measure the risk of a security by its beta(s) on some systematic factor(s), and they each argue that the expected excess return must be proportional to the beta(s). While we have seen that this is intuitively appealing and has a strong basis in theory, there are alternative approaches.

Most of these alternatives can be lumped under the broad heading of parametric or **empirical models.** The word *empirical* refers to the fact that these approaches are based less on some theory of how financial markets work and more on simply looking for regularities and relations in the history of market data. In these approaches the researcher specifies some parameters or attributes associated with the securities in question and then examines the data directly for a relation between these attributes and expected returns. For example, an extensive amount of research has been done on whether the expected return on a firm is related to its size. Is it true that small firms have higher average returns than large firms? Researchers have also examined a variety of accounting measures such as the ratio of the price of a stock to the accounting earnings, the P/E ratio, and the closely related ratio of the market value of the stock to the book value of the company, the M/B ratio. Here it might be argued that companies with low P/E's or low M/B's are "undervalued" and can be expected to have higher returns in the future.

To use the empirical approach to determine the expected return, we would estimate the following equation:

$$\overline{R}_i = R_F + k_{P/E}(P/E)_i + k_{M/B}(M/B)_i + k_{size}(size)_P$$

where $\overline{R}_i$ is the expected return of firm *i,* and where the k's are coefficients that we estimate from stock market data. Notice that this is the same form as equation (11.6) with the firm's attributes in place of betas and with the k's in place of the excess factor portfolio returns.

When tested with data, these parametric approaches seem to do quite well. In fact, when comparisons are made between using parameters and using betas to predict stock returns, the parameters, such as P/E and M/B, seem to work better. There are a variety of possible explanations for these results, and the issues have certainly not been settled. Critics of the empirical approach are skeptical of what they call *data mining.* The particular parameters that researchers work with are often chosen because they have been shown to be related to returns. For instance, suppose that you were asked to explain the change in SAT test scores over the past 40 years in some particular state. Suppose that to do this you searched through all of the data series you could find. After much searching, you might discover, for example, that the change in the scores was directly related to the jackrabbit population in Arizona. We know that any such relation is purely accidental but if you search long enough and have enough choices, you will find something even if it is not really there. It's a bit like staring at clouds. After a while you will see clouds that look like anything you want, clowns, bears, or whatever, but all you are really doing is data mining.

Needless to say, the researchers on these matters defend their work by arguing that they have not mined the data and have been very careful to avoid such traps by not snooping at the data to see what will work.

Of course, as a matter of pure theory, since anyone in the market can easily look up the P/E ratio of a firm, one would certainly not expect to find that firms with low P/E's did better than firms with high P/E's simply because they were undervalued. In an efficient market, such public measures of undervaluation would be quickly exploited and would not expect to last.

Perhaps a better explanation for the success of empirical approaches lies in a synthesis of the risk-based approaches and the empirical methods. In an efficient market, risk and return are related, hence perhaps the parameters or attributes which appear to be related to returns are also better measures of risk. For example, if we were to find that low P/E firms outperformed high P/E firms and that this was true even for firms that had the same beta(s), then we have at least two possible explanations. First, we could simply discard the risk-based theories as incorrect. Furthermore, we could argue that markets are inefficient and that buying low P/E stocks provides us with an opportunity to make higher than predicted returns. Second, we could argue that *both* views of the world are correct and that the P/E is really just a better way to measure systematic risk, i.e., beta(s), than directly estimating beta from the data.

Style Portfolios

In addition to their use as a platform for estimating expected returns, stock attributes are also widely used as a way of characterizing money management styles. For example, a portfolio that has a P/E ratio much in excess of the market average might be characterized as a high P/E or a **growth stock portfolio.** Similarly, a portfolio made up of stocks with an average P/E less than that for a market index might be characterized as a low P/E or a **value portfolio.**

To evaluate how well a portfolio manager is doing, often their performance is compared with the performance of some basic indexes. For example, the portfolio returns of a manager who purchases large U.S. stocks might be compared to the performance of the S&P 500 Index. In such a case the S&P 500 is said to be the **benchmark** against which their performance is measured. Similarly, an international manager might be compared against some common index of international stocks. In choosing an appropriate benchmark, care should be taken to identify a benchmark that contains only those types of stocks that the manager targets as representative of his or her style and that are also available to be purchased. A manager who was told not to purchase any stocks in the S&P 500 Index would not consider it legitimate to be compared against the S&P 500.

Increasingly, too, managers are compared not only against an index, but also against a peer group of similar managers. The performance of a fund that advertises itself as a growth fund might be measured against the performance of a large sample of similar funds. For instance, the performance over some period commonly is assigned to quartiles. The top 25 percent of the funds are said to be in the first quartile, the next 25 percent in the second quartile, the next 25 percent in the third quartile, and the worst performing 25 percent of the funds in the last quartile. If the fund we are examining happens to have a performance that falls in the second quartile, then we speak of it as a second quartile manager.

Similarly, we call a fund that purchases low M/B stocks a value fund and would measure its performance against a sample of similar value funds. These approaches to measuring performance are relatively new, and they are part of an active and exciting effort to refine our ability to identify and use investment skills.

CONCEPT QUESTIONS

- Empirical models are sometimes called factor models. What is the difference between a factor as we have used it previously in this chapter and an attribute as we use it in this section?
- What is data mining and why might it overstate the relation between some stock attribute and returns?
- What is wrong with measuring the performance of a U.S. growth stock manager against a benchmark composed of English stocks?

11.8 SUMMARY AND CONCLUSIONS

The previous chapter developed the capital-asset-pricing model (CAPM). As an alternative, this chapter develops the arbitrage pricing theory (APT).

1. The APT assumes that stock returns are generated according to factor models. For example, we might describe a stock's return as

$$R = \bar{R} + \beta_I F_I + \beta_{GNP} F_{GNP} + \beta_r F_r = \epsilon$$

where I, GNP, and r stand for inflation, gross national product, and the interest rate, respectively. The three factors F_I, F_{GNP}, and F_r represent systematic risk because these factors affect many securities. The term ϵ is considered unsystematic risk because it is unique to each individual security.

2. For convenience, we frequently describe a security's return according to a one-factor model:

$$R = \bar{R} + \beta F + \epsilon$$

3. As securities are added to a portfolio, the unsystematic risks of the individual securities offset each other. A fully diversified portfolio has no unsystematic risk but still has systematic risk. This result indicates that diversification can eliminate some, but not all, of the risk of individual securities.

4. Because of this, the expected return on a stock is positively related to its systematic risk. In a one-factor model, the systematic risk of a security is simply the beta of the CAPM. Thus, the implications of the CAPM and the one-factor APT are identical. However, each security has many risks in a multifactor model. The expected return on a security is positively related to the beta of the security with each factor.

5. Empirical or parametric models that capture the relations between returns and stock attributes such as P/E or M/B ratios can be estimated directly from the data without any appeal to theory. These ratios are also used to measure the style of a portfolio manager and to construct benchmarks and samples against which they are measured.

KEY TERMS

SUGGESTED READINGS

Complete treatments of the APT can be found in both of the following articles:

Ross, S. A. "Return, Risk and Arbitrage." In Friend and Bicksler, eds., *Risk and Return in Finance*. New York: Heath Lexington, 1974.

Ross, S. A. "The Arbitrage Theory of Asset Pricing." *Journal of Economic Theory* (December 1976).

Two less technical discussions of APT are:

Bower, D. H.; R. S. Bower; and D. Logue. "A Primer on Arbitrage Pricing Theory." *Midland Corporate Finance Journal* (Fall 1984).

Roll, R., and S. Ross. "The Arbitrage Pricing Theory Approach to Strategic Portfolio Planning." *Financial Analysts Journal* (May/June 1984).

The following article describes the idea of style portfolios:

Roll, R. "Style Return Differentials: Illusions, Risk Premia, or Investment Opportunities." In Fabozzi (ed.), *Handbook of Equity Style Management.* New Hope, PA: Frank Fabozzi Associates, 1995.

QUESTIONS AND PROBLEMS

Factor Models and Risk

11.1 You own stock in the Lewis-Striden Drug Company. Suppose you had expected the following events to occur last month.

a. The government would announce that real GNP would have grown 1.2 percent during the previous quarter. The returns of Lewis-Striden are positively related to real GNP.

b. The government would announce that inflation over the previous quarter was 3.7 percent. The returns of Lewis-Striden are negatively related to inflation.

c. Interest rates would rise 2.5 percentage points. The returns of Lewis-Striden are negatively related to interest rates.

d. The president of the firm would announce his retirement. The retirement would be effective six months from the announcement day. The president is well liked: in general he is considered an asset to the firm.

e. Research data would conclusively prove the efficacy of an experimental drug. Completion of the efficacy testing means the drug will be on the market soon.

Suppose the following events actually occurred.

a. The government announced that real GNP grew 2. 3 percent during the previous quarter.

b. The government announced that inflation over the previous quarter was 3.7 percent.

c. Interest rates rose 2.1 percentage points.

d. The president of the firm died suddenly of a heart attack.

e. Research results in the efficacy testing were not as strong as expected. The drug must be tested another six months and the efficacy results must be resubmitted to the FDA.

f. Lab researchers had a breakthrough with another drug.

g. A competitor announced that it will begin distribution and sale of a medicine that will compete directly with one of Lewis-Striden's top-selling products.

   i. Discuss how each of the actual occurrences affects the returns on your Lewis-Striden stock.

   ii. Which events represent systematic risk?

   iii. Which events represent unsystematic risk?

11.2 Suppose a three-factor model is appropriate to describe the returns of a stock. Information about those three factors is presented in the following chart. Suppose this is the only information you have concerning the factors.

Factor	Beta of Factor	Expected Value	Actual Value
GNP	0.0042	$4,416	$4,480
Inflation	−1.40	3.1%	4.3%
Interest rate	−0.67	9.5%	11.8%

a. What is the systematic risk of the stock return?

b. Suppose unexpected bad news about the firm was announced that dampens the returns by 2.6 percentage points. What is the unsystematic risk of the stock return?

c. Suppose the expected return of the stock is 9.5 percent. What is the total return on this stock?

11.3 Suppose a factor model is appropriate to describe the returns on a stock. Information about those factors is presented in the following chart.

Factor	Beta of Factor	Expected Value (%)	Actual Value (%)
Growth in GNP	2.04	3.5%	4.8%
Interest rates	−1.90	14.0	15.2
Stock return		10.0	

a. What is the systematic risk of the stock return?

b. The firm announced that its market share had unexpectedly increased from 23 percent to 27 percent. Investors know from their past experience that the stock return will increase by 0.36 percent per an increase of 1 percent in its market share. What is the unsystematic risk of the stock?

c. What is the total return on this stock?

11.4 The following three stocks are available in the market.

	Expected Return (%)	Beta
Stock A	10.5%	1.20
Stock B	13.0	0.98
Stock C	15.7	1.37
Market	14.2	1.00

Assume the market model is valid.

a. Write the market-model equation for each stock.

b. What is the return on a portfolio that is 30-percent stock A, 45-percent stock B, and 25-percent stock C?

c. Suppose the return on the market is 15 percent and there are no unsystematic surprises in the returns.

  i. What is the return on each stock?

  ii. What is the return on the portfolio?

11.5 You are forming an equally weighted portfolio of stocks. There are many stocks that all have the same beta of 0.84 for factor 1 and the same beta of 1.69 for factor 2. All stocks also have the same expected return of 11 percent. Assume a two-factor model describes the returns on each of these stocks.

a. Write the equation of the returns on your portfolio if you place only five stocks in it.

b. Write the equation of the returns on your portfolio if you place in it a very large number of stocks that all have the same expected returns and the same betas.

The APT

11.6 There are two stock markets, each driven by the same common force F with an expected value of zero and standard deviation of 10 percent. There are a large number of securities in each market; thus, you can invest in as many stocks as you wish. Due to restrictions, however, you can invest in only one of the two markets. The expected return on every security in both markets is 10 percent.

The returns for each security i in the first market are generated by the relationship

$$R_{1i} = 0.10 + 1.5F + \epsilon_{1i}$$

where ϵ_{1i} is the term that measures the surprises in the returns of stock i in market 1. These surprises are normally distributed; their mean is zero. The returns for security j in the second market are generated by the relationship

$$R_{2j} = 0.10 + 0.5F + \epsilon_{2j}$$

where ϵ_{2j} is the term that measures the surprises in the returns of stock j in market 2.

These surprises are normally distributed; their mean is zero. The standard deviation of ϵ_{1i} and ϵ_{2j} for any two stocks, i and j, is 20 percent.

a. If the correlation between the surprises in the returns of any two stocks in the first market is zero, and if the correlation between the surprises in the returns of any two stocks in the second market is zero, in which market would a risk-averse person prefer to invest? (Note: The correlation between ϵ_{1i} and ϵ_{1j} for any i and j is zero, and the correlation between ϵ_{2i} and ϵ_{2j} for any i and j is zero.)

b. If the correlation between ϵ_{1i} and ϵ_{1j} in the first market is 0.9 and the correlation between ϵ_{2i} and ϵ_{2j} in the second market is zero, in which market would a risk-averse person prefer to invest?

c. If the correlation between ϵ_{1i} and ϵ_{1j} in the first market is zero and the correlation between ϵ_{2i} and ϵ_{2j} in the second market is 0.5, in which market would a risk-averse person prefer to invest?

d. In general, what is the relationship between the correlations of the disturbances in the two markets that would make a risk-averse person equally willing to invest in either of the two markets?

11.7 Assume that the following market model adequately describes the return-generating behavior of risky assets.

$$R_{it} = \alpha_i + \beta_i R_{Mt} + \epsilon_{it}$$

where

$$R_{it} = \text{The return for the } i\text{th asset at time } t$$

and

$$R_{Mt} = \text{The return on a portfolio containing all risky}$$
$$\text{assets in some proportion, at time } t$$

R_{Mt} and ϵ_{it} are statistically independent.
Suppose the following data are true.

Asset	β_i	$E(R_i)$	$Var(\epsilon_i)$
A	0.7	8.41%	1.00%
B	1.2	12.06	1.44
C	1.5	13.95	2.25

$Var(R_{Mt}) = 1.21\%$

a. Calculate the standard deviation of returns for each asset.

b. Assume short selling is allowed.

   i. Calculate the variance of return of three portfolios containing an infinite number of asset types A, B, or C, respectively.

   ii. Assume: $R_F = 3.3\%$ and $\bar{R}_M = 10.6\%$. Which asset will not be held by rational investors?

   iii. What equilibrium state will emerge such that no arbitrage opportunities exist? Why?

11.8 Assume that the returns of individual securities are generated by the following two-factor model:

$$R_{it} = E(R_{it}) + \beta_{i1}F_{1t} + \beta_{i2}F_{2t}$$

R_{it} is the return for security i at time t. F_{1t} and F_{2t} are market factors with zero expectation and zero covariance. In addition, assume that there is a capital market for four securities, where each one has the following characteristics:

Security	β_1	β_2	$E(R_{it})$
1	1.0	1.5	20%
2	0.5	2.0	20
3	1.0	0.5	10
4	1.5	0.75	10

The capital market for these four assets is perfect in the sense that there are no transactions costs and short sales can take place.

a. Construct a portfolio containing (long or short) securities *1* and *2,* with a return that does not depend on the market factor, F_{1t}, in any way. (Hint: Such a portfolio will have $\beta_1 = 0$.) Compute the expected return and β_2 coefficient for this portfolio.

b. Following the procedure in (*a*), construct a portfolio containing securities *3* and *4* with a return that does not depend on the market factor, F_{1t}. Compute the expected return and β_2 coefficient for this portfolio.

c. Consider a risk-free asset with expected return equal to 5 percent, $\beta_1 = 0$, and $\beta_2 = 0$. Describe a possible arbitrage opportunity in such detail that an investor could implement it.

d. What effect would the existence of these kinds of arbitrage opportunities have on the capital markets for these securities in the short and long run? Graph your analysis.

Risk, Cost of Capital, and Capital Budgeting

EXECUTIVE SUMMARY

O ur text has devoted a number of chapters to net present value (NPV) analysis. We pointed out that a dollar to be received in the future is worth less than a dollar received today for two reasons. First, there is the simple time-value-of-money argument in a riskless world. If you have a dollar today, you can invest it in the bank and receive more than a dollar by some future date. Second, a risky dollar is worth less than a riskless dollar. Consider a firm expecting a $1 cash flow. If actuality exceeds expectations (revenues are especially high or expenses are especially low), perhaps $1.10 or $1.20 will be received. If actuality falls short of expectations, perhaps only $0.80 or $0.90 will be received. This risk is unattractive to the typical firm.

Our work on NPV allowed us to value riskless cash flows precisely. That is, we discounted by the riskless interest rate. However, because most real-world cash flows in the future are risky, business demands a procedure for discounting risky cash flows. This chapter applies the concept of net present value to risky cash flows.

Let us review what previous work in the text has to say about NPV. In earlier chapters we learned that the basic NPV formula for an investment that generates cash flows (C_t) in future periods is

$$NPV = C_0 + \sum_{t=1}^{T} \frac{C_t}{(1 + r)^t}$$

For risky projects, expected incremental cash flows $\overline{C_t}$ are placed in the numerator, and the NPV formula becomes

$$NPV = C_0 + \sum_{t=1}^{T} \frac{\overline{C_t}}{(1 + r)^t}$$

In this chapter, we will learn that the discount rate used to determine the NPV of a risky project can be computed from the CAPM (or APT). For example, if an all-equity firm is seeking to value a risky project, such as renovating a warehouse, the firm will determine the required return, r_S, on the project by using the SML. We call r_S the firm's **cost of equity** capital.

When firms finance with both debt and equity, the discount rate to use is the project's overall cost of capital. The overall cost of capital is a weighted average of the cost of debt and the cost of equity.

12.1 THE COST OF EQUITY CAPITAL

Whenever a firm has extra cash, it can take one of two actions. On the one hand, it can pay out the cash immediately as a dividend. On the other hand, the firm can invest extra cash in a project, paying out the future cash flows of the project as dividends. Which procedure would the stockholders prefer? If a stockholder can reinvest the dividend in a financial asset (a stock or bond) with the same risk as that of the project, the stockholders would desire the

■ Figure 12.1 Choices of a Firm with Extra Cash

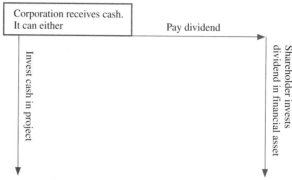

Stockholders want the firm to invest in a project only if the
expected return on the project is at least as great as that of a
financial asset of comparable risk.

alternative with the highest expected return. In other words, the project should be undertaken
only if its expected return is greater than that of a financial asset of comparable risk. This is
illustrated in Figure 12.1. This discussion implies a very simple capital-budgeting rule:

> The discount rate of a project should be the expected return on a financial asset of comparable risk.

From the firm's perspective, the expected return is the cost of equity capital. Under the
CAPM, the expected return on the stock is

$$\overline{R} = R_F + \beta \times (\overline{R}_M - R_F) \tag{12.1}$$

where R_F is the risk-free rate and $\overline{R}_M - R_F$ is the difference between the expected return on
the market portfolio and the riskless rate. This difference is often called the expected *excess*
market return.[1]

We now have the tools to estimate a firm's cost of equity capital. To do this, we need
to know three things:

- The risk-free rate, R_F
- The market-risk premium, $\overline{R}_M - R_F$
- The company beta, β_i

Example

Suppose the stock of the Quatram Company, a publisher of college textbooks, has
a beta (β) of 1.3. The firm is 100-percent equity financed; that is, it has
no debt. Quatram is considering a number of capital-budgeting projects that will
double its size. Because these new projects are similar to the firm's existing ones,
the average beta on the new projects is assumed to be equal to Quatram's existing
beta. The risk-free rate is 7 percent. What is the appropriate discount rate for these
new projects, assuming a market-risk premium of 9.5 percent?

We estimate the cost of equity r_S for Quatram as

$$
\begin{aligned}
r_S &= 7\% + (9.5\% \times 1.3) \\
&= 7\% + 12.35\% \\
&= 19.35\%
\end{aligned}
$$

---

[1]Of course, we can use the *k*-factor APT model (Chapter 11) and estimate several beta coefficients. However,
for our purposes it is sufficient to estimate a single beta.

Two key assumptions were made in this example: (1) The beta risk of the new projects is the same as the risk of the firm, and (2) The firm is all-equity financed. Given these assumptions, it follows that the cash flows of the new projects should be discounted at the 19.35-percent rate.

EXAMPLE

Suppose Alpha Air Freight is an all-equity firm with a beta of 1.21. Further suppose the market-risk premium is 9.5 percent, and the risk-free rate is 5 percent. We can determine the expected return on the common stock of Alpha Air Freight by using the SML of equation (12.1). We find that the expected return is

$$5\% + (1.21 \times 9.5\%) = 16.495\%$$

Because this is the return that shareholders can expect in the financial markets on a stock with a β of 1.21, it is the return they expect on Alpha Air Freight's stock.

Further suppose Alpha is evaluating the following non-mutually exclusive projects:

Project	Project's Beta (β)	Project's Expected Cash Flows Next Year	Project's Internal Rate of Return	Project's NPV When Cash Flows Are Discounted at 16.495%	Accept or Reject
A	1.21	$140	40%	$20.2	Accept
B	1.21	120	20	3.0	Accept
C	1.21	110	10	−5.6	Reject

Each project initially costs $100. All projects are assumed to have the same risk as the firm as a whole. Because the cost of equity capital is 16.495 percent, projects in an all-equity firm are discounted at this rate. Projects A and B have positive NPVs, and C has a negative NPV. Thus, only A and B will be accepted.[2] This is illustrated in Figure 12.2.

---

[2]In addition to the SML, the dividend-valuation model presented earlier in the text can be used to represent the firm's cost of equity capital. Using this model, the present value (P) of the firm's expected dividend payments can be expressed as

$$P = \frac{\text{Div}_1}{(1 + r_S)} + \frac{\text{Div}_2}{(1 + r_S)^2} + \ldots + \frac{\text{Div}_N}{(1 + r_S)^N} + \ldots \tag{a}$$

where r_S is the required return of shareholders and the firm's cost of equity capital. If the dividends are expected to grow at a constant rate, g, equation (a) reduces to

$$P = \frac{\text{Div}_1}{r_S - g} \tag{b}$$

Equation (b) can be reformulated as

$$r_S = \frac{\text{Div}_1}{P} + g \tag{c}$$

We can use equation (c) to estimate r_S. Div_1/P is the dividend yield expected over the next year. An estimate of the cost of equity capital is determined from an estimate of Div_1/P and g.

The dividend-valuation model is generally considered both less theoretically sound and more difficult to apply practically than the SML. In addition, J. R. Graham and C. R. Harvey, "The Theory and Practice of Corporate Finance: Evidence from the Field," unpublished paper, Duke University (April, 2000) present evidence that only about 15 percent of real-world companies use the dividend-valuation model, a far smaller percentage than use the SML approach. Hence, examples in this chapter calculate cost of equity capital using the SML approach.

◼ FIGURE 12.2   **Using the Security-Market Line to Estimate the Risk-Adjusted Discount Rate for Risky Projects**

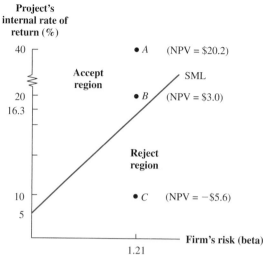

The diagonal line represents the relationship between the cost of equity capital and the firm's beta. An all-equity firm should accept a project whose internal rate of return is greater than the cost of equity capital, and should reject a project whose internal rate of return is less than the cost of equity capital. (The above graph assumes that all projects are as risky as the firm.)

12.2 ESTIMATION OF BETA

In the previous section we assumed that the beta of the company was known. Of course, beta must be estimated in the real world. We pointed out earlier that the beta of a security is the standardized covariance of a security's return with the return on the market portfolio. The formula for security i, first given in Chapter 10, is

$$\text{Beta of security } i = \frac{\text{Cov}(R_i, R_M)}{\text{Var}(R_M)} = \frac{\sigma_{i,M}}{\sigma_M^2}$$

In words, the beta is the covariance of a security with the market, divided by the variance of the market. Because we calculated both covariance and variance in earlier chapters, calculating beta involves no new material.

EXAMPLE (ADVANCED)

Suppose we sample the returns on the stock of the General Tool Company and the returns on the S&P 500 Index for four years. They are tabulated as follows:

Year	General Tool Company R_G	S&P 500 Index R_M
1	−10%	−40%
2	3	−30
3	20	10
4	15	20

We can calculate beta in six steps.

TABLE 12.1 **Calculating Beta**

(1) Year	(2) Rate of Return on General Tool (R_G)	(3) General Tool's Deviation from Average Return* $(R_G - \bar{R}_G)$	(4) Rate of Return on Market Portfolio	(5) Market Portfolio's Deviation from Average Return† $(R_M - \bar{R}_M)$	(6) Deviation of General Tool Multiplied by Deviation of Market Portfolio	(7) Squared Deviation of Market Portfolio
1	−0.10	−0.17 (−0.10 − 0.07)	−0.40	−0.30	0.051 [(−0.17) × (−0.30)]	0.090 [(−0.30) × (−0.30)]
2	0.03	−0.04	−0.30	−0.20	0.008	0.040
3	0.20	0.13	0.10	0.20	0.026	0.040
4	0.15	0.08	0.20	0.30	0.024	0.090
	Avg = 0.07		Avg = −0.10		Sum: 0.109	Sum: 0.260

Beta of General Tool: $0.419 = \dfrac{0.109}{0.260}$.

*Average return for General Tool is 0.07.
†Average return for market is −0.10.

1. Calculate average return on each asset:

   Average Return on General Tool:

   $$\frac{-\,0.10 + 0.03 + 0.20 + 0.15}{4} = 0.07 \ (7\%)$$

   Average Return on Market Portfolio:

   $$\frac{-\,0.40 - 0.30 + 0.10 + 0.20}{4} = -\,0.10 \ (-\,10\%)$$

2. For each asset, calculate the deviation of each return from the asset's average return determined above. This is presented in columns 3 and 5 of Table 12.1.

3. Multiply the deviation of General Tool's return by the deviation of the market's return. This is presented in column 6. This procedure is analogous to our calculation of covariance in an earlier chapter. The procedure will be used in the numerator of the beta calculation.

4. Calculate the squared deviation of the market's return. This is presented in column 7. This procedure is analogous to our calculation of variance in Chapter 9. This procedure will be used in the denominator of the beta calculation.

5. Take the sum of column 6 and the sum of column 7. They are

Sum of Deviation of General Tool Multiplied by Deviation of Market Portfolio:

$$0.051 + 0.008 + 0.026 + 0.024 = 0.109$$

Sum of Squared Deviation of Market Portfolio:

$$0.090 + 0.040 + 0.040 + 0.090 = 0.260$$

MEASURING COMPANY BETAS

The basic method of measuring company betas is to estimate:

$$\frac{\text{Cov}(R_{it}, R_{Mt})}{\text{Var}(R_{Mt})}$$

using $t = 1, 2, \ldots, T$ observations

Problems
1. Betas may vary over time.
2. The sample size may be inadequate.
3. Betas are influenced by changing financial leverage and business risk.

Solutions
1. Problems 1 and 2 (above) can be moderated by more sophisticated statistical techniques.
2. Problem 3 can be lessened by adjusting for changes in business and financial risk.
3. Look at average beta estimates of several comparable firms in the industry.

---

6. The beta is the sum of column 6 divided by the sum of column 7. This is

Beta of General Tool:

$$0.419 = \frac{0.109}{0.260}$$

Real-World Betas

The General Tool Company discussed in the previous example is fictional. It is instructive to see how betas are determined for actual real-world companies. Figure 12.3 plots monthly returns for four large firms against monthly returns on the Standard & Poor's (S&P) 500 Index. As mentioned in Chapter 10, each firm has its own characteristic line. The slope of the characteristic line is beta, as estimated using the technique of Table 12.1. This technique is called *regression*. Though we have not shown it in the table, one can also determine the intercept (commonly called alpha) of the characteristic line by regression. Since a line can be created from its intercept and slope, the regression allows one to estimate the characteristic line of a firm.

We use five years of monthly data for each plot. While this choice is arbitrary, it is in line with calculations performed in the real world. Practitioners know that the accuracy of the beta coefficient is suspect when too few observations are used. Conversely, since firms may change their industry over time, observations from the distant past are out-of-date.

We stated in Chapter 10 that the average beta across all stocks in an index is 1. Of course, this need not be true for a subset of the index. For example, of the four securities in our figure, three have betas above 1 and one has a beta below 1. Since beta is a measure of the risk of a single security for someone holding a large, diversified portfolio, our results indicate that Coca-Cola has relatively low risk and Philip Morris has relatively high risk. A more detailed discussion of the determinants of beta is presented in Section 12.3.

Stability of Beta

We stated above that the beta of a firm is likely to change if the firm changes its industry. It is also interesting to ask the reverse question: Does the beta of a firm stay the same if its industry stays the same?

■ FIGURE 12.3   **Plots of Five Years of Monthly Returns on Four Individual Securities against Five Years of Monthly Returns on the Standard & Poor's (S&P) 500 Index**

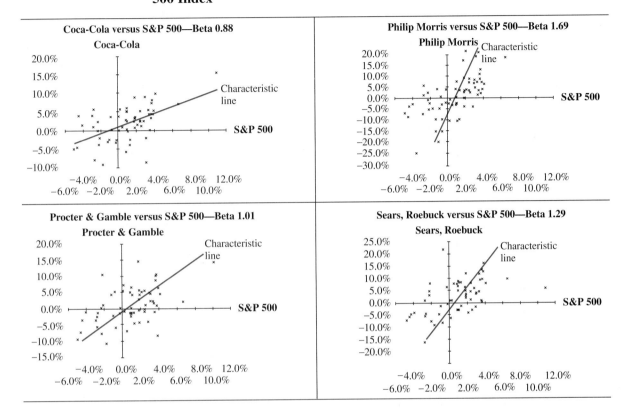

Take the case of General Electric, a large, diversified firm that for the most part has stayed in the same industries for many decades. Figure 12.4 plots the returns on General Electric and the returns on the S&P 500 for four successive five-year periods. As can be seen from the figure, GE's beta has increased slightly from the first to the third subperiod while falling in the last subperiod. However, this movement in beta is probably nothing more than random variation.[3] Thus, for practical purposes, GE's beta has been approximately constant over the two decades covered in the figure. While GE is just one company, most analysts argue that betas are generally stable for firms remaining in the same industry.

However, this is not to say that, as long as a firm stays in the same industry, its beta will *never* change. Changes in product line, changes in technology, or changes in the market may affect a firm's beta. For example, the deregulation of the airline industry has increased the betas of airline firms. Furthermore, as we will show in a later section, an increase in the leverage of a firm (i.e., the amount of debt in its capital structure) will increase the firm's beta.

Using an Industry Beta

Our approach of estimating the beta of a company from its own past data may seem commonsensical to you. However, it is frequently argued that one can better estimate a firm's beta by involving the whole industry. Consider Table 12.2, which shows the betas of some

---

[3]More precisely, one can say that the beta coefficients over the four periods are not statistically different from each other.

■ FIGURE 12.4   **Plots of Monthly Returns on General Electric and on the Standard & Poor's 500 Index for Four Five-Year Periods**

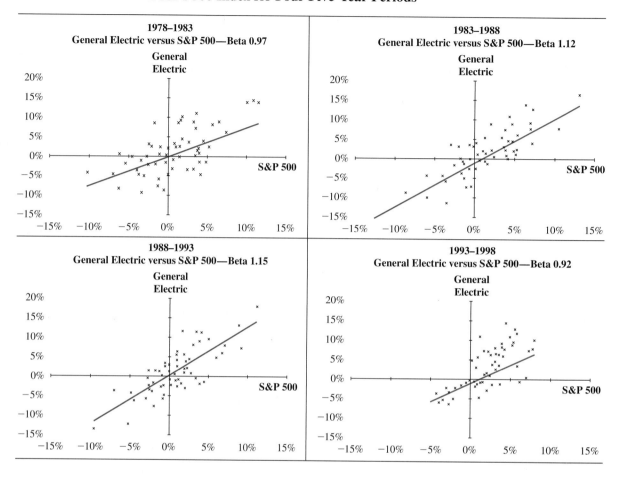

■ TABLE 12.2   **Betas for Firms in the Software Industry**

Company	Beta
Adobe Systems Inc.	1.51
BMC Software Inc.	0.96
Cadence Design	0.98
Cerner Corp.	1.87
Citrix Systems Inc.	1.29
Comshare Inc.	1.22
Informix Corp.	2.09
Int. Lottery & Totalizator Sys. Inc.	3.34
Microsoft Corp.	1.11
Oracle Corp.	1.63
Symantec Corp.	1.82
Veritas Software	1.94
Equally weighted portfolio	1.65

of the more prominent firms in the software industry. The average beta across all of the firms in the table is 1.65. Imagine a financial executive at Oracle Corp. trying to estimate the firm's beta. Because beta-estimation is subject to large random variation in this volatile industry, the executive may be uncomfortable with the estimate of 1.63. However, the error in beta-estimation on a single stock is much higher than the error for a portfolio of securities. Thus, the executive of Oracle may use the industry beta of 1.65 as the estimate of its own firm's beta. (As it turns out, the choice is unimportant here, since the industry beta is so close to that of the firm.)

By contrast, consider Cadence Design. Assuming a risk-free rate of 6 percent and a risk-premium of 9.5 percent, Cadence might estimate its cost of equity capital as:

$$6\% + 0.98 \times 9.5\% = 15.31\%$$

However, if Cadence believed that the industry beta contained less estimation error, it could estimate its cost of equity capital as:

$$6\% + 1.65 \times 9.5\% = 21.67\%$$

The difference is substantial here, perhaps presenting a difficult choice for a financial executive at Cadence.

While there is no formula for selecting the right beta, there is a very simple guideline. If one believes that the operations of the firm are similar to the operations of the rest of the industry, one should use the industry beta simply to reduce estimation error.[4] However, if an executive believes that the operations of the firm are fundamentally different from those in the rest of the industry, the firm's beta should be used.

QUESTIONS

• What is the disadvantage of using too few observations when estimating beta?
• What is the disadvantage of using too many observations when estimating beta?
• What is the disadvantage of using the industry beta as the estimate of the beta of an individual firm?

12.3 Determinants of Beta

The regression analysis approach in the previous section doesn't tell us where beta comes from. The beta of a stock does not come out of thin air. Rather, it is determined by the characteristics of the firm. We consider three factors: the cyclical nature of revenues, operating leverage, and financial leverage.

Cyclicality of Revenues

The revenues of some firms are quite cyclical. That is, these firms do well in the expansion phase of the business cycle and do poorly in the contraction phase. Empirical evidence suggests high-tech firms, retailers, and automotive firms fluctuate with the business cycle. Firms in industries such as utilities, railroads, food, and airlines are less dependent upon the cycle. Because beta is the standardized covariability of a stock's return with the market's return, it is not surprising that highly cyclical stocks have high betas. For example, Sears's beta, as shown in Figure 12.3, is high because its sales are dependent on the market cycle.

---

[4]As we will see later, an adjustment must be made when the debt level in the industry is different from that of the firm. However, we ignore this adjustment here, since firms in the software industry generally have little debt.

It is worthwhile to point out that cyclicality is not the same as variability. For example, a movie-making firm has highly variable revenues because hits and flops are not easily predicted. However, because the revenues of a studio are more dependent on the quality of its releases than upon the phase of the business cycle, motion-picture companies are not particularly cyclical. In other words, stocks with high standard deviations need not have high betas, a point we have stressed before.

Operating Leverage

We distinguished fixed costs from variable costs earlier in the text. At that time, we mentioned that fixed costs do not change as quantity changes. Conversely, variable costs increase as the quantity of output rises. This difference between variable and fixed costs allows us to define operating leverage.

EXAMPLE

Consider a firm that can choose either technology *A* or technology *B* when making a particular product. The relevant differences between the two technologies are displayed below:

Technology A	Technology B
Fixed cost: $1,000/year	Fixed cost: $2,000/year
Variable cost: $8/unit	Variable cost: $6/unit
Price: $10/unit	Price: $10/unit
Contribution margin: $2 ($10 − $8)	Contribution margin: $4 ($10 − $6)

Technology *A* has lower fixed costs and higher variable costs than does technology *B*. Perhaps technology *A* involves less mechanization than does *B*. Or, the equipment in *A* may be leased whereas the equipment in *B* must be purchased. Alternatively, perhaps technology *A* involves few employees but many subcontractors, whereas *B* involves only highly skilled employees who must be retained in bad times. Because technology *B* has both lower variable costs and higher fixed costs, we say that it has higher **operating leverage.**[5]

Figure 12.5 graphs the costs under both technologies. The slope of each total-cost line represents variable costs under a single technology. The slope of *A*'s line is steeper, indicating greater variable costs.

Because the two technologies are used to produce the same products, a unit price of $10 applies for both cases. We mentioned in an earlier chapter that contribution margin is the difference between price and variable cost. It measures the incremental profit from one additional unit. Because the contribution margin in *B* is greater, its technology is riskier. An unexpected sale increases profit by $2 under *A* but increases profit by $4 under *B*. Similarly, an unexpected sale cancellation reduces profit by $2 under *A* but reduces profit by $4 under *B*. This is

---

[5]The actual definition of operating leverage is

$$\frac{\text{Change in EBIT}}{\text{EBIT}} \times \frac{\text{Sales}}{\text{Change in sales}}$$

where EBIT is the earnings before interest and taxes. That is, operating leverage measures the percentage change in EBIT for a given percentage change in sales or revenues. It can be shown that operating leverage increases as fixed costs rise and as variable costs fall.

■ FIGURE 12.5 **Illustration of Two Different Technologies**

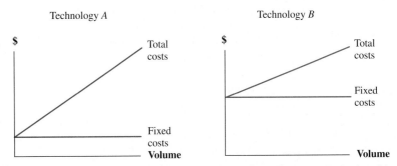

Technology *B* has higher variable costs and lower fixed costs than does technology *B*. Technology *B* has higher operating leverage.

■ FIGURE 12.6 **Illustration of the Effect of a Change in Volume on the Change in Earnings before Interest and Taxes (EBIT)**

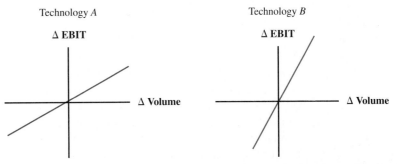

Technology *B* has lower variable costs than A, implying a higher contribution margin. The profits of the firm are more responsive to changes in volume under technology *B* than under *A*.

illustrated in Figure 12.6. This figure shows the change in earnings before interest and taxes for a given change in volume. The slope of the right-hand graph is greater, indicating that technology *B* is riskier.

The cyclicality of a firm's revenues is a determinant of the firm's beta. Operating leverage magnifies the effect of cyclicality on beta. As mentioned earlier, business risk is generally defined as the risk of the firm without financial leverage. Business risk depends both on the responsiveness of the firm's revenues to the business cycle and on the firm's operating leverage.

Although the preceding discussion concerns firms, it applies to projects as well. If one cannot estimate a project's beta in another way, one can examine the project's revenues and operating leverage. Those projects whose revenues appear strongly cyclical and whose operating leverage appears high are likely to have high betas. Conversely, weak cyclicality and low operating leverage implies low betas. As mentioned earlier, this approach is unfortunately qualitative in nature. Because start-up projects have little data, quantitative estimates of beta generally are not feasible.

Financial Leverage and Beta

As suggested by their names, operating leverage and financial leverage are analogous concepts. Operating leverage refers to the firm's fixed costs of *production*. Financial leverage is the extent to which a firm relies on debt and a levered firm is a firm with some debt in its capital structure. Because a *levered* firm must make interest payments regardless of the firm's sales, financial leverage refers to the firm's fixed costs of *finance*.

Consider our discussion in Section 10.8 concerning the beta of Jelco, Inc. In that example, we estimated beta from the returns on Jelco *stock*. Similarly, we estimated General Tool's beta in Section 12.1 from stock returns. Furthermore, the betas in Figures 12.3 and 12.4 from real-world firms were estimated from returns on stock. Thus, in each case, we estimated the firm's stock or **equity beta.** The beta of the assets of a levered firm is different from the beta of its equity. As the name suggests, the **asset beta** is the beta of the assets of the firm. The asset beta could also be thought of as the beta of the common stock had the firm been financed only with equity.

Imagine an individual who owns all the firm's debt and all its equity. In other words, this individual owns the entire firm. What is the beta of her portfolio of the firm's debt and equity?

As with any portfolio, the beta of this portfolio is a weighted average of the betas of the individual items in the portfolio. Hence, we have

$$\beta_{\text{Asset}} = \frac{\text{Debt}}{\text{Debt} + \text{Equity}} \times \beta_{\text{Debt}} + \frac{\text{Equity}}{\text{Debt} + \text{Equity}} \times \beta_{\text{Equity}} \qquad (12.2)$$

where β_{Equity} is the beta of the stock of the *levered* firm. Notice that the beta of debt is multiplied by debt/(debt + equity), the percentage of debt in the capital structure. Similarly, the beta of equity is multiplied by the percentage of equity in the capital structure. Because the portfolio contains both the debt of the firm and the equity of the firm, the beta of the portfolio is the *asset beta*. As we said above, the asset beta can also be viewed as the beta of the common stock had the firm been all equity.

The beta of debt is very low in practice. If we make the commonplace assumption that the beta of debt is zero, we have

$$\beta_{\text{Asset}} = \frac{\text{Equity}}{\text{Debt} + \text{Equity}} \times \beta_{\text{Equity}} \qquad (12.3)$$

Because equity/(debt + equity) must be below 1 for a levered firm, it follows that $\beta_{\text{Asset}} < \beta_{\text{Equity}}$. Rearranging this equation, we have

$$\beta_{\text{Equity}} = \beta_{\text{Asset}} \left(1 + \frac{\text{Debt}}{\text{Equity}}\right)$$

The equity beta will always be greater than the asset beta with financial leverage.[6]

EXAMPLE

Consider a tree-growing company, Rapid Cedars, Inc., which is currently all equity and has a beta of 0.8. The firm has decided to move to a capital structure of one part debt to two parts equity. Because the firm is staying in the same industry,

---

[6]It can be shown that the relationship between a firm's asset beta and its equity beta with corporate taxes is

$$\beta_{\text{Equity}} = \beta_{\text{Asset}} \left[1 + (1 - T_C)\frac{\text{Debt}}{\text{Equity}}\right]$$

See Chapter 17 for more details.

its asset beta should remain at 0.8. However, assuming a zero beta for its debt, its equity beta would become

$$\beta_{\text{Equity}} = \beta_{\text{Asset}} \left(1 + \frac{\text{Debt}}{\text{Equity}} \right)$$

$$1.2 = 0.8 \left(1 + \frac{1}{2} \right)$$

If the firm had one part debt to one part equity in its capital structure, its equity beta would be

$$1.6 = 0.8 \, (1 + 1)$$

However, as long as it stayed in the same industry, its asset beta would remain at 0.8. The effect of leverage, then, is to increase the equity beta.

CONCEPT QUESTIONS

?

- What are determinants of equity betas?
- What is the difference between an asset beta and an equity beta?

12.4 EXTENSIONS OF THE BASIC MODEL

The Firm versus the Project: Vive la Différence

We now assume that the risk of a project differs from that of the firm, while going back to the all-equity assumption. We began the chapter by pointing out that each project should be paired with a financial asset of comparable risk. If a project's beta differs from that of the firm, the project should be discounted at the rate commensurate with its own beta. This is a very important point because firms frequently speak of a *corporate discount rate.* (*Hurdle rate, cutoff rate, benchmark,* and *cost of capital* are frequently used synonymously.) Unless all projects in the corporation are of the same risk, choosing the same discount rate for all projects is incorrect.

EXAMPLE

D. D. Ronnelley Co., a publishing firm, may accept a project in computer software. Noting that computer software companies have high betas, the publishing firm views the software venture as more risky than the rest of its business. It should discount the project at a rate commensurate with the risk of software companies. For example, it might use the average beta of a portfolio of publicly traded software firms. Instead, if all projects in D. D. Ronnelley Co. were discounted at the same rate, a bias would result. The firm would accept too many high-risk projects (software ventures) and reject too many low-risk projects (books and magazines). This point is illustrated in Figure 12.7.

The D. D. Ronnelley example assumes that the proposed project has identical risk to that of the software industry, allowing the industry beta to be used. However, the beta of a new project may be greater than the beta of existing firms in the same industry because the very newness of the project likely increases its responsiveness to economy wide movements. For

■ FIGURE 12.7 **Relationship between the Firm's Cost of Capital and the Security Market Line**

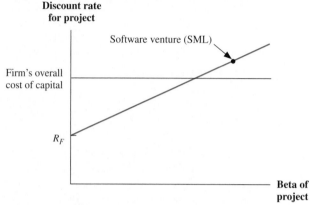

Use of a firm's cost of capital in calculations may lead to incorrect capital-budgeting decisions. Projects with high risk, such as the software venture for D. D. Ronnelley Co., should be discounted at a high rate. By using the firm's cost of equity, the firm is likely to accept too many high-risk projects.

Projects with low risk should be discounted at a low rate. By using the firm's cost of capital, the firm is likely to reject too many low-risk projects.

example, a start-up computer venture may fail in a recession while IBM, Compaq, or Hewlett-Packard will still be around. Conversely, in an economywide expansion, the venture may grow much faster than the old-line computer firms.

Fortunately, a slight adjustment is all that is needed here. The new venture should be assigned a somewhat higher beta than that of the industry to reflect added risk. The adjustment is necessarily ad hoc, so no formula can be given. Our experience indicates that this approach is widespread in practice today.

However, a problem does arise for the rare project constituting its own industry. For example, consider the firms providing consumer shopping by television. Today, one can obtain a reasonable estimate for the beta of this industry, since a few of the firms have publicly traded stock. However, when the ventures began in the 1980s, any beta estimate was suspect. At that time, no one knew whether shopping by TV belonged in the television industry, the retail industry, or in an entirely new industry.

What beta should be used in the rare case when an industrywide beta is not appropriate? One approach, which considers the determinants of the project's beta, was treated earlier in this chapter. Unfortunately, that approach is only qualitative in nature.

The Cost of Capital with Debt

Section 12.1 showed how to choose the discount rate when a project is all-equity financed. In this section, we discuss an adjustment when the project is financed with both debt and equity.

Suppose a firm uses both debt and equity to finance its investments. If the firm pays r_B for its debt financing and r_S for its equity, what is the overall or average cost of its capital? The cost of equity is r_S, as discussed in earlier sections. The cost of debt is the firm's borrowing rate, r_B. If a firm uses both debt and equity, the cost of capital is a weighted average of each. This works out to be

$$\frac{S}{S + B} \times r_S + \frac{B}{S + B} \times r_B$$

The weights in the formula are, respectively, the proportion of total value represented by the equity

$$\left(\frac{S}{S + B}\right)$$

and the proportion of total value represented by debt

$$\left(\frac{B}{S + B}\right)$$

This is only natural. If the firm had issued no debt and was therefore an all-equity firm, its average cost of capital would equal its cost of equity, r_S. At the other extreme, if the firm had issued so much debt that its equity was valueless, it would be an all-debt firm, and its average cost of capital would be its cost of debt, r_B.

Of course, interest is tax deductible at the corporate level, a point to be treated in more detail in Chapter 15. The after-tax cost of debt is

$$\text{Cost of debt (after corporate tax)} = r_B \times (1 - T_C)$$

where T_C is the corporation's tax rate.

Assembling these results, we get the average cost of capital (after tax) for the firm:

$$\text{Average cost of capital} = \left(\frac{S}{S + B}\right) \times r_S + \left(\frac{B}{S + B}\right) \times r_B \times (1 - T_C) \quad (12.4)$$

Because the average cost of capital is a weighting of its cost of equity and its cost of debt, it is usually referred to as the **weighted average cost of capital, r$_{\text{WACC}}$,** and from now on we will use this term.

EXAMPLE

Consider a firm whose debt has a market value of $40 million and whose stock has a market value of $60 million (3 million outstanding shares of stock, each selling for $20 per share). The firm pays a 15-percent rate of interest on its new debt and has a beta of 1.41. The corporate tax rate is 34 percent. (Assume that the SML holds, that the risk premium on the market is 9.5 percent, and that the current Treasury bill rate is 11 percent.) What is this firm's r_{WACC}?

To compute the r_{WACC} using equation (12.4), we must know (1) the after-tax cost of debt, $r_B \times (1 - T_C)$, (2) the cost of equity, r_S, and (3) the proportions of debt and equity used by the firm. These three values are computed below.

1. The pretax cost of debt is 15 percent, implying an after-tax cost of 9.9 percent [15% × (1 − 0.34)].

2. The cost of equity capital is computed by using the SML:

$$r_S = R_F + \beta \times [\overline{R}_M - R_F]$$
$$= 11\% + 1.41 \times 9.5\%$$
$$= 24.40\%$$

3. The proportions of debt and equity are computed from the market values of debt and equity. Because the market value of the firm is $100 million ($40 million + $60 million), the proportions of debt and equity are 40 and 60 percent, respectively.

The cost of equity, r_S, is 24.40 percent, and the after-tax cost of debt, $r_B \times (1 - T_C)$, is 9.9 percent. B is $40 million and S is $60 million. Therefore,

$$r_{WACC} = \frac{B}{B + S} \times r_B \times (1 - T_C) + \frac{S}{B + S} \times r_S$$

$$= \left(\frac{40}{100} \times 9.9\%\right) + \left(\frac{60}{100} \times 24.40\%\right) = 18.60\%$$

This procedure is presented in chart form next:

(1) Financing Components	(2) Market Values	(3) Weight	(4) Cost of Capital (after corporate tax)	(5) Weighted Cost of Capital
Debt	$ 40,000,000	0.40	15% × (1 − 0.34) = 9.9%	3.96%
Equity	60,000,000	0.60	11% + 1.41 × 9.5% = 24.40%	14.64
	$100,000,000	1.00		18.60%

The weights we used in the previous example were market-value weights. Market-value weights are more appropriate than book-value weights because the market values of the securities are closer to the actual dollars that would be received from their sale. Actually it is usually useful to think in terms of "target" market weights. These are the market weights expected to prevail over the life of the firm or project.

EXAMPLE

Suppose that a firm has both a current and a target debt-equity ratio of 0.6, a cost of debt of 15.15 percent, and a cost of equity of 20 percent. The corporate tax rate is 34 percent.

Our first step calls for transforming the debt-to-equity (B/S) ratio to a debt-to-value ratio. A B/S ratio of 0.6 implies 6 parts debt for 10 parts equity. Since value is equal to the sum of the debt plus the equity, the debt-to-value ratio is $\frac{6}{6 + 10} = 0.375$. Similarly, the equity-to-value ratio is $\frac{10}{6 + 10} = 0.625$. The r_{WACC} will then be

$$r_{WACC} = \left(\frac{S}{S + B}\right) \times r_S + \left(\frac{B}{S + B}\right) \times r_B \times (1 - T_C)$$

$$= .625 \times 20\% + .375 \times 15.15\% \times (.66) = 16.25\%$$

Suppose the firm is considering taking on a warehouse renovation costing $50 million that is expected to yield cost savings of $12 million a year for six years. Using the NPV equation and discounting the six years of expected cash flows from the renovation at the r_{WACC}, we have[7]

$$NPV = -\$50 + \frac{\$12}{(1 + r_{WACC})} + \ldots + \frac{\$12}{(1 + r_{WACC})^6}$$
$$= -\$50 + \$12 \times A_{.1625}^6$$
$$= -\$50 + (12 \times 3.66)$$
$$= -\$6.07$$

Should the firm take on the warehouse renovation? The project has a negative NPV using the firm's r_{WACC}. This means that the financial markets offer superior projects in the same risk class (namely, the firm's risk class). The answer is clear: The firm should reject the project.

12.5 ESTIMATING INTERNATIONAL PAPER'S COST OF CAPITAL

In the previous section, we calculated the cost of capital in two examples. Now, we will do the same thing for a real-world company. Table 12.3 lists nine large and well-known firms in the paper and pulp mills industry. We will calculate the cost of capital for one of them, International Paper (IP).

From the previous section, we know that there are two steps in the calculation of the cost of capital. First, we estimate the cost of equity and cost of debt. Second, we determine the weighted average cost of capital by weighting these two costs appropriately.

■ TABLE 12.3   **Betas for Firms in the Pulp and Paper Mills Industry**

Company	Beta
Abitibi-Price Inc.	0.74
American Israeli Paper Mills, Ltd.	0.41
Boise Cascade Corp.	0.97
Glatfelter, P. H., Co.	0.57
International Paper Co.	0.83
Kimberly-Clark Corp.	0.90
Mead Corp.	1.14
Union Camp Corp.	0.85
Westvaco Corp.	0.97
Equally weighted portfolio	0.82

---

[7]This discussion of WACC has been implicitly based on perpetual cash flows. However, an important paper by J. Miles and R. Ezzel, "The Weighted Average Cost of Capital, Perfect Capital Markets and Project Life: A Clarification," *Journal of Financial and Quantitative Analysis* (September 1980), shows that the WACC is appropriate even when cash flows are not perpetual.

Cost of Equity and Debt

We will tackle the cost of equity first. We need a beta estimate to determine International Paper's cost of equity and Table 12.3 shows the betas of the nine firms in the industry. The table tells us that IP's beta is 0.83 and the industry's average beta is 0.82. Which number should we use? We argued earlier in the chapter that there is less measurement error with the industry beta. Therefore, we will work with 0.82, though IP's beta is so close to the average of the industry that either number would have been fine.

As discussed in Chapter 9, 9.5 percent is our best estimate of the market's risk premium. If the risk-free rate is 6 percent, our best estimate of International Paper's cost of equity capital is:

$$R_F + \beta \times [\overline{R}_M - R_F]$$
$$= 6\% + 0.82 \times 9.5\%$$
$$= 13.79\%$$

The yield on the company's debt is about 8 percent, which we will use as the (pretax) cost of debt capital, r_B.

Determining r_{WACC}

Now that we have estimates of both r_S, the cost of equity, and r_B, the cost of debt, we are ready to determine the weighted average cost of capital. However, we still need the percentages of debt and equity in IP's capital structure and the tax rate. We find that the ratio of debt-to-value is 32 percent and the ratio of equity-to-value is 68 percent. The tax rate is 37 percent.[8] These inputs allow us to calculate the weighted average cost of capital:

$$r_{\text{WACC}} = \left(\frac{S}{S+B}\right) \times r_S + \left(\frac{B}{S+B}\right) \times r_B \times (1 - T_c)$$
$$= 0.68 \times 13.79\% + 0.32 \times 8\% \times (1 - .37)$$
$$= 10.99\%$$

Thus, 10.99 percent is International Paper's cost of capital. It should be used to discount any project where one believes that the project's risk is equal to the risk of the firm as a whole, and the project has the same leverage as the firm as a whole.

12.6 Reducing the Cost of Capital

Chapters 9–12 develop the idea that both the expected return on a stock and the cost of capital of the firm are positively related to risk. Recently, a number of academics have argued that expected return and cost of capital are negatively related to liquidity as well.[9] In addition, these scholars make the interesting point that, although it is quite difficult to lower the risk of a firm, it is much easier to increase the liquidity of the firm's stock. Therefore, they suggest that a firm can actually lower its cost of capital through liquidity enhancement. We develop this idea next.

---

[8] These numbers were taken from *Value Line Investment Survey*. The tax rate includes both federal and local taxes.

[9] For example, see Y. Amihud and H. Mendelson, "The Liquidity Route to a Lower Cost of Capital," *Journal of Applied Corporate Finance* (Winter 2000) and M. J. Brennan and C. Tamarowski, "Investor Relations, Liquidity, and Stock Prices," *Journal of Applied Corporate Finance* (Winter 2000).

What Is Liquidity?

Anyone who owns his or her own home probably thinks of liquidity in terms of the time it takes to buy or sell the home. For example, condominiums in large metropolitan areas are generally quite liquid. Particularly in good times, a condominium may sell within days of being placed on the market. By contrast, single-family homes in suburban areas may take weeks or months to sell. Special properties such as multimillion dollar mansions may take longer still.

The concept of liquidity is similar, but not identical, in stocks. Here, we speak of the *cost* of buying and selling instead. That is, those stocks that are expensive to trade are considered less liquid than those that trade cheaply. What do we mean by the cost to trade? We generally think of three costs here: brokerage fees, the bid-ask spread, and market-impact costs.

Brokerage fees are the easiest to understand, because you must pay a broker to execute a trade. More difficult is the bid-ask spread. Consider the New York Stock Exchange (NYSE), where all trades on a particular stock must go through the stock's specialist, who is physically on the floor of the exchange. If you want to trade 100 shares of XYZ Co., your broker must get the *quote* from XYZ's specialist. Suppose the specialist provides a quote of 100–100⅛. This means that you can buy from the specialist at $100⅛ per share and sell to the specialist at $100 per share. Note that the specialist makes money here, since she buys from you at $100 and sells to you (or to someone else) at $100⅛. The gain to the specialist is a cost to you, because you are losing ⅛ dollar per share over a round-trip transaction (over a purchase and a subsequent sale).

Finally, we have *market-impact costs.* Suppose that a trader wants to sell 10,000 shares instead of just 100 shares. Here, the specialist has to take on extra risk when buying. First, she has to pay out $100,000 (10,000 × $100), cash which may not be easily available to her. Second, the trader may be selling this large amount because she has special information that the stock will fall imminently. The specialist bears the risk of losing a lot of money on that trade. Consequently, to compensate for these risks, the specialist may not buy at $100/share but at a lower price. Similarly, the specialist may be willing to sell a large block of stock only at a price above $100⅛. The price drop associated with a large sale and the price rise associated with a large purchase are the market-impact costs.

Liquidity, Expected Returns, and the Cost of Capital

The cost of trading a nonliquid stock reduces the total return that an investor receives. That is, if one buys a stock for $100 and sells it later for $105, the gain before trading costs is $5. If one must pay a dollar of commission when buying and another dollar when selling, the gain after trading costs is only $3. Both the bid-ask spread and market-impact costs would reduce this gain still further.

As we will see later, trading costs vary across securities. In the last four chapters, we have stressed that investors demand a high expected return as compensation when investing in high risk, e.g., high-beta, stocks. Because the expected return to the investor is the cost of capital to the firm, the cost of capital is positively related to beta. Now, we are saying the same thing for trading costs. Investors demand a high expected return when investing in stocks with high trading costs, i.e., low liquidity. And, this high expected return implies a high cost of capital to the firm. This idea is illustrated in Figure 12.8.

Liquidity and Adverse Selection

Liquidity varies across stocks, because the factors determining liquidity vary across stocks. Although there are a number of factors, we focus on just one, *adverse selection.* As mentioned before, the specialist will lose money on a trade if the trader has information that the

■ FIGURE 12.8 **Liquidity and the Cost of Capital**

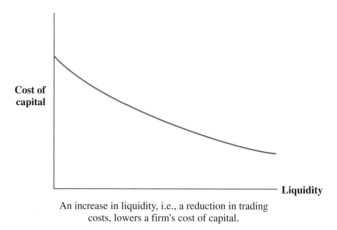

An increase in liquidity, i.e., a reduction in trading
costs, lowers a firm's cost of capital.

specialist does not have. If you have special information that the stock is worth $110 in the preceding example, you will want to buy shares at $100⅛. The specialist is obligated to sell to you at this price, which is considerably below the true price of $110. Conversely, if you know that the stock is worth only $90 and you currently own 100 shares, you will be happy to sell these shares to the specialist at $100. Again, the specialist loses, since he pays $100/share for a stock worth only $90. In either of these cases, we say that the specialist has been *picked off,* or has been subject to adverse selection.

The specialist must protect himself in some way here. Of course, he can not forbid informed individuals from trading, because he does not know ahead of time who these investors are. His next best alternative is to widen the bid-ask spread, thereby increasing the costs of trading to *all* traders—both informed and uninformed. That is, if the spread is widened to, say 99⅞–100¼, each trader pays a round-trip cost of $⅜ per share.

The key here is that the spread should be positively related to the ratio of informed to uninformed traders. That is, informed traders will pick off the specialist and uninformed traders will not. Thus, informed traders in a stock raise the required return on equity, thereby increasing the cost of capital.

What the Corporation Can Do

The corporation has an incentive to lower trading costs because—given the preceding discussion—a lower cost of capital should result. Amihud and Mendelson identify two general strategies for corporations. First, they argue that firms should try to bring in more uninformed investors. Stock splits may be a useful tool here. Imagine that a company has 1 million shares outstanding with a price per share of $100. Because investors generally buy in round lots of 100 shares, these investors would need $10,000 ($100 × 100 shares) for a purchase. A number of small investors might be "priced out" of the stock, although large investors would not be. Thus, the ratio of large investors to small investors would be high. Because large investors are generally more likely than small investors to be informed, the ratio of informed investors to uninformed investors will likely be high.

A 2:1 stock split would give two shares of stock for every one that the investor previously held. Because every investor would still hold the same proportional interest in the firm, each investor would be no better off than before. Thus, it is likely that the price per share will fall to $50 from $100. Here, an individual with 100 shares worth $10,000 ($100 × 100 shares) finds herself still worth $10,000 (= $50 × 200 shares) after the split.

However, a round lot becomes more affordable, thereby bringing more small and uninformed investors into the firm. Consequently, the adverse selection costs are reduced, allowing the specialist to lower the bid-ask spread. In turn, it is hoped that the expected return on the stock, and the cost of equity capital, will fall as well. If this happens, the stock might actually trade at a price slightly above $50.

This idea is a new one and empirical evidence is not yet in. Amihud and Mendelson themselves point out the possibility that this strategy might backfire, because brokerage commissions are often higher on lower-priced securities. We must await confirmation of this intriguing suggestion.

Companies can also attract small investors by facilitating stock purchases through the Internet. Direct stock purchase plans and dividend reinvestment programs handled online allow small investors the opportunity to buy securities cheaply. In addition, Amihud and Mendelson state, "And when these plans are administered over the Internet using web sites like Stockpower.com, moneypaper.com and Netstockdirect.com, the process is fast and efficient for both the company and the investor."[10]

Secondly, companies can disclose more information. This narrows the gap between uninformed and informed investors, thereby lowering the cost of capital. Suggestions include providing greater financial data on corporate segments and more management forecasts. An interesting study by Coller and Yohn[11] concludes that the bid-ask spread is reduced after the release of these forecasts.

This section would not be complete without a discussion of security analysts. These analysts are employed by brokerage houses to follow the companies in individual industries. For example, an analyst for a particular brokerage house might follow all the firms in, say, the auto industry. This analyst distributes reports and other information to the clients of the brokerage house. Virtually all brokerage houses have analysts following the major industries. Again, through dissemination of the information, these analysts narrow the gap between the informed and the uninformed investors, thereby tending to reduce the bid-ask spread.

Although all major industries are covered, the smaller firms in these industries are often ignored, implying a higher bid-ask spread and a higher cost of capital for these firms. Analysts frequently state that they avoid following companies that release little information, pointing out that these companies are more trouble than they are worth. Thus, it behooves companies that are not followed to release as much information as possible to security analysts in the hopes of attracting their interest. Friendliness toward security analysts would be very helpful as well. The argument here is not to get the analysts to make buy recommendations. Rather, it is simply to interest the analysts in following the company, thereby reducing the information asymmetry between informed and uninformed investors.

Concept Questions

- What is liquidity?
- What is the relation between liquidity and expected returns?
- What is adverse selection?
- What can a corporation do to lower its cost of capital?

---

[10]Ibid., p. 19.

[11]M. Coller and T. Yohn, "Management Forecasts and Information Asymmetry: An Examination of Bid-Ask Spreads," *Journal of Accounting Research* (Fall 1997).

12.7 SUMMARY AND CONCLUSIONS

Earlier chapters on capital budgeting assumed that projects generate riskless cash flows. The appropriate discount rate in that case is the riskless interest rate. Of course, most cash flows from real-world capital-budgeting projects are risky. This chapter discusses the discount rate when cash flows are risky.

1. A firm with excess cash can either pay a dividend or make a capital expenditure. Because stockholders can reinvest the dividend in risky financial assets, the expected return on a capital-budgeting project should be at least as great as the expected return on a financial asset of comparable risk.

2. The expected return on any asset is dependent upon its beta. Thus, we showed how to estimate the beta of a stock. The appropriate procedure employs regression analysis on historical returns.

3. We considered the case of a project whose beta risk was equal to that of the firm. If the firm is unlevered, the discount rate on the project is equal to

$$R_F + \beta \times (\overline{R}_M - R_F)$$

where $\overline{R}_M$ is the expected return on the market portfolio and R_F is the risk-free rate. In words, the discount rate on the project is equal to the CAPM's estimate of the expected return on the security.

4. If the project's beta differs from that of the firm, the discount rate should be based on the project's beta. The project's beta can generally be estimated by determining the average beta of the project's industry.

5. The beta of a company is a function of a number of factors. Perhaps the three most important are
   - Cyclicality of revenues
   - Operating leverage
   - Financial leverage

6. Sometimes one cannot use the average beta of the project's industry as an estimate of the beta of the project. For example, a new project may not fall neatly into any existing industry. In this case, one can estimate the project's beta by considering the project's cyclicality of revenues and its operating leverage. This approach is qualitative in nature.

7. If a firm uses debt, the discount rate to use is the r_{WACC}. In order to calculate r_{WACC}, the cost of equity and the cost of debt applicable to a project must be estimated. If the project is similar to the firm, the cost of equity can be estimated using the SML for the firm's equity. Conceptually, a dividend-growth model could be used as well, though it is likely to be far less accurate in practice.

8. A number of academics have argued that expected returns are negatively related to liquidity, where high liquidity is equivalent to low costs of trading. These scholars have further suggested that firms can reduce their cost of capital by lowering these trading costs. Practical suggestions include stock splits, more complete dissemination of information, and more effective assistance to security analysts.

KEY TERMS

Asset beta   318
Cost of equity   307
Equity beta   318

Operating leverage   316
Weighted average cost of capital (r_{WACC})   321

SUGGESTED READINGS

The following article contains a superb discussion of some of the subtleties of using WACC for project evaluation:

Miles, J., and R. Ezzel. "The Weighted Average Cost of Capital, Perfect Capital Markets and Project Life: A Clarification." *Journal of Financial and Quantitative Analysis* 15 (September 1980).

The following article provides a comprehensive survey of capital budgeting in practice, including the determination of the cost of capital:

Graham, J. R., and C. R. Harvey, "The Theory and Practice of Corporate Finance: Evidence from the Field," unpublished paper, Duke University (April, 2000).

Estimates of the cost of capital under both the capital asset pricing model and the arbitrage pricing theory are contained in:

Fama, E. F., and K. R. French, "Industry Cost of Capital," *Journal of Financial Economics* (February 1997).

One of the best "how-to" guides is:

Copeland, T.; T. Koller; and J. Murrin. *Valuation: Measuring and Managing the Value of Companies.* 2nd ed. New York: John Wiley & Sons, 1995.

QUESTIONS AND PROBLEMS

Beta and the Cost of Equity

12.1 Furniture Depot, Inc., is an all-equity firm with a beta of 0.95. The market-risk premium is 9 percent and the risk-free rate is 5 percent. The company must decide whether or not to undertake the project that requires an immediate investment of $1.2 million and will generate annual after-tax cash flows of $340,000 at year-end for five years. If the project has the same risk as the firm as a whole, should Furniture Depot undertake the project?

12.2 The returns for the past five years on Douglas stock and the New York Stock Exchange Composite Index (NYSE) are listed below:

Douglas	NYSE
−0.05	−0.12
0.05	0.01
0.08	0.06
0.15	0.10
0.10	0.05

  a. What are the average returns on Douglas stock and on the market?
  b. Compute the beta of Douglas stock.

12.3 Mitsubishi Inc. is a levered firm with a debt-to-equity ratio of 0.25. The beta of common stock is 1.15, while the beta of debt is 0.3. The market-risk premium is 10 percent and the risk-free rate is 6 percent. The corporate tax rate is 35 percent. The SML holds for the company.
  a. If a new project of the company has the same risk as the common stock of the firm, what is the cost of equity on the project?
  b. If a new project of the company has the same risk as the overall firm, what is the weighted average cost of capital on the project?

12.4 The correlation between the returns on Ceramics Craftsman, Inc., and the returns on the S&P 500 is 0.675. The variance of the returns on Ceramics Craftsman, Inc., is 0.004225, and the variance of the returns on the S&P 500 is 0.001467. What is the beta of Ceramics Craftsman stock?

12.5 The returns from the past 13 quarters on Mercantile Bank Corporation and the market are listed below.

Mercantile	Market
−0.009	0.023
0.051	0.058
−0.001	−0.020
−0.045	−0.050
0.085	0.071
0.000	0.012
−0.080	−0.075
0.020	0.050
0.125	0.120
0.110	0.049
−0.100	−0.030
0.040	0.028

a. What is the beta of Mercantile Bank Corporation stock?
b. Is Mercantile's beta higher or lower than the beta of the average stock?

12.6 The following table lists possible rates of return on two risky assets, M and J. The table also lists their joint probabilities, that is, the probabilities that they will occur simultaneously.

R_M	R_J	Prob(R_M, R_J)
0.16	0.16	0.10
0.16	0.18	0.06
0.16	0.22	0.04
0.18	0.18	0.12
0.18	0.20	0.36
0.18	0.22	0.12
0.20	0.18	0.02
0.20	0.20	0.04
0.20	0.22	0.04
0.20	0.24	0.10

a. List the possible values for R_M and the probabilities that correspond to those values.
b. Compute the following items for R_M.
   i. Expected value
   ii. Variance
   iii. Standard deviation
c. List the possible values for R_J and the probabilities that correspond to those values.
d. Compute the following items for R_J.
   i. Expected value
   ii. Variance
   iii. Standard deviation
e. Calculate the covariance and correlation coefficient of R_M and R_J.
f. Assume M is the market portfolio. Calculate the beta coefficient for security J.

12.7 If you use the stock beta and the security market line to compute the discount rate for a project, what assumptions are you implicitly making?

12.8 Pacific Cosmetics is evaluating a project to produce a perfume line. Pacific currently produces no body-scent products. Pacific Cosmetics is an all-equity firm.
   a. Should Pacific Cosmetics use its stock beta to evaluate the project?
   b. How should Pacific Cosmetics compute the beta to evaluate the project?

12.9 The following table lists possible rates of return on Compton Technology's stock and debt, and on the market portfolio. The corporate tax rate is 35 percent. The corresponding probabilities are also listed.

State	Probability	Return on Equity (%)	Return on Debt (%)	Return on the Market (%)
1	0.1	3%	8%	5%
2	0.3	8	8	10
3	0.4	20	10	15
4	0.2	15	10	20

   a. What is the beta of Compton Technology debt?
   b. What is the beta of Compton Technology stock?
   c. If the debt-to-equity ratio of Compton Technology is 0.5, what is the asset beta of Compton Technology?

12.10 Is the discount rate for the projects of a levered firm higher or lower than the cost of equity computed using the security market line? Why? (Consider only projects that have similar risk to that of the firm.)

12.11 What factors determine the beta of a stock? Define and describe each.

Weighted Average Cost of Capital

12.12 The equity beta for Adobe Online Company is 1.29. Adobe Online has a debt-to-equity ratio of 1.0. The expected return on the market is 13 percent. The risk-free rate is 7 percent. The cost of debt capital is 7 percent. The corporate tax rate is 35 percent.
   a. What is Adobe Online's cost of equity?
   b. What is Adobe Online's weighted average cost of capital?

12.13 Calculate the weighted average cost of capital for the Luxury Porcelain Company. The book value of Luxury's outstanding debt is $60 million. Currently, the debt is trading at 120 percent of book value and is priced to yield 12 percent. The 5 million outstanding shares of Luxury stock are selling for $20 per share. The required return on Luxury stock is 18 percent. The tax rate is 25 percent.

12.14 First Data Co. has 20 million shares of common stock outstanding that are currently being sold for $25 per share. The firm's debt is publicly traded at 95 percent of its face value of $180 million. The cost of debt is 10 percent and the cost of equity is 20 percent. What is the weighted average cost of capital for the firm? Assume the corporate tax rate is 40 percent.

12.15 Calgary Industries, Inc., is considering a new project that costs $25 million. The project will generate after-tax (year-end) cash flows of $7 million for five years. The firm has a debt-to-equity ratio of 0.75. The cost of equity is 15 percent and the cost of debt is 9 percent. The corporate tax rate is 35 percent. It appears that the project has the same risk as that of the overall firm. Should Calgary take on the project?

12.16 Suppose Garageband.com has a 28 percent cost of equity capital and a 10 percent before-tax cost of debt capital. The firm's debt-to-equity ratio is 1.0. Garageband is interested in investing in a telecomm project that will cost $1,000,000 and will provide $600,000 pretax annual earnings for 5 years. Given the project is an extension of its core business, the project risk is similar to the overall risk of the firm. What is the net present value of this project if Garageband's tax rate is 35%?

Minicase: AlliedProducts

AlliedProducts, Inc., has recently won approval from the Federal Aviation Administration (FAA) for its Enhanced Ground Proximity Warning System (GPWS). This system is designed to give airplane pilots additional warning of approaching ground danger and thus help prevent crashes. AlliedProducts has spent $10 million in research and development the past four years developing GPWS. The GPWS will be put on the market beginning this year and AlliedProducts expects it to stay on the market for a total of five years.

As a financial analyst specializing in the aerospace industry for USC Pension & Investment, Inc., you are asked by your managing partner, Mr. Adam Smith, to evaluate the potential of this new GPWS project.

Initially, AlliedProducts will need to acquire $42 million in production equipment to make the GPWS. The equipment is expected to have a seven-year useful life. This equipment can be sold for $12 million at the end of five years. AlliedProducts intends to sell two different versions of the GPWS:

1. *New GPWS*—intended for installation in new aircraft. The selling price is $70,000 per system and the variable cost of production is $50,000 per system. (Assume cash flows occur at year-end.)
2. *Upgrade GPWS*—intended for installation on existing aircraft with an older version ground proximity radar in place. The selling price of the Upgrade system is $35,000 per system and the variable cost to produce it is $22,000 per system.

AlliedProducts intends to raise prices at the same rate as inflation. Variable costs will also increase with inflation. In addition, the GPWS project will also incur $3 million in marketing and general administration costs the first year (expected to increase at the same rate as inflation).

AlliedProducts' corporate tax rate is 40 percent. Assume that the equity beta listed in *Value Line Investment Survey* (the latest edition) is the best estimate of AlliedProducts' beta. A five-year U.S. Treasury Bond has a rate of 6.20 percent and the S&P 500 recent years' historical average excess return (i.e., the market return less the Treasury bond rate) is 8.3 percent. Annual inflation is expected to remain constant at 3 percent. Further, suppose AlliedProducts' cost of debt is 6.2 percent and (although somewhat unrealistic) its debt-to-equity ratio is 50 percent and will remain at 50 percent for at least five years.

Commercial Aircraft Market

The state of the economy has a major impact on the airplane manufacturing industry. Airline industry analysts have the following production expectations, depending on the annual state of the economy for the next five years:

■ Table 12.4

State of Economy	Probability of State	New Aircraft (year 1)	Annual Growth
Strong growth	.15	350	.15
Moderate growth	.45	250	.10
Mild recession	.30	150	.06
Severe recession	.10	50	.03

While probabilities of each state of the economy will not change during the next five years, airplane production for each category will increase, as shown in Table 12.4, each year after year 1. The FAA requires that these planes have new ground proximity warning systems, of which there are a number of manufacturers besides AlliedProducts.

AlliedProducts estimates that there are approximately 12,500 existing aircraft that comprise the market for its GPWS Upgrade package. Due to FAA regulations, all existing aircraft will be required to get an upgraded ground proximity warning system within the next five years, again, not necessarily from AlliedProducts. AlliedProducts believes the upgrades of the existing aircraft fleet will be spread evenly over the five years (the time value of money would suggest manufacturers defer purchasing upgrades until the fifth year; however, consumer demand for the additional safety will induce earlier upgrades).

AlliedProducts uses the MACRS depreciation schedule (seven-year property class). The immediate initial working capital requirement is $2 million and thereafter the net working capital requirements will be 5 percent of sales.

AlliedProducts has a number of competitors both in the new GPWS and upgrade GPWS markets but expects to dominate the market with a 45 percent share.

Assignment:

First, use the CAPM to determine the appropriate discount rate for this product. Then, use computer spreadsheets such as Excel or Lotus 1-2-3 to analyze the project.

Will the GPWS project improve the wealth of AlliedProducts' shareholders, such as your firm—USC Pension & Investment, Inc.?

Economic Value Added and the Measurement of Financial Performance

Chapter 12 shows how to calculate the appropriate discount rate for capital budgeting and other valuation problems. We now consider the measurement of financial performance. We introduce the concept of economic value added, which uses the same discount rate developed for capital budgeting. We begin with a simple example.

Many years ago, Henry Bodenheimer started Bodie's Blimps, one of the largest high-speed blimp manufacturers. Because growth was so rapid, Henry put most of his effort into capital budgeting. His approach to capital budgeting paralleled that of Chapter 12. He forecasted cash flows for various projects and discounted them at the cost of capital appropriate to the beta of the blimp business. However, these projects have grown rapidly, in some cases becoming whole divisions. He now needs to evaluate the performance of these divisions in order to reward his division managers. How does he perform the appropriate analysis?

Henry is aware that capital budgeting and performance measurement are essentially mirror images of each other. Capital budgeting is forward-looking by nature because one must estimate future cash flows to value a project. By contrast, performance measurement is backward-looking. As Henry stated to a group of his executives, "Capital budgeting is like looking through the windshield while driving a car. You need to know what lies further down the road to calculate a net present value. Performance measurement is like looking into the rearview mirror. You find out where you have been."

Henry first measured the performance of his various divisions by return on assets (ROA), an approach, which we treated in the appendix to Chapter 2. For example, if a division had earnings after tax of $1,000 and had assets of $10,000, the ROA would be[12]

$$\frac{\$1,000}{\$10,000} = 10\%.$$

He calculated the ROA ratio for each of his divisions, paying a bonus to each of his division managers based on the size of that division's ROA. However, while ROA was generally effective in motivating his managers, there were a number of situations where it appeared that ROA was counterproductive.

For example, Henry always believed that Sharon Smith, head of the supersonic division, was his best manager. The ROA of Smith's division was generally in the high double digits, but the best estimate of the weighted average cost of capital for the division was only 20%. Furthermore, the division had been growing rapidly. However, as soon as Henry paid bonuses based on ROA, the division stopped growing. At that time, Smith's division had after tax earnings of $2,000,000 on an asset base of $2,000,000, for an ROA of 100% ($2 million/$2 million).

Henry found out why the growth stopped when he suggested a project to Smith that would earn $1,000,000 per year on an investment of $2,000,000. This was clearly an attractive project with an ROA of 50% ($1 million/$2 million). He thought that Smith would jump at the chance to place his project into her division, because the ROA of the project was much higher than the cost of capital of 20%. However, Smith did everything she could to kill the project. And, as Henry later figured out, Smith was rational to do so. Smith must have realized that if the project were accepted, the division's ROA would become

$$\frac{\$2,000,000 + \$1,000,000}{\$2,000,000 + \$2,000,000} = 75\%$$

Thus, the ROA of Smith's division would fall from 100% to 75% if the project were accepted, with Smith's bonus falling in tandem.

Henry was later exposed to the economic-value-added (EVA) approach,[13] which seems to obviate this particular problem. The formula for EVA is

[ROA − Weighted average cost of capital] × Total capital

Without the new project, the EVA of Smith's division would be:

[100% − 20%] × $2,000,000 = $1,600,000

This is an annual number. That is, the division would bring in $1.6 million above and beyond the cost of capital to the firm each year.

With the new project included, the EVA jumps to

[75% − 20%] × $4,000,000 = $2,200,000

If Sharon Smith knew that her bonus was based on EVA, she would now have an incentive to accept, not reject, the project. Although ROA appears in the EVA formula, EVA differs substantially from ROA. The big difference is that ROA is a percentage number and

---

[12]Earnings after tax is EBIT $(1 - T_c)$ where EBIT is earnings before interest and taxes and T_c is the tax rate.

[13]Stern Stewart & Company have a copyright on the terms economic value added and EVA. Details on the Stern Steward & Company EVA can be found in J. M. Stern, G. B. Stewart, and D. A. Chew, "The EVA Financial Management System," *Journal of Applied Corporate Finance* (Summer 1999).

EVA is a dollar value. In the preceding example, EVA increased when the new project was added even though the ROA actually decreased. In this situation, EVA correctly incorporates the fact that a high return on a large division may be better than a very high return on a smaller division. The situation here is quite similar to the scale problem in capital budgeting that we discussed in Section 6.6.

Further understanding of EVA can be achieved by rewriting the EVA formula. Because ROA × total capital is equal to earnings after tax, we can write the EVA formula as:

$$\text{Earnings after tax} - \text{Weighted average cost of capital} \times \text{Total capital}$$

Thus, EVA can simply be viewed as earnings after capital costs. Although accountants subtract many costs (including depreciation) to get the earnings number shown in financial reports, they do not subtract out capital costs. One can see the logic of accountants, because the cost of capital is very subjective. By contrast, costs such as COGS (cost of goods sold), SGA (sales, general and administration), and even depreciation can be measured more objectively. However, even if the cost of capital is difficult to estimate, it is hard to justify ignoring it completely. After all, this textbook argues that the cost of capital is a necessary input to capital budgeting. Shouldn't it also be a necessary input to performance measurement?

This example argues that EVA can increase investment for those firms that are currently underinvesting. However, there are many firms in the reverse situation; the managers are so focused on increasing earnings that they take on projects for which the profits do not justify the capital outlays. These managers either are unaware of capital costs or, knowing these costs, choose to ignore them. Because the cost of capital is right in the middle of the EVA formula, managers will not easily ignore these costs when evaluated on an EVA system.

One other advantage of EVA is that it is so stark; the number is either positive or it is negative. Plenty of divisions have negative EVAs for a number of years. Because these divisions are destroying more value than they are creating, a strong point can be made for liquidating these divisions. Although managers are generally emotionally opposed to this type of action, EVA analysis makes liquidation harder to ignore.

The preceding discussion puts EVA in a very positive light. However, one can certainly find much to criticize with EVA as well. We now focus on two well-known problems with EVA. First, the preceding example uses EVA for performance measurement, where we believe it properly belongs. To us, EVA seems a clear improvement over ROA and other financial ratios. However, EVA has little to offer for capital budgeting because EVA focuses only on current earnings. By contrast, net-present-value analysis uses projections of all future cash flows, where the cash flows will generally differ from year to year. Thus, as far as capital budgeting is concerned, NPV analysis has a richness that EVA does not have. Although supporters may argue that EVA correctly incorporates the weighted average cost of capital, one must remember that the discount rate in NPV analysis is the same weighted average cost of capital. That is, both approaches take the cost of equity capital based on beta and combine it with the cost of debt to get an estimate of this weighted average.

A second problem with EVA is that it may increase the shortsightedness of managers. Under EVA, a manager will be well rewarded today if earnings are high today. Future losses may not harm the manager, because there is a good chance that she will be promoted or have left the firm by then. Thus, the manager has an incentive to run a division with more regard for short-term than long-term value. By raising prices or cutting quality, the manager may increase current profits (and, therefore, current EVA). However, to the extent that customer satisfaction is reduced, future profits (and therefore future EVA) are likely to fall. However, one should not be too harsh with EVA here, because the same problem occurs with ROA. A manager who raises prices or cuts quality will increase current ROA at the expense of future ROA. The problem, then, is not EVA per se but with the use of accounting numbers in general. Because stockholders want the discounted present value of all cash flows to be maximized, managers with bonuses based on some function of current profits or current cash flows are likely to behave in a shortsighted way.

EXAMPLE

Assume the following figures for the International Trade Corporation

$$\text{EBIT} = \$2.5 \text{ billion}$$
$$T_c = .4$$
$$r_{\text{WACC}} = 11\%$$
$$\text{Total capital contributed} = \text{Total debt} + \text{Equity}$$
$$= \$10 \text{ billion} + \$10 \text{ billion}$$
$$= \$20 \text{ billion}$$

Now we can calculate International Trade's EVA:

$$\text{EVA} = \text{EBIT} (1 - T_c) - r_{\text{WACC}} \times \text{Total capital}$$
$$= (\$2.5 \text{ billion} \times .6) - (.11 \times \$20 \text{ billion})$$
$$= \$1.5 \text{ billion} - \$2.2 \text{ billion}$$
$$= -\$700 \text{ million}$$

Capital Structure and Dividend Policy

PART II discussed the capital budgeting decisions of the firm. We argued that the objective of the firm should be to create value from its capital budgeting decisions. To do this the firm must find investments with a positive net present value. In Part IV we concentrate on financing decisions. As with capital budgeting decisions, the firm seeks to create value with its financing decisions. To do this the firm must find positive NPV financing arrangements. However, financial markets do not provide as many opportunities for positive NPV transactions as do nonfinancial markets. We show that the sources of NPV in financing are taxes, bankruptcy costs, and agency costs.

Chapter 13 introduces the concept of efficient markets, where current market prices reflect available information. We describe several forms of efficiency: the weak form, the semistrong form, and the strong form. The chapter offers a number of important lessons for the corporate financial manager in understanding the logic behind efficient financial markets.

In Chapter 14 we describe the basic types of long-term financing: common stock, preferred stock, and bonds. We then briefly analyze the major trends and patterns of long-term financing.

We consider the firm's overall capital-structure decision in Chapters 15 and 16. In general, a firm can choose any capital structure it desires: common stocks, bonds, preferred stocks, and so on. How should a firm choose its capital structure? Changing the capital structure of the firm changes the way the firm pays out its cash flows. Firms that borrow pay lower taxes than firms that do not. Because of corporate taxes, the value of a firm that borrows may be higher than the value of one that does not. However, with costly bankruptcy, a firm that borrows may have lower value. The combined effects of taxes and bankruptcy costs can produce an optimal capital structure.

Chapter 17 discusses capital budgeting for firms with some debt in their capital structures. It extends some of the material of Chapter 12. This chapter presents three alternative valuation methods: the weighted-average-cost-of-capital approach, the flows-to-equity approach, and the adjusted-present-value approach.

We discuss dividend policy in Chapter 18. It seems surprising that much empirical evidence and logic suggest that dividend policy does not matter. There are some good reasons for firms to pay low levels of dividends: lower taxes and costs of issuing new equity. However, there are also some good reasons to pay high levels of dividends: to reduce agency costs and to satisfy low-tax, high-income clienteles.

CHAPTER 13

Corporate-Financing Decisions and Efficient Capital Markets

EXECUTIVE SUMMARY

The section on value concentrated on the firm's capital budgeting decisions—the left-hand side of the balance sheet of the firm. This chapter begins our analysis of corporate-financing decisions—the right-hand side of the balance sheet. We take the firm's capital budgeting decision as fixed in this section of the text.

The point of this chapter is to introduce the concept of *efficient capital markets* and its implications for corporate finance. Efficient capital markets are those in which current market prices reflect available information. This means that current market prices reflect the underlying present value of securities, and there is no way to make unusual or excess profits by using the available information.

This concept has profound implications for financial managers, because market efficiency eliminates many value-enhancing strategies of firms. In particular, we show that in an efficient market

1. Financial managers cannot time issues of bonds and stocks.
2. The issuance of additional stock should not depress the stock's market price.
3. Stock and bond prices should not be affected by a firm's choice of accounting method.

Ultimately, whether or not capital markets are efficient is an empirical question. We will describe several of the important studies that have been carried out to examine efficient markets.

13.1 CAN FINANCING DECISIONS CREATE VALUE?

Earlier parts of the book show how to evaluate projects according to the net present value criterion. The real world is a competitive one where projects with positive net present value are not always easy to come by. However, through hard work or through good fortune, a firm can identify winning projects. For example, to create value from capital budgeting decisions, the firm is likely to

1. Locate an unsatisfied demand for a particular product or service.
2. Create a barrier to make it more difficult for other firms to compete.
3. Produce products or services at lower cost than the competition.
4. Be the first to develop a new product.

The next five chapters concern *financing* decisions. Typical financing decisions include how much debt and equity to sell, what types of debt and equity to sell, and when to sell debt and equity. Just as the net present value criterion was used to evaluate capital budgeting projects, we now want to use the same criterion to evaluate financing decisions.

Though the procedure for evaluating financing decisions is identical to the procedure for evaluating projects, the results are different. It turns out that the typical firm has many more capital-expenditure opportunities with positive net present values than financing opportunities with positive net present values. In fact, we later show that some plausible financial models imply that no valuable financial opportunities exist at all.

Though this dearth of profitable financing opportunities will be examined in detail later, a few remarks are in order now. We maintain that there are basically three ways to create valuable financing opportunities:

1. *Fool Investors.* Assume that a firm can raise capital either by issuing stock or by issuing a more complex security, say, a combination of stock and warrants. Suppose that, in truth, 100 shares of stock are worth the same as 50 units of our complex security. If investors have a misguided, overly optimistic view of the complex security, perhaps the 50 units can be sold for more than the 100 shares of stock can be. Clearly this complex security provides a valuable financing opportunity because the firm is getting more than fair value for it.

Financial managers try to package securities to receive the greatest value. A cynic might view this as attempting to fool investors. However, empirical evidence suggests that investors cannot easily be fooled. Thus, one must be skeptical that value can easily be created here.

The theory of efficient capital markets expresses this idea. In its extreme form, it says that all securities are appropriately priced at all times, implying that the market as a whole is very shrewd indeed. Thus, corporate managers should not attempt to create value by fooling investors. Instead, managers must create value in other ways.

2. *Reduce Costs or Increase Subsidies.* We show later in the book that certain forms of financing have greater tax advantages than other forms. Clearly, a firm packaging securities to minimize taxes can increase firm value. In addition, any financing technique involves other costs. For example, investment bankers, lawyers, and accountants must be paid. A firm packaging securities to minimize these costs can also increase its value. Finally, any financing vehicle that provides subsidies is valuable. This last possibility is illustrated below.

EXAMPLE

Suppose Vermont Electronics Company is thinking about relocating its plant to Mexico where labor costs are lower. In the hope that it can stay in Vermont, the company has submitted an application to the State of Vermont to issue $2 million in five-year, tax-exempt industrial bonds. The coupon rate on industrial revenue bonds in Vermont is currently 5 percent. This is an attractive rate because the normal cost of debt capital for Vermont Electronics Company is 10 percent. What is the NPV of this potential financing transaction?

If the application is accepted and the industrial revenue bonds are issued by the Vermont Electronics Company, the NPV (ignoring corporate taxes) is

$$NPV = \$2{,}000{,}000 - \left[\frac{\$100{,}000}{1.1} + \frac{\$100{,}000}{(1.1)^2} + \frac{\$100{,}000}{(1.1)^3} + \frac{\$100{,}000}{(1.1)^4} + \frac{\$2{,}100{,}000}{(1.1)^5} \right]$$
$$= \$2{,}000{,}000 - \$1{,}620{,}921$$
$$= \$379{,}079$$

This transaction has a positive NPV. The Vermont Electronics Company obtains subsidized financing where the amount of the subsidy is $379,079.

3. *Create a New Security.* There has been a surge in financial innovation in recent years. For example, in a speech on financial innovation, Nobel laureate Merton Miller asked the rhetorical question, "Can any twenty-year period in recorded history have witnessed even a tenth as much new development? Where corporations once issued only straight debt and straight common stock, they now issue zero-coupon bonds, adjustable-rate notes, floating-

rate notes, putable bonds, credit-enhanced debt securities, receivable-backed securities, adjusted-rate preferred stock, convertible adjustable preferred stock, auction-rate preferred stock, single-point adjustable-rate stock, convertible exchangeable preferred stock, adjustable-rate convertible debt, zero-coupon convertible debt, debt with mandatory common-stock-purchase contracts—to name just a few!"[1] And, financial innovation has occurred even more rapidly in the years following Miller's speech.

Though the advantage of each instrument is different, one general theme is that these new securities cannot easily be duplicated by combinations of existing securities. Thus, a previously unsatisfied clientele may pay extra for a specialized security catering to its needs. For example, putable bonds let the purchaser sell the bond at a fixed price back to the firm. This innovation creates a price floor, allowing the investor to reduce his or her downside risk. Perhaps risk-averse investors or investors with little knowledge of the bond market would find this feature particularly attractive.

Corporations gain from developing unique securities by issuing these securities at high prices. However, we believe that the value captured by the innovator is small in the long run because the innovator usually cannot patent or copyright his idea. Soon many firms are issuing securities of the same kind, forcing prices down as a result.[2]

This brief introduction sets the stage for the next five chapters of the book. The rest of this chapter examines the efficient-capital-markets hypothesis. We show that if capital markets are efficient, corporate managers cannot create value by fooling investors. This is quite important, because managers must create value in other, perhaps more difficult, ways. The following four chapters concern the costs and subsidies of various forms of financing. A discussion of new financing instruments is postponed until later chapters of the text.

CONCEPT QUESTION

?

• List three ways financing decisions can create value.

13.2 A DESCRIPTION OF EFFICIENT CAPITAL MARKETS

An efficient capital market is one in which stock prices fully reflect available information. To illustrate how an efficient market works, suppose the F-stop Camera Corporation (FCC) is attempting to develop a camera that will double the speed of the auto-focusing system now available. FCC believes this research has positive NPV.

---

[1]M. Miller, "Financial Innovation: The Last Twenty Years and the Next," *Journal of Financial and Quantitative Analysis* (December 1986). However, Peter Tufano, "Securities Innovations: A Historical and Functional Perspective," *Journal of Applied Corporate Finance* (Winter 1995), shows that many securities commonly believed to have been invented in the 1970s and 1980s can be traced as far back as the 1830s.

[2]Most financial innovations originally come from investment banks and are then sold to firms. Peter Tufano, "Financial Innovation and First-Mover Advantages," *Journal of Financial Economics* 25 (1990), pp. 213–40, looked at 58 financial innovations (including original-issue deep-discount bonds) to examine how well investment banks are compensated for developing new financial products. He finds investment banks underwrite significantly more public offerings of the products they create. His study does not directly address the question of whether investment banks or corporations obtain most of the benefits of new financial products. However, it is clear that investment banks benefit substantially from creating new products.

Raj Varma and Donald Chambers, "The Role of Financial Innovation in Raising Capital," *Journal of Financial Economics* 26 (1990), pp. 289–98, look at how firms have benefited from issuing original-issue deep-discount bonds after TEFRA. They report no gains.

Now consider a share of stock in FCC. What determines the willingness of investors to hold shares of FCC at a particular price? One important factor is the probability that FCC will be the company to develop the new auto-focusing system first. In an efficient market we would expect the price of the shares of FCC to increase if this probability increases.

Suppose a well-known engineer is hired by FCC to help develop the new auto-focusing system. In an efficient market, what will happen to FCC's share price when this is announced? If the well-known scientist is paid a salary that fully reflects his or her contribution to the firm, the price of the stock will not necessarily change. Suppose, instead, that hiring the scientist is a positive NPV transaction. In this case, the price of shares in FCC will increase because the firm can pay the scientist a salary below his or her true value to the company.

When will the increase in the price of FCC's shares take place? Assume that the hiring announcement is made in a press release on Wednesday morning. In an efficient market, the price of shares in FCC will *immediately* adjust to this new information. Investors should not be able to buy the stock on Wednesday afternoon and make a profit on Thursday. This would imply that it took the stock market a day to realize the implication of the FCC press release. The efficient-market hypothesis predicts that the price of shares of FCC stock on Wednesday afternoon will already reflect the information contained in the Wednesday morning press release.

The **efficient-market hypothesis** (EMH) has implications for investors and for firms.

- Because information is reflected in prices immediately, investors should only expect to obtain a normal rate of return. Awareness of information when it is released does an investor no good. The price adjusts before the investor has time to trade on it.
- Firms should expect to receive the fair value for securities that they sell. *Fair* means that the price they receive for the securities they issue is the present value. Thus, valuable financing opportunities that arise from fooling investors are unavailable in efficient capital markets.

Some people spend their entire careers trying to pick stocks that will outperform the average. For any given stock, they can learn not only what has happened in the past to the stock price and dividends, but also what the company earnings have been, how much debt it owes, what taxes it pays, what businesses it is in, what market share it has for its products, how well it is doing in each of its businesses, what new investments it has planned, how sensitive it is to the economy, and so on.

If you want to learn about a given company and its stock, an enormous amount of information is available to you. The preceding list only scratches the surface. Not only is there a lot to know about any given company, there is also a powerful motive for doing so, the profit motive. If you know more about a company than other investors in the marketplace, you can profit from that knowledge by investing in the company's stock if you have good news or selling it if you have bad news.

There are other ways to use your information. If you could convince investors that you have reliable information about the fortunes of the companies, you might start a newsletter and sell investors that information. You could even charge a varying rate depending on how fresh the information is. You could sell the monthly standard report for a subscription price of $100 per year, but for an extra $300 a subscriber could get special interim once-a-week reports. For $5,000 per year you could offer to telephone the customer as soon as you had a new idea or a new piece of information. This may sound a bit farfetched, but it is what many sellers of market information actually do.

The logical consequence of all of this information being available, studied, sold, and used in an effort to make profits from stock market trading is that the market becomes *efficient*. A market is efficient with respect to information if there is no way to make unusual or excess profits by using that information. When a market is efficient with respect to information, we say that prices *incorporate* the information. Without knowing anything special about a stock, an investor in an efficient market expects to earn an equilibrium required return from an investment, and a company expects to pay an equilibrium cost of capital.[3]

EXAMPLE

Suppose IBM announces it has invented a microprocessor that will make its computer 30 times faster than existing computers. The price of a share of IBM should increase immediately to a new equilibrium level.

Figure 13.1 presents several possible adjustments in stock prices. The solid line represents the path taken by the stock in an efficient market. In this case the price adjusts immediately to the new information so that further changes take place in the price of the stock. The dotted line depicts a delayed reaction. Here it takes the market 30 days to fully absorb the information. Finally, the broken line illustrates an overreaction and subsequent correction back to the true price. The broken line and the dotted line show the paths that the stock price might take in an inefficient market. If the price of the stock takes several days to adjust, trading profits would be available to investors who bought at the date of the announcement and sold once the price settled back to the equilibrium.[4]

QUESTION
CONCEPT
?
• Can you define an efficient market?

13.3 THE DIFFERENT TYPES OF EFFICIENCY

In our previous discussion, we assumed that the market responds immediately to all available information. In actuality, certain information may affect stock prices more quickly than other information. To handle differential response rates, researchers separate information into different types. The most common classification system speaks of three types: information on past prices, publicly available information, and all information. The effect of these three information sets on prices is examined next.

The Weak Form

Imagine a trading strategy that recommends buying a stock when it has gone up three days in a row and recommends selling a stock when it has gone down three days in a row. This strategy uses information based only on past prices. It does not use any other information,

---

[3]In Chapter 10 we analyzed how the required return on a risky asset is determined.

[4]Now you should understand the following short story. A student was walking down the hall with his finance professor when they both saw a $20 bill on the ground. As the student bent down to pick it up, the professor shook his head slowly and, with a look of disappointment on his face, said patiently to the student, "Don't bother. If it was really there, someone else would have already picked it up."

The moral of the story reflects the logic of the efficient-market hypothesis: If you think you have found a pattern in stock prices or a simple device for picking winners, you probably have not. If there were such a simple way to make money, someone else would have found it before. Furthermore, if people tried to exploit the information, their efforts would become self-defeating and the pattern would disappear.

■ FIGURE 13.1   **Reaction of Stock Price to New Information in Efficient and Inefficient Markets**

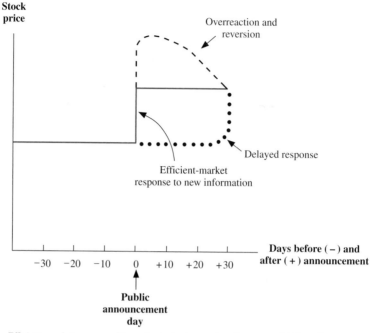

Efficient-market response: The price instantaneously adjusts to and fully reflects new information; there is no tendency for subsequent increases and decreases.
Delayed response: The price adjusts slowly to the new information; 30 days elapse before the price completely reflects the new information.
Overreaction: The price overadjusts to the new information; there is a bubble in the price sequence.

such as earnings, forecasts, merger announcements, or money-supply figures. A capital market is said to be *weakly efficient* or to satisfy **weak-form efficiency** if it fully incorporates the information in past stock prices. Thus, the above strategy would not be able to generate profits if weak-form efficiency holds.

Often weak-form efficiency is represented mathematically as

$$P_t = P_{t-1} + \text{Expected return} + \text{Random error}_t \qquad (13.1)$$

Equation (13.1) states that the price today is equal to the sum of the last observed price plus the expected return on the stock plus a random component occurring over the interval. The last observed price could have occurred yesterday, last week, or last month, depending on one's sampling interval. The expected return is a function of a security's risk and would be based on the models of risk and return in previous chapters. The random component is due to new information on the stock. It could be either positive or negative and has an expectation of zero. The random component in any one period is unrelated to the random component in any past period. Hence, this component is not predictable from past prices. If stock prices follow equation (13.1), they are said to follow a **random walk.**[5]

---

[5]For purposes of this text, the random walk can be considered synonymous with weak-form efficiency. Technically, the random walk is a slightly more restrictive hypothesis because it assumes that stock returns are identically distributed through time.

■ FIGURE 13.2   Investor Behavior Tends to Eliminate Cyclical Patterns

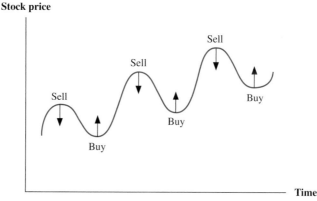

If a stock's price has followed a cyclical pattern, the pattern will be quickly eliminated in an efficient market. A random pattern will emerge as investors buy at the trough and sell at the peak of a cycle.

Weak-form efficiency is about the weakest type of efficiency that we would expect a financial market to display because historical price information is the easiest kind of information about a stock to acquire. If it were possible to make extraordinary profits simply by finding the patterns in the stock price movements, everyone would do it, and any profits would disappear in the scramble.

The effect of competition can be seen in Figure 13.2. Suppose the price of a stock displayed a cyclical pattern, as indicated by the wavy curve. Shrewd investors would buy at the low points, forcing those prices up. Conversely, they would sell at the high points, forcing prices down. Via competition, the cyclical regularities would be eliminated, leaving only random fluctuations.

By denying that future market movements can be predicted from past movements, we are denying the profitability of a host of techniques falling under the heading of technical analysis. The term **technical analysis** refers to attempts to predict the future from the patterns of past price movements. Furthermore, we are denigrating the work of all of their followers, who are called *technical analysts.*

To provide some flavor to technical analysis, consider two commonly used approaches. First, many technical analysts believe that stock prices are likely to follow a *head-and-shoulders* pattern. This is presented in the left-hand side of Figure 13.3. An analyst at point *A,* anticipating a head-and-shoulders pattern, might very well buy the stock and hopefully hold it for a short-term gain. An analyst at point *B,* anticipating the completion of the pattern, would sell the stock.

Second, other analysts believe that stocks making three tops are likely to fall in price. This *triple-tops* pattern is presented in the right-hand side of Figure 13.3. An analyst who, at point *C,* discovers that the pattern has occurred, might sell the stock.

At this point, one might wonder why anyone would restrict his or her information to the set of past prices. Surprisingly, many technical analysts do just that, saying that all relevant information on a security's future price movement is contained in the security's past movement. Other information is considered distracting. John Magee,[6] one of the most renowned of technical analysts, took this approach to an extreme. He reportedly worked on his stock market charts in an office with boarded-up windows. To him, weather was superfluous information that could only impede his task of stock selection.

---

[6]His book (John Magee and Robert Davis Edwards, *Technical Analysis of Stock Trends,* 7th ed., New York: AMACON, 1997) is considered by many to be the bible of technical analysis.

■ FIGURE 13.3 **Two Widely Believed Technical Patterns**

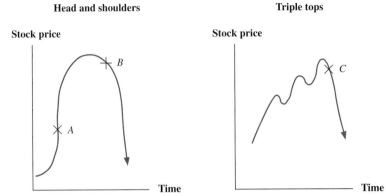

Technical analysts frequently claim that the price of a stock is likely to follow a head-and-shoulders pattern or a triple-tops pattern. According to a technical analyst, if a head-and-shoulders pattern can be identified early enough, an investor might like to buy at point *A* and sell at point *B*. A triple-tops pattern occurs when three highs are followed by a precipitous drop. If a triple-tops pattern can be identified early enough, an investor might like to sell at point *C*.

The Semistrong and Strong Forms

If weak-form efficiency is controversial, even more contentious are the two stronger types of efficiency, **semistrong-form efficiency** and **strong-form efficiency.** A market is semi-strong-form efficient if prices reflect (incorporate) all publicly available information, including information such as published accounting statements for the firm as well as historical price information. A market is strong-form efficient if prices reflect all information, public or private.

The information set of past prices is a subset of the information set of publicly available information, which in turn is a subset of all information. This is shown in Figure 13.4. Thus, strong-form efficiency implies semistrong-form efficiency, and semistrong-form efficiency implies weak-form efficiency. The distinction between semistrong-form efficiency and weak-form efficiency is that semistrong-form efficiency requires not only that the market be efficient with respect to historical price information, but that *all* of the information available to the public be reflected in price.

To illustrate the different forms of efficiency, imagine an investor who always sold a particular stock after its price had risen. A market that was only weak-form efficient and not semistrong-form efficient would still prevent such a strategy from generating positive profits. According to weak-form efficiency, a recent price rise does not imply that the stock is overvalued.

Now consider a firm reporting increased earnings. An individual might consider investing in the stock after hearing of the news release giving this information. However, if the market is semistrong efficient, the price should rise immediately upon the news release. Thus, the investor would end up paying the higher price, eliminating all chance for profit.

At the furthest end of the spectrum is strong-form efficiency, which incorporates the other two types of efficiency. This form says that anything that is pertinent to the value of the stock and that is known to at least one investor is, in fact, fully incorporated into the stock value. A strict believer in strong-form efficiency would deny that an insider who knew whether a company mining operation had struck gold could profit from that information. Such a devotee of the strong-form efficient-market hypothesis might argue that as soon as the insider tried to trade on his or her information, the market would recognize what was

■ FIGURE 13.4 **Relationship among Three Different Information Sets**

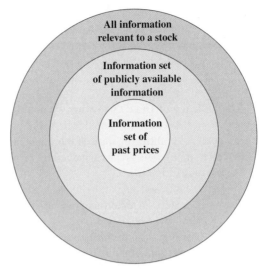

The information set of past prices is a subset of the information set of publicly available information, which in turn is a subset of all information. If today's price reflects only information on past prices, the market is weak-form efficient. If today's price reflects all publicly available information, the market is semistrong-form efficient. If today's price reflects all information, both public and private, the market is strong-form efficient.

Semistrong-form efficiency implies weak-form efficiency and strong-form efficiency implies semistrong-form efficiency.

happening, and the price would shoot up before he or she could buy any of the stock. Alternatively, sometimes believers in strong-form efficiency take the view that there are no such things as secrets and that as soon as the gold is discovered, the secret gets out.

Are the hypotheses of semistrong-form efficiency and strong-form efficiency good descriptions of how markets work? Expert opinion is divided here. The evidence in support of semistrong-form efficiency is, of course, more compelling than that in support of strong-form efficiency, and for many purposes it seems reasonable to assume that the market is semistrong-form efficient. The extreme of strong-form efficiency seems more difficult to accept. Before we look at the evidence on market efficiency, we will summarize our thinking on the versions of the efficient-market hypothesis in terms of basic economic arguments.

One reason to expect that markets are weak-form efficient is that it is so cheap and easy to find patterns in stock prices. Anyone who can program a computer and knows a little bit of statistics can search for such patterns. It stands to reason that if there were such patterns, people would find and exploit them, in the process causing them to disappear.

Semistrong-form efficiency, though, uses much more sophisticated information and reasoning than weak-form efficiency. An investor must be skilled at economics and statistics, and steeped in the idiosyncrasies of individual industries and companies. Furthermore, to acquire and use such skills requires talent, ability, and time. In the jargon of the economist, such an effort is costly and the ability to be successful at it is probably in scarce supply.

As for strong-form efficiency, this is just farther down the road than semistrong-form efficiency. It is difficult to believe that the market is so efficient that someone with true and valuable inside information cannot prosper by using it. It is also difficult to find direct evidence concerning strong-form efficiency. What we have tends to be unfavorable to this hypothesis of market efficiency.

Some Common Misconceptions about the Efficient-Market Hypothesis

No idea in finance has attracted as much attention as that of efficient markets, and not all of the attention has been flattering. To a certain extent this is because much of the criticism has been based on a misunderstanding of what the hypothesis does and does not say. We illustrate three misconceptions below.

The Efficacy of Dart Throwing   When the notion of market efficiency was first publicized and debated in the popular financial press, it was often characterized by the following quote: ". . . throwing darts at the financial page will produce a portfolio that can be expected to do as well as any managed by professional security analysts."[7, 8] This is almost, but not quite, true.

All the efficient-market hypothesis really says is that, on average, the manager will not be able to achieve an abnormal or excess return. The excess return is defined with respect to some benchmark expected return that comes from the security market line of Chapter 10 (SML). The investor must still decide how risky a portfolio he or she wants and what expected return it will normally have. A random dart thrower might wind up with all of the darts sticking into one or two high-risk stocks that deal in genetic engineering. Would you really want all of your stock investments in two such stocks? (Beware, though—a professional portfolio manager could do the same.)

The failure to understand this has often led to a confusion about market efficiency. For example, sometimes it is wrongly argued that market efficiency means that it does not matter what you do because the efficiency of the market will protect the unwary. However, someone once remarked, "The efficient market protects the sheep from the wolves, but nothing can protect the sheep from themselves."

What efficiency does say is that the price that a firm will obtain when it sells a share of its stock is a fair price in the sense that it reflects the value of that stock given the information that is available about it. Shareholders need not worry that they are paying too much for a stock with a low dividend or some other characteristic, because the market has already incorporated it into the price. However, investors still have to worry about such things as their level of risk exposure and their degree of diversification.

Price Fluctuations   Much of the public is skeptical of efficiency because stock prices fluctuate from day to day. However, daily price movement is in no way inconsistent with efficiency; a stock in an efficient market adjusts to new information by changing price. A great deal of new information comes into the stock market each day. In fact, the absence of daily price movements in a changing world might suggest an inefficiency.

Stockholder Disinterest   Many laypersons are skeptical that the market price can be efficient if only a fraction of the outstanding shares changes hands on any given day. However, the number of traders in a stock on a given day is generally far less than the number of people following the stock. This is true because an individual will trade only when his appraisal of the value of the stock differs enough from the market price to justify incurring brokerage commissions and other transaction costs. Furthermore, even if the number of traders following a stock is small relative to the number of outstanding shareholders, the

---

[7]B. G. Malkiel, *A Random Walk Down Wall Street,* 7th ed. (New York: Norton, 1999).

[8]Older articles often referred to the benchmark of "dart-throwing monkeys." As government involvement in the securities industry grew, the benchmark was oftentimes restated as "dart-throwing congressmen."

stock can be expected to be efficiently priced as long as a number of interested traders use the publicly available information. That is, the stock price can reflect the available information even if many stockholders never follow the stock and are not considering trading in the near future, and even if some stockholders trade with little or no information. Thus, the empirical findings suggesting that the stock market is predominantly efficient need not be surprising.

QUESTIONS

- Can you describe the three forms of the efficient-market hypothesis?
- What kinds of things could make markets inefficient?
- Does market efficiency mean you can throw darts at *The Wall Street Journal* listing of New York Stock Exchange stocks to pick a portfolio?
- What does it mean to say the price you pay for a stock is fair?

13.4 THE EVIDENCE

The record on the efficient-market hypothesis is extensive, and in large measure it is reassuring to advocates of the efficiency of markets. The studies done by academicians fall into broad categories. First, there is evidence as to whether changes of stock prices are random. Second are *event studies*. Third is the record of professionally managed investment firms.

The Weak Form

The random-walk hypothesis, as expressed in equation (13.1), implies that a stock's price movement in the past is unrelated to its price movement in the future. The work of Chapter 10 allows us to test this implication. In that chapter, we discussed the concept of correlation between the returns on two different stocks. For example, the correlation between the return on General Motors and the return on Ford is likely to be high because both stocks are in the same industry. Conversely, the correlation between the return on General Motors and the return on the stock of, say, a European fast-food chain is likely to be low.

Financial economists frequently speak of **serial correlation,** which involves only one security. This is the correlation between the current return on a security and the return on the same security over a later period. A positive coefficient of serial correlation for a particular stock indicates a tendency toward *continuation*. That is, a higher-than-average return today is likely to be followed by higher-than-average returns in the future. Similarly, a lower-than-average return today is likely to be followed by lower-than-average returns in the future.

A negative coefficient of serial correlation for a particular stock indicates a tendency toward *reversal*. A higher-than-average return today is likely to be followed by lower-than-average returns in the future. Similarly, a lower-than-average return today is likely to be followed by higher-than-average returns in the future. Both significantly positive and significantly negative serial-correlation coefficients are indications of market inefficiencies; in either case, returns today can be used to predict future returns.

Serial correlation coefficients for stock returns near zero would be consistent with the random-walk hypothesis. Thus, a current stock return that is higher than average is as likely to be followed by lower-than-average returns as by higher-than-average returns. Similarly, a current stock return that is lower than average is as likely to be followed by higher-than-average returns as by lower-than-average returns.

Table 13.1 shows the serial correlation for daily stock-price changes for 8 large U.S. companies. These coefficients indicate whether or not there are relationships between yesterday's return and today's return. As can be seen, the correlation coefficients are predominantly

■ TABLE 13.1   **Serial Correlation Coefficients for 8 Large U.S. Companies**

Company	Serial Correlation Coefficient
Boeing Co.	0.038
Bristol-Myers Squibb Co.	0.064
Coca-Cola Co.	0.041
IBM Corporation	−0.004
Philip Morris Companies Inc.	0.075
Procter & Gamble Co.	0.030
Sears, Roebuck & Co.	0.046
Texaco Inc.	0.005

Boeing's coefficient of 0.038 is slightly positive, implying that a positive return today makes a positive return tomorrow slightly more likely. IBM's coefficient is negative, implying that a negative return today makes a positive return tomorrow slightly more likely. However, the coefficients are so small relative to estimation error and transaction costs that the results are generally considered to be consistent with efficient capital markets.

positive, implying that a higher-than-average return today makes a higher-than-average return tomorrow slightly more likely. Conversely, IBM's coefficient is slightly negative, implying that a lower-than-average return today makes a higher-than-average return tomorrow slightly more likely.

However, because correlation coefficients can, in principle, vary between −1 and 1, the reported coefficients are quite small. In fact, the coefficients are so small relative to both estimation errors and to transactions costs that the results are generally considered to be consistent with weak-form efficiency.

The weak form of the efficient-market hypothesis has been tested in many other ways as well. Our view of the literature is that the evidence, taken as a whole, is strongly consistent with weak-form efficiency.

This finding raises an interesting thought: If price changes are truly random, why do so many believe that prices follow patterns? The work of both psychologists and statisticians suggests that most people simply do not know what randomness looks like. For example, consider Figure 13.5. The top graph was generated by a computer using random numbers and equation (13.1). Because of this it must follow a random walk. Yet, we have found that people examining the chart generally see patterns. Different people will see different patterns and will forecast different future price movements. However, in our experience, viewers are all quite confident of the patterns they see.

Next, consider the bottom graph, which tracks actual movements in Sears, Roebuck's stock price. This graph may look quite nonrandom to some, suggesting weak-form inefficiency. However, it also bears a close visual resemblance to the simulated series above, and statistical tests indicate that it indeed behaves like a purely random series. Thus, in our opinion, people claiming to see patterns in stock-price data are probably seeing optical illusions.

The Semistrong Form

The semistrong form of the efficient-market hypothesis implies that prices should reflect all publicly available information. We present two types of tests of this form.

■ FIGURE 13.5   **Simulated and Actual Stock-Price Movements**

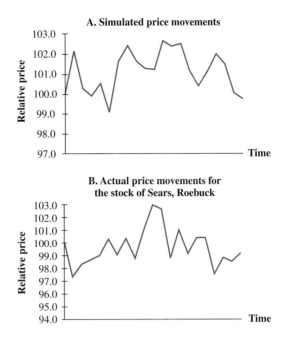

A. Simulated price movements

B. Actual price movements for the stock of Sears, Roebuck

Event Studies   The *abnormal return* (AR) on a given stock for a particular day can be calculated by subtracting the market's return on the same day (R_m)—as measured by a broad-based index such as the S&P composite index—from the actual return (R) on the stock for that day.[9] We write this algebraically as:

$$AR = R - R_m$$

A way to think of the tests of the semistrong form is to examine the following system of relationships:

Information released at time $t - 1 \rightarrow AR_{t-1}$
Information released at time $t \rightarrow AR_t$
Information released at time $t + 1 \rightarrow AR_{t+1}$

The arrows indicate that the return in any time period is related only to the information released during that period.

According to the efficient-market hypothesis, a stock's abnormal return at time t, AR_t, should reflect the release of information at the same time, t. Any information released before then, though, should have no effect on abnormal returns in this period, because all of its influence should have been felt before. In other words, an efficient market would already have incorporated previous information into prices. Because a stock's return today cannot depend on what the market does not yet know, the information that will be known only in the future cannot influence the stock's return either. Hence the arrows point in the direction that is shown, with information in any one time period affecting only that period's abnormal return. *Event studies* are statistical studies that examine whether the arrows are as shown or whether the release of information influences returns on other days.

---

[9]The abnormal return can also be measured by using the market model. In this case the abnormal return is

$$AR = R - (\alpha + \beta R_m)$$

■ FIGURE 13.6   Cumulative Abnormal Returns for Companies Announcing Dividend Omissions

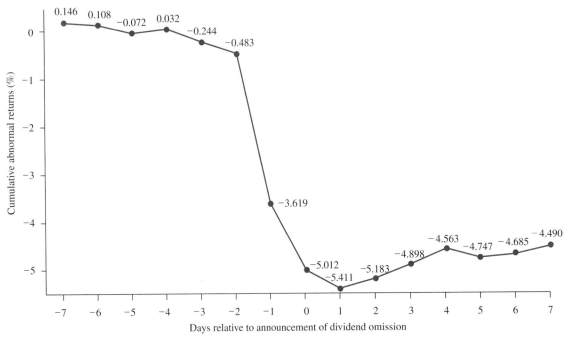

Cumulative abnormal returns (CARs) fall on both the day before the announcement and the day of the announcement of dividend omissions. CARs have very little movement after the announcement date. This pattern is consistent with market efficiency.

From Exhibit 2 in S. H. Szewczyk, George P. Tsetsekos, and Zaher Zantout, "Do Dividend Omissions Signal Future Earnings or Past Earnings?" *Journal of Investing* (Spring 1997).

As an example, consider the study by Szewczyk, Tsetsekos, and Zantout[10] on dividend omissions. Figure 13.6 shows the plot of *cumulative abnormal returns* (CARs) for a sample of companies announcing dividend omissions. Since dividend omissions are generally considered to be bad events, we would expect that abnormal returns would be negative around the time of the announcements. They are, as evidenced by a drop in the CAR on both the day before the announcement (day −1) and the day of the announcement (day 0).[11] However, note that there is virtually no movement in the CARs in the days following the announcement. This implies that the bad news is fully incorporated into the stock price by the announcement day, a result consistent with market efficiency.

---

[10]Samuel H. Szewczyk, George P. Tsetsekos, and Zaher Z. Zantout, "Do Dividend Omissions Signal Future Earnings or Past Earnings?" *Journal of Investing* (Spring 1997).

[11]An astute reader may wonder why the abnormal return is negative on day −1, as well as on day 0. To see why, first note that the announcement date is generally taken in academic studies to be the publication date of the story in *The Wall Street Journal (WSJ)*. Then consider a company announcing a dividend omission via a press release at noon on Tuesday. The stock should fall on Tuesday. The announcement will be reported in the *WSJ* on Wednesday, because the Tuesday edition of the *WSJ* has already been printed. For this firm, the stock price falls on the day *before* the announcement in the *WSJ*.

Alternatively, imagine another firm announcing a dividend omission via a press release on Tuesday at 8 P.M. Since the stock market is closed at that late hour, the stock price will fall on Wednesday. Because the *WSJ* will report the announcement on Wednesday, the stock price falls on the day of the announcement in the *WSJ*.

Since firms may either make announcements during trading hours or after trading hours, stocks should fall on both day −1 and day 0 relative to publication in the *WSJ*.

Over the years this type of methodology has been applied to a large number of events. Announcements of dividends, earnings, mergers, capital expenditures, and new issues of stock are a few examples of the vast literature in the area.[12] Although there are exceptions, the event-study tests generally support the view that the market is semistrong-form (and therefore also weak-form) efficient. In fact, the tests even tend to support the view that the market is gifted with a certain amount of foresight. By this we mean that news tends to leak out and be reflected in stock prices even before the official release of the information.

Tests of market efficiency can be found in the oddest places. The price of frozen orange juice depends to a large extent on the weather in Orlando, Florida, where many of the oranges that are frozen for juice are grown. One researcher found that he could actually use frozen-orange-juice prices to improve the U.S. Weather Bureau's forecast of the temperature for the following night.[13] Clearly the market knows something that the weather forecasters do not.

Another group of researchers found that, as expected, stock prices generally fall on the date when the *sudden* death of a chief executive is announced.[14] However, the stock price generally rises for the sudden death of a company's founder if he was still heading up the firm prior to his death. The implication is that many of these individuals have outlived their usefulness to their firms.

The Record of Mutual Funds   If the market is efficient in the semistrong form, then no matter what publicly available information mutual-fund managers rely on to pick stocks, their average returns should be the same as those of the average investor in the market as a whole. We can test efficiency, then, by comparing the performance of these professionals with that of a market index.

Consider Figure 13.7, which presents the performance of various types of mutual funds relative to the stock market as a whole. The far left of the figure shows that the universe of all funds covered in the study underperforms the market by 2.13 percent per year, after an appropriate adjustment for risk.[15] Thus, rather than outperforming the market, the evidence shows underperformance. This underperformance holds for a number of types of funds as well. Returns in this study are net of fees, expenses, and commissions, so fund returns would be higher if these costs were added back. However, the study shows no evidence that funds, as a whole, are *beating* the market.

Perhaps nothing rankles successful stock market investors more than to have some professor tell them that they are not necessarily smart, just lucky. However, while Figure 13.7 represents only one study, there have been many papers on mutual funds. The overwhelming evidence here is that mutual funds, on average, do not beat broad-based indices. This does not mean that no individual investor can beat the market average or that he or she lacks a special insight, only that proof seems difficult to find.

By and large, mutual-fund managers rely on publicly available information. Thus the finding that they do not outperform the market indices is consistent with semistrong-form

---

[12]In academic finance nothing is ever completely resolved, and some event studies suggest that stock market prices respond to information too slowly for the market to be efficient. For example, Eli Bartov, Suresh Radhakrishnan, and Itzhak Krinsky, "Investor Sophistication and Patterns in Stock Returns after Earnings Announcements," *The Accounting Review* 75 (January 2000).

[13]These findings are reported in R. Roll, "Orange Juice and Weather," *American Economic Review* (December 1984).

[14]W. B. Johnson, R. P. Magee, N. J. Nagarajan, and H. A. Newman, "An Analysis of the Stock Price Reaction to Sudden Executive Deaths: Implications for the Managerial Labor Market," *Journal of Accounting and Economics* (April 1985).

[15]This finding is similar to those reported by R. Wermers, "Mutual Fund Performance: An Empirical Decomposition into Stock-Picking, Talent, Style, Transactions Costs, and Expenses," *Journal of Finance* (August 2000).

■ FIGURE 13.7   **Annual Return Performance* of Different Types of U.S. Mutual Funds Relative to a Broad-Based Market Index (1963–1998)**

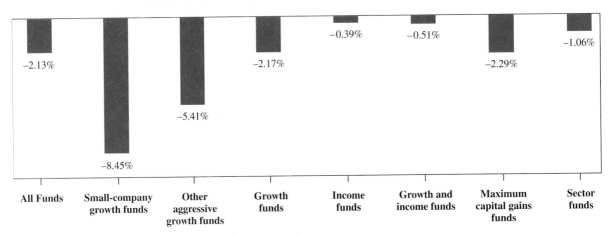

On average, mutual funds do not appear to be outperforming the market.

Taken from Table 2 of Lubos Pastor and Robert F. Stambaugh, "Mutual Fund Performance and Seemingly Unrelated Assets," unpublished paper, Graduate School of Business, University of Chicago (February, 2001), forthcoming *Journal of Financial Economics*.

*Performance is relative to the market-model.

and weak-form efficiency. This does not imply that mutual funds are bad investments for individuals. Though these funds fail to achieve better returns than some indices of the market, they do permit the investor to buy a portfolio that has a large number of stocks in it (the phrase "a well-diversified portfolio" is often used). They might also be very good at providing a variety of services such as keeping custody and records of all the stocks.

Some Contrary Views   Although the bulk of the evidence supports the view that markets are efficient, we would not be fair if we did not note the existence of contrary results. We begin with three areas of academic research.

1. *Size.* In 1981, two important papers presented evidence that, in the United States, the returns on stocks with small **market capitalizations**[16] were greater than the returns on stocks with large market capitalizations over most of the 20th century.[17] The studies have since been replicated over different time periods and in different countries. For example, Figure 13.8 shows average returns over the period from 1963 to 1995 for five portfolios of U.S. stocks ranked on size. As can be seen, the average return on small stocks is quite a bit higher than the average return on large stocks. Although much of the differential performance is merely compensation for the extra risk of small stocks, researchers have generally argued that not all of it can be explained by risk differences. In addition, Donald Keim[18] presented evidence that most of the 5 percent per year difference in performance occurs in the month of January.

2. *Temporal Anomalies.* After Keim's surprising results in January, researchers examined returns over various time intervals. For example, studies indicate that average stock returns in January are higher than in other months for both large and small capitalization securities.

---

[16]Market capitalization is the price per share of stock multiplied by the number of shares outstanding.

[17]See R. W. Banz, "The Relationship between Return and Market Value of Common Stocks," *Journal of Financial Economics* (March 1981), and M. R. Reinganum, "Misspecification of Capital Asset Pricing: Empirical Anomalies Based on Earnings Yields and Market Values," *Journal of Financial Economics* (March 1981).

[18]D. B. Keim, "Size-Related Anomalies and Stock Return Seasonality: Further Empirical Evidence," *Journal of Financial Economics* (June 1983).

■ FIGURE 13.8 Annual Stock Returns on Portfolios Sorted by Size (Market Capitalization)

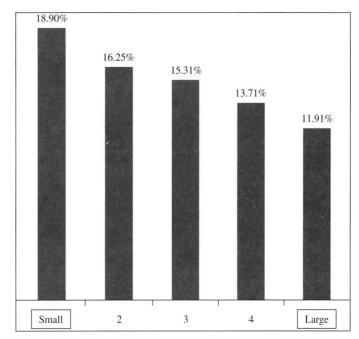

Historically, the average return on small stocks has been above the average return on large stocks.

Source: Tim Loughran, "Book-to-Market across Firm Size, Exchange and Seasonality," *Journal of Financial and Quantitative Analysis* 32 (1997).

Average stock returns are significantly higher over the first half of the month than they are over the second half of the month.[19] Returns are particularly high on the day before a holdiay.[20]

Across days of the week, stock returns are highest on Wednesdays and Fridays and are lowest on Mondays.[21] In fact, researchers generally conclude that the average return on Monday is negative. This finding is inconsistent with market efficiency since rational investors should never be willing to lose money on average—and to take risk to boot. Consider Figure 13.9, which shows average returns for Monday and for the other days of the week for five different countries. For each country, average daily returns on Monday are negative while they are positive for the rest of the week.

The evidence on temporal anomalies is quite convincing, with results being replicated in other time periods and in other countries. However, the implications are few because the return differences generally do not exceed transaction costs. For example, an individual who bought a stock every Tuesday morning and sold the stock every Friday evening in order to avoid the negative Monday return would have a lower return after commissions than an individual who bought the same stock and held it for months or years without trading.

3. *Value versus Growth.* A number of papers have argued that stocks with high book-value-to-stock-price ratios and/or high earnings-to-price ratios (generally called value stocks)

---

[19]R. A. Ariel, "A Monthly Effect on Stock Returns," *Journal of Financial Economics,* (1987).

[20]R. A. Ariel, "High Stock Returns before Holidays: Existence and Evidence on Possible Causes," *Journal of Finance,* (December 1990).

[21]One of the original articles to observce "day of the week" anomalies is M. R. Gibbons and P. Hess, "Day of the Week Effects and Asset Returns," *Journal of Business* (1981).

■ FIGURE 13.9   **Average Daily Returns (in percent) for Monday and for Rest of the Week for Stock Market Indices in Selected Countries**

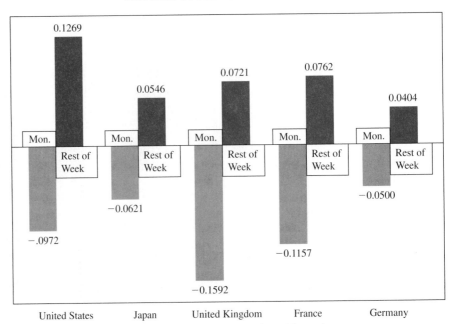

Returns on Monday are lower than the returns on the other days of the week.

Source: Adapted from Table 3 of Wilson Tong, "International Evidence on Weekend Anomalies," unpublished paper, Hong Kong University of Science and Engineering (1999).

outperform stocks with low ratios (growth stocks). For example, Fama and French[22] find that, for twelve of thirteen major international stock markets, the average return on stocks with high book-value-to-stock-price ratios is above the average return on stocks with low book-value-to-stock-price ratios. Figure 13.10 shows these returns for the world's five largest stock markets. Value stocks have outperformed growth stocks in each of these five markets.

Because the return difference is so large and because the above ratios can be obtained so easily for individual stocks, the results may constitute strong evidence against market efficiency. However, a number of current papers suggest that the unusual returns are due to biases in the commercial databases or to differences in risk, not to a true inefficiency.[23] Since the debate revolves around arcane statistical issues, we will not pursue the issue further. However, it is safe to say that no conclusion is warranted at this time. As with so many other topics in finance and economics, further research is needed.

In addition, the stock market crash of October 19, 1987, is extremely puzzling. The market dropped between 20 percent and 25 percent on a Monday following a weekend during which little surprising news was released. A drop of this magnitude for no apparent reason is not consistent with market efficiency. Because the crash of 1929 is still an enigma, it

---

[22]Taken from Table III of Eugene F. Fama and Kenneth R. French, "Value versus Growth: The International Evidence," *Journal of Finance* 53 (December, 1998).

[23]For example, see S. P. Kothari, J. Shanken, and R. G. Sloan, "Another Look at the Cross Section of Expected Stock Returns," *Journal of Finance* (March 1995), and E. F. Fama and K. R. French, "Multifactor Explanations of Asset Pricing Anomalies," *Journal of Finance* 51 (March 1996).

■ FIGURE 13.10   **Annual Dollar Returns* (in percent) on Low Book-to-Price Firms and High Book-to-Price Firms in Selected Countries**

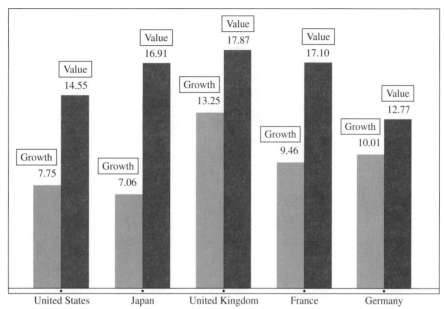

High book-to-price stocks (frequently called value stocks) outperform low book-to-price (growth) stocks in different countries.

Source: Eugene F. Fama and Kenneth R. French, "Value versus Growth: The International Evidence," *Journal of Finance* (December 1998).

*Dollar returns are expressed as the excess over the return on U.S. Treasury bills.

is doubtful that the more recent debacle will be explained anytime soon. The recent comments of an eminent historian are apt here: When asked what, in his opinion, the effect of the French Revolution of 1789 was, he replied that it was too early to tell.

Perhaps the two stock market crashes are evidence consistent with the **bubble theory** of speculative markets. That is, security prices sometimes move wildly above their true values. Eventually prices fall back to their original level, causing great losses for investors. The tulip craze of the 17th century in Holland and the South Sea Bubble in England the following century are perhaps the two best-known bubbles. In the first episode, tulips rose to unheard-of prices. For example:

> A single bulb of the Harlaem species was exchanged for twelve acres of building ground. . . . Another variety fetched 4,600 florins, a new carriage and two gray horses, plus nine complete sets of harnesses. A bulb of the Viceroy species commanded the sum of all the following items in exchange: seventeen bushels of wheat, thirty-four bushels of rye, four fat oxen, eight fat swine, twelve fat sheep, two hogshead of wine, four tons of beer, two tons of butter, 1,000 pounds of cheese, a complete bed, a suit of clothes, and a silver drinking cup thrown in for good measure.[24]

It seems speculative fervor hit England a century later. Fantastic schemes of all types were paraded before a public eager to invest. Most of them provided good evidence for the dictums: "A sucker is born every minute" and "A fool and his money are soon parted."

---

[24]B. G. Malkiel, *A Random Walk Down Wall Street,* college ed. (New York: Norton, 1975), pp. 31–32.

WERE THE JAPANESE STOCK PRICES TOO HIGH?

This is the question investors have been asking about the Japanese stock market. As can be seen from the chart below, an investment of one yen, placed in a diversified portfolio of Japanese stocks on the last day of 1969, would have grown to about 18 yen by 1988. By contrast, the tables in Chapter 9 can be used to show that a $1 investment in American stocks would have only risen to under $7 over the same time period. During this time period, the average price-earnings ratio for Japanese stocks was much higher than that for American stocks. For example, the Japanese P/E ratio was 54.3 in 1988, while the United States P/E ratio was 12.9 at the same time.*

However, as can be seen from the chart below, Japanese stocks took quite a fall after 1988. By the end of 1993, the 18:1 ratio had dropped to 9:1. It has stayed at about 9:1 over the ensuing years. By contrast, the U.S. ratio had risen from 7:1 to over 22. Not surprisingly, the P/E ratios had moved closer together. By the middle of 1997, the Japanese P/E ratio was approximately 44, while the American P/E ratio was about 21. This pattern has persisted into the year 2001.

Worth of an Investment of One Yen Made at the End of 1969 in Japanese Stocks

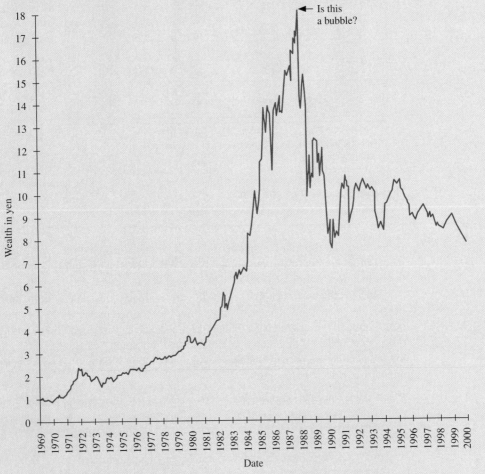

Data for this chart supplied by Yasushi Hamao. Reinvestment of dividends is assumed.

*Actually, this disparity is partly due to differences in accounting treatments for the two countries. Kenneth R. French and James M. Poterba ("Were Japanese Stock Prices Too High?" *Journal of Financial Economics* 29 (October 1991), pp. 337–64) estimate that in 1988 the price-earnings ratio of Japanese firms would have been 32.1 instead of 54.3 had U.S. accounting practices been adopted.

According to Malkiel,

The prize, however, must surely go to the unknown soul who started "A Company for carrying on an undertaking of great advantage, but nobody to know what it is." The prospectus promises unheard-of rewards. At nine o'clock in the morning, when the subscription books opened, crowds of people from all walks of life practically beat down the doors in an effort to subscribe. Within five hours a thousand investors handed over their money for shares in the company. Not being greedy himself, the promoter promptly closed up shop and set off for the Continent. He was never heard from again.[25]

The Strong Form

Even the strongest adherents to the efficient-market hypothesis would not be surprised to find that markets are inefficient in the strong form. After all, if an individual has information that no one else has, it is likely that he can profit from it.

One group of studies of strong-form efficiency investigates insider trading. Insiders in firms have access to information that is not generally available. But if the strong form of the efficient-market hypothesis holds, they should not be able to profit by trading on their information. A government agency, the Securities and Exchange Commission, requires insiders in companies to reveal any trading they might do in their own company's stock. By examining the record of such trades, we can see whether they made abnormal returns. A number of studies support the view that these trades were abnormally profitable. Thus, strong-form efficiency does not seem to be substantiated by the evidence.[26]

13.5 IMPLICATIONS FOR CORPORATE FINANCE

Accounting and Efficient Markets

The accounting profession provides firms with a significant amount of leeway in their reporting practices. For example, companies may choose between the last-in–first-out (LIFO) or first-in–first-out (FIFO) method in valuing inventories. They may choose either the percentage-of-completion or the completed-contract method for construction projects. They may depreciate physical assets by either accelerated or straight-line depreciation.

Accountants have frequently been accused of misusing this leeway in the hopes of boosting earnings and stock prices. For example, U.S. Steel (now USX Corporation) switched from straight-line to accelerated depreciation after World War II, because their high reported profits at the time attracted much governmental scrutiny. They switched back to straight-line depreciation in the 1960s after years of low reported earnings.

However, accounting choice should not affect stock price if two conditions hold. First, enough information must be provided in the annual report so that financial analysts can construct earnings under the alternative accounting methods. This appears to be the case for many, though not necessarily all, accounting choices. For example, most skilled analysts can create *pro forma* financial statements under a LIFO assumption if they are provided with actual statements prepared under FIFO. Second, the market must be efficient in the semistrong form. In other words, the market must appropriately use all of this accounting information in determining the market price.

Of course, the issue of whether accounting choice affects stock price is ultimately an empirical matter. A number of academic papers have addressed this issue. Kaplan and Roll

---

[25]B. G. Malkiel, *A Random Walk Down Wall Street.*

[26]H. N. Seyhun, *Investor Intelligence from Insider Trading,* MIT Press: Cambridge, Mass., 1998.

found that the switch from accelerated to straight-line depreciation generally did not significantly affect stock prices.[27] Kaplan and Roll also looked at changes from the deferral method of accounting for the investment tax credit to the flow-through method.[28] They found that a switch would increase accounting earnings but had no effect on stock prices.

Several other accounting procedures have been studied. Hong, Kaplan, and Mandelker found no evidence that the stock market was affected by the artificially higher earnings reported using the pooling method, compared to the purchase method, for reporting mergers and acquisitions.[29] Biddle and Lindahl found that firms switching to the LIFO method of costing inventory experienced an increase in stock price.[30] This is to be expected in inflationary environments because LIFO inventory costing can reduce taxes, compared to FIFO inventory costing. They found that the larger the tax decrease resulting from the use of LIFO, the greater was the increase in stock price. In summary, the above empirical evidence suggests that accounting changes do not fool the market.

However, a recent study reaches different conclusions.[31] Sloane points out that a firm's earnings can be broken up into the following two components:

$$\text{Earnings} = \text{Cash flow} + \text{Accruals}$$

This relationship implies that a firm with no cash flow but high earnings must have a high level of accruals. An increase in inventories, an increase in accounts receivable, and a reduction in accounts payable would all be examples of a buildup in accruals. Conversely, accruals could be negative if either current assets are being reduced or if there is substantial depreciation.

Accountants have long argued that the "quality" of earnings is high for firms with low (or even negative) accruals, while the quality of earnings is low for firms with high accruals. Sloane finds that the one-year stock returns on firms that recently had a reduction in accruals is quite high, while the one-year returns on firms experiencing an increase in accruals is negative. In fact, a strategy of buying stocks following a reduction in accruals and simultaneously selling stocks following a buildup in accruals would have generated an average return of about 10 percent per year. These results are not consistent with market efficiency. Thus, the Sloane paper suggests that investors react slowly to this type of accounting information.

Accountants also argue that the quality of earnings is higher for firms with hidden reserves, such as the reserve generated by companies on LIFO. Penman and Zhang[32] find that a strategy of buying stocks experiencing an increase in these reserves and simultaneously selling stocks experiencing a decrease would have created an average return of about 9 percent a year. Both Sloane and Penman-Zhang show that an analysis of the quality of earnings can yield stock market profits.

---

[27]R. S. Kaplan and R. Roll, "Investor Evaluation of Accounting Information: Some Empirical Evidence," *Journal of Business* 45 (April 1972).

[28]Before 1987, U.S. tax law allowed a 10-percent tax credit on the purchase of most kinds of capital equipment.

[29]H. Hong, R. S. Kaplan, and G. Mandelker. "Pooling vs. Purchase: The Effects of Accounting for Mergers on Stock Prices," *Accounting Review* 53 (1978).

[30]G. C. Biddle and F. W. Lindahl, "Stock Price Reactions to LIFO Adoptions: The Association between Excess Returns and LIFO Tax Savings," *Journal of Accounting Research* (1982).

[31]Richard G. Sloane, "Do Stock Prices Fully Reflect Information in Accruals and Cash Flows about Future Earnings?" *The Accounting Review* (July 1996).

[32]Stephen H. Penman and Xiao-Jun Zhang, "Accounting Conservatism, the Quality of Earnings and Stock Returns," unpublished paper, University of California, Berkeley (December 1999).

■ FIGURE 13.11   **Three Stock Price Adjustments**

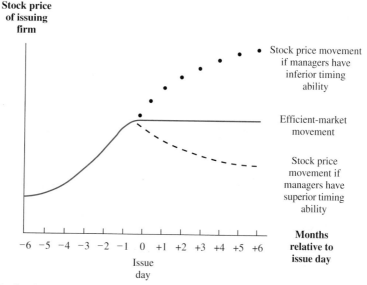

Studies show that stock is more likely to be issued after stock prices have increased. No inferences on market efficiency can be drawn from this result. Rather, market efficiency implies that the stock price of the issuing firm, on average, neither rises nor falls *after* issuance of stock.

The Timing Decision

Imagine a firm whose managers are contemplating the date to issue equity. This decision is frequently called the *timing* decision. If managers believe that their stock is overpriced, they are likely to issue equity immediately. Here, they are creating value for their current stockholders because they are selling stock for more than it is worth. Conversely, if the managers believe that their stock is underpriced, they are more likely to wait, hoping that the stock price will eventually rise to its true value.

However, if markets are efficient, securities are always correctly priced. Since efficiency implies that stock is always sold for its true worth, the timing decision becomes unimportant. Figure 13.11 shows three possible stock price adjustments to the issuance of new stock.

Of course, market efficiency is ultimately an empirical issue. Surprisingly, a recent paper has called market efficiency into question. Loughran and Ritter[33] present evidence that annual returns over the five years following an initial public offering (IPO) are, on average, approximately 7 percent less for the issuing company than the return on a non-issuing company of similar market capitalization. In addition, Loughran and Ritter examine seasoned equity offerings (SEOs), i.e., issuances of common stock for publicly traded companies. They find that, over the five years following an SEO, the annualized return on the issuing firm's stock is, on average, 8 percent less than the return on a comparable nonissuing company. The upper half of Figure 13.12 shows the average annual returns of both IPOs and their control group, and the lower half of Figure 13.12 shows the average annual returns of both SEOs and their control group. The evidence of the Loughran and Ritter paper suggests that corporate managers issue stock when it is overpriced. In other words, they are successfully able to time the market.

---

[33]T. Loughran and J. R. Ritter, "The Timing and Subsequent Performance of New Issue," *Journal of Finance* (1995).

■ FIGURE 13.12   **Returns on Initial Public Offerings (IPOs) and Seasoned Equity Offerings (SEOs) in Years Following Issue**

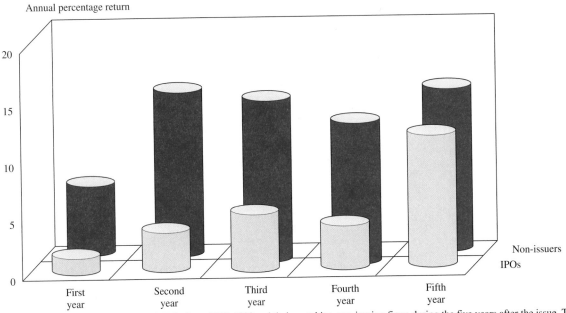

The average annual raw returns for 4,753 IPOs from 1970–1990 and their matching non-issuing firms during the five years after the issue. The first-year return does not include the return on the day of issue.

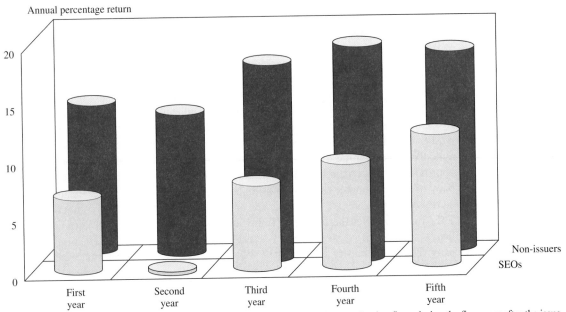

The average annual raw returns for 3,702 SEOs from 1970–1990 and their matching non-issuing firms during the five years after the issue. On average, IPOs and SEOs underperform their control groups by 7% and 8% per year, respectively, in the five years following issuance.
Source: See T. Loughran and J. R. Ritter, "The Timing and Subsequent Performance of New Issues," *Journal of Finance* (1995).

EFFICIENT-MARKET HYPOTHESIS: A SUMMARY

Does Not Say

Prices are uncaused.

Investors are foolish and too stupid to be in the market.

All shares of stock have the same expected returns.

Investors should throw darts to select stocks.

There is no upward trend in stock prices.

Does Say

Prices reflect underlying value.

Financial managers cannot time stock and bond sales.

Sales of stock and bonds will not depress prices.

You cannot cook the books.

Why Doesn't Everybody Believe It?

There are optical illusions, mirages, and apparent patterns in charts of stock market returns.

The truth is less interesting.

There is some evidence against efficiency:

• Seasonality.
• Small versus large stocks.
• Value versus growth stocks.

The tests of market efficiency are weak.

Three Forms

Weak form (random walk): Prices reflect past prices; chartism (technical analysis) is useless.

Semistrong form: Prices reflect all public information; most financial analysis is useless.

Strong form: Prices reflect all that is knowable; nobody consistently makes superior profits.

If firms can time the issuance of common stock, perhaps they can also time the repurchase of stock. Here, a firm would like to repurchase when its stock is undervalued. Ikenberry, Lakonishok, and Vermaelen[34] find that stock returns of repurchasing firms are abnormally high in the two years following the repurchase, suggesting that timing is effective here.

As is always the case, empirical research is never ultimately settled. However, in our opinion, the evidence of the Loughran and Ritter paper and the evidence of the Ikenberry, Lakonishok, and Vermaelen paper, taken together, suggests that managers successfully engage in timing. These papers, if they stand the test of time, constitute evidence against market efficiency.[35]

---

[34]D. Ikenberry, J. Lakonishok, and T. Vermaelen, "Market Underreaction to Open Market Share Repurchases," *Journal of Financial Economics* (October–November 1995).

[35]There is a vigorous academic debate on Loughran and Ritter's findings. Two papers with contrary conclusions are A. Brav, C. Geczy, and P. A. Gompers, "Is the Abnormal Return Following Equity Issues Anomalous?" unpublished paper, Duke University (August 1999), and E. B. Eckbo, R. W. Masulis, and O. Norli, "Seasoned Public Offerings: Resolution of the 'New Issues' Puzzle," unpublished paper, Vanderbilt University (1999). Two papers supporting Loughran and Ritter are D. Ahn and A. Shivdasani, "Long-Term Returns Following Seasoned Equity Issues: Bad Performance or Bad Models," unpublished paper, University of North Carolina (July 1999) and T. Loughran and J. R. Ritter, "Uniformly Least Powerful Tests of Market Efficiency," *Journal of Financial Economics* 5 (March 2000).

■ FIGURE 13.13 **Price Impacts of Block Trading**

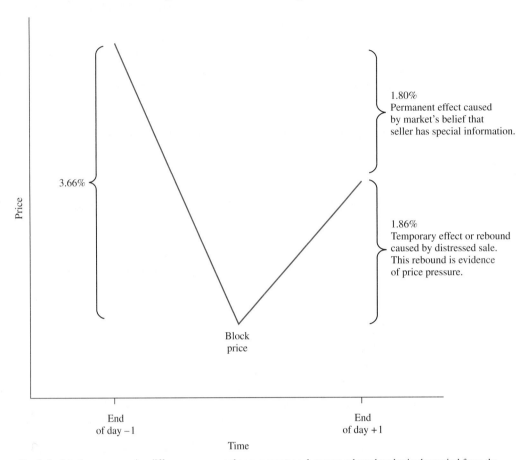

Graph depicts the average price difference, expressed as a percentage, between selected trades in the period from the close of trading on day −1 to the close of trading on day +1. Day 0 is the day on which a block sale occurred. The drop in price from a block trade and subsequent rebound is evidence of a price-pressure effect.

From D. Keim and A. Madhavan, "The Upstairs Market for Large Block Transactions: Analysis and Measurement of Price Effects," *Review of Financial Studies* (Spring 1996).

Price-Pressure Effects

Suppose a firm wants to sell a large block of stock. Can it sell as many shares as it wants without depressing the price? If capital markets are efficient, a firm should be able to sell as many shares as it desires without depressing the price. Scholes was one of the first to examine this question empirically.[36] He found that the market's ability to absorb large blocks of stock was virtually unlimited. His findings were surprising to real-world practitioners because the sale of large blocks of shares is generally believed to temporarily depress the price of a company's stock.

Keim and Madhavan[37] also study the price impact of large block trades, as shown in Figure 13.13. Their conclusions differ from those of Scholes. For New York Stock Exchange

---

[36]M. Scholes, "The Market for Securities: Substitution versus Price Pressure and the Effects of Information on Share Prices," *Journal of Business* (April 1972).

[37]D. Keim and A. Madhavan, "The Upstairs Market for Block Transactions: Analysis and Measurement of Price Effects," *Review of Financial Studies* (Spring 1996).

and American Stock Exchange securities, they find that the stock price drops, on average, about 3.66 percent from the closing trade on the previous day to the block trade itself. However, the stock rebounds by 1.86 percent by the close of the day after the block trade. Keim and Madhavan argue that the difference of 1.80 percent (= 3.66% − 1.86%) reflects the market's belief that the block seller has special (negative) information concerning the stock. This drop of 1.80 percent is a permanent effect. In addition, the block trader sells at a still lower price because of his need to sell quickly. This temporary or rebound effect (1.86% in this example) is similar to real estate sales at distressed prices when the seller needs cash immediately. This drop in price and subsequent rebound of 1.86 percent is evidence of price pressure.

The preceding are just two of a large number of studies in the area. Because the magnitude of the price-pressure effect varies across the existing research, more work is needed to resolve the conflicting results.

• What are three implications of the efficient-market hypothesis for corporate finance?

13.6 SUMMARY AND CONCLUSIONS

1. An efficient financial market processes the information available to investors and incorporates it into the prices of securities. Market efficiency has two general implications. First, in any given time period, a stock's abnormal return depends on information or news received by the market in that period. Second, an investor who uses the same information as the market cannot expect to earn abnormal returns. In other words, systems for playing the market are doomed to fail.

2. What information does the market use to determine prices? The weak form of the efficient-market hypothesis says that the market uses the past history of prices and is therefore efficient with respect to these past prices. This implies that stock selection based on patterns of past stock-price movements is not better than random stock selection.

3. A stronger theory of efficiency is semistrong-form efficiency, which states that the market uses all publicly available information in setting prices.

4. The strongest theory of efficiency, strong-form efficiency, states that the market has available to it and uses all of the information that anybody knows about stocks, even inside information.

5. The evidence from different financial markets supports weak-form and semistrong-form efficiency but not strong-form efficiency. This is no consolation to the army of investors that uses publicly available information in attempts to beat the market.

6. In our study of efficient markets we stress the importance of distinguishing between the actual return on a stock and the expected return. The difference is called the *abnormal return* and comes from the release of news to the market.

7. Not everybody completely believes the efficient-market hypothesis. It is a misunderstood theory. The boxed material (on page 363) summarizes what it does and does not say.

8. Three implications of efficient markets for corporate finance are listed below:
   a. The price of a company's stock cannot be affected by a change in accounting.
   b. Financial managers cannot time issues of stocks and bonds using publicly available information.
   c. A firm can sell as many bonds or shares of stock as it desires without depressing prices. There is conflicting empirical evidence on all three points.

9. Do we have a better theory? At the present time, we think the answer is no. However, over time the theory will no doubt improve.

KEY TERMS

Bubble theory 357	Serial correlation 349
Efficient-market hypothesis 342	Strong-form efficiency 346
Market capitalization 354	Technical analysis 345
Random walk 344	Weak-form efficiency 344
Semistrong-form efficiency 346	

SUGGESTED READINGS

The concept of market efficiency is an important one. Perhaps the classic review articles are
Fama, E. F. "Efficient Capital Markets: A Review of Theory and Empirical Work." *Journal of Finance* (May 1970).
Fama, E. F. "Efficient Capital Markets: II." *Journal of Finance* (December 1991).
Fama, E. F. "Market Efficiency, Long-Term Returns, and Behavioral Finance." *Journal of Financial Economics* (1998).

An entertaining, yet quite informative, book on efficient markets is
Malkiel, B. G. *A Random Walk Down Wall Street.* 7th ed. New York: Norton, 1999.

QUESTIONS AND PROBLEMS

Can Financing Decisions Create Value?

13.1   *a.*   What rule should a firm follow when making financing decisions?

      b.   How can firms create valuable financing opportunities?

A Description of Efficient Capital Markets

13.2   Define the three forms of market efficiency.

13.3   Which of the following statements are true about the efficient-market hypothesis?

      a.   It implies perfect forecasting ability.

      b.   It implies that prices reflect all available information.

      c.   It implies an irrational market.

      d.   It implies that prices do not fluctuate.

      e.   It results from keen competition among investors.

13.4   Aerotech, an aerospace-technology research firm, announced this morning that it has hired the world's most knowledgeable and prolific space researchers. Before today, Aerotech's stock had been selling for $100.

      a.   What do you expect will happen to Aerotech's stock?

      b.   Consider the following scenarios:

         i.   The stock price jumps to $118 on the day of the announcement. In subsequent days it floats up to $123 then falls back to $116.

         ii.   The stock price jumps to $116 and remains there.

         iii.   The stock price gradually climbs to $116 over the next week.

      Which scenario(s) indicate market efficiency? Which do not? Why?

13.5   When the 56-year-old founder of Gulf & Western, Inc., died of a heart attack, the stock price jumped from $18.00 a share to $20.25, a 12.5-percent increase. This is evidence of market inefficiency, because an efficient stock market would have anticipated his death and adjusted the price beforehand. Is this statement true or false? Explain.

13.6   On January 10, 1985, the following announcement was made: "Early today the Justice Department reached a decision in the Universal Product Care (UPC) case. UPC has been found guilty of discriminatory practices in hiring. For the next five years, UPC must pay $2 million each year to a fund representing victims of UPC's policies." Should investors not buy UPC stock after the announcement because the litigation will cause an abnormally low rate of return? Why?

13.7   Newtech Corp. is going to adopt a new chip testing device that can greatly improve its production efficiency. Do you think the lead engineer of this device can profit from purchasing the firm's stock before the news release on the implementation of the new technology? What if you rush to call your broker to buy the stock right after you learn of the announcement in *The Wall Street Journal?*

13.8   Trans Trust Corp. has changed how it accounts for inventory. The change does not change tax, but the resulting earnings report released this quarter is 20 percent higher than what it would have been under the old accounting system. There is no other surprise in this earnings report. Will the stock price be higher when the market learns that the earnings are higher?

13.9   Many empirical studies have documented that firms that issue stock usually experience a period of price run-up before the public stock offering. Alex Johnson invests primarily in firms that have just carried out new stock offerings. Based on the evidence that these firms have generally performed very well before the stock offering, can Alex make money using this strategy?

13.10   Sooners Investing Agency has been the hottest stock picker for the past two years. Before the rise to fame occurred, subscribers to the Sooners newsletter totaled only 200. Those subscribers beat the market consistently; they earned substantially higher returns after adjustment for risk and transaction costs. Subscriptions have now skyrocketed to 10,000. Now when Sooners recommends a stock, the stock price instantly rises several points. The subscribers now earn only a normal return when they buy recommended stock because the price rises before anybody can act on the information. Briefly explain this phenomenon.

13.11   In a recent discussion with you, your broker commented that well-managed firms are not necessarily more profitable than firms with average management. To convince you of this, she presented you with evidence from a recent study conducted by the firm for which she works. The study examined the returns on 17 small manufacturing firms that, eight years earlier, an industry magazine had listed as the best-managed small manufacturers in the country. In the eight years since the publication of that issue of the magazine, the 17 firms have not earned more than the market. Your broker concluded that if they were well-managed, they should have produced better-than-average returns. Do you agree with your broker?

13.12   A famous economist just announced his findings that the recession is over and the economy is entering the expansion stage once again. Can you profit from investing in the stock market after you learned this study result from reading *The Wall Street Journal?*

13.13   Many investors (sometimes called technical analysts) claim to observe patterns in stock market prices. Is technical analysis consistent with EMH? If the stock price follows a random walk model, can technical analysts systematically profit from trading rules based on patterns in the historical stock prices? If so, what form of market efficiency is violated?

The Evidence

13.14   Some people argue that the EMH can't explain the 1987 market crash or the high price-to-earnings ratio of the Japanese stock market. What alternative hypothesis is currently used for these two phenomena?

13.15   Prospectors, Inc., is a small publicly traded gold-prospecting company in Alaska. Usually its searches prove fruitless; however, occasionally the prospectors find a rich vein of ore.

  a. What pattern would you expect to observe for Prospectors' cumulative abnormal returns?

   b. Is this a random walk? Explain.

   c. Is this consistent with an efficient market? Explain.

13.16 You are conducting a cumulative average residual study on the effect of airline companies' buying new planes. The announcement dates for the purchase of the planes were July 18 (7/18) for Delta, February 12 (2/12) for United, and October 7 (10/7) for American. Construct a cumulative abnormal return (CAR) for these stocks as a group, chart it, and explain it. All stocks have a beta of 1.

| | Delta | | | United | | | American | |
Date	Market Return	Company Return	Date	Market Return	Company Return	Date	Market Return	Company Return
7/12	−0.3	−0.5	2/8	−0.9	−1.1	10/1	0.5	0.3
7/13	0.0	0.2	2/9	−1.0	−1.1	10/2	0.4	0.6
7/16	0.5	0.7	2/10	0.4	0.2	10/3	1.1	1.1
7/17	−0.5	−0.3	2/11	0.6	0.8	10/6	0.1	−0.3
7/18	−2.2	1.1	2/12	−0.3	−0.1	10/7	−2.2	−0.3
7/19	−0.9	−0.7	2/15	1.1	1.2	10/8	0.5	0.5
7/20	−1.0	−1.1	2/16	0.5	0.5	10/9	−0.3	−0.2
7/23	0.7	0.5	2/17	−0.3	−0.2	10/10	0.3	0.1
7/24	0.2	0.1	2/18	0.3	0.2	10/13	0.0	−0.1

13.17 The following diagram shows the cumulative abnormal returns on the stock prices of 386 oil- and gas-exploration companies that announced oil discoveries in month 0. The sample was drawn from 1950 to 1980, and no single month had more than six announcements. Is the diagram consistent with market efficiency? Why or why not?

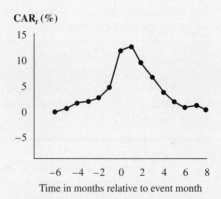

CAR$_t$ (%)

Time in months relative to event month

13.18 The following diagram represents the hypothetical results of a study of the behavior of the stock prices of firms that lost antitrust cases. Included are all firms that lost the initial court decision, even if it was later overturned on appeal. Is the diagram consistent with market efficiency? Why or why not.?

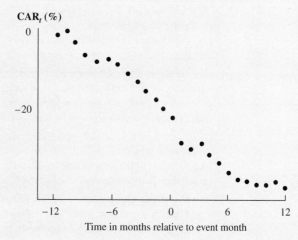

Time in months relative to event month

13.19 The following figures present the results of four cumulative-average-residual studies conducted to test the semistrong form of the efficient-market hypothesis. Indicate in each case whether the results of the study support, reject, or are inconclusive about the hypothesis. In each figure, time 0 is the date of an event.

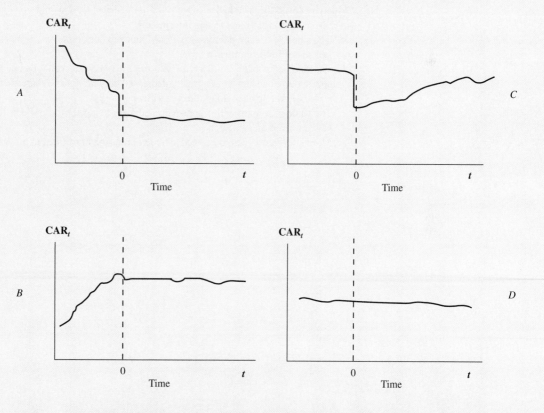

13.20 Several years ago, just before Arco purchased the firm, Kennecott Copper Corporation had large amounts of marketable securities as a consequence of receiving compensation for some overseas expropriations and other factors. For a period of time before Arco's purchase, the market value of Kennecott was actually *less* than the market value of the marketable securities alone. Is this evidence of market inefficiency?

13.21 Suppose the market is semistrong-form efficient. Can you expect to earn excess returns if you make trades based on:
  a. Your broker's information about record earnings for a stock?
  b. Rumors about a merger of a firm?
  c. Yesterday's announcement of a successful test of a new product?

13.22 Consider an efficient capital market in which a particular macroeconomic variable that influences your firm's net earnings is positively serially correlated. Would you expect price changes in your stock to be serially correlated? Why or why not?

13.23 Although mutual fund managers frequently claim that they have investing strategies, under the EMH, mutual fund managers should obtain the same returns after adjusting for the risk level of their respective investments. Therefore, we can simply pick mutual funds at random. Is this statement true or false? Explain.

13.24 A pension manager intends to unload a large block of Bob's Toy Inc. shares.
  a. What are the general empirical findings on the price effect of block trading?
  b. Do you consider it a good idea for the pension manager to break up the trades to several lots instead of one big block at a time?
  c. What is the expected price effect if we assume that EMH holds?

13.25 Assume that markets are efficient. Suppose that during a trading day, important new information is released for the first time concerning American Golf Inc. This information indicates that the firm has lost a contract for a large golf-course project that the market widely believed the firm had secured prior to the news. How would you expect the price of a share of stock to react to this information?
  a. The value of a share decreases over an extended period of time as investors begin to sell shares in the company.
  b. The value of a share will decrease to a price above what would be considered appropriate, because of the greatly decreased demand for the shares. Eventually the price would rise back up to the correct level.
  c. The value of a share will decrease immediately to a price that reflects the value of the new information.
  d. More information would be needed to determine the movement in the price of the stock.

CHAPTER 14

Long-Term Financing: An Introduction

EXECUTIVE SUMMARY

This chapter introduces the basic sources of long-term financing: common stock, preferred stock, and long-term debt. Later chapters discuss these topics in more detail. Perhaps no other area of corporate finance is more perplexing to new students of finance than corporate securities such as shares of stock, bonds, and debentures. Whereas the concepts are simple and logical, the language is strange and unfamiliar.

The purpose of this chapter is to describe the basic features of long-term financing. We begin with a look at common stock, preferred stock, and long-term debt and then briefly consider patterns of the different kinds of long-term financing. Discussion of nonbasic forms of long-term finance, such as convertibles and leases, is reserved for later chapters.

14.1 COMMON STOCK

The term **common stock** has no precise meaning. It usually is applied to stock that has no special preference either in dividends or in bankruptcy. A description of the common stock of Anheuser-Busch in 1996 is presented below.

ANHEUSER-BUSCH
Common Stock and Other Shareholders' Equity
December 31, 1999
(in millions)

Common stock, $1 par value, authorized 1.6 billion shares, issued 716.1 million shares	$ 716.1
Capital in excess of par value	1,241.0
Retained earnings	9,181.2
Treasury stock, at cost	(6,831.3)
Other	
ESOP debt guarantee	(210.5)
Foreign currency translation adjustment	(175.0)
Total Equity	$3,921.5

Par and No-Par Stock

Owners of common stock in a corporation are referred to as *shareholders* or *stockholders*. They receive stock certificates for the *shares* they own. There is usually a stated value on each stock certificate called the *par value*. However, some stocks have no-par value. The par value of each share of the common stock of Anheuser-Busch is $1.

The total par value is the number of shares issued multiplied by the par value of each share and is sometimes referred to as the *dedicated capital* of a corporation. The dedicated capital of Anheuser-Busch is $1 × 716.1 million shares = $716.1 million.

Authorized versus Issued Common Stock

Shares of common stock are the fundamental ownership units of the corporation. The articles of incorporation of a new corporation must state the number of shares of common stock the corporation is authorized to issue.

The board of directors of the corporation, after a vote of the shareholders, can amend the articles of incorporation to increase the number of shares authorized; there is no limit to the number of shares that can be authorized. In 1999 Anheuser-Busch had authorized 1.6 billion shares and had issued 716.1 million shares. There is no requirement that all of the authorized shares actually be issued. Although there are no legal limits to authorizing shares of stock, some practical considerations may exist:

1. Some states impose taxes based on the number of authorized shares.
2. Authorizing a large number of shares may create concern on the part of investors, because authorized shares can be issued later *with* the approval of the board of directors but without a vote of the shareholders.

Capital Surplus

Capital surplus usually refers to amounts of directly contributed equity capital in excess of the par value.

EXAMPLE

Suppose 100 shares of common stock have a par value of $2 each and are sold to shareholders for $10 per share. The capital surplus would be ($10 − $2) × 100 = $8 × 100 = $800, and the total par value would be $2 × 100 = $200. What difference does it make if the total capital contribution is reported as par value or capital surplus?

About the only difference is that in most states the par value is locked in and cannot be distributed to stockholders except upon the liquidation of the corporation.

The capital surplus of Anheuser-Busch is $1,241 million. This figure indicates that the price of new shares issued by Anheuser-Busch has exceeded the par value and the difference has been entered as *capital in excess of par value.* In most states shares of stock cannot be issued below par value, implying that capital in excess of par value cannot be negative.

Retained Earnings

Anheuser-Busch usually pays out less than one half of its net income as dividends; the rest is retained in the business and is called **retained earnings.** The cumulative amount of retained earnings (since original incorporation) was $9,181.2 million in 1999.

The sum of the par value, capital surplus, and accumulated retained earnings is the *common equity* of the firm, which is usually referred to as the firm's **book value.** The book value represents the amount contributed directly and indirectly to the corporation by equity investors.

EXAMPLE

Suppose Western Redwood Corporation was formed in 1906 with 10,000 shares of stock issued and sold at its $1 par value. Because the stock was sold for $1, the first balance sheet showed a zero amount for capital surplus. By 1998 the company had become very profitable and had retained profits of $100,000. The stockholders' equity of Western Redwood Corporation in 1998 is as follows:

WESTERN REDWOOD CORPORATION
Equity Accounts
January 1, 1998

Common stock, $1 par, 10,000 shares outstanding	$ 10,000
Capital surplus	0
Retained earnings	100,000
Total stockholders' equity	$110,000

$$\text{Book value per share} = \frac{\$110,000}{10,000} = \$11$$

Suppose the company has profitable investment opportunities and decides to sell 10,000 shares of new stock. The current market price is $20 per share. The effect of the sale of stock on the balance sheet will be

WESTERN REDWOOD CORPORATION
Equity Accounts
December 31, 1998

Common stock, $1 par, 20,000 shares outstanding	$ 20,000
Capital surplus ($20 − $1) × 10,000 shares	190,000
Retained earnings	100,000
Total stockholders' equity	$310,000

$$\text{Book value per share} = \frac{\$310,000}{20,000} = \$15.5$$

What happened?

1. Because 10,000 shares of new stock were issued with par value of $1, the par value rose $10,000.
2. The total amount raised by the new issue was $20 × 10,000 = $200,000, and $190,000 was entered into capital surplus.
3. The book value per share increased because the market price of the new stock was higher than the book value of the old stock.

Market Value, Book Value, and Replacement Value

The book value of Anheuser-Busch in 1999 was $3,921.5 million. This figure is based on the number of shares outstanding. The company had issued 716.1 million shares and bought back approximately 263.4 million shares, so that the total number of outstanding shares was 716.1 million − 263.4 million = 452.7 million. The shares bought back are called *treasury stock*.

The book value per share was equal to

$$\frac{\text{Total common shareholders' equity}}{\text{Shares outstanding}} = \frac{\$3,921.5 \text{ million}}{452.7 \text{ million}} = \$8.66$$

Anheuser-Busch is a publicly owned company. Its common stock trades on the New York Stock Exchange (NYSE), and thousands of shares change hands every day. The recent market prices of Anheuser-Busch were between $75 and $84 per share. Thus the market prices were above the book value.

In addition to market and book values, you may hear the term *replacement value.* This refers to the current cost of replacing the assets of the firm. Market, book, and replacement value are equal at the time when a firm purchases an asset. After that time, these values will diverge. The *market-to-book-value* ratio of common stock and *Tobin's Q* (market value of assets/replacement value of assets) introduced in the appendix to Chapter 2 are indicators of the success of the firm. A market-to-book or Tobin's Q ratio greater than 1 indicates the firm has done well with its investment decisions.

Shareholders' Rights

The conceptual structure of the corporation assumes that shareholders elect directors who in turn elect corporate officers—more generally, the management—to carry out their directives. It is the right to elect the directors of the corporation by vote that constitutes the most important control device of shareholders.

Directors are elected each year at an annual meeting by a vote of the holders of a majority of shares who are present and entitled to vote. The exact mechanism for electing differs among different companies. The most important difference is whether shares must be voted cumulatively or must be voted straight.

EXAMPLE

Imagine that a corporation has two shareholders: Smith with 25 shares and Marshall with 75 shares. Both want to be on the board of directors. Marshall does not want Smith to be a director. Let us assume that there are four directors to be elected and each shareholder nominates four candidates.

Cumulative Voting   The effect of **cumulative voting** is to permit minority participation. If cumulative voting is permitted, the total number of votes that each shareholder may cast is determined first. That number is usually calculated as the number of shares (owned or controlled) multiplied by the number of directors to be elected. Each shareholder can distribute these votes as he or she wishes over one or more candidates. Smith will get $25 \times 4 = 100$ votes, and Marshall is entitled to $75 \times 4 = 300$ votes. If Smith gives all his votes to himself, he is assured of a directorship. It is not possible for Marshall to divide 300 votes among the four candidates in such a way as to preclude Smith's election to the board.

Straight Voting   If **straight voting** is permitted, Smith may cast 25 votes for each candidate and Marshall may cast 75 votes for each. As a consequence, Marshall will elect all of the candidates.

Straight voting can freeze out minority shareholders; that is the reason many states have mandatory cumulative voting. In states where cumulative voting is mandatory, devices have been worked out to minimize its impact. One such device is to *stagger* the voting for the board of directors. Staggering permits a fraction of the directorships to come to a vote at a particular time. It has two basic effects:

1. Staggering makes it more difficult for a minority to elect a director when there is cumulative voting.
2. Staggering makes successful takeover attempts less likely by making the election of new directors more difficult.

Proxy Voting   A **proxy** is the legal grant of authority by a shareholder to someone else to vote his or her shares. For convenience, the actual voting in large public corporations usually is done by proxy.

Many companies such as Anheuser-Busch have hundreds of thousands of shareholders. Shareholders can come to the annual meeting and vote in person, or they can transfer their right to vote to another party by proxy.

Obviously, management always tries to get as many proxies transferred to it as possible. However, if shareholders are not satisfied with management, an outside group of shareholders can try to obtain as many votes as possible via proxy. They can vote to replace management by adding enough directors. This is called a *proxy fight.*

Other Rights   The value of a share of common stock in a corporation is directly related to the general rights of shareholders. In addition to the right to vote for directors, shareholders usually have the following rights:

1. The right to share proportionally in dividends paid.
2. The right to share proportionally in assets remaining after liabilities have been paid in a liquidation.
3. The right to vote on matters of great importance to stockholders, such as a merger, usually decided at the annual meeting or a special meeting.
4. The right to share proportionally in any new stock sold. This is called the *preemptive right* and will be discussed in detail in later chapters.

Dividends

A distinctive feature of corporations is that they issue shares of stock and are authorized by law to pay dividends to the holders of those shares. **Dividends** paid to shareholders represent a return on the capital directly or indirectly contributed to the corporation by the shareholders. The payment of dividends is at the discretion of the board of directors.

Here are some important characteristics of dividends:

1. Unless a dividend is declared by the board of directors of a corporation, it is not a liability of the corporation. A corporation cannot *default* on an undeclared dividend. As a consequence, corporations cannot become *bankrupt* because of nonpayment of dividends. The amount of the dividend—and even whether or not it is paid—are decisions based on the business judgment of the board of directors.
2. The payment of dividends by the corporation is not a business expense. Dividends are not deductible for corporate tax purposes. In short, dividends are paid out of after-tax profits of the corporation.
3. Dividends received by individual shareholders are for the most part considered ordinary income by the IRS and are fully taxable. However, corporations that own stock in other corporations are permitted to exclude 70 percent of the amounts they receive as dividends. In other words, they are taxed only on the remaining 30 percent.

Classes of Stock

Some firms issue more than one class of common stock. The classes are usually created with unequal voting rights. The Ford Motor Company has Class B common stock, which is not publicly traded (it is held by Ford family interests and trusts). This class has about 40 percent of the voting power, but these shares comprise only about 15 percent of the total outstanding stock.

Many companies issue dual classes of common stock. The reason has to do with control of the firm. Management of a firm can raise equity capital by issuing nonvoting common stock while maintaining voting control. Harry and Linda DeAngelo found that managements' holdings of common stock are usually tilted toward the stock with the superior voting rights.[1] Thus, managerial vote ownership is an important element of corporate control structure.

Lease, McConnell, and Mikkelson found the market prices of stocks with superior voting rights to be about 5 percent higher than the prices of otherwise identical stocks with inferior voting rights.[2] However, DeAngelo and DeAngelo found some evidence that the market value of differences in voting rights may be much higher when control of the firm is involved.

CONCEPT QUESTIONS

- What is a company's book value?
- What rights do stockholders have?
- What is a proxy?

14.2 CORPORATE LONG-TERM DEBT: THE BASICS

Securities issued by corporations may be classified roughly as *equity* securities and *debt* securities. The distinction between equity and debt is basic to much of the modern theory and practice of corporate finance.

At its crudest level, debt represents something that must be repaid; it is the result of borrowing money. When corporations borrow, they promise to make regularly scheduled interest payments and to repay the original amount borrowed (that is, the *principal*). The person or firm making the loan is called a *creditor* or *lender*.

Interest versus Dividends

The corporation borrowing the money is called a *debtor* or *borrower*. The amount owed the creditor is a liability of the corporation; however, it is a liability of limited value. The corporation can legally default at any time on its liability.[3] This can be a valuable option. The creditors benefit if the assets have a value greater than the value of the liability, but this would happen only if management were foolish. On the other hand, the corporation and the equity investors benefit if the value of the assets is less than the value of the liabilities, because equity investors are able to walk away from the liabilities and default on their payment.

From a financial point of view, the main differences between debt and equity are the following:

1. Debt is not an ownership interest in the firm. Creditors do not usually have voting power. The device used by creditors to protect themselves is the loan contract (that is, the *indenture*).

2. The corporation's payment of interest on debt is considered a cost of doing business and is fully tax-deductible. Thus interest expense is paid out to creditors before the corporate tax liability is computed. Dividends on common and preferred stock are paid to share-

---

[1] H. DeAngelo and L. DeAngelo, "Managerial Ownership of Voting Rights: A Study of Public Corporations with Dual Classes of Common Stock," *Journal of Financial Economics* 14 (1985).

[2] R. C. Lease, J. J. McConnell, and W. H. Mikkelson, "The Market Value of Control in Publicly Traded Corporations," *Journal of Financial Economics* (April 1983).

[3] In practice, creditors can make a claim against the assets of the firm and a court will administer the legal remedy.

holders after the tax liability has been determined. Dividends are considered a return to shareholders on their contributed capital. Because interest expense can be used to reduce taxes, the government (that is, the IRS) is providing a direct tax subsidy on the use of debt when compared to equity. This point is discussed in detail in the next two chapters.

3. Unpaid debt is a liability of the firm. If it is not paid, the creditors can legally claim the assets of the firm. This action may result in *liquidation* and *bankruptcy.* Thus one of the costs of issuing debt is the possibility of *financial failure,* which does not arise when equity is issued.

Is It Debt or Equity?

Sometimes it is not clear whether a particular security is debt or equity. For example, suppose a 50-year bond is issued with interest payable solely from corporate income if and only if earned, and repayment is subordinate to all other debts of the business. Corporations are very adept at creating hybrid securities that look like equity but are called *debt.* Obviously, the distinction between debt and equity is important for tax purposes. When corporations try to create a debt security that is really equity, they are trying to obtain the tax benefits of debt while eliminating its bankruptcy costs.

Basic Features of Long-Term Debt

Long-term corporate debt usually is denominated in units of $1,000 called the *principal* or *face value.*[4] Long-term debt is a promise by the borrowing firm to repay the principal amount by a certain date, called the *maturity date.* Long-term debt almost always has a par value equal to the face value, and debt price is often expressed as a percentage of the par value. For example, it might be said that General Motors debt is selling at 90, which means that a bond with a par value of $1,000 can be purchased for $900. In this case the debt is selling at a discount because the market price is less than the par value. Debt can also sell at a premium with respect to par value. The borrower using long-term debt generally pays interest at a rate expressed as a fraction of par value. Thus, at $1,000 par value, General Motors' 7-percent debt means that $70 of interest is paid to holders of the debt, usually in semi-annual installments (for example, $35 on June 30 and December 31). The payment schedules are in the form of coupons that are detached from the debt certificates and sent to the company for payment.

Different Types of Debt

Typical debt securities are called *notes, debentures,* or *bonds.* A debenture is an unsecured corporate debt, whereas a bond is secured by a mortgage on the corporate property. However, in common usage the word *bond* is used indiscriminately and often refers to both secured and unsecured debt. A note usually refers to an unsecured debt with a maturity shorter than that of a debenture, perhaps under 10 years.

Debentures and bonds are long-term debt. *Long-term debt* is any obligation that is payable more than one year from the date it was originally issued. Sometimes long-term debt—debentures and bonds—is called *funded debt.* Debt that is due in less than one year is unfunded and is accounted for as a current liability. Some debt is perpetual and has no specific maturity. This type of debt is referred to as a *consol.*

---

[4]Many government bonds have larger principal denominations, up to $10,000 or $25,000, and most municipal bonds come in denominations of $5,000.

Repayment

Long-term debt is typically repaid in regular amounts over the life of the debt. The payment of long-term debt by installments is called *amortization*. At the end of the amortization the entire indebtedness is said to be *extinguished*. Amortization is typically arranged by a *sinking fund*. Each year the corporation places money into a sinking fund, and the money is used to buy back the bonds.

Debt may be extinguished before maturity by a call. Historically, almost all publicly issued corporate long-term debt has been *callable*.[5] These are debentures or bonds for which the firm has the right to pay a specific amount, the *call price,* to retire (extinguish) the debt before the stated maturity date. The call price is always higher than the par value of the debt. Debt that is callable at 105 is debt that the firm can buy back from the holder at a price of $1,050 per debenture or bond, regardless of what the market value of the debt might be. Call prices are always specified when the debt is originally issued. However, lenders are given a 5-year to 10-year call-protection period during which the debt cannot be called away. Recently there has been a higher incidence of noncallable offerings.

Seniority

In general terms **seniority** indicates preference in position over other lenders. Some debt is **subordinated.** In the event of default, holders of subordinated debt must give preference to other specified creditors. Usually, this means that the subordinated lenders will be paid off only after the specified creditors have been compensated. However, debt cannot be subordinated to equity.

Security

Security is a form of attachment to property; it provides that the property can be sold in the event of default to satisfy the debt for which security is given. A mortgage is used for security in tangible property; for example, debt can be secured by mortgages on plant and equipment. Holders of such debt have prior claim on the mortgaged assets in case of default. Debentures are not secured by a mortgage. Thus, if mortgaged property is sold in the event of default, debenture holders will obtain something only if the mortgage bondholders have been fully satisfied.

Indenture

The written agreement between the corporate debt issuer and the lender, setting forth maturity date, interest rate, and all other terms, is called an *indenture*. We treat this in detail in later chapters. For now, we note that

1. The indenture completely describes the nature of the indebtedness.
2. It lists all restrictions placed on the firm by the lenders. These restrictions are placed in *restrictive covenants.*

Some typical restrictive covenants are the following:

1. Restrictions on further indebtedness.
2. A maximum on the amount of dividends that can be paid.
3. A minimum level of working capital.

---

[5]When issued, callable industrial corporate debt typically has 10-year protection against being called.

EXAMPLE

The following table shows some of the many long-term debt securities of Anheuser-Busch at the end of 1999 (in millions).

Commercial paper (weighted average interest rates
    between 5.1% and 5.5%).. $1,000.0
Medium-term notes due 2000 to 2001 (interest rates
    from 5.1% to 8.0%) 32.5
4.1% dual-currency notes due 2001 .... 162.8
6.9% notes due 2002... 200.0
6.75% notes due 2003.. 200.0
6.75% notes due 2005.. 200.0
7% notes due 2005 .... 100.0
6.75% notes due 2006.. 250.0
9% debentures due 2009.. 350.0
7.25% debentures due 2015 .... 150.0
7.375% debentures due 2023 .... 200.0
7% debentures due 2025.. 200.0
Industrial revenue bonds....................................... 157.4
ESOP debt guarantee 210.5
Other long-term debt 33.9

Anheuser-Busch has many different notes and debentures. As can be seen, there is $1 billion of commercial paper. Commercial paper refers to short-term unsecured notes. It is listed as long-term debt because it will be maintained on a long-term basis by "rolling it over." Anheuser-Busch has $162.8 million of Japanese yen/Australian dollar notes. The company will have the choice of using Japanese yen or Australian dollars for both interest and principal payments on these notes. There is also a $210.5 million guarantee of Employee Stock Option Plan (ESOP) debt.

CONCEPT QUESTIONS

- What is corporate debt? Describe its general features.
- Why is it sometimes difficult to tell whether a particular security is debt or equity?

14.3 PREFERRED STOCK

Preferred stock represents equity of a corporation, but it is different from common stock because it has preference over common stock in the payment of dividends and in the assets of the corporation in the event of bankruptcy. *Preference* means only that the holder of the preferred share must receive a dividend (in the case of an ongoing firm) before holders of common shares are entitled to anything.

Stated Value

Preferred shares have a stated liquidating value, usually $100 per share. The dividend preference is described in terms of dollars per share. For example, General Motors "$5 preferred" translates into a dividend yield of 5 percent of stated value.

Cumulative and Noncumulative Dividends

A preferred dividend is not like interest on a bond. The board of directors may decide not to pay the dividends on preferred shares, and their decision may not have anything to do with current net income of the corporation. Dividends payable on preferred stock are either *cumulative* or *noncumulative.* If preferred dividends are cumulative and are not paid in a particular year, they will be carried forward. Usually both the cumulated (past) preferred dividends plus the current preferred dividends must be paid before the common shareholders can receive anything. Unpaid preferred dividends are *not* debts of the firm. Directors elected by the common shareholders can defer preferred dividends indefinitely. However, if so,

1. Common shareholders must forgo dividends.
2. Though holders of preferred shares do not always have voting rights, they will typically be granted these rights if preferred dividends have not been paid for some time.

Because preferred stockholders receive no interest on the cumulated dividends, some have argued that firms have an incentive to delay paying preferred dividends.

Is Preferred Stock Really Debt?

A good case can be made that preferred stock is really debt in disguise. Preferred shareholders receive a stated dividend only, and if the corporation is liquidated, preferred shareholders get a stated value. In recent years, many new issues of preferred stock have had obligatory sinking funds.

For all these reasons, preferred stock seems like debt, but, unlike debt, preferred stock dividends cannot be deducted as interest expense when determining taxable corporate income. From the individual investor's point of view, preferred dividends are ordinary income for tax purposes. For corporate investors, however, 70 percent of the amounts they receive as dividends from preferred stock are exempt from income taxes.

The yields on preferred stock are typically very low. For example, Citigroup has a Series F preferred stock with a stated $3.18 dividend. This dividend is perpetual, that is, it will be paid each year by Citigroup forever unless called. However, holders of Series F preferred stock have no voting rights. Recently, the market price of the Citigroup preferred stock was $46. The current dividend yield on the Citigroup preferred of 6.9 percent ($3.18/46) was slightly more than U.S. government bond yields on the same date. In fact, it was less than the yield on Citigroup's long-term debt.

Corporate investors have an incentive to hold the preferred stock issued by other corporations over holding their debt because of the 70-percent income tax exemption they receive on preferred stock dividends. Because of this tax exclusion, corporate investors pay a premium for preferred stock; as a consequence, the yields are low. Because individual investors do not receive this tax break, most preferred stock in the United States is owned by corporate investors.

Thus, there are two offsetting tax effects to consider in evaluating preferred stock:

a. Dividends are not deducted from corporate income in computing the tax liability of the issuing corporation. This is the bad news.
b. When a corporation purchases preferred stock, 70 percent of the dividends received are exempt from corporate taxation. This is the good news.

The Preferred-Stock Puzzle

Effect (*a*) on page 380 represents a clear tax disadvantage to the issuance of preferred stock. While (*b*) represents a tax advantage, both academics and practitioners generally agree that (*b*) does *not* fully offset (*a*). In addition, preferred stock requires a regular dividend payment and thus lacks the flexibility of common stock. For these reasons, some have argued that preferred stock should not exist.

Why then do firms issue preferred stock? While the nondeductibility of dividends from taxable corporate income is the most serious obstacle to issuing preferred stock, there are several reasons why preferred stock is issued.

1. Because of the way utility rates are determined in regulatory environments, regulated public utilities can pass the tax disadvantage of issuing preferred stock on to their customers. Consequently, a substantial amount of straight preferred stock is issued by utilities.

2. Companies reporting losses to the IRS may issue preferred stock. Because they have no taxable income from which interest on debt can be deducted, preferred stock imposes no tax penalty relative to debt. In other words, (*a*) does not apply.

3. Firms issuing preferred stock can avoid the threat of bankruptcy that exists with debt financing. Unpaid preferred dividends are not debts of a corporation, and preferred shareholders cannot force a corporation into bankruptcy because of unpaid dividends.

- What is preferred stock?
- Do you think it is more like debt or equity?
- What are three reasons why preferred stock is issued?

EQUITY VERSUS DEBT

Feature	Equity	Debt
Income	Dividends	Interest
Tax status	Dividends are taxed as personal income. Dividends are not a business expense.	Interest is taxed as personal income. Interest is a business expense, and corporations can deduct interest when computing corporate tax liability.
Control	Common stock and preferred stock usually have voting rights.	Control is exercised with loan agreement.
Default	Firms cannot be forced into bankruptcy for nonpayment of dividends.	Unpaid debt is a liability of the firm. Nonpayment results in bankruptcy.

Bottom line: Tax status favors debt, but default favors equity. Control features of debt and equity are different, but one is not better than the other.

14.4 Patterns of Financing

Firms use cash flow for capital spending and net working capital. Historically, U.S. firms have spent about 80 percent of cash flow on capital spending and 20 percent on net working capital. Table 14.1 summarizes the patterns of long-term financing for U.S. industrial firms from 1979 to 1999. Here we observe **internal financing,** debt financing, and external equity financing as a percentage of total financing. For example, in 1999 capital spending by U.S. industrial firms was $859.9 billion and increases in net working capital were $207 billion. In other words, total business investment spending was $1,066.9 billion ($859.9 + 207 = 1,066.9$). Capital spending was $\frac{859.9}{1,066.9} = 80.6\%$ of the total, whereas net working capital was $\frac{207}{1,066.9} = 19.4\%$ of the total.

In 1999, U.S. industrial firms generated $750.5 billion of internal cash flow. Because total business spending exceeded internally generated cash flow (i.e., $1,066.9 > 750.5$), there was a *financial gap*. This is very typical of U.S. business finance. The financial gap in 1999 was $316.4 billion (i.e., $1,066.9 - 750.5 = 316.4$). The financial gap is made up by external financing. The financial gap was 29.6% of total business spending, because internal cash flow was only 70.4% of total business spending.

One of the challenges of the financial manager is to finance the gap. In 1999, this meant issuing $469.3 billion of new debt because net new equity actually shrank (by $153 billion) due to stock buybacks. Figure 14.1 charts these patterns of finance.

Internal financing comes from internally generated cash flow and is defined as net income plus depreciation minus dividends. External financing is net new debt and new shares of equity net of buybacks.

Several features of long-term financing seem clear from Table 14.1.

1. Internally generated cash flow has dominated as a source of financing. Typically, between 70 and 90 percent of long-term financing comes from cash flows that corporations generate internally.

2. Typically, total firm spending is greater than internally generated cash flow. A financial deficit is created by the difference between total firm spending and internally generated cash flow. For example, 70 percent of financing came from internal cash flow in 1999, implying a financial deficit in that year of 30 percent ($100\% - 70\%$). Debt was 47 percent of total financing and -17 percent was financed from new stock issues. This financial deficit has averaged about 30 percent in recent years (Figure 14.2).

3. In general, the financial deficit is covered by (1) borrowing and (2) issuing new equity, the two sources of external financing. However, one of the most prominent aspects of external financing is that new issues of equity (both common stock and preferred stock) in the aggregate seem to be unimportant. Net new issues of equity typically account for a small part of total financing; in the late 1980s and very recently, this figure was negative.

4. Table 14.2 shows that firms in the United States generate more financing from internally generated cash than firms in other countries. Firms in other countries rely to a greater extent than U.S. firms on external equity.

These data are consistent with the results of a survey conducted by Gordon Donaldson on the way firms establish long-term financing strategies.[6] He found that:

---

[6]G. G. Donaldson, *Corporate Debt Capacity: A Study of Corporate Debt Policy and Determination of Corporate Debt Capacity* (Boston: Harvard Graduate School of Business Administration, 1961). See also S. C. Myers, "The Capital Structure Puzzle," *Journal of Finance* (July 1984).

■ TABLE 14.1 Historical U.S. Financing Patterns (percent), 1979 to 1999

	1979	1980	1981	1982	1983	1984	1985	1986	1987	1988	1989	1990	1991	1992	1993	1994	1995	1996	1997	1998	1999
Uses of funds																					
Capital spending	84%	80%	66%	86%	65%	64%	78%	72%	67%	70%	71%	76%	87%	72%	84%	76%	80%	92%	81%	92%	80%
Net working capital	16	20	34	14	35	36	22	28	33	30	29	24	13	28	16	24	20	8	19	8	20
Total uses	100	100	100	100	100	100	100	100	100	100	100	100	100	100	100	100	100	100	100	100	100
Sources of funds																					
Internal financing	79	65	66	80	74	71	83	77	79	80	79	77	97	86	84	72	67	87	79	81	70
External financing	21	35	34	20	26	29	17	23	21	20	21	23	3	14	16	28	33	13	21	19	30
New debt	18	31	37	18	20	45	36	41	37	46	45	36	−1	9	12	34	42	23	35	51	47
New stock	3	4	−3	2	6	−16	−19	−18	−16	−26	−24	−13	4	5	4	−6	−9	−10	−14	−32	−17

Source: Board of Governors of the Federal Reserve System, *Flow of Funds Accounts.*

■ FIGURE 14.1 **Financing Decisions by U.S. Nonfinancial Corporations**

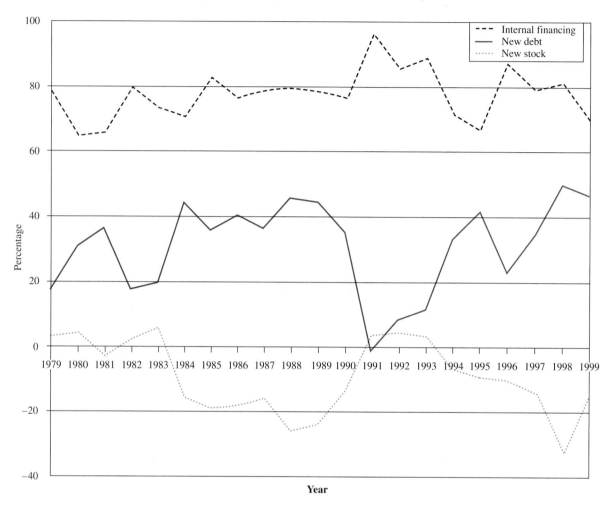

1. The first form of financing used by firms for positive NPV projects is internally generated cash flow: net income plus depreciation minus dividends.

2. As a last resort a firm will use externally generated cash flow. First, debt is used. Common stock is used last.

These observations, when taken together, suggest a **pecking order** to long-term financing strategy. At the top of the pecking order is using internally generated cash flow, and at the bottom is issuing new equity.

QUESTIONS
- What is the difference between internal financing and external financing?
- What are the major sources of corporate financing?
- What factors influence a firm's choices of external versus internal equity financing?
- What pecking order can be observed in the historical patterns of long-term financing?

■ FIGURE 14.2 **The Long-Term Financial Deficit (1999)**

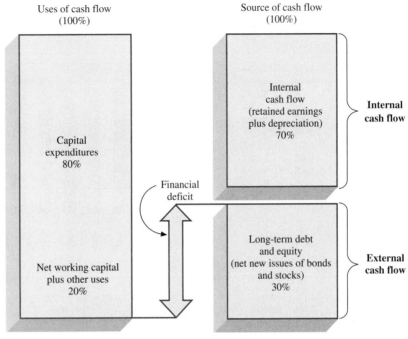

The deficit is the difference between long-term financing uses and internal financing.

■ TABLE 14.2 **International Financing Patterns: 1991–1996 (sources of funds as a percent of total sources)**

	United States	Japan	United Kingdom	Germany	Canada	France
Internally generated funds	82.8	49.3	68.3	65.5	58.3	54.0
Externally generated funds	17.2	50.8	31.7	34.5	41.7	46.0
Increase in long-term debt	17.4	35.9	7.4	31.4	37.5	6.9
Increase in short-term debt	−3.7	9.7	6.1	—	3.8	10.6
Increase in stock	3.5	5.1	16.9	—	10.3	12.4

Source: OECD, *Financial Statements of Nonfinancial Enterprises.*

14.5 RECENT TRENDS IN CAPITAL STRUCTURE

The previous section of this chapter established that U.S. firms from 1984 to 1990 and after 1993 issued large amounts of new debt to finance the retirement of shares of stock. This pattern of financing suggests the question: Did the capital structure of firms change significantly in the 1980s and the mid 1990s? Unfortunately there is no precise answer to this important question. If we use book values (i.e., balance sheet values) the answer would be yes. Figure 14.3 charts the book value of debt to the book value of debt plus equity for U.S.

■ FIGURE 14.3   **Book Debt Ratio: Total Debt as a Percentage of Equity and Debt for U.S. Nonfarm, Nonfinancial Firms from 1988 to 1999**

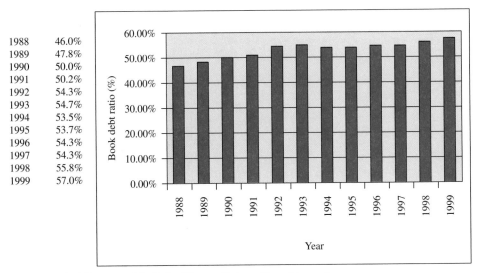

1988	46.0%
1989	47.8%
1990	50.0%
1991	50.2%
1992	54.3%
1993	54.7%
1994	53.5%
1995	53.7%
1996	54.3%
1997	54.3%
1998	55.8%
1999	57.0%

Source: Board of Governors of the Federal Reserve System, *Flow of Accounts.*

nonfinancial firms. There is an upward trend throughout the 1990s. However, if we used market values instead of book values, this would not have been the case. As can be seen in Figure 14.4, when we use market values there is no upward trend in the use of debt by U.S. firms. From 1988 to 1999 the amount of debt increased by 350 percent. The market value of equity increased by almost 600 percent. Therefore, when observing the capital structures of firms, it is important to distinguish between market values and book values. For example, suppose a firm buys back shares of its own stock and finances the purchase with new debt. This would seem to suggest that the firm's reliance on debt should go up and its reliance on equity should go down. After all, the firm has fewer shares of stock outstanding and more debt. The analysis is more complicated than it seems because the market value of the firm's remaining shares of stock may go up and offset the effect of the increased debt. In fact, the market debt ratio is remarkably stable over time and has trended downward in recent years.

Which Are Best: Book or Market Values?

In general, financial economists prefer the use of market values when measuring debt ratios. This is true because market values reflect current rather than historical values. Most financial economists believe that current market values better reflect true intrinsic values than do historically based values. However, the use of market values contrasts with the perspective of many corporate practitioners.

Our conversations with corporate treasurers suggest to us that the use of book values is popular because of the volatility of the stock market. It is frequently claimed that the inherent volatility of the stock market makes market-based debt ratios move around too much.

■ FIGURE 14.4 Market Debt Ratio: Total Debt as a Percentage of the Market Value of Equity and Debt for U.S. Nonfarm, Nonfinancial Firms from 1988 to 1999

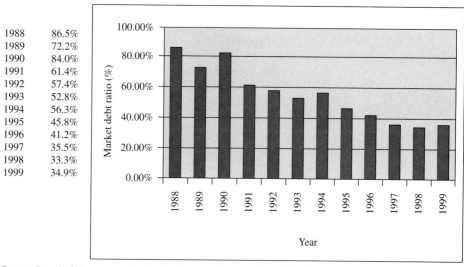

1988	86.5%
1989	72.2%
1990	84.0%
1991	61.4%
1992	57.4%
1993	52.8%
1994	56.3%
1995	45.8%
1996	41.2%
1997	35.5%
1998	33.3%
1999	34.9%

Source: Board of Governors of the Federal Reserve System, *Flow of Funds.*

It is also true that restrictions of debt in bond covenants are usually expressed in book values rather than market values. Moreover, firms such as Standard & Poor's and Moody's use debt ratios expressed in book values to measure credit worthiness.

A key fact is that whether we use book or market values, debt ratios for U.S. nonfinancial firms generally have been below 60 percent of total financing in recent years.

14.6 SUMMARY AND CONCLUSIONS

The basic sources of long-term financing are long-term debt, preferred stock, and common stock. This chapter describes the essential features of each.

1. We emphasize that common shareholders have
   - Residual risk and return in a corporation.
   - Voting rights.
   - Limited liability if the corporation elects to default on its debt and must transfer some or all of the assets to the creditors.
2. Long-term debt involves contractual obligations set out in indentures. There are many kinds of debt, but the essential feature is that debt involves a stated amount that must be

repaid. Interest payments on debt are considered a business expense and are tax deductible.

3. Preferred stock has some of the features of debt and some of the features of common equity. Holders of preferred stock have preference in liquidation and in dividend payments compared to holders of common equity.

4. Firms need financing for capital expenditures, working capital, and other long-term uses. Most of the financing is provided from internally generated cash flow. In the U.S., only about 25 percent of financing comes from new debt and new equity. Only firms in Japan have historically relied more on external financing than on internal financing.

5. In the 1980s and recently, U.S. firms retired massive amounts of equity. These share buy-backs have been financed with new debt.

Key Terms

Book value 372	Preferred stock 379
Capital surplus 372	Proxy 375
Common stock 371	Retained earnings 372
Cumulative voting 374	Seniority 378
Dividends 375	Straight voting 374
Internal financing 382	Subordinated 378
Pecking order 384	

Suggested Reading

The following provides some data on the financial structure of industrial corporations:
Cost of Capital Quarterly. 1999 Yearbook. Ibbotson Associates, 2000.

Questions and Problems

Common Stock

14.1 Following are the equity accounts for Kerch Manufacturing.

Common stock, $2 par	$ 135,430
Capital surplus	203,145
Retained earnings	2,370,025
Total	$2,708,600

    a. How many shares are outstanding?
    b. At what average price were the shares sold?
    c. What is the book value of Kerch stock?

14.2 The Eastern Spruce equity accounts for last year are as follows:

Common stock, $1 par, 500	
shares outstanding	(1)
Capital surplus	$ 50,000
Retained earnings	100,000
Total	(2)

    a. Fill in the missing numbers.
    b. Eastern decided to issue 1,000 shares of new stock. The current price is $30 per share. Show the effects of the new issue upon the equity accounts.

14.3 Ulrich Inc.'s articles of incorporation authorize the firm to issue 500,000 shares of $5 par-value common stock, of which 325,000 shares have been issued. Those shares were sold at an average of 12 percent over par. In the quarter that ended last week, Ulrich earned $260,000 net income; 4 percent of that income was paid as a dividend. Prior to the close of the books, Ulrich had $3,545,000 in retained earnings. The company owns no treasury stock.
   a. Create the equity statement for Ulrich.
   b. Create a new equity statement that reflects the sale of 25,000 authorized but unissued shares at the price of $4 per share.

14.4 The shareholders of the Unicorn Company need to elect seven new directors. There are 2 million shares outstanding. How many shares do you need to be certain that you can elect at least one director if
   a. Unicorn has straight voting?
   b. Unicorn has cumulative voting?

14.5 Power Inc. is going to elect six board members next month. Betty Brown owns 17.3 percent of the total shares outstanding. How confident can she be to have one of her candidate friends be elected under the cumulative voting rule? And will her friend be elected for certain if the voting procedure is changed to the staggering rule, under which shareholders vote on three board members at a time?

14.6 *a.* An election is being held to fill two seats on the board of directors of a firm in which you hold stock. There is a total of 420 shares outstanding. If the election is conducted under cumulative voting and you own 120 shares, how many more shares must you buy to be assured of earning a seat on the board?
   b. The shareholders of Motive Power Corp. need to elect three new directors to the board. There are 2,000,000 shares of common stock outstanding and current share price is $5. If Motive Power uses cumulative voting procedures, how much will it cost to guarantee yourself one seat on the Motive Power's board?

Preferred Stock

14.7 What are the differences between preferred stock and debt?

14.8 Preferred stock doesn't offer corporate tax shield on the dividends paid. Why do we still observe some firms issuing preferred stock?

14.9 The yields on nonconvertible preferred stock are lower than the yields on corporate bonds.
   a. Why is there a difference?
   b. Which investors are the primary holders of preferred stock? Why?

Patterns of Financing

14.10 What are the main differences between corporate debt and equity? Why do some firms try to issue equity in the guise of debt?

Recent Trends in Capital Structure

14.11 The Cable Company has $1 million of positive NPV projects it would like to take advantage of. If Cable's managers follow the historical pattern of long-term financing for U.S. industrial firms, what will their financing strategy be?

CHAPTER 15

Capital Structure: Basic Concepts

EXECUTIVE SUMMARY

Previous chapters of this book examined the capital-budgeting decision. We pointed out that this decision concerns the left-hand side of the balance sheet. The last two chapters began our discussion of the capital-structure decision,[1] which deals with the right-hand side of the balance sheet.

In general, a firm can choose among many alternative capital structures. It can issue a large amount of debt or it can issue very little debt. It can issue floating-rate preferred stock, warrants, convertible bonds, caps, and callers. It can arrange lease financing, bond swaps, and forward contracts. Because the number of instruments is so large, the variations in capital structures are endless. We simplify the analysis by considering only common stock and straight debt in this chapter. The "bells and whistles," as they are called on Wall Street, must await later chapters of the text. The capital-structure decision we consider is the decision to rely on debt. We examine the factors that are important in the choice of a firm's debt-to-equity ratio.

Our results in this chapter are basic. First we discuss the capital-structure decision in a world with neither taxes nor other capital-market imperfections. Surprisingly, we find that the capital-structure decision is a matter of *indifference* in this world. We next argue that there is a quirk in the U.S. tax code that subsidizes debt financing. Finally, we show that an increase in the firm's value from debt financing leads to an increase in the value of the equity.

15.1 THE CAPITAL-STRUCTURE QUESTION AND THE PIE THEORY

How should a firm choose its debt-equity ratio? We call our approach to the capital-structure question the **pie model.** If you are wondering why we chose this name, just take a look at Figure 15.1. The pie in question is the sum of the financial claims of the firm, debt and equity in this case. We *define* the value of the firm to be this sum. Hence, the value of the firm, V, is

$$V \equiv B + S \tag{15.1}$$

where B is the market value of the debt and S is the market value of the equity. Figure 15.1 presents two possible ways of slicing this pie between stock and debt: 40 percent–60 percent and 60 percent–40 percent. If the goal of the management of the firm is to make the firm as valuable as possible, then the firm should pick the debt-equity ratio that makes the pie—the total value—as big as possible.

---

[1]It is conventional to refer to choices regarding debt and equity as *capital-structure decisions.* However, the term *financial-structure decisions* would be more accurate, and we use the terms interchangeably.

■ FIGURE 15.1 **Two Pie Models of Capital Structure**

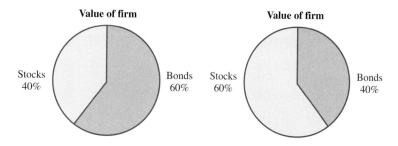

This discussion begs two important questions:

1. Why should the stockholders in the firm care about maximizing the value of the entire firm? After all, the value of the firm is, by definition, the sum of both the debt and the equity. Instead, why should the stockholders not prefer the strategy that maximizes their interests only?

2. What is the ratio of debt to equity that maximizes the shareholders' interests?

Let us examine each of the two questions in turn.

CONCEPT QUESTION
?

• What is the pie model of capital structure?

15.2 MAXIMIZING FIRM VALUE VERSUS MAXIMIZING STOCKHOLDER INTERESTS

The following example illustrates that the capital structure that maximizes the value of the firm is the one that financial managers should choose for the shareholders.

EXAMPLE

Suppose the market value of the J. J. Sprint Company is $1,000. The company currently has no debt, and each of J. J. Sprint's 100 shares of stock sells for $10. A company such as J. J. Sprint with no debt is called an *unlevered* company. Further suppose that J. J. Sprint plans to borrow $500 and pay the $500 proceeds to shareholders as an extra cash dividend of $5 per share. After the issuance of debt, the firm becomes *levered*. The investments of the firm will not change as a result of this transaction. What will the value of the firm be after the proposed restructuring?

Management recognizes that, by definition, only one of three outcomes can occur from restructuring. Firm value after restructuring can be either (1) greater than the original firm value of $1,000, (2) equal to $1,000, or (3) less than $1,000. After consulting with investment bankers, management believes that restructuring will not change firm value more than $250 in either direction. Thus, they view firm values of $1,250, $1,000, and $750 as the relevant range. The original capital structure and these three possibilities under the new capital structure are presented next.

	No Debt (original capital structure)	Value of Debt plus Equity after Payment of Dividend (three possibilities)		
		I	II	III
Debt	$ 0	$ 500	$ 500	$500
Equity	1,000	750	500	250
Firm value	$1,000	$1,250	$1,000	$750

Note that the value of equity is below $1,000 under any of the three possibilities. This can be explained in one of two ways. First, the chart shows the value of the equity *after* the extra cash dividend is paid. Since cash is paid out, a dividend represents a partial liquidation of the firm. Consequently, there is less value in the firm for the equityholders after the dividend payment. Second, in the event of a future liquidation, stockholders will be paid only after bondholders have been paid in full. Thus, the debt is an encumbrance of the firm, reducing the value of the equity.

Of course, management recognizes that there are infinite possible outcomes. The above three are to be viewed as *representative* outcomes only. We can now determine the payoff to stockholders under the three possibilities.

	Payoff to Shareholders after Restructuring		
	I	II	III
Capital gains	−$250	−$500	−$750
Dividends	500	500	500
Net gain or loss to stockholders	$250	$ 0	−$250

No one can be sure ahead of time which of the three outcomes will occur. However, imagine that managers believe that outcome *I* is most likely. They should definitely restructure the firm because the stockholders would gain $250. That is, although the price of the stock declines by $250 to $750, they receive $500 in dividends. Their net gain is $250 = −$250 + $500. Also, notice that the value of the firm would rise by $250 = $1,250 − $1,000.

Alternatively, imagine that managers believe that outcome *III* is most likely. In this case they should not restructure the firm because the stockholders would expect a $250 loss. That is, the stock falls by $750 to $250 and they receive $500 in dividends. Their net loss is −$250 = −$750 + $500. Also, notice that the value of the firm would change by −$250 = $750 − $1,000.

Finally, imagine that the managers believe that outcome *II* is most likely. Restructuring would not affect the stockholders' interest because the net gain to stockholders in this case is zero. Also, notice that the value of the firm is unchanged if outcome *II* occurs.

This example explains why managers should attempt to maximize the value of the firm. In other words, it answers question (1) in Section 15.1. We find in this example that:

Changes in capital structure benefit the stockholders *if and only if* the value of the firm increases.

Conversely, these changes hurt the stockholders if and only if the value of the firm decreases. This result holds true for capital-structure changes of many different types.[2] As a corollary, we can say:

> Managers should choose the capital structure that they believe will have the highest firm value, because this capital structure will be most beneficial to the firm's stockholders.

Note however that the example does not tell us which of the three outcomes is most likely to occur. Thus, it does not tell us whether debt should be added to J. J. Sprint's capital structure. In other words, it does not answer question (2) in section 15.1. This second question is treated in the next section.

QUESTION
?
CONCEPT
- Why should financial managers choose the capital structure that maximizes the value of the firm?

15.3 FINANCIAL LEVERAGE AND FIRM VALUE: AN EXAMPLE

Leverage and Returns to Shareholders

The previous section shows that the capital structure producing the highest firm value is the one that maximizes shareholder wealth. In this section, we wish to determine that optimal capital structure. We begin by illustrating the effect of capital structure on returns to stockholders. We will use a detailed example which we encourage students to study carefully. Once we have this example under our belts, we will be ready to determine the optimal capital structure.

Trans Am Corporation currently has no debt in its capital structure. The firm is considering issuing debt to buy back some of its equity. Both its current and proposed capital structures are presented in Table 15.1. The firm's assets are $8,000. There are 400 shares of the all-equity firm, implying a market value per share of $20. The proposed debt issue is for $4,000, leaving $4,000 in equity. The interest rate is 10 percent.

■ TABLE 15.1 **Financial Structure of Trans Am Corporation**

	Current	Proposed
Assets	$8,000	$8,000
Debt	$0	$4,000
Equity (market and book)	$8,000	$4,000
Interest rate	10%	10%
Market value/share	$20	$20
Shares outstanding	400	200

The proposed capital structure has leverage, whereas the current structure is all equity.

---

[2]This result may not hold exactly in a more complex case where debt has a significant possibility of default. Issues of default are treated in the next chapter.

■ TABLE 15.2 **Trans Am's Current Capital Structure: No Debt**

	Recession	Expected	Expansion
Return on assets (ROA)	5%	15%	25%
Earnings	$400	$1,200	$2,000
Return on equity (ROE) = Earnings/Equity	5%	15%	25%
Earnings per share (EPS)	$1.00	$3.00	$5.00

■ TABLE 15.3 **Trans Am's Proposed Capital Structure: Debt = $4,000**

	Recession	Expected	Expansion
Return on assets (ROA)	5%	15%	25%
Earnings before interest (EBI)	$400	$1,200	$2,000
Interest	−400	−400	−400
Earnings after interest	$ 0	$ 800	$1,600
Return on equity (ROE) = Earnings after interest/Equity	0	20%	40%
Earnings per share (EPS)	0	$4.00	$8.00

The effect of economic conditions on earnings per share is shown in Table 15.2 for the current capital structure (all-equity). Consider first the middle column where earnings are *expected* to be $1,200. Since assets are $8,000, the return on assets (ROA) is 15 percent (= $1,200/$8,000). Because assets equal equity for this all-equity firm, return on equity (ROE) is also 15 percent. Earnings per share (EPS) is $3.00 (= $1,200/400). Similar calculations yield EPS of $1.00 and $5.00 in the cases of recession and expansion, respectively.

The case of leverage is presented in Table 15.3. ROA in the three economic states is identical in Tables 15.2 and 15.3, because this ratio is calculated before interest is considered. Since debt is $4,000 here, interest is $400 (= .10 × $4,000). Thus, earnings after interest is $800 (= $1,200 − $400) in the middle (expected) case. Since equity is $4,000, ROE is 20 percent ($800/$4,000). Earnings per share is $4.00 (= $800/200). Similar calculations yield earnings of $0 and $8.00 for recession and expansion, respectively.

Tables 15.2 and 15.3 show that the effect of financial leverage depends on the company's earnings before interest. If earnings before interest is equal to $1,200, the return on equity (ROE) is higher under the proposed structure. If earnings before interest is equal to $400, the ROE is higher under the current structure.

This idea is represented in Figure 15.2. The solid line represents the case of no leverage. The line begins at the origin, indicating that earnings per share (EPS) would be zero if earnings before interest (EBI) were zero. The EPS rises in tandem with a rise in EBI.

The dotted line represents the case of $4,000 of debt. Here, EPS is negative if EBI is zero. This follows because $400 of interest must be paid regardless of the firm's profits.

Now consider the slopes of the two lines. The slope of the dotted line (the line with debt) is higher than the slope of the solid line. This occurs because the levered firm has *fewer* shares of stock outstanding than does the unlevered firm. Therefore, any increase in EBI leads to a greater rise in EPS for the levered firm because the earnings increase is distributed over fewer shares of stock.

■ FIGURE 15.2 Financial Leverage: EPS and EBI for the Trans Am Corporation

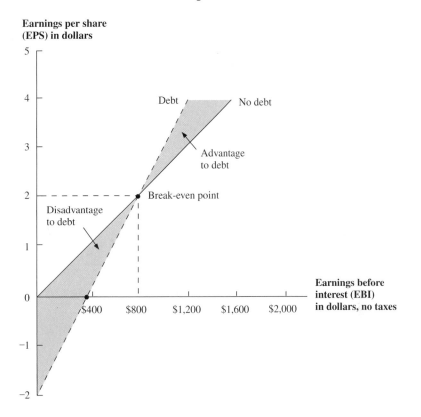

Because the dotted line has a lower intercept but a higher slope, the two lines must intersect. The *break-even* point occurs at $800 of EBI. Were earnings before interest to be $800, both firms would produce $2 of earnings per share (EPS). Because $800 is break-even, earnings above $800 lead to greater EPS for the levered firm. Earnings below $800 lead to greater EPS for the unlevered firm.

The Choice between Debt and Equity

Tables 15.2 and 15.3 and Figure 15.2 are important because they show the effect of leverage on earnings per share. Students should study the tables and figure until they feel comfortable with the calculation of each number in them. However, we have not yet presented the punch line. That is, we have not yet stated which capital structure is better for Trans Am.

At this point, many students believe that leverage is beneficial, because EPS is expected to be $4.00 with leverage and only $3.00 without leverage. However, leverage also creates *risk.* Note that in a recession, EPS is higher ($1.00 versus 0) for the unlevered firm. Thus, a risk-averse investor might prefer the all-equity firm, while a risk-neutral (or less risk-averse) investor might prefer leverage. Given this ambiguity, which capital structure *is* better?

Modigliani and Miller (MM) have a convincing argument that a firm cannot change the total value of its outstanding securities by changing the proportions of its capital structure. In other words, the value of the firm is always the same under different capital structures.

■ TABLE 15.4 **Payoff and Cost to Shareholders of Trans Am Corporation under the Proposed Structure and under the Current Structure with Homemade Leverage**

Strategy A: Buy 100 Shares of Levered Equity			
	Recession	Expected	Expansion
EPS of *levered* equity (taken from last line of Table 15.3)	$0	$ 4	$ 8
Earnings per 100 shares	$0	$400	$800
Initial cost = 100 shares @ $20/share = $2,000			

Strategy B: Homemade Leverage			
	Recession	Expected	Expansion
Earnings per 200 shares in current *unlevered* Trans Am	$1 × 200 = $ 200	$3 × 200 = $ 600	$5 × 200 = $1,000
Interest at 10% on $2,000	−200	−200	−200
Net earnings	$ 0	$ 400	$ 800
Initial cost = 200 shares @ $20/share − $2,000 = $2,000			
Cost of stock Amount borrowed			

Investor receives the same payoff whether she (1) buys shares in a levered corporation or (2) buys shares in an unlevered firm and borrows on personal account. Her initial investment is the same in either case. Thus, the firm neither helps nor hurts her by adding debt to capital structure.

In *still* other words, no capital structure is any better or worse than any other capital structure for the firm's stockholders. This rather pessimistic result is the famous **MM Proposition I.**[3]

Their argument compares a simple strategy, which we call Strategy *A*, with a two-part strategy, which we call Strategy *B*. Both of these strategies for shareholders of Trans Am are illuminated in Table 15.4. Let us now examine the first strategy.

Strategy A—Buy 100 shares of the levered equity.

The first line in the top panel of Table 15.4 shows EPS for the proposed levered equity in the three economic states. The second line shows the earnings in the three states for an individual buying 100 shares. The next line shows that the cost of these 100 shares is $2,000.

Let us now consider the second strategy, which has two parts to it.

Strategy B:

1. Borrow $2,000 from either a bank or, more likely, a brokerage house. (If the brokerage house is the lender, we say that this is *going on margin*.)

2. Use the borrowed proceeds plus your own investment of $2,000 (a total of $4,000) to buy 200 shares of the current unlevered equity at $20 per share.

The bottom panel of Table 15.4 shows payoffs under Strategy *B*, which we call the *homemade leverage* strategy. First, observe the middle column, which indicates that 200 shares of the unlevered equity are *expected* to generate $600 of earnings. Assuming that the

---

[3]The original paper is F. Modigliani and M. Miller, "The Cost of Capital, Corporation Finance and the Theory of Investment," *American Economic Review* (June 1958).

$2,000 is borrowed at a 10 percent interest rate, the interest expense is $200 (= 0.10 × $2,000). Thus, the net earnings are expected to be $400. A similar calculation generates net earnings of either $0 or $800 in recession or expansion, respectively.

Now, let us compare these two strategies, both in terms of earnings per year and in terms of initial cost. The top panel of the table shows that Strategy *A* generates earnings of $0, $400, and $800 in the three states. The bottom panel of the table shows that Strategy *B* generates the *same* net earnings in the three states.

The top panel of the table shows that Strategy *A* involves an initial cost of $2,000. Similarly, the bottom panel shows an *identical* net cost of $2,000 for Strategy *B*.

This shows a very important result. Both the cost and the payoff from the two strategies are the same. Thus, one must conclude that Trans Am is neither helping nor hurting its stockholders by restructuring. In other words, an investor is not receiving anything from corporate leverage that he or she could not receive on their own.

Note that, as shown in Table 15.1, the equity of the unlevered firm is valued at $8,000. Since the equity of the levered firm is $4,000 and its debt is $4,000, the value of the levered firm is also $8,000. Now suppose that, for whatever reason, the value of the levered firm were actually greater than the value of the unlevered firm. Here, Strategy *A* would cost more than Strategy *B*. In this case, an investor would prefer to borrow on his own account and invest in the stock of the unlevered firm. He would get the same net earnings each year as if he had invested in the stock of the levered firm. However, his cost would be less. The strategy would not be unique to our investor. Given the higher value of the levered firm, no rational investor would invest in the stock of the levered firm. Anyone desiring shares in the levered firm would get the same dollar return more cheaply by borrowing to finance a purchase of the unlevered firm's shares. The equilibrium result would be, of course, that the value of the levered firm would fall, and the value of the unlevered firm would rise until they became equal. At this point, individuals would be indifferent between Strategy *A* and Strategy *B*.

This example illustrates the basic result of Modigliani-Miller (MM) and is commonly called their Proposition I. We state this proposition as:

> MM Proposition I (no taxes): The value of the levered firm is the same as the value of the unlevered firm.

This is perhaps the most important result in all of corporate finance. In fact, it is generally considered the beginning point of modern managerial finance. Before MM, the effect of leverage on the value of the firm was considered complex and convoluted. Modigliani and Miller show a blindingly simple result: If levered firms are priced too high, rational investors will simply borrow on their personal accounts to buy shares in unlevered firms. This substitution is oftentimes called *homemade leverage*. As long as individuals borrow (and lend) on the same terms as the firms, they can duplicate the effects of corporate leverage on their own.

The example of Trans Am Corporation shows that leverage does not affect the value of the firm. Since we showed earlier that stockholders' welfare is directly related to the firm's value, the example indicates that changes in capital structure cannot affect the stockholders' welfare.

A Key Assumption

The MM result hinges on the assumption that individuals can borrow as cheaply as corporations. If, alternatively, individuals can only borrow at a higher rate, one can easily show that corporations can increase firm value by borrowing.

Is this assumption of equal borrowing costs a good one? Individuals who want to buy stock and borrow can do so by establishing a margin account with the broker. Under this arrangement, the broker loans the individual a portion of the purchase price. For example, the individual might buy $10,000 of stock by investing $6,000 of her own funds and borrowing $4,000 from the broker. Should the stock be worth $9,000 on the next day, the individual's net worth or equity in the account would be $5,000 = $9,000 − $4,000.[4]

The broker fears that a sudden price drop will cause the equity in the individual's account to be negative, implying that the broker may not get her loan repaid in full. To guard against this possibility, stock exchange rules require that the individual make additional cash contributions (replenish her margin account) as the stock price falls. Because (1) the procedures for replenishing the account have developed over many years, and (2) the broker holds the stock as collateral, there is little default risk to the broker.[5] In particular, if margin contributions are not made on time, the broker can sell the stock in order to satisfy her loan. Therefore, brokers generally charge low interest, with many rates being only slightly above the risk-free rate.

By contrast, corporations frequently borrow using illiquid assets (e.g., plant and equipment) as collateral. The costs to the lender of initial negotiation and ongoing supervision, as well as of working out arrangements in the event of financial distress, can be quite substantial. Thus, it is difficult to argue that individuals must borrow at higher rates than can corporations.[6]

CONCEPT QUESTIONS
- Describe financial leverage.
- What is levered equity?
- How can a shareholder of Trans Am undo the company's financial leverage?

15.4 MODIGLIANI AND MILLER: PROPOSITION II (NO TAXES)

Risk to Equityholders Rises with Leverage

At a Trans Am corporate meeting, a corporate officer said, "Well, maybe it does not matter whether the corporation or the individual levers—as long as some leverage takes place. Leverage benefits investors. After all, an investor's expected return rises with the amount of the leverage present." He then pointed out that, as shown in Tables 15.2 and 15.3, the expected return on unlevered equity is 15 percent while the expected return on levered equity is 20 percent.

However, another officer replied, "Not necessarily. Though the expected return rises with leverage, the *risk* rises as well." This point can be seen from an examination of Tables 15.2 and 15.3. With earnings before interest (EBI) varying between $400 and $2,000, earnings per share (EPS) for the stockholders of the unlevered firm vary between $1.00 and $5.00. EPS for the stockholders of the levered firm vary between $0 and $8.00. This greater range for the EPS of the levered firm implies greater risk for the levered firm's stockholders. In other words, levered stockholders have better returns in good times than do unlevered stockholders but have worse returns in bad times. The two tables also show greater range for the ROE of the levered firm's stockholders. The above interpretation concerning risk applies here as well.

---

[4]We are ignoring the one-day interest charge on the loan.

[5]Had this text been published before October 19, 1987, when stock prices declined by more than 20 percent, we might have used the phrase "virtually no" risk instead of "little."

[6]One caveat is in order. Initial margin or borrowing is currently limited by law to 50 percent of value. Certain companies, like financial institutions, borrow over 90 percent of their firm's market value. Individuals borrowing against the stock of all-equity corporations cannot duplicate the debt of these highly levered corporations.

The same insight can be taken from Figure 15.2. The slope of the line for the levered firm is greater than the slope of the line for the unlevered firm. This means that the levered stockholders have better returns in good times than do unlevered stockholders but have worse returns in bad times, implying greater risk with leverage. In other words, the slope of the line measures the risk to stockholders, since the slope indicates the responsiveness of ROE to changes in firm performance (earnings before interest).

Proposition II: Required Return to Equityholders Rises with Leverage

Since levered equity has greater risk, it should have a greater expected return as compensation. In our example, the market *requires* only a 15-percent expected return for the unlevered equity, but it requires a 20-percent expected return for the levered equity.

This type of reasoning allows us to develop **MM Proposition II.** Here, MM argue that the expected return on equity is positively related to leverage, because the risk to equityholders increases with leverage.

To develop this position recall from Chapter 12 that the firm's weighted average cost of capital, r_{WACC}, can be written as:[7]

$$\frac{B}{B + S} \times r_B + \frac{S}{B + S} \times r_S \qquad (15.2)$$

where

r_B is the interest rate, also called the cost of debt

r_S is the expected return on equity or stock, also called the *cost of equity* or the *required return on equity*

r_{WACC} is the firm's weighted average cost of capital

B is the value of the firm's debt or bonds

S is the value of the firm's stock or equity

Formula (15.2) is quite intuitive. It simply says that a firm's weighted average cost of capital is a weighted average of its cost of debt and its cost of equity. The weight applied to debt is the proportion of debt in the capital structure, and the weight applied to equity is the proportion of equity in the capital structure. Calculations of r_{WACC} from formula (15.2) for both the unlevered and the levered firm are presented in Table 15.5.

An implication of MM Proposition I is that r_{WACC} is a constant for a given firm, regardless of the capital structure.[8] For example, Table 15.5 shows that r_{WACC} for Trans Am is 15 percent, with or without leverage.

Let us now define r_0 to be the *cost of capital for an all-equity firm.* For the Trans Am Corp., r_0 is calculated as:

$$r_0 = \frac{\text{Expected earnings to unlevered firm}}{\text{Unlevered equity}} = \frac{\$1,200}{\$8,000} = 15\%$$

As can be seen from Table 15.5, r_{WACC} is equal to r_0 for Trans Am. In fact, r_{WACC} must *always* equal r_0 in a world without corporate taxes.

---

[7]Since we do not have taxes here, the cost of debt is r_B, not $r_B(1 - T_C)$ as it was in Chapter 12.

[8]This statement holds in a world of no taxes. It does not hold in a world with taxes, a point to be brought out later in this chapter (see Figure 15.6).

■ TABLE 15.5 Cost of Capital Calculations for Trans Am

$$r_{\text{WACC}} = \frac{B}{B+S} \times r_B + \frac{S}{B+S} \times r_S$$

Unlevered firm:
$$15\% = \frac{0}{\$8,000} \times 10\%^* + \frac{\$8,000}{\$8,000} \times 15\%†$$

Levered firm:
$$15\% = \frac{\$4,000}{\$8,000} \times 10\%^* + \frac{\$4,000}{\$8,000} \times 20\%‡$$

*10% is the interest rate.
†From the "Expected" column in Table 15.2, we learn that expected earnings after interest for the unlevered firm are $1,200. From Table 15.1, we learn that equity for the unlevered firm is $8,000. Thus, r_S for the unlevered firm is:

$$\frac{\text{Expected earnings after interest}}{\text{Equity}} = \frac{\$1,200}{\$8,000} = 15\%$$

‡From the "Expected" column in Table 15.3, we learn that expected earnings after interest for the levered firm are $800. From Table 15.1, we learn that equity for the levered firm is $4,000. Thus r_S for the levered firm is:

$$\frac{\text{Expected earnings after interest}}{\text{Equity}} = \frac{\$800}{\$4,000} = 20\%$$

Proposition II states the expected return of equity, r_S, in terms of leverage. The exact relationship, derived by setting $r_{\text{WACC}} = r_0$ and then rearranging formula (15.2), is[9]

MM Proposition II (no taxes):

$$r_S = r_0 + \frac{B}{S}(r_0 - r_B) \tag{15.3}$$

Equation (15.3) implies that the required return on equity is a linear function of the firm's debt-to-equity ratio. Examining equation (15.3), we see that if r_0 exceeds the debt rate, r_B, then the cost of equity rises with increases in the debt-equity ratio, B/S. Normally, r_0 should exceed r_B. That is, because even unlevered equity is risky, it should have an expected return greater than that of riskless debt. Note that equation (15.3) holds for Trans Am in its levered state:

$$0.20 = 0.15 + \frac{\$4,000}{\$4,000}(0.15 - 0.10)$$

---

[9]This can be derived from formula (15.2) by setting $r_{\text{WACC}} = r_0$, yielding:

$$\frac{B}{B+S}r_B + \frac{S}{B+S}r_S = r_0. \tag{15.2}$$

Multiplying both sides by $(B+S)/S$ yields:

$$\frac{B}{S}r_B + r_S = \frac{B+S}{S}r_0.$$

We can rewrite the right-hand side as

$$\frac{B}{S}r_B + r_S = \frac{B}{S}r_0 + r_0.$$

Moving $(B/S)r_B$ to the right-hand side and rearranging yields:

$$r_S = r_0 + \frac{B}{S}(r_0 - r_B). \tag{15.3}$$

■ FIGURE 15.3   **The Cost of Equity, the Cost of Debt, and the**
Weighted Average Cost of Capital:
MM Proposition II with No Corporate Taxes

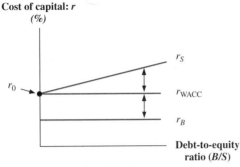

$$r_S = r_0 + (r_0 - r_B)B/S$$

r_S is the cost of equity

r_B is the cost of debt

r_0 is the cost of capital for an all-equity firm

r_{WACC} is a firm's weighted average cost of capital. In a world
with no taxes, r_{WACC} for a levered firm is equal to r_0.

r_0 is a single point while r_S, r_B, and r_{WACC} are all entire lines.

The cost of equity capital, r_S, is positively related to the firm's debt-
equity ratio. The firm's weighted average cost of capital, r_{WACC}, is
invariant to the firm's debt-equity ratio.

Figure 15.3 graphs equation (15.3). As you can see, we have plotted the relation between the cost of equity, r_S, and the debt-equity ratio, B/S, as a straight line. What we witness in equation (15.3) and illustrate in Figure 15.3 is the effect of leverage on the cost of equity. As the firm raises the debt-equity ratio, each dollar of equity is levered with additional debt. This raises the risk of equity and therefore the required return, r_S, on the equity.

Figure 15.3 also shows that r_{WACC} is unaffected by leverage, a point we made above. (It is important for students to realize that r_0, the cost of capital for an all-equity firm, is represented by a single dot on the graph. By contrast, r_{WACC} is an entire line.)

Example Illustrating Proposition I and Proposition II

EXAMPLE

Luteran Motors, an all-equity firm, has expected earnings of $10 million per year in perpetuity. The firm pays all of its earnings out as dividends, so that the $10 million may also be viewed as the stockholders' expected cash flow. There are 10 million shares outstanding, implying expected annual cash flow of $1 per share. The cost of capital for this unlevered firm is 10 percent. In addition, the firm will soon build a new plant for $4 million. The plant is expected to generate additional cash flow of $1 million per year. These figures can be described as

Current Company	New Plant
Cash flow: $10 million	Initial outlay: $4 million
Number of outstanding shares: 10 million	Additional annual cash flow: $1 million

The project's net present value is

$$- \$4 \text{ million} + \frac{\$1 \text{ million}}{0.1} = \$6 \text{ million}$$

assuming that the project is discounted at the same rate as the firm as a whole. Before the market knows of the project, the *market-value* balance sheet of the firm is

LUTERAN MOTORS
Balance Sheet (all equity)

Old assets: $\dfrac{\$10 \text{ million}}{0.1} = \$100 \text{ million}$	Equity:	$100 million
		(10 million shares of stock)

The value of the firm is $100 million, because the cash flow of $10 million per year is capitalized at 10 percent. A share of stock sells for $10 ($100 million/10 million) because there are 10 million shares outstanding.

The market-value balance sheet is a useful tool of financial analysis. Because students are often thrown off guard by it initially, we recommend extra study here. The key is that the market-value balance sheet has the same form as the balance sheet that accountants use. That is, assets are placed on the left-hand side whereas liabilities and owners' equity are placed on the right-hand side. In addition, the left-hand side and the right-hand side must be equal. The difference between a market-value balance sheet and the accountant's balance sheet is in the numbers. Accountants value items in terms of historical cost (original purchase price less depreciation), whereas financial people value items in terms of market value.

The firm will either issue $4 million of equity or debt. Let us consider the effect of equity and debt financing in turn.

Stock Financing   Imagine that the firm announces that, in the near future, it will raise $4 million in equity in order to build a new plant. The stock price, and therefore the value of the firm, will rise to reflect the positive net present value of the plant. According to efficient markets, the increase occurs immediately. That is, the rise occurs on the day of the announcement, not on the date of either the onset of construction of the power plant or the forthcoming stock offering. The market-value balance sheet becomes

LUTERAN MOTORS
Balance Sheet
(upon announcement of equity issue to construct plant)

Old assets	$100 million	Equity	$106 million
			(10 million shares of stock)
NPV of plant:			
$-4 \text{ million} + \dfrac{\$1 \text{ million}}{0.1} =$ 6 million			
Total assets	$106 million		

Note that the NPV of the plant is included in the market-value balance sheet. Because the new shares have not yet been issued, the number of outstanding shares remains 10 million. The price per share has now risen to $10.60 ($106 million/10 million) to reflect news concerning the plant.

Shortly thereafter, $4 million of stock is issued or *floated*. Because the stock is selling at $10.60 per share, 377,358 ($4 million/$10.60) shares of stock are issued. Imagine that funds are put in the bank *temporarily* before being used to build the plant. The market-value balance sheet becomes

LUTERAN MOTORS
Balance Sheet
(upon issuance of stock but before construction begins on plant)

Old assets	$100 million	Equity	$110 million
			(10,377,358 shares of stock)
NPV of plant	6 million		
Proceeds from new issue			
of stock (currently			
placed in bank)	4 million		
Total assets	$110 million		

The number of shares outstanding is now 10,377,358 because 377,358 new shares were issued. The price per share is $10.60 ($110,000,000/10,377,358). Note that the price has not changed. This is consistent with efficient capital markets, because the stock price should only move due to new information.

Of course, the funds are placed in the bank only temporarily. Shortly after the new issue, the $4 million is given to a contractor who builds the plant. To avoid problems in discounting, we assume that the plant is built immediately. The balance sheet then becomes

LUTERAN MOTORS
Balance Sheet
(upon completion of the plant)

Old assets	$100 million	Equity	$110 million
			(10,377,358 shares of stock)
PV of plant: $\dfrac{\$1\text{ million}}{0.1} =$	10 million		
Total assets	$110 million		

Though total assets do not change, the composition of the assets does change. The bank account has been emptied to pay the contractor. The present value of cash flows of $1 million a year from the plant are reflected as an asset worth $10 million. Because the building expenditures of $4 million have already been paid, they no longer represent a future cost. Hence, they no longer reduce the value of the plant. According to efficient capital markets, the price per share of stock remains $10.60.

Expected yearly cash flow from the firm is $11 million, $10 million of which comes from the old assets and $1 million from the new. The expected return to equityholders is

$$r_S = \frac{\$11\text{ million}}{\$110\text{ million}} = 0.10$$

Because the firm is all equity, $r_S = r_0 = 0.10$.

Debt Financing   Alternatively, imagine that the firm announces that, in the near future, it will borrow $4 million at 6 percent to build a new plant. This implies yearly interest payments of $240,000 ($4,000,000 × 6%). Again the stock price rises immediately to reflect the positive net present value of the plant. Thus, we have

LUTERAN MOTORS
Balance Sheet
(upon announcement of debt issue to construct plant)

Old assets	$100 million	Equity	$106 million
			(10 million shares of stock)
NPV of plant:			
$-\$4 \text{ million} + \dfrac{\$1 \text{ million}}{0.1} =$ 6 million			
Total assets	$106 million		

The value of the firm is the same as in the equity financing case because (1) the same plant is to be built and (2) MM prove that debt financing is neither better nor worse than equity financing.

At some point, $4 million of debt is issued. As before, the funds are placed in the bank temporarily. The market-value balance sheet becomes

LUTERAN MOTORS
Balance Sheet
(upon debt issuance but before construction begins on plant)

Old assets	$100 million	Debt	$4 million
NPV of plant	6 million	Equity	106 million
			(10 million shares of stock)
Proceeds from debt issue (currently invested in bank)	4 million		
Total assets	$110 million	Debt plus equity	$110 million

Note that debt appears on the right-hand side of the balance sheet. The stock price is still $10.60, in accordance with our discussion of efficient capital markets.

Finally, the contractor receives $4 million and builds the plant. The market-value balance sheet becomes

LUTERAN MOTORS
Balance Sheet
(upon completion of the plant)

Old assets	$100 million	Debt	$ 4 million
PV of plant	10 million	Equity	106 million
			(10 million shares of stock)
Total assets	$110 million	Debt plus equity	$110 million

The only change here is that the bank account has been depleted to pay the contractor. The equityholders expect yearly cash flow after interest of

$$\underset{\substack{\text{Cash flow on}\\\text{old assets}}}{\$10,000,000} + \underset{\substack{\text{Cash flow on}\\\text{new assets}}}{\$1,000,000} - \underset{\substack{\text{Interest:}\\\$4 \text{ million} \times 6\%}}{\$240,000} = \$10,760,000$$

The equityholders expect to earn a return of

$$\frac{\$10,760,000}{\$106,000,000} = 10.15\%$$

This return of 10.15 percent for levered equityholders is higher than the 10 percent return for the unlevered equityholders. This result is sensible because, as we argued earlier, levered equity is riskier. In fact, the return of 10.15 percent should be exactly what MM Proposition II predicts. This prediction can be verified by plugging values into

$$r_S = r_0 + \frac{B}{S} \times (r_0 - r_B) \tag{15.3}$$

We obtain

$$10.15\% = 10\% + \frac{\$4,000,000}{\$106,000,000} \times (10\% - 6\%)$$

This example was useful for two reasons. First, we wanted to introduce the concept of market-value balance sheets, a tool that will prove useful elsewhere in the text. Among other things, this technique allows one to calculate the price per share of a new issue of stock. Second, the example illustrates three aspects of Modigliani and Miller:

1. The example is consistent with MM Proposition I because the value of the firm is $110 million after either equity or debt financing.
2. Students are often more interested in stock price than in firm value. We show that the stock price is always $10.60, regardless of whether debt or equity financing is used.
3. The example is consistent with MM Proposition II. The expected return to equityholders rises from 10 to 10.15 percent, just as formula (15.3) states. This rise occurs because the equityholders of a levered firm face more risk than do the equityholders of an unlevered firm.

MM: An Interpretation

The Modigliani-Miller results indicate that managers cannot change the value of a firm by repackaging the firm's securities. Though this idea was considered revolutionary when it was originally proposed in the late 1950s, the MM model and arbitrage proof have since met with wide acclaim.[10]

MM argue that the firm's overall cost of capital cannot be reduced as debt is substituted for equity, even though debt appears to be cheaper than equity. The reason for this is that as the firm adds debt, the remaining equity becomes more risky. As this risk rises, the cost of equity capital rises as a result. The increase in the cost of the remaining equity capital offsets the higher proportion of the firm financed by low-cost debt. In fact, MM prove that the two effects exactly offset each other, so that both the value of the firm and the firm's overall cost of capital are invariant to leverage.

MM use an interesting analogy to food. They consider a dairy farmer with two choices. On the one hand, he can sell whole milk. On the other hand, by skimming he can sell a combination of cream and low-fat milk. Though the farmer can get a high price for the cream, he gets a low price for the low-fat milk, implying no net gain. In fact, imagine that the proceeds from the whole-milk strategy were less than those from the cream–low-fat-milk strategy. Arbitrageurs would buy the whole milk, perform the skimming operation themselves, and

---

[10]Both Merton Miller and Franco Modigliani were awarded separate Nobel Prizes, in part for their work on capital structure.

IN THEIR OWN WORDS

In Professor Miller's Words . . .

The Modigliani-Miller results are not easy to understand fully. This point is related in a story told by Merton Miller.[11]

"How difficult it is to summarize briefly the contribution of the [Modigliani-Miller] papers was brought home to me very clearly last October after Franco Modigliani was awarded the Nobel Prize in Economics in part—but, of course, only in part—for the work in finance. The television camera crews from our local stations in Chicago immediately descended upon me. 'We understand,' they said, 'that you worked with Modigliani some years back in developing these M and M theorems and we wonder if you could explain them briefly to our television viewers.'

" 'How briefly?' I asked.

" 'Oh, take ten seconds,' was the reply.

"Ten seconds to explain the work of a lifetime! Ten seconds to describe two carefully reasoned articles, each running to more than thirty printed pages and each with sixty or so long footnotes! When they saw the look of dismay on my face, they said, 'You don't have to go into details. Just give us the main points in simple, common-sense terms.'

"The main point of the first or cost-of-capital article was, in principle at least, simple enough to make. It said that in an economist's ideal world of complete and perfect capital markets and with full and symmetric information among all market participants, the total market value of all the securities issued by a firm was governed by the earning power and risk of its underlying real assets and was independent of how the mix of securities issued to finance it was divided between debt instruments and equity capital. . . .

"Such a summary, however, uses too many shorthanded terms and concepts, like perfect capital markets, that are rich in connotations to economists but hardly so to the general public. So I thought, instead, of an analogy that we ourselves had invoked in the original paper. . . .

" 'Think of the firm,' I said, 'as a gigantic tub of whole milk. The farmer can sell the whole milk as is. Or he can separate out the cream and sell it at a considerably higher price than the whole milk would bring. (That's the analog of a firm selling low-yield and hence high-priced debt securities.) But, of course, what the farmer would have left would be skim milk with low butterfat content and that would sell for much less than whole milk. That corresponds to the levered equity. The M and M proposition says that if there were no costs of separation (and, of course, no government dairy support programs), the cream plus the skim milk would bring the same price as the whole milk.'

"The television people conferred among themselves and came back to inform me that it was too long, too complicated, and too academic.

" 'Don't you have anything simpler?' they asked. I thought of another way that the M and M proposition is presented these days, which emphasizes the notion of market completeness and stresses the role of securities as devices for 'partitioning' a firm's payoffs in each possible state of the world among the group of its capital suppliers.

" 'Think of the firm,' I said, 'as a gigantic pizza, divided into quarters. If now you cut each quarter in half into eighths, the M and M proposition says that you will have more pieces but not more pizza.'

"Again there was a whispered conference among the camera crew, and the director came back and said:

" 'Professor, we understand from the press release that there were two M and M propositions. Can we try the other one?' "

[Professor Miller tried valiantly to explain the second proposition, though this was apparently even more difficult to get across. After his attempt:]

"Once again there was a whispered conversation. They shut the lights off. They folded up their equipment. They thanked me for giving them the time. They said that they'd get back to me. But I knew that I had somehow lost my chance to start a new career as a packager of economic wisdom for TV viewers in convenient ten-second bites. Some have the talent for it . . . and some just don't."

resell the cream and low-fat milk separately. Competition between arbitrageurs would tend to boost the price of whole milk until proceeds from the two strategies became equal. Thus, the value of the farmer's milk is invariant to the way in which the milk is packaged.

Food found its way into this chapter earlier, when we viewed the firm as a pie. MM argue that the size of the pie does not change, no matter how stockholders and bondholders divide it. MM say that a firm's capital structure is irrelevant; it is what it is by some histor-

---

[11]Taken from *GSB Chicago,* University of Chicago (Autumn 1986).

SUMMARY OF MODIGLIANI-MILLER
PROPOSITIONS WITHOUT TAXES

Assumptions:
- No taxes
- No transaction costs
- Individuals and corporations borrow at same rate

Results:
Proposition I: $V_L = V_U$ (Value of levered firm equals value of unlevered firm)

Proposition II: $r_S = r_0 + \dfrac{B}{S}(r_0 - r_B)$

Intuition:
Proposition I: Through homemade leverage, individuals can either duplicate or undo the effects of corporate leverage.
Proposition II: The cost of equity rises with leverage, because the risk to equity rises with leverage.

ical accident. The theory implies that firms' debt-equity ratios could be anything. They are what they are because of whimsical and random managerial decisions about how much to borrow and how much stock to issue.

Although scholars are always fascinated with far-reaching theories, students are perhaps more concerned with real-world applications. Do real-world managers follow MM by treating capital-structure decisions with indifference? Unfortunately for the theory, virtually all companies in certain industries, such as banking, choose high debt-to-equity ratios. Conversely, companies in other industries, such as pharmaceuticals, choose low debt-to-equity ratios. In fact, almost any industry has a debt-to-equity ratio to which companies in that industry adhere. Thus, companies do not appear to be selecting their degree of leverage in a frivolous or random manner. Because of this, financial economists (including MM themselves) have argued that real-world factors may have been left out of the theory.

Though many of our students have argued that individuals can only borrow at rates above the corporate borrowing rate, we disagreed with this argument earlier in the chapter. But when we look elsewhere for unrealistic assumptions in the theory, we find two:[12]

1. Taxes were ignored.
2. Bankruptcy costs and other agency costs were not considered.

We turn to taxes in the next section. Bankruptcy costs and other agency costs will be treated in the next chapter. A summary of the main Modigliani-Miller results without taxes is presented in the accompanying boxed section.

QUESTIONS
CONCEPT
?

- Why does the expected return on equity rise with firm leverage?
- What is the exact relationship between the expected return on equity and firm leverage?
- How are market-value balance sheets set up?

---

[12]MM were aware of both of these issues, as can be seen in their original paper.

■ FIGURE 15.4   **Two Pie Models of Capital Structure under Corporate Taxes**

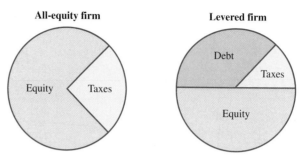

The levered firm pays less in taxes than does the all-equity firm.
Thus, the sum of the debt plus the equity of the levered firm is
greater than the equity of the unlevered firm.

15.5 TAXES

The Basic Insight

The previous part of this chapter showed that firm value is unrelated to debt in a world without taxes. We now show that, in the presence of corporate taxes, the firm's value is positively related to its debt. The basic intuition can be seen from a pie chart, such as the one in Figure 15.4. Consider the all-equity firm on the left. Here, both equityholders and the IRS have claims on the firm. The value of the all-equity firm is, of course, that part of the pie owned by the equityholders. The proportion going to taxes is simply a cost.

The pie on the right for the levered firm shows three claims: equityholders, debtholders, and taxes. The value of the levered firm is the sum of the value of the debt and the value of the equity. In selecting between the two capital structures in the picture, a financial manager should select the one with the higher value. Assuming that the total area is the same for both pies,[13] value is maximized for that capital structure paying the least in taxes. In other words, the manager should choose the capital structure that the IRS hates the most.

We will show that, due to a quirk in U.S. tax law, the proportion of the pie allocated to taxes is less for the levered firm than it is for the unlevered firm. Thus, managers should select high leverage.

The Quirk in the Tax Code

EXAMPLE

The Water Products Company has a corporate tax rate, T_C, of 35 percent and expected earnings before interest and taxes (EBIT) of $1 million each year. Its entire earnings after taxes are paid out as dividends.

The firm is considering two alternative capital structures. Under plan *I*, Water Products would have no debt in its capital structure. Under plan *II*, the company would have $4,000,000 of debt, *B*. The cost of debt, r_B, is 10 percent.

---

[13]Under the MM propositions developed earlier, the two pies should be of the same size.

The chief financial officer for Water Products makes the following calculations:

	Plan I	Plan II
Earnings before interest and corporate taxes (EBIT)	$1,000,000	$1,000,000
Interest ($r_B B$)	0	(400,000)
Earnings before taxes (EBT) = (EBIT − $r_B B$)	1,000,000	600,000
Taxes ($T_C = 0.35$)	(350,000)	(210,000)
Earnings after corporate taxes (EAT) = [(EBIT − $r_B B$) × (1 − T_C)]	650,000	390,000
Total cash flow to both stockholders and bondholders [EBIT × (1 − T_C) + $T_C r_B B$]	$ 650,000	$ 790,000

The most relevant numbers for our purposes are the two on the bottom line. Dividends, which are equal to earnings after taxes in this example, are the cash flow to stockholders, and interest is the cash flow to bondholders. Here, we see that more cash flow reaches the owners of the firm (both stockholders and bondholders) under plan *II*. The difference is $140,000 = $790,000 − $650,000. It does not take one long to realize the source of this difference. The IRS receives less taxes under plan *II* ($210,000) than it does under plan *I* ($350,000). The difference here is $140,000 = $350,000 − $210,000.

This difference[14] occurs because the IRS treats interest differently than it does earnings going to stockholders. Interest totally escapes corporate taxation, whereas earnings after interest but before corporate taxes (EBT) are taxed at the 35-percent rate.

Present Value of the Tax Shield

The discussion above shows a tax advantage to debt or, equivalently, a tax disadvantage to equity. We now want to value this advantage. The dollar interest is:

$$\text{Interest} = \underbrace{r_B}_{\text{Interest rate}} \times \underbrace{B}_{\text{Amount borrowed}}$$

This interest is $400,000 (10% × $4,000,000) for Water Products. All this interest is tax-deductible. That is, whatever the taxable income of Water Products would have been without the debt, the taxable income is now $400,000 *less* with the debt.

Because the corporate tax rate is 0.35 in our example, the reduction in corporate taxes is $140,000 (0.35 × $400,000). This number is identical to the reduction in corporate taxes calculated previously.

Algebraically, the reduction in corporate taxes is:

$$\underbrace{T_C}_{\text{Corporate tax rate}} \times \underbrace{r_B \times B}_{\text{Dollar amount of interest}} \tag{15.4}$$

---

[14]Note that stockholders actually receive more under plan *I* ($650,000) than under plan *II* ($390,000). Students are often bothered by this since it seems to imply that stockholders are better off without leverage. However, remember that there are more shares outstanding in plan *I* than in plan *II*. A full-blown model would show that earnings *per share* are higher with leverage.

That is, whatever the taxes that a firm would pay each year without debt, the firm will pay $T_C r_B B$ less with the debt of B. Expression (15.4) is often called the *tax shield from debt*. Note that it is an *annual* amount.

As long as the firm expects to be in a positive tax bracket, we can assume that the cash flow in expression (15.4) has the same risk as the interest on the debt. Thus, its value can be determined by discounting at the interest rate, r_B. Assuming that the cash flows are perpetual, the present value of the tax shield is

$$\frac{T_C r_B B}{r_B} = T_C B$$

Value of the Levered Firm

We have just calculated the present value of the tax shield from debt. Our next step is to calculate the value of the levered firm. The annual after-tax cash flow of an unlevered firm is

$$\text{EBIT} \times (1 - T_C),$$

where EBIT is earnings before interest and taxes. The value of an unlevered firm (that is, a firm with no debt) is the present value of $\text{EBIT} \times (1 - T_C)$,

$$V_U = \frac{\text{EBIT} \times (1 - T_C)}{r_0}$$

where

$$
\begin{aligned}
V_U &= \text{Present value of an unlevered firm} \\
\text{EBIT} \times (1 - T_C) &= \text{Firm cash flows after corporate taxes} \\
T_C &= \text{Corporate tax rate} \\
r_0 &= \text{The cost of capital to an all-equity firm. As can be seen from} \\
&\quad \text{the formula, } r_0 \text{ now discounts } \textit{after-tax} \text{ cash flows.}
\end{aligned}
$$

As shown previously, leverage increases the value of the firm by the tax shield, which is $T_C B$ for perpetual debt. Thus, we merely add this tax shield to the value of the unlevered firm to get the value of the levered firm.

We can write this algebraically as:[15]

MM Proposition I (corporate taxes):

$$V_L = \frac{\text{EBIT} \times (1 - T_C)}{r_0} + \frac{T_C r_B B}{r_B} \tag{15.5}$$

$$= V_U + T_C B$$

Equation (15.5) is MM Proposition I under corporate taxes. The first term in equation (15.5) is the value of the cash flows of the firm with no debt tax shield. In other words, this term is equal to V_U, the value of the all-equity firm. The value of the levered firm is the value of an all-equity firm plus $T_C B$, the tax rate times the value of the debt. $T_C B$ is the present value

---

[15]This relationship holds when the debt level is assumed to be constant through time. A different formula would apply if the debt-equity ratio was assumed to be a non-constant over time. For a deeper treatment of this point, see J. A. Miles and J. R. Ezzel, "The Weighted Average Cost of Capital, Perfect Capital Markets and Project Life," *Journal of Financial and Quantitative Analysis* (September 1980).

of the tax shield in the case of perpetual cash flows.[16] Because the tax shield increases with the amount of debt, the firm can raise its total cash flow and its value by substituting debt for equity.

EXAMPLE

Divided Airlines is currently an unlevered firm. The company expects to generate $153.85 in earnings before interest and taxes (EBIT), in perpetuity. The corporate tax rate is 35 percent, implying after-tax earnings of $100. All earnings after tax are paid out as dividends.

The firm is considering a capital restructuring to allow $200 of debt. Its cost of debt capital is 10 percent. Unlevered firms in the same industry have a cost of equity capital of 20 percent. What will the new value of Divided Airlines be?

The value of Divided Airlines will be equal to[17]

$$V_L = \frac{\text{EBIT} \times (1 - T_C)}{r_0} + T_C B$$
$$= \frac{\$100}{0.20} + (0.35 \times \$200)$$
$$= \$500 + \$70$$
$$= \$570$$

The value of the levered firm is $570, which is greater than the unlevered value of $500. Because $V_L = B + S$, the value of levered equity, S, is equal to $570 − $200 = $370. The value of Divided Airlines as a function of leverage is illustrated in Figure 15.5.

Expected Return and Leverage under Corporate Taxes

MM Proposition II under no taxes posits a positive relationship between the expected return on equity and leverage. This result occurs because the risk of equity increases with

---

[16]The following example calculates the present value if we assume the debt has a finite life. Suppose the Maxwell Company has $1 million in debt with an 8-percent coupon rate. If the debt matures in two years and the cost of debt capital, r_B, is 10 percent, what is the present value of the tax shields if the corporate tax rate is 35 percent? The debt is amortized in equal installments over two years.

Year	Loan Balance	Interest	Tax Shield	Present Value of Tax Shield
0	$1,000,000			
1	500,000	$80,000	0.35 × $80,000	$25,454.54
2	0	40,000	0.35 × $40,000	11,570.25
				$37,024.79

The present value of the tax savings is

$$\text{PV} = \frac{0.35 \times \$80,000}{1.10} + \frac{0.35 \times \$40,000}{(1.10)^2} = \$37,024.79$$

The Maxwell Company's value is higher than that of a comparable unlevered firm by $37,024.79.

[17]Note that, in a world with taxes, r_0 is used to discount *after-tax* cash flows.

■ FIGURE 15.5   The Effect of Financial Leverage on Firm Value: MM with Corporate Taxes in the Case of Divided Airlines

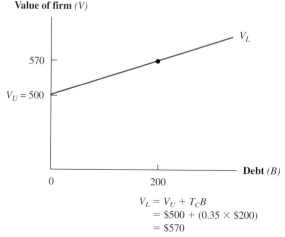

$$V_L = V_U + T_C B$$
$$= \$500 + (0.35 \times \$200)$$
$$= \$570$$

Debt reduces Divided's tax burden. As a result, the value of the firm is positively related to debt.

leverage. The same intuition also holds in a world of corporate taxes. The exact formula in a world of corporate taxes is[18]

MM Proposition II (corporate taxes):

$$r_S = r_0 + \frac{B}{S} \times (1 - T_C) \times (r_0 - r_B) \tag{15.6}$$

---

[18]This relationship can be shown as follows: Given MM Proposition I under taxes, a levered firm's market-value balance sheet can be written as

V_U = Value of unlevered firm	B = Debt
$T_C B$ = Tax shield	S = Equity

The value of the unlevered firm is simply the value of the assets without benefit of leverage. The balance sheet indicates that the firm's value increases by $T_C B$ when debt of B is added. The expected cash flow *from* the left-hand side of the balance sheet can be written as

$$V_U r_0 + T_C B r_B \tag{a}$$

Because assets are risky, their expected rate of return is r_0. The tax shield has the same risk as the debt, so its expected rate of return is r_B.

The expected cash *to* bondholders and stockholders together is

$$S r_S + B r_B \tag{b}$$

Expression (b) reflects the fact that stock earns an expected return of r_S and debt earns the interest rate r_B.

Because all cash flows are paid out as dividends in our no-growth perpetuity model, the cash flows going into the firm equal those going to stockholders. Hence (a) and (b) are equal:

$$S r_S + B r_B = V_U r_0 + T_C B r_B \tag{c}$$

Dividing both sides of (c) by S, subtracting $B r_B$ from both sides, and rearranging yields

$$r_S = \frac{V_U}{S} \times r_0 - (1 - T_C) \times \frac{B}{S} r_B \tag{d}$$

Because the value of the levered firm, V_L, equals $V_U + T_C B = B + S$, it follows that $V_U = S + (1 - T_C) \times B$. Thus, (d) can be rewritten as

$$r_S = \frac{S + (1 - T_C) \times B}{S} \times r_0 - (1 - T_C) \times \frac{B}{S} r_B \tag{e}$$

Bringing the terms involving $(1 - T_C) \times \frac{B}{S}$ together produces formula (15.6).

■ FIGURE 15.6 **The Effect of Financial Leverage on the Cost of Debt and Equity Capital**

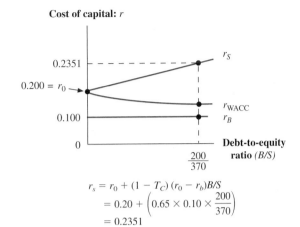

$$r_s = r_0 + (1 - T_C)(r_0 - r_b)B/S$$
$$= 0.20 + \left(0.65 \times 0.10 \times \frac{200}{370}\right)$$
$$= 0.2351$$

Financial leverage adds risk to the firm's equity. As compensation, the cost of equity rises with the firm's risk. Note that r_0 is a single point, while r_S, r_B, and r_{WACC} are all entire lines.

Applying the formula to Divided Airlines, we get

$$r_S = 0.2351 = 0.20 + \frac{200}{370} \times (1 - 0.35) \times (0.20 - 0.10)$$

This calculation is illustrated in Figure 15.6.

Whenever $r_0 > r_B$, r_S increases with leverage, a result that we also found in the no-tax case. As stated earlier in this chapter, r_0 should exceed r_B. That is, since equity (even unlevered equity) is risky, it should have an expected return greater than that on the less risky debt.

Let's check our calculations by determining the value of the levered equity in another way. The algebraic formula for the value of levered equity is

$$S = \frac{(\text{EBIT} - r_B B) \times (1 - T_C)}{r_S}$$

The numerator is the expected cash flow to levered equity after interest and taxes. The denominator is the rate at which the cash flow to equity is discounted.

For Divided Airlines we get[19]

$$\frac{(\$153.85 - 0.10 \times \$200)(1 - 0.35)}{0.2351} = \$370$$

the same result we obtained earlier.

The Weighted Average Cost of Capital r_{WACC} and Corporate Taxes

In Chapter 12, we defined the weighted average cost of capital (with corporate taxes) as

$$r_{WACC} = \frac{B}{V_L} r_B (1 - T_C) + \frac{S}{V_L} r_S$$

---

[19]The calculation suffers slightly from rounding error because we only carried the discount rate, 0.2351, out to four decimal places.

Note that the cost of debt capital, r_B, is multiplied by $(1 - T_C)$ because interest is tax-deductible at the corporate level. However, the cost of equity, r_S, is not multiplied by this factor because dividends are not deductible. In the no-tax case, r_{WACC} is not affected by leverage. This result is reflected in Figure 15.3, which we discussed earlier. However, since debt is tax-advantaged relative to equity, it can be shown that r_{WACC} declines with leverage in a world with corporate taxes. This result can be seen in Figure 15.6.

For Divided Airlines, r_{WACC} is equal to

$$r_{WACC} = \left(\frac{200}{570} \times 0.10 \times 0.65\right) + \left(\frac{370}{570} \times 0.2351\right)$$
$$= .1754$$

Divided Airlines has reduced its r_{WACC} from 0.20 (with no debt) to 0.1754 with reliance on debt. This result is intuitively pleasing because it suggests that, when a firm lowers its r_{WACC}, the firm's value will increase. Using the r_{WACC} approach, we can confirm that the value of Divided Airlines is $570.

$$V_L = \frac{\text{EBIT} \times (1 - T_C)}{r_{WACC}} = \frac{\$100}{.1754}$$
$$= \$570$$

Stock Price and Leverage under Corporate Taxes

At this point, students often believe the numbers—or at least are too intimidated to dispute them. However, they sometimes think we have asked the wrong question. "Why are we choosing to maximize the value of the firm?" they will say. "If managers are looking out for the stockholder's interest, why aren't they trying to maximize stock price?" If this question occurred to you, you have come to the right section.

Our response is twofold: First, we showed in the first section of this chapter that the capital structure that maximizes firm value is also the one that most benefits the interests of the stockholders.[20]

However, that general explanation is not always convincing to students. As a second procedure, we calculate the stock price of Divided Airlines both before and after the exchange of debt for stock. We do this by presenting a set of market-value balance sheets. The market-value balance sheet for the company in its all-equity form can be represented as

DIVIDED AIRLINES
Balance Sheet
(all-equity firm)

Physical assets: $\frac{\$153.85}{0.20} \times (1 - 0.35) = \$500$	Equity $500 (100 shares)

Assuming that there are 100 shares outstanding, each share is worth $5 = $500/100.

Next imagine that the company announces that, in the near future, it will issue $200 of debt to buy back $200 of stock. We know from our previous discussion that the value of the firm will rise to reflect the tax shield of debt. If we assume that capital markets efficiently price securities, the increase occurs immediately. That is, the rise occurs on the day of the announcement, not on the date of the debt-for-equity exchange. The market-value balance sheet now becomes

---

[20]At that time, we pointed out that this result may not exactly hold in the more complex case where debt has a significant possibility of default. Issues of default are treated in the next chapter.

DIVIDED AIRLINES
Balance Sheet
(upon announcement of debt issue)

Physical assets:	$500	Equity	$570
			(100 shares)
Present value of tax shield:			
$T_C B = 35\% \times \$200 =$	70		
Total Assets	$570		

Note that the debt has not yet been issued. Therefore, only equity appears on the right-hand side of the balance sheet. Each share is now worth $570/100 = $5.70, implying that the stockholders have benefited by $70. The equityholders gain because they are the owners of a firm that has improved its financial policy.

The introduction of the tax shield to the balance sheet is perplexing to many students. Although physical assets are tangible, the ethereal nature of the tax shield bothers these students. However, remember that an asset is any item with value. The tax shield has value because it reduces the stream of future taxes. The fact that one cannot touch the shield in the way that one can touch a physical asset is a philosophical, not a financial, consideration.

At some point, the exchange of debt for equity occurs. Debt of $200 is issued, and the proceeds are used to buy back shares. How many shares of stock are repurchased? Because shares are now selling at $5.70 each, the number of shares that the firm acquires is $200/$5.70 = 35.09. This leaves 64.91 (100 − 35.09) shares of stock outstanding. The market-value balance sheet is now

DIVIDED AIRLINES
Balance Sheet
(after exchange has taken place)

Physical assets:	$500	Equity	$370
		(100 − 35.09 = 64.91 shares)	
Present value of tax shield	70	Debt	200
Total assets	$570	Debt plus equity	$570

Each share of stock is worth $370/64.91 = $5.70 after the exchange. Notice that the stock price does not change on the exchange date. As we mentioned above, the stock price moves on the date of the announcement only. Because the shareholders participating in the exchange receive a price equal to the market price per share after the exchange, they do not care whether they exchange their stock or not.

This example was provided for two reasons. First, it shows that an increase in the value of the firm from debt financing leads to an increase in the price of the stock. In fact, the stockholders capture the entire $70 tax shield. Second, we wanted to provide more work with market-value balance sheets.

A summary of the main results of Modigliani-Miller with corporate taxes is presented in the accompanying boxed section.

CONCEPT QUESTIONS

- What is the quirk in the tax code making a levered firm more valuable than an otherwise identical unlevered firm?
- What is MM Proposition I under corporate taxes?
- What is MM Proposition II under corporate taxes?

SUMMARY OF MODIGLIANI-MILLER PROPOSITIONS WITH CORPORATE TAXES

Assumptions:
- Corporations are taxed at the rate T_C, on earnings after interest.
- No transaction costs.
- Individuals and corporations borrow at same rate.

Results:
Proposition I: $V_L = V_U + T_C B$
   (for a firm with perpetual debt)

Proposition II: $r_S = r_0 + \dfrac{B}{S}(1 - T_C)(r_0 - r_B)$

Intuition:
Proposition I: Since corporations can deduct interest payments but not dividend payments, corporate leverage lowers tax payments.
Proposition II: The cost of equity rises with leverage, because the risk to equity rises with leverage.

15.6 SUMMARY AND CONCLUSIONS

1. We began our discussion of the capital-structure decision by arguing that the particular capital structure that maximizes the value of the firm is also the one that provides the most benefit to the stockholders.

2. In a world of no taxes, the famous Proposition I of Modigliani and Miller proves that the value of the firm is unaffected by the debt-to-equity ratio. In other words, a firm's capital structure is a matter of indifference in that world. The authors obtain their results by showing that either a high or a low corporate ratio of debt to equity can be offset by homemade leverage. The result hinges on the assumption that individuals can borrow at the same rate as corporations, an assumption we believe to be quite plausible.

3. MM's Proposition II in a world without taxes states

$$r_S = r_0 + \frac{B}{S}(r_0 - r_B)$$

This implies that the expected rate of return on equity (also called the *cost of equity* or the *required return on equity*) is positively related to the firm's leverage. This makes intuitive sense, because the risk of equity rises with leverage, a point illustrated by the different sloped lines of Figure 15.2.

4. While the above work of MM is quite elegant, it does not explain the empirical findings on capital structure very well. MM imply that the capital-structure decision is a matter of indifference, while the decision appears to be a weighty one in the real world. To achieve real-world applicability, we next considered corporate taxes.

5. In a world with corporate taxes but no bankruptcy costs, firm value is an increasing function of leverage. The formula for the value of the firm is

$$V_L = V_U + T_C B$$

Expected return on levered equity can be expressed as

$$r_S = r_0 + (1 - T_C) \times (r_0 - r_B) \times \frac{B}{S}$$

Here, value is positively related to leverage. This result implies that firms should have a capital structure almost entirely composed of debt. Because real-world firms select more moderate levels of debt, the next chapter considers modifications to the results of this chapter.

KEY TERMS

MM Proposition I   396
MM Proposition II   399
MM Proposition I (corporate taxes)   410

MM Proposition II (corporate taxes)   412
Pie model   390

SUGGESTED READINGS

The classic papers by Modigliani and Miller are
Modigliani, F., and M. H. Miller. "The Cost of Capital, Corporation Finance, and the Theory of Investment." *American Economic Review* (June 1958).
Modigliani, F., and M. H. Miller. "Corporate Income Taxes and the Cost of Capital: A Correction." *American Economic Review* (June 1963).

A more recent perspective on the above papers is provided by
Miller, M. "The Modigliani-Miller Propositions after 30 Years" in D. Chew, ed., *The New Corporate Finance: Where Theory Meets Practice* (New York: McGraw-Hill, 1993).

QUESTIONS AND PROBLEMS

Capital Structure without Taxes

15.1 Nadus Corporation and Logis Corporation are identical in every way except their capital structures. Nadus Corporation, an all-equity firm, has 5,000 shares of stock outstanding; each share sells for $20. Logis Corporation uses leverage in its capital structure. The market value of Logis Corporation's debt is $25,000. Logis's cost of debt is 12 percent. Each firm is expected to have earnings before interest of $350,000. Neither firm pays taxes.

Suppose you want to purchase the same portion of the equity of each firm. Assume you can borrow money at 12 percent.

  a. What is the value of Nadus's stock?
  b. What is the value of Logis's stock?
  c. What will your costs and returns be if you buy 20 percent of each firm's equity?
  d. Which investment is riskier? Why?
  e. Construct an investment strategy for Nadus stock that replicates the investment returns of Logis stock.
  f. What is the value of Logis Corporation?
  g. If the value of Logis's assets is $135,000 and you can invest in up to 20 percent of the Logis stock, what should you do?

15.2 Acetate, Inc., has common stock with a market value of $20 million and debt with a market value of $10 million. The cost of the debt is 14 percent. The current Treasury-bill rate is 8 percent, and the expected market premium is 10 percent. The beta on Acetate's equity is 0.9.

  a. What is Acetate's debt-equity ratio?
  b. What is the firm's overall required return?

15.3 You invest $100,000 in the stock of the Liana Rope Company. To make the investment, you borrowed $75,000 from a friend at a cost of 10 percent. You expect your equity investment to return 20 percent. There are no taxes. What would your return be if you did not use leverage?

15.4 Levered, Inc., and Unlevered, Inc., are identical companies with identical business risk. Their earnings are perfectly correlated. Each company is expected to earn $96 million per year in perpetuity, and each company distributes all its earnings. Levered's debt has a market value of $275 million and provides a return of 8 percent. Levered's stock sells for $100 per share, and there are 4.5 million outstanding shares. Unlevered has only 10 million outstanding shares worth $80 each. Unlevered has no debt. There are no taxes. Which stock is a better investment?

15.5 The Veblen Company and the Knight Company are identical in every respect except that Veblen Company is not levered. The market value of Knight Company's 6-percent bonds is $1 million. The financial statistics for the two firms appear below. Neither firm pays taxes.

	Veblen	Knight
Net operating income	$ 300,000	$ 300,000
Interest on debt	0	60,000
Earnings available to common stock	$ 300,000	$ 240,000
Required return on equity	0.125	0.140
Market value of stock	$2,400,000	$1,714,000
Market value of debt	0	$1,000,000
Market value of the firm	$2,400,000	$2,714,000
Overall required return	0.125	0.110
Debt-equity ratio	0	0.584

a. An investor who is also able to borrow at 6 percent owns $10,000 worth of Knight stock. Can he increase his net return by borrowing money to buy Veblen stock? If so, show the strategy.

b. According to Modigliani and Miller, what kind of investors will attempt this strategy? When will the process cease?

15.6 No Lights At Wrigley, Inc. (NLAW), is a Hong Kong–based corporation that sells sunglasses. The firm pays no corporate taxes, and its shareholders pay no personal income taxes. NLAW currently has 100,000 shares outstanding worth $50 each; the firm has no debt.

Consider three stockholders of NLAW, Ms. *A*, Ms. *B*, and Ms. *C*. All three women have good access to capital markets, so they can lend and borrow at 20 percent, the same rate at which the firm lends and borrows. The value of their holdings and their overall borrowing and lending positions are listed below.

	Value of NLAW Shares	Total Borrowing	Total Lending
Ms. *A*	$10,000	$ 2,000	$ 0
Ms. *B*	50,000	0	6,000
Ms. *C*	20,000	0	0

NLAW desires a ratio of debt to total capital of 0.20. To meet that desire, suppose the firm issues $1 million in risk-free debt and uses the funds to repurchase 20,000 shares.

The three stockholders wish to keep the risk of their portfolios unchanged. Show the value of their holdings and their borrowing and lending positions after they have adjusted their portfolios.

15.7 Rayburn Manufacturing is currently an all-equity firm. The firm's equity is worth $2 million. The cost of that equity is 18 percent. Rayburn pays no taxes.

Rayburn plans to issue $400,000 in debt and to use the proceeds to repurchase stock. The cost of debt is 10 percent.

a. After Rayburn repurchases the stock, what will the firm's overall cost of capital be?

b. After the repurchase, what will the cost of equity be?

c. Explain your result in (*b*).

15.8 Strom, Inc., has 250,000 outstanding shares of stock that sell for $20 per share. Strom, Inc., currently has no debt. The appropriate discount rate for the firm is 15 percent. Strom's earnings last year were $750,000. The management expects that if no changes affect the assets of the firm, the earnings will remain $750,000 in perpetuity. Strom pays no taxes.

Strom plans to buy out a competitor's business at a cost of $300,000. Once added to Strom's current business, the competitor's facilities will generate earnings of $120,000 in perpetuity. The competitor has the same risk as Strom, Inc.

a. Construct the market-value balance sheet for Strom before the announcement of the buyout is made.

b. Suppose Strom uses equity to fund the buyout.

i. According to the efficient-market hypothesis, what will happen to Strom's price?

ii. Construct the market-value balance sheet as it will look after the announcement.

iii. How many shares did Strom sell?

iv. Once Strom sells the new shares of stock, how will its accounts look?

v. After the purchase is finalized, how will the market-value balance sheet look?

vi. What is the return to Strom's equityholders?

c. Suppose Strom uses 10-percent debt to fund the buyout.

i. Construct the market-value balance sheet as it will look after the announcement.

ii. Once Strom sells the bonds, how will its accounts look?

iii. What is the cost of equity?

iv. Explain any difference in the cost of equity between the two plans.

v. Use MM Proposition II to verify the answer in (*iii*).

15.9 The Gulf Power Company is an electric utility that is planning to build a new conventional power plant. The company has traditionally paid out all earnings to the stockholders as dividends, and has financed capital expenditures with new issues of common stock. There is no debt or preferred stock presently outstanding. Data on the company and the new power plant follow. Assume all earnings streams are perpetuities.

Company Data
Current annual earnings: $27 million
Number of outstanding shares: 10 million

New Power Plant
Initial outlay: $20 million
Added annual earnings: $3 million

Management considers the power plant to have the same risk as existing assets. The current required rate of return on equity is 10 percent. Assume there are no taxes and no costs of bankruptcy.

a. What will the total market value of Gulf Power be if common stock is issued to finance the plant?

b. What will the total market value of the firm be if $20 million in bonds with an interest rate of 8 percent are issued to finance the plant? Assume the bonds are perpetuities.

c. Suppose Gulf Power issues the bonds. Calculate the rate of return required by stockholders after the financing has occurred and the plant has been built.

15.10 Suppose there are no taxes, no transaction costs, and no costs of financial distress. In such a world, are the following statements true, false, or uncertain? Explain your answers.

   a. If a firm issues equity to repurchase some of its debt, the price of the remaining shares will rise because those shares are less risky.

   b. Moderate borrowing does not significantly affect the probability of financial distress or bankruptcy. Hence, moderate borrowing will not increase the required return on equity.

15.11 *a.* List the three assumptions that lie behind the Modigliani-Miller theory.

   b. *Briefly* explain the effect of each upon the conclusions of the theory for the real world.

15.12 The Digital Sound Corporation has 1 million shares of common stock outstanding at $10 per share. It is an all-equity firm. Susan Wang is CEO at Wang Finance Ltd. She wants to acquire a stake of 1 percent of the firm but has not decided among the three possible financing choices. She can borrow 20 percent, 40 percent, or 60 percent of the money she needs at a constant interest rate of 10 percent a year. The return on equity of the Digital Sound Corporation is 15 percent. Assume that she is in an MM no-tax world.

   a. How much dollar return can Susan expect to earn from her investment each year under each of the three financing alternatives, respectively?

   b. What are Susan's returns on equity on each financing choice, respectively?

   c. From parts (*a*) and (*b*), what inference can she draw about the return on equity of a leveraged firm?

15.13 Old Fashion Corp. is an all-equity firm famous for its antique furniture business. If the firm uses 36-percent leverage through issuance of long-term debt, the CFO predicts that there is a 20-percent chance that the ROE will be 10 percent, a 40-percent chance that the ROE will be 15 percent, and a 40-percent chance that the ROE will be 20 percent. The firm is tax exempt. Explain whether the firm should change its capital structure if the forecast of the CFO changes to 30-percent, 50-percent, and 20-percent chances, respectively, for the three ROE possibilities.

15.14 Sunrise Industries Corp. is planning to repurchase part of its common stock in the open market by issuing corporate debt. As a result, the debt-to-equity ratio is expected to rise from 40 percent to 50 percent. The annual interest payment on its outstanding debt amounts to $0.75 million with an interest rate at 10 percent. The expected earnings before interest are $3.75 million. There are no taxes in the country where Sunrise operates. (Treat the debt and earnings as perpetuities to simplify calculation.)

   a. What is the total value of Sunrise Industries Corp.?

   b. What is the expected return on equity before and after the announcement of the stock repurchase plan?

   c. How would the stock price change at the announcement of the repurchase?

Capital Structure with Corporate Taxes

15.15 The market value of a firm with $500,000 of debt is $1,700,000. EBIT is expected to be a perpetuity. The pretax interest rate on debt is 10 percent. The company is in the 34-percent tax bracket. If the company was 100-percent equity financed, the equityholders would require a 20-percent return.

   a. What would the value of the firm be if it was financed entirely with equity?

   b. What is the net income to the stockholders of this levered firm?

15.16 An all-equity firm is subject to a 30-percent corporate tax rate. Its equityholders require a 20-percent return. The firm's initial market value is $3,500,000, and there are 175,000 shares outstanding. The firm issues $1 million of bonds at 10 percent and uses the proceeds to repurchase common stock. Assume there is no change in the cost of financial distress for the firm. According to MM, what is the new market value of the equity of the firm?

15.17 Streiber Publishing Company, an all-equity firm, generates perpetual earnings before interest and taxes (EBIT) of $2.5 million per year. Streiber's after-tax, all-equity discount rate is 20 percent. The company's tax rate is 34 percent.

   a. What is the value of Streiber Publishing?

   b. If Streiber adjusts its capital structure to include $600,000 of debt, what is the value of the firm?

    c. Explain any difference in your answers.

    d. What assumptions are you making when you are valuing Streiber?

15.18 Olbet, Inc., is a nongrowth company in the 35-percent tax bracket. Olbet's perpetual EBIT is $1.2 million per annum. The firm's pretax cost of debt is 8 percent and its interest expense per year is $200,000. Company analysts estimate that the unlevered cost of Olbet's equity is 12 percent.

    a. What is the value of this firm?

    b. What does the calculation in (*a*) imply about the correct level of debt?

    c. Is the conclusion correct? Why or why not?

15.19 Green Manufacturing, Inc., plans to announce that it will issue $2,000,000 of perpetual bonds. The bonds will have a 6-percent coupon rate. Green Manufacturing currently is an all-equity firm. The value of Green's equity is $10,000,000 and there are 500,000 shares outstanding. After the sale of the bonds, Green will maintain the new capital structure indefinitely. The expected annual pretax earnings of Green are $1,500,000. Those earnings are also expected to remain constant into the foreseeable future. Green is in the 40-percent tax bracket.

    a. What is Green's current overall required return?

    b. Construct Green Manufacturing's market-value balance sheet as it looks before the announcement of the debt issue.

    c. What is the market-value balance sheet after the announcement?

    d. How many shares of stock will Green retire?

    e. What will the accounts show after the restructuring has taken place?

    f. What is Green's cost of equity after the capital restructuring?

15.20 The Nikko Company has perpetual EBIT of $4 million per year. The after-tax, all-equity discount rate r_0 is 15 percent. The company's tax rate is 35 percent. The cost of debt capital is 10 percent, and Nikko has $10 million of debt in its capital structure.

    a. What is Nikko's value?

    b. What is Nikko's r_{WACC}?

    c. What is Nikko's cost of equity?

15.21 AT&B has a debt-equity ratio of 2.5. Its r_{WACC} is 15 percent and its cost of debt is 11 percent. The corporate tax rate is 35 percent.

    a. What is AT&B's cost of equity capital?

    b. What is AT&B's unlevered cost of equity capital?

    c. What would the weighted average cost of capital be if the debt-to-equity ratio was .75? What if it were 1.5?

15.22 General Tools (GT) expects EBIT to be $100,000 every year, in perpetuity. The firm can borrow at 10 percent. GT currently has no debt. Its cost of equity is 25 percent. If the corporate tax rate is 40 percent, what is the value of the firm? What will the value be if GT borrows $500,000 and uses the proceeds to repurchase shares?

15.23 Eureka Space Technology Group (an all-equity firm) is announcing a $100 million R&D project, which is expected to drastically improve its satellite launching technology by reducing its annual launching costs from $500 million to $475 million. The firm can finance the project through either retained earnings or a new bond issue. The firm's cost of equity capital is 12.5 percent. The prevailing market rate of interest for comparable corporate bonds is 8 percent. Currently, the firm has 15 million shares of stock outstanding at $32.5 a share. The firm has sufficient earnings to fully utilize the corporate tax shield if the project is debt financed. Assume the relevant marginal corporate tax rate is 35 percent.

    a. Which financing method, retained earnings or external debt financing, would you recommend to the management and why?

    b. What is the resulting PV of the firm from each of these two financing methods?

    c. What do you expect will be the stock market stock price response to the two different methods?

    d. Explain the intuition behind the results in part (*c*).

CHAPTER 16

Capital Structure: Limits to the Use of Debt

EXECUTIVE SUMMARY

One question a student might ask is, "Does the MM theory with taxes predict the capital structure of typical firms?" The answer is, unfortunately, "no." The theory states that $V_L = V_U + T_C B$. According to this equation, one can always increase firm value by increasing leverage, implying that firms should issue maximum debt. This is inconsistent with the real world, where firms generally employ only moderate amounts of debt.

However, the MM theory tells us *where to look* when searching for the determinants of capital structure. For example, the theory ignores bankruptcy and its attendant costs. Because these costs are likely to get out of hand for a highly levered firm, the moderate leverage of most firms can now easily be explained. Our discussion leads quite naturally to the idea that a firm's capital structure can be thought of as a trade-off between the tax benefits of debt and the costs of financial distress and bankruptcy. This trade-off of benefits and costs leads to an optimum amount of debt.

In addition, the MM theory ignores personal taxes. In the real world, the *personal* tax rate on interest is higher than the *effective* personal tax rate on equity distributions. Thus, the personal tax penalties to bondholders tend to offset the tax benefits to debt at the corporate level. Even when bankruptcy costs are ignored, this idea can be shown to imply that there is an optimal amount of debt for the economy as a whole. The implications of bankruptcy costs and personal taxes are examined in this chapter.

16.1 COSTS OF FINANCIAL DISTRESS

Bankruptcy Risk or Bankruptcy Cost?

As mentioned throughout the previous chapter, debt provides tax benefits to the firm. However, debt puts pressure on the firm, because interest and principal payments are obligations. If these obligations are not met, the firm may risk some sort of financial distress. The ultimate distress is *bankruptcy,* where ownership of the firm's assets is legally transferred from the stockholders to the bondholders. These debt obligations are fundamentally different from stock obligations. While stockholders like and expect dividends, they are not legally entitled to dividends in the way bondholders are legally entitled to interest and principal payments.

We show below that bankruptcy costs, or more generally financial distress costs, tend to offset the advantages to debt. We begin by positing a simple example of bankruptcy. All taxes are ignored to focus only on the costs of debt.

EXAMPLE

The Knight Corporation plans to be in business for one more year. It forecasts a cash flow of either $100 or $50 in the coming year, each occurring with 50-percent probability. The firm has no other assets. Previously issued debt requires payments of $49 of interest and principal. The Day Corporation has identical cash flow prospects but has $60 of interest and principal obligations. The cash flows of these two firms can be represented as

	Knight Corporation		Day Corporation	
	Boom Times (prob. 50%)	Recession (prob. 50%)	Boom Times (prob. 50%)	Recession (prob. 50%)
Cash flow	$100	$50	$100	$50
Payment of interest and principal on debt	49	49	60	50
Distribution to stockholders	$ 51	$ 1	$ 40	$ 0

For Knight Corporation in both boom times and recession and for Day Corporation in boom times, cash flow exceeds interest and principal payments. In these situations, the bondholders are paid in full and the stockholders receive any residual. However, the most interesting of the four columns involves Day Corporation in a recession. Here, the bondholders are owed $60, but the firm has only $50 in cash. Since we assumed that the firm has no other assets, the bondholders cannot be satisfied in full. If bankruptcy occurs, the bondholders will receive all of the firm's cash, and the stockholders will receive nothing. Importantly, the stockholders do not have to come up with the additional $10 (= $60 − $50). Corporations have limited liability in America and most other countries, implying that bondholders cannot sue the stockholders for the extra $10.[1]

We assume that (1) both bondholders and stockholders are risk-neutral and (2) the interest rate is 10 percent. Due to this risk neutrality, cash flows to both stockholders and bondholders are to be discounted at the 10-percent rate.[2] We can evaluate the debt, the equity, and the entire firm for both Knight and Day as follows:

$$S_{\text{KNIGHT}} = \$23.64 = \frac{\$51 \times \frac{1}{2} + \$1 \times \frac{1}{2}}{1.10} \qquad S_{\text{DAY}} = \$18.18 = \frac{\$40 \times \frac{1}{2} + 0 \times \frac{1}{2}}{1.10}$$

$$B_{\text{KNIGHT}} = \$44.54 = \frac{\$49 \times \frac{1}{2} + \$49 \times \frac{1}{2}}{1.10} \qquad B_{\text{DAY}} = \$50 \quad = \frac{\$60 \times \frac{1}{2} + \$50 \times \frac{1}{2}}{1.10}$$

$$V_{\text{KNIGHT}} = \$68.18 \qquad\qquad V_{\text{DAY}} = \$68.18$$

Note that the two firms have the same value, even though Day runs the risk of bankruptcy. Furthermore, notice that Day's bondholders are valuing the bonds with their eyes open. Though the promised payment of principal and interest is

---

[1]There are situations where the limited liability of corporation can be "pierced." Typically, fraud or misrepresentation must be present.

[2]Normally, one assumes that investors are *averse* to risk. In that case, the cost of debt capital, r_B, is less than the cost of equity capital, r_S, which rises with leverage as shown in the previous chapter. In addition, r_B may rise when the increase in leverage allows the possibility of default.

For simplicity, we assume *risk neutrality* in this example. This means that investors are indifferent to whether risk is high, low, or even absent. Here, $r_S = r_B$, because risk-neutral investors do not demand compensation for bearing risk. In addition, neither r_S nor r_B rises with leverage. Because the interest rate is 10 percent, our assumption of risk neutrality implies that $r_S = 10\%$ as well.

Though financial economists believe that investors are risk-averse, they frequently develop examples based on risk-neutrality to isolate a point unrelated to risk. This is our approach, because we want to focus on bankruptcy costs—not bankruptcy risk. The same qualitative conclusions from this example can be drawn in a world of risk aversion, albeit with *much* more difficulty for the reader.

$60, the bondholders are willing to pay only $50. Hence, their *promised* return or yield is

$$\frac{\$60}{\$50} - 1 = 20\%$$

Day's debt can be viewed as a *junk bond,* because the probability of default is so high. As with all junk bonds, bondholders demand a high promised yield.

Day's example is not realistic because it ignores an important cash flow to be discussed below. A more realistic set of numbers might be

DAY CORPORATION

	Boom times (prob. 50%)	Recession (prob. 50%)	
Earnings	$100	$50	$S_{DAY} = \$18.18 = \dfrac{\$40 \times \frac{1}{2} + 0 \times \frac{1}{2}}{1.10}$
Debt repayment	60	35	$B_{DAY} = \$43.18 = \dfrac{\$60 \times \frac{1}{2} + \$35 \times \frac{1}{2}}{1.10}$
Distribution to stockholders	$ 40	$ 0	$V_{DAY} = \$61.36$

Why do the bondholders receive only $35 in a recession? If cash flow is only $50, bondholders will be informed that they will not be paid in full. These bondholders are likely to hire lawyers to negotiate or even to sue the company. Similarly, the firm is likely to hire lawyers to defend itself. Further costs will be incurred if the case gets to a bankruptcy court. These fees are always paid before the bondholders get paid. In this example, we are assuming that bankruptcy costs total $15 ($50 − 35).

The value of the firm is now $61.36, an amount below the $68.18 figure calculated earlier. By comparing Day's value in a world with no bankruptcy costs to Day's value in a world with these costs, we conclude

> The possibility of bankruptcy has a negative effect on the value of the firm. However, it is not the *risk* of bankruptcy itself that lowers value. Rather it is the *costs* associated with bankruptcy that lower value.

The explanation follows from our pie example. In a world without bankruptcy costs, the bondholders and the stockholders share the entire pie. However, bankruptcy costs eat up some of the pie in the real world, leaving less for the stockholders and bondholders.

Because the bondholders are aware that they would receive little in a recession, they pay a low price. In this case, their promised return is

$$\frac{\$60}{\$43.18} - 1 = 39.0\%$$

The bondholders are paying a fair price if they are realistic about both the probability and the cost of bankruptcy. It is the *stockholders* who bear these future bankruptcy costs. To see this, imagine that Day Corporation was originally all equity. The stockholders want the firm to issue debt with a promised payment of $60 and use the proceeds to pay a dividend. If there had been no bankruptcy costs, our results show that bondholders would pay $50 to purchase debt with a promised payment of $60. Hence, a dividend of $50 could be paid to the stockholders. However, if bankruptcy costs exist, bondholders would only pay $43.18 for the debt. In that case, only a dividend of $43.18 could be paid to the stockholders. Because the dividend is smaller when bankruptcy costs exist, the stockholders are hurt by bankruptcy costs.

CONCEPT QUESTIONS

?

- What does risk neutrality mean?
- Can one have bankruptcy risk without bankruptcy costs?
- Why do we say that stockholders bear bankruptcy costs?

16.2 DESCRIPTION OF COSTS

The preceding example showed that bankruptcy costs can lower the value of the firm. In fact, the same general result holds even if a legal bankruptcy is prevented. Thus, *financial distress costs* may be a better phrase than *bankruptcy costs*. It is worthwhile to describe these costs in more detail.

Direct Costs of Financial Distress: Legal and Administrative Costs of Liquidation or Reorganization

As mentioned earlier, lawyers are involved throughout all the stages before and during bankruptcy. With fees often in the hundreds of dollars an hour, these costs can add up quickly. A wag once remarked that bankruptcies are to lawyers what blood is to sharks. In addition, administrative and accounting fees can substantially add to the total bill. And if a trial takes place, we must not forget expert witnesses. Each side may hire a number of these witnesses to testify about the fairness of a proposed settlement. Their fees can easily rival those of lawyers or accountants. (However, we personally look upon these witnesses more kindly, because they are frequently drawn from the ranks of finance professors.)

Perhaps one of the most well-publicized bankruptcies in recent years concerned a municipality, Orange County, California, not a corporation. This bankruptcy followed large bond-trading losses in the county's financial portfolio. The Los Angeles Times stated:

> Orange County taxpayers lost $1.69 billion, and their government, one year ago today, sank into bankruptcy. Now they are spending millions more to get out of it.
>
> Accountants pore over fiscal ledgers at $325 an hour. Lawyers toil into the night—at $385 an hour. Financial advisors from one of the nation's most prominent investment houses labor for the taxpayers at $150,000 a month. Clerks stand by the photocopy machines, running up bills that sometimes exceed $3,000.
>
> Total so far: $29 million. And it's nowhere near over.
>
> The multi-pronged effort to lift Orange County out of the nation's worst municipal bankruptcy has become a money-eating machine, gobbling up taxpayer funds at a rate of $2.4 million a month. That's $115,000 a day.
>
> County administrators are not alarmed.
>
> They say Orange County's bankruptcy was an epic disaster that will require equally dramatic expenditures of taxpayer cash to help it survive. While they have refused to pay several thousand dollars worth of claimed expenses—lavish dinners, big hotel bills—they have rarely questioned the sky-high hourly fees. They predict the costs could climb much higher.
>
> Indeed, participants in the county's investment pool have agreed to create a separate $50 million fund to pay the costs of doing legal battle with Wall Street.[3]

---

[3]"The High Cost of Going Bankrupt," *Los Angeles Times Orange County Edition,* December 6, 1995. Taken from Lexis/Nexis.

A number of academic studies have measured the direct costs of financial distress. While large in absolute amount, these costs are actually small as a percentage of firm value. White, Altman, and Weiss estimate the direct costs of financial distress to be about 3 percent of the market value of the firm.[4] In a study of direct financial distress costs of 20 railroad bankruptcies, Warner finds that net financial distress costs were, on average, 1 percent of the market value of the firm seven years before bankruptcy and were somewhat larger percentages as bankruptcy approached (for example, 2.5 percent of the market value of the firm three years before bankruptcy).[5] Of course, few firms end up in bankruptcy. Thus, the preceding cost estimates must be multiplied by the probability of bankruptcy to yield the *expected* cost of bankruptcy. Warner states:

> Suppose, for example, that a given railroad picks a level of debt such that bankruptcy would occur on average once every 20 years (i.e., the probability of going bankrupt is 5 percent in any given year). Assume that when bankruptcy occurs, the firm would pay a lump sum penalty equal to 3 percent of its now current market value. . . .
>
> [Then], the firm's expected cost of bankruptcy is equal to fifteen one-hundredths of one percent of its now current market value.

Indirect Costs of Financial Distress

Impaired Ability to Conduct Business   Bankruptcy hampers conduct with customers and suppliers. Sales are frequently lost because of both fear of impaired service and loss of trust. For example, many loyal Chrysler customers switched to other manufacturers when Chrysler skirted insolvency in the 1970s. These buyers questioned whether parts and servicing would be available were Chrysler to fail. Sometimes the taint of impending bankruptcy is enough to drive customers away. For example, gamblers avoided Atlantis casino in Atlantic City after it became technically insolvent. Gamblers are a superstitious bunch. Many reasoned, "If the casino itself cannot make money, how can I expect to make money there?" A particularly outrageous story concerned two unrelated stores both named Mitchells in New York City. When one Mitchells declared bankruptcy, customers stayed away from both stores. In time, the second store was forced to declare bankruptcy as well.

Though these costs clearly exist, it is quite difficult to measure them. Altman estimates that both direct and indirect costs of financial distress are frequently greater than 20 percent of firm value.[6] Andrade and Kaplan[7] estimate total distress costs to be between 10 percent and

---

[4]M. J. White, "Bankruptcy Costs and the New Bankruptcy Code," *Journal of Finance* (May 1983); and E. I. Altman, " A Further Empirical Investigation of the Bankruptcy Cost Question," *Journal of Finance* (September 1984). More recently, Lawrence A. Weiss, "Bankruptcy Resolution: Direct Costs and Violation of Priority of Claims," *Journal of Financial Economics* 27 (1990), estimates that direct costs of bankruptcy are 3.1 percent of the value of the firm.

[5]J. B. Warner, "Bankruptcy Costs: Some Evidence," *Journal of Finance* (May 1977).

[6]Altman, op. cit. "A Further Empirical Investigation."

A fascinating and provacative set of articles by Robert Haugen and Lemma Senbet ("The Insignificance of Bankruptcy Costs to the Theory of Optimal Capital Structure." *Journal of Finance* (May 1978); "New Perspectives on Information Asymmetry and Agency Relationships." *Journal of Financial and Quantitative Analysis* (November 1979); "Bankruptcy and Agency Costs: Their Significance to the Theory of Optimal Capital Structure," *Journal of Financial and Quantitative Analysis* (March 1988)) argue that financial distress should, at most, only slightly impair the firm's ability to conduct business. They say that customers, employees, and so on, are concerned with the tenure of the *firm,* which is fundamentally a function of its asset characteristics. This tenure should not be dependent on the way the assets are financed.

[7]Gregor Andrade and Steven N. Kaplan, "How Costly is Financial (Not Economic) Distress? Evidence from Highly Leveraged Transactions that Became Distressed," *Journal of Finance* (October 1998).

20 percent of firm value. Bar-Or[8] estimates expected future distress costs for firms that are currently healthy to be 8 to 10 percent of operating value, a number below the estimates of either Altman or Andrade and Kaplan. However, unlike Bar-Or, these authors consider distress costs for firms already in distress, not expected distress costs for currently healthy firms.

Cutler and Summers[9] examine the costs of the well-publicized Texaco bankruptcy. In January of 1984, Pennzoil reached what it believed to be a binding agreement to acquire three-sevenths of Getty Oil. However, less than a week later, Texaco acquired all of Getty at a higher per-share price. Pennzoil then sued Getty for breach of contract. Because Texaco had previously indemnified Getty against litigation, Texaco became liable for damages.

In November 1985, the Texas State Court awarded damages of $12 billion to Pennzoil, although this amount was later reduced. As a result, Texaco filed for bankruptcy. Cutler and Summers identify nine important events over the course of the litigation. They find that Texaco's market value (stock price times number of shares outstanding) fell a cumulative $4.1 billion over these events, whereas Pennzoil rose only $682 million. Thus, Pennzoil gained about one-sixth of what Texaco lost, resulting in a net loss to the two firms of almost $3½ billion.

What could explain this net loss? Cutler and Summers suggest that it is likely due to costs that Texaco and Pennzoil incurred from the litigation and subsequent bankruptcy. The authors argue that direct bankruptcy fees represent only a small part of these costs, estimating Texaco's after-tax legal expenses to be about $165 million. Legal costs to Pennzoil were more difficult to assess, because Pennzoil's lead lawyer, Joe Jamail, stated publicly that he had no set fee. However, using a clever statistical analysis, the authors estimate his fee to be about $200 million. Thus, one must search elsewhere for the bulk of the costs.

Indirect costs of financial distress may be the culprit here. An affidavit by Texaco stated that, following the lawsuit, some of its suppliers were demanding cash payment. Other suppliers halted or canceled shipments of crude oil. Certain banks restricted Texaco's use of futures contracts on foreign exchange. The affidavit stressed that these constraints were reducing Texaco's ability to run its business, leading to deterioration of its financial condition. Could these sorts of indirect costs explain the $3½ billion disparity between Texaco's drop and Pennzoil's rise in market value? Unfortunately, although it is quite likely that indirect costs play a role here, there is simply no way to obtain a decent, quantitative estimate for them.

Agency Costs

When a firm has debt, conflicts of interest arise between stockholders and bondholders. Because of this, stockholders are tempted to pursue selfish strategies. These conflicts of interest, which are magnified when financial distress is incurred, impose **agency costs** on the firm. We describe three kinds of selfish strategies that stockholders use to hurt the bondholders and help themselves. These strategies are costly because they will lower the market value of the whole firm.

Selfish Investment Strategy 1: *Incentive to Take Large Risks*   Firms near bankruptcy oftentimes takes great chances, because they believe that they are playing with someone else's money. To see this, imagine a levered firm considering two *mutually exclusive* projects, a low-risk one and a high-risk one. There are two equally likely outcomes, recession and boom. The firm is in such dire straits that should a recession hit, it will come near to bankruptcy with one project and actually fall into bankruptcy with the other. The cash flows for the entire firm if the low-risk project is taken can be described as

---

[8]Yuval Bar-Or, "An Investigation of Expected Financial Distress Costs," unpublished paper, Wharton School, University of Pennsylvania (March 2000).

[9]David M. Cutler and Lawrence H. Summers, "The Costs of Conflict Resolution and Financial Distress: Evidence from the Texaco-Pennzoil Litigation," *Rand Journal of Economics* (Summer 1988).

Value of Entire Firm if Low-Risk Project Is Chosen

	Probability	Value of Firm	=	Stock	+	Bonds
Recession	0.5	$100	=	$ 0	+	$100
Boom	0.5	200	=	100	+	100

If recession occurs, the value of the firm will be $100, and if boom obtains, the value of the firm will be $200. The expected value of the firm is $150 (0.5 × $100 + 0.5 × $200).

The firm has promised to pay bondholders $100. Shareholders will obtain the difference between the total payoff and the amount paid to the bondholders. In other words, the bondholders have the prior claim on the payoffs, and the shareholders have the residual claim.

Now suppose that another, riskier project can be substituted for the low-risk project. The payoffs and probabilities are as follows:

Value of Entire Firm if High-Risk Project Is Chosen

	Probability	Value of Firm	=	Stock	+	Bonds
Recession	0.5	$ 50	=	$ 0	+	$ 50
Boom	0.5	240	=	140	+	100

The expected value of the *firm* is $145 (0.5 × $50 + 0.5 × $240), which is lower than the expected value of the firm with the low-risk project. Thus, the low-risk project would be accepted if the firm were all equity. However, note that the expected value of the *stock* is $70 (0.5 × 0 + 0.5 × $140) with the high-risk project, but only $50 (0.5 × 0 + 0.5 × $100) with the low-risk project. Given the firm's present levered state, stockholders will select the high-risk project.

The key is that, relative to the low-risk project, the high-risk project increases firm value in a boom and decreases firm value in a recession. The increase in value in a boom is captured by the stockholders, because the bondholders are paid in full (they receive $100) regardless of which project is accepted. Conversely, the drop in value in a recession is lost by the bondholders, because they are paid in full with the low-risk project but receive only $50 with the high-risk one. The stockholders will receive nothing in a recession anyway, whether the high-risk or low-risk project is selected. Thus, financial economists argue that stockholders expropriate value from the bondholders by selecting high-risk projects.

A story, perhaps apocryphal, illustrates this idea. It seems that Federal Express was near financial collapse within a few years of its inception. The founder, Frederick Smith, took $20,000 of corporate funds to Las Vegas in despair. He won at the gaming tables, providing enough capital to allow the firm to survive. Had he lost, the banks would simply have received $20,000 less when the firm reached bankruptcy.

Selfish Investment Strategy 2: *Incentive toward Underinvestment*   Stockholders of a firm with a significant probability of bankruptcy often find that new investment helps the bondholders at the stockholders' expense. The simplest case might be a real estate owner facing imminent bankruptcy. If he took $100,000 out of his own pocket to refurbish the building, he could increase the building's value by, say, $150,000. Though this investment has a positive net present value, he will turn it down if the increase in value cannot prevent bankruptcy. "Why," he asks, "should I use my own funds to improve the value of a building that the bank will soon repossess?"

This idea is formalized by the following simple example. Consider a firm with $4,000 of principal and interest payments due at the end of the year. It will be pulled into bankruptcy by a recession because its cash flows will be only $2,400 in that state. The firm's

■ TABLE 16.1   **Example Illustrating Incentive to Underinvest**

	Firm without Project		Firm with Project	
	Boom	Recession	Boom	Recession
Firm cash flows	$5,000	$2,400	$6,700	$4,100
Bondholders' claim	4,000	2,400	4,000	4,000
Stockholders' claim	$1,000	$ 0	$2,700	$ 100

The project has positive NPV. However, much of its value is captured by bondholders. Rational managers, acting in the stockholders' interest, will reject the project.

cash flows are presented in the left-hand side of Table 16.1. The firm could avoid bankruptcy in a recession by raising new equity to invest in a new project. The project costs $1,000 and brings in $1,700 in either state, implying a positive net present value. Clearly it would be accepted in an all-equity firm.

However, the project hurts the stockholders of the levered firm. To see this, imagine the old stockholders contribute the $1,000 *themselves.*[10] The expected value of the stockholders' interest without the project is $500 ($0.5 \times \$1,000 + 0.5 \times 0$). The expected value with the project is $1,400 ($0.5 \times \$2,700 + 0.5 \times \$100$). The stockholders' interest rises by only $900 ($\$1,400 - \$500$) while costing $1,000.

The key is that the stockholders contribute the full $1,000 investment, but the stockholders and bondholders *share* the benefits. The stockholders take the entire gain if boom times occur. Conversely, the bondholders reap most of the cash flow from the project in a recession.

The discussion of selfish strategy 1 is quite similar to the discussion of selfish strategy 2. In both cases, an investment strategy for the levered firm is different from the one for the unlevered firm. Thus, leverage results in distorted investment policy. Whereas the unlevered corporation always chooses projects with positive net present value, the levered firm may deviate from this policy.

Selfish Investment Strategy 3: *Milking the Property*   Another strategy is to pay out extra dividends or other distributions in times of financial distress, leaving less in the firm for the bondholders. This is known as *milking the property,* a phrase taken from real estate. Strategies 2 and 3 are very similar. In strategy 2, the firm chooses not to raise new equity. Strategy 3 goes one step further, because equity is actually withdrawn through the dividend.

Summary of Selfish Strategies   The above distortions occur only when there is a probability of bankruptcy or financial distress. Thus, these distortions *should not* affect, say, General Electric because bankruptcy is not a realistic possibility for a diversified blue-chip firm such as this. In other words, General Electric's debt will be virtually risk-free, regardless of the projects it accepts. The same argument could be made for regulated companies that are protected by state utility commissions. However, firms such as Intel or Intuit might be very much affected by these distortions. Both Intel and Intuit are firms with significant potential future investment opportunities as compared to assets in place and both firms face intense competition and uncertain future revenues. Because the distortions are related to financial distress, we have included them in our discussion of the "Indirect Costs of Financial Distress."

---

[10]The same qualitative results will obtain if the $1,000 is raised from new stockholders. However, the arithmetic becomes much more difficult since we must determine how many new shares are issued.

Who pays for the cost of selfish investment strategies? We argue that it is ultimately the stockholders. Rational bondholders know that, when financial distress is imminent, they cannot expect help from stockholders. Rather, stockholders are likely to choose investment strategies that reduce the value of the bonds. Bondholders protect themselves accordingly by raising the interest rate that they require on the bonds. Because the stockholders must pay these high rates, they ultimately bear the costs of selfish strategies. The relationship between stockholders and bondholders is very similar to the relationship between Erroll Flynn and David Niven, good friends and movie stars in the 1930s. Niven reportedly said that the good thing about Flynn was that you knew exactly where you stood with him. When you needed his help, you could always count on him to let you down.

For firms that face these distortions, debt will be difficult and costly to obtain. These firms will have low leverage ratios.

QUESTIONS
CONCEPT
?

- What is the main direct cost of financial distress?
- What are the indirect costs of financial distress?
- Who pays the costs of selfish strategies?

16.3 CAN COSTS OF DEBT BE REDUCED?

As U.S. senators are prone to say, "A billion here, a billion there. Pretty soon it all adds up."[11] Each of the costs of financial distress we mentioned above is substantial in its own right. The sum of them may well affect debt financing severely. Thus, managers have an incentive to reduce these costs. We now turn to some of their methods. However, it should be mentioned at the outset that the methods below can, at most, reduce the costs of debt. They cannot *eliminate* them entirely.

Protective Covenants

Because the stockholders must pay higher interest rates as insurance against their own selfish strategies, they frequently make agreements with bondholders in hopes of lower rates. These agreements, called **protective covenants,** are incorporated as part of the loan document (or *indenture*) between stockholders and bondholders. The covenants must be taken seriously since a broken covenant can lead to default. Protective covenants can be classified into two types: negative covenants and positive covenants.

A **negative covenant** limits or prohibits actions that the company may take. Here are some typical negative covenants:

1. Limitations are placed on the amount of dividends a company may pay.
2. The firm may not pledge any of its assets to other lenders.
3. The firm may not merge with another firm.
4. The firm may not sell or lease its major assets without approval by the lender.
5. The firm may not issue additional long-term debt.

---

[11]The original quote is generally attributed to Senator Everett Dirksen. In the 1950s, he reportedly said, "A *million* here, a *million* there. Pretty soon it all adds up." Government spending has increased since that time.

■ TABLE 16.2 **Loan Covenants**

Covenant Type	Shareholder Action or Firm Circumstances	Reason for Covenant

Financial-statement signals
  1. Working capital requirement
  2. Interest coverage
  3. Minimum net worth
	As firm approaches financial distress, shareholders may want firm to make high-risk investments.	Shareholders lose value before bankruptcy; bondholders are hurt much more in bankruptcy than shareholders (limited liability); bondholders are hurt by *distortion of investment that leads to increases in risk.*

Restrictions on asset disposition
  1. Limit dividends
  2. Limit sale of assets
  3. Collateral and mortgages
	Shareholders attempt to transfer corporate assets to themselves.	This limits the ability of shareholders to transfer assets to themselves and to *underinvest.*

Restrictions on switching assets	Shareholders attempt to increase risk of firm.	Increased firm risk helps shareholders; bondholders hurt by *distortion of investment that leads to increases in risk.*

Dilution
  1. Limit on leasing
  2. Limit on further borrowing
	Shareholders may attempt to issue new debt of equal or greater priority.	This restricts *dilution of the claim of existing bondholders.*

A **positive covenant** specifies an action that the company agrees to take or a condition the company must abide by. Here are some examples:

1. The company agrees to maintain its working capital at a minimum level.

2. The company must furnish periodic financial statements to the lender.

These lists of covenants are not exhaustive. We have seen loan agreements with more than 30 covenants.

Smith and Warner examined public issues of debt and found that 91 percent of the bond indentures included covenants that restricted the issuance of additional debt, 23 percent restricted dividends, 39 percent restricted mergers, and 36 percent limited the sale of assets.[12]

Protective covenants should reduce the costs of bankruptcy, ultimately increasing the value of the firm. Thus, stockholders are likely to favor all reasonable covenants. To see this, consider three choices by stockholders to reduce bankruptcy costs.

1. *Issue No Debt.* Because of the tax advantages to debt, this is a very costly way of avoiding conflicts.

2. *Issue Debt with No Restrictive and Protective Covenants.* In this case, bondholders will demand high interest rates to compensate for the unprotected status of their debt.

3. *Write Protective and Restrictive Covenants into the Loan Contracts.* If the covenants are clearly written, the creditors may receive protection without large costs being imposed on the shareholders. They will happily accept a lower interest rate.

Thus, bond covenants, even if they reduce flexibility, can increase the value of the firm. They can be the lowest-cost solution to the stockholder-bondholder conflict. A list of typical bond covenants and their uses appears in Table 16.2.

---

[12]C. W. Smith and J. B. Warner, "On Financial Contracting: An Analysis of Bond Covenants," *Journal of Financial Economics* 7 (1979).

■ FIGURE 16.1 **The Optimal Amount of Debt and the Value of the Firm**

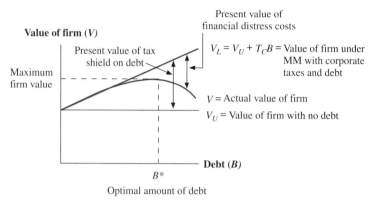

The tax shield increases the value of the levered firm. Financial distress costs lower the value of the levered firm. The two offsetting factors produce an optimal amount of debt at B^*.

Consolidation of Debt

One reason bankruptcy costs are so high is that different creditors (and their lawyers) contend with each other. This problem can be alleviated by proper arrangement of bondholders and stockholders. For example, perhaps one, or at most a few, lenders can shoulder the entire debt. Should financial distress occur, negotiating costs are minimized under this arrangement. In addition, bondholders can purchase stock as well. In this way, stockholders and debtholders are not pitted against each other, because they are not separate entities. This appears to be the approach in Japan where large banks generally take significant stock positions in the firms to which they lend money.[13] Debt-equity ratios in Japan are far higher than those in the United States.

16.4 INTEGRATION OF TAX EFFECTS AND FINANCIAL DISTRESS COSTS

Modigliani and Miller argue that the firm's value rises with leverage in the presence of corporate taxes. Because this implies that all firms should choose maximum debt, the theory does not predict the behavior of firms in the real world. Other authors have suggested that bankruptcy and related costs reduce the value of the levered firm.

The integration of tax effects and distress costs appears in Figure 16.1. The diagonal straight line in the figure represents the value of the firm in a world without bankruptcy costs. The ∩-shaped curve represents the value of the firm with these costs. The ∩-shaped curve rises as the firm moves from all-equity to a small amount of debt. Here, the present value of the distress costs is minimal because the probability of distress is so small. However, as more and more debt is added, the present value of these costs rises at an *increasing* rate. At some point, the increase in the present value of these costs from an additional dollar of debt equals the increase in the present value of the tax shield. This is the

---

[13]Legal limitations may prevent this practice in the United States.

debt level maximizing the value of the firm and is represented by B^* in Figure 16.1. In other words, B^* is the optimal amount of debt. Bankruptcy costs increase faster than the tax shield beyond this point, implying a reduction in firm value from further leverage.

The preceding discussion presents two factors that affect the degree of leverage. Unfortunately, no formula exists at this time to exactly determine the optimal debt level for a particular firm. This is primarily because financial distress costs cannot be expressed in a precise way. However, our discussion leads naturally to the idea that a firm's capital structure decisions can be thought of as a trade-off between the tax benefits of debt and the costs of financial distress. In fact, this approach is frequently called the *trade-off* or the *static trade-off* theory of capital structure. The implication is that there is an optimum amount of debt for any individual firm. The optimum amount of debt becomes the firm's target debt level. (In the real world of finance, this optimum is frequently referred to as the firm's *debt capacity.*) The last section of this chapter offers some rules of thumb for selecting a debt-equity ratio in the real world.

Our situation reminds one of a quote of John Maynard Keynes. He reputedly said that, although most historians would agree that Queen Elizabeth I was both a better monarch and an unhappier woman than Queen Victoria, no one has yet been able to express the statement in a precise and rigorous formula.

Pie Again

Critics of the MM theory often say that MM fails when we add such real-world issues as taxes and bankruptcy costs. Taking that view, however, blinds critics to the real value of the MM theory. The pie approach offers a more constructive way of thinking about these matters and the role of capital structure.

Taxes are just another claim on the cash flows of the firm. Let G (for government and taxes) stand for the market value of the government's claim to the firm's taxes. Bankruptcy costs are also another claim on the cash flows. Let us label their value with an L (for lawyers?). The bankruptcy costs are cash flows paid from the firm's cash flows in a bankruptcy. The cash flows to the claim L rise with the debt-equity ratio.

The pie theory says that all these claims are paid from only one source, the cash flows (CF) of the firm. Algebraically, we must have

$$CF = \text{Payments to stockholders}$$
$$+$$
$$\text{Payments to bondholders}$$
$$+$$
$$\text{Payments to the government}$$
$$+$$
$$\text{Payments to lawyers}$$
$$+$$
$$\text{Payments to any and all other claimants}$$
$$\text{to the cash flows of the firm}$$

Figure 16.2 shows the new pie. No matter how many slices we take and no matter who gets them, they must still add up to the total cash flow. The value of the firm, V_T, is unaltered by the capital structure. Now, however, we must be broader in our definition of the firm's value

$$V_T = S + B + G + L$$

We previously wrote the firm's value as

$$S + B$$

when we ignored taxes and bankruptcy costs.

■ FIGURE 16.2   **The Pie Model with Real-World Factors**

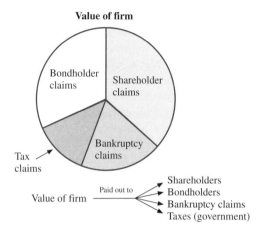

Nor have we even begun to exhaust the list of financial claims to the firm's cash flows. To give an unusual example, everyone reading this book has an economic claim to the cash flows of General Motors. After all, if you are injured in an accident, you might sue GM. Win or lose, GM will expend resources dealing with the matter. If you think this is farfetched and unimportant, ask yourself what GM might be willing to pay every man, woman, and child in the country to have them promise that they would never sue GM, no matter what happened. The law does not permit such payments, but that does not mean that a value to all of those potential claims does not exist. We guess that it would run into the billions of dollars, and, for GM or any other company, there should be a slice of the pie labeled *LS* for "potential lawsuits."

This is the essence of the MM intuition and theory: *V* is V(CF) and depends on the total cash flow of the firm. The capital structure cuts it into slices.

There is, however, an important difference between claims such as those of stockholders and bondholders on the one hand and those of government and potential litigants in lawsuits on the other. The first set of claims are **marketed claims,** and the second set are **nonmarketed claims.** One difference is that the marketed claims can be bought and sold in financial markets, and the nonmarketed claims cannot.

When we speak of the value of the firm, generally we are referring just to the value of the marketed claims, V_M, and not the value of nonmarketed claims, V_N. What we have shown is that the total value,

$$V_T = S + B + G + L$$
$$= V_M + V_N$$

is unaltered. But, as we saw, the value of the marketed claims, V_M, can change with changes in the capital structure in general and the debt-equity ratio in particular.

By the pie theory, any increase in V_M must imply an identical decrease in V_N. In an efficient market we showed that the capital structure will be chosen to maximize the value of the marketed claims, V_M. We can equivalently think of the efficient market as working to minimize the value of the nonmarketed claims, V_N. These are taxes and bankruptcy costs in the previous example, but they also include all the other nonmarketed claims such as the *LS* claim.

QUESTIONS
CONCEPT ?

- List all the claims to the firm's assets.
- Describe marketed claims and nonmarketed claims.
- How can a firm maximize the value of its marketed claims?

16.5 SHIRKING, PERQUISITES, AND BAD INVESTMENTS: A NOTE ON AGENCY COST OF EQUITY

The previous section introduced the static trade-off model, where a rise in debt increases both the tax shield and the costs of distress. We now extend the trade-off model by considering an important agency cost of equity. A discussion of this cost of equity is contained in a well-known quote from Adam Smith.[14]

> The directors of such [joint-stock] companies, however, being the managers of other people's money than of their own, it cannot well be expected that they should watch over it with the same anxious vigilance with which the partners in a private copartnery frequently watch over their own. Like the stewards of a rich man, they are apt to consider attention to small matters as not for their master's honor, and very easily give themselves a dispensation from having it. Negligence and profusion, therefore, must always prevail, more or less, in the management of the affairs of such a company.

This elegant prose can be restated in modern-day vocabulary. An individual will work harder for a firm if she is one of its owners than if she is just an employee. In addition, the individual will work harder if she owns a large percentage of the company than if she owns a small percentage. This idea has an important implication for capital structure, which we illustrate with the following example.

EXAMPLE

Ms. Pagell is an owner-entrepreneur running a computer-services firm worth $1 million. She currently owns 100 percent of the firm. Because of the need to expand, she must raise another $2 million. She can either issue $2 million of debt at 12-percent interest or issue $2 million in stock. The cash flows under the two alternatives are presented below:

	Debt Issue				**Stock Issue**			
	Cash Flow	Interest	Cash Flow to Equity	Cash Flow to Ms. Pagell (100% of equity)	Cash Flow	Interest	Cash Flow to Equity	Cash Flow to Ms. Pagell (33⅓% of equity)
6-hour days	$300,000	$240,000	$ 60,000	$ 60,000	$300,000	0	$300,000	$100,000
10-hour days	400,000	240,000	160,000	160,000	400,000	0	400,000	133,333

Like any entrepreneur, Ms. Pagell can choose the degree of intensity with which she works. In our example, she can either work a 6- or a 10-hour day. With the debt issue, the extra work brings her $100,000 ($160,000 − $60,000) more income. However, let's assume that with a stock issue she retains only a one-third interest in the equity. Here, the extra work brings her merely $33,333 ($133,333 − $100,000). Being only human, she is likely to work harder if she issues debt. In other words, she has more incentive to *shirk* if she issues equity.

---

[14]Adam Smith, *The Wealth of Nations* [1776], Cannon edition (New York: Modern Library, 1937), p. 700, as quoted in M. C. Jensen and W. Meckling, "Theory of the Firm: Managerial Behavior, Agency Costs, and Ownership Structure," *Journal of Financial Economics* 3 (1978).

In addition, she is likely to obtain more *perquisites* (a big office, a company car, more expense-account meals) if she issues stock. If she is a one-third stockholder, two-thirds of these costs are paid for by the other stockholders. If she is the sole owner, any additional perquisites reduce her equity stake.

Finally, she is more likely to take on capital-budgeting projects with negative net present values. It might seem surprising that a manager with any equity interest at all would take on negative NPV projects, since stock price would clearly fall here. However, managerial salaries generally rise with firm size, indicating that managers have an incentive to accept some unprofitable projects after all the profitable ones have been taken on. That is, when an unprofitable project is accepted, the loss in stock value to a manager with only a small equity interest may be less than the increase in salary. In fact, it is our opinion that losses from accepting bad projects are far greater than losses from either shirking or excessive perquisites. Hugely unprofitable projects have bankrupted whole firms, something that even the largest of expense accounts is unlikely to do.

Thus, as the firm issues more equity, our entrepreneur will likely increase leisure time, work-related perquisites, and unprofitable investments. These three items are called agency costs, because managers of the firm are agents of the stockholders.[15]

This example is quite applicable to a small company considering a large stock offering. Because a manager-owner will greatly dilute his or her share in the total equity in this case, a significant drop in work intensity or a significant increase in fringe benefits is possible. However, the example may be less applicable for a large corporation with many stockholders. For example, consider a large company such as General Motors going public for the umpteenth time. The typical manager there already has such a small percentage stake in the firm that any temptation for negligence has probably been experienced before. An additional offering cannot be expected to increase this temptation.

Who bears the burden of these agency costs? If the new stockholders invest with their eyes open, they do not. Knowing that Ms. Pagell may work shorter hours, they will pay only a low price for the stock. Thus, it is the owner who is hurt by agency costs. However, Ms. Pagell can protect herself to some extent. Just as stockholders reduce bankruptcy costs through protective covenants, an owner may allow monitoring by new stockholders. However, though proper reporting and surveillance may reduce the agency costs of equity, these techniques are unlikely to eliminate them.

It is commonly suggested that leveraged buyouts (LBOs) significantly reduce the above cost of equity. In an LBO, a purchaser (usually a team of existing management) buys out the stockholders at a price above the current market. In other words, the company goes private since the stock is placed in the hands of only a few people. Because the managers now own a substantial chunk of the business, they are likely to work harder than when they were simply hired hands.[16]

---

[15]As previously discussed, agency costs are generally defined as the costs from the conflicts of interest among stockholders, bondholders, and managers.

[16]One professor we know introduces his classes to LBOs by asking the students three questions:

1. How many of you have ever owned your own car?
2. How many of you have ever rented a car?
3. How many of you took better care of the car you owned than the car you rented?

Just as it is human nature to take better care of your own car, it is human nature to work harder when you own more of the company.

Effect of Agency Costs of Equity on Debt-Equity Financing

The preceding discussion on the agency costs of equity should be viewed as an extension of the static trade-off model. That is, we stated in Section 16.4 that the change in the value of the firm when debt is substituted for equity is the difference between (1) the tax shield on debt and (2) the increase in the costs of financial distress (including the agency costs of debt). Now, the change in the value of the firm is (1) the tax shield on debt plus (2) the reduction in the agency costs of equity minus (3) the increase in the costs of financial distress (including the agency costs of debt). The optimal debt-equity ratio would be higher in a world with agency costs of equity than in a world without these costs. However, because costs of financial distress are so significant, the costs of equity do not imply 100-percent debt financing.

Free Cash Flow

Any reader of murder mysteries knows that a criminal must have both motive and opportunity. The above discussion was about motive. Managers with only a small ownership interest have an incentive for wasteful behavior. For example, they bear only a small portion of the costs of, say, excessive expense accounts, and reap all of the benefits.

Now let's talk about opportunity. A manager can only pad his expense account if the firm has the cash flow to cover it. Thus, we might expect to see more wasteful activity in a firm with a capacity to generate large cash flows than in one with a capacity to generate only small flows. This very simple idea, which is formally called the *free cash flow hypothesis*, has recently attracted the attention of the academic community.[17]

A fair amount of academic work supports the hypothesis. For example, a frequently cited paper found that firms with high free cash flow are more likely to make bad acquisitions than firms with low free cash flow.[18]

The hypothesis has important implications for capital structure. Since dividends leave the firm, they reduce free cash flow. Thus, according to the free cash flow hypothesis, an increase in dividends should benefit the stockholders by reducing the ability of managers to pursue wasteful activities. Furthermore, since interest and principal also leave the firm, debt reduces free cash flow as well. In fact, interest and principal should have a greater effect than dividends have on the free-spending ways of managers, because bankruptcy will occur if the firm is unable to make future debt payments. By contrast, a future dividend reduction will cause fewer problems to the managers, since the firm has no legal obligation to pay dividends. Because of this, the free cash flow hypothesis argues that a shift from equity to debt will boost firm value.

In summary, the free cash flow hypothesis provides still another reason for firms to issue debt. We previously discussed the cost of equity; new equity dilutes the holdings of managers with equity interests, increasing their *motive* to waste corporate resources. We now state that debt reduces free cash flow, because the firm must make interest and principal payments. The free cash flow hypothesis implies that debt reduces the *opportunity* for managers to waste resources.

CONCEPT QUESTIONS

• What are agency costs?
• Why are shirking and perquisites considered an agency cost of equity?
• How do agency costs of equity affect the firm's debt-equity ratio?
• What is the free cash flow hypothesis?

[17]The seminal article is Michael C. Jensen, "Agency Costs of Free Cash Flow, Corporate Finance Takeovers," *American Economic Review* 76 (1986), pp. 323–39.

[18]L. Lang, R. Stulz, and R. Walkling, "Managerial Performance, Tobin's *Q* and the Gains in Tender Offers," *Journal of Financial Economics* (1989).

16.6 THE PECKING-ORDER THEORY

Although the trade-off theory has dominated corporate finance circles for a long time, attention is also being paid to the *pecking-order theory*.[19] To understand this view of the world, let's put ourselves in the position of a corporate financial manager whose firm needs new capital. The manager faces a choice between issuing debt and issuing equity. Previously, we evaluated the choice in terms of tax benefits, distress costs, and agency costs. However, there is one consideration that we have so far neglected: timing.

Imagine the manager saying:

> I want to issue stock in one situation only—when it is overvalued. If the stock of my firm is selling at $50 per share, but I think that it is actually worth $60, I will not issue stock. I would actually be giving new stockholders a gift, because they would receive stock worth $60, but would only have to pay $50 for it. More importantly, my current stockholders would be upset, because the firm would be receiving $50 in cash, but giving away something worth $60. So if I believe that my stock is undervalued, I would issue bonds. Bonds, particularly those with little or no risk of default, are likely to be priced correctly. Their value is primarily determined by the marketwide interest rate, a variable that is publicly known.
>
> But, suppose that our stock is selling at $70. Now I'd like to issue stock. If I can get some fool to buy our stock for $70 while the stock is really only worth $60, I will be making $10 for our current shareholders.

Now, although this may strike you as a cynical view, it seems to square well with reality. Before the United States adopted insider trading and disclosure laws, many managers were alleged to have unfairly trumpeted their firm's prospects prior to equity issuance. And, even today, managers seem more willing to issue equity after the price of their stock has risen than after their stock has fallen in price. Thus, timing might be an important motive in equity issuance, perhaps even more important than those motives in the trade-off model. After all, the firm in the preceding example *immediately* makes $10 by properly timing the issuance of equity. Ten dollars worth of agency costs and bankruptcy cost reduction might take many years to realize.

The key that makes the example work is asymmetric information; the manager must know more about his firm's prospects than does the typical investor. If the manager's estimate of the true worth of the company is no better than the estimate of a typical investor, any attempts by the manager to time will fail. This assumption of asymmetry is quite plausible. Managers should know more about their company than do outsiders, because managers work at the company every day. (One caveat is that some managers are perpetually optimistic about their firm, blurring good judgment.)

But we are not done with this example yet; we must consider the investor. Imagine an investor saying:

> I make investments carefully, because it involves my hard-earned money. However, even with all the time I put into studying stocks, I can't possibly know what the managers themselves know. After all, I've got a day job to be concerned with. So, I watch what the managers do. If a firm issues stock, the firm was likely overvalued beforehand. If a firm issues debt, it was likely overvalued.

When we look at both issuers and investors, we see a kind of poker game, with each side trying to outwit the other. There are two prescriptions to the issuer in this poker game. The first one, which is fairly straightforward, is to issue debt instead of equity when the

---

[19]The pecking order theory is generally attributed to S. C. Myers, "The Capital Structure Puzzle," *Journal of Finance* 39 (July 1984).

stock is undervalued. The second, which is more subtle, is to issue debt also when the firm is *overvalued*. After all, if a firm issues equity, investors will infer that the stock is overvalued. They will not buy it until the stock has fallen enough to eliminate any advantage from equity issuance. In fact, only the most overvalued firms have any incentive to issue equity. Should even a moderately overpriced firm issue equity, investors will infer that this firm is among the *most* overpriced, causing the stock to fall more than is deserved. Thus, the end result is that virtually no one will issue equity.[20]

This result that essentially all firms should issue debt is clearly an extreme one. It is as extreme as (1) the Modigliani-Miller (MM) result that, in a world without taxes, firms are indifferent to capital structure and (2) the MM result that, in a world of corporate taxes but no financial distress costs, all firms should be 100 percent debt-financed. Perhaps we in finance have a penchant for extreme models!

But, just as one can temper MM's conclusions by combining financial distress costs with corporate taxes, we can temper those of the pure pecking-order theory. This pure version assumes that timing is the financial manager's only consideration. In reality, a manager must consider taxes, financial distress costs, and agency costs as well. Thus, a firm may issue debt only up to a point. If financial distress becomes a real possibility beyond that point, the firm may issue equity instead.

Rules of the Pecking Order

For expository purposes, we have oversimplified by comparing equity to *riskless* debt. Managers cannot use special knowledge of their firm to determine if this type of debt is mispriced, because the price of riskless debt is determined solely by the marketwide interest rate. However, in reality, corporate debt has the possibility of default. Thus, just as managers have a tendency to issue equity when they think it is overvalued, managers also have a tendency to issue debt when they think it is overvalued.

When would managers view their debt as overvalued? Probably in the same situations when they think their equity is overvalued. For example, if the public thinks that the firm's prospects are rosy but the managers see trouble ahead, these managers would view their debt—as well as their equity—as being overvalued. That is, the public might see the debt as nearly risk-free, whereas the managers see a strong possibility of default.

Thus, investors are likely to price a debt issue with the same skepticism that they have when pricing an equity issue. The way managers get out of this box is to finance projects out of retained earnings. You don't have to worry about investor skepticism if you can avoid going to investors in the first place. Thus, the first rule of the pecking order is:

Rule 1
Use internal financing.

However, although investors fear mispricing of both debt and equity, the fear is much greater for equity. Corporate debt still has relatively little risk compared to equity because, if financial distress is avoided, investors receive a fixed return. Thus, the pecking-order theory implies that, if outside financing is required, debt should be issued before equity. Only when the firm's debt capacity is reached should the firm consider equity.

Of course, there are many types of debt. For example, because convertible debt is more risky than straight debt, the pecking-order theory implies that one should issue straight debt before issuing convertibles. Thus, the second rule of pecking-order theory is:

---

[20]In the interest of simplicity, we have not presented our results in the form of a rigorous model. To the extent that a reader wants a deeper explanation, we refer him or her to S. C. Myers. "The Capital Structure Puzzle," *Journal of Finance* (July 1984).

Rule 2

Issue the safest securities first.

Implications

There are a number of implications associated with the pecking-order theory that are at odds with the trade-off theory.

1. *There is no target amount of leverage.* According to the trade-off model, each firm balances the benefits of debt, such as the tax shield, with the costs of debt, such as distress costs. The optimal amount of leverage occurs where the marginal benefit of debt equals the marginal cost of debt.

By contrast, the pecking-order theory does not imply a target amount of leverage. Rather, each firm chooses its leverage ratio based on financing needs. Firms first fund projects out of retained earnings. This should lower the percentage of debt in the capital structure, because profitable, internally funded projects raise both the book value and the market value of equity. Additional cash needs are met with debt, clearly raising the debt level. However, at some point the debt capacity of the firm may be exhausted, giving way to equity issuance. Thus, the amount of leverage is determined by the happenstance of available projects. Firms do not pursue a target ratio of debt to equity.

2. *Profitable firms use less debt.* Profitable firms generate cash internally, implying less need for outside financing. Because firms desiring outside capital turn to debt first, profitable firms end up relying on less debt. The trade-off model does not have this implication. The greater cash flow of more profitable firms creates greater debt capacity. These firms will use that debt capacity to capture the tax shield and the other benefits of leverage. Two recent papers find that in the real world, more profitable firms are less levered,[21] a result consistent with the pecking-order theory.

3. *Companies like financial slack.* The pecking-order theory is based on the difficulties of obtaining financing at a reasonable cost. A skeptical investing public thinks a stock is overvalued if the managers try to issue more of it, thereby leading to a stock-price decline. Because this happens with bonds only to a lesser extent, managers rely first on bond financing. However, firms can only issue so much debt before encountering the potential costs of financial distress.

Wouldn't it be easier to have the cash ahead of time? This is the idea behind *financial slack.* Because firms know that they will have to fund profitable projects at various times in the future, they accumulate cash today. They are then not forced to go to the capital markets when a project comes up. However, there is a limit to the amount of cash a firm will want to accumulate. As mentioned earlier in this chapter, too much free cash may tempt managers to pursue wasteful activities.

CONCEPT QUESTIONS

- What is the pecking-order theory?
- What are the problems of issuing equity according to this theory?
- What is financial slack?

---

[21] See L. S. Sunder and S. C. Myers, "Testing Static Trade-off Against Pecking Order Models of Capital Structure," *Journal of Financial Economics* (February 1999), and E. F. Fama and K. R. French, "Testing Trade-off and Pecking Order Predictions about Dividends and Debt," unpublished paper, University of Chicago (November 1999). Most recently Armen Hovakimian, Tim Opler and Sheridan Titman, "The Debt-Equity Choice," *Journal of Financial and Quantitative Analysis* (March 2001) find that while pecking order considerations affect firm debt levels in the short run, firms tend to move to target debt ratios in a manner consistent with the trade-off model.

16.7 GROWTH AND THE DEBT-EQUITY RATIO

While the trade-off between the tax shield and bankruptcy costs (as illustrated in Figure 16.1) is often viewed as the "standard model" of capital structure, it has its critics. For example, some point out that bankruptcy costs in the real world appear to be much smaller than the tax subsidy. Thus, the model implies that the optimal debt/value ratio should be near 100 percent, an implication at odds with reality.[22]

Perhaps the pecking-order theory is more consistent with the real world here. That is, firms are likely to have more equity in their capital structure than implied by the static trade-off theory, because internal financing is preferred to external financing.

In addition, a relatively recent article argues that growth implies significant equity financing, even in a world with low bankruptcy costs.[23] To explain the idea, we first consider an example of a no-growth firm. Next, we examine the effect of growth on firm leverage.

No-Growth

Imagine a world of perfect certainty[24] where a firm has earnings before interest and taxes (EBIT) of $100. In addition, the firm has issued $1,000 of debt at an interest rate of 10 percent, implying interest payments of $100 per year. The cash flows to the firm are:

Date	1	2	3	4 ...
Earnings before interest and taxes (EBIT)	$100	$100	$100	$100 ...
Interest	−100	−100	−100	−100 ...
Taxable income	$ 0	$ 0	$ 0	$ 0

The firm has issued just enough debt so that all EBIT is paid out as interest. Since interest is tax-deductible, the firm pays no taxes. In this example, the equity is worthless because stockholders receive no cash flows. Since debt is worth $1,000, the firm is also valued at $1,000. Therefore, the debt-to-value ratio is 100 percent (= $1,000/$1,000).

Had the firm issued less than $1,000 of debt, the corporation would have positive taxable income and, consequently, would have ended up paying some taxes. Had the firm issued more than $1,000 of debt, interest would have exceeded EBIT, causing default. Consequently, the optimal debt-to-value ratio is 100 percent.

Growth

Now imagine another firm that also has EBIT of $100 at date 1 but is growing at 5 percent per year.[25] To eliminate taxes, this firm also wants to issue enough debt so that interest equals EBIT. Since EBIT is growing at 5 percent per year, interest must also grow

---

[22]See Merton Miller's Presidential Address to the American Finance Association, reprinted as "Debt and Taxes," *Journal of Finance* (May 1977).

[23]This new idea is introduced and analyzed in J. L. Berens and C. L. Cuny, "Inflation, Growth and Capital Structure," *Review of Financial Studies* 8 (Winter 1995).

[24]The same qualitative results occur under uncertainty, though the mathematics is more troublesome.

[25]For simplicity, assume that growth is achieved without earnings retention. The same conclusions would be reached with retained earnings, though the arithmetic would become more involved. Of course, growth without earnings retention is less realistic than growth with retention.

at this rate. This is achieved by increasing debt by 5 percent per year.[26] The debt and income levels are:

Date	0	1	2	3	4 . . .
Debt	$1,000	$1,050	$1,102.50	$1,157.63 . . .	
New debt issued		50	52.50	55.13 . . .	
EBIT		$ 100	$ 105	$ 110.25	$115.76 . . .
Interest		−100	−105	−110.25	−115.76 . . .
Taxable income		$ 0	$ 0	$ 0	$ 0

Note that interest on a particular date is always 10 percent of the debt on the previous date. Debt is set so that interest is exactly equal to EBIT. As in the no-growth case, the levered firm has the maximum amount of debt at each date. Default would occur if interest payments were increased.

Because growth is 5 percent per year, the value of the firm is:[27]

$$V_{\text{Firm}} = \frac{\$100}{0.10 - 0.05} = \$2,000$$

The equity at date 0 is the difference between the value of the firm at that time, $2,000, and the debt of $1,000. Hence, equity must be equal to $1,000,[28] implying a debt-to-value ratio of 50 percent (= $1,000/$2,000). Note the important difference between the no-growth and the growth example. The no-growth example has no equity; the value of the firm is simply the value of the debt. With growth, there is equity as well as debt.

We can also value the equity in another way. It may appear at first glance that the stockholders receive nothing, because the EBIT is paid out as interest each year. However, the new debt issued each year can be paid as a dividend to the stockholders. Because the new debt is $50 at date 1 and grows at 5 percent per year, the value of the stockholders' interest is

$$\frac{\$50}{0.10 - 0.05} = \$1,000$$

the same number that we obtained in the previous paragraph.

As we mentioned earlier, any further increase in debt above $1,000 at date 0 would lower the value of the firm in a world with bankruptcy costs. Thus, with growth, the optimal amount of debt is less than 100 percent. Note, however, that bankruptcy costs need not be as large as the tax subsidy. In fact, even with infinitesimally small bankruptcy costs, firm value would decline if promised interest rose above $100 in the first year. The key to this example is that *today's* interest is set equal to *today's* income. While the introduction of future growth opportunities increases firm value, it does not increase the current level of debt needed to shield today's income from today's taxes. Since equity is the difference between firm value and debt, growth increases the value of equity.

---

[26]Since the firm makes no real investment, the new debt is used to buy back shares of stock.

[27]The firm can also be valued by a variant of (15.7):

$$V_L = V_U + PVTS$$

$$= \frac{\$100(1 - T_C)}{0.10 - 0.05} + \frac{T_C \times \$100}{0.10 - 0.05} = \$2,000$$

Because of firm growth, both V_U and $PVTS$ are growing perpetuities.

[28]Students are often surprised that equity has value when taxable income is zero. Actually, the equityholders are receiving cash flow each period, since new debt is used to buy back stock.

The preceding example captures an essential feature of the real world: growth. The same conclusion is reached in a world of inflation but with no growth opportunities. The result of this section, that 100 percent debt financing is suboptimal, holds whether growth opportunities and/or inflation is present. Since most firms have growth opportunities and since inflation has been with us for most of this century, this section's example is based on realistic assumptions.[29] The basic point is this: High-growth firms will have lower debt ratios than low-growth firms.

QUESTION

CONCEPT ?

- How do growth opportunities decrease the advantage of debt financing?

16.8 PERSONAL TAXES

So far in the chapter, we have considered corporate taxes only. Unfortunately, the IRS does not let us off that easily. Income to individuals is taxed at marginal rates up to 39.6 percent. To see the effect of personal taxes on capital structure, we have reproduced our Water Products example (from Section 15.5) below.

	Plan I	Plan II
EBIT	$1,000,000	$1,000,000
Interest ($r_B B$)	0	(400,000)
Earnings before taxes (EBT = EBIT − $r_B B$)	1,000,000	600,000
Taxes ($T_C = 0.35$)	(350,000)	(210,000)
Earnings after taxes [EAT = (EBIT − $r_B B$) × (1 − T_C)]	650,000	390,000
Add back interest ($r_B B$)	0	400,000
Total cash flow to all investors [EBIT × (1 − T_C) + $T_C r_B B$]	$ 650,000	$ 790,000

As presented above, this example considers corporate but not personal taxes. To treat these personal taxes, we first assume that all earnings after taxes are paid out as dividends. Because dividends and interest are both taxed at the same personal rate (we assume 28 percent), we have

	Plan I		Plan II	
Dividends	$650,000		$390,000	
Personal taxes on dividends (Personal rate = 28%)	(182,000)		(109,200)	
Dividends after personal taxes		$468,000		$280,800
Interest	0		400,000	
Personal taxes on interest	0		(112,000)	
Interest after personal taxes		0		288,000
Total cash flow to both bondholders and stockholders after personal taxes		$468,000		$568,800

[29]Our example assumes a single perpetual bond with level coupon payments. Berens and Cuny (BC) point out (p. 1201) that, with a number of different bonds, a firm might be able to construct an equally optimal capital structure with a greater debt-to-value (D/V) ratio. Because both capital structures are equally optimal, a firm might choose either one.

Although the analysis with many financing instruments is more complex, a firm can still choose a low D/V with no ill effect. Thus, BC's conclusion that firms *can* employ a significant amount of equity in a world with a low level of bankruptcy costs still holds.

Total taxes paid at both corporate and personal levels are

Plan *I*: $350,000   + $182,000   = $532,000
                 Corporate taxes   Personal taxes
                                          on dividends

Plan *II*: $210,000   + $109,200   + $112,000   = $431,200
                 Corporate taxes   Personal taxes   Personal taxes
                                          on dividends   on interest

Total cash flow to all investors after personal taxes is greater under plan *II*. This must be the case because (1) total cash flow was higher when personal taxes were ignored and (2) all cash flows (both interest and dividends) are taxed at the same personal tax rate. Thus, the conclusion that debt increases the value of the firm still holds. Note that the difference between the two plans in the total cash flow to all investors, $100,800 (= 568,800 − 468,000), is exactly equal to the difference in taxes of $100,800 (= 532,000 − 431,200). Thus, the effect of leverage on cash flow is totally explained by taxes.

The above analysis assumed that all earnings are paid out in dividends. In reality, a firm may repurchase shares in lieu of dividends, a strategy resulting in lower personal taxes than would have occurred with dividends.[30] Alternatively, dividends may be deferred through retention of earnings. Thus, the effective personal tax rate on distributions to stockholders is likely to be below the personal tax rate on interest.

To illustrate this tax rate differential, let us assume that the effective personal tax rate on distributions to stockholders, T_S, is 10 percent and the personal tax rate on interest, T_B, is 50 percent.[31] The cash flows for the two plans are

	Plan I		Plan II	
Distributions to stockholders	$650,000		$390,000	
Personal taxes on stockholder distributions (at 10% tax rate)	(65,000)		(39,000)	
Distribution to stockholders after personal taxes		$585,000		$351,000
Interest	0		400,000	
Personal taxes on interest (at 50% tax rate)	0		(200,000)	
Interest after personal taxes		0		200,000
Total cash flow to both bondholders and stockholders after personal taxes		$585,000		$551,000

---

[30]Under the current U.S. tax code, dividends are taxed at an individual's marginal tax rate. Long-term capital gains are taxed at the lower of (*a*) the individual's marginal tax bracket or (*b*) 28 percent.

Interestingly, individuals face higher taxes on a dividend than on a long-term capital gain of equal size, even if tax rates on the two forms of income are the same. To see this, imagine a firm where all stockholders own 10 shares, each selling for $20. On the one hand, the firm can pay out a $2 dividend per share. Here, each stockholder would receive $20 of dividends and pay taxes of

$$T_S \times \$20$$

where T_S is the tax rate on both dividends and capital gains. On the other hand, the firm could repurchase one tenth of all the outstanding shares at the market price. Assuming that all shareholders participate in the repurchase, each shareholder would sell one share of stock. Because a share sells for $20, total payout from the firm is the same for the repurchase as it is for the dividend. Upon receiving $20, the shareholder's gain on the sale would be $20 − P_0$. Here P_0 is the price at which the share was originally purchased. This implies a capital gains tax of

$$(\$20 - P_0) \times T_S$$

[31]This 50-percent tax rate was possible under previous tax codes, where the highest marginal rate was 70 percent. However, it is not possible today.

Total taxes paid at both personal and corporate levels are

Plan *I*: $350,000   + $65,000   = $415,000
              Corporate taxes   Personal taxes
                                       on dividends

Plan *II*: $210,000   + $39,000   + $200,000   = $449,000
              Corporate taxes   Personal taxes   Personal taxes
                                       on dividends   on interest

In this scenario, the total cash flows are higher under plan *I* than under plan *II*. Though this example is expressed in terms of cash flows, we would expect the value of the firm to be higher under plan *I* than under plan *II*. Which plan does the IRS dislike the most? Clearly, the IRS dislikes plan *I* more because total taxes are lower. The increase in corporate taxes under the all-equity plan is more than offset by the decrease in personal taxes.

Interest receives a tax deduction at the corporate level. Equity distributions may be taxed at a lower rate than interest at the personal level. The above examples illustrate that total tax at all levels may either increase or decrease with debt, depending on the tax rates in effect.

The Miller Model

Valuation under Personal and Corporate Taxes   The previous example calculated *cash flows* for the two plans under personal and corporate taxes. However, we have made no attempt to determine firm *value* so far. It can be shown that the value of the levered firm can be expressed in terms of an unlevered firm as[32]

$$V_L = V_U + \left[1 - \frac{(1 - T_C) \times (1 - T_S)}{(1 - T_B)} \right] \times B \tag{16.1}$$

T_B is the personal tax rate on ordinary income, such as interest, and T_S is the personal tax rate on equity distributions.

If we set $T_B = T_S$, (16.1) reduces to

$$V_L = V_U + T_C B \tag{16.2}$$

---

[32]Stockholders receive

$$(EBIT - r_B B) \times (1 - T_C) \times (1 - T_S)$$

Bondholders receive

$$r_B B \times (1 - T_B)$$

Thus, the total cash flow to all investors is

$$(EBIT - r_B B) \times (1 - T_C) \times (1 - T_S) + r_B B \times (1 - T_B)$$

which can be rewritten as

$$EBIT \times (1 - T_C) \times (1 - T_S) + r_B B \times (1 - T_B) \times \left[1 - \frac{(1 - T_C) \times (1 - T_S)}{1 - T_B} \right] \tag{a}$$

The first term in (a) is the cash flow from an unlevered firm after all taxes. The value of this stream must be V_U, the value of an unlevered firm. An individual buying a bond for B receives $r_B B \times (1 - T_B)$ after all taxes. Thus, the value of the second term in (a) must be

$$B \times \left[1 - \frac{(1 - T_C) \times (1 - T_S)}{1 - T_B} \right]$$

Therefore, the value of the stream in (a), which is the value of the levered firm, must be

$$V_U + \left[1 - \frac{(1 - T_C) \times (1 - T_S)}{1 - T_B} \right] \times B$$

■ FIGURE 16.3   **Effect of Financial Leverage on Firm Value with Both Corporate and Personal Taxes**

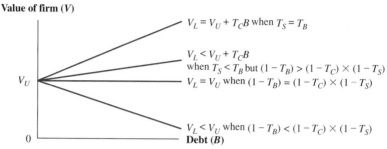

T_C is the corporate tax rate.
T_B is the personal tax rate on interest.
T_S is the personal tax rate on dividends and other equity distributions.
Both personal taxes and corporate taxes are included. Bankruptcy costs and agency costs are ignored.
The effect of debt on firm value depends on T_S, T_C, and T_B.

which is the result we calculated for a world of no personal taxes. Hence, the introduction of personal taxes does not affect our valuation formula as long as equity distributions are taxed identically to interest at the personal level.

However, the gain from leverage is reduced when $T_S < T_B$. Here, more taxes are paid at the personal level for a levered firm than for an unlevered firm. In fact, imagine that $(1 - T_C) \times (1 - T_S) = 1 - T_B$. Formula (16.1) tells us there is no gain from leverage at all! In other words, the value of the levered firm is equal to the value of the unlevered firm. This lack of gain occurs because the lower corporate taxes for a levered firm are *exactly* offset by higher personal taxes. The above results are presented in Figure 16.3. The Miller model is further examined in Appendix B of this chapter.

EXAMPLE

Acme Industries anticipates a perpetual pretax earnings stream of $100,000 and faces a 35-percent corporate tax rate. Investors discount the earnings stream after corporate taxes at 15 percent. The personal tax rate on equity distributions is 12 percent, and the personal tax rate on interest is 28 percent. Acme currently has an all-equity capital structure but is considering borrowing $120,000 at 10 percent.

The value of the all-equity firm is[33]

$$V_U = \frac{\$100,000 \times (1 - 0.35)}{0.15} = \$433,333$$

The value of the levered firm is

$$V_L = \$433,333 + \left[1 - \frac{(1 - 0.35) \times (1 - 0.12)}{(1 - 0.28)}\right] \times \$120,000 = \$458,000$$

---

[33]Alternatively, we could have said that investors discount the earnings stream after *both* corporate and personal taxes at 13.20 percent [15% × (1 − 0.12)]:

$$V_U = \frac{\$100,000 \times (1 - 0.35) \times (1 - 0.12)}{0.1320} = \$433,333$$

Thus, the same value for the unlevered firm would apply.

The advantage to leverage here is $458,000 - $433,333 = $24,677$. This is much smaller than $42,000 = 0.35 \times $120,000 = T_C B$, which would have been the gain in a world with no personal taxes.

Acme had previously considered the choice years earlier when $T_B = 50\%$ and $T_S = 18\%$. Here,

$$V_L = \$433,333 + \left[1 - \frac{(1 - 0.35) \times (1 - 0.18)}{(1 - 0.50)} \right] \times \$120,000 = \$425,413$$

In this case, $V_L < V_U$. Hence, Acme was wise not to increase leverage years ago. This inequality occurred because the personal tax rate on interest was much higher than the personal tax rate on equity distributions. In other words, the reduction in corporate taxes from leverage was more than offset by the increase in taxes from leverage at the personal level.

The Miller model provides an elegant description of the capital-structure decision. However, critics of the model commonly focus on two related areas:

1. *Tax Rates in the Real World.* Both Figure 16.3 and the previous example show that the relationship between firm value and leverage depends on personal and corporate tax rates. Consider 2001, when the marginal corporate tax rate in the United States was 35 percent and the highest personal tax rate was 39.6 percent. Under the assumption that $T_S = 20\%$ (a somewhat arbitrary assumption), equation (16.1) becomes

$$V_L = V_U + \left[1 - \frac{(1 - 0.35) \times (1 - .20)}{1 - 0.396} \right] \times B = V_U + 0.139B$$

Since $0.139 > 0$, there is a gain from leverage. And, while the corporate tax rate of 35 percent applied to essentially all large corporations, most individuals were in tax brackets well below 39.6 percent, so the gain from leverage was likely even greater still. Thus, assuming that $T_S = 20$ percent, the Miller model predicted *all*-debt financing in 2000, clearly a result at odds with reality.

However, as stated before, our assumption that $T_S = 20\%$ is arbitrary. Depending on the distribution of both T_B and T_S across individuals, leverage today may increase, decrease, or have no effect on firm value. Graham[34] analyzes empirically the effect of both personal and corporate taxes on the leverage decision. He finds that, for almost every year of his sample period of 1980–1994, the personal tax rate disadvantage of debt reduces, but does not eliminate, the corporate tax incentive to use debt. Thus, the Miller model implies all-debt financing over Graham's sample period.

2. *Unlimited Tax Deductibility.* The above discussion casts doubt on an empirical prediction of Miller's work. One problem is that we have not considered financial distress costs. Another problem lies in a missing assumption in the model. For example, critics point out that corporations have unlimited interest deductibility in the model. In reality, firms can deduct interest only to the extent of profits. Thus, the expected tax benefits of debt financing under this real-world assumption are clearly less than under the assumption of unlimited deductibility. Two effects are likely to result. First, corporations should supply less debt, reducing the interest rate. Second, the first unit of debt should increase firm value more than the last unit, because the interest on later units may not be deductible.

---

[34]John R. Graham, "Do Personal Taxes Affect Corporate Financing Decisions?" *Journal of Public Economics* 73 (1999).

■ FIGURE 16.4   **Value of the Firm under the Miller Model when Interest Deductibility Is Limited to Earnings**

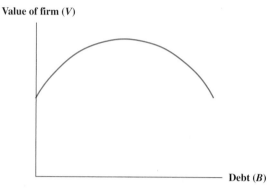

The Miller model with limited deductibility of interest leads to a ∩-shaped graph similar to the one presented in Figure 16.1. The ∩-shape in Figure 16.1 arose from the trade-off between corporate taxes and bankruptcy costs.

The results of limited deductibility are provided in Figure 16.4. Because the interest rate is now lower than that in the strict Miller model, firm value should rise when debt is first added to the capital structure. However, as more and more debt is issued, the full deductibility of the interest becomes less likely. Firm value still increases, but at a lower and lower rate. At some point, the probability of tax deductibility is low enough that an incremental dollar of debt is as costly to the firm as an incremental dollar of equity. Firm value then decreases with further leverage.[35]

This graph looks surprisingly like the curve in Figure 16.1 where the trade-off between the tax shield and bankruptcy costs is illustrated. Thus, a key change in assumptions may explain why firms are never all-debt financed, even when T_C is high relative to T_B.

16.9 How Firms Establish Capital Structure

The theories of capital structure are among the most elegant and sophisticated in the field of finance. Financial economists should (and do!) pat themselves on the back for contributions in this area. However, the practical applications of the theories are less than fully satisfying. Consider that our work on net present value produced an *exact* formula for evaluating projects. Prescriptions for capital structure under either the trade-off model or the pecking-order theory are vague by comparison. No exact formula is available for evaluating the optimal debt-equity ratio. Because of this, we turn to evidence from the real world.

The following empirical regularities are worthwhile to consider when formulating capital-structure policy.

1. *Most Corporations Have Low Debt-Asset Ratios.* In fact, historically, most U.S. corporations use less debt than equity financing. Many of these corporations pay substantial amounts in taxes, and the corporate tax has been an important source of government revenue. Figures 14.3 and 14.4 show the debt-to-value ratios for U.S. industrial firms in both book

---

[35]H. DeAngelo and R. Masulis, "Optimal Capital Structure under Corporate and Personal Taxation," *Journal of Financial Economics* (March 1980), posit a model where interest on debt is not the firm's only tax shield. Investment tax credits, depreciation, and depletion are examples of other tax shields. The authors show results similar to those in this section.

■ FIGURE 16.5 **Estimated Ratios of Debt to Total Value (accounting value) of Nonfinancial Firms, Various Countries**

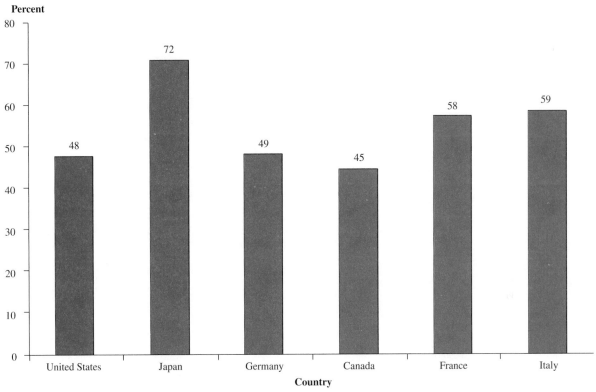

Definition: Debt is short-term debt plus long-term debt. Total value is debt plus equity (in book-value terms).

Source: OECD financial statistics.

and market values for the years 1988 to 1999. Notice that the debt ratios are usually less than 50 percent. Nevertheless firms pay substantial taxes. For example, corporate taxes were almost $200 billion in 1996. It is clear that corporations do not issue debt up to the point that tax shelters are completely used up.[36] Figure 16.5 shows the debt-to-total-value ratios of firms in several countries in recent years. Differences in accounting procedures make these figures difficult to interpret. However, the debt ratios of U.S. and Canadian firms are the lowest. In all of the countries, firms have debt ratios considerably less than 100 percent. There are clearly limits to the amount of debt corporations actually issue.

2. *A number of firms use no debt.* In a fascinating study, Agrawal and Nagarajan[37] examined approximately 100 firms on the New York Stock Exchange without long-term debt. They found that these firms are averse to leverage of any kind, with little short-term debt as well. In addition, they have levels of cash and marketable securities well above their levered counterparts. Typically, the managers of these firms have high equity ownership. Furthermore, there is significantly greater family involvement in all-equity firms than in levered firms.

---

[36]John Graham estimates that the average value of the tax benefit of debt is no more than 10 percent of the firm's value. He asks the question: Is money left in the table? His answer is a tentative yes. He concludes that either firms use debt too conservatively or that the financial distress costs (and related costs) are very large. "How Big Are the Tax Benefits of Debt?" Unpublished manuscript, Duke University (June 2002).

[37]Anup Agrawal and Nandu Nagarajan, "Corporate Capital Structure, Agency Costs, and Ownership Control: The Case of All-Equity Firms," *Journal of Finance* 45 (September 1990).

■ FIGURE 16.6   **Stock Returns at the Time of Announcements of Exchange Offers**

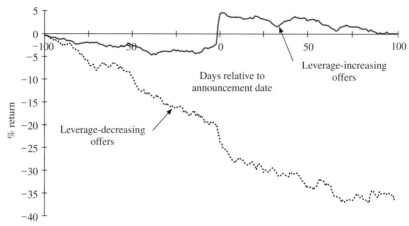

Exchange offers change the debt-to-equity ratios of firms. The graph shows that stock prices increase for firms whose exchange offers increase leverage. Conversely, stock prices decrease for firms whose offers decrease leverage.

Source: K. Shah, "The Nature of Information Conveyed by Pure Capital Structure Changes," *Journal of Financial Economics* 36 (August 1994).

Thus, a story emerges. Managers of all-equity firms are less diversified than the managers of similar, but levered, firms. Because of this, significant leverage represents an added risk that the managers of all-equity firms are loathe to accept.

3. *Changes in Financial Leverage Affect Firm Value.* In an important study, Shah[38] examines the effect of announcements of changes in capital structure on stock prices. His results, which are presented in Figure 16.6, show the stock price behavior of firms that change their proportions of debt and equity via exchange offers. The solid line in the figure indicates that stock prices rise substantially on the date when an exchange offer increasing leverage is announced. (This date is referred to in the figure as date 0.) Conversely, the dotted line in the figure indicates that stock price falls substantially when an offer decreasing leverage is announced.

Shah's results are consistent with a *signaling* version of the trade-off model. That is, managers are likely to raise the amount of debt if they believe that the probability of bankruptcy has been decreased and lower debt if they believe that the probability has been increased.

The market infers from an increase in debt that the firm is better off, leading to a stock-price rise. Conversely, the market infers the reverse from a decrease in debt, implying a stock-price fall. Thus, we say that managers signal information when they change leverage. Shah's results are also consistent with the pecking-order theory. Here, managers are more likely to turn debt into equity through an exchange offer when they believe the equity is overvalued. The market understands this motive, leading to a stock-price decline.

---

[38]K. Shah, "The Nature of Information Conveyed by Pure Capital Structure Changes," *Journal of Financial Economics* 36 (1994), has examined exchange offers; see also, R. Masulis, "The Effects of Capital Structure Change on Security Prices: A Study of Exchange Offers," *Journal of Financial Economics* 8 (1980); M. Cornett and N. Travlos, "Information Effects Associated with Debt-in-Equity and Equity-in-Debt Exchange Offers," *Journal of Finance* 44 (1989); and T. Copeland and Won Heum Lee, "Exchange Offers and Swaps: New Evidence," *Financial Management* 20 (1991).

■ TABLE 16.3 **Capital Structure Ratios for Selected U.S. Nonfinancial Firms (medians), 5-Year Average**

	Debt as a Percentage of the Market Value of Equity and Debt
High leverage	
Building construction	61.5
Hotels and lodging	55.5
Air transport	40.8
Primary metals	36.2
Paper	30.3
Low leverage	
Drugs and chemicals	3.1
Electronics	11.1
Biological products	2.3
Computers	9.3
Catalog and mail-order stores	12.1

Definition: Debt is the total of short-term debt and long-term debt.
Source: Ibbotson Associates 1999, *Cost of Capital Quarterly,* 1999 Yearbook.

4. *There Are Differences in the Capital Structures of Different Industries.* There are very significant interindustry differences in debt ratios that persist over time. As can be seen in Table 16.3, debt ratios tend to be very low in high growth industries with ample future investment opportunities such as the drugs and electronics industries. This is true even when the need for external financing is great. Industries such as primary metals and paper, with relatively few investment opportunities and slow growth, tend to use the most debt.

No formula can establish a debt-equity ratio for all companies. However, there is evidence that firms behave as if they had target debt-equity ratios.[39] We present three important factors affecting the target debt-equity ratio:

1. *Taxes.* If a company has (and will continue to have) taxable income, an increased reliance on debt will reduce taxes paid by the company and increase taxes paid by some bondholders. If corporate tax rates are higher than bondholder tax rates, there is value from using debt.

2. *Types of Assets.* Financial distress is costly, with or without formal bankruptcy proceedings. The costs of financial distress depend on the types of assets that the firm has. For example, if a firm has a large investment in land, buildings, and other tangible assets, it will have smaller costs of financial distress than a firm with a large investment in research and development. Research and development typically has less resale value than land; thus, most of its value disappears in financial distress.

3. *Uncertainty of Operating Income.* Firms with uncertain operating income have a high probability of experiencing financial distress, even without debt. Thus, these firms must finance mostly with equity. For example, pharmaceutical firms have uncertain operating income

---

[39]The classic studies showing that firms may have target debt ratios are P. Marsh, "The Choice between Equity and Debt: An Empirical Study," *Journal of Finance* (March 1981); and R. A. Taggart, "A Model of Corporate Financing Decisions," *Journal of Finance* (December 1977).

because no one can predict whether today's research will generate new drugs. Consequently, these firms issue little debt. By contrast, the operating income of utilities generally has little uncertainty. Relative to other industries, utilities use a great deal of debt.

One final note is in order. Because no formula supports them, the preceding points may seem too nebulous to assist financial decision making. Instead, many real-world firms simply base their capital structure decisions on industry averages. While this may strike some as a cowardly approach, it at least keeps firms from deviating far from accepted practice. After all, the existing firms in any industry are the survivors. Therefore, one should at least pay some attention to their decisions.

CONCEPT QUESTIONS

- List the empirical regularities we observe for corporate capital structure.
- What are the factors to consider in establishing a debt-equity ratio?

16.10 SUMMARY AND CONCLUSIONS

1. We mentioned in the last chapter that, according to theory, firms should create all-debt capital structures under corporate taxation. Because firms generally assume moderate amounts of debt in the real world, the theory must have been missing something at that point. We point out in this chapter that costs of financial distress cause firms to restrain their issuance of debt. These costs are of two types: direct and indirect. Lawyers' and accountants' fees during the bankruptcy process are examples of direct costs. We mention four examples of indirect costs:

   Impaired ability to conduct business.

   Incentive to take on risky projects.

   Incentive toward underinvestment.

   Distribution of funds to stockholders prior to bankruptcy.

2. Because the above costs are substantial and the stockholders ultimately bear them, firms have an incentive for cost reduction. We suggest three cost-reduction techniques:

   Protective covenants.

   Repurchase of debt prior to bankruptcy.

   Consolidation of debt.

3. Because costs of financial distress can be reduced but not eliminated, firms will not finance entirely with debt. Figure 16.1 illustrates the relationship between firm value and debt. In the figure, firms select the debt-to-equity ratio at which firm value is maximized.

4. The pecking-order theory implies that managers prefer internal to external financing. If external financing is required, managers tend to choose the safest securities, such as debt. Firms may accumulate slack to avoid external equity.

5. Berens and Cuny argue that significant equity financing can be explained by real growth and inflation, even in a world of low bankruptcy costs.

6. The results so far have ignored personal taxes. If distributions to equityholders are taxed at a lower effective personal tax rate than are interest payments, the tax advantage to debt at the corporate level is partially offset. In fact, the corporate tax advantage to debt is eliminated if

$$(1 - T_C) \times (1 - T_S) = (1 - T_B)$$

EDISON INTERNATIONAL: A CASE FOR HIGH DEBT

Edison International is the parent firm of Southern California Edison (SCE) and five nonutility companies. Southern California Edison is the nation's second largest electric utility in terms of number of customers. SCE currently operates in a highly regulated environment in which it has an obligation to provide electric service to customers in return for a monopoly franchise in Southern California. SCE generated about 90 percent of the total operating revenue for Edison International. Traditionally, long-term debt has been a very prominent part of Edison International's capital structure. Its capital structure in 1999, based on market values, is illustrated next:

1999	$ (in millions)	Percentage
Debt	$16,906	67.2%
Preferred stock	1,659	6.6
Market value of stock	6,600	26.2
Total	$25,165	100.0%

In many ways Edison International is the opposite of Marshall Industries. It has grown slowly over the past several years in a regulated, noncompetitive environment. The company pays out significant dividends. Most of its assets are tangible in the form of transmission, distribution, and generating systems. The following questions were asked of Alan J. Fohrer, Executive Vice President and Chief Financial Officer of Edison International (as well as Southern California Edison):

RWJ: Traditionally, Edison International has relied on high leverage—why?
AJF: It is a low cost source of funding and we have significant borrowing capacity with a stable revenue stream, high quality assets in place, and for SCE regulatory framework. As you know, the interest on debt is tax-deductible. If we didn't have taxes, it would be much different, but the tax deduction is very important.

RWJ: Does Edison International have a target leverage ratio?
AJF: Not precisely. We want each subsidiary to have ready access to the debt markets. Thus, ratings of BBB and above are important. A rating below BBB would make new borrowing more difficult. The spreads today are minimal. The biggest issue today is availability.

Edison International is a mature, mostly regulated firm with cash flow that has not been used to keep leverage low. Instead, the company has established a high dividend payout ratio that has given the cash flow back to its investors and kept leverage high. This behavior is consistent with a target debt ratio and the trade-off theory of capital structure. A high percentage of Edison's assets are tangible and state regulatory commissions reduce the possibility that managers can engage in some of the selfish strategies described earlier in this chapter. As a consequence, financial distress costs have been lower for firms like Edison International than for nonregulated firms.

EDISON INTERNATIONAL
1999
(in $ millions except as noted)

Revenues	$9,670
Net income	$777
Long-term debt	$13,391
Market value of stock	$6,600
Dividend payout ratio	53%
Rate of return on equity	113%
Debt to total capital	67%
Five-year compound annual growth rate for revenues	8.5%
Market-to-book value ratio	1.7

Postscript: On January 5, 2001, because of skyrocketing wholesale electricity prices, Standard & Poor's lowered the credit rating for Edison International to the lowest investment grade. The stock price of Edison plummeted and was trading at $10¾, about one-half of the price a year earlier.

QUALCOMM: A CASE FOR LOW DEBT

Qualcomm is a supplier of digital wireless communications products and services. It is the innovator and implementer of the proprietary code-division multiple access (CDMA), a digital wireless technology. CDMA generates licensing fees, royalties, and chip sales. In addition, Qualcomm has a new high-data-rate (HDR) technology that it expects to transmit data at very high speeds for Internet use and access. Its primary U.S. competitor uses another wireless technology called TDMA. It competes with suppliers of alternative wireless technologies, such as GSM used by Pac Bell and TDMA used by AT&T.

Qualcomm employs about 7,000 people and is headquartered in San Diego. By March 2000, Qualcomm had redeemed all its convertible preferred securities and had very little long-term debt. Its capital structure was:

Long-term debt	Nil
Market value of stock	$112 billion

Why does Qualcomm rely so little on long-term debt? This question was asked of Anthony S. Thornley, Executive Vice President and Chief Financial Officer of Qualcomm.

RWJ: One thing that stands out from a financial point of view about Qualcomm is that it has almost no long-term debt. Why?
AST: There currently isn't any reason to leverage the company. We can finance our growth from retained earnings and outside equity.
RWJ: Outside equity?
AST: With our high P/E ratio we have a very low cost of equity.
RWJ: Qualcomm is in a very competitive business. Is this a factor in the capital structure?
AST: We are conservative financially and have relied largely on equity to finance the company. However, we have used debt at times when the relative cost was lower than equity.

RWJ: Many of the assets of Qualcomm are intangible, such as the value of its patents and its highly skilled engineers. Does this limit Qualcomm's debt capacity?
AST: Intangible assets have less collateral value than bricks and mortar, but Qualcomm's patents throw off a steady stream of cash flow. Qualcomm has a great deal of debt capacity. We just prefer flexibility at this time.
RWJ: Thanks.

What Can We Learn from Qualcomm?
First, Qualcomm is a firm with very uncertain future outcomes in a very competitive business and with significant intangible assets. This would suggest Qualcomm has a relatively low debt capacity when compared to, say, Edison International. Moreover, the financial management of Qualcomm is conservative by nature. Qualcomm's patents generate a steady stream of cash flow, which enhances debt capacity, but the competitive and fast-paced nature of the telecommunications industry suggests a need for financial slack and flexibility. Second, Qualcomm has experienced a rapid growth in profit and sales over the past five years—greater than 60 percent per annum. As a consequence, the tax potential benefits of debt have only recently materialized. Finally, Qualcomm's very high stock price and price-earnings ratio suggest (to its financial management) that this is an opportune time to rely more on equity financing than debt.

**A Financial Profile of Qualcomm
(April 2000)
(in $ millions except as noted)**

Revenues	3,937.3
Net income	391.9
Long-term debt	—
Dividend payout (%)	0
Return on equity (ROE) (%)	13.6
Five-year compound annual growth in revenues	62.5%
Recent price-to-earnings ratio	40–100

7. Debt-to-equity ratios vary across industries. We present three factors determining the target debt-to-equity ratio:

   a. *Taxes.* Firms with high taxable income should rely more on debt than firms with low taxable income.

   b. *Types of Assets.* Firms with a high percentage of intangible assets such as research and development should have low debt. Firms with primarily tangible assets should have higher debt.

   c. *Uncertainty of Operating Income.* Firms with high uncertainty of operating income should rely mostly on equity.

Key Terms

Agency costs 427	Nonmarketed claims 434
Marketed claims 434	Positive covenant 431
Negative covenant 430	Protective covenants 430

Suggested Readings

An excellent collection of recent articles appears in
Chew, D. *The New Corporate Finance: Where Theory Meets Practice* (New York: McGraw-Hill, 1993).

Merton Miller's Nobel lecture is reprinted as
Miller, M. "Leverage." *Journal of Finance* (June 1991).

An extremely influential set of articles arguing that bankruptcy costs are low are
Haugen, R. A., and L. Senbet. "The Insignificance of Bankruptcy Costs to the Theory of Optimal Capital Structure." *Journal of Finance* (May 1978).
Haugen, R. A., and L. Senbet. "Bankruptcy and Agency Costs: Their Significance to the Theory of Optimal Capital Structure." *Journal of Financial and Quantitative Analysis* (March 1988).

The following excellent paper surveys the various capital-structure theories:
Rajan, Raghuram G., and Luigi Zingales. "What Do We Know about Capital Structure?" *Journal of Finance* (December 1995).

In several recent articles, John R. Graham estimates effective corporate tax rates and their input on corporate financing policy.
"Do Personal Taxes Affect Corporate Financing Decisions." *Journal of Public Economics* 73 (1999).
"Debt and the MTR." *Journal of Financial Economics* 4 (1996).
Graham, John R.; Michael Lemmon; and James Schollheirn. "Debt, Leases, Taxes and the Endogeneity of Corporate Tax Status." *Journal of Finance* 53 (1998).

Questions and Problems

Costs of Financial Distress

16.1 Good Time Co. is a regional chain department store. It will remain in business for one more year. The estimated probability of a boom year is 60 percent and that of a recession is 40 percent. It is projected that Good Time will have total cash flow of $250 million in a boom year and $100 million in a recession. Its required debt payment is $150 million per annum. Assume a one-period model.

Assume risk neutrality and an annual discount rate of 12 percent for both the stock and the bond.

   a. What is the total stock value of the firm?

   b. If the total value of bonds outstanding of Good Time is $108.93 million, what is the expected bankruptcy cost in case of recession?

   c. What is the total value of the firm?

   d. What is the promised return on the bond?

16.2 VanSant Corporation and Matta, Inc., are identical firms except that Matta, Inc., is more levered than VanSant. The companies' economists agree that the probability of a recession next year is 20 percent and the probability of a continuation of the current expansion is 80 percent. If the expansion continues, each firm will have EBIT of $2 million. If a recession occurs, each firm will have EBIT of $0.8 million. VanSant's debt obligation requires the firm to make $750,000 in payments. Because Matta carries more debt, its debt payment obligations are $1 million.

   Assume that the investors in these firms are risk-neutral and that they discount the firms' cash flows at 15 percent. Assume a one-period example. Also assume there are no taxes.

   a. Duane, the president of VanSant, commented to Matta's president, Deb, that his firm has a higher value than Matta, Inc., because VanSant has less debt and, therefore, less bankruptcy risk. Is Duane correct?

   b. Using the data of the two firms, prove your answer to (*a*).

   c. What might cause the firms to be valued differently?

Description of Costs

16.3 What are the direct and indirect costs of bankruptcy? Briefly explain each.

16.4 Chrysler's financial structure in August 1983 was as follows:

Security	Number of Units Outstanding	Price per Unit	Market Value
Common stock	115,000,000	$ 26.00	$2,990,000,000
Preferred stock	10,000,000	32.50	325,000,000
Warrants	14,400,000	13.50	194,400,000
Bonds	2,000,000	650.00	1,300,000,000

Due to large losses incurred during 1978–1981, Chrysler had $2 billion in tax-loss carryforwards; therefore, the next $2 billion of income was free from corporate income taxes. At the time, the consensus of security analysts was that Chrysler would not have cumulative profits in excess of $2 billion over the next five years.

   Most of the preferred stock was held by banks. Chrysler had agreed to retire the preferred stock over the next few years. Chrysler had to decide whether to issue debt or sell common equity to raise the funds needed to retire the preferred stock.

   If you were Lee Iacocca, what would you have done? Why?

16.5 Fountain Corporation economists estimate that the probability of a good business environment next year is equal to the probability of a bad environment. Knowing that, the managers of Fountain must choose between two mutually exclusive projects. Suppose the project that Fountain chooses will be the only business it does next year. Therefore, the payoff of the project will determine the value of the firm. Fountain is obliged to make a $500 payment to its bondholders. The first project is one of low risk.

Low-risk Project

Economy	Probability	Project Payoff	Value of Firm		Value of Stock		Value of Bonds
Bad	0.5	$500	$500	=	$ 0	+	$500
Good	0.5	700	700	=	200	+	500

If the firm does not undertake the low-risk project, it will choose the following high-risk project.

High-risk Project

Economy	Probability	Project Payoff	Value of Firm		Value of Stock		Value of Bonds
Bad	0.5	$100	$100	=	$ 0	+	$100
Good	0.5	800	800	=	300	+	500

Which project would the stockholders prefer? Why?

16.6 Do you agree or disagree with the following statement? Explain your answer.
   A firm's stockholders would never want the firm to invest in projects with negative NPVs.

16.7 Refer to the selfish strategy in section 16.5. Suppose the bondholders are fully aware of the discrepancy between maximizing the firm value and the stock value. To minimize the agency costs, bondholders use a bond covenant to stipulate that when the firm takes on high-risk projects, bondholders can demand a higher debt payment. By how much would the bondholders need to raise the debt payment so that the stockholders would be indifferent between the two projects? What is the corporate finance implication of this postulated example?

Can Costs of Debt Be Reduced?
16.8 What measures do stockholders undertake to minimize the costs of debt?

Integration of Tax Effect and Financial Distress Costs
16.9 How would the consideration of financial distress costs and agency costs affect the MM proposition in a world where corporations pay taxes?

Shirking and Perquisites: A Note on Agency Cost of Equity
16.10 What are the sources of the agency costs of equity?

Personal Taxes
16.11 Fortune Enterprises (FE) is an all-equity firm that is considering issuing $13,500,000 in 10-percent debt. The firm will use the proceeds of the bond sale to repurchase equity. FE has a 100-percent payout policy. Because FE is a nongrowth firm, its earnings and debt would be perpetual. FE's income statement under each of the financial structures is shown below.

	All Equity	Debt
EBIT	$3,000,000	$3,000,000
Interest	0	1,350,000
EBT	3,000,000	1,650,000
Taxes ($T_C = 0.4$)	1,200,000	660,000
Net income	$1,800,000	$ 990,000

   a. If the personal tax rate is 30 percent, which plan offers the investors the higher cash flows? Why?
   b. Which plan does the IRS prefer?
   c. Suppose stockholders demand a 20-percent return after personal taxes. What is the value of the firm under each plan?
   d. Suppose $T_S = 0.2$ and $T_B = 0.55$. What are the investors' returns under each plan?

16.12 The general expression for the value of a leveraged firm in a world in which $T_S = 0$ is

$$V_L = V_U + \left[\frac{1 - (1 - T_C)}{(1 - T_B)}\right] \times B - C(B)$$

   where

V_U = Value of an unlevered firm

T_C = Effective corporate tax rate for the firm

T_B = Personal tax rate of the marginal bondholder

B = Debt level of the firm

$C(B)$ = Present value of the costs of financial distress for the firm as a function of its debt level. [Note: $C(B)$ encompasses all non–tax-related effects of leverage on the firm's value.]

Assume all investors are risk-neutral.

a. In their no-tax model, what do Modigliani and Miller assume about T_C, T_B, and $C(B)$? What do these assumptions imply about a firm's optimal debt-equity ratio?

b. In their model that includes corporate taxes, what do Modigliani and Miller assume about T_C, T_B, and $C(B)$? What do these assumptions imply about a firm's optimal debt-equity ratio?

c. Assume that IBM is certain to be able to use its interest deductions to reduce its corporate tax bill. What would the change in the value of IBM be if the company issued $1 billion in debt and used the proceeds to repurchase equity? Assume that the personal tax rate on bond income is 20 percent, the corporate tax rate is 34 percent, and the costs of financial distress are zero.

d. Assume that USX is virtually certain not to be able to use interest deductions. What would the change in the value of the company be from adding $1 of perpetual debt rather than $1 of equity? Assume that the personal tax rate on bond income is 20 percent, the corporate tax rate is 35 percent, and the costs of financial distress are zero.

e. For companies that may or may not be able to use the interest deduction, what would the change in the value of the company be from adding $1 of perpetual debt rather than $1 of equity? Assume that the personal tax rate on bond income is 20 percent, the corporate tax rate is 35 percent, and the costs of financial distress are zero. Also assume the probability of using the incremental deduction is 65 percent.

16.13 Because of the large cash inflows from the sales of its cookbook, *Fear of Frying,* the Overnight Publishing Company (OPC) has decided to retire all of its outstanding debt. The debt is made up of consul bonds; its maturity date is indefinitely far away. The debt is also considered risk-free. It carries a 10-percent coupon rate and has a book value of $3 million. Because market rates on long-term bonds are 15 percent, the market value of the bonds is only $2 million. All of the debt is held by one institution that will sell it back to OPC for $2 million cash. The institution will not charge OPC any transaction costs, and there are no tax consequences from retiring the debt. Once OPC becomes an all-equity firm, it will remain unlevered forever.

If OPC does not return the debt, the company will use the $2 million in cash to buy back some of its stock on the open market. Repurchasing stock also has no transaction costs. Investors expect OPC to repurchase some stock, so they will be completely surprised when the debt-retirement plan is announced.

The required rate of return of the equity holders after OPC becomes all equity will be 20 percent. The expected annual earnings before interest and taxes for the firm are $1,100,000; those earnings are expected to remain constant in perpetuity. OPC has no growth opportunities, and the company is subject to a 35-percent corporate tax rate. Assume that $T_B = 10\%$ and $T_S = 0$. Also assume that bankruptcy costs do not change for OPC as a result of this capital-structure change. How much does the market value of the company change?

16.14 The EXES Company is assessing its present capital structure and that structure's implications for the welfare of its investors. EXES is currently financed entirely with common stock, of which 1,000 shares are outstanding. Given the risk of the underlying cash flows (EBIT) generated by EXES, investors currently require a 20-percent return on the EXES common stock. The company pays out all earnings as dividends to common stockholders.

EXES estimates that operating income may be $1,000, $2,000, or $4,200 with respective probabilities of 0.1, 0.4, and 0.5. Assume the firm's expectations about earnings will be met and that they will be unchanged in perpetuity. Also, assume that the corporate and personal tax rates are equal to zero.

a. What is the value of EXES Company?

b. The president of EXES has decided that shareholders would be better off if the company had equal proportions of debt and equity. He therefore proposes to issue $7,500 of debt at an interest rate of 10 percent. He will use the proceeds to repurchase 500 shares of common stock.

  i. What will the new value of the firm be?

  ii. What will the value of EXES's debt be?

  iii. What will the value of EXES's equity be?

c. Suppose the president's proposal is implemented.

  i. What is the required rate of return on equity?

  ii. What is the firm's overall required return?

d. Suppose the corporate tax rate is 40 percent.

  i. Use the Modigliani-Miller framework that includes taxes to find the value of the firm.

  ii. Does the presence of taxes increase or decrease the value of the firm? Why?

  iii. Verbally explain how the presence of bankruptcy costs would change the effect of taxes on the value of the firm, if at all.

e. Suppose interest income is taxed at 40 percent while the effective tax on returns to equityholders is zero. Assume that the introduction of the personal tax rate does not affect the required return on equity.

  i. What is the value of EXES in a world with personal taxes?

  ii. Under the Miller model, what will happen to the value of the firm as the tax on interest income rises?

16.15 Mueller Brewing Company has been ordered by the EPA to stop polluting the Menomenie River. It must now spend $100 million on pollution-control equipment. The company has three alternatives for obtaining the needed $100 million.

  1. Sell $100 million of perpetual, taxable corporate bonds with a 20-percent coupon rate.

  2. Sell $100 million of perpetual pollution-control bonds with a 10-percent coupon rate. The interest on these bonds is not taxable to investors.

  3. Sell $100 million of common stock with a 9.5-percent current dividend yield. Mueller Brewing Company is in the 35-percent tax bracket.

  The president of Mueller Brewing wants to sell the common stock because it has the lowest rate. Mr. Daniels, the company's treasurer, suggests bond financing because of the tax shield offered by the debt. His analysis shows that the value of the firm would increase $r_B B T_C / r_B$ = ($100 million) × (0.35) = $35 million if Mueller issues bonds instead of equity. A newly hired financial analyst, Ms. Harris, argues that it does not matter which type of bond is issued. She claims that the yields will be bid up to reflect taxes and, thus, the financing choice will not matter.

a. Comment on the analyses of the president, Mr. Daniels, and Ms. Harris.

b. Should Mueller be indifferent about which financing plan it chooses? If not, rank the three alternatives and give the benefits and costs of each.

16.16 Melvin Clark, CFO of the Matsushita Corp., is evaluating the value of the firm's current capital structure. Being conservative, he expects that Matsushita will have a perpetual EBIT of $800,000, with an after-tax discount rate of 10 percent if it is all-equity financed. Currently, the firm has $1.2 million debt. The corporate tax rate is 35 percent. The uniform personal tax rate in the economy is 15 percent. Personal tax rates on equity income are effectively zero because of the possibility of infinite deferral of the realization of capital gains. The combined financial distress and agency costs associated with the debt are approximately 5 percent of the total debt value.

a. What is the added value of the debt?

b. What is the firm value of Matsushita?

Integrative Questions

16.17 The Gulf Power Company is an electric utility planning to build a new power-generating plant of conventional design. The company has traditionally paid out all earnings to the stockholders as dividends and financed capital expenditures with new issues of common stock. There is no debt or preferred stock presently outstanding. Data on the company and the new power plant follow. Assume all earnings streams are perpetuities that are constant.

Company Data
Current annual earnings: $27 million
Number of outstanding shares: 10 million

New Power Plant
Initial outlay: $20 million
Added annual earnings: $3 million

Management estimates the rate of return currently required by stockholders to be 10 percent per year and considers the power plant to have the same risk as existing assets. Assume there are no taxes, no costs of bankruptcy, and perfect capital markets.

a. What will be the total market value of Gulf Power if common stock is issued to finance the plant?

b. What will be the total value (stocks plus bonds) of the firm if $20 million in bonds at an interest rate of 8 percent is issued to finance the plant, assuming the bonds are perpetuities?

c. Given that bonds will be issued as in (b), calculate the rate of return required by stockholders after the financing has occurred and the plant has been built.

16.18 The management of New England Textile Corporation (NETC) has decided to relocate the firm to North Carolina after four more years of operating its factory in Cotton Mather, Massachusetts. Because of transportation costs and a nonexistent secondary market for used textile machines, all of NETC's machines will be worthless after four years.

Mr. Rayon, plant engineer, recommends that a Spool Pfitzer machine be purchased. His analysis of the only two available models shows that:

	Heavy-Duty Model	Light-Weight Model
Annual savings in costs	$340	$316
Economic life	4 years	2 years
Price of machine	$1,000	$500

NETC's accountant, Mr. Wool, must decide on two actions.

a. Purchase the Heavy-Duty Spool Pfitzer now, or

b. Purchase one Light-Weight Spool Pfitzer now and replace it after two years with a second Light-Weight Spool Pfitzer.

The manufacturer of the Spool Pfitzers is willing to guarantee that the prices he charges to NETC won't change during the next four years. The annual cost savings are known with certainty because of NETC's backlog of orders to supply the Slobovian Army and because of NETC's long-term contracts with its workers and suppliers. Only straight-line depreciation over their economic life is allowed for Spool Pfitzer machines. NETC's tax rate is 34 percent.

Mr. Wool, being a sophisticated USC MBA, obtained the following information for his analysis of various investment and financial proposals:

Asset	Expected Value	Variance	Covariance with Market Return
Risk-free asset	0.10		
Market portfolio	0.20	0.04	0.04
NETC common stock			0.048

As a matter of company policy, NETC has never borrowed in the past; it is 100 percent equity financed. The market value of NETC common stock is $10 million.

a. What is the cost of capital for NETC?

b. Which of the two Spool Pfitzers should NETC purchase? If Spool Pfitzers are a bad investment, show why.

c. Assuming that the Heavy-Duty Spool Pfitzer will be purchased, what is the minimum annual savings in costs necessary for the Heavy-Duty Spool Pfitzer to be an acceptable investment?

d. Mr. Wool has long believed that NETC's capital structure is not optimal; however, he was afraid to suggest changing the company's traditional all-equity financing policy. He believes in the Miller-Modigliani analysis and thinks that by selling $2 million of 10 percent perpetual bonds (no maturity) at par ("par" = "face" or "principal" amount) and using the proceeds to repurchase NETC stock, the total value of the firm would increase.
   If Mr. Wool is correct and if his financial plan is adopted, what would be the new:
   i. Total value of the firm
   ii. Total value of NETC stock
   iii. Weighted average cost of capital for NETC

e. Ms. Nylon says that Mr. Wool is mistaken. Because NETC is a high-risk firm in a declining industry, it would have to pay a 20 percent interest rate on its bonds, and the "increase in the value of the firm would be much *less.*" Mr. Rayon says that a 20 percent interest rate "would mean that the value of the firm would increase *more* than Mr. Wool expects because of a larger tax shield." Mr. Orlon, chairman of the board of NETC, says that Wool, Nylon, and Rayon are all wrong and that the total value of the firm would remain at $10 million "because bond investors are risk-averse too!" Discuss the arguments given by Wool, Rayon, Nylon, and Orlon.

f. Suppose that, because of the new debt, there are new costs associated with possible financial distress. These costs can be expressed as 2 percent of the new firm value. Does this new information change the analysis?

g. Mr. Buck, loan officer at the First Cotton Mather National Bank (FCMNB), received an application for a 20-year $2 million loan from NETC. FCMNB is one of the few banks in the United States that make long-term loans. Although NETC is a well-known and respected local firm, Mr. Buck is worried about whether he should approve the loan. Does he have any reason to examine this loan application more carefully than (for example) one from Cotton Mather Electric Utility Company? What (if any) are the risks of making the loan to NETC?

Appendix 16A Some Useful Formulas of Financial Structure

Definitions

$E(EBIT)$ = A perpetual expectation of cash operating income before interest and taxes

V_U = Value of an unlevered firm

V_L = Value of levered firm

B = Present value of debt

S = Present value of equity

r_S = Cost of equity

r_B = Cost of debt capital

r_0 = Cost of capital to an all-equity firm. In a world of no corporate taxes, the weighted average cost of capital to a levered firm, r_{WACC}, is also equal to r_0. However, with corporate taxes, r_0 is above r_{WACC} for a levered firm.

Model I (No Tax)

$$V_L = V_U = \frac{\text{E(EBIT)}}{r_0}$$

$$r_S = r_0 + (r_0 - r_B) \times B/S$$

Model II (Corporate Tax, $T_C > 0$; No Personal Taxes, $T_S = T_B = 0$)

$$V_L = \frac{\text{E[EBIT]} \times (1 - T_C)}{r_0} + \frac{T_C r_B B}{r_B} = V_U + T_C B$$

$$r_S = r_0 + (1 - T_C) \times (r_0 - r_B) \times B/S$$

Model III (Corporate Tax, $T_C > 0$; Personal Tax, $T_B > 0$; $T_S > 0$)

$$V_L = V_U + \left[1 - \frac{(1 - T_C) \times (1 - T_S)}{(1 - T_B)} \right] \times B$$

Appendix 16B THE MILLER MODEL AND THE GRADUATED INCOME TAX

In our previous discussion, we assumed a flat personal income tax on interest income. In other words, we assumed that all individuals are subject to the same personal tax rate on interest income. Merton Miller derived the results of the previous section in a classic paper.[40] However, the genius of his paper was to consider the implications of personal taxes when tax rates differ across individuals.

This *graduated* income tax is consistent with the real world. For example, individuals are currently taxed at rates of 0, 15, 28, 31, 36, and 39.6 percent in the United States, depending on income. In addition, other entities, such as corporate pension funds, individual retirement accounts (IRAs), and universities, are tax-exempt.

To illustrate Miller's model with graduated taxes, we consider a world where *all* firms initially only issue equity. We assume that $T_C = 35\%$ and $T_S = 0$.[41] The required return on stock, r_S, is 10 percent. In addition, we posit a graduated personal income tax, where tax rates vary between 0 and 50 percent. All individuals are risk-neutral.

Now consider a courageous firm contemplating a $1,000 issue of debt. What is the interest rate that the firm can pay and still be as well off as if it issued equity? Because debt is tax deductible, the after–corporate tax cost of debt is $(1 - T_C) \times r_B$. However, equity is not deductible at the corporate level, so the after-tax cost of equity is r_S. Thus, the firm is indifferent to whether it issues debt or equity when

$$(1 - T_C) \times r_B = r_S \tag{16.3}$$

Because $T_C = 35\%$ and $r_S = 10\%$, the firm could afford to pay a rate on debt as high as 15.38 percent.

Miller argues that those in the lowest tax brackets (tax-exempt in our example) will buy the debt because they pay the least personal tax on interest. These tax-exempt investors will be indifferent to whether they buy the stock or purchase bonds also yielding 10 percent.

---

[40]M. Miller, "Debt and Taxes," *Journal of Finance* (May 1977). Yes, this is the same Miller of MM.

[41]The assumption that $T_S = 0$ is perhaps an extreme one. However, it is commonly made in the literature, justified by the investor's ability to defer realization of capital gains indefinitely. Besides, the same qualitative conclusions hold if $T_S > 0$, though the explanation would be more involved.

Thus, if this firm is the *only* one issuing debt, it can pay an interest rate well below its break-even rate of 15.38 percent.

Noticing the gain to the first firm, many other firms are likely to issue debt. However, if there are only a fixed number of tax-exempt investors, new debt issues must attract people in higher brackets. Because these individuals are taxed on interest at a higher rate than they are taxed on equity distributions, they will only buy debt if its yield is greater than 10 percent. For example, an individual in the 15-percent bracket has an interest rate after personal tax of $r_B \times (1 - 0.15)$. He will be indifferent to whether he buys bonds or stock if $r_B = 11.765\%$, because $0.11765 \times 0.85 = 10\%$. Because 11.765 percent is less than the 15.38 percent rate of equation (16.3), corporations gain by issuing debt to investors in the 15-percent bracket.

Now consider investors in the 35-percent bracket. A return on bonds of 15.38 percent provides them with a $10\% = 15.38\% \times (1 - 0.35)$ interest rate after personal tax. Thus, they are indifferent to whether they earn a 15.38-percent return on bonds or a 10-percent return on stock. Miller argues that, in equilibrium, corporations will issue enough debt so that investors with personal tax brackets up to and including 35 percent will hold debt.[42] Additional debt will not be issued because the interest rate needed to attract investors in higher tax brackets is above the 15.38-percent rate that corporations can afford to pay.

The beauty of competition is that other companies can so capitalize on someone's innovation that all value to the courageous first entrant is eliminated. According to the Miller model, firms will issue enough debt so that individuals up to and including the 35-percent bracket hold it. In order to induce these investors to hold bonds, the competitive interest rate becomes 15.38 percent. No firm profits from issuing debt in equilibrium. Rather, all firms are indifferent to whether they issue debt or equity in equilibrium.

Miller's work produces three results:

1. In aggregate, the corporate sector will issue just enough debt so that individuals with tax brackets equal to and below the corporate tax rate, T_C, will hold debt, and individuals with higher tax brackets will not hold debt. Thus, individuals in these higher brackets will hold stock.

2. Because people in tax brackets equal to the corporate rate hold debt, there is no gain or loss to corporate leverage. Therefore, the capital-structure decision is a matter of indifference to an individual firm. Though the Miller model is quite sophisticated, this conclusion is identical to that reached by MM in a world without any taxes.

3. As given in equation (16.3), the return on bonds will be higher than the return on stocks of comparable risk. (An adjustment to (16.3) must be made to reflect the greater risk of stocks in the real world.)

EXAMPLE

Consider an economy in which there are four groups of investors and no others:

Group	Marginal Tax Rate (%) on Bonds (T_B)	Personal Wealth (in $ millions)
Finance majors	50%	$1,200
Accounting majors	35	300
Marketing majors	20	150
Management majors	0	50

---

[42]All investors with $T_B < 35$ percent hold bonds. Because investors with $T_B = 35$ percent are indifferent to whether they hold stocks or bonds, only some of them are likely to choose bonds.

We assume that investors are risk-neutral and that equity income is untaxed at the personal level for all investors (i.e., $T_S = 0$). All investors can earn a tax-free return of 5.4 percent by investing in foreign real estate; therefore, this is the return on equity. The corporate tax rate is 35 percent. Interest payments are tax deductible at the corporate level and taxable at the individual level. Corporations receive a total of $120 million in cash flow before tax and interest. There are no growth opportunities, and every year is the same in perpetuity. What is the range of possible debt-equity ratios?

The return on equity, r_S, will be set equal to the return on foreign real estate, which is 0.054. In a Miller equilibrium, $r_S = (1 - T_C) \times r_B$. Therefore,

$$r_B = \frac{0.054}{1 - 0.35} = 0.0831$$

Given the tax brackets of the different groups of investors, we would expect that finance majors would hold equity and foreign real estate, and accounting majors would be indifferent to whether they held equity or debt. Marketing and management majors would hold bonds because their personal tax rates are below 0.35. Because accounting majors are indifferent to whether they hold bonds or stocks, we must learn what happens if they invest in bonds or equity. If accounting majors use their $300 to buy bonds, $B = \$300 + \$150 + \$50 = \$500$. Then the following calculations can be made.

$$S = \frac{(\text{EBIT} - r_B B) \times (1 - T_C)}{r_S} = \frac{[\$120 - (0.0831 \times \$500)] \times (1 - 0.35)}{0.054}$$

$$= \$944$$

$$B = \frac{r_B B}{r_B} = \$500$$

$$V_L = S + B = \$944 + \$500 = \$1,444$$

$$\frac{B}{S} = \frac{\$500}{\$944} = 0.530$$

If accounting majors buy stocks and foreign real estate ($B = \$150 + \$50 = \$200$),

$$S = \frac{(\text{EBIT} - r_B B) \times (1 - T_C)}{r_S} = \frac{[\$120 - (0.0831 \times \$200)] \times (1 - 0.35)}{0.054}$$

$$= \$1,244$$

$$B = \$200$$

$$V_L = S + B = \$1,244 + \$200 = \$1,444$$

$$\frac{B}{S} = \frac{\$200}{\$1,244} = 0.161$$

Thus, depending on the amount of bonds held by accounting majors, the debt-equity ratio in the economy can lie in the range of 0.161 to 0.530.

QUESTIONS AND PROBLEMS

The Miller Model and the Graduated Income Tax

16.19 Consider an economy with three investor groups with marginal personal tax rate of 10 percent, 20 percent, and 40 percent, respectively. The corporate tax rate is 35 percent. Assume zero personal tax rate on equity income. The required rate of return on all-equity financed projects is 11 percent.

   a. What is the prevailing equilibrium interest rate?

   b. What is the investment pattern for each of the three investor groups?

   c. If Quantex Corp. has an EBIT of $1 million in perpetuity, what is its firm value? Does the firm value vary with different capital structure choices?

16.20 Assume that there are three groups of investors with the following tax rates and investable funds:

Group	Investable Funds (in $ millions)	Tax Rate (percent)
A	375	50
B	220	32.5
C	105	10

Each group requires a minimum after-tax return of 8.1 percent on any security. The only types of securities available are common stock and perpetual corporate bonds. Income from corporate bonds is subject to a personal tax, but it is deductible for corporate tax purposes. Capital gains from common stock are untaxed at the personal level. In equilibrium, common stock yields an 8.1 percent pretax return; foreign real estate also earns this rate. All funds not invested in stocks or bonds will be invested in foreign real estate. Assume the common stock and the bonds are both risk-free.

   Corporate earnings before interest and taxes total $85 million each year in perpetuity. The corporate tax rate is 35 percent.

   a. What is the equilibrium market rate of interest on corporate bonds, r_B?

   b. In equilibrium, what is the composition of each of the groups' portfolios?

   c. What is the total market value of all companies?

   d. What is the total tax bill?

16.21 Consider an economy in which there are four groups of people:

Group	Marginal Tax Rate (percent)	Wealth (in $ millions)
L	50	700
M	40	300
N	20	200
O	0	500

All investors can earn a tax-free return of 6 percent by investing in foreign real estate. Interest payments are taxable at the individual level, but equity income is untaxed at the personal level for all investors.

   Corporations receive pretax cash flows of interest totaling $150 million. Interest payments are tax deductible at the corporate level. There are no depreciation deductions. Firms have no growth opportunities, and their plants are everlasting. The corporate tax rate is 40 percent.

   a. What is the range of possible aggregate debt-equity ratios in the economy?

   b. What would your answer to (*a*) be if the corporate tax rate is 30 percent?

APPENDIX 16C

CASE STUDY   *The Decision to Use More Debt: The Case of Goodyear Tire and Rubber*[43]

■■■■■ What actually happens when a particular firm abruptly decides to use more debt? We look at the experience of Goodyear Tire and Rubber to try to answer this question. Goodyear's increased reliance on debt illustrates many of the important points of this chapter.

Goodyear Tire and Rubber is a well-known manufacturer of rubber products. Automotive products account for about 60 percent of its sales. By 1986 Goodyear Tire and Rubber had become the world's largest manufacturer of tires. Goodyear had worked hard to obtain a reputation for outstanding quality in "high performance" tires. Although Goodyear was the world's leader in making tires, it had encountered difficulties when it tried to diversify into oil and gas and to build an oil pipeline from Texas to California.

In December 1986, Goodyear Tire and Rubber started a cash tender offer for 40 million of its shares at $50 per share. This represented a 50 percent premium over its share price two months earlier. The stock market's reaction was to substantially increase Goodyear's stock price. Why did Goodyear buy back almost one half of its outstanding stock? One reason was the threat of a takeover. Several weeks earlier, the company had reached an agreement with a group headed by feared raider Sir James Goldsmith to acquire his stake in Goodyear for $49.50 per share. The purpose of Goodyear's acquisition of its own stock was to buy out the Goldsmith group's position and to make Goodyear more "shark repellent" for other raiders. The buyout was financed with new debt and with cash from sales of major assets. The result was to significantly increase Goodyear's reliance on debt.

Goodyear's type of financial restructuring is often called a levered recapitalization. Recapitalization is an imprecise term that refers to changes on the right-hand side of a firm's balance sheet. When the effect is to increase a firm's reliance on debt, it is called a levered recapitalization, and usually it involves repurchasing stock and new borrowing. The net effect of Goodyear's recapitalization on its balance sheet was to increase its long-term debt-to-equity ratio from 28.4 percent in 1985 to 150.2 percent in 1988 (see the following table).

GOODYEAR TIRE AND RUBBER
(in $ millions)

	1985	1986	1987	1988	1989	1990
Long-term debt	$997.5	$2,487.5	$3,282.4	$3,044.8	$2,963.4	$3,286.4
Equity	$3,507.4	$3,002.6	$1,834.4	$2,027.1	$2,143.8	$2,097.9
Shares outstanding	216.2	194.2	114.0	114.9	115.6	117.0
Return on equity (ROE)	8.6%	9.2%	24.0%	17.7%	13.8%	negative

Was Goodyear's levered recapitalization a good decision? There are benefits and costs from any levered recapitalization. Clues can be gleaned from the stock market. The stock market's reaction to Goodyear's levered recapitalization was very positive. On the day Goodyear's levered recapitalization was announced, Goodyear's stock jumped by over 20 percent.

Benefits

1. *Tax Benefits.* It is well known that new debt can increase a firm's value by reducing its taxes. There is no doubt that Goodyear's tax burden has been substantially reduced due to increased reliance on debt. Goodyear's interest expense increased from $101 million in 1985 to $282 million in 1987, and Goodyear's taxable income was reduced.

---

[43]Alan Shapiro writes about the Goodyear Tire and Rubber Company in "Corporate Stockholders and Corporate Responsibility," *USC Business* (Summer 1991). See also "Goodyear Tire and Rubber: 1988," Harvard Business School Case 284-177, for a description of Goodyear Tire and Rubber's restructuring and the aftermath. An upbeat article on Goodyear's current prospects appears in "Gault on Fixing Goodyear's Flat," *Fortune,* July 15, 1991.

2. *Lower Agency Costs.* It is often argued that leverage reduces the agency costs arising between management and shareholders. Therefore, the new debt from the levered recapitalization can be thought of as a type of a control device for the shareholders of Goodyear. In 1982 Goodyear had embarked on a diversification program by acquiring Celeron, an oil and gas company. The acquisition of Celeron was followed by several other diversification attempts. Most importantly, Goodyear decided to construct a crude oil pipeline from Texas to California. Shareholders did not react favorably to Goodyear's diversification program, and its stock price fell 65 percent (relative to the S&P 500 Index) over the three and one-half years after 1982. It can be argued that this is a classic case of management pursuing selfish shortsighted goals at the expense of shareholders. Goodyear's diversification program imposed agency costs on its shareholders. Goodyear's levered recapitalization probably prevented it from further diversification because Goodyear was forced to sell most of its non-tire assets to service its new debt. It sold Celeron Oil in December 1987. By borrowing an amount equal to the present value of Goodyear's excess cash flow that could be used to acquire other firms, Goodyear's management has been effectively prevented from further diversification.

Costs

1. *Financial Distress.* When firms such as Goodyear increase their reliance on debt, they also increase the likelihood of financial distress. Financial distress can be formal bankruptcy. So far, Goodyear has not filed for bankruptcy. However, financial distress may occur without bankruptcy. After the levered recapitalization, Goodyear's debt was downgraded by Moody's and Standard & Poor's. This may be evidence of financial distress. Goodyear lost money in 1990 and its ROE was negative. More importantly, financial distress means doing particularly harmful things such as the selfish strategies that we talked about previously. Goodyear has said that it has been forced to cut down on planned research and development and capital spending because of its reliance on debt. Its level of capital spending decreased from about $1.5 billion in 1986 to $754 million in 1988. This may be evidence of financial distress. If so, this is one of the costs imposed upon Goodyear because of its levered recapitalization.
2. *Financial Slack.* The new debt has increased Goodyear's leverage well beyond traditional industry norms. Up to 1985 Goodyear had relied on little debt, leading some industry analysts in 1985 to contend that Goodyear had excess debt capacity (i.e., *financial slack*). However, the excess cash flows that supported Goodyear's borrowing in 1986 and 1987 disappeared in 1988. By the end of 1988 Goodyear had used up all of its financial slack. Loss of financial slack can preclude strategic options if competitors increase capital spending or lower prices. Many analysts believe this is what happened when in 1989 Bridgestone, Goodyear's main competitor, announced its intention to increase its capital spending in the North American tire market. Goodyear could not counter by increasing its own level of capital spending. The only way Goodyear could do so would have been by issuing new equity. But firms do not like to issue new equity because it is very expensive and it is the lowest financing option on the pecking order.

Part of Goodyear's decision to use more debt can be analyzed in terms of a trade-off between the tax benefits of debt and the costs of financial distress. However, the Goodyear experience shows that agency costs and financial slack are also factors in a firm's decision to use debt.

Postscript

Goodyear almost went broke in 1990–1991 and was forced to cut its dividend for the first time since the 1930s. In 1991 it hired a new CEO, Stanley Gault, who was hailed as CEO of the year in 1992 (by *Financial World*). In 1997 Goodyear's ROE was close to 20 percent and its long-term debt reduced to about $1 billion. Capital spending remained very low at about $620 million. Its oil pipeline was profitable for the first time in 1994. (But, in 1997 Goodyear finally found a buyer for its pipeline.) Today Goodyear is still the world's largest rubber manufacturer. Its market capitalization is about $3 billion and it has increased its dividend payout from 20¢ in 1991 to $1.20 in 1999. Its ROE is 10%.

CHAPTER 17

Valuation and Capital Budgeting for the Levered Firm

EXECUTIVE SUMMARY

Instructors often structure the basic course in corporate finance around the two sides of the balance sheet. The left-hand side of the balance sheet contains assets. Chapters 4, 5, 6, 7, and 8 of this textbook treat the capital-budgeting decision, which is a decision concerning the assets of the firm. Chapters 9, 10, 11, and 12 treat the discount rate for a project, so those chapters also concern the left-hand side of the balance sheet. The right-hand side of the balance sheet contains liabilities and owner's equity. Chapters 13, 14, 15, and 16 of this textbook examine the debt-versus-equity decision, which is a decision about the right-hand side of the balance sheet.

While the preceding chapters of this textbook have, for the most part, treated the capital-budgeting decision separately from the capital-structure decision, the two decisions are actually related. As we will see, a project of an all-equity firm might be rejected, while the same project might be accepted for a levered but otherwise identical firm. This occurs because the cost of capital frequently decreases with leverage, thereby turning some negative NPV projects into positive NPV projects.

Chapters 4 through 8 implicitly assumed that the firm is financed with only equity. The goal of this chapter is to value a project, or the firm itself, when leverage is employed. We point out that there are three standard approaches to valuation under leverage: the adjusted-present-value (APV) method, the flow-to-equity (FTE) method, and the weighted-average-cost-of-capital (WACC) method. These three approaches may seem, at first glance, to be quite different. However, we show that, if applied correctly, all three approaches provide the same value estimate.

The three methods discussed next can be used to value either the firm as a whole or a project. The example below discusses project value, though everything we say applies to an entire firm as well.

17.1 ADJUSTED-PRESENT-VALUE APPROACH

The **adjusted-present-value (APV)** method is best described by the following formula:

$$APV = NPV + NPVF$$

In words, the value of a project to a levered firm (APV) is equal to the value of the project to an unlevered firm (NPV) plus the net present value of the financing side effects (NPVF). One can generally think of four side effects:

1. *The Tax Subsidy to Debt.* This was discussed in Chapter 15, where we pointed out that, for perpetual debt, the value of the tax subsidy is $T_C B$. (T_C is the corporate tax rate, and B is the value of the debt.) The material on valuation under corporate taxes in Chapter 15 is actually an application of the APV approach.

2. *The Costs of Issuing New Securities.* As we will discuss in detail in Chapter 20, investment bankers participate in the public issuance of corporate debt. These bankers must be compensated for their time and effort, a cost that lowers the value of the project.

3. *The Costs of Financial Distress.* The possibility of financial distress, and bankruptcy in particular, arises with debt financing. As stated in the previous chapter, financial distress imposes costs, thereby lowering value.

4. *Subsidies to Debt Financing.* The interest on debt issued by state and local governments is not taxable to the investor. Because of this, the yield on tax-exempt debt is generally substantially below the yield on taxable debt. Frequently, corporations are able to obtain financing from a municipality at the tax-exempt rate because the municipality can borrow at that rate as well. As with any subsidy, this subsidy adds value.

While each of the preceding four side effects is important, the tax deduction to debt almost certainly has the highest dollar value in practice. For this reason, the following example considers the tax subsidy, but not the other three side effects.[1]

Consider a project of the P. B. Singer Co. with the following characteristics:

Cash inflows: $500,000 per year for the indefinite future
Cash costs: 72% of sales
Initial investment: $475,000
$T_C = 34\%$
$r_0 = 20\%$, where r_0 is the cost of capital for a project of an all-equity firm.

If both the project and the firm are financed with only equity, the project's cash flow is

Cash inflows	$500,000
Cash costs	−360,000
Operating income	140,000
Corporate tax (.34 tax rate)	−47,600
Unlevered cash flow (UCF)	$92,400

The distinction in Chapter 4 between present value and net present value is important for this example. As pointed out in Chapter 4, the *present value* of a project is determined before the initial investment at date 0 is subtracted. The initial investment is subtracted for the calculation of *net* present value.

Given a discount rate of 20 percent, the present value of the project is

$$\frac{\$92,400}{0.20} = \$462,000$$

The net present value (NPV) of the project, that is, the value of the project to an all-equity firm, is

$$\$462,000 - \$475,000 = -\$13,000$$

Since the NPV is negative, the project would be rejected by an all-equity firm.

Now imagine that the firm finances the project with exactly $126,229.50 in debt, so that the remaining investment of $348,770.50 ($475,000 − $126,229.50) is financed with equity. The net present value of the project under leverage, which we call the adjusted present value, or the APV, is

$$APV = NPV + T_C \times B$$
$$\$29,918 = -\$13,000 + 0.34 \times \$126,229.50$$

---

[1]The Bicksler Enterprises example of Section 17.6 handles both flotation costs and interest subsidies.

That is, the value of the project when financed with some leverage is equal to the value of the project when financed with all equity plus the tax shield from the debt. Since this number is positive, the project should be accepted.

You may be wondering why we chose such a precise amount of debt. Actually, we chose it so that the ratio of debt to the present value of the project under leverage is 0.25.[2]

In this example, debt is a fixed proportion of the present value of the project, not a fixed proportion of the initial investment of $475,000. This is consistent with the goal of a target debt-to-*market*-value ratio, which we find in the real world. For example, commercial banks typically lend to real estate developers a fixed percentage of the market value of a project, not a fixed percentage of the initial investment.

QUESTIONS
- How is the APV method applied?
- What additional information beyond NPV does one need to calculate APV?

17.2 FLOW-TO-EQUITY APPROACH

The **flow-to-equity (FTE)** approach is an alternative capital-budgeting approach. The formula simply calls for discounting the cash flow from the project to the equityholders of the levered firm at the cost of equity capital, r_S. For a perpetuity, this becomes

$$\frac{\text{Cash flow from project to equityholders of the levered firm}}{r_S}$$

There are three steps to the FTE approach.

Step 1: Calculating Levered Cash Flow (LCF)[3]

Assuming an interest rate of 10 percent, the perpetual cash flow to equityholders in our example is

Cash inflows	$500,000.00
Cash costs	−360,000.00
Interest (10% × $126,229.50)	−12,622.95
Income after interest	127,377.05
Corporate tax (.34 tax rate)	−43,308.20
Levered cash flow (LCF)	$ 84,068.85

---

[2]That is, the present value of the project after the initial investment has been made is $504,918 ($29,918 + $475,000). Thus, the debt-to-value ratio of the project is 0.25 ($126,229.50/$504,918).

This level of debt can be calculated directly. Note that

$$\text{Present value of levered project} = \text{Present value of unlevered project} + T_C \times B$$

$$V_{\text{With debt}} = \$462,000 \qquad\qquad + 0.34 \times .25 \times V_{\text{With debt}}$$

Rearranging the last line, we have

$$V_{\text{With debt}}(1 - 0.34 \times 0.25) = \$462,000$$
$$V_{\text{With debt}} = \$504,918$$

Since debt is 0.25 of value, debt is $126,229.50 (0.25 × $504,918).

[3]We use the term *levered cash flow* (LCF) for simplicity. A more complete term would be *cash flow from the project to the equityholders of a levered firm*. Similarly, a more complete term for *unlevered cash flow* (UCF) would be *cash flow from the project to the equityholders of an unlevered firm*.

Alternatively, one can calculate levered cash flow (LCF) directly from unlevered cash flow (UCF). The key here is that the difference between the cash flow that equityholders receive in an unlevered firm and the cash flow that equityholders receive in a levered firm is the after-tax interest payment. (Repayment of principal does not appear in this example, since the debt is perpetual.) One writes this algebraically as

$$\text{UCF} - \text{LCF} = (1 - T_C)r_B B$$

The term on the right-hand side of this expression is the after-tax interest payment. Thus, since cash flow to the unlevered equityholders (UCF) is $92,400 and the after-tax interest payment is $8,331.15 [(.66).10 × $126,229.50], cash flow to the levered equityholders (LCF) is

$$\$92,400 - \$8,331.15 = \$84,068.85$$

which is exactly the number we calculated earlier.

Step 2: Calculating r_S

The next step is to calculate the discount rate, r_S. Note that we assumed that the discount rate on unlevered equity, r_0, is .20. As we saw in Chapter 15, the formula for r_S is

$$r_S = r_0 + \frac{B}{S}(1 - T_C)(r_0 - r_B)$$

Note that our target debt-to-value ratio of 1/4 implies a target debt-to-equity ratio of 1/3. Applying the preceding formula to this example, we have

$$r_S = .222 = .20 + \frac{1}{3}(.66)(.20 - .10)$$

Step 3: Valuation

The present value of the project's LCF is

$$\frac{\text{LCF}}{r_S} = \frac{\$84,068.85}{.222} = \$378,688.50$$

Since the initial investment is $475,000 and $126,299.50 is borrowed, the firm must advance the project $348,770.50 ($475,000 − $126,229.50) out of its own cash reserves. The *net* present value of the project is simply the difference between the present value of the project's LCF and the investment not borrowed. Thus, the NPV is

$$\$378,688.50 - \$348,770.50 = \$29,918$$

which is identical to the result found with the APV approach.

QUESTIONS
?
CONCEPT

- How is the FTE method applied?
- What information is needed to calculate FTE?

17.3 WEIGHTED-AVERAGE-COST-OF-CAPITAL METHOD

Finally, one can value a project using the **weighted-average-cost-of-capital** (WACC) method. While this method was discussed in Chapters 12 and 15, it is worthwhile to review it here. The WACC approach begins with the insight that projects of levered firms are simultaneously financed with both debt and equity. The cost of capital is a weighted average of the cost of debt and the cost of equity. As seen in Chapters 12 and 15, the cost of equity is r_S. Ignoring taxes, the cost of debt is simply the borrowing rate, r_B. However, with corporate taxes, the appropriate cost of debt is $(1 - T_C)r_B$, the after-tax cost of debt.

The formula for determining the weighted average cost of capital, r_{WACC}, is

$$r_{WACC} = \frac{S}{S + B} r_S + \frac{B}{S + B} r_B(1 - T_C)$$

The weight for equity, $\frac{S}{S + B}$, and the weight for debt, $\frac{B}{S + B}$, are target ratios. Target ratios are generally expressed in terms of market values, not accounting values. (Recall that another phrase for accounting value is *book value*.)

The formula calls for discounting the *unlevered* cash flow of the project (UCF) at the weighted average cost of capital, r_{WACC}. The net present value of the project can be written algebraically as

$$\sum_{t=1}^{\infty} \frac{UCF_t}{(1 + r_{WACC})^t} - \text{Initial investment}$$

If the project is a perpetuity, the net present value is

$$\frac{UCF}{r_{WACC}} - \text{Initial investment}$$

We previously stated that the target debt-to-value ratio of our project is 1/4 and the corporate tax rate is .34, implying that the weighted average cost of capital is

$$r_{WACC} = \frac{3}{4} \times 0.222 + \frac{1}{4} \times 0.10(0.66) = 0.183$$

Note that r_{WACC}, 0.183, is lower than the cost of equity capital for an all-equity firm, 0.20. This must always be the case, since debt financing provides a tax subsidy that lowers the average cost of capital.

We previously determined the UCF of the project to be $92,400, implying that the present value of the project is

$$\frac{\$92,400}{0.183} = \$504,918$$

Since this initial investment is $475,000, the NPV of the project is

$$\$504,918 - \$475,000 = \$29,918$$

In this example, all three approaches yield the same value.

CONCEPT QUESTION
?
• How is the WACC method applied?

17.4 A Comparison of the APV, FTE, and WACC Approaches

Capital-budgeting techniques in the early chapters of this text applied to all-equity firms. Capital budgeting for the levered firm could not be handled early in the book because the effects of debt on firm value were deferred until the previous two chapters. We learned there that debt increases firm value through tax benefits but decreases value through bankruptcy and related costs.

In this chapter we provide three approaches to capital budgeting for the levered firm. The adjusted-present-value (APV) approach first values the project on an all-equity basis. That is, the project's after-tax cash flows under all-equity financing (called unlevered cash flows, or UCF) are placed in the numerator of the capital-budgeting equation. The discount rate, assuming all-equity financing, appears in the denominator. At this point, the calculation is identical to that performed in the early chapters of this book. We then add the net present value of the debt. We point out that the net present value of the debt is likely to be the sum of four parameters: tax effects, flotation costs, bankruptcy costs, and interest subsidies.

The flow-to-equity (FTE) approach discounts the after-tax cash flow from a project going to the equityholders of a levered firm (LCF). LCF, which stands for levered cash flow, is the residual to equityholders after interest has been deducted. The discount rate is r_S, the cost of capital to the equityholders of a levered firm. For a firm with leverage, r_S must be greater than r_0, the cost of capital for an unlevered firm. This follows from our material in Chapter 15 showing that leverage raises the risk to the equityholders.

The last approach is the weighted-average-cost-of-capital (WACC) method. This technique calculates the project's after-tax cash flows assuming all-equity financing (UCF). The UCF is placed in the numerator of the capital-budgeting equation. The denominator, r_{WACC}, is a weighted average of the cost of equity capital and the cost of debt capital. The tax advantage of debt is reflected in the denominator because the cost of debt capital is determined net of corporate tax. The numerator does not reflect debt at all.

All three approaches perform the same task: valuation in the presence of debt financing. And, as illustrated by the previous example, all three provide the same valuation estimate. However, as we saw before, the approaches are markedly different in technique. Because of this, students often ask questions of the following sort: "How can this be? How can the three approaches look so different and yet give the same answer?" We believe that the best way to handle questions like these is through the following two points.

1. *APV versus WACC.* Of the three approaches, APV and WACC display the greatest similarity. After all, both approaches put the unlevered cash flow (UCF) in the numerator. However, the APV approach discounts these flows at r_0, yielding the value of the unlevered project. Adding the present value of the tax shield gives the value of the project under leverage. The WACC approach discounts UCF at r_{WACC}, which is lower than r_0.

    Thus, both approaches adjust the basic NPV formula for unlevered firms in order to reflect the tax benefit of leverage. The APV approach makes this adjustment directly. It simply adds in the present value of the tax shield as a separate term. The WACC approach makes the adjustment in a more subtle way. Here, the discount rate is lowered below r_0. Although we do not provide a proof in the textbook, it can be shown that these two adjustments always have the same quantitative effect.

2. *Entity Being Valued.* The FTE approach appears at first glance to be far different from the other two. For both the APV and the WACC approaches, the initial investment is subtracted out in the final step ($475,000 in our example). However, for the FTE approach, only the firm's contribution to the initial investment ($348,770.50 = $475,000 − $126,229.50) is subtracted out. This occurs because under the FTE approach, only the future cash flows to the levered equityholders (LCF) are valued. By contrast, future cash flows to the unlevered equityholders (UCF) are valued in both the APV and WACC approaches. Thus, since LCFs are net of interest payments, whereas UCFs are not, the initial investment under the FTE approach is correspondingly reduced by debt financing. In this way, the FTE approach produces the same answer that the other two approaches do.

A Suggested Guideline

The net present value of our project is exactly the same under each of the three methods. In theory, this should always be the case.[4] However, one method usually provides an easier computation than another, and, in many cases, one or more of the methods are virtually impossible computationally. We first consider when it is best to use the WACC and FTE approaches.

If the risk of a project stays constant throughout its life, it is plausible to assume that r_0 remains constant throughout the project's life. This assumption of constant risk appears to be reasonable for most real-world projects. In addition, if the debt-to-value ratio remains constant over the life of the project, both r_S and r_{WACC} will remain constant as well. Under this latter assumption, either the FTE or the WACC approach is easy to apply. However, if the debt-to-value ratio varies from year to year, both r_S and r_{WACC} vary from year to year as well. Using the FTE or the WACC approach when the denominator changes every year is computationally quite complex, and when computations become complex, the error rate rises. Thus, both the FTE and WACC approaches present difficulties when the debt-to-value *ratio* changes over time.

The APV approach is based on the *level* of debt in each future period. Consequently, when the debt level can be specified precisely for future periods, the APV approach is quite easy to use. However, when the debt level is uncertain, the APV approach becomes more problematic. For example, when the debt-to-value ratio is constant, the debt level varies with the value of the project. Since the value of the project in a future year cannot be easily forecast, the level of debt cannot be easily forecast either.

Thus, we suggest the following guideline:

Use WACC or FTE if the firm's target debt-to-value *ratio* applies to the project over its life. Use APV if the project's *level* of debt is known over the life of the project.

There are a number of situations where the APV approach is preferred. For example, in a leveraged buyout (LBO) the firm begins with a large amount of debt but rapidly pays down the debt over a number of years. Since the schedule of debt reduction in the future is known when the LBO is arranged, tax shields in every future year can be easily forecast. Thus, the APV approach is easy to use here. (An illustration of the APV approach applied to LBOs is provided in the appendix to this chapter.) By contrast, the WACC and FTE approaches are virtually impossible to apply here, since the debt-to-equity value cannot be expected to be constant over time. In addition, situations involving interest subsidies and flotation costs are much easier to handle with the APV approach. (The Bicksler Enterprises

---

[4]See I. Inselbag and H. Kaufold, "Two DCF Approaches for Valuing Companies under Alternative Financial Strategies (and How to Choose Between Them)" *Journal of Applied Corporate Finance* (Spring 1997).

THE THREE METHODS OF CAPITAL BUDGETING WITH LEVERAGE

1. Adjusted-Present-Value (APV) Method

$$\sum_{t=1}^{\infty} \frac{UCF_t}{(1 + r_0)^t} + \text{Additional effects of debt} - \text{Initial investment}$$

UCF_t = The project's cash flow at date t to the equityholders of an unlevered firm
r_0 = Cost of capital for project in an unlevered firm

2. Flow-to-Equity (FTE) Method

$$\sum_{t=1}^{\infty} \frac{LCF_t}{(1 + r_S)^t} - (\text{Initial investment} - \text{Amount borrowed})$$

LCF_t = The project's cash flow at date t to the equityholders of a levered firm
r_S = Cost of equity capital with leverage

3. Weighted-Average-Cost-of-Capital (WACC) Method

$$\sum_{t=1}^{\infty} \frac{UCF_t}{(1 + r_{\text{WACC}})^t} - \text{Initial investment}$$

r_{WACC} = Weighted average cost of capital

Notes:

1. The middle term in the APV formula implies that the value of a project with leverage is greater than the value of the project without leverage. Since $r_{\text{WACC}} < r_0$, the WACC formula implies that the value of a project with leverage is greater than the value of the project without leverage.

2. In the FTE method, cash flow *after interest* (LCF) is used. Initial investment is reduced by *amount borrowed* as well.

Guidelines:

1. Use WACC or FTE if the firm's target debt-to-value *ratio* applies to the project over its life.

2. Use APV if the project's *level* of debt is known over the life of the project.

example in Section 17.6 applies the APV approach to subsidies and flotation costs.) Finally, the APV approach handles the lease-versus-buy decision much more easily than does either the FTE or the WACC approach. (A full treatment of the lease-versus-buy decision appears in Chapter 24.)

The preceding examples are special cases. Typical capital budgeting situations are more amenable to either the WACC or the FTE approach than to the APV approach. Financial managers generally think in terms of target debt-value *ratios*. If a project does better than expected, both its value and its debt capacity will likely rise. The manager will increase debt correspondingly here. Conversely, the manager would be likely to reduce debt if the value of the project were to decline unexpectedly. Of course, because financing is a time-consuming task, the ratio cannot be adjusted on a day-to-day or a month-to-month basis. Rather, the adjustment can be expected to occur over the long run. As mentioned before, the WACC and FTE approaches are more appropriate than is the APV approach when a firm focuses on a target debt-value ratio.

Because of this, we recommend that the WACC and the FTE approaches, rather than the APV approach, be used in most real-world situations. In addition, frequent discussions with business executives have convinced us that the WACC is the most widely used method in the real world, by far. Thus, practitioners seem to agree with us that, outside of the special situations mentioned above, the APV approach is a less important method of capital budgeting.

CONCEPT QUESTIONS

?
- What is the main difference between APV and WACC?
- What is the main difference between the FTE approach and the other two approaches?
- When should the APV method be used?
- When should the FTE and WACC approaches be used?

17.5 Capital Budgeting When the Discount Rate Must Be Estimated

The previous sections of this chapter introduced APV, FTE, and WACC—the three basic approaches to valuing a levered firm. However, one important detail remains. The example in Sections 17.1 through 17.3 *assumed* a discount rate. We now want to show how this rate is determined for real-world firms with leverage, with an application to the three preceding approaches. The example in this section brings together the work in Chapters 9–12 on the discount rate for unlevered firms with that in Chapter 15 on the effect of leverage on the cost of capital.

Example

World-Wide Enterprises (WWE) is a large conglomerate thinking of entering the widget business, where it plans to finance projects with a debt-to-value ratio of 25 percent (or, alternatively, a debt-to-equity ratio of 1/3). There is currently one firm in the widget industry, American Widgets (AW). This firm is financed with 40-percent debt and 60-percent equity. The beta of AW's equity is 1.5. AW has a borrowing rate of 12 percent, and WWE expects to borrow for its widget venture at 10 percent. The corporate tax rate for both firms is 0.40, the market-risk premium is 8.5 percent, and the riskless interest rate is 8 percent. What is the appropriate discount rate for WWE to use for its widget venture?

As shown in Sections 17.1–17.3, a corporation may use one of three capital budgeting approaches: APV, FTE, or WACC. The appropriate discount rates for these three approaches are r_0, r_S, and r_{WACC}, respectively. Since AW is WWE's only competitor in widgets, we look at AW's cost of capital to calculate r_0, r_S, and r_{WACC} for WWE's widget venture. The four-step procedure below will allow us to calculate all three discount rates.

1. *Determining AW's Cost of Equity Capital.* First, we determine AW's cost of equity capital, using the security market line (SML) of Chapter 10:

AW's Cost of Equity Capital:

$$r_S = R_F + \beta \times (\bar{R}_M - R_F)$$
$$20.75\% = 8\% + 1.5 \times 8.5\%$$

where $\bar{R}_M$ is the expected return on the market portfolio and R_F is the risk-free rate.

2. *Determining AW's Hypothetical All-Equity Cost of Capital.* We must standardize the preceding number in some way, since AW and WWE's widget venture have different target debt-to-value ratios. The easiest approach is to calculate the hypothetical cost of equity capital for AW, assuming all-equity financing. This can be determined from MM's Proposition II under taxes (see Chapter 15):

AW's Cost of Capital if All-Equity:

$$r_S = r_0 + \frac{B}{S}(1 - T_C)(r_0 - r_B)$$

$$20.75\% = r_0 + \frac{0.4}{0.6}(0.60)(r_0 - 12\%)$$

In the examples of Chapter 15, the unknown in this equation was r_S. However, for this example, the unknown is r_0. By solving the equation, one finds that $r_0 = 0.1825$. Of course, r_0 is less than r_S because the cost of equity capital would be less when the firm employs no leverage.

At this point, firms in the real world generally make the assumption that the business risk of their venture is about equal to the business risk of the firms already in the business. Applying this assumption to our problem, we assert that the hypothetical discount rate of WWE's widget venture if all-equity financed is also 0.1825.[5] This discount rate would be employed if WWE uses the APV approach, since the APV approach calls for r_0, the project's cost of capital in a firm with no leverage.

3. *Determining* r$_S$ *for WWE's Widget Venture.* Alternatively, WWE might use the FTE approach, where the discount rate for levered equity is determined from:

Cost of Equity Capital for WWE's Widget Venture:

$$r_S = r_0 + \frac{B}{S}(1 - T_C)(r_0 - r_B)$$

$$19.9\% = 18.25\% + \frac{1}{3}(0.60)(18.25\% - 10\%)$$

Note that the cost of equity capital for WWE's widget venture, 0.199, is less than the cost of equity capital for AW, 0.2075. This occurs because AW has a higher debt-to-equity ratio. (As mentioned above, both firms are assumed to have the same business risk.)

4. *Determining* r$_{WACC}$ *for WWE's Widget Venture.* Finally, WWE might use the WACC approach. The appropriate calculation here is

r_{WACC} **for WWE's Widget Venture:**

$$r_{\text{WACC}} = \frac{B}{S + B}r_B(1 - T_C) + \frac{S}{S + B}r_S$$

$$16.425\% = \frac{1}{4}10\%(0.60) + \frac{3}{4}19.9\%$$

---

[5]Alternatively, a firm might assume that its venture would be somewhat riskier since it is a new entrant. Thus, the firm might select a discount rate slightly higher than 0.1825. Of course, no exact formula exists for adjusting the discount rate upwards.

The preceding example shows how the three discount rates, r_0, r_S, and r_{WACC}, are determined in the real world. These are the appropriate rates for the APV, FTE, and WACC approaches, respectively. Note that r_S for American Widgets is determined first, because the cost of equity capital can be determined from the beta of the firm's stock. As discussed in Chapter 12, beta can easily be estimated for any publicly traded firm, such as AW.

17.6 APV EXAMPLE

As mentioned earlier in this chapter, firms generally set a target debt-to-equity ratio, allowing the use of WACC and FTE for capital budgeting. APV does not work as well here. However, as we also mentioned earlier, APV is the preferred approach when there are side benefits and side costs to debt. Because the analysis here can be tricky, we now devote an entire section to an example where, in addition to the tax subsidy to debt, both flotation costs and interest subsidies come into play.

EXAMPLE

Bicksler Enterprises is considering a $10 million project that will last five years, implying straight-line depreciation per year of $2 million. The cash revenues less cash expenses per year are $3,500,000. The corporate tax bracket is 34 percent. The risk-free rate is 10 percent, and the cost of unlevered equity is 20 percent.

The cash flow projections each year are

	C_0	C_1	C_2	C_3	C_4	C_5
Initial outlay	−$10,000,000					
Depreciation tax shield		0.34 × $2,000,000 = $680,000	$680,000	$680,000	$680,000	$680,000
Revenue less expenses		(1−0.34) × $3,500,000 = $2,310,000	$2,310,000	$2,310,000	$2,310,000	$2,310,000

We stated before that the APV of a project is the sum of its all-equity value plus the additional effects of debt. We examine each in turn.

All-Equity Value

Assuming the project is financed with all equity, the value of the project is

$$\underbrace{-\$10,000,000}_{\text{Initial cost}} + \underbrace{\frac{\$680,000}{0.10} \times \left[1 - \left(\frac{1}{1.10}\right)^5\right]}_{\text{Depreciation tax shield}} +$$

$$\underbrace{\frac{\$2,310,000}{0.20} \times \left[1 - \left(\frac{1}{1.20}\right)^5\right]}_{\text{Present value of (Cash revenues − Cash expenses)}} = -\$513,951$$

This calculation uses the techniques presented in the early chapters of this book. Notice that the depreciation tax shield is discounted at the riskless rate of 10 percent. The revenues and expenses are discounted at the higher rate of 20 percent.

An all-equity firm would clearly *reject* this project, because the NPV is −$513,951. And equity-flotation costs (not mentioned in the example) would only make the NPV more negative. However, debt financing may add enough value to the project to justify acceptance. We consider the effects of debt next.

Additional Effects of Debt

Bicksler Enterprises can obtain a five-year, nonamortizing loan for $7,500,000 after flotation costs at the risk-free rate of 10 percent. Flotation costs are fees paid when stock or debt is issued. These fees may go to printers, lawyers, and investment bankers, among others. Bicksler Enterprises is informed that flotation costs will be 1 percent of the gross proceeds of its loan. The previous chapter indicates that debt financing alters the NPV of a typical project. We look at the effects of debt next.

Flotation Costs   Given that flotation costs are 1 percent of the gross proceeds, we have

$$\$7,500,000 = (1 - 0.01) \times \text{Gross proceeds} = 0.99 \times \text{Gross proceeds}$$

Thus, the gross proceeds are

$$\frac{\$7,500,000}{1 - 0.01} = \frac{\$7,500,000}{0.99} = \$7,575,758$$

This implies flotation costs of $75,758 (1% × $7,575,758). To check the calculation, note that net proceeds are $7,500,000 ($7,575,758 − $75,758). In other words, Bicksler Enterprises receives only $7,500,000. The flotation costs of $75,758 are received by intermediaries, e.g., investment bankers.

Flotation costs are paid immediately but are deducted from taxes by amortizing on a straight-line basis over the life of the loan. The cash flows from flotation costs are

	Date 0	Date 1	Date 2	Date 3	Date 4	Date 5
Flotation costs	−$75,758					
Deduction		$15,152 = \dfrac{\$75,758}{5}$	$15,152	$15,152	$15,152	$15,152
Tax shield from flotation costs		$0.34 \times \$15,152$ = **$5,152**	**$5,152**	**$5,152**	**$5,152**	**$5,152**

The relevant cash flows from flotation costs are in boldface. When discounting at 10 percent, the tax shield has a net present value of

$$\$5,152 \times A^5_{0.10} = \$19,530$$

This implies a net cost of flotation of

$$-\$75,758 + \$19,530 = -\$56,228$$

The net present value of the project after the flotation costs of debt but before the benefits of debt is

$$-\$513,951 - \$56,228 = -\$570,179$$

Tax Subsidy   Interest must be paid on the gross proceeds of the loan, even though intermediaries receive the flotation costs. Since the gross proceeds of the loan are $7,575,578, annual interest is $757,576 ($7,575,758 × 0.10). The interest cost after taxes is $500,000 [$757,576 $\times$ (1 $-$ 0.34)]. Because the loan is nonamortizing, the entire debt of $7,575,758 is repaid at date 5. These terms are indicated below:

	Date 0	Date 1	Date 2	Date 3	Date 4	Date 5
Loan (gross proceeds)	**$7,575,758**					
Interest paid		10% $\times$ $7,575,758 = $757,576	$757,576	$757,576	$757,576	$ 757,576
Interest cost after taxes		(1 $-$ 0.34) $\times$ $757,576 = **$500,000**	**$500,000**	**$500,000**	**$500,000**	**$ 500,000**
Repayment of debt						**$7,575,758**

The relevant cash flows are listed in boldface in the above table. They are (1) loan received, (2) annual interest cost after taxes, and (3) repayment of debt. Note that we include the *gross* proceeds of the loan as an inflow, since the flotation costs have previously been subtracted.

In Chapter 15 we mentioned that the financing decision can be evaluated in terms of net present value. The net present value of the loan is simply the net present value of each of the three cash flows. This can be represented as

$$\text{NPV(Loan)} = + \begin{array}{c}\text{Amount} \\ \text{borrowed}\end{array} - \begin{array}{c}\text{Present value} \\ \text{of after-tax} \\ \text{interest payments}\end{array} - \begin{array}{c}\text{Present value} \\ \text{of loan} \\ \text{repayments}\end{array} \qquad (17.1)$$

The calculations for this example are

$$\$976,415 = + \$7,575,758 - \frac{\$500,000}{0.10} \times \left[1 - \left(\frac{1}{1.10}\right)^5\right] - \frac{\$7,575,758}{(1.10)^5} \quad (17.1')$$

The NPV(Loan) is positive, reflecting the interest tax shield.[6]

The adjusted present value of the project with this financing is

$$\text{APV} = \text{All-equity value} - \text{Flotation costs of debt} + \text{NPV(Loan)} \qquad (17.2)$$
$$\$406,236 = -\$513,951 - \$56,228 + \$976,415 \qquad (17.2')$$

Though we previously saw that an all-equity firm would reject the project, a firm would *accept* the project if a $7,500,000 (net) loan could be obtained.

Because the loan discussed above was at the market rate of 10 percent, we have considered only two of the three additional effects of debt (flotation costs and tax subsidy) so far. We now examine another loan where the third effect arises.

Non–Market-Rate Financing   A number of companies are fortunate enough to obtain subsidized financing from a governmental authority. Suppose that the project of Bicksler Enterprises is deemed socially beneficial and the state of New Jersey

---

[6]The NPV (Loan) must be zero in a no-tax world, because interest provides no tax shield there. To check this intuition, we calculate

$$\text{No-tax case: } 0 = +\$7,575,758 - \frac{\$757,576}{0.10} \times \left[1 - \left(\frac{1}{1.10}\right)^5\right] - \frac{\$7,575,758}{(1.10)^5}$$

grants the firm a $7,500,000 loan at 8-percent interest. In addition, all flotation costs are absorbed by the state. Clearly, the company will choose this loan over the one we previously calculated. The cash flows from the loan are

	Date 0	Date 1	Date 2	Date 3	Date 4	Date 5
Loan received	**$7,500,000**					
Interest paid		8% × $7,500,000 = $600,000	$600,000	$600,000	$600,000	$ 600,000
After-tax interest		(1 − 0.34) × $600,000 = **$396,000**	**$396,000**	**$396,000**	**$396,000**	**$ 396,000**
Repayment of debt						**$ 7,500,000**

The relevant cash flows are listed in boldface in the preceding table. Using equation (17.1), the NPV(Loan) is

$$\$1,341,939 = +\$7,500,000 - \frac{\$396,000}{0.10} \times \left[1 - \left(\frac{1}{1.10} \right)^5 \right] - \frac{\$7,500,000}{(1.10)^5} \qquad (17.1'')$$

Why do we discount the cash flows in equation (17.1″) at 10 percent when the firm is borrowing at 8 percent? We discount at 10 percent because that is the fair or marketwide rate. That is, 10 percent is the rate at which one could borrow *without* benefit of subsidization. The net present value of the subsidized loan is larger than the net present value of the earlier loan because the firm is now borrowing at the below-market rate of 8 percent. Note that the NPV(Loan) calculation in equation (17.1″) captures both the tax effect *and* the non–market-rate effect.

The net present value of the project with subsidized debt financing is

$$\text{APV} = \text{All-equity value} - \text{Flotation costs of debt} + \text{NPV(Loan)} \qquad (17.2)$$
$$+\$827,988 = \quad -\$513,951 \quad - \quad 0 \quad +\$1,341,939 \qquad (17.2'')$$

The preceding example illustrates the adjusted-present-value (APV) approach. The approach begins with the present value of a project for the all-equity firm. Next, the effects of debt are added in. The approach has much to recommend it. It is intuitively appealing because individual components are calculated separately and added together in a simple way. And, if the debt from the project can be specified precisely, the present value of the debt can be calculated precisely.

17.7 BETA AND LEVERAGE

Chapter 12 provides the formula for the relationship between the beta of the common stock and leverage of the firm in a world without taxes. We reproduce this formula here:

The No-Tax Case:

$$\beta_{\text{Equity}} = \beta_{\text{Asset}} \left(1 + \frac{\text{Debt}}{\text{Equity}} \right) \qquad (17.3)$$

As pointed out in Chapter 12, this relationship holds under the assumption that the beta of debt is zero.

Since firms must pay corporate taxes in practice, it is worthwhile to provide the relationship in a world with corporate taxes. It can be shown that the relationship between the beta of the unlevered firm and the beta of the levered equity is[7]

The Corporate-Tax Case:

$$\beta_{\text{Equity}} = \left(1 + \frac{(1 - T_C)\text{Debt}}{\text{Equity}}\right)\beta_{\text{Unlevered firm}} \tag{17.4}$$

when (1) the corporation is taxed at the rate of T_C and (2) the debt has a zero beta.

Because $[1 + (1 - T_C)\text{debt/equity}]$ must be more than 1 for a levered firm, it follows that $\beta_{\text{Unlevered firm}} < \beta_{\text{Equity}}$. The corporate-tax case of equation (17.4) is quite similar to the no-tax case of equation (17.3), because the beta of levered equity must be greater than the beta of the unlevered firm in either case. The intuition that leverage increases the risk of equity applies in both cases.

However, notice that the two equations are not equal. It can be shown that leverage increases the equity beta less rapidly under corporate taxes. This occurs because, under taxes, leverage creates a *riskless* tax shield, thereby lowering the risk of the entire firm.

---

[7]This result holds only if the beta of debt equals zero. To see this, note that

$$V_U + T_C B = V_L = B + S \tag{a}$$

where

V_U = Value of unlevered firm
V_L = Value of levered firm
B = Value of debt in a levered firm
S = Value of equity in a levered firm

As we stated in the text, the beta of the levered firm is a weighted average of the debt beta and the equity beta:

$$\frac{B}{B + S} \times \beta_B + \frac{S}{B + S} \times \beta_S$$

where β_B and β_S are the betas of the debt and the equity of the levered firm, respectively. Because $V_L = B + S$, we have

$$\frac{B}{V_L} \times \beta_B + \frac{S}{V_L} \times \beta_S \tag{b}$$

The beta of the levered firm can *also* be expressed as a weighted average of the beta of the unlevered firm and the beta of the tax shield:

$$\frac{V_U}{V_U + T_C B} \times \beta_U + \frac{T_C B}{V_U + T_C B} \times \beta_B$$

where β_U is the beta of the unlevered firm. This follows from equation (a). Because $V_L = V_U + T_C B$, we have

$$\frac{V_U}{V_L} \times \beta_U + \frac{T_C B}{V_L} \times \beta_B \tag{c}$$

We can equate (b) and (c) because both represent the beta of a levered firm. Equation (a) tells us that $V_U = S + (1 - T_C) \times B$. Under the assumption that $\beta_B = 0$, equating (b) and (c) and using equation (a) yields equation (17.4).

The generalized formula for the levered beta (where β_B is not zero) is:

$$\beta_S = \beta_U + (1 - T_C)(\beta_U - \beta_B)\frac{B}{S}$$

and

$$\beta_U = \frac{S}{B(1 - T_C) + S}\beta_S + \frac{B(1 - T_C)}{B(1 - T_C) + S}\beta_B$$

EXAMPLE

C. F. Lee Incorporated is considering a scale-enhancing project. The market value of the firm's debt is $100 million, and the market value of the firm's equity is $200 million. The debt is considered riskless. The corporate tax rate is 34 percent. Regression analysis indicates that the beta of the firm's equity is 2. The risk-free rate is 10 percent, and the expected market premium is 8.5 percent. What would the project's discount rate be in the hypothetical case that C. F. Lee, Inc., is all-equity?

We can answer this question in two steps.

1. *Determining Beta of Hypothetical All-Equity Firm.* Rearranging equation (17.4), we have

Unlevered Beta:

$$\frac{\text{Equity}}{\text{Equity} + (1 - T_C) \times \text{Debt}} \times \beta_{\text{Equity}} = \beta_{\text{Unlevered firm}} \qquad (17.5)$$

$$\frac{\$200 \text{ million}}{\$200 \text{ million} + (1 - 0.34) \times \$100 \text{ million}} \times 2 = 1.50$$

2. *Determining Discount Rate.* We calculate the discount rate from the security market line (SML) as

Discount Rate:

$$r_S = R_F + \beta \times [\bar{R}_M - R_F]$$
$$22.75\% = 10\% + 1.50 \times 8.5\%$$

The Project Is Not Scale-Enhancing

Because the above example assumed that the project is scale-enhancing, we began with the beta of the firm's equity. If the project is not scale-enhancing, one could begin with the equity betas of firms in the industry of the project. For each firm, the hypothetical beta of the unlevered equity could be calculated by equation (17.5). The SML could then be used to determine the project's discount rate from the average of these betas.

EXAMPLE

The J. Lowes Corporation, which currently manufactures staples, is considering a $1 million investment in a project in the aircraft adhesives industry. The corporation estimates unlevered after-tax cash flows (UCF) of $300,000 per year into perpetuity from the project. The firm will finance the project with a debt-to-value ratio of 0.5 (or, equivalently, a debt-to-equity ratio of 1:1).

The three competitors in this new industry are currently unlevered, with betas of 1.2, 1.3, and 1.4. Assuming a risk-free rate of 5 percent, a market-risk premium of 9 percent, and a corporate tax rate of 34 percent, what is the net present value of the project?

We can answer this question in five steps.

1. *Calculating the Average Unlevered Beta in the Industry.* The average un-levered beta across all three existing competitors in the aircraft adhesives industry is

$$\frac{1.2 + 1.3 + 1.4}{3} = 1.3$$

2. *Calculating the Levered Beta for J. Lowes's New Project.* Assuming the same unlevered beta for this new project as for the existing competitors, we have, from equation (17.4),

Levered Beta:

$$\beta_{\text{Equity}} = (1 + \frac{(1 - T_C)\text{Debt}}{\text{Equity}})\beta_{\text{Unlevered firm}}$$

$$2.16 = (1 + \frac{0.66 \times 1}{1}) \times 1.3$$

3. *Calculating the Cost of Levered Equity for the New Project.* We calculate the discount rate from the security market line (SML) as

Discount Rate:

$$r_S = R_F + \beta \times [\overline{R}_M - R_F]$$

$$0.244 = 0.05 + 2.16 \times 0.09$$

4. *Calculating the WACC for the New Project.* The formula for determining the weighted average cost of capital, r_{WACC}, is

$$r_{\text{WACC}} = \frac{B}{V}r_B(1 - T_C) + \frac{S}{V}r_S$$

$$0.139 = \frac{1}{2} \times 0.05 \times 0.66 + \frac{1}{2} \times 0.244$$

5. *Determining the Project's Value.* Because the cash flows are perpetual, the NPV of the project is

$$\frac{\text{Unlevered cash flows (UCF)}}{r_{\text{WACC}}} - \text{Initial investment}$$

$$\frac{\$300,000}{0.139} - \$1\text{ million} = \$1.16\text{ million}$$

17.8 Summary and Conclusions

Earlier chapters of this text showed how to calculate net present value for projects of all-equity firms. We pointed out in the last two chapters that the introduction of taxes and bankruptcy costs changes a firm's financing decisions. Rational corporations should employ some debt in a world of this type. Because of the benefits and costs associated with debt, the capital-budgeting decision is different for levered firms than for unlevered firms. The present chapter has discussed three methods for capital budgeting by levered firms: the adjusted-present-value (APV), flows-to-equity (FTE), and weighted-average-cost-of-capital (WACC) approaches.

1. The APV formula can be written as

$$\sum_{t=1}^{\infty} \frac{\text{UCF}_t}{(1 + r_0)^t} + \text{Additional effects of debt} - \text{Initial investment}$$

There are four additional effects of debt:
    - Tax shield from debt financing
    - Flotation costs
    - Bankruptcy costs
    - Benefit of non–market-rate financing

2. The FTE formula can be written as

$$\sum_{t=1}^{\infty} \frac{\text{LCF}_t}{(1 + r_S)^t} - (\text{Initial investment} - \text{Amount borrowed})$$

3. The WACC formula can be written as

$$\sum_{t=1}^{\infty} \frac{\text{UCF}_t}{(1 + r_{\text{WACC}})^t} - \text{Initial investment}$$

4. Corporations frequently follow the guideline:
    Use WACC or FTE if the firm's target debt-to-value *ratio* applies to the project over its life. Use APV if the project's *level* of debt is known over the life of the project.

5. The APV method is used frequently for special situations like interest subsidies, LBOs, and leases. The WACC and FTE methods are commonly used for more typical capital-budgeting situations. The APV approach is a rather unimportant method for typical capital-budgeting situations.

6. The beta of the equity of the firm is positively related to the leverage of the firm.

KEY TERMS

Adjusted present value (APV) 468	Weighted average cost of capital 471
Flow to equity (FTE) 470	

SUGGESTED READINGS

The following article contains a superb discussion of some of the subtleties of using WACC for project valuation:

Miles, J., and R. Ezzel. "The Weighted Average Cost of Capital, Perfect Capital Markets and Project Life: A Clarification." *Journal of Financial and Quantitative Analysis* 15 (September 1980).

The following article presents the practical aspects of the APV approach:

T. A. Luehrman. "Using APV: A Better Tool for Valuing Operations." *Harvard Business Review* (May/June 1997).

A fascinating article on the merits of the APV and WACC approaches is:

Inselbag, I., and H. Kaufold. "Two DCF Approaches in Valuing Companies under Alternative Financing Strategies (and How to Choose between Them)." *Journal of Applied Corporate Finance* (Summer 1997).

Questions and Problems

Adjusted-Present-Value Approach

17.1 Honda and GM are competing to sell a fleet of cars to Hertz. Hertz's policies on its rental cars include use of straight-line depreciation and disposing of the cars after five years. Hertz expects that the autos will have no salvage value. The firm expects a fleet of 25 cars to generate $100,000 per year in pretax income. Hertz is in the 34-percent tax bracket, and the firm's overall required return is 10 percent. The addition of the new fleet will not add to the risk of the firm. Treasury bills are priced to yield 6 percent.

a. What is the maximum price that Hertz should be willing to pay for the fleet of cars?

b. Suppose the price of the fleet (in U.S. dollars) is $325,000; both suppliers are charging this price. Hertz is able to issue $200,000 in debt to finance the project. The bonds can be issued at par and will carry an 8-percent interest rate. Hertz will incur no costs to issue the debt and no costs of financial distress. What is the APV of this project if Hertz uses debt to finance the auto purchase?

c. To entice Hertz to buy the cars from Honda, the Japanese government is willing to lend Hertz $200,000 at 5 percent. Now what is the maximum price that Hertz is willing to pay Honda for the fleet of cars?

17.2 Peatco, Inc., is considering a $2.1 million project that will be depreciated according to the straight-line method over the three-year life of the project. The project will generate pretax earnings of $900,000 per year, and it will not change the risk level of the firm. Peatco can obtain a three-year, 12.5-percent loan to finance the project; the bank will charge Peatco flotation fees of 1 percent of the gross proceeds of the loan. The fee must be paid up front, not from the loan proceeds. If Peatco financed the project with all equity, its cost of capital would be 18 percent. The tax rate is 30 percent, and the risk-free rate is 6 percent.

a. Using the APV method, determine whether or not Peatco should undertake the project.

b. After hearing that Peatco would not be initiating the project in their town, the city council voted to subsidize Peatco's loan. Under the city's proposal, Peatco will pay the same flotation costs, but the rate on the loan will be 10 percent. Should Peatco accept the city's offer and begin the project?

17.3 MEO Foods, Inc., has made cat food for over 20 years. The company currently has a debt-equity ratio of 25 percent, borrows at a 10-percent interest rate, and is in the 40-percent tax bracket. Its shareholders require an 18-percent return.

MEO is planning to expand cat food production capacity. The equipment to be purchased would last three years and generate the following unlevered cash flows (UCF):

Unlevered Cash Flows by Year (in $ millions)				
0	1	2	3	4+
−15	5	8	10	0

MEO has also arranged a $6 million debt issue to partially finance the expansion. Under the loan, the company would pay 10 percent annually on the outstanding balance. The firm would also make year-end principal payments of $2 million per year, completely retiring the issue at the end of the third year.

Ignoring costs of financial distress and issue costs, should MEO proceed with the expansion plan?

17.4 Roller and Decker Corp. has established a joint venture with Malaysia Road Construction Company to build a toll road in Malaysia. The initial investment in paving equipment is $20 million. Straight-line depreciation will be used, and the equipment has an economic life of five years with no salvage value. The annual construction costs are estimated to be $10 million. The project will be finished in two years. Net toll revenue collected from the usage of the road is projected to be $6 million per annum for 20 years starting from the end of the first year of usage. The local preferential corporate tax rate for joint ventures is

25 percent. There are no other taxes. The required rate of return for the project under all-equity financing is 12 percent. The prevailing market interest rate is 9 percent a year. To encourage foreign capital participation in the infrastructure sector, the Malaysian government will subsidize the project with $10 million of a 15-year, long-term loan, at an interest rate of 5 percent a year. What is the NPV of this project?

Flow-to-Equity Approach

17.5 Milano Pizza Club owns a chain of three identical restaurants popular for their Milan style pizza. Comparable stores have an equity value of $900,000 and debt-to-equity ratio of 30 percent. The prevailing market interest rate is 9.5 percent. An equivalent all-equity-financed store would have a discount rate of 15 percent. For each Milano store, the estimated annual sales are $1,000,000, costs of goods sold $400,000, and general and administrative costs $300,000. (Every cash flow stream is assumed to be a perpetuity.) The marginal tax rate is 40 percent. What is the value of the Milano Pizza Club?

Weighted-Average-Cost-of-Capital Approach

17.6 The overall firm beta for Wild Widgets, Inc., (WWI) is 0.9. WWI has a target debt-equity ratio of 1/2. The expected return on the market is 16 percent, and Treasury bills are currently selling to yield 8 percent. WWI one-year bonds that carry a 7-percent coupon are selling for $972.72. The corporate tax rate is 34 percent.
  a. What is WWI's cost of equity?
  b. What is WWI's cost of debt?
  c. What is WWI's weighted average cost of capital?

17.7 Value Company has compiled the following information on its financing costs:

Type of Financing	Book Value	Market Value	Before-Tax Cost
Long-term debt	$ 5,000,000	$ 2,000,000	10%
Short-term debt	5,000,000	5,000,000	8
Common stock	10,000,000	13,000,000	15
Total	$20,000,000	$20,000,000	

Value is in the 34-percent tax bracket and has a target debt-equity ratio of 100 percent. Value's managers would like to keep the market values of short-term and long-term debt equal.
  a. Calculate the weighted average cost of capital for Value Company using
    i. Book-value weights
    ii. Market-value weights
    iii. Target weights
  b. Explain the differences between the WACCs. What are the correct weights to use in the WACC calculation?

17.8 Baber Corporation's stock returns have a covariance with the market of 0.031. The standard deviation of the market returns is 0.16, and the historical market premium is 8.5 percent. Baber bonds carry a 13-percent coupon rate and are priced to yield 11 percent. The market value of the bonds is $24 million. Baber stock, of which 4 million shares are outstanding, sells for $15 per share. Baber's CFO considers the firm's current debt-equity ratio optimal. The tax rate is 34 percent, and the Treasury bill rate is 7 percent.

Baber Corp. must decide whether to purchase additional capital equipment. The cost of the equipment is $27.5 million. The expected cash flows from the new equipment are $9 million a year for five years. Purchasing the equipment will not change the risk level of Baber Corp. Should Baber purchase the equipment?

17.9 National Electric Company (NEC) is considering a $20 million modernization expansion project in the power systems division. Tom Edison, the company's chief financial officer, has evaluated the project; he determined that the project's after-tax cash flows will be $8 million, in perpetuity. In addition, Mr. Edison has devised two possibilities for raising the necessary $20 million:

• Issue 10-year, 10-percent debt.

• Issue common stock.

NEC's cost of debt is 10 percent, and its cost of equity is 20 percent. The firm's target debt-equity ratio is 200 percent. The expansion project has the same risk as the existing business, and it will support the same amount of debt. NEC is in the 34-percent tax bracket.

Mr. Edison has advised the firm to undertake the expansion. He suggests they use debt to finance the project because it is cheaper and its issuance costs are lower.

a. Should NEC accept the project? Support your answer with the appropriate calculations.

b. Do you agree with Mr. Edison's opinion of the expense of the debt? Why or why not?

17.10 Refer to question 17.8.

Baber Corporation has chosen to purchase the additional equipment. If Baber funds the project entirely with debt, what is the firm's weighted average cost of capital? Explain your answer.

A Comparison of the APV, FTE, and WACC Approaches

17.11 ABC, Inc., is an unlevered firm with expected perpetual annual before-tax cash flows of $30 million and required return on equity of 18 percent. It has 1 million shares outstanding. ABC is paying tax at a marginal rate of 34 percent. The firm is planning a recapitalization under which it will issue $50 million of perpetual debt bearing a 10-percent interest rate and use the proceeds to buy back shares. Calculate the post-recap share price, earnings per share, and required return on equity.

17.12 Kinedyne, Inc., has decided to divest one of its divisions. The assets of the group have the same operating risk characteristics as those of the parent firm. The capital structure for the parent has been stable at 40-percent debt/60-percent equity (in market-value terms), the level determined to be optimal given the firm's assets. The required return on Kinedyne's assets is 16 percent, and the firm (and the division) borrows at a rate of 10 percent.

Sales revenue for the division is expected to remain stable indefinitely at last year's level of $19,740,000. Variable costs amount to 60 percent of sales. Annual depreciation of $1.8 million is exactly matched each year by new investment in the division's equipment. The division would be taxed at the parent's current rate of 40 percent.

a. How much is the division worth in unleveraged form?

b. If the division had the same capital structure as the parent firm, how much would it be worth?

c. At this optimal capital structure, what return will the equityholders of the division require?

d. Show that the market value of the equity of the division would be justified by the earnings to shareholders and the required return on equity.

17.13 Folgers Air Transport (FAT) is currently an unleveraged firm. It is considering a capital restructuring to allow $500 in debt. The company expects to generate $151.52 in cash flows before interest and taxes, in perpetuity. Its cost of debt capital is 10 percent and the corporate tax rate is 34 percent. Unleveraged firms in the same industry have a cost of equity capital of 20 percent.

Using WACC, APV, and FTE, what will be the new value of FAT?

Capital Budgeting for Projects That Are Not Scale-Enhancing

17.14 Schwartz & Brothers Inc. is in the process of deciding whether to make an equity investment in a project of holiday gifts production and sales. Arron Buffet is in charge of the feasibility study of the project. To better assess the risk of the project, he used the average of 10 other firms in the holiday gift industry with similar operational scales as the benchmark. The figures that he has are as follows:

	Project	Benchmark
Debt-equity ratio	35%	30%
β	?	1.5
r_B	10%	10%

The expected market return is 17 percent, and the risk-free interest rate is 9 percent. Corporate tax rate is 40 percent. The initial investment in the project is estimated at $325,000, and the cash flow at the end of the first year is $55,000. Annual cash flow will grow at a constant rate of 5 percent till the end of the fifth year and remain constant forever thereafter. Should Schwartz & Brothers invest in this project (assume that the bond beta is zero)?

APV Example

17.15 Brenda Lynch, CFO of Hunter Enterprises, is evaluating a 10-year, 9-percent loan. The projected net proceeds after flotation costs to be raised by the loan are $4,250,000. The flotation costs are estimated to be 1.25 percent of the gross proceeds and will be amortized using a straight-line schedule over the life of the loan. The cost of similar debt is 9.4 percent. The applicable corporate tax is 40 percent. Suppose that the loan will not increase the financial distress cost of the firm. What is the net present value of this loan?

Beta and Leverage

17.16 North Pole Fishing Equipment Corp. and South Pole Fishing Equipment Corp. would have identical β of 1.2 if both of them were all-equity financed. The capital structures of the two firms are as follows:

	North Pole Fishing Equipment Corp.	South Pole Fishing Equipment Corp.
Debt	$1,000,000	$1,500,000
Equity	1,500,000	1,000,000

The expected market rate of return is 12.75 percent, and the three-month Treasury bill rate is 4.25 percent. Corporate tax rate is 35 percent (assume that bond beta is zero).

a. What are the βs of the two firms, respectively?

b. What are the required rates of return on the two firms' equity?

c. Try to give an intuitive explanation of the different βs and the returns on equity obtained in parts (*a*) and (*b*).

APPENDIX 17A   THE ADJUSTED-PRESENT-VALUE APPROACH TO VALUING LEVERAGED BUYOUTS[8]

Introduction

A leveraged buyout (LBO) is the acquisition by a small group of equity investors of a public or private company financed primarily with debt. The equityholders service the heavy interest and principal payments with cash from operations and/or asset sales. The shareholders generally hope to reverse the LBO within three to seven years by way of a public offering or sale of the company to another firm. A buyout is therefore likely to be successful only if the firm generates enough cash to serve the debt in the early years, and if the company is attractive to other buyers as the buyout matures.

In a leveraged buyout, the equity investors are expected to pay off outstanding principal according to a specific timetable. The owners know that the firm's debt-equity ratio will fall and can forecast the dollar amount of debt needed to finance future operations. Under

---

[8]This appendix has been adapted by Isik Inselbag and Howard Kaufold. The Wharton School, University of Pennsylvania, from their unpublished manuscript entitled "Analyzing the RJR Nabisco Buyout: An Adjusted Present Value Approach."

these circumstances, the adjusted-present-value (APV) approach is more practical than the weighted-average-cost-of-capital (WACC) approach because the capital structure is changing. In this appendix, we illustrate the use of this procedure in valuing the RJR Nabisco transaction, the largest LBO in history.

The RJR Nabisco Buyout   In the summer of 1988, the price of RJR stock was hovering around $55 a share. The firm had $5 billion of debt. The firm's CEO, acting in concert with some other senior managers of the firm, announced a bid of $75 per share to take the firm private in a management buyout. Within days of management's offer, Kohlberg, Kravis and Roberts (KKR) entered the fray with a $90 bid of their own. By the end of November, KKR emerged from the ensuing bidding process with an offer of $109 a share, or $25 billion total. We now use the APV technique to analyze KKR's winning strategy.

The APV method as described in this chapter can be used to value companies as well as projects. Applied in this way, the maximum value of a levered firm (V_L) is its value as an all-equity entity (V_U) plus the discounted value of the interest tax shields from the debt its assets will support (PVTS).[9] This relation can be stated as

$$V_L = V_U + \text{PVTS}$$
$$= \sum_{t=1}^{\infty} \frac{\text{UCF}_t}{(1 + r_0)^t} + \sum_{t=1}^{\infty} \frac{T_C r_B B_{t-1}}{(1 + r_B)^t}$$

In the second part of this equation, UCF_t is the unlevered cash flow from operations for year t. Discounting these cash flows by the required return on assets, r_0, yields the all-equity value of the company. B_{t-1} represents the debt balance remaining at the end of year $(t - 1)$. Because interest in a given year is based on the debt balance remaining at the end of the previous year, the interest paid in year t is $r_B B_{t-1}$. The numerator of the second term, $T_C r_B B_{t-1}$, is therefore the tax shield for year t. We discount this series of annual tax shields using the rate at which the firm borrows, r_B.[10]

KKR planned to sell several of RJR's food divisions and operate the remaining parts of the firm more efficiently. Table 17A.1 presents KKR's projected unlevered cash flows for RJR under the buyout, adjusting for planned asset sales and operational efficiencies.

With respect to financial strategy, KKR planned a significant increase in leverage with accompanying tax benefits. Specifically, KKR issued almost $24 billion of new debt to complete the buyout, raising annual interest costs to more than $3 billion.[11] Table 17A.2 presents the projected interest expense and tax shields for the transaction.

---

[9]One should also deduct from this value any costs of financial distress. However, we would expect these costs to be small in the case of RJR for two reasons. As a firm in the tobacco and food industries, its cash flows are relatively stable and recession resistant. Furthermore, the firm's assets are divisible and attractive to a number of potential buyers, allowing the firm to receive full value if disposition is required.

[10]The pretax borrowing rate, r_B, represents the appropriate discount rate for the interest tax shields when there is a precommitment to a specific debt repayment schedule under the terms of the LBO. If debt covenants require that the entire free cash flow be dedicated to debt service, the amount of debt outstanding and, therefore, the interest tax shield at any point in time are a direct function of the operating cash flows of the firm. Since the debt balance is then as risky as the cash flows, the required return on assets should be used to discount the interest tax shields.

[11]A significant portion of this debt was of the payment in kind (PIK) variety, which offers lenders additional bonds instead of cash interest. This PIK debt financing provided KKR with significant tax shields while allowing it to postpone the cash burden of debt service to future years. For simplicity of presentation, Table 17A.2 does not separately show cash versus noncash interest charges.

■ TABLE 17A.1　**RJR Operating Cash Flows (in $ millions)**

	1989	1990	1991	1992	1993
Operating income	$2,620	$3,410	$3,645	$3,950	$4,310
Tax on operating income	891	1,142	1,222	1,326	1,448
After-tax operating income	1,729	2,268	2,423	2,624	2,862
Add back depreciation	449	475	475	475	475
Less capital expenditures	522	512	525	538	551
Less change in working capital	(203)	(275)	200	225	250
Add proceeds from asset sales	3,545	1,805			
Unlevered cash flow (UCF)	$5,404	$4,311	$2,173	$2,336	$2,536

■ TABLE 17A.2　**Projected Interest Expenses and Tax Shields (in $ millions)**

	1989	1990	1991	1992	1993
Interest expenses	$3,384	$3,004	$3,111	$3,294	$3,483
Interest tax shields ($T_C = 34\%$)	1,151	1,021	1,058	1,120	1,184

■ TABLE 17A.3　**RJR LBO Valuation (in $ millions except share data)**

	1989	1990	1991	1992	1993
Unlevered cash flow (UCF)	$ 5,404	$4,311	$2,173	$2,336	$ 2,536
Terminal value: (3% growth after 1993)					
Unlevered terminal value (UTV)					23,746
Terminal value at target debt					26,654
Tax shield in terminal value					2,908
Interest tax shields	1,151	1,021	1,058	1,120	1,184
PV of UCF 1989–93 at 14%	12,224				
PV of UTV at 14%	12,333				
Total unlevered value	$24,557				
PV of tax shields 1989–93 at 13.5%	3,877				
PV of tax shield in TV at 13.5%	1,544				
Total value of tax shields	5,421				
Total value	29,978				
Less value of assumed debt	5,000				
Value of equity	$24,978				
Number of shares	229 million				
Value per share	$109.07				

We now use the data from Tables 17A.1 and 17A.2 to calculate the APV of the RJR buyout. This valuation process is presented in Table 17A.3.

The valuation presented in Table 17A.3 involves four steps.

Step 1: *Calculating the present value of unlevered cash flows for 1989–93*   The unlevered cash flows for 1989–93 are shown in the last line of Table 17A.1 and the first line of Table 17A.3. These flows are discounted by the required asset return, r_0, which at the time of the buyout was approximately 14 percent. The value as of the end of 1988 of the unlevered cash flows expected from 1989 through 1993 is

$$\frac{5.404}{1.14} + \frac{4.311}{1.14^2} + \frac{2.173}{1.14^3} + \frac{2.336}{1.14^4} + \frac{2.536}{1.14^5} = \$12.224 \text{ billion}$$

Step 2: *Calculating the present value of the unlevered cash flows beyond 1993 (unlevered terminal value)*   We assume the unlevered cash flows grow at the modest annual rate of 3 percent after 1993. The value, as of the end of 1993, of these cash flows is equal to the following discounted value of a growing perpetuity:

$$\frac{2.536(1.03)}{0.14 - 0.03} = \$23.746 \text{ billion}$$

This translates to a 1988 value of

$$\frac{23.746}{1.14^5} = \$12.333 \text{ billion}$$

As in Step 1, the discount rate is the required asset rate of 14 percent.

The total unlevered value of the firm is therefore ($12.224 + $12.333 =) $24.557 billion.

To calculate the total buyout value, we must add the interest tax shields expected to be realized by debt financing.

Step 3: *Calculating the present value of interest tax shields for 1989–93*   Under the prevailing U.S. tax laws in 1989, every dollar of interest reduces taxes by 34 cents. The present value of the interest tax shield for the period from 1989–93 can be calculated by discounting the annual tax savings at the pretax average cost of debt, which was approximately 13.5 percent. Using the tax shields from Table 17A.2, the discounted value of these tax shields is calculated as

$$\frac{1.151}{1.135} + \frac{1.021}{1.135^2} + \frac{1.058}{1.135^3} + \frac{1.120}{1.135^4} + \frac{1.184}{1.135^5} = \$3.877 \text{ billion}$$

Step 4: *Calculating the present value of interest tax shields beyond 1993*   Finally, we must calculate the value of tax shields associated with debt used to finance the operations of the company after 1993. We assume that debt will be reduced and maintained at 25 percent of the value of the firm from that date forward.[12] Under this assumption it is appropriate to use the WACC method to calculate a terminal value for the firm at the target capital structure. This in turn can be decomposed into an all-equity value and a value from tax shields.

---

[12]This 25-percent figure is consistent with the debt utilization in industries in which RJR Nabisco is involved. In fact, that was the debt-to-total-market-value ratio for RJR immediately before management's initial buyout proposal. The firm can achieve this target by 1993 if a significant portion of the convertible debt used to finance the buyout is exchanged for equity by that time. Alternatively, KKR could issue new equity (as would occur, for example, if the firm were taken public) and use the proceeds to retire some of the outstanding debt.

If, after 1993, RJR uses 25-percent debt in its capital structure, its WACC at this target capital structure would be approximately 12.8 percent.[13] Then the levered terminal value as of the end of 1993 can be estimated as

$$\frac{2.536(1.03)}{0.128 - 0.03} = \$26.654 \text{ billion}$$

Since the levered value of the company is the sum of the unlevered value plus the value of interest tax shields, it is the case that

$$\text{Value of tax shields (end 1993)} = V_L \text{ (end 1993)} - V_U \text{ (end 1993)}$$
$$= \$26.654 \text{ billion} - \$23.746 \text{ billion}$$
$$= \$2.908 \text{ billion}$$

To calculate the value, as of the end of 1988, of these future tax shields, we again discount by the borrowing rate of 13.5 percent to get[14]

$$\frac{2.908}{1.135^5} = \$1.544 \text{ billion}$$

The total value of interest tax shields therefore equals ($3.877 + $1.544) $5.421 billion.

Adding all of these components together, the total value of RJR under the buyout proposal is $29.978 billion. Deducting the $5 billion market value of assumed debt yields a value for equity of $24.978 billion, or $109.07 per share.

---

[13]To calculate this rate, use the weighted average cost of capital from this chapter:

$$r_{\text{WACC}} = \frac{S}{S + B} r_S + \frac{B}{S + B} r_B (1 - T_C)$$

and substitute the appropriate values for the proportions of debt and equity used, as well as their respective costs. Specifically, at the target debt-value ratio, $\frac{B}{S + B} = 25\%$, and $\frac{S}{S + B} = \left(1 - \frac{B}{S + B}\right) = 75\%$. Given this blend,

$$r_S = r_0 + \frac{B}{S}(1 - T_C)(r_0 - r_B)$$

$$= 0.14 + \frac{0.25}{0.75}(1 - 0.34)(0.14 - 0.135) = 0.141$$

Using these findings plus the borrowing rate of 13.5 percent in r_{WACC}, we find

$$r_{\text{WACC}} = 0.75(0.141) + 0.25(0.135)(1 - 0.34) = 0.128$$

In fact, this value is an approximation to the true weighted average cost of capital when the market debt-value blend is constant, or when the cash flows are growing. For a detailed discussion of this issue, see Isik Inselbag and Howard Kaufold, "A Comparison of Alternative Discounted Cash Flow Approaches to Firm Valuation." The Wharton School, University of Pennsylvania (June 1990), unpublished paper.

[14]A good argument can be made that since post-1993 debt levels are proportional to firm value, the tax shields are as risky as the firm and should be discounted at the rate r_0.

Concluding Comments on LBO Valuation Methods   As mentioned earlier in this chapter, the WACC method is by far the most widely applied approach to capital budgeting. One could analyze an LBO and generate the results of the second section of this appendix using this technique, but it would be a much more difficult process. We have tried to show that the APV approach is the preferred way to analyze a transaction in which the capital structure is not stable over time.

Consider the WACC approach to valuing the KKR bid for RJR. One could discount the operating cash flows of RJR by a set of weighted average costs of capital and arrive at the same $30 billion total value for the company. To do this, one would need to calculate the appropriate rate for each year since the WACC rises as the buyout proceeds. This occurs because the value of the tax subsidy declines as debt principal is repaid. In other words, there is no single return that represents the cost of capital when the firm's capital structure is changing.

There is also a theoretical problem with the WACC approach to valuing a buyout. To calculate the changing WACC, one must know the market value of a firm's debt and equity. But if the debt and equity values are already known, the total market value of the company is also known. That is, one must know the value of the company to calculate the WACC. One must therefore resort to using book-value measures for debt and equity, or make assumptions about the evolution of their market values, in order to implement the WACC method.

CHAPTER 18

Dividend Policy: Why Does It Matter?

EXECUTIVE SUMMARY

In recent years, U.S. corporations have paid out about 50 percent of their net income as cash dividends. However, a significant number of corporations pay no cash dividends and many pay more dividends than their net income.

Corporations view the dividend decision as quite important because it determines what funds flow to investors and what funds are retained by the firm for reinvestment. Dividend policy can also provide information to the stockholder concerning the firm's performance. The bulk of this chapter considers the rationale both for a policy of high dividend payout and for a policy of low dividend payout.

In part, all discussions of dividends are plagued by the "two-handed lawyer" problem. President Truman, while discussing the legal implications of a possible presidential decision, asked his staff to set up a meeting with a lawyer. Supposedly Mr. Truman said, "But I don't want one of those two-handed lawyers." When asked what a two-handed lawyer was, he replied, "You know, a lawyer who says, 'On the one hand I recommend you do so-and-so because of the following reasons, but on the other hand I recommend that you don't do it because of these other reasons.' " Unfortunately, any sensible treatment of dividend policy will appear to be written by a two-handed lawyer. On the one hand there are many good reasons for corporations to pay high dividends, but on the other hand there are many good reasons to pay low dividends.

We begin this chapter with a discussion of some practical aspects of dividend payments. Next we treat dividend policy. Before delineating the pros and cons of different dividend levels, we examine a benchmark case in which the choice of the level of dividends is not important. Surprisingly, we will see that this conceptual setup is not merely an academic curiosity but, instead, quite applicable to the real world. Next we consider personal taxes, an imperfection generally inducing a low level of dividends. This is followed by reasons justifying a high dividend level. Finally, we study the history of dividends of the Apple Computer Company. The case provides some clues as to why firms pay dividends.

18.1 DIFFERENT TYPES OF DIVIDENDS

The term *dividend* usually refers to a cash distribution of earnings. If a distribution is made from sources other than current or accumulated retained earnings, the term *distribution* rather than dividend is used. However, it is acceptable to refer to a distribution from earnings as a *dividend* and a distribution from capital as a *liquidating dividend*. More generally, any direct payment by the corporation to the shareholders may be considered part of dividend policy.

The most common type of dividend is in the form of cash. Public companies usually pay **regular cash dividends** four times a year. Sometimes firms will pay a regular cash dividend and an *extra cash dividend*. Paying a cash dividend reduces the corporate cash and retained earnings shown in the balance sheet—except in the case of a liquidating dividend (where paid-in capital may be reduced).

■ FIGURE 18.1   **Example of Procedure for Dividend Payment**

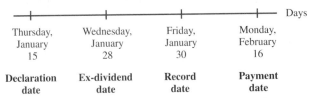

1. *Declaration Date:* The board of directors declares a payment of dividends.
2. *Record Date:* The declared dividends are distributable to shareholders of record on a specific date.
3. *Ex-dividend Date:* A share of stock becomes ex-dividend on the date the seller is entitled to keep the dividend; under NYSE rules, shares are traded ex-dividend on and after the second business day before the record date.
4. *Payment Date:* The dividend checks are mailed to shareholders of record.

Another type of dividend is paid out in shares of stock. This dividend is referred to as a **stock dividend.** It is not a true dividend, because no cash leaves the firm. Rather, a stock dividend increases the number of shares outstanding, thereby reducing the value of each share. A stock dividend is commonly expressed as a ratio; for example, with a 2-percent stock dividend a shareholder receives one new share for every 50 currently owned.

When a firm declares a **stock split,** it increases the number of shares outstanding. Because each share is now entitled to a smaller percentage of the firm's cash flow, the stock price should fall. For example, if the managers of a firm whose stock is selling at $90 declare a 3:1 stock split, the price of a share of stock should fall to about $30. A stock split strongly resembles a stock dividend except it is usually much larger.

18.2 STANDARD METHOD OF CASH DIVIDEND PAYMENT

The decision whether or not to pay a dividend rests in the hands of the board of directors of the corporation. A dividend is distributable to shareholders of record on a specific date. When a dividend has been declared, it becomes a liability of the firm and cannot be easily rescinded by the corporation. The amount of the dividend is expressed as dollars per share (*dividend per share*), as a percentage of the market price (*dividend yield*), or as a percentage of earnings per share (*dividend payout*).

The mechanics of a dividend payment can be illustrated by the example in Figure 18.1 and the following chronology.

1. **Declaration date.** On January 15 (the declaration date), the board of directors passes a resolution to pay a dividend of $1 per share on February 16 to all holders of record on January 30.

2. **Date of record.** The corporation prepares a list on January 30 of all individuals believed to be stockholders as of this date. The word *believed* is important here, because the dividend will not be paid to those individuals whose notification of purchase is received by the company after January 30.

3. **Ex-dividend date.** The procedure on the date of record would be unfair if efficient brokerage houses could notify the corporation by January 30 of a trade occurring on January 29, whereas the same trade might not reach the corporation until February 2 if executed by a less efficient house. To eliminate this problem, all brokerage firms entitle stockholders to receive the dividend if they purchased the stock three business days before

■ FIGURE 18.2   Price Behavior around the Ex-dividend Date for a $1 Cash Dividend

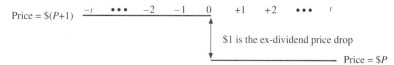

Perfect-world case

Ex-date

The stock price will fall by the amount of the dividend on the ex-date (time 0). If the dividend is $1 per share, the price will be equal to P on the ex-date.

Before ex-date (−1)   Price = $(P + 1)$

Ex-date (0)   Price = P

the date of record. The second day before the date of record, which is Wednesday, January 28, in our example, is called the *ex-dividend date.* Before this date the stock is said to trade *cum dividend.*

4. **Date of payment.** The dividend checks are mailed to the stockholders on February 16.

Obviously, the ex-dividend date is important, because an individual purchasing the security before the ex-dividend date will receive the current dividend, whereas another individual purchasing the security on or after this date will not receive the dividend. The stock price should fall on the ex-dividend date.[1] It is worthwhile to note that this drop is an indication of efficiency, not inefficiency, because the market rationally attaches value to a cash dividend. In a world with neither taxes nor transaction costs, the stock price would be expected to fall by the amount of the dividend:

Before ex-dividend date   Price = $(P + 1)$

On or after ex-dividend date   Price = P

This is illustrated in Figure 18.2.

The amount of the price drop is a matter for empirical investigation. Elton and Gruber have argued that, due to personal taxes, the stock price should fall by less than the dividend.[2] For example, consider the case with no capital gains taxes. On the day before a stock goes ex-dividend, shareholders must decide either (1) to buy the stock immediately and pay tax on the forthcoming dividend, or (2) to buy the stock tomorrow, thereby missing the dividend. If all investors are in the 28-percent bracket and the quarterly dividend is $1, the stock price should fall by $0.72 on the ex-dividend date. That is, if the stock price falls by this amount on the ex-dividend date, purchasers will receive the same return from either strategy.[3]

---

[1]Empirically, the stock price appears to fall within the first few minutes of the ex-dividend day.

[2]N. Elton and M. Gruber, "Marginal Stockholder Tax Rates and the Clientele Effect," *Review of Economics and Statistics* 52 (February 1970). See also R. Bali and G. L. Hite, "Ex-Dividend Day Stock Price Behavior: Discreteness or Tax-Induced Clienteles?" *Journal of Financial Economics* (February 1998) and M. Frank and R. Jagannathan, "Why Do Stock Prices Drop by Less than the Value of the Dividend? Evidence from a Country without Taxes," *Journal of Financial Economics* (February 1998).

[3]The situation is more complex when capital gains are considered. The individual pays capital gains taxes upon a subsequent sale. Because the price drops on the ex-dividend date, the original purchase price is higher if the purchase is made before the ex-dividend date, and the individual will reap, and pay taxes on, lower capital gains. Elton and Gruber show that the price drop should be somewhat more than 72¢ when capital gains are considered.

QUESTIONS
CONCEPT
?
• Describe the procedure of a dividend payment.
• Why should the price of a stock change when it goes ex-dividend?

18.3 THE BENCHMARK CASE: AN ILLUSTRATION OF THE IRRELEVANCE OF DIVIDEND POLICY

A powerful argument can be made that dividend policy does not matter. This will be illustrated with the Bristol Corporation. Bristol is an all-equity firm that has existed for 10 years. The current financial managers know at the present time (date 0) that the firm will dissolve in one year (date 1). At date 0 the managers are able to forecast cash flows with perfect certainty. The managers know that the firm will receive a cash flow of $10,000 immediately and another $10,000 next year. They believe that Bristol has no additional positive NPV projects it can use to its advantage.[4]

Current Policy: Dividends Set Equal to Cash Flow

At the present time, dividends (Div) at each date are set equal to the cash flow of $10,000. The value of the firm can be calculated by discounting these dividends. This value is expressed as

$$V_0 = \text{Div}_0 + \frac{\text{Div}_1}{1 + r_s}$$

where Div_0 and Div_1 are the cash flows paid out in dividends, and r_s is the discount rate. The first dividend is not discounted because it will be paid immediately.

Assuming $r_S = 10\%$, the value of the firm is

$$\$19,090.91 = \$10,000 + \frac{\$10,000}{1.1}$$

If 1,000 shares are outstanding, the value of each share is

$$\$19.09 = \$10 + \frac{\$10}{1.1} \tag{18.1}$$

To simplify the example, we assume that the ex-dividend date is the same as the date of payment. After the imminent dividend is paid, the stock price will immediately fall to $9.09 ($19.09 − $10). Several members of the board of Bristol have expressed dissatisfaction with the current dividend policy and have asked you to analyze an alternative policy.

Alternative Policy: Initial Dividend Is Greater than Cash Flow

Another policy is for the firm to pay a dividend of $11 per share immediately, which is, of course, a total dividend payout of $11,000. Because the cash runoff is only $10,000, the extra $1,000 must be raised in one of a few ways. Perhaps the simplest would be to issue $1,000 of bonds or stock now (at date 0). Assume that stock is issued and the new stockholders will desire enough cash flow at date 1 to let them earn the

---

[4]Bristol's investment in physical assets is fixed.

required 10-percent return on their date 0 investment.[5] The new stockholders will demand $1,100 of the date 1 cash flow,[6] leaving only $8,900 to the old stockholders. The dividends to the old stockholders will be

	Date 0	Date 1
Aggregate dividends to old stockholders	$11,000	$8,900
Dividends per share	$ 11.00	$ 8.90

The present value of the dividends per share is therefore

$$\$19.09 = \$11 + \frac{\$8.90}{1.1} \tag{18.2}$$

Students often find it instructive to determine the price at which the new stock is issued. Because the new stockholders are not entitled to the immediate dividend, they would pay $8.09 ($8.90/1.1) per share. Thus, 123.61 ($1,000/$8.09) new shares are issued.

The Indifference Proposition

Note that the values in equations (18.1) and (18.2) are equal. This leads to the initially surprising conclusion that the change in dividend policy did not affect the value of a share of stock. However, upon reflection, the result seems quite sensible. The new stockholders are parting with their money at date 0 and receiving it back with the appropriate return at date 1. In other words, they are taking on a zero NPV investment. As illustrated in Figure 18.3, old stockholders are receiving additional funds at date 0 but must pay the new stockholders their money with the appropriate return at date 1. Because the old stockholders must pay back principal plus the appropriate return, the act of issuing new stock at date 0 will not increase or decrease the value of the old stockholders' holdings. That is, they are giving up a zero NPV investment to the new stockholders. An increase in dividends at date 0 leads to the necessary reduction of dividends at date 1, so the value of the old stockholders' holdings remains unchanged.

This illustration is based on the pioneering work of Miller and Modigliani (MM).[7] Although our presentation is in the form of a numerical example, the MM paper proves that investors are indifferent to dividend policy in the general algebraic case. MM make the following assumptions:

1. There are neither taxes nor brokerage fees, and no single participant can affect the market price of the security through his or her trades. Economists say that perfect markets exist when these conditions are met.

2. All individuals have the same beliefs concerning future investments, profits, and dividends. As mentioned in Chapter 10, these individuals are said to have *homogeneous expectations.*

3. The investment policy of the firm is set ahead of time, and is not altered by changes in dividend policy.

---

[5]The same results would occur after an issue of bonds, though the argument would be less easily resolved.

[6]Because the new stockholders buy at date 0, their first (and only) dividend is at date 1.

[7]M. H. Miller and F. Modigliani, "Dividend Policy, Growth and the Valuation of Shares," *Journal of Business* (October 1961). Yes, this is the same MM who gave us a capital-structure theory.

■ FIGURE 18.3 **Current and Alternative Dividend Policies**

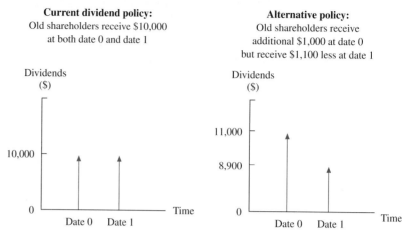

Current dividend policy:
Old shareholders receive $10,000
at both date 0 and date 1

Alternative policy:
Old shareholders receive
additional $1,000 at date 0
but receive $1,100 less at date 1

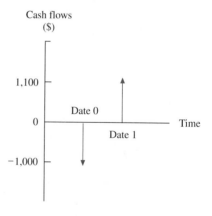

Alternative policy:
New shareholders pay in $1,000
at date 0 and receive $1,100 in
dividends at date 1

Homemade Dividends

To illustrate the indifference investors have toward dividend policy in our example, we used present-value equations. An alternative and perhaps more intuitively appealing explanation avoids the mathematics of discounted cash flows.

Suppose individual investor *X* prefers dividends per share of $10 at both dates 0 and 1. Would she be disappointed when informed that the firm's management is adopting the alternative dividend policy (dividends of $11 and $8.90 on the two dates, respectively)? Not necessarily, because she could easily reinvest the $1 of unneeded funds received on date 0, yielding an incremental return of $1.10 at date 1. Thus, she would receive her desired net cash flow of $11 − $1 = $10 at date 0 and $8.90 + $1.10 = $10 at date 1.

Conversely, imagine investor *Z* preferring $11 of cash flow at date 0 and $8.90 of cash flow at date 1, who finds that management will pay dividends of $10 at both dates 0 and 1. Here he can sell off shares of stock at date 0 to receive the desired amount of cash flow. That is, if he sells off shares (or fractions of shares) at date 0 totaling $1, his cash flow at date 0 becomes $10 + $1 = $11. Because a sale of $1 stock at date 0 will reduce his dividends by $1.10 at date 1, his net cash flow at date 1 would be $10 − $1.10 = $8.90.

■ FIGURE 18.4 **Homemade Dividends: A Trade-Off between Dividends at Date 0 and Dividends at Date 1**

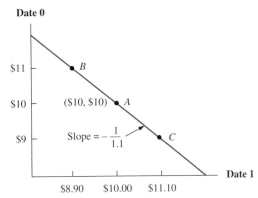

The graph illustrates both (1) how managers can vary dividend policy and (2) how individuals can undo the firm's dividend policy.
   Managers varying dividend policy. A firm paying out all cash flows immediately is at point *A* on the graph. The firm could achieve point *B* by issuing stock to pay extra dividends or achieve point *C* by buying back old stock with some of its cash.
   Individuals undoing the firm's dividend policy. Suppose the firm adopts the dividend policy represented by point *B:* dividends of $11 at date 0 and $8.90 at date 1. An investor can reinvest $1 of the dividends at 10 percent, which will place her at point *A.* Suppose, alternatively, the firm adopts the dividend policy represented by point *A.* An individual can sell off $1 of stock at date 0, placing him at point *B.* No matter what dividend policy the firm establishes, a sharholder can undo it.

The example illustrates how investors can make **homemade dividends.** In this instance, corporate dividend policy is being undone by a potentially dissatisfied stockholder. This homemade dividend is illustrated by Figure 18.4. Here the firm's cash flows of $10 at both dates 0 and 1 are represented by point *A.* This point also represents the initial dividend payout. However, as we just saw, the firm could alternatively pay out $11 at date 0 and $8.90 at date 1, a strategy represented by point *B.* Similarly, by either issuing new stock or buying back old stock, the firm could achieve a dividend payout represented by any point on the diagonal line.

The previous paragraph describes the choices available to the managers of the firm. The same diagonal line also represents the choices available to the shareholder. For example, if the shareholder receives a dividend distribution of ($11, $8.90), he or she can either reinvest some of the dividends to move down and to the right on the graph or sell off shares of stock and move up and to the left.

The implications of the graph can be summarized in two sentences:

1. By varying dividend policy, the managers can achieve any payout along the diagonal line in Figure 18.4.
2. Either by reinvesting excess dividends at date 0 or by selling off shares of stock at this date, any individual investor can achieve any net cash payout along the diagonal line.

Thus, because both the corporation and the individual investor can move only along the diagonal line, dividend policy in this model is irrelevant. The changes the managers make in dividend policy can be undone by an individual who, by either reinvesting dividends or selling off stock, can move to a desired point on the diagonal line.

A Test

You can test your knowledge of this material by examining these true statements:

1. Dividends are relevant.
2. Dividend policy is irrelevant.

The first statement follows from common sense. Clearly, investors prefer higher dividends to lower dividends at any single date if the dividend level is held constant at every other date. In other words, if the dividend per share at a given date is raised while the dividend per share for each other date is held constant, the stock price will rise. This act can be accomplished by management decisions that improve productivity, increase tax savings, or strengthen product marketing. In fact, you may recall in Chapter 5 we argued that the value of a firm's equity is equal to the discounted present value of all its future dividends.

The second statement is understandable once we realize that dividend policy cannot raise the dividend per share at one date while holding the dividend level per share constant at all other dates. Rather, dividend policy merely establishes the trade-off between dividends at one date and dividends at another date. As we saw in Figure 18.4, an increase in date 0 dividends can be accomplished only by a decrease in date 1 dividends. The extent of the decrease is such that the present value of all dividends is not affected.

Thus, in this simple world, dividend policy does not matter. That is, managers choosing either to raise or to lower the current dividend do not affect the current value of their firm. The above theory is a powerful one, and the work of MM is generally considered a classic in modern finance. With relatively few assumptions, a rather surprising result is shown to be perfectly true.[8] Because we want to examine many real-world factors ignored by MM, their work is only a starting point in this chapter's discussion of dividends. The next part of the chapter investigates these real-world considerations.

Dividends and Investment Policy

The preceding argument shows that an increase in dividends through issuance of new shares neither helps nor hurts the stockholders. Similarly, a reduction in dividends through share repurchase neither helps nor hurts stockholders.

What about reducing capital expenditures to increase dividends? Earlier chapters show that a firm should accept all positive net-present-value projects. To do otherwise would reduce the value of the firm. Thus, we have an important point:

> Firms should never give up a positive NPV project to increase a dividend (or to pay a dividend for the first time).

This idea was implicitly considered by Miller and Modigliani. As we pointed out, one of the assumptions underlying their dividend-irrelevance proposition was, "The investment policy of the firm is set ahead of time and is not altered by changes in dividend policy."

CONCEPT QUESTIONS

?

- How can an investor make homemade dividends?
- Are dividends irrelevant?
- What assumptions are needed to show that dividend policy is irrelevant?

---

[8]One of the real contributions of MM has been to shift the burden of proof. Before MM, firm value was believed to be influenced by its dividend policy. After MM, it became clear that establishing a correct dividend policy was not obvious at all.

■ FIGURE 18.5   Firm Issues Stock in Order to Pay a Dividend

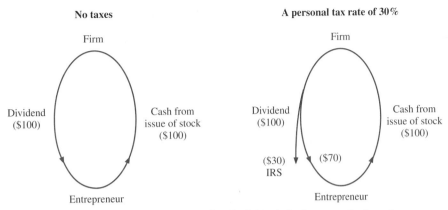

In the no-tax case, the entrepreneur receives the $100 in dividends that he gave to the firm when purchasing stock. The entire operation is called a *wash;* in other words, it has no economic effect. With taxes, the entrepreneur still receives $100 in dividends. However, he must pay $30 in taxes to the IRS. The entrepreneur loses and the IRS wins when a firm issues stock to pay a dividend.

18.4 TAXES, ISSUANCE COSTS, AND DIVIDENDS

The model we used to determine the level of dividends assumed that there were no taxes, no transactions costs, and no uncertainty. It concluded that dividend policy is irrelevant. Although this model helps us to grasp some fundamentals of dividend policy, it ignores many factors that exist in reality. It is now time to investigate these real-world considerations. We first examine the effect of taxes on the level of a firm's dividends.

Cash dividends received are taxed as ordinary income. Capital gains are generally taxed at somewhat lower rates. In addition, dividends are taxable when distributed, whereas taxes on capital gains are deferred until the stock is sold. Thus, for individual shareholders, the *effective* tax rate on dividend income is higher than the tax rate on capital gains. A discussion of dividend policy in the presence of personal taxes is facilitated by classifying firms into two types, those without sufficient cash to pay a dividend and those with sufficient cash to do so.

Firms without Sufficient Cash to Pay a Dividend

It is simplest to begin with a firm without cash and owned by a single entrepreneur. If this firm should decide to pay a dividend of $100, it must raise capital. The firm might choose among a number of different stock and bond issues in order to pay the dividend. However, for simplicity, we assume that the entrepreneur contributes cash to the firm by issuing stock to himself. This transaction, diagrammed in the left-hand side of Figure 18.5, would clearly be a *wash* in a world of no taxes. $100 cash goes into the firm when stock is issued and is immediately paid out as a dividend. Thus, the entrepreneur neither benefits nor loses when the dividend is paid, a result consistent with Miller-Modigliani.

Now assume that dividends are taxed at the owner's personal tax rate of 30 percent. The firm still receives $100 upon issuance of stock. However, the $100 dividend is not fully credited to the entrepreneur. Instead, the dividend payment is taxed, implying that the owner receives only $70 net after tax. Thus, the entrepreneur loses $30.

Though the example is clearly contrived and unrealistic, similar results can be reached for more plausible situations. Thus, financial economists generally agree that, in a world of personal taxes, one should not issue stock to pay a dividend.

The direct costs of issuance will add to this effect. Investment bankers must be paid when new capital is raised. Thus, the net receipts due to the firm from a new issue are less than 100 percent of total capital raised. These costs are examined in a later chapter. Because the size of new issues can be lowered by a reduction in dividends, we have another argument in favor of a low-dividend policy.

An increase in dividends may lead to a decline in stock price for still another reason. The market price of a stock is determined by the interaction of the demand for and the supply of stock. New issues increase the outstanding supply of the stock, putting downward pressure on the market price of existing shares. Therefore, to the extent that dividends are financed by new issues, an increase in dividends may well contribute to a stock-price reduction. However, in an efficient stock market, changes in the supply of stock should have a negligible effect on stock price.

Of course, our advice not to finance dividends through new stock issues might need to be modified somewhat in the real world. A company with a large and steady cash flow for many years in the past might be paying a regular dividend. If the cash flow unexpectedly dried up for a single year, should new stock be issued so that dividends could be continued? While our above discussion would imply that new stock should not be issued, many managers might issue the stock anyway for practical reasons. In particular, stockholders appear to prefer dividend stability. Thus, managers might be forced to issue stock to achieve this stability, knowing full well the adverse tax consequences.

Firms with Sufficient Cash to Pay a Dividend

The previous discussion argues that, in a world with personal taxes, one should not issue stock to pay a dividend. Does the tax disadvantage of dividends imply the stronger policy, "Never pay dividends in a world with personal taxes"?

We argue below that this prescription does not necessarily apply to firms with excess cash. To see this, imagine a firm with $1 million in extra cash after selecting all positive NPV projects and determining the level of prudent cash balances. The firm might consider the following alternatives to a dividend:

1. *Select Additional Capital-Budgeting Projects.* Because the firm has taken all the available positive NPV projects already, it must invest its excess cash in negative NPV projects. This is clearly a policy at variance with principles of corporate finance. In spite of our distaste for this strategy, Professor Michael Jensen of Harvard University has suggested that many managers choose to take on negative NPV projects in lieu of paying dividends, doing their stockholders a disservice in the process.[9] Oil companies and tobacco companies appear to be particularly guilty of this policy. It is frequently argued that managers who adopt negative NPV projects are ripe for takeover, leveraged buyouts, and proxy fights.

2. *Acquire Other Companies.* To avoid the payment of dividends, a firm might use excess cash to acquire another company. This strategy has the advantage of acquiring profitable assets. However, a firm often incurs heavy costs when it embarks on an acquisition program. In addition, acquisitions are invariably made above the market price. Premiums of 20 to 80 percent are not uncommon. Because of this, a number of researchers have argued that mergers are not generally profitable to the acquiring company, even when

---

[9]M. C. Jensen, "Agency Costs of Free Cash Flows, Corporate Finance and Takeovers," *American Economic Review* (May 1986).

firms are merged for a valid business purpose.[10] Therefore, a company making an acquisition merely to avoid a dividend is unlikely to succeed.

3. *Purchase Financial Assets.* The strategy of purchasing financial assets in lieu of a dividend payment can be illustrated with the following example.

EXAMPLE

The Regional Electric Company has $1,000 of extra cash. It can retain the cash and invest it in Treasury bills yielding 10 percent, or it can pay the cash to shareholders as a dividend. Shareholders can also invest in Treasury bills with the same yield. Suppose the corporate tax rate is 34 percent, and the individual tax rate is 28 percent. How much cash will investors have after five years under each policy?

If dividends are paid now, shareholders will receive

$$\$1,000 \times (1 - 0.28) = \$720$$

today after personal tax. Because their return after personal tax is 7.2 percent, they will have

$$\$720 \times (1.072)^5 = \$1,019.31 \tag{18.3}$$

in five years. If Regional Electric Company retains the cash to invest in Treasury bills and pays out the proceeds five years from now, the firm will have

$$\$1,000 \times (1.066)^5 = \$1,376.53$$

in five years.

If this is paid as a dividend, the stockholders will receive

$$\$1,376.53 \times (1 - 0.28) = \$991.10 \tag{18.4}$$

after personal taxes at date 5. The result in formula (18.3) is greater than that in (18.4), implying that cash to stockholders will be greater if the firm pays the dividend now.

This example shows that, for a firm with extra cash, the dividend-payout decision will depend on personal and corporate tax rates. If personal tax rates are higher than corporate tax rates, a firm will have an incentive to reduce dividend payouts. However, if personal tax rates are lower than corporate tax rates, a firm will have an incentive to pay out any excess cash as dividends.

There is a quirk in the tax law benefiting firms that invest in stock rather than bonds. For a company investing in less than 20 percent of the stock of other firms, 70 percent of the dividends received are excluded from corporate tax.[11] If Regional Electric invested $1,000 in a one-year preferred stock yielding 10 percent, only $30 of the $100 in dividends would be subject to tax. Corporate tax would be

$$\$30 \times 0.34 = \$1,000 \times 0.10 \times 0.3 \times 0.34 = \$10.20$$

Thus, Regional Electric would have

$$\begin{aligned}\$1,000 \times 1.10 - \$1,000 &\times 0.10 \times 0.3 \times 0.34 \\ = \$1,000 \times [1 + 0.10 &\times (1 - 0.3 \times 0.34)] \\ = \$1,100 - \$10.20 &= \$1,089.80\end{aligned}$$

---

[10]Richard Roll, "The Hubris Hypothesis of Corporate Takeovers," *Journal of Business* (1986), pp. 197–216, explores this idea in depth.

[11]The exclusion is 100 percent if a company owns 80 percent or more of the stock of another firm. It is 80 percent if a company holds more than 20 percent and less than 80 percent of another company.

at the end of one year. Regional is being taxed at an effective rate of $0.30 \times 0.34 = 10.2\%$. At the end of five years, Regional would have

$$\$1,000 \times [1 + 0.10 \times (1 - 0.30 \times 0.34)]^5$$
$$= \$1,000 \times [1 + 0.10 \times (1 - 0.1020)]^5$$
$$= \$1,537.21$$

If this is paid as a dividend, the stockholders would receive

$$\$1,537.21 \times (1 - 0.28) = \$1,106.79 \tag{18.5}$$

at that time.

Because individual investors are not allowed this dividend exclusion, they would receive the same amount whether they invested date 0 dividends in 10-percent T-bills or 10-percent preferred stock. Because the result in equation (18.5) is greater than the one in (18.4), Regional should invest in preferred stock rather than pay a dividend at date 0.

Because this dividend-exclusion percentage is so large, most real-world examples favor retention rather than payment of dividends. However, there appear to be very few, if any, companies that hoard cash in this manner without limit. This occurs because Section 532 of the Internal Revenue Code penalizes firms with "improper accumulation of surplus."

The above example suggests that, because of personal taxes, firms have an incentive to reduce their payment of dividends. For example, they might increase capital expenditures, repurchase shares, acquire other firms, or buy financial assets. However, due to financial considerations and legal constraints, rational firms at some point may bite the bullet and pay some dividends. In other words, we are arguing that firms with large cash flows may pay dividends simply because they have run out of better things to do with their funds.

Summary on Taxes

Miller and Modigliani argue that dividend policy is irrelevant in a perfect capital market. However, because dividends are taxed as ordinary income, the MM irrelevance principle does not hold in the presence of personal taxes.

We make three points for a regime of personal taxes:

1. A firm should not issue stock to pay a dividend.
2. Managers have an incentive to seek alternative uses for funds to reduce dividends.
3. Though personal taxes mitigate against the payment of dividends, these taxes are not sufficient to lead firms to eliminate all dividends.

We argue that a manager should only avoid dividends if the alternative use of the funds is less costly. Though this point may seem obvious to some, it has been missed by many financial people. A number of them have argued, incorrectly in our view, that personal taxes imply that no firm should ever pay dividends.

18.5 REPURCHASE OF STOCK

Instead of paying cash dividends, a firm can rid itself of excess cash by repurchasing shares of its own stock. Recently share repurchase has become an important way of distributing earnings to shareholders.[12] The repurchase of stock is a potentially useful adjunct to divi-

---

[12]Adam Dunsby, "Share Repurchases, Dividends, and Corporate Distribution Policy," unpublished manuscript, The Wharton School, University of Pennsylvania, November 29, 1994, shows a dramatic increase in share repurchase since 1983. See also Laurie S. Bagwell and John B. Shoven, "Cash Distribution to Shareholders," *Journal of Economic Perspective* 3 (1989).

■ TABLE 18.1 Dividend versus Repurchase Example

	For Entire Firm	Per Share
Extra Dividend		**(100,000 shares outstanding)**
Proposed dividend	$ 300,000	$ 3.00
Forecasted annual earnings after dividend	450,000	4.50
Market value of stock after dividend	2,700,000	27.00
Repurchase		**(90,000 shares outstanding)**
Forecasted annual earnings after repurchase	$ 450,000	$ 5.00
Market value of stock after repurchase	2,700,000	30.00

dend policy, when tax avoidance is important. We first consider an example presented in the theoretical world of a perfect capital market. We next discuss the real-world factors involved in the repurchase decision.

Dividend versus Repurchase

Imagine a company with excess cash of $300,000 (or $3 per share) that is considering an immediate payment of this amount as an extra dividend. The firm forecasts that, after the dividend, earnings will be $450,000 per year, or $4.50 for each of the 100,000 shares outstanding. Because the price-earnings ratio is 6 for comparable companies, the shares of the firm should sell for $27. These figures are presented in the top half of Table 18.1.

Alternatively, the firm could use the excess cash to repurchase some of its own stock. Imagine that a tender offer of $30 a share is made. Here, 10,000 shares are repurchased so that the total number of shares remaining is 90,000. With fewer shares outstanding, the earnings per share will rise to $5. The price-earnings ratio remains at 6, since both the business and financial risks of the firm are the same in the repurchase case as they were for the dividend case. Thus the price of a share after the repurchase is $30.

If commissions, taxes, and other imperfections are ignored in our example, the stockholders are indifferent between a dividend and a repurchase. With dividends, each stockholder owns a share worth $27 and receives $3 in dividends, so that the total value is $30. This figure is the same as both the amount received by the selling stockholders and the value of the stock for the remaining stockholders in the repurchase case.

This example illustrates the important point that, in a perfect market, the firm is indifferent between a dividend payment and a share repurchase. This result is quite similar to the indifference propositions established by MM for debt versus equity financing and for dividends versus capital gains.

Relationship between EPS and Market Value

You may often read in the popular financial press that a repurchase agreement is beneficial because earnings per share increase. Earnings per share do rise in the preceding example where repurchase is substituted for a cash dividend: the EPS is $4.50 after a dividend and $5 after the repurchase. This result holds because the drop in shares after a repurchase implies a reduction in the denominator of the EPS ratio.

However, the financial press may place undue emphasis on EPS figures in a repurchase agreement. Given the irrelevance propositions we have discussed, an increase in EPS need not be beneficial. When a repurchase is financed by excess cash, we showed that in a perfect capital market the total value to the stockholder is the same under the dividend payment strategy as under the repurchase agreement strategy.

Taxes

The examples we have just described show that repurchase does not raise the wealth of the remaining shareholders in a world without taxes and transactions costs. However, stockholders generally prefer a repurchase to a dividend under current tax law. For example, a dividend of $1 per share is taxed at ordinary income rates. Investors in the 28 percent tax bracket who own 100 shares of the security would pay as much as $28 in taxes. Selling stockholders would pay far lower taxes under a repurchase of $100 of existing shares. This is because taxes are paid only on the profit from a sale. Thus the gain on a sale would be only $40 if the shares sold at $100 were originally purchased at $60. In addition, the capital gains tax rate is usually lower than the ordinary income tax rate. In this example, the capital gains tax rate is 20 percent. The capital gains tax would be $(0.20 \times \$40) = \$8$.

If the example strikes you as being too good to be true, you are quite likely right. The IRS is aware that the stockholders of a corporation engaging in a continuous repurchasing program pay far less in taxes than stockholders receiving dividends. Thus the IRS is likely to penalize corporations repurchasing their own stocks if the only reason is to avoid the taxes that would be levied on dividends. However, a one-time-only repurchase of shares will most often avoid IRS scrutiny.

Targeted Repurchase

Our previous discussion concerned companies that make nonselective repurchases, usually executed through tender offers[13] or open-market purchases. In addition, firms have repurchased shares from specific individual stockholders. This procedure has been called a "targeted repurchase." For example, suppose the International Biotechnology Corporation purchased approximately 10 percent of the outstanding stock of the Prime Robotics Company (P-R Co.) in April at around $38 per share. At that time, International Biotechnology announced to the Securities and Exchange Commission that it might eventually try to take control of P-R Co. In May, P-R Co. repurchased the International Biotechnology holdings at $48 per share, well above the market price at that time. This offer was not extended to other shareholders.

Companies engage in this type of repurchase for a variety of reasons. In some rare cases a single large stockholder can be bought out at a price lower than that in a tender offer. The legal fees in a targeted repurchase may also be lower than those in a more typical buyback. More frequently, the repurchasing firm has argued that certain stockholders had been nuisances. Though targeted repurchases executed for these reasons are in the interest of the remaining shareholders, the shares of large stockholders are often repurchased to avoid a takeover unfavorable to management.

Repurchase as Investment

Many companies buy back stock because they believe that a repurchase is their best investment. This occurs more frequently when managers believe that the stock price is temporarily depressed. Here, it is likely thought that (1) investment opportunities in nonfinancial assets are few, and (2) the firm's own stock price should rise with the passage of time.

The fact that some companies repurchase their stock when they believe it is undervalued does not imply that the management of the company must be correct; only empirical studies can make this determination. The immediate stock market reaction to the announcement of a

---

[13]In a tender offer, shareholders send in (tender) their shares in exchange for a specified price per share.

stock repurchase is usually quite favorable. In addition, recent empirical work has shown that the long-term stock price performance of securities after a buyback is significantly better than the stock price performance of comparable companies that do not repurchase.[14]

QUESTIONS

CONCEPT   ?

- Why does a stock repurchase make more sense than paying dividends?
- Why don't all firms use stock repurchases?

18.6 EXPECTED RETURN, DIVIDENDS, AND PERSONAL TAXES

The material presented so far in this chapter can properly be called a discussion of *dividend policy*. That is, it is concerned with the level of dividends chosen by a firm. A related, but distinctly different, question is, "What is the relationship between the expected return on a security and its dividend yield?" To answer this question, we consider an extreme situation where dividends are taxed as ordinary income and capital gains are not taxed. Corporate taxes are ignored.

Suppose every shareholder is in a 25-percent tax bracket and is considering the stocks of firm g and firm d. Firm g pays no dividend; firm d does. Suppose the current price of the stock of firm g is $100 and next year's price is expected to be $120. The shareholder in firm g expects a $20 capital gain, implying a 20-percent return. If capital gains are not taxed, the pretax and after-tax returns must be the same.[15]

Suppose firm d will pay a $20 dividend per share next year. The price of firm d's stock is expected to be $100 after the dividend payment. If the stocks of firm g and firm d are equally risky, the market prices must be set so that their *after-tax* expected returns are equal, in this case, to 20 percent. What will the current price of stock in firm d equal?

The current market price of a share in firm d can be calculated as follows:

$$P_0 = \frac{\$100 + \$20(1 - T_d)}{1.20}$$

The first term in the numerator is $100, the expected price of the stock at date 1. The second term represents the dividend after personal tax, where T_d is the personal tax rate on dividends. (The tax on capital gains is ignored under our assumption of no capital gains tax.) By discounting at 20 percent, we are ensuring that the after-tax rate on stock d is 20 percent, the same as the rate of return (both pre- and post-tax) for firm g. Setting $T_d = 0.25$, $P_0 = \$95.83$.

Because the investor receives $120 from firm d at date 1 ($100 in value of stock plus $20 in dividends) before personal taxes, the expected pretax return on the security equals

$$\frac{\$120}{\$95.83} - 1 = 25.22\%$$

These calculations are presented in Table 18.2.

---

[14]For example, see David Ikenberry, Joseph Lakonishok, and Theo Vermaelen, "Market Underreaction to Open Market Share Repurchases," *Journal of Financial Economics* 39 (1995).

[15]Under current tax law, taxes on capital gains are not paid until the owner sells. Because the owner may wait indefinitely, the effective tax on capital gains in the real world is quite low. For example, A. Protopapadakis ("Some Indirect Evidence on Effective Capital Gains Tax Rates," *Journal of Business,* April 1983) finds that "the effective marginal tax rates on capital gains fluctuated between 3.4 percent and 6.6 percent between 1960 and 1978 and that capital gains are held, on average, between 24 and 31 years before they are reported" (p. 127).

■ TABLE 18.2   **Effect of Dividend Yield on Pretax Expected Returns**

	Firm g (no dividend)	Firm d (all dividend)
Assumptions:		
Expected price at date 1	$120	$100
Dividend at date 1 (before tax)	0	$ 20
Dividend at date 1 (after tax)	0	$ 15
Price at date 0	$100	(to be solved)
Analysis:		
We solve that the price of firm *d* at date 0 is $95.83,* allowing us to calculate		
Capital gain	$20	$100 − $95.83 = $4.17
Total gain before tax (both dividend and capital gain)	$20	$20 + $4.17 = $24.17
Total percentage return (before tax)	$\dfrac{\$20}{\$100} = 0.20$	$\dfrac{\$24.17}{\$95.83} = 0.252$
Total gain after tax	$20	$15 + $4.17 = $19.17
Total percentage return (after tax)	$\dfrac{\$20}{\$100} = 0.20$	$\dfrac{\$19.17}{\$95.83} = 0.20$

Stocks with high-dividend yields will have higher pretax expected returns than stocks with low-dividend yields. This is referred to as the *grossing up effect.*

*We solve for the price of firm *d* at date 0 as

$$P_0 = \frac{\$100 + \$20 \times (1 - 0.25)}{1.20} = \$95.83$$

This example shows that the expected *pretax* return on a security with a high dividend yield is greater than the expected *pretax* return on an otherwise identical security with a low dividend yield.[16] The result is graphed in Figure 18.6. Our conclusion is consistent with efficient capital markets because much of the pretax return for a security with a high dividend yield is taxed away. One implication is that an individual in a zero tax bracket should invest in securities with high dividend yields. There is at least casual evidence that pension funds, which are not subject to taxes, select securities with high dividend yields.

Does the above example suggest that corporate managers should avoid paying dividends? One might think so at first glance, because firm *g* sells at a higher price at date 0 than does firm *d*. However, by deferring a potential $20 dividend, firm *d* might increase its stock price at date 0 by far less than $20. For example, this is likely to be the case if firm *d*'s best use for its cash is to pay $20 for a company whose market price is far below $20. Moreover, our previous discussion showed that deferment of dividends to purchase either bonds or shares of stock is justified only when personal taxes go down by more than corporate taxes rise. Thus, this example does *not* imply that dividends should be avoided.

Empirical Evidence

As explained above, financial theory indicates that the expected return on a security should be related to its dividend yield. Although this issue has been researched thoroughly, the empirical results are not generally consistent with each other. On the one hand, Brennan as well as Litzenberger and Ramaswamy (LR) find a positive association between expected

---

[16]Dividend yield is defined as $\dfrac{\text{Annual dividends per share}}{\text{Current price per share}}$.

■ FIGURE 18.6 **Relationship between Expected Return and
                 Dividend Yield**

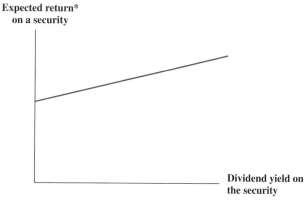

**Expected return*
on a security**

**Dividend yield on
the security**

Because the tax rate on dividends at the personal level is higher than the
effective rate on capital gains, stockholders demand higher expected
returns on high-dividend stocks than on low-dividend stocks.
*Expected return includes both expected capital gain and dividend.

pretax returns and dividend yields.[17,18,19] In particular, LR find that a 1-percent increase in
dividend yield requires an extra 23 percent in expected return. On the other hand, both
Black and Scholes and Miller and Scholes find no relationship between expected pretax returns and dividend yields.[20,21]

Fama and French develop a third point of view.[22] They present evidence that expected
returns are positively related to a number of variables, such as dividend yield, the earnings-
to-price ratio, and the ratio of book equity to market equity (BEME). However, they argue
that the underlying relationship is between returns and BEME. In their view, a relationship
between returns and the dividend yield is observed only because dividend yield is correlated with BEME. Their work has had a big impact, with the field generating little, if any,
research on expected returns and dividend yields in recent years.

CONCEPT QUESTION

• What is the relationship between expected returns and dividend yield?

[17]M. Brennan, "Taxes: Market Valuation and Corporate Financial Policy," *National Tax Journal* (December 1970).

[18]R. Litzenberger and K. Ramaswamy, "The Effect of Personal Taxes and Dividends on Capital Asset Prices:
Theory and Empirical Evidence," *Journal of Financial Economics* (June 1979).

[19]R. Litzenberger and K. Ramaswamy, "The Effects of Dividends on Common Stock Prices: Tax Effects or
Information Effect?" *Journal of Finance* (May 1982).

[20]F. Black and M. Scholes, "The Effects of Dividend Yield and Dividend Policy on Common Stock Prices and
Returns," *Journal of Financial Economics* (May 1974).

[21]M. Miller and M. Scholes, "Dividends and Taxes: Some Empirical Evidence," *Journal of Political Economics*
(December 1982).

[22]See, for example, E. F. Fama and K. R. French, "The Cross-Section of Expected Returns," *Journal of Finance*
(June 1992).

18.7 REAL-WORLD FACTORS FAVORING A HIGH-DIVIDEND POLICY

In a previous section, we pointed out that dividends are taxed at the personal level. This implies that financial managers will seek out ways to reduce dividends, though a complete elimination of dividends would be unlikely for firms with strong cash flow. We also pointed out that share repurchase is a way financial managers can convey many of the same benefits of a dividend without the tax disadvantage. In this section, we consider reasons why a firm might pay its shareholders high dividends, even in the presence of high personal taxes on dividends.

Desire for Current Income

It has been argued that many individuals desire current income. The classic example is the group of retired people and others living on a fixed income, proverbially known as "widows and orphans." The argument further states that these individuals would bid up the stock price should dividends rise and bid down the stock price should dividends fall.

Miller and Modigliani point out that this argument is not relevant to their theoretical model. An individual preferring high current cash flow but holding low-dividend securities could easily sell off shares to provide the necessary funds. Thus, in a world of no transactions costs, a high–current-dividend policy would be of no value to the stockholder. However, the current income argument does have relevance in the real world. Here the sale of low-dividend stocks would involve brokerage fees and other transactions costs—direct cash expenses that could be avoided by an investment in high-dividend securities. In addition, the expenditure of the stockholder's own time when selling securities and the natural (but not necessarily rational) fear of consuming principal might further lead many investors to buy high-dividend securities.

However, to put this argument in perspective, it should be remembered that financial intermediaries such as mutual funds can perform these repackaging transactions for individuals at very low cost. Such intermediaries could buy low-dividend stocks and, by a controlled policy of realizing gains, pay their investors at a higher rate.

Uncertainty Resolution

We have just pointed out that investors with substantial needs for current consumption will prefer high current dividends. Gordon originally argued that a high-dividend policy also benefits stockholders because it resolves uncertainty.[23] He states that investors price a security by forecasting and discounting future dividends. According to Gordon, forecasts of dividends to be received in the distant future have greater uncertainty than do forecasts of near-term dividends. Because the discount rate is positively related to the degree of uncertainty surrounding dividends, the stock price should be low for those companies that pay small dividends now in order to remit higher dividends at later dates.

Dividends are easier to predict than capital gains; however, it would be false to conclude that increased dividends can make the firm less risky. A firm's overall cash flows are not necessarily affected by dividend policy—as long as capital spending and borrowing are not changed. It is hard to see how the risks of the overall cash flows can be changed with a change in dividend policy.

---

[23]M. Gordon, *The Investment, Financing, and Valuation of the Corporation* (Homewood, Ill.: Richard D. Irwin, 1961).

Tax Arbitrage

Miller and Scholes (MS) argue that a two-step procedure eliminates the taxes ordinarily due on investments in high-yield securities.[24] The MS strategy is as follows. First, buy stocks with high dividend yields, borrowing enough of the purchase price so that the interest paid is equal to the dividends received. The benefit of this strategy is that no taxes would be due because dividends are taxable whereas interest is deductible. The problem with the strategy is that the resulting position is quite risky due to the leverage involved. Second, to offset the leverage, invest an amount equivalent to the debt already incurred in a tax-deferred account (such as a Keogh account). Because income in a tax-deferred account avoids taxes, no taxes are paid when the two steps are done simultaneously.

If enough investors are able to take advantage of the strategy, corporate managers need not view dividends as tax-disadvantaged. Thus, only a slight preference for current income and for resolution of uncertainty among investors causes responsive managers to provide high dividends.

Agency Costs

Although stockholders, bondholders, and management form firms for mutually beneficial reasons, one party may later gain at the other's expense. For example, take the potential conflict between bondholders and stockholders. Bondholders would like stockholders to leave as much cash as possible in the firm so that this cash would be available to pay the bondholders during times of financial distress. Conversely, stockholders would like to keep this extra cash for themselves. That's where dividends come in. Managers, acting on behalf of the stockholders, may pay dividends simply to keep the cash away from the bondholders. In other words, a dividend can be viewed as a wealth transfer from bondholders to stockholders. There is empirical evidence for this view of things. For example, DeAngelo and DeAngelo[25] find that firms in financial distress are reluctant to cut dividends. Of course, bondholders know of the propensity of stockholders to transfer money out of the firm. To protect themselves, bondholders frequently create loan agreements stating that dividends can be paid only if the firm has earnings, cash flow, and working capital above prespecified levels.

Although the managers may be looking out for the stockholders in any conflict with bondholders, the managers may pursue selfish goals at the expense of stockholders in other situations. For example, as discussed in Chapter 16, managers might pad expense accounts, take on pet projects with negative NPVs, or, more simply, not work very hard. Managers find it easier to pursue these selfish goals when the firm has plenty of free cash flow. After all, one can not squander funds if the funds are not available in the first place. And, that is where dividends come in. Several scholars have suggested that dividends can serve as a way to reduce agency costs.[26] By paying dividends equal to the amount of "surplus" cash flow, a firm can reduce management's ability to squander the firm's resources.

CONCEPT QUESTION

• What are the real-world factors favoring a high-dividend policy?

---

[24]M. Miller and M. Scholes, "Dividends and Taxes," *Journal of Financial Economics* (December 1978).

[25]H. De Angelo and L. De Angelo, "Dividend Policy and Financial Distress: An Empirical Investigation of Troubled NYSE Firms," *Journal of Finance* 45 (1990).

[26]Michael Rozeff, "How Companies Set Their Dividend Payout Ratios," in *The Revolution in Corporate Finance,* edited by Joel M. Stern and Donald H. Chew (New York: Basel Blackwell, 1986). See also Robert S. Hansen, Raman Kumar, and Dilip K. Shome, "Dividend Policy and Corporate Monitoring: Evidence from the Regulated Electric Utility Industry," *Financial Management* (Spring 1994).

18.8 A Resolution of Real-World Factors?

In the previous sections, we pointed out that the existence of personal taxes favors a low-dividend policy after all positive NPV projects are taken, whereas other factors favor high dividends. The financial profession had hoped that it would be easy to determine which of these sets of factors dominates. Unfortunately, after years of research, no one has been able to conclude which of the two is more important. Thus, the dividend-policy question is not resolved.

A discussion of two important concepts—the information content of dividends and the clientele effect—will give the reader an appreciation of some of the relevant issues. The first topic both illustrates the difficulty in interpreting empirical results on dividends and provides another reason for dividends. The second topic suggests that the dividend-payout ratio may not be as important as we originally imagined.

Information Content of Dividends: A Brainteaser with Practical Applications

The present topic is fascinating, because it is a brainteaser. To begin let us quickly review some of our earlier discussion. Previously, we examined three different positions on dividends:

1. From the homemade-dividend argument of MM, dividend policy is irrelevant, given that future earnings are held constant.
2. Because of tax effects, a firm's stock price may be negatively related to the current dividend when future earnings are held constant.
3. Because of the desire for current income and related factors, a firm's stock price may be positively related to its current dividend, even when future earnings are held constant.

It has been empirically established that the price of a firm's stock will generally rise when its current dividend is increased and fall when its current dividend has been reduced or omitted. For example, Asquith and Mullins estimate that stock prices rise about 3 percent following announcements of dividend initiations. Healy and Palepu[27] and Michaely, Thaler, and Womack[28] find that stock prices fall about 7 percent following announcements of dividend omissions.

At first glance, this observation may seem consistent with position 3 and inconsistent with positions 1 and 2. In fact, many writers have argued this. However, other authors have countered that the observation itself is consistent with all three positions. They point out that companies do not like to cut a dividend. Thus, firms will raise the dividend only when future earnings, cash flow, and so on are expected to rise enough so that the dividend is not likely to be reduced later to its original level. A dividend increase is management's signal to the market that the firm is expected to do well.

It is the expectation of good times, and not only the stockholder's affinity for current income, that raises stock price. The rise in the stock price following the dividend signal is called the **information-content effect** of the dividend. To recapitulate, imagine that the stock price is unaffected or negatively affected by the level of dividends, given that future

---

[27]P. Asquith and D. Mullins, Jr., "The Impact of Initiating Dividend Payments on Shareholder Wealth," *Journal of Business* (January 1983).

[28]P. M. Healy and K. G. Palepu, "Earnings Information Conveyed by Dividend Initiations and Omissions," *Journal of Financial Economics* 21 (1988); and R. Michaely, R. H. Thaler, and K. Womack, "Price Reactions to Dividend Initiations and Omissions: Overreactions or Drift," *Journal of Finance* 50 (1995).

earnings are held constant. Nevertheless, the information-content effect implies that stock price may rise when dividends are raised—if dividends simultaneously cause stockholders to upwardly adjust their expectations of future earnings.

Several theoretical models of dividend policy incorporate managerial incentive to communicate information via dividends.[29] Here, dividends serve to signal to shareholders the firm's current and future performance.

The Clientele Effect

In the first part of this chapter we established the MM proposition that dividend policy is irrelevant when certain conditions hold. Later sections dealt with those imperfections likely to make dividend policy relevant. Because many imperfections were presented there, the reader might be skeptical that the imperfections could cancel each other out so perfectly that dividend policy would become irrelevant. However, the argument presented below suggests the irrelevance of dividend policy in the real world.

Those individuals in high tax brackets are likely to prefer either no or low dividends. We can classify low–tax-bracket investors into three types. First, there are individual investors in low brackets. They are likely to prefer some dividends if they desire current income or favor resolution of uncertainty. Second, pension funds pay no taxes on either dividends or capital gains. Because they face no tax consequences, pension funds will also prefer dividends if they have a preference for current income. Finally, corporations can exclude at least 70 percent of their dividend income but cannot exclude any of their capital gains. Thus, corporations would prefer to invest in high-dividend stocks, even without a desire to resolve uncertainty or a preference for current income.

Suppose that 40 percent of all investors prefer high dividends and 60 percent prefer low dividends, yet only 20 percent of firms pay high dividends while 80 percent pay low dividends. Here, the high-dividend firms will be in short supply; thus their stock should be bid up while the stock of low-dividend firms should be bid down.

However, the dividend policies of all firms need not be fixed in the long run. In this example, we would expect enough low-dividend firms to increase their payout so that 40 percent of the firms pay high dividends and 60 percent of the firms pay low dividends. After this has occurred, no type of firm will be better off from changing its dividend policy. Once payouts of corporations conform to the desires of stockholders, no single firm can affect its market value by switching from one dividend strategy to another.

Clienteles are likely to form in the following way:

Group	Stocks
Individuals in high tax brackets	Zero-to-low-payout stocks
Individuals in low tax brackets	Low-to-medium-payout stocks
Tax-free institutions	Medium-payout stocks
Corporations	High-payout stocks

---

[29]S. Bhattacharya, "Imperfect Information, Dividend Policy, and 'the Bird in the Hand' Fallacy," *Bell Journal of Economics* 10 (1979); S. Bhattacharya, "Nondissipative Signaling Structure and Dividend Policy," *Quarterly Journal of Economics* 95 (1980), p. 1; S. Ross, "The Determination of Financial Structure: The Incentive Signalling Approach," *Bell Journal of Economics* 8 (1977), p. 1; M. Miller and K. Rock, "Dividend Policy under Asymmetric Information," *Journal of Finance* (1985).

An interesting case for the clientele effect on dividend policy is made by John Childs of Kidder Peabody in the following exchange:[30]

> *Joseph T. Willet:* John, you've been around public utilities for a good many years. Why do you think that utilities have such high dividend payout ratios?
>
> *John Childs:* They're raising dividends so they can raise capital. . . . If you take the dividends out of utilities today, you'll never sell another share of stock. That's how important it is. In fact, if a few major utilities (with no special problems) cut their dividends, small investors would lose faith in the utility industry and that would finish the sales of utility stocks.
>
> *John Childs (again):* What you are trying to do with dividend policy is to enhance and strengthen the natural interest of investors in your company. The type of stockholders you attract will depend on the type of company you are. If you're Genentech, you are going to attract the type of stockholders who have absolutely no interest in dividends. In fact, you would hurt the stockholders if you paid dividends. On the other hand, you go over to the other extreme such as utilities' and the yield bank's stocks. There the stockholders are extremely interested in dividends, and these dividends have an effect on market price.

However, despite the preceding exchange, a desire for dividends on the part of existing shareholders should not be sufficient to justify a high-dividend payout policy.

To see if you understand the clientele effect, consider the following question: "In spite of the theoretical argument that dividend policy is irrelevant or that firms should not pay dividends, many investors like high dividends. Because of this fact, a firm can boost its share price by having a higher dividend payout ratio." True or false?

The statement is likely to be false. As long as enough high-dividend firms satisfy dividend-loving investors, a firm will not be able to boost its share price by paying high dividends. A firm can boost its stock price only if an unsatisfied clientele exists. There is no evidence that this is the case.

Our discussion on clienteles followed from the fact that tax brackets vary across investors. If shareholders care about taxes, stock should attract tax clienteles based on dividend yield. This appears to be true. Surveys by Blume, Crockett, and Friend, and by Lewellen, Stanley, Lease, and Schlarbaum in Table 18.3, show that stocks with the highest dividend yields tend to be held by individual investors in low tax brackets.[31]

CONCEPT QUESTIONS

- Do dividends have information content?
- What are tax clienteles?

18.9 WHAT WE KNOW AND DO NOT KNOW ABOUT DIVIDEND POLICY

Corporate Dividends Are Substantial

We pointed out earlier in the chapter that dividends are tax-disadvantaged relative to capital gains for two reasons. First, dividends are taxed at the ordinary income-tax rate, whereas capital gains are taxed at a lower rate. Second, taxes on dividends are paid in the year in

---

[30]Joseph T. Willett, moderator, "A Discussion of Corporate Dividend Policy," in *Six Roundtable Discussions of Corporate Finance with Joel Stern,* ed. by D. H. Chew (New York: Basel Blackwell, 1986). The panelists included Robert Litzenberger, Pat Hess, Bill Kealy, John Childs, and Joel Stern.

[31]M. Blume, J. Crockett, and I. Friend, "Stockownership in the United States: Characteristics and Trends," *Survey of Current Business* 54 (1974), p. 11. W. Lewellen, K. L. Stanley, R. C. Lease, and G. C. Schlarbaum, "Some Direct Evidence on the Dividend Clientele Phenomenon," *Journal of Finance* 33 (December 1978), p. 5.

■ TABLE 18.3   **Relationship between Dividend Yield and Marginal Tax Rate from Direct Observation of Individual Investors' Portfolios**

Decile	Dividend Yield (% per annum)	Marginal Tax* Rate (%)
1	7.9%	36%
2	5.4	35
3	4.4	38
4	3.5	39
5	2.7	38
6	1.8	41
7	0.6	40
8	0.0	41
9	0.0	42
10	0.0	41

Stockholders in high marginal tax brackets buy securities with low-dividend yield and vice versa.

*Lewellen et al. use several alternative methods to calculate the marginal tax rate from data on income. The results are broadly similar, and above we give the results for their "Tax-1" definition.

From W. Lewellen, K. L. Stanley, R. C. Lease, and G. C. Schlarbaum, "Some Direct Evidence on the Dividend Clientele Phenomenon," *Journal of Finance* 33 (December 1978), p. 5.

which the dividend is received while taxes on capital gains are deferred until the year of sale. Nevertheless, dividends in the U.S. economy are substantial. For example, consider Figure 18.7, which shows the ratio of aggregate dividends to aggregate earnings for firms on the New York Stock Exchange (NYSE), the American Stock Exchange (AMEX), and NASDAQ over various time periods. The ratio is approximately 43 percent for the period from 1963 to 1998. This ratio varies from a low of 33.95 percent in the 1973–77 period to a high of 56.86 percent from 1988 to 1992.

One might argue that the taxation on dividends is actually minimal, perhaps because dividends are paid primarily to individuals in low tax brackets or because institutions such as pension funds, which pay no taxes, are the primary recipients. However, Peterson, Peterson and Ang[32] conducted an in-depth study of dividends for one representative year, 1979. They found that about two-thirds of dividends went to individuals and that the average marginal tax bracket for these individuals was about 40 percent. Thus, we must conclude that large amounts of dividends are paid, even in the presence of substantial taxation.

Fewer Companies Pay Dividends

In a recent and fascinating paper, Fama and French[33] (FF) point out that the percentage of companies paying dividends has fallen in recent years. This insight is illustrated in Figure 18.8 for NYSE, AMEX, and NASDAQ firms. FF argue that the decline was caused primarily by an explosion of small, currently unprofitable companies that have recently

---

[32]P. Peterson, D. Peterson, and J. Ang, "Direct Evidence on the Marginal Rate of Taxation on Dividend Income," *Journal of Financial Economics* 14 (1985).

[33]E. F. Fama and K. R. French, "Disappearing Dividends: Changing Firm Characteristics or Lower Propensity to Pay?," *Journal of Financial Economics* (April 2001).

■ FIGURE 18.7   **Ratio of Aggregate Dividends to Aggregate Earnings in the United States**

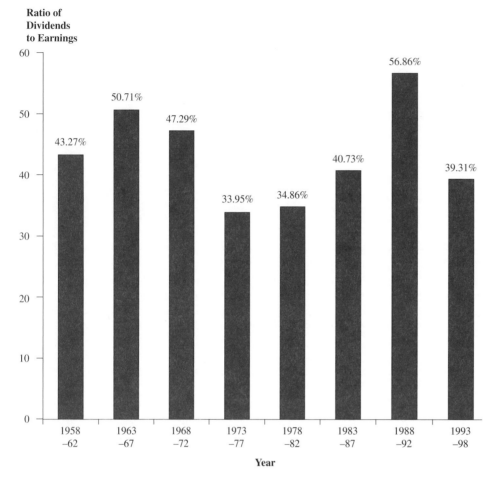

Corporations pay a significant amount of earnings out as dividends.
Source: Table 11 of E. F. Fama and K. R. French, "Disappearing Dividends: Changing Firm Characteristics or Lower Propensity to Pay,"
Journal of Financial Economics (Apr. 2001).

listed on the different exchanges. For the most part, firms of this type do not pay dividends. In addition, the authors argue that the percentage of firms of all types paying dividends has declined in recent years.

Corporations Smooth Dividends

In 1956, John Lintner[34] made two important observations concerning dividend policy. First, real-world companies typically set long-run target ratios of dividends to earnings. A firm is likely to set a low target ratio if it has many positive NPV projects relative to available cash flow and a high

---

[34]J. Lintner, "Distribution and Incomes of Corporations among Dividends, Retained Earnings and Taxes,"
American Economic Review (May 1956).

■ FIGURE 18.8 **Percent of CRSP Firms Paying Dividends**

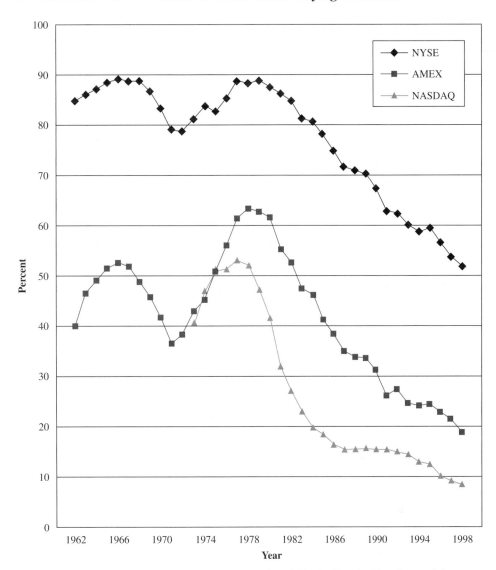

Source: Figure 5 of E. F. Fama and K. R. French, "Disappearing Dividends: Changing Firm Characteristics or Lower Propensity to Pay," unpublished paper, Graduate School of Business, University of Chicago (March 1999).

ratio if it has few positive NPV projects. Second, managers know that only part of any change in earnings is likely to be permanent. Because managers need time to assess the permanence of any earnings rise, dividend changes appear to lag earnings changes by a number of periods.

Taken together, Lintner's observations suggest that two parameters describe dividend policy: the target payout ratio (t) and the speed of adjustment of current dividends to the target (s). Dividend changes will tend to conform to the following model:

$$\text{Div}_1 - \text{Div}_0 = s \cdot (t\text{EPS}_1 - \text{Div}_0)$$

where Div_1 and Div_0 are dividends in the next year and dividends in the current year, respectively. EPS_1 is earnings per share in the next year.

The limiting cases occur when $s = 1$ and $s = 0$. If $s = 1$, the actual change in dividends will be equal to the target change in dividends. Here, the full adjustment occurs immediately.

Anthony S. Thornley on Why Qualcomm Pays No Dividends

Qualcomm has consistently been able to generate for its shareholders a significantly higher return than the shareholders could get from being paid a dividend. It has no "excess" cash for dividends. If Qualcomm paid a dividend, our shareholders would view it very negatively. Qualcomm would be saying, "We have run out of good profit opportunities." Our shareholders don't like dividends as much as they like the capital gains from Qualcomm's growth and profitability.

Anthony S. Thornley is Executive Vice President and Chief Financial Officer of Qualcomm. Qualcomm trades on NASDAQ and is part of the Standard & Poor's 500 Index. Its average annual growth rate in earnings over the past five years has been 65 percent.

Alan J. Fohrer on Why Edison International Pays Dividends

Utility investors like dividends. Historically, Edison International has paid out considerably more than 50 percent of its earnings as dividends. Investors have viewed utilities such as Edison as defensive stocks where dividends are a cushion against stock market volatility. As a utility, Edison has had limited growth opportunities and has been able to finance their growth out of retained earnings and new stock. In 1994, Edison reduced its dividend reflecting changes in the utility business and Edison's increasing participation in higher growth, nonutility business.

Alan J. Fohrer is Executive Vice President and Chief Financial Officer of Edison International.

If $s = 0$, $\text{Div}_1 = \text{Div}_0$. In other words, there is no change in dividends at all. Real-world companies can be expected to set s between 0 and 1.

An implication of Lintner's model is that the dividends-to-earnings ratio rises when a company begins a period of bad times, and the ratio falls when a company reaches a period of good times. Thus, dividends display less variability than do earnings. In other words, firms smooth dividends.

Dividends Provide Information to the Market

We previously observed that the price of a firm's stock frequently rises when its current dividend is increased. Conversely, the price of a firm's stock can fall significantly when its dividend is cut. In other words, there is information content in dividend changes. For example, consider what happened to Pacific Enterprises a number of years ago. Faced with poor operating results, Pacific Enterprises omitted its regular quarterly dividend. The next day the common stock dropped from 24⅞ to 18⅞. One reason may be that investors are looking at current dividends for clues concerning the level of future earnings and dividends.

A Sensible Dividend Policy

The knowledge of the finance profession varies across topic areas. For example, capital-budgeting techniques are both powerful and precise. A single net-present-value equation can accurately determine whether a multimillion dollar project should be accepted or rejected. The capital-asset-pricing model and the arbitrage-pricing model provide empirically validated relationships between expected return and risk.

Conversely, the field has less knowledge of capital-structure policy. Though a number of elegant theories relate firm value to the level of debt, no formula can be used to calculate the firm's optimum debt-equity ratio. Our profession is forced too frequently to employ

THE PROS AND CONS OF PAYING DIVIDENDS

Pros	Cons
1. Cash dividends can underscore good results and provide support to stock price.	1. Dividends are taxed as ordinary income.
2. Dividends may attract institutional investors who prefer some return in the form of dividends. A mix of institutional and individual investors may allow a firm to raise capital at lower cost because of the ability of the firm to reach a wider market.	2. Dividends can reduce internal sources of financing. Dividends may force the firm to forgo positive NPV projects or to rely on costly external equity financing.
3. Stock price usually increases with the announcement of a new or increased dividend.	3. Once established, dividend cuts are hard to make without adversely affecting a firm's stock price.
4. Dividends absorb excess cash flow and may reduce agency costs that arise from conflicts between management and shareholders.	

rules of thumb, such as treating the industry's average ratio as the optimal one for the firm. The field's knowledge of dividend policy is, perhaps, similar to its knowledge of capital-structure policy. We do know that:

1. Firms should avoid having to cut back on positive NPV projects to pay a dividend, with or without personal taxes.
2. Firms should avoid issuing stock to pay a dividend in a world with personal taxes.
3. Repurchases should be considered when there are few positive new investment opportunities and there is a surplus of unneeded cash.

The preceding recommendations suggest that firms with many positive NPV projects relative to available cash flow should have low payout ratios. Firms with fewer positive NPV projects relative to available cash flow might want to consider higher payouts. In addition, there is some benefit to dividend stability, and unnecessary changes in dividend payout are avoided by most firms. However, there is no formula for calculating the optimal dividend-to-earnings ratio.

CASE STUDY: *How Firms Make the Decision to Pay Dividends:*
The Case of Apple Computer

■ ■ ■ ■ ■   Perhaps the most important dividend decisions a firm must make are when to pay dividends for the first time and when to omit them once they have started. We study the case of Apple Computer for clues to why firms pay dividends and later on omit them.

In 1976 two young friends, Stephen Wozniak and Steven Jobs, built the Apple I Computer in Jobs's garage in the "Silicon Valley" area of Northern California and founded Apple Computer, Inc. The first Apple was built and sold without a monitor, or keyboard. The Apple II was introduced in 1977 and was targeted at the home and educational markets as a personal computer. The Apple II was very successful, and by 1980 over 130,000 units had been sold and Apple's revenues were $117 million. In 1980 Apple "went public" with an initial public offering (IPO) of common stock. Shortly thereafter, Wozniak left Apple and John Scully was hired from Pepsi to become president. Apple did not do well with its Lisa (1983) and Apple III computers, but the Macintosh (1984) was a huge hit—primarily in the home and educational markets. In 1985, after a widely publicized struggle for power with Scully, Jobs left to start another computer company called Next.

In many ways 1986 was a watershed year for Apple. By the end of 1986, Apple had revenues of $1.9 billion and net income of $154 million. From 1980 to 1986 its annual growth rate in net income was 53 percent. In 1986, with Mac Plus, Apple launched an aggressive effort to penetrate the expanding office computer market—the domain of its main rival IBM. However, its future prospects were not necessarily bright. Much depended on Apple's ability to do well in the business market. Competition was very intense in early 1987, and Sun Microsystems slashed the price of its least costly computer workstation to try to stop encroachment by the Apple Mac. However, Apple surprised everyone with large earnings gains in the final quarter of 1987 and by disclosing the fact that the sales on Macintosh models had increased by 41 percent.

To demonstrate its faith in its future, to underscore the recent success of the Mac, and to attract more institutional investors, on April 23, 1987, Apple declared its first ever quarterly dividend of $.12 per share. It also announced a two-for-one stock split. The stock market reacted very positively to the announcement of Apple's initial dividend. On the day of the announcements, its stock increased by $1.75. Over a four-day time span the stock rose by about 8 percent.

The initial dividend turned out to be a positive portent, and the next four years were good years for Apple. At the end of 1990, Apple's revenues, profits, and capital spending had achieved record highs.

	1986	1990	Growth per Annum from 1986 to 1990	1997	Growth per Annum from 1990 to 1997
Revenues (in millions)	$1,902	$5,558	31%	$7,081	4%
Net income (in millions)	154	475	33	−379	NA
Capital spending (in millions)	66	223	36	63	−16
Stock price	$ 20	$ 48	24	$ 24	−10
Long-term debt (in millions)	0	0	0	950	NA
Dividends per share	0	$ .45		0	−100

Why do firms like Apple decide to pay dividends? There is no single answer to this question. In Apple's case, one part of the answer can be traced to Apple's attempt to "signal" the stock market about the potential growth and positive NPV prospects of its attempt to penetrate the office computer market. The payment of dividends can also "ratify" good results. Apple's initial dividend served to convince the market that Apple's success was not temporary.

Why did Apple announce a two-for-one stock split at the same time of its announcement of an initial cash dividend? It is often said that a stock split without a cash dividend is like giving shareholders two five-dollar bills for a $10 bill. Your wallet feels thicker but you are no better off. However, a stock split accompanied by a cash dividend can amplify the positive signal and pack a more powerful message than would be true otherwise. In addition, firms sometimes split their shares, because they believe a low stock price may attract more individual investors and as a consequence increase liquidity. However, the evidence is not clear on this point, and some firms like Berkshire Hathaway disdain stock splits. (Its stock was recently selling at $67,000 a share.)

Was Apple's decision to offer an initial dividend the best decision for the company? This is an impossible question to answer precisely. However, the stock market's positive reaction and Apple's subsequent performance suggest it was a good decision. Unfortunately, the years since 1990 have not been as good for Apple. Its revenue growth has moderated and its profits have declined due to a difficult transition from a high-priced, high-quality producer of personal computers to a more competitively priced producer. It experienced losses in 1996 and 1997. Apple's small market share has become a problem because software developers have been more interested in producing products that could run on Intel-based machines. At the end of 1997, Apple's stock price was at $24 per share—lower than in 1990. In Figure 18.9, we plot Apple's earnings per share and dividends per share from

■ FIGURE 18.9   Dividend Pattern of Apple Computer from 1983 to 2000

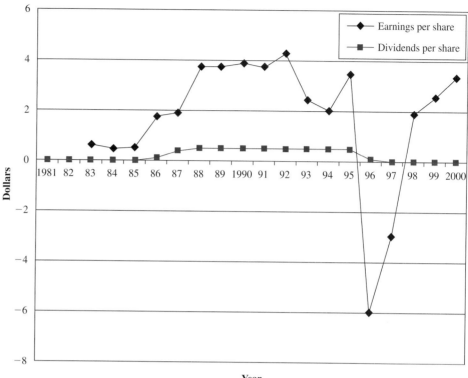

1981 to 1997. As can be seen, dividend changes have tended to lag earnings changes. In 1992, when earnings per share increased from $3.74 to $4.33 there was no change in dividend payouts. And when in 1993, earnings per share declined to $2.45, Apple did not change its dividend payouts. However, Apple's dividend was completely omitted in 1996.

Now we have another question, why did Apple omit its dividend in 1996? The firm had experienced several market setbacks. It was forced to retreat from its much heralded "cloning" strategy. In an important shift in strategic thinking, Apple had started licensing its Mac operating system to other manufacturers. Unfortunately, instead of attracting new buyers, this policy was eroding its own base and sales fell sharply. As a consequence, Apple experienced operating losses of $742 million in 1996 and $379 million in 1997.

Looking back at Figure 18.9, it can be seen that Apple's dividends have been more stable over time than its earnings. This is typical of the dividend policy of most firms. Stability cannot be maintained forever in the face of huge operating losses and most companies ultimately slash dividends if the losses continue.

Apple has not yet resumed its dividend, despite the fact that its earnings per share climbed to $3.45 in 2000. Its recent stock price was $109—a record high. Current sales appear strong, especially for its iMac consumer product. The market has responded well to its iBook and Power Book portables. A deal with EarthLink could make Apple the exclusive internet access provider bundled with Macs. Now we ask the question: Should Apple resume its dividend payout? ■ ■ ■ ■ ■

18.10 SUMMARY AND CONCLUSIONS

1. The dividend decision is important because it determines the payout received by shareholders and the funds retained by the firm for investment. Dividend policy is usually reflected by the current dividend-to-earnings ratio. This is referred to as the payout ratio. Unfortunately, the optimal payout *ratio* cannot be determined quantitatively. Rather, one can only indicate qualitatively what factors lead to low- or high-dividend policies.
2. The dividend policy of the firm is irrelevant in a perfect capital market because the shareholder can effectively undo the firm's dividend strategy. If a shareholder receives a greater dividend than desired, he or she can reinvest the excess. Conversely, if the shareholder receives a smaller dividend than desired, he or she can sell off extra shares of stock. This argument is due to MM and is similar to their homemade-leverage concept, discussed in Chapter 15.
3. Even in a perfect capital market, a firm should not reject positive NPV projects to increase dividend payments.
4. Although the MM argument is useful in introducing the topic of dividends, it ignores many factors in practice. We show that personal taxes and new-issue costs are real-world considerations that favor low dividend payouts. With personal taxes and new-issue costs, the firm should not issue stock to pay a dividend. However, our discussion does not imply that all firms should avoid dividends. Rather, those with high cash flow relative to positive NPV opportunities might pay dividends due to legal constraints and/or a dearth of investment opportunities.
5. The expected return on a security is positively related to its dividend yield in a world with personal taxes. This result suggests that individuals in low or zero tax brackets should consider investing in high-yielding stocks. However, the result does not imply that firms should avoid all dividends.
6. The general consensus among financial analysts is that the tax effect is the strongest argument in favor of low dividends and the preference for current income is the strongest argument in favor of high dividends. Unfortunately, no empirical work has determined which of these two factors dominates, perhaps because the clientele effect argues that dividend policy is quite responsive to the needs of stockholders. For example, if 40 percent of the stockholders prefer low dividends and 60 percent prefer high dividends, approximately 40 percent of companies will have a low dividend payout, and 60 percent will have a high payout. This sharply reduces the impact of an individual firm's dividend policy on its market price.
7. Research has shown that many firms appear to have a long-run target dividend-payout policy. Firms that have few (many) positive NPV projects relative to available cash flow will have high (low) payouts. In addition, firms try to reduce the fluctuations in the level of dividends. There appears to be some value in dividend stability and smoothing.
8. The stock market reacts positively to increases in dividends (or an initial dividend payment) and negatively to decreases in dividends. This suggests that there is information content in dividend payments.

KEY TERMS

Clienteles   515
Date of payment   497
Date of record   496
Declaration date   496
Ex-dividend date   496

Homemade dividends   501
Information-content effect   514
Regular cash dividends   495
Stock dividend   496
Stock split   496

SUGGESTED READINGS

The breakthrough in the theory of dividend policy is contained in
Miller, M., and F. Modigliani. "Dividend Policy, Growth and the Valuation of Shares." *Journal of Business* (October 1961).

A survey of dividend policy can be found in
Allen, Franklin, and Roni Michaely. "Dividend Policy." In R. A. Jarrow, V. Maksimovic, and W. T. Ziemba (eds.). *Handbooks in Operations Research and Management Science: Finance.* Amsterdam: Elsevier Science (1995), 793–838.

Current trends in dividend policy are examined in
Fama, Eugene F., and Kenneth R. French. "Disappearing Dividends: Changing Firm Characteristics or Lower Propensity to Pay?" (March 1999). Graduate School of Business, University of Chicago, Unpublished paper.

QUESTIONS AND PROBLEMS

The Mechanics of Dividend Payouts

18.1 Identify and describe each of the following dates that are associated with a dividend payment on common stock:

February 16
February 24
February 26
March 14

18.2 On April 5, the board of directors of Capital City Golf Club declared a dividend of $.75 per share payable on Tuesday, May 4, to shareholders of record as of Tuesday, April 20. Suppose you bought 350 shares of Capital City stock on April 6 for $8.75 a share. Assume there are no taxes, no transaction costs, and no news between your purchase and sale of the stock. If you were to sell your stocks on April 16, how much would you be able to sell your stock for?

18.3 The Mann Company belongs to a risk class for which the appropriate discount rate is 10 percent. Mann currently has 100,000 outstanding shares selling at $100 each. The firm is contemplating the declaration of a $5 dividend at the end of the fiscal year that just began. Answer the following questions based on the Miller and Modigliani model, which is discussed in the text.
  a. What will be the price of the stock on the ex-dividend date if the dividend is declared?
  b. What will be the price of the stock at the end of the year if the dividend is not declared?
  c. If Mann makes $2 million of new investments at the beginning of the period, earns net income of $1 million, and pays the dividend at the end of the year, how many shares of new stock must the firm issue to meet its funding needs?
  d. Is it realistic to use the MM model in the real world to value stock? Why or why not?

18.4 On February 17, the board of directors of Exertainment Corp. declared a dividend of $1.25 per share payable on March 18 to all holders of record on March 1. All investors are in the 31-percent tax bracket.
  a. What is the ex-dividend date?
  b. Ignoring personal taxes, how much should the stock price drop on the ex-dividend date?

The Benchmark Case: An Illustration of the Irrelevance of Dividend Policy

18.5 The growing-perpetuity model expresses the value of a share of stock as the present value of the expected dividends from that stock. How can you conclude that dividend policy is irrelevant when this model is valid?

18.6 Andahl Corporation stock, of which you own 500 shares, will pay a $2-per-share dividend one year from today. Two years from now Andahl will close its doors; stockholders will receive liquidating dividends of $17.5375 per share. The required rate of return on Andahl stock is 15 percent.

    a. What is the current price of Andahl stock?

    b. You prefer to receive equal amounts of money in each of the next two years. How will you accomplish this?

18.7 The net income of Novis Corporation, which has 10,000 outstanding shares and a 100-percent payout policy, is $32,000. The expected value of the firm one year hence is $1,545,600. The appropriate discount rate for Novis is 12 percent.

    a. What is the current value of the firm?

    b. What is the ex-dividend price of Novis's stock if the board follows its current policy?

    c. At the dividend declaration meeting, several board members claimed that the dividend is too meager and is probably depressing Novis's price. They proposed that Novis sell enough new shares to finance a $4.25 dividend.

        i. Comment on the claim that the low dividend is depressing the stock price. Support your argument with calculations.

        ii. If the proposal is adopted, at what price will the new shares sell and how many will be sold?

18.8 Gibson Co. has a current period cash flow of $1.2 million and pays no dividends, and the present value of forecasted future cash flows is $15 million. It is an all-equity-financed company with 1 million shares outstanding. Assume the effective personal tax rate is zero.

    a. What is the share price of the Gibson stock?

    b. Suppose the board of directors of Gibson Co. announces its plan to pay out 50 percent of its current cash flow as cash dividends to its shareholders. How can Jeff Miller, who owns 1,000 shares of Gibson stock, achieve a zero payout policy on his own?

Taxes, Issuances Costs, and Dividends

18.9 National Business Machine Co. (NBM) has $2 million of extra cash. NBM has two choices to make use of this cash. One alternative is to invest the cash in financial assets. The resulted investment income will be paid out as a special dividend at the end of three years. In this case, the firm can invest in Treasury bills yielding 7 percent, or an 11 percent preferred stock. Only 30 percent of the dividends from investing in preferred stock would be subject to corporate taxes. Another alternative is to pay out the cash as dividends and let the shareholders invest on their own in Treasury bills with the same yield. The corporate tax rate is 35 percent, and the individual tax rate is 31 percent. Should the cash be paid today or in three years? Which of the two options generates the highest after-tax income for the shareholders?

18.10 The University of Pennsylvania pays no taxes on capital gains, dividend income, or interest payments. Would you expect to find low-dividend, high-growth stock in the university's portfolio? Would you expect to find tax-free municipal bonds in the portfolio?

18.11 In their 1970 paper on dividends and taxes, Elton and Gruber reported that the ex-dividend–date drop in a stock's price as a percentage of the dividend should equal the ratio of 1 minus the ordinary income tax rate to 1 minus the capital gains rate; that is,

$$\frac{P_e - P_b}{D} = \frac{1 - T_o}{1 - T_c}$$

where

    P_e = The ex-dividend stock price
    P_b = The stock price before it trades ex-dividend
    D = The amount of the dividend
    T_o = The tax rate on ordinary income
    T_c = The effective tax rate on capital gains

Note: As we pointed out in the text, effective tax rate of capital gains is less than the actual tax rate, because their realization may be postponed. Indeed, because investors could postpone their realizations indefinitely, the effective rate could be zero.

a. If $T_o = T_c = 0$, how much will the stock's price fall?

b. If $T_o \neq 0$ and $T_c = 0$, how much will it fall?

c. Explain the results you found in (*a*) and (*b*).

d. Do the results of Elton and Gruber's study imply that firms will maximize shareholder wealth by not paying dividends?

18.12 After completing its capital spending for the year, Carlson Manufacturing has $1,000 extra cash. Carlson's managers must choose between investing the cash in Treasury bonds that yield 8 percent or paying the cash out to investors who would invest in the bonds themselves.

a. If the corporate tax rate is 35 percent, what tax rate on ordinary income would make the investors equally willing to receive the dividend and to let Carlson invest the money?

b. Is the answer to part (*a*) reasonable? Why or why not?

c. Suppose the only investment choice is stock that yields 12 percent. What personal tax rate will make the stockholders indifferent to the outcome of Carlson's dividend decision?

d. Is this a compelling argument for a low dividend payout ratio? Why or why not?

Expected Return, Dividends, and Personal Taxes

18.13 A political advisory committee recently recommended wage and price controls to prevent the spiraling inflation that was experienced in the 1970s. Members of the investment community and several labor unions have sent the committee reports that discuss whether or not dividends should be under the controls.

The reports from the investment community demonstrated that the value of a share of stock is equal to the discounted value of its expected dividend stream. Thus, they argued that any legislation that caps dividends will also hold down share prices, thereby increasing companies' costs of capital.

The union reports conceded that dividend policy is important to firms that are trying to control costs. They also felt that dividends are important to stockholders, but only because the dividend is the shareholder's wage. In order to be fair, the unions argued, if the government controls labor's wage, it should also control dividends.

Discuss these arguments and explain the fallacy in them.

18.14 Deaton Co. and Grebe, Inc., are in the same risk class. Shareholders expect Deaton to pay a $4 dividend next year when the stock will sell for $20. Grebe has a no-dividend policy. Currently, Grebe stock is selling for $20 per share. Grebe shareholders expect a $4 capital gain over the next year. Capital gains are not taxed, but dividends are taxed at 25 percent.

a. What is the current price of Deaton Co. stock?

b. If capital gains are also taxed at 25 percent, what is the price of Deaton Co. stock?

c. Explain the result you found in part (*b*).

18.15 Payall Inc., Payless Inc., and Paynone Inc. are equally risky. They follow a 100-percent, 50-percent, and zero payout policy, respectively. The expected share prices at dates 0 and 1 for Paynone Inc. are $100 and $125. The market prices are set so that their after-tax expected returns are equal. What should the current share prices of Payless Inc. and Payall Inc. be? Assume the marginal personal tax rate on dividends is 25 percent, and the effective tax rate on capital gain is zero.

18.16 Suppose the Du Pont Company currently has outstanding series 4.50, nonconvertible preferred stock that pays an annual dividend of $4.50. Du Pont has also issued 11-percent bonds that will mature in 10 years. The stock and bonds have about the same risk.

a. The current price of the 4.50 preferred stock is 50½. What is its dividend yield?

b. The bonds were sold at par. What is their yield to maturity?

    c. As a financial consultant, you want to know the after-tax yields for each of these investments. The corporate tax rate is 34 percent and the personal tax rate is 28 percent. Compute the after-tax yields on Du Pont's preferred stock and its bonds for each of the following groups:

        i. General Motors's tax-exempt pension.

        ii. General Motors Corporation.

    d. Which group do you believe owns the most Du Pont stock?

Real-World Factors Favoring a High-Dividend Policy

18.17 The bird-in-the-hand argument, which states that a dividend today is safer than the uncertain prospect of a capital gain tomorrow, is often used to justify high dividend-payout ratios. Explain the fallacy behind the argument.

18.18 The desire for current income is not a valid explanation for preference for high-current-dividend policy, as investors can always create homemade dividends by selling a portion of their stocks. Comment.

18.19 Your aunt is in a high tax bracket and would like to minimize the tax burden of her investment portfolio. She is willing to buy and sell in order to maximize her after-tax returns and she has asked for your advice. What would you suggest she do?

A Resolution of Real-World Factors?

18.20 In the May 4, 1981, issue of *Fortune,* an article entitled "Fresh Evidence That Dividends Don't Matter" stated, "All told, 115 companies of the 500 [largest industrial corporations] raised their payout every year during the period [1970–1989]. Investors in this . . . group would have fared somewhat better than investors in the 500 as a whole: the median total [annual compound] return of the 115 was 10.7% during the decade versus 9.4% for the 500."

    Is this evidence that investors prefer dividends to capital gains? Why or why not?

18.21 Last month Central Virginia Power Company, which had been having trouble with cost overruns on a nuclear plant that it had been building, announced that it was "temporarily suspending dividend payments due to the cash flow crunch associated with its investment program." When the announcement was made, the company's stock price dropped from 28½ to 25. What do you suspect caused the change in the stock price?

18.22 Southern Established Inc. has been paying out regular quarterly dividends ever since 1983. It just slashed the dividend by half in the current fiscal quarter and a more severe cut is to be underway. Southern's stock price dropped from $35.25 to $31.75 when the dividend cut was announced. Explain the possible reasons for this price drop.

18.23 Cap Henderson owns Neotech stock because its price has been steadily rising over the past few years and he expects its performance to continue. Cap is trying to convince Widow Jones to purchase some Neotech stock, but she is reluctant because Neotech has never paid a dividend. She depends on steady dividends to provide her with income.

    a. What preferences are these two investors demonstrating?

    b. What argument should Cap use to convince Widow Jones that Neotech stock is the stock for her?

    c. Why might Cap's argument not convince Widow Jones?

18.24 If the market places the same value on $1 of dividends as on $1 of capital gains, then firms with different payout ratios will appeal to different clienteles of investors. One clientele is as good as another; therefore, a firm cannot increase its value by changing its dividend policy. Yet empirical investigations reveal a strong correlation between dividend payout ratios and other firm characteristics. For example, small, rapidly growing firms that have recently gone public almost always have payout ratios that are zero; all earnings are reinvested in the business. Explain this phenomenon if dividend policy is irrelevant.

18.25 In spite of the theoretical argument that dividend policy should be irrelevant, the fact remains that many investors like high dividends. If this preference exists, a firm can boost its share price by increasing its dividend-payout ratio. Explain the fallacy in this argument.

What We Know and Do Not Know about Dividend Policy

18.26 The Sharpe Co. has a period 0 dividend of $1.25. Its target payout ratio is 40 percent. The period 1 EPS is expected to be $4.5.

    a. If the adjustment rate is 0.3 as defined in the Lintner Model, what will be the Sharpe Co. dividend in period 1?

    b. If the adjustment rate is 0.6 instead, what is the dividend in period 1?

18.27 Empirical research found that there have been significant increases in stock price on the day an initial dividend (i.e., the first time a firm pays a cash dividend) is announced. What does this finding imply about the information content of initial dividends?

Appendix 18A STOCK DIVIDENDS AND STOCK SPLITS

In addition to the cash dividend, companies may issue stock dividends or split their stock. Since stock dividends and stock splits are quite similar, we treat them together. We begin with examples of these two strategies. Next, their benefits and costs to the firm are discussed.

Example of a Stock Dividend

Imagine a company with 10,000 shares of stock, each selling at $60. With a stock dividend of 10 percent, each stockholder receives one additional share for each 10 that he or she originally owned. Therefore the total number of shares outstanding after the dividend is 11,000. Note that the stockholders receive no cash and that each shareholder's percentage of the total outstanding stock remains the same. Thus a case can be made that a stock dividend is of no value to the firm. More will be said on this later.

Imagine that, before the stock dividend, the equity portion of the firm's balance sheet looks like this:

Common stock (par value set at $12 per share)	$120,000
Capital in excess of par value	200,000
Retained earnings	180,000
Total owner's equity	**$500,000**

A seemingly arbitrary accounting procedure is used to adjust the balance sheet after the stock dividend. Since 1,000 new shares are issued, $12,000 (1,000 × $12) is transferred to common stock after the dividend. The market price of $60 is $48 above the par value. Thus $48 × 1,000 = $48,000 is shifted to the excess capital account. Because the total value of owner's equity is unchanged by a stock dividend, $60,000 is withdrawn from retained earnings.

After the stock dividend, owner's equity for the firm is represented as:

Common stock (par value set at $12 per share)	$132,000
Capital in excess of par value	248,000
Retained earnings	120,000
Total owner's equity	**$500,000**

There is actually a good reason behind this procedure. Accountants fear that stock dividends could be used to impress a naive stockholder, even if the firm is doing poorly. This type of accounting treatment limits this possibility, since a stock dividend can never be greater than retained earnings.

Example of a Stock Split

A stock split is similar conceptually to a stock dividend. In a three-for-one split, each shareholder receives two additional shares of stock for each one held originally. Again, no cash is paid out, and the percentage of the entire firm that each shareholder owns is unaffected. However, the accounting of splits differs from the accounting of stock dividends. Imagine in our previous example that a three-for-one-split occurs, raising the number of shares to 30,000. The owner's equity after the split is represented as:

Common stock (30,000 shares with par value set at $4 per share)	$120,000
Capital in excess of par value	200,000
Retained earnings	180,000
Total owner's equity	**$500,000**

Note that for three of the categories the figures on the right are completely unaffected by the split. Only the par value is changed, being reduced here to $4 per share.

Since stock dividends and stock splits are similar, the dividing point between them is arbitrary.

Value of Stock Splits and Stock Dividends

The laws of logic tell us that stock splits and stock dividends can (1) leave the firm's value unaffected, (2) increase the value of the firm, or (3) decrease its value. Unfortunately, the issues are complex enough that one cannot easily determine which of the three relationships holds.

The Benchmark Case

A strong case can be made that stock dividends and splits do not change either the wealth of any shareholder or the wealth of the firm as a whole. For example, imagine a firm with $100 of earnings and 100 shares outstanding, implying EPS of $1. With a price-earnings ratio of 10, the price per share is $10 and the total market value of the firm is $1,000. Now imagine a 2-for-1 stock split where the number of shares rises to 200 and EPS falls to $0.50. Given the same P/E ratio of 10, the value of each share of stock is now $5. However, with twice the number of shares, the value of the entire firm is still $1,000. The wealth of each stockholder remains the same since the doubling in the number of shares is offset by the halving of the stock price. This result is sensible because (1) total earnings of the firm are held constant, and (2) the percentage of the firm owned by each investor is unchanged.

The same results would hold for a stock dividend. Imagine that the total number of shares is increased by 10 percent to 110. Given that EPS drops to $100/110 = $0.90909, the price per share should fall to $9.0909. Therefore the total value of the firm should remain at $1,000. The wealth of each stockholder should not change because, as with a split, the percentage of the firm that each investor owns remains the same.

Although these results are relatively obvious, they are developed in the idealized world of a perfect capital market. The typical financial manager is aware of many real-world complexities, and for that reason the stock split or stock dividend decision is not treated lightly in practice.

Popular Trading Range

Proponents of stock dividends and stock splits frequently argue that a security has a proper **trading range.** When the security is priced above this level, many investors do not have the funds to buy the common trading unit of 100 shares, called a *round lot*. Although securities can be purchased in *odd-lot* form (fewer than 100 shares), the commissions are more expensive here. Thus firms will split the stock to keep its price in this trading range.

Although this argument is a popular one, its validity has recently been questioned.[35] Mutual funds, pension funds, and other institutions have steadily increased their trading activity since World War II and now handle a sizable percentage of total trading volume. Because these institutions can buy and sell in such huge amounts, they would not regard securities in the popular trading range with any special favor. In fact, whether because of the rise of institutions or some other factor, odd-lot trades comprise a quite small proportion of the market today.

Costs with Stock Splits or Stock Dividends

The reasoning in the previous paragraph minimizes the benefits of a stock split or dividend. In addition, some authors state that there are costs associated with these financial procedures. For example, Copeland argues that two types of transaction costs rise following a stock split. He further reasons that both of these cost increases ultimately reduce the liquidity of the stock, an unexpected result because a rise in liquidity through a broadening of the stockholder base often is given as a reason for a split.[36]

Copeland finds that brokerage fees, measured in percentages, increase after a split. This result is not surprising, since most published price lists of commissions show that brokerage fees for low-priced securities are a larger percentage of sales price than they are for high-priced securities. For example, commissions are generally higher for 400 shares of a security selling at $10 than for 100 shares of a security selling at $40.

The bid-ask spread is the difference between the price at which you sell a security to a dealer and the price at which you buy a security from a dealer. For example, a bid-ask spread of 49 1/2–50 means that an individual can sell a share to the dealer at $49.50 and buy a share at $50, implying a round-trip loss to the investor of $0.50. Copeland finds that the bid-ask spread, expressed as a percentage of sales price, rises after a stock split. This finding is consistent with other work showing that the bid-ask spread is higher in percentage terms for lower-proceed securities.[37] The data suggest that the benefits to the stockholder associated with a stock dividend or stock split are not clearly greater than the costs to him.

Reverse Split

A less frequently encountered financial maneuver is the **reverse split.** In a one-for-three reverse split, each investor exchanges three old shares for one new share. The par value is tripled in the process. As mentioned previously with stock splits and stock dividends, a case can be made that, in a theoretical model, a reverse split changes nothing substantial about the company.

Given real-world imperfections, three related reasons are cited for reverse splits. First, transactions costs to shareholders are often less after the reverse split. This follows the conclusions of Copeland that brokerage commissions per dollar traded rise as the price of the stock falls. Second, the liquidity and marketability of a company's stock are improved when its price is raised to the "popular trading range." Third, stocks selling below a certain level are not considered "respectable," implying that investors bias downward their estimates of these firms' earnings, cash flow, growth, and stability. Some financial analysts argue that a reverse split can achieve instant respectability.

---

[35]For example, see T. Copeland, "Liquidity Changes Following Stock Splits," *Journal of Finance* (March 1979).

[36]Although Copeland's empirical work included only stock splits, the same factors should apply to the stock dividend case.

[37]See H. Demsetz, "The Cost of Transacting," *Quarterly Journal of Economics* 82 (February 1968); and H. Stoll, "The Supply of Dealer Services in Securities Markets," *Journal of Finance* 33 (September 1978).

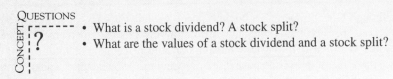

- What is a stock dividend? A stock split?
- What are the values of a stock dividend and a stock split?

KEY TERMS

Reverse split   531
Trading range   530

SUGGESTED READING

New evidence on how the market reacts to stock splits and stock dividends is in
Ranking, G., and Earl Stice. "The Market Reaction to the Choice of Accounting Method for
Stock Splits and Large Stock Dividends." *Journal of Financial and Quantitative Analysis*
(June 1997).

Long-Term Financing

■ ■ ■ ■ ■

Part IV discussed capital structure; we determined the relationship between the firm's debt-equity ratio and the firm's value. The debt we used in Part IV was stylized. In fact, there are many different types of debt. In Part V we discuss how financial managers choose the type of debt that makes the most sense, including straight debt, debt with options, and leasing.

In Chapter 19 we describe the ways firms sell securities to the public. In general, a public issue can be sold as a general cash offer to investors at large, as a privately placed issue with a few institutions, or as a privileged subscription (in the case of equities). We describe the features of these methods and point out some puzzling trends.

In Chapter 20 we describe some basic features of long-term debt. One of the special features of most long-term bonds is that they can be called by the firms before the maturity date. We try to explain why call provisions exist. There are many types of long-term debt, including floating-rate bonds, income bonds, and original-issue discount bonds. We discuss why they exist.

Chapter 21 describes a special form of long-term debt called *leasing.* In general, a rental agreement that lasts for more than one year is a lease. Leases are a source of financing and displace debt in the balance sheet. Many silly reasons are given for leasing, and we present some of them. The major reason for long-term leasing is to lower taxes.

CHAPTER 19

Issuing Securities to the Public

EXECUTIVE SUMMARY

T his chapter looks at how corporations issue securities to the investing public. The general procedures for debt and equity are quite similar. This chapter focuses on equity, but the procedures for debt and equity are basically the same.

Before securities can be traded on a securities market, they must be issued to the public. A firm making an issue to the public must satisfy requirements set out in various federal legislation and statutes and enforced by the Securities and Exchange Commission (SEC). In general, investors must be given all material information in the form of a registration statement and prospectus. In the first part of this chapter we discuss what this entails.

A public issue of equity can be sold directly to the public with the help of underwriters. This is called a *general cash offer.* Alternatively, a public equity issue can be sold to the firm's existing stockholders by what is called a *rights offer.* This chapter examines the difference between a general cash offer and a rights offer.

Stock of companies going public for the first time is typically underpriced. We describe this unusual phenomenon and provide a possible explanation.

19.1 THE PUBLIC ISSUE

The basic steps in a public offering are depicted in Table 19.1. The Securities Act of 1933 sets forth the federal regulation for all new interstate securities issues. The Securities Exchange Act of 1934 is the basis for regulating securities already outstanding. The SEC administers both acts.

The Basic Procedure for a New Issue

1. Management's first step in any issue of securities to the public is to obtain approval from the board of directors.

2. Next, the firm must prepare and file a **registration statement** with the SEC. This statement contains a great deal of financial information, including a financial history, details of the existing business, proposed financing, and plans for the future. It can easily run to 50 or more pages. The document is required for all public issues of securities with two principal exceptions:

   a. Loans that mature within nine months.

   b. Issues that involve less than $5.0 million.

The second exception is known as the *small-issues exemption.* Issues of less than $5.0 million are governed by **Regulation A,** for which only a brief offering statement—rather than the above registration statement—is needed. For Regulation A to be operative, no more than $1.5 million may be sold by insiders.

3. The SEC studies the registration statement during a *waiting period.* During this time, the firm may distribute copies of a preliminary **prospectus.** The preliminary prospectus is called a **red herring** because bold red letters are printed on the cover. A prospectus

■ TABLE 19.1   **The Process of Raising Capital**

Steps in Public Offering	Time	Activities
1. Preunderwriting conferences	Several months	The amount of money to be raised and the type of security to be issued are discussed. The underwriting syndicate and selling group are put together. The underwriting contract is negotiated. Board approval is obtained.
2. Registration statements filed and approved	A 20-day waiting period	The registration statement contains all relevant financial and business information.
3. Pricing the issue	Usually not before the last day of the registration period	For seasoned offerings the price is set close to the prevailing market price. For initial public offerings intensive research and analysis are required.
4. Public offering and sale	Shortly after the last day of the registration period	In a typical firm commitment contract, the underwriter buys a stipulated amount of stock from the firm and sells it at a higher price. The selling group assists in the sale.
5. Market stabilization	Usually 30 days after the offering	The underwriter stands ready to place orders to buy at a specified price on the market.

contains much of the information put into the registration statement, and it is given to potential investors by the firm. The company cannot sell the securities during the waiting period. However, oral offers can be made.

A registration statement will become effective on the 20th day after its filing unless the SEC sends a *letter of comment* suggesting changes. After the changes are made, the 20-day waiting period starts anew.

4. The registration statement does not initially contain the price of the new issue. On the effective date of the registration statement, a price is determined and a full-fledged selling effort gets under way. A final prospectus must accompany the delivery of securities or confirmation of sale, whichever comes first.

5. **Tombstone** advertisements are used during and after the waiting period. An example is reproduced in Figure 19.1.

CONCEPT QUESTIONS
• Describe the basic procedures in a new issue.
• What is a registration statement?

19.2 ALTERNATIVE ISSUE METHODS

When a company decides to issue a new security, it can sell it as a public issue or a private issue. If it is a public issue, the firm is required to register the issue with the SEC. If the issue is sold to fewer than 35 investors, it can be treated as a private issue. A registration statement is not required in this case.[1]

There are two kinds of public issues: the *general cash offer* and the *rights offer.* Cash offers are sold to all interested investors, and rights offers are sold to existing shareholders. Equity is sold by both the cash offer and the rights offer, though almost all debt is sold by cash offer.

---

[1]However, regulation significantly restricts the resale of unregistered securities. The purchaser must hold the securities at least two years.

■ FIGURE 19.1   **An Example of a Tombstone Advertisement**

58,750,000 Shares

Consolidated Rail Corporation

Common Stock
(per value $1.00 per share)

Price $28 Per Share

The shares are being sold by the United States Government pursuant to the Conrail Privatization Act. The Company will not receive any proceeds from the sale of the shares.

Upon request, a copy of the Prospectus describing these securities and the business of the Company may be obtained within any state from any Underwriter who may legally distribute it within such State. The securities are offered only by means of the Prospectus, and this announcement is neither an offer to sell nor a solicitation of any offer to buy.

52,000,000 Shares

This portion of the offering is being offered in the United States and Canada by the undersigned.

Goldman, Sachs & Co.

The First Boston Corporation

Merrill Lynch Capital Markets

Morgan Stanley & Co.
Incorporated

Salomon Brothers Inc.

Shearson Lehman Brothers Inc.

Alex, Brown & Sons	Dillion, Read & Co. Inc.	Donaldson, Lufkin & Jenrette	Drexel Burnham Lambert	Hambrecht & Quist E.F. Hutton & Company Inc.

Alex, Brown & Sons   Dillion, Read & Co. Inc.   Donaldson, Lufkin & Jenrette   Drexel Burnham Lambert   Hambrecht & Quist   E.F. Hutton & Company Inc.
Incorporated   Securities Corporation   Incorporated   Incorporated
Kidder, Peabody & Co.   Lazard Freres & Co.   Montgomery Securities   Prudential-Bache Capital Funding   Robertson, Colman & Stephens
Incorporated
L.F. Rothschild, Unterberg, Towbin, Inc.   Smith Barney, Harris Upham & Co.   Wertheim Schroder & Co.   Dean Witter Reynolds Inc.
                                                            Incorporated   Incorporated
William Blair & Company   J.C. Bradford & Co.   Dain Bosworth   A.G. Edwards & Sons, Inc.   McDonald & Co.   Oppenheimer & Co., Inc.
                                 Incorporated   Securities, Inc.
Piper, Jaffray & Hopwood   Prescott, Ball & Turben, Inc.   Thomson McKinnon Securities Inc.   Wheat, First Securities, Inc.
Incorporated   Incorporated
Advest, Inc.   American Securities Corporation   Arnhold and S. Bleichroeder, Inc.   Robert W. Baird & Co.   Bateman Eichier, Hill Richards
Sanford C. Bernstein & Co., Inc.   Blunt Ellis & Loewi   Boettcher & Company, Inc.   Burns Fry and Timmins Inc.   Butcher & Singer Inc.   Cowen & Company
                                        Incorporated   Incorporated   Incorporated
Dominion Securities Corporation   Eberstadt Fleming Inc.   Eppler, Guerin & Tuner, Inc.   First of Michigan Corporation   First Southwest Company
Furman Seiz Mager Dietz & Birney   Gruntal & Co., Incorporated   Howard, Well, Labouisse, Friedrichs   Interstate Securities Corporation
Janney Montgomery Scott Inc.   Johnson, Lane, Space, Smith & Co., Inc.   Jonston, Lemon & Co.   Josephthal & Co.   Ladenburg, Thalman & Co.
                                                                                               Incorporated   Incorporated
Cyrus J. Lawrence   Legg Mason Wood Walker   Morgan Keegan & Company, Inc.   Moseley Securities Corporation   Needham & Company, Inc.
Incorporated   Incorporated
Neuberger & Berman   The Ohio Company   Rauscher Pierce Refsnes, Inc.   The Robinson-Humphrey Company, Inc.   Rothschild Inc.   Stephens Inc.
Stifel, Nicolaus & Company   Sutro & Co.   Tucker, Anthony & R. L. Day, Inc.   Underwood, Neuhaus & Co.   Wood Gundy Corp.
Incorporated

This special bracket of minority-owned and controlled firms assisted the Co-Lead
Managers in the United States Offering pursuant to the Conrail Privatization Act.

AIBC Investment Services Corporation   **Daniels & Bell, Inc.**   **Doley Securities, Inc.**
WR Lazard Securities Corporations   **Pryon, Govan, Counts & Co. Inc.**   **Muriel Siebert & Co., Inc.**

6,750,000 Shares

This Portion of the offering is being offered outside the United States and Canada by the undersigned.

Goldman Sachs International Corp.

First Boston International Limited

Merrill Lynch Capital Markets

Morgan Stanley International

Salomon Brothers International Limited

Shearson Lehman Brothers International

Algemene Bank Nederland N.V.   Banque Bruxelles Lambert S.A.   Banque Nationale de Paris   Cazenove & Co.   The Nikko Securities Co., (Europe) Ltd.
Nomura International   N. M. Rothschild & Sons   J. Henry Schroder Wagg & Co.   Soclété Générate   S. G. Warburg Securities
Limited   Limited
ABC International Ltd.   Banque Paribas Capital Markets Limited   Caisse Nationale de Credit Agricole   Campagnie de Banque et dinvestissements, CBI
Crédit Lyonnais   Daiwa Europe   IMI Capital Markets (UK) Ltd.   Joh. Berenberg, Gossler & Co.   Leu Securities Limited
                            Limited
Morgan Grenfell & Co.   Peterbroeck, van Campenhout & Cie SCS   Swiss Volksbank   Vereins- und Westbank
Limited   Aktiengesellschaft
J. Vontobel & Co. Ltd   M.M. Warburg-Brinckmann, Wirtz & Co.   Westdeutsche Landesbank   Yamaichi International (Europe)
                                                                      Girozentrale   Limited

March 27, 1987

■ TABLE 19.2 **The Methods of Issuing New Securities**

Method	Type	Definition
Public		
Traditional negotiated cash offer	Firm-commitment cash offer	Company negotiates an agreement with an investment banker to underwrite and distribute the new stocks or bonds. A specified number of shares is bought by underwriters and sold at a higher price.
	Best-efforts cash offer	Company has investment bankers sell as many of the new shares as possible at the agreed-upon price. There is no guarantee concerning how much cash will be raised.
Privileged subscription	Direct rights offer	Company offers new stock directly to its existing shareholders.
	Standby rights offer	Like the direct rights offer, this contains a privileged subscription arrangement with existing shareholders. The net proceeds are guaranteed by the underwriters.
Nontraditional cash offer	Shelf cash offer	Qualifying companies can authorize all shares they expect to sell over a two-year period and sell them when needed.
	Competitive firm cash offer	Company can elect to award underwriting contract through a public auction instead of negotiation.
Private	Direct placement	Securities are sold directly to purchaser, who cannot resell securities for at least two years.

The first public equity issue that is made by a company is referred to as an **initial public offering (IPO)** or an **unseasoned new issue.** All initial public offerings are cash offers because, if the firm's existing shareholders wanted to buy the shares, the firm would not need to sell them publicly. More than $5 billion was raised in 116 IPOs in 1994. A **seasoned new issue** refers to a new issue where the company's securities have been previously issued. A seasoned new issue of common stock may be made by using a cash offer or a rights offer.

These methods of issuing new securities are shown in Table 19.2 and discussed in the next few sections.

19.3 THE CASH OFFER

As mentioned above, stock is sold to all interested investors in a **cash offer.** If the cash offer is a public one, **investment banks** are usually involved. Investment banks are financial intermediaries who perform a wide variety of services. In addition to aiding in the sale of securities, they may facilitate mergers and other corporate reorganizations, act as brokers to both individual and institutional clients, and trade for their own accounts. You may very well have heard of large Wall Street investment banking houses such as Goldman Sachs, Merrill Lynch, and Salomon Smith Barney. Table 19.3 lists the leading investment bankers for U.S. public security offerings.

For corporate issuers, investment bankers perform services such as the following:

Formulating the method used to issue the securities.
Pricing the new securities.
Selling the new securities.

■ **TABLE 19.3   The Leading U.S. Underwriters—1997**

Top Underwriters of U.S. Debt and Equity
Manager
Merrill Lynch
Salomon Smith Barney
Morgan Stanley Dean Witter
Goldman, Sachs
Lehman Brothers
JP Morgan
Credit Suisse First Boston
Bear, Stearns
Donaldson, Lufkin & Jenrette
Chase Manhattan

There are two basic methods of issuing securities for cash.

1. **Firm commitment.** Under this method, the investment bank (or a group of investment banks) buys the securities for less than the offering price and accepts the risk of not being able to sell them. Because this function involves risk, we say that the investment banker *underwrites* the securities in a firm commitment. In other words, when participating in a firm-commitment offering, the investment banker acts as an *underwriter.* (Because firm commitments are so prevalent, we will use *investment banker* and *underwriter* interchangeably in this chapter.)

To minimize the risks here, investment bankers combine to form an underwriting group (**syndicate**) to share the risk and to help sell the issue. In such a group, one or more managers arrange or co-manage the deal. The manager is designated as the lead manager or principal manager. The lead manager typically has responsibility for all aspects of the issue. The other investment bankers in the syndicate serve primarily to sell the issue to their clients.

The difference between the underwriter's buying price and the offering price is called the *spread* or *discount.* It is the basic compensation received by the underwriter. Sometimes the underwriter will get noncash compensation in the form of warrants or stock in addition to the spread.

Firm-commitment underwriting is really just a purchase-sale arrangement, and the syndicate's fee is the spread. The issuer receives the full amount of the proceeds less the spread, and all the risk is transferred to the underwriter. If the underwriter cannot sell all of the issue at the agreed-upon offering price, it may need to lower the price on the unsold shares. However, because the offering price usually is not set until the underwriters have investigated how receptive the market is to the issue, this risk is usually minimal. This is particularly true with seasoned new issues because the price of the new issue can be based on prior trades in the security.

2. **Best efforts.** The underwriter bears risk with a firm commitment because it buys the entire issue. Conversely, the syndicate avoids this risk under a best-efforts offering because it does not purchase the shares. Instead, it merely acts as an agent, receiving a commission for each share sold. The syndicate is legally bound to use its best efforts to sell the securities at the agreed-upon offering price. If the issue cannot be sold at the offering price, it is usually withdrawn.

This form is more common for initial public offerings than for seasoned new issues. In addition, a recent study by Jay Ritter shows that best-efforts offerings are generally used for small IPOs and firm-commitment offerings are generally used for large IPOs. His results are reproduced in our Table 19.4. The last column in the table best illustrates his finding.

■ TABLE 19.4   **Initial Public Offerings of Stock Categorized by Gross Proceeds: 1977–1982**

Gross Proceeds ($)	All Offerings	Firm Commitment	Best Efforts	Fraction Best Efforts
100,000–1,999,999	243	68	175	0.720
2,000,000–3,999,999	311	165	146	0.469
4,000,000–5,999,999	156	133	23	0.147
6,000,000–9,999,999	137	122	15	0.109
10,000,000–120,174,195	180	176	4	0.022
All offerings	1,027	664	363	0.353

From J. R. Ritter, "The Costs of Going Public," *Journal of Financial Economics* 19 (1987). © Elsevier Science Publishers B. V. (North-Holland).

For either firm-commitment or best-efforts issues, the principal underwriter is permitted to buy shares if the market price falls below the offering price. The purpose is to *support* the market and *stabilize* the price from temporary downward pressure. If the issue remains unsold after a time (for example, 30 days), members may leave the group and sell their shares at whatever price the market will allow.

Many underwriting contracts contain a **Green Shoe provision,** which gives the members of the underwriting group the option to purchase additional shares at the offering price.[2] The stated reason for the Green Shoe option is to cover excess demand and oversubscription. Green Shoe options usually last for about 30 days and involve no more than 15 percent of the newly issued shares. The Green Shoe option is a benefit to the underwriting syndicate and a cost to the issuer. If the market price of the new issue goes above the offering price within 30 days, the underwriters can buy shares from the issuer and immediately resell the shares to the public.

Investment Banks

Investment banks are at the heart of new security issues. They provide advice, market the securities (after investigating the market's receptiveness to the issue), and underwrite the proceeds. They accept the risk that the market price may fall between the date the offering price is set and the time the issue is sold.

In addition, investment banks have the responsibility of pricing fairly. When a firm goes public, particularly for the first time, the buyers know relatively little about the firm's operations. After all, it is not rational for a buyer of, say, only 1,000 shares of stock to study the company at length. Instead, the buyer must rely on the judgment of the investment bank, who has presumably examined the firm in detail. Given this asymmetry of information, what prevents the investment banker from pricing the issued securities too high? While the underwriter has a short-run incentive to price high, it has a long-run incentive to make sure that its customers do not pay too much; they might desert the underwriter in future deals if they lose money on this one. Thus, as long as investment banks plan to stay in business over time, it is in their self-interest to price fairly.

---

[2]The Green Shoe Corp. was the first firm to allow this provision.

IN THEIR OWN WORDS

Robert S. Hansen on The Economic Rationale for the Firm Commitment Offer

Underwriters provide four main functions: certification, monitoring, marketing, and risk bearing.

Certification assures investors that the offer price is fair. Investors have concerns about whether the offer price is unfairly above the stock's intrinsic value. Certification increases issuer value by reducing investor doubt about fairness, making a better offer price possible.

Monitoring of issuing firm management and performance builds value because it adds to shareholders' ordinary monitoring. Underwriters provide collective monitoring on behalf of both capital suppliers and current shareholders. Individual shareholder monitoring is limited because the shareholder bears the entire cost, whereas all owners collectively share the benefit, pro rata. By contrast, in underwriter monitoring all stockholders share both the costs and benefits, pro rata.

Due diligence and legal liability for the proceeds give investors assurance. However, what makes certification and monitoring credible is lead bank reputation in competitive capital markets, where they are disciplined over time. Evidence that irreputable behavior is damaging to a bank's future abounds. Capital market participants punish poorly performing banks by refusing to hire them. The participants pay banks for certification and meaningful monitoring in "quasi-rents" in the spread, which represent the fair cost of "renting" the reputations.

Marketing is finding long-term investors who can be persuaded to buy the securities at the offer price. This would not be needed if demand for new shares were "horizontal." There is much evidence that issuers and syndicates repeatedly invest in costly marketing practices, such as expensive road shows to identify and expand investor interest. Another is organizing members to avoid redundant pursuit of the same customers. Lead banks provide trading support in the issuer's stock for several weeks after the offer.

Underwriting risk is like the risk of selling a put option. The syndicate agrees to buy all new shares at the offer price and resell them at that price or at the market price, whichever is lower. Thus, once the offer begins, the syndicate is exposed to potential losses on unsold inventory should the market price fall below the offer price. The risk is likely to be small, because offerings are typically well prepared for quick sale.

Robert S. Hansen is the Freeman Senior Research Professor of Finance at Tulane University.

In other words, financial economists argue that each investment bank has a reservoir of "reputation capital."[3] Mispricing of new issues, as well as unethical dealings, is likely to reduce this reputation capital.

One measure of this reputation capital is the pecking order among the investment banks. MBA students are aware of this order because they know that accepting a job with a top-tier firm is universally regarded as more prestigious than accepting a job with a lower-tier firm. This pecking order can be seen in Figure 19.1. The investment banks listed diagonally in the figure are considered the most prestigious. These appear alphabetically so that one cannot distinguish the relative status of these firms from the figure. The next set of firms, running from Alex. Brown & Sons to Dean Witter Reynolds, is also in alphabetical order. By noting when the alphabetical order begins anew, one can determine the number of firms in each tier.

Investment banks put great importance in their relative rankings and view downward movement in their placement with much distaste. While this jockeying for position may seem as unimportant as the currying of royal favor in the court of Louis XVI, it is explained by the above discussion. In any industry where reputation is so important, the firms in the industry must guard theirs with great vigilance.

---

[3]For example, see R. Carter and S. Manaster, "Initial Public Offerings and Underwriter Reputation," unpublished Iowa State and University of Utah working paper (1988); and R. Beatty and J. Ritter, "Investment Banking, Reputation and the Underpricing of Initial Public Offerings," *Journal of Financial Economics* (1986).

There are two basic methods for selecting the syndicate. In a **competitive offer,** the issuing firm can offer its securities to the underwriter bidding highest. In a **negotiated offer,** the issuing firm works with one underwriter. Because the firm generally does not negotiate with many underwriters concurrently, negotiated deals may suffer from lack of competition.

While competitive bidding occurs frequently in other areas of commerce, it may surprise you that negotiated deals in investment banking occur with all but the largest issuing firms. Investment bankers argue that they must expend much time and effort learning about the issuer before setting an issue price and a fee schedule. Except in the case of large issues, these underwriters could not expend the time and effort without the near certainty of receiving the contract.

Studies generally show that issuing costs are higher in negotiated deals than in competitive ones. However, many financial economists argue that issuing firms are not necessarily hurt by negotiated deals. They point out that the underwriter gains much information about the issuing firm through negotiation, information likely to increase the probability of a successful offering.[4]

The Offering Price

Determining the correct offering price is the most difficult thing the lead investment bank must do for an initial public offering. The issuing firm faces a potential cost if the offering price is set too high or too low. If the issue is priced too high, it may be unsuccessful and be withdrawn. If the issue is priced below the true market price, the issuer's existing shareholders will experience an opportunity loss.

Ibbotson has found that unseasoned new equity issues typically have been offered at 11 percent below their true market price.[5] Underpricing helps new shareholders earn a higher return on the shares they buy. However, the existing shareholders of the issuing firm are not necessarily helped by underpricing. To them it is an indirect cost of issuing new securities.

Several studies have confirmed the early research of Ibbotson. For example, Ritter examined approximately 1,030 firms that went public from 1977 through 1982 in the United States.[6] He finds that the average firm-commitment IPO rose in price 14.8 percent in the first day of trading following issuance. The comparable figure is 47.8 percent for best-efforts IPOs. These figures are not annualized! Both of these results are clearly consistent with substantial underpricing.

Another recent dramatic example of underpricing came with the IPO of Shiva Corporation. Shiva makes hardware and software that allow desktop and laptop computers to hook directly into a local area network from outside the office. The initial offering, on November 18, 1994, of 2.76 million shares priced at $15 rose $16½ to $31½ by the end of the first trading day. Goldman Sachs, head of the underwriting syndicate that underwrote

---

[4]This choice has been studied recently by Robert S. Hansen and Naveen Khanna, "Why Negotiation with a Single Syndicate May Be Preferred to Making Syndicates Compete: The Problem of Trapped Bidders," *Journal of Business* 67 (1994) and S. Bhagat, "The Effect of Management's Choice between Negotiated and Competitive Equity Offerings on Shareholder Wealth," *Journal of Financial and Quantitative Analysis* (1986); and D. Logue and R. Jarrow, "Negotiation vs. Competitive Bidding in the Sales of Securities by Public Utilities," *Financial Management* 7 (1978).

[5]R. Ibbotson, "Price Performance of Common Stock New Issues," *Journal of Financial Economics* 2 (1975).

[6]J. R. Ritter, "The Costs of Going Public," *Journal of Financial Economics* (1987). Underpricing also exists for new issues of seasoned stock, but to a much smaller extent. See J. Parsons and A. Raviv, "Underpricing of Seasoned Issues," *Journal of Financial Economics* 14 (1985).

Jay R. Ritter on IPO Underpricing around the World

The United States is not the only country in which initial public offerings of common stock (IPOs) are underpriced. The phenomenon exists in every country with a stock market, although the amount of underpricing varies from country to country.

The 1980s and 1990s have seen thousands of companies go public. Outside of the United States, certain industries, such as airlines and telephone companies, were almost entirely owned by governments 20 years ago. In the last two decades, firms in these industries have been "privatized" in many countries.

In many emerging markets, many of the firms going public have been old family businesses or government-owned enterprises, and their IPOs haven't always gone smoothly. The extreme example is China, where "A" shares, which can only be owned by Chinese citizens, have frequently seen first day price jumps (initial returns) of several hundred percent.

The table below gives a summary of the average initial returns on IPOs for 32 countries around the world, with the figures collected from many studies by various authors.

Country	Source	Sample Size	Time Period	Average Initial Return
Australia	Lee, Taylor & Walter	266	1976–89	11.9%
Austria	Aussenegg	61	1984–95	6.5
Belgium	Rogiers, Manigart & Ooghe	28	1984–90	10.1
Brazil	Aggarwal, Leal & Hernandez	62	1979–90	78.5
Canada	Jog & Riding; Jog & Srivastava	258	1971–92	5.4
Chile	Aggarwal, Leal & Hernandez	19	1982–90	16.3
China	Datar and Mao	226	1990–96	388.0
Denmark	Bisgard	29	1989–97	8.0
Finland	Keloharju	85	1984–92	9.6
France	Husson & Jacquillat; Leleux & Muzyka; Paliard & Belletante	187	1983–92	4.2
Germany	Ljungqvist	170	1978–92	10.9
Greece	Kazantzis and Levis	79	1987–91	48.5
Hong Kong	McGuinness; Zhao and Wu	334	1980–96	15.9
India	Krishnamurti and Kumar	98	1992–93	35.3
Israel	Kandel, Sarig & Wohl	28	1993–94	4.5
Italy	Cherubini & Ratti	75	1985–91	27.1
Japan	Fukuda; Dawson & Hiraki; Hebner & Hiraki; Pettway & Kaneko; Hamao, Packer, & Ritter	975	1970–96	24.0
Korea	Dhatt, Kim & Lim	347	1980–90	78.1
Malaysia	Isa	132	1980–91	80.3
Mexico	Aggarwal, Leal & Hernandez	37	1987–90	33.0
Netherlands	Wessels; Eijgenhuijsen & Buijs	72	1982–91	7.2
New Zealand	Vos & Cheung	149	1979–91	28.8
Portugal	Alpalhao	62	1986–87	54.4
Singapore	Lee, Taylor & Walter	128	1973–92	31.4
Spain	Rahnema, Fernandez & Martinez	71	1985–90	35.0
Sweden	Rydqvist	251	1980–94	34.1
Switzerland	Kunz & Aggarwal	42	1983–89	35.8
Taiwan	Chen	168	1971–90	45.0
Thailand	Wethyavivorn & Koo-smith	32	1988–89	58.1
Turkey	Kiymaz	138	1990–96	13.6
United Kingdom	Dimson; Levis	2,133	1959–90	12.0
United States	Ibbotson, Sindelar & Ritter	13,308	1960–96	15.8%

Jay R. Ritter is Cordell Professor of Finance at the University of Florida. An outstanding scholar, he is well-respected for his insightful analyses of new issues and companies going public.

the issue, was quoted as saying that pricing an IPO is not just about what the market will bear at the time, but "we are trying to get the company launched for the long term and build a good investor base."[7]

Underpricing: A Possible Explanation

When the price of a new issue is too low, the issue is often *oversubscribed*. This means investors will not be able to buy all of the shares they want, and the underwriters will allocate the shares among investors. The average investor will find it difficult to get shares in an oversubscribed offering because there will not be enough shares to go around. While initial public offerings have positive initial returns on average, a significant fraction of them have price drops. An investor submitting an order for all new issues may find that he or she will be allocated more shares in issues that go down in price.

Consider this tale of two investors. Ms. Smarts knows precisely what companies are worth when their shares are offered. Mr. Average knows only that prices usually rise one month after the IPO. Armed with this information, Mr. Average decides to buy 1,000 shares of every IPO. Does Mr. Average actually earn an abnormally high average return across all initial offerings?

The answer is no, and at least one reason is Ms. Smarts. For example, because Ms. Smarts knows that company *XYZ* is underpriced, she invests all her money in its IPO. When the issue is oversubscribed, the underwriters must allocate the shares between Ms. Smarts and Mr. Average. If they do it on a pro rata basis and if Ms. Smarts has bid for twice as many shares as Mr. Average, she will get two shares for each one Mr. Average receives. The net result is that when an issue is underpriced, Mr. Average cannot buy as much of it as he wants.

Ms. Smarts also knows that company *ABC* is overpriced. In this case she avoids its IPO altogether, and Mr. Average ends up with a full 1,000 shares. To summarize, Mr. Average receives fewer shares when more knowledgeable investors swarm to buy an underpriced issue, but he gets all he wants when the smart money avoids the issue.

This is called the *winner's curse,* and it explains much of the reason why IPOs have such a large average return. When the average investor wins and gets his allocation, it is because those who knew better avoided the issue. To counteract the winner's curse and attract the average investor, underwriters underprice issues.[8]

- Describe a firm-commitment underwriting and a best-efforts underwriting.
- Suppose that a stockbroker calls you up out of the blue and offers to sell you some shares of a new issue. Do you think the issue will do better or worse than average?

19.4 THE ANNOUNCEMENT OF NEW EQUITY AND THE VALUE OF THE FIRM

It seems reasonable to believe that new long-term financing is arranged by firms after positive net present value projects are put together. As a consequence, when the announcement of external financing is made, the firm's market value should go up. As we mentioned in an earlier chapter, this is precisely the opposite of what actually happens in the case of new equity

---

[7]*The New York Times,* February 19, 1995, "Anatomy of a High Flying IPO, Problems and All," p. 7.

[8]This explanation was first suggested in K. Rock, "Why New Issues Are Underpriced," *Journal of Financial Economics* 15 (1986).

financing. Asquith and Mullins, Masulis and Korwar, and Mikkelson and Partch have all found that the market value of existing equity drops on the announcement of a new issue of common stock.[9] Plausible reasons for this strange result include:

1. *Managerial Information.* If managers have superior information about the market value of the firm, they may know when the firm is overvalued. If they do, they might attempt to issue new shares of stock when the market value exceeds the correct value. This will benefit existing shareholders. However, the potential new shareholders are not stupid. They will infer overvaluation from the new issue, thereby bidding down the stock price on the announcement date of the issue.

2. *Debt Capacity.* The stereotypical firm chooses a debt-to-equity ratio that balances the tax shield from the debt with the cost of financial distress. When the managers of a firm have special information that the probability of financial distress has risen, the firm is more likely to raise capital through stock than through debt. If the market infers this chain of events, the stock price should fall on the announcement date of an equity issue.

3. *Falling Earnings.*[10] When managers raise capital in amounts that are unexpectedly large (as most unanticipated financings will be) and if investors have a reasonable fix on the firm's upcoming investments and dividend payouts (as they do because capital expenditure announcements are often well known, as are future dividends), the unanticipated financings are roughly equal to unanticipated shortfalls in earnings (this follows directly from the firm's sources and uses of funds identity). Therefore, an announcement of a new stock issue will also reveal a future earnings shortfall.

- What are some reasons that the price of stock drops on the announcement of a new equity issue?

19.5 THE COST OF NEW ISSUES

Issuing securities to the public is not free, and the costs of different issuing methods are important determinants of which will be used. The costs fall into six categories.

1. Spread or underwriting discount	The spread is the difference between the price the issue receives and the price offered to the public.
2. Other direct expenses	These are costs incurred by the issuer that are not part of the compensation to underwriters. They include filing fees, legal fees, and taxes—all reported in the prospectus.
3. Indirect expenses	These costs are not reported in the prospectus and include management time on the new issue.

---

[9]P. Asquith and D. Mullins, "Equity Issues and Offering Dilution," *Journal of Financial Economics* 15 (1986); R. Masulis and A. N. Korwar, "Seasoned Equity Offerings: An Empirical Investigation," *Journal of Financial Economics* 15 (1986); and W. H. Mikkelson and M. M. Partch, "The Valuation Effects of Security Offerings and the Issuance Process," *Journal of Financial Economics* 15 (1986).

[10]Robert S. Haugen and Claire Crutchley, "Corporate Earnings and Financings, An Empirical Analysis," *Journal of Business* 20 (1990).

4. Abnormal returns | In a seasoned issue of stock, the price drops by 3 percent to 4 percent upon the announcement of the issue. The drop protects new shareholders against the firm's selling overpriced stock to new shareholders.

5. Underpricing | For initial public offerings, the stock typically rises substantially after the issue date. This is a cost to the firm because the stock is sold for less than its efficient price in the aftermarket.[11]

6. Green Shoe option | The Green Shoe option gives the underwriters the right to buy additional shares at the offer price to cover overallotments. This is a cost to the firm because the underwriter will only buy additional shares when the offer price is below the price in the aftermarket.

An interesting study by Lee, Lockhead, Ritter, and Zhao reports two of these six costs: underwriting discount and other direct expenses.[12] Their findings for both equity offerings and debt offerings are reproduced in Table 19.5. Three conclusions emerge from the table.

1. The costs in each category, for both equity offerings and debt offerings, decline as the gross proceeds of the offering increase. Thus, it appears that issuance costs are subject to substantial economies of scale.[13]

2. The bottom line of Table 19.5 indicates that, across all offerings, direct expenses are higher for equity offers than for debt offers.

3. Last, and perhaps most important, the costs of issuing securities to the public are quite large. For example, total direct expenses are approximately 17 percent for an initial public offering of less than $10,000,000. In addition, Table 19.6 establishes that underpricing costs are another 16.36 percent. This implies that going public for the first time is a weighty decision. While there are many benefits, such as raising needed capital and spreading ownership, the costs cannot be ignored.

QUESTIONS
CONCEPT **?**

• Describe the costs of a new issue of common stock.
• What conclusions emerge from analyses of Tables 19.6 and 19.7?

---

[11]Some people have argued that the price in the aftermarket is not efficient after all. However, R. Ibbotson, "Price Performance of Common Stock New Issues," *Journal of Financial Economics* 2 (1975), shows that, on average, new issues exhibit no abnormal price performance over the first five years following issuance. This result is generally viewed as being consistent with market efficiency. That is, the stock obtains an efficient price immediately following issuance and remains at an efficient price.

[12]The notion of economies of scale has been contested by Oya Altinkilic and Robert S. Hansen "Are There Scale Economies in Underwriting Spreads? Evidence of Rising External Financing Costs," *Review of Financial Studies* 13 (2000). They provide data and analysis that underwriter cost will be U-shaped.

[13]Among the most interesting developments in the initial public offering market is that almost all underwriter spreads in recent offerings have been exactly 7 percent. This is documented in H. C. Chen and Jay R. Ritter, "The Seven-Percent Solution," *Journal of Finance* (June 2000); and Robert S. Hansen, "Do Investment Banks Compete in IPO's? The Advent of the 7% Plus Contract," *Journal of Financial Economics* (forthcoming).

■ TABLE 19.5 Direct Costs as a Percentage of Gross Proceeds for Equity (IPOs and SEOs) and Straight and Convertible Bonds Offered by Domestic Operating Companies: 1990–94*

Proceeds ($ in millions)	Equity								Bonds							
	IPOs				SEOs				Convertible Bonds				Straight Bonds			
	Number of Issues	Gross Spread	Other Direct Expense	Total Direct Cost	Number of Issues	Gross Spread	Other Direct Expense	Total Direct Cost	Number of Issues	Gross Spread	Other Direct Expense	Total Direct Cost	Number of Issues	Gross Spread	Other Direct Expense	Total Direct Cost
2– 9.99	337	9.05%	7.91%	16.96%	167	7.72%	5.56%	13.28%	4	6.07%	2.68%	8.75%	32	2.07%	2.32%	4.39%
10– 19.99	389	7.24	4.39	11.63	310	6.23	2.49	8.72	14	5.48	3.18	8.66	78	1.36	1.40	2.76
20– 39.99	533	7.01	2.69	9.70	425	5.60	1.33	6.93	18	4.16	1.95	6.11	89	1.54	.88	2.42
40– 59.99	215	6.96	1.76	8.72	261	5.05	.82	5.87	28	3.26	1.04	4.30	90	.72	.60	1.32
60– 79.99	79	6.74	1.46	8.20	143	4.57	.61	5.18	47	2.64	.59	3.23	92	1.76	.58	2.34
80– 99.99	51	6.47	1.44	7.91	71	4.25	.48	4.73	13	2.43	.61	3.04	112	1.55	.61	2.16
100–199.99	106	6.03	1.03	7.06	152	3.85	.37	4.22	57	2.34	.42	2.76	409	1.77	.54	2.31
200–499.99	47	5.67	.86	6.53	55	3.26	.21	3.47	27	1.99	.19	2.18	170	1.79	.40	2.19
500 and up	10	5.21	.51	5.72	9	3.03	.12	3.15	3	2.00	.09	2.09	20	1.39	.25	1.64
Total	1,767	7.31%	3.69%	11.00%	1,593	5.44%	1.67%	7.11%	211	2.92%	.87%	3.79%	1,092	1.62%	.62%	2.24%

*IPO refers to initial public offering and SEO refers to seasoned equity offering.
Source: Inmoo Lee, Scott Lockhead, Jay Ritter, and Quanshui Zhao, "The Costs of Raising Capital," *Journal of Financial Research* 1 (Spring 1996).

■ TABLE 19.6   **Direct and Indirect Costs, in Percentages,
of Equity IPOs: 1990–94**

Proceeds ($ in millions)	Number of Issues	Gross Spread	Other Direct Expense	Total Direct Cost	Underpricing
2– 9.99	337	9.05%	7.91%	16.96%	16.36%
10– 19.99	389	7.24	4.39	11.63	9.65
20– 39.99	533	7.01	2.69	9.70	12.48
40– 59.99	215	6.96	1.76	8.72	13.65
60– 79.99	79	6.74	1.46	8.20	11.31
80– 99.99	51	6.47	1.44	7.91	8.91
100–199.99	106	6.03	1.03	7.06	7.16
200–499.99	47	5.67	.86	6.53	5.70
500 and up	10	5.21	.51	5.72	7.53
Total	1,767	7.31%	3.69%	11.00%	12.05%

As we have discussed, the underpricing of IPOs is an additional cost to the issuer. To give a better idea of the total cost of going public, Table 19.6 combines the information in Table 19.5 for IPOs with data on the underpricing experience by these firms. Comparing the total direct costs (in the fifth column) to the underpricing (in the sixth column), we see that they are roughly the same size, so the direct costs are only about half of the total. Overall, across all size groups, the total direct costs amount to 11 percent of the amount raised and the underpricing amounts to 12 percent.

Source: Inmoo Lee, Scott Lockhead, Jay Ritter, and Quanshui Zhao, "The Costs of Raising Capital," *Journal of Financial Research* 1 (Spring 1996).

19.6 RIGHTS

When new shares of common stock are offered to the general public, the proportionate ownership of existing shareholders is likely to be reduced. However, if a preemptive right is contained in the firm's articles of incorporation, the firm must first offer any new issue of common stock to existing shareholders. This assures each owner his or her proportionate owner's share.

An issue of common stock to existing stockholders is called a *rights offering*. Here, each shareholder is issued an *option* to buy a specified number of new shares from the firm at a specified price within a specified time, after which the rights expire. For example, a firm whose stock is selling at $30 may let current stockholders buy a fixed number of shares at $10 per share within two months. The terms of the option are evidenced by certificates known as *share warrants* or *rights*. Such rights are often traded on securities exchanges or over the counter.

The Mechanics of a Rights Offering

The various considerations confronting a financial manager in a rights offering are illustrated by the situation of the National Power Company, whose initial financial statements are given in Table 19.7.

National Power earns $2 million after taxes and has 1 million shares outstanding. Earnings per share are $2, and the stock sells at 10 times earnings (that is, its price-earnings ratio is 10). The market price of each share is therefore $20. The company plans to raise $5 million of new equity funds by a rights offering.

■ TABLE 19.7   **Financial Statement before Rights Offering**

NATIONAL POWER COMPANY
Balance Sheet and Income Statement

Balance Sheet		
Assets	Shareholder Equity	
	Common stock	$10,000,000
	Retained earnings	10,000,000
Total $20,000,000	Total	$20,000,000
Income Statement		
Earnings before taxes	$ 3,030,303	
Taxes (34%)	1,030,303	
Net income	$ 2,000,000	
Earnings per share	2	
Shares outstanding	1,000,000	
Market price per share	20	
Total market value	$20,000,000	

The process of issuing rights differs from the process of issuing shares of stock for cash. Existing stockholders are notified that they have been given one right for each share of stock they own. Exercise occurs when a shareholder sends payment to the firm's subscription agent (usually a bank) and turns in the required number of rights. Shareholders of National Power will have several choices: (1) subscribe for the full number of entitled shares, (2) order all the rights sold, or (3) do nothing and let the rights expire.

The financial management of National Power must answer the following questions:

1. What price should the existing shareholders be allowed to pay for a share of new stock?
2. How many rights will be required to purchase one share of stock?
3. What effect will the rights offering have on the existing price of the stock?

Subscription Price

In a rights offering, the **subscription price** is the price that existing shareholders are allowed to pay for a share of stock. A rational shareholder will only subscribe to the rights offering if the subscription price is below the market price of the stock on the offer's expiration date. For example, if the stock price at expiration is $13 and the subscription price is $15, no rational shareholder will subscribe. Why pay $15 for something worth $13? National Power chooses a price of $10, which is well below the current market price of $20. As long as the market price does not fall by half before expiration, the rights offering will succeed.

Number of Rights Needed to Purchase a Share

National Power wants to raise $5 million in new equity. With a subscription price of $10, it must issue 500,000 new shares. This can be determined by dividing the total amount to be raised by the subscription price:

$$\text{Number of new shares} = \frac{\text{Funds to be raised}}{\text{Subscription price}} = \frac{\$5,000,000}{\$10} = 500,000 \text{ shares}$$

Because stockholders typically get one right for each share of stock they own, 1 million rights will be issued by National Power. To determine how many rights must be exercised to get one share of stock, we can divide the number of existing outstanding shares of stock by the number of new shares:

$$\text{Number of rights needed to buy a share of stock} = \frac{\text{"Old" shares}}{\text{"New" shares}} = \frac{1,000,000}{500,000} = 2 \text{ rights}$$

Thus, a shareholder must give up two rights plus $10 to receive a share of new stock. If all the stockholders do this, National Power will raise the required $5 million.

It should be clear that the subscription price, the number of new shares, and the number of rights needed to buy a new share of stock are interrelated. If National Power lowers the subscription price, it must issue more new shares to raise $5 million in new equity. Several alternatives appear here:

Subscription Price	Number of New Shares	Number of Rights Needed to Buy a Share of Stock
$20	250,000	4
10	500,000	2
5	1,000,000	1

Effect of Rights Offering on Price of Stock

Rights clearly have value. In the case of National Power, the right to be able to buy a share of stock worth $20 for $10 is valuable.

Suppose a shareholder of National Power owns two shares of stock just before the rights offering. This situation is depicted in Table 19.8. Initially, the price of National Power is $20 per share, so the shareholder's total holding is worth 2 × $20 = $40. The stockholder who has two shares will receive two rights. The National Power rights offer gives shareholders with two rights the opportunity to purchase one additional share for $10. The holding of the shareholder who exercises these rights and buys the new share would increase to three shares. The value of the new holding would be $40 + $10 = $50 (the $40 initial value plus the $10 paid to the company). Because the stockholder now holds three shares, the price per share would drop to $50/3 = $16.67 (rounded to two decimal places).

The difference between the old share price of $20 and the new share price of $16.67 reflects the fact that the old shares carried rights to subscribe to the new issue. The difference must be equal to the value of one right, that is, $20 − $16.67 = $3.33.

Just as we learned of an ex-dividend date in the previous chapter, there is an **ex-rights date** here. An individual buying the stock prior to the ex-rights date will receive the rights when distributed. An individual buying the stock on or after the ex-rights date will not receive the rights. In our example, the price of the stock prior to the ex-rights date is $20. An individual buying on or after the ex-rights date is not entitled to the rights. The price on or after the ex-rights date is $16.67.

Table 19.9 shows what happens to National Power. If all shareholders exercise their rights, the number of shares will increase to 1.5 million and the value of the firm will increase to $25 million. After the rights offering the value of each share will drop to $16.67 (= $25 million/1.5 million).

An investor holding no shares of National Power stock who wants to subscribe to the new issue can do so by buying rights. An outside investor buying two rights will pay $3.33 × 2 = $6.67 (to account for previous rounding). If the investor exercises the rights

■ TABLE 19.8 **The Value to the Individual Shareholder of National Power's Rights**

	The Shareholder
Initial position	
Number of shares	2
Share price	$20
Value of holding	$40
Terms of offer	
Subscription price	$10
Number of rights issued	2
Number of rights for a share	2
After offer	
Number of shares	3
Value of holding	$50
Share price	$16.67
Value of a right	
Old price − New price	$20 − $16.67 = $3.33
$\dfrac{\text{New price} - \text{Subscription price}}{\text{Number of rights for a share}}$	($16.67 − $10)/2 = $3.33

■ TABLE 19.9 **National Power Company Rights Offering**

Initial position	
Number of shares	1 million
Share price	$20
Value of firm	$20 million
Terms of offer	
Subscription price	$10
Number of rights issued	1 million
Number of rights for a share	2
After offer	
Number of shares	1.5 million
Share price	$16.67
Value of firm	$25 million
Value of one right	$20 − $16.67 = $3.33
	or ($16.67 − $10)/2 = $3.33

at a subscription cost of $10, the total cost would be $10 + $6.67 = $16.67. In return for this expenditure, the investor will receive a share of the new stock, which is worth $16.67.

Of course, outside investors can also buy National Power stock directly at $16.67 per share. In an efficient stock market it will make no difference whether new stock is obtained via rights or via direct purchase.

Effects on Shareholders

Shareholders can exercise their rights or sell them. In either case, the stockholder will neither win nor lose by the rights offering. The hypothetical holder of two shares of National Power has a portfolio worth $40. On the one hand, if the shareholder exercises the rights, he or she ends up with three shares worth a total of $50. In other words, by spending $10, the investor increases the value of the holding by $10, which means that he or she is neither better nor worse off.

On the other hand, a shareholder who sells the two rights for $3.33 each obtains $3.33 × 2 = $6.67 in cash. Because the two shares are each worth $16.67, the holdings are valued at

$$
\begin{aligned}
\text{Shares} &= &2 \times \$16.67 &= \$33.33 \\
\text{Sold rights} &= 2 \times \$ &3.33 &= \underline{\$\ 6.67} \\
\text{Total} & & &= \$40.00
\end{aligned}
$$

The new $33.33 market value plus $6.67 in cash is exactly the same as the original holding of $40. Thus, stockholders can neither lose nor gain from exercising or selling rights.

It is obvious that the new market price of the firm's stock will be lower after the rights offering than it was before the rights offering. The lower the subscription price, the greater the price decline of a rights offering. However, our analysis shows that the stockholders have suffered no loss because of the rights offering.

The Underwriting Arrangements

Undersubscription can occur if investors throw away rights or if bad news causes the market price of the stock to fall below the subscription price. To ensure against these possibilities, rights offerings are typically arranged by **standby underwriting.** Here, the underwriter makes a firm commitment to purchase the unsubscribed portion of the issue at the subscription price less a take-up fee. The underwriter usually receives a **standby fee** as compensation for his risk-bearing function.

In practice, the subscription price is usually set well below the current market price, making the probability of a rights failure quite small. Though a small percentage (less than 10 percent) of shareholders fail to exercise valuable rights, shareholders are usually allowed to purchase unsubscribed shares at the subscription price. This **oversubscription privilege** makes it unlikely that the corporate issuer would need to turn to its underwriter for help.

- Describe the details of a rights offering.
- What are the questions that financial management must answer in a rights offering?
- How is the value of a right determined?

19.7 THE RIGHTS PUZZLE

Smith calculated the issuance costs from three alternative methods: an equity issue with underwriting, a rights issue with standby underwriting, and a pure rights issue.[14] The results of his study, which appear in Table 19.10, suggest that a pure rights issue is the cheapest of the three alternatives. The bottom line of the table shows that total costs as a percentage of proceeds is 6.17 percent, 6.05 percent, and 2.45 percent for the three alternatives, respectively. As the body of the table indicates, this disparity holds when issues of different sizes are separated.

---

[14]C. W. Smith, Jr., "Alternative Methods for Raising Capital: Rights versus Underwritten Offerings," *Journal of Financial Economics* 5 (December 1977).

■ TABLE 19.10 Costs of Flotation as a Percentage of Proceeds*

Size of Issue (in $ millions)	Underwriting				Rights with Standby Underwriting				Pure Rights	
	Number	Compensation as a Percentage of Proceeds	Other Expenses as a Percentage of Proceeds	Total Cost as a Percentage of Proceeds	Number	Compensation as a Percentage of Proceeds	Other Expenses as a Percentage of Proceeds	Total Cost as a Percentage of Proceeds	Number	Total Cost as a Percentage of Proceeds
Under 0.50	—	—	—	0	—	—	—	8.99	3	4.59
0.50 to 0.99	6	6.96	6.78	13.74	2	3.43	4.80	8.24	2	4.90
1.00 to 1.99	18	10.40	4.89	15.29	5	6.36	4.15	10.51	5	2.85
2.00 to 4.99	61	6.59	2.87	9.47	9	5.20	2.85	8.06	7	1.39
5.00 to 9.99	66	5.50	1.53	7.03	4	3.92	2.18	6.10	6	0.72
10.00 to 19.99	91	4.84	0.71	5.55	10	4.14	1.21	5.35	3	0.52
20.00 to 49.99	156	4.30	0.37	4.67	12	3.84	0.90	4.74	1	0.21
50.00 to 99.99	70	3.97	0.21	4.18	9	3.96	0.74	4.70	2	0.13
100.00 to 500.00	16	3.81	0.14	3.95	5	3.50	0.50	4.00	9	
Total/average	484	5.02	1.15	6.17	56	4.32	1.73	6.05	38	2.45

*Based on 578 common stock issues registered under the Securities Act of 1933 during 1971–1975. The issues are subdivided by size of issue and method of financing: underwriting, rights with standby underwriting, and pure rights offering.

Issues are included only if the company's stock was listed on the NYSE, AMEX, or regional exchanges before the offering; any associated secondary distribution represents less than 10 percent of the total proceeds of the issue, and the offering contains no other types of securities. The costs reported are: (1) compensation received by investment bankers for underwriting services rendered, (2) legal fees, (3) accounting fees, (4) engineering fees, (5) trustees' fees, (6) printing and engraving expenses, (7) SEC registration fees, (8) federal revenue stamps, and (9) state taxes.

Modified from C. W. Smith, Jr., "Costs of Underwritten versus Rights Issues," *Journal of Financial Economics* 5 (December 1977), p. 277 (Table 1).

If corporate executives are rational, they will raise equity in the cheapest manner. Thus, the above evidence suggests that issues of pure rights should dominate. Surprisingly, Smith points out that over 90 percent of new issues are underwritten. This is generally viewed as an anomaly in the finance profession, though a few explanations have been advanced.[15]

1. Underwriters increase the stock price. This is supposedly accomplished because of increased public confidence or by the selling effort of the underwriting group. However, Smith could find no evidence of this in an examination of 52 rights offerings and 344 underwritten offerings.

2. Because the underwriter buys the shares at the agreed-upon price, it is providing insurance to the firm. That is, the underwriter loses if it is unable to sell all the shares to the public. This potential loss might mean that the underwriter's effective compensation is less than that measured in Table 19.10. However, the potential economic loss is probably not large. In most cases, the offer price is set within 24 hours of the offering, by which time the underwriter has usually made a careful assessment of the market for the shares.

3. Other arguments include (*a*) the proceeds of underwritten issues are available sooner than are the proceeds from a rights offer, (*b*) underwriters provide a wider distribution of ownership than would be true with a rights offering, (*c*) consulting advice from investment bankers may be beneficial, and (*d*) stockholders find exercising rights a nuisance.

All of the preceding arguments are pieces of the puzzle, but none seems very convincing. Recently, Booth and Smith identified a function of the underwriter that had not been taken into account in previous cost studies.[16] They argue that the underwriter *certifies* that the offering price is consistent with the true value of the issue. This certification is implied in the underwriting relationship and is provided when the underwriting firm gets access to inside information and puts its reputation for correct pricing on the line.

CONCEPT QUESTION ?

- Why might a firm prefer a general cash offering to a rights offering?

19.8 SHELF REGISTRATION

To simplify the procedures for issuing securities, the SEC currently allows **shelf registration.** Shelf registration permits a corporation to register an offering that it reasonably expects to sell within the next two years. A master registration statement is filed at the time of registration. The company is permitted to sell the issue whenever it wants over those two years as long as it distributes a short-form statement.

Not all companies are allowed shelf registration. The major qualifications are as follows:

1. The company must be rated *investment* grade.
2. The firm cannot have defaulted on its debt in the past 12 months.
3. The aggregate market value of the firm's outstanding stock must be more than $75 million.
4. The firm must not have violated the Securities Act of 1934 in the past 12 months.

---

[15]It is even more anomalous because rights offerings are used around the world. In fact, they are required by law in many other countries.

[16]Booth and R. Smith, "The Certification Role of the Investment Banker in New Issue Pricing," *Midland Corporate Finance Journal* (Spring 1986).

Hershman reports on the use of the *dribble* method of new equity issuance.[17] With dribbling, a company registers the issue and hires an underwriter to be its selling agent. The company sells shares in small amounts from time to time via a stock exchange. Companies that have dribble programs include Middle South Utilities, Niagara Mohawk, Pacific Gas and Electric, and the Southern Company. However, the evidence is that shelf registration is almost never used for equity but is used about one-half of the time for debt.[18]

The rule has been very controversial. Several arguments have been made against shelf registration.

1. The timeliness of disclosure is reduced with shelf registration, because the master registration statement may have been prepared up to two years before the actual issue occurs.

2. Some investment bankers have argued that shelf registration will cause a market overhang, because registration informs the market of future issues. It has been suggested that this overhang will depress market prices. However, an empirical analysis by Bhagat, Marr, and Thompson found that shelf registration is less costly than conventional underwriting and found no evidence to suggest a market-overhang effect.[19] Surprisingly, few eligible companies are currently selling equity by using shelf registration.[20]

CONCEPT QUESTIONS

- Describe shelf registration.
- What are the arguments against shelf registration?

19.9 THE PRIVATE EQUITY MARKET

The previous sections of this chapter assumed that a company is big enough, successful enough, and old enough to raise capital in the public equity market. Of course, there are many firms that have not reached this stage and cannot use the public equity market. For start-up firms or firms in financial trouble, the public equity market is often not available. The market for **venture capital** is part of the private equity market.[21]

Private Placement

Private placements avoid the costly procedures associated with the registration requirements that are part of public issues. The Securities and Exchange Commission (SEC) restricts private placement issues to no more than a couple of dozen knowledgeable investors including institutions such as insurance companies and pension funds. The biggest drawback of privately placed securities is that the securities cannot be easily resold. Most private placements involve debt securities, but equity securities can also be privately placed.

---

[17]A. Hershman, "New Strategies in Equity Financing," *Dunn's Business Monthly* (June 1983).

[18]D. J. Dennis, "Shelf Registration and the Market in Seasonal Equity Offerings," *Journal of Business* 64 (1991).

[19]S. Bhagat, M. W. Marr, and G. R. Thompson, "The Rule 415 Experiment: Equity Markets," *Journal of Finance* 19 (December 1985).

[20]R. Rogowski and E. Sorenson, "Deregulation in Investment Banking: Shelf Registration, Structure, and Performance," *Financial Management* (Spring 1985).

[21]S. E. Pratt, "Overview and Introduction to the Venture Capital Industry," *Guide to Venture Capital Sources,* 10th ed., 1987 (Venture Economics. Laurel Avenue, Box 348, Wellesley Hills, MA 02181).

■ FIGURE 19.2   **Corporate Equity Security Offerings: 1997**

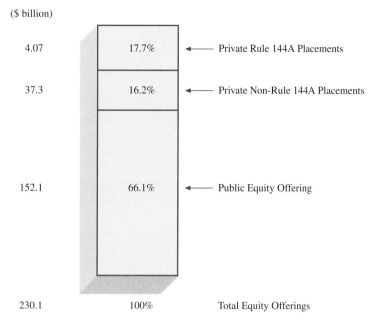

Source: Jennifer E. Bethal and Erik R. Sirri, "Express Lane or Toll Booth in the Desert: The Sec of Framework for Securities Issuance," *Journal of Applied Corporate Finance* (Spring 1998).

In 1990, Rule 144A was adopted by the SEC and established a framework for the issuance of private securities to certain qualified institutional investors. The rule has generated a substantial market for privately underwritten issues. Largely because of Rule 144A, companies raise about one-sixth of the proceeds from all new issues without registration with the SEC. To qualify to buy Rule 144A offerings, investors must have at least $100 million in assets under management. Most private placements are in straight bonds or convertible bonds. However, preferred stock is frequently issued as a private placement.

The Private Equity Firm

A large amount of private equity investment is undertaken by professional private equity managers representing large institutional investors such as mutual funds and pension funds. The limited partnership is the dominant form of intermediation in this market. Typically, the institutional investors act as the limited partners and the professional managers act as general partners. The general partners are firms that specialize in funding and managing equity investments in closely held private firms. The private equity market has been important for both traditional start-up companies and established public firms. Thus, the private equity market can be divided into venture equity and nonventure equity markets. A large part of the nonventure market is made up of firms in financial distress. Firms in financial distress are not likely to be able to issue public equity and typically cannot use traditional forms of debt such as bank loans or public debt. For these firms, the best alternative is to find a private equity market firm.

Suppliers of Venture Capital

As we have pointed out, venture capital is an important part of the private equity market. There are at least four types of suppliers of venture capital. First, a few old-line, wealthy families have traditionally provided start-up capital to promising businesses. For example, over the years, the Rockefeller family has made the initial capital contribution to a number of successful businesses. These families have been involved in venture capital for the better part of this century, if not longer.

Second, a number of private partnerships and corporations have been formed to provide investment funds. The organizer behind the partnership might raise capital from institutional investors, such as insurance companies and pension funds. Alternatively, a group of individuals might provide the funds to be ultimately invested with budding entrepreneurs.

Of the early partnerships, the most well-known is clearly American Research and Development (ARD), which was formed in 1946. Though ARD invested in many companies, its success was largely due to its investment in Digital Equipment Company (DEC). When Textron acquired ARD in 1972, over 85 percent of the shareholders' distribution was due to the investment in DEC.[22] Among the more recent venture capitalists, Arthur Rock & Co. of San Francisco may very well be the best known. Because of its huge success with Apple Computer and other high-tech firms, it has achieved near mythic stature in the venture-capital industry.

Recent estimates put the number of venture-capital firms at about 2,000. Pratt's *Guide to Venture Capital* (Venture Economics) provides a list of the names of many of these firms.[23] The average amount invested per venture has been estimated to be between $1 million and $2 million. However, one should not make too much of this figure, because the amount of financing varies considerably with the venture to be funded.

Stories used to abound about how easily an individual could obtain venture capital. Though that may have been the case in an earlier era, it is certainly not the case today. Venture-capital firms employ various screening procedures to prevent inappropriate funding. For example, because of the large demand for funds, many venture capitalists have at least one employee whose full-time job consists of reading business plans. Only the very best plans can expect to attract funds. Maier and Walker indicate that only about 2 percent of requests actually receive financing.[24]

Third, large industrial or financial corporations have established venture-capital subsidiaries. The Lambda Fund of Drexel Burnham Lambert, Manufacturers Hanover Venture Capital Corp., Citicorp Venture Capital, and Chemical Venture Capital Corporation of Chemical Bank are examples of this type. However, subsidiaries of this type appear to make up only a small portion of the venture-capital market.

Fourth, participants in an informal venture-capital market have recently been identified.[25] Rather than belonging to any venture-capital firm, these investors (often referred to as *angels*) act as individuals when providing financing. However, they should not, by any means, be viewed as isolated. Wetzel and others indicate that there is a rich network of angels, continually relying on each other for advice. A number of researchers have stressed that, in any informal network, there is likely one knowledgeable and trustworthy individual who, when backing a venture, brings a few less experienced investors in with him.

---

[22]H. Stevenson, D. Muzka, and J. Timmons, "Venture Capital in Transition: A Monte-Carlo Simulation of Changes in Investment Patterns," *Journal of Business Venturing* (Spring 1987).

[23]Pratt, "Overview and Introduction to the Venture Capital Industry."

[24]J. B. Maier and D. Walker, "The Role of Venture Capital in Financing Small Business," *Journal of Business Venturing* (Summer 1987).

[25]See W. E. Wetzel, "The Informal Venture Capital Market: Aspects of Scale and Market Efficiency," *Journal of Business Venturing* (Fall 1987).

The venture-capital community has unfortunately chosen to refer to these individuals as "dumb dentists." Although a number indeed may be dentists, their intelligence should not be called into question. Wetzel argues that the prototypical angel has income over $100,000, net worth over $1,000,000, and substantial business experience and knowledge. As one might expect, the informal venture capitalist is able to tolerate high risks.

Though this informal market may seem small and unimportant, it is perhaps the largest of all sources of venture capital. Wetzel argues that aggregate investments from this source total around $50 billion, about twice the amount invested by more professional venture capitalists. The size of each contribution is smaller here. Perhaps, on average, only $250,000 per venture is raised when the informal market is tapped.

Stages of Financing

A. V. Bruno and T. T. Tyebjee identify six stages in venture-capital financing:[26]

1. *Seed-Money Stage.* A small amount of financing needed to prove a concept or develop a product. Marketing is not included in this stage.
2. *Start-Up.* Financing for firms that started within the past year. Funds are likely to pay for marketing and product development expenditures.
3. *First-Round Financing.* Additional money to begin sales and manufacturing after a firm has spent its start-up funds.
4. *Second-Round Financing.* Funds earmarked for working capital for a firm that is currently selling its product but still losing money.
5. *Third-Round Financing.* Financing for a company that is at least breaking even and is contemplating an expansion. This is also known as mezzanine financing.
6. *Fourth-Round Financing.* Money provided for firms that are likely to go public within half a year. This round is also known as bridge financing.

Although these categories may seem vague to the reader, we have found that the terms are well-accepted within the industry. For example, the venture-capital firms listed in Pratt's *Guide to Venture Capital* indicate which of the above stages they are interested in financing.

The penultimate stage in venture capital finance is the initial public offering.[27] Venture capitalists are very important participants in initial public offerings. Venture capitalists rarely sell all of the shares they own at the time of the initial public offering. Instead, they usually sell out in subsequent public offerings. However, there is considerable evidence that venture capitalists can successfully time IPOs by taking firms public when the market values are at the highest. Figure 19.3 shows the number of IPOs of privately held venture-capital-backed biotechnology companies in each month from 1978 to 1992. The venture-capital-backed IPOs clearly coincide with the ups and downs in the biotech market index in the top panel.

CONCEPT QUESTIONS

? • What are the different sources of venture-capital financing?
• What are the different stages for companies seeking venture-capital financing?
• What is the private equity market?
• What is Rule 144A?

---

[26]A. V. Bruno and T. T. Tyebjee, "The Entrepreneur's Search for Capital," *Journal of Business Venturing* (Winter 1985).

[27]A very influential paper by Christopher Barry, Chris J. Muscarella, John W. Peavey III, and Michael R. Vetsuypens, "The Role of Venture Capital in the Creation of Public Companies: Evidence from the Going Public Process," *Journal of Financial Economics* 27 (1990), shows that venture capitalists do not usually sell shares at the time of the initial public offering, but they usually have board seats and act as advisors to managers.

■ FIGURE 19.3   **Initial Public Offerings by Venture-Capital-Backed Biotechnology Firms, January 1978 to January 1992**

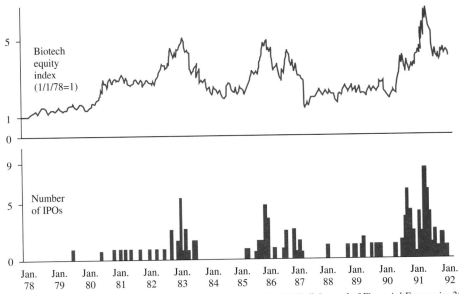

Source: Joshua Lerner, "Venture Capitalists and the Decision to Go Public," *Journal of Financial Economics* 35 (June 1994).

CASE STUDY: *The Decision to Do an Initial Public Offering (IPO): The Case of Medstone International, Inc.*

■■■■■   Most firms initially raise equity financing with private placements in the venture-capital market from a small number of investor capitalists. If a firm does well and needs to raise more equity financing, it may decide to sell stock with an initial public offering. We see how this occurs with the case of Medstone International, Inc.

Medstone International, Inc., was created in 1984 to manufacture and sell medical products using the new technology of shockwave lithotripsy. Initially, Medstone raised its cash from contributions from its founders and from banks. From 1984 to 1986 Medstone spent most of its available cash on research and development of the technology of shockwave lithotripsy. Eventually, in 1986, the company developed a product called the Medstone 1050 ST. The purpose of the Medstone 1050 ST was for nonsurgical disintegration of kidney stones and gallstones.

However, it wasn't until 1987 that the company actually generated profits from the Medstone 1050 ST (as follows).

	Summary of Financial Information (in thousands)	
	1986	1987
Revenues	$ 25	$ 6,562
Income	(1,698)	680
Assets	865	3,205
Liabilities	6,062	5,517
Equity	(5,197)	(2,312)

By January 1988 Medstone International had obtained an investigative new drug permit from the Food and Drug Administration (FDA) and had entered into an agreement to sell and install the Medstone System in seven U.S. states. In early 1988 the firm's prospects seemed excellent and its founders had reason to be optimistic. But Medstone needed additional cash and its founders wanted the opportunity to cash out, so it hired the Weeden Co., a well-known investment banking firm, to arrange for an initial public offering (IPO) of common stock. In June 1988, Medstone went public with an IPO and sold 1 million shares of stock at $13 per share and raised $11,700,000. Immediately after the IPO there were 4,500,000 shares of Medstone stock outstanding. Insiders owned 3,500,000 shares, and outsiders owned 1,000,000 shares.

	Price to Public	Underwriting Discount	Proceeds to Company
Per share	$13,000,000	$1,300,000	$11,700,000
Total	13,000,000	1,300,000	11,700,000

Although the stock was offered at $13 per share, by the end of the first day, it was selling for $18 (this is a 38.5 percent increase).

As is typical in IPOs, the proceeds from the sale of stock had two purposes: to reduce indebtedness to banks and to cash out insiders, and to finance present and future operations and growth opportunities.

In 1984 when Medstone was formed, it was a "start-up" with no operating history and virtually no manufacturing and marketing experience. Moreover, when Medstone did its IPO, its product had not yet received final FDA approval. The company's potential was great and so were its risks of failure. The company's ultimate success depended upon its ability to form a new business, introduce new products, and successfully compete in the marketplace. However, in the case of medical products, success depends on obtaining FDA approval. Obtaining FDA approval for a new product can be a time-consuming process, and there is no guarantee that final clearance will ever be granted. Unfortunately, Medstone was never able to obtain final FDA approval.

When the company announced that it would no longer try to sell the Medstone 1050 ST, the market for its stock collapsed and the firm was forced to reorganize. Were investors in Medstone too optimistic? If so, they were not alone. The stocks of many IPOs have performed poorly after the offering.

Every IPO is unique but there are some familiar themes.

1. *Underpricing.* Firms going through an IPO usually have their shares underpriced. This means that the initial market price is usually significantly less than their market price prevailing at the end of the first trading day. This is one of the indirect costs of IPOs, and Medstone's underpricing was typical.
2. *Underperformance.* The Medstone IPO did not work out very well for many of the outside investors because the firm ultimately could not sell its Medstone 1050 ST. The Medstone IPO is typical in that the average firm performs very poorly after an IPO. Three years after an IPO, the stock price of firms doing IPOs has typically fallen below the initial price. Interestingly, it is also true for seasoned equity issues. This is a puzzle and several reasons have been put forth to explain it.
3. *Going Public.* Many IPOs such as Medstone are to give inside equity investors an opportunity to exchange their private equity for public equity and cash out their stakes in the firm. Usually only a fraction of the inside equity is sold in the IPO. Later in subsequent common stock sales, the rest of the inside ownership is sold. ■ ■ ■ ■ ■

19.10 SUMMARY AND CONCLUSIONS

This chapter looks closely at how equity is issued. The main points follow.

1. Large issues have proportionately much lower costs of issuing equity than small ones.
2. Firm-commitment underwriting is far more prevalent for large issues than is best-efforts underwriting. Smaller issues probably primarily use best efforts because of the greater uncertainty of these issues. For an offering of a given size, the direct expenses of best-efforts underwriting and firm-commitment underwriting are of the same magnitude.
3. Rights offerings are cheaper than general cash offers and eliminate the problem of underpricing. Yet, most new equity issues are underwritten general cash offers.
4. Shelf registration is a new method of issuing new debt and equity. The direct costs of shelf issues seem to be substantially lower than those of traditional issues.
5. Venture capitalists are an increasingly important influence in start-up firms and subsequent financing.

KEY TERMS

Best efforts   538
Cash offer   537
Competitive offer   541
Ex-rights date   549
Firm commitment   538
Green Shoe provision   539
Initial public offering (IPO)   537
Investment banks   537
Negotiated offer   541
Oversubscription privilege   551
Prospectus   534
Red herring   534

Registration statement   534
Regulation A   534
Seasoned new issue   537
Shelf registration   553
Standby fee   551
Standby underwriting   551
Subscription price   548
Syndicate   538
Tombstone   535
Unseasoned new issue   537
Venture capital   554

SUGGESTED READINGS

Here are several significant recent articles that have helped shape our understanding of how capital is raised.

Altinkilic, Oya, and Robert S. Hansen. "Are There Economies of Scale in Underwriting Fees? Evidence of Rising External Financing Costs." *Review of Financial Studies* 13 (2000).

Ellis, Katrina, Roni Michaely, and Maureen O'Hara. "When the Underwriter is the Market Maker: An Examination of Trading in the IPO After Market." *Journal of Finance* (June 2000).

Chen, Hsuan-Chi, and Jay R. Ritter. "The Seven Percent Solution," *Journal of Finance* (June 2000).

Aggarwal, Reena. "Stabilization Activities by Underwriters After Initial Public Offerings." *Journal of Finance* (June 2000).

QUESTIONS AND PROBLEMS

The Public Issue

19.1 Define the following terms related to the issuance of public securities.
   a. General cash offer
   b. Rights offer

     c. Registration statement

     d. Prospectus

     e. Initial public offering

     f. Seasoned new issue

     g. Shelf registration

19.2 *a.* What does the Securities Exchange Act of 1933 regulate?

     b. What does the Securities Exchange Act of 1934 regulate?

The Cash Offer

19.3 What are the comparative advantages of a competitive offer and a negotiated offer, respectively?

19.4 Define the following terms related to underwriting.

     a. Firm commitment

     b. Syndicate

     c. Spread

     d. Best efforts

19.5 *a.* Who bears the risk in firm-commitment underwriting? Explain.

     b. Who bears the risk in best-efforts underwriting? Explain.

19.6 Suppose the Newton Company has 10,000 shares of stock. Each share is worth $40, and the company's market value of equity is $400,000. Suppose the firm issues 5,000 shares of the new stock at the following prices: $40, $20, and $10. What will be the effect of each of the alternative offering prices on the existing price per share?

19.7 In 1980 a certain assistant professor of finance bought 12 initial public offerings of common stock. He held each of these for approximately one month and then sold them. The investment rule he followed was to submit a purchase order for every firm-commitment initial public offering of oil- and gas-exploration companies. There were 22 such offerings, and he submitted a purchase order for approximately $1,000 of stock for each one. With 10 of these, no shares were allocated to this assistant professor. With five of the 12 offerings that were purchased, fewer than the requested number of shares were allocated.

     The year 1980 was very good for oil- and gas-exploration company owners. For the 22 stocks that went public, the stock was selling on average for 80 percent above the offering price within a month. Yet, this assistant professor looked at his performance record and found the $8,400 invested in 12 companies had grown to only $10,100, a return of only about 20 percent. (Commissions were negligible.) Did he have bad luck, or should he have expected to do worse than the average initial-public-offering investor? Explain.

The Announcement of New Equity and the Value of the Firm

19.8 What are the possible reasons for why the stock price typically drops on the announcement of a seasoned new equity issue?

The Cost of New Issues

19.9 What are the costs of new issues?

Rights

19.10 Bountiful Beef Processors (BBP) wants to raise equity through a rights offering. BBP has 2,400,000 shares of common stock outstanding, and must raise $12,000,000. The subscription price of the rights will be $15.

     a. How many new shares of stock must BBP issue?

     b. How many rights will be necessary to purchase one share of stock?

     c. What must a shareholder remit to receive one share of stock?

19.11 Jelly Beans, Inc., is proposing a rights offering. There are 100,000 outstanding shares at $25 each. There will be 10,000 new shares issued at a $20 subscription price.

     a. What is the value of a right?

     b. What is the ex-rights price?

     c. What is the new market value of the company?

     d. Why might a company have a rights offering rather than a common stock offering?

19.12 Superior, Inc., is a manufacturer of beta-blockers. Management has concluded that additional equity financing is required to increase production capacity, and that these funds are best attained through a rights offering. It has correctly concluded that, as a result of the rights offering, share price will fall from $50 to $45 ($50 is the rights-on price; $45 is the ex-rights price, also known as the *when-issued* price). The company is seeking $5 million in additional funds with a per-share subscription price equal to $25.

  a. How many shares were there before the offering?

19.13 A company's stock currently sells for $45 per share. Last week the firm issued rights to raise new equity. To purchase a new share, a stockholder must remit $10 and three rights.

  a. What is the ex-rights stock price?
  b. What is the price of one right?
  c. When will the price drop occur? Why will it occur then?

19.14 Summit Corp.'s stock is currently selling at $13 per share. There are 1 million shares outstanding. The firm is planning to raise $2 million to finance a new project. What is the ex-right stock price, the value of a right, and the appropriate subscription prices, if

  a. Two shares of outstanding stock are entitled to purchase one additional share of the new issue.
  b. Four shares of outstanding stock are entitled to purchase one additional share of the new issue.
  c. How does the stockholders' wealth change from *a* to *b?*

The New Issue Puzzle

19.15 Megabucks Industries is planning to raise fresh equity capital by selling a large new issue of common stock. Megabucks is a publicly traded corporation, and is trying to choose between an underwritten cash offer and a rights offering (not underwritten) to current shareholders. Megabucks' management is interested in maximizing the wealth of current shareholders and has asked you for advice on the choice of issue methods. What is your recommendation? Why?

Shelf Registration

19.16 Explain why shelf registration has been used by many firms instead of syndication.

Venture Capital

19.17 Who are the different suppliers of venture capital?

The Decision to Do an Initial Public Offering (IPO): The Case of Medstone International, Inc.

19.18 What are the uses for the proceeds from an IPO?

19.19 Every IPO is unique, but what are the basic empirical regularities in IPOs?

CHAPTER 20

Long-Term Debt

EXECUTIVE SUMMARY

The previous chapter introduced the mechanics of new long-term financing, with an emphasis on equity. This chapter takes a closer look at long-term debt instruments.

The chapter begins with a review of the basic features of long-term debt, and a description of some important aspects of publicly issued long-term bonds. We also discuss forms of long-term financing that are not publicly issued: term loans and private-placement bonds. These are directly placed with lending institutions, such as a commercial bank or a life insurance company.

All bond agreements have protective covenants. These are restrictions on the firm that protect the bondholder. We present several types of protective covenants in this chapter.

A large number of publicly issued industrial bonds have call provisions, which enable a company to buy back its bonds at a predetermined call price. This chapter attempts to answer two questions about call provisions.

1. Should firms issue callable bonds?
2. When should such bonds be called?

There are many different kinds of long-term bonds. We discuss three—floating-rate bonds, income bonds, and deep-discount bonds—and analyze what types of bonds are best in different circumstances.

20.1 LONG-TERM DEBT: A REVIEW

Long-term debt securities are promises by the issuing firm to pay interest and principal on the unpaid balance. The *maturity* of a long-term debt instrument refers to the length of time the debt remains outstanding with some unpaid balance. Debt securities can be *short-term* (maturities of one year or less) or *long-term* (maturities of more than one year).[1] Short-term debt is sometimes referred to as *unfunded debt* and long-term debt as *funded debt.*[2]

The two major forms of long-term debt are public issue and privately placed debt. We discuss public-issue bonds first, and most of what we say about them holds true for privately placed long-term debt as well. The main difference between publicly issued and privately placed debt is that private debt is directly placed with a lending institution.

There are many other attributes to long-term debt, including security, call features, sinking funds, ratings, and protective covenants. The boxed material illustrates these attributes.

---

[1]In addition, people often refer to intermediate-term debt, which has a maturity of more than one year and less than three to five years.

[2]The word *funding* generally implies long-term. Thus, a firm planning to *fund* its debt requirements may be replacing short-term debt with long-term debt.

FEATURES OF A HYPOTHETICAL BOND

	Terms	Explanations
Amount of issue	$100 million	The company issued $100 million of bonds.
Date of issue	10/21/95	The bonds were sold on 10/21/95.
Maturity	12/31/24	The principal will be paid in 30 years.
Denomination	$1,000	Each individual bond will pay $1,000 at maturity.
Annual coupon	10.50	Because the denomination of each bond is $1,000, each bondholder will receive $105 per bond per year.
Offer price	100	The offer price was 100 percent of the denomination, or $1,000 per bond.
Yield to maturity	10.50%	If the bond is held to maturity, bondholders will receive a stated annual rate of return equal to 10.5 percent.
Dates of coupon payments	12/31, 6/30	Coupons of $52.50 will be paid on these dates.
Security	None	The bonds are debentures.
Sinking funds	Annual; begins in 2005	The sinking funds will be sufficient to pay 80 percent of principal, the balance to be paid at maturity.
Call provision	Not callable before 12/31/05. Call price: $1,100	The bonds have a deferred call feature. After 12/31/05 the company can buy back the bonds for $1,100 per bond.
Rating	Moody's Aaa	This is Moody's highest rating. The bonds have the lowest probability of default.

20.2 THE PUBLIC ISSUE OF BONDS

The general procedures followed for a **public issue** of bonds are the same as those for stocks, as described in the previous chapter. First, the offering must be approved by the board of directors. Sometimes a vote of stockholders is also required. Second, a registration statement is prepared for review by the Securities and Exchange Commission. Third, if accepted, the registration statement becomes *effective* 20 days later, and the securities are sold.

However, the registration statement for a public issue of bonds must include an indenture, a document not relevant for the issue of common stock. An **indenture** is a written agreement between the corporation (the borrower) and a trust company. It is sometimes referred to as the *deed of trust*.[3] The trust company is appointed by the corporation to represent the bondholders. The trust company must (1) be sure the terms of the indenture are obeyed, (2) manage the sinking fund, and (3) represent bondholders if the company defaults on its payments.

The typical bond indenture can be a document of several hundred pages, and it generally includes the following provisions:

1. The basic terms of the bonds.
2. A description of property used as security.

---

[3]The terms *loan agreement* or *loan contract* are usually used for privately placed debt and term loans.

3. Details of the protective covenants.
4. The sinking-fund arrangements.
5. The call provision.

Each of these is discussed next.

The Basic Terms

Bonds usually have a *face value* of $1,000. This is also called the *principal value* or the *denomination* and it is stated on the bond certificate. In addition, the *par value* (i.e., initial accounting value) of a bond is almost always the same as the face value.

Transactions between bond buyers and bond sellers determine the market value of the bond. Actual bond-market values depend on the general level of interest rates, among other factors, and need not equal the face value. The bond price is quoted as a percentage of the denomination. Though interest is paid only twice a year, interest *accrues* continually over the year, and the quoted prices of a bond usually include accrued interest. This is illustrated in the example below.

EXAMPLE

Suppose the Black Corporation has issued 100 bonds. The amount stated on each bond certificate is $1,000. The total face value or principal value of the bonds is $100,000. Further suppose the bonds are currently *priced* at 100, which means 100 percent of $1,000. This means that buyers and sellers are holding bonds at a price per bond of $1,000. If interest rates rise, the price of the bond might fall to, say, 97, which means 97 percent of $1,000, or $970.

Suppose the bonds have a stated interest rate of 12 percent due on January 1, 2050. The bond indenture might read as follows:

> The bond will mature on January 1, 2050, and will be limited in aggregate principal amount to $100,000. Each bond will bear interest at the rate of 12.0% per annum from January 1, 1990, or from the most recent Interest Payment Date to which interest has been paid or provided for. Interest is payable semiannually on July 1 and January 1 of each year.

Suppose an investor buys the bonds on April 1. Since the last interest payment, on January 1, three months of interest at 12 percent per year would have accrued. Because interest of 12 percent a year works out to 1 percent per month, interest over the three months is 3 percent. Therefore, the buyer of the bond must pay a price of 100 percent plus the 3 percent of accrued interest ($30). On July 1 the buyer will receive an interest payment of $60. This can be viewed as the sum of the $30 he or she paid the seller plus the three months of interest, $30, for holding the bond from April 1 to July 1.

As is typical of industrial bonds, the Black bonds are registered. The indenture might read as follows:

> Interest is payable semiannually on July 1 and January 1 of each year to the person in whose name the bond is registered at the close of business on June 15 or December 15, respectively.

This means that the company has a registrar who will record the ownership of each bond. The company will pay the interest and principal by check mailed directly to the address of the owner of record.

When a bond is registered with attached coupons, the bondholder must separate a coupon from the bond certificate and send it to the company registrar (paying agent). Some bonds are in **bearer** form. This means that ownership is not recorded in the company books. As with a registered bond with attached coupons, the holder of the bond certificate separates the coupon and sends it in to the company to receive payment.

There are two drawbacks to bearer bonds. First, they can be easily lost or stolen. Second, because the company does not know who owns its bonds, it cannot notify bondholders of important events. Consider, for example, Mr. and Mrs. Smith, who go to their safe-deposit box and clip the coupon on their 12-percent, $1,000 bond issued by the Black Corporation. They send the coupon to the paying agent and feel richer. A few days later, a notice comes from the paying agent that the bond was retired and its principal paid off one year earlier. In other words, the bond no longer exists. Mr. and Mrs. Smith must forfeit one year of interest. (Of course, they can turn their bond in for $1,000.)

However, bearer bonds have the advantage of secrecy because even the issuing company does not know who the bond's owners are. This secrecy is particularly vexing to taxing authorities because tax collection on interest is difficult if the holder is unknown.

Security

Debt securities are also classified according to the *collateral* protecting the bondholder. Collateral is a general term for the assets that are pledged as a security for payment of debt. For example, *collateral trust bonds* involve a pledge of common stock held by the corporation.

EXAMPLE

Suppose Railroad Holding Company owns all of the common stock of Track, Inc.; that is, Track, Inc., is a wholly owned subsidiary of the Railroad Holding Company. Railroad issues debt securities that pledge the common stock of Track, Inc., as collateral. The debts are collateral trust bonds; U.S. Sur Bank will hold them. If Railroad Holding Company defaults on the debt, U.S. Sur Bank will be able to sell the stock of Track, Inc., to satisfy Railroad's obligation.

Mortgage securities are secured by a mortgage on real estate or other long-term assets of the borrower.[4] The legal document that describes that mortgage is called a *mortgage-trust indenture* or *trust deed.* The mortgage can be *closed-end,* so that there is a limit as to the amount of bonds that can be issued. More frequently it is *open-end,* without limit to the amount of bonds that may be issued.

EXAMPLE

Suppose the Miami Bond Company has buildings and land worth $10 million and a $4 million mortgage on these properties. If the mortgage is closed-end, the Miami Bond Company cannot issue more bonds on this property.

If the bond indenture contains no clause limiting the amount of additional bonds that can be issued, it is an open-end mortgage. In this case the Miami Bond Company can issue additional bonds on its property, making the existing bonds riskier. For example, if additional mortgage bonds of $2 million are issued, the

---

[4]A set of railroad cars is an example of "other long-term assets" used as security.

property has been pledged for a total of $6 million of bonds. If Miami Bond Company must liquidate its property for $4 million, the original bondholders will receive ⅔, or 67 percent, of their investment. If the mortgage had been closed-end, they would have received 100 percent of the stated value.

The value of a mortgage depends on the market value of the underlying property. Because of this, mortgage bonds sometimes require that the property be properly maintained and insured. Of course, a building and equipment bought in 1914 for manufacturing slide rules might not have much value no matter how well the company maintains it. The value of any property ultimately depends on its next best economic use. Bond indentures cannot easily insure against losses in economic value.

Sometimes mortgages are on specific property, for example, a single building. More often, blanket mortgages are used. A blanket mortgage pledges many assets owned by the company.

Some bonds represent unsecured obligations of the company. A **debenture** is an unsecured bond, where no specific pledge of property is made. Debenture holders have a claim on property not otherwise pledged: the property that remains after mortgages and collateral trusts are taken into account. At the current time, almost all public bonds issued by industrial and finance companies are debentures. However, most utility and railroad bonds are secured by a pledge of assets.

Protective Covenants

A **protective covenant** is that part of the indenture or loan agreement that limits certain actions of the borrowing company. Protective covenants can be classified into two types: negative covenants and positive covenants. A **negative covenant** limits or prohibits actions that the company may take. Here are some typical examples:

1. Limitations are placed on the amount of dividends a company may pay.
2. The firm cannot pledge any of its assets to other lenders.
3. The firm cannot merge with another firm.
4. The firm may not sell or lease its major assets without approval by the lender.
5. The firm cannot issue additional long-term debt.

A **positive covenant** specifies an action that the company agrees to take or a condition the company must abide by. Here are some examples:

1. The company agrees to maintain its working capital at a minimum level.
2. The company must furnish periodic financial statements to the lender.

The financial implications of protective covenants were treated in detail in the chapters on capital structure. In that discussion, we argued that protective covenants can benefit stockholders because, if bondholders are assured that they will be protected in times of financial stress, they will accept a lower interest rate.

The Sinking Fund

Bonds can be entirely repaid at maturity, at which time the bondholder will receive the stated value of the bond, or they can be repaid before maturity. Early repayment is more typical.

In a direct placement of debt the repayment schedule is specified in the loan contract. For public issues, the repayment takes place through the use of a sinking fund and a call provision.

A *sinking fund* is an account managed by the bond trustee for the purpose of repaying the bonds. Typically, the company makes yearly payments to the trustee. The trustee can purchase bonds in the market or can select bonds randomly using a lottery and purchase them, generally at face value. There are many different kinds of sinking-fund arrangements:

- Most sinking funds start between 5 and 10 years after the initial issuance.
- Some sinking funds establish equal payments over the life of the bond.
- Most high-quality bond issues establish payments to the sinking fund that are not sufficient to redeem the entire issue. As a consequence, there is the possibility of a large *balloon* payment at maturity.

Sinking funds have two opposing effects on bondholders:

1. *Sinking Funds Provide Extra Protection to Bondholders.* A firm experiencing financial difficulties would have trouble making sinking-fund payments. Thus, sinking-fund payments provide an early warning system to bondholders.

2. *Sinking Funds Give the Firm an Attractive Option.* If bond prices fall below the face value, the firm will satisfy the sinking fund by buying bonds at the lower market prices. If bond prices rise above the face value, the firm will buy the bonds back at the lower face value.

The Call Provision

A *call provision* lets the company repurchase or *call* the entire bond issue at a predetermined price over a specified period.

Generally, the call price is above the bond's face value of $1,000. The difference between the call price and the face value is the **call premium.** For example, if the call price is 105, that is, 105 percent of $1,000, the call premium is 50. The amount of the call premium usually becomes smaller over time. One typical arrangement is to set the call premium initially equal to the annual coupon payment and then make it decline to zero over the life of the bond.

Call provisions are not usually operative during the first few years of a bond's life. For example, a company may be prohibited from calling its bonds for the first 10 years. This is referred to as a **deferred call.** During this period the bond is said to be **call-protected.**

CONCEPT QUESTIONS ?

- Do bearer bonds have any advantage? Why might Mr. "I Like to Keep My Affairs Private" prefer to hold bearer bonds?
- What advantages and what disadvantages do bondholders derive from provisions of sinking funds?
- What is a call provision? What is the difference between the call price and the stated price?

20.3 Bond Refunding

Replacing all or part of an issue of outstanding bonds is called bond **refunding.** Usually, the first step in a typical bond refunding is to call the entire issue of bonds at the call price. Bond refunding raises two questions:

1. Should firms issue callable bonds?
2. Given that callable bonds have been issued, when should the bonds be called?

We attempt to answer these questions in this section.

Should Firms Issue Callable Bonds?

Common sense tells us that call provisions have value. First, many publicly issued bonds have call provisions. Second, it is obvious that a call works to the advantage of the issuer. If interest rates fall and bond prices go up, the option to buy back the bonds at the call price is valuable. In bond refunding, firms will typically replace the called bonds with a new bond issue. The new bonds will have a lower coupon rate than the called bonds.

However, bondholders will take the call provision into account when they buy the bond. For this reason, we can expect that bondholders will demand higher interest rates on callable bonds than on noncallable bonds. In fact, financial economists view call provisions as being zero-sum in efficient capital markets.[5] Any expected gains to the issuer from being allowed to refund the bond at lower rates will be offset by higher initial interest rates. We illustrate the zero-sum aspect to callable bonds in the following example.

EXAMPLE

Suppose Kraus Intercable Company intends to issue perpetual bonds of $1,000 face value at a 10-percent interest rate.[6] Annual coupons have been set at $100. There is an equal chance that by the end of the year interest rates will do one of the following:

1. Fall to 6 2/3 percent. If so, the bond price will increase to $1,500.
2. Increase to 20 percent. If so, the bond price will fall to $500.

Noncallable Bond   Suppose the market price of the noncallable bond is the expected price it will have next year plus the coupon, all discounted at the current 10-percent interest rate.[7] The value of the noncallable bond is

Value of Noncallable Bond:

$$\frac{\text{First-year coupon} + \text{Expected price at end of year}}{1 + r}$$
$$= \frac{\$100 + (0.5 \times \$1,500) + (0.5 \times \$500)}{1.10}$$
$$= \$1,000$$

Callable Bond   Now suppose the Kraus Intercable Company decides to issue callable bonds. The call premium is set at $100 over par value and the bonds can be called *only* at the end of the first year.[8] In this case, the call provision will allow the company to buy back its bonds at $1,100 ($1,000 par value plus the $100 call premium). Should interest rates fall, the company will buy a bond for $1,100 that would be worth $1,500 in the absence of a call provision. Of course, if interest rates rise, Kraus would not want to call the bonds for $1,100 because they are worth only $500 on the market.

---

[5]See A. Kraus, "An Analysis of Call Provisions and the Corporate Refunding Decision," *Midland Corporate Finance Journal* 1 (Spring 1983), p. 1.

[6]Recall that perpetual bonds have no maturity date.

[7]We are assuming that the current price of the noncallable bonds is the expected value discounted at the risk-free rate of 10 percent. This is equivalent to assuming that the risk is unsystematic and carries no risk premium.

[8]Normally, bonds can be called over a period of many years. Our assumption that the bond can only be called at the end of the first year was introduced for simplicity.

Suppose rates fall and Kraus calls the bonds by paying $1,100. If the firm simultaneously issues new bonds with a coupon of $100, it will bring in $1,500 ($100/0.0667) at the 6 2/3-percent interest rate. This will allow Kraus to pay an extra dividend to shareholders of $400 ($1,500 − $1,100). In other words, if rates fall from 10 percent to 6 2/3 percent, exercise of the call will transfer $400 of potential bondholder gains to the shareholders.

When investors purchase callable bonds, they realize that they will forfeit their anticipated gains to shareholders if the bonds are called. As a consequence, they will not pay $1,000 for a callable bond with a coupon of $100.

How high must the coupon on the callable bond be so that it can be issued at the par value of $1,000? We can answer this in three steps.

Step 1: Determining End-of-Year Value if Interest Rates Drop   If the interest rate drops to 6 2/3 percent by the end of the year, the bond will be called for $1,100. The bondholder will receive both this and the annual coupon payment. If we let C represent the coupon on the callable bond, the bondholder gets the following at the end of the year:

$$\$1,100 + C$$

Step 2: Determining End-of-Year Value if Interest Rates Rise   If interest rates rise to 20 percent, the value of the bondholder's position at the end of the year is:

$$\frac{C}{0.20} + C$$

That is, the perpetuity formula tells us that the bond will sell at $C/0.20$. In addition, the bondholder receives the coupon payment at the end of the year.

Step 3: Solving for C   Because interest rates are equally likely to rise or to fall, the expected value of the bondholder's end-of-year position is

$$(\$1,100 + C) \times 0.5 + \left(\frac{C}{0.20} + C\right) \times 0.5$$

Using the current interest rate of 10 percent, we set the present value of these payments equal to par:

$$\$1,000 = \frac{(\$1,100 + C) \times 0.5 + \left(\dfrac{C}{0.20} + C\right) \times 0.5}{1.10}$$

C is the unknown in the equation. The equation holds if $C = \$157.14$. In other words, callable bonds can sell at par only if their coupon rate is 15.714 percent.

The Paradox Restated   If Kraus issues a noncallable bond, it will only need to pay a 10-percent interest rate. By contrast, Kraus must pay an interest rate of 15.7 percent on a callable bond. The interest-rate differential makes an investor indifferent whether she buys one of the two bonds in our example or the other. Because the return to the investor is the same with either bond, the cost of debt capital is the same to Kraus with either bond. Thus, our example suggests that there is neither an advantage nor a disadvantage from issuing callable bonds.

Why, therefore, are callable bonds issued in the real world? This question has vexed financial economists for a long time. We now consider four specific reasons why a company might use a call provision:

1. Superior interest-rate predictions.
2. Taxes.

3. Financial flexibility for future investment opportunities.

4. Less interest-rate risk.

Superior Interest-Rate Forecasting   Company insiders may know more about interest-rate changes on its bonds than does the investing public. For example, managers may be better informed about potential changes in the firm's credit rating. Thus, a company may prefer the call provision at a particular time because it believes that the expected fall in interest rates (the probability of a fall multiplied by the amount of the fall) is greater than the bondholders believe.

Although this is possible, there is reason to doubt that inside information is the rationale for call provisions. Suppose firms really had superior ability to predict changes that would affect them. Bondholders would infer that a company expected an improvement in its credit rating whenever it issued callable bonds. Bondholders would require an increase in the coupon rate to protect them against a call if this occurred. As a result, we would expect that there would be no financial advantage to the firm from callable bonds over non-callable bonds.

Of course, there are many non–company-specific reasons why interest rates can fall. For example, the interest-rate level is connected to the anticipated inflation rate. But it is difficult to see how companies could have more information about the general level of interest rates than other participants in the bond markets.

Taxes   Call provisions may have tax advantages if the bondholder is taxed at a lower rate than the company. We have seen that callable bonds have higher coupon rates than noncallable bonds. Because the coupons provide a deductible interest expense to the corporation and are taxable income to the bondholder, the corporation will gain more than a bondholder in a low tax bracket will lose. Presumably, some of the tax saving can be passed on to the bondholders in the form of a high coupon.

Future Investment Opportunities   As we have explained, bond indentures contain protective covenants that restrict a company's investment opportunities. For example, protective covenants may limit the company's ability to acquire another firm or to sell certain assets (for example, a division of the company). If the covenants are sufficiently restrictive, the cost to the shareholders in lost net present value can be large. However, if bonds are callable, the company can buy back the bonds at the call price and take advantage of a superior investment opportunity.[9]

Less Interest-Rate Risk   The call provision will reduce the sensitivity of a bond's value to changes in the level of interest rates. As interest rates increase, the value of a noncallable bond will fall. Because the callable bond has a higher coupon rate, the value of a callable bond will fall less than the value of a noncallable bond. Kraus has argued that, by reducing the sensitivity of a bond's value to changes in interest rates, the call provision may reduce the risk of shareholders as well as bondholders.[10] He argues that, because the bond is a liability of the corporation, the equityholders bear risk as the bond changes value over time. Thus, it can be shown that, under certain conditions, reducing the risk of bonds through a call provision will also reduce the risk of equity.

---

[9]This argument is from Z. Bodie and R. A. Taggart, "Future Investment Opportunities and the Value of the Call Provision on a Bond," *Journal of Finance* 33 (1978), p. 4.

[10]A. Kraus, "An Analysis of Call Provisions and the Corporate Refunding Decision," *Midland Corporate Finance Journal* 1 (Spring 1983). Kraus points out that the call provision will not always reduce the equity's interest-rate risk. If the firm as a whole bears interest-rate risk, more of this risk may be shifted from equityholders to bondholders with noncallable debt. In this case, equityholders may actually bear more risk with callable debt.

Calling Bonds: When Does It Make Sense?

The value of the company is the value of the stock plus the value of the bonds. From the Modigliani-Miller theory and the pie model in earlier chapters, we know that firm value is unchanged by how it is divided between these two instruments. Therefore, maximizing shareholder wealth means minimizing the value of the callable bond. In a world with no transaction costs, it can be shown that the company should call its bonds whenever the callable-bond value exceeds the call price. This policy minimizes the value of the callable bonds.

The preceding analysis is modified slightly by including the costs from issuing new bonds. These extra costs change the refunding rule to allow bonds to trade at prices above the call price. The objective of the company is to minimize the sum of the value of the callable bonds plus new issue costs. It has been observed that many real-world firms do not call their bonds when the market value of the bonds reaches the call price. Instead, they wait until the market value of the bonds exceeds the call price. Perhaps these issue costs are an explanation. Also, when a bond is called, the holder has about 30 days to surrender the bond and receive the call price in cash. In 30 days the market value of the bonds could fall below the call price. If so, the firm is giving away money. To forestall this possibility, it can be argued that firms should wait until the market value of the bond exceeds the call price before calling bonds.

CONCEPT QUESTIONS

- What are the advantages to a firm of having a call provision?
- What are the disadvantages to bondholders of having a call provision?

20.4 BOND RATINGS

Firms frequently pay to have their debt rated. The two leading bond-rating firms are Moody's Investors Service and Standard & Poor's. The debt ratings depend upon (1) the likelihood that the firm will default and (2) the protection afforded by the loan contract in the event of default. The ratings are constructed from information supplied by the corporation, primarily the financial statements of the firm. The rating classes are shown in the accompanying box.

The highest rating debt can have is AAA or Aaa. Debt rated AAA or Aaa is judged to be the best quality and to have the lowest degree of risk. The lowest rating is D, which indicates that the firm is in default. Since the 1980s, a growing part of corporate borrowing has taken the form of *low-grade bonds*. These bonds are also known as either *high-yield bonds* or *junk bonds.* Low-grade bonds are corporate bonds that are rated below *investment grade* by the major rating agencies (that is, below BBB for Standard & Poor's or Baa for Moody's).

Bond ratings are important, because bonds with lower ratings tend to have higher interest costs. However, the most recent evidence is that bond ratings merely reflect bond risk. There is no conclusive evidence that bond ratings affect risk.[11] It is not surprising that the stock prices and bond prices of firms do not show any unusual behavior on the days around a rating change. Because the ratings are based on publicly available information, they probably do not, in themselves, supply new information to the market.[12]

---

[11]M. Weinstein, "The Systematic Risk of Corporate Bonds," *Journal of Financial and Quantitative Analysis* (September 1981); J. P. Ogden, "Determinants of Relative Interest Rate Sensitivity of Corporate Bonds," *Financial Management* (Spring 1987); and F. Reilly and M. Joehnk, "The Association between Market-Based Risk Measures for Bonds and Bond Ratings," *Journal of Finance* (December 1976).

[12]M. Weinstein, "The Effect of a Ratings Change Announcement on Bond Price," *Journal of Financial Economics* 5 (1977). However, Robert W. Holthausen and Richard W. Leftwich, "The Effect of Bond Rating Changes on Common Stock Prices," *Journal of Financial Economics* 17 (September 1986), find that bond rating downgrades are associated with abnormal negative returns of the stock of the issuing firm.

BOND RATINGS

	Very High Quality	High Quality	Specu-lative	Very Poor
Standard & Poor's	AAA AA	A BBB	BB B	CCC CC C D
Moody's	Aaa Aa	A Baa	Ba B	Caa Ca C D

At times both Moody's and Standard & Poor's adjust these ratings. S&P uses plus and minus signs: A+ is the strongest A rating and A− the weakest. Moody's uses a 1, 2, or 3 designation, with 1 indicating the strongest.

Moody's	S&P	
Aaa	AAA	Debt rated Aaa and AAA has the highest rating. Capacity to pay interest and principal is extremely strong.
Aa	AA	Debt rated Aa and AA has a very strong capacity to pay interest and repay principal. Together with the highest rating, this group comprises the high-grade bond class.
A	A	Debt rated A has a strong capacity to pay interest and repay principal. However, it is somewhat more susceptible to adverse changes in circumstances and economic conditions.
Baa	BBB	Debt rated Baa and BBB is regarded as having an adequate capacity to pay interest and repay principal. Whereas it normally exhibits adequate protection parameters, adverse economic conditions or changing circumstances are more likely to lead to a weakened capacity to pay interest and repay principal for debt in this category than in higher-rated categories. These bonds are medium grade obligations.
Ba	BB	Debt rated in these categories is regarded, on balance, as
B	B	predominantly speculative. Ba and BB indicate the lowest degree of
Caa	CCC	speculation, and Ca and CC the highest. Although such debt is likely
Ca	CC	to have some quality and protective characteristics, these are outweighed by large uncertainties or major risk exposure to adverse conditions.
C	C	This rating is reserved for income bonds on which no interest is being paid.
D	D	Debt rated D is in default, and payment of interest and/or repayment of principal is in arrears.

Data from various editions of *Standard & Poor's Bond Guide* and *Moody's Bond Guide*.

Junk Bonds

The investment community has labeled bonds with a Standard & Poor's rating of BB and below or a Moody's rating of Ba and below as **junk bonds.** These bonds are also called *high-yield* or *low-grade* and we shall use all three terms interchangeably. Issuance of junk bonds has grown greatly in recent years, leading to increased public interest in this form of financing.

Table 20.1 presents data on junk-bond financing in the recent past. Column (1) shows the great growth in junk-bond issuance over a 27-year period. Column (3) shows the default rate on junk bonds increased from 1.24 percent in 1971 to 10.27 percent in 1991. In 1999 the default rate was 4.1 percent. Table 20.2 presents data on default rates by Standard & Poor's on cumulative bases for 10 years. It shows that junk bonds can have a 10-year cumulative (if rated CCC) rate of 48.4 percent.

■ TABLE 20.1 **Junk bonds: 1971–1999**

Year	Par Value Outstanding (a)	Par Value Defaults	Default Rates
1999	$567,400	$23,532	4.147%
1998	$465,500	$ 7,464	1.603%
1997	$335,400	$ 4,200	1.252%
1996	$271,000	$ 3,336	1.231%
1995	$240,000	$ 4,551	1.896%
1994	$235,000	$ 3,418	1.454%
1993	$206,907	$ 2,287	1.105%
1992	$163,000	$ 5,545	3.402%
1991	$183,600	$18,862	10.273%
1990	$181,000	$18,354	10.140%
1989	$189,258	$ 8,110	4.285%
1988	$148,187	$ 3,944	2.662%
1987	$129,557	$ 7,486	5.778%
1986	$ 90,243	$ 3,156	3.497%
1985	$ 58,088	$ 992	1.708%
1984	$ 40,939	$ 344	0.840%
1983	$ 27,492	$ 301	1.095%
1982	$ 18,109	$ 577	3.186%
1981	$ 17,115	$ 27	0.158%
1980	$ 14,935	$ 224	1.500%
1979	$ 10,356	$ 20	0.193%
1978	$ 8,946	$ 119	1.330%
1977	$ 8,157	$ 381	4.671%
1976	$ 7,735	$ 30	0.388%
1975	$ 7,471	$ 204	2.731%
1974	$ 10,894	$ 123	1.129%
1973	$ 7,824	$ 49	0.626%
1972	$ 6,928	$ 193	2.786%
1971	$ 6,602	$ 82	1.242%

Source: Edward I. Altman's compilation and Salomon Smith Barney estimates.

In our opinion, the growth in junk-bond financing in the 1970s and 1980s can better be explained by the activities of one man than by a number of economic factors. While a graduate student at the Wharton School in the 1970s, Michael Milken observed a large difference between the return on high-yield bonds and the return on safer bonds. Believing that this difference was greater than what the extra default risk would justify, he concluded that institutional investors would benefit from purchases of junk bonds.

His later employment at Drexel Burnham Lambert allowed him to develop the junk-bond market. Milken's salesmanship simultaneously increased the demand for junk bonds among institutional investors and the supply of junk bonds among corporations. Corporations were particularly impressed with Drexel's vast network of institutional clients, allowing capital to be raised quickly. However, with the demise of the junk-bond market and with Michael Milken's conviction of securities fraud, Drexel found it necessary to declare bankruptcy.

The junk-bond market took on increased importance when these bonds were used to finance mergers and other corporate restructurings. Whereas a firm can only issue a small amount of high-grade debt, the same firm can issue much more debt if low-grade financing is allowed as well. Therefore, the use of junk bonds lets acquirers effect takeovers that they

Edward I. Altman on Junk Bonds

One of the most important developments in corporate finance over the last 20 years has been the reemergence of publicly owned and traded low-rated corporate debt. Originally offered to the public in the early 1900s to help finance some of our emerging growth industries, these high-yield/high-risk bonds virtually disappeared after the rash of bond defaults during the Depression. Recently, however, the junk-bond market has been catapulted from an insignificant element in the corporate fixed income market to one of the fastest growing and most controversial types of financing mechanisms.

The term *junk* emanates from the dominant type of low-rated bond issues outstanding prior to 1977 when the "market" consisted almost exclusively of original-issue investment-grade bonds that fell from their lofty status to a higher default risk, speculative-grade level. These so-called "fallen angels" amounted to about $8.5 billion in 1977. At the beginning of 1998, fallen angels comprised about 10 percent of the $450 billion publicly owned junk-bond market.

Beginning in 1977, issuers began to go directly to the public to raise capital for growth purposes. Early users of junk bonds were energy-related firms, cable TV companies, airlines, and assorted other industrial companies. The emerging growth company rationale, coupled with relatively high returns to early investors, helped legitimize this sector. Most investment banks ignored junk bonds until 1983–1984, when their merits and profit potential became more evident.

Synonymous with the market's growth was the emergence of the investment banking firm Drexel Burnham Lambert, and its junk-bond wizard, Michael Milken. Drexel established a potent network of issuers and investors and rode the wave of new financing and the consequent surge in secondary trading to become one of the powerful investment banks in the late 1980s. The incredible rise in power of this firm was followed by an equally incredible fall, resulting first in government civil and criminal convictions and huge fines for various misdealings and, finally, the firm's total collapse and bankruptcy in February 1990.

By far the most controversial aspect of junk-bond financing was its role in the corporate restructuring movement from 1985–1989. High-leverage transactions, such as leveraged buyouts (LBOs), which occur when a firm is taken private, transformed the face of corporate America, leading to a heated debate as to the economic and social consequences of corporate control changes with debt/equity ratios of at least 6:1.

These transactions involved increasingly large companies, and the multibillion dollar takeover became fairly common, capped by the huge $25 billion RJR Nabisco LBO in 1989. LBOs were typically financed with 60-percent senior bank and insurance company debt, about 25–30-percent subordinated public debt (junk bonds), and 10–15-percent equity. The junk-bond segment is sometimes referred to as "mezzanine" financing because it lies between the "balcony" senior debt and the "basement" equity.

These restructurings resulted in large fees to advisors and underwriters and huge premiums to the old shareholders, and they continued as long as the market was willing to buy these new debt offerings at what appeared to be a favorable risk/return trade-off. The bottom fell out of the market in the last six months of 1989 due to a number of factors including a marked increase in defaults, government regulation against S&Ls holding junk bonds, higher interest rates, a recession, and, finally, the growing realization of the leverage excesses of certain ill-conceived restructurings.

The default rate rose dramatically to over 4 percent in 1989 and then skyrocketed in 1990 and 1991 to over 10 percent each year, with about $19 billion of defaults in 1991. Throughout 1990, the pendulum of growth in the new junk-bond issues and returns to investors swung dramatically downward as prices plummeted and the new issue market all but dried up. The following year (1991) was a pivotal period in that despite record defaults, bond prices and new issues rebounded strongly as the prospects for the future brightened.

In the early 1990s, the financial market was questioning the very survival of the junk-bond market. The answer was a resounding "Yes," as the amount of new issuance soared to record annual levels of $38 billion in 1992 and has steadily grown to an incredible $120 billion in 1997! Coupled with plummeting annual default rates (under 2.0 percent from 1993–1997 compared to 3.5 percent for 1971–1997) and returns in these years between 10–20 percent, the risk-return characteristics have been extremely favorable. Newer dimensions of the junk-bond market include the pooling of large numbers of bonds into collateralized bond obligations (CBOs), the establishment of emerging market international issuance, and the now common use of the nonregistered 144A new issuance mechanism. The junk-bond market in the late 1990s is a quieter one compared to the 1980s, but, in terms of growth and returns, it is healthier than ever before.

Dr. Edward I. Altman is Max L. Heine Professor of Finance and Vice Director of the Salomon Center at the Stern School of Business of New York University. He is widely recognized as one of the world's experts on bankruptcy and credit analysis as well as the high-yield or junk-bond market.

■ TABLE 20.2   **Defaults by Original Rating—All Rated Corporate Bonds***

| | | \(1971–1999\)\\Years after Issuance | | | | | | | | | |
		1	2	3	4	5	6	7	8	9	10
AAA	Yearly	0.00%	0.00%	0.00%	0.00%	0.04%	0.00%	0.00%	0.00%	0.00%	0.00%
	Cumulative	0.00%	0.00%	0.00%	0.00%	0.04%	0.04%	0.04%	0.04%	0.04%	0.04%
AA	Yearly	0.00%	0.00%	0.36%	0.20%	0.00%	0.00%	0.00%	0.00%	0.03%	0.03%
	Cumulative	0.00%	0.00%	0.36%	0.56%	0.56%	0.56%	0.57%	0.57%	0.60%	0.62%
A	Yearly	0.00%	0.00%	0.03%	0.08%	0.04%	0.08%	0.05%	0.09%	0.07%	0.00%
	Cumulative	0.00%	0.00%	0.03%	0.11%	0.15%	0.23%	0.29%	0.38%	0.45%	0.45%
BBB	Yearly	0.07%	0.25%	0.27%	0.53%	0.32%	0.32%	0.35%	0.06%	0.06%	0.24%
	Cumulative	0.07%	0.32%	0.58%	1.12%	1.43%	1.75%	2.09%	2.15%	2.20%	2.44%
BB	Yearly	0.71%	0.81%	2.65%	1.41%	2.35%	0.80%	1.71%	0.30%	1.45%	3.03%
	Cumulative	0.71%	1.51%	4.12%	5.47%	7.69%	8.44%	10.00%	10.27%	11.58%	14.25%
B	Yearly	1.58%	3.92%	4.88%	5.78%	4.62%	3.65%	2.38%	1.77%	1.54%	0.92%
	Cumulative	1.58%	5.43%	10.05%	15.25%	19.17%	22.12%	23.98%	25.33%	26.48%	27.15%
CCC	Yearly	1.63%	13.60%	15.16%	8.27%	3.05%	8.96%	4.02%	3.36%	0.00%	3.56%
	Cumulative	1.63%	15.01%	27.89%	33.86%	36.07%	42.21%	44.53%	46.39%	46.39%	48.38%

*Rated by S & P at issuance.
Based on 802 issues.
Source: Standard & Poor's (New York) and Edward I. Altman's compilation.

could not do with only traditional bond-financing techniques. Drexel was particularly successful with this technique, primarily because their huge base of institutional clients allowed them to raise large sums of money quickly.

At this time, it is not clear how the great growth in junk-bond financing has altered the returns on these instruments. On the one hand, financial theory indicates that the expected returns on an asset should be negatively related to its marketability.[13] Because trading volume in junk bonds has greatly increased in recent years, the marketability has risen as well. This should lower the expected return on junk bonds, thereby benefiting corporate issuers. On the other hand, the increased interest in junk-bond financing by corporations (the increase in the supply schedule of junk bonds) is likely to raise the expected returns on these assets. The net effect of these two forces is unclear.[14]

Junk-bond financing has recently created much controversy. First, because the use of junk bonds increases the firm's interest deduction, Congress and the IRS have registered strong disapproval. Several legislators have suggested denying interest deductibility on

---

[13]For example, see Y. Amihud and H. Mendelson, "Asset Pricing and the Bid-Ask Spread," *Journal of Financial Economics* (December 1986).

[14]The actual risk of junk bonds is not known with certainty because it is not easy to measure default rate. Paul Asquith, David W. Mullins, Jr., and Eric D. Wolff, "Original Issue High Yield Bonds: Aging Analysis of Defaults, Exchanges, and Calls," *Journal of Finance* (September 1989), show that the default rate on junk bonds can be greater than 30 percent over the life of the bond. They look at cumulative default rates and find that of all junk bonds issued in 1977 and 1978, 34 percent had defaulted by December 31, 1988. Table 20.1 shows yearly default rates. Edward I. Altman, "Setting the Record Straight on Junk Bonds: A Review of the Research on Default Rates and Returns," *Journal of Applied Corporate Finance* (Summer 1990), shows that yearly default rates of 5 percent are consistent with cumulative default rates of over 30 percent.

TABLE 20.3 Average Gross Spreads and Total Direct Costs for Domestic Debt Issues: 1990–94

Proceeds ($ in millions)	Convertible Bonds						Straight Bonds					
	Investment Grade			Noninvestment Grade			Investment Grade			Noninvestment Grade		
	Number of Issues	Gross Spread	Total Direct Cost	Number of Issues	Gross Spread	Total Direct Cost	Number of Issues	Gross Spread	Total Direct Cost	Number of Issues	Gross Spread	Total Direct Cost
2– 9.99	0	—	—	0	—	—	14	.58%	2.19%	0	—%	—%
10– 19.99	0	—	—	1	4.00%	5.67%	56	.50	1.19	2	5.13%	7.41%
20– 39.99	1	1.75%	2.75%	9	3.29	4.92	64	.86	1.48	9	3.11	4.42
40– 59.99	3	1.92	2.43	19	3.37	4.58	78	.47	.94	9	2.48	3.35
60– 79.99	4	1.31	1.76	41	2.76	3.37	49	.61	.98	43	3.07	3.84
80– 99.99	2	1.07	1.34	10	2.83	3.48	65	.66	.94	47	2.78	3.75
100– 199.99	20	2.03	2.33	37	2.51	3.00	181	.57	.81	222	2.75	3.44
200– 499.99	17	1.71	1.87	10	2.46	2.70	60	.50	.93	105	2.56	2.96
500 and up	3	2.00	2.09	0	—	—	11	.39	.57	9	2.60	2.90
Total	50	1.81%	2.09%	127	2.81%	3.53%	578	.58%	.94%	446	2.75%	3.42%

Source: Inmoo Lee, Scott Lochhead, Jay Ritter, and Quanshui Zhao, "The Costs of Raising Capital," *Journal of Financial Research* 1 (Spring 1996).

junk bonds, particularly when the bonds are used to finance mergers. Second, the media has focused on the effect of junk-bond financing on corporate solvency. Clearly, this form of financing permits the possibility of higher debt-equity ratios. Whether or not this increased leverage will lead to wholesale defaults in an economic downturn, as some commentators have suggested, remains to be seen. Third, the recent wave of mergers has often resulted in dislocations and loss of jobs. Because junk-bond financing has played a role in mergers, it has come under much criticism. The social policy implications of mergers are quite complex, and any final judgment on them is likely to be reserved for the distant future. At any rate, junk-bond financing should not be implicated too strongly in either the social benefits or the social costs of the recent wave of mergers. Perry and Taggart point out that, contrary to popular belief, this form of financing accounts for only a few percent of all mergers.[15]

We discussed the costs of issuing securities in Chapter 19 and established that the costs of issuing debt are substantially less than the costs of issuing equity. Table 20.3 clarifies several questions regarding the costs of issuing debt securities. It contains a breakdown of direct costs for bond issues after the investment and noninvestment grades have been separated.

First, there are substantial economies of scale here as well. Second, investment-grade issues have much lower direct costs, particularly for straight bonds. Finally, there are relatively few noninvestment-grade issues in the smaller size categories, reflecting the fact that such issues are more commonly handled as private placements, which we discuss in a later section.

CONCEPT QUESTIONS

- List and describe the different bond-rating classes.
- Why don't bond prices change when bond ratings change?
- Are the costs of bond issues related to their ratings?

20.5 SOME DIFFERENT TYPES OF BONDS

Until now we have considered "plain vanilla" bonds. In this section we look at some more unusual types: floating-rate bonds, deep-discount bonds, and income bonds.

Floating-Rate Bonds

The conventional bonds we have discussed in this chapter have *fixed-dollar obligations.* That is, the coupon rate is set as a fixed percentage of the par value.

With **floating-rate bonds,** the coupon payments are adjustable. The adjustments are tied to an *interest-rate index* such as the Treasury-bill interest rate or the 30-year Treasury-bond rate. For example, in 1974 Citibank issued $850 million of floating-rate notes maturing in 1989. The coupon rate was set at 1 percent above the 90-day Treasury-bill rate and adjusted semiannually.

In most cases the coupon adjusts with a lag to some base rate. For example, suppose a coupon-rate adjustment is made on June 1. The adjustment may be from a simple average of yields on six-month Treasury bills issued during March, April, and May. In addition, the majority of these *floaters* have put provisions and floor-and-ceiling provisions:

1. With a *put provision* the holder has the right to redeem his or her note at par on the coupon payment date. Frequently, the investor is prohibited from redeeming at par during the first few years of the bond's life.

2. With floor-and-ceiling provisions the coupon rate is subject to a minimum and maximum. For example, the minimum coupon rate might be 8 percent and the maximum rate might be 14 percent.

---

[15]K. Perry and R. Taggart, "The Growing Role of Junk Bonds in Corporate Finance," *Journal of Applied Corporate Finance* (Spring 1988).

The popularity of floating-rate bonds is connected to *inflation risk*. When inflation is higher than expected, issuers of fixed-rate bonds tend to make gains at the expense of lenders, and when inflation is less than expected, lenders make gains at the expense of borrowers. Because the inflation risk of long-term bonds is borne by both issuers and bondholders, it is in their interests to devise loan agreements that minimize inflation risk.[16]

Floaters reduce inflation risk because the coupon rate is tied to the current interest rate, which, in turn, is influenced by the rate of inflation. This can most clearly be seen by considering the formula for the present value of a bond. As inflation increases the interest rate (the denominator of the formula), inflation increases a floater's coupon rate (the numerator of the formula). Hence, bond value is hardly affected by inflation. Conversely, the coupon rate of fixed-rate bonds cannot change, implying that the prices of these bonds are at the mercy of inflation.

As an alternative, an individual who is concerned with inflation risk can invest in short-term notes, such as Treasury bills, and *roll them over*.[17] The investor can accomplish essentially the same objective by buying a floater that is adjusted to the Treasury-bill rate. However, the purchaser of a floater can reduce transactions costs relative to rolling over short-term Treasury bills because floaters are long-term bonds. The same type of reduction in transactions costs makes floaters attractive to some corporations.[18] They benefit from issuing a floater instead of issuing a series of short-term notes.

In an earlier section, we discussed callable bonds. Because the coupon on floaters varies with marketwide interest rates, floaters always sell at or near par. Therefore, it is not surprising that floaters do not generally have call features.

Deep-Discount Bonds

A bond that pays no coupon must be offered at a price that is much lower than its face value. Such bonds are known as **original-issue discount bonds, deep-discount bonds, pure-discount bonds,** or **zero-coupon bonds.** They are frequently called *zeros* for short.

Suppose the DDB Company issues $1,000 of five-year deep-discount bonds when the marketwide interest rate is 10 percent. These bonds do not pay any coupons. The initial price is set at $621 because $621 = $1,000/(1.10)^5$.

Because these bonds have no intermediate coupon payments, they are quite attractive to certain investors and quite unattractive to others. For example, consider an insurance company forecasting death-benefit payments of $1,000,000 five years from today. The company would like to be sure that it will have the funds to pay off the liability in five years' time. The company could buy five-year zero-coupon bonds with a face value of $1,000,000. The company is matching assets with liabilities here, a procedure that eliminates interest-rate risk. That is, regardless of the movement of interest rates, the firm's set of zeros will always be able to pay off the $1,000,000 liability.

Conversely, the firm would be at risk if it bought coupon bonds instead. For example, if it bought five-year coupon bonds, it would need to reinvest the coupon payments through to the fifth year. Because interest rates in the future are not known with certainty today, one cannot be sure if these bonds will be worth more or less than $1,000,000 by the fifth year.

Now, consider a couple saving for their child's college education in 15 years. They *expect* that, with inflation, four years of college should cost $150,000 in 15 years. Thus, they

---

[16]See B. Cornell, "The Future of Floating Rate Bonds," in *The Revolution in Corporate Finance,* ed. by J. M. Stern and D. H. Chew, Jr. (New York: Basil Blackwell, 1986).

[17]That is, the investor could buy a bill, receive the face value at maturity, use these proceeds to buy a second bill, receive the face value from the second bill at maturity, and so on.

[18]Cox, Ingersoll, and Ross developed a framework for pricing floating-rate notes; see J. Cox, J. Ingersoll, and S. A. Ross, "An Analysis of Variable Rate Loan Contracts," *Journal of Finance* 35 (May 1980).

buy 15-year zero-coupon bonds with a face value of $150,000.[19] If they have forecasted inflation perfectly (and if college costs keep pace with inflation), their child's tuition will be fully funded. However, if inflation rises more than expected, the tuition would be more than $150,000. Because the zero-coupon bonds produce a shortfall, the child might end up working his way through school. As an alternative, the parents might have considered rolling over Treasury bills. Because the yields on Treasury bills rise and fall with the inflation rate, this simple strategy is likely to cause less risk than the strategy with zeros.

The key to these examples concerns the distinction between nominal and real quantities. The insurance company's liability is $1,000,000 in *nominal* dollars. Because the face value of a zero-coupon bond is a nominal quantity, the purchase of zeros eliminates risk. However, it is easier to forecast college costs in real terms than in nominal terms. Thus, a zero-coupon bond is a poor choice to reduce the financial risk of a child's college education.

Income Bonds

Income bonds are similar to conventional bonds, except that coupon payments are dependent on company income. Specifically, coupons are paid to bondholders only if the firm's income is sufficient.

Income bonds are a financial puzzle because, from the firm's standpoint, they appear to be a cheaper form of debt than conventional bonds. Income bonds provide the same tax advantage to corporations from interest deductions that conventional bonds do. However, a company that issues income bonds is less likely to experience financial distress. When a coupon payment is omitted because of insufficient corporate income, an income bond is not in default.

Why don't firms issue more income bonds? Two explanations have been offered:

1. *The "Smell of Death" Explanation.* Firms that issue income bonds signal the capital markets of their increased prospect of financial distress.

2. *The "Dead-Weight Costs" Explanation.* The calculation of corporate income is crucial to determining the status of bondholders' income, and stockholders and bondholders will not necessarily agree on how to calculate the income. This creates agency costs associated with the firm's accounting methods.

Although these are possibilities, the work of McConnell and Schlarbaum suggests that no truly satisfactory reason exists for the lack of more investor interest in income bonds.[20]

- Create an idea of an unusual bond and analyze its features.

20.6 Direct Placement Compared to Public Issues

Earlier in this chapter, we described the mechanics of issuing debt to the public. However, more than 50 percent of all debt is privately placed. There are two basic forms of direct private long-term financing: term loans and private placement.

Term loans are direct business loans with maturities of between 1 year and 15 years. The typical term loan is amortized over the life of the loan. That is, the loan is repaid by equal

---

[19]A more precise strategy would be to buy zeros maturing in years 15, 16, 17, and 18, respectively. In this way, the bonds might mature just in time to meet tuition payments.

[20]J. McConnell and G. Schlarbaum, "The Income Bond Puzzle," in *The Revolution in Corporate Finance.* ed. by J. M. Stern and D. H. Chew, Jr. (New York: Basil Blackwell, 1986).

annual payments of interest and principal. The lenders are commercial banks and insurance companies. A **private placement,** which also involves the sale of a bond or loan directly to a limited number of investors, is very similar to a term loan except that the maturity is longer.

Some important differences between direct long-term financing and public issues are:

1. A direct long-term loan avoids the cost of registration with the Securities and Exchange Commission.

2. Direct placement is likely to have more restrictive covenants.

3. It is easier to renegotiate a term loan and a private placement in the event of a default. It is harder to renegotiate a public issue because hundreds of holders are usually involved.

4. Life insurance companies and pension funds dominate the private-placement segment of the bond market. Commercial banks are significant participants in the term-loan market.

5. The costs of distributing bonds are lower in the private market.

The interest rates on term loans and private placements are usually higher than those on an equivalent public issue. Hayes, Joehnk, and Melicher found that the yield to maturity on private placements was 0.46 percent higher than on similar public issues.[21] This finding reflects the trade-off between a higher interest rate and more flexible arrangements in the event of financial distress, as well as the lower transaction costs associated with private placements.

CONCEPT QUESTIONS

• What are the differences between private and public bond issues?
• A private placement is more likely to have restrictive covenants than is a public issue. Why?

20.7 LONG-TERM SYNDICATED BANK LOANS

Most bank loans are for less than a year. They serve as a short-term "bridge" for the acquisition of inventory and are typically self-liquidating—that is, when the firm sells the inventory, the cash is used to repay the bank loan. We talk about the need for short-term bank loans in the next section of the text. Now we focus on long-term bank loans.

First, we introduce the concept of commitment. Most bank loans are made with a commitment to a firm. That commitment establishes a line of credit and allows the firm to borrow up to a predetermined limit. Most commitments are in the form of a revolving credit commitment (i.e., a revolver) with a fixed term of up to three years or more. Revolving credit commitments are drawn or undrawn depending on whether the firm has a current need for the funds.

Now we turn to the concept of syndication. Very large banks such as Citigroup typically have a larger demand for loans than they can supply, and small regional banks frequently have more funds on hand than they can profitably lend to existing customers. Basically, they cannot generate enough good loans with the funds they have available. As a result, a very large bank may arrange a loan with a firm or country and then sell portions of it to a syndicate of other banks. With a syndicated loan, each bank has a separate loan agreement with the borrowers.

A syndicated loan is a corporate loan made by a group (or syndicate) of banks and other institutional investors. A syndicated loan may be publicly traded. It may be a line of credit and be "undrawn" or it may be drawn and be used by a firm. Syndicated loans are always rated investment grade. However, a *leveraged* syndicated loan is rated speculative grade (i.e., it is "junk"). Every week, *The Wall Street Journal* reports on the number of syndicated

---

[21]P. A. Hayes, M. D. Joehnk, and R. W. Melicher, "Determinants of Risk Premiums in the Public and Private Bond Market," *Journal of Financial Research* (Fall 1979).

Syndicated Loans / *Trends & Prices*

Syndicated loans are corporate loans made by a group, or syndicate, of banks and institutional investors. 'Undrawn' loans are lines of credit made available to corporations as backing for commercial paper or for general corporate purposes. A basis point is 1/100th of a percentage point.

Deal Flow

A leading indicator of activity, showing new deals mandated or in the market. Deals tallied are transactions priced at or below Libor+150 basis points.

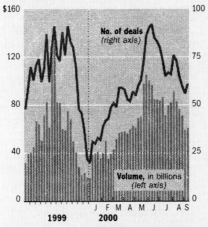

Credit Costs

Average new-issue fees paid by investment-grade issuers on undrawn loans*; in basis points, by credit rating of issuer.

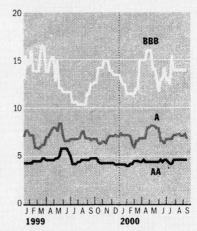

*These loans are assumed to be 100% undrawn. Fees include the facility fee, paid to have a line of credit open and/or the commitment fee, paid to retain the portion of the money that's undrawn.

The Week's Biggest Movers

Biggest gainers and losers among widely-quoted syndicated loans in secondary trading, in the week ended Monday. Listed are the biggest movers among the 105 loans with at least five bids. All loans listed are B-term, or sold to institutional investors.

	LOAN RATING MOODY'S/S&P	COUPON	MATURITY	AVERAGE BID (pct. pts.)	WEEKLY CHANGE (pct. pts.)
Adelphia Commun.	Ba3/N.R.*	L+250	March 21, '09	99.93	+0.07
Allied Waste	Ba3/BB	L+275	July 1, '06	95.86	+0.16
Casella Waste Sys.	B1/BB–	L+350	Jan. 26, '07	99.05	+1.55
Federal-Mogul	Ba2/BB	L+225	Dec. 18, '05	92.79	–0.04
Global Crossing	Ba1/BBB–	L+275	July 6, '06	100.38	+0.04
Huntsman Pkg.	B1/BB–	L+300	April 15, '08	97.34	–0.14
Integrated Health	N.R.*/N.R.*	L+200	Sept. 30, '04	27.67	–0.17
Kansas City So. Rail	Ba1/BB+	L+350	Dec.17, '06	100.29	+0.05
Laidlaw/Safety-Kleen	N.R./CC	L+312.5	May 15, '04	30.57	–0.43
Lincoln Electric	Ba3/BB+	L+300	May 30, '08	100.55	+0.05
Magellan Health	B2/B+	L+250	Feb. 12, '05	85.67	+0.50
McLeod	Ba2/BB–	L+300	April 12, '08	100.04	+0.05
Nextel Finance	Ba2/BB–	L+337.5	April 10, '08	100.44	+0.07

	LOAN RATING MOODY'S/S&P	COUPON	MATURITY	AVERAGE BID (pct. pts.)	WEEKLY CHANGE (pct. pts.)
Nextlink	B1/B+	L+350	June 30, '07	99.92	+0.05
Pillowtex	B3/CCC	L+275	Dec. 31, '04	68.38	+0.13
Safelite Glass	Caa1/D	L+200	Dec. 29, '04	41.25	+0.25
Superior TeleCom	Ba3/B+	L+375	Nov. 27, '05	98.89	–0.04
Tenneco Auto.	Ba3/BB	L+275	August 5, '07	98.82	–0.17
Thermadyne	B1/B	L+275	May 22, '05	92.90	–0.2
Total Renal Care	B1/B+(a)	L+375	March 31, '08	96.30	+0.20
U.S. Office Prod.	Caa1/CCC+	L+250	April 22, '06	58.75	–2
VenTrust-Ventas	N.R.*/N.R.*	L+375	Dec. 31, '05	89.00	+1.50
Voicestream Wrlss	B1/B+	L+350	Jan. 31, '09	99.49	+0.05
Winstar Commun.	B2/B+	L+400	Sept. 10, '07	97.05	–0.34
Wyndham Intl.		L+350	June 18, '06	98.49	+0.28

*Not rated

Advancers 93

Decliners 97

Unchanged 1,557

Total loans with at least one bid: 1,747
Average change in bids: –0.04 percentage point

Note: These are the averages of indicative bid prices provided by bank-loan traders, excluding the highest bid and expressed as a percentage of the par, or face, value. Coupon, or interest rate, is in 1/100s of a percentage point over Libor, the benchmark London Interbank Offered Rate. All ratings are for specific loans and not for the company itself except as noted with an (a). These prices do not represent actual trades nor are they offers to trade; rather they are estimated values provided by dealers.

loan deals, credit costs, and yields, as seen in Table 20.4. In addition, syndicated loan prices are reported for a group of publicly traded loans. Altman and Suggitt report slightly higher default rates for syndicated loans when compared to comparable corporate bonds.[22]

20.8 SUMMARY AND CONCLUSIONS

This chapter describes some important aspects of long-term debt financing.

1. The written agreement describing the details of the long-term debt contract is called an *indenture.* Some of the main provisions are security, repayment, protective covenants, and call provisions.
2. There are many ways that shareholders can take advantage of bondholders. Protective covenants are designed to protect bondholders from management decisions that favor stockholders at bondholders' expense.
3. Unsecured bonds are called *debentures* or *notes.* They are general claims on the company's value. Most public industrial bonds are unsecured. In contrast, utility bonds are usually secured. Mortgage bonds are secured by tangible property, and collateral trust bonds are secured by financial securities such as stocks and bonds. If the company defaults on secured bonds, the trustee can repossess the assets. This makes secured bonds more valuable.
4. Long-term bonds usually provide for repayment of principal before maturity. This is accomplished by a sinking fund. With a sinking fund, the company retires a certain number of bonds each year. A sinking fund protects bondholders because it reduces the average maturity of the bond, and its payment signals the financial condition of the company.
5. Most publicly issued bonds are callable. A callable bond is less attractive to bondholders than a noncallable bond. A callable bond can be bought back by the company at a call price that is less than the true value of the bond. As a consequence, callable bonds are priced to obtain higher stated interest rates for bondholders than noncallable bonds.

   Generally, companies should exercise the call provision whenever the bond's value is greater than the call price.

   There is no single reason for call provisions. Some sensible reasons include taxes, greater flexibility, management's ability to predict interest rates, and the fact that callable bonds are less sensitive to interest-rate changes.
6. There are many different types of bonds, including floating-rate bonds, deep-discount bonds, and income bonds. This chapter also compares private placement with public issuance.

KEY TERMS

---

[22]Edward I. Altman and Heather J. Suggitt, "Default Rates in the Syndicated Bank Loan Market: A Longitudinal Analysis," *Journal of Banking and Finance* 24 (2000).

Suggested Reading

The following provides a complete coverage of bonds and the bond market:
Fabozzi, F. J., and T. D. Fabozzi, eds. *The Handbook of Fixed Income Securities.* 4th ed. Homewood, Ill.: Irwin Professional Publishing, 1995.

Questions and Problems

The Public Issue of Bonds

20.1 Raeo Corp. bonds trade at 100 today. The bonds pay semiannual interest that is paid on January 1 and July 1. The coupon on the bonds is 10 percent. How much will you pay for a Raeo bond if today is
  a. March 1.
  b. October 1.
  c. July 1.
  d. August 15.

20.2 Define the following terms:
  a. Protective covenant
  b. Negative covenant
  c. Positive covenant
  d. Sinking fund

20.3 Sinking funds have both positive and negative characteristics to the bondholders. Why?

20.4 Which is riskier to a prospective creditor, an open-end mortgage or closed-end mortgage? Why?

20.5 What is call premium? During what period of time is a bond said to be call-protected?

Bond Refunding

20.6 KIC, Inc., plans to issue $5 million of perpetual bonds. The face value of each bond is $1,000. The annual coupon on the bonds is 12 percent. Market interest rates on one-year bonds are 11 percent. With equal probability, the long-term market interest rate will be either 14 percent or 7 percent next year. Assume investors are risk-neutral.
  a. If the KIC bonds are noncallable, what is the price of the bonds?
  b. If the bonds are callable one year from today at $1,450, will their price be greater than or less than the price you computed in part (*a*)? Why?

20.7 Bowdeen Manufacturing intends to issue callable, perpetual bonds. The bonds are callable at $1,250. One-year interest rates are 12 percent. There is a 60-percent probability that long-term interest rates one year from today will be 15 percent. With a 40-percent probability, long-term interest rates will be 8 percent. To simplify the firm's accounting, Bowdeen would like to issue the bonds at par ($1,000). What must the coupon on the bonds be for Bowdeen to be able to sell them at par?

20.8 Illinois Industries has decided to borrow money by issuing perpetual bonds. The face value of the bonds will be $1,000. The coupon will be 8 percent, payable annually. The one-year interest rate is 8 percent. It is known that next year there is a 65-percent chance that interest rates will decline to 6 percent, and that there is a 35-percent chance that they will rise to 9 percent.
  a. What will the market value of these bonds be if they are noncallable?
  b. If the company instead decides to make the bonds callable, what coupon will be demanded by the bondholders for the bonds to sell at par? Assume that the bonds can be called in one year (i.e., the call date is one year from now) and that the call premium is equal to the annual coupon.
  c. What will be the value of the call provision to Illinois Industries?

20.9 New Business Ventures, Inc., has an outstanding perpetual bond with a face value equal to $1,000 and a 9-percent coupon rate. The bond cannot be called for one year. The call premium is set at $150 over par value. It is forecasted that there is a 40-percent chance that the interest rate will rise to 12-percent, and a 60-percent chance that the interest rate will fall down to 6 percent next year. The current interest rate is 10 percent. What is the current market price of this callable bond?

20.10 Hudson River Electronics has $500 million of 9-percent perpetual bonds outstanding. These bonds can be called at a price of $1,090 for each $1,000 of face value. Under present market conditions, the outstanding bonds can be replaced by $500 million of 7-percent perpetual bonds. The underwriting and legal expenses of this new issue would be $80 million. What would be the net present value of this refunding? Assume that there are no taxes.

20.11 An outstanding issue of Public Express Airlines debentures has a call provision attached. The total principal value of the bonds is $250 million, and the bonds pay an annual coupon of $80 for each $1,000 of face value. The total cost of refunding would be 12 percent of the principal amount raised. The appropriate tax rate for the company is 35 percent. How low does the borrowing cost of Public Express need to drop to justify refunding with a new bond issue?

20.12 Margret Kimberly, CFO of Charles River Associates, is considering whether or not to refinance the two currently outstanding corporate bonds of the firm. The first one is an 8-percent perpetual bond with a $1,000 face value with $75 million outstanding. The second one is a 9-percent perpetual bond with the same face value with $87.5 million outstanding. The call premiums for the two bonds are 8.5 percent and 9.5 percent of the face value, respectively. The transaction costs of the refundings are $10 million and $12 million, respectively. The current interest rates for the two bonds are 7 percent and 7.25 percent, respectively. Which bond should Ms. Kimberly recommend be refinanced? What is the NPV of the refunding?

Some Different Types of Bonds

20.13 What is a "junk bond"? What are some of the controversies created by junk-bond financing?

20.14 Describe the following types of bonds:
   a. Floating rate
   b. Deep discount
   c. Income

Direct Placement Compared to Public Issues

20.15 Which of the following are characteristics of public issues, and which are characteristics of direct financing?
   a. SEC registration required
   b. Higher interest cost
   c. Higher fixed cost
   d. Quicker access to funds
   e. Active secondary market
   f. Easily renegotiated
   g. Lower flotation costs
   h. Regular amortization required
   i. Ease of repurchase at favorable prices
   j. High total cost to small borrowers
   k. Flexible terms
   l. Less intensive investigation required

General Topics

20.16 *a.* In an efficient market callable and noncallable bonds will be priced in such a way that there will be no advantage or disadvantage to the call provision. Comment.
   b. If interest rates fall, will the price of noncallable bonds move up higher than that of callable bonds? Why or why not?

CHAPTER 21

Leasing

EXECUTIVE SUMMARY

Almost any asset that can be purchased can be leased, from aircraft to zithers. When we take vacations or business trips, renting a car for a few days frequently seems a convenient thing to do. This is an example of a short-term lease. After all, buying a car and selling it a few days later would be a great nuisance.

Corporations lease both short-term and long-term, but this chapter is primarily concerned with long-term leasing over a term of more than five years. Long-term leasing is a method of financing property, plant, and equipment. More equipment is financed today by long-term leases than by any other method of equipment financing.[1]

Every lease contract has two parties: the lessee and the lessor. The **lessee** is the user of the equipment, and the **lessor** is the owner. Typically, the lessee first decides on the asset needed and then negotiates a lease contract with a lessor. From the lessee's standpoint, long-term leasing is similar to buying the equipment with a secured loan. The terms of the lease contract are compared to what a banker might arrange with a secured loan. Thus, long-term leasing is a form of financing.

Many questionable advantages are claimed for long-term leasing, such as "leasing provides 100-percent financing," or "leasing conserves capital." However, the principal benefit of long-term leasing is tax reduction. Leasing allows the transfer of tax benefits from those who need equipment but cannot take full advantage of the tax benefits associated with ownership to a party who can. If the corporate income tax were repealed, long-term leasing would virtually disappear.

21.1 TYPES OF LEASES

The Basics

A *lease* is a contractual agreement between a lessee and lessor. The agreement establishes that the lessee has the right to use an asset and in return must make periodic payments to the lessor, the owner of the asset. The lessor is either the asset's manufacturer or an independent leasing company. If the lessor is an independent leasing company, it must buy the asset from a manufacturer. Then the lessor delivers the asset to the lessee, and the lease goes into effect.

As far as the lessee is concerned, it is the use of the asset that is most important, not who owns the asset. The use of an asset can be obtained by a lease contract. Because the user can also buy the asset, leasing and buying involve alternative financing arrangements for the use of an asset. This is illustrated in Figure 21.1.

---

[1]P. K. Nevitt and F. J. Fabozzi, *Equipment Leasing,* 2nd ed. (Homewood, Ill.: Dow Jones-Irwin, 1985).

■ FIGURE 21.1   **Buying versus Leasing**

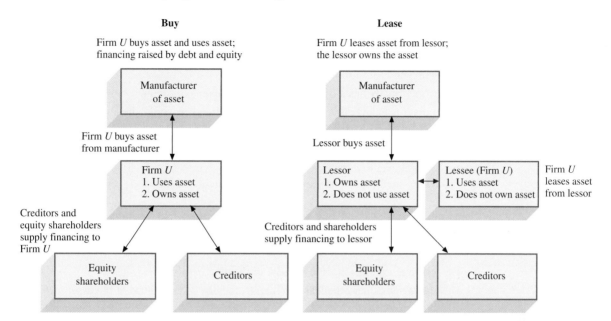

The specific example in Figure 21.1 happens often in the computer industry. Firm *U*, the lessee, might be a hospital, a law firm, or any other firm that uses computers. The lessor is an independent leasing company who purchased the equipment from a manufacturer such as IBM or Apple. Leases of this type are called **direct leases.** In the figure, the lessor issued both debt and equity to finance the purchase.

Of course, a manufacturer like IBM could lease its *own* computers, though we do not show this situation in the example. Leases of this type are called **sales-type leasing.** In this case, IBM would compete with the independent computer-leasing company.

Operating Leases

Years ago, a lease where the lessee received an operator along with the equipment was called an **operating lease.** Though the operating lease defies an exact definition today, this form for leasing has several important characteristics.

1. Operating leases are usually not fully amortized. This means that the payments required under the terms of the lease are not enough to recover the full cost of the asset for the lessor. This occurs because the term or life of the operating lease is usually less than the economic life of the asset. Thus, the lessor must expect to recover the costs of the asset by renewing the lease or by selling the asset for its residual value.

2. Operating leases usually require the lessor to maintain and insure the leased assets.

3. Perhaps the most interesting feature of an operating lease is the cancellation option. This option gives the lessee the right to cancel the lease contract before the expiration date. If the option to cancel is exercised, the lessee must return the equipment to the lessor. The value of a cancellation clause depends on whether future technological and/or economic conditions are likely to make the value of the asset to the lessee less than the value of the future lease payments under the lease.

To leasing practitioners, the above characteristics constitute an operating lease. However, accountants use the term in a slightly different way, as we will see shortly.

Financial Leases

Financial leases are the exact opposite of operating leases, as is seen from their important characteristics:

1. Financial leases do not provide for maintenance or service by the lessor.
2. Financial leases are fully amortized.
3. The lessee usually has a right to renew the lease on expiration.
4. Generally, financial leases cannot be canceled. In other words, the lessee must make all payments or face the risk of bankruptcy.

Because of the above characteristics, particularly (2), this lease provides an alternative method of financing to purchase. Hence, its name is a sensible one. Two special types of financial leases are the sale and lease-back arrangement and the leveraged lease.

Sale and Lease-Back   A **sale and lease-back** occurs when a company sells an asset it owns to another firm and immediately leases it back. In a sale and lease-back, two things happen:

1. The lessee receives cash from the sale of the asset.
2. The lessee makes periodic lease payments, thereby retaining use of the asset.

An example of a sale and lease-back occurred when the city of Oakland, California, used the proceeds of a sale of its city hall and 23 other buildings to help meet the liabilities of the $150 million Police and Retirement System. As part of the same transaction, Oakland leased back the buildings to obtain their continued use.

Leveraged Leases   A **leveraged lease** is a three-sided arrangement among the lessee, the lessor, and the lenders:

1. As in other leases, the lessee uses the assets and makes periodic lease payments.
2. As in other leases, the lessor purchases the assets, delivers them to the lessee, and collects the lease payments. However, the lessor puts up no more than 40 to 50 percent of the purchase price.
3. The lenders supply the remaining financing and receive interest payments from the lessor. Thus, the arrangement on the right-hand side of Figure 24.1 would be a leveraged lease if the bulk of the financing was supplied by creditors.

The lenders in a leveraged lease typically use a nonrecourse loan. This means that the lessor is not obligated to the lender in case of a default. However, the lender is protected in two ways:

1. The lender has a first lien on the asset.
2. In the event of loan default, the lease payments are made directly to the lender.

The lessor puts up only part of the funds but gets the lease payments and all the tax benefits of ownership. These lease payments are used to pay the debt service of the nonrecourse loan. The lessee benefits because, in a competitive market, the lease payment is lowered when the lessor saves taxes.

CONCEPT QUESTIONS

- What are some reasons that assets like automobiles would be leased with operating leases, whereas machines or real estate would be leased with financial leases?
- What are the differences between an operating lease and a financial lease?

■ TABLE 21.1   **Example of Balance Sheet under FAS 13**

Balance Sheet			
Truck is purchased with debt (the company owns a $100,000 truck)			
Truck	$100,000	Debt	$100,000
Land	100,000	Equity	100,000
Total assets	$200,000	Total debt plus equity	$200,000
Operating lease (the company has an operating lease for the truck)			
Truck	$0	Debt	$0
Land	100,000	Equity	100,000
Total assets	$100,000	Total debt plus equity	$100,000
Capital lease (the company has a capital lease for the truck)			
Assets under capital lease	$100,000	Obligations under capital lease	$100,000
Land	100,000	Equity	100,000
Total assets	$200,000	Total debt plus equity	$200,000

21.2 ACCOUNTING AND LEASING

Before November 1976, a firm could arrange to use an asset through a lease and not disclose the asset or the lease contract on the balance sheet. Lessees needed only to report information on leasing activity in the footnotes of their financial statements. Thus, leasing led to **off–balance-sheet financing.**

In November 1976, the Financial Accounting Standards Board (FASB) issued its Statement of Financial Accounting Standards No. 13 (FAS 13), "Accounting for Leases." Under FAS 13, certain leases are classified as capital leases. (We present the criteria later in this section.) For a capital lease, the present value of the lease payments appears on the right-hand side of the balance sheet. The identical value appears on the left-hand side of the balance sheet as an asset.

FASB classifies all other leases as operating leases, though FASB's definition differs from that of nonaccountants. (The use of operating leases by nonaccountants was discussed in an earlier section of this chapter.) No mention of the lease appears on the balance sheet for operating leases.

The accounting implications of this distinction are illustrated in Table 21.1. Imagine a firm that, years ago, issued $100,000 of equity in order to purchase land. It now wants to use a $100,000 truck, which it can either purchase or lease. The balance sheet reflecting purchase of the truck is shown at the top of the table. (We assume that the truck is financed entirely with debt.) Alternatively, imagine that the firm leases the truck. If the lease is judged to be an operating one, the middle balance sheet is created. Here, neither the lease liability nor the truck appears on the balance sheet. The bottom balance sheet reflects a capital lease. The truck is shown as an asset and the lease is shown as a liability.

Accountants generally argue that a firm's financial strength is inversely related to the amount of its liabilities. Since the lease liability is hidden with an operating lease, the balance sheet of a firm with an operating lease *looks* stronger than the balance sheet of a firm with an otherwise-identical capital lease. Given the choice, firms would probably classify all their leases as operating ones. Because of this tendency, FAS 13 states that a lease must be classified as a capital one if at least one of the following four criteria is met:

1. The present value of the lease payments is at least 90 percent of the fair market value of the asset at the start of the lease.
2. The lease transfers ownership of the property to the lessee by the end of the term of the lease.
3. The lease term is 75 percent or more of the estimated economic life of the asset.
4. The lessee can purchase the asset at a price below fair market value when the lease expires. This is frequently called a *bargain-purchase-price option.*

These rules capitalize those leases that are similar to purchases. For example, the first two rules capitalize leases where the asset is likely to be purchased at the end of the lease period. The last two rules capitalize long-term leases.

Some firms have tried to cook the books by exploiting this classification scheme. Suppose a trucking firm wants to lease a $200,000 truck that it expects to use for 15 years. A clever financial manager could try to negotiate a lease contract for 10 years with lease payments having a present value of $178,000. These terms would get around criteria (1) and (3). If criteria (2) and (4) could be circumvented, the arrangement would be an operating lease and would not show up on the balance sheet.

Does this sort of gimmickry pay? The semistrong form of the efficient-capital-markets hypothesis implies that stock prices reflect all publicly available information. As we discussed earlier in this text, the empirical evidence generally supports this form of the hypothesis. Though operating leases do not appear in the firm's balance sheet, information on these leases must be disclosed elsewhere in the annual report. Because of this, attempts to keep leases off the balance sheet will not affect stock price in an efficient capital market.

QUESTIONS

• Define capital lease.
• Define operating lease.

21.3 TAXES, THE IRS, AND LEASES

The lessee can deduct lease payments for income tax purposes if the lease is qualified by the Internal Revenue Service. Because tax shields are critical to the economic viability of any lease, all interested parties generally obtain an opinion from the IRS before agreeing to a major lease transaction. The opinion of the IRS will reflect the following guidelines:

1. The term of the lease must be less than 30 years. If the term is greater than 30 years, the transaction will be regarded as a conditional sale.
2. The lease should not have an option to acquire the asset at a price below its fair market value. This type of bargain option would give the lessee the asset's residual scrap value, implying an equity interest.
3. The lease should not have a schedule of payments that is very high at the start of the lease term and thereafter very low. Early *balloon* payments would be evidence that the lease was being used to avoid taxes and not for a legitimate business purpose.
4. The lease payments must provide the lessor with a fair market rate of return. The profit potential of the lease to the lessor should be apart from the deal's tax benefits.
5. The lease should not limit the lessee's right to issue debt or pay dividends while the lease is operative.

6. Renewal options must be reasonable and reflect fair market value of the asset. This requirement can be met by granting the lessee the first option to meet a competing outside offer.

   The reason the IRS is concerned about lease contracts is that many times they appear to be set up solely to avoid taxes. To see how this could happen, suppose that a firm plans to purchase a $1 million bus that has a five-year class life. Depreciation expense would be $200,000 per year, assuming straight-line depreciation. Now suppose that the firm can lease the bus for $500,000 per year for two years and buy the bus for $1 at the end of the two-year term. The present value of the tax benefits from acquiring the bus would clearly be less than if the bus were leased. The speedup of lease payments would greatly benefit the firm and *de facto* give it a form of accelerated depreciation. If the tax rates of the lessor and lessee are different, leasing can be a form of tax avoidance.

CONCEPT QUESTION

?

- What are the IRS guidelines for treating a lease contract as a lease for tax purposes?

21.4 THE CASH FLOWS OF LEASING

In this section we identify the basic cash flows used in evaluating a lease. Consider the decision confronting the Xomox corporation, which manufactures pipe. Business has been expanding, and Xomox currently has a five-year backlog of pipe orders for the Trans-Honduran Pipeline.

The International Boring Machine Corporation (IBMC) makes a pipe-boring machine that can be purchased for $10,000. Xomox has determined that it needs a new machine, and the IBMC model will save Xomox $6,000 per year in reduced electricity bills for the next five years. These savings are known with certainty because Xomox has a long-term electricity purchase agreement with State Electric Utilities, Inc.

Xomox has a corporate tax rate of 34 percent. We assume that five-year straight-line depreciation is used for the pipe-boring machine, and the machine will be worthless after five years.[2]

However, Friendly Leasing Corporation has offered to lease the same pipe-boring machine to Xomox for $2,500 per year for five years. With the lease, Xomox would remain responsible for maintenance, insurance, and operating expenses.[3]

Simon Smart, a recently hired MBA, has been asked to calculate the incremental cash flows from leasing the IBMC machine in lieu of buying it. He has prepared Table 21.2, which shows the direct cash flow consequences of buying the pipe-boring machine and also signing the lease agreement with Friendly Leasing.

To simplify matters, Simon Smart has prepared Table 21.3, which subtracts the direct cash flows of buying the pipe-boring machine from those of leasing it. Noting that only the net advantage of leasing is relevant to Xomox, he concludes the following from his analysis:

---

[2]This is a simplifying assumption because current tax law allows the accelerated method as well. The accelerated method will almost always be the best choice.

[3]For simplicity, we have assumed that lease payments are made at the end of each year. Actually, most leases require lease payments to be made at the beginning of the year.

■ TABLE 21.2   **Cash Flows to Xomox from Using the IBMC Pipe-Boring Machine: Buy versus Lease**

	Year 0	Year 1	Year 2	Year 3	Year 4	Year 5
Buy						
Cost of machine	−$10,000					
After-tax operating savings [$3,960 = $6,000 × (1 − 0.34)]		$3,960	$3,960	$3,960	$3,960	$3,960
Depreciation tax benefit		680	680	680	680	680
	−$10,000	$4,640	$4,640	$4,640	$4,640	$4,640
Lease						
Lease payments		−$2,500	−$2,500	−$2,500	−$2,500	−$2,500
Tax benefits of lease payments ($850 = $2,500 × 0.34)		850	850	850	850	850
After-tax operating savings		3,960	3,960	3,960	3,960	3,960
Total		$2,310	$2,310	$2,310	$2,310	$2,310

Depreciation is straight-line. Because the depreciable base is $10,000, depreciation expense per year is $10,000/5 = $2,000.

The depreciation tax benefit per year is equal to

$$\text{Tax rate} \times \text{Depreciation expense per year} = \text{Depreciation tax benefit}$$
$$0.34 \quad \times \quad \$2,000 \quad = \quad \$680$$

■ TABLE 21.3   **Incremental Cash Flow Consequences for Xomox from Leasing instead of Purchasing**

Lease Minus Buy	Year 0	Year 1	Year 2	Year 3	Year 4	Year 5
Lease						
Lease payment		−$2,500	−$2,500	−$2,500	−$2,500	−$2,500
Tax benefit of lease payment		850	850	850	850	850
Buy (minus)						
Cost of machine	−(−$10,000)					
Lost depreciation tax benefit		−680	−680	−680	−680	−680
Total	$10,000	−$2,330	−$2,330	−$2,330	−$2,330	−$2,330

The bottom line presents the cash flows from leasing relative to the cash flows from purchase. The cash flows would be exactly the *opposite* if we considered the purchase relative to the lease.

1. Operating costs are not directly affected by leasing. Xomox will save $3,960 (after taxes) from use of the IBMC boring machine regardless of whether the machine is owned or leased. Thus, this cash flow stream does not appear in Table 21.3.

2. If the machine is leased, Xomox will save the $10,000 it would have used to purchase the machine. This saving shows up as an initial cash *inflow* of $10,000 in year 0.

3. If Xomox leases the pipe-boring machine, it will no longer own this machine and must give up the depreciation tax benefits. These tax benefits show up as an *outflow*.

4. If Xomox chooses to lease the machine, it must pay $2,500 per year for five years. The first payment is due at the end of the first year. (This is a break, because sometimes the first payment is due immediately.) The lease payments are tax-deductible and, as a consequence, generate tax benefits of $850 (0.34 × $2,500).

The net cash flows have been placed in the bottom line of Table 21.3. These numbers represent the cash flows from *leasing* relative to the cash flows from the purchase. It is arbitrary that we express the flows in this way. We could have expressed the cash flows from the *purchase* relative to the cash flows from leasing. These cash flows would be

	Year 0	Year 1	Year 2	Year 3	Year 4	Year 5
Net cash flows from purchase alternative relative to lease alternative	−$10,000	$2,330	$2,330	$2,330	$2,330	$2,330

Of course, the cash flows here are the opposite of those in the bottom line of Table 21.3. Depending on our purpose, we may look at either the purchase relative to the lease or vice versa. Thus, the student should become comfortable with either viewpoint.

Now that we have the cash flows, we can make our decision by discounting the flows properly. However, because the discount rate is tricky, we take a detour in the next section before moving back to the Xomox case. In this next section, we show that cash flows in the lease-versus-buy decision should be discounted at the *after-tax* interest rate (i.e., the after-tax cost of debt capital).

21.5 A Detour on Discounting and Debt Capacity with Corporate Taxes

The analysis of leases is difficult, and both financial practitioners and academics have made conceptual errors. These errors revolve around taxes. We hope to avoid their mistakes by beginning with the simplest type of example, a loan for one year. Though this example is unrelated to our lease-versus-buy situation, principles developed here will apply directly to lease-buy analysis.

Present Value of Riskless Cash Flows

Consider a corporation that lends $100 for a year. If the interest rate is 10 percent, the firm will receive $110 at the end of the year. Of this amount, $10 is interest and the remaining $100 is the original principal. A corporate tax rate of 34 percent implies taxes on the interest of $3.40 (0.34 × $10). Thus, the firm ends up with $106.60 ($110 − $3.40) after taxes on a $100 investment.

Now, consider a company that borrows $100 for a year. With a 10-percent interest rate, the firm must pay $110 to the bank at the end of the year. However, the borrowing firm can take the $10 of interest as a tax deduction. The corporation pays $3.40 (0.34 × $10) less in taxes than it would have paid had it not borrowed the money at all. Thus, considering this reduction in taxes, the firm must pay $106.60 ($110 − $3.40) on a $100 loan. The cash flows from both lending and borrowing are displayed in Table 21.4.

■ TABLE 21.4 Lending and Borrowing in a World with Corporate Taxes (interest rate is 10 percent and corporate tax rate is 34 percent)

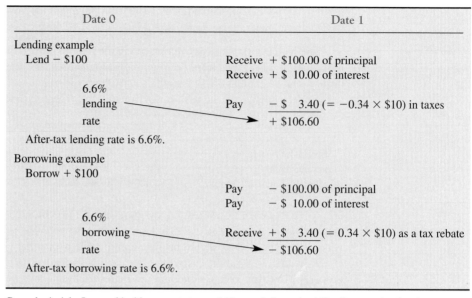

Date 0	Date 1
Lending example	
Lend − $100	Receive + $100.00 of principal
	Receive + $ 10.00 of interest
6.6% lending rate	Pay − $ 3.40 (= −0.34 × $10) in taxes
	+ $106.60
After-tax lending rate is 6.6%.	
Borrowing example	
Borrow + $100	
	Pay − $100.00 of principal
	Pay − $ 10.00 of interest
6.6% borrowing rate	Receive + $ 3.40 (= 0.34 × $10) as a tax rebate
	− $106.60
After-tax borrowing rate is 6.6%.	

General principle: In a world with corporate taxes, riskless cash flows should be discounted at the after-tax interest rate.

The above two paragraphs show a very important result: the firm could not care less whether it received $100 today or $106.60 next year.[4] If it received $100 today, it could lend it out, thereby receiving $106.60 after corporate taxes at the end of the year. Conversely, if it knows today that it will receive $106.60 at the end of the year, it could borrow $100 today. The after-tax interest and principal payments on the loan would be paid with the $106.60 that the firm will receive at the end of the year. Because of the interchangeability illustrated above, we say that a payment of $106.60 next year has a present value of $100. Because $100 = $106.60/1.066, a riskless cash flow should be discounted at the after-tax interest rate of 0.066 [0.10 × (1 − 0.34)].

Of course, the above discussion considered a specific example. The general principle is

In a world with corporate taxes, the firm should discount riskless cash flows at the after-tax riskless rate of interest.

Optimal Debt Level and Riskless Cash Flows (Advanced)

In addition, our simple example can illustrate a related point concerning optimal debt level. Consider a firm that has just determined that the current level of debt in its capital structure is optimal. Immediately following that determination, it is surprised to learn that it will receive a guaranteed payment of $106.60 in one year from, say, a tax-exempt government lottery. This future windfall is an asset that, like any asset, should raise the firm's optimal debt level. How much does this payment raise the firm's optimal level?

---

[4]For simplicity, assume that the firm received $100 or $106.60 *after* corporate taxes. Since 0.66 = 1 − 0.34, the pretax inflows would be $151.52 ($100/0.66) and $161.52 ($106.60/0.66), respectively.

Our preceding analysis implies that the firm's optimal debt level must be $100 more than it previously was. That is, the firm could borrow $100 today, perhaps paying the entire amount out as a dividend. It would owe the bank $110 at the end of the year. However, because it receives a tax rebate of $3.40 (0.34 × $10), its net repayment will be $106.60. Thus, its borrowing of $100 today is fully offset by next year's government lottery proceeds of $106.60. In other words, the lottery proceeds act as an irrevocable trust that can service the increased debt. Note that we need not know the optimal debt level before the lottery was announced. We are merely saying that, whatever this prelottery optimal level was, the optimal debt level is $100 more after the lottery announcement.

Of course, this is just one example. The general principle is[5]

> In a world with corporate taxes, one determines the increase in the firm's optimal debt level by discounting a future guaranteed after-tax inflow at the after-tax riskless interest rate.

Conversely, suppose that a second and unrelated firm is surprised to learn that it must pay $106.60 next year to the government for back taxes. Clearly, this additional liability impinges on the second firm's debt capacity. By the above reasoning, it follows that the second firm's optimal debt level must be lowered by exactly $100.

CONCEPT QUESTION

- How should one discount a riskless cash flow?

21.6 NPV ANALYSIS OF THE LEASE-VERSUS-BUY DECISION

The detour leads to a simple method for evaluating leases: discount all cash flows at the after-tax interest rate. From the bottom line of Table 21.3, Xomox's incremental cash flows from leasing versus purchasing are

	Year 0	Year 1	Year 2	Year 3	Year 4	Year 5
Net cash flows from lease alternative relative to purchase alternative	$10,000	−$2,330	−$2,330	−$2,330	−$2,330	−$2,330

Let us assume that Xomox can either borrow or lend at the interest rate of 7.57575 percent. If the corporate tax rate is 34 percent, the correct discount rate is the after-tax rate of 5 percent [7.57575% × (1 − 0.34)]. When 5 percent is used to compute the NPV of the lease, we have

$$NPV = \$10,000 - \$2,330 \times A_{0.05}^{5} = -\$87.68 \qquad (21.1)$$

Because the net present value of the incremental cash flows from leasing relative to purchasing is negative, Xomox prefers to purchase.

Equation (21.1) is the correct approach to lease-versus-buy analysis. However, students are often bothered by two things. First, they question whether the cash flows in Table 21.3 are truly riskless. We examine this issue below. Second, they feel that this approach lacks intuition. We address this concern a little later.

---

[5]This principle holds for riskless or guaranteed cash flows only. Unfortunately, there is no easy formula for determining the increase in optimal debt level from a *risky* cash flow.

The Discount Rate

Because we discounted at the after-tax riskless rate of interest, we have implicitly assumed that the cash flows in the Xomox example are riskless. Is this appropriate?

A lease payment is like the debt service on a secured bond issued by the lessee, and the discount rate should be approximately the same as the interest rate on such debt. In general, this rate will be slightly higher than the riskless rate considered in the previous section. The various tax shields could be somewhat riskier than the lease payments for two reasons. First, the value of the depreciation tax benefits depends on the ability of Xomox to generate enough taxable income to use them. Second, the corporate tax rate may change in the future, just as it fell in 1986 and increased in 1993. For these two reasons, a firm might be justified in discounting the depreciation tax benefits at a rate higher than that used for the lease payments. However, our experience is that real-world companies discount both the depreciation shield and lease payments at the same rate. This implies that financial practitioners view the above two risks as minor. We adopt the real-world convention of discounting the two flows at the same rate. This rate is the after-tax interest rate on secured debt issued by the lessee.

At this point some students still ask the question: Why not use r_{WACC} as the discount rate in lease-versus-buy analysis? Of course, r_{WACC} should not be used for lease analysis because the cash flows are more like debt-service cash flows than operating cash flows and, as such, the risk is much less. The discount rate should reflect the risk of the incremental cash flows.

21.7 Debt Displacement and Lease Valuation

The Basic Concept of Debt Displacement (Advanced)

The previous analysis allows one to calculate the right answer in a simple manner. This clearly must be viewed as an important benefit. However, the analysis has little intuitive appeal. To remedy this, we hope to make lease-buy analysis more intuitive by considering the issue of debt displacement.

A firm that purchases equipment will generally issue debt to finance the purchase. The debt becomes a liability of the firm. A lessee incurs a liability equal to the present value of all future lease payments. Because of this, we argue that leases displace debt. The balance sheets in Table 21.5 illustrate how leasing might affect debt.

Suppose a firm initially has $100,000 of assets and a 150-percent optimal debt-equity ratio. The firm's debt is $60,000, and its equity is $40,000. As in the Xomox case, suppose the firm must use a new $10,000 machine. The firm has two alternatives:

1. *The Firm Can Purchase the Machine.* If it does, it will finance the purchase with a secured loan and with equity. The debt capacity of the machine is assumed to be the same as for the firm as a whole.

2. *The Firm Can Lease the Asset and Get 100-Percent Financing.* That is, the present value of the future lease payments will be $10,000.

If the firm finances the machine with both secured debt and new equity, its debt will increase by $6,000 and its equity by $4,000. Its optimal debt-equity ratio of 150 percent will be maintained.

Conversely, consider the lease alternative. Because the lessee views the lease payment as a liability, the lessee thinks in terms of a *liability-to-equity* ratio, not just a debt-to-equity ratio. As mentioned above, the present value of the lease liability is $10,000. If the leasing

■ TABLE 21.5   **Debt Displacement Elsewhere in the Firm When a Lease Is Instituted**

Assets		Liabilities	
Initial situation			
Current	$50,000	Debt	$60,000
Fixed	50,000	Equity	40,000
Total	$100,000	Total	$100,000
Buy with secured loan			
Current	$50,000	Debt	$66,000
Fixed	50,000	Equity	44,000
Machine	10,000		
Total	$110,000	Total	$110,000
Lease			
Current	$50,000	Lease	$10,000
Fixed	50,000	Debt	56,000
Machine	10,000	Equity	44,000
Total	$110,000	Total	$110,000

This example shows that leases reduce the level of debt elsewhere in the firm. Though the example illustrates a point, it is not meant to show a *precise* method for calculating debt displacement.

firm is to maintain a liability-to-equity ratio of 150 percent, debt elsewhere in the firm must fall by $4,000 when the lease is instituted. Because debt must be repurchased, net liabilities only rise by $6,000 ($10,000 − $4,000) when $10,000 of assets are placed under lease.[6]

Debt displacement is a hidden cost of leasing. If a firm leases, it will not use as much regular debt as it would otherwise. The benefits of debt capacity will be lost, particularly the lower taxes associated with interest expense.

Optimal Debt Level in the Xomox Example (Advanced)

The previous section showed that leasing displaces debt. Though the section illustrated a point, it was not meant to show the *precise* method for calculating debt displacement. Below, we describe the precise method for calculating the difference in optimal debt levels between purchase and lease in the Xomox example.

From the last line of Table 21.3, we know that the cash flows from the *purchase* alternative relative to the cash flows from the lease alternative are[7]

	Year 0	Year 1	Year 2	Year 3	Year 4	Year 5
Net cash flows from purchase alternative relative to lease alternative	−$10,000	$2,330	$2,330	$2,330	$2,330	$2,330

[6]Growing firms in the real world will not generally repurchase debt when instituting a lease. Rather, they will issue less debt in the future than they would have without the lease.

[7]The last line of Table 21.3 presents the cash flows form the lease alternative relative to the purchase alternative. As pointed out earlier, our cash flows are now reversed because we are now presenting the cash flows from the purchase alternative relative to the lease alternative.

An increase in the optimal debt level at year 0 occurs because the firm learns at that time of guaranteed cash flows beginning at year 1. Our detour on discounting and debt capacity told us to calculate this increased debt level by discounting the future riskless cash inflows at the after-tax interest rate.[8] Thus, additional debt level of the purchase alternative relative to the lease alternative is

Increase in optimal debt level from purchase alternative relative to lease alternative:

$$\$10,087.68 = \frac{\$2,330}{1.05} + \frac{\$2,330}{(1.05)^2} + \frac{\$2,330}{(1.05)^3} + \frac{\$2,330}{(1.05)^4} + \frac{\$2,330}{(1.05)^5}$$

That is, whatever the optimal amount of debt would be under the lease alternative, the optimal amount of debt would be $10,087.68 more under the purchase alternative.

This result can be stated in another way. Imagine there are two identical firms except that one firm purchases the boring machine and the other leases it. From Table 21.3, we know that the purchasing firm generates $2,330 more cash flow after taxes in each of the five years than does the leasing firm. Further imagine that the same bank lends money to both firms. The bank should lend the purchasing firm more money because it has a greater cash flow each period. How much extra money should the bank loan the purchasing firm so that the incremental loan can be paid off by the extra cash flows of $2,330 per year? The answer is exactly $10,087.68, the increase in the optimal debt level we calculated earlier.

To see this, let us work through the example on a year-by-year basis. Because the purchasing firm borrows $10,087.68 more at year 0 than does the leasing firm, the purchasing firm will pay interest of $764.22 ($10,087.68 × 0.0757575) at year 1 on the additional debt. The interest allows the firm to reduce its taxes by $259.83 ($764.22 × 0.34), leaving an after-tax outflow of $504.39 ($764.22 − $259.83) at year 1.

We know from Table 21.3 that the purchasing firm generates $2,330 more cash at year 1 than does the leasing firm. Because the purchasing firm has the extra $2,330 coming in at year 1 but must pay interest on its loan, how much of the loan can the firm repay at year 1 and still have the same cash flow as the leasing firm has? The purchasing firm can repay $1,825.61 ($2,330 − $504.39) of the loan at year 1 and still have the same net cash flow that the leasing firm has. After the repayment, the purchasing firm will have a remaining balance of $8,262.07 ($10,087.68 − $1,825.61) at year 1. For each of the five years, this sequence of cash flows is displayed in Table 21.6. The outstanding balance goes to zero over the five years. Thus, the annual cash flow of $2,330, which represents the extra cash from purchasing instead of leasing, fully amortizes the loan of $10,087.68.

Our analysis on debt capacity has two purposes. First, we want to show the additional debt capacity from purchasing. We just completed this task. Second, we want to determine whether or not the lease is preferred to the purchase. This decision rule follows easily from the above discussion. By leasing the equipment and having $10,087.68 less debt than under the purchase alternative, the firm has exactly the same cash flow in years 1 to 5 that it would have through a levered purchase. Thus, we can ignore cash flows beginning in year 1 when comparing the lease alternative with the purchase with debt alternative. However, the cash flows differ between the alternatives at year 0. These differences are

1. *The Purchase Cost at Year 0 of $10,000 Is Avoided by Leasing.* This should be viewed as a cash inflow under the leasing alternative.

---

[8]Though our detour considered only riskless cash flows, the cash flows in a leasing example are not necessarily riskless. As we explained earlier, we therefore adopt the real-world convention of discounting at the after-tax interest rate on secured debt issued by the lessee.

■ TABLE 21.6 **Calculation of Increase in Optimal Debt Level if Xomox Purchases instead of Leases**

	Year 0	Year 1	Year 2	Year 3	Year 4	Year 5
Outstanding balance of loan	$10,087.68	$8,262.07*	$6,345.17	$4,332.42	$2,219.05	$ 0
Interest		764.22	625.91	480.69	328.22	168.11
Tax deduction on interest		259.83	212.81	163.44	111.59	57.16
After-tax interest expense		$ 504.39	$ 413.10	$ 317.25	$ 216.63	$110.95
Extra cash that purchasing firm generates over leasing firm (from Table 24.2)		$2,330.00	$2,330.00	$2,330.00	$2,330.00	$2,330.00
Repayment of loan		$1,825.61†	$1,916.90	$2,012.75	$2,113.37	$2,219.05

Assume that there are two otherwise-identical firms where one leases and the other purchases. The purchasing firm can borrow $10,087.68 more than the leasing firm. The extra cash flow each year of $2,330 from purchasing instead of leasing can be used to pay off the loan in five years.
*$8,262.07 = $10,087.68 − $1,825.61.
†$1,825.61 = $2,330 − $504.39.

2. *The Firm Borrows $10,087.68 Less at Year 0 under the Lease Alternative Than It Can under the Purchase Alternative.* This should be viewed as a cash outflow under the leasing alternative.

Because the firm borrows $10,087.68 less by leasing but saves only $10,000 on the equipment, the lease alternative requires an extra cash outflow at year 0 relative to the purchase alternative of −$87.68 ($10,000 − $10,087.68). Because cash flows in later years from leasing are identical to those from purchasing with debt, the firm should purchase.

This is exactly the same answer we got when, earlier in this chapter, we discounted all cash flows at the after-tax interest rate. Of course, this is no coincidence because the increase in the optimal debt level is also determined by discounting all flows at the after-tax interest rate. The accompanying box presents both methods. (The numbers in the box are in terms of the NPV of the lease relative to the purchase. Thus, a negative NPV indicates that the purchase alternative should be taken.)

TWO METHODS FOR CALCULATING NET PRESENT VALUE OF LEASE RELATIVE TO PURCHASE*

Method 1: Discount all cash flows at the after-tax interest rate

$$-\$87.68 = \$10,000 - \$2,330 \times A^5_{0.05}$$

Method 2: Compare purchase price with reduction in optimal debt level under leasing alternative

$$-\$87.68 = \underset{\substack{\text{Purchase} \\ \text{price}}}{\$10,000} - \underset{\substack{\text{Reduction in} \\ \text{optimal debt} \\ \text{level if leasing}}}{\$10,087.68}$$

*Because we are calculating the NPV of the lease relative to the purchase, a negative value indicates that the purchase alternative is preferred.

■ TABLE 21.7   **Cash Flows to Friendly Leasing as Lessor of IBMC Pipe-Boring Machine**

	Year 0	Year 1	Year 2	Year 3	Year 4	Year 5
Cash for machine	−$10,000					
Depreciation tax benefit ($680 = $2,000 × 0.34)		$ 680	$ 680	$ 680	$ 680	$ 680
After-tax lease payment [$1,650 = $2,500 × (1 − 0.34)]		1,650	1,650	1,650	1,650	1,650
Total	−$10,000	$2,330	$2,330	$2,330	$2,330	$2,330

These cash flows are the opposite of the cash flows to Xomox, the lessee (see the bottom line of Table 21.3).

21.8 DOES LEASING EVER PAY: THE BASE CASE

We previously looked at the lease-buy decision from the point of view of the potential lessee, Xomox. Let's now look at the decision from the point of view of the lessor, Friendly Leasing. This firm faces three cash flows, all of which are displayed in Table 21.7. First, Friendly purchases the machine for $10,000 at year 0. Second, because the asset is depreciated straight-line over five year, the depreciation expense at the end of each of the five years is $2,000 ($10,000/5). The yearly depreciation tax shield is $680 ($2,000 × 0.34). Third, because the yearly lease payment is $2,500, the after-tax lease payment is $1,650 [$2,500 × (1 − 0.34)].

Now examine the total cash flows to Friendly Leasing, as displayed in the bottom line of Table 21.7. Those of you with a healthy memory will notice something very interesting. These cash flows are exactly the *opposite* of those of Xomox, as displayed in the bottom line of Table 21.3. Those of you with a healthy sense of skepticism may be thinking something very interesting: "If the cash flows of the lessor are exactly the opposite of those of the lessee, the combined cash flow of the two parties must be zero each year. Thus, there does not seem to be any joint benefit to this lease. Because the net present value to the lessee was −$87.68, the NPV to the lessor must be $87.68. The joint NPV is $0 (−$87.68 + $87.68). There does not appear to be any way for the NPV of both the lessor and the lessee to be positive at the same time. Because one party would inevitably lose money, the leasing deal could never fly."

This is one of the most important results of leasing. Though Table 21.7 concerns one particular leasing deal, the principle can be generalized. As long as (1) both parties are subject to the same interest and tax rates and (2) transaction costs are ignored, there can be no leasing deal that benefits both parties. However, there is a lease payment for which both parties would calculate an NPV of zero. Given that fee, Xomox would be indifferent to whether it leased or bought, and Friendly Leasing would be indifferent to whether it leased or not.[9]

---

[9]The break-even lease payment is $2,469.32 in our example. Both the lessor and lessee can solve for this as

$$\$10,000 = \$680 \times A^5_{0.05} + L \times (1 - 0.34) \times A^5_{0.05}$$

In this case, $L = \$2,469.32$.

A student with an even healthier sense of skepticism might be thinking, "This textbook appears to be arguing that leasing is not beneficial. Yet, we know that leasing occurs frequently in the real world. Maybe, just maybe, the textbook is wrong." Although we will not admit to being wrong (what textbook would?!), we freely admit to being incomplete at this point. The next section considers factors that give benefits to leasing.

21.9 REASONS FOR LEASING

Proponents of leasing make many claims about why firms should lease assets rather than buy them. Some of the reasons given to support leasing are good, and some are not. We discuss here the reasons for leasing we think are good and some of the ones we think aren't.

Good Reasons for Leasing

If leasing is a good choice, it will be because one or more of the following will be true:

1. Taxes may be reduced by leasing.
2. The lease contract may reduce certain types of uncertainty.
3. Transactions costs can be higher for buying an asset and financing it with debt or equity than for leasing the asset.

Tax Advantages   The most important reason for long-term leasing is tax reduction. If the corporate income tax were repealed, long-term leasing would probably disappear. The tax advantages of leasing exist because firms are in different tax brackets.

Should a user in a low tax bracket purchase, he will receive little tax benefit from depreciation and interest deductions. Should the user lease, the lessor will receive the depreciation shield and the interest deductions. In a competitive market, the lessor must charge a low lease payment to reflect these tax shields. Thus, the user is likely to lease rather than purchase.

In our example with Xomox and Friendly Leasing, the value of the lease to Friendly was $87.68. That is,

$$\$87.68 = -\$10,000 + \$2,330 \times A_{0.05}^{5}$$

However, the value of the lease to Xomox was exactly the opposite (−$87.68). Because the lessor's gains came at the expense of the lessee, no deal could be arranged.

However, if Xomox pays no taxes and the lease payments are reduced to $2,475 from $2,500, both Friendly and Xomox will find there is positive NPV in leasing. Xomox can rework Table 21.3 with $T_c = 0$, finding that its cash flows from leasing are

	Year 0	Year 1	Year 2	Year 3	Year 4	Year 5
Cost of machine	$10,000					
Lease payment		−$2,475	−$2,475	−$2,475	−$2,475	−$2,475

The value of the lease to Xomox is

$$\text{Value of lease} = \$10,000 - \$2,475 \times A_{0.0757575}^{5}$$
$$= \$6.55$$

Notice that the discount rate is the interest rate of 7.57575 percent because tax rates are zero. In addition, the full lease payment of $2,475—and not some lower, after-tax number—is used since there are no taxes. Finally, note that depreciation is ignored, also because no taxes apply.

Given a lease payment of $2,475, the cash flows to Friendly Leasing are

	Year 0	Year 1	Year 2	Year 3	Year 4	Year 5
Cost of machine	−$10,000					
Depreciation tax shield ($680 = $2,000 × 0.34)		$ 680	$ 680	$ 680	$ 680	$ 680
After-tax lease payment [$1,633.50 = $2,475 × (1 − 0.34)]		$1,633.50	$1,633.50	$1,633.50	$1,633.50	$1,633.50
Total		$2,313.50	$2,313.50	$2,313.50	$2,313.50	$2,313.50

The value of the lease to Friendly is

$$\text{Value of lease} = -\$10,000 + \$2,313.50 \times A^5_{0.05}$$
$$= -\$10,000 + \$10,016.24$$
$$= \$16.24$$

As a consequence of different tax rates, the lessee (Xomox) gains $6.55 and the lessor (Friendly) gains $16.24. Both the lessor and the lessee can gain if their tax rates are different, because the lessor uses the depreciation and interest tax shields that cannot be used by the lessee. The IRS loses tax revenue, and some of the tax gains to the lessor are passed on to the lessee in the form of lower lease payments.

Because both parties can gain when tax rates differ, the lease payment is agreed upon through negotiation. Before negotiation begins, each party needs to know the *reservation payment* of both parties. This is the payment such that one party will be indifferent to whether it entered the lease deal or not. In other words, this is the payment such that the value of the lease is zero. These payments are calculated below.

Reservation Payment of Lessee   We now solve for L_{MAX}, the payment such that the value of the lease to the lessee is zero. When the lessee is in a zero tax bracket, his cash flows, in terms of L_{MAX}, are

	Year 0	Year 1	Year 2	Year 3	Year 4	Year 5
Cost of machine	$10,000					
Lease payment		$-L_{MAX}$	$-L_{MAX}$	$-L_{MAX}$	$-L_{MAX}$	$-L_{MAX}$

This chart implies that

$$\text{Value of lease} = \$10,000 - L_{MAX} \times A^5_{0.0757575}$$

The value of the lease equals zero when

$$L_{MAX} = \frac{\$10,000}{A^5_{0.0757575}} = \$2,476.62$$

After performing this calculation, the lessor knows that he will never be able to charge a payment above $2,476.62.

Reservation Payment of Lessor   We now solve for L_{MIN}, the payment such that the value of the lease to the lessor is zero. The cash flows to the lessor, in terms of L_{MIN}, are

	Year 0	Year 1	Year 2	Year 3	Year 4	Year 5
Cost of machine	−$10,000					
Depreciation tax shield ($680 = $2,000 × 0.34)		$680	$680	$680	$680	$680
After-tax lease payment ($T_c = 0.34$)		$L_{MIN} \times (0.66)$	$L_{MIN} \times (0.66)$	$L_{MIN} \times (0.66)$	$L_{MIN} \times (0.66)$	$L_{MIN} \times (0.66)$

This chart implies that

$$\text{Value of lease} = -\$10,000 + \$680 \times A_{0.05}^5 + L_{MIN} \times (0.66) \times A_{0.05}^5$$

The value of the lease equals zero when

$$L_{MIN} = \frac{\$10,000}{0.66 \times A_{0.05}^5} - \frac{\$680}{0.066}$$

$$= \$3,499.62 - \$1,030.30$$

$$= \$2,469.32$$

After performing this calculation, the lessee knows that the lessor will never agree to a lease payment below $2,469.32.

A Reduction of Uncertainty   We have noted that the lessee does not own the property when the lease expires. The value of the property at this time is called the *residual value,* and the lessor has a firm claim to it. When the lease contract is signed, there may be substantial uncertainty as to what the residual value of the asset will be. Thus, under a lease contract, this residual risk is borne by the lessor. Conversely, the user bears this risk when purchasing.

It is common sense that the party best able to bear a particular risk should do so. If the user has little risk aversion, he will not suffer by purchasing. However, if the user is highly averse to risk, he should find a third-party lessor more capable of assuming this burden.

This latter situation frequently arises when the user is a small and/or newly formed firm. Because the risk of the entire firm is likely to be quite high and because the principal stockholders are likely to be undiversified, the firm desires to minimize risk wherever possible. A potential lessor, such as a large and publicly held financial institution, is far more capable of bearing the risk. Conversely, this situation is not expected to happen when the user is a blue chip corporation. That potential lessee is more able to bear risk.

Transactions Costs   The costs of changing an asset's ownership are generally greater than the costs of writing a lease agreement. Consider the choice that confronts a person who lives in Los Angeles but must do business in New York for two days. It will clearly be cheaper to rent a hotel room for two nights than it would be to buy an apartment condominium for two days and then to sell it.

Unfortunately, leases generate agency costs as well. For example, the lessee might misuse or overuse the asset, since she has no interest in the asset's residual value. This cost will be implicitly paid by the lessee through a high lease payment. Although the lessor can reduce these agency costs through monitoring, monitoring itself is costly.

Thus, leasing is most beneficial when the transaction costs of purchase and resale outweigh the agency costs and monitoring costs of a lease. Flath argues that this occurs in short-term leases but not in long-term leases.[10]

---

[10]D. Flath, "The Economics of Short Term Leasing," *Economic Inquiry* 18 (April 1980).

Bad Reasons for Leasing

Leasing and Accounting Income   In our discussion on "Accounting and Leasing," we pointed out that a firm's balance sheet shows fewer liabilities with an operating lease than with either a capitalized lease or a purchase financed with debt. We indicated that a firm desiring to project a strong balance sheet might select an operating lease. In addition, the firm's return on assets (ROA) is generally higher with an operating lease than with either a capitalized lease or a purchase. To see this, we look at the numerator and denominator of the ROA formula in turn.

With an operating lease, lease payments are treated as an expense. If the asset is purchased, both depreciation and interest charges are expenses. At least in the early part of the asset's life, the yearly lease payment is generally less than the sum of yearly depreciation and yearly interest. Thus, accounting income, the numerator of the ROA formula, is higher with an operating lease than with a purchase. Because accounting expenses with a capitalized lease are analogous to depreciation and interest with a purchase, the increase in accounting income does not occur when a lease is capitalized.

In addition, leased assets do not appear on the balance sheet with an operating lease. Thus, the total asset value of a firm, the denominator of the ROA formula, is less with an operating lease than it is with either a purchase or a capitalized lease. The two preceding effects imply that the firm's ROA should be higher with an operating lease than with either a purchase or a capitalized lease.

Of course, in an efficient capital market, accounting information cannot be used to fool investors. It is unlikely, then, that leasing's impact on accounting numbers should create value for the firm. Savvy investors should be able to see through attempts by management to improve the firm's financial statements.

One Hundred-Percent Financing   It is often claimed that leasing provides 100-percent financing, whereas secured equipment loans require an initial down payment. However, we argued earlier that leases tend to displace debt elsewhere in the firm. Our earlier analysis suggests that leases do not permit a greater level of total liabilities than do purchases with borrowing.

Other Reasons   There are, of course, many special reasons that some companies find advantages in leasing. In one celebrated case, the U.S. Navy leased a fleet of tankers instead of asking Congress for appropriations. Thus, leasing may be used to circumvent capital-expenditure control systems set up by bureaucratic firms.

CONCEPT QUESTION

• Summarize the good and bad arguments for leasing.

21.10 SOME UNANSWERED QUESTIONS

Our analysis suggests that the primary advantage of long-term leasing results from the differential tax rates of the lessor and the lessee. Other valid reasons for leasing are lower contracting costs and risk reduction. There are several questions our analysis has not specifically answered.

Are the Uses of Leases and of Debt Complementary?

Ang and Peterson find that firms with high debt tend to lease frequently as well.[11] This result should not be puzzling. The corporate attributes that provide high debt capacity may also make leasing advantageous. Thus, even though leasing displaces debt (that is, leasing and borrowing are substitutes) for an individual firm, high debt and high leasing can be positively associated when one looks at a number of firms.

Why Are Leases Offered by Both Manufacturers and Third-Party Lessors?

The offsetting effects of taxes can explain why both manufacturers (for example, computer firms) and third-party lessors offer leases.

1. For manufacturer lessors, the basis for determining depreciation is the manufacturer's cost. For third-party lessors, the basis is the sales price that the lessor paid to the manufacturer. Because the sales price is generally greater than the manufacturer's cost, this is an advantage to third-party lessors.

2. However, the manufacturer must recognize a profit for tax purposes when selling the asset to the third-party lessor. The manufacturer's profit for some equipment can be deferred if the manufacturer becomes the lessor. This provides an incentive for manufacturers to lease.

Why Are Some Assets Leased More than Others?

Certain assets appear to be leased more frequently than others. Smith and Wakeman have looked at nontax incentives affecting leasing.[12] Their analysis suggests many asset and firm characteristics that are important in the lease-or-buy decision. The following are among the things they mention:

1. The more sensitive the value of an asset is to use and maintenance decisions, the more likely it is that the asset will be purchased instead of leased. They argue that ownership provides a better incentive to minimize maintenance costs than does leasing.

2. Price-discrimination opportunities may be important. Leasing may be a way of circumventing laws against charging too *low* a price.

21.11 SUMMARY AND CONCLUSIONS

A large fraction of America's equipment is leased rather than purchased. This chapter both describes the institutional arrangements surrounding leases and shows how to evaluate leases financially.

1. Leases can be separated into two polar types. Though operating leases allow the lessee to use the equipment, ownership remains with the lessor. Although the lessor in a financial lease legally owns the equipment, the lessee maintains effective ownership because financial leases are fully amortized.

---

[11]J. Ang and P. P. Peterson, "The Leasing Puzzle," *Journal of Finance* 39 (September 1984).

[12]C. W. Smith, Jr., and L. M. Wakeman, "Determinants of Corporate Leasing Policy," *Journal of Finance* (July 1985)

2. When a firm purchases an asset with debt, both the asset and the liability appear on the firm's balance sheet. If a lease meets at least one of a number of criteria, it must be capitalized. This means that the present value of the lease appears as both an asset and a liability. A lease escapes capitalization if it does not meet any of these criteria. Leases not meeting the criteria are called *operating leases,* though the accountant's definition differs somewhat from the practitioner's definition. Operating leases do not appear on the balance sheet. For cosmetic reasons, many firms prefer that a lease be called *operating.*

3. Firms generally lease for tax purposes. To protect its interests, the IRS allows financial arrangements to be classified as leases only if a number of criteria are met.

4. We showed that risk-free cash flows should be discounted at the after-tax risk-free rate. Because both lease payments and depreciation tax shields are nearly riskless, all relevant cash flows in the lease-buy decision should be discounted at a rate near this after-tax rate. We use the real-world convention of discounting at the after-tax interest rate on the lessee's secured debt.

5. Though this method is simple, it lacks certain intuitive appeal. In an optional section, we presented an alternative method in the hopes of increasing the reader's intuition. Relative to a lease, a purchase generates debt capacity. This increase in debt capacity can be calculated by discounting the difference between the cash flows of the purchase and the cash flows of the lease by the after-tax interest rate. The increase in debt capacity from a purchase is compared to the extra outflow at year 0 from a purchase.

6. If the lessor is in the same tax bracket as the lessee, the cash flows to the lessor are exactly the opposite of the cash flows to the lessee. Thus, the sum of the value of the lease to the lessee plus the value of the lease to the lessor must be zero. While this suggests that leases can never fly, there are actually at least three good reasons for leasing:

   a. Differences in tax brackets between lessor and lessee.

   b. Shift of risk-bearing to the lessor.

   c. Minimization of transaction costs.

   We also document a number of bad reasons for leasing.

Key Terms

Debt displacement 597	Leveraged lease 588
Direct leases 587	Off–balance-sheet financing 589
Financial leases 588	Operating lease 587
Lessee 586	Sales and lease-back 588
Lessor 586	Sales-type leases 587

Suggested Readings

Some evidence on the determination of discount rates used in leasing is found in
Schallheim, J. S.; R. E. Johnson; R. C. Lease; and J. J. McConnell. "The Determinants of Yields on Financial Leasing Contracts." *Journal of Financial Economics* (1987).

Other good articles on leasing are
Bowman, R. G. "The Debt Equivalence of Leases: An Empirical Investigation." *Accounting Review* 55 (April 1980).

Crawford, P. J.; C. P. Harper; and J. J. McConnell. "Further Evidence on the Terms of Financial Leases." *Financial Management* 10 (Autumn 1981).

Franks, J. R., and S. D. Hodges. "Valuation of Financial Lease Contracts: A Note." *Journal of Finance* (May 1978).

Myers, S.; D. A. Dill; and A. J. Bautista. "Valuation of Financial Lease Contracts." *Journal of Finance* (June 1976).

Other important readings are

Ang, J., and P. P. Peterson. "The Leasing Puzzle." *Journal of Finance* 39 (September 1984).

McConnell, J. J., and J. S. Schallheim. "Valuation of Asset Leasing Contracts." *Journal of Financial Economics* 12 (August 1983).

Schall, L. D. "The Lease-or-Buy and Asset Acquisition Decisions." *Journal of Finance* 29 (September 1974).

Sivarama, K. V., and R. C. Moyer. "Bankruptcy Costs and Financial Leasing Decisions." *Financial Management* (1994).

Smith, C. W., Jr., and L. M. Wakeman. "Determinations of Corporate Leasing Policy." *Journal of Finance* (July 1985).

Sorenson, I. W., and R. E. Johnson. "Equipment Financial Leasing Practices and Costs: An Empirical Study." *Financial Management* (Spring 1977).

A complete guide to the lease-versus-buy decision is in

Schallheim, James S. *Lease or Buy.* Boston, Mass.: Harvard Business School Press, 1994.

Questions and Problems

21.1 Discuss the validity of each of the following statements.
   a. Leasing reduces risk and can reduce a firm's cost of capital.
   b. Leasing provides 100-percent financing.
   c. Firms that do a large amount of leasing will not do much borrowing.
   d. If the tax advantages of leasing were eliminated, leasing would disappear.

21.2 Quartz Corporation is a relatively new firm. Quartz has experienced enough losses during its early years to provide it with at least eight years of tax-loss carryforwards. Thus, Quartz's effective tax rate is zero. Quartz plans to lease equipment from New Leasing Company. The term of the lease is five years. The purchase cost of the equipment is $250,000. New Leasing Company is in the 35-percent tax bracket. There are no transaction costs to the lease. Each firm can borrow at 8 percent.
   a. What is Quartz's reservation price?
   b. What is New Leasing Company's reservation price?
   c. Explain why these reservation prices determine the negotiating range of the lease.

21.3 Super Sonics Entertainment is considering borrowing money at 11 percent and purchasing a machine that costs $350,000. The machine will be depreciated over five years by the straight-line method and will be worthless in five years. Super Sonics can lease the machine with the year-end payments of $94,200. The corporate tax rate is 35 percent. Should Super Sonics buy or lease?

21.4 Maxwell, Inc., is entering negotiations for the lease of equipment that has a $200,000 purchase price. Maxwell's effective tax rate is zero. Maxwell will be negotiating the lease with Mercer Leasing Corp. The term of the lease is five years. Mercer Leasing Corp. is in the 35-percent tax bracket. There are no transaction costs to the lease. Each firm can borrow at 10 percent. What is the negotiating range of the lease?

21.5 Raymond Rayon Corporation wants to expand its manufacturing facilities. Liberty Leasing Corporation has offered Raymond Rayon the opportunity to lease a machine for $100,000 for five years. The machine will be fully depreciated by the straight-line method. The corporate tax rate for Raymond Rayon is 25 percent, while Liberty Leasing's corporate tax rate is 35 percent. The appropriate before-tax interest rate is 8 percent. Assume lease payments occur at year-end. What is Raymond's reservation price? What is Liberty's reservation price? What is the negotiating range of the lease?

21.6 An asset costs $86.87. Only straight-line depreciation is allowed for this asset. The asset's useful life is two years. It will have no salvage value. The corporate tax rate on ordinary income is 34 percent. The interest rate on risk-free cash flows is 10 percent.

     a. What set of lease payments will make the lessee and the lessor equally well off?

     b. Show the general condition that will make the value of a lease to the lessor the negative of the value to the lessee.

     c. Assume that the lessee pays no taxes and the lessor is in the 34-percent tax bracket. For what range of lease payments does the lease have a positive NPV for both parties?

21.7 High electricity costs have made Farmer Corporation's chicken-plucking machine economically worthless. There are only two machines available to replace it.

     The International Plucking Machine (IPM) model is available only on a lease basis. The annual, end-of-year payments are $2,100 for five years. This machine will save Farmer $6,000 per year through reductions in electricity costs in each of the five years.

     As an alternative, Farmer can purchase a more energy-efficient machine from Basic Machine Corporation (BMC) for $15,000. This machine will save $9,000 per year in electricity costs. A local bank has offered to finance the machine with a $15,000 loan. The interest rate on the loan will be 10 percent on the remaining balance and five annual principal payments of $3,000.

     Farmer has a target debt-to-asset ratio of 67 percent. Farmer is in the 34-percent tax bracket. After five years, both machines are worthless. Only straight-line depreciation is allowed for chicken-plucking machines. The savings that Farmer will enjoy are known with certainty, because Farmer has a long-term chicken purchase agreement with State Food Products, Inc., and a four-year backlog of orders.

     a. Should Farmer lease the IPM machine or purchase the more efficient BMC machine?

     b. Does your answer depend on the form of financing for direct purchase?

     c. How much debt is displaced by this lease?

21.8 Redwood Timberland Corporation is a furniture manufacturer that is considering installing a milling machine for $420,000. The machine will be straight-line depreciated over seven years and will be worthless after its economic life. Redwood has been financially distressed and thus the company does not appear to get tax shields over the next seven years. American Leasing Company has offered to lease the machine over seven years. The corporate tax rate for Redwood is 35 percent. The appropriate before-tax interest rate is 6 percent for both firms. Lease payments occur at the beginning of the year. What is Redwood's reservation price? What is American's reservation price? What is the negotiating range of the lease?

21.9 Wolfson Corporation has decided to purchase a new machine that costs $3 million. The machine will be worthless after three years. Only straight-line method is allowed by the IRS for this type of machine. Wolfson is in the 35-percent tax bracket.

     The Sur Bank has offered Wolfson a three-year loan for $3 million. The repayment schedule is three yearly principal repayments of $1 million and an interest charge of 12 percent on the outstanding balance of the loan at the beginning of each year. Twelve percent is the marketwide rate of interest. Both principal repayments and interest are due at the end of each year.

     Cal Leasing Corporation offers to lease the same machine to Wolfson. Lease payments of $1.2 million per year are due at the end of each of the three years of the lease.

     a. Should Wolfson lease the machine or buy it with bank financing?

     b. What is the annual lease payment that will make Wolfson indifferent to whether it leases the machine or purchases it?

Appendix 21A APV Approach to Leasing

The box that appeared earlier in this chapter showed two methods for calculating the NPV of the lease relative to the purchase:

1. Discount all cash flows at the after-tax interest rate.

2. Compare the purchase price with reduction in optimal debt level under the leasing alternative.

Surprisingly (and perhaps unfortunately) there is still another method. We feel compelled to present this third method, because it has important links with the adjusted present value (APV) approach discussed earlier in this text. We illustrate this approach using the Xomox example developed in Table 21.3.

In a previous chapter, we learned that the APV of any project can be expressed as

$$APV = \text{All-equity value} + \text{Additional effects of debt}$$

In other words, the adjusted present value of a project is the sum of the net present value of the project when financed by all equity plus the additional effects from debt financing. In the context of the lease-versus-buy decision, the APV method can be expressed as

$$
\begin{array}{ccc}
\text{Adjusted present value} & \text{Net present value of} & \\
\text{of the lease relative to} = & \text{the lease relative to the} & \text{Additional effects when} \\
\text{the purchase} & \text{purchase when} \quad - & \text{purchase is financed} \\
& \text{purchase is financed} & \text{with some debt} \\
& \text{by all equity} &
\end{array}
$$

All-Equity Value

From an earlier chapter, we know that the all-equity value is simply the NPV of the cash flows discounted at the *pretax* interest rate. For the Xomox example, we know from Table 21.3 that this value is

$$\$592.03 = \$10,000 - \$2,330 \times A^5_{0.0757575}$$

This calculation is identical to method 1 in the earlier box except that we are now discounting at the pretax interest rate. The calculation states that the lease is preferred over the purchase by $592.03 if the purchase is financed by all equity. Because debt financing generates a tax subsidy, it is not surprising that the lease alternative would be preferred by almost $600 over the purchase alternative if debt were not allowed.

Additional Effects of Debt

We learned earlier in the text that the interest tax shield in any year is the interest multiplied by the corporate tax rate. Taking the interest in each of the five years from Table 21.6, the present value of the interest tax shield is

$$\$679.71 = 0.34\left[\frac{\$764.22}{1.0757575} + \frac{\$625.91}{(1.0757575)^2} + \frac{\$480.69}{(1.0757575)^3}\right.$$
$$\left. + \frac{\$328.21}{(1.0757575)^4} + \frac{\$168.11}{(1.0757575)^5}\right]$$

This tax shield must be subtracted from the NPV of the lease because it represents interest deductions not available under the lease alternative. The adjusted present value of the lease relative to the purchase is

$$-\$87.68 = \$592.03 - \$679.71$$

This value is the same as our calculations from the previous two approaches, implying that all three approaches are equivalent. The accompanying box presents the APV approach.

A Third Method for Calculating Net Present Value of Lease Relative to Purchase*†

Method 3: Calculate APV:

$$\text{All-equity value: } \$592.03 = \$10,000 - \$2,330 \times A^5_{0.0757575}$$

Additional effects of debt:‡

$$-\$679.71 = -0.34\left[\frac{\$764.22}{1.0757575} + \frac{\$625.91}{(1.0757575)^2} + \frac{\$480.69}{(1.0757575)^3}\right.$$
$$\left. + \frac{\$328.21}{(1.0757575)^4} + \frac{\$168.11}{(1.0757575)^5}\right]$$

$$\text{APV} = -\$87.68 = \$592.03 - \$679.71$$

---

*Because we are calculating the NPV of the lease relative to the purchase, a negative value indicates that the purchase alternative is preferred.

†The first two methods are shown in the earlier box appearing in this chapter.

‡The firm misses the interest deductions if it leases. Because we are calculating the NPV of the lease relative to the purchase, the additional effect of debt is a negative number.

Which approach is easiest to calculate? The first approach is easiest because one need only discount the cash flows at the after-tax interest rate. Though the second and third approaches (in the two boxes) look easy, the extra step of calculating the increased debt capacity is needed for both of them.

Which approach is more intuitive? Our experience is that students generally find the third method the most intuitive. This is probably because they have already learned the APV method from a previous chapter. The second method is generally straightforward to those students who have taken the time to understand the increased-debt-level concept. However, the first method seems to have the least intuitive appeal because it is merely a mechanical approach.

Which approach should the practitioner use? The practitioner should use the simplest approach, which is the first. We included the others only for intuitive appeal.

Options, Futures, and Corporate Finance

THE public has often viewed options and futures as exotic and risky instruments that individuals enter into at their peril. Although these derivatives can increase risk, they also have important uses to corporations. In Part VI, we discuss these instruments in detail, showing three basic ideas: Recent advances allow options and futures to be easily priced. Options are frequently embedded or hidden in the everyday activities of corporations. Firms can actually use derivatives to reduce risk.

In Chapter 22 we examine options. First we describe the options that trade on organized exchanges. Options are contingent claims on the value of an underlying asset. Every issue of corporate security has option features. Later in the chapter we present a formal model that can be used to value options. The model bears no resemblance to net present value (NPV). Our goal is to present the underlying logic of option valuation. This is important because NPV does not work well for contingent claims.

In Chapter 23, we describe some extensions of option pricing theory. There are option-like features in most investing and financing decisions.

In Chapter 24 we look at bonds with special option features. These bonds are sold as bonds with warrants and as bonds convertible into common stock. A warrant gives the holder a right to buy shares of common stock for cash, and a convertible bond gives the holder the right to exchange it for shares of common stock.

Previous chapters of this text assume that the volatility of the firm is fixed. Chapter 25 shows how firms can use financial instruments to reduce their risk, specifically discussing financial futures.

CHAPTER 22

Options and Corporate Finance: Basic Concepts

EXECUTIVE SUMMARY

In the summer of 2000, General Mills (GM) made an offer to acquire the Pillsbury division of Diageo PLC. Although the offer was generous, the managers of Diageo were worried about the possibility of a decline in GM's stock price. The deal eventually went through, due to a creative financing technique called a contingent value rights (CVR). Although CVRs may seem arcane, they are really straightforward applications of options, a topic to be examined in this chapter.

Options are special contractual arrangements giving the owner the right to buy or sell an asset at a fixed price anytime on or before a given date. Stock options, the most familiar type, are options to buy and sell shares of common stock. Ever since 1973, stock options have been traded on organized exchanges.

Corporate securities are very similar to the stock options that are traded on organized exchanges. Almost every issue of corporate bonds and stocks has option features. In addition, capital-structure decisions and capital-budgeting decisions can be viewed in terms of options.

We start this chapter with a description of different types of publicly traded options. We identify and discuss the factors that determine their values. Next, we show how common stocks and bonds can be thought of as options on the underlying value of the firm. This leads to several new insights concerning corporate finance. For example, we show how certain corporate decisions can be viewed as options. General Mills' issuance of a CVR is one of these corporate decisions.

22.1 OPTIONS

An **option** is a contract giving its owner the right to buy or sell an asset at a fixed price on or before a given date. For example, an option on a building might give the buyer the right to buy the building for $1 million on or anytime before the Saturday prior to the third Wednesday in January 2010. Options are a unique type of financial contract because they give the buyer the right, but not the *obligation,* to do something. The buyer uses the option only if it is advantageous to do so; otherwise the option can be thrown away.

There is a special vocabulary associated with options. Here are some important definitions:

1. **Exercising the Option.** The act of buying or selling the underlying asset via the option contract is referred to as *exercising the option.*
2. **Striking or Exercise Price.** The fixed price in the option contract at which the holder can buy or sell the underlying asset is called the *striking price* or *exercise price.*
3. **Expiration Date.** The maturity date of the option is referred to as the *expiration date.* After this date, the option is dead.
4. **American and European Options.** An American option may be exercised anytime up to the expiration date. A European option differs from an American option in that it can be exercised only on the expiration date.

22.2 CALL OPTIONS

The most common type of option is a **call option.** A call option gives the owner the right to buy an asset at a fixed price during a particular time period. There is no restriction on the kind of asset, but the most common ones traded on exchanges are options on stocks and bonds.

For example, call options on IBM stock can be purchased on the Chicago Board Options Exchange. IBM does not issue (that is, sell) call options on its common stock. Instead, individual investors are the original buyers and sellers of call options on IBM common stock. A representative call option on IBM stock enables an investor to buy 100 shares of IBM on or before July 15, at an exercise price of $100. This is a valuable option if there is some probability that the price of IBM common stock will exceed $100 on or before July 15.

The Value of a Call Option at Expiration

What is the value of a call-option contract on common stock at expiration? The answer depends on the value of the underlying stock at expiration.

Let's continue with the IBM example. Suppose the stock price is $130 at expiration. The buyer[1] of the call option has the right to buy the underlying stock at the exercise price of $100. In other words, he has the right to exercise the call. Having the right to buy something for $100 when it is worth $130 is obviously a good thing. The value[2] of this right is $30 ($130–$100) on the expiration day.

The call would be worth even more if the stock price were higher on expiration day. For example, if IBM were selling for $150 on the date of expiration, the call would be worth $50 ($150–$100) at that time. In fact, the call's value increases $1 for every $1 rise in the stock price.

If the stock price is greater than the exercise price, we say that the call is *in the money.* Of course, it is also possible that the value of the common stock will turn out to be less than the exercise price. In this case, we say that the call is *out of the money.* The holder will not exercise in this case. For example, if the stock price at the expiration date is $90, no rational investor would exercise. Why pay $100 for stock worth only $90? Because the option holder has no obligation to exercise the call, she can *walk away* from the option. As a consequence, if IBM's stock price is less than $100 on the expiration date, the value of the call option will be 0. In this case the value of the call option is not the difference between IBM's stock price and $100, as it would be if the holder of the call option had the *obligation* to exercise the call.

The payoff of a call option at expiration is

<table>
<thead>
<tr><th></th><th colspan="2" style="text-align:center">Payoff on the Expiration Date</th></tr>
<tr><th></th><th>If Stock Price Is Less Than $100</th><th>If Stock Price Is Greater Than $100</th></tr>
</thead>
<tbody>
<tr><td>Call-option value:</td><td>0</td><td>Stock price −$100</td></tr>
</tbody>
</table>

Figure 22.1 plots the value of the call at expiration against the value of IBM's stock. It is referred to as the *hockey-stick diagram* of call-option values. If the stock price is less than $100, the call is out of the money and worthless. If the stock price is greater than $100, the call is in the money and its value rises one-for-one with increases in the stock price. Notice that the call can never have a negative value. It is a *limited-liability instrument,* which means that all the holder can lose is the initial amount she paid for it.

---

[1] We use *buyer, owner,* and *holder* interchangeably.

[2] This example assumes that the call lets the holder purchase one share of stock at $100. In reality, a call lets the holder purchase 100 shares @ $100 per share. The profit would then equal $3000 [($130 − $100) × 100].

■ FIGURE 22.1   **The Value of a Call Option on the Expiration Date**

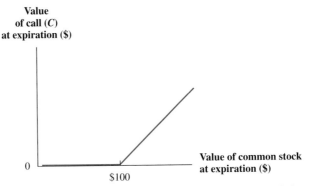

A call option gives the owner the right to buy an asset at a fixed price during a particular time period. If IBM's stock price is greater than $100 at the expiration date, the call's value is

Stock price −$100

If IBM's stock price is less than $100 at this time, the value of the call is zero.

EXAMPLE

Suppose Mr. Optimist holds a one-year call option on TIX common stock. It is a European call option and can be exercised at $150. Assume that the expiration date has arrived. What is the value of the TIX call option on the expiration date? If TIX is selling for $200 per share, Mr. Optimist can exercise the option—purchase TIX at $150—and then immediately sell the share at $200. Mr. Optimist will have made $50 ($200 − $150).

Instead, assume that TIX is selling for $100 per share on the expiration date. If Mr. Optimist still holds the call option, he will throw it out. The value of the TIX call on the expiration date will be zero in this case.

QUESTIONS
CONCEPT
?
- What is a call option?
- How is a call option's price related to the underlying stock price at the expiration date?

22.3 PUT OPTIONS

A **put option** can be viewed as the opposite of a call option. Just as a call gives the holder the right to buy the stock at a fixed price, a put gives the holder the right to *sell* the stock for a fixed exercise price.

The Value of a Put Option at Expiration

The circumstances that determine the value of the put are the opposite of those for a call option, because a put option gives the holder the right to sell shares. Let us assume that the exercise price of the put is $50 and the stock price at expiration is $40. The owner of this put option has the right to sell the stock for *more* than it is worth, something that is clearly

■ FIGURE 22.2 **The Value of a Put Option on the Expiration Date**

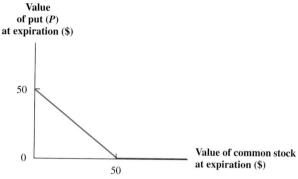

A put option gives the owner the right to sell an asset at a fixed price during a
particular time period. If the stock price is greater than the exercise price of $50,
the put value is zero. If the stock price is less than $50, the put value is

$50 — Stock price

profitable. That is, he can buy the stock at the market price of $40 and immediately sell it
at the exercise price of $50, generating a profit of $10 ($50 − $40). Thus, the value of the
option at expiration must be $10.

The profit would be greater still if the stock price were lower. For example, if the stock
price were only $30, the value of the option would be $20 ($50 − $30). In fact, for every
$1 that the stock price declines at expiration, the value of the put rises by $1.

However, suppose that the stock at expiration is trading at $60—or any price above the
exercise price of $50. The owner of the put would not want to exercise here. It is a losing
proposition to sell stock for $50 when it trades in the open market at $60. Instead, the owner
of the put will walk away from the option. That is, he will let the put option expire.

The payoff of this put option is

	Payoff on the Expiration Date Stock	
	If Stock Price Is Less Than $50	If Stock Price Is Greater Than $50
Put-option value	$50 − stock price	0

Figure 22.2 plots the values of a put option for all possible values of the underlying stock.
It is instructive to compare Figure 22.2 with Figure 22.1 for the call option. The call option
is valuable whenever the stock is above the exercise price, and the put is valuable when the
stock price is below the exercise price.

EXAMPLE ───

Ms. Pessimist feels quite certain that BMI will fall from its current $160-per-share
price. She buys a put. Her put-option contract gives her the right to sell a share of
BMI stock at $150 one year from now. If the price of BMI is $200 on the expiration date, she will tear up the put option contract because it is worthless. That is,
she will not want to sell stock worth $200 for the exercise price of $150.

On the other hand, if BMI is selling for $100 on the expiration date, she will
exercise the option. In this case, she can buy a share of BMI in the market for $100

per share and turn around and sell the share at the exercise price of $150. Her profit will be $50 ($150 − $100). The value of the put option on the expiration date therefore will be $50.

CONCEPT QUESTIONS

- What is a put option?
- How is a put option's price related to the underlying stock price at expiration date?

22.4 SELLING OPTIONS

An investor who sells (or *writes*) a call on common stock promises to deliver shares of the common stock if required to do so by the call-option holder. Notice that the seller is *obligated* to do so.

If, at expiration date, the price of the common stock is greater than the exercise price, the holder will exercise the call and the seller must give the holder shares of stock in exchange for the exercise price. The seller loses the difference between the stock price and the exercise price. For example, assume that the stock price is $60 and the exercise price is $50. Knowing that exercise is imminent, the option seller buys stock in the open market at $60. Because she is obligated to sell at $50, she loses $10 ($50 − $60). Conversely, if at the expiration date, the price of the common stock is below the exercise price, the call option will not be exercised and the seller's liability is zero.

Why would the seller of a call place himself in such a precarious position? After all, the seller loses money if the stock price ends up above the exercise price and he merely avoids losing money if the stock price ends up below the exercise price. The answer is that the seller is paid to take this risk. On the day that the option transaction takes place, the seller receives the price that the buyer pays.

Now, let's look at the seller of puts. An investor who sells a put on common stock agrees to purchase shares of common stock if the put holder should so request. The seller loses on this deal if the stock price falls below the exercise price and the holder puts the stock to the seller. For example, assume that the stock price is $40 and the exercise price is $50. The holder of the put will exercise in this case. In other words, he will sell the underlying stock at the exercise price of $50. This means that the seller of the put must buy the underlying stock at the exercise price of $50. Because the stock is only worth $40, the loss here is $10 ($40 − $50).

The values of the "sell-a-call" and "sell-a-put" positions are depicted in Figure 22.3. The graph on the left-hand side of the figure shows that the seller of a call loses nothing when the stock price at expiration date is below $50. However, the seller loses a dollar for every dollar that the stock rises above $50. The graph in the center of the figure shows that the seller of a put loses nothing when the stock price at expiration date is above $50. However, the seller loses a dollar for every dollar that the stock falls below $50.

It is worthwhile to spend a few minutes comparing the graphs in Figure 22.3 to those in Figures 22.1 and 22.2. The graph of selling a call (the graph in the left-hand side of Figure 22.3) is the mirror image[3] of the graph of buying a call (Figure 22.1). This occurs because options are a zero-sum game. The seller of a call loses what the buyer makes. Similarly, the graph of selling a put (the middle graph in Figure 22.3) is the mirror image of the graph of buying a put (Figure 22.2). Again, the seller of a put loses what the buyer makes.

---

[3]Actually, because of differing exercise prices, the two graphs are not quite mirror images of each other. The exercise price in Figure 22.1 is $100 and the exercise price in Figure 22.3 is $50.

■ FIGURE 22.3 **The Payoffs to Sellers of Calls and Puts, and to Buyers of Common Stock**

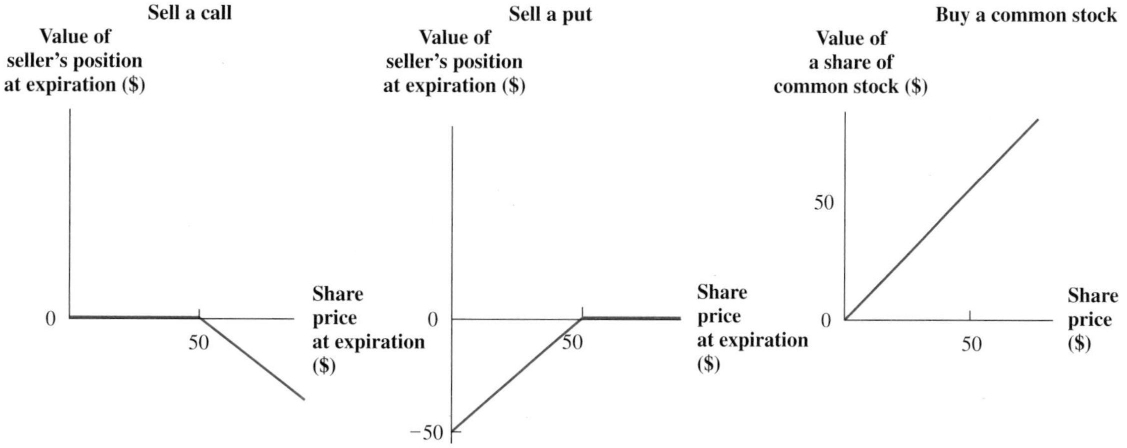

Figure 22.3 also shows the value at expiration of simply buying common stock. Notice that buying the stock is the same as buying a call option on the stock with an exercise price of zero. This is not surprising. If the exercise price is 0, the call holder can buy the stock for nothing, which is really the same as owning it.

22.5 READING *THE WALL STREET JOURNAL*

Now that we understand the definitions for calls and puts, let's see how these options are quoted. Table 22.1 presents information on the options of Microsoft Corporation from a recent issue of *The Wall Street Journal* (WSJ). The options are traded on the Chicago Board Options Exchange, one of a number of options exchanges. The first column tells us that the stock of Microsoft closed at \$90⅜ per share on the previous day. Now consider the second and third columns. The closing price for an option maturing at the end of April with a strike price of \$85 was \$6⅛. Because the option is sold as a 100-share contract, the cost of the contract is \$612.5 (100 × \$6⅛) before commissions. The call maturing in April with an exercise price of \$90 closed at \$2 9/16. The call with an exercise price of \$85 maturing in October did not trade during the day, as indicated by —.

■ TABLE 22.1 **Information on the Options of Microsoft Corporation**

		Chicago Board					
		Calls—Last			Puts—Last		
Option and NY Close	Strike Price	April	July	Oct.	April	July	Oct.
Microsoft							
90⅜	85	6⅛	9¾	—	9/16	3½	—
90⅜	90	2 9/16	7¼	9⅞	2	5	7
90⅜	95	11/16	4¾	—	5	8	—

■ FIGURE 22.4   **Payoff to the Combination of Buying a Put and Buying the Underlying Stock**

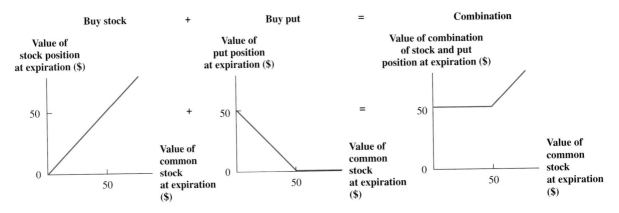

The last three columns display quotes on puts. For example, a put maturing in April with an exercise price of $95 sells at $5.

22.6 COMBINATIONS OF OPTIONS

Puts and calls can serve as building blocks for more complex option contracts. For example, Figure 22.4 illustrates the payoff from buying a put option on a stock and simultaneously buying the stock.

If the share price is greater than the exercise price, the put option is worthless, and the value of the combined position is equal to the value of the common stock. If instead the exercise price is greater than the share price, the decline in the value of the shares will be exactly offset by the rise in value of the put.

The strategy of buying a put and buying the underlying stock is called a *protective put*. It is as if one is buying insurance for the stock. The stock can always be sold at the exercise price, regardless of how far the market price of the stock falls.

Note that the combination of buying a put and buying the underlying stock has the same *shape* in Figure 22.4 as the call purchase in Figure 22.1. To pursue this point, let's consider the graph for buying a call, which is shown at the far left of Figure 22.5. This graph is the same as Figure 22.1, except that the exercise price is $50 here. Now, let's try the strategy of:

(Leg A) Buying a call.
(Leg B) Buying a zero-coupon bond with a face value of $50 that matures on the same day that the option expires.

We have drawn the graph of Leg A of this strategy at the far left of Figure 22.5, but what does the graph of Leg B look like? It looks like the middle graph of the figure. That is, anyone buying this zero-coupon bond will be guaranteed to get $50, regardless of the price of the stock at expiration.

What does the graph of *simultaneously* buying both Leg A and Leg B of this strategy look like? It looks like the far right graph of Figure 22.5. That is, the investor receives a guaranteed $50 from the bond, regardless of what happens to the stock. In addition, the investor receives a payoff from the call of $1 for every $1 that the price of the stock rises above the exercise price of $50.

■ FIGURE 22.5 **Payoff to the Combination of Buying a Call and Buying a Zero-Coupon Bond**

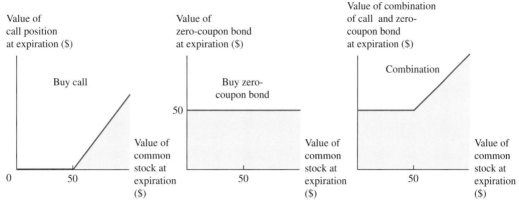

The graph of buying a call and buying a zero-coupon bond is the same as the graph of buying a put and buying the stock in Figure 22.4

The far-right graph of Figure 22.5 looks *exactly* like the far-right graph of Figure 22.4. Thus, an investor gets the same payoff from the strategy of Figure 22.4, and the strategy of Figure 22.5, regardless of what happens to the price of the underlying stock. In other words, the investor gets the same payoff from

1. Buying a put and buying the underlying stock.
2. Buying a call and buying a zero-coupon bond.

If investors have the same payoffs from the two strategies, the two strategies must have the *same* cost. Otherwise, all investors will choose the strategy with the lower cost and avoid the strategy with the higher cost. This leads to the interesting result that:

Price of underlying stock + Price of put = Price of call + Present value of exercise price.   (22.1)
    Cost of first strategy   Cost of second strategy

This relationship is known as **put-call parity** and is one of the most fundamental relationships concerning options. It says that there are two ways of buying a protective put. You can buy a put and buy the underlying stock simultaneously. Here, your total cost is the price of the underlying stock plus the price of the put. Or, you can buy the call and buy a zero-coupon bond. Here, your total cost is the price of the call plus the price of the zero-coupon bond. The price of the zero-coupon bond is equal to the present value of the exercise price, i.e., the present value of $50 in our example.

Equation (22.1) is a very precise relationship. It holds only if the put and the call have both the same exercise price and the same expiration date. In addition, the maturity date of the zero-coupon bond must be the same as the expiration date of the options.

To see how fundamental put-call parity is, let's rearrange the formula, yielding:

Price of underlying stock = Price of call − Price of put + Present value of exercise price

This relationship now states that you can replicate the purchase of a share of stock by buying a call, selling a put, and buying a zero-coupon bond. (Note that, because a minus sign comes before "Price of put," the put is sold, not bought.) Investors in this three-legged strategy are said to have purchased a *synthetic* stock.

■ FIGURE 22.6   **Payoff to the Combination of Buying a Stock and Writing a Call**

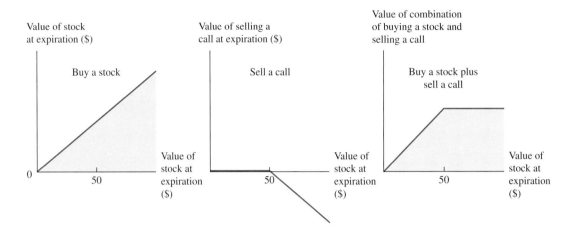

Let's do one more transformation:

Covered-call Strategy

Price of underlying stock − Price of call = −Price of put + Present value of exercise price

Many investors like to buy a stock and write the call on the stock simultaneously. This is a conservative strategy known as *selling a covered call.* The preceding put-call parity relationship tells us that this strategy is equivalent to selling a put and buying a zero-coupon bond. Figure 22.6 develops the graph for the covered call. You can verify that the covered call can be replicated by selling a put and simultaneously buying a zero-coupon bond.

Of course, there are other ways of rearranging the basic put-call relationship. For each rearrangement, the strategy on the left-hand side is equivalent to the strategy on the right-hand side. The beauty of put-call parity is that it shows how any strategy in options can be achieved in two different ways.

CONCEPT QUESTION

• What is put-call parity?

22.7 VALUING OPTIONS

In the last section we determined what options are worth on the expiration date. Now we wish to determine the value of options when you buy them well before expiration.[4] We begin by considering the lower and upper bounds on the value of a call.

---

[4]Our discussion in this section is of American options, because they are traded in the real world. As necessary, we will indicate differences for European options.

■ FIGURE 22.7   **The Upper and Lower Boundaries of Call-Option Values**

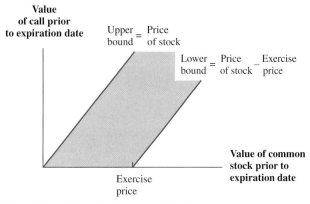

Value of the call must lie in the colored region.

Bounding the Value of a Call

Lower Bound   Consider an American call that is in the money prior to expiration. For example, assume that the stock price is $60 and the exercise price is $50. In this case, the option cannot sell below $10. To see this, note the simple strategy if the option sells at, say, $9.

Date			Transaction	
Today	(1)		Buy call.	−$ 9
Today	(2)		Exercise call, that is, buy underlying stock at exercise price.	−$50
Today	(3)		Sell stock at current market price.	+$60
Arbitrage profit				+$ 1

The type of profit that is described in this transaction is an *arbitrage* profit. Arbitrage profits come from transactions that have no risk or cost and cannot occur regularly in normal, well-functioning financial markets. The excess demand for these options would quickly force the option price up to at least $10 ($60 − $50).[5]

Of course, the price of the option is likely to sell above $10. Investors will rationally pay more than $10 because of the possibility that the stock will rise above $60 before expiration.

Upper Bound   Is there an upper boundary for the option price as well? It turns out that the upper boundary is the price of the underlying stock. That is, an option to buy common stock cannot have a greater value than the common stock itself. A call option can be used to buy common stock with a payment of an exercise price. It would be foolish to buy stock this way if the stock could be purchased directly at a lower price.

The upper and lower bounds are represented in Figure 22.7. In addition, these bounds are summarized in the bottom half of Table 22.2.

---

[5]It should be noted that this lower bound is strictly true for an American option but not for a European option.

The Factors Determining Call-Option Values

The previous discussion indicated that the price of a call option must fall somewhere in the shaded region of Figure 22.7. We now will determine more precisely where in the shaded region it should be. The factors that determine a call's value can be broken into two sets. The first set contains the features of the option contract. The two basic contractual features are the expiration price and the exercise date. The second set of factors affecting the call price concerns characteristics of the stock and the market.

Exercise Price   An increase in the exercise price reduces the value of the call. For example, imagine that there are two calls on a stock selling at $60. The first call has an exercise price of $50 and the second one has an exercise price of $40. Which call would you rather have? Clearly, you would rather have the call with an exercise price of $40, because that one is $20 ($60 − $40) in the money. In other words, the call with an exercise price of $40 should sell for more than an otherwise-identical call with an exercise price of $50.

Expiration Date   The value of an American call option must be at least as great as the value of an otherwise identical option with a shorter term to expiration. Consider two American calls: One has a maturity of nine months and the other expires in six months. Obviously, the nine-month call has the same rights as the six-month call, and also has an additional three months within which these rights can be exercised. It cannot be worth less and will generally be more valuable.[6]

Stock Price   Other things being equal, the higher the stock price, the more valuable the call option will be. For example, if a stock is worth $80, a call with an exercise price of $100 isn't worth very much. If the stock soars to $120, the call becomes much more valuable.

Now consider Figure 22.8, which shows the relationship between the call price and the stock price prior to expiration. The curve indicates that the call price increases as the stock price increases. Furthermore, it can be shown that the relationship is represented, not by a straight line, but by a *convex* curve. That is, the increase in the call price for a given change in the stock price is greater when the stock price is high than when the stock price is low.

There are two special points on the curve in Figure 22.8:

1. *The Stock Is Worthless.* The call must be worthless if the underlying stock is worthless. That is, if the stock has no chance of attaining any value, it is not worthwhile to pay the exercise price in order to obtain the stock.
2. *The Stock Price Is* Very *High Relative to the Exercise Price.* In this situation, the owner of the call knows that he will end up exercising the call. He can view himself as the owner of the stock now, with one difference. He must pay the exercise price at expiration.

Thus, the value of his position, i.e., the value of the call, is:

$$\text{Stock price} - \text{Present value of exercise price}$$

These two points on the curve are summarized in the bottom half of Table 22.2.

---

[6]This relationship need not hold for a European call option. Consider a firm with two otherwise identical European call options, one expiring at the end of May and the other expiring a few months later. Further assume that a *huge* dividend is paid in early June. If the first call is exercised at the end of May, its holder will receive the underlying stock. If he does not sell the stock, he will receive the large dividend shortly thereafter. However, the holder of the second call will receive the stock through exercise after the dividend is paid. Because the market knows that the holder of this option will miss the dividend, the value of the second call option could be less than the value of the first.

■ FIGURE 22.8 **Value of an American Call as a Function of Stock Price**

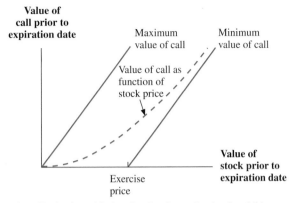

The call price is positively related to the stock price. In addition, the change in the call price for a given change in the stock price is greater when the stock price is high than when it is low.

The Key Factor: The Variability of the Underlying Asset   The greater the variability of the underlying asset, the more valuable the call option will be. Consider the following example. Suppose that just before the call expires, the stock price will be either $100 with probability 0.5 or $80 with probability 0.5. What will be the value of a call with an exercise price of $110? Clearly, it will be worthless because no matter what happens to the stock, its price will always be below the exercise price.

Now let us see what happens if the stock is more variable. Suppose that we add $20 to the best case and take $20 away from the worst case. Now the stock has a one-half chance of being worth $60 and a one-half chance of being worth $120. We have spread the stock returns, but, of course, the expected value of the stock has stayed the same:

$$(1/2 \times \$80) + (1/2 \times \$100) = \$90 = (1/2 \times \$60) + (1/2 \times \$120)$$

Notice that the call option has value now because there is a one-half chance that the stock price will be $120, or $10 above the exercise price of $110. This illustrates a very important point. There is a fundamental distinction between holding an option on an underlying asset and holding the underlying asset. If investors in the marketplace are risk-averse, a rise in the variability of the stock will decrease its market value. However, the holder of a call receives payoffs from the positive tail of the probability distribution. As a consequence, a rise in the variability in the underlying stock increases the market value of the call.

This result can also be seen from Figure 22.9. Consider two stocks, *A* and *B,* each of which is normally distributed. For each security, the figure illustrates the probability of different stock prices on the expiration date.[7] As can be seen from the figures, stock *B* has more volatility than does stock *A*. This means that stock *B* has higher probability of both abnormally high returns and abnormally low returns. Let us assume that options on each of the two securities have the same exercise price. To option holders, a return much below average on stock *B* is no worse than a return only moderately below average on stock *A*. In either situation, the option expires out of the money. However, to option holders, a return

---

[7]This graph assumes that, for each security, the exercise price is equal to the expected stock price. This assumption is employed merely to facilitate the discussion. It is not needed to show the relationship between a call's value and the volatility of the underlying stock.

■ FIGURE 22.9   **Distribution of Common-Stock Price at Expiration for Both Security *A* and Security *B*. Options on the Two Securities Have the Same Exercise Price.**

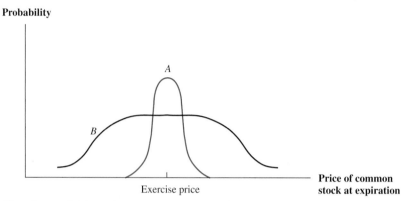

The call on stock *B* is worth more than the call on stock *A* because stock *B* is more volatile. At expiration, a call that deep in the money is more valuable than a call that is only slightly in the money. However, at expiration, a call way out of the money is worth zero, just as is a call only slightly out of the money.

much above average on stock *B* is better than a return only moderately above average on stock *A*. Because a call's price at the expiration date is the difference between the stock price and the exercise price, the value of the call on *B* at expiration will be higher in this case.

The Interest Rate   Call prices are also a function of the level of interest rates. Buyers of calls do not pay the exercise price until they exercise the option, if they do so at all. The ability to delay payment is more valuable when interest rates are high and less valuable when interest rates are low. Thus, the value of a call is positively related to interest rates.

A Quick Discussion of Factors Determining Put-Option Values

Given our extended discussion of the factors influencing a call's value, we can examine the effect of these factors on puts very easily. Table 22.2 summarizes the five factors influencing the prices of both American calls and American puts. The effect of three factors on puts are the opposite of the effect of these three factors on calls:

1. The put's market value *decreases* as the stock price increases because puts are in the money when the stock sells below the exercise price.

2. The value of a put with a high exercise price is *greater* than the value of an otherwise identical put with a low exercise price for the reason given in (1).

3. A high interest rate *adversely* affects the value of a put. The ability to sell a stock at a fixed exercise price sometime in the future is worth less if the present value of the exercise price is diminished by a high interest rate.

The effect of the other two factors on puts is the same as the effect of these factors on calls:

4. The value of an American put with a distant expiration date is greater than an otherwise identical put with an earlier expiration.[8] The longer time to maturity gives the put holder more flexibility, just as it did in the case of a call.

---

[8]Though this result must hold in the case of an American put, it need not hold for a European put.

■ TABLE 22.2 **Factors Affecting American Option Values**

Increase in	Call Option*	Put Option*
Value of underlying asset (stock price)	+	−
Exercise price	−	+
Stock volatility	+	+
Interest rate	+	−
Time to exercise date	+	+

In addition to the preceding, we have presented the following four relationships for American calls:

1. The call price can never be greater than the stock price (*upper bound*).
2. The call price can never be less than either zero or the difference between the stock price and the exercise price (*lower bound*).
3. The call is worth zero if the stock is worth zero.
4. When the stock price is much greater than the exercise price, the call price tends toward the difference between the stock price and the present value of the exercise price.

*The signs (+, −) indicate the effect of the variables on the value of the option. For example, the two +s for stock volatility indicate that an increase in volatility will increase both the value of a call and the value of a put.

5. Volatility of the underlying stock increases the value of the put. The reasoning is analogous to that for a call. At expiration, a put that is way in the money is more valuable than a put only slightly in the money. However, at expiration, a put way out of the money is worth zero, just as is a put only slightly out of the money.

QUESTIONS
CONCEPT
?

- List the factors that determine the value of options.
- Why does a stock's variability affect the value of options written on it?

22.8 AN OPTION-PRICING FORMULA

We have explained *qualitatively* that the value of a call option is a function of five variables:

1. The current price of the underlying asset, which for stock options is the price of a share of common stock.
2. The exercise price.
3. The time to expiration date.
4. The variance of the underlying asset.
5. The risk-free interest rate.

It is time to replace the qualitative model with a precise option-valuation model. The model we choose is the famous Black-Scholes option-pricing model. You can put numbers into the Black-Scholes model and get values back.

The Black-Scholes model is represented by a rather imposing formula. A derivation of the formula is simply not possible in this textbook, as the students will be happy to learn. However, some appreciation for the achievement as well as some intuitive understanding is in order.

In the early chapters of this book, we showed how to discount capital-budgeting projects using the net-present-value formula. We also used this approach to value stocks and bonds. Why, students sometimes ask, can't the same NPV formula be used to value puts and calls? It is a good question because the earliest attempts at valuing options used NPV. Unfortunately, the attempts were simply not successful because no one could determine the appropriate discount rate. An option is generally riskier than the underlying stock but no one knew exactly how much riskier.

Black and Scholes attacked the problem by pointing out that a strategy of borrowing to finance a stock purchase duplicates the risk of a call. Then, knowing the price of a stock already, one can determine the price of a call such that its return is identical to that of the stock-with-borrowing alternative.

We illustrate the intuition behind the Black-Scholes approach by considering a simple example where a combination of a call and a stock eliminates all risk. This example works because we let the future stock price be one of only *two* values. Hence, the example is called a *two-state option model.* By eliminating the possibility that the stock price can take on other values, we are able to duplicate the call exactly.

A Two-State Option Model

Consider the following example. Suppose the current market price of a stock is $50 and the stock will either be $60 or $40 at the end of the year. Further, imagine a call option on this stock with a one-year expiration date and a $50 exercise price. Investors can borrow at 10 percent. Our goal is to determine the value of the call.

In order to value the call correctly, we need to examine two strategies. The first is to simply buy the call. The second is to:

a. Buy one-half a share of stock.
b. Borrow $18.18, implying a payment of principal and interest at the end of the year of $20 ($18.18 × 1.10).

As you will see shortly, the cash flows from the second strategy exactly match the cash flows from buying a call. (A little later we will show how we came up with the exact fraction of a share of stock to buy and the exact borrowing amount.) Because the cash flows match, we say that we are *duplicating* the call with the second strategy.

At the end of the year, the future payoffs are set out as follows:

| | **Future Payoffs** | | | |
Initial Transactions	If Stock Price Is $60		If Stock Price Is $40	
1. Buy a call	$60 − $50 =	$10		0
2. Buy ½ share of stock	½ × $60 =	$30	½ × $40 =	$20
Borrow $18.18 at 10%	−($18.18 × 1.10) =	−$20		−$20
Total from stock and borrowing strategy		$10		0

Note that the future payoff structure of the "buy-a-call" strategy is duplicated by the strategy of "buy stock" and "borrow." That is, under either strategy, an investor would end up with $10 if the stock price rose and $0 if the stock price fell. Thus, these two strategies are equivalent as far as traders are concerned.

Now, if two strategies always have the same cash flows at the end of the year, how must their initial costs be related? The two strategies must have the *same* initial cost. Otherwise, there will be an arbitrage possibility. We can easily calculate this cost for our strategy of buying stock and borrowing. This cost is:

$$
\begin{array}{lrr}
\text{Buy } \frac{1}{2} \text{ share of stock} & \frac{1}{2} \times \$50 = & \$25.00 \\
\text{Borrow } \$18.18 & & -\$18.18 \\
\hline
& & \$6.82
\end{array}
$$

Because the call option provides the same payoffs at expiration as does the strategy of buying stock and borrowing, the call must be priced at $6.82. This is the value of the call option in a market without arbitrage profits.

We left two issues unexplained in the preceding example.

Determining the Delta   How did we know to buy one-half share of stock in the duplicating strategy? Actually, the answer is easier than it might at first appear. The call price at the end of the year will be either $10 or $0, whereas the stock price will be either $60 or $40. Thus, the call price has a potential swing of $10 ($10 − $0) next period, whereas the stock price has a potential swing of $20 ($60 − $40). We can write this in terms of the following ratio:

Delta

$$
\frac{\text{Swing of call}}{\text{Swing of stock}} = \frac{\$10 - \$0}{\$60 - \$40} = \frac{1}{2}
$$

This ratio is called the *delta* of the call. In words, a $1 swing in the price of the stock gives rise to a $1/2 swing in the price of the call. Because we are trying to duplicate the call with the stock, it seems sensible to buy one-half share of stock instead of buying one call. In other words, the risk of buying one-half share of stock should be the same as the risk of buying one call.

Determining the Amount of Borrowing   How did we know how much to borrow? Buying one-half share of stock brings us either $30 or $20 at expiration, which is exactly $20 more than the payoffs of $10 and $0, respectively, from the call. To duplicate the call through a purchase of stock, we should also borrow enough money so that we have to pay back exactly $20 of interest and principal. This amount of borrowing is merely the present value of $20, which is $18.18 ($20/1.10).

Now that we know how to determine both the delta and the borrowing, we can write the value of the call as:

$$
\begin{array}{rcccccc}
\text{Value of call} & = & \text{Stock price} & \times & \text{Delta} & - & \text{Amount borrowed} \\
\$6.82 & = & \$50 & \times & \frac{1}{2} & - & \$18.18
\end{array}
\qquad (22.2)
$$

We will find this intuition very useful in explaining the Black-Scholes model.

Risk-Neutral Valuation   Before leaving this simple example, we should comment on a remarkable feature. We found the exact value of the option without even knowing the probability that the stock would go up or down! If an optimist thought the probability of an up move was very high and a pessimist thought it was very low, they would still agree on the option value. How could that be? The answer is that the current $50 stock price already balances the views of the optimists and the pessimists. The option reflects that balance because its value depends on the stock price.

This insight provides us with another approach to valuing the call. If we don't need the probabilities of the two states to value the call, perhaps we can select *any* probabilities we want and still come up with the right answer. Suppose we selected probabilities such that the return on the stock is equal to the risk-free rate of 10 percent. We know that the stock return given a rise is 20 percent ($60/$50 − 1) and the stock return given a fall is −20 percent ($40/$50 − 1). Thus, we can solve for the probability of a rise necessary to achieve an expected return of 10 percent as:

$$10\% = \text{Probability of a rise} \times 20\% + (1 - \text{Probability of rise}) \times -20\%$$

Solving this formula, we find that the probability of a rise is 3/4 and the probability of a fall is 1/4. If we apply these probabilities to the call, we can value it as:

$$\text{Value of call} = \frac{^{3}\!/_{4} \times \$10 + {}^{1}\!/_{4} \times \$0}{1.10} = \$6.82$$

the same value that we got from the duplicating approach.

Why did we select probabilities such that the expected return on the stock is 10 percent? We wanted to work with the special case where investors are *risk-neutral*. This case occurs where the expected return on *any* asset (including both the stock and the call) is equal to the risk-free rate. In other words, this case occurs when investors demand no additional compensation beyond the risk-free rate, regardless of the risk of the asset in question.

What would have happened if we had assumed that the expected return on a stock was greater than the risk-free rate? The value of the call would still be $6.82. However, the calculations would be difficult. For example, if we assumed that the expected return on the stock was, say, 11 percent, we would have had to derive the expected return on the call. Although the expected return on the call would be higher than 11 percent, it would take a lot of work to determine it precisely. Why do any more work than you have to? Because we can't think of any good reason, we (and most other financial economists) choose to assume risk-neutrality.

Thus, the preceding material allows us to value a call in the following two ways:

1. Determine the cost of a strategy to duplicate the call. This strategy involves an investment in a fractional share of stock financed by partial borrowing.

2. Calculate the probabilities of a rise and a fall under the assumption of risk-neutrality.

Use those probabilities, in conjunction with the risk-free rate, to discount the payoffs of the call at expiration.

The Black-Scholes Model

The preceding example illustrates the duplicating strategy. Unfortunately, a strategy such as this will not work in the real world over, say, a one-year time frame, because there are many more than two possibilities for next year's stock price. However, the number of possibilities is reduced as the time period is shortened. In fact, the assumption that there are only two possibilities for the stock price over the next infinitesimal instant is quite plausible.[9]

In our opinion, the fundamental insight of Black and Scholes is to shorten the time period. They show that a specific combination of stock and borrowing can indeed duplicate a call over an infinitesimal time horizon. Because the price of the stock will change over the first instant, another combination of stock and borrowing is needed to duplicate the call over the second instant and so on. By adjusting the combination from moment to moment, they can continually duplicate the call. It may boggle the mind that a formula can (1) determine the duplicating combination at any moment and (2) value the option based on this duplicating strategy. Suffice it to say that their dynamic strategy allows them to value a call in the real world just as we showed how to value the call in the two-state model.

---

[9]A full treatment of this assumption can be found in John C. Hull, *Options, Futures and Other Derivatives,* 4th ed. Upper Saddle River, N.J.: Prentice Hall (1999).

This is the basic intuition behind the Black-Scholes (BS) model. Because the actual derivation of their formula is, alas, far beyond the scope of this text, we simply present the formula itself. The formula is

Black-Scholes Model:

$$C = SN(d_1) - Ee^{-rt} N(d_2)$$

where

$$d_1 = [\ln(S/E) + (r + 1/2\sigma^2)t]/\sqrt{\sigma^2 t}$$

$$d_2 = d_1 - \sqrt{\sigma^2 t}$$

This formula for the value of a call, C, is one of the most complex in finance. However, it involves only five parameters:

1. S = Current stock price
2. E = Exercise price of call
3. r = Annual risk-free rate of return, continually compounded
4. σ^2 = Variance (per year) of the continuous return on the stock
5. t = Time (in years) to expiration date

In addition, there is the statistical concept:

$N(d)$ = Probability that a standardized, normally distributed,
random variable will be less than or equal to d

Rather than discuss the formula in its algebraic state, we illustrate the formula with an example.

EXAMPLE

Consider Private Equipment Company (PEC). On October 4, of year 0, the PEC April 49 call option had a closing value of $4. The stock itself is selling at $50. On October 4 the option had 199 days to expiration (maturity date = April 21, Year 1). The annual risk-free interest rate, continually compounded, is 7 percent.

This information determines three variables directly:

1. The stock price, S, is $50.
2. The exercise price, E, is $49.
3. The risk-free rate, r, is 0.07.

In addition, the time to maturity, t, can be calculated quickly: The formula calls for t to be expressed in *years*.

4. We express the 199-day interval in years as $t = 199/365$.

In the real world, an option trader would know S and E exactly. Traders generally view U.S. Treasury bills as riskless, so a current quote from *The Wall Street Journal* or a similar newspaper would be obtained for the interest rate. The trader would also know (or could count) the number of days to expiration exactly. Thus, the fraction of a year to expiration, t, could be calculated quickly.

The problem comes in determining the variance of the stock's return. The formula calls for the variance in operation between the purchase date of October 4 and the expiration date. Unfortunately, this represents the future, so the correct value for variance is simply not available. Instead, traders frequently estimate variance from past data, just as we calculated variance in an earlier chapter. In addition, some traders may use intuition to adjust their estimate. For example, if anticipation of an upcoming event is currently increasing the volatility of the stock, the trader might adjust her estimate of variance upward to reflect this. (This problem was most severe right after the October 19, 1987, crash. The stock market was quite risky in the aftermath, so estimates using precrash data were too low.)

The above discussion was intended merely to mention the difficulties in variance estimation, not to present a solution. For our purposes, we assume that a trader has come up with an estimate of variance:

5. The variance of Private Equipment Co. has been estimated to be 0.09 per year.

Using the above five parameters, we calculate the Black-Scholes value of the PEC option in three steps:

Step 1: *Calculate d_1 and d_2.* These values can be determined by a straightforward, albeit tedious, insertion of our parameters into the basic formula. We have

$$d_1 = \left[\ln\left(\frac{S}{E}\right) + (r + 1/2\sigma^2)t\right]/\sqrt{\sigma^2 t}$$
$$= \left[\ln\left(\frac{50}{49}\right) + (0.07 + 1/2 \times 0.09) \times \frac{199}{365}\right]/\sqrt{0.09 \times \frac{199}{365}}$$
$$= [0.0202 + 0.0627]/0.2215 = 0.3742$$
$$d_2 = d_1 - \sqrt{\sigma^2 t}$$
$$= 0.1527$$

Step 2: *Calculate $N(d_1)$ and $N(d_2)$.* The values $N(d_1)$ and $N(d_2)$ can best be understood by examining Figure 22.10. The figure shows the normal distribution with an expected value of 0 and a standard deviation of 1. This is frequently called the **standardized normal distribution.** We mentioned in an earlier chapter that the probability that a drawing from this distribution will be between -1 and $+1$ (within one standard deviation of its mean, in other words) is 68.26 percent.

Now, let us ask a different question. What is the probability that a drawing from the standardized normal distribution will be *below* a particular value? For example, the probability that a drawing will be below 0 is clearly 50 percent because the normal distribution is symmetric. Using statistical terminology, we say that the **cumulative probability** of 0 is 50 percent. Statisticians also say that $N(0) = 50\%$. It turns out that

$$N(d_1) = N(0.3742) = 0.6459$$
$$N(d_2) = N(0.1527) = 0.5607$$

■ FIGURE 22.10 **Graph of Cumulative Probability**

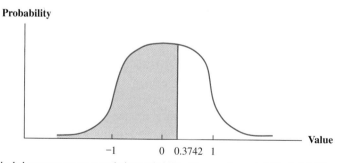

Shaded area represents cumulative probability. Because the probability is 0.6459 that a drawing from the standard normal distribution will be below 0.3742, we say that N(0.3742) = 0.6459. That is, the cumulative probability of 0.3742 is 0.6459.

The first value means that there is a 64.59-percent probability that a drawing from the standardized normal distribution will be below 0.3742. The second value means that there is a 56.07-percent probability that a drawing from the standardized normal distribution will be below 0.1527. More generally, $N(d)$ is the notation that a drawing from the standardized normal distribution will be below d. In other words, $N(d)$ is the cumulative probability of d. Note that d_1 and d_2 in our example are slightly above zero, so $N(d_1)$ and $N(d_2)$ are slightly greater than 0.50.

Perhaps the easiest way to determine $N(d_1)$ and $N(d_2)$ is from the EXCEL function NORMSDIST. In our example, NORMSDIST (0.3742) and NORMSDIST (0.1527) are 0.6459 and 0.5607, respectively.

We can also determine the cumulative probability from Table 22.3. For example, consider $d = 0.37$. This can be found in the table as 0.3 on the vertical and 0.07 on the horizontal. The value in the table for $d = 0.37$ is 0.1443. This value is *not* the cumulative probability of 0.37. One must first make an adjustment to determine cumulative probability. That is,

$$N(0.37) = 0.50 + 0.1443 = 0.6443$$
$$N(-0.37) = 0.50 - 0.1443 = 0.3557$$

Unfortunately, our table handles only two significant digits, whereas our value of 0.3742 has four significant digits. Hence, we must interpolate to find $N(0.3742)$. Because $N(0.37) = 0.6443$ and $N(0.38) = 0.6480$, the difference between the two values is 0.0037 ($0.6480 - 0.6443$). Because 0.3742 is 42 percent of the way between 0.37 and 0.38, we interpolate as[10]

$$N(0.3742) = 0.6443 + 0.42 \times 0.0037 = 0.6459$$

Step 3: *Calculate C.* We have

$$
\begin{aligned}
C &= S \times [N(d_1)] - Ee^{-rt} \times [N(d_2)] \\
&= \$50 \times [N(d_1)] - \$49 \times [e^{-0.07 \times (199/365)}] \times N(d_2) \\
&= (\$50 \times 0.6459) - (\$49 \times 0.9626 \times 0.5607) \\
&= \$32.295 - \$26.447 \\
&= \$5.85
\end{aligned}
$$

The estimated price of $5.85 is greater than the $4 actual price, implying that the call option is underpriced. A trader believing in the Black-Scholes model would buy a call. Of course, the Black-Scholes model is fallible. Perhaps the disparity between the model's estimate and the market price reflects error in the trader's estimate of variance.

The previous example stressed the calculations involved in using the Black-Scholes formula. Is there any intuition behind the formula? Yes, and that intuition follows from the stock purchase and borrowing strategy in our binomial example. The first line of the Black-Scholes equation is:

$$C = S \times N(d_1) - Ee^{-rt} N(d_2)$$

which is exactly analogous to equation (22.2):

$$\text{Value of call} = \text{Stock price} \times \text{Delta} - \text{Amount borrowed} \qquad (22.2)$$

---

[10]This method is called *linear interpolation*. It is only one of a number of possible methods of interpolation.

■ TABLE 22.3   **Cumulative Probabilities of the Standard Normal Distribution Function**

d	0.00	0.01	0.02	0.03	0.04	0.05	0.06	0.07	0.08	0.09
0.0	0.0000	0.0040	0.0080	0.0120	0.0160	0.0199	0.0239	0.0279	0.0319	0.0359
0.1	0.0398	0.0438	0.0478	0.0517	0.0557	0.0596	0.0636	0.0675	0.0714	0.0753
0.2	0.0793	0.0832	0.0871	0.0910	0.0948	0.0987	0.1026	0.1064	0.1103	0.1141
0.3	0.1179	0.1217	0.1255	0.1293	0.1331	0.1368	0.1406	0.1443	0.1480	0.1517
0.4	0.1554	0.1591	0.1628	0.1664	0.1700	0.1736	0.1772	0.1808	0.1844	0.1879
0.5	0.1915	0.1950	0.1985	0.2019	0.2054	0.2088	0.2123	0.2157	0.2190	0.2224
0.6	0.2257	0.2291	0.2324	0.2357	0.2389	0.2422	0.2454	0.2486	0.2517	0.2549
0.7	0.2580	0.2611	0.2642	0.2673	0.2704	0.2734	0.2764	0.2794	0.2823	0.2852
0.8	0.2881	0.2910	0.2939	0.2967	0.2995	0.3023	0.3051	0.3078	0.3106	0.3133
0.9	0.3159	0.3186	0.3212	0.3238	0.3264	0.3289	0.3315	0.3340	0.3365	0.3389
1.0	0.3413	0.3438	0.3461	0.3485	0.3508	0.3531	0.3554	0.3577	0.3599	0.3621
1.1	0.3643	0.3665	0.3686	0.3708	0.3729	0.3749	0.3770	0.3790	0.3810	0.3830
1.2	0.3849	0.3869	0.3888	0.3907	0.3925	0.3944	0.3962	0.3980	0.3997	0.4015
1.3	0.4032	0.4049	0.4066	0.4082	0.4099	0.4115	0.4131	0.4147	0.4162	0.4177
1.4	0.4192	0.4207	0.4222	0.4236	0.4251	0.4265	0.4279	0.4292	0.4306	0.4319
1.5	0.4332	0.4345	0.4357	0.4370	0.4382	0.4394	0.4406	0.4418	0.4429	0.4441
1.6	0.4452	0.4463	0.4474	0.4484	0.4495	0.4505	0.4515	0.4525	0.4535	0.4545
1.7	0.4554	0.4564	0.4573	0.4582	0.4591	0.4599	0.4608	0.4616	0.4625	0.4633
1.8	0.4641	0.4649	0.4656	0.4664	0.4671	0.4678	0.4686	0.4693	0.4699	0.4706
1.9	0.4713	0.4719	0.4726	0.4732	0.4738	0.4744	0.4750	0.4756	0.4761	0.4767
2.0	0.4773	0.4778	0.4783	0.4788	0.4793	0.4798	0.4803	0.4808	0.4812	0.4817
2.1	0.4821	0.4826	0.4830	0.4834	0.4838	0.4842	0.4846	0.4850	0.4854	0.4857
2.2	0.4861	0.4866	0.4830	0.4871	0.4875	0.4878	0.4881	0.4884	0.4887	0.4890
2.3	0.4893	0.4896	0.4898	0.4901	0.4904	0.4906	0.4909	0.4911	0.4913	0.4916
2.4	0.4918	0.4920	0.4922	0.4925	0.4927	0.4929	0.4931	0.4932	0.4934	0.4936
2.5	0.4938	0.4940	0.4941	0.4943	0.4945	0.4946	0.4948	0.4949	0.4951	0.4952
2.6	0.4953	0.4955	0.4956	0.4957	0.4959	0.4960	0.4961	0.4962	0.4963	0.4964
2.7	0.4965	0.4966	0.4967	0.4968	0.4969	0.4970	0.4971	0.4972	0.4973	0.4974
2.8	0.4974	0.4975	0.4976	0.4977	0.4977	0.4978	0.4979	0.4979	0.4980	0.4981
2.9	0.4981	0.4982	0.4982	0.4982	0.4984	0.4984	0.4985	0.4985	0.4986	0.4986
3.0	0.4987	0.4987	0.4987	0.4988	0.4988	0.4989	0.4989	0.4989	0.4990	0.4990

$N(d)$ represents areas under the standard normal distribution function. Suppose that $d_1 = 0.24$. This table implies a cumulative probability of $0.5000 + 0.0948 = 0.5948$. If d_1 is equal to 0.2452, we must estimate the probability by interpolating between $N(0.25)$ and $N(0.24)$.

that we presented in the binomial example. It turns out that $N(d_1)$ is the delta in the Black-Scholes model. $N(d_1)$ is 0.6459 in the previous example. In addition, $Ee^{-rt}N(d_1)$ is the amount that an investor must borrow to duplicate a call. In the previous example, this value is \$26.45 (\$49 × 0.9626 × 0.5607). Thus, the model tells us that we can duplicate the call of the preceding example by both:

1. Buying 0.6459 share of stock.
2. Borrowing \$26.45.

It is no exaggeration to say that the Black-Scholes formula is among the most important contributions in finance. It allows anyone to calculate the value of an option given a few parameters. The attraction of the formula is that four of the parameters are observable: the current price of stock, *S,* the exercise price, *E,* the interest rate, *r,* and the time to expiration date, *t.* Only one of the parameters must be estimated: the variance of return, σ^2.

To see how truly attractive this formula is, note what parameters are not needed. First, the investor's risk aversion does not affect value. The formula can be used by anyone, regardless of willingness to bear risk. Second, it does not depend on the expected return on the stock! Investors with different assessments of the stock's expected return will nevertheless agree on the call price. As in the two-state example, this is because the call depends on the stock price and that price already balances investors' divergent views.

CONCEPT QUESTIONS

?

- How does the two-state option model work?
- What is the formula for the Black-Scholes option-pricing model?

22.9 STOCKS AND BONDS AS OPTIONS

The previous material in this chapter described, explained, and valued publicly traded options. This is important material to any finance student because much trading occurs in these listed options. The study of options has another purpose for the student of corporate finance.

You may have heard the one-liner about the elderly gentleman who was surprised to learn that he had been speaking prose all of his life. The same can be said about the corporate finance student and options. Although options were formally defined for the first time in this chapter, many corporate policies discussed earlier in the text were actually options in disguise. Though it is beyond the scope of this chapter to recast all of corporate finance in terms of options, the rest of the chapter considers the implicit options in three topics:

1. Stocks and bonds as options.
2. Capital-structure decisions as options.
3. Capital-budgeting decisions as options.

We begin by illustrating the implicit options in stocks and bonds through a simple example.

EXAMPLE

The Popov Company has been awarded the concessions at next year's Olympic Games in Antarctica. Because the firm's principals live in Antarctica and because there is no other concession business in that continent, their enterprise will disband after the games. The firm has issued debt to help finance this venture. Interest and principal due on the debt next year will be $800, at which time the debt will be paid off in full. The firm's cash flows next year are forecasted as

	Popov's Cash-Flow Schedule			
	Very Successful Games	Moderately Successful Games	Moderately Unsuccessful Games	Outright Failure
Cash flow before interest and principal	$1,000	$850	$700	$550
−Interest and principal	−800	−800	−700	−550
Cash flow to stockholders	$ 200	$ 50	$ 0	$ 0

As can be seen, the principals forecasted four equally likely scenarios. If either of the first two scenarios occurs, the bondholders will be paid in full. The extra cash flow goes to the stockholders. However, if either of the last two scenarios occurs, the bondholders will not be paid in full. Instead, they will receive the firm's entire cash flow, leaving the stockholders with nothing.

This example is similar to the bankruptcy examples presented in our chapters on capital structure. Our new insight is that the relationship between the common stock and the firm can be expressed in terms of options. We consider call options first because the intuition is easier. The put-option scenario is treated next.

The Firm Expressed in Terms of Call Options

The Stockholders   We now show that stock can be viewed as a call option on the firm. To illustrate this, Figure 22.11 graphs the cash flow to the stockholders as a function of the cash flow to the firm. The stockholders receive nothing if the firm's cash flows are less than $800; here, all of the cash flows go to the bondholders. However, the stockholders earn a dollar for every dollar that the firm receives above $800. The graph looks exactly like the call-option graphs that we considered earlier in this chapter.

But what is the underlying asset upon which the stock is a call option? The underlying asset is the firm itself. That is, we can view the *bondholders* as owning the firm. However, the stockholders have a call option on the firm with an exercise price of $800.

If the firm's cash flow is above $800, the stockholders would choose to exercise this option. In other words, they would buy the firm from the bondholders for $800. Their net cash flow is the difference between the firm's cash flow and their $800 payment. This would be $200 ($1,000 − $800) if the games are very successful and $50 ($850 − $800) if the games are moderately successful.

Should the value of the firm's cash flows be less than $800, the stockholders would not choose to exercise their option. Instead, they walk away from the firm, as any call-option holder would do. The bondholders then receive the firm's entire cash flow.

■ FIGURE 22.11   **Cash Flow to Stockholders of Popov Company as a Function of Cash Flow of Firm**

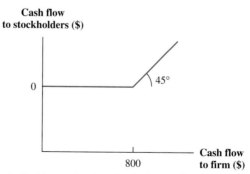

The stockholders can be viewed as having a call option on the firm. If the cash flows of the firm exceed $800, the stockholders pay $800 in order to receive the firm. If the cash flows of the firm are less than $800, the stockholders do not exercise their option. They walk away from the firm, receiving nothing.

■ FIGURE 22.12   **Cash Flow to Bondholders as a Function of Cash Flow of Firm**

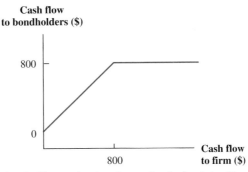

The bondholders can be viewed as owning the firm but writing a call option to the stockholders as well. If the cash flows of the firm exceed $800, the call is exercised against the bondholders. The bondholders give up the firm and receive $800. If the cash flows are less than $800, the call expires. The bondholders receive the cash flows of the firm in this case.

This view of the firm is a novel one, and students are frequently bothered by it on first exposure. However, we encourage students to keep looking at the firm in this way until the view becomes second nature to them.

The Bondholders   What about the bondholders? Our earlier cash flow schedule showed that they would get the entire cash flow of the firm if the firm generates less cash than $800. Should the firm earn more than $800, the bondholders would receive only $800. That is, they are entitled only to interest and principal. This schedule is graphed in Figure 22.12.

In keeping with our view that the stockholders have a call option on the firm, what does the bondholders' position consist of? The bondholders' position can be described by two claims:

1. They own the firm.
2. They have written a call against the firm with an exercise price of $800.

As we mentioned before, the stockholders walk away from the firm if cash flows are less than $800. Thus, the bondholders retain ownership in this case. However, if the cash flows are greater than $800, the stockholders exercise their option. They call the stock away from the bondholders for $800.

The Firm Expressed in Terms of Put Options

The preceding analysis expresses the positions of the stockholders and the bondholders in terms of call options. We can now express the situation in terms of put options.

The Stockholders   The stockholders' position can be expressed by three claims:

1. They own the firm.
2. They owe $800 in interest and principal to the bondholders.

If the debt were risk-free, these two claims would fully describe the stockholders' situation. However, because of the possibility of default, we have a third claim as well.

3. The stockholders own a put option on the firm with an exercise price of $800. The group of bondholders is the seller of the put.

Now consider two possibilities.

Cash Flow Is Less than $800   Because the put has an exercise price of $800, the put is in the money. The stockholders "put," that is, sell, the firm to the bondholders. Normally, the holder of a put receives the exercise price when the asset is sold. However, the stockholders already owe $800 to the bondholders. Thus, the debt of $800 is simply canceled—and no money changes hands—when the stock is delivered to the bondholders. Because the stockholders give up the stock in exchange for extinguishing the debt, the stockholders end up with nothing if the cash flow is below $800.

Cash Flow Is Greater than $800   Because the put is out of the money here, the stockholders do not exercise. Thus, the stockholders retain ownership of the firm but pay $800 to the bondholders as interest and principal.

The Bondholders   The bondholders' position can be described by two claims:

1. The bondholders are owed $800.
2. They have sold a put option on the firm to the stockholders with an exercise price of $800.

Cash Flow Is Less than $800   As mentioned before, the stockholders will exercise the put in this case. This means that the bondholders are obligated to pay $800 for the firm. Because they are owed $800, the two obligations offset each other. Thus, the bondholders simply end up with the firm in this case.

Cash Flow Is Greater than $800   Here, the stockholders do not exercise the put. Thus, the bondholders merely receive the $800 that is due them.

Expressing the bondholders' position in this way is illuminating. With a riskless default-free bond, the bondholders are owed $800. Thus, we can express the risky bond in terms of a riskless bond and a put:

$$
\begin{matrix}
\text{Value of} \\
\text{risky bond}
\end{matrix}
=
\begin{matrix}
\text{Value of} \\
\text{default-free bond}
\end{matrix}
-
\begin{matrix}
\text{Value of} \\
\text{put option}
\end{matrix}
$$

That is, the value of the risky bond is the value of the default-free bond less the value of the stockholders' option to sell the company for $800.

A Resolution of the Two Views

We have argued above that the positions of the stockholders and the bondholders can be viewed either in terms of calls or in terms of puts. These two viewpoints are summarized in Table 22.4.

We have found from past experience that it is generally harder for students to think of the firm in terms of puts than in terms of calls. Thus, it would be helpful if there were a way to show that the two viewpoints are equivalent. Fortunately there is *put-call parity*. In an earlier section we presented the put-call parity relationship as equation (22.1), which we now repeat:

Price of underlying stock + Price of put = Price of call + Present value of exercise price (22.1)

Using the results of this section, equation (22.1) can be rewritten as:

■ TABLE 22.4 **Positions of Stockholders and Bondholders in Popov Company in Terms of Calls and Puts**

Stockholders	Bondholders
Positions viewed in terms of call options	
1. Stockholders own a call on the firm with exercise price of $800.	1. Bondholders own the firm.
	2. Bondholders have sold a call on the firm to the stockholders.
Positions viewed in terms of put options	
1. Stockholders own the firm.	1. Bondholders are owed $800 in interest and principal.
2. Stockholders owe $800 in interest and principal to bondholders.	2. Bondholders have sold a put on the firm to the stockholders.
3. Stockholders own a put option on the firm with exercise price of $800.	

$$\underbrace{\text{Value of call on firm}}_{\substack{\text{Stockholders'} \\ \text{position in terms} \\ \text{of call options}}} = \underbrace{\text{Value of firm} + \text{Value of put on firm} - \text{Value of default-free bond}}_{\substack{\text{Stockholders' position} \\ \text{in terms of put options}}} \qquad (22.3)$$

Going from equation (22.1) to equation (22.3) involves a few steps. First, we treat the firm, not the stock, as the underlying asset in this section. (In keeping with common convention, we refer to the *value* of the firm and the *price* of the stock.) Second, the exercise price is now $800, the principal and interest on the firm's debt. Taking the present value of this amount at the riskless rate yields the value of a default-free bond. Third, the order of the terms in equation (22.1) is rearranged in equation (22.3).

Note that the left-hand side of equation (22.3) is the stockholders' position in terms of call options, as shown in Table 22.4. The right-hand side of equation (22.3) is the stockholders' position in terms of put options, as shown in the table. Thus, put-call parity shows that viewing the stockholders' position in terms of call options is equivalent to viewing the stockholders' position in terms of put options.

Now, let's rearrange terms in equation (22.3) to yield

$$\underbrace{\text{Value of firm} - \text{Value of call on firm}}_{\substack{\text{Bondholders' position in} \\ \text{terms of call options}}} = \underbrace{\text{Value of default-free bond} - \text{Value of put on firm}}_{\substack{\text{Bondholders' position in} \\ \text{terms of put options}}} \qquad (22.4)$$

The left-hand side of equation (22.4) is the bondholders' position in terms of call options, as shown in Table 22.4. The right-hand side of the equation is the bondholders' position in terms of put options, as shown in Table 22.4. Thus, put-call parity shows that viewing the bondholders' position in terms of call options is equivalent to viewing the bondholders' position in terms of put options.

A Note on Loan Guarantees

In the Popov example given earlier, the bondholders bore the risk of default. Of course, bondholders generally ask for an interest rate that is enough to compensate them for bearing risk. When firms experience financial distress, they can no longer attract new debt at moderate interest rates. Thus, firms experiencing distress have frequently sought loan guarantees from the government. Our framework can be used to understand these guarantees.

If the firm defaults on a guaranteed loan, the government must make up the difference. In other words, a government guarantee converts a risky bond into a riskless bond. What is the value of this guarantee?

Recall that, with option pricing,

$$
\begin{array}{c}
\text{Value of} \\
\text{default-free bond}
\end{array}
=
\begin{array}{c}
\text{Value of} \\
\text{risky bond}
\end{array}
+
\begin{array}{c}
\text{Value of} \\
\text{put option}
\end{array}
$$

This equation shows that the government is assuming an obligation that has a cost equal to the value of a put option.

This analysis differs from that of either politicians or company spokespeople. They generally say that the guarantee will cost the taxpayer nothing because the guarantee enables the firm to attract debt, thereby staying solvent. However, it should be pointed out that, although solvency may be a strong possibility, it is never a certainty. Thus, at the time the guarantee is made, the government's obligation has a cost in terms of present value. To say that a government guarantee costs the government nothing is like saying a put on the stock of Microsoft has no value because the stock is *likely* to rise in price.

Actually, the government has had good fortune with loan guarantees. Its two biggest guarantees were to the Lockheed Corporation in 1971 and the Chrysler Corporation in 1980. Both firms nearly ran out of cash and defaulted on loans. In both cases the U.S. government came to the rescue by agreeing to guarantee new loans. Under the guarantees, if Lockheed and Chrysler had defaulted on new loans, the lenders could have obtained the full value of their claims from the U.S. government. From the lender's point of view, the loans became as risk-free as Treasury bonds. These guarantees enabled Lockheed and Chrysler to borrow large amounts of cash and to get through a difficult time. As it turned out, neither firm defaulted.

Who benefits from a typical loan guarantee?

1. If existing risky bonds are guaranteed, all gains accrue to the existing bondholders. The stockholders gain nothing because the limited liability of corporations absolves the stockholders of any obligation in bankruptcy.

2. If new debt is being issued and guaranteed, the new debtholders do not gain. Rather, in a competitive market, they must accept a low interest rate because of the debt's low risk. The stockholders gain here because they are able to issue debt at a low interest rate. In addition, some of the gains accrue to the old bondholders because the firm's value is greater than would otherwise be true. Therefore, if shareholders want all the gains from loan guarantees, they should renegotiate or retire existing bonds before the guarantee is in place. This happened in the Chrysler case.

QUESTIONS

CONCEPT

?

- How can the value of the firm be expressed in terms of call options?
- How can the value of the firm be expressed in terms of put options?
- How does put-call parity relate these two expressions?

22.10 CAPITAL-STRUCTURE POLICY AND OPTIONS

Recall our chapters on capital structure where we showed how managers, acting on behalf of the stockholders, can take advantage of bondholders. A number of these strategies can be explained in terms of options. As an illustration, this section examines one such strategy, the choice between a high-risk project and a low-risk project.

Selecting High-Risk Projects

Imagine a levered firm considering two mutually exclusive projects, a low-risk one and a high-risk one. There are two equally likely outcomes, recession and boom. The firm is in such dire straits that, should a recession hit, it will come near to bankruptcy if the low-risk project is selected and actually fall into bankruptcy if the high-risk project is selected. The cash flows for the firm if the low-risk project is undertaken can be described as

Low-Risk Project

	Probability	Value of Firm	=	Stock	+	Bonds
Recession	0.5	$400	=	0	+	$400
Boom	0.5	$800	=	$400	+	$400

If recession occurs, the value of the firm will be $400, and if boom occurs, the value of the firm will be $800. The expected value of the firm is $600 (0.5 × $400 + 0.5 × $800). The firm has promised to pay the bondholders $400. Shareholders will obtain the difference between the total payoff and the amount paid to the bondholders. The bondholders have the prior claim on the payoffs, and the shareholders have the residual claim.

Now suppose that another, riskier project can be substituted for the low-risk project. The payoffs and probabilities are as follows:

High-Risk Project

	Probability	Value of Firm	=	Stock	+	Bonds
Recession	0.5	$ 200	=	0	+	$200
Boom	0.5	$1,000	=	$600	+	$400

The expected value of the firm is $600 (0.5 × $200 + 0.5 × $1,000), which is identical to the value of the firm with the low-risk project. However, note that the expected value of the stock is $300 (0.5 × 0 + 0.5 × $600) with the high-risk project, but only $200 (0.5 × 0 + 0.5 × $400) with the low-risk project. Given the firm's present levered state, stockholders will select the high-risk project.

The stockholders benefit at the expense of the bondholders when the high-risk project is accepted. The explanation is quite clear: The bondholders suffer dollar for dollar when the firm's value falls short of the $400 bond obligation. However, the bondholders' payments are capped at $400 when the firm does well.

This can be explained in terms of call options. We argued earlier in this chapter that the value of a call rises with an increase in the volatility of the underlying asset. Because the stock is a call option on the firm, a rise in the volatility of the firm increases the value of the stock. In our example, the value of the stock is higher if the high-risk project is accepted.

Table 22.4 showed that the value of a risky bond can be viewed as the difference between the value of the firm and the value of a call on the firm. Because a call's value rises with the risk of the underlying asset, the value of the bond should decline if the firm increases its risk. In our example, the bondholders are hurt when the high-risk project is accepted.

22.11 MERGERS AND OPTIONS

Mergers are structured either as *cash-for-stock* transactions or as *stock-for-stock* transactions. The selling stockholders receive cash from the buyer in the first type of transaction and receive stock in the buying company in the second type of transaction. In the first half of 2000, General Mills (GM) was attempting to acquire the Pillsbury division of Diageo PLC. GM wanted a stock-for-stock transaction and initially offered Diageo 141,000,000 shares of GM's stock. Given that GM was trading at that time at $42.55 per share, the stockholders of Diageo would receive consideration of about $6 billion ($42.55 × 141 million). Although this amount was more than satisfactory to Diageo's management, they were upset with the risk inherent in stock-for-stock transactions. That is, General Mills' shares might be overpriced at $42.55, implying the possibility of a price decline at a later date.

To allay these fears, GM decided to "insure" Diageo's stockholders with a contingent value rights (CVR) plan of up to $642 million or $4.55 ($642 million/141 million) per share. Under this plan, each of the 141 million GM shares issued to Diageo's stockholders would receive in cash the difference between $42.55 and the price of GM's stock one year after the deal's closing date, up to a maximum of $4.55. For example, if GM's stock traded at $40 one year after closing, each newly issued share of GM would receive $2.55 ($42.55 − $40) in cash. Thus, because the cash payment of $2.55 goes with each newly issued share worth $40, the total package is still worth $42.55. However, because the maximum payment is $4.55, no additional insurance is provided for stock price drops below $38 ($42.55 − $4.55). For example, if the stock falls to $36, the total package is worth only $40.55 ($36 + $4.55). In Figure 22.13 the cash payment per share of newly issued GM stock is graphed as a function of GM's stock price one year after the closing date. The total package (price of one share of GM's stock plus the cash payment) is shown in Figure 22.14.

The contingent value rights plan can be viewed in terms of puts. That is, the CVR plan implies that each newly issued share of GM's stock receives a put on GM's stock with an exercise price of $42.55 while selling a put on GM with an exercise price of $38. This idea is illustrated in Figure 22.15. If GM's stock price ends up below $42.55, the cash payoff from each put with an exercise price of $42.55 is equal to the difference between $42.55 and the ending price of GM. However, should the price fall below $38, the put with an exercise price of $38 will also be in the money. Each newly issued share of GM's stock receives a put with an exercise price of $42.55 and writes a put with an exercise price of $38, so each share receives cash of $4.55 ($42.55 − $38) should GM's stock price drop below $38.

Diageo's management liked the contingent value rights plan enough to accept the merger with the CVR agreement attached. This example shows that creative financing techniques, such as the use of puts in this case, can be used to accommodate a buyer who would otherwise be reluctant.

Cash Payment to Each Newly Issued Share of GM Stock in Acquisition of Pillsbury Division of Diageo PLC

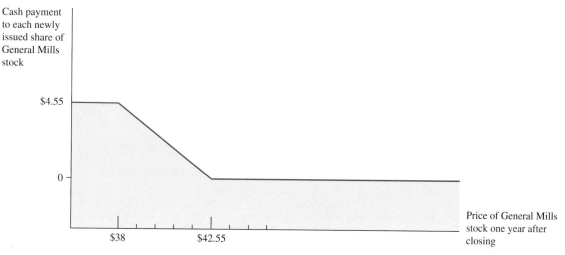

Cash payment to each newly issued share of General Mills stock

$4.55

0

$38 $42.55

Price of General Mills stock one year after closing

Each newly issued share of GM stock receives a cash payment equal to the difference between $42.55 and the price of GM stock one year after closing, up to a maximum of $4.55. For example:

Price one year after closing	Cash payment per share
$42.55 or above	0
$41	$1.55 = $42.55 − $41
$38 or below	$4.55 = $42.55 − $38

■ FIGURE 22.14   **Total Value of a Newly Issued Share of GM Stock, Including the Cash Payment**

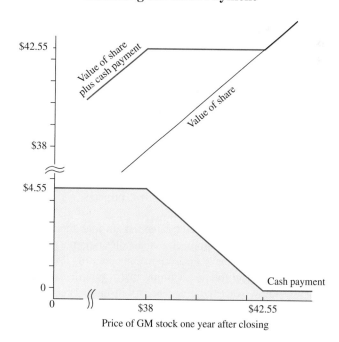

$42.55

Value of share plus cash payment

Value of share

$38

$4.55

0

Cash payment

0     $38 $42.55

Price of GM stock one year after closing

■ FIGURE 22.15   **Payoffs to Implied Puts in General Mills' Acquisition of Pillsbury**

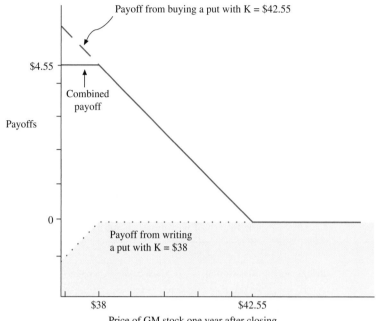

Combined payoff from buying a put with K = $42.55 and selling a put with K = $38 is identical to payoff from contingent value rights plan

22.12 Investment in Real Projects and Options

Let us quickly review the material on capital budgeting presented earlier in the text. We first considered projects where forecasts for future cash flows were made at date 0. The expected cash flow in each future period was discounted at an appropriate risky rate, yielding an NPV calculation. For independent projects, a positive NPV meant acceptance and a negative NPV meant rejection.

This approach treated risk through the discount rate. We later considered decision-tree analysis, an approach that handles risk in a more sophisticated way. We pointed out that the firm will make investment and operating decisions on a project over its entire life. We value a project today, assuming that future decisions will be optimal. However, we do not yet know what these decisions will be, because much information remains to be discovered. The firm's ability to delay its investment and operating decisions until the release of information is an option. We now illustrate this option through an example.

EXAMPLE

Exoff Oil Corporation is considering the purchase of an oil field in a remote part of Alaska. The seller has listed the property for $10,000 and is eager to sell immediately. Initial drilling costs are $500,000. The firm anticipates that 10,000 barrels of oil can be extracted each year for many decades. Because the termination date is so far in the future and so hard to estimate, the firm views the cash flow stream from the oil as a perpetuity. With oil prices at $20 per barrel and extraction costs at $16 a barrel, the firm anticipates a net margin of $4 per barrel. Because oil prices are expected to rise at the inflation rate, the firm assumes that its cash flow per barrel will always be $4 in real terms. The appropriate real discount rate is 10 percent. The firm has enough tax credits from bad years in the past that it will not need to pay taxes on any profits from the oil field. Should Exoff buy the property?

The NPV of the oil field to Exoff is

$$- \$110,000 = -\$10,000 - \$500,000 + \frac{\$4 \times 10,000}{0.10}$$

According to this analysis, Exoff should not purchase the land.

Though this approach uses the standard capital-budgeting techniques of this and other textbooks, it is actually inappropriate for this situation. To see this, consider the analysis of Kirtley Thornton, a consultant to Exoff. He agrees that the price of oil is *expected* to rise at the rate of inflation. However, he points out that the next year is quite perilous for oil prices. On the one hand, OPEC is considering a long-term agreement that would raise oil prices to $35 per barrel in real terms for many years in the future. On the other hand, National Motors recently indicated that cars using a mixture of sand and water for fuel are currently being tested. Thornton argues that oil will be priced at $5 in real terms for many years, should this development prove successful. Full information on both these developments will be released in exactly one year.

Should oil prices rise to $35 a barrel, the NPV of the project would be

$$\$1,390,000 = -\$10,000 - \$500,000 + \frac{(\$35 - \$16) \times 10,000}{0.10}$$

However, should oil prices fall to $5 a barrel, the NPV of the oil field will be even more negative than it is today.

Mr. Thornton makes two recommendations to Exoff's board. He argues that

1. The land should be purchased.
2. The drilling decision should be delayed until information on both OPEC's new agreement and National Motors' new automobile is released.

Kirtley explains his recommendations to the board by first assuming that the land has already been purchased. He argues that, under this assumption, the drilling decision should be delayed. Second, he investigates his assumption that the land should have been purchased in the first place. This approach of examining the second decision (whether to drill) after assuming that the first decision (to buy the land) had been made was also used in our earlier presentation on decision trees. Let us now work through Mr. Thornton's analysis.

Assume the land has already been purchased. If the land has already been purchased, should drilling begin immediately? If drilling begins immediately, the NPV is −$110,000. If the drilling decision is delayed until new information is released in a year, the optimal choice can be made at that time. If oil prices drop to

$5 a barrel, Exoff should not drill. Instead, the firm should walk away from the project, losing nothing beyond its $10,000 purchase price for the land. If oil prices rise to $35, drilling should begin.

Mr. Thornton points out that, by delaying, the firm will only invest the $500,000 of drilling costs if oil prices rise. Thus, by delaying, the firm saves $500,000 in the case where oil prices drop. Kirtley concludes that, once the land is purchased, the drilling decision should be delayed.[11]

Should the land have been purchased in the first place? We now know that if the land had been purchased, it is optimal to defer the drilling decision until the release of information. Given that we know this optimal decision concerning drilling, should the land be purchased in the first place? Without knowing the exact probability that oil prices will rise, Mr. Thornton is nevertheless confident that the land should be purchased. The NPV of the project at $35 oil prices is $1,390,000 whereas the cost of the land is only $10,000. Kirtley believes that an oil price rise is possible, though by no means probable. Even so, he argues that the high potential return is clearly worth the risk.

This example presents an approach that is similar to our decision-tree analysis of the Solar Equipment Company in a previous chapter. Our purpose in this section is to discuss this type of decision in an option framework. When Exoff purchases the land, it is actually purchasing a call option. That is, once the land has been purchased, the firm has an option to buy an active oil field at an exercise price of $500,000. As it turns out, one should generally not exercise a call option immediately.[12] In this case, the firm should delay exercise until relevant information concerning future oil prices is released.

This section points out a serious deficiency in classical capital budgeting; net-present-value calculations typically ignore the flexibility that real-world firms have. In our example, the standard techniques generated a negative NPV for the land purchase. Yet, by allowing the firm the option to change its investment policy according to new information, the land purchase can easily be justified.

We entreat the reader to look for hidden options in projects. Because options are beneficial, managers are shortchanging their firm's projects if capital-budgeting calculations ignore flexibility.

CONCEPT QUESTION

?

- Why are the hidden options in projects valuable?

---

[11]Actually, there are three separate effects here. First, the firm avoids drilling costs in the case of low oil prices by delaying the decision. This is the effect discussed by Mr. Thornton. Second, the present value of the $500,000 payment is less when the decision is delayed, even if drilling eventually takes place. Third, the firm loses one year of cash inflows through delay.

The first two arguments support delaying the decision. The third argument supports immediate drilling. In this example, the first argument greatly outweighs the other two arguments. Thus, Mr. Thornton avoided the second and third arguments in his presentation.

[12]Actually, it can be shown that a call option that pays no dividend should *never* be exercised before expiration. However, for a dividend-paying stock, it may be optimal to exercise prior to the ex-dividend date. The analogy applies to our example of an option in real assets.

The firm would receive cash flows from oil earlier if drilling begins immediately. This is equivalent to the benefit from exercising a call on a stock prematurely in order to capture the dividend. However, in our example, this dividend effect is far outweighed by the benefits from waiting.

22.13 SUMMARY AND CONCLUSIONS

This chapter serves as an introduction to options.

1. The most familiar options are puts and calls. These options give the holder the right to sell or buy shares of common stock at a given exercise price. American options can be exercised any time up to and including the expiration date. European options can be exercised only on the expiration date.
2. We showed that a strategy of buying a stock and buying a put is equivalent to a strategy of buying a call and buying a zero-coupon bond. From this, the put-call–parity relationship was established:

$$\text{Value of stock} + \text{Value of put} - \text{Value of call} = \text{Present value of exercise price}$$

3. The value of an option depends on five factors:
   - The price of the underlying asset.
   - The exercise price.
   - The expiration date.
   - The variability of the underlying asset.
   - The interest rate on risk-free bonds.

   The Black-Scholes model can determine the intrinsic price of an option from these five factors.
4. Much of corporate financial theory can be presented in terms of options. In this chapter we pointed out that
   a. Common stock can be represented as a call option on the firm.
   b. Stockholders enhance the value of their call by increasing the risk of their firm.
   c. Real projects have hidden options that enhance value.

KEY TERMS

American options 612	Option 612
Call option 613	Put-call parity 619
Cumulative probability 630	Put option 614
European options 612	Standardized normal distribution 630
Exercising the option 612	Striking or exercise price 612
Expiration date 612	

SUGGESTED READINGS

The path-breaking article on options is:
Black, Fischer, and Myron Scholes. "The Pricing of Options and Corporate Liabilities." *Journal of Political Economy* 81 (May–June 1973).

For a detailed discussion of options, read
Hull, John C. *Options, Futures, and Other Derivatives,* 4th Ed. Upper Saddle River, N.J.: Prentice Hall, 1999.

QUESTIONS AND PROBLEMS

Options: General

22.1 Define the following terms associated with options:
  a. Option
  b. Exercise
  c. Strike price
  d. Expiration date
  e. Call option
  f. Put option

22.2 What is the difference between American options and European options?

22.3 Mr. Goodie holds American put options on Delta Triangle stock. The exercise price of the put is $40 and Delta stock is selling for $35 per share. If the put sells for $4½, what is the best strategy for Mr. Goodie?

22.4 A call option on Futura Corporation stock currently trades for $4. The expiration date is February 18 of next year. The exercise price of the option is $45.
  a. If this is an American option, on what dates can the option be exercised?
  b. If this is a European option, on what dates can the option be exercised?
  c. Suppose the current price of Futura Corporation stock is $35. Is this option worthless?

22.5 Mrs. Gerard sold 10 IBM put contracts and bought 5 IBM call contracts with the proceeds of the sales. Both options have the same exercise price of $80 and the same expiration date. Draw the payoff diagram of her zero-investment portfolio.

22.6 The strike price of a call option on Simpsons Entertainment common stock is $50.
  a. What is the payoff at expiration of this call if, on the expiration date, Simpsons stock sells for $55?
  b. What is the payoff at expiration of this call if, on the expiration date, Simpsons stock sells for $45?
  c. Draw the payoff diagram for this option.

22.7 A put is trading on Simpsons Entertainment stock. It has a strike price of $50.
  a. What is the payoff at expiration of this put if, on the expiration date, Simpsons stock sells for $55?
  b. What is the payoff at expiration of this put if, on the expiration date, Simpsons stock sells for $45?
  c. Draw the payoff diagram for this option.

22.8 Suppose you bought two Xerox call contracts and one Xerox put contract, both of which will expire in three months. The exercise price of the call is $70 and the exercise price of the put is $75. Each option is sold as a 100-share contract.
  a. What is your payoff at expiration of your investment if Xerox stock sells for $65 on the expiration date? What if it sells for $72? What if it sells for $80?
  b. Draw the payoff diagram for the investment.

22.9 You hold a six-month European call-option contract on Sertile stock. The exercise price of the call is $100 per share. The option will expire in moments. Assume there are no transactions costs or taxes associated with this contract.
  a. What is your profit on this contract if the stock is selling for $130?
  b. If Sertile stock is selling for $90, what will you do?

22.10 General Furnishings, Inc., has both call and put options traded on the Chicago Board Options Exchange. Both options have the same exercise price of $40 and the same expiration date. The options will expire in one year. The call is currently selling for $8 per share and the put is selling for $2 per share. The interest rate is 10 percent. What should the stock price of General Furnishings be in order to prevent arbitrage opportunities?

22.11 Piersol Paper Mill's common stock currently sells for $145. Both puts and calls on Piersol Paper are being traded. These options all expire eight months from today, and they have a strike price of $160. Eight months from today, Piersol Paper common stock will sell for $172 with a probability of 0.5. It will sell for $138 with a probability of 0.5. You own a put on Piersol Paper. Now, you are becoming nervous about the risk to which you are exposed.
  a. What other transactions should you make to eliminate this risk?
  b. What is the expected payoff at expiration of the strategy you developed in (a)?

22.12 Suppose you observe the following market prices:

| American call (Strike = $50) | $8 |
| Stock | $60 |

  a. What should you do?
  b. What is your profit or loss?
  c. What do opportunities such as this imply about the lower bound on the price of American calls?
  d. What is the upper bound on the price of American calls? Explain.

22.13 List the factors that determine the value of an American call option. State how a change in each factor alters the option's value.

22.14 List the factors that determine the value of an American put option. State how a change in each factor alters the option's value.

22.15 a. If the risk of a stock increases, what is likely to happen to the prices of call options on the stock? Why?
  b. If the risk of a stock increases, what is likely to happen to the price of put options on the stock? Why?

The Two-State Option Model

22.16 You bought a 100-share call contract three weeks ago. The expiration date of the calls is five weeks from today. On that date, the price of the underlying stock will be either $120 or $95. The two states are equally likely to occur. Currently, the stock sells for $96; its strike price is $112. You are able to purchase 32 shares of stock. You are able to borrow money at 10 percent per annum.
     What is the value of your call contract?

22.17 Wellington Company stock is currently selling for $30 per share. It is expected that the stock price will be either $25 or $35 in six months. Treasury bills that will mature in six months yield 5 percent. What is the price of Wellington put option per share that has an exercise price of $32? Wellington put is a European option.

22.18 Assume only two states will exist one year from today when a call on Delta Transportation, Inc., stock expires. The price of Delta stock will be either $60 or $40 on that date. Today, Delta stock trades for $55. The strike price of the call is $50. The rate at which you can borrow is 9 percent. How much are you willing to pay for a contract of this call?

The Black-Scholes Option Model

22.19 Use the Black-Scholes model to price a call with the following characteristics:

Stock price = $62
Strike price = $70
Time to expiration = 4 weeks
Stock-price variance = 0.35
Risk-free interest rate = 0.05

22.20 Use the Black-Scholes model to price a call with the following characteristics:

> Stock price = $52
> Strike price = $48
> Time to expiration = 120 days
> Stock-price variance = 0.04
> Risk-free interest rate = 0.05

22.21 *a.* Use the Black-Scholes model to price a call with the following characteristics:

> Stock price = $45
> Strike price = $52
> Time to expiration = 6 months
> Stock-price variance = 0.40
> Risk-free interest rate = 0.065

  b. What does put-call parity imply the price of the corresponding put will be?

22.22 *a.* Use the Black-Scholes model to price a call with the following characteristics:

> Stock price = $70
> Strike price = $90
> Time to expiration = 6 months
> Stock-price variance = 0.25
> Risk-free interest rate = 0.06

  b. What does put-call parity imply the price of the corresponding put will be?

22.23 Consider a call option on Computer Plus Company stock. The option will expire one year from today and the exercise price is $35. The risk-free rate is 7 percent. Computer Plus stock is selling for $37 per share and your estimate of variance of the return on the stock is 0.004.

  a. Use the Black-Scholes model to price the call.

  b. You have found out that the estimate of the variance should be revised to 0.0064. What should the new price of the call be?

  c. The stock price dropped to $35 after the announcement that the company is about to shut down three factories in California. Using the result in part (*b*), what should the new price of the call be?

22.24 You have been asked by a client to determine the maximum price he should be willing to pay to purchase a Kingsley call. The options have an exercise price of $25, and they expire in 120 days. The current price of Kingsley stock is $27, the annual risk-free rate is 7 percent, and the estimated variance of the stock is 0.0576. No dividends are expected to be declared over the next six months. What is the maximum price your client should pay?

Application of Options to Corporate Finance

22.25 It is said that the equity in a levered firm is like a call option on the underlying assets. Explain what is meant by this statement.

22.26 Global Real Estate Partners, LTD., is undertaking a new project. If the project is successful, the value of the firm in a year will be $650 million, but if it turns out to be a failure, the firm will be worth only $250 million. The current value of the firm is $400 million. The firm has outstanding bonds due in a year with a face value of $300 million. The T-bill rate is 7 percent. What is the value of the equity? What is the value of the debt?

22.27 Suppose Global Real Estate Partners, LTD., in the above problem decided to undertake a riskier project: The value of the firm in a year will be either $800 million or $100 million, depending on the success of the project. What is the value of the equity? What is the value of the debt? Which project is preferred by bondholders?

CHAPTER 23

Options and Corporate Finance: Extensions and Applications

EXECUTIVE SUMMARY

This chapter extends the analysis of options contained in Chapter 22. We describe four different types of options found in common corporate finance decisions.

- Executive stock options and compensation.
- The embedded option in a start-up company.
- The option in simple business contracts.
- The option to shut down and reopen a project.

Option features are pervasive in corporate finance decisions. They are involved in decisions of whether to build, expand, or close a factory, to buy productive assets like trucks or machines, to drill for oil or mine for gold, or to build a building. Sometimes they are involved in decisions about how to pay managers and other employees. In this chapter we do not argue that the NPV approach should be completely jettisoned. In fact, many decisions have few embedded options and, in these cases, optionality can be ignored. However, in many cases, options are an important aspect of the decision and must be separately valued. In practice, there is a decision continuum. At one end of the continuum are decisions with little optionality and at the other are decisions with significant optionality.

In the previous chapter, we presented a few examples of options in corporate finance. We saw that stock is a call option on the firm. We showed that the value of this option could be increased by selecting high-risk rather than low-risk projects. We discussed the embedded option in oil exploration.

However, although the previous chapter presented these options, we made no attempt to *value* them. In this chapter, we will value four embedded options. The first two are handled with the Black-Scholes model. We use the binomial model to value the last two options. Although the Black-Scholes model is more well known, the binomial model is probably used more frequently in the real world. The Black-Scholes model works well on only a narrow set of problems. The flexibility of the binomial model allows it to be applied to a wider range of situations. However, binomial approaches often use complex numerical analyses involving large amounts of computer time. In this regard, binomial approaches are less elegant than the Black-Scholes approach.

23.1 EXECUTIVE STOCK OPTIONS

Why Options?

Executive compensation is usually made up of base salary plus some or all of the following elements:

1. Long-term compensation

■ TABLE 23.1 **1999 Top 15 Option Grants (a)**

Company	CEO	Number of Options Granted (in thousands) (b)	Stock Price	Face Value of Options Granted (in thousands) (c)
Citigroup Inc.	**Sanford I. Weill**	**6,868.4**	**$51.15**	**$351,318**
American Express Company	**Harvey Golub**	**1,089.2**	**$123.12**	**$134,102**
Cisco Systems, Inc.	**John T. Chambers**	**2,500.0**	**$52.84**	**$132,100**
Bank of America Corporation	Hugh L. McColl, Jr.	1,400.0	$74.50	$104,300
Honeywell Inc.	**Michael R. Bosignore**	**1,781.2**	**$58.21**	**$103,683**
ALCOA Inc.	**Paul O'Neill**	**1,928.6**	**$49.96**	**$96,352**
American General Corporation	**Robert M. Devlin**	**1,350.0**	**$68.06**	**$91,881**
Sprint Corporation	**William T. Esrey**	**2,473.4**	**$34.91**	**$86,346**
UnitedHealth Group Incorporated	**William W. McGuire, M.D.**	**2,075.0**	**$40.93**	**$84,929**
WorldCom, Inc.	**Bernard J. Ebbers**	**1,800.0**	**$46.58**	**$83,844**
General Electric Company	**John F. Welch, Jr.**	**625.0**	**$119.19**	**$74,493**
U.S. Bancorp	**John Grundhofer**	**1,919.3**	**$36.73**	**$70,495**
Hewlett-Packard Company	Carleton S. Fiorina	600.0	$113.03	$67,818
McKesson HBOC, Inc.	John H. Hammergree	2,300.0	$28.60	$65,780
Conseco, Inc.	**Stephen C. Hibert**	**2,047.4**	**$30.81**	**$63,080**

Source: Pearl Meyer & Partners.

(a) Based on the 200 largest U.S. industrial and service corporations. Companies in bold awarded "mega options" to the same CEO in fiscal year 1998 as well as in fiscal year 1999.

(b) Stock option award includes reload/restoration options.

(c) Face value of options granted is the number of options times the stock price.

2. Annual bonuses

3. Retirement contributions

4. Options

The final component of compensation, options, is by far the biggest part of total compensation for many top executives. Table 23.1 lists the 15 CEOs who received the largest stock option grants during 1999. The rank is in terms of the *face value* of the options granted. This is the number of options times the current stock price.

Knowing the face value of an option does not automatically allow us to determine the market value of the option. We also need to know the exercise price before valuing the option according to either the Black-Scholes model or the binomial model. However, the exercise price is generally set equal to the market price of the stock on the date the executive receives the options. In the next section, we value options under the assumption that the exercise price is equal to the market price.

Options in the stock of the company are increasingly being granted to executives as an alternative to increases in base pay. Some of the reasons given for using options are:

1. Options make executives share the same interests as the stockholders. By aligning their interests, it is argued that executives will make better decisions for the benefit of the stockholders.

2. Using options allows the company to lower the executive's base pay. This removes pressures on morale caused by great disparities between the salaries of executives and those of other employees.

3. Options put an executive's pay at risk, rather than guaranteeing it independent of the performance of the firm.

4. Options are a tax-efficient way to pay employees. Under current tax law, if an executive is given options to purchase company stock and the options are "at the money," they are not considered part of taxable income. The options are taxed only when and if they are eventually exercised.

EXAMPLE

The granting of stock options is not restricted to the highest ranking executives. Starbucks, the coffee chain that started in Seattle, has pushed stock options down to the lowest level employees. To quote its founder, Howard Schultz, "Even though we were a private company, we would grant stock options to every employee companywide, from the top managers to the baristas, in proportion to their level of base pay. They could then, through their efforts, help make Starbucks more successful every year, and if Starbucks someday went public, their options could eventually be worth a good sum of money."

Valuing Executive Compensation

We now attempt to value the options granted to executives. Not surprisingly, the complexity of the total compensation package often makes this a very difficult task. The actual economic value of the options depends on other factors such as the volatility of the underlying stock and the exact terms of the option grant.

Using Table 23.1, we will attempt to estimate the economic value of the options held by the executives listed. To do so we will employ the Black-Scholes option pricing formula from Chapter 22. Of course, we are missing many features of the particular plans and the best we can hope for is a rough estimate. Simple matters such as requiring the executive to hold the option for a fixed period, the freeze-out period, before exercising, can significantly diminish the value of a standard option. Equally important, the Black-Scholes formula has to be modified if the stock pays dividends. Intuitively, a call option on a dividend-paying stock is worth less than a call on a stock that pays no dividends, since, all other things being equal, the dividends will lower the stock price. Nevertheless, let us see what we can do.

We will assume that all of the options are "at the money," so that their exercise prices are the current stock values. The total exercise prices are thus equal to the reported face value. We will take the risk-free interest rate as 7 percent and assume that the options all have a maturity of five years. Finally, we will ignore the dilution from exercising them as warrants and value them as call options. The last required input, the volatility or standard deviation of the stock, σ, was estimated from the historical returns on each of the stocks. Table 23.2 lists the volatilities for each stock and the estimated value of the stock grants. As can be seen, these values, while large by ordinary standards, are significantly less than the corresponding face values. Notice that the ordering by face value is not the same as that by economic value. For example, the high volatility of Conseco raises its option value to over $37 million, the tenth highest in the table, even though its rank by face value alone is fifteenth.

EXAMPLE

Consider Sandy Weill, the chief executive officer (CEO) of Citigroup, who was granted 6.8684 million options. The stock price at the time of the options grant was 51.15. We will assume that his options are at the money. The risk-free rate is 7 percent and the options expire in five years. The preceding information implies that:

■ TABLE 23.2 Value of 1999 Top 15 Option Grants

Company	CEO	Face Value of Options Granted (in thousands)	Annual Stock Standard Deviation (%/year)	Black-Scholes Value (in thousands)
Citigroup Inc.	Sanford I. Weill	$351,318	38.26	$158,646
American Express Company	Harvey Golub	$134,102	30.69	$54,201
Cisco Systems, Inc.	John T. Chambers	$132,100	38.99	$60,259
Bank of America Corporation	Hugh L. McColl, Jr.	$104,300	36.30	$45,814
Honeywell Inc.	Michael R. Bosignore	$103,683	38.29	$54,886
ALCOA Inc.	Paul O'Neill	$ 96,352	35.96	$42,115
American General Corporation	Robert M. Devlin	$ 91,881	26.14	$34,578
Sprint Corporation	William T. Esrey	$ 86,346	34.92	$37,178
UnitedHealth Group Incorporated	William W. McGuire, M.D.	$ 84,929	39.08	$38,789
WorldCom, Inc.	Bernard J. Ebbers	$ 83,844	40.28	$38,925
General Electric Company	John F. Welch, Jr.	$ 74,493	25.39	$27,702
U.S. Bancorp	John Grundhofer	$ 70,495	40.28	$32,727
Hewlett-Packard Company	Carleton S. Fiorina	$ 67,818	42.60	$32,472
McKesson HBOC, Inc.	John H. Hammergree	$ 65,780	50.26	$34,609
Conseco, Inc.	Stephen C. Hibert	$ 63,080	60.56	$37,042

Source: Pearl Meyer & Partners.

1. The stock price (*S*) of $51.15 equals the exercise price (*E*).
2. The risk-free rate (*r*) is 0.07.
3. The five-year time interval is *t* = 5.

In addition, the variance of Citigroup stock is estimated to be $(0.3826)^2 = 0.1464$.

The above information allows us to estimate the value of Sandy Weill's options using the Black-Scholes model.

$$C = SN(d_1) - Ee^{-rt}N(d_2)$$
$$d_1 = [(r + 1/2\sigma^2)t]/\sqrt{\sigma^2 t} = 0.8369$$
$$d_2 = d_1 - \sqrt{\sigma^2 t} = -0.0186$$
$$N(d_1) = 0.7987$$
$$N(d_2) = 0.4926$$
$$e^{-.07 \times 5} = 0.7047$$
$$C = \$51.15 \times 0.7987 - \$51.15 \times (0.7047 \times 0.4926) = \$23.098$$

Thus, the value of a call option on one share of Citigroup stock was $23.098. Since Mr. Weill was granted options on 6.8684 million shares, his grant has a market value of $158,646,000 (6.8684 million × $23.098).

The values we have computed in Table 23.2 are the economic values of the options if they were to trade in the market. The real question is, whose value are we talking about? Are these the costs of the options to the company? Are they the values of the options to the executives?

Suppose that a company computes the fair market value of the options as we have done in Table 23.2. For purposes of illustration, assume that the options are in the money, and that they are worth $25 each. Suppose, too, that the CEO holds 1 million such options for a total value of $25 million. This is the amount that the options would trade at in the financial markets and that traders and investors would be willing to pay for them.[1] If the company were very large, it would not be unreasonable for it to view this as the cost of granting the options to the CEO. Of course, in return, the company would expect the CEO to improve the value of the company to its shareholders by more than this amount. As we have seen, perhaps the main purpose of options is to align the interests of management with those of the shareholders of the firm. Under no circumstances, though, is the $25 million necessarily a fair measure of what the options are worth to the CEO.

As an illustration, suppose that the CEO of ABC has options on $1 million in shares with an exercise price of $30 per share, and the current price of ABC stock is $50 per share. If the options were exercised today, they would be worth $20 million (an underestimation of their market value). Suppose, in addition, that the CEO owns $5 million in company stock and has $5 million in other assets. The CEO clearly has a very undiversified personal portfolio. By the standards of modern portfolio theory having 25/30 or about 83 percent of your personal wealth in one stock and its options is unnecessarily risky.

While the CEO is wealthy by most standards, significant shifts in the stock value will have dramatic impacts on the CEO's economic well-being. If the value drops from $50 per share to $30 per share, the current exercise value of the options on 1 million shares drops from $20 million down to zero. Ignoring the fact that if the options would have more time to mature they will not lose all of this value, we nevertheless have a rather startling decline in the CEO's net worth from about $30 million to $8 million ($5 million in other assets plus stock that is now worth $3 million). But that is the purpose of giving the options and the

---

[1]We ignore warrant dilution in this example. See Chapter 24 for a discussion of warrant dilution.

stock holdings to the CEO, namely, to make the CEO's fortunes rise and fall with those of the company. It is why the company requires the executive to hold the options, at least for a freeze-out period, rather than letting the executive sell them to realize their value.

The implication is that when options are a large portion of an executive's net worth and the executive is forced by the company to be undiversified, the total value of the position is worth less to the executive than the fair financial market value. As a purely financial matter, an executive might by happier with $5 million in cash rather than $20 million in options. At the least, the executive could then diversify his personal portfolio.

QUESTION

?

CONCEPT

- Why do companies issue options to executives if they cost the company more than they are worth to the executive? Why not just give cash and split the difference? Wouldn't that make both the company and the executive better off?

23.2 VALUING A START-UP

Ralph Simmons was not your typical MBA student. Since childhood, he had had one ambition, to open a restaurant that sold alligator meat. He went to business school because he realized that, although he knew 101 ways to cook alligators, he didn't have the business skills necessary to run a restaurant. He was extremely focused, with each course at graduate school being important to him only to the extent that it could further his dream.

While taking his school's course in entrepreneurship, he began to develop a business plan for his restaurant, which he now called Alligator Alley. He thought about marketing, he thought about raising capital, he thought about dealing with future employees. He even devoted a great deal of time to designing the physical layout of the restaurant. Against the advice of his professor in the entrepreneurship class, he decided to design the restaurant in the shape of an alligator, where the front door went through the animal's mouth. Of course, his business plan would not be complete without financial projections. After much thought, he came up with the projections shown in Table 23.3

The table starts with sales projections, which rise from $300,000 in the first year to a steady state of $1 million a year. Cash Flows from Operations are shown in the next line, although we leave out the intermediate calculations needed to move from line (1) to line

■ TABLE 23.3 **Financial Projections for Alligator Alley**

	Year 1	Year 2	Year 3	Year 4	All Future Years
(1) Sales	$300,000	$600,000	$900,000	$1,000,000	$1,000,000
(2) Cash flows from operations	−$100,000	−$ 50,000	+$ 75,000	+$ 250,000	+$ 250,000
(3) Increase in working capital	$ 50,000	$ 20,000	$ 10,000	$ 10,000	0
Net cash flows (2) − (3)	−$150,000	−$ 70,000	$ 65,000	$ 240,000	$ 250,000

Present value of net cash flows in years 1–4 (discounted at 20%)	−$20,255

$$\text{Present value of terminal value} \left[\frac{\$250,000}{0.20} \times \frac{1}{(1.20)^4} \right] = \quad +\$602,816$$

Present value of restaurant	$582,561
− Cost of building	−$700,000
Net present value of restaurant	−$117,439

(2). After subtracting Working Capital, the table shows Net Cash Flows in line 4. Net Cash Flows are negative initially, as is quite common in start-ups, but they become positive by Year 3. However, the rest of the table presents the unfortunate truth. The cash flows from the restaurant yield a present value of $582,561, assuming a discount rate of 20 percent. Unfortunately, the cost of the building is greater, at $700,000, implying a negative *net* present value of −$117,439.

The projections indicate that Ralph's lifelong dream may not come to pass. He cannot expect to raise the capital needed to open his restaurant, and if he did obtain the funding, the restaurant would likely go under anyway. Ralph checked and rechecked the numbers, hoping vainly to discover either a numerical error or a cost-saving omission that would move his venture from the red to the black. In fact, Ralph saw that, if anything, his forecasts are generous, because a 20 percent discount rate and an infinitely lived building are on the optimistic side.

It wasn't until Ralph took a course in corporate strategy that he realized the hidden value in his venture. In that course, his instructor repeatedly stated the importance of positioning a firm to take advantage of new opportunities. Although Ralph didn't see the connection at first, he finally realized the implications for Alligator Alley. His financial projections were based on expectations. There was a 50 percent probability that alligator meat would be more popular than he thought, in which case actual cash flows would exceed projections. And, there was a 50 percent probability that the meat would be less popular, in which case the actual flows would fall short of projections.

If the restaurant did poorly, it would probably fold in a few years, because he would not want to keep losing money forever. However, if the restaurant did well, he would be in a position to expand. If alligator meat proved popular in one locale, it would likely prove popular in other locales as well. Thus, he noticed two options, the option to abandon under bad conditions and the option to expand under good conditions. Although both options can be valued according to the principles of the previous chapter, we focus on the option to expand because it is probably much more valuable.

Ralph reasoned that, as much as he personally liked alligator meat, there were whole regions of the country where consumer resistance would doom Alligator Alley. So he developed a strategy of catering only to those regions where alligator meat is somewhat popular already. He forecast that, although he could expand quickly if the first restaurant proved successful, the market would limit him to 30 additional restaurants.

Ralph believes that this expansion will occur about four years from now. He believes that he will need three years of operating the first restaurant to (1) get the initial restaurant running smoothly and (2) have enough information to place an accurate value on the restaurant. If the first restaurant is successful enough, he will need another year to obtain outside capital. Thus, he will be ready to build the 30 additional units around the fourth year.

Ralph will value his enterprise, including the option to expand, according to the Black-Scholes model. From Table 23.3, we see that each unit cost $700,000, implying a total cost over the 30 additional units of $21,000,000 (30 × $700,000). The present value of the cash inflows from these 30 units is $17,476,830 (30 × $582,561), according to the table. However, because the expansion will occur around the fourth year, this present-value calculation is provided from the point of view of four years in the future. The present value as of today is $8,428,255 ($17,476,830/(1.20)^4), assuming a discount rate of 20 percent per year. Thus, Ralph views his potential restaurant business as an option, where the exercise price is $21,000,000 and the value of the underlying asset is $8,428,255. The option is currently out of the money, a result that follows from the negative value of a typical restaurant, as calculated in Table 23.3. Of course, Ralph is hoping that the option will move into the money within four years.

Ralph needs three additional parameters to use the Black-Scholes model: r, the continuously compounded interest rate; t, the time to maturity; and σ, the standard deviation of the underlying asset. Ralph uses the yield on a four-year zero-coupon bond, which is 3.5

■ TABLE 23.4   **Valuing a Start-Up Firm (Alligator Alley) as an Option**

Facts
1. The value of a single restaurant is negative, as indicated by the net-present-value calculation in Table 23.3 of −$117,439. Thus, the restaurant would not be funded if there were no possibility of expansion.
2. If the pilot restaurant is successful, Ralph Simmons plans to create 30 additional restaurants around year 4. This leads to the following observations:
   a. The total cost of 30 units is $21,000,000 (30 × $700,000).
   b. The present value of future cash flows as of year 4 is $17,476,830 (30 × $582,561).
   c. The present value of these cash flows today is $8,428,255 ($17,476,830/(1.20)^4).

Here, we assume that cash flows from the project are discounted at 20% per annum.
   Thus, the business is essentially a call option, where the exercise price is $21,000,000 and the underlying asset is worth $8,428,255.

3. Ralph Simmons estimates the standard deviation of the return on Alligator Alley's stock to be 0.50.

Parameters of the Black-Scholes model:
$$S \text{ (stock price)} = \$8,428,255$$
$$E \text{ (exercise price)} = \$21,000,000$$
$$t \text{ (time to maturity)} = 4 \text{ years}$$
$$\sigma \text{ (standard deviation)} = 0.50$$
$$r \text{ (continuously compounded interest rate)} = 3.5\%$$

Calculation from the Black-Scholes model:
$$C = SN(d_1) - Ee^{-rt}N(d_2)$$
$$d_1 = [\ln(S/E) + (r + 1/2\ \sigma^2)t]/\sqrt{\sigma^2 t}$$
$$d_2 = d_1 - \sqrt{\sigma^2 t}$$
$$d_1 = \left[\ln\frac{8,428,255}{21,000,000} + \left(0.035 + \tfrac{1}{2}(0.50)^2\right)4\right]/\sqrt{(0.50)^2 \cdot 4} = -0.27293$$
$$d_2 = -0.27293 - \sqrt{(0.50)^2 \cdot 4} = -1.27293$$
$$N(d_1) = N(-0.27293) = 0.3936$$
$$N(d_2) = N(-1.27293) = 0.1020$$
$$C = \$8,428,255 \times 0.3936 - \$21,000,000 \times e^{-0.035 \times 4} \times 0.1020$$
$$= \$1,455,196$$

Value of business including cost of pilot restaurant = $1,455,196 − $117,439
$$= \$1,337,757$$

percent, as the estimate of the interest rate. The time to maturity is four years. The estimate of standard deviation is a little trickier, because there is no historical data on alligator restaurants. Ralph finds that the average annual standard deviation of the returns on publicly traded restaurants is 0.35. Because Alligator Alley is a new venture, he reasons that the risk here would be somewhat greater. He finds that the average annual standard deviation for restaurants that have gone public in the last few years is 0.45. Because Ralph's restaurant is newer still, he uses a standard deviation of 0.50.

   There is now enough data to value Ralph's venture. The value according to the Black-Scholes model is $1,455,196. The actual calculations are shown in Table 23.4. Of course, Ralph must start his pilot restaurant before he can take advantage of this option. Thus, the net value of the call option less the negative present value of the pilot restaurant is $1,337,757 ($1,455,196 − $117,439). Because this value is large and positive, Ralph decides to stay with his dream of Alligator Alley. He knows that the probability that the restaurant will fail is greater than 50%. Nevertheless, the option to expand is important enough that his restaurant business has value. And, if he needs outside capital, he probably can attract the necessary investors.

This finding leads to the appearance of a paradox. If Ralph approaches investors to invest in a single restaurant with no possibility of expansion, he will probably not be able to attract capital. After all, Table 23.3 shows a net present value of −$117,439. However, if Ralph thinks bigger, he will likely be able to attract all the capital that he needs. But this is really not a paradox at all. By thinking bigger, Ralph is offering investors the option, not the obligation, to expand.

The example we have chosen may seem frivolous and, certainly, we added offbeat characteristics for interest. However, if you think that business situations involving options are unusual or unimportant, let us state emphatically that nothing can be further from the truth. The notion of embedded options is at the heart of business. There are two possible outcomes for virtually every business idea. On the one hand, the business may fail, in which case the managers will probably try to shut it down in the most cost-efficient way. On the other hand, the business may prosper, in which case the managers will try to expand. Thus, virtually every business has both the option to abandon and the option to expand. You may have read pundits claiming that the net-present-value approach to capital budgeting is wrong or incomplete. Although criticism of this type frequently irritates the finance establishment, the pundits definitely have a point. If virtually all projects have embedded options, only an approach such as the one we have outlined can be appropriate. Ignoring the options is likely to lead to serious undervaluation.

CONCEPT QUESTIONS

?

- What are the two options that many businesses have?
- Why does a strict NPV calculation typically understate the value of a firm or project?

23.3   MORE ON THE BINOMIAL MODEL

Earlier in this chapter, we examined two applications of options, executive compensation and the start-up decision. In both cases we valued an option using the Black-Scholes model. Although this model is justifiably well known, it is not the only approach to option valuation. As mentioned in the previous chapter, the binomial model is an alternative and—in some situations—a superior approach to valuation. The rest of this chapter examines two applications under this binomial model.

Heating Oil

Two-Date Example   Consider Anthony Meyer, a typical heating-oil distributor, whose business consists of buying heating oil at the wholesale level and reselling the oil to homeowners at a slightly higher price. Most of his revenue comes from sales during the winter. Today, September 1, heating oil sells for $1.00 per gallon. Of course, this price is not fixed. Rather, oil prices will vary from September 1 until December 1, the time when his customers will probably be making their big winter purchases of heating oil. Let's simplify the situation by assuming that Anthony believes that oil prices will either be at $1.37 or $0.73 on December 1. Figure 23.1 portrays this possible price movement. This potential price range represents a great deal of uncertainty, because Anthony has no idea which of the two possible prices will actually occur. However, this price variability does not translate into that much risk, because he is able to pass price changes on to his customers. That is, he will charge his customers more if he ends up paying $1.37 per gallon than if he ends up paying $0.73 per gallon.

■ FIGURE 23.1   Movement of Heating-Oil Prices from September 1 to December 1 in a Two-Date Example

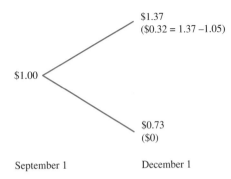

$1.00

$1.37
($0.32 = 1.37 −1.05)

$0.73
($0)

September 1   December 1

The price of heating oil on December 1 will either be $1.37 or $0.73. Because the price on September 1 is $1.00, we say that $u = 1.37$ ($1.37 / $1.00) and $d = 0.73$ ($0.73 / $1.00). The loss per gallon to Anthony (or, equivalently, the gain per gallon to CECO) of $0.32 in the up-state and $0 in the down-state are shown in parentheses.

Of course, Anthony is avoiding risk by passing on that risk to his customers. His customers accept this risk, perhaps because they are each too small to negotiate a better deal with Anthony. This is not the case with CECO, a large electric utility in his area. CECO approaches Anthony with the following proposition. The utility would like to be able to buy *up to* 6 million gallons of oil from him at $1.05 per gallon on December 1.

Although this arrangement represents a lot of oil, both Mr. Meyer and CECO know that Anthony can expect to lose money on it. If prices rise to $1.37 per gallon, the utility will happily buy all 6 million gallons from Anthony at only $1.05 per gallon, clearly creating a loss for the distributor. However, if oil prices decline to $0.73 per gallon, the utility will not buy any oil from Anthony. After all, why should CECO pay $1.05 per gallon to Anthony when the utility can buy all the oil it wants at $0.73 per gallon in the open market? In other words, CECO is asking for a *call option* on heating oil. To compensate Anthony for the risk of loss, the two parties agree that CECO will pay him $500,000 up front for the right to buy up to 6 million gallons of oil at $1.05 per gallon.

Is this a fair deal? Although small distributors may evaluate a deal like this by "gut feel," we can evaluate it more quantitatively using the binomial model described in the previous chapter. In that chapter, we pointed out that option problems can be handled most easily by assuming *risk-neutral pricing*. Under this approach, we first note that oil will either rise 37 percent ($1.37/$1.00 − 1) or fall −27 percent ($0.73/$1.00 − 1) from September 1 to December 1. We can think of these two numbers as the possible returns on heating oil. In addition, we introduce two new terms, u and d. We define u as $1 + 0.37 = 1.37$ and d as $1 − 0.27 = 0.73$.[2] Using the methodology of the previous chapter, we value the contract in the following two steps.

Step 1: Determining the Risk-Neutral Probabilities   We determine the probability of a price rise such that the expected return on oil exactly equals the risk-free rate. Assuming an 8 percent annual interest rate, which implies a 2 percent rate over the next three months, we can solve for the probability of a rise as[3]:

$$2\% = \text{Probability of rise} \times 0.37 + (1 - \text{Probability of rise}) \times (-0.27)$$

---

[2]As we will see later, here u and d are consistent with a standard deviation of the annual return on heating oil of 0.63.

[3]For simplicity, we ignore both storage costs and a convenience yield.

Solving this equation, we find that the probability of a rise is approximately 45 percent, implying that the probability of a fall is 55 percent. In other words, if the probability of a price rise is 45 percent, the expected return on heating oil is 2 percent. In accordance with what we said in the previous chapter, these are the probabilities that are consistent with a world of risk-neutrality. That is, under risk-neutrality, the expected return on any asset would equal the riskless rate of interest. No one would demand an expected return above this riskless rate, because risk-neutral individuals do not need to be compensated for risk-bearing.

Step 2: Valuing the Contract   If the price of oil rises to $1.37 on December 1, CECO will want to buy oil from Anthony at $1.05 per gallon. Anthony will lose $0.32 per gallon, because he buys oil in the open market at $1.37 per gallon, only to resell it to CECO at $1.05 per gallon. This loss of $0.32 is shown in parentheses in Figure 23.1. Conversely, if the market price of heating oil falls to $0.73 per gallon, CECO will not buy any oil from Anthony at all. That is, CECO would not want to pay $1.05 per gallon to Anthony when the utility could buy heating oil in the open market at $0.73 per gallon. Thus, we can say that Anthony neither gains nor loses if the price drops to $0.73. The gain or loss of zero is placed in parentheses under the price of $0.73 in Figure 23.1. In addition, as mentioned earlier, Anthony receives $500,000 up front.

Given these numbers, the value of the contract to Anthony can be calculated as:

$$\underbrace{[0.45 \times (\$1.05 - \$1.37) \times 6 \text{ million} + 0.55 \times 0]/1.02}_{\text{Value of the call option}} + \$500,000 = -\$347,000. \quad (23.1)$$

As in the previous chapter, we are valuing an option using risk-neutral pricing. The cash flows of −$0.32 ($1.05 − $1.37) and $0 per gallon are multiplied by their risk-neutral probabilities. The entire first term in equation (23.1) is then discounted at $1.02 because the cash flows in that term occur on December 1. The $500,000 is not discounted, because Anthony receives it today, September 1. Because the present value of the contract is negative, Anthony would be wise to reject the contract.

As stated before, the distributor has sold a call option to CECO. The first term in the preceding equation, which equals −$847,000, can be viewed as the value of this call option. It is a negative number because the equation looks at the option from Anthony's point of view. Therefore, the value of the call option would be +$847,000 to CECO. On a per-gallon basis, the value of the option to CECO is:

$$[0.45 (\$1.37 - \$1.05) + 0.55 \times 0]/1.02 = \$0.141 \quad (23.2)$$

Equation (23.2) shows that CECO will gain $0.32 ($1.37 − $1.05) per gallon in the up-state, because CECO can buy heating oil worth $1.37 for only $1.05 under the contract. By contrast, the contract is worth nothing to CECO in the down-state, because the utility will not pay $1.05 for oil selling for only $0.73 in the open market. Using risk-neutral pricing, the formula tells us that the value of the call option on 1 gallon of heating oil is $0.141.

Three-Date Example   Although the preceding example captures a number of aspects of the real world, it has one deficiency. It assumes that the price of heating oil can take on only two values on December 1. This is clearly not plausible, because oil can take on essentially any value in reality. Although this deficiency seems glaring at first glance, it actually is quite correctable; all one has to do is to introduce more intervals over the three-month period of our example.

■ FIGURE 23.2   **Movement of Heating-Oil Prices in a Three-Date Model**

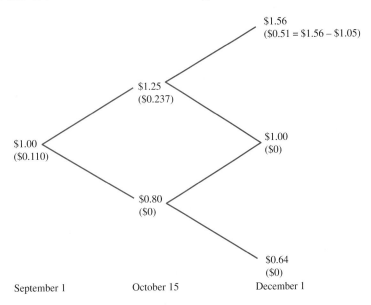

$1.56
($0.51 = $1.56 − $1.05)

$1.25
($0.237)

$1.00
($0)

$1.00
($0.110)

$0.80
($0)

$0.64
($0)

September 1   October 15   December 1

The figure shows the prices of a gallon of heating oil on three dates, given $u = 1.25$ and $d = 0.80$. There are three possible prices for heating oil on December 1. For each one of these three prices, we calculate the price on December 1 of a call option on a gallon of heating oil with an exercise price of $1.05. These numbers are in parentheses. Call prices at earlier dates are determined by the binomial model and are also shown in parentheses.

For example, consider Figure 23.2, which shows the price movement of heating oil over two intervals of 1½ months each.[4] As shown in the figure, the price will be either $1.25 or $0.80 on October 15. We refer to $1.25 as the price in the *up-state* and $0.80 as the price in the *down-state*. Thus, heating oil has returns of 25 percent ($1.25/$1) and −20 percent ($0.80/$1) in the two states.

We assume the same variability as we move forward from October 15 to December 1. That is, given a price of $1.25 on October 15, the price on December 1 will be either $1.56 ($1.25 × 1.25) or $1 ($1.25 × 0.80). Similarly, given a price of $0.80 on October 15, the price on December 1 will be either $1 ($0.80 × 1.25) or $0.64 ($0.80 × 0.80). This assumption of constant variability is quite plausible, because the rate of new information impacting heating oil (or most commodities or assets) is likely to be similar from month to month.

Note that there are three possible prices on December 1, but there are two possible prices on October 15. Also note that there are two paths, both generating a price of $1 on December 1. The price could rise to $1.25 on October 15 before falling back down to $1 on December 1 or, alternatively, the price could fall to $0.80 on October 15 before going back up to $1 on December 1. In other words, the model has symmetry, where an up-movement followed by a down-movement yields the same price on December 1 as a down-movement followed by an up-movement.

---

[4]Though it is not apparent at first glance, we will see later that the price movement in Figure 23.2 is consistent with the price movement in Figure 23.1.

How do we value CECO's option in this three-date example? We employ the same procedure that we used in the two-date example, although we will now need an extra step because of the extra date:

Step 1: Determining the Risk-Neutral Probabilities   As we did in the two-date example, we determine what the probability of a price rise would be such that the expected return on heating oil exactly equals the riskless rate. However, in this case, we work with an interval of 1½ months. Assuming an 8 percent annual rate of interest, which implies a 1 percent rate over a 1½ month interval,[5] we can solve for the probability of a rise as:

$$1\% = \text{Probability of rise} \times 0.25 + (1 - \text{Probability of rise}) \times (-0.20)$$

Solving the equation, we find that the probability of a rise here is 47 percent, implying that the probability of a fall is 53 percent. In other words, if the probability of a rise is 47 percent, the expected return on heating oil is 1 percent per each 1½-month interval. Again, these probabilities are determined under the assumption of risk-neutral pricing.

Note that the probabilities of 47 percent and 53 percent hold for both the interval from September 1 to October 15 and the interval from October 15 to December 1. This is the case because the return in the up-state is 25 percent and the return in the down-state is −20 percent for each of the two intervals. Thus, the preceding equation must apply to each of the intervals separately.

Step 2: Valuing the Option as of October 15   As indicated in Figure 23.2, the option to CECO will be worth $0.51 per gallon on December 1 if the price of heating oil has risen to $1.56 on that date. That is, CECO can buy oil from Anthony at $1.05 when it would otherwise have to pay $1.56 in the open market. However the option will be worthless on December 1 if the price of a gallon of heating oil is either $1 or $0.64 on that date. Here, the option is out of the money because the exercise price of $1.05 is above either $1 or $0.64.

Using these implicit option prices on December 1, we can calculate the value of the call option on October 15. If the price of a gallon of heating oil is $1.25 on October 15, Figure 23.2 shows us that the call option will either be worth $0.51 or $0 on December 1. Thus, if the price of heating oil is $1.25 on October 15, the value of the option on 1 gallon of heating oil at that time is:

$$[0.47 \times 0.51 + 0.53 \times 0]/1.01 = \$0.237$$

Here, we are valuing an option using the same risk-neutral pricing approach that we used in the earlier two-date example. This value of $0.237 is shown in parentheses in Figure 23.2

We also want to value the option on October 15 if the price at that time is $0.80. However, the value here is clearly zero, as indicated by the calculation:

$$[0.47 \times \$0 + 0.53 \times \$0]/1.01 = 0$$

This is obvious, once one looks at Figure 23.2. We see from the figure that the call must end up out of the money on December 1 if the price of heating oil is $0.80 on October 15. Thus, the call must have zero value on October 15 if the price of heating oil is $0.80 on that date.

Step 3: Valuing the Option on September 1   In the previous step, we saw that the price of the call on October 15 would be $0.237 if the price of a gallon of heating oil were $1.25 on that date. Similarly, the price of the option on October 15 would be $0 if oil were selling at $0.80 on that date. From these values, we can calculate the call option value on September 1 as:

$$[0.47 \times \$0.237 + 0.53 \times \$0]/1.01 = \$0.110$$

---

[5]For simplicity, we ignore interest compounding.

Notice that this calculation is completely analogous to the calculation of the option value in the previous step, as well as the calculation of the option value in the two-date example that we presented earlier. In other words, the same approach applies regardless of the number of intervals used. As we will see later, we can move to many intervals, which produces greater realism, yet still maintain the same basic methodology.

The previous calculation has given us the value of CECO of its option on 1 gallon of heating oil. Now we are ready to calculate the value of the contract to Anthony. Given the calculations from the previous equation, the contract's value can be written as:

$$-\$0.110 \times 6,000,000 + \$500,000 = -\$160,000$$

That is, Anthony is giving away an option worth $0.110 for each of the 6 million gallons of heating oil. In return, he is receiving only $500,000 up front. On balance, he is losing $160,000. Of course, the value of the contract to CECO is the opposite, so the value to this utility is $160,000.

Extension to Many Dates   We have looked at the contract between CECO and Anthony using both a two-date example and a three-date example. The three-date case is more realistic because more possibilities for price movements are allowed here. However, why stop at just three dates? Moving to 4 dates, 5 dates, 50 dates, 500 dates, and so on, should give us ever more realism. Note that, as we move to more dates, we are merely shortening the interval between dates without increasing the overall time period of three months (September 1 to December 1).

For example, imagine a model with 90 dates over the three months. Here, each interval is approximately one day long, because there are about 90 days in a three-month period. The assumption of two possible outcomes in the binomial model is more plausible over a one-day interval than it is over a 1½-month interval, let alone a three-month interval. Of course, we could probably achieve greater realism still by going to an interval of, say, one hour or one minute.

How does one adjust the binomial model in order to accommodate increases in the number of intervals? It turns out that two simple formulas relate u and d to the standard deviation of the return of the underlying asset[6]:

$$u = e^{\sigma/\sqrt{n}} \quad \text{and} \quad d = 1/u$$

where σ is the standard deviation of the annualized return on the underlying asset (heating oil, in this case) and n is the number of intervals over a year.

When we created the heating oil example, we assumed that the annualized standard deviation of the return on heating oil was 0.63 (or, equivalently, 63 percent). Because there are four quarters in a year, $u = e^{0.63/\sqrt{4}} = 1.37$ and $d = 1/1.37 = 0.73$, as shown in the two-date example of Figure 23.1. In the three-date example of Figure 23.2, where each interval is 1½ months long, $u = e^{0.63/\sqrt{8}} = 1.25$ and $d = 1/1.25 = 0.80$. Thus, the binomial model can be applied in practice if the standard deviation of the return of the underlying asset can be estimated.

We stated earlier that the value of the call option on a gallon of heating oil was estimated to be $0.141 in the two-date model and $0.110 in the three-date model. How does the value of the option change as we increase the number of intervals, while keeping the time period constant at three months (from September 1 to December 1)? We have calcu-

---

[6]See John C. Hull, *Options, Futures, and Other Derivatives,* 4th ed. (Upper Saddle River, N.J.: Prentice Hall, 1999) for a derivation of these formulas.

■ TABLE 23.5 **Value of a Call on One Gallon of Heating Oil**

	Number of Intervals*	Call Value
	1	$0.141
	2	0.110
	3	0.122
	4	0.116
	6	0.114
	10	0.114
	20	0.114
	30	0.114
	40	0.114
	50	0.113
	99	0.113
Black-Scholes	Infinity	0.113

In this example, the value of the call according to the binomial model varies as the number of intervals increases. However, the value of the call converges rapidly to the Black-Scholes value. Thus, the binomial model, even with only a few intervals, appears to be a good approximation to Black-Scholes.
*The number of intervals is always one less than the number of dates.

lated the value of the call for various time intervals[7] in Table 23.5. The realism increases with the number of intervals, because the restriction of only two possible outcomes is more plausible over a short interval than over a long one. Thus, the value of the call when the number of intervals is 99 or infinity is likely more realistic than this value when the number of intervals is, say, 1 or 2. However, a very interesting phenomenon can be observed from the table. Although the value of the call changes as the number of intervals increases, convergence occurs quite rapidly. The call's value when the number of intervals is 6 is almost identical to the value when there are 99 intervals. Thus, a small number of intervals appears serviceable for the binomial model.

What happens when the number of intervals goes to infinity, implying that the length of the interval goes to zero? It can be proved mathematically that one ends up with the value of the Black-Scholes model. This value is also presented in Table 23.5. Thus, one can argue that the Black-Scholes model is the best approach to value the heating-oil option. It is also quite easy to apply. We can use a calculator to value options with Black-Scholes, whereas we must generally use a computer program for the binomial model. However, as shown in Table 23.5, the values from the binomial model, even with relatively few intervals, are quite close to the Black-Scholes value. Thus, although Black-Scholes may save us time, it does not materially affect our estimate of value.

At this point it seems as if the Black-Scholes model is preferable to the binomial model. Who wouldn't want to save time and still get a slightly more accurate value? However, such is not always the case. There are plenty of situations where the binomial model is preferred to the Black-Scholes model. One such situation is presented in the next section.

---

[7]In this discussion we have used both *intervals* and *dates.* To keep the terminology straight, remember that the number of intervals is always one less than the number of dates. For example, if a model has two dates, it only has one interval.

23.4 SHUTDOWN AND REOPENING DECISIONS

Some of the earliest and most important examples of special options occur in the natural resources and mining industries.

Valuing a Gold Mine

The "Woe Is Me" gold mine was founded in 1878 on one of the richest veins of gold in the West. Thirty years later, by 1908, the mine had been played out, but occasionally, depending on the price of gold, it is reopened. Currently gold is not actively mined at Woe Is Me, but its stock is still traded on the exchange under the ticker symbol, WOE. WOE has no debt and, with about 20 million outstanding shares, it has a market value (stock price times number of shares outstanding) well above $1 billion. WOE owns about 160 acres of land surrounding the mine and has a 100-year government lease to mine gold there. However, land in the desert has a market value of only a few thousand dollars. WOE holds cash and securities and other assets worth about $30 million. What could possibly explain why a company with $30 million in assets and a closed gold mine that is producing no cash flow whatsoever has the market value that WOE has?

The answer lies in the options that WOE implicitly owns in the form of a gold mine. Assume that the current price of gold is about $320 per ounce and the cost of extraction and processing at the mine is about $350 per ounce. It is no wonder that the mine is closed. Every ounce of gold extracted costs $350 and can be sold for only $320 for a loss of $30 per ounce. Presumably, if the price of gold were to rise, the mine could be opened. It costs $2 million to open the mine and when it is opened, production is 50,000 ounces per year. Geologists believe that the amount of gold in the mine is essentially unlimited, and WOE has the right to mine it for the next 100 years. Under the terms of its lease, WOE cannot stockpile gold and must sell each year all the gold it mines that year. Closing the mine requires equipment to be mothballed and some environmental precautions to be put in place and costs $1 million. We will refer to the $2 million required to open the mine as the entry fee or investment and the $1 million to close it as the closing or abandonment cost. (There is no way to avoid the abandonment cost by simply keeping the mine open and not operating.)

From a financial perspective, WOE is really just a package of options on the price of gold disguised as a company and a mine. The basic option is a call on the price of gold where the exercise price is the $350 extraction cost. The option is complicated by having an exercise fee of $2 million—the opening cost—whenever it is exercised and a closing fee of $1 million when it is abandoned. It is also complicated by the fact that it is a perpetual option with no final maturity.

The Abandonment and Opening Decisions

Before trying to figure out the exact value of the option implicit in WOE or, for that matter, in any real option problem, it is useful to see what we can say by just applying common sense. To begin with, the mine should only be opened when the price of gold is sufficiently above the extraction cost of $350 per ounce. Because it costs $2 million to open the mine, the mine should not be opened whenever the price of gold is only slightly above $350. At a gold price of, say, $350.10, the mine wouldn't be opened because the ten-cent profit per ounce translates into $5,000 per year (50,000 ounces × $0.10/ounce). This would not begin to cover the $2 million opening costs. More significantly, though, the mine probably would not be opened if the price rose to $360 per ounce even though a $10 profit per ounce—$500,000 per year—would pay the $2 million opening costs at any reasonable discount rate. The reason is that here, as in all option problems, volatility, in this case the volatility of gold, plays a significant role. Because the gold price is volatile the price has to rise sufficiently above $350 per ounce to make it worth opening the mine. If the price at which the mine is opened is too close to the extraction price of $350 per ounce, say at $360 per ounce, for example, then we would wind up opening the mine every time the price jogged above $360 and finding ourselves operating at a loss or facing a closing decision whenever the gold price jogged down $10 per ounce or only 3 percent down.

The estimated volatility of the return on gold is about 15 percent per year. This means that a single annual standard deviation movement in the gold price is 15 percent of $320 or $48 per year. Surely with this amount of random movement in the gold price, a threshold of $352 is much too low at which to open the mine. A similar logic applies to the closing decision. If the mine is open, then we will clearly keep it open as long as the gold price is above the extraction cost of $350 per ounce since we are profiting on every ounce of gold mined. But, we also won't close the mine down simply because the gold price drops below $350 per ounce. We will tolerate a running loss to keep alive the possibility that the gold price will rise above $350 and to avoid the necessity of having to pay the $1 million abandonment cost only to have to pay another $2 million to reopen the mine.

To summarize, if the mine is currently closed, then it will be opened—at a cost of $2 million—whenever the price of gold rises sufficiently above the extraction cost of $350 per ounce. If the mine is currently operating, then it will be closed down—at a cost of $1 million—whenever the price of gold falls sufficiently below the extraction cost of $350 per ounce. WOE's problem is to find these two threshold prices at which it opens a closed mine and closes an open mine. We call these prices *popen* and *pclose,* respectively, where

$$popen > \$350/ounce > pclose$$

In other words, WOE will open the mine if the gold price option is sufficiently in the money and will close it when the option is sufficiently out of the money.

We know that the more volatile the gold price, the further away popen and pclose will be from $350 per ounce. We also know that the greater the cost of opening the mine the higher popen will be and the greater the cost of abandoning the mine the lower will be pclose. Interestingly, we should also expect that popen will be higher if the abandonment cost is increased. After all, if it costs more to abandon the mine WOE will need to be more assured that the price will stay above the extraction cost when it decides to open the mine. Otherwise, WOE might soon face the costly choice between abandonment and operating at a loss if the price falls below $350 per ounce. Similarly, raising the cost of opening the mine will make WOE more reluctant to close an open mine. As a result, pclose will be lower.

The above arguments have enabled us to reduce the problem of valuing WOE to two stages. First, we have to determine the threshold prices, popen and pclose. Second, given the best choices for these thresholds, we must determine the value of a gold option that is exercised for a cost of $2 million when the gold price rises above popen and is shut down for a cost of $1 million whenever the gold price is below pclose.

When the mine is open, i.e., when the option is exercised, the annual cash flow is equal to the difference between the gold price and the extraction cost of $350 per ounce times 50,000 ounces. When the mine is shut down, it generates no cash flow.

The following diagram describes the decisions available at each point in time.

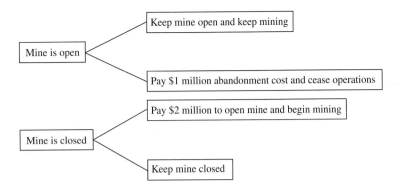

How do we determine the critical values for popen and pclose and then the value of the mine? It is possible to get a good approximation by using the tools we have currently developed.

Valuing the Simple Gold Mine

Here is what has to be done in order both to determine popen and pclose and to value the mine:

Step 1   Find the risk-free interest rate and the volatility. We will use a semiannual interest rate of 3.4 percent and a volatility of 15 percent per year for gold.

Step 2   Construct a binomial tree and fill it out with gold prices. Suppose, for example, that we set the steps of the tree six months apart. If the annual volatility is 15 percent, u is equal to $e^{0.15/\sqrt{2}}$, which is approximately equal to 1.11. The other parameter, $d,$ is 0.90 (1/1.11). Figure 23.3 illustrates the tree. Starting at the current price of $320, the first 11 percent increase takes the price to $355 in six months. The first 10 percent decrease takes the price to $288. Subsequent steps are up 11 percent or down 10 percent from the previous price. The tree extends for the 100-year life of the lease or 200 six-month steps.

Using our analysis from the previous section, we now compute the risk-adjusted probabilities for each step. Given a semiannual interest rate of 3.4 percent, we have

$$3.4\% = \text{Probability of a rise} \times 0.11 + (1 - \text{Probability of a rise}) \times -0.10.$$

Solving this equation gives us 0.64 for the probability of a rise, implying that the probability of a fall is 0.36. These probabilities are the same for each six-month interval. In other words, if the probability of a rise is 0.64, the expected return on gold is 3.4 percent per each six-month interval. These probabilities are determined under the assumption of risk-neutral pricing. In other words, if investors are risk-neutral, they will be satisfied with an expected return equal to the risk-free rate, because the extra risk of gold will not concern them.

Step 3   Now we turn the computer on and let it simulate, say, 5,000 possible paths through the tree. At each node, the computer has a 0.64 probability of picking an "up" movement in the price and a corresponding 0.36 probability of picking a "down" movement in the price. A typical path might be represented by whether the price rose or fell each six-month period over the next 100 years and it would be a list like

up, up, down, up, down, down, . . . , down

where the first "up" meant the price rose from $320 to $355 in the first six months, the next "up" meant it again went up in the second half of the year from $355 to $394, and so on, ending with a down move in the last half of year 100.

■ FIGURE 23.3   **A Binomial Tree for Gold Prices**

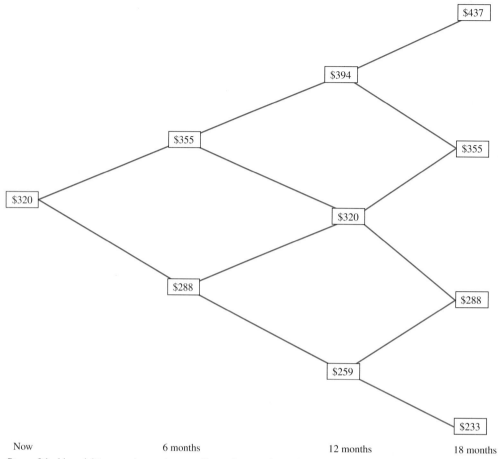

| Now | 6 months | 12 months | 18 months |

Steps of the binomial tree are six months apart. For each step, *u* is equal to 1.11 and *d* is equal to 0.90.

With 5,000 such paths we will have a good sample of all the future possibilities for movement in the gold price.

Step 4   Next we consider possible choices for the threshold prices, popen and pclose. For popen, we let the possibilities be

$$popen = \$360 \text{ or } \$370 \text{ or } \ldots \text{ or } \$500$$

a total of 15 values. For pclose we let the probabilities be

$$pclose = \$340 \text{ or } \$330 \text{ or } \ldots \text{ or } \$100$$

a total of 25 values.

We picked these choices because they seemed reasonable and because increments of $10 for each seemed sensible. To be precise, though, we should let the threshold prices change as we move through the tree and get closer to the 100 year-end. Presumably, for example, if we decided to open the mine with one year left on the lease, the price of gold should be at least high enough to cover the $2 million-dollar opening costs in the coming year. Since we mine 50,000 ounces per year, in year 99 we will only open the mine if the gold price is at least $40 above the extraction cost, or $390.

■ FIGURE 23.4   **A Possible Path for the Price of Gold**

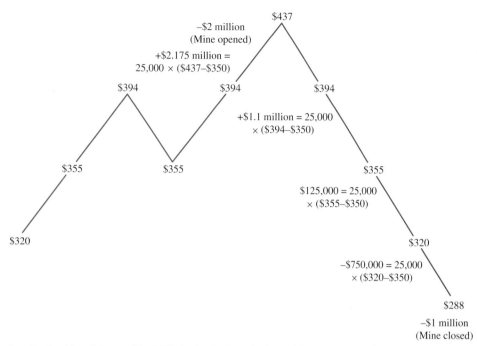

Imagine that this path is one of the 5,000 simulated price paths for gold. Because popen = $410 and pclose = $290, the mine is opened when the price reaches $437. The mine is closed when the price reaches $288.

While this will become important at the end of the lease, using a constant threshold shouldn't have too big an impact on the value with 100 years to go and we will stick with our approximation of constant threshold prices.

Step 5   We calculate the value of the mines for each pair of choices of popen and pclose. For example, if popen = $410 and pclose = $290, we use the computer to keep track of the cash flows if we opened the mine whenever it was closed and the gold price rose to $410, and closed the mine whenever it was open and the gold price fell to $290. We do this for each of the 5,000 paths we simulated in Step 4.

For example, consider the path illustrated in Figure 23.4 of

up, up, down, up, up, down, down, down, down

As can be seen from the figure, the price reaches a peak of $437 in 2½ years, only to fall to $288 over the following four six-month intervals. If popen = $410 and pclose = $290, the mine will be opened when the price reaches $437, necessitating a cost of $2 million. However, the firm can sell 25,000 ounces of gold at $437 at that time, producing a cash flow of $2.175 million (25,000 × ($437 − $350)). When the price falls to $394 six months later, the firm sells another 25,000 ounces, yielding a cash flow of $1.1 million (25,000 × ($394 − $350)). The price continues to fall, with the price reaching $320 a year later. Here, the firm realizes a cash outflow, because production costs are $350 per ounce. Next, the price falls to $288. Because this is below pclose of $290, the mine is closed at a cost of $1 million. Of course, the price of gold will fluctuate in further years, leading to the possibility of future mine openings and closings.

■ TABLE 23.6 **Valuation of Woe Is Me (WOE) Gold Mine for the 20 Best Choices of popen and pclose**

popen	pclose	Estimated Value of Gold Mine
$400	$140	$1,466,720,900
460	300	1,459,406,200
380	290	1,457,838,700
370	100	1,455,131,900
360	190	1,449,708,200
420	150	1,448,711,400
430	340	1,448,450,200
430	110	1,445,396,500
470	200	1,435,687,400
500	320	1,427,512,000
410	290	1,426,483,500
420	290	1,423,865,300
400	160	1,423,061,900
360	320	1,420,748,700
360	180	1,419,112,000
380	280	1,417,405,400
450	310	1,416,238,000
450	280	1,409,709,800
440	220	1,408,269,100
440	240	1,403,398,100

For our simulation, WOE opens the mine whenever the gold price rises above popen and closes the mine whenever the gold price falls below pclose.

This path is just a possibility. It may or may not occur in any simulation of 5,000 paths. For each of these 5,000 paths that the computer simulated, we have a sequence of semiannual cash flows using a popen of $410 and a pclose of $290. We calculate the present value of each of these cash flows, discounting at the interest rate of 3.4 percent. Summing up across all the cash flows, we have the present value of the gold mine for one path.

We then take the average present value of the gold mine across all the 5,000 simulated paths. This number is the expected value of the mine from following a policy of opening the mine whenever the gold price hits $410 and closing it at a price of $290.

Step 6 The final step is to compare the different expected discounted cash flows from Step 5 for the range of possible choices for popen and pclose and to pick the highest one. This is the best estimate of the expected value of the mine. The value for pclose and popen corresponding to this estimate is our best estimate (within $10) of the points at which to open a closed mine and to shut an open one.

As mentioned in Step 3, there are 15 different values for popen and 25 different values for pclose, implying 375 (15 × 25) different pairs. Consider Table 23.6, which shows the present values associated with the 20 best pairs. The table indicates that the best pair is popen = $400 and pclose = $140, with a present value of $1.467 billion. This number represents the average present value across 5,000 simulations, all assuming the preceding values of popen and pclose. The next best pair is popen = $460 and pclose = $300, with a present value of $1.459 billion. The third best pair has a somewhat lower present value still, and so on.

Of course, our estimate of the value of the mine is $1.467 billion, the present value of the best pair of choices. The market capitalization (price × number of shares outstanding) of WOE should reach this value if the market makes the same assumptions that we did. Note that the value of the firm is quite high using an option framework. However, as stated earlier, WOE would appear worthless if a regular discounted cash-flow approach were used. This occurs because the initial price of gold of $320 is below the extraction cost of $350.

This example is not easy, either in terms of concepts or in terms of implementation. However, we believe that the extra work involved in mastering this example is worth it, because it illustrates the type of modeling that actually occurs in corporate finance departments in the real world.

Furthermore, the example illustrates the benefits of the binomial approach. One merely calculates the cash flows associated with each of a number of simulations, discounts the cash flows from each simulation, and averages present values across the simulations. Because the Black-Scholes model is not amenable to simulations, it cannot be used for this type of problem. In addition, there are a number of other situations where the binomial model is more appropriate than is the Black-Scholes model. For example, it is well known that the Black-Scholes model cannot properly handle options with dividend payments prior to the expiration date. This model also does not adequately handle the valuation of an American put. By contrast, the binomial model can easily handle both these situations.

Thus, any student of corporate finance should be well versed with both models. The Black-Scholes model should be used whenever appropriate, because it is simpler to use than is the binomial model. However, for the more complex situations where the Black-Scholes model breaks down, the binomial model becomes a necessary tool.

23.5 SUMMARY AND CONCLUSIONS

This chapter extends the intuitions of one of the most significant concepts in finance: option pricing theory. We describe four different types of special options:

Executive stock options.
The embedded option in a start-up company.
The option in simple business contracts.
The option to shut down and reopen a project.

We try to keep the presentation simple and straightforward from a mathematical point of view. We extend the binomial approach to option pricing in Chapter 22 to many periods. This adjustment brings us closer to the real world, because the assumption of only two prices at the end of an interval is more plausible when the interval is short.

SUGGESTED READINGS

An excellent practical treatment of real options can be found in:
Amran, Martha, and Nalin Kulatilaka. *Real Options.* Cambridge: Harvard Business School
    Press, 1999.

A more academic treatment can be found in:

Brennan, Michael, and L. Trigeorgis, eds. *Flexibility, Natural Resources, and Strategic Options.* Oxford: Oxford University Press, 1998.

Copeland, Tom, and Vladimir Antikarov. *Real Options: A Practitioner's Guide.* Texere LLC, 2001.

QUESTIONS AND PROBLEMS

Executive Stock Options

23.1 William Hurt is the Chief Executive Officer of the First Pacific Trading Company (FPTC). His annual straight salary is $1 million.

The current value of FPTC stock is $50 per share. Mr. Hurt has just been granted options on $1 million in shares of FPTC stock *at the money* by FPTC's board of directors. The risk-free rate is 6 percent. The options have a maturity of four years. The volatility of FPTC stock has been about 25 percent on an annual basis. Determine the value of Mr. Hurt's stock options.

23.2 Mr. Hurt has been quoted as saying that he doesn't want stock options. He has said he would be satisfied with straight pay of $1.25 million. The board of directors disagrees. Who is right?

Flexible Production

23.3 The market for golf putters is notoriously fickle. One year mallet head putters can be the hottest seller and the next it can be blade putters that are in demand. Tims Golf Company (TGC) has a difficult decision to make. It can build a flexible plant that can produce either blade or mallet head putters. The plant would have a capacity of 150,000 putters a year and could produce either type but not both at the same time. In fact, it could be switched only once, one year from now, and the lifetime of the plant is ten years. Currently, there is a high demand for blade putters and TGC forecasts it will need to produce 150,000 for the next year. One year from now there is a 50-50 chance that the company will need to produce mallet head putters rather than blade putters. The company can also build a plant that could only produce blade putters. Both plants would have the same capacity. The profit for the flexible plant is $10 per blade putter and $15 per mallet putter. A fixed putter plant could produce only blade putters but could do so more efficiently. The profit from having a fixed plant produce blade putters is $20 per unit. The relevant discount rate is 12 percent.

In one year, it will be known if the demand for blade putters will continue for nine more years or it will drop by 50 percent.

The company has a choice. It can either invest $1 million in a fixed plant that will produce blade putters only or it can invest $1.5 million in a flexible plant capable of switching from blades to mallets. What should TGC's decision be?

Waiting to Invest

23.4 John Lusk is a real estate developer who owns the right to put up an office building on a parcel of land in downtown Los Angeles. The office building will cost $50 million. John Lusk does not actually plan to own and run the office building but instead he will build it, rent it, and then sell it to a long-term investor at the end of one year. John Lusk estimates that the building can be sold one year from now for $55 million. The IRR of the project is 10 percent and so John Lusk has determined that this is a zero NPV project. However, one year from now there is a 50-50 chance that the cost of capital will be either 11 percent or 9 percent. John Lusk has received an offer on his option for $500. Should he take it?

The Option to Shut Down or Reopen a Project

23.5 We are examining a new project. We expect to sell 10,000 units a year of a new golf video at $200 net cash flow each for the next five years. The relevant discount is 15 percent and the initial required investment is $7 million.

   a. What is the base case NPV?

   b. After the first year, the golf video project can be abandoned and the machinery sold for $100,000. At what level of sales would it make sense to abandon the project?

23.6 Suppose in the previous problem, you think it is likely that expected sales will be revised upward to 15,000 units if the first year is a success and downward to zero units if the first year is a failure. Success or failure are equally likely. What is the NPV of the project?

CHAPTER 24

Warrants and Convertibles

EXECUTIVE SUMMARY

We study two financing instruments in this chapter, warrants and convertibles. A warrant gives the holder the right to buy common stock for cash. In this sense, it is very much like a call. Warrants are generally issued with privately placed bonds, though they are also combined with new issues of common stock and preferred stock. In the case of new issues of common stock, warrants are sometimes given to investment bankers as compensation for underwriting services.

A convertible bond gives the holder the right to exchange the bond for common stock. Therefore, it is a mixed security blurring the traditional line between stocks and bonds. There is also convertible preferred stock.

The chapter describes the basic features of warrants and convertibles. Here are some of the most important questions concerning warrants and convertibles:

1. How can warrants and convertibles be valued?
2. What impact do warrants and convertibles have on the value of the firm?
3. What are the differences between warrants, convertibles, and call options?
4. Why do some companies issue bonds with warrants and convertible bonds?
5. Under what circumstances are warrants and convertibles converted into common stock?

24.1 WARRANTS

Warrants are securities that give holders the right, but not the obligation, to buy shares of common stock directly from a company at a fixed price for a given period of time. Each warrant specifies the number of shares of stock that the holder can buy, the exercise price, and the expiration date.

From the preceding description of warrants, it is clear that they are similar to call options. The differences in contractual features between warrants and the call options that trade on the Chicago Board Options Exchange are small. For example, warrants have longer maturity periods.[1] Some warrants are actually perpetual, meaning that they never expire at all.

Warrants are referred to as *equity kickers* because they are usually issued in combination with privately placed bonds.[2] In most cases, warrants are attached to the bonds when issued. The loan agreement will state whether the warrants are detachable from the bond, that is, whether they can be sold separately. Usually the warrant can be detached immediately.

---

[1] Warrants are usually protected against stock splits and dividends in the same way that call options are.

[2] Warrants are also issued with publicly distributed bonds and new issues of common stock.

EXAMPLE

Safeway, Inc., is one of the nation's largest supermarket chains. On November 24, 1986, Safeway was acquired in a levered buyout by the private investment firm Kohlberg Kravis Roberts and Co. (KKR). Each share of old common stock was converted into a junior subordinated debenture (i.e., junk bond) and a "merger" warrant. Each warrant gave the holder the right to purchase .279 shares of new common stock for $1.052 per warrant. To purchase one share of common stock, a holder had to give up 3.584 warrants and pay an amount of $3.7691 per warrant. This made the exercise price of the Safeway warrants equal to $13.5085 (3.584 × $3.7691 = $13.5085). The warrants expired on November 24, 1996. They are called *merger warrants* because Safeway issued the warrants in a buyout of old shares.

When Safeway was acquired by KKR, it was a private firm with no publicly traded common stock or warrants. However, KKR took Safeway public on April 26, 1990, by issuing 10 million shares in a new issue of common stock. The stock was listed on the New York Stock Exchange. On that day, several thousand warrants were traded at a closing price of 3⅛. The price of the Safeway common stock was 12⅛.

The relationship between the value of Safeway's warrants and its stock price can be viewed like the relationship between a call option and its stock price, described in a previous chapter. Figure 24.1 depicts the relationship for Safeway warrants. The lower limit on the value of the warrants is zero if Safeway's stock price is below $13.5085 per share. If the price of Safeway's common stock rises above $13.5085 per share, the lower limit is the stock price minus $13.5085 divided by 3.584.[3] The upper limit is the price of Safeway's common stock divided by 3.584. A warrant to buy one share of common stock cannot sell at a price above the price of the underlying common stock.

The price of Safeway warrants on April 26, 1990, was higher than the lower limit. The height of the warrant price above the lower limit will depend on the following:

1. The variance of Safeway's stock returns.
2. The time to expiration date.

■ FIGURE 24.1 **Safeway Warrants on April 26, 1990**

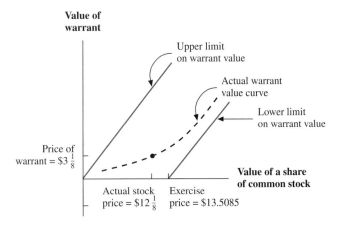

----
[3]We need to divide by 3.584 because it takes 3.584 warrants to purchase one share of stock.

3. The risk-free rate of interest.

4. The stock price of Safeway.

5. The exercise price.

These are the same factors that determine the value of a call option.

24.2   THE DIFFERENCE BETWEEN WARRANTS AND CALL OPTIONS

From the holder's point of view, warrants are similar to call options on common stock. A warrant, like a call option, gives its holder the right to buy common stock at a specified price. Warrants usually have an expiration date, though in most cases they are issued with longer lives than call options. From the firm's point of view, however, a warrant is very different from a call option on the company's common stock.

The most important difference between call options and warrants is that call options are issued by individuals and warrants are issued by firms. When a warrant is exercised, a firm must issue new shares of stock. Each time a warrant is exercised, then, the number of shares outstanding increases.

To illustrate, suppose the Endrun Company issues a warrant giving holders the right to buy one share of common stock at $25. Further suppose the warrant is exercised. Endrun must print one new stock certificate. In exchange for the stock certificate, it receives $25 from the holder.

In contrast, when a call option is exercised, there is no change in the number of shares outstanding. Suppose Ms. Eager holds a call option on the common stock of the Endrun Company. The call option gives Ms. Eager the right to buy one share of the common stock of the Endrun Company for $25. If Ms. Eager chooses to exercise the call option, a seller, say Mr. Swift, is obligated to give her one share of Endrun's common stock in exchange for $25. If Mr. Swift does not already own a share, he must enter the stock market and buy one. The call option is a side bet between buyers and sellers on the value of the Endrun Company's common stock. When a call option is exercised, one investor gains and the other loses. The total number of shares outstanding of the Endrun Company remains constant, and no new funds are made available to the company.

EXAMPLE

To see how warrants affect the value of the firm, imagine that Mr. Gould and Ms. Rockefeller are two investors who have together purchased six ounces of platinum. At the time they bought the platinum, Mr. Gould and Ms. Rockefeller each contributed one-half of the cost, which we will assume was $3,000 for six ounces, or $500 an ounce (they each contributed $1,500). They incorporated, printed two stock certificates, and named the firm the GR Company. Each certificate represents a one-half claim to the platinum. Mr. Gould and Ms. Rockefeller each own one certificate. Mr. Gould and Ms. Rockefeller have formed a company with platinum as its only asset.

A Call Is Issued   Suppose Mr. Gould later decides to sell to Mrs. Fiske a call option issued on Mr. Gould's share. The call option gives Mrs. Fiske the right to buy Mr. Gould's share for $1,800 within the next year. If the price of platinum rises above $600 per ounce, the firm will be worth more than $3,600 and each share will be worth more than $1,800. If Mrs. Fiske decides to exercise her option, Mr. Gould must turn over his stock certificate and receive $1,800.

How would the firm be affected by the exercise? The number of shares will remain the same. There will still be two shares, now owned by Ms. Rockefeller and Mrs. Fiske. If the price of platinum rises to $700 an ounce, each share will be worth $2,100 ($4,200/2). If Mrs. Fiske exercises her option at this price, she will profit by $300.

A Warrant Is Issued Instead   This story changes if a warrant is issued. Suppose that Mr. Gould does not sell a call option to Mrs. Fiske. Instead, Mr. Gould and Ms. Rockefeller have a stockholders' meeting. They vote that GR Company will issue a warrant and sell it to Mrs. Fiske. The warrant will give Mrs. Fiske the right to receive a share of the company at an exercise price of $1,800.[4] If Mrs. Fiske decides to exercise the warrant, the firm will issue another stock certificate and give it to Mrs. Fiske in exchange for $1,800.

From Mrs. Fiske's perspective, the call option and the warrant *seem* to be the same. The exercise prices of the warrant and the call are the same: $1,800. It is still advantageous for Mrs. Fiske to exercise the option when the price of platinum exceeds $600 per ounce. However, we will show that Mrs. Fiske actually makes less in the warrant situation due to dilution.

The GR Company must also consider dilution. Suppose the price of platinum increases to $700 an ounce and Mrs. Fiske exercises her warrant. Two things will occur:

1. Mrs. Fiske will pay $1,800 to the firm.
2. The firm will print one stock certificate and give it to Mrs. Fiske. The stock certificate will represent a one-third claim on the platinum of the firm.

Because Mrs. Fiske contributes $1,800 to the firm, the value of the firm increases. It is now worth

New value of firm = Value of platinum + Contribution to the firm by Mrs. Fiske
= $4,200   + $1,800
= $6,000

Because Mrs. Fiske has a one-third claim on the firm's value, her share is worth $2,000 ($6,000/3). By exercising the warrant, Mrs. Fiske gains $2,000 − $1,800 = $200. This is illustrated in Table 24.1.

Dilution   Why does Mrs. Fiske only gain $200 in the warrant case while gaining $300 in the call option case? The key is dilution, that is, the creation of another share. In the call option case, she contributes $1,800 and receives one of the two outstanding shares. That is, she receives a share worth $2,100 (½ × $4,200). Her gain is $300 ($2,100 − $1,800). We rewrite this gain as

Gain on Exercise of Call:

$$\frac{\$4,200}{2} - \$1,800 = \$300 \tag{24.1}$$

---

[4]The sale of the warrant brings cash into the firm. We assume that the sale proceeds immediately leave the firm through a cash dividend to Mr. Gould and Ms. Rockefeller. This simplifies the analysis, because the firm with warrants then has the same total value as the firm without warrants.

■ TABLE 24.1 **Effect of Call Option and Warrant on the GR Company***

	Price of Platinum per Share	
Value of Firm if:	$700	$600
No Warrant		
Mr. Gould's share	$2,100	$1,800
Ms. Rockefeller's share	2,100	1,800
Firm	$4,200	$3,600
Call option		
Mr. Gould's claim	$ 0	$1,800
Ms. Rockefeller's claim	2,100	1,800
Mrs. Fiske's claim	2,100	0
Firm	$4,200	$3,600
Warrant		
Mr. Gould's share	$2,000	$1,800
Ms. Rockefeller's share	2,000	1,800
Mrs. Fiske's share	2,000	0
Firm	$6,000	$3,600

*If the price of platinum is $700, the value of the firm is equal to the value of six ounces of platinum plus the excess dollars paid into the firm by Mrs. Fiske. This amount is $4,200 + $1,800 = $6,000.

In the warrant case, she contributes $1,800 and receives a newly created share. She now owns one of the three outstanding shares. Because the $1,800 remains in the firm, her share is worth $2,000 [($4,200 + $1,800)/3]. Her gain is $200 ($2,000 − $1,800). We rewrite this gain as

Gain on Exercise of Warrant:

$$\frac{\$4,200 + \$1,800}{2 + 1} - \$1,800 = \$200 \tag{24.2}$$

Warrants also affect accounting numbers. Warrants and (as we shall see) convertible bonds cause the number of shares to increase. This causes the firm's net income to be spread over a larger number of shares, thereby decreasing earnings per share. Firms with significant amounts of warrants and convertible issues must report earnings on a *primary* basis and a *fully diluted* basis.

How the Firm Can Hurt Warrant Holders

The platinum firm owned by Mr. Gould and Ms. Rockefeller has issued a warrant to Mrs. Fiske that is *in the money* and about to expire. One way that Mr. Gould and Ms. Rockefeller can hurt Mrs. Fiske is to pay themselves a large dividend. This could be funded by selling a substantial amount of platinum. The value of the firm would fall, and the warrant would be worth much less.

CONCEPT QUESTIONS

?
• What is the key difference between a warrant and a traded call option?
• Why does dilution occur when warrants are exercised?
• How can the firm hurt warrant holders?

24.3 WARRANT PRICING AND THE BLACK-SCHOLES MODEL (ADVANCED)

We now wish to express the gains from exercising a call and a warrant in more general terms. The gain on a call can be written as

Gain from Exercising a Single Call:

$$\frac{\text{Firm's value net of debt}}{\#} - \text{Exercise price} \qquad (24.3)$$

(Value of a share of stock)

Equation (24.3) generalizes equation (24.1). We define the *firm's value net of debt* to be the total firm value less the value of the debt. The total firm value is $4,200 in our example and there is no debt. The # stands for the number of shares outstanding, which is 2 in our example. The ratio on the left is the value of a share of stock. The gain on a warrant can be written as

Gain from Exercising a Single Warrant:

$$\frac{\text{Firm's value net of debt} + \text{Exercise price} \times \#_w}{\# + \#_w} = \text{Exercise price} \qquad (24.4)$$

(Value of a share of stock after warrant is exercised)

Equation (24.4) generalizes (24.2). The numerator of the left-hand term is the firm's value net of debt *after* the warrant is exercised. It is the sum of the firm's value net of debt *prior* to the warrant's exercise plus the proceeds the firm receives from the exercise. The proceeds equal the product of the exercise price multiplied by the number of warrants. The number of warrants appears as $\#_w$. (Our analysis uses the plausible assumption that all warrants in the money will be exercised.) Note that $\#_w = 1$ in our numerical example. The denominator, $\# + \#_w$, is the number of shares outstanding *after* the exercise of the warrants. The ratio on the left is the value of a share of stock after exercise. By rearranging terms, equation (24.4) can be rewritten as[5]

Gain from Exercising a Single Warrant:

$$\frac{\#}{\# + \#_w} \times \left(\frac{\text{Firm's value net of debt}}{\#} - \text{Exercise price} \right) \qquad (24.5)$$

(Gain from a call on a firm with no warrants)

Formula (24.5) relates the gain on a warrant to the gain on a call. Note that the term within parentheses is (24.3). Thus, the gain from exercising a warrant is a proportion of the gain from exercising a call in a firm without warrants. The proportion $\#/(\# + \#_w)$ is the ratio of the number of shares in the firm without warrants to the number of shares after all the warrants have been exercised. This ratio must always be less than 1. Thus, the gain on a warrant must be less than the gain on an identical call in a firm without warrants. Note that $\#/(\# + \#_w) = \frac{2}{3}$ in our example, which explains why Mrs. Fiske gains $300 on her call yet gains only $200 on her warrant.

---

[5]To derive formula (24.5), one should separate "Exercise price" in (24.4). This yields

$$\frac{\text{Firm's value net of debt}}{\# + \#_w} - \frac{\#}{\# + \#_w} \times \text{Exercise price}$$

By rearranging terms, one can obtain formula (24.5).

The preceding implies that the Black-Scholes model must be adjusted for warrants. When a call option is issued to Mrs. Fiske, we know that the exercise price is $1,800 and the time to expiration is one year. Though we have posited neither the price of the stock, the variance of the stock, nor the interest rate, we could easily provide these data for a real-world situation. Thus, we could use the Black-Scholes model to value Mrs. Fiske's call.

Suppose that the warrant is to be issued tomorrow to Mrs. Fiske. We know the number of warrants to be issued, the warrant's expiration date, and the exercise price. Using our assumption that the warrant proceeds are immediately paid out as a dividend, we could use the Black-Scholes model to value the warrant. We would first calculate the value of an identical call. The warrant price is the call price multiplied by the ratio $\#/(\# + \#_w)$. As mentioned earlier, this ratio is $\frac{2}{3}$ in our example.

24.4 Convertible Bonds

A **convertible bond** is similar to a bond with warrants. The most important difference is that a bond with warrants can be separated into distinct securities and a convertible bond cannot. A convertible bond gives the holder the right to exchange it for a given number of shares of stock anytime up to and including the maturity date of the bond.

Preferred stock can frequently be converted into common stock. A convertible preferred stock is the same as a convertible bond except that it has an infinite maturity date.

Example

Seagate Technology is one of the most important manufacturers of rigid magnetic disk drives for computers. Its stock is traded on the New York Stock Exchange.

On November 1, 1993, Seagate raised $300 million by issuing 6.75 percent convertible subordinated debentures due in 2012. It planned to use the proceeds to invest in new plant and equipment. Like typical debentures, they had a sinking fund and were callable. Seagate's bonds differed from other debentures in their convertible feature: Each bond was convertible into 23.53 shares of common stock of Seagate anytime before maturity. The number of shares received for each bond (23.53 in this example) is called the **conversion ratio.**

Bond traders also speak of the **conversion price** of the bond. This is calculated as the ratio of the face value of the bond to the conversion ratio. Because the face value of each Seagate bond was $1,000, the conversion price was $42.5 ($1,000/23.53). The bondholders of Seagate could give up bonds with a face value of $1,000 and receive 23.53 shares of Seagate common stock. This was equivalent to paying $42.5 ($1,000/23.53) for each share of Seagate common stock received.

When Seagate issued its convertible bonds, its common stock was trading at $22.625 per share. The conversion price of $42.5 was 88 percent higher than the actual common stock price. This 88 percent is referred to as the **conversion premium.** It reflects the fact that the conversion option in Seagate convertible bonds was *out of the money*. This conversion premium is typical.

Convertibles are almost always protected against stock splits and stock dividends. If Seagate's common stock had been split two for one, the conversion ratio would have been increased from 23.53 to 47.06.

Conversion ratio, conversion price, and conversion premium are well-known terms in the real world. For that reason alone, the student should master the concepts. However, conversion price and conversion premium implicitly assume that the bond is selling at par. If the bond is selling at another price, the terms have little meaning. By contrast, conversion ratio can have a meaningful interpretation regardless of the price of the bond.

CONCEPT QUESTION

?

• What are the conversion ratio, the conversion price, and the conversion premium?

24.5 THE VALUE OF CONVERTIBLE BONDS

The value of a convertible bond can be described in terms of three components: straight bond value, conversion value, and option value.[6] We examine these three components below.

Straight Bond Value

The straight bond value is what the convertible bonds would sell for if they could not be converted into common stock. It will depend on the general level of interest rates and on the default risk. Suppose that straight debentures issued by Seagate had been rated A, and A-rated bonds were priced to yield 4 percent on November 1, 1995. The straight bond value of Seagate convertible bonds can be determined by discounting the $33.75 semiannual coupon payment and principal amount at 4 percent.[7]

$$
\begin{aligned}
\text{Straight bond} &= \sum_{t=1}^{37} \frac{\$33.75}{1.04^t} + \frac{\$1,000}{(1.04)^{37}} \\
&= \$33.75 \times A_{0.04}^{37} + \frac{\$1,000}{(1.04)^{37}} \\
&= \$646.06 + \$234.3 \\
&= \$880.36
\end{aligned}
$$

The straight bond value of a convertible bond is a minimum value. The price of Seagate's convertible could not have gone lower than the straight bond value.

Figure 24.2 illustrates the relationship between straight bond value and stock price. In Figure 24.2 we have been somewhat dramatic and implicitly assumed that the convertible bond is default free. In this case the straight bond value does not depend on the stock price and so it is graphed as a straight line.

Conversion Value

The value of convertible bonds depends on conversion value. **Conversion value** is what the bonds would be worth if they were immediately converted into the common stock at current prices. Typically, conversion value is computed by multiplying the number of shares of common stock that will be received when the bond is converted by the current price of the common stock.

---

[6]For a similar treatment see Richard Brealey and Stewart Myers, *Principles of Corporate Finance*, 2nd ed. (New York: McGraw-Hill, 1984), Chapter 23; and James C. Van Horne, *Financial Markets and Flows*, 2nd ed. (Englewood Cliffs, N.J.: Prentice Hall, 1987) Chapter 11.

[7]This formula assumes that coupons are paid annually.

■ FIGURE 24.2 **Minimum Value of a Convertible Bond versus the Value of the Stock for a Given Interest Rate**

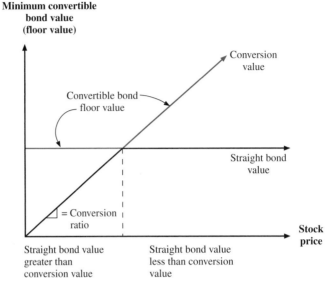

As shown, the minimum, or floor, value of a convertible bond is either its straight bond value or its conversion value, whichever is greater.

On November 1, 1993, each Seagate convertible bond could have been converted into 23.53 shares of Seagate common stock. Seagate common was selling for $22.625. Thus, the conversion value was 23.53 × $22.625 = $532.37. A convertible cannot sell for less than its conversion value. Arbitrage prevents this from happening. If Seagate's convertible sold for less than $532.37, investors would have bought the bonds and converted them into common stock and sold the stock. The profit would have been the difference between the value of the stock sold and the bond's conversion value.

Thus, convertible bonds have two minimum values: the straight bond value and the conversion value. The conversion value is determined by the value of the firm's underlying common stock. This is illustrated in Figure 24.2. As the value of common stock rises and falls, the conversion price rises and falls with it. When the value of Seagate's common stock increased by $1, the conversion value of its convertible bonds increased by $23.53.

Option Value

The value of a convertible bond will generally exceed both the straight bond value and the conversion value.[8] This occurs because holders of convertibles need not convert immediately. Instead, by waiting they can take advantage of whichever is greater in the future, the straight bond value or the conversion value. This option to wait has value, and it raises the value over both the straight bond value and the conversion value.

---

[8]The most plausible exception is when conversion would provide the investor with a dividend much greater than the interest available prior to conversion. The optimal strategy here could very well be to convert immediately, implying that the market value of the bond would exactly equal the conversion value. Other exceptions occur when the firm is in default or the bondholders are forced to convert.

■ FIGURE 24.3   **Value of a Convertible Bond versus the Value of the Stock for a Given Interest Rate**

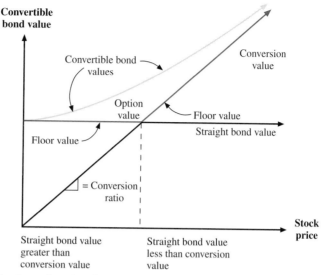

As shown, the value of a convertible bond is the sum of its floor value and its option value (highlighted region).

When the value of the firm is low, the value of convertible bonds is most significantly influenced by their underlying value as straight debt. However, when the value of the firm is very high, the value of convertible bonds is mostly determined by their underlying conversion value. This is illustrated in Figure 24.3.

The bottom portion of the figure implies that the value of a convertible bond is the maximum of its straight bond value and its conversion value, plus its option value:

$$\begin{array}{rl} \text{Value of convertible} = & \text{The greater of (Straight bond value, Conversion value)} \\ \text{bond} & + \text{Option value} \end{array}$$

EXAMPLE

Suppose the Moulton Company has outstanding 1,000 shares of common stock and 100 bonds. Each bond has a face value of $1,000 at maturity. They are discount bonds and pay no coupons. At maturity each bond can be converted into 10 shares of newly issued common stock.

What are the circumstances that will make it advantageous for the holders of Moulton convertible bonds to convert to common stock at maturity?

If the holders of the convertible bonds convert, they will receive $100 \times 10 = 1,000$ shares of common stock. Because there were already 1,000 shares, the total number of shares outstanding becomes 2,000 upon conversion. Thus, converting bondholders own 50 percent of the value of the firm, V. If they do not convert, they will receive $100,000 or V, whichever is less. The choice for the holders of the

Moulton bonds is obvious. They should convert if 50 percent of *V* is greater than $100,000. This will be true whenever *V* is greater than $200,000. This is illustrated as follows:

Payoff to Convertible Bondholders and Stockholders of the Moulton Company

	(1) $V \le \$100,000$	(2) $\$100,000 < V \le \$200,000$	(3) $V > \$200,000$
Decision:	Bondholders will not convert	Bondholders will not convert	Bondholders will convert
Convertible bondholders	*V*	$100,000	0.5*V*
Stockholders	0	*V* − $100,000	0.5*V*

CONCEPT QUESTIONS

?

• What three elements make up the value of a convertible bond?
• Describe the payoff structure of convertible bonds.

24.6 REASONS FOR ISSUING WARRANTS AND CONVERTIBLES

Probably there is no other area of corporate finance where real-world practitioners get as confused as they do on the reasons for issuing convertible debt. In order to separate fact from fantasy, we present a rather structured argument. We first compare convertible debt with straight debt. Then we compare convertible debt with equity. For each comparison, we ask in what situations is the firm better off with convertible debt and in what situations is it worse off.

Convertible Debt versus Straight Debt

Convertible debt pays a lower interest rate than does otherwise identical straight debt. For example, if the interest rate is 10 percent on straight debt, the interest rate on convertible debt might be 9 percent. Investors will accept a lower interest rate on a convertible because of the potential gain from conversion.

Imagine a firm that seriously considers both convertible debt and straight debt, finally deciding to issue convertibles. When would this decision have benefited the firm and when would it have hurt the firm? We consider two situations.

The Stock Price Later Rises So That Conversion Is Indicated   The firm clearly likes to see the stock price rise. However, it would have benefited even more had it previously issued straight debt instead of a convertible. While the firm paid out a lower interest rate than it would have with straight debt, it was obligated to sell the convertible holders a chunk of the equity at a below-market price.

The Stock Price Later Falls or Does Not Rise Enough to Justify Conversion   The firm hates to see the stock price fall. However, as long as the stock price does fall, it is glad that it had previously issued convertible debt instead of straight debt. This is because the interest rate on convertible debt is lower. Because conversion does not take place, our comparison of interest rates is all that is needed.

Summary   Compared to straight debt, the firm is worse off having issued convertible debt if the underlying stock subsequently does well. The firm is better off having issued convertible debt if the underlying stock subsequently does poorly. In an efficient market, one cannot predict future stock price. Thus, we cannot argue that convertibles either dominate or are dominated by straight debt.

Convertible Debt versus Common Stock

Next, imagine a firm that seriously considers both convertible debt and common stock finally decides to issue convertibles. When would this decision benefit the firm and when would it hurt the firm? We consider our two situations.

The Stock Price Later Rises So That Conversion Is Indicated   The firm is better off having previously issued a convertible instead of equity. To see this, consider the Seagate case. The firm could have issued stock for $22. Instead, by issuing a convertible, the firm effectively received $42.50 for a share upon conversion.

The Stock Price Later Falls or Does Not Rise Enough to Justify Conversion   No firm wants to see the stock price fall. However, given that the price did fall, the firm would have been better off if it had previously issued stock instead of a convertible. The firm would have benefited by issuing stock above its later market price. That is, the firm would have received more than the subsequent worth of the stock. However, the drop in stock price did not affect the value of the convertible much because the straight bond value serves as a floor.

Summary   Compared with equity, the firm is better off having issued convertible debt if the underlying stock subsequently does well. The firm is worse off having issued convertible debt if the underlying stock subsequently does poorly. One cannot predict future stock price in an efficient market. Thus, we cannot argue that issuing convertibles is better or worse than issuing equity. The above analysis is summarized in Table 24.2.

Modigliani-Miller (MM) pointed out that, abstracting from taxes and bankruptcy costs, the firm is indifferent to whether it issues stock or issues debt. The MM relationship is a quite general one. Their pedagogy could be adjusted to show that the firm is indifferent to

■ TABLE 24.2   **The Case for and against Convertible Bonds (CBs)**

	If Firm Subsequently Does Poorly	If Firm Subsequently Prospers
Convertible bonds (CBs)	No conversion because of low stock price	Conversion because of high stock price
Compared to:		
Straight bonds	CBs provide cheap financing because coupon rate is lower.	CBs provide expensive financing because bonds are converted, which dilutes existing equity.
Common stock	CBs provide expensive financing because firm could have issued common stock at high prices.	CBs provide cheap financing because firm issues stock at high prices when bonds are converted.

whether it issues convertibles or issues other instruments. To save space (and the patience of students), we have omitted a full-blown proof of MM in a world with convertibles. However, the above results are perfectly consistent with MM. Now we turn to the real-world view of convertibles.

The "Free Lunch" Story

The preceding discussion suggests that issuing a convertible bond is no better and no worse than issuing other instruments. Unfortunately, many corporate executives fall into the trap of arguing that issuing convertible debt is actually better than issuing alternative instruments. This is a free lunch type of explanation, of which we are quite critical.

EXAMPLE

The stock price of RW Company is $20. Suppose this company can issue subordinated debentures at 10 percent. It can also issue convertible bonds at 6 percent with a conversion value of $800. The conversion value means that the holders can convert a convertible bond into 40 ($800/$20) shares of common stock.

A company treasurer who believes in free lunches might argue that convertible bonds should be issued because they represent a cheaper source of financing than either subordinated bonds or common stock. The treasurer will point out that if the company does poorly and the price does not rise above $20, the convertible bondholders will not convert the bonds into common stock. In this case, the company will have obtained debt financing at below-market rates by attaching worthless equity kickers. On the other hand, if the firm does well and the price of its common stock rises to $25 or above, convertible holders will convert. The company will issue 40 shares. The company will receive a bond with face value of $1,000 in exchange for issuing 40 shares of common stock, implying a conversion price of $25. The company will have issued common stock *de facto* at $25 per share, or 20 percent above the $20 common-stock price prevailing when the convertible bonds were issued. This enables it to lower its cost of equity capital. Thus, the treasurer happily points out, regardless of whether the company does well or poorly, convertible bonds are the cheapest form of financing.

Although this argument may sound quite plausible at first glance, there is a flaw. The treasurer is comparing convertible financing *with straight debt* when the stock subsequently falls. However, the treasurer compares convertible financing *with common stock* when the stock subsequently rises. This is an unfair mixing of comparisons. By contrast, our analysis of Table 24.2 was fair, because we examined both stock increases and decreases when comparing a convertible with each alternative instrument. We found that no single alternative dominated convertible bonds in *both* up and down markets.

The "Expensive Lunch" Story

Suppose we stand the treasurer's argument on its head by comparing (1) convertible financing with straight debt when the stock rises and (2) convertible financing with equity when the stock falls.

From Table 24.2, we see that convertible debt is more expensive than straight debt when the stock subsequently rises. The firm's obligation to sell convertible holders a chunk of the equity at a below-market price more than offsets the lower interest rate on a convertible.

Also from Table 24.2, we see that convertible debt is more expensive than equity when the stock subsequently falls. Had the firm issued stock, it would have received a price higher than its subsequent worth. Therefore, the expensive lunch story implies that convertible debt is an inferior form of financing. Of course, we dismiss both the free lunch and the expensive lunch arguments.

A Reconciliation

In an efficient financial market there is neither a free lunch nor an expensive lunch. Convertible bonds can be neither cheaper nor more expensive than other instruments. A convertible bond is a package of straight debt and an option to buy common stock. The difference between the market value of a convertible bond and the value of a straight bond is the price investors pay for the call-option feature. In an efficient market this is a fair price.

In general, if a company prospers, issuing convertible bonds will turn out to be worse than issuing straight bonds and better than issuing common stock. In contrast, if a company does poorly, convertible bonds will turn out to be better than issuing straight bonds and worse than issuing common stock.

CONCEPT QUESTIONS
?

- What is wrong with the simple view that it is cheaper to issue a bond with a warrant or a convertible feature because the required coupon is lower?
- What is wrong with the Free Lunch story?
- What is wrong with the Expensive Lunch story?

24.7 WHY ARE WARRANTS AND CONVERTIBLES ISSUED?

From studies it is known that firms that issue convertible bonds are different from other firms. Here are some of the differences:

1. The bond ratings of firms using convertibles are lower than those of other firms.[9]
2. Convertibles tend to be used by smaller firms with high growth rates and more financial leverage.[10]
3. Convertibles are usually subordinated and unsecured.

The kind of company that uses convertibles provides clues to why they are issued. Here are some explanations that make sense.

Matching Cash Flows

If financing is costly, it makes sense to issue securities whose cash flows match those of the firm. A young, risky, and, it hopes, growing firm might prefer to issue convertibles or bonds with warrants because these will have lower initial interest costs. When the firm is successful, the convertibles (or warrants) will be converted. This causes expensive dilution, but it occurs when the firm can most afford it.

Risk Synergy

Another argument for convertible bonds and bonds with warrants is that they are useful when it is very costly to assess the risk of the issuing company. Suppose you are evaluating

---

[9]E. F. Brigham, "An Analysis of Convertible Debentures," *Journal of Finance* 21 (1966).

[10]W. H. Mikkelson, "Convertible Calls and Security Returns," *Journal of Financial Economics* 9 (September 1981), p. 3.

■ TABLE 24.3 **A Hypothetical Case of the Yields on Convertible Bonds***

	Firm Risk	
	Low	High
Straight bond yield	10%	15%
Convertible bond yield	6	7

*The yields on straight bonds reflect the risk of default. The yields on convertibles are not sensitive to default risk.

a new product by a start-up company. The new product is a biogenetic virus that may increase the yields of corn crops in northern climates. It may also cause cancer. This type of product is difficult to value properly. Thus, the risk of the company is very hard to determine: it may be high, or it may be low. If you could be sure the risk of the company was high, you would price the bonds for a high yield, say 15 percent. If it was low, you would price them at a lower yield, say 10 percent.

Convertible bonds and bonds with warrants can protect somewhat against mistakes of risk evaluation. Convertible bonds and bonds with warrants have two components: straight bonds and call options on the company's underlying stock. If the company turns out to be a low-risk company, the straight bond component will have high value and the call option will have low value. However, if the company turns out to be a high-risk company, the straight bond component will have low value and the call option will have high value. This is illustrated in Table 24.3.

However, although risk has effects on value that cancel each other out in convertibles and bonds with warrants, the market and the buyer nevertheless must make an assessment of the firm's potential to value securities, and it is not clear that the effort involved is that much less than is required for a straight bond.

Agency Costs

Convertible bonds can resolve agency problems associated with raising money. In a previous chapter we showed that straight bonds are like risk-free bonds minus a put option on the assets of the firm. This creates an incentive for creditors to force the firm into low-risk activities. In contrast, holders of common stock have incentives to adopt high-risk projects. High-risk projects with negative NPV transfer wealth from bondholders to stockholders. If these conflicts cannot be resolved, the firm may be forced to pass up profitable investment opportunities. However, because convertible bonds have an equity component, less expropriation of wealth can occur when convertible debt is issued instead of straight debt.[11] In other words, convertible bonds mitigate agency costs. One implication is that convertible bonds have less-restrictive debt covenants than do straight bonds in the real world. Casual empirical evidence seems to bear this out.

Backdoor Equity

A popular theory of convertibles views them as backdoor equity.[12] The basic story is that young, small, high-growth firms cannot usually issue debt on reasonable terms due to high

---

[11]A. Barnea, R. A. Haugen, and L. Senbet, *Agency Problems and Financial Contracting,* Prentice Hall Foundations of Science Series (New York: Prentice Hall, 1985), Chapter VI.

[12]J. Stein, "Convertible Bonds as Backdoor Equity Financing," *Journal of Financial Economics,* 32 (1992). See also Craig M. Lewis, Richard J. Ragolski, and James K. Seward, "Understanding the Design of Convertible Debt," *The Journal of Applied Corporate Finance* (Spring, 1998).

financial distress costs. However, the owners may be unwilling to issue equity if current stock prices are too low.

Lewis, Ragolski, and Sewart examine the risk shifting and backdoor equity theories of convertible bond debt. They find evidence for both theories.

QUESTION
CONCEPT
?

• Why do firms issue convertible bonds and bonds with warrants?

24.8 CONVERSION POLICY

There is one aspect of convertible bonds that we have omitted so far. Firms are frequently granted a call option on the bond. The typical arrangements for calling a convertible bond are simple. When the bond is called, the holder has about 30 days to choose between the following:

1. Converting the bond to common stock at the conversion ratio.
2. Surrendering the bond and receiving the call price in cash.

What should bondholders do? It should be obvious that if the conversion value of the bond is greater than the call price, conversion is better than surrender; and if the conversion value is less than the call price, surrender is better than conversion. If the conversion value is greater than the call price, the call is said to **force conversion.**

What should financial managers do? Calling the bonds does not change the value of the firm as a whole. However, an optimal call policy can benefit the stockholders at the expense of the bondholders. Because we are speaking of dividing a pie of fixed size, the optimal call policy is very simple: Do whatever the bondholders do not want you to do.

Bondholders would love the stockholders to call the bonds when the bond's market value is below the call price. Shareholders would be giving bondholders extra value. Alternatively, should the value of the bonds rise above the call price, the bondholders would love the stockholders not to call the bonds, because bondholders would be allowed to hold onto a valuable asset.

There is only one policy left. This is the policy that maximizes shareholder value and minimizes bondholder value. This policy is

Call the bond when its value is equal to the call price.

It is a puzzle that firms do not always call convertible bonds when the conversion value reaches the call price. Ingersoll examined the call policies of 124 firms between 1968 and 1975.[13] In most cases he found that the company waited to call the bonds until the conversion value was much higher than the call price. The median company waited until the conversion value of its bonds was 44 percent higher than the call price. This is not even close to the above optimal strategy. Why?

One reason is that if firms attempt to implement the above optimal strategy, it may not be truly optimal. Recall that bondholders have 30 days to decide whether to convert bonds to common stock or to surrender bonds for the call price in cash. In 30 days, the stock price could drop, forcing the conversion value below the call price. If so, the convertible is "out of the money"

---

[13]J. Ingersoll, "An Examination of Corporate Call Policies on Convertible Bonds," *Journal of Finance* (May 1977). See also M. Harris and A. Raviv, "A Sequential Signalling Model of Convertible Debt Policy," *Journal of Finance* (December 1985). Harris and Raviv describe a signal equilibrium that is consistent with Ingersoll's result. They show that managers with favorable information will delay calls to avoid depressing stock prices.

and the firm is giving away money. The firm would be giving up cash for common stock worth much less. Because of this possibility, firms in the real world usually wait until the conversion value is substantially above the call price before they trigger the call.[14] This is sensible.

CONCEPT QUESTIONS

• Why will convertible bonds not be voluntarily converted to stock before expiration?
• When should firms force conversion of convertibles? Why?

24.9 SUMMARY AND CONCLUSIONS

1. A warrant gives the holder the right to buy shares of common stock at an exercise price for a given period of time. Typically, warrants are issued in a package with privately placed bonds. Afterward they become detached and trade separately.

2. A convertible bond is a combination of a straight bond and a call option. The holder can give up the bond in exchange for shares of stock.

3. Convertible bonds and warrants are like call options. However, there are some important differences:

   a. Warrants and convertible securities are issued by corporations. Call options are traded between individual investors.

      i. Warrants are usually issued privately and are combined with a bond. In most cases the warrants can be detached immediately after the issue. In some cases warrants are issued with preferred stock, with common stock, or in executive compensation programs.

      ii. Convertibles are usually bonds that can be converted into common stock.

      iii. Call options are sold separately by individual investors (called *writers* of call options).

   b. Warrants and call options are exercised for cash. The holder of a warrant gives the company cash and receives new shares of the company's stock. The holder of a call option gives another individual cash in exchange for shares of stock. When someone converts a bond, it is exchanged for common stock. As a consequence, bonds with warrants and convertible bonds have different effects on corporate cash flow and capital structure.

   c. Warrants and convertibles cause dilution to the existing shareholders. When warrants are exercised and convertible bonds converted, the company must issue new shares of common stock. The percentage ownership of the existing shareholders will decline. New shares are not issued when call options are exercised.

4. Many arguments, both plausible and implausible, are given for issuing convertible bonds and bonds with warrants. One plausible rationale for such bonds has to do with risk. Convertibles and bonds with warrants are associated with risky companies. Lenders can do several things to protect themselves from high-risk companies:

---

[14]See Paul Asquith, "Convertible Bonds Are Not Called Late," *Journal of Finance* (September 1995). On the other hand, the stock market usually reacts negatively to the announcement of a call. For example, see A. K. Singh, A. R. Cowan, and N. Nayan, "Underwritten Calls of Convertible Bonds," *Journal of Financial Economics* (March 1991) and M. A. Mazzeo and W. T. Moore, "Liquidity Costs and Stock Price Response to Convertible Security Calls," *Journal of Business* (July 1992).

Most recently, Ederington, Caton, and Campbell test various theories on when it is optimal to call convertibles. They find evidence consistent for the preceding 30-day "safety margin" theory. They also find that calls of in-the-money convertibles are highly unlikely if dividends to be received (after conversion) exceed the company's interest payment. See Louis H. Ederington, Gary L. Caton, and Cynthia J. Campbell, "To Call or Not to Call Convertible Debt," *Financial Management* (Spring 1997).

a. They can require high yields.

b. They can lend less or not at all to firms whose risk is difficult to assess.

c. They can impose severe restrictions on such debt.

Another useful way to protect against risk is to issue bonds with equity kickers. This gives the lenders the chance to benefit from risks and reduces the conflicts between bondholders and stockholders concerning risk.

5. A puzzle particularly vexes financial researchers: Convertible bonds usually have call provisions. Companies appear to delay calling convertibles until the conversion value greatly exceeds the call price. From the shareholders' standpoint, the optimal call policy would be to call the convertibles when the conversion value equals the call price.

KEY TERMS

Conversion premium 680	Convertible bond 680
Conversion price 680	Force conversion 689
Conversion ratio 680	Warrants 674
Conversion value 681	

SUGGESTED READINGS

The following articles analyze when it is optimal to force conversion of convertible bonds:

Asquith, P. "Convertible Bonds Are Not Called Late." *Journal of Finance* (September 1995).

Brennan, M., and E. Schwartz. "Convertible Bonds: Valuation and Optimal Strategies for Call Conversion." *Journal of Finance* (December 1977).

Michael Brennan examines the conventional arguments for and against convertible bonds and offers a new "risk synergy" rationale:

Brennan, M. "The Case for Convertibles." In J. M. Stern and D. H. Crew, eds. *The Revolution in Corporate Finance.* New York: Basil Blackwell, 1986.

QUESTIONS AND PROBLEMS

24.1 Define:

    a. Warrants

    b. Convertibles

Warrants

24.2 Explain why the following limits on warrant prices exist.

    a. The lower limit is zero if the stock price is below the exercise price.

    b. The lower limit is stock price less exercise price if the stock price is above the exercise price.

    c. The upper limit is the price of the stock.

24.3 *a.* What is the primary difference between warrants and calls?

    b. What is the implication of that difference?

24.4 Suppose the GR Company, which was discussed in the text, sells Mrs. Fiske a warrant. Prior to the sale, the company has two shares outstanding. Mr. Gould owns one share and Ms. Rockefeller owns the other share. The assets of the firm are seven ounces of platinum, which were purchased at $500 per ounce. The exercise price of the warrant is $1,800. All funds that enter the firm are used to purchase more platinum. Mrs. Fiske is sold the warrant moments after incorporation for $500.

    a. What is the price of GR stock before the warrant is sold?

    b. At what price for platinum will Mrs. Fiske exercise her warrant?

    c. Suppose the price of platinum suddenly rises to $520 per ounce.

        i. What is the value of GR?

        ii. What will Mrs. Fiske do?

        iii. What is the new price per share of GR stock?

        iv. What was Mrs. Fiske's gain from the exercise?

    d. What would Mrs. Fiske's gain have been if Mr. Gould had sold her a call?

    e. Why are Mrs. Fiske's gains different?

24.5 General Autos has its warrants traded in the market and they will expire five years from today. Each warrant is entitled to purchase 0.25 shares of General Autos common stock at $10 per share.

    a. Suppose General Autos stock is currently selling for $8. What is the lower limit on the warrant value? What is the upper limit?

    b. Suppose General Autos stock is currently selling for $12. What is the lower limit on the warrant value? What is the upper limit?

24.6 Pace Western Crystal, Inc., has outstanding 10 million common shares and 200,000 warrants. Each warrant can purchase five shares of common stock at $15 per share. Warrant holders exercised all of their warrants today. Pace Western's stock price before the exercise was $17. What should the new stock price be after the exercise? Assume there is no information content on the exercise of the warrants.

24.7 A warrant entitles the holder to buy 10 shares of common stock at $21 per share. When the market price of the stock is $15, will the market price of the warrant equal zero? Why or why not?

24.8 Grand Mills Corporation has 4 million shares of common stock outstanding. The company has 500,000 warrants being traded in the market. Each warrant has the right to buy one share of common stock at $20 per share. The warrant will expire one year from today. Grand Mills stock is selling for $22 per share and the variance of the return on the stock is 0.005. The risk-free rate is 5 percent. Use the Black-Scholes model to price the warrant.

24.9 Express Transportation's current market-balance sheet shows assets of the firm are $150 million. The market value of the debt Express has issued is $47 million. Express has 1.5 million shares of common stock outstanding. Tomorrow, Express will issue 100,000 warrants. Each warrant has the option to buy five shares of Express common stock for one year. The proceeds of the issue will be used to pay the dividend that is due tomorrow. Call options on the firm's stock with similar terms are currently selling for $4.70. What will be the price of Express warrants?

24.10 Consider the following warrants.

        Warrant X: For each warrant held, three shares of common stock can be purchased at an exercise price of $20 per share.

        Warrant Y: For each warrant held, two shares of common stock can be purchased at an exercise price of $30 per share.

The current market price of stock X is $30 per share. The current market price of stock Y is $40 per share.

    a. What is the minimum value of warrant X?

    b. What is the minimum value of warrant Y?

Convertibles

24.11 At issuance of McArthur Corp.'s convertible bonds, one of the two following sets of characteristics was true.

	A	B
Offering price of bond	$900	$1,000
Bond value (straight debt)	$900	$ 950
Stock price	$ 20	$ 30
Conversion ratio	50	30

Which of the relationships do you believe was more likely to have prevailed? Why?

24.12 The following facts apply to a convertible security:

Conversion price	$25/share
Coupon rate	6%
Par value	$1,000
Yield on nonconvertible debenture of same quality	10%
Market value of straight bond of same quality with coupon rate of 10%	$950
Stock price	$24/share

a. What is the minimum price at which the convertible should sell?

b. What accounts for any premium in the market price of the convertible over the value of the common stock into which it can be converted?

24.13 Ms. Mary Malone is a CEO of Malone, Inc., and owns 500,000 shares of the common stock. The company's total number of common shares outstanding is 4 million. The company also has $20 million of convertible bond outstanding. The face value of the bond is $1,000 and its conversion price is $20. Malone's common stock is currently selling for $25, and the company has decided to call the bond to force conversion. Calculate Ms. Malone's ownership changes between, before, and after the call. Assume that Ms. Malone does not hold any of the company's convertible bond.

24.14 Ryan Home Products, Inc., issued $430,000 of 8-percent convertible debentures. Each bond is convertible into 28 shares of common stock anytime before maturity.

a. Suppose the current price of the bonds is $1,000 and the current price of Ryan common is $31.25.
  i. What is the conversion ratio?
  ii. What is the conversion price?
  iii. What is the conversion premium?

b. Suppose the current price of the bonds is $1,180 and the current price of Ryan common is $31.25.
  i. What is the conversion ratio?
  ii. What is the conversion price?
  iii. What is the conversion premium?

c. What is the conversion value of the debentures?

d. If the value of Ryan common increases by $2, what will the conversion value be?

24.15 Acme Medical Supplies, Inc., issued a zero coupon convertible bond due 10 years from today. The bond has a face value of $1,000 at maturity. Each bond can be converted into 25 shares of Acme's common stock. The appropriate interest rate is 10 percent. The company's stock is selling for $12 per share. Each convertible bond is traded at $400 in the market.

a. What is the straight bond value?

b. What is the conversion value?

c. What is the option value of the bond?

24.16 A $1,000 par convertible debenture has a conversion price for common stock of $180 per share. With the common stock selling at $60, what is the conversion value of the bond?

24.17 You are a financial analyst hired to value a new 30-year callable, convertible bond. The bond has a 6-percent coupon payable annually. The conversion price is $125. The stock currently sells for $35. The stock price is expected to rise 15 percent per year. The bond is callable at $1,100. The required return on the bond is 10 percent.

   a. What is the straight bond value?

   b. What is the conversion value?

   c. How long would it take for the conversion value to exceed a call price?

CHAPTER 25

Derivatives and Hedging Risk

EXECUTIVE SUMMARY

Hardly a day seems to go by without a story in the popular press about some firm that has taken a major hit to its bottom line from its activities in the derivatives markets. Perhaps the largest losses due to derivative trading involved the U.S. firm MG Refining and Marketing (MGRM) and its German parent Metallgesellschaft (MGAG).[1] In late 1993 and early 1994, the financial press reported more than $1 billion of losses from MGRM's trading in oil futures. MGAG is one of Germany's largest industrial firms, generating more than $17 billion in sales revenue in 1993. It has been a closely held firm with 65 percent of its ownership in the hands of seven large institutional owners including the Deutsche Bank, one of the largest banks in the world.

MGRM's derivatives were a central element in its marketing strategy in which it attempted to offset customers' long-term price guarantees (up to 10 years) on gasoline, heating oil, and diesel fuel purchased from MGRM with futures trading. How did MGRM hedge its resulting exposure to spot price increases? Why did MGRM lose so much money? These are some of the questions that we will address in this chapter.

MGRM is not the only firm with reportedly large losses because of derivatives. Procter & Gamble and Gibson Greeting Cards have allegedly lost hundreds of millions of dollars in trading derivatives. The trading of derivatives by Nicholas Leeson is widely credited with having brought down the venerable international merchant bank of Barings. In addition, we have the Piper Jaffrey funds in which investors in a supposedly secure medium-term government bond fund lost 50 percent of their value, and Orange County (California), whose investments lost so much that there was concern about whether basic public services would be disrupted. Whether all of these really happened because of the use or misuse of derivatives will probably be settled years later in the courts, but in the court of public opinion, the culprit has been named—derivatives—and regulators and politicians are deciding on the sentence.

In this chapter we take a close look at derivatives—what they are, how they work, and the uses to which they can be put. When we are done, you will understand how financial derivatives are designed, and you will be able to decide for yourself in an informed fashion what is happening when the next derivatives scandal erupts.

Derivatives, Hedging, and Risk

The name *derivatives* is self-explanatory. A derivative is a financial instrument whose payoffs and values are derived from, or depend on, something else. Often we speak of the thing that the derivative depends on as the *primitive* or the *underlying*. For example, in Chapter 22 we studied how options work. An option is a derivative. The value of a call option depends on the value of the underlying stock on which it is written. Actually, call options are

---

[1] C. Culp and M. Miller, "Metallgesellschaft and the Economics of Synthetic Storage," *Journal of Applied Corporate Finance* (Winter 1995), discuss the MGRM derivative losses.

quite complicated examples of derivatives. The vast majority of derivatives are simpler than call options. Most derivatives are forward or futures agreements or what are called swaps, and we will study each of these in some detail.

Why do firms use derivatives? The answer is that derivatives are tools for changing the firm's risk exposure. Someone once said that derivatives are to finance what scalpels are to surgery. By using derivatives, the firm can cut away unwanted portions of risk exposure and even transform the exposures into quite different forms. A central point in finance is that risk is undesirable. In our chapters on risk and return, we pointed out that individuals would choose risky securities only if the expected return compensated for the risk. Similarly, a firm will accept a project with high risk only if the return on the project compensates for this risk. Not surprisingly, then, firms are usually looking for ways to reduce their risk. When the firm reduces its risk exposure with the use of derivatives, it is said to be **hedging.** Hedging offsets the firm's risk, such as the risk in a project, by one or more transactions in the financial markets.

Derivatives can also be used to merely change or even increase the firm's risk exposure. When this occurs, the firm is **speculating** on the movement of some economic variables—those that underlie the derivative. For example, if a derivative is purchased that will rise in value if interest rates rise, and if the firm has no offsetting exposure to interest rate changes, then the firm is speculating that interest rates will rise and give it a profit on its derivatives position. Using derivatives to translate an opinion about whether interest rates or some other economic variable will rise or fall is the opposite of hedging—it is risk enhancing. Speculating on your views on the economy and using derivatives to profit if that view turns out to be correct is not necessarily wrong, but the speculator should always remember that sharp tools cut deep, and if the opinions on which the derivatives position is based turn out to be incorrect, then the consequences can prove costly. Efficient market theory teaches how difficult it is to predict what markets will do. Most of the sad experiences with derivatives have occurred not from their use as instruments for hedging and offsetting risk, but, rather, from speculation.

25.1 FORWARD CONTRACTS

We can begin our discussion of hedging by considering forward contracts. One frequently hears the one-liner about the gentleman who was shocked to find he had been speaking prose all his life. Forward contracts are a lot like that; you have probably been dealing in them your whole life without knowing it. Suppose you walk into a bookstore on, say, February 1 to buy the best-seller *Eating Habits of the Rich and Famous.* The cashier tells you that the book is currently sold out, but he takes your phone number, saying that he will re-order it for you. He says the book will cost $10.00. If you agree on February 1 to pick up and pay $10.00 for the book when called, you and the cashier have engaged in a **forward contract.** That is, you have agreed both to pay for the book and to pick it up when the bookstore notifies you. Since you are agreeing to buy the book at a later date, you are *buying* a forward contract on February 1. In commodity parlance, you will be **taking delivery** when you pick up the book. The book is called the **deliverable instrument.**

The cashier, acting on behalf of the bookstore, is selling a forward contract. (Alternatively, we say that he is writing a forward contract.) The bookstore has agreed to turn the book over to you at the predetermined price of $10.00 as soon as the book arrives. The act of turning the book over to you is called **making delivery.** Table 25.1 illustrates the book purchase. Note that the agreement takes place on February 1. The price is set and the

■ TABLE 25.1   **Illustration of Book Purchase as a Forward Contract**

February 1	Date When Book Arrives
Buyer	**Buyer:**
Buyer agrees to:	1. Pays purchase price of $10.00.
1. Pay the purchase price of $10.00.	2. Receives book.
2. Receive book when book arrives.	
Seller	
Seller agrees to:	**Seller:**
1. Give up book when book arrives.	1. Gives up book.
2. Accept payment of $10.00 when book arrives.	2. Accepts payment of $10.00.

Note that cash does not change hands on February 1. Cash changes hands when the book arrives.

conditions for sale are set at that time. In this case, the sale will occur when the book arrives. In other cases, an exact date of sale would be given. However, *no* cash changes hands on February 1; cash changes hands only when the book arrives.

Though forward contracts may have seemed exotic to you before you began this chapter, you can see that they are quite commonplace. Dealings in your personal life probably have involved forward contracts. Similarly, forward contracts occur all the time in business. Every time a firm orders an item that cannot be delivered immediately, a forward contract takes place. Sometimes, particularly when the order is small, an oral agreement will suffice. Other times, particularly when the order is larger, a written agreement is necessary.

Note that a forward contract is not an option. Both the buyer and the seller are obligated to perform under the terms of the contract. Conversely, the buyer of an option *chooses* whether or not to exercise the option.

A forward contract should be contrasted with a **cash transaction,** that is, a transaction where exchange is immediate. Had the book been on the bookstore's shelf, your purchase of it would constitute a cash transaction.

CONCEPT QUESTIONS
?
• What is a forward contract?
• Give examples of forward contracts in your life.

25.2 FUTURES CONTRACTS

A variant of the forward contract takes place on financial exchanges. Contracts on exchanges are usually called **futures contracts.** For example, consider Table 25.2, which provides data on trading in wheat for Thursday, September 15, 20X1. Let us focus on the September futures contract, which is illustrated in the first row of the table. The first trade of the day in the contract was for $4.11 per bushel. The price reached a high of $4.16 ¼ during the day and reached a low of $4.07. The last trade was also at $4.07. In other words, the contract *closed* or *settled* at $4.07. The price dropped 6¼ cents per bushel during the day, indicating that the price closed the previous day at $4.13¼ ($4.07 + $0.0625). The contract had been trading for slightly less than a year. During that time, the price reached a high of $4.21 per bushel and a low of $2.72 per bushel. The open interest indicates the number of *contracts outstanding.* The number of contracts outstanding at the close of September 15 was 423.

■ TABLE 25.2 **Data on Wheat Futures Contracts, Thursday, September 15, 20X1**

						Lifetime		
	Open	High	Low	Settle	Change	High	Open Low	Interest
Sept	411	416¼	407	407	−6¼	421	272	423
Oct	427	432¼	422	423¼	−5½	432¼	289	47,454
Mar X2	430½	436	426½	427	−4¼	436	323	42,823
May	409	443½	404	405	−5½	420	330	3,422
July	375	376½	369	370¾	−6¾	395	327	4,805

Though we are discussing a futures contract, let us work with a forward contract first. Suppose you wrote a *forward* contract for September wheat at $4.07. From our discussion on forward contracts, this would mean that you would agree to turn over an agreed-upon number of wheat bushels for $4.07 per bushel on some specified date in the remainder of the month of September.

A futures contract differs somewhat from a forward contract. First, the seller can choose to deliver the wheat on any day during the delivery month, that is, the month of September. This gives the seller leeway that he would not have with a forward contract. When the seller decides to deliver, he notifies the exchange clearinghouse that he wants to do so. The clearinghouse then notifies an individual who bought a September wheat contract that she must stand ready to accept delivery within the next few days. Though each exchange selects the buyer in a different way, the buyer is generally chosen in a random fashion. Because there are so many buyers at any one time, the buyer selected by the clearinghouse to take delivery almost certainly did not originally buy the contract from the seller now making delivery.

Second, futures contracts are traded on an exchange whereas forward contracts are generally traded off an exchange. Because of this, there is generally a liquid market in futures contracts. A buyer can net out her futures position with a sale. A seller can net out his futures position with a purchase. This procedure is analogous to the *netting-out* process in the options markets. However, the buyer of an options contract can also walk away from the contract by not exercising it. If a buyer of a futures contract does not subsequently sell her contract, she must take delivery.

Third, and most important, the prices of futures contracts are **marked to the market** on a daily basis. That is, suppose that the price falls to $4.05 on Friday's close. Because all buyers lost two cents per bushel on that day, they each must turn over the two cents per bushel to their brokers within 24 hours, who subsequently remit the proceeds to the clearinghouse. Because all sellers gained two cents per bushel on that day, they each receive two cents per bushel from their brokers. Their brokers are subsequently compensated by the clearinghouse. Because there is a buyer for every seller, the clearinghouse must break even every day.

Now suppose that the price rises to $4.12 on the close of the following Monday. Each buyer receives seven cents ($4.12 − $4.05) per bushel and each seller must pay seven cents per bushel. Finally, suppose that, on Monday, a seller notifies his broker of his intention to deliver.[2] The delivery price will be $4.12, which is Monday's close.

There are clearly many cash flows in futures contracts. However, after all the dust settles, the *net price* to the buyer must be the price at which she bought originally. That is, an individual buying at Thursday's closing price of $4.07 and being called to take delivery on Monday

[2]He will deliver on Wednesday, two days later.

ILLUSTRATION OF EXAMPLE INVOLVING MARKING TO MARKET IN FUTURES CONTRACTS

Both buyer and seller originally transact at Thursday's closing price. Delivery takes place at Monday's closing price.*

	Thursday, September 19	Friday, September 20	Monday, September 23	Delivery (notification given by seller on Monday)
Closing price:	$4.07	$4.05	$4.12	
BUYER	Buyer purchases futures contract at closing price of $4.07/bushel.	Buyer must pay two cents/ bushel to clearinghouse within one business day.	Buyer receives seven cents/ bushel from clearinghouse within one business day.	Buyer pays $4.12 per bushel and receives grain within one business day.

Buyer's net payment of −$4.07 (−$0.02 + $0.07 − $4.12) is the same as if buyer purchased a forward contract for $4.07/bushel.

SELLER	Seller sells futures contract at closing price of $4.07/bushel.	Seller receives two cents/ bushel from clearinghouse within one business day.	Seller pays seven cents/ bushel to clearinghouse within one business day.	Seller receives $4.12 per bushel and delivers grain within one business day.

Seller's net receipts of $4.07 ($0.02 − $0.07 + $4.12) are the same as if seller sold a forward contract for $4.07/bushel.

---

*For simplicity, we assume that buyer and seller both (1) initially transact at the same time and (2) meet in delivery process. This is actually very unlikely to occur in the real world because the clearinghouse assigns the buyer to take delivery in a random manner.

pays two cents per bushel on Friday, receives seven cents per bushel on Monday, and takes delivery at $4.12. Her net outflow per bushel is −$4.07 (−$0.02 + $0.07 − $4.12), which is the price at which she contracted on Thursday. (Our analysis ignores the time value of money.) Conversely, an individual selling at Thursday's closing price of $4.07 and notifying his broker concerning delivery the following Monday receives two cents per bushel on Friday, pays seven cents per bushel on Monday and makes delivery at $4.12. His net inflow per bushel is $4.07 ($0.02 − $0.07 + $4.12), which is the price at which he contracted on Thursday.

These details are presented in the adjacent box. For simplicity, we assumed that the buyer and seller who initially transact on Thursday's close meet in the delivery process.[3] The point in the example is that the buyer's net payment of $4.07 per bushel is the same as if she purchased a forward contract for $4.07. Similarly, the seller's net receipt of $4.07 per bushel is the same as if he sold a forward contract for $4.07 per bushel. The only difference

---

[3]As pointed out earlier, this is actually very unlikely to occur in the real world.

is the timing of the cash flows. The buyer of a forward contract knows that he will make a single payment of $4.07 on the expiration date. He will not need to worry about any other cash flows in the interim. Conversely, though the cash flows to the buyer of a futures contract will net to exactly $4.07 as well, the pattern of cash flows is not known ahead of time.

The mark-to-the-market provision on futures contracts has two related effects. The first concerns differences in net present value. For example, a large price drop immediately following purchase means an immediate outpayment for the buyer of a futures contract. Though the net outflow of $4.07 is still the same as under a forward contract, the present value of the cash outflows is greater to the buyer of a futures contract. Of course, the present value of the cash outflows is less to the buyer of a futures contract if a price rise followed purchase.[4] Though this effect could be substantial in certain theoretical circumstances, it appears to be of quite limited importance in the real world.[5]

Second, the firm must have extra liquidity to handle a sudden outflow prior to expiration. This added risk may make the futures contract less attractive.

Students frequently ask, "Why in the world would managers of the commodity exchanges ruin perfectly good contracts with these bizarre mark-to-the-market provisions?" Actually, the reason is a very good one. Consider the forward contract of Table 25.1 concerning the bookstore. Suppose that the public quickly loses interest in *Eating Habits of the Rich and Famous*. By the time the bookstore calls the buyer, other stores may have dropped the price of the book to $6.00. Because the forward contract was for $10.00, the buyer has an incentive not to take delivery on the forward contract. Conversely, should the book become a hot item selling at $15.00, the bookstore may simply not call the buyer.

As indicated, forward contracts have a very big flaw. Whichever way the price of the deliverable instrument moves, one party has an incentive to default. There are many cases where defaults have occurred in the real world. One famous case concerned Coca-Cola. When the company began in the early 20th century, Coca-Cola made an agreement to supply its bottlers and distributors with cola syrup at a constant price *forever*. Of course, subsequent inflation would have caused Coca-Cola to lose large sums of money had they honored the contract. After much legal effort, Coke and its bottlers put an *inflation-escalator clause* in the contract. Another famous case concerned Westinghouse. It seems the firm had promised to deliver uranium to certain utilities at a fixed price. The price of uranium skyrocketed in the 1970s, making Westinghouse lose money on every shipment. Westinghouse defaulted on its agreement. The utilities took Westinghouse to court but did not recover amounts anything near what Westinghouse owed them.

The mark-to-the-market provisions minimize the chance of default on a futures contract. If the price rises, the seller has an incentive to default on a forward contract. However, after paying the clearinghouse, the seller of a futures contract has little reason to default. If the price falls, the same argument can be made for the buyer. Because changes in the value of the underlying asset are recognized daily, there is no accumulation of loss, and the incentive to default is reduced.

Because of this default issue, forward contracts generally involve individuals and institutions who know and can trust each other. But as W. C. Fields said, "Trust everybody, but cut the cards." Lawyers earn a handsome living writing supposedly air-tight forward contracts, even among friends. The genius of the mark-to-the-market system is that is can prevent default where it is most likely to occur—among investors who do not

---

[4]The direction is reversed for the seller of a futures contract. However, the general point that the net present value of cash flows may differ between forward and futures contracts holds for sellers as well.

[5]See John C. Cox, John E. Ingersoll, and Steven A. Ross. "The Relationship between Forward and Future Prices," *Journal of Financial Economics* (1981).

know each other. Textbooks on futures contracts from one or two decades ago usually include a statement such as "No major default has ever occurred on the commodity exchanges." No textbook published after the Hunt Brothers defaulted on silver contracts in the 1970s can make that claim. Nevertheless, the extremely low default rate in futures contracts is truly awe-inspiring.

Futures contracts are traded in three areas: agricultural commodities, metals and petroleum, and financial assets. The extensive array of futures contracts is listed in Table 25.3.

CONCEPT QUESTIONS
?
- What is a futures contract?
- How is a futures contract related to a forward contract?
- Why do exchanges require futures contracts to be marked to the market?

■ TABLE 25.3 **Futures Contracts Listed in** *The Wall Street Journal*

Contract	Contract Size	Exchange
Agricultural (grain and oilseeds)		
Corn	5,000 bushels	Chicago Board of Trade (CBT)
Oats	5,000 bushels	CBT
Soybeans	5,000 bushels	CBT
Soybean meal	400 tons	CBT
Soybean oil	60,000 lbs.	CBT
Wheat	5,000 bushels	CBT
Wheat	5,000 bushels	Kansas City (KC)
Wheat	5,000 bushels	Minneapolis
Barley	20 metric tons	Winnipeg (WPG)
Flaxseed	20 metric tons	WPG
Rapeseed	20 metric tons	WPG
Wheat	20 metric tons	WPG
Rye	20 metric tons	WPG
Agricultural (livestock and meat)		
Cattle (feeder)	44,000 lbs.	Chicago Mercantile Exchange (CME)
Cattle (live)	40,000 lbs.	CME
Hogs	30,000 lbs.	CME
Pork bellies	40,000 lbs.	CME
Agricultural (food, fiber, and wood)		
Cocoa	10 metric tons	Coffee, Sugar and Cocoa Exchange (CSCE)
Coffee	37,500 lbs.	CSCE
Cotton	50,000 lbs.	New York Cotton Exchange (CTN)
Orange juice	15,000 lbs.	CTN
Sugar (world)	112,000 lbs.	CSCE
Sugar (domestic)	142,000 lbs.	CSCE
Lumber	150,000 board feet	CME

■ TABLE 25.3   (*concluded*)

Contract	Contract Size	Exchange
Metals and petroleum		
Copper (standard)	25,000 lbs.	Commodity Exchange in New York (CMX)
Gold	100 troy oz.	CMX
Platinum	50 troy oz.	New York Mercantile (NYM)
Palladium	100 troy oz.	NYM
Silver	5,000 troy oz.	CMX
Silver	1,000 troy oz.	CBT
Crude oil (light sweet)	1,000 barrels	NYM
Heating oil no. 2	42,000 gallons	NYM
Gas oil	100 metric tons	International Petroleum Exchange of London (IPEL)
Gasoline unleaded	42,000 gallons	NYM
Financial		
British pound	62,500 pounds	International Monetary Market in Chicago (IMM)
Australian dollar	100,000 dollars	IMM
Canadian dollar	100,000 dollars	IMM
Japanese yen	12.5 million yen	IMM
Swiss franc	125,000 francs	IMM
German mark	125,000 marks	IMM
Eurodollar	$1 million	London International Financial Futures Exchange (LIFFE)
Financial		
Sterling	500,000 pounds	LIFFE
Treasury bonds	$1 million	LIFFE
Long gilt	250,000 pounds	LIFFE
Eurodollar	$1 million	IMM
U.S. Dollar Index	500 times Index	Financial Instrument Exchange in New York (FINEX)
CRB Index	500 times Index	New York Futures Exchange (NYFE)
Treasury bonds	$100,000	CBT
Treasury notes	$100,000	CBT
5-year Treasury notes	$100,000	CBT
5-year Treasury notes	$100,000	FINEX
Treasury bonds	$50,000	MCE
Treasury bonds	$1 million	IMM
Financial indexes		
Municipal bonds	1,000 times Bond Buyer Index	CBT
S&P 500 Index	500 times Index	CME
NYSE Composite	500 times Index	NYFE
Kansas City Value Line Index	500 times Index	KC
Major Market Index	250 times Index	CBT

25.3 HEDGING

Now that we have determined how futures contracts work, let us talk about hedging. There are two types of hedges, long and short. We discuss the short hedge first.

EXAMPLE

In June, Bernard Abelman, a Midwestern farmer, anticipates a harvest of 50,000 bushels of wheat at the end of September. He has two alternatives.

1. *Write Futures Contracts against His Anticipated Harvest.* The September wheat contract on the Chicago Board of Trade is trading at $3.75 a bushel on June 1. He executes the following transaction:

Date of Transaction	Transaction	Price per Bushel
June 1	Write 10 September futures contracts	$3.75

He notes that transportation costs to the designated delivery point in Chicago are 30 cents/bushel. Thus, his net price per bushel is $3.45 = $3.75 − $0.30.

2. *Harvest the Wheat without Writing a Futures Contract.* Alternatively, Mr. Abelman could have harvested the wheat without benefit of a futures contract. The risk would be quite great here since no one knows what the cash price in September will be. If prices rise, he will profit. Conversely, he will lose if prices fall.

We say that strategy 2 is an unhedged position because there is no attempt to use the futures markets to reduce risk. Conversely, strategy 1 involves a hedge. That is, a position in the futures market offsets the risk of a position in the physical, that is, in the actual, commodity.

Though hedging may seem quite sensible to you, it should be mentioned that not everyone hedges. Mr. Abelman might reject hedging for at least two reasons.

First, he may simply be uninformed about hedging. We have found that not everyone in business understands the hedging concept. Many executives have told us that they do not want to use futures markets for hedging their inventories because the risks are too great. However, we disagree. While there are large price fluctuations in these markets, hedging actually reduces the risk that an individual holding inventories bears.

Second, Mr. Abelman may have a special insight or some special information that commodity prices will rise. He would not be wise to lock in a price of $3.75 if he expects the cash price in September to be well above this price.

The hedge of strategy 1 is called a **short hedge,** because Mr. Abelman reduces his risk by *selling* a futures contract. The short hedge is very common in business. It occurs whenever someone either anticipates receiving inventory or is holding inventory. Mr. Abelman was anticipating the harvest of grain. A manufacturer of soybean meal and oil may hold large quantities of raw soybeans, which are already paid for. However, the price to be received for meal and oil are not known because no one knows what the market price will be when the meal and oil are produced. The manufacturer may write futures contracts in meal and oil to lock in a sales price. An oil company may hold large inventories of petroleum to be processed into heating oil. The firm could sell futures contracts in heating oil in order to lock in the sales price. A mortgage banker may assemble mortgages slowly before selling them in bulk to a financial institution. Movements of interest rates affect the value of the mortgages during the time they are in inventory. The mortgage banker could sell Treasury-bond futures contracts in order to offset this interest-rate risk. (This last example is treated later in this chapter.)

EXAMPLE

On April 1, Moon Chemical agreed to sell petrochemicals to the U.S. government in the future. The delivery dates and prices have been determined. Because oil is a basic ingredient of the production process, Moon Chemical will need to have large quantities of oil on hand. The firm can get the oil in one of two ways:

1. *Buy the Oil As the Firm Needs It.* This in an unhedged position because, as of April 1, the firm does not know the prices it will later have to pay for the oil. Oil is quite a volatile commodity, so Moon Chemical is bearing a good bit of risk. The key to this risk-bearing is that the sales price to the U.S. government has already been fixed. Thus, Moon Chemical cannot pass on increased costs to the consumer.

2. *Buy Futures Contracts.*[6] The firm can buy futures contracts with expiration months corresponding to the dates the firm needs inventory. The futures contract locks in the purchase price to Moon Chemical. Because there is a crude-oil futures contract for every month, selecting the correct futures contract is not difficult. Many other commodities have only five contracts per year, frequently necessitating buying contracts one month away from the month of production.

As mentioned earlier, Moon Chemical is interested in hedging the risk of fluctuating oil prices because it cannot pass any cost increases on to the consumer. Suppose, alternatively, that Moon Chemical was not selling petrochemicals on fixed contract to the U.S. government. Instead, imagine that the petrochemicals were to be sold to private industry at currently prevailing prices. The price of petrochemicals should move directly with oil prices, because oil is a major component of petrochemicals. Because cost increases are likely to be passed on to the consumer, Moon Chemical would probably not want to hedge in this case. Instead, the firm is likely to choose strategy 1, buying the oil as it is needed. If oil prices increase between April 1 and September 1, Moon Chemical will, of course, find that its inputs have become quite costly. However, in a competitive market, its revenues are likely to rise as well.

Strategy 2 is called a **long hedge** because one *purchases* a futures contract to reduce risk. In other words, one takes a long position in the futures market. In general, a firm institutes a long hedge when it is committed to a fixed sales price. One class of situations involves actual written contracts with customers, such as Moon Chemical had with the U.S. government. Alternatively, a firm may find that it cannot easily pass on costs to consumers or does not want to pass on these costs. For

---

[6]Alternatively, the firm could buy the oil on April 1 and store it. This would eliminate the risk of price movement, because the firm's oil costs would be fixed upon the immediate purchase. However, this strategy would be inferior to strategy 2 in the common case where the difference between the futures contract quoted on April 1 and the April 1 cash price is less than storage costs.

example, a group of students opened a small meat market called *What's Your Beef* near the University of Pennsylvania in the late 1970s.[7] You may recall that this was a time of volatile consumer prices, especially food prices. Knowing that their fellow students were particularly budget-conscious, the owners vowed to keep food prices constant, regardless of price movements in either direction. They accomplished this by purchasing futures contracts in various agricultural commodities.

CASE STUDY

■■■■■

Making the Decision to Use Derivatives: The Case of Metallgesellschaft

Earlier in the chapter we introduced MG Refining and Marketing (MGRM), a U.S. subsidiary of Metallgesellschaft AG (MGAG).[8] MGRM reportedly lost more than $1 billion from trading derivatives. Essentially, MGRM sold gasoline, heating oil, and diesel fuel at fixed prices for up to 10 years in the future. This is called "selling forward." In 1993 MGRM had sold forward more than 150 million barrels of petroleum products. As in any "selling forward program," MGRM would lose if the prices of petroleum products rose over time. For example, suppose MGRM had agreed to sell 150 million barrels of heating oil 10 years from now at $25 per barrel. In 10 years, if the actual price of heating oil turned out to be $35 per barrel, MGRM would stand to lose $10 for every barrel it must sell.

There are several things that MGRM could do to hedge this exposure.

1. MGRM could have attempted to acquire 150 million barrels of oil for forward delivery 10 years from now. If the 10-year forward price had been $25 per barrel, MGRM would have broken even. In theory, this would have been a perfect hedge. Unfortunately, it is almost impossible to find firms who will commit to buying or selling 150 million barrels of oil 10 years in the future. There is no organized 10-year forward market in petroleum products.
2. MGRM could have tried to buy a futures contract that would guarantee delivery of 150 million barrels of oil 10 years from now at $25 per barrel. But, as with forward trading, there is no 10-year futures market for petroleum products.
3. Because no 10-year futures contract existed, MGRM employed a "rolling stack" strategy. That is, they first bought a short-term, say, a one-year, futures contract instead of the 10-year contract. At the end of one year, when the futures contract matured, MGRM wrote another one-year futures contract. The strategy called for a series of 10 one-year futures contracts over the 10 years.

The strategy can be best understood in a two-year example. At date 0, MGRM would sell oil forward 10 years, at, say, $25 a barrel, to its customers. Simultaneously, MGRM would buy a one-year futures contract, also at $25 a barrel.[9] Now assume that the spot price of oil, i.e., the price for immediate delivery, rises to $30 a barrel at date 1. Also, at date 2, the price of the one-year futures contract sells at $30 a barrel. Here, MGRM would break even and at date 1, would gain $5 on its first one-year futures contract. That is, its futures contract issued at date 0 requires it to pay $25 for a barrel of oil

---

[7]Ordinarily, an unusual firm name in this textbook is a tip-off that it is fictional. This, however, is a true story.

[8]For a spirited debate on what caused the MGRM derivative trading losses, please read: F. R. Edwards and M. S. Canter, "The Collapse of Metallgesellschaft: Unhedgeable Risks, Poor Hedging Strategy or Just Bad Luck," *Journal of Applied Corporate Finance* (Spring 1995); A. S. Mello and J. E. Parsons, "Maturity Structure of a Hedge Matters: Lessons from the Metallgesellschaft Debacle," *Journal of Applied Corporate Finance* (Spring 1995); C. Culp and M. Miller, "Hedging in the Theory of Corporate Finance: A Reply to Our Critics," *Journal of Applied Corporate Finance* (Spring 1995).

[9]For simplicity, we assume a level "term structure" of oil prices. A case of nonlevel prices, while more complex, would lead to the same conclusion. We also use the term of one year when rolling stacks are usually in terms of months.

at date 1. It could immediately sell this oil in the spot market at $30 a barrel. However, at date 2, it would lose $5. That is, its futures contract issued at date 1 requires it to buy oil at $30 a barrel at date 2. This oil must be sold to its customers for only $25 at date 2.

Unfortunately, there are two potential problems with this hedge. First, the entire term structure of oil prices need not move together. For example, if the spot price of oil was only $29 at date 1 while the one-year futures contract was quoted at $30 on that date, the firm would lose $1. That is, the gain on the first contract of $4 ($29 − $25) would be less than the loss of $5 ($30 − $25) on the second contract.

Second, the first contract must be settled before the second contract, necessitating liquidity problems. For example, if oil prices fell at date 1, the loss on the first contract would be settled to that date. The gain on the second contract would occur at date 2.[10] In fact, oil prices did fall over much of the 10-year life of MGRM's hedge, causing large liquidity problems.

The above shows that risks arise even when a position is hedged. However, MGRM created a third risk (and perhaps greater risk) by eliminating their hedge in the middle. Suppose, in our example, that MGRM bought the first futures contract at date 0 but did not buy the second futures contract at date 1. That is, they did not "roll over" their hedge. Since the firm had previously sold oil forward for two years, they would be unhedged over the second year. A rise in oil prices over the second year to pay $35 would mean that MGRM would have to buy oil in the spot market at $35 on date 2 in order to simultaneously sell oil to its customers at $25. While MGRM in the real world had a 10-year contract, the effect was similar. After MGRM failed to roll over its stacked hedge, i.e., failed to buy futures contracts in later years, oil prices rose. MGRM suffered great losses because of this.

Was the decision to terminate the right one? No one can really know the answer to this important question. It may be that the funding requirements from margin calls forced MGRM into liquidating the futures leg of the hedge, precipitating the collapse. It is possible that the rolling stack hedge was not well designed and had more risks than was initially perceived. It is also possible that the program was terminated prematurely and, had MGRM hung on, the hedge would have been operative. Nevertheless, it must be pointed out that MGRM incurred quite a bit of bad luck. Oil prices fell when MGRM was hedged, leading to liquidity problems. Oil prices rose after the hedge was lifted, leading to losses. ■ ■ ■ ■ ■

- Define short and long hedges.
- Under what circumstances is each of the two hedges used?
- What is a rolling stack strategy?

25.4 INTEREST-RATE FUTURES CONTRACTS

In this section we consider interest-rate futures contracts. Our examples deal with futures contracts on Treasury bonds because of their high popularity. We first price Treasury bonds and Treasury-bond forward contracts. Differences between futures and forward contracts are explored. Hedging examples are provided next.

Pricing of Treasury Bonds

As mentioned earlier in the text, a Treasury bond pays semiannual interest over its life. In addition, the face value of the bond is paid at maturity. Consider a 20-year, 8-percent coupon bond that was issued on March 1. The first payment is to occur in six months, that is, on September 1. The value of the bond can be determined as

---

[10]In addition, since futures contracts are marked-to-the-market daily, gains and losses on the first contract must be settled each day over the first year. If oil prices fell, margin calls would have occurred over the first year.

■ FIGURE 25.1   **Cash Flows for Both a Treasury Bond and a Forward Contract on a Treasury Bond**

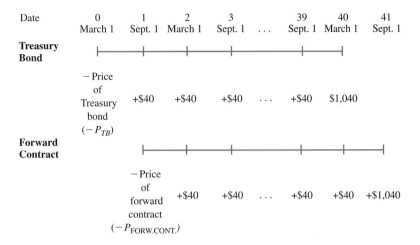

Pricing of a Treasury Bond:

$$P_{TB} = \frac{\$40}{1 + r_1} + \frac{\$40}{(1 + r_2)^2} + \frac{\$40}{(1 + r_3)^3} + \ldots + \frac{\$40}{(1 + r_{39})^{39}} + \frac{\$1,040}{(1 + r_{40})^{40}} \quad (25.1)$$

Because an 8-percent coupon bond pays interest of $80 a year, the semiannual coupon is $40. Principal and the semiannual coupons are both paid at maturity. As we mentioned in a previous chapter, the price of the Treasury bond, P_{TB}, is determined by discounting each payment on a bond at the appropriate spot rate. Because the payments are semiannual, each spot rate is expressed in semiannual terms. That is, imagine a horizontal term structure where the effective annual yield is 12 percent for all maturities. Because each spot rate, r, is expressed in semiannual terms, each spot rate is $\sqrt{1.12} - 1 = 5.83\%$. Because coupon payments occur every six months, there are 40 spot rates over the 20-year period.

Pricing of Forward Contracts

Now, imagine a *forward* contract where, on March 1, you agree to buy a new 20-year, 8-percent coupon Treasury bond in six months, that is, on September 1. As with typical forward contracts, you will pay for the bond on September 1, not March 1. The cash flows from both the Treasury bond issued on March 1 and the forward contract that you purchase on March 1 are presented in Figure 25.1. The cash flows on the Treasury bond begin exactly six months earlier than do the cash flows on the forward contract. The Treasury bond is purchased with cash on March 1 (date 0). The first coupon payment occurs on September 1 (date 1). The last coupon payment occurs at date 40, along with the face value of $1,000. The forward contract compels you to pay $P_{FORW.CONT.}$, the price of the forward contract, on September 1 (date 1). You receive a new Treasury bond at that time. The first coupon payment from the bond you receive occurs on March 1 of the following year (date 2). The last coupon payment occurs at date 41, along with the face value of $1,000.

Given the 40 spot rates, equation (25.1) showed how to price a Treasury bond. How does one price the forward contract on a Treasury bond? Just as we saw earlier in the text that net-present-value analysis can be used to price bonds, we will now show that net-present-value analysis can be used to price forward contracts. Given the cash flows for the forward contract in Figure 25.1, the price of the forward contract must satisfy the following equation:

$$\frac{P_{\text{FORW.CONT.}}}{1 + r_1} = \frac{\$40}{(1 + r_2)^2} + \frac{\$40}{(1 + r_3)^3} + \frac{\$40}{(1 + r_4)^4}$$

$$+ \ldots + \frac{\$40}{(1 + r_{40})^{40}} + \frac{\$1,040}{(1 + r_{41})^{41}} \qquad (25.2)$$

The right-hand side of equation (25.2) discounts all the cash flows from the delivery instrument (the Treasury bond issued on September 1) back to date 0 (March 1). Because the first cash flow occurs at date 2 (March 1 of the subsequent year), it is discounted by $1/(1 + r_2)^2$. The last cash flow of \$1,040 occurs at date 41, so it is discounted by $1/(1 + r_{41})^{41}$. The left-hand side represents the cost of the forward contract as of date 0. Because the actual outpayment occurs at date 1, it is discounted by $1/(1 + r_1)$.

Students often ask, "Why are we discounting everything back to date 0, when we are actually paying for the forward contract on September 1?" The answer is simply that we apply the same techniques to equation (25.2) that we apply to all capital-budgeting problems; we want to put everything in today's (date 0's) dollars. Given that the spot rates are known in the marketplace, traders should have no more trouble pricing a forward contract by equation (25.2) than they would have pricing a Treasury bond by (25.1).

Forward contracts are similar to the underlying bonds themselves. If the entire term structure of interest rates unexpectedly shifts upward on March 2, the Treasury bond issued the previous day should fall in value. This can be seen from equation (25.1). A rise in each of the spot rates lowers the present value of each of the coupon payments. Hence, the value of the bond must fall. Conversely, a fall in the term structure of interest rates increases the value of the bond.

The same relationship holds with forward contracts, as can be seen from rewriting (25.2) as

$$P_{\text{FORW.CONT.}} = \frac{\$40 \times (1 + r_1)}{(1 + r_2)^2} + \frac{\$40 \times (1 + r_1)}{(1 + r_3)^3} + \frac{\$40 \times (1 + r_1)}{(1 + r_4)^4}$$

$$+ \ldots + \frac{\$40 \times (1 + r_1)}{(1 + r_{40})^{40}} + \frac{\$1,040 \times (1 + r_1)}{(1 + r_{41})^{41}} \qquad (25.3)$$

We went from (25.2) to (25.3) by multiplying both the left- and the right-hand sides by $(1 + r_1)$. If the entire term structure of interest rates unexpectedly shifts upward on March 2, the *first* term on the right-hand side of equation (25.3) should fall in value.[11] That is, both r_1 and r_2 will rise an equal amount. However, r_2 enters as a *squared* term, $1/(1 + r_2)^2$, so an increase in r_2 more than offsets the increase in r_1. As we move further to the right, an increase in any spot rate, r_i, more than offsets an increase in r_1. Here r_i enters as the ith power, $1/(1 + r_i)^i$. Thus, as long as the entire term structure shifts upward an equal amount on March 2, the value of a forward contract must fall on that date. Conversely, as long as the entire term structure shifts downward an equal amount on March 2, the value of a forward contract must rise.

---

[11]We are assuming that each spot rate shifts the same amount. For example, suppose that, on March 1, $r_1 = 5\%$, $r_2 = 5.4\%$, and $r_3 = 5.8\%$. Assuming that all rates increase by 1/2 percent on March 2, r_1 becomes 5.5 percent (5% + 1/2%), r_2 becomes 5.9 percent, and r_3 becomes 6.3 percent.

Futures Contracts

The above discussion concerned a forward contract in U.S. Treasury bonds, that is, a forward contract where the deliverable instrument is a U.S. Treasury bond. What about a futures contract on a Treasury bond?[12] We mentioned earlier that futures contracts and forward contracts are quite similar, though there are a few differences between the two. First, futures contracts are generally traded on exchanges, whereas forward contracts are not traded on an exchange. In this case, the Treasury-bond futures contract is traded on the Chicago Board of Trade. Second, futures contracts generally allow the seller a period of time in which to deliver, whereas forward contracts generally call for delivery on a particular day. The seller of a Treasury-bond futures contract can choose to deliver on any business day during the delivery month.[13] Third, futures contracts are subject to the mark-to-the-market convention, whereas forward contracts are not. Traders in Treasury-bill futures contracts must adhere to this convention. Fourth, there is generally a liquid market for futures contracts allowing contracts to be quickly netted out. That is, a buyer can sell his futures contract at any time, and a seller can buy back her futures contract at any time. Conversely, because forward markets are generally quite illiquid, traders cannot easily net out their positions. The popularity of the Treasury-bond futures contract has produced liquidity even higher than that on other futures contracts. Positions in that contract can be netted out quite easily.

The above discussion is not intended to be an exhaustive list of differences between the Treasury-bond forward contract and the Treasury-bond futures contract. Rather, it is intended to show that both contracts share fundamental characteristics. Though there are differences, the two instruments should be viewed as variations of the same species, not different species. Thus, the pricing equation of (25.3), which is exact for the forward contract, should be a decent approximation for the futures contract.

Hedging in Interest-Rate Futures

Now that we have the basic institutional details under our belt, we are ready for examples of hedging using either futures contracts or forward contracts on Treasury bonds. Because the T-bond futures contract is extremely popular whereas the forward contract is traded sporadically, our examples use the futures contract.

EXAMPLE

Ron Cooke owns a mortgage-banking company. On March 1, he made a commitment to loan a total of $1 million to various homeowners on May 1. The loans are 20-year mortgages carrying a 12-percent coupon, the going interest rate on mortgages at the time. Thus, the mortgages are made at par. Though homeowners would not use the term, we could say that he is buying a *forward contract* on a mortgage. That is, he agrees on March 1 to give $1 million to his borrowers on May 1 in exchange for principal and interest from them every month for the next 20 years.

Like many mortgage bankers, he has no intention of paying the $1 million out of his own pocket. Rather, he intends to sell the mortgages to an insurance company. Thus, the insurance company will actually loan the funds and will receive principal and interest over the next 20 years. Mr. Cooke does not currently have an

---

[12]Futures contracts on bonds are also called *interest-rate futures contracts.*

[13]Delivery occurs two days after the seller notifies the clearinghouse of her intention to deliver.

■ TABLE 25.4   **Effects of Changing Interest Rate on Ron Cooke, Mortgage Banker**

Mortgage interest rate on April 15	Above 12%	Below 12%
Sale price to Acme Insurance Company	Below $1 million (We assume $940,000)	Above $1 million (We assume $1.05 million)
Effect on mortgage banker	He loses because he must loan full $1 million to borrowers.	He gains because he loans only $1 million to borrowers.
Dollar gain or loss	Loss of $60,000 ($1 million − $940,000)	Gain of $50,000 ($1.05 million − $1 million)

The interest rate on March 1, the date when the loan agreement was made with the borrowers, was 12 percent. April 15 is the date the mortgages were sold to Acme Insurance Company.

insurance company in mind. He plans to visit the mortgage departments of insurance companies over the next 60 days to sell the mortgages to one or many of them. He sets April 30 as a deadline for making the sale because the borrowers expect the funds on the following day.

Suppose that Mr. Cooke sells the mortgages to the Acme Insurance Co. on April 15. What price will Acme pay for the bonds?

You may think that the insurance company will obviously pay $1 million for the loans. However, suppose interest rates have risen above 12 percent by April 15. The insurance company will buy the mortgage at a discount. For example, suppose the insurance company agrees to pay only $940,000 for the mortgages. Because the mortgage banker agreed to loan a full $1 million to the borrowers, the mortgage banker must come up with the additional $60,000 ($1 million − $940,000) out of his own pocket.

Alternatively, suppose that interest rates fall below 12 percent by April 15. The mortgages can be sold at a premium under this scenario. If the insurance company buys the mortgages at $1.05 million, the mortgage banker will have made an unexpected profit of $50,000 ($1.05 million − $1 million).

Because Ron Cooke is unable to forecast interest rates, this risk is something that he would like to avoid. The risk is summarized in Table 25.4.

Seeing the interest-rate risk, students at this point may ask, "What does the mortgage banker get out of this loan to offset his risk-bearing?" Mr. Cooke wants to sell the mortgages to the insurance company so that he can get two fees. The first is an *origination fee,* which is paid to the mortgage banker from the insurance company on April 15, that is, on the date the loan is sold. An industry standard in certain locales is 1 percent of the value of the loan, that is $10,000 (1% × $1 million). In addition, Mr. Cooke will act as a collection agent for the insurance company. For this service, he will receive a small portion of the outstanding balance of the loan each month. For example, if he is paid 0.03 percent of the loan each month, he will receive $300 (0.03% × $1 million) in the first month. As the outstanding balance of the loan declines, he will receive less.

Though Mr. Cooke will earn profitable fees on the loan, he bears interest-rate risk. He loses money if interest rates rise after March 1, and he profits if interest rates fall after March 1. To hedge this risk, he writes June Treasury-bond futures contracts on March 1. As with mortgages, Treasury-bond futures contracts fall in value if interest rates rise. Because he *writes* the contract, he makes money on

■ TABLE 25.5 **Illustration of Hedging Strategy for Ron Cooke,**
                    Mortgage Banker

	Cash Markets	Futures Markets
March 1	Mortgage banker makes forward contracts to loan $1 million at 12 percent for 20 years. The loans are to be funded on May 1. No cash changes hands on March 1.	Mortgage banker writes 10 June Treasury-bond futures contracts.
April 15	Loans are sold to Acme Insurance Company. Mortgage banker will receive sale price from Acme on the May 1 funding date.	Mortgage banker buys back all the futures contracts.
If interest rates rise:	Loans are sold at a price below $1 million. Mortgage banker *loses* because he receives less than the $1 million he must give to borrowers.	Each futures contract is bought back at a price below the sales price, resulting in *profit*. Mortgage banker's profit in futures market offsets loss in cash market.
If interest rates fall:	Loans are sold at a price above $1 million. Mortgage banker *gains* because he receives more than the $1 million he must give to borrowers.	Each futures contract is bought back at a price above the sales price, resulting in *loss*. Mortgage banker's loss in futures market offsets gain in cash market.

these contracts if they fall in value. Therefore, with an interest-rate rise, the loss he endures in the mortgages is offset by the gain he earns in the futures market. Conversely, Treasury-bond futures contracts rise in value if interest rates fall. Because he writes the contracts, he suffers losses on them when rates fall. With an interest-rate fall, the profit he makes on the mortgages is offset by the loss he suffers in the futures markets.

The details of this hedging transaction are presented in Table 25.5. The column on the left is labeled "Cash markets," because the deal in the mortgage market is transacted off an exchange. The column on the right shows the offsetting transactions in the futures market. Consider the first row. The mortgage banker enters into a forward contract on March 1. He simultaneously writes Treasury-bond futures contracts. Ten contracts are written because the deliverable instrument on each contract is $100,000 of Treasury bonds. The total is $1 million (10 × $100,000), which is equal to the value of the mortgages. Mr. Cooke would prefer to write May Treasury-bond futures contracts. Here, Treasury bonds would be delivered on the futures contract during the same month that the loan is funded. Because there is no May T-bond futures contract, Mr. Cooke achieves the closest match through a June contract.

If held to maturity, the June contract would obligate the mortgage banker to deliver Treasury bonds in June. Interest-rate risk ends in the cash market when the loans are sold. Interest-rate risk must be terminated in the futures market at that time. Thus, Mr. Cooke nets out his position in the futures contract as soon as the loan is sold to Acme Insurance.

Risk is clearly reduced via an offsetting transaction in the futures market. However, is risk totally eliminated? Risk would be totally eliminated if losses in the cash markets were *exactly* offset in the futures markets and vice versa. This is unlikely to happen because mortgages and Treasury bonds are not identical instruments. First, mortgages may have different maturities than Treasury bonds. Second, Treasury bonds have a different payment stream than do mortgages. Principal is only paid at maturity on T-bonds, whereas principal is paid every month on mortgages. Because mortgages pay principal continuously, these instruments have a shorter *effective* time to maturity than do Treasury bonds of equal maturity.[14] Third, mortgages have default risk whereas Treasury bonds do not. The term structure applicable to instruments with default risk may change even when the term structure for risk-free assets remains constant. Fourth, mortgages may be paid off early and hence have a shorter *expected maturity* than Treasury bonds of equal maturity.

Because mortgages and Treasury bonds are not identical instruments, they are not identically affected by interest rates. If Treasury bonds are less volatile than mortgages, financial consultants may advise Mr. Cooke to write more than 10 T-bond futures contracts. Conversely, if these bonds are more volatile, the consultant may state that less than 10 futures contracts are indicated. An optimal ratio of futures to mortgages will reduce risk as much as possible. However, because the price movements of mortgages and Treasury bonds are not *perfectly correlated,* Mr. Cooke's hedging strategy cannot eliminate all risk.

The above strategy is called a *short hedge* because Mr. Cooke sells futures contracts in order to reduce risk. Though it involves an interest-rate futures contract, this short hedge is analogous to short hedges in agricultural and metallurgical futures contracts. We argued at the beginning of this chapter that individuals and firms institute short hedges to offset inventory price fluctuation. Once Mr. Cooke makes a contract to loan money to borrowers, the mortgages effectively become his inventory. He writes a futures contract to offset the price fluctuation of his inventory.

We now consider an example where a mortgage banker institutes a long hedge.

Example

Margaret Boswell is another mortgage banker. Her firm faces problems similar to those facing Mr. Cooke's firm. However, she tackles the problems through the use of **advance commitments,** a strategy the opposite of Mr. Cooke's. That is, she promises to deliver loans to a financial institution *before* she lines up borrowers. On March 1, her firm agreed to sell mortgages to No-State Insurance Co. The agreement specifies that she must turn over 12-percent coupon mortgages with a face value of $1 million to No-State by May 1. No-State is buying the mortgages at par, implying that they will pay Ms. Boswell $1 million on May 1. As of March 1, Ms. Boswell had not signed up any borrowers. Over the next two months, she will seek out individuals who want mortgages beginning May 1.

As with Mr. Cooke, changing interest rates will affect Ms. Boswell. If interest rates fall before she signs up a borrower, the borrower will demand a premium on a 12-percent coupon loan. That is, the borrower will receive more than par on May 1.[15] Because Ms. Boswell receives par from the insurance company, she must make up the difference.

---

[14]Alternatively, we can say that mortgages have shorter duration than do Treasury bonds of equal maturity. A precise definition of duration is provided later in this chapter.

[15]Alternatively, the mortgage would still be at par if a coupon rate below 12 percent were used. However, this is not done since the insurance company only wants to buy 12-percent mortgages.

■ TABLE 25.6 **Illustration of Advance Commitment for**
Margaret Boswell, Mortgage Banker

	Cash Markets	Futures Markets
March 1	Mortgage banker makes a forward contract (advance commitment) to deliver $1 million of mortgages to No-State Insurance. The insurance company will pay par to Ms. Boswell for the loans on May 1. The borrowers are to receive their funding from mortgage banker on May 1. The mortgages are to be 12-percent coupon loans for 20 years.	Mortgage banker buys 10 June Treasury-bond futures contracts.
April 15	Mortgage banker signs up borrowers to 12-percent coupon, 20-year mortgages. She promises that the borrowers will receive funds on May 1.	Mortgage banker sells all futures contracts.
If interest rates rise:	Mortgage banker issues mortgages to borrowers at a discount. Mortgage banker *gains* because she receives par from insurance company.	Futures contract is sold at a price below purchase price, resulting in *loss.* Mortgage banker's loss in futures market offsets gain in cash market.
If interest rates fall:	Loans to borrowers are issued at a premium. Mortgage banker *loses* because she receives only par from insurance company.	Futures contract is sold at a price above purchase price, resulting in *gain.* Mortgage banker's gain in futures market offsets loss in cash market.

Conversely, if interest rates rise, a 12-percent coupon loan will be made at a discount. That is, the borrower will receive less than par on May 1. Because Ms. Boswell receives par from the insurance company, the difference is pure profit to her.

The details are provided in the left-hand column of Table 25.6. As did Mr. Cooke, Ms. Boswell finds the risk burdensome. Therefore, she offsets her advance commitment with a transaction in the futures markets. Because she *loses* in the cash market when interest rates fall, she *buys* futures contracts to reduce the risk. When interest rates fall, the value of her futures contracts increases. The gain in the futures market offsets the loss in the cash market. Conversely, she gains in the cash markets when interest rates rise. The value of her futures contracts decreases when interest rates rise, offsetting her gain.

We call this a *long hedge* because Ms. Boswell offsets risk in the cash markets by buying a futures contract. Though it involves an interest-rate futures contract, this long hedge is analogous to long hedges in agricultural and metallurgical futures contracts. We argued at the beginning of this chapter that individuals and firms institute long hedges when their finished goods are to be sold at a fixed price. Once Ms. Boswell makes the advance commitment with No-State Insurance, she has fixed her sales price. She buys a futures contract to offset the price fluctuation of her raw materials, that is, her mortgages.

CONCEPT

?

- How are forward contracts on bonds priced?
- What are the differences between forward contracts on bonds and futures contracts on bonds?
- Give examples of hedging with futures contracts on bonds.

25.5 DURATION HEDGING

The last section concerned the risk of interest-rate changes. We now want to explore this risk in a more precise manner. In particular, we want to show that the concept of duration is a prime determinant of interest-rate risk. We begin by considering the effect of interest-rate movements on bond prices.

The Case of Zero-Coupon Bonds

Imagine a world where the interest rate is 10 percent across all maturities. A one-year pure discount bond pays $110 at maturity. A five-year pure discount bond pays $161.05 at maturity. Both of these bonds are worth $100, as given by[16]

Value of One-Year Pure Discount Bond:

$$\$100 = \frac{\$110}{1.10}$$

Value of Five-Year Pure Discount Bond:

$$\$100 = \frac{\$161.05}{(1.10)^5}$$

Which bond will change more when interest rates move? To find out, we calculate the value of these bonds when interest rates are either 8 or 12 percent. The results are presented in Table 25.7. As can be seen, the five-year bond has greater price swings than does the one-year bond. That is, both bonds are worth $100 when interest rates are 10 percent. The five-year bond is worth more than the one-year bond when interest rates are 8 percent and worth less than the one-year bond when interest rates are 12 percent. We state that the five-year bond is subject to more price volatility. This point, which was mentioned in passing in an earlier section of the chapter, is not difficult to understand. The interest-rate term in the denominator, $1 + r$, is taken to the fifth power for a five-year bond and only to the first power for the one-year bond. Thus, the effect of a changing interest rate is magnified for the five-year bond. The general rule is

The percentage price changes in long-term pure discount bonds are greater than the percentage price changes in short-term pure discount bonds.

The Case of Two Bonds with the Same Maturity but with Different Coupons

The previous example concerned pure discount bonds of different maturities. We now want to see the effect of different coupons on price volatility. To abstract from the effect of differing maturities, we consider two bonds with the same maturity but with different coupons.

---

[16]Alternatively, we could have chosen bonds that pay $100 at maturity. Their values would be $90.91 ($100/1.10) and $62.09 [$100/(1.10)^5]. However, our comparisons to come are made easier if both have the same initial price.

■ TABLE 25.7 Value of a Pure Discount Bond as a Function of Interest Rate

Interest Rate	One-Year Pure Discount Bond	Five-Year Pure Discount Bond
8%	$101.85 = \dfrac{\$110}{1.08}$	$109.61 = \dfrac{\$161.05}{(1.08)^5}$
10%	$100.00 = \dfrac{\$110}{1.10}$	$100.00 = \dfrac{\$161.05}{(1.10)^5}$
12%	$98.21 = \dfrac{\$110}{1.12}$	$91.38 = \dfrac{\$161.05}{(1.12)^5}$

For a given interest rate change, a five-year pure discount bond fluctuates more in price than does a one-year pure discount bond.

Consider a five-year, 10-percent coupon bond and a five-year, 1-percent coupon bond. When interest rates are 10 percent, the bonds are priced at

Value of Five-Year, 10-Percent Coupon Bond:

$$\$100 = \frac{\$10}{1.10} + \frac{\$10}{(1.10)^2} + \frac{\$10}{(1.10)^3} + \frac{\$10}{(1.10)^4} + \frac{\$110}{(1.10)^5}$$

Value of Five-Year, 1-Percent Coupon Bond:

$$\$65.88 = \frac{\$1}{1.10} + \frac{\$1}{(1.10)^2} + \frac{\$1}{(1.10)^3} + \frac{\$1}{(1.10)^4} + \frac{\$101}{(1.10)^5}$$

Which bond will change more in *percentage terms* if interest rates change?[17] To find out, we first calculate the value of these bonds when interest rates are either 8 or 12 percent. The results are presented in Table 25.8. As we would expect, the 10-percent coupon bond always sells for more than the 1-percent coupon bond. Also, as we would expect, each bond is worth more when the interest rate is 8 percent than when the interest rate is 12 percent.

We calculate percentage price changes for both bonds as the interest rate changes from 10 to 8 percent and from 10 to 12 percent. These percentage price changes are

	10% Coupon Bond	1% Coupon Bond
Interest rate changes from 10% to 8%:	$7.99\% = \dfrac{\$107.99}{\$100} - 1$	$9.37\% = \dfrac{\$72.05}{\$65.88} - 1$
Interest rate changes from 10% to 12%:	$-7.21\% = \dfrac{\$92.79}{\$100} - 1$	$-8.39\% = \dfrac{\$60.35}{\$65.88} - 1$

As can be seen, the 1-percent coupon bond has a greater percentage price increase than does the 10-percent coupon bond when the interest rate falls. Similarly, the 1-percent coupon bond has a greater percentage price decrease than does the 10-percent coupon bond when the interest rate rises. Thus, we say that the percentage price changes on the 1-percent coupon bond are greater than are the percentage price changes on the 10-percent coupon bond.

---

[17]The bonds are at different prices initially. Thus, we are concerned with percentage price changes, not absolute price changes.

■ **TABLE 25.8** **Value of Coupon Bonds at Different Interest Rates**

Interest Rate	Five-Year, 10% Coupon Bond
8%	$\$107.99 = \dfrac{\$10}{1.08} + \dfrac{\$10}{(1.08)^2} + \dfrac{\$10}{(1.08)^3} + \dfrac{\$10}{(\$1.08)^4} + \dfrac{\$110}{(1.08)^5}$
10%	$\$100.00 = \dfrac{\$10}{1.10} + \dfrac{\$10}{(1.10)^2} + \dfrac{\$10}{(1.10)^3} + \dfrac{\$10}{(1.10)^4} + \dfrac{\$110}{(1.10)^5}$
12%	$92.79 = \dfrac{\$10}{1.12} + \dfrac{\$10}{(1.12)^2} + \dfrac{\$10}{(1.12)^3} + \dfrac{\$10}{(1.12)^4} + \dfrac{\$110}{(1.12)^5}$

Interest Rate	Five-Year, 1% Coupon Bond
8%	$\$72.05 = \dfrac{\$1}{1.08} + \dfrac{\$1}{(1.08)^2} + \dfrac{\$1}{(1.08)^3} + \dfrac{\$1}{(1.08)^4} + \dfrac{\$101}{(1.08)^5}$
10%	$\$65.88 = \dfrac{\$1}{1.10} + \dfrac{\$1}{(1.10)^2} + \dfrac{\$1}{(1.10)^3} + \dfrac{\$1}{(1.10)^4} + \dfrac{\$101}{(1.10)^5}$
12%	$\$60.35 = \dfrac{\$1}{1.12} + \dfrac{\$1}{(1.12)^2} + \dfrac{\$1}{(1.12)^3} + \dfrac{\$1}{(1.12)^4} + \dfrac{\$101}{(1.12)^5}$

Duration

The question, of course, is "Why?" We can answer this question only after we have explored a concept called **duration.** We begin by noticing that any coupon bond is actually a combination of pure discount bonds. For example, the five-year, 10-percent coupon bond is made up of five pure discount bonds:

1. A pure discount bond paying $10 at the end of year 1.
2. A pure discount bond paying $10 at the end of year 2.
3. A pure discount bond paying $10 at the end of year 3.
4. A pure discount bond paying $10 at the end of year 4.
5. A pure discount bond paying $110 at the end of year 5.

Similarly, the five-year, 1-percent coupon bond is made up of five pure discount bonds. Because the price volatility of a pure discount bond is determined by its maturity, we would like to determine the average maturity of the five pure discount bonds that make up a five-year coupon bond. This leads us to the concept of duration.

   We calculate average maturity in three steps. For the 10-percent coupon bond, we have these:

   1. *Calculate Present Value of Each Payment.* We do this as

Year	Payment	Present Value of Payment by Discounting at 10%
1	$ 10	$ 9.091
2	10	8.264
3	10	7.513
4	10	6.830
5	110	68.302
		$100.00

2. *Express the Present Value of Each Payment in Relative Terms.* We calculate the relative value of a single payment as the ratio of the present value of the payment to the value of the bond. The value of the bond is $100. We have

Year	Payment	Present Value of Payment	Relative Value $=$ $\dfrac{\text{Present Value of Payment}}{\text{Value of Bond}}$
1	$ 10	$ 9.091	$9.091/$100 = 0.09091
2	10	8.264	0.08264
3	10	7.513	0.07513
4	10	6.830	0.06830
5	110	68.302	0.68302
		$100.00	1.0

The bulk of the relative value, 68.302 percent, occurs at year 5 because the principal is paid back at that time.

3. *Weight the Maturity of Each Payment by Its Relative Value.* We have

$$4.1699 \text{ years} = 1 \text{ year} \times 0.09091 + 2 \text{ years} \times 0.08264 + 3 \text{ years}$$
$$\times 0.07513 + 4 \text{ years} \times 0.06830 + 5 \text{ years} \times 0.68302$$

There are many ways to calculate the average maturity of a bond. We have calculated it by weighting the maturity of each payment by the payment's present value. We find that the *effective* maturity of the bond is 4.1699 years. *Duration* is a commonly used word for effective maturity. Thus, the bond's duration is 4.1699 years. Note that duration is expressed in units of time.[18]

Because the five-year, 10-percent coupon bond has a duration of 4.1699 years, its percentage price fluctuations should be the same as those of a zero-coupon bond with a duration of 4.1699 years.[19] It turns out that the five-year, 1-percent coupon bond has a duration of 4.8742 years. Because the 1-percent coupon bond has a higher duration than the 10-percent bond, the 1-percent coupon bond should be subject to greater price fluctuations. This is exactly what we found earlier. In general, we say:

> The percentage price changes of a bond with high duration are greater than the percentage price changes of a bond with low duration.

A final question: Why *does* the 1-percent bond have a greater duration than the 10-percent bond, even though they both have the same five-year maturity? As mentioned earlier, duration is an average of the maturity of the bond's cash flows, weighted by the present

---

[18]The mathematical formula for duration is

$$\text{Duration} = \frac{\text{PV}(C_1)1 + \text{PV}(C_2)2 + \ldots + \text{PV}(C_T)T}{\text{PV}}$$

and

$$\text{PV} = \text{PV}(C_1) + \text{PV}(C_2) + \ldots + \text{PV}(C_T)$$

$$\text{PV}(C_T) = \frac{C_T}{(1 + r)^T}$$

where C_T is the cash to be received in time T and r is the current discount rate.

  Also note that in the above numerical example we discounted each payment by the interest rate of 10 percent. This was done because we wanted to calculate the duration of the bond before a change in the interest rate occurred. After a change in the rate to, say, 8 or 12 percent, all three of our steps would need to reflect the new interest rate. In other words, the duration of a bond is a function of the current interest rate.

[19]Actually, this relationship only exactly holds in the case of a one-time shift in a flat yield curve, where the change in the spot rate is identical for all different maturities.

value of each cash flow. The 1-percent coupon bond receives only $1 in each of the first four years. Thus, the weights applied to years 1 through 4 in the duration formula will be low. Conversely, the 10-percent coupon bond receives $10 in each of the first four years. The weights applied to years 1 through 4 in the duration formula will be higher.

Matching Liabilities with Assets

Earlier in this chapter we argued that firms can hedge risk by trading in futures. Because some firms are subject to interest-rate risk, we showed how they can hedge with interest-rate futures contracts. Firms may also hedge interest-rate risk by matching liabilities with assets. This ability to hedge follows from our discussion of duration.

EXAMPLE

The Physical Bank of New York has the following market-value balance sheet:

PHYSICAL BANK OF NEW YORK
Market-Value Balance Sheet

	Market Value	Duration
Assets		
Overnight money	$ 35 million	0
Accounts-receivable–backed loans	500 million	3 months
Inventory loans	275 million	6 months
Industrial loans	40 million	2 years
Mortgages	150 million	14.8 years
	$1,000 million	
Liabilities and Owners' Equity		
Checking and savings accounts	$ 400 million	0
Certificates of deposit	300 million	1 year
Long-term financing	200 million	10 years
Equity	100 million	
	$1,000 million	

The bank has $1,000 million of assets and $900 million of liabilities. Its equity is the difference between the two: $100 million ($1,000 million − $900 million). Both the market value and the duration of each individual item is provided in the balance sheet. Both overnight money and checking and savings accounts have a duration of zero. This is because the interest paid on these instruments adjusts immediately to changing interest rates in the economy.

The bank's managers think that interest rates are likely to move quickly in the coming months. Because they do not know the direction of the movement, they are worried that their bank is vulnerable to changing rates. They call in a consultant, James Charest, to determine hedging strategy.

Mr. Charest first calculates the duration of the assets and the duration of the liabilities.[20]

---

[20]Note that the duration of a group of items is an average of the duration of the individual items, weighted by the market value of each item. This is a simplifying step that greatly increases duration's practicality.

Duration of Assets:

$$2.56 \text{ years} = 0 \text{ years} \times \frac{\$35 \text{ million}}{\$1,000 \text{ million}} + \tfrac{1}{4} \text{ year} \times \frac{\$500 \text{ million}}{\$1,000 \text{ million}} \quad (25.4)$$

$$+ \tfrac{1}{2} \text{ year} \times \frac{\$275 \text{ million}}{\$1,000 \text{ million}} + 2 \text{ years} \times \frac{\$40 \text{ million}}{\$1,000 \text{ million}}$$

$$+ 14.8 \text{ years} \times \frac{\$150 \text{ million}}{\$1,000 \text{ million}}$$

Duration of Liabilities:

$$2.56 = 0 \text{ years} \times \frac{\$400 \text{ million}}{\$900 \text{ million}} + 1 \text{ year} \times \frac{\$300 \text{ million}}{\$900 \text{ million}} \quad (25.5)$$

$$+ 10 \text{ years} \times \frac{\$200 \text{ million}}{\$900 \text{ million}}$$

The duration of the assets, 2.56 years, equals the duration of the liabilities. Because of this, Mr. Charest argues that the firm is immune to interest-rate risk.

Just to be on the safe side, the bank calls in a second consultant, Gail Ellert. Ms. Ellert argues that it is incorrect to simply match durations, because assets total $1,000 million and liabilities total only $900 million. If both assets and liabilities have the same duration, the price change on a *dollar* of assets should be equal to the price change on a dollar of liabilities. However, the *total* price change will be greater for assets than for liabilities, because there are more assets than liabilities in this bank. The firm will be immune from interest-rate risk only when the duration of the liabilities is greater than the duration of the assets. Ms. Ellert states that the following relationship must hold if the bank is to be **immunized,** that is, immune to interest-rate risk:

$$\begin{array}{c} \text{Duration of} \\ \text{assets} \end{array} \times \begin{array}{c} \text{Market value of} \\ \text{assets} \end{array} = \begin{array}{c} \text{Duration of} \\ \text{liabilities} \end{array} \times \begin{array}{c} \text{Market value} \\ \text{of liabilities} \end{array} \quad (25.6)$$

She says that the bank should not *equate* the duration of the liabilities with the duration of the assets. Rather, using equation (25.6), the bank should match the duration of the liabilities to the duration of the assets. She suggests two ways to achieve this match.

1. *Increase the Duration of the Liabilities without Changing the Duration of the Assets.* Ms. Ellert argues that the duration of the liabilities could be increased to

$$\text{Duration of assets} \times \frac{\text{Market value of assets}}{\text{Market value of liabilities}}$$

$$= 2.56 \text{ years} \times \frac{\$1,000 \text{ million}}{\$900 \text{ million}}$$

$$= 2.84 \text{ years}$$

Equation (25.5) then becomes:

$$2.56 \times \$1 \text{ billion} = 2.84 \times \$900 \text{ million}$$

2. *Decrease the Duration of the Assets without Changing the Duration of the Liabilities.* Alternatively, Ms. Ellert points out that the duration of the assets could be decreased to

$$\text{Duration of liabilities} \times \frac{\text{Market value of liabilities}}{\text{Market value of assets}}$$

$$= 2.56 \text{ years} \times \frac{\$900 \text{ million}}{\$1,000 \text{ million}}$$

$$= 2.30 \text{ years}$$

Equation (25.6) then becomes:

$$2.30 \times \$1 \text{ billion} = 2.56 \times \$900 \text{ million}$$

Though we agree with Ms. Ellert's analysis, the bank's current mismatch was small anyway. Huge mismatches have occurred for real-world financial institutions, particularly savings and loans. S&Ls have frequently invested large portions of their assets in mortgages. The durations of these mortgages would clearly be above 10 years. Much of the funds available for mortgage lending were financed by short-term credit, especially savings accounts. As we mentioned, the duration of such instruments is quite small. A thrift institution in this situation faces a large amount of interest-rate risk, because any increase in interest rates would greatly reduce the value of the mortgages. Because an interest-rate rise would only reduce the value of the liabilities slightly, the equity of the firm would fall. As interest rates rose over much of the 1960s and the 1970s, many S&Ls found that the market value of their equity approached zero.[21]

Duration and the accompanying immunization strategies are useful in other areas of finance. For example, many firms establish pension funds to meet obligations to retirees. If the assets of a pension fund are invested in bonds and other fixed-income securities, the duration of the assets can be computed. Similarly, the firm views the obligations to retirees as analogous to interest payments on debt. The duration of these liabilities can be calculated as well. The manager of a pension fund would commonly choose pension assets so that the duration of the assets is matched with the duration of the liabilities. In this way, changing interest rates would not affect the net worth of the pension fund.

Life insurance companies receiving premiums today are legally obligated to provide death benefits in the future. Actuaries view these future benefits as analogous to interest and principal payments of fixed-income securities. The duration of these expected benefits can be calculated. Insurance firms frequently invest in bonds where the duration of the bonds is matched to the duration of the future death benefits.

The business of a leasing company is quite simple. The firm issues debt to purchase assets, which are then leased. The lease payments have a duration, as does the debt. Leasing companies frequently structure debt financing so that the duration of the debt matches the duration of the lease. If the firm did not do this, the market value of its equity could be eliminated by a quick change in interest rates.

CONCEPT QUESTIONS

?

- What is duration?
- How is the concept of duration used to reduce interest-rate risk?

---

[21] Actually, the market value of the equity could easily be negative in this example. However, S&Ls in the real world have an asset not shown on our market-value balance sheet: the ability to generate new, profitable loans. This should increase the market value of a thrift above the market value of its outstanding loans less its existing debt.

25.6 SWAPS CONTRACTS

Swaps are close cousins to forwards and futures contracts. Swaps are arrangements between two counterparts to exchange cash flows over time. There is enormous flexibility in the forms that swaps can take, but the two basic types are **interest-rate swaps** or **currency swaps.** Often these are combined when interest received in one currency is swapped for interest in another currency.

Interest-Rate Swaps

Like other derivatives, swaps are tools that firms can use to easily change their risk exposures and their balance sheets.[22] Consider a firm that has borrowed and carried on its books an obligation to repay a 10-year loan for $100 million of principal with a 9-percent coupon rate paid annually. Ignoring the possibility of calling the loan, the firm expects to have to pay coupons of $9 million every year for 10 years and a balloon payment of $100 million at the end of the 10 years. Suppose, though, that the firm is uncomfortable with having this large fixed obligation on its books. Perhaps the firm is in a cyclical business where its revenues vary and could, conceivably, fall to a point where it would be difficult to make the debt payment.

Suppose, too, that the firm earns a lot of its revenue from financing the purchase of its products. Typically, for example, a manufacturer might help its customers finance their purchase of its products through a leasing or credit subsidiary. Usually these loans are for relatively short time periods and are financed at some premium over the prevailing short-term rate of interest. This puts the firm in the position of having revenues that move up and down with interest rates while its costs are relatively fixed.

This is a classic situation where a swap can be used to offset the risk. When interest rates rise, the firm would have to pay more on the loan, but it would be making more on its product financing. What the firm would really prefer is to have a floating-rate loan rather than a fixed-rate loan. It can use a swap to accomplish this.

Of course, the firm could also just go into the capital markets and borrow $100 million at a variable interest rate and then use the proceeds to retire its outstanding fixed-rate loan. While this is possible, it is generally quite expensive, requiring underwriting a new loan and the repurchase of the existing loan. The ease of entering into a swap is its inherent advantage.

The particular swap would be one that exchanged its fixed obligation for an agreement to pay a floating rate. Every six months it would agree to pay a coupon based on whatever the prevailing interest rate was at the time in exchange for an agreement from a counterparty to pay the firm's fixed coupon.

A common reference point for floating-rate commitments is called LIBOR. LIBOR stands for the London Interbank Offered Rate, and it is the rate that most international banks charge one another for dollar-denominated loans in the London market. LIBOR is commonly used as the reference rate for a floating-rate commitment, and, depending on the creditworthiness of the borrower, the rate can vary from LIBOR to LIBOR plus one point or more over LIBOR.

If we assume that our firm has a credit rating that requires it to pay LIBOR plus 50 basis points, then in a swap it would be exchanging its fixed 9-percent obligation for the obligation to pay whatever the prevailing LIBOR rate is plus 50 basis points. Figure 25.2 displays how the cash flows on this swap would work. In the figure we have assumed that LIBOR starts at 8 percent and rises for four years to 11 percent and then drops to 7 percent. As the figure

---

[22]Under current accounting rules, most derivatives do not usually show up on firms' balance sheets since they do not have an historical cost (i.e., the amount a dealer would pay on the initial transaction day).

■ FIGURE 25.2   **Fixed-for-Floating a Swap: Cash Flows ($ million)**

		Coupons									
	Year	1	2	3	4	5	6	7	8	9	10
A. Swap											
Fixed obligation	9	9	9	9	9	9	9	9	9	9	9
LIBOR floating	−8.5	−9.5	−10.5	−11.5	−7.5	−7.5	−7.5	−7.5	−7.5	−7.5	−7.5
B. Original Loan											
Fixed obligation	−9	−9	−9	−9	−9	−9	−9	−9	−9	−9	109
Net effect	−8.5	−9.5	10.5	11.5	7.5	7.5	7.5	7.5	7.5	7.5	−107.5

illustrates, the firm would owe a coupon of 8.5% × $100 million = $8.5 million in year 1, $9.5 million in year 2, $10.5 million in year 3, and $11.5 million in year 4. The precipitous drop to 7 percent lowers the annual payments to $7.5 million thereafter. In return, the firm receives the fixed payment of $9 million each year. Actually, rather than swapping the full payments, the cash flows would be netted. Since the firm is paying variable and receiving fixed—which it uses to pay its lender—in the first year, for example, the firm owes $8.5 million and is owed by its counterparty, who is paying fixed, $9 million. Hence, net, the firm would receive a payment of $.5 million. Since the firm has to pay its lender $9 million, but gets a net payment from the swap of $.5 million, it really only pays out the difference, or $8.5 million. In each year, then, the firm would effectively pay only LIBOR plus 50 basis points.

Notice, too, that the entire transaction can be carried out without any need to change the terms of the original loan. In effect, by swapping, the firm has found a counterparty who is willing to pay its fixed obligation in return for the firm paying a floating obligation.

Currency Swaps

FX stands for foreign exchange, and currency swaps are sometimes called FX swaps. Currency swaps are swaps of obligations to pay cash flows in one currency for obligations to pay in another currency.

Currency swaps arise as a natural vehicle for hedging the risk in international trade. For example, suppose a U.S. firm sells a broad range of its product line in the German market. Every year the firm can count on receiving revenue from Germany in the German currency, Deutschemarks, or DM for short. We will study international finance later in this book, but for now we can just observe that, because exchange rates fluctuate, this subjects the firm to considerable risk.

If the firm produces its products in the United States and exports them to Germany, then the firm has to pay its workers and its suppliers in dollars. But, it is receiving some of its revenues in DM. The exchange rate between $ and DM changes over time. As the DM rises in value, the German revenues are worth more $, but as it falls they decline. Suppose that the firm can count on selling 100 million DM of goods each year in Germany. If the exchange rate is 2 DM for each $, then the firm will receive $50 million. But, if the exchange rate were to rise to 3 DM for each $, the firm would only receive $33.333 million for its 100 million DM. Naturally the firm would like to protect itself against these currency swings.

To do so the firm can enter into a currency swap. We will learn more about exactly what the terms of such a swap might be, but for now we can assume that the swap is for five years at a fixed term of 100 million DM for $50 million each year. Now, no matter what happens to the exchange rate between DM and $ over the next five years, as long as the firm makes 100 million DM each year from the sale of its products, it will swap this for $50 million each year.

We have not addressed the question of how the market sets prices for swaps, either interest-rate swaps or currency swaps. In the fixed-for-floating example and in the currency swap, we just quoted some terms. We won't go into great detail on exactly how it is done, but we can stress the most important points.

Swaps, like forwards and futures, are essentially zero-sum transactions, which is to say that in both cases the market sets prices at a fair level, and neither party has any substantial bargain or loss at the moment the deal is struck. For example, in the currency swap, the swap rate is some average of the market expectation of what the exchange rate will be over the life of the swap. In the interest-rate swap, the rates are set as the fair floating and fixed rates for the creditor, taking into account the creditworthiness of the counterparties. We can actually price swaps fairly once we know how to price forward contracts. In our interest-rate swap example, the firm swapped LIBOR plus 50 basis points for a 9-percent fixed rate, all on a principal amount of $100 million. This is equivalent to a series of forward contracts extending out the life of the swap. In year 1, for example, having made the swap, the firm is in the same position that it would be if it had sold a forward contract entitling the buyer to receive LIBOR plus 50 basis points on $100 million in return for a fixed payment of $9 million (9 percent on $100 million). Similarly, the currency swap can also be viewed as a series of forward contracts.

QUESTION
CONCEPT
?

• Show that a currency swap is equivalent to a series of forward contracts.

Exotics

Up to now we have dealt with the meat and potatoes of the derivatives markets, swaps, options, forwards, and futures. **Exotics** are the complicated blends of these that often produce the surprising results for the buyers.

One of the more interesting types of exotics is called an *inverse floater.* In our fixed-for-floating swap, the floating payments fluctuated with LIBOR. An inverse floater is one that fluctuates inversely with some rate such as LIBOR. For example, the floater might pay an interest rate of 20 percent minus LIBOR. IF LIBOR is 9 percent, then the inverse pays 11 percent, and if LIBOR rises to 12 percent, the payments on the inverse would fall to 8 percent. Clearly the purchaser of an inverse profits from the inverse if interest rates fall.

Both floaters and inverse floaters have a supercharged version called *superfloaters* and *superinverses* that fluctuate more than one for one with movements in interest rates. As an example of a superinverse floater, consider a floater that pays an interest rate of 30 percent minus *twice* LIBOR. When LIBOR is 10 percent, the inverse pays

$$30\% - 2 \times 10\% = 30\% - 20\% = 10\%$$

and if LIBOR falls by 3 percent to 7 percent, then the return on the inverse rises by 6 percent from 10 percent to 16 percent,

$$30\% - 2 \times 7\% = 30\% - 14\% = 16\%$$

Sometimes derivatives are combined with options to bound the impact of interest rates. The most important of these instruments are called *caps* and *floors*. A cap is so named because it puts an upper limit or a cap on the impact of a rise in interest rates. A floor, conversely, provides a floor below which the interest rate impact is insulated.

To illustrate the impact of these, consider a firm that is borrowing short-term and is concerned that interest rates might rise. For example, using LIBOR as the reference interest rate, the firm might purchase a 7 percent cap. The cap pays the firm the difference between LIBOR and 7 percent on some principal amount, provided that LIBOR is greater than 7 percent. As long as LIBOR is below 7 percent, the holder of the cap receives no payments.

By purchasing the cap the firm has assured itself that even if interest rates rise above 7 percent, it will not have to pay more than a 7 percent rate. Suppose that interest rates rise to 9 percent. While the firm is borrowing short-term and paying 9 percent rates, this is offset by the cap, which is paying the firm the difference between 9 percent and the 7 percent limit. For any LIBOR rate above 7 percent, the firm receives the difference between LIBOR and 7 percent, and, as a consequence, it has capped its cost of borrowing at 7 percent.

On the other side, consider a financial firm that is in the business of lending short-term and is concerned that interest rates—and, consequently, its revenues—might fall. The firm could purchase a floor to protect itself from such declines. If the limit on the floor is 7 percent, then the floor pays the difference between 7 percent and LIBOR whenever LIBOR is below 7 percent, and nothing if LIBOR is above 7 percent. Thus, if interest rates were to fall to, say, 5 percent while the firm is only receiving 5 percent from its lending activities, the floor is paying it the difference between 7 percent and 5 percent, or an additional 2 percent. By purchasing the floor, the firm has assured itself of receiving no less than 7 percent from the combination of the floor and its lending activities.

We have only scratched the surface of what is available in the world of derivatives. Derivatives are designed to meet marketplace needs, and the only binding limitation is the human imagination. Nowhere should the buyer's warning *caveat emptor* be taken more seriously than in the derivatives markets, and this is especially true for the exotics. If swaps are the meat and potatoes of the derivatives markets, then caps and floors are the meat and potatoes of the exotics. As we have seen, they have obvious value as hedging instruments. But, much attention has been focused on truly exotic derivatives, some of which appear to have arisen more as the residuals that were left over from more straightforward deals. We won't examine these in any detail, but suffice it to say that some of these are so volatile and unpredictable that market participants have dubbed them "toxic waste."

25.7 ACTUAL USE OF DERIVATIVES

Because derivatives do not usually appear in financial statements, it is much more difficult to observe the use of derivatives by firms when compared to, say, bank debt. Much of our knowledge of corporate derivative use comes from academic surveys. Most surveys report that the use of derivatives appears to vary widespread among large publically traded firms. It appears that about one-half of all publically traded nonfinancial firms use derivatives of some kind.[23] Large firms are far more likely to use derivatives than small firms. Table 25.9 shows that for firms that use derivatives, foreign-currency and interest-rate derivatives are the most frequently used.[24]

---

[23]Gordon M. Bodnar, Gregory S. Hayt, and Richard Marston, "1998 Wharton Survey of Finance Risk Management by U.S. Non-Financial Firms," *Financial Management* (Winter 1998).

[24]Howton and Perfect report that interest rate derivatives are the most frequently used derivatives. Shawn D. Howton and Steven B. Perfect, "Currency and Interest-Rate Derivatives Use in U.S. Firms," *Financial Management* (Winter 1998).

■ TABLE 25.9 **Derivative Usage by Firms Using Derivatives**

	Exposure Managed with Derivatives	Exposure Not Managed with Derivatives
Foreign exchange	88%	12%
Interest rate	77%	23%
Commodity	55%	45%
Equity	30%	70%

Source: Gordon M. Bodnar, Gregory S. Hayt, and Richard Marston, "1998 Wharton Survey of Financial Risk Management of U.S. Non-Financial Firms," *Financial Management* (Winter 1998). Survey included 400 firms; 50 percent of the firms reported using derivatives.

The prevailing view is that derivatives can be very helpful in reducing the variability of firm cash flows, which, in turn, reduces the various costs associated with financial distress. Therefore, it is somewhat puzzling that large firms use derivatives more often than small firms—because large firms tend to have less cash flow variability than small firms. Also some surveys report that firms occasionally use derivatives when they want to speculate about future prices and not just to hedge risks.[25]

However, most of the evidence is consistent with the theory that derivatives are most frequently used by firms where financial distress costs are high and access to the capital markets is constrained.[26]

25.8 SUMMARY AND CONCLUSIONS

1. Firms hedge to reduce risk. This chapter shows a number of hedging strategies.
2. A forward contract is an agreement by two parties to sell an item for cash at a later date. The price is set at the time the agreement is signed. However, cash changes hands on the date of delivery. Forward contracts are generally not traded on organized exchanges.
3. Futures contracts are also agreements for future delivery. They have certain advantages, such as liquidity, that forward contracts do not. An unusual feature of futures contracts is the mark-to-the-market convention. If the price of a futures contract falls on a particular day, every buyer of the contract must pay money to the clearinghouse. Every seller of the contract receives money from the clearinghouse. Everything is reversed if the price rises. The mark-to-the-market convention prevents defaults on futures contracts.
4. We divided hedges into two types: short hedges and long hedges. An individual or firm that sells a futures contract to reduce risk is instituting a short hedge. Short hedges are generally appropriate for holders of inventory. An individual or firm that buys a futures contract to

[25]Walter Dolde, "The Trajectory of Corporate Financial Risk Management," *Journal of Applied Corporate Finance* (Fall 1993).

[26]Shawn D. Howton and Steven B. Perfect, "Currency and Interest-Rate Derivatives Use in U.S. Firms," *Financial Management* (Winter 1998). See also H. Berkman and M. E. Bradbury, "Empirical Evidence on the Corporate Use of Derivatives," *Financial Management* (Summer 1996).

reduce risk is instituting a long hedge. Long hedges are typically used by firms with contracts to sell finished goods at a fixed price.

5. An interest-rate futures contract employs a bond as the deliverable instrument. Because of their popularity, we worked with Treasury-bond futures contracts. We showed that Treasury-bond futures contracts can be priced using the same type of net-present-value analysis that is used to price Treasury bonds themselves.

6. Many firms are faced with interest-rate risk. They can reduce this risk by hedging with interest-rate futures contracts. As with other commodities, a short hedge involves the sale of a futures contract. Firms that are committed to buying mortgages or other bonds are likely to institute short hedges. A long hedge involves the purchase of a futures contract. Firms that have agreed to sell mortgages or other bonds at a fixed price are likely to institute long hedges.

7. Duration measures the average maturity of all the cash flows in a bond. Bonds with high duration have high price variability. Firms frequently try to match the duration of their assets with the duration of their liabilities.

8. Swaps are agreements to exchange cash flows over time. The first major type is an interest-rate swap in which one pattern of coupon payments, say, fixed payments, is exchanged for another, say, coupons that float with LIBOR. The second major type is a currency swap in which an agreement is struck to swap payments denominated in one currency for payments in another currency over time.

Key Terms

Advance commitments 712	Immunized 719
Cash transaction 697	Interest-rate swaps 721
Currency swaps 721	Long hedge 704
Deliverable instrument 696	Making delivery 696
Duration 716	Marked to the market 698
Exotics 723	Short hedge 703
Forward contract 696	Speculating 696
Futures contract 697	Swaps 721
Hedging 696	Taking delivery 696

Suggested Readings

Several cases that illustrate the concepts, tools, and markets for hedging can be found in
Tufano, Peter. "How Financial Engineering Can Advance Corporate Strategy." *Harvard Business Review* (January–February 1996).

An advanced article on the empirical implications of very recent models for pricing swaps contracts is in
Minton, Bernadette A. "An Empirical Examination of Basic Valuation Models for Plain Vanilla U.S. Interest Rate Swaps." *Journal of Financial Economics* 44 (Winter 1997).

Questions and Problems

Futures and Forward Contracts

25.1 Define:
   a. Forward contract
   b. Futures contract

25.2 Explain the three ways in which futures contracts and forward contracts differ.

25.3 The following table lists the closing prices for wheat futures contracts. Suppose you bought one contract at $5.00 at the opening of trade on March 15.

March 15	$5.03
March 16	$5.08
March 17	$5.12
March 18	$5.10
March 19	$4.98

    a. Suppose that on March 18 you receive from your broker a notice of delivery on that day.
       i. What is the delivery price?
      ii. What price did you pay for wheat?
     iii. List the cash flows associated with this contract.
    b. Suppose that on March 19 you receive from your broker a notice of delivery on that day.
       i. What is the delivery price?
      ii. What price did you pay for wheat?
     iii. List the cash flows associated with this contract.

25.4 Two days ago, you agreed to buy a 10-year, zero-coupon bond that would be issued in a year. Today, both the 1-year and 11-year spot rates unexpectedly shifted downward an equal amount. What should today's price of the forward contract be?

25.5 *a.* How is a short hedge created?
    b. In what type of situation is a short hedge a wise strategy?
    c. How is a long hedge created?
    d. In what type of situation is a long hedge a wise strategy?

25.6 A speculator is an investor who uses his or her private information to profit from futures contracts. Mary Johnson is a speculator, who believes that wheat futures prices will fall in a month. What position would Mary Johnson take?

25.7 A classmate of yours recently entered the import/export business. During a visit with him last week, he said to you, "If you play the game right, this is the safest business in the world. By hedging all my transactions in the foreign-exchange futures market, I eliminate all risk."

      Do you agree with your friend's assessment of hedging? Why or why not?

25.8 This morning you agreed to buy a two-year Treasury bond six months from today. The bond carries a 10-percent coupon rate and has a $1,000 face. Below are listed the expected spot rates of interest for the life of the bond. These rates are semiannual rates.

Time from Today	Semiannual Rate
6 months	0.048
12 months	0.050
18 months	0.052
24 months	0.055
30 months	0.057

    a. How much should you have paid for this forward contract?
    b. Suppose that shortly after you purchased the forward contract, all semiannual rates increased 30 *basis points;* that is, the six-month rate increased from 0.048 to 0.051.
       i. State what you expect will happen to the value of the forward contract.
      ii. What is the value of the forward contract?

25.9 Derive the relationship between the spot price (S_0) and the futures price (F) by comparing the following two strategies:

      Strategy 1: Buy the silver at S_0 today and hold it for one month.
      Strategy 2: Take a long position on the silver futures contract expiring in one month. Lend money that will be equal to the futures price in one month. The lending rate for the period is the risk-free rate, r_f.

25.10 Aiko Miyazawa is a Japanese student who is planning a one-year stay in America for studying English. She expects to leave for America in eight months. Since she is worried about the unstable exchange rates, she has decided to lock in the current exchange rates. What should Aiko's hedging position be?

25.11 After reading the text's example about Ron Cooke, the mortgage banker, you decide to enter the business. You begin small; you agree to provide $300,000 to an old college roommate to finance the purchase of her home. The loan is a 20-year loan and has a 10-percent interest rate. Ten percent is the current market rate of interest. For ease of computation, assume the mortgage payments are made annually. Your former roommate needs the money four months from today. You do not have $300,000, but you intend to sell the mortgage to MAX Insurance Corp. The president of MAX is also an old friend, so you know with certainty that he will buy the mortgage. Unfortunately, he is unavailable to meet with you until three months from today.
   a. What is your former roommate's mortgage payment?
   b. What is the most significant risk you face in this deal?
   c. How can you hedge this risk?

25.12 Refer to question 25.11. There are four-month T-bond futures available. A single contract is for $100,000 of T-bonds.
   a. Suppose that between today and your meeting with the president of MAX, the market rate of interest rises to 12 percent.
      i. How much is MAX's president willing to pay you for the mortgage?
      ii. What will happen to the value of the T-bond futures contract?
      iii. What is your net gain or loss if you wrote a futures contract?
   b. Suppose that between today and your meeting with the president of MAX, the market rate of interest falls to 9 percent.
      i. How much is MAX's president willing to pay you for the mortgage?
      ii. What will happen to the value of the T-bond futures contract?
      iii. What is your net gain or loss if you wrote a futures contract?

Duration

25.13 Available are three zero-coupon, $1,000 face-value bonds. All of these bonds are initially priced using an 11-percent interest rate. Bond *A* matures one year from today, bond *B* matures five years from today, and bond *C* matures 10 years from today.
   a. What is the current price of each bond?
   b. If the market rate of interest rises to 14 percent, what will be the prices of these bonds?
   c. Which bond experienced the greatest percentage change in price?

25.14 Calculate the duration of a perpetuity that pays $100 at each year-end. Assume the annual discount rate of 12 percent. What if the discount rate is 10 percent?

25.15 Consider two four-year bonds. Each bond has a $1,000 face value. Bond *A*'s coupon rate is 7 percent, while bond *B*'s coupon rate is 11 percent.
   a. What is the price of each bond when the market rate of interest is 10 percent?
   b. What is the price of each bond when the market rate of interest is 7 percent?
   c. Which bond experienced the greatest percentage change in price?
   d. Explain your (*c*) result.

25.16 Calculate the duration of a three-year, $1,000 face-value bond with a 9-percent coupon rate, selling at par.

25.17 Calculate the duration of a four-year, $1,000 face-value bond with a 9-percent coupon rate, selling at par.

25.18 Calculate the duration of a four-year, $1,000 face-value bond with a 5-percent coupon rate, selling at par.

25.19 Mr. and Mrs. Chaikovski have a son who is going to enter a music college three years from today. Annual school expenses of $20,000 will occur at the beginning of each year for four years. What is the duration of Mr. and Mrs. Chaikovski's liability as parents? Assume the annual borrowing rate of 15 percent.

25.20 The following balance sheet is for Besdall Community Bank.

	Market Value	Duration
Assets		
Federal funds deposits	$ 43 million	0
Accounts-receivable loans	615 million	4 months
Short-term loans	345 million	9 months
Long-term loans	55 million	5 years
Mortgages	197 million	15 years
Liabilities and Equity		
Checking and savings deposits	$490 million	0
Certificates of deposit	370 million	18 months
Long-term financing	250 million	10 years
Equity	145 million	

    a. What is the duration of Besdall's assets?

    b. What is the duration of Besdall's liabilities?

    c. Is Besdall Community Bank immune from interest-rate risk?

25.21 Refer to the previous problem. To what values must the durations of Besdall Community Bank change to make the bank immune from interest-rate risk if

    a. Only the durations of the liabilities change?

    b. Only the durations of the assets change?

25.22 Consider the following balance sheet for California Commercial Bank.

CALIFORNIA COMMERCIAL BANK
Market Value Balance Sheet

	Market Value ($ million)	Duration
Assets		
Overnight money	$ 100	0
Loans	500	1 year
Mortgages	1,200	12 years
	$1,800	
Liabilities and Equity		
Checking and savings accounts	$ 300	0
Certificates of deposit	400	1.1 year
Long-term debt	500	18.9 years
Equity	600	
	$1,800	

    a. What is the duration of California's assets? What is the duration of liabilities?

    b. Is the bank immunized from interest-rate risk?

Swaps

25.23 The Miller Company and the Edwards Company both need to raise money to fund facilities improvements at their manufacturing plants in New York. Miller has been in business for 40 years and has a very good credit rating. It can borrow money at either 10 percent or at the LIBOR + .03 percent floating rate. The Edwards Company has experienced some financial distress recently and does not have a strong credit history. It can borrow funds at 15 percent or 2 percent over the LIBOR rate.

    a. Is there an opportunity for the Miller Company and the Edwards Company to benefit from a swap?

    b. Show how you would structure a swap transaction between Miller and Edwards.

Financial Planning and Short-Term Finance

Financial planning establishes the blueprint for change in a firm. It is necessary because (1) it includes putting forth the firm's goals to motivate the organization and provide benchmarks for performance measurement, (2) the firm's financing and investment decisions are not independent and their interaction must be identified, and (3) the firm must anticipate changing conditions and surprises.

Most of Chapter 26 is devoted to long-term financial planning. Long-term financial planning incorporates decisions such as capital budgeting, capital structure, and dividend policy. An important part of Chapter 26 is the discussion of building corporate financial models. Here we introduce the concept of sustainable growth and show that a firm's growth rate depends on its operating characteristics (profit margin and asset turnover) and financial policies (dividend policy and capital structure).

In Chapter 27 we introduce short-term financial planning, which involves short-lived assets and liabilities. We discuss two aspects of short-term financial planning: (1) the size of the firm's investment in current assets, such as cash, accounts receivable, and inventory, and (2) how to finance short-term assets. We describe the primary tool for short-term financial planning, the cash budget. It incorporates the short-term financial goals of the firm and tells the financial manager the amount of necessary short-term financing.

In Chapter 28 we describe the management of a firm's investment in cash. The chapter divides cash management into three separate areas:

1. Determining the appropriate target cash balance.
2. Collecting and disbursing cash.
3. Investing the excess cash in marketable securities.

Chapter 29 describes what is involved when a firm makes the decision to grant credit to its customers. This decision involves three types of analysis:

1. A firm must decide on the conditions under which it sells its goods and services for credit. These conditions are the terms of the sale.
2. Before granting credit, the firm must analyze the risk that the customer will not pay; this is called *credit analysis.*
3. After credit is extended, the firm must determine how to collect its cash.

CHAPTER 26

Corporate Financial Models and Long-Term Planning

EXECUTIVE SUMMARY

Financial planning establishes guidelines for change in the firm. These guidelines should include (1) an identification of the firm's financial goals, (2) an analysis of the differences between these goals and the current financial status of the firm, and (3) a statement of the actions needed for the firm to achieve its financial goals. In other words, as one member of GM's board was heard to say, "Planning is a process that at best helps the firm avoid stumbling into the future backwards."

The basic policy elements of financial planning have been put forth in various chapters in this book. They comprise (1) the investment opportunities the firm elects to take advantage of, (2) the degree of financial leverage the firm chooses to employ, and (3) the amount of cash the firm thinks is necessary and appropriate to pay shareholders. These are the financial policies that the firm must decide upon for its growth and profitability.

Almost all firms use an explicit, companywide growth rate as a major component of their long-run financial planning. In one famous case International Business Machines' stated growth goal was simple but typical: to match the growth of the computer industry, which was projected to 15 percent per year through the end of the 1990's.[1] Though we may have had some doubts about IBM's ability to sustain a 15-percent growth rate, we are certain there are important financial implications of the strategies that IBM will adopt to achieve that rate. There are direct connections between the growth that a company can achieve and its financial policy. One purpose of this chapter is to look at the financial aspects of strategic decisions.

The chapter first describes what is usually meant by corporate financial planning. Mostly we talk about long-term financial planning. Short-term financial planning is discussed in the next chapter. We examine what the firm can accomplish by developing a long-term financial plan. This enables us to make an important point: Investment and financing decisions frequently interact. The different interactions of investment and financing decisions can be analyzed in the planning model.

Finally, financial planning forces the corporation to think about goals. The goal most frequently espoused by corporations is growth. Indeed, one of the consequences of accepting positive NPV projects is growth. We show how financial-planning models can be used to better understand how growth is achieved.

---

[1] See *The Wall Street Journal*, June 12, 1985. IBM's actual annual growth rate in revenues was considerably lower than 15 percent. From 1985 to 1994, IBM's growth in annual revenues was closer to 6 percent. In the last five years, its revenues have grown at an annual rate of 2.5 percent.

26.1 WHAT IS CORPORATE FINANCIAL PLANNING?

Financial planning formulates the method by which financial goals are to be achieved. It has two dimensions: a time frame and a level of aggregation.

A financial plan is a statement of what is to be done in a future time. The GM board member was right on target when he explained the virtues of financial planning. Most decisions have long lead times, which means they take a long time to implement. In an uncertain world, this requires that decisions be made far in advance of their implementation. If a firm wants to build a factory in 2003, it may need to line up contractors in 2001. It is sometimes useful to think of the future as having a short run and a long run. The short run, in practice, is usually the coming 12 months. Initially, we focus our attention on financial planning over the long run, which is usually taken to be a two-year to five-year period of time.

Financial plans are compiled from the capital-budgeting analyses of each of a firm's projects. In effect, the smaller investment proposals of each operational unit are added up and treated as a big project. This process is called **aggregation.**

Financial plans always entail alternative sets of assumptions. For example, suppose a company has two separate divisions: one for consumer products and one for gas turbine engines. The financial-planning process might require each division to prepare three alternative business plans for the next three years.

1. *A Worst Case.* This plan would require making the worst possible assumptions about the company's products and the state of the economy. It could mean divestiture and liquidation.

2. *A Normal Case.* This plan would require making the most likely assumptions about the company and the economy.

3. *A Best Case.* Each division would be required to work out a case based on the most optimistic assumptions. It could involve new products and expansion.

Because the company is likely to spend a lot of time preparing proposals on different scenarios that will become the basis for the company's financial plan, it seems reasonable to ask what the planning process will accomplish.

1. *Interactions.* The financial plan must make the linkages between investment proposals for the different operating activities of the firm and the financing choices available to the firm explicit. IBM's 15-percent growth target goes hand in hand with its financing program.

2. *Options.* The financial plan provides the opportunity for the firm to work through various investment and financing options. The firm addresses questions of what financing arrangements are optimal, and evaluates options of closing plants or marketing new products.

3. *Feasibility.* The different plans must fit into the overall corporate objective of maximizing shareholder wealth.

4. *Avoiding Surprises.* Financial planning should identify what may happen in the future if certain events take place. Thus, one of the purposes of financial planning is to avoid surprises.

CONCEPT QUESTIONS

? • What are the two dimensions of the financial planning process?
  • Why should firms draw up financial plans?

26.2 A FINANCIAL-PLANNING MODEL: THE INGREDIENTS

Just as companies differ in size and products, financial plans are not the same for all companies. However, there are some common elements:

1. **Sales forecast.** All financial plans require a sales forecast. Perfectly accurate sales forecasts are not possible, because sales depend on the uncertain future state of the economy. Firms can get help from businesses specializing in macroeconomic and industry projections.

2. **Pro forma statements.** The financial plan will have a forecast balance sheet, an income statement, and a sources-and-uses statement. These are called *pro forma statements,* or *pro formas.*

3. **Asset requirements.** The plan will describe projected capital spending. In addition, it will discuss the proposed uses of net working capital.

4. **Financial requirements.** The plan will include a section on financing arrangements. This part of the plan should discuss dividend policy and debt policy. Sometimes firms will expect to raise equity by selling new shares of stock. In this case the plan must consider what kinds of securities must be sold and what methods of issuance are most appropriate.

5. **Plug.** Suppose a financial planner assumes that sales, costs, and net income will rise at a particular rate, g_1. Further suppose that the planner wants assets and liabilities to grow at a different rate, g_2. These two different growth rates may be incompatible unless a third variable is also adjusted. For example, compatibility may only be reached if outstanding stock grows at a different rate, g_3. In this example, we treat the growth in outstanding stock as the *plug* variable. That is, the growth rate in outstanding stock is chosen to make the growth rate in income-statement items consistent with the growth rate in balance-sheet items. Surprisingly, even if the income-statement items grow at the *same* rate as the balance-sheet items, consistency might be achieved only if outstanding stock grows at a different rate.

   Of course, the growth rate in outstanding stock need not be the plug variable. One could have income-statement items grow at g_1, and assets, long-term debt, and outstanding stock grow at g_2. In this case, compatibility between g_1 and g_2 might be achieved by letting short-term debt grow at a rate of g_3.

6. **Economic assumptions.** The plan must explicitly state the economic environment in which the firm expects to reside over the life of the plan. Among the economic assumptions that must be made is the level of interest rates.

EXAMPLE

The Computerfield Corporation's 20X1 financial statements are as follows:

Income Statement 20X1		Balance Sheet Year-End 20X1			
Sales	$1,000	Assets	$500	Debt	$250
Costs	800			Equity	250
Net income	$ 200	Total	$500	Total	$500

In 20X1, Computerfield's profit margin is 20 percent, and it has never paid a dividend. Its debt-equity ratio is 1. This is also the firm's *target* debt-equity ratio. Unless otherwise stated, the financial planners at Computerfield assume that all variables are tied directly to sales and that current relationships are optimal.

Suppose that sales increase by 20 percent from 20X1 to 20X2. Because the planners would then also forecast a 20-percent increase in costs, the pro forma income statement would be

Income Statement
20X2

Sales	$1,200
Costs	960
Net income	$ 240

The assumption that all variables will grow by 20 percent will enable us to construct the pro forma balance sheet as well:

Balance Sheet
Year-End 20X2

Assets	$600	Debt	$300
		Equity	300
Total	$600	Total	$600

Now we must reconcile these two pro formas. How, for example, can net income be equal to $240 and equity increase by only $50? The answer is that Computerfield must have paid a dividend or repurchased stock equal to $190. In this case dividends are the plug variable.

Suppose Computerfield does not pay a dividend and does not repurchase its own stock. With these assumptions, Computerfield's equity will grow to $490, and debt must be retired to keep total assets equal to $600. In this case the debt-to-equity ratio is the plug variable. This example shows the interaction of sales growth and financial policy. The next example focuses on the need for external funds. It identifies a six-step procedure for constructing the pro forma balance sheet.

EXAMPLE

The Rosengarten Corporation is thinking of acquiring a new machine. With this new machine the company expects sales to increase from $20 million to $22 million—10-percent growth. The corporation believes that its assets and liabilities vary directly with its level of sales. Its profit margin on sales is 10 percent, and its dividend-payout ratio is 50 percent.

The company's current balance sheet (reflecting the purchase of the new machine) is as follows:

Current Balance Sheet		Pro Forma Balance Sheet	
			Explanation
Current assets	$ 6,000,000	$ 6,600,000	30% of sales
Fixed assets	24,000,000	26,400,000	120% of sales
Total assets	$30,000,000	$33,000,000	150% of sales
Short-term debt	$10,000,000	$11,000,000	50% of sales
Long-term debt	6,000,000	6,600,000	30% of sales
Common stock	4,000,000	4,000,000	Constant
Retained earnings	10,000,000	11,100,000	Net income
Total financing	$30,000,000	$32,700,000	
		$ 300,000	Funds needed (the difference between total assets and total financing)

From this information we can determine the pro forma balance sheet, which is on the right-hand side. The change in retained earnings will be

$$\text{Net income} \quad - \quad \text{Dividends} \quad = \quad \text{Change in retained earnings}$$
$$(0.10 \times \$22 \text{ million}) - (0.5 \times 0.10 \times \$22 \text{ million}) = \$1.1 \text{ million}$$

In this example the plug variable is new shares of stock. The company must issue $300,000 of new stock. The equation that can be used to determine if external funds are needed is

External Funds Needed (EFN):

$$\left(\frac{\text{Assets}}{\text{Sales}}\right) \times \Delta \text{Sales} - \frac{\text{Debt}}{\text{Sales}} \times \Delta \text{Sales} - (p \times \text{Projected sales}) \times (1 - d)$$
$$= (1.5 \times \$2 \text{ million}) - (0.80 \times \$2 \text{ million}) - (0.10 \times \$22 \text{ million} \times 0.5)$$
$$= \$1.4 \text{ million} \qquad\qquad - \$1.1 \text{ million}$$
$$= \$0.3 \text{ million}$$

where

$$\frac{\text{Assets}}{\text{Sales}} = 1.5$$
$$\frac{\text{Debt}}{\text{Sales}} = 0.8$$
$$p = \text{Net profit margin} = 0.10$$
$$d = \text{Dividend payout ratio} = 0.5$$
$$\Delta \text{Sales} = \text{Projected change in sales}$$

The steps in the estimation of the pro forma sheet for the Rosengarten Corporation and the external funds needed (EFN) are as follows:

1. Express balance-sheet items that vary with sales as a percentage of sales.
2. Multiply the percentages determined in step (1) by projected sales to obtain the amount for the future period.
3. Where no percentage applies, simply insert the previous balance-sheet figure in the future period.

4. Compute projected retained earnings as follows:

Projected retained earnings = Present retained earnings
+ Projected net income − Cash dividends

5. Add the asset accounts to determine projected assets. Next, add the liabilities and equity accounts to determine the total financing; any difference is the *shortfall*. This equals external funds needed (EFN).
6. Use the plug to fill EFN.

Table 26.1 computes EFN for several different growth rates. For low growth rates, Rosengarten will run a surplus, and for high growth rates, it will run a deficit. The "break-even" growth rate is 7.7 percent. Figure 26.1 illustrates the relation between projected sales

■ **TABLE 26.1 Projected Sales Growth and EFN for the Rosengarten Corporation**

Projected Sales Growth	Increase in Assets Required	Addition to Retained Earnings	External Financing Needed (EFN)	Projected Debt-to-Equity Ratio
0%	$ 0	$1,000,000	−$1,000,000	83.6%
5	1,500,000	1,050,000	−350,000	86.8
7.7	2,310,000	1,077,000	—	89.2
10	3,000,000	1,100,000	300,000	91.2
20	6,000,000	1,200,000	1,600,000	100.0

■ **FIGURE 26.1 Growth and EFN for the Rosengarten Corporation**

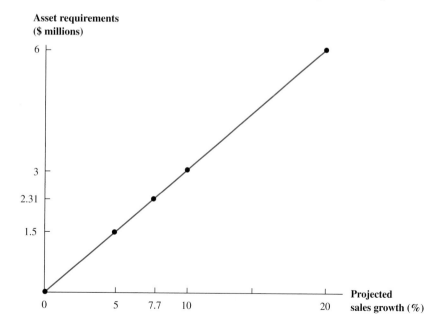

growth and EFN. As can be seen, the need for new assets from projected sales growth grows much faster than the additions to retained earnings plus new debt. Eventually, a deficit is created and a need for external financing becomes evident.

26.3 WHAT DETERMINES GROWTH?

Firms frequently make growth forecasts an explicit part of financial planning. Donaldson reports on the pervasiveness of stating corporate goals in terms of growth rates.[2] This may seem puzzling in the light of our previous emphasis on maximizing the firm's value as the central goal of management. One way to reconcile the difference is to think of growth as an intermediate goal that leads to higher value. Rappaport correctly points out that, in applying the NPV approach, growth should not be a goal but must be a consequence of decisions that maximize NPV.[3] In fact, if the firm is willing to accept negative NPV projects just to grow in size, growth will probably make the stockholders (but perhaps not the managers) worse off.

Donaldson also concludes that most major industrial companies are very reluctant to use external equity as a regular part of their financial planning. To illustrate the linkages between the ability of a firm to grow and its financial policy when the firm does not issue equity, we can make some planning assumptions.

1. The firm's assets will grow in proportion to its sales.
2. Net income is a constant proportion of its sales.
3. The firm has a given dividend-payout policy and a given debt-equity ratio.
4. The firm will not change the number of outstanding shares of stock.

There is only one growth rate that is consistent with the preceding assumptions. In effect, with these assumptions, growth has been made a plug variable. To see this, recall that a change in assets must always be equal to a change in debt plus a change in equity:

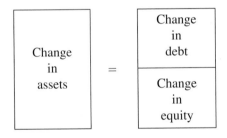

Now we can write the conditions that ensure this equality and solve for the growth rate that will give it to us.

---

[2]G. Donaldson, *Managing Corporation Wealth: The Operations of a Comprehensive Financial Goals System* (New York: Praeger, 1984).

[3]A. Rappaport, *Creating Shareholder Value: The New Standard for Business Performance* (New York: Free Press, 1986).

The variables used in this demonstration are the following:

T = The ratio of total assets to sales
p = The net profit margin on sales
d = The dividend-payout ratio
L = The debt-equity ratio
S_0 = Sales this year
ΔS = The change in sales ($S_1 - S_0 = \Delta S$)
S_1 = Next year's projected sales
RE = Retained earnings = Net income $\times$ Retention ratio = $S_1 \times p \times (1 - d)$
NI = Net income = $S_1 \times p$

If the firm is to increase sales by ΔS during the year, it must increase assets by $T\Delta S$. The firm is assumed not to be able to change the number of shares of stock outstanding, so the equity financing must come from retained earnings. Retained earnings will depend on next year's sales, the payout ratio, and the profit margin. The amount of borrowing will depend on the amount of retained earnings and the debt-equity ratio.

$$
\begin{array}{ll}
\text{New equity:} & S_1 \times p \times (1 - d) \\
\text{plus} & \\
\text{Borrowing:} & [S_1 \times p \times (1 - d)] \times L \\
\text{equals} & \\
\text{Capital spending:} & T\Delta S
\end{array}
$$

Moving things around a little gives the following:

$$T\Delta S = [S_1 \times p \times (1 - d)] + [S_1 \times p \times (1 - d) \times L]$$

and

$$\frac{\Delta S}{S_0} = \frac{p \times (1 - d) \times (1 + L)}{T - (p \times (1 - d) \times (1 + L))} = \text{Growth rate in sales} \qquad (26.1)$$

This is the growth-rate equation. Given the profit margin (p), the payout ratio (d), the debt-equity ratio (L), and the asset-requirement ratio (T), the growth rate can be determined.[4] It is the only growth possible with the preset values for the four variables. Higgins has referred to this growth rate as the firm's **sustainable growth rate.**[5]

EXAMPLE

Table 26.2 shows the current income statement, the sources-and-uses-of-funds statement, and the balance sheet for the Hoffman Corporation. Net income for the corporation was 16.5 percent ($1,650/$10,000) of sales revenue. The company paid out 72.4 percent ($1,195/$1,650) of its net income in dividends. The interest rate on debt was 10 percent, and the long-term debt was 50 percent ($5,000/$10,000) of assets. (Notice that, for simplicity, we use the single term *net working capital,* in

---

[4]This is approximately equal to the rate of return on equity (ROE) multiplied by the retention rate (RR): ROE $\times$ RR. This expression is only precisely equal to equation (26.1) above in continuous time; otherwise it is an approximation. More precisely,

$$\text{Growth rate in sales} = \frac{\text{ROE} \times \text{RR}}{1 - (\text{ROE} \times \text{RR})}$$

[5]R. C. Higgins, "Sustainable Growth under Inflation," *Financial Management* (Autumn 1981). The definition of sustainable growth was popularized by the Boston Consulting Group and others.

■ TABLE 26.2 **Current Financial Statements:**
The Hoffman Corporation (in thousands)

THE HOFFMAN CORPORATION
Income Statement

	This Year
Net sales (S)	$10,000
Cost of sales	7,000
Earnings before taxes and interest	3,000
Interest expense	500
Earnings before taxes	2,500
Taxes	850
Net income (NI)	$ 1,650

Sources and Uses of Cash

	This Year
Sources:	
Net income (NI)	$ 1,650
Depreciation	500
Operating cash flow	2,150
Borrowing	455
New stock issue	0
Total sources	$ 2,605
Uses:	
Increase in net working capital	455
Capital spending	955
Dividends	1,195
Total uses	$ 2,605

Balance Sheet

	This Year	*Last Year*	*Change*
Assets			
Net working capital	$ 5,000	$4,545	$455
Fixed assets	5,000	4,545	455
Total assets	$10,000	$9,090	$910
Liabilities and Stockholders' Equity			
Debt	$ 5,000	$4,545	$455
Equity	5,000	4,545	455
Total liabilities and stockholders' equity	$10,000	$9,090	$910

Table 26.2, instead of separating current assets from current liabilities.) Hoffman's assets grew at the rate of 10 percent ($910/$9,090). In addition, sales grew at 10 percent, though this increase is not shown in Table 26.2.

The cash flow generated by Hoffman was enough not only to pay a dividend but also to increase net working capital and fixed assets by $455 each. The company did not issue any shares of stock during the year. Its debt-equity ratio and dividend-payout ratio remained constant throughout the year.

The sustainable growth rate for the Hoffman Corporation is 10 percent, or

$$\frac{0.165 \times 0.276 \times 2}{1 - (0.165 \times 0.276 \times 2)} = 0.1$$

However, suppose its desired growth rate was to be 20 percent. It is possible for Hoffman's desired growth to exceed its sustainable growth because Hoffman is able to issue new shares of stock. A firm can do several things to increase its sustainable growth rate as seen from the Hoffman example:

1. Sell new shares of stock.
2. Increase its reliance on debt.
3. Reduce its dividend-payout ratio.
4. Increase profit margins.
5. Decrease its asset-requirement ratio.

Now we can see the use of a financial-planning model to test the feasibility of the planned growth rate. If sales are to grow at a rate higher than the sustainable growth rate, the firm must improve operating performance, increase financial leverage, decrease dividends, or sell new shares. Of course, the planned rates of growth should be the result of a complete NPV-based planning process.

QUESTIONS
CONCEPT

- When might the goals of growth and value maximization be in conflict, and when would they be aligned?
- What are the determinants of growth?

26.4 SOME CAVEATS OF FINANCIAL-PLANNING MODELS

Financial-planning models suffer from a great deal of criticism. We present two commonly voiced attacks below.

First, financial-planning models do not indicate which financial policies are the best. For example, our model could not tell us whether Hoffman's decision to issue new equity to achieve a higher growth rate raises the NPV of the firm.

Second, financial-planning models are too simple. In reality, costs are not always proportional to sales, assets need not be a fixed percentage of sales, and capital-budgeting involves a sequence of decisions over time. These assumptions are generally not incorporated into financial plans.

Financial-planning models are necessary to assist in planning the future investment and financial decisions of the firm. Without some sort of long-term financial plan, the firm may find itself adrift in a sea of change without a rudder for guidance. But, because of the assumptions and the abstractions from reality necessary in the construction of the financial plan, we also think that they should carry the label: Let the user beware!

IN THEIR OWN WORDS

Robert C. Higgins on Sustainable Growth

Most financial officers know intuitively that it takes money to make money. Rapid sales growth requires increased assets in the form of accounts receivable, inventory, and fixed plant, which, in turn, require money to pay for assets. They also know that if their company does not have the money when needed, it can literally "grow broke." The sustainable growth equation states these intuitive truths explicitly.

Sustainable growth is often used by bankers and other external analysts to assess a company's credit-worthiness. They are aided in this exercise by several sophisticated computer software packages that provide detailed analyses of the company's past financial performance, including its annual sustainable growth rate.

Bankers use this information in several ways. Quick comparison of a company's actual growth rate to its sustainable rate tells the banker what issues will be at the top of management's financial agenda. If actual growth consistently exceeds sustainable growth, management's problem will be where to get the cash to finance growth. The banker thus can anticipate interest in loan products. Conversely, if sustainable growth consistently exceeds actual, the banker had best be prepared to talk about investment products, because management's problem will be what to do with all the cash that keeps piling up in the till.

Bankers also find the sustainable growth equation useful for explaining to financially inexperienced small business owners and overly optimistic entrepreneurs that, for the long-run viability of their business, it is necessary to keep growth and profitability in proper balance.

Finally, comparison of actual to sustainable growth rates helps a banker understand why a loan applicant needs money and for how long the need might continue. In one instance, a loan applicant requested $100,000 to pay off several insistent suppliers and promised to repay in a few months when he collected some accounts receivable that were coming due. A sustainable growth analysis revealed that the firm had been growing at four to six times its sustainable growth rate and that this pattern was likely to continue in the foreseeable future. This alerted the banker that impatient suppliers were only a symptom of the much more fundamental disease of overly rapid growth, and that a $100,000 loan would likely prove to be only the down payment on a much larger, multiyear commitment.

Robert C. Higgins is Professor of Finance at the University of Washington. He pioneered the use of sustainable growth as a tool for financial analysis.

26.5 SUMMARY AND CONCLUSIONS

Financial planning forces the firm to think about and forecast the future. It involves the following:

1. Building a corporate financial model.
2. Describing different scenarios of future development from worst to best cases.
3. Using the models to construct pro forma financial statements.
4. Running the model under different scenarios (conducting sensitivity analysis).
5. Examining the financial implications of ultimate strategic plans.

Corporate financial planning should not become a purely mechanical activity. If it does, it will probably focus on the wrong things. In particular, plans are formulated all too often in terms of a growth target with an explicit linkage to creation of value. Nonetheless, the alternative to financial planning is stumbling into the future.

Key Terms

Suggested Readings

Approaches to building a financial planning model are contained in:

Carleton, W. T., and C. L. Dick, Jr. "Financial Policy Models: Theory and Practice." *Journal of Financial and Quantitative Analysis* 8 (1973).

Francis, J. C., and D. R. Rowell. "A Simultaneous-Equation Model of the Firm for Financial Analysis and Planning." *Financial Management* (Spring 1978).

Myers, S. C., and G. A. Pogue. "A Programming Approach to Corporate Financial Management." *Journal of Finance* 29 (May 1974).

Warren, J. M., and J. R. Shelton. "A Simultaneous-Equation Approach to Financial Planning." *Journal of Finance* (December 1971).

The most extensive textbook treatment of financial planning:

Lee, C. F. *Financial Analysis and Planning: Theory and Application.* Reading, Mass.: Addison-Wesley, 1985.

For a critical discussion of sustainable growth, see:

Rappaport, A. *Creating Shareholder Value: The New Standard for Business Performance.* New York: Free Press, 1986.

Questions and Problems

Financial-Planning Models: The Ingredients

26.1 After examining patterns from recent years, management found the following regression-estimated relationships between some company balance sheets and income statement accounts and sales.

$$CA = 0.5 \text{ million} + 0.25S$$
$$FA = 1.0 \text{ million} + 0.50S$$
$$CL = 0.1 \text{ million} + 0.10S$$
$$NP = 0.0 \text{ million} + 0.02S$$

where

CA = Current assets
FA = Fixed assets
CL = Current liabilities
NP = Net profit after taxes
S = Sales

The company's sales for last year were $10 million. The year-end balance sheet is reproduced below.

Current assets	$3,000,000	Current liabilities	$1,100,000
Fixed assets	6,000,000	Bonds	2,500,000
		Common stock	2,000,000
		Retained earnings	3,400,000
Total	$9,000,000	Total	$9,000,000

Management further found that the company's sales bear a relationship to GNP. That relationship is

$$S = 0.00001 \times \text{GNP}$$

The forecast of GNP for next year is $2.05 trillion. The firm pays out 34 percent of net profits after taxes in dividends.

Create a pro forma balance sheet for this firm.

26.2 Cheryl Colby, the CFO of Charming Florist Ltd. has created the firm's pro forma balance sheet for the next fiscal year. Sales are projected to grow at 10 percent to the level of $330 million. Current assets, fixed assets, short-term debt, and long-term debt are 25 percent, 150 percent, 40 percent, and 45 percent of the total sales, respectively. Charming Florist pays out 40 percent of net income. The value of common stock is constant at $50 million. The profit margin on sales is 12 percent.

   a. Based on Ms. Colby's forecast, how much external fund does Charming Florist need?

   b. Reconstruct the current balance sheet based on the projected figures.

   c. Lay out the firm's pro forma balance sheet for the next fiscal year.

What Determines Growth?

26.3 The Stieben Company has determined that the following will be true next year:

T = Ratio of total assets to sales = 1
P = Net profit margin on sales = 5%
d = Dividend-payout ratio = 50%
L = Debt-equity ratio = 1

   a. What is Stieben's sustainable growth rate in sales?

   b. Can Stieben's actual growth rate in sales be different from its sustainable growth rate? Why or why not?

   c. How can Stieben change its sustainable growth?

26.4 The Optimal Scam Company would like to see its sales grow at 20 percent for the foreseeable future. Its financial statements for the current year are presented below.

Income Statement ($ millions)		Balance Sheet ($ millions)	
Sales	32.00	Current assets	16
Costs	28.97	Fixed assets	16
Gross profit	3.03	Total assets	32
Taxes	1.03		
Net income	2.00	Current debt	10
		Long-term debt	4
Dividends	1.40	Total debt	14
Retained earnings	0.60	Common stock	14
		Ret. earnings	4
		Total liabilities and equity	32

The current financial policy of the Optimal Scam Company includes

Dividend-payout ratio (d) = 70%
Debt-to-equity ratio (L) = 77.78%
Net profit margin (P) = 6.25%
Assets-sales ratio (T) = 1

   a. Determine Optimal Scam's need for external funds next year.

   b. Construct a pro forma balance sheet for Optimal Scam.

   c. Calculate the sustainable growth rate for the Optimal Scam Company.

   d. How can Optimal Scam change its financial policy to achieve its growth objective?

26.5 The MBI Company does not want to grow. The company's financial management believes it has no positive NPV projects. The company's operating financial characteristics are

> Profit margin $= 10\%$
> Assets-sales ratio $= 150\%$
> Debt-equity ratio $= 100\%$
> Dividend-payout ratio $= 50\%$

> *a.* Calculate the sustainable growth rate for the MBI Company.
> *b.* How can the MBI Company achieve its stated growth goal?

26.6 Throughout this text, you have learned that financial managers should select positive net-present-value projects. How does this project-selection criterion relate to financial-planning models?

26.7 Your firm recently hired a new MBA. She insists that your firm is incorrectly computing its sustainable growth rate. Your firm computes the sustainable growth rate using the following formula:

$$\frac{P \times (1 - d) \times (1 + L)}{T - P \times (1 - d) \times (1 - L)}$$

> $P =$ Net profit margin on sales
> $d =$ Dividend-payout ratio
> $L =$ Debt-equity ratio
> $T =$ Ratio of total assets to sales

Your new employee claims that the correct formula is ROE $\times (1 - d)$ where ROE is net profit divided by net worth and d is dividends divided by net profit. Is your new employee correct?

26.8 Atlantic Transportation Co. has a payout ratio of 60 percent, debt-equity ratio of 50 percent, return on equity of 16 percent, and an assets-sales ratio of 175 percent.
> *a.* What is its sustainable growth rate?
> *b.* What must its profit margin be in order to achieve its sustainable growth rate?

Some Caveats of Financial-Planning Models

26.9 What are the shortcomings of financial-planning models that we should be aware of?

CHAPTER 27

Short-Term Finance and Planning

EXECUTIVE SUMMARY

Up to now we have described many of the decisions of long-term finance: capital budgeting, dividend policy, and capital structure. This chapter introduces short-term finance. Short-term finance is an analysis of decisions that affect current assets and current liabilities and will frequently have an impact on the firm within a year.

The term *net working capital* is often associated with short-term financial decision making. Net working capital is the difference between current assets and current liabilities. The focus of short-term finance on net working capital seems to suggest that it is an accounting subject. However, making net working capital decisions still relies on cash flow and net present value.

There is no universally accepted definition of short-term finance. The most important difference between short-term and long-term finance is the timing of cash flows. Short-term financial decisions involve cash inflows and outflows within a year or less. For example, a short-term financial decision is involved when a firm orders raw materials, pays in cash, and anticipates selling finished goods in one year for cash, as illustrated in Figure 27.1. A long-term financial decision is involved when a firm purchases a special machine that will reduce operating costs over the next five years, as illustrated in Figure 27.2.

Here are some questions of short-term finance:

1. What is a reasonable level of cash to keep on hand (in a bank) to pay bills?
2. How much raw material should be ordered?
3. How much credit should be extended to customers?

This chapter introduces the basic elements of short-term financial decisions. First, we describe the short-term operating activities of the firm, and then we identify alternative short-term financial policies. Finally, we outline the basic elements in a short-term financial plan and describe short-term financing instruments.

27.1 TRACING CASH AND NET WORKING CAPITAL

In this section we trace the components of cash and net working capital as they change from one year to the next. Our goal is to describe the short-term operating activities of the firm and their impact on cash and working capital.

Current assets are cash and other assets that are expected to be converted to cash within the year. Current assets are presented in the balance sheet in order of their accounting **liquidity**—the ease with which they can be converted to cash at a fair price and the time it takes to do so. Table 27.1 gives the balance sheet and income statement of the Tradewinds Manufacturing Corporation for 20X2 and 20X1. The four major items found in the current asset section of the Tradewinds balance sheet are cash, marketable securities, accounts receivable, and inventories.

■ FIGURE 27.1 **Short-Term Financial Decision**

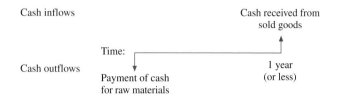

■ FIGURE 27.2 **Long-Term Financial Decision**

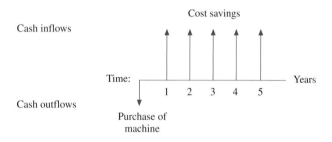

Analogous to their investment in current assets, firms use several kinds of short-term debt, called current liabilities. Current liabilities are obligations that are expected to require cash payment within one year or within the operating cycle, whichever is shorter.[1] The three major items found as *current liabilities* are accounts payable; accrued wages, taxes, and other expenses payable; and notes payable.

27.2 DEFINING CASH IN TERMS OF OTHER ELEMENTS

Now we will define cash in terms of the other elements of the balance sheet. The balance sheet equation is

$$\text{Net working capital} + \text{Fixed assets} = \text{Long-term debt} + \text{Equity} \qquad (27.1)$$

Net working capital is cash plus the other elements of net working capital; that is,

$$\frac{\text{Net working}}{\text{capital}} = \text{Cash} + \frac{\text{Other current}}{\text{assets}} - \frac{\text{Current}}{\text{liabilities}} \qquad (27.2)$$

Substituting equation (27.2) into (27.1) yields

$$\text{Cash} + \frac{\text{Other current}}{\text{assets}} - \frac{\text{Current}}{\text{liabilities}} = \frac{\text{Long-term}}{\text{debt}} + \text{Equity} - \frac{\text{Fixed}}{\text{assets}} \qquad (27.3)$$

and rearranging, we find that

$$\text{Cash} = \frac{\text{Long-term}}{\text{debt}} + \text{Equity} - \frac{\text{Net working capital}}{\text{(excluding cash)}} - \frac{\text{Fixed}}{\text{assets}} \qquad (27.4)$$

---

[1]As we will learn in this chapter, the operating cycle begins when inventory is received and ends when cash is collected from the sale of inventory.

■ TABLE 27.1 **Financial Statements**

TRADEWINDS MANUFACTURING CORPORATION
December 31, 20X2, and December 31, 20X1
Balance Sheet

	20X2	20X1
Assets		
Current assets:		
Cash	$ 500,000	$ 500,000
Marketable securities (at cost)	500,000	450,000
Accounts receivable less allowance for bad debts	2,000,000	1,600,000
Inventories	3,000,000	2,000,000
Total current assets	$ 6,000,000	$4,550,000
Fixed assets (property, plant, and equipment):		
Land	450,000	450,000
Building	4,000,000	4,000,000
Machinery	1,500,000	800,000
Office equipment	50,000	50,000
Less: Accumulated depreciation	2,000,000	1,700,000
Net fixed assets	4,000,000	3,600,000
Prepayments and deferred charges	400,000	300,000
Intangibles	100,000	100,000
Total assets	$10,500,000	$8,550,000
Liabilities		
Current liabilities:		
Accounts payable	$ 1,000,000	$ 750,000
Notes payable	1,500,000	500,000
Accrued expenses payable	250,000	225,000
Taxes payable	250,000	225,000
Total current liabilities	$ 3,000,000	$1,700,000
Long-term liabilities:		
First mortgage bonds, 5% interest, due 2025	3,000,000	3,000,000
Deferred taxes	600,000	600,000
Total liabilities	$ 6,600,000	$5,300,000

The natural interpretation of equation (27.4) is that increasing long-term debt and equity and decreasing fixed assets and net working capital (excluding cash) will increase cash to the firm.

The Sources-and-Uses-of-Cash Statement

From the right-hand side of equation (27.4), we can see an increase in long-term debt and/or equity leads to an increase in cash. Moreover, a decrease in net working capital and/or fixed assets leads to a decrease in cash. In addition, the sum of net income and depreciation increases cash, whereas dividend payments decrease cash. This reasoning allows an accountant to create a sources-and-uses-of-cash statement, which shows all the transactions that affect a firm's cash position.

■ TABLE 27.1 *(concluded)*

TRADEWINDS MANUFACTURING CORPORATION
December 31, 20X2, and December 31, 20X1

	20X2	20X1
Stockholders' Equity		
Common stock, $5 par value each; authorized,		
issued, and outstanding 300,000 shares	$ 1,500,000	$ 1,500,000
Capital surplus	500,000	500,000
Accumulated retained earnings	1,900,000	1,250,000
Total stockholders' equity	3,900,000	3,250,000
Total liabilities and stockholders' equity	$10,500,000	$ 8,550,000
Consolidated Income Statement		
Net sales	$11,500,000	$10,700,000
Cost of sales and operating expenses:		
Cost of goods sold	8,200,000	7,684,000
Depreciation	300,000	275,000
Selling and administration expenses	1,400,000	1,325,000
Operating profit	1,600,000	1,416,000
Other income:		
Dividends and interest	50,000	50,000
Total income from operations	1,650,000	1,466,000
Less: Interest on bonds and other liabilities	300,000	150,000
Income before provision for income tax	1,350,000	1,316,000
Provision for income tax	610,000	600,000
Net profit	$ 740,000	$ 716,000
Dividends paid out	$ 90,000	$ 132,000
Retained earnings	$ 650,000	$ 584,000

Let us trace the changes in cash for Tradewinds during the year. Notice that Tradewinds' cash balance remained constant during 20X2, even though cash flow from operations was $1.04 million (net income plus depreciation). Why did cash remain the same? The answer is simply that the sources of cash were equal to the uses of cash. From the firm's sources-and-uses-of-cash statement (Table 27.2), we find that Tradewinds generated cash as follows:

1. It generated cash flow from operations of $1.04 million.
2. It increased its accounts payable by $250,000. This is the same as increasing borrowing from suppliers.
3. It increased its borrowing from banks by $1 million. This shows up as an increase in notes payable.
4. It increased accrued expenses by $25,000.
5. It increased taxes payable by $25,000, in effect borrowing from the IRS.

Tradewinds used cash for the following reasons:

1. It invested $700,000 in fixed assets.
2. It increased prepayments by $100,000.

■ TABLE 27.2

TRADEWINDS MANUFACTURING CORPORATION	
Sources and Uses of Cash	
(in thousands)	
Sources of Cash:	
Cash flow from operations:	
Net income	$ 740
Depreciation	300
Total cash flow from operations	$1,040
Decrease in net working capital:	
Increase in accounts payable	250
Increase in notes payable	1,000
Increase in accrued expenses	25
Increase in taxes payable	25
Total sources of cash	$2,340
Uses of cash:	
Increase in fixed assets	$ 700
Increase in prepayments	100
Dividends	90
Increase in net working capital:	
Investment in inventory	1,000
Increase in accounts receivable	400
Increase in marketable securities	50
Total uses of cash	$2,340
Change in cash balance	0

3. It paid a $90,000 dividend.

4. It invested in inventory worth $1 million.

5. It lent its customers additional money. Hence, accounts receivable increased by $400,000.

6. It purchased $50,000 worth of marketable securities.

    This example illustrates the difference between a firm's cash position on the balance sheet and cash flows from operations.

QUESTIONS
CONCEPT ?

- What is the difference between net working capital and cash?
- Will net working capital always increase when cash increases?
- List the potential uses of cash.
- List the potential sources of cash.

27.3 THE OPERATING CYCLE AND THE CASH CYCLE

Short-term finance is concerned with the firm's **short-run operating activities.** A typical manufacturing firm's short-run operating activities consist of a sequence of events and decisions:

■ FIGURE 27.3   **Cash Flow Time Line and the Short-Term Operating Activities of a Typical Manufacturing Firm**

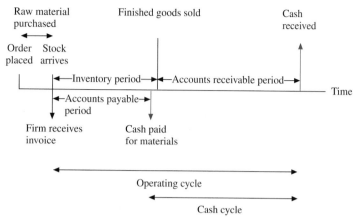

The *operating cycle* is the time period from the arrival of stock until the receipt of cash. (Sometimes the operating cycle is defined to include the time from placement of the order until arrival of the stock.) The *cash cycle* begins when cash is paid for materials and ends when cash is collected from receivables.

Events	Decisions
1. Buying raw materials	1. How much inventory to order?
2. Paying cash for purchases	2. To borrow, or draw down cash balance?
3. Manufacturing the product	3. What choice of production technology?
4. Selling the product	4. To offer cash terms or credit terms to customers?
5. Collecting cash	5. How to collect cash?

These activities create patterns of cash inflows and cash outflows that are both unsynchronized and uncertain. They are unsynchronized because the payments of cash for raw materials does not happen at the same time as the receipt of cash from selling the product. They are uncertain because future sales and costs are not known with certainty.

Figure 27.3 depicts the short-term operating activities and cash flows for a typical manufacturing firm along the **cash flow time line.** The **operating cycle** is the time interval between the arrival of inventory stock and the date when cash is collected from receivables. The **cash cycle** begins when cash is paid for materials and ends when cash is collected from receivables. The cash flow time line consists of an operating cycle and a cash cycle. The need for short-term financial decision making is suggested by the gap between the cash inflows and cash outflows. This is related to the lengths of the operating cycle and the accounts payable period. This gap can be filled either by borrowing or by holding a liquidity reserve for marketable securities. The gap can be shortened by changing the inventory, receivable, and payable periods. Now we take a closer look at the operating cycle.

The length of the operating cycle is equal to the sum of the lengths of the inventory and accounts receivable periods. The inventory period is the length of time required to order, produce, and sell a product. The accounts receivable period is the length of time required to collect cash receipts.

The cash cycle is the time between cash disbursement and cash collection. It can be thought of as the operating cycle less the accounts payable period, that is

$$\text{Cash cycle} = \text{Operating cycle} - \text{Accounts payable period}$$

The accounts payable period is the length of time the firm is able to delay payment on the purchase of various resources, such as wages and raw materials.

In practice, the inventory period, the accounts receivable period, and the accounts payable period are measured by days in inventory, days in receivables, and days in payables, respectively. We illustrate how the operating cycle and the cash cycle can be measured in the following example.

EXAMPLE

Tradewinds Manufacturing is a diversified manufacturing firm with the balance sheet and income statement shown in Table 27.1 for 20X1 and 20X2. The operating cycle and the cash cycle can be determined for Tradewinds after calculating the appropriate ratios for inventory, receivables, and payables. Consider inventory first. The average inventory is

$$\text{Average inventory} = \frac{\$3 \text{ million} + \$2 \text{ million}}{2} = \$2.5 \text{ million}$$

The terms in the numerator are the ending inventory in the second and first years, respectively.

We next calculate the inventory-turnover ratio:

$$\frac{\text{Inventory-}}{\text{turnover ratio}} = \frac{\text{Cost of goods sold}}{\text{Average inventory}} = \frac{\$8.2 \text{ million}}{\$2.5 \text{ million}} = 3.3$$

This implies that the inventory cycle occurs 3.3 times a year. Finally, we calculate days in inventory:

$$\text{Days in inventory} = \frac{365 \text{ days}}{3.3} = 110.6 \text{ days}$$

Our calculation implies that the inventory cycle is slightly more than 110 days.

We perform analogous calculations for receivables and payables.[2]

$$\frac{\text{Average}}{\text{accounts receivable}} = \frac{\$2.0 \text{ million} + \$1.6 \text{ million}}{2} = \$1.8 \text{ million}$$

$$\frac{\text{Average}}{\text{receivable turnover}} = \frac{\text{Credit sales}}{\text{Average accounts receivable}} = \frac{\$11.5 \text{ million}}{\$1.8 \text{ million}} = 6.4$$

$$\frac{\text{Days in}}{\text{receivables}} = \frac{365}{6.4} = 57 \text{ days}$$

$$\frac{\text{Average}}{\text{payables}} = \frac{\$1.0 \text{ million} + \$0.75 \text{ million}}{2} = \$0.875 \text{ million}$$

$$\frac{\text{Accounts payable}}{\text{deferral period}} = \frac{\text{Cost of goods sold}}{\text{Average payables}} = \frac{\$8.2 \text{ million}}{\$0.875 \text{ million}} = 9.4$$

$$\frac{\text{Days in}}{\text{payables}} = \frac{365}{9.4} = 38.8 \text{ days}$$

---

[2]We assume that Tradewinds Manufacturing makes no cash sales.

The preceding calculations allow us to determine both the operating cycle and the cash cycle.

$$\frac{\text{Operating}}{\text{cycle}} = \frac{\text{Days in}}{\text{inventory}} + \frac{\text{Days in}}{\text{receivables}}$$

$$= 110.6 \text{ days} + 57 \text{ days} = 167.6 \text{ days}$$

$$\frac{\text{Cash}}{\text{cycle}} = \frac{\text{Operating}}{\text{cycle}} - \frac{\text{Days in}}{\text{payables}}$$

$$= 167.6 \text{ days} - 38.8 \text{ days} = 128.8 \text{ days}.$$

The need for short-term financial decision making is suggested by the gap between the cash inflows and cash outflows. This is related to the lengths of the operating cycles and accounts payable period. This gap can be filled either by borrowing or by holding a liquidity reserve for marketable securities. The gap can be shortened by changing the inventory, receivable, and payable periods. Now we take a closer look at this aspect of short-term financial policy.

CONCEPT QUESTIONS

- What does it mean to say that a firm has an inventory-turnover ratio of four?
- Describe the operating cycle and the cash cycle. What are the differences between them?

27.4 SOME ASPECTS OF SHORT-TERM FINANCIAL POLICY

The policy that a firm adopts for short-term finance will be composed of at least two elements:

1. *The Size of the Firm's Investment in Current Assets.* This is usually measured relative to the firm's level of total operating revenues. A flexible or accommodative short-term financial policy would maintain a high ratio of current assets to sales. A restrictive short-term financial policy would entail a low ratio of current assets to sales.

2. *The Financing of Current Assets.* This is measured as the proportion of short-term debt to long-term debt. A restrictive short-term financial policy means a high proportion of short-term debt relative to long-term financing, and a flexible policy means less short-term debt and more long-term debt.

The Size of the Firm's Investment in Current Assets

Flexible short-term financial policies include:

1. Keeping large balances of cash and marketable securities.
2. Making large investments in inventory.
3. Granting liberal credit terms, which results in a high level of accounts receivable.

Restrictive short-term financial policies are:

1. Keeping low cash balances and no investment in marketable securities.
2. Making small investments in inventory.
3. Allowing no credit sales and no accounts receivable.

Determining the optimal investment level in short-term assets requires an identification of the different costs of alternative short-term financing policies. The objective is to trade off the cost of restrictive policies against those of the flexible ones to arrive at the best compromise.

Current asset holdings are highest with a flexible short-term financial policy and lowest with a restrictive policy. Thus, flexible short-term financial policies are costly in that they require higher cash outflows to finance cash and marketable securities, inventory, and accounts receivable. However, future cash inflows are highest with a flexible policy. Sales are stimulated by the use of a credit policy that provides liberal financing to customers. A large amount of inventory on hand ("on the shelf") provides a quick delivery service to customers and increases in sales.[3] In addition, the firm can probably charge higher prices for the quick delivery service and the liberal credit terms of flexible policies. A flexible policy also may result in fewer production stoppages because of inventory shortages.[4]

Managing current assets can be thought of as involving a trade-off between costs that rise with the level of investment and costs that fall with the level of investment. Costs that rise with the level of investment in current assets are called **carrying costs.** Costs that fall with increases in the level of investment in current assets are called **shortage costs.**

Carrying costs are generally of two types. First, because the rate of return on current assets is low compared with that of other assets, there is an opportunity cost. Second, there is the cost of maintaining the economic value of the item. For example, the cost of warehousing inventory belongs here.

Shortage costs are incurred when the investment in current assets is low. If a firm runs out of cash, it will be forced to sell marketable securities. If a firm runs out of cash and cannot readily sell marketable securities, it may need to borrow or default on an obligation. (This general situation is called *cash-out.*) If a firm has no inventory (a *stock-out*) or if it cannot extend credit to its customers, it will lose customers.

There are two kinds of shortage costs:

1. *Trading or Order Costs.* Order costs are the costs of placing an order for more cash (*brokerage costs*) or more inventory (*production set-up costs*).
2. *Costs Related to Safety Reserves.* These are costs of lost sales, lost customer goodwill, and disruption of production schedule.

Figure 27.4 illustrates the basic nature of carrying costs. The total costs of investing in current assets are determined by adding the carrying costs and the shortage costs. The minimum point on the total cost curve (CA*) reflects the optimal balance of current assets. The curve is generally quite flat at the optimum, and it is difficult, if not impossible, to find the precise optimal balance of shortage and carrying costs. Usually we are content with a choice near the optimum.

If carrying costs are low and/or shortage costs are high, the optimal policy calls for substantial current assets. In other words, the optimal policy is a flexible one. This is illustrated in the middle graph of Figure 27.4.

If carrying costs are high and/or shortage costs are low, the optimal policy is a restrictive one. That is, the optimal policy calls for modest current assets. This is illustrated in the bottom graph of the figure.

---

[3]This is true of some types of finished goods.

[4]This is true of inventory of raw material but not of finished goods.

■ FIGURE 27.4   **Carrying Costs and Shortage Costs**

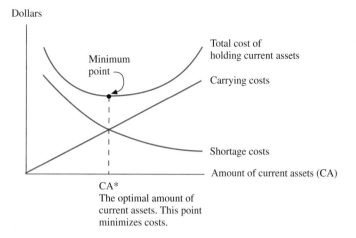

CA*
The optimal amount of
current assets. This point
minimizes costs.

Flexible policy

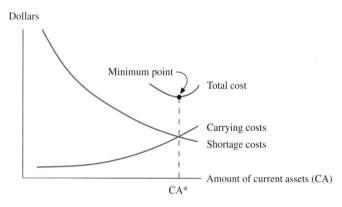

Restrictive policy

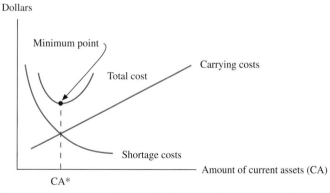

Carrying costs increase with the level of investment in current assets. They
include both opportunity costs and the costs of maintaining the asset's
economic value. *Shortage costs* decrease with increases in the level of
investment in current assets. They include trading costs and the costs of
running out of the current asset (for example, being short of cash).

DETERMINANTS OF CORPORATE LIQUID ASSET HOLDINGS

Firms with High Holdings of Liquid Assets Will Have	Firms with Low Holdings of Liquid Assets Will Have
High-growth opportunities	Low-growth opportunities
High-risk investments	Low-risk investments
Small firms	Large firms
Low-credit firms	High-credit firms

Firms will hold more liquid assets (i.e., cash and marketable securities) to ensure that they can continue investing when cash flow is low relative to positive NPV investment opportunities. Firms that have good access to capital markets will hold less-liquid assets.

Source: Tim Opler, Lee Pinkowitz, René Stultz, and Rohan Williamson, "The Determinants and Implication of Corporate Cash Holdings," *Journal of Finance Economics,* 62 (1999).

Opler, Pinkowitz, Stulz, and Williamson[5] examine the determinants of holdings of cash and marketable securities by publically traded firms. They find evidence that firms behave according to the static trade-off model described earlier. Their study focuses only on liquid assets (i.e., cash and market securities), so that carrying costs are the opportunity costs of holding liquid assets and shortage costs are the risks of not having cash when investment opportunities are good.

Alternative Financing Policies for Current Assets

In the previous section we examined the level of investment in current assets. Now we turn to the level of current liabilities, assuming the investment in current assets is optimal.

An Ideal Model   In an ideal economy, short-term assets can always be financed with short-term debt, and long-term assets can be financed with long-term debt and equity. In this economy, net working capital is always zero.

Imagine the simple case of a grain-elevator operator. Grain-elevator operators buy crops after harvest, store them, and sell them during the year. They have high inventories of grain after the harvest and end with low inventories just before the next harvest.

Bank loans with maturities of less than one year are used to finance the purchase of grain. These loans are paid with the proceeds from the sale of grain.

The situation is shown in Figure 27.5. Long-term assets are assumed to grow over time, whereas current assets increase at the end of the harvest and then decline during the year. Short-term assets end at zero just before the next harvest. These assets are financed by short-term debt, and long-term assets are financed with long-term debt and equity. Net working capital—current assets minus current liabilities—is always zero.

---

[5]Tim Opler, Lee Pinkowitz, René Stulz, and Rohan Williamson, "The Determinants and Implication of Corporate Cash Holdings," *Journal of Financial Economics,* 52 (1999).

■ FIGURE 27.5 **Financing Policy for an Idealized Economy**

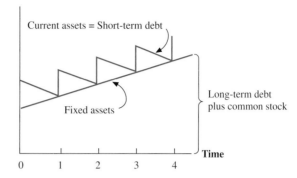

In an ideal world, net working capital is always zero because short-term assets are financed by short-term debt.

■ FIGURE 27.6 **The Total Asset Requirement over Time**

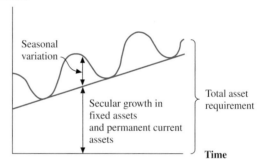

Different Strategies in Financing Current Assets   Current assets cannot be expected to drop to zero in the real world, because a long-term rising level of sales will result in some permanent investment in current assets. A growing firm can be thought of as having both a permanent requirement for current assets and one for long-term assets. This total asset requirement will exhibit balances over time reflecting (1) a secular growth trend, (2) a seasonal variation around the trend, and (3) unpredictable day-to-day and month-to-month fluctuations. This is depicted in Figure 27.6. (We have not tried to show the unpredictable day-to-day and month-to-month variations in the total asset requirement.)

Now, let us look at how this asset requirement is financed. First, consider the strategy (strategy *F* in Figure 27.7) where long-term financing covers more than the total asset requirement, even at seasonal peaks. The firm will have excess cash available for investment in marketable securities when the total asset requirement falls from peaks. Because this approach implies chronic short-term cash surpluses and a large investment in net working capital, it is considered a flexible strategy.

When long-term financing does not cover the total asset requirement, the firm must borrow short-term to make up the deficit. This restrictive strategy is labeled strategy *R* in Figure 27.7.

■ FIGURE 27.7 **Alternative Asset-Financing Policies**

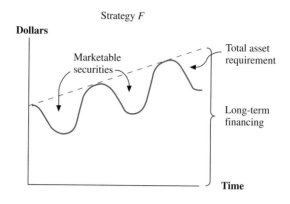

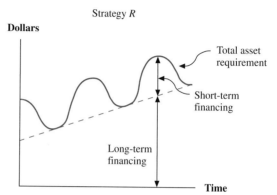

Strategy *F* always implies a short-term cash surplus and a large investment in cash and marketable securities.
Strategy *R* uses long-term financing for secular asset requirements only, and short-term borrowing for seasonal variations.

Which Is Best?

What is the most appropriate amount of short-term borrowing? There is no definitive answer. Several considerations must be included in a proper analysis:

1. *Cash Reserves.* The flexible financing strategy implies surplus cash and little short-term borrowing. This strategy reduces the probability that a firm will experience financial distress. Firms may not need to worry as much about meeting recurring, short-run obligations. However, investments in cash and marketable securities are zero net-present-value investments at best.

2. *Maturity Hedging.* Most firms finance inventories with short-term bank loans and fixed assets with long-term financing. Firms tend to avoid financing long-lived assets with short-term borrowing. This type of maturity mismatching would necessitate frequent financing and is inherently risky, because short-term interest rates are more volatile than longer rates.

3. *Term Structure.* Short-term interest rates are normally lower than long-term interest rates. This implies that, on average, it is more costly to rely on long-term borrowing than on short-term borrowing.

QUESTIONS
CONCEPT

- What keeps the real world from being an ideal one where net working capital could always be zero?
- What considerations determine the optimal compromise between flexible and restrictive net working capital policies?

27.5 CASH BUDGETING

The **cash budget** is a primary tool of short-run financial planning. It allows the financial manager to identify short-term financial needs (and opportunities). It will tell the manager the required borrowing for the short term. It is the way of identifying the cash-flow gap on the cash-flow time line. The idea of the cash budget is simple: It records estimates of cash receipts and disbursements. We illustrate cash budgeting with the following example of Fun Toys.

EXAMPLE

All of Fun Toys' cash inflows come from the sale of toys. Cash budgeting for Fun Toys starts with a sales forecast for the next year, by quarter:

	First Quarter	Second Quarter	Third Quarter	Fourth Quarter
Sales ($ millions)	$100	$200	$150	$100

Fun Toys' fiscal year starts on July 1. Fun Toys' sales are seasonal and are usually very high in the second quarter, due to Christmastime sales. But Fun Toys sells to department stores on credit, and sales do not generate cash immediately. Instead, cash comes later from collections on accounts receivable. Fun Toys has a 90-day collection period, and 100 percent of sales are collected the following quarter. In other words,

$$\text{Collections} = \text{Last quarter's sales}$$

This relationship implies that

$$\frac{\text{Accounts receivable}}{\text{at end of last quarter}} = \frac{\text{Last quarter's}}{\text{sales}} \qquad (27.5)$$

We assume that sales in the fourth quarter of the previous fiscal year were $100 million. From equation (27.5), we know that accounts receivable at the end of the fourth quarter of the previous fiscal year were $100 million and collections in the first quarter of the current fiscal year are $100 million.

The first quarter sales of the current fiscal year of $100 million are added to the accounts receivable, but $100 million of collections are subtracted. Therefore, Fun Toys ended the first quarter with accounts receivable of $100 million. The basic relation is

$$\frac{\text{Ending accounts}}{\text{receivable}} = \frac{\text{Starting accounts}}{\text{receivable}} + \text{Sales} - \text{Collections}$$

Table 27.3 shows cash collections for Fun Toys for the next four quarters. Though collections are the only source of cash here, this need not always be the case. Other sources of cash could include sales of assets, investment income, and long-term financing.

■ TABLE 27.3 **Sources of Cash (in millions)**

	First Quarter	Second Quarter	Third Quarter	Fourth Quarter
Sales	$100	$200	$150	$100
Cash collections	100	100	200	150
Starting receivables	100	100	200	150
Ending receivables	100	200	150	100

■ TABLE 27.4 **Disbursement of Cash (in millions)**

	First Quarter	Second Quarter	Third Quarter	Fourth Quarter
Sales	$100	$200	$150	$100
Purchases	100	75	50	50
Uses of cash				
Payments of accounts payable	50	100	75	50
Wages, taxes, and other expenses	20	40	30	20
Capital expenditures	0	0	0	100
Long-term financing expenses: interest and dividends	10	10	10	10
Total uses of cash	$ 80	$150	$115	$180

Cash Outflow

Next, we consider the cash disbursements. They can be put into four basic categories, as shown in Table 27.4.

1. *Payments of Accounts Payable.* These are payments for goods or services, such as raw materials. These payments will generally be made after purchases. Purchases will depend on the sales forecast. In the case of Fun Toys, assume that

   Payments = Last quarter's purchases
   Purchases = 1/2 next quarter's sales forecast

2. *Wages, Taxes, and Other Expenses.* This category includes all other normal costs of doing business that require actual expenditures. Depreciation, for example, is often thought of as a normal cost of business, but it requires no cash outflow.

3. *Capital Expenditures.* These are payments of cash for long-lived assets. Fun Toys plans a major capital expenditure in the fourth quarter.

4. *Long-Term Financing.* This category includes interest and principal payments on long-term outstanding debt and dividend payments to shareholders.

The total forecasted outflow appears in the last line of Table 27.4.

■ TABLE 27.5   **The Cash Balance (in millions)**

	First Quarter	Second Quarter	Third Quarter	Fourth Quarter
Total cash receipts	$100	$100	$200	$150
Total cash disbursements	80	150	115	180
Net cash flow	20	(50)	85	(30)
Cumulative excess cash balance	20	(30)	55	25
Minimum cash balance	5	5	5	5
Cumulative finance surplus (deficit) requirement	15	(35)	50	20

The Cash Balance

The net cash balance appears in Table 27.5, and a large net cash outflow is forecast in the second quarter. This large outflow is not caused by an inability to earn a profit. Rather, it results from delayed collections on sales. This results in a cumulative cash shortfall of $30 million in the second quarter.

Fun Toys had established a minimum operating cash balance equal to $5 million to facilitate transactions, protect against unexpected contingencies, and maintain compensating balances at its commercial banks. This means that it has a cash shortfall in the second quarter equal to $35 million.

QUESTIONS
- How would you conduct a sensitivity analysis for Fun Toys' net cash balance?
- What could you learn from such an analysis?

27.6 THE SHORT-TERM FINANCIAL PLAN

Fun Toys has a short-term financing problem. It cannot meet the forecasted cash outflows in the second quarter from internal sources. Its financing options include: (1) unsecured bank borrowing, (2) secured borrowing, and (3) other sources.

Unsecured Loans

The most common way to finance a temporary cash deficit is to arrange a short-term unsecured bank loan. Firms that use short-term bank loans usually ask their bank for either a noncommitted or a committed *line of credit*. A *noncommitted* line is an informal arrangement that allows firms to borrow up to a previously specified limit without going through the normal paperwork. The interest rate on the line of credit is usually set equal to the bank's prime lending rate plus an additional percentage. Most of the time, banks will also require that compensating balances be kept at the bank by the firm. For example, a firm might be required to keep an amount equal to 5 percent on the line of credit.

Committed lines of credit are formal legal arrangements and usually involve a commitment fee paid by the firm to the bank (usually the fee is approximately 0.25 percent of the total committed funds per year). For larger firms the interest rate is often tied to the London Interbank Offered Rate (LIBOR) or to the bank's cost of funds, rather than the prime rate. Midsized and smaller firms often are required to keep compensating balances in the bank.

Compensating balances are deposits the firm keeps with the bank in low-interest or noninterest-bearing accounts. Compensating balances are commonly on the order of 2 to 5 percent of the amount used. By leaving these funds with the bank without receiving interest, the firm increases the effective interest earned by the bank on the line of credit. For example, if a firm borrowing $100,000 must keep $5,000 as a compensating balance, the firm effectively receives only $95,000. A stated interest rate of 10 percent implies yearly interest payments of $10,000 ($100,000 × 0.10). The effective interest rate is 10.53 percent ($10,000/$95,000).

Secured Loans

Banks and other finance companies often require *security* for a loan. Security for short-term loans usually consists of accounts receivable or inventories.

Under **accounts receivable financing,** receivables are either *assigned* or *factored.* Under assignment, the lender not only has a lien on the receivables but also has recourse to the borrower. Factoring involves the sale of accounts receivable. The purchaser, who is called a *factor,* must then collect on the receivables. The factor assumes the full risk of default on bad accounts.

As the name implies, an **inventory loan** uses inventory as collateral. Some common types of inventory loans are

1. *Blanket Inventory Lien.* The blanket inventory lien gives the lender a lien against all the borrower's inventories.
2. *Trust Receipt.* Under this arrangement, the borrower holds the inventory in trust for the lender. The document acknowledging the loan is called the trust receipt. Proceeds from the sale of inventory are remitted immediately to the lender.
3. *Field-Warehouse Financing.* In field-warehouse financing, a public warehouse company supervises the inventory for the lender.

Other Sources

There are a variety of other sources of short-term funds employed by corporations. The most important of these are the issuance of **commercial paper** and financing through **banker's acceptances.** Commercial paper consists of short-term notes issued by large and highly rated firms. Typically these notes are of short maturity, ranging up to 270 days (beyond that limit the firm must file a registration statement with the SEC). Because the firm issues these directly and because it usually backs the issue with a special bank line of credit, the rate the firm obtains is often significantly below the prime rate the bank would charge it for a direct loan.

A banker's acceptance is an agreement by a bank to pay a sum of money. These agreements typically arise when a seller sends a bill or draft to a customer. The customer's bank *accepts* this bill and notes the acceptance on it, which makes it an obligation of the bank. In this way a firm that is buying something from a supplier can effectively arrange for the bank to pay the outstanding bill. Of course, the bank charges the customer a fee for this service.

CONCEPT QUESTIONS

?

- What are the two basic forms of short-term financing?
- Describe two types of secured loans.

27.7 SUMMARY AND CONCLUSIONS

1. This chapter introduces the management of short-term finance. Short-term finance involves short-lived assets and liabilities. We trace and examine the short-term sources and uses of cash as they appear on the firm's financial statements. We see how current assets and current liabilities arise in the short-term operating activities and the cash cycle of the firm. From an accounting perspective, short-term finance involves net working capital.

2. Managing short-term cash flows involves the minimization of costs. The two major costs are carrying costs—the interest and related costs incurred by overinvesting in short-term assets such as cash—and shortage costs, the cost of running out of short-term assets. The objective of managing short-term finance and short-term financial planning is to find the optimal trade-off between these two costs.

3. In an ideal economy the firm could perfectly predict its short-term uses and sources of cash, and net working capital could be kept at zero. In the real world, net working capital provides a buffer that lets the firm meet its ongoing obligations. The financial manager seeks the optimal level of each of the current assets.

4. The financial manager can use the cash budget to identify short-term financial needs. The cash budget tells the manager what borrowing is required or what lending will be possible in the short run. The firm has available to it a number of possible ways of acquiring funds to meet short-term shortfalls, including unsecured and secured loans.

KEY TERMS

Accounts receivable financing   762
Banker's acceptances   762
Carrying costs   754
Cash budget   759
Cash cycle   751
Cash flow time line   751
Commercial paper   762

Compensating balance   762
Inventory loan   762
Liquidity   746
Operating cycle   751
Shortage costs   754
Short-run operating activities   750

SUGGESTED READINGS

A book that describes working capital management is:
Fabozzi, F., and L. N. Masonson. *Corporate Cash Management Techniques and Analyses.* Homewood, Ill.: Dow Jones–Irwin, 1985.
Kallberg, J. G., and K. Parkinson. *Corporate Liquidity: Management and Measurement.* Burr Ridge, IL: Irwin/McGraw Hill, 1996.

QUESTIONS AND PROBLEMS

Tracing Cash and Net Working Capital

27.1 Derive the cash equation from the basic balance sheet equation: assets = liabilities + equity.

27.2 Indicate whether the following corporate actions increase, decrease, or cause no change to cash.

a. Cash is paid for raw materials purchased for inventory.
b. A dividend is paid.
c. Merchandise is sold on credit.
d. Common stock is issued.
e. Raw material is purchased for inventory on credit.
f. A piece of machinery is purchased and paid for with long-term debt.
g. Payments for previous sales are collected.
h. Accumulated depreciation is increased.
i. Merchandise is sold for cash.
j. Payment is made for a previous purchase.
k. A short-term bank loan is received.
l. A dividend is paid with funds received from a sale of common stock.
m. Allowance for bad debts is decreased.
n. A piece of office equipment is purchased and paid for with a short-term note.
o. Marketable securities are purchased with retained earnings.
p. Last year's taxes are paid.
q. This year's tax liability is increased.
r. Interest on long-term debt is paid.

Defining Cash in Terms of Other Elements

27.3 Below are the 20X2 balance sheet and income statement for Country Kettles, Inc. Use this information to construct a sources-and-uses-of-cash statement.

COUNTRY KETTLES, INC.
Balance Sheet
December 31, 20X2

	20X2	20X1
Assets		
Cash	$ 42,000	$ 35,000
Accounts receivable	94,250	84,500
Inventory	78,750	75,000
Property, plant, equipment	181,475	168,750
Less: Accumulated depreciation	61,475	56,250
Total assets	$335,000	$307,000
Liabilities and Equity		
Accounts payable	$ 60,500	$ 55,000
Accrued expenses	5,150	8,450
Long-term debt	15,000	30,000
Common stock	28,000	25,000
Retained earnings	226,350	188,550
Total liabilities and equity	$335,000	$307,000

COUNTRY KETTLES, INC.
Income Statement
20X2

Net sales	$765,000
Cost of goods sold	459,000
Sales, general, and administrative costs	91,800
Advertising	26,775
Rent	45,000
Depreciation	5,225
Profit before taxes	137,200
Taxes	68,600
Net profit	$ 68,600
Dividends	$ 30,800
Retained earnings	$ 37,800

27.4 Following are the 20X2 balance sheet and income statement for the S/B Corporation. Use them to construct a sources-and-uses-of-cash statement.

S/B CORPORATION
Balance Sheet
December 31, 20X2
(in thousands)

	20X2	20X1
Assets		
Cash	$ 388	$ 375
Accounts receivable	1,470	1,219
Inventories	2,663	2,777
Net fixed assets	9,314	9,225
Total assets	$13,835	$13,596
Liabilities and Equity		
Accounts payable	$ 282	$ 259
Bank loan payable	1,300	924
Taxes payable	(33)	99
Accrued expenses payable	95	106
Mortgage	4,000	4,000
Common stock	4,000	4,000
Retained earnings	4,191	4,208
Total liabilities and equity	$13,835	$13,596

S/B CORPORATION
Income Statement
20X2
(in thousands)

Net sales	$1,030
Cost of goods sold:	
Materials	652
Overhead	64
Depreciation	50
Gross profit	264
Selling and administrative costs	98
Profit before taxes	166
Taxes	83
Net profit	$ 83
Dividends paid	$ 100

The Operating Cycle and Cost Cycle

27.5 On Eastern Printing Machines Co.'s income statement of 20X1, the cost of goods sold and the credit sales are $200 million and $240 million, respectively. The following data are from its balance sheets.

	($ millions)	
	Dec. 31, 20X1	Dec. 31, 20X2
Inventory	$40	$60
Accounts receivable	30	50
Accounts payable	10	30

    a. How many days is Eastern Printing Machines' operating cycle?

    b. How many days is Eastern Printing Machines' cash cycle?

27.6 Define:

    a. Operating cycle

    b. Cash cycle

    c. Accounts payable period

27.7 Indicate whether the following company actions increase, decrease, or cause no change to the cash cycle and the operating cycle.

    a. The use of discounts offered by suppliers is decreased.

    b. More finished goods are being produced for orders instead of for inventory.

    c. A greater percentage of raw materials purchases is paid for with cash.

    d. The terms of discounts offered to customers are made more favorable for the customers.

    e. A larger than usual amount of raw materials is purchased as a result of a price decline.

    f. An increased number of customers pays with cash instead of credit.

Some Aspects of Short-Term Financial Policy

27.8 *a.* Define flexible short-term financing.

    b. Define restrictive short-term financing.

    c. When is flexible short-term financing optimal?

    d. When is restrictive short-term financing optimal?

27.9 What are the costs of shortages? Describe them.

27.10 Cleveland Compressor and Pnew York Pneumatic are competing manufacturing firms. Their financial statements are printed below.

   a. How are the current assets of each firm financed?

   b. Which firm has the larger investment in current assets? Why?

   c. Which firm is more likely to incur carrying costs, and which is more likely to incur shortage costs? Why?

CLEVELAND COMPRESSOR
Balance Sheet
December 31, 20X1

	20X2	20X1
Assets		
Cash	$ 13,862	$ 16,339
Net accounts receivable	23,887	25,778
Inventory	54,867	43,287
Total current assets	$ 92,616	$ 85,404
Fixed assets:		
Plant, property, and equipment	101,543	99,615
Less: Accumulated depreciation	34,331	31,957
Net fixed assets	$ 67,212	$ 67,658
Prepaid expenses	1,914	1,791
Other assets	13,052	13,138
Total assets	$174,794	$167,991

	20X2	20X1
Liabilities and Equity		
Current liabilities:		
Accounts payable	$ 6,494	$ 4,893
Notes payable	10,483	11,617
Accrued expenses	7,422	7,227
Other taxes payable	9,924	8,460
Total current liabilities	34,323	32,197
Long-term debt	22,036	22,036
Total liabilities	$ 56,359	$ 54,233
Equity:		
Common stock	38,000	38,000
Paid-in capital	12,000	12,000
Retained earnings	68,435	63,758
Total equity	118,435	113,758
Total liabilities and equity	$174,794	$167,991

CLEVELAND COMPRESSOR
Income Statement
20X2

Income:	
Sales	$162,749
Other income	1,002
Total income	$163,751
Operating expenses:	
Cost of goods sold	103,570
Selling and administrative expenses	28,495
Depreciation	2,274
Total expenses	$134,339
Pretax earnings	29,412
Taxes	14,890
Net earnings	$ 14,522
Dividends	$ 9,845
Retained earnings	$ 4,677

PNEW YORK PNEUMATIC
Balance Sheet
December 31, 20X2

	20X2	20X1
Assets		
Cash	$ 5,794	$ 3,307
Net accounts receivable	26,177	22,133
Inventory	46,463	44,661
Total current assets	78,434	70,101
Fixed assets:		
Plant, property, and equipment	31,842	31,116
Less: Accumulated depreciation	19,297	18,143
Net fixed assets	12,545	12,973
Prepaid expenses	763	688
Other assets	1,601	1,385
Total assets	$93,343	$85,147
Liabilities and Equity		
Current liabilities:		
Accounts payable	$ 6,008	$ 5,019
Bank loans	3,722	645
Accrued expenses	4,254	3,295
Other taxes payable	5,688	4,951
Total current liabilities	19,672	13,910
Equity:		
Common stock	20,576	20,576
Paid-in capital	5,624	5,624
Retained earnings	48,598	46,164
Less: Treasury stock	1,127	1,127
Total equity	73,671	71,237
Total liabilities and equity	$93,343	$85,147

PNEW YORK PNEUMATIC
Income Statement
20X2

Income:
    Sales $91,374
    Other income 1,067
        Total income 92,441
Operating expenses:
    Cost of goods sold 59,042
    Selling and administrative expenses 18,068
    Depreciation 1,154
        Total expenses 78,264
Pretax earnings 14,177
Taxes 6,838
Net earnings .... $ 7,339

Dividends .... $ 4,905
Retained earnings .... $ 2,434

27.11 In an ideal economy, net working capital is always zero. Why might net working capital be greater than zero in the real world?

Cash Budgeting

27.12 The following is the sales budget for the Smithe and Wreston Company for the first quarter of 20X1.

	January	February	March
Sales budget	$90,000	$100,000	$120,000

The aging of credit sales is

    30 percent collected in the month of sale
    40 percent collected in the month after sale

The accounts receivable balance at the end of the previous quarter is $36,000. $30,000 of that amount is uncollected December sales.

a. Compute the sales for December.

b. Compute the cash collections from sales for each month from January through March.

27.13 The sales budget for your company in the coming year is based on a 20-percent quarterly growth rate with the first quarter projection at $100 million. In addition to this basic trend, the seasonal adjustments for the four quarters are 0, −10, −5, and 15 million dollars, respectively. Generally, 30 percent of the sales can be collected within the month and 50 percent in the following month; the rest of the sales are bad debt. All sales are credit sales. Compute the cash collections from sales for each quarter from the second to the fourth quarter.

27.14 Below are some important figures from the budget of Pine Mulch Company for the second quarter of 20X2.

	April	May	June
Credit sales	$160,000	$140,000	$192,000
Credit purchases	68,000	64,000	80,000
Cash disbursements:			
Wages, taxes, and expenses	8,000	7,000	8,400
Interest	3,000	3,000	3,000
Equipment purchases	50,000		4,000

The company predicts that 10 percent of its sales will never be collected; 50 percent of its sales will be collected in the month of the sale; and the rest of its sales will be collected in the following month. Purchases on trade accounts will be paid in the month following the purchase. In March 20X2 the sales were $180,000.

Use this information to complete the following cash budget:

	April	May	June
Beginning cash balance	$200,000		
Cash receipts:			
Cash collections from credit sales			
Total cash available			
Cash disbursements:			
Pay credit purchases	$ 65,000		
Wages, taxes, and expenses			
Interest			
Equipment purchases			
Total cash disbursed			
Ending cash balance			

27.15 What are the most important considerations in deciding the most appropriate amount of short-term borrowing?

The Short-Term Financial Plan

27.16 List several short-term external financing options.

CHAPTER 28

Cash Management

EXECUTIVE SUMMARY

The balance sheet of Singapore Airlines showed total assets of $8.7 billion in March 1994. On this basis, Singapore Airlines was one of the largest transportation firms in the world. In addition, Singapore Airlines held $62.4 million in cash. This cash included currency, demand deposits at commercial banks, and undeposited checks.[1]

Since cash earns no interest, why would Singapore Airlines hold cash? It would seem more sensible for Singapore Airlines to put its cash into marketable securities, such as Treasury bills, and get some investment income. Of course, one reason Singapore Airlines holds cash is to pay for goods and services. Singapore Airlines might prefer to pay its employees in Treasury bills, but the minimum denomination of Treasury bills is $10,000! The firm must use cash because cash is more divisible than Treasury bills.[2]

This chapter is about how firms manage cash. The basic objective in cash management is to keep the investment in cash as low as possible while still operating the firm's activities efficiently and effectively. This chapter separates cash management into three steps:

1. Determining the appropriate target cash balance.
2. Collecting and disbursing cash efficiently.
3. Investing excess cash in marketable securities.

Determining the appropriate target cash balance involves an assessment of the trade-off between the benefit and cost of liquidity. The benefit of holding cash is the convenience in liquidity it gives the firm. The cost of holding cash is the interest income that the firm could have received from investing in Treasury bills and other marketable securities. If the firm has achieved its target cash balance, the value it gets from the liquidity provided by its cash will be exactly equal to the value forgone in interest on an equivalent holding of Treasury bills. In other words, a firm should increase its holding of cash until the net present value from doing so is zero. The incremental liquidity value of cash should decline as more of it is held.

After the optimal amount of liquidity is determined, the firm must establish procedures so that cash is collected and disbursed as efficiently as possible. This usually reduces to the dictum, "collect early and pay late."

Firms must invest temporarily idle cash in short-term marketable securities. These securities can be bought and sold in the *money market*. Money-market securities have very little risk of default and are highly marketable.

---

[1] It was somewhat unusual for Singapore Airlines to report cash in this way. Usually, a firm's reported cash includes cash equivalents, such as Treasury bills.

[2] Cash is liquid. One property of liquidity is divisibility, that is, how easily an asset can be divided into parts.

28.1 REASONS FOR HOLDING CASH

The term cash is a surprisingly imprecise concept. The economic definition of cash includes currency, checking account deposits at commercial banks, and undeposited checks. However, financial managers often use the term cash to include short-term marketable securities. Short-term marketable securities are frequently referred to as "cash equivalents" and include Treasury bills, certificates of deposit, and repurchase agreements. (Several different types of short-term marketable securities are described at the end of this chapter.) The balance sheet item "cash" usually includes cash equivalents.[3]

The previous chapter discussed the management of net working capital. Net working capital includes both cash and cash equivalents. This chapter is concerned with cash, not net working capital, and it focuses on the narrow economic definition of cash.

The basic elements of net working capital management such as carrying costs, shortage costs, and opportunity costs are relevant for cash management. However, cash management is more concerned with how to minimize cash balances by collecting and disbursing cash effectively.

There are two primary reasons for holding cash. First, cash is needed to satisfy the **transactions motive.** Transactions-related needs come from normal disbursement and collection activities of the firm. The disbursement of cash includes the payment of wages and salaries, trade debts, taxes, and dividends. Cash is collected from sales from operations, sales of assets, and new financing. The cash inflows (*collections*) and outflows (*disbursements*) are not perfectly synchronized, and some level of cash holdings is necessary to serve as a buffer. If the firm maintains too small a cash balance, it may run out of cash. If so, it must sell marketable securities or borrow. Selling marketable securities and borrowing involve *trading costs.*

Another reason to hold cash is for **compensating balances.** Cash balances are kept at commercial banks to compensate for banking services rendered to the firm. A minimum required compensating balance at banks providing credit services to the firm may impose a lower limit on the level of cash a firm holds.

The cash balance for most firms can be thought of as consisting of transactions balances and compensating balances. However, it would not be correct for a firm to add the amount of cash required to satisfy its transactions needs to the amount of cash needed to satisfy its compensatory balances to produce a target cash balance. The same cash can be used to satisfy both requirements.

The cost of holding cash is, of course, the opportunity cost of lost interest. To determine the target cash balance, the firm must weigh the benefits of holding cash against the costs. It is generally a good idea for firms to figure out first how much cash to hold to satisfy the transactions needs. Next, the firm must consider compensating-balance requirements, which will impose a lower limit on the level of the firm's cash holdings. Because compensating balances merely provide a lower limit, we shall ignore compensating balances for the following discussion of the target cash balance.

---

[3]Many firms hold very large balances of cash and cash equivalents. In 1997 the largest balances included:

	(in $ billions)
Ford	$18.5
General Motors	10.1
Microsoft	9.1
Intel	8.5
IBM	6.5

The reasons firms hold large balances of cash and equivalents include precautionary balances such as in the case of a recession or large anticipated spending on dividends, stock repurchases, stock options, or capital investment.

• What is the transactions motive, and how does it lead firms to hold cash?
• What is a compensating balance?

28.2 Determining the Target Cash Balance

The **target cash balance** involves a trade-off between the opportunity costs of holding too much cash and the trading costs of holding too little. Figure 28.1 presents the problem graphically. If a firm tries to keep its cash holdings too low, it will find itself selling marketable securities (and perhaps later buying marketable securities to replace those sold) more frequently than if the cash balance was higher. Thus, trading costs will tend to fall as the cash balance becomes larger. In contrast, the opportunity costs of holding cash rise as the cash holdings rise. At point C^* in Figure 28.1, the sum of both costs, depicted as the total cost curve, is at a minimum. This is the target or optimal cash balance.

The Baumol Model

William Baumol was the first to provide a formal model of cash management incorporating opportunity costs and trading costs.[4] His model can be used to establish the target cash balance.

Suppose the Golden Socks Corporation began week 0 with a cash balance of $C = \$1.2$ million, and outflows exceed inflows by $600,000 per week. Its cash balance will drop to zero at the end of week 2, and its average cash balance will be $C/2 = \$1.2$ million$/2 = \$600,000$ over the two-week period. At the end of week 2, Golden Socks must replace its cash either by selling marketable securities or by borrowing. Figure 28.2 shows this situation.

 FIGURE 28.1   **Costs of Holding Cash**

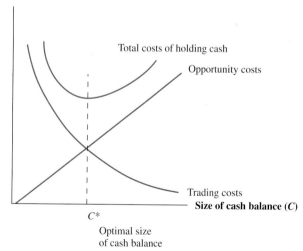

Cost in dollars
of holding cash

Total costs of holding cash

Opportunity costs

Trading costs

Size of cash balance (C)

C^*

Optimal size
of cash balance

Trading costs are increased when the firm must sell securities to establish a cash balance. Opportunity costs are increased when there is a cash balance because there is no return to cash.

---

[4]W. S. Baumol, "The Transactions Demand for Cash: An Inventory Theoretic Approach," *Quarterly Journal of Economics* 66 (November 1952).

■ FIGURE 28.2   **Cash Balances for the Golden Socks Corporation**

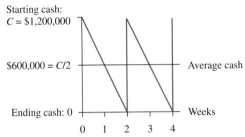

The Golden Socks Corporation begins week 0 with cash of $1,200,000. The balance drops to zero by the second week. The average cash balance is $C/2 = \$1,200,000/2 = \$600,000$ over the period.

If C were set higher, say, at $2.4 million, cash would last four weeks before the firm would need to sell marketable securities, but the firm's average cash balance would increase to $1.2 million (from $600,000). If C were set at $600,000, cash would run out in one week and the firm would need to replenish cash more frequently, but its average cash balance would fall from $600,000 to $300,000.

Because transactions costs must be incurred whenever cash is replenished (for example, the brokerage costs of selling marketable securities), establishing large initial cash balances will lower the trading costs connected with cash management. However, the larger the average cash balance, the greater the opportunity cost (the return that could have been earned on marketable securities).

To solve this problem, Golden Socks needs to know the following three things:

F = The fixed cost of selling securities to replenish cash

T = The total amount of new cash needed for transactions purposes over the relevant planning period, say, one year

and

K = The opportunity cost of holding cash; this is the interest rate on marketable securities

With this information, Golden Socks can determine the total costs of any particular cash-balance policy. It can then determine the optimal cash-balance policy.

The Opportunity Costs   The total opportunity costs of cash balances, in dollars, must be equal to the average cash balance multiplied by the interest rate, or

$$\text{Opportunity costs (\$)} = (C/2) \times K$$

The opportunity costs of various alternatives are given here:

Initial Cash Balance	Average Cash Balance	Opportunity Costs (K = 0.10)
C	$C/2$	$(C/2) \times K$
$4,800,000	$2,400,000	$240,000
2,400,000	1,200,000	120,000
1,200,000	600,000	60,000
600,000	300,000	30,000
300,000	150,000	15,000

The Trading Costs   Total trading costs can be determined by calculating the number of times that Golden Socks must sell marketable securities during the year. The total amount of cash disbursement during the year is $600,000 \times 52$ weeks $= \$31.2$ million. If the initial cash balance is set at $1.2 million, Golden Socks will sell $1.2 million of marketable securities every two weeks. Thus, trading costs are given by

$$\frac{\$31.2 \text{ million}}{\$1.2 \text{ million}} \times F = 26F$$

The general formula is

$$\text{Trading costs (\$)} = (T/C) \times F$$

A schedule of alternative trading costs follows:

Total Disbursements during Relevant Period	Initial Cash Balance	Trading Costs (F = $1,000)
T	*C*	$(T/C) \times F$
$31,200,000	$4,800,000	$ 6,500
31,200,000	2,400,000	13,000
31,200,000	1,200,000	26,000
31,200,000	600,000	52,000
31,200,000	300,000	104,000

The Total Cost   The total cost of cash balances consists of the opportunity costs plus the trading costs:

$$\text{Total cost} = \text{Opportunity costs} + \text{Trading costs}$$
$$= (C/2) \times K + (T/C) \times F$$

Cash Balance	Total Cost	=	Opportunity Costs	+	Trading Costs
$4,800,000	$246,500		$240,000		$ 6,500
2,400,000	133,000		120,000		13,000
1,200,000	86,000		60,000		26,000
600,000	82,000		30,000		52,000
300,000	119,000		15,000		104,000

The Solution   We can see from the preceding schedule that a $600,000 cash balance results in the lowest total cost of the possibilities presented: $82,000. But what about $700,000 or $500,000 or other possibilities? To determine minimum total costs precisely, Golden Socks must equate the marginal reduction in trading costs as balances rise with the marginal increase in opportunity costs associated with cash balance increases. The target cash balance should be the point where the two offset each other. This can be calculated by using either numerical iteration or calculus. We will use calculus, but if you are unfamiliar with such an analysis, you can skip to the solution.

Recall that the total cost equation is

$$\text{Total cost (TC)} = (C/2) \times K + (T/C) \times F$$

If we differentiate the TC equation with respect to the cash balance and set the derivative equal to zero, we will find that

$$\frac{d\text{TC}}{dC} = \frac{K}{2} - \frac{TF}{C^2} = 0$$

$$\begin{array}{ccc} \text{Marginal} & & \text{Marginal} & \text{Marginal}^{5} \\ \text{total} & = & \text{opportunity} + & \text{trading} \\ \text{cost} & & \text{costs} & \text{costs} \end{array}$$

The solution for the general cash balance, C^*, is obtained by solving this equation for C:

$$\frac{K}{2} = \frac{TF}{C^2}$$
$$C^* = \sqrt{2TF/K}$$

If $F = \$1,000$, $T = \$31,200,000$, and $K = 0.10$, then $C^* = \$789,936.71$. Given the value of C^*, opportunity costs are

$$(C^*/2) \times K = \frac{\$789,936.71}{2} \times 0.10 = \$39,496.84$$

Trading costs are

$$(T/C^*) \times F = \frac{\$31,200,000}{\$789,936.71} \times \$1,000 = \$39,496.84$$

Hence, total costs are

$$\$39,496.84 + \$39,496.84 = \$78,993.68$$

Limitations   The Baumol model represents an important contribution to cash management. The limitations of the model include the following:

1. *The Model Assumes the Firm Has a Constant Disbursement Rate.* In practice, disbursements can be only partially managed, because due dates differ and costs cannot be predicted with certainty.

2. *The Model Assumes There Are No Cash Receipts during the Projected Period.* In fact, most firms experience both cash inflows and outflows on a daily basis.

3. *No Safety Stock Is Allowed For.* Firms will probably want to hold a safety stock of cash designed to reduce the possibility of a cash shortage or *cash-out.* However, to the extent that firms can sell marketable securities or borrow in a few hours, the need for a safety stock is minimal.

The Baumol model is possibly the simplest and most stripped-down sensible model for determining the optimal cash position. Its chief weakness is that it assumes discrete, certain cash flows. We next discuss a model designed to deal with uncertainty.

The Miller-Orr Model

Merton Miller and Daniel Orr developed a cash-balance model to deal with cash inflows and outflows that fluctuate randomly from day to day.[6] In the Miller-Orr model, both cash inflows and cash outflows are included. The model assumes that the distribution of daily

---

[5]Marginal trading costs are negative because trading costs are *reduced* when C is increased.

[6]M. H. Miller and D. Orr, "A Model of the Demand for Money by Firms," *Quarterly Journal of Economics* (August 1966).

■ FIGURE 28.3   **The Miller-Orr Model**

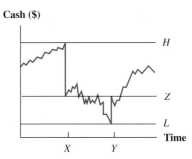

H is the upper control limit. *L* is the lower control
limit. The target cash balance is *Z*. As long as
cash is between *L* and *H*, no transaction is made.

net cash flows (cash inflow minus cash outflow) is normally distributed. On each day the
net cash flow could be the expected value or some higher or lower value. We will assume
that the expected net cash flow is zero.

Figure 28.3 shows how the Miller-Orr model works. The model operates in terms of
upper (*H*) and lower (*L*) control limits, and a target cash balance (*Z*). The firm allows its
cash balance to wander randomly within the lower and upper limits. As long as the cash balance is between *H* and *L*, the firm makes no transaction. When the cash balance reaches *H*,
such as at point *X*, then the firm buys $H - Z$ units (or dollars) of marketable securities. This
action will decrease the cash balance to *Z*. In the same way, when cash balances fall to *L*,
such as at point *Y* (the lower limit), the firm should sell $Z - L$ securities and increase the
cash balance to *Z*. In both situations, cash balances return to *Z*. Management sets the lower
limit, *L*, depending on how much risk of a cash shortfall the firm is willing to tolerate.

Like the Baumol model, the Miller-Orr model depends on trading costs and opportunity costs. The cost per transaction of buying and selling marketable securities, *F*, is assumed to be fixed. The percentage opportunity cost per period of holding cash, *K*, is the
daily interest rate on marketable securities. Unlike the Baumol model, the number of transactions per period is a random variable that varies from period to period, depending on the
pattern of cash inflows and outflows.

As a consequence, trading costs per period are dependent on the expected number of
transactions in marketable securities during the period. Similarly, the opportunity costs of
holding cash are a function of the expected cash balance per period.

Given *L*, which is set by the firm, the Miller-Orr model solves for the target cash balance, *Z*, and the upper limit, *H*. Expected total costs of the cash-balance–return policy (*Z*,
H) are equal to the sum of expected transactions costs and expected opportunity costs. The
values of *Z* (the return-cash point) and *H* (the upper limit) that minimize the expected total
cost have been determined by Miller and Orr:

$$Z^* = \sqrt[3]{3F\sigma^2/4K} + L$$
$$H^* = 3Z^* - 2L$$

where * denotes optimal values, and σ2 is the variance of net daily cash flows.

The average cash balance in the Miller-Orr model is

$$\text{Average cash balance} = \frac{4Z - L}{3}$$

EXAMPLE

To clarify the Miller-Orr model, suppose $F = \$1,000$, the interest rate is 10 percent annually, and the standard deviation of daily net cash flows is $2,000. The daily opportunity cost, K, is

$$(1 + K)^{365} - 1.0 = 0.10$$
$$1 + K = \sqrt[365]{1.10} = 1.000261$$
$$K = 0.000261$$

The variance of daily net cash flows is

$$\sigma^2 = (2,000)^2 = 4,000,000$$

Let us assume that $L = 0$:

$$Z^* = \sqrt[3]{(3 \times \$1,000 \times 4,000,000)/(4 \times 0.000261)} + 0$$
$$= \sqrt[3]{(\$11,493,900,000,000)} = \$22,568$$
$$H^* = 3 \times \$22,568 = \$67,704$$
$$\text{Average cash balance} = \frac{4 \times \$22,568}{3} = \$30,091$$

Implications of the Miller-Orr Model   To use the Miller-Orr model, the manager must do four things.

1. Set the lower control limit for the cash balance. This lower limit can be related to a minimum safety margin decided on by management.
2. Estimate the standard deviation of daily cash flows.
3. Determine the interest rate.
4. Estimate the trading costs of buying and selling marketable securities.

These four steps allow the upper limit and return point to be computed. Miller and Orr tested their model using nine months of data for cash balances for a large industrial firm. The model was able to produce average daily cash balances much lower than the averages actually obtained by the firm.[7]

The Miller-Orr model clarifies the issues of cash management. First, the model shows that the best return point, Z^*, is positively related to trading costs, F, and negatively related to K. This finding is consistent with and analogous to the Baumol model. Second, the Miller-Orr model shows that the best return point and the average cash balance are positively related to the variability of cash flows. That is, firms whose cash flows are subject to greater uncertainty should maintain a larger average cash balance.

Other Factors Influencing the Target Cash Balance

Borrowing   In our previous examples, the firm has obtained cash by selling marketable securities. Another alternative is to borrow cash. Borrowing introduces additional considerations to cash management.

---

[7]D. Mullins and R. Hamonoff discuss tests of the Miller-Orr model in "Applications of Inventory Cash Management Models," in *Modern Developments in Financial Management*, ed. by S. C. Myers (New York: Praeger, 1976). They show that the model works very well when compared to the actual cash balances of several firms. However, simple rules of thumb do as good a job as the Miller-Orr model.

1. Borrowing is likely to be more expensive than selling marketable securities because the interest rate is likely to be higher.

2. The need to borrow will depend on management's desire to hold low cash balances. A firm is more likely to need to borrow to cover an unexpected cash outflow the greater its cash flow variability and the lower its investment in marketable securities.

Compensating Balance   The costs of trading securities are well below the lost income from holding cash for large firms. Consider a firm faced with either selling $2 million of Treasury bills to replenish cash or leaving the money idle overnight. The daily opportunity cost of $2 million at a 10-percent annual interest rate is 0.10/365 = 0.027 percent per day. The daily return earned on $2 million is 0.00027 × $2 million = $540. The cost of selling $2 million of Treasury bills is much less than $540. As a consequence, a large firm will buy and sell securities many times a day before it will leave substantial amounts idle overnight.

However, most large firms hold more cash than cash-balance models imply. Here are some possible reasons.

1. Firms have cash in the bank as a compensating balance in payment for banking services.

2. Large corporations have thousands of accounts with several dozen banks. Sometimes it makes more sense to leave cash alone than to manage each account on a daily basis.

QUESTIONS

- What is a target cash balance?
- What are the strengths and weaknesses of the Baumol model and the Miller-Orr model?

28.3 MANAGING THE COLLECTION AND DISBURSEMENT OF CASH

A firm's cash balance as reported in its financial statements (*book cash* or *ledger cash*) is not the same thing as the balance shown in its bank account (*bank cash* or *collected bank cash*). The difference between bank cash and book cash is called **float** and represents the net effect of checks in the process of collection.

EXAMPLE

Imagine that General Mechanics, Inc., (GMI) currently has $100,000 on deposit with its bank. It purchases some raw materials, paying its vendors with a check written on July 8 for $100,000. The company's books (that is, ledger balances) are changed to show the $100,000 reduction in the cash balance. But the firm's bank will not find out about this check until it has been deposited at the vendor's bank and has been presented to the firm's bank for payment on, say, July 15. Until the check's presentation, the firm's bank cash is greater than its book cash, and it has *positive float.*

Position Prior to July 8:

$$\text{Float} = \text{Firm's bank cash} - \text{Firm's book cash}$$
$$= \$100,000 \qquad - \qquad \$100,000$$
$$= \qquad 0$$

Position from July 8 through July 14:

$$
\begin{aligned}
\text{Disbursement float} &= \text{Firm's bank cash} - \text{Firm's book cash} \\
&= \$100,000 \qquad - \qquad 0 \\
&= \$100,000
\end{aligned}
$$

During the period of time that the check is *clearing,* GMI has a balance with the bank of $100,000. It can obtain the benefit of this cash while the check is clearing. For example, the bank cash could be invested in marketable securities. Checks written by the firm generate *disbursement float,* causing an immediate decrease in book cash but no immediate change in bank cash.

EXAMPLE

Imagine that GMI receives a check from a customer for $100,000. Assume, as before, that the company has $100,000 deposited at its bank and has a *neutral float position.* It deposits the check and increases its book cash by $100,000 on November 8. However, the cash is not available to GMI until its bank has presented the check to the customer's bank and received $100,000 on, say, November 15. In the meantime, the cash position at GMI will reflect a collection float of $100,000.

Position Prior to November 8:

$$
\begin{aligned}
\text{Float} &= \text{Firm's bank cash} - \text{Firm's book cash} \\
&= \$100,000 \qquad - \qquad \$100,000 \\
&= \qquad 0
\end{aligned}
$$

Position from November 8 through November 14:

$$
\begin{aligned}
\text{Collection float} &= \text{Firm's bank cash} - \text{Firm's book cash} \\
&= \$100,000 \qquad - \qquad \$200,000 \\
&= -\$100,000
\end{aligned}
$$

Checks received by the firm represent *collection float,* which increases book cash immediately but does not immediately change bank cash. The firm is helped by disbursement float and is hurt by collection float. The sum of disbursement float and collection float is *net float.*

A firm should be more concerned with net float and bank cash than with book cash. If a financial manager knows that a check will not clear for several days, he or she will be able to keep a lower cash balance at the bank than might be true otherwise. Good float management can generate a great deal of money. For example, the average daily sales of Exxon are about $248 million. If Exxon speeds up the collection process or slows down the disbursement process by one day, it frees up $248 million, which can be invested in marketable securities. With an interest rate of 10 percent, this represents overnight interest of approximately $68,000 [($248 million/365) $\times$ 0.10].

Float management involves controlling the collection and disbursement of cash. The objective in cash collection is to reduce the lag between the time customers pay their bills and the time the checks are collected. The objective in cash disbursement is to slow down payments, thereby increasing the time between when checks are written and when checks are presented. In other words, collect early and pay late. Of course, to the extent that the firm succeeds in doing this, the customers and suppliers lose money, and the trade-off is the effect on the firm's relationship with them.

Collection float can be broken down into three parts: mail float, in-house processing float, and availability float:

1. *Mail Float* is the part of the collection and disbursement process where checks are trapped in the postal system.
2. *In-House Processing Float* is the time it takes the receiver of a check to process the payment and deposit it in a bank for collection.
3. *Availability Float* refers to the time required to clear a check through the banking system. The clearing process takes place using the Federal Reserve check collection service, using correspondent banks, or using local clearinghouses.

EXAMPLE

A check for $1,000 is mailed from a customer on Monday, September 1. Because of mail, processing, and clearing delays, it is not credited as available cash in the firm's bank until the following Monday, seven days later. The float for this check is

$$\text{Float} = \$1,000 \times 7 \text{ days} = \$7,000$$

Another check for $7,000 is mailed on September 1. It is available on the next day. The float for this check is

$$\text{Float} = \$7,000 \times 1 \text{ day} = \$7,000$$

The measurement of float depends on the time lag and the dollars involved. The cost of float is an opportunity cost, because the cash is unavailable for use during the time checks are tied up in the collection process. The cost of float can be determined by (1) estimating the average daily receipts, (2) calculating the average delay in obtaining the receipts, and (3) discounting the average daily receipts by the *delay-adjusted cost of capital.*

EXAMPLE

Suppose that Concepts, Inc., has two receipts each month:

	Amount	Number of Days' Delay	Float
Item 1	$5,000,000	× 3 =	$15,000,000
Item 2	3,000,000	× 5 =	15,000,000
Total	$8,000,000		$30,000,000

The average daily float over the month is equal to

Average Daily Float:

$$\frac{\text{Total float}}{\text{Total days}} = \frac{\$30,000,000}{30} = \$1,000,000$$

Another procedure that can be used to calculate average daily float is to determine average daily receipts and multiply by the average daily delay.

Average Daily Receipts:

$$\frac{\text{Total receipts}}{\text{Total days}} = \frac{\$8,000,000}{30} = \$266,666.67$$

$$\text{Weighted average delay} = (5/8) \times 3 + (3/8) \times 5$$
$$= 1.875 + 1.875 = 3.75 \text{ days}$$

$$\text{Average daily float} = \text{Average daily receipts} \times \text{Weighted average delay}$$
$$= \$266,666.67 \times 3.75 = \$1,000,000$$

EXAMPLE

Suppose Concepts, Inc., has average daily receipts of $266,667. The float results in this amount being delayed 3.75 days. The present value of the delayed cash flow is

$$V = \frac{\$266,667}{1 + r_B}$$

where r_B is the cost of debt capital for Concepts, adjusted to the relevant time frame. Suppose the annual cost of debt capital is 10 percent. Then

$$r_B = 0.1 \times (3.75/365) = 0.00103$$

and

$$V = \frac{\$266,667}{1 + 0.00103} = \$266,392.62$$

Thus, the net present value of the delay float is $266,392.62 − $266,667 = −$274.38 per day. For a year, this is −$274.38 × 365 = −$100,148.70.

Accelerating Collections

The following is a depiction of the basic parts of the cash collection process.

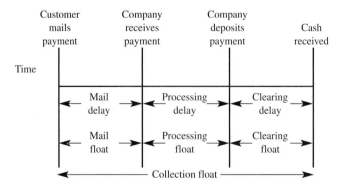

The total time in this process is made up of mailing time, check-processing time, and check-clearing time. The amount of time cash spends in each part of the cash collection process depends on where the firm's customers and banks are located and how efficient the firm is at collecting cash. Some of the techniques used to accelerate collections and reduce collection time are lockboxes, concentration banking, and wire transfers.

■ FIGURE 28.4 **Overview of Lockbox Processing**

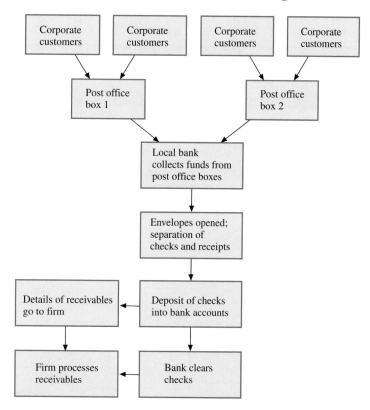

The flow starts when a corporate customer mails remittances to a post office box number instead of to the corporation. Several times a day the bank collects the lockbox receipts from the post office. the checks are then put into the company bank accounts.

Lockboxes   The **lockbox** is the most widely used device to speed up collections of cash. It is a special post office box set up to intercept accounts receivable payments.

Figure 28.4 illustrates the lockbox system.[8] The collection process is started by customers mailing their checks to a post office box instead of sending them to the firm. The lockbox is maintained by a local bank and is typically located no more than several hundred miles away. Large corporations may maintain more than 20 lockboxes around the country. In the typical lockbox system, the local bank collects the lockbox checks from the post office several times a day. The bank deposits the checks directly to the firm's account. Details of the operation are recorded (in some computer-usable form) and sent to the firm.

A lockbox system reduces mailing time because checks are received at a nearby post office instead of at corporate headquarters. Lockboxes also reduce the firm's processing time because they reduce the time required for a corporation to physically handle receivables and to deposit checks for collection. A bank lockbox should enable a firm to get its receipts processed, deposited, and cleared faster than if it were to receive checks at its headquarters and deliver them itself to the bank for deposit and clearing.

---

[8]Two types of lockboxes are offered by banks. Wholesale lockboxes are used in processing a small number of large-dollar checks. Retail lockboxes are used for processing a large number of smaller checks.

■ FIGURE 28.5   **Lockboxes and Concentration Banks in a Cash-Management System**

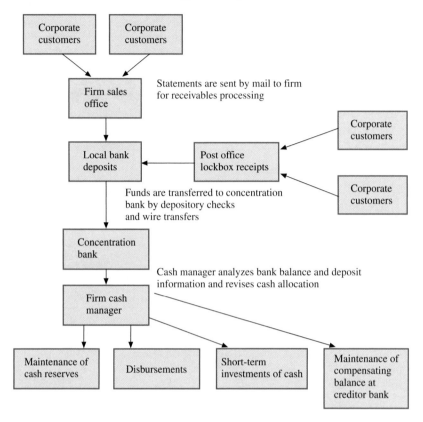

Concentration Banking   Using lockboxes is one way firms can collect checks from customers and get them into deposit banks. Another way to speed up collection is to get the cash from the deposit banks to the firm's main bank more quickly. This is done by a method called **concentration banking.**

With a concentration-banking system, the firm's sales offices are usually responsible for the collection and processing of customer checks. The sales office deposits the checks into a local deposit bank account. Surplus funds are transferred from the deposit bank to the concentration bank. The purpose of concentration banking is to obtain customer checks from nearby receiving locations. Concentration banking reduces mailing time because the firm's sales office is usually nearer than corporate headquarters to the customer. Furthermore, bank clearing time will be reduced because the customer's check is usually drawn on a local bank. Figure 28.5 illustrates this process, where concentration banks are combined with lockboxes in a total cash-management system.

The corporate cash manager uses the pools of cash at the concentration bank for short-term investing or for some other purpose. The concentration banks usually serve as the source of short-term investments. They also serve as the focal point for transferring funds to disbursement banks.

Wire Transfers   After the customers' checks get into the local banking network, the objective is to transfer the surplus funds (funds in excess of required compensating balances) from the local deposit bank to the concentration bank. The fastest and most expensive way is by **wire transfer.**[9] Wire transfers take only a few minutes, and the cash becomes available to the firm upon receipt of a wire notice at the concentration bank. Wire transfers take place electronically, from one computer to another, and eliminate the mailing and check-clearing times associated with other cash-transfer methods.

Two wire services are available—Fedwire, the Federal Reserve wire service (that is operated by the Federal Reserve bank system), and CHIPS (Clearing House Interbank Payments System)—as well as the proprietary wire systems of the major investment banks. A typical wire transfer cost is $10, which is split between the originating bank and the receiving bank.

EXAMPLE

The decision to use a bank cash-management service incorporating lockboxes and concentration banks depends on where a firm's customers are located and the speed of the U.S. postal system. Suppose Atlantic Corporation, located in Philadelphia, is considering a lockbox system. Its collection delay is currently eight days. It does business in the southwestern part of the country (New Mexico, Arizona, and California). The proposed lockbox system will be located in Los Angeles and operated by Pacific Bank. Pacific Bank has analyzed Atlantic's cash-gathering system and has concluded it can decrease collection float by two days. Specifically, the bank has come up with the following information on the proposed lockbox system:

Reduction in mailing time	= 1.0 day
Reduction in clearing time	= 0.5 day
Reduction in firm's processing time	= 0.5 day
Total reduction	2.0 days
Daily interest on Treasury bills	= 0.03%
Average number of daily payments to lockboxes	= 200
Average size of payment	= $5,000

The cash flows for the current collection are shown in the following cash flow time chart:

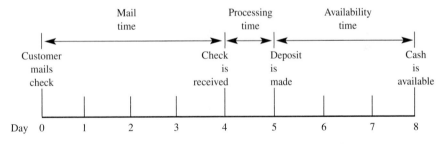

The cash flows for the lockbox collection operation will be as follows:

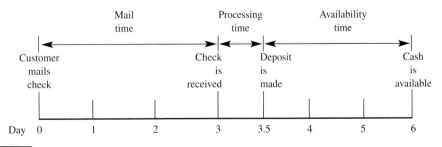

[9]A slower and cheaper way is a depository transfer check. This is an unsigned, nonnegotiable check drawn on the local collection bank and payable to the concentration bank.

The average daily collections from the southwestern region are $1 million (200 × $5,000). The Pacific Bank has agreed to operate a lockbox system for an annual fee of $20,000 and $0.30 per check processed.

On this basis the lockbox would increase the collected bank balance by $1 million × 2 = $2 million. The lockbox, in effect, releases $2 million to the firm by reducing processing, mailing, and clearing time by two days.

The Atlantic Corporation can expect to realize a daily return of 0.0003 × $2 million = $600. The yearly savings would be $600 × 365 days = $219,000 under the lockbox system.

The Pacific Bank's charge for this lockbox service would be

Annual variable fee	365 days × 200 checks × $0.30 = $21,900
Annual fixed fee	$20,000
Total	$41,900

Because the return on released funds exceeds the lockbox system costs, Atlantic should employ Pacific Bank. (We should note, however, that this example has ignored the cost of moving funds into the concentration account).

Delaying Disbursements

Accelerating collections is one method of cash management; paying more slowly is another. The cash disbursement process is illustrated in Figure 28.6. Techniques to slow down disbursement will attempt to increase mail time and check-clearing time.

■ FIGURE 28.6 **Cash Disbursement**

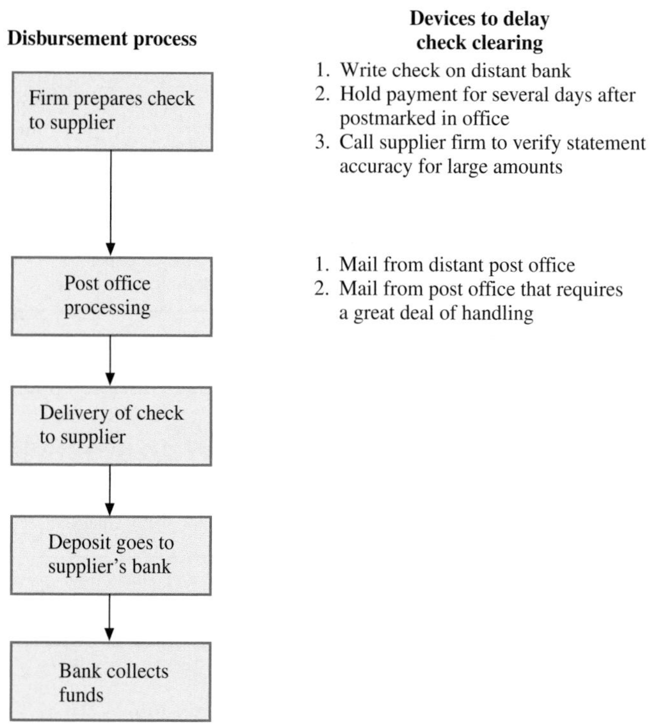

Disbursement Float ("Playing the Float Game")

Even though the cash balance at the bank may be $1 million, a firm's books may show only $500,000 because it has written $500,000 in payment checks. The disbursement float of $500,000 is available for the corporation to use until the checks are presented for payment. Float in terms of slowing down payment checks comes from mail delivery, check-processing time, and collection of funds. This is illustrated in Figure 28.6. Disbursement float can be increased by writing a check on a geographically distant bank. For example, a New York supplier might be paid with checks drawn on a Los Angeles bank. This will increase the time required for the checks to clear through the banking system.

Zero-Balance Accounts

Some firms set up a **zero-balance account (ZBA)** to handle disbursement activity. The account has a zero balance as checks are written. As checks are presented to the zero-balance account for payment (causing a negative balance), funds are automatically transferred in from a central control account. The master account and the ZBA are located in the same bank. Thus, the transfer is automatic and involves only an accounting entry in the bank.

Drafts

Firms sometimes use drafts instead of checks. Drafts differ from checks because they are not drawn on a bank but on the issuer (the firm) and are payable by the issuer. The bank acts only as an agent, presenting the draft to the issuer for payment. When a draft is transmitted to a firm's bank for collection, the bank must present the draft to the issuing firm for acceptance before making payment. After the draft has been accepted, the firm must deposit the necessary cash to cover the payment. The use of drafts rather than checks allows a firm to keep lower cash balances in its disbursement accounts because cash does not need to be deposited until the drafts are presented to it for payment.

Ethical and Legal Questions

The cash manager must work with cash balances collected by the bank and not the firm's book balance, which reflects checks that have been deposited but not collected. If not, a cash manager could be drawing on uncollected cash as a source for making short-term investments. Most banks charge a penalty for use of uncollected funds. However, banks may not have good enough accounting and control procedures to be fully aware of the use of uncollected funds. This raises some ethical and legal questions for the firm.

In May 1985, Robert Fomon, chairman of E. F. Hutton, pleaded guilty to 2,000 charges of mail and wire fraud in connection with a scheme the firm had operated from 1980 to 1982. E. F. Hutton employees wrote checks totaling hundreds of millions of dollars in uncollected cash, which were invested in short-term money-market assets. E. F. Hutton's systematic overdrafting of accounts is apparently not a widespread practice among corporations, and since the E. F. Hutton affair, firms have been much more careful in managing their cash accounts. Generally, firms are scrupulous in investing only the cash they actually have on hand. E. F. Hutton paid a $2 million fine, reimbursed the government (the U.S. Department of Justice) $750,000, and reserved $8 million for restitution to defrauded banks.

CONCEPT QUESTIONS

? • Describe collection and disbursement float.
   • What are lockboxes? Concentration banks? Wire transfers?
   • Suppose an overzealous financial manager writes checks on uncollected funds. Aside from legal issues, who is the financial loser in this situation?

28.4 INVESTING IDLE CASH

If a firm has a temporary cash surplus, it can invest in short-term marketable securities. The market for short-term financial assets is called the *money market.* The maturity of short-term financial assets that trade in the money market is one year or less.

Most large firms manage their own short-term financial assets, transacting through banks and dealers. Some large firms and many small firms use money-market funds. These are funds that invest in short-term financial assets for a management fee. The management fee is compensation for the professional expertise and diversification provided by the fund manager. Among the many money-market mutual funds, some specialize in corporate customers. Banks also offer *sweep accounts,* where the bank takes all excess available funds at the close of each business day and invests them for the firm.

Firms have temporary cash surpluses for these reasons: to help finance seasonal or cyclical activities of the firm, to help finance planned expenditures of the firm, and to provide for unanticipated contingencies.

Seasonal or Cyclical Activities

Some firms have a predictable cash flow pattern. They have surplus cash flows during part of the year and deficit cash flows the rest of the year. For example, Toys "R" Us, a retail toy firm, has a seasonal cash flow pattern influenced by Christmas. Such a firm may buy marketable securities when surplus cash flows occur and sell marketable securities when deficits occur. Of course, bank loans are another short-term financing device. Figure 28.7 illustrates the use of bank loans and marketable securities to meet temporary financing needs.

Planned Expenditures

Firms frequently accumulate temporary investments in marketable securities to provide the cash for a plant-construction program, dividend payment, and other large expenditures. Thus, firms may issue bonds and stocks before the cash is needed, investing the proceeds in short-term marketable securities, and then selling the securities to finance the expenditures.

The important characteristics of short-term marketable securities are their maturity, default risk, marketability, and taxability.

■ FIGURE 28.7 **Seasonal Cash Demands**

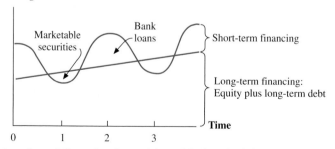

Time 1: A surplus cash flow exists. Seasonal demand for investing is low. The surplus cash flow is invested in short-term marketable securities. Time 2: A deficit cash flow exists. Seasonal demand for investing is high. The financial deficit is financed by selling marketable securities and by bank borrowing.

Maturity   *Maturity* refers to the time period over which interest and principal payments are made. For a given change in the level of interest rates, the prices of longer-maturity securities will change more than those for shorter-maturity securities. As a consequence, firms that invest in long-term maturity securities are accepting greater risk than firms that invest in securities with short-term maturities. This type of risk is usually called *interest-rate risk.* Most firms limit their investments in marketable securities to those maturing in less than 90 days. Of course, the expected return on securities with short-term maturities is usually less than the expected return on securities with longer maturities.

Default Risk   *Default risk* refers to the probability that interest or principal will not be paid on the due date and in the promised amount. In previous chapters we observed that various financial reporting agencies, such as Moody's Investors Service and Standard & Poor's, compile and publish ratings of various corporate and public securities. These ratings are connected to default risk. Of course, some securities have negligible default risk, such as U.S. Treasury bills. Given the purposes of investing idle corporate cash, firms typically avoid investing in marketable securities with significant default risk.

Marketability   *Marketability* refers to how easy it is to convert an asset to cash. Sometimes marketability is referred to as *liquidity.* It has two characteristics:

1. *No Price-Pressure Effect.* If an asset can be sold in large amounts without changing the market price, it is marketable. Price-pressure effects are those that come about when the price of an asset must be lowered to facilitate the sale.
2. *Time.* If an asset can be sold quickly at the existing market price, it is marketable. In contrast, a Renoir painting or antique desk appraised at $1 million will likely sell for much less if the owner must sell on short notice.

In general, marketability is the ability to sell an asset for its face market value quickly and in large amounts. Perhaps the most marketable of all securities are U.S. Treasury bills.

Taxability   Several kinds of securities have varying degrees of tax exemption.

1. The interest on the bonds of state and local governments is exempt from federal taxes, and usually from the state and local taxes where the bonds are issued. Pretax expected returns on state and local bonds must be lower than on similar taxable investments and therefore are more attractive to corporations in high marginal tax brackets.
2. Seventy percent of the dividend income on preferred and common stock is exempt from corporate income taxes.

The market price of securities will reflect the total demand and supply of tax influences. The position of the firm may be different from that of the market.

Different Types of Money-Market Securities

Money-market securities are generally highly marketable and short term. They usually have low risk of default. They are issued by the U.S. government (for example, U.S. Treasury bills), domestic and foreign banks (for example, certificates of deposit), and business corporations (commercial paper, for example).

U.S. Treasury bills are obligations of the U.S. government that mature in 90, 180, 270, or 360 days. They are pure discount securities. The 90-day and 180-day bills are sold by auction every week, and 270-day and 360-day bills are sold every month.

U.S. Treasury notes and bonds have original maturities of more than one year. They are interest-bearing securities. The interest is exempt from state and local taxes.

Federal agency securities are securities issued by corporations and agencies created by the U.S. government, such as the Federal Home Loan Bank Board and the Government National Mortgage Association (*Ginnie Mae*). The interest rates on agency issues are higher than those on comparable U.S. Treasury issues. This is true because agency issues are not as marketable as U.S. Treasury issues, and they have more default risk.

Short-term tax exempts are short-term securities issued by states, municipalities, local housing agencies, and urban renewal agencies. They have more default risk than U.S. Treasury issues and are less marketable. The interest is exempt from federal income tax. As a consequence, the pretax yield on tax exempts is lower than those on comparable securities, such as U.S. Treasury bills.

Commercial paper refers to short-term securities issued by finance companies, banks, and corporations. Commercial paper typically is unsecured notes. Maturities range from a few weeks to 270 days. There is no active secondary market in commercial paper. As a consequence, their marketability is low. (However, firms that issue commercial paper will directly repurchase before maturity.) The default risk of commercial paper depends on the financial strength of the issuer. Moody's and Standard & Poor's publish quality ratings for commercial paper.

Certificates of deposit (CDs) are short-term loans to commercial banks. There are active markets in CDs of 3-month, 6-month, 9-month, and 12-month maturities.

Repurchase agreements are sales of government securities (for example, U.S. Treasury bills) by a bank or securities dealer with an agreement to repurchase. An investor typically buys some Treasury securities from a bond dealer and simultaneously agrees to sell them back at a later date at a specified higher price. Repurchase agreements are usually very short term—overnight to a few days.

Eurodollar CDs are deposits of dollars with foreign banks.

Banker's acceptances are time drafts (orders to pay) issued by a business firm (usually an importer) that have been accepted by a bank that guarantees payment.

CONCEPT QUESTIONS

- Why do firms find themselves with idle cash?
- What are the types of money-market securities?

28.5 SUMMARY AND CONCLUSIONS

The chapter discussed how firms manage cash.

1. A firm holds cash to conduct transactions and to compensate banks for the various services they render.
2. The optimal amount of cash for a firm to hold depends on the opportunity cost of holding cash and the uncertainty of future cash inflows and outflows. The Baumol model and the Miller-Orr model are two transactions models that provide rough guidelines for determining the optimal cash position.
3. The firm can make use of a variety of procedures to manage the collection and disbursement of cash in such a way as to speed up the collection of cash and slow down payments. Some methods to speed up collection are lockboxes, concentration banking, and wire transfers. The financial manager must always work with collected company cash balances and not with the company's book balance. To do otherwise is to use the bank's cash without the bank knowing it, raising ethical and legal questions.

4. Because of seasonal and cyclical activities, to help finance planned expenditures, or as a reserve for unanticipated needs, firms temporarily find themselves with cash surpluses. The money market offers a variety of possible vehicles for parking this idle cash.

KEY TERMS

Compensating balances   772
Concentration banking   784
Float   779
Lockbox   783

Target cash balance 773
Transactions motive   772
Wire transfer   785
Zero-balance account (ZBA)   787

SUGGESTED READINGS

The following are general readings in cash management:

Hill, Ned. C., and William L. Sartoris. *Short-Term Financial Management.* New York: Macmillan Publishing Company, 1992.

Maness, Terry S., and John T. Zietlow. *Short-Term Financial Management.* Minneapolis/St. Paul: West Publishing Company, 1993.

QUESTIONS AND PROBLEMS

Reasons for Holding Cash

28.1 What are the reasons for holding cash?

Determining the Target Cash Balance

28.2 Indicate whether the following actions increase, decrease, or cause no change in a company's cash balance.
  a. Interest rates paid on money-market securities rise.
  b. Commissions charged by brokers increase.
  c. The compensating-balance requirement of a bank is lowered.
  d. The cost of borrowing decreases.
  e. The firm's credit rating declines.
  f. Direct fees for banking services are established.

28.3 A company's weekly average cash balances are as follows:

Week 1	$24,000
Week 2	34,000
Week 3	10,000
Week 4	15,000

If the annual interest rate is 12 percent, what return can be earned on the average cash balances?

28.4 The Casablanca Piano Company is currently holding $800,000 in cash. It projects that over the next year its cash outflows will exceed its cash inflows by $345,000 per month. Each time securities are bought or sold through a broker, the company pays a fee of $500. The annual interest rate on money-market securities is 7 percent.
  a. How much of this cash should be retained and how much should be used to increase the company's holdings of marketable securities?
  b. After the initial investment of excess cash, how many times during the next 12 months will securities be sold?

28.5 Lisa Tylor, CFO of Purple Rain Co., concluded from the Baumol model that the optimal cash balance for the firm is $20 million. The annual interest rate on marketable securities is 7.5 percent. The fixed cost of selling securities to replenish cash is $5,000. Purple Rain's cash flow pattern is well approximated by the Baumol model. What can you infer about Purple Rain's average weekly cash disbursement?

28.6 The variance of the daily net cash flows for the Tseneg Asian Import Company is $1.44 million. The opportunity cost to the firm of holding cash is 8 percent per year. The fixed cost of buying and selling securities is $600 per transaction.

   What should the target cash level and upper limit be, if the tolerable lower limit has been established at $20,000?

28.7 Gold Star Co. and Silver Star Co. both manage their cash flows according to the Miller-Orr model. Gold Star's daily cash flow is controlled between $100,000 and $200,000, whereas Silver Star's daily cash flow is controlled between $150,000 and $300,000. The annual interest rates Gold Star and Silver Star can get are 10 percent and 9 percent, respectively, and the costs per transaction of trading securities are $2,000 and $2,500, respectively.

   a. What are their respective target cash balances?

   b. Which firm's daily cash flow is more volatile?

Managing the Collection and Disbursement of Cash

28.8 Garden Groves, Inc., a Florida-based company, has determined that a majority of its customers are located in the New York City area. Therefore, it is considering using a lockbox system offered by a bank located in New York. The bank has estimated that use of the system will reduce collection float by three days. Based on the following information, should the lockbox system be adopted?

> Average number of payments per day: 150
> Average value of payment: $15,000
> Fixed annual lockbox fee: $80,000
> Variable lockbox fee: $0.50/transaction
> Annual interest rate on money-market securities: 7.5 percent

28.9 A large New England lumber producer, Salisbury Stakes, Inc., is planning to use a lockbox system to speed collections from its customers located in the midwestern United States. A Chicago-area bank will provide this service for an annual fee of $15,000 plus $0.25 per transaction. The estimated reduction in collection and processing time is two days. Treasury bills are currently yielding 6 percent per year.

   If the average customer payment in this region is $4,500, how many customers each day, on average, must use the system to make it profitable?

28.10 Each business day, on average, a company writes checks totaling $12,000 to pay its suppliers. The usual clearing time for these checks is five days. Each day, the company receives payments from its customers in the form of checks totaling $15,000. The cash from the payments is available to the firm after three days.

   Calculate the company's disbursement float, collection float, and net float.

   How would these values change if the collected funds were available in four days instead of three?

28.11 It takes the Herman Company about seven days to receive and deposit checks from customers. The top management of the Herman Company is considering a lockbox system. It is expected that the lockbox system will reduce float time to four days. Average daily collections are $100,000. The marketwide interest rate is 12 percent.

   a. What would the reduction in outstanding cash balances be as a result of implementing the lockbox system?

   b. What is the return that could be earned on these savings?

   c. What is the maximum monthly charge the Herman Company should pay for this lockbox system?

28.12 The Walter Company disburses checks every two weeks that average $200,000 in total and take three days to clear. How much cash can the Walter Company save annually if it delays the transfer of funds from an interest-bearing account that pays 0.04 percent per day for these three days?

28.13 The Miller Company has an agreement with the First National Bank by which the bank handles $4 million in collections each day and requires a $500,000 compensating balance. Miller is contemplating canceling the agreement and dividing its eastern region so that two other banks will handle its business. Banks 1 and 2 will each handle $2 million of collections each day, requiring a compensating balance of $300,000. Miller's financial management expects that collections will be accelerated by one day if the eastern region is divided. The T-bill rate is 7 percent. Should the Miller Company implement the new system? What will the annual net savings be?

28.14 Anthony Marino, CFO of Thousand Years Inc., is evaluating two alternatives of float management: lockbox and concentration banking. The average number of daily payments to lockboxes is 250 with the average size of each payment at $7,500. The lockbox system can reduce the collection float by 1.5 days and concentration banking can reduce the collection float by 1 day. However, the bank charges an annual fee of $30,000 and $0.30 per check processed for the lockbox service. Which method is more economical for Thousand Years, the lockbox system or the concentration-banking system? Assume daily interest on Treasury bills is 0.03 percent.

Investing Idle Cash

28.15 What are the important characteristics of short-term marketable securities?

Appendix 28A ADJUSTABLE-RATE PREFERRED STOCK, AUCTION-RATE PREFERRED STOCK, AND FLOATING-RATE CERTIFICATES OF DEPOSIT

Corporate cash managers are continually seeking new ways to improve the return on their surplus cash. Many of the sophisticated investment vehicles developed over the last decade are too illiquid or too risky or have an inappropriate time horizon for use in cash management. However, three instruments—adjustable-rate preferred stock, auction-rate preferred stock, and floating-rate CDs or notes—offer substantial benefits and are currently employed by corporations in their cash-management activities.

Adjustable-Rate Preferred Stock

Adjustable-rate preferred stock (ARPS) is designed to offer rates of return competitive with more traditional money-market instruments while still affording the corporate investor the 80-percent tax exclusion on dividend income—a tax advantage that makes equity investments extremely attractive.

Agencies such as Moody's or Standard & Poor's give issues credit ratings, so the cash manager has a gauge to judge the creditworthiness of the instruments relative to other investments. The dividend rate on these issues is adjusted quarterly at a fixed spread over or under the highest of the 90-day T-bill rate, the 10-year T-note rate, or the 20-year T-bond rate prevailing on the reset date. The spread is specified by each issuer. ARPS issues have *collars*—minimum and maximum dividend-rate levels—that, when hit, result in the issue taking on the characteristics of a fixed-rate preferred instrument.

The floating-rate feature keeps the dividend rate (and thus the overall pretax return) in line with alternative investments and reduces price volatility caused solely by changes in interest rates. The floating rate does not, however, eliminate all of the incremental risk associated with these instruments.

Risk is present in the ARPS market and can be broken down into three categories. Cash managers must continually reevaluate the market in light of changes that might occur in any of the three areas.

The greatest risk in the ARPS market is derived from the limited number of issuers and their clustering in certain industry groups, most notably banking, and the ever-present risk of downgraded ratings. Like any other credit instrument, ARPS is subject to volatility based on the market's perceptions of the strength of the issuer and industry group. The possibility of impaired principal is a real one for ARPS purchasers, because concerns about credit could govern the floating-rate dividend between and on reset dates. The cash manager must be aware that substantial month-to-month volatility (the normal time horizon for corporate evaluation of their cash portfolios) could exist with ARPS investments.

A second risk factor centers around the narrowness of the primary and secondary markets for ARPS. The demand for these issues comes primarily from corporate investors, and the limited nature of this investment base is a factor in evaluating the depth of the market. If a cash manager must liquidate a position quickly, a thin market could exacerbate price pressure. As a result, most corporate investors employ mutual-fund managers who specialize in the ARPS market to run their portfolios. Liquidity is normally next-day with the funds (although principal is by no means guaranteed), and mutual-fund managers represent the most active players in the market.

Finally, changes in the tax code have a great impact on the price of ARPS issues, because their main feature is the tax advantage of the dividend exclusion. The Tax Reform Act of 1986 reduced this exclusion from 85 to 70 percent. Assuming a 46-percent tax rate, a corporate investor in the ARPS market would have found its dividend income being taxed at 13.8 percent (30 percent taxed at 46 percent) instead of 6.9 percent (15 percent taxed at 46 percent). Such an increase would have undoubtedly resulted in substantial price declines for existing issues. Luckily for both ARPS issuers and purchasers, the top corporate tax rate is now lower than 46 percent, resulting in only a small change for recipients of dividend income. The issue of tax advantage is crucial, because ARPS as an investment is evaluated on an after-tax risk-adjusted basis relative to other instruments. If the added risk inherent in the instrument begins to eclipse the tax advantage, the instrument will become increasingly unattractive.

The adjustable-rate preferred market has not fared as well as early proponents had hoped, primarily because the floating-rate dividend failed to compensate for credit concerns about the issuers. This has resulted in many issues trading below par and has prompted the development of several related instruments. The most successful of these new vehicles is auction-rate preferred stock.

Auction-Rate Preferred Stock

The similarity between ARPS and *auction-rate preferred stock* extends only to the fact that both have a floating dividend rate and afford the corporate investor the same exclusion of taxes on dividends. Auction rates differ from ARPS in the way the dividend is set and in the way these portfolios are managed.

The dividend rate for auction-rate preferred is set not by the issuers but by the market through a process called a *Dutch auction*. The auction permits investors to determine the dividend yield for the 49-day period that is standard between reset dates. The Internal Revenue Service requires that a corporate investor hold dividend-paying stock for at least

45 days to be eligible for the dividend exclusion; 49 days was chosen so the auctions will always occur on the same day of the week for the life of individual issues.

An auction-rate preferred stock is auctioned as follows. Each bidder (someone who already owns shares and wishes to continue to hold them, or a new purchaser) submits to the agent in charge of the auction the number of shares desired and at what dividend level. The lowest rate that sells out the available shares will be the dividend for the 49 days until the next reset/auction. Investors who already own shares going into the auction have the option to take their shares at whatever dividend is set (called *rolling*) or bid the lowest rate they would accept and risk losing some or all of the shares to another bidder who would be willing to take a lower dividend. Of course, shareholders also have the right to simply sell all of their shares at the auction. Although the process is essentially independent, the dividend rate for most issues is usually set at approximately 60 to 80 percent of the 60-day AA commercial paper rate prevailing on auction day.

Auction-rate preferred stock offers the corporate investor several important features:

1. The 49-day reset period is shorter than the 90-day period found in the ARPS market, reducing the potential for price volatility resulting from both interest-rate movement and credit concerns.

2. The auction method of determining the dividend level makes it more likely that the issue will trade at par, minimizing principal impairment. The shorter reset period also offers the cash manager increased liquidity in the event funds are needed for corporate operations between auctions. The auction-rate investor sacrifices some return relative to ARPS because of these features, but still garners a substantial after-tax benefit relative to alternative money-market investments.

3. The auction-rate preferred market is more accessible to the corporate investor, allowing it to invest individually rather than through a mutual fund. Many cash managers prefer the added control this gives them over their portfolios.

The risks associated with auction-rate preferred stock are smaller than those associated with ARPS but must still be considered substantial for the cash manager who may need immediate liquidity or who faces strict return criteria. These risks include the following:

1. *Failed Auctions.* If the agent supervising an auction does not receive enough bids to match offers to sell for existing shares of a particular issue, the auction is considered to have failed. There have been several auction failures, but it is not as catastrophic as it sounds. It means that the dividend rate for the subsequent 49-day period will be set at 110 percent of the 60-day AA commercial paper rate. A seller would therefore be faced with a capital loss if it wished to liquidate.

2. *Issuer Credit Quality.* As with ARPS, all auction-rate preferred issues receive a rating from Moody's or Standard & Poor's. They remain susceptible to perceived or actual changes in that credit quality between reset periods. To facilitate the new market, some large brokers were even guaranteeing to redeem auction-rate preferred at par between reset periods to generate investor participation.

3. *Changes in the Tax Code.* Major changes in the tax code will affect the auction-rate preferred market in much the same manner as they would the APRS market. Once again, it is crucial to remember that these instruments are judged on an after-tax risk-adjusted basis relative to alternative investments.

Auction-rate preferred stock has been extremely well received by the corporate marketplace. The key to its continued success will be diversification of issuers, orderly and successful auctions, and an ongoing after-tax yield advantage relative to other money-market investments.

Floating-Rate Certificates of Deposit

A third investment available to the cash manager looking to increase the return on surplus cash is the *floating-rate certificate of deposit* or note. Our discussion centers on the CD, but the same argument applies to the short-term note, adjusting for time-horizon considerations.

The floating-rate certificate of deposit (FRCD) market presents substantial investment opportunities for the manager of short-term cash. Frequently reset coupons, the hallmark of the FRCD, allow the investor to combine the yield of an intermediate-term instrument with the liquidity of a short-term one. This combination also reduces interest-rate risk and provides for capital maintenance, while continuing to provide attractive returns.

Two issues must be addressed when evaluating the FRCD market:

1. How are the issues priced?
2. Which base rate should be selected?

Floating-rate CDs are priced at a spread above or below a well-known market index such as the London Interbank Offered Rate (LIBOR), T-bills, or commercial paper. The width of the spread reflects the issuer's credit, the maturity of the issue, its liquidity, and the overall level of rates at the time of issuance. In general, this spread is fixed over the life of the security, but some new issues do have a floating spread. When the market perception of credit quality changes significantly from that implied in the spread to the base rate, the price of the security will decline as the market compensates investors for the increased risk.

The actual coupon paid (the index rate plus or minus the predetermined spread) to the investor will be reset periodically, usually monthly, quarterly, or semiannually. It is the floating nature of the coupon that keeps most FRCDs within one to two points of par at all times, as the issue is continually repriced relative to existing market conditions. Price stability will increase with the frequency of reset.

Most FRCDs also feature redemption specifications in the form of call or put options. In the case of a call, the issuer has the option to call the security back from an investor at par, usually within three to five years of issuance. The security can be called on any coupon-payment date, and, as would be expected, the option is usually exercised when the security is trading at a premium. For the put option, the investor has the right to sell the security back to the issuer at par before maturity. The option is usually exercised when the security is trading at a discount. These features must be incorporated into yield calculations, with the call or put dates generally substituted for the maturity date.

The initial price of the FRCD will adapt to reflect market demand for the issue, liquidity, and favorable aspects of the issue's structure. Whether the security trades at a premium or discount to par depends on changes in the market's perception of these and the other factors discussed previously. However, given frequently reset coupons, only drastic changes in issuer quality or quality spreads will prompt significant deterioration of principal.

The price of an FRCD will also be affected if a change occurs in the relationship between index rates, such as a widening of the T-bill/Eurodollar spread. Assume that two FRCDs are priced to identical yields, one at a spread over LIBOR and the other at a spread above T-bills. If the T-bill/Eurodollar spread widens, the FRCDs indexed to LIBOR will experience a price decline. This will occur regardless of the absolute level of interest rates or any shift in market perception of specific credit risk.

In evaluating an FRCD, the selection of an issue based on its index rate can be as important as selection of an issue based on the issuer's credit ratings or maturity. The choice of an index reflects the perception of how the issuer's industry fundamentals will behave relative to that index. For instance, the choice of T-bills as the base implies an analysis of how the issuer will perform relative to a risk-free measure; the choice of commercial paper implies an analysis of the issuer's prospects relative to companies with access to that market.

The base rate will also be important when general quality concerns arise in the market. A LIBOR index will reflect those concerns, and the price of an FRCD indexed to LIBOR should not change drastically, because its coupon is linked directly to a market-determined cost of funds. An FRCD indexed to T-bills, however, might exhibit substantial price volatility over the same time period. The greater the index's sensitivity to market movement, the greater the issue's price stability.

Although the FRCD does not offer the tax advantage of ARPS or auction-rate preferred stock, it gives the cash manager an opportunity to keep returns on excess cash in line with changing interest rates. The secondary market for FRCDs is still developing but is considerably deeper than that for preferred securities.

All of these investments were designed for cash-management activities that allow for investment of cash for longer periods of time. Generally, a cash manager will be using at least a 9-month to 12-month horizon before considering investing in these vehicles. Money should not be committed to these investments unless the manager can be reasonably sure that it will not be needed for corporate operations for at least one year.

CHAPTER 29

Credit Management

EXECUTIVE SUMMARY

When a firm sells goods and services it can (1) be paid in cash immediately or (2) wait for a time to be paid, that is, extend credit to customers. Granting credit is investing in a customer, an investment tied to the sale of a product or service. This chapter examines the firm's decision to grant credit.

An account receivable is created when credit is granted. These receivables include credit granted to other firms, called *trade credit,* and credit granted consumers, called *consumer credit.* About one-sixth of all the assets of industrial firms are in the form of accounts receivable. Trade credit extended by a firm's supplier to the firm appears as an accounts payable. Figure 29.1 illustrates this aspect of trade credit.

The investment in accounts receivable for any firm depends on both the amount of credit sales and the average collection period. For example, if a firm's credit sales per day equal $1,000 and its average collection period is 30 days, its accounts receivable will be equal to $30,000. Thus, a firm's investment in accounts receivable depends on factors influencing credit sales and collection. A firm's credit policy affects these factors.

The following are the components of credit policy:

1. **Terms of the sale.** A firm must decide on certain conditions when selling its goods and services for credit. For example, the terms of sale may specify the credit period, the cash discount, and the type of credit instrument.

2. **Credit analysis.** When granting credit, a firm tries to distinguish between customers that will pay and customers that will not pay. Firms use a number of devices and procedures to determine the probability that customers will pay.

3. **Collection policy.** Firms that grant credit must establish a policy for collecting the cash when it becomes due.

This chapter discusses each of the components of credit policy that makes up the decision to grant credit.

In some ways, the decision to grant credit is connected to the cash collection process described in the previous chapter. This is illustrated in Figure 29.2 with a cash-flow diagram.

The typical sequence of events when a firm grants credit is (1) the credit sale is made, (2) the customer sends a check to the firm, (3) the firm deposits the check, and (4) the firm's account is credited for the amount of the check.

29.1 TERMS OF THE SALE

The terms of sale refer to the period for which credit is granted, the cash discount, and the type of credit instrument. For example, suppose a customer is granted credit with terms of 2/10, net 30. This means that the customer has 30 days from the **invoice** date within which

■ FIGURE 29.1 **Trade Credit**

Trade credit extended to a customer by a firm appears as an accounts receivable.
Trade credit extended by the firm's supplier to the firm appears as an accounts payable.

■ FIGURE 29.2 **The Cash Flows of Granting Credit**

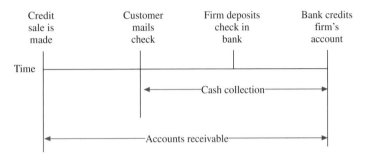

to pay.[1] In addition, a cash discount of 2 percent from the stated sales price is to be given if payment is made in 10 days. If the stated terms are net 60, the customer has 60 days from the invoice date to pay and no discount is offered for early payment.

When sales are seasonal, a firm might use seasonal dating. O. M. Scott and Sons is a manufacturer of lawn and garden products with a seasonal dating policy that is tied to the growing season. Payments for winter shipments of fertilizer might be due in the spring or summer. A firm offering 3/10, net 60, May 1 dating, is making the effective invoice date May 1. The stated amount must be paid on June 30, regardless of when the sale is made. The cash discount of 3 percent can be taken until May 10.

Credit Period

Credit periods vary among different industries. For example, a jewelry store may sell diamond engagement rings for 5/30, net 4 months. A food wholesaler, selling fresh fruit and produce, might use net 7. Generally a firm must consider three factors in setting a credit period:

1. *The Probability That the Customer Will Not Pay.* A firm whose customers are in high-risk businesses may find itself offering restrictive credit terms.
2. *The Size of the Account.* If the account is small, the credit period will be shorter. Small accounts are more costly to manage, and small customers are less important.
3. *The Extent to Which the Goods Are Perishable.* If the collateral values of the goods are low and cannot be sustained for long periods, less credit will be granted.

Lengthening the credit period effectively reduces the price paid by the customer. Generally this increases sales.

---

[1]An *invoice* is a bill written by a seller of goods or services and submitted to the buyer. The invoice date is usually the same as the shipping date.

Cash Discounts

Cash discounts are often part of the terms of sale. One reason they are offered is to speed up the collection of receivables. The firm must trade this off against the cost of the discount.

EXAMPLE

Edward Manalt, the chief financial officer of Ruptbank Company, is considering the request of the company's largest customer, who wants to take a 3-percent discount for payment within 20 days on a $10,000 purchase. In other words, he intends to pay $9,700 [$10,000 × (1 − 0.03)]. Normally, this customer pays in 30 days with no discount. The cost of debt capital for Ruptbank is 10 percent. Edward has worked out the cash flow implications illustrated in Figure 29.3. He assumes that the time required to cash the check when the customer receives it is the same under both credit arrangements. He has calculated the present value of the two proposals:

Current Policy:

$$PV = \frac{\$10,000}{1 + (0.1 \times 30/365)} = \$9,918.48$$

Proposed Policy:

$$PV = \frac{\$9,700}{1 + (0.1 \times 20/365)} = \$9,647.14$$

His calculation shows that granting the discount would cost the Ruptbank firm $271.34 ($9,918.48 − $9,647.14) in present value. Consequently, Ruptbank is better off with the current credit arrangement.

■ FIGURE 29.3   **Cash Flows for Different Credit Terms**

Current situation: Customers usually pay 30 days from the sale date and receive no discount.
Proposed situation: Customer will pay 20 days from the sale date at a 3-percent discount from the $10,000 purchase price.

In the previous example, we implicitly assumed that granting credit had no side effects. However, the decision to grant credit may generate higher sales and involve a different cost structure. The next example illustrates the impact of changes in the level of sales and costs in the credit decision.

EXAMPLE

Suppose that Ruptbank Company has variable costs of $0.50 per $1 of sales. If offered a discount of 3 percent, customers will increase their order size by 10 percent. This new information is shown in Figure 29.4. That is, the customer will increase the order size to $11,000 and, with the 3-percent discount, will remit $10,670 [$11,000 $\times$ (1 − 0.03)] to Ruptbank in 20 days. It will cost more to fill the larger order because variable costs are $5,500. The net present values are worked out here:

Current Policy:

$$\text{NPV} = -\$5,000 + \frac{\$10,000}{1 + (0.1 \times 30/365)} = \$4,918.48$$

Proposed Policy:

$$\text{NPV} = -\$5,500 + \frac{\$10,670}{1 + (0.1 \times 20/365)} = \$5,111.85$$

Now it is clear that the firm is better off with the proposed credit policy. This increase is the net effect of several different factors including the larger initial costs, the earlier receipt of the cash inflows, the increased sales level, and the discount.

Credit Instruments

Most credit is offered on *open account*. This means that the only formal **credit instrument** is the invoice, which is sent with the shipment of goods, and which the customer signs as evidence that the goods have been received. Afterward, the firm and its customers record the exchange on their accounting books.

■ FIGURE 29.4 **Cash Flows for Different Credit Terms: The Impact of New Sales and Costs**

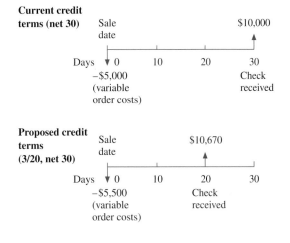

At times, the firm may require that the customer sign a *promissory note,* or IOU. This is used when the order is large and when the firm anticipates a problem in collections. Promissory notes can eliminate controversies later about the existence of a credit agreement.

One problem with promissory notes is that they are signed after delivery of the goods. One way to obtain a credit commitment from a customer before the goods are delivered is through the use of a *commercial draft.* The selling firm typically writes a commercial draft calling for the customer to pay a specific amount by a specified date. The draft is then sent to the customer's bank with the shipping invoices. The bank has the buyer sign the draft before turning over the invoices. The goods can then be shipped to the buyer. If immediate payment is required, it is called a *sight draft.* Here, funds must be turned over to the bank before the goods are shipped.

Frequently, even the signed draft is not enough for the seller. In this case, he might demand that the banker pay for the goods and collect the money from the customer. When the banker agrees to do so in writing, the document is called a *banker's acceptance.* That is, the banker *accepts* responsibility for payment. Because banks generally are well-known and well-respected institutions, the banker's acceptance becomes a liquid instrument. In other words, the seller can then sell (*discount*) the banker's acceptance in the secondary market.

A firm can also use a *conditional sales contract* as a credit instrument. This is an arrangement where the firm retains legal ownership of the goods until the customer has completed payment. Conditional sales contracts usually are paid off in installments and have interest costs built into them.

QUESTION
CONCEPT
?

- What considerations enter into the determination of the terms of sale?

29.2 THE DECISION TO GRANT CREDIT: RISK AND INFORMATION

Locust Industries has been in existence for two years. It is one of several successful firms that develop computer programs. The present financial managers have set out two alternative credit strategies: The firm can offer credit, or the firm can refuse credit.

Suppose Locust has determined that, if it offers no credit to its customers, it can sell its existing computer software for $50 per program. It estimates that the costs to produce a typical computer program are equal to $20 per program.

The alternative is to offer credit. In this case, customers of Locust will pay one period later. With some probability, Locust has determined that if it offers credit, it can charge higher prices and expect higher sales.

Strategy 1: Refuse Credit   If Locust refuses to grant credit, cash flows will not be delayed, and period 0 net cash flows, NCF, will be

$$P_0Q_0 - C_0Q_0 = \text{NCF}$$

The subscripts denote the time when the cash flows are incurred, where

P_0 = Price per unit received at time 0

C_0 = Cost per unit received at time 0

Q_0 = Quantity sold at time 0

The net cash flows at period 1 are zero, and the net present value to Locust of refusing credit will simply be the period 0 net cash flow:

$$NPV = NCF$$

For example, if credit is not granted and $Q_0 = 100$, the NPV can be calculated as

$$(\$50 \times 100) - (\$20 \times 100) = \$3,000$$

Strategy 2: Offer Credit   Alternatively, let us assume that Locust grants credit to all customers for one period. The factors that influence the decision are listed below.

	Strategy 1 Refuse Credit	Strategy 2 Offer Credit
Price per unit	$P_0 = \$50$	$P_0' = \$50$
Quantity sold	$Q_0 = 100$	$Q_0' = 200$
Cost per unit	$C_0 = \$20$	$C_0' = \$25$
Probability of payment	$h = 1$	$h = 0.90$
Credit period	0	1 period
Discount rate	0	$r_B = 0.01$

The prime (′) denotes the variables under the second strategy. If the firm offers credit and the new customers pay, the firm will receive revenues of $P_0' Q_0'$ one period hence, but its costs, $C_0' Q_0'$, are incurred in period 0. If new customers do not pay, the firm incurs costs $C_0' Q_0'$ and receives no revenues. The probability that customers will pay, h, is 0.90 in the example. Quantity sold is higher with credit, because new customers are attracted. The cost per unit is also higher with credit because of the costs of operating a credit policy.

The expected cash flows for each policy are set out as follows:

	Expected Cash Flows	
	Time 0	Time 1
Refuse credit	$P_0 Q_0 - C_0 Q_0$	0
Offer credit	$-C_0' Q_0'$	$h \times P_0' Q_0'$

Note that granting credit produces delayed expected cash inflows equal to $h \times P_0' Q_0'$. The costs are incurred immediately and require no discounting. The net present value if credit is offered is

$$
\begin{aligned}
NPV(\text{offer}) &= \frac{h \times P_0' Q_0'}{1 + r_B} - C_0' Q_0' \\
&= \frac{0.9 \times \$50 \times 200}{1.01} - \$5,000 = \$3,910.89
\end{aligned}
$$

Locust's decision should be to adopt the proposed credit policy. The NPV of granting credit is higher than that of refusing credit. This decision is very sensitive to the probability of payment. If it turns out that the probability of payment is 81 percent, Locust Software is indifferent to whether it grants credit or not. In this case the NPV of granting credit is $3,000, which we previously found to be the NPV of not granting credit:

$$\$3,000 = h \times \frac{\$50 \times 200}{1.01} - \$5,000$$

$$\$8,000 = h \times \frac{\$50 \times 200}{1.01}$$

$$h = 80.8\%$$

The decision to grant credit depends on four factors:

1. The delayed revenues from granting credit, $P_0'Q_0'$.
2. The immediate costs of granting credit, $C_0'Q_0'$.
3. The probability of payment, h.
4. The appropriate required rate of return for delayed cash flows, r_B.

The Value of New Information about Credit Risk

Obtaining a better estimate of the probability that a customer will default can lead to a better decision. How can a firm determine when to acquire new information about the creditworthiness of its customers?

It may be sensible for Locust to determine which of its customers are most likely not to pay. The overall probability of nonpayment is 10 percent. But credit checks by an independent firm show that 90 percent of Locust's customers (computer stores) have been profitable over the last five years and that these customers have never defaulted on payments. The less profitable customers are much more likely to default. In fact, 100 percent of the less profitable customers have defaulted on previous obligations.

Locust would like to avoid offering credit to the deadbeats. Consider its projected number of customers per year of $Q_0' = 200$ if credit is granted. Of these customers, 180 have been profitable over the last five years and have never defaulted on past obligations. The remaining 20 have not been profitable. Locust Software expects that all of these less profitable customers will default. This information is set out in a table:

Type of Customer	Number	Probability of Nonpayment	Expected Number of Defaults
Profitable	180	0%	0
Less profitable	20	100	20
Total customers	200	10%	20

The NPV of granting credit to the customers who default is

$$\frac{hP_0'Q_0'}{1 + r_B} - C_0'Q_0' = \frac{0 \times \$50 \times 20}{1.01} - \$25 \times 20 = -\$500$$

This is the cost of providing them with the software. If Locust can identify these customers without cost, it would certainly deny them credit.

In fact, it actually costs Locust \$3 per customer to figure out whether a customer has been profitable over the last five years. The expected payoff of the credit check on its 200 customers is then

$$\begin{array}{cc} \text{Gain from not} & \text{Cost of} \\ \text{extending credit} - \text{credit checks} \\ \$500 \quad - \quad \$3 \times 200 \quad = -\$100 \end{array}$$

For Locust, credit is not worth checking. It would need to pay \$600 to avoid a \$500 loss.

Future Sales

Up to this point, Locust has not considered the possibility that offering credit will permanently increase the level of sales in future periods (beyond next month). In addition, payment and nonpayment patterns in the current period will provide credit information that is useful for the next period. These two factors should be analyzed.

■ FIGURE 29.5   **Future Sales and the Credit Decision**

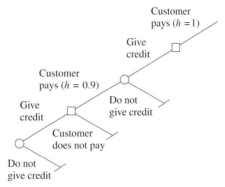

There is a 90-percent probability that a customer
will pay in period 1. However, if payment is made,
there will be another sale in period 2. The
probability that the customer will pay in period 2 is
100 percent—if the customer has paid in period 1.

In the case of Locust, there is a 90-percent probability that the customer will pay in period 1. But, if payment is made, there will be another sale in period 2. The probability that
the customer will pay in period 2, if the customer has paid in period 1, is 100 percent. Locust
can refuse to offer credit in period 2 to customers that have refused to pay in period 1. This
is diagrammed in Figure 29.5.

• List the factors that influence the decision to grant credit.

29.3 OPTIMAL CREDIT POLICY

So far we have discussed how to compute net present value for two alternative credit policies. However, we have not discussed the optimal amount of credit. At the optimal amount
of credit, the incremental cash flows from increased sales are exactly equal to the carrying
costs from the increase in accounts receivable.

Consider a firm that does not currently grant credit. This firm has no bad debts, no
credit department, and relatively few customers. Now consider another firm that grants
credit. This firm has lots of customers, a credit department, and a bad-debt expense account.

It is useful to think of the decision to grant credit in terms of carrying costs and opportunity costs:

1. *Carrying costs* are the costs associated with granting credit and making an investment
   in receivables. Carrying costs include the delay in receiving cash, the losses from bad
   debts, and the costs of managing credit.
2. *Opportunity costs* are the lost sales from refusing to offer credit. These costs drop as
   credit is granted.

We represent these costs in Figure 29.6.

■ FIGURE 29.6   **The Costs of Granting Credit**

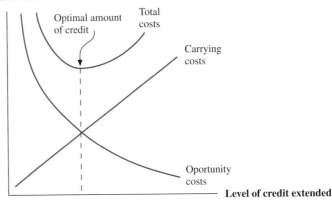

Carrying costs are the costs that must be incurred when credit is granted. They are positively related to the amount of credit extended.
Opportunity costs are the lost sales from refusing credit. These costs drop when credit is granted.

The sum of the carrying costs and the opportunity costs of a particular credit policy is called the *total-credit-cost curve*. A point is identified as the minimum of the total-credit-cost curve. If the firm extends more credit than the minimum, the additional net cash flow from new customers will not cover the carrying costs of this investment in receivables.

The concept of optimal credit policy in the context of modern principles of finance should be somewhat analogous to the concept of the optimal capital structure discussed earlier in the text. In perfect financial markets there should be no optimal credit policy. Alternative amounts of credit for a firm should not affect the value of the firm. Thus, the decision to grant credit would be a matter of indifference to financial managers.

Just as with optimal capital structure, we could expect taxes, monopoly power, bankruptcy costs, and agency costs to be important in determining an optimal credit policy in a world of imperfect financial markets. For example, customers in high tax brackets would be better off borrowing and taking advantage of cash discounts offered by firms than would customers in low tax brackets. Corporations in low tax brackets would be less able to offer credit, because borrowing would be relatively more expensive than for firms in high tax brackets.

In general, a firm will extend trade credit if it has a comparative advantage in doing so. Trade credit is likely to be advantageous if the selling firm has a cost advantage over other potential lenders, if the selling firm has monopoly power it can exploit, if the selling firm can reduce taxes by extending credit, and if the product quality of the selling firm is difficult to determine. Firm size may be important if there are size economies in managing credit.

The optimal credit policy depends on characteristics of particular firms. Assuming that the firm has more flexibility in its credit policy than in the prices it charges, firms with excess capacity, low variable operating costs, high tax brackets, and repeat customers should extend credit more liberally than others.

THE DECISION TO GRANT CREDIT

Trade credit is more likely to be granted by the selling firm if

1. The selling firm has a cost advantage over other lenders.

    Example: The American Manufacturing Co. produces widgets. In a default, it is easier for the American Manufacturing Co. to repossess widgets and resell them than for a finance company to arrange for it with no experience in selling widgets.

2. The selling firm can engage in price discrimination.

    Example: National Motors can offer below-market interest rates to lower income customers that must finance a large portion of the purchase price of cars. Higher income customers pay the list price and do not generally finance a large part of the purchase.

3. The selling firm can obtain favorable tax treatment.

    Example: The A.B. Production Company offers long-term credit to its best customers. This form of financing may qualify as an installment plan and allow the A.B. Production Co. to book profits of the sale over the life of the loan. This may save taxes because the present value of the tax payments will be lower if spread over time.

4. The selling firm has no established reputation for quality products or services.

    Example: Advanced Micro Instruments (AMI) manufactures sophisticated measurement instruments for controlling electrical systems on commercial airplanes. The firm was founded by two engineering graduates from the University of Pennsylvania in 1997. It became a public firm in 1998. To hedge their bets, aircraft manufacturers will ask for credit from AMI. It is very difficult for customers of AMI to assess the quality of its instruments until the instruments have been in place for some time.

5. The selling firm perceives a long-term strategic relationship.

    Example: Food.com is a fast-growing, cash-constrained Internet food distributor. It is currently not profitable. Acme Food will grant Food.com credit for food purchased, because Food.com will generate profits in the future.

Source: Shezad I. Mian and Clifford W. Smith, "Extending Trade Credit and Financing Receivables," *Journal of Applied Corporate Finance* (Spring 1994); Marc Deloof and Marc Jegers, "Trade Credit, Product Quality and Intragroup Trade: Some European Evidence," *Financial Management* (Autumn 1996); and Michael Long, I. B. Malitz, and S. A. Ravid, "Trade Credit, Quality Guarantees, and Product Marketability," *Financial Management* (Winter 1993); Mitchell A. Petersen and Raghuram G. Rajan, "Trade Credit: Theories and Evidence," *The Review of Financial Studies* 10 (1997).

29.4 CREDIT ANALYSIS

When granting credit, a firm tries to distinguish between customers that will pay and customers that will not pay. There are a number of sources of information for determining creditworthiness.

Credit Information

Information commonly used to assess creditworthiness includes the following:

1. *Financial Statements.* A firm can ask a customer to supply financial statements. Rules of thumb based on financial ratios can be calculated.
2. *Credit Reports on Customer's Payment History with Other Firms.* Many organizations sell information on the credit strength of business firms. The best known and largest firm of this type is Dun & Bradstreet, which provides subscribers with a credit-reference book and credit reports on individual firms. The reference book has credit ratings on many thousands of businesses.
3. *Banks.* Banks will generally provide some assistance to their business customers in acquiring information on the creditworthiness of other firms.
4. *The Customer's Payment History with the Firm.* The most obvious way to obtain an estimate of a customer's probability of nonpayment is whether he or she has paid previous bills.

Credit Scoring

Once information has been gathered, the firm faces the hard choice of either granting or refusing credit. Many firms use the traditional and subjective guidelines referred to as the "five Cs of credit":

1. *Character.* The customer's willingness to meet credit obligations.
2. *Capacity.* The customer's ability to meet credit obligations out of operating cash flows.
3. *Capital.* The customer's financial reserves.
4. *Collateral.* A pledged asset in the case of default.
5. *Conditions.* General economic conditions.

Conversely, firms such as credit-card issuers have developed elaborate statistical models (called **credit-scoring** models) for determining the probability of default. Usually all the relevant and observable characteristics of a large pool of customers are studied to find their historic relation to default. Because these models determine who is and who is not creditworthy, not surprisingly they have been the subject of government regulation. For example, if a model were to find that women default more than men, it might be used to deny women credit. This regulation removes such models from the domain of the statistician and makes them the subject of politicians.

QUESTIONS
CONCEPT
?

- What is credit analysis?
- What are the five Cs of credit?

29.5 COLLECTION POLICY

Collection refers to obtaining payment of past-due accounts. The credit manager keeps a record of payment experiences with each customer.

Average Collection Period

Acme Compact Disc Players sells 100,000 compact disc players a year at $300 each. All sales are for credit with terms of 2/20, net 60.

Suppose that 80 percent of Acme's customers take the discounts and pay on day 20; the rest pay on day 60. The **average collection period (ACP)** measures the average amount of time required to collect an account receivable. The ACP for Acme is 28 days:

$$0.8 \times 20 \text{ days} + 0.2 \times 60 \text{ days} = 28 \text{ days}$$

(The average collection period is frequently referred to as *days' sales outstanding* or *days in receivables.*)

Of course, this is an idealized example where customers pay on either one of two dates. In reality, payments arrive in a random fashion, so that the average collection period must be calculated differently.

To determine the ACP in the real world, firms first calculate average daily sales. The **average daily sales (ADS)** equal annual sales divided by 365. The ADS of Acme are

$$\text{Average daily sales} = \frac{\$300 \times 100,000}{365 \text{ days}} = \$82,192$$

If receivables today are $2,301,376, the average collection period is

$$\text{Average collection period} = \frac{\text{Accounts receivable}}{\text{Average daily sales}}$$

$$= \frac{\$2,301,736}{\$82,192}$$

$$= 28 \text{ days}$$

In practice, firms observe sales and receivables on a daily basis. Consequently, an average collection period can be computed and compared to the stated credit terms. For example, suppose Acme had computed its ACP at 40 days for several weeks, versus its credit terms of 2/20, net 60. With a 40-day ACP, some customers are paying later than usual. It may be that some accounts are overdue.

However, firms with seasonal sales will often find the *calculated* ACP changing during the year, making the ACP a somewhat flawed tool. This occurs because receivables are low before the selling season and high after the season. Thus, firms may keep track of seasonal movement in the ACP over past years. In this way, they can compare the ACP for today's date with the average ACP for that date in previous years. To supplement the information in the ACP, the credit manager may make up an accounts receivable aging schedule.

Aging Schedule

The **aging schedule** tabulates receivables by age of account. In the following schedule, 75 percent of the accounts are on time, but a significant number are more than 60 days past due. This signifies that some customers are in arrears.

Aging Schedule

Age of Account	Percentage of Total Value of Accounts Receivable
0–20 days	50%
21–60 days	25
61–80 days	20
Over 80 days	5
	100%

The aging schedule changes during the year. Comparatively, the ACP is a somewhat flawed tool because it only gives the yearly average. Some firms have refined it so that they can examine how it changes with peaks and valleys in their sales. Similarly, the aging schedule is often augmented by the payments pattern. The *payments pattern* describes the lagged collection pattern of receivables. Like a mortality table that describes the probability that a 23-year-old will live to be 24, the payments pattern describes the probability that a 67-day-old account will still be unpaid when it is 68 days old.

Collection Effort

The firm usually employs the following procedures for customers that are overdue:

1. Sends a delinquency letter informing the customer of the past-due status of the account.
2. Makes a telephone call to the customer.
3. Employs a collection agency.
4. Takes legal action against the customer.

At times, a firm may refuse to grant additional credit to customers until arrearages are paid. This may antagonize a normally good customer and points to a potential conflict of interest between the collections department and the sales department.

Factoring

Factoring refers to the sale of a firm's accounts receivable to a financial institution known as a *factor*. The firm and the factor agree on the basic credit terms for each customer. The customer sends payment directly to the factor, and the factor bears the risk of nonpaying customers. The factor buys the receivables at a discount, which usually ranges from 0.35 to 4 percent of the value of the invoice amount. The average discount throughout the economy is probably about 1 percent.

One point should be stressed. We have presented the elements of credit policy as though they were somewhat independent of each other. In fact, they are closely interrelated. For example, the optimal credit policy is not independent of collection and monitoring policies. A tighter collection policy can reduce the probability of default and this in turn can raise the NPV of a more liberal credit policy.

CONCEPT QUESTION

? • What tools can a manager use to analyze a collection policy?

29.6 How to Finance Trade Credit

In addition to unsecured debt instruments described earlier in this chapter, there are three general ways of financing accounting receivables: secured debt, a captive finance company, and securitization.

Use of secured debt is usually referred to as asset-based receivables financing. This is the predominant form of receivables financing. Many lenders will not lend without security to firms with substantive uncertainty or little equity. With secured debt, if the borrower gets into financial difficulty, the lender can repossess the asset and sell it for its fair market value.

Many large firms with good credit ratings use captive finance companies. The captive finance companies are subsidiaries of the parent firm. This is similar to the use of secured debt because the creditors of the captive finance company have a claim on its assets and, as a consequence, the accounts receivable of the parent firm. A captive finance company is attractive if economies of scale are important and if an independent subsidiary with limited liability is warranted.

Securitization occurs when the selling firm sells its accounts receivable to a financial institution. The financial institution pools the receivables with other receivables and issues securities to finance items.

29.7 Summary and Conclusions

1. The components of a firm's credit policy are the terms of sale, the credit analysis, and the collection policy.
2. The terms of sale describe the amount and period of time for which credit is granted and the type of credit instrument.
3. The decision to grant credit is a straightforward NPV decision, and can be improved by additional information about the payment characteristics of the customers. Additional information about the customers' probability of defaulting is valuable, but this value must be traded off against the expense of acquiring the information.
4. The optimal amount of credit the firm offers is a function of the competitive conditions in which it finds itself. These conditions will determine the carrying costs associated with granting credit and the opportunity costs of the lost sales from refusing to offer credit. The optimal credit policy minimizes the sum of these two costs.
5. We have seen that knowledge of the probability that customers will default is valuable. To enhance its ability to assess customers' default probability, a firm can score credit. This relates the default probability to observable characteristics of customers.
6. The collection policy is the method of dealing with past-due accounts. The first step is to analyze the average collection period and to prepare an aging schedule that relates the age of accounts to the proportion of the accounts receivable they represent. The next step is to decide on the collection method and to evaluate the possibility of factoring, that is, selling the overdue accounts.

KEY TERMS

Aging schedule 809	Credit instrument 801
Average collection period (ACP) 809	Credit periods 799
Average daily sales (ADS) 809	Credit scoring 808
Cash discounts 800	Factoring 810
Collection policy 798	Invoice 798
Credit analysis 798	Terms of the sale 798

SUGGESTED READINGS

The following articles are important for an understanding of how to make short-term financial decisions:

Sartoris, W. L., and N. C. Hill. "Evaluating Credit Policy Alternatives: A Present Value Framework." *Journal of Financial Research* 4 (Spring 1981), p. 1.

_____ "A Generalized Cash Flow Approach to Short-Term Financial Decisions." *Journal of Finance* 38 (May 1983), p. 3.

Our treatment of the credit decision owes much to:

Bierman, H., Jr., and W. H. Hausman. "The Credit Granting Decision." *Management Science* 16 (April 1970), and Mian, Shezad I., and Clifford W. Smith. "Extending Trade Credit and Financial Receivables." *Journal of Applied Corporate Finance* (Spring 1994).

Three recent articles that establish a theoretical framework and some empirical work on trade credit:

Mian, S. I., and C. Smith. "Extending Trade Credit and Financing Receivables." *Journal of Applied Corporate Finance* (Spring 1994).

Long, M. S.; I. B. Malitz; and S. A. Ravid. "Trade Credit, Quality Guarantees, and Product Marketability." *Financial Management* (Winter 1993).

Lee, Y. W., and J. D. Stowe. "Product Risk, Asymmetric Introduction and Trade Credit." *Journal of Financial and Quantitative Analysis* (June 1993).

An interesting normative article on how to establish trade credit limits is:

Scherr, F. C. "Optimal Trade Credit Limits." *Financial Management* (Spring 1996).

QUESTIONS AND PROBLEMS

Terms of the Sale

29.1 The North County Publishing Company has provided the following data:

> Annual credit sales = $10 million
>
> Average collection period = 60 days
>
> Terms: Net 30
>
> Interest rate = 10%

North County Publishing proposes to offer a discount policy of 2/10, net 30. It anticipates that 50 percent of its customers will take advantage of this new policy. As a result, the collection period will be reduced to 30 days. Should the North County Publishing Company offer the new credit terms?

29.2 The Webster's Company sells on credit terms of net 45. Its accounts are on average 45 days past due. If annual credit sales are $5 million, what is the company's balance in accounts receivable?

29.3 The Tropeland Company has obtained the following information:

> Annual credit sales = $30 million
>
> Collection period = 60 days
>
> Terms: Net 30
>
> Interest rate = 12%

The company is considering offering terms of 4/10, net 30. It anticipates that 50 percent of its customers will take advantage of the discount. The collection period is expected to decrease by one month. Should the new credit policy be adopted?

The Decision to Grant Credit: Risk and Information

29.4 Berkshire Sports, Inc., operates a mail-order running-shoe business. Management is considering dropping its policy of no credit. The credit policy under consideration by Berkshire follows:

	No Credit	Credit
Price per unit	$35	$40
Cost per unit	$25	$32
Quantity sold	2,000	3,000
Probability of payment	100%	85%
Credit period	0	1
Discount rate	0	3%

a. Should Berkshire offer credit to its customers?

b. What must the probability of payment be before Berkshire would adopt the policy?

29.5 The Theodore Bruin Corporation, a manufacturer of high-quality stuffed animals, does not extend credit to its customers. A study has shown that, by offering credit, the company can increase sales from the current 750 units to 1,000 units. The cost per unit, however, will increase from $43 to $45, reflecting the expense of managing accounts receivable. The current price of a toy is $48. The probability of a customer making a payment on a credit sale is 92 percent, and the appropriate discount rate is 2.7 percent.

By how much should Theodore Bruin increase the price to make offering credit an attractive strategy?

29.6 Fast Typing Co. is in the business of manufacturing and selling Fast-Line Typewriters. It does not offer any credit sales currently. The per unit price and cost of each Fast-Line typewriter are $900 and $600, respectively. Fast Typing Co. is considering the possibility of credit sales. The market price of the typewriter will stay the same with credit sales, but it is expected that the annual sales will increase from 5,000 units to 9,000 units and the per unit cost will go up by $50 due to implementation cost of credit sales. The credit period will be two months and the appropriate discount rate for the credit period is 1.5 percent. What is the minimum probability of repayment that can make Fast Typing Co. indifferent between whether or not to implement the new credit policy?

29.7 The Silver Spokes Bicycle Shop has decided to offer credit to its customers during the spring selling season. Sales are expected to be 300 cycles. The average cost to the shop of a cycle is $240. The owner knows that only 95 percent of the customers will be able to make their payments. To identify the remaining 5 percent, she is considering subscribing to a credit agency. The initial charge for this service is $500, with an additional charge of $4 per individual report. Should she subscribe to the agency?

Optimal Credit Policy

29.8 In principle, how should we decide the optimal credit policy?

Credit Analysis

29.9 What is the information commonly used to assess creditworthiness of a client?

Collection Policy

29.10 Major Electronics sells 85,000 personal stereos each year at a price per unit of $55. All sales are on credit; the terms are 3/15, net 40. The discount is taken by 40 percent of the customers. What is the investment in accounts receivable?

In reaction to a competitor, Major Electronics is considering changing its credit terms to 5/15, net 40, to preserve its sales level. Describe qualitatively how this policy change will affect the company's investment in accounts receivable.

29.11 The Allen Company has monthly credit sales of $600,000. The average collection period is 90 days. The cost of production is 70 percent of the selling price. What is the Allen Company's average investment in accounts receivable?

29.12 The factoring department of Inter American Bank (IAB) is processing 100,000 invoices per year with average invoice value of $1,500. IAB buys the accounts receivable at 4 percent off the invoice value. The average collection period is 30 days. Currently 2 percent of the accounts receivable turns out to be bad debt. The annual interest rate is 10 percent. The annual operating expense of this department is $400,000. What is the gross profit before interest and tax for the factoring department of IAB?

Special Topics

I$_N$ Part VIII we discuss three special topics: mergers and acquisitions, financial distress, and international corporate finance.

Chapter 30 describes the corporate finance of mergers and acquisitions. The acquisition of one firm by another is a capital-budgeting decision, and the basic principles of NPV apply; that is, a firm should be acquired if it generates positive NPV to the shareholders of the acquiring firm. The purpose of Chapter 30 is to discuss how to value an acquisition candidate. However, the NPV of an acquisition candidate is more difficult to determine than that of a typical investment project because of complex accounting, tax, and legal effects.

Chapter 31 discusses what happens when a firm experiences financial distress. Financial distress is a special circumstance when a firm's cash flow falls below its contractually required payments. Financial restructuring involving private workouts or formal bankruptcy usually follows financial distress.

Our last chapter concerns international corporate finance. Many firms have significant foreign operations and must consider special financial factors that do not directly affect purely domestic firms. These factors include foreign exchange rates, interest rates that vary from country to country, and complex accounting, legal, and tax rules.

PART VIII

CHAPTER 30

Mergers and Acquisitions

EXECUTIVE SUMMARY

There is no more dramatic or controversial activity in corporate finance than the acquisition of one firm by another or the merger of two firms. This chapter addresses two basic questions: Why does a firm choose to merge with or acquire another firm and how does it happen?

The acquisition of one firm by another is, of course, an investment made under uncertainty. The basic principle of valuation applies: a firm should be acquired if it generates a positive net present value to the shareholders of the acquiring firm. However, because the NPV of an acquisition candidate is very difficult to determine, mergers and acquisitions are interesting topics in their own right. Here are some of the special features of this area of finance:

1. The benefits from acquisitions are called *synergies*. It is hard to estimate synergies using discounted cash flow techniques.

2. There are complex accounting, tax, and legal effects when one firm is acquired by another.

3. Acquisitions are an important control device of shareholders. It appears that some acquisitions are a consequence of an underlying conflict between the interests of existing managers and of shareholders. Acquisition by another firm is one way that shareholders can remove managers with whom they are unhappy.

4. Acquisition analysis frequently focuses on the total value of the firms involved. But usually an acquisition will affect the relative values of stocks and bonds, as well as their total value.

5. Mergers and acquisitions sometimes involve unfriendly transactions. Thus, when one firm attempts to acquire another, it does not always involve quiet, gentlemanly negotiations. The sought-after firm may use defensive tactics, including poison pills, greenmail, and white knights.

This chapter starts by introducing the basic legal, accounting, and tax aspects of acquisitions. When one firm acquires another, it must choose the legal framework, the accounting method, and tax status. These choices will be explained throughout the chapter.

The chapter discusses how to determine the NPV of an acquisition candidate. The NPV of an acquisition candidate is the difference between the synergy from the merger and the premium to be paid. We consider the following types of synergy: (1) revenue enhancement, (2) cost reduction, (3) lower taxes, and (4) lower cost of capital. The premium paid for an acquisition is the price paid minus the market value of the acquisition prior to the merger. The premium depends on whether cash or securities are used to finance the offer price.

30.1 THE BASIC FORMS OF ACQUISITIONS

There are three basic legal procedures that one firm can use to acquire another firm: (1) merger or consolidation, (2) acquisition of stock, and (3) acquisition of assets.

Merger or Consolidation

A **merger** refers to the absorption of one firm by another. The acquiring firm retains its name and its identity, and it acquires all of the assets and liabilities of the acquired firm. After a merger, the acquired firm ceases to exist as a separate business entity.

A **consolidation** is the same as a merger except that an entirely new firm is created. In a consolidation, both the acquiring firm and the acquired firm terminate their previous legal existence and become part of the new firm. In a consolidation, the distinction between the acquiring and the acquired firm is not important. However, the rules for mergers and consolidations are basically the same. Acquisitions by merger and consolidation result in combinations of the assets and liabilities of acquired and acquiring firms.

EXAMPLE

Suppose firm *A* acquires firm *B* in a merger. Further, suppose firm *B*'s shareholders are given one share of firm *A*'s stock in exchange for two shares of firm *B*'s stock. From a legal standpoint, firm *A*'s shareholders are not directly affected by the merger. However, firm *B*'s shares cease to exist. In a consolidation, the shareholders of firm *A* and firm *B* would exchange their shares for the share of a new firm (e.g., firm *C*). Because the differences between mergers and consolidations are not all that important for our purposes, we shall refer to both types of reorganizations as mergers.

There are some advantages and some disadvantages to using a merger to acquire a firm:

1. A merger is legally straightforward and does not cost as much as other forms of acquisition. It avoids the necessity of transferring title of each individual asset of the acquired firm to the acquiring firm.
2. A merger must be approved by a vote of the stockholders of each firm.[1] Typically, votes of the owners of two-thirds of the shares are required for approval. In addition, shareholders of the acquired firm have *appraisal rights*. This means that they can demand that their shares be purchased at a fair value by the acquiring firm. Often the acquiring firm and the dissenting shareholders of the acquired firm cannot agree on a fair value, which results in expensive legal proceedings.

Acquisition of Stock

A second way to acquire another firm is to purchase the firm's voting stock in exchange for cash, shares of stock, or other securities. This may start as a private offer from the management of one firm to another. At some point the offer is taken directly to the selling firm's stockholders. This can be accomplished by use of a tender offer. A **tender offer** is a public offer to buy shares of a target firm. It is made by one firm directly to the shareholders of another firm.

---

[1]Mergers between corporations require compliance with state laws. In virtually all states the shareholders of each corporation must give their assent.

The offer is communicated to the target firm's shareholders by public announcements such as newspaper advertisements. Sometimes a general mailing is used in a tender offer. However, a general mailing is very difficult because it requires the names and addresses of the stockholders of record, which are not usually available.

The following are factors involved in choosing between an acquisition of stock and a merger:

1. In an acquisition of stock, no shareholder meetings must be held and no vote is required. If the shareholders of the target firm do not like the offer, they are not required to accept it and they will not tender their shares.

2. In an acquisition of stock, the bidding firm can deal directly with the shareholders of a target firm by using a tender offer. The target firm's management and board of directors can be bypassed.

3. Acquisition of stock is often unfriendly. It is used in an effort to circumvent the target firm's management, which is usually actively resisting acquisition. Resistance by the target firm's management often makes the cost of acquisition by stock higher than the cost by merger.

4. Frequently a minority of shareholders will hold out in a tender offer, and thus the target firm cannot be completely absorbed.

5. Complete absorption of one firm by another requires a merger. Many acquisitions of stock end with a formal merger later.

Acquisition of Assets

One firm can acquire another firm by buying all of its assets. A formal vote of the shareholders of the selling firm is required. This approach to acquisition will avoid the potential problem of having minority shareholders, which can occur in an acquisition of stock. Acquisition of assets involves transferring title to assets. The legal process of transferring assets can be costly.

A Classification Scheme

Financial analysts have typically classified acquisitions into three types:

1. *Horizontal Acquisition.* This is an acquisition of a firm in the same industry as the acquiring firm. The firms compete with each other in their product market.

2. *Vertical Acquisition.* A vertical acquisition involves firms at different steps of the production process. The acquisition by an airline company of a travel agency would be a vertical acquisition.

3. *Conglomerate Acquisition.* The acquiring firm and the acquired firm are not related to each other. The acquisition of a food-products firm by a computer firm would be considered a conglomerate acquisition.

A Note on Takeovers

Takeover is a general and imprecise term referring to the transfer of control of a firm from one group of shareholders to another.[2] A firm that has decided to take over another firm is usually referred to as the **bidder.** The bidder offers to pay cash or securities to obtain the stock or assets of another company. If the offer is accepted, the target firm will give up control over its stock or assets to the bidder in exchange for *consideration* (i.e., its stock, its debt, or cash).

---

[2]*Control* may be defined as having a majority vote on the board of directors.

■ FIGURE 30.1   **Varieties of Takeovers**

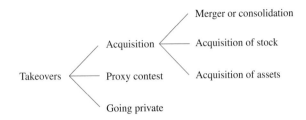

For example, when a bidding firm acquires a target firm, the right to control the operating activities of the target firm is transferred to a newly elected board of directors of the acquiring firm. This is a takeover by acquisition.

Takeovers can occur by acquisition, proxy contests, and going-private transactions. Thus, takeovers encompass a broader set of activities than acquisitions. Figure 30.1 depicts this.

If a takeover is achieved by acquisition, it will be by merger, tender offer for shares of stock, or purchase of assets. In mergers and tender offers, the acquiring firm buys the voting common stock of the acquired firm.

Takeovers can occur with *proxy contests.* Proxy contests occur when a group of shareholders attempts to gain controlling seats on the board of directors by voting in new directors. A *proxy* authorizes the proxy holder to vote on all matters in a shareholders' meeting. In a proxy contest, proxies from the rest of the shareholders are solicited by an insurgent group of shareholders.

In *going-private transactions,* all the equity shares of a public firm are purchased by a small group of investors. The group usually includes members of incumbent management and some outside investors. The shares of the firm are delisted from stock exchanges and can no longer be purchased in the open market.

CONCEPT QUESTIONS
?
- What is a merger? How does a merger differ from other forms of acquisition?
- What is a takeover?

30.2 THE TAX FORMS OF ACQUISITIONS

If one firm buys another firm, the transaction may be taxable or tax-free. In a *taxable acquisition,* the shareholders of the acquired firm are considered to have sold their shares, and they have realized capital gains or losses that will be taxed. In a taxable transaction, the *appraised value* of the assets of the selling firm may be revalued, as we explain below.

In a *tax-free acquisition,* the selling shareholders are considered to have exchanged their old shares for new ones of equal value, and they have experienced no capital gains or losses. In a tax-free acquisition, the assets are not revalued.

EXAMPLE ────────────────

Suppose that 15 years ago Bill Evans started Samurai Machinery (SM) and purchased plant and equipment costing $80,000. These have been the only assets of SM, and the company has no debts. Bill is the sole proprietor of SM and owns all the shares. For tax purposes the assets of SM have been depreciated using the straight-line method over 10 years, and have no salvage value. The annual depreciation expense has been $8,000 ($80,000/10). The machinery has no accounting value today (i.e., it has been written off the books). However, because of inflation, the fair market value of the machinery is $200,000. As a consequence, the S. A. Steel Company has bid $200,000 for all of the outstanding stock of Samurai.

Tax-Free Transaction   If Bill Evans receives *shares* of S. A. Steel worth $200,000, the IRS will treat the sale as a tax-free transaction. Thus, Bill will not have to pay taxes on any gain received from the stock. In addition, S. A. Steel will be allowed the same depreciation deduction that Samurai Machinery was allowed. Because the asset has already been fully depreciated, S. A. Steel will receive no depreciation deduction.

Taxable Transaction   If S. A. Steel pays $200,000 in *cash* for Samurai Machinery, it will be a taxable transaction. There will be a number of tax consequences:

1. In the year of the merger, Bill Evans must pay taxes on the difference between the merger price of $200,000 and his initial contribution to the firm of $80,000. Thus, his taxable income is $120,000 ($200,000 − $80,000).

2. S. A. Steel may *elect* to *write up* the value of the machinery. In this case, S. A. Steel will be able to depreciate the machinery from an initial tax basis of $200,000. If S. A. Steel depreciates straight-line over 10 years, depreciation will be $20,000 ($200,000/10) per year.

   If S. A. Steel elects to write up the machinery, S. A. Steel must treat the $200,000 write-up as taxable income immediately.[3]

3. Should S. A. Steel *not* elect the write-up, there is no increase in depreciation. Thus, depreciation remains zero in this example. In addition, because there is no write-up, S. A. Steel does not need to recognize any additional taxable income.

   Because the tax benefits from depreciation occur slowly over time and the taxable income is recognized immediately, the acquirer generally elects *not* to write up the value of the machinery in a taxable transaction.

Because the write-up is not allowed for tax-free transactions and generally not chosen for taxable ones, the only real tax difference between the two types of transactions concerns the taxation of the selling shareholders. Because these individuals can defer taxes under a tax-free situation but must pay taxes immediately under a taxable situation, the tax-free transaction has better tax consequences. The tax implications for both types of transactions are displayed in Table 30.1.

30.3 ACCOUNTING FOR ACQUISITIONS

Earlier in this text we mentioned that firms keep two distinct sets of books: the stockholders' books and the tax books. The previous section concerned the effect of acquisitions on the tax books. We now consider the stockholders' books. When one firm acquires another firm, the acquisition will be treated as either a purchase or a pooling of interests on the stockholders' books.

---

[3]Technically, Samurai Machinery pays this tax. However, because Samurai is now a subsidiary of S. A. Steel, S. A. Steel is the effective taxpayer.

■ TABLE 30.1   **The Incremental Tax Consequences of S. A. Steel Company's Acquisition of Samurai Machinery**

Buyer or Seller	Type of Acquisition	
	Taxable Acquisition	Tax-Free Acquisition
Bill Evans	Immediate tax on $120,000 ($200,000 − $80,000)	Capital gain tax not paid until Evans sells shares of S. A. Steel
S. A. Steel	S. A. Steel may elect to write up assets. Here: 1. Assets of Samurai written up to $200,000 (with useful life of 10 years). Annual depreciation expense is $20,000. 2. Immediate tax on $200,000 write-up of assets. Alternatively, S. A. Steel may elect not to write up assets. Here, there is neither additional depreciation nor immediate tax. Typically, acquirer elects *not* to write up assets.	No additional depreciation

S. A. Steel acquires Samurai Machinery for $200,000, which is the market value of Samurai's equipment. The book value of the equipment is $0. Bill Evans started Samurai Steel 15 years ago with a contribution of $80,000.

The tax consequences of a tax-free acquisition are better than the tax consequences of a taxable acquisition, because the seller pays no immediate tax on a tax-free acquisition.

The Purchase Method

The **purchase** method of reporting acquisitions requires that the assets of the acquired firm be reported at their fair market value on the books of the acquiring firm. This allows the acquiring firm to establish a new cost basis for the acquired assets.

In a purchase, an accounting term called *goodwill* is created. **Goodwill** is the excess of the purchase price over the sum of the fair market values of the individual assets acquired.

EXAMPLE

Suppose firm *A* acquires firm *B*, creating a new firm, *AB*. Firm *A*'s and firm *B*'s financial positions at the date of the acquisition are shown in Table 30.2. The book value of firm *B* on the date of the acquisition is $10 million. This is the sum of $8 million in buildings and $2 million in cash. However, an appraiser states that the sum of the fair market values of the individual buildings is $14 million. With $2 million in cash, the sum of the market values of the individual assets in firm *B* is $16 million. This represents the value to be received if the firm is liquidated by selling off the individual assets separately. However, the whole is often worth more than the sum of the parts in business. Firm *A* pays $19 million in cash for firm *B*. This difference of $3 million ($19 million − $16 million) is goodwill. It represents the increase in value by keeping the firm intact as an ongoing business. Firm *A* issued $19 million in new debt to finance the acquisition. The last balance sheet in Table 30.2 shows what happens under purchase accounting.

■ TABLE 30.2   Accounting for Acquisitions: Purchase (in $ millions)

Firm A				Firm B			
Cash	$ 4	Equity	$20	Cash	$2	Equity	$10
Land	16			Land	0		
Buildings	0			Buildings	8		
Total	$20		$20	Total	$10		$10

Firm AB			
Cash	$ 6	Debt	$19
Land	16	Equity	20
Buildings	14		
Goodwill	3		
Total	$39		$39

When the purchase method is used, the assets of the acquired firm (firm *B*) appear in the combined firm's books at their fair market value.

1. The total assets of firm *AB* increase to $39 million. The buildings of firm *B* appear in the new balance sheet at their current market value. That is, the market value of the assets of the acquired firm becomes part of the book value of the new firm. However, the assets of the acquiring firm (firm *A*) remain at their old book value. They are not revalued upwards when the new firm is created.
2. The excess of the purchase price over the sum of the fair market values of the individual assets acquired is $3 million. This amount is reported as goodwill. Goodwill will be amortized over a period of years on the stockholders' books. However, the amortization expenses are *not tax-deductible*.

Pooling of Interests

Under a **pooling of interests,** the assets of the new firm are valued at the same level at which they were carried on the books of the acquired and acquiring firms. Using the previous example, assume that firm *A* issues common stock with a market value of $19 million to acquire firm *B*. Table 30.3 illustrates this merger.

The new firm is owned jointly by all the stockholders of the previously separate firms. The total assets and the total equity are unchanged by the acquisition. No goodwill is created. Furthermore, the $19 million used to acquire firm *B* does not appear in Table 30.3.

Purchase or Pooling of Interests: A Comparison

Pooling of interests is used when the acquiring firm issues voting stock in exchange for at least 90 percent of the outstanding voting stock of the acquired firm. Purchase accounting is generally used under other financing arrangements. Though there are many possible arrangements, the most common is that the acquiring firm distributes cash and bonds to obtain the assets or stock of the acquired firm.

We mentioned above that, in purchase accounting, goodwill is amortized over a period of years on the stockholders' books. Therefore, just like depreciation, the amortization expense reduces income on the stockholders' books. In addition, the assets of the acquired firm are written up on the stockholders' books in purchase accounting. This creates a higher

■ TABLE 30.3   **Accounting for Acquisitions: Pooling of Interests (in $ millions)**

Firm A				Firm B			
Cash	$ 4	Equity	$20	Cash	$2	Equity	$10
Land	16			Land	0		
Buildings	0			Buildings	8		
Total	$20		$20	Total	$10		$10

Firm AB			
Cash	$ 6	Equity	$30
Land	16		
Buildings	8		
Total	$30		$30

In a pooling of interests, the assets appear in the combined firm's books at the same value that they had in each separate firm's books prior to the merger.

depreciation expense for the combined firm than would be the case for a pooling. Due to both goodwill and asset write-ups, purchase accounting will usually result in lower reported income on the stockholders' books than will pooling.

The previous paragraph concerns effects on the stockholders' books, not the tax books. Because the amount of tax-deductible expenses is not affected by the method of acquisition accounting, cash flows are not affected. Hence, the net present value of the acquisition should be the same whether pooling or purchase accounting is used.[4]

QUESTION
• What is the difference between purchase accounting and pooling-of-interests accounting?

30.4 DETERMINING THE SYNERGY FROM AN ACQUISITION

Suppose firm A is contemplating acquiring firm B. The value of firm A is V_A and the value of firm B is V_B. (It is reasonable to assume that, for public companies, V_A and V_B can be determined by observing the market price of the outstanding securities.) The difference between the value of the combined firm (V_{AB}) and the sum of the values of the firms as separate entities is the *synergy* from the acquisition:

$$\text{Synergy} = V_{AB} - (V_A + V_B)$$

---

[4]It is widely believed that chief financial officers prefer the pooling-of-interests accounting method because of its advantageous treatment of earnings. However, Eric Lindenberg and Michael P. Ross, "To Purchase or to Pool? Does it Matter?" *Journal of Applied Corporate Finance* (Summer 1999), find it really doesn't matter which method is used. In any case, on April 21, 1999, the Financial Accounting Standards Board (FASB) announced its intent to eliminate the pooling-of-interests accounting method. It is widely expected that the ruling will take effect in early 2001.

The acquiring firm must generally pay a premium for the acquired firm. For example, if stock of the target is selling for $50, the acquirer might need to pay $60 a share, implying a premium of $10 or 20 percent. Firm *A* will want to determine the synergy before entering into negotiations with firm *B* on the premium.

The synergy of an acquisition can be determined from the usual discounted cash flow model:

$$\text{Synergy} = \sum_{t=1}^{T} \frac{\Delta \text{CF}_t}{(1 + r)^t}$$

where ΔCF_t is the difference between the cash flows at date t of the combined firm and the sum of the cash flows of the two separate firms. In other words, ΔCF_t is the incremental cash flow at date t from the merger. The term, r, is the risk-adjusted discount rate appropriate for the incremental cash flows. This is generally considered to be the required rate of return on the equity of the target.

From the chapters on capital budgeting we know that the incremental cash flows can be separated into four parts:

$$\Delta \text{CF}_t = \Delta \text{Rev}_t - \Delta \text{Costs}_t - \Delta \text{Taxes}_t - \Delta \text{Capital Requirements}_t$$

where ΔRev_t is the incremental revenue of the acquisition, ΔCosts_t is the incremental costs of the acquisition, ΔTaxes_t is the incremental acquisition taxes, and $\Delta \text{Capital Requirements}_t$ is the incremental new investment required in working capital and fixed assets.

30.5 Source of Synergy from Acquisitions

It follows from our classification of incremental cash flows that the possible sources of synergy fall into four basic categories: revenue enhancement, cost reduction, lower taxes, and lower cost of capital.[5]

Revenue Enhancement

One important reason for acquisitions is that a combined firm may generate greater revenues than two separate firms. Increased revenues may come from marketing gains, strategic benefits, and market power.

Marketing Gains   It is frequently claimed that mergers and acquisitions can produce greater operating revenues from improved marketing. Improvements can be made in the following:

---

[5]Many reasons are given by firms to justify mergers and acquisitions. When two firms merge, the boards of directors of the two firms adopt an *agreement of merger.* The agreement of merger of U.S. Steel and Marathon Oil is typical. It lists the economic benefits that shareholders can expect from the merger (key words have been italicized):

> U.S Steel believes that the acquisition of Marathon provides U.S. Steel with an attractive opportunity to *diversify* into the energy business. Reasons for the merger include, but are not limited to, the facts that consummation of the merger will allow U.S. Steel to consolidate Marathon into U.S. Steel's federal *income tax return,* will also contribute to *greater efficiency,* and will enhance the ability to manage capital by permitting the movement of cash between U.S. Steel and Marathon. Additionally, the merger will eliminate the possibility of conflicts of interests between the interests of minority and majority shareholders and will enhance management flexibility. The acquisition will provide Marathon shareholders with a substantial premium over historical market prices for their shares. However, shareholders will no longer continue to share in the future prospects of the company.

1. Previously ineffective media programming and advertising efforts.
2. A weak existing distribution network.
3. An unbalanced product mix.

Strategic Benefits   Some acquisitions promise a *strategic* advantage.[6] This is an opportunity to take advantage of the competitive environment if certain situations materialize. In this regard, a strategic benefit is more like an option than it is a standard investment opportunity. For example, imagine that a sewing machine company acquired a computer company. The firm will be well positioned if technological advances allow computer-driven sewing machines in the future. Michael Porter has used the word *beachhead* in his description of the process of entering a new industry to exploit perceived opportunities.[7] The beachhead is used to spawn new opportunities based on *intangible* relationships. He uses the example of Procter & Gamble's initial acquisition of the Charmin Paper Company as a beachhead that allowed Procter & Gamble to develop a highly interrelated cluster of paper products—disposable diapers, paper towels, feminine hygiene products, and bathroom tissue.

Market or Monopoly Power   One firm may acquire another to reduce competition. If so, prices can be increased and monopoly profits obtained. Mergers that reduce competition do not benefit society and may be challenged by the U.S. Department of Justice or the Federal Trade Commission.

   The empirical evidence does not suggest that increased market power is a significant reason for mergers. If monopoly power is increased through an acquisition, all firms in the industry should benefit as the price of the industry's product is increased. However, Stillman's and Eckbo's examination of the share prices of firms that compete with the merger target when a merger announcement is made indicate that this is not the case.[8] They find no consistent tendency for the share prices of rivals to increase, and, thus, the Stillman-Eckbo data do not support the monopoly-power theory.

Cost Reduction

One of the most basic reasons for merger is that a combined firm may operate more efficiently than two separate firms. Thus, when Bank of America agreed to acquire Security Pacific, lower costs were cited as the primary reason. A firm can obtain greater operating efficiency in several different ways through a merger or an acquisition.

Economies of Scale   If the average cost of production falls while the level of production increases, there is said to be an economy of scale. Figure 30.2 illustrates that economies of scale result while the firm grows to its optimal size. After this point, diseconomies of scale occur. In other words, average cost increases with further firm growth.

   Though the precise nature of economy of scale is not known, it is one obvious benefit of horizontal mergers. The phrase *spreading overhead* is frequently used in connection with economies of scale. This refers to the sharing of central facilities such as corporate headquarters, top management, and a large mainframe computer.

---

[6]For a discussion of the financial side of strategic planning, see S. C. Myers, "Finance Theory and Finance Strategy," *Interfaces* 14 (January–February 1984), p. 1.

[7]M. Porter, *Competitive Advantage* (New York: Free Press, 1985).

[8]R. Stillman, "Examining Antitrust Policy toward Horizontal Mergers," *Journal of Financial Economics* 11 (April 1983); and E. B. Eckbo, "Horizontal Mergers, Collusion and Stockholder Wealth," *Journal of Financial Economics* 11 (April 1983).

■ FIGURE 30.2   **Economies of Scale and the Optimal Size of the Firm**

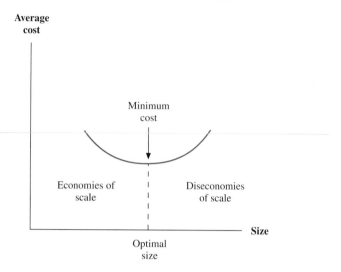

Economies of Vertical Integration   Operating economies can be gained from vertical combinations as well as from horizontal combinations. The main purpose of vertical acquisitions is to make coordination of closely related operating activities easier. This is probably the reason why most forest product firms that cut timber also own sawmills and hauling equipment. Economies from vertical integration probably explain why most airline companies own airplanes; it also may explain why some airline companies have purchased hotels and car-rental companies.

Technology transfers are another reason for vertical integration. Consider the merger of General Motors and Hughes Aircraft in 1985. An automobile manufacturer might well acquire an advanced electronics firm if the special technology of the electronics firm can improve the quality of the automobile.

Complementary Resources   Some firms acquire others to make better use of existing resources or to provide the missing ingredient for success. Think of a ski-equipment store that could merge with a tennis-equipment store to produce more even sales over both the winter and summer seasons—and better use of store capacity.

Elimination of Inefficient Management   There are firms whose value could be increased with a change in management. For example, Jensen and Ruback argue that acquisitions can occur because of changing technology or market conditions that require a restructuring of the corporation.[9] Incumbent managers in some cases do not understand changing conditions. They have trouble abandoning strategies and styles they have spent years formulating.

The oil industry is an example of managerial inefficiency cited by Jensen. In the late 1970s, changes in the oil industry included reduced expectations of the future price of oil, increased exploration and development costs, and increased real interest rates. As a result of these changes, substantial reductions in exploration and development were called for. However, many oil company managers were unable to "downsize" their firms. For exam-

---

[9]M. C. Jensen and R. S. Ruback, "The Market for Corporate Control: The Scientific Evidence," *Journal of Financial Economics* 11 (April 1983); and M. C. Jensen, "Agency Costs of Free Cash Flow, Corporate Finance and Takeovers," *American Economic Review* (May 1986).

■ TABLE 30.4   **Tax Effect of Merger of Firms *A* and *B***

	Before Merger				After Merger	
	Firm A		Firm B		Firm AB	
	If State 1	If State 2	If State 1	If State 2	If State 1	If State 2
Taxable income	$200	−$100	−$100	$200	$100	$100
Taxes	68	0	0	68	34	34
Net income	$132	−$100	−$100	$132	$ 66	$ 66

Neither firm will be able to deduct its losses prior to the merger. The merger allows the losses from *A* to offset the taxable profits from *B*—and vice versa.

ple, a study by McConnell and Muscarella reports that the stock prices of oil companies tended to decrease with announcements of increases in exploration and development expenditures in the period of 1975–1981.[10]

Acquiring companies sought out oil firms in order to reduce the investment levels of these oil companies.[11] For example, T. Boone Pickens of Mesa Petroleum perceived the changes taking place in the oil industry and attempted to buy several oil companies: Unocal, Phillips, and Getty. The results of these attempted acquisitions have been reduced expenditures on exploration and development and huge gains to the shareholders of the affected firms.

Mergers and acquisitions can be viewed as part of the labor market for top management. Jensen and Ruback have used the phrase *market for corporate control,* in which alternative management teams compete for the rights to manage corporate activities.

Tax Gains

Tax gains may be a powerful incentive for some acquisitions. The possible tax gains that can come from an acquisition are the following:

1. The use of tax losses from net operating losses.
2. The use of unused debt capacity.
3. The use of surplus funds.

Net Operating Losses   Sometimes firms have tax losses they cannot take advantage of. These tax losses are referred to as NOL (an acronym for net operating losses). Consider the situation of firm *A* and firm *B*.

Table 30.4 shows the pretax income, taxes, and after-tax income for firms *A* and *B*. Firm *A* will earn $200 under state 1 but will lose money under state 2. The firm will pay taxes under state 1 but is not entitled to a tax rebate under state 2. Conversely, firm *B* will pay taxes of $68 under state 2. Thus, if firms *A* and *B* are separate, the IRS will obtain $68 in taxes, regardless of which state occurs. However, if *A* and *B* merge, the combined firm will pay $34 in taxes under both state 1 and state 2.

---

[10]J. J. McConnell and C. J. Muscarella, "Corporate Capital Expenditure Decisions and the Market Value of the firm," *Journal of Financial Economics* 14 (1985).

[11]More than 26 percent of the total valuation of all takeover transactions involved a selling firm in the oil and gas industry in 1981–1984 [W. T. Grimm, *Mergerstat Review* (1985), p. 41].

It is obvious that if firms *A* and *B* merge, they will pay lower taxes than if they remain separate. Without merger, they do not take advantage of potential tax losses.

The message of the preceding example is that firms need taxable profits to take advantage of potential tax losses. Mergers can sometimes accomplish this. However, there are two qualifications to the previous example:

1. The federal tax laws permit firms that experience alternating periods of profits and losses to equalize their taxes by carryback and carryforward provisions. A firm that has been profitable but has a loss in the current year can get refunds of income taxes paid in *three previous years* and can carry the loss *forward for 15 years.* Thus, a merger to exploit unused tax shields must offer tax savings over and above what can be accomplished by firms via carryovers.[12]

2. The IRS may disallow an acquisition if the principal purpose of the acquisition is to avoid federal tax. This is one of the Catch 22s of the Internal Revenue Code.

Unused Debt Capacity   We argued earlier in the text that the optimal debt-equity ratio is the one where the marginal tax benefit from additional debt is equal to the marginal increase in the financial distress costs from additional debt. Because some diversification occurs when firms merge, the cost of financial distress is likely to be less for the combined firm than is the sum of these present values for the two separate firms. Thus, the acquiring firm might be able to increase its debt-equity ratio after a merger, creating additional tax benefits—and additional value.[13,14]

Surplus Funds   Another quirk in the tax laws involves surplus funds. Consider a firm that has *free cash flow.* That is, it has cash flow available after payment of all taxes and after all positive net present value projects have been provided for. In this situation, aside from purchasing fixed-income securities, the firm has several ways to spend the free cash flow, including

1. Pay dividends.
2. Buy back its own shares.
3. Acquire shares in another firm.

We have already seen in our previous discussion of dividend policy that an extra dividend will increase the income tax paid by some investors. Investors pay lower taxes in a share repurchase. However, this is not a legal option if the sole purpose is to avoid taxes that would otherwise have been paid by shareholders.

The firm can buy the shares of another firm. This accomplishes two objectives. First, the firm's shareholders avoid taxes from dividends that would have been paid. Second, the firm pays little corporate tax on dividends received from the shares of the firm it has purchased, because 70 percent of the dividend income received from the acquired firm is excluded from the corporate income tax. However, under Section 532 of the tax code the IRS might disallow the tax benefits from a continual strategy of this type.

---

[12]Under the 1986 Tax Reform Act a corporation's ability to carry forward net operating losses (and other tax credits) is limited when more than 50 percent of the stock changes hands over a three-year period.

[13]Unused debt capacity is cited as a benefit in many mergers. An example was the proposed merger of Hospital Corporation of America and American Hospital Supply Corporation in 1985. Insiders were quoted as saying that the combined companies could borrow as much as an additional $1 billion, 10 times the usual borrowing capacity of Hospital Corporation alone (*The Wall Street Journal,* April 1, 1985). (The merger never took place.)

[14]Michael C. Jensen ["Agency Costs of Free Cash Flow, Corporate Finance and Takeovers," *American Economic Review* (May 1986)] offers another reason why debt is frequently used in mergers and acquisitions. He argues that using more debt provides incentives for the new management to create efficiencies so that debt can be repaid.

Instead, the firm might make acquisitions with its excess funds. In a merger no taxes at all are paid on dividends remitted from the acquired firm, and the IRS would not question mergers of this type.

The Cost of Capital

The cost of capital can often be reduced when two firms merge because the costs of issuing securities are subject to economies of scale. As we observed in earlier chapters, the costs of issuing both debt and equity are much lower for larger issues than for smaller issues.

30.6 CALCULATING THE VALUE OF THE FIRM AFTER AN ACQUISITION

Now that we have listed the possible sources of synergy from a merger, let us see how one would value these sources. Consider two firms. Gamble, Inc., manufactures and markets soaps and cosmetics. The firm has a reputation for its ability to attract, develop, and keep talented people. The firm has successfully introduced several major products in the past two years. It would like to enter the over-the-counter drug market to round out its product line. Shapiro, Inc., is a well-known maker of cold remedies. Al Shapiro, the great-grandson of the founder of Shapiro, Inc., became chairman of the firm last year. Unfortunately, Al knows nothing about cold remedies, and as a consequence, Shapiro, Inc., has had lackluster financial performance. For the most recent year, pretax cash flow fell by 15 percent. The firm's stock price is at an all-time low.

The financial management of Gamble finds Shapiro an attractive acquisition candidate. It believes that the cash flows from the combined firms would be far greater than what each firm would have alone. The cash flows and present values from the acquisition are shown in Table 30.5. The increased cash flows (ΔCF_t) would come from three benefits:

1. *Tax Gains.* If Gamble acquires Shapiro, Gamble will be able to use some tax-loss carryforwards to reduce its tax liability. The additional cash flows from tax gains should be discounted at the cost of debt capital because they can be determined with very little uncertainty. The financial management of Gamble estimates that the acquisition will reduce taxes by $1 million per year in perpetuity. The relevant discount rate is 5 percent, and the present value of the tax reduction is $20 million.

■ TABLE 30.5 **Acquisition of Shapiro, Inc., by Gamble, Inc.**

	Net Cash Flow per Year (perpetual)	Discount Rate	Value
Gamble, Inc.	$10.0 million	0.10	$100 million
Shapiro, Inc.	4.5 million	0.15	30 million*
Benefits from acquisition:	5.5 million	0.122	45 million
Strategic fit	3.0 million	0.20	15 million
Tax shelters	1.0 million	0.05	20 million
Operating efficiencies	1.5 million	0.15	10 million
Gamble-Shapiro	20.0 million	0.114	175 million

*The market value of Shapiro's outstanding common stock is $30 million; 1 million shares are outstanding.

2. *Operating Efficiencies.* The financial management of Gamble has determined that Gamble can take advantage of some of the unused production capacity of Shapiro. At times Gamble has been operating at full capacity with a large backlog of orders. Shapiro's manufacturing facilities, with a little reconfiguration, can be used to produce Gamble's soaps. Thus, more soaps and cold remedies can be produced without adding to the combined firm's capacity and cost. These operating efficiencies will increase after-tax cash flows by $1.5 million per year. Using Shapiro's discount rate and assuming perpetual gains, the PV of the unused capacity is determined to be $10 million.

3. *Strategic Fit.* The financial management of Gamble has determined that the acquisition of Shapiro will give Gamble a strategic advantage. The management of Gamble believes that the addition of the Shapiro Bac-Rub ointment for sore backs to its existing product mix will give it a better chance to launch successful new skin care cosmetics if these markets develop in the future. Management of Gamble estimates that there is a 50-percent probability that $6 million in after-tax cash flow can be generated with the new skin care products. These opportunities are contingent on factors that cannot be easily quantified. Because of the lack of precision here, the managers decided to use a high discount rate. Gamble chooses a 20-percent rate, and it estimates that the present value of the strategic factors is $15 million ($0.50 \times \$6$ million/0.20).

Avoiding Mistakes

The Gamble-Shapiro illustration is very simple and straightforward. It is deceptive because the incremental cash flows have already been determined. In practice an analyst must estimate these cash flows and determine the proper discount rate. Valuing the benefits of a potential acquisition is harder than valuing benefits for standard capital-budgeting projects. Many mistakes can be made. The following are some of the general rules:

1. *Do Not Ignore Market Values.* In many cases it is very difficult to estimate values using discounted cash flows. Because of this, an expert at valuation should know the market prices of comparable opportunities. In an efficient market, prices should reflect value. Because the market value of Shapiro is $30 million, we use this to estimate Shapiro's existing value.

2. *Estimate Only Incremental Cash Flows.* Only incremental cash flows from an acquisition will add value to the acquiring firm. Thus, it is important to estimate the cash flows that are incremental to the acquisition.

3. *Use the Correct Discount Rate.* The discount rate should be the required rate of return for the incremental cash flows associated with the acquisition.[15] It should reflect the risk associated with the *use* of funds, not their *source.* It would be a mistake for Gamble to use its own cost of capital to value the cash flows from Shapiro.

4. *If Gamble and Shapiro Combine, There Will Be Transactions Costs.* These will include fees to investment bankers, legal fees, and disclosure requirements.

30.7 A Cost to Stockholders from Reduction in Risk

The previous section discussed gains to the firm from a merger. In a firm with debt, these gains are likely to be shared by both bondholders and stockholders. We now consider a benefit to the bondholders from a merger, which occurs at the expense of the stockholders.

---

[15]Recall that the required rate of return is sometimes referred to as the *cost of capital,* or the *opportunity cost of capital.*

IN THEIR OWN WORDS

Michael C. Jensen on Mergers and Acquisitions

Economic analysis and evidence indicate that takeovers, LBOs, and corporate restructurings are playing an important role in helping the economy adjust to major competitive changes in the last two decades. The competition among alternative management teams and organizational structures for control of corporate assets has enabled vast economic resources to move more quickly to their highest-valued use. In the process, substantial benefits for the economy as a whole as well as for shareholders have been created. Overall gains to selling-firm shareholders from mergers, acquisitions, leveraged buyouts, and other corporate restructurings in the 12-year period 1977–1988 total over $500 billion in 1988 dollars. I estimate gains to buying-firm shareholders to be at least $50 billion for the same period. These gains equal 53 percent of the total cash dividends (valued in 1988 dollars) paid to investors by the entire corporate sector in the same period.

Mergers and acquisitions are a response to new technologies or market conditions which require a strategic change in a company's direction or use of resources. Compared to current management, a new owner is often better able to accomplish major change in the existing organizational structure. Alternatively, leveraged buyouts bring about organizational change by creating entrepreneurial incentives for management and by eliminating the centralized bureaucratic obstacles to maneuverability that are inherent in large public corporations.

When managers have a substantial ownership interest in the organization, the conflicts of interest between shareholders and managers over the payout of the company's free cash flow are reduced. Management's incentives are focused on maximizing the value of the enterprise, rather than building empires—often through poorly conceived diversification acquisitions—without regard to shareholder value. Finally, the required repayment of debt replaces management's discretion in paying dividends and the tendency to overretain cash. Substantial increases in efficiency are thereby created.

Michael C. Jensen is Edsel Bryant Ford Professor of Business Administration at Harvard University. An outstanding scholar and researcher, he is famous for his path-breaking analysis of the modern corporation and its relations with its stockholders.

When two firms merge, the variability of their combined values is usually less than would be true if the firms remained separate entities. A reduction of the variability of firm values can occur if the values of the two firms are less than perfectly correlated. The reduction in variability can reduce the cost of borrowing and make the creditors better off than before. This will occur if the probability of financial distress is reduced by the merger.

Unfortunately, the shareholders are likely to be worse off. The gains to creditors are at the expense of the shareholders if the total value of the firm does not change. The relationship among the value of the merged firm, debt capacity, and risk is very complicated. We now consider two examples.

The Base Case

Consider a base case where two all-equity firms merge. Table 30.6 gives the net present values of firm *A* and firm *B* in three possible states of the economy—prosperity, average, and depression. The market value of firm *A* is $60, and the market value of firm *B* is $40. The market value of each firm is the weighted average of the values in each of the three states. For example, the value of firm *A* is

$$\$60 = \$80 \times 0.5 + \$50 \times 0.3 + \$25 \times 0.2$$

The values in each of the three states for firm *A* are $80, $50, and $25, respectively. The probabilities of each of the three states occurring are 0.5, 0.3, and 0.2, respectively.

■ TABLE 30.6 **Stock-Swap Mergers**

	NPV			
	State 1	State 2	State 3	Market Value
Base case: two all-equity firms before merger				
Firm *A*	$ 80	$50	$25	$ 60
Firm *B*	$ 50	$40	$15	$ 40
Probability	0.5	0.3	0.2	
After merger*				
Firm *AB*	$130	$90	$40	$100
Firm *A*, equity and risky debt before merger				
Firm *B*, all-equity before merger				
Firm *A*	$ 80	$50	$25	$ 60
Debt	$ 40	$40	$25	$ 37
Equity	$ 40	$10	$ 0	$ 23
Firm *B*	$ 50	$40	$15	$ 40
After merger†				
Firm *AB*	$130	$90	$40	$100
Debt	$ 40	$40	$40	$ 40
Equity	$ 90	$50	$ 0	$ 60

Value of debt rises after merger. Value of original stock in acquiring firm falls correspondingly.

*Stockholders in *B* receive stock value of $40. Therefore, stockholders of *A* have a value of $100 − $40 = $60 and are *indifferent to merger.*

†Because firm *B*'s stockholders receive stock in firm *A* worth $40, original stockholders in firm *A* have stock worth $20 ($60 − $40). Gains and losses from merger are

$20 − $23 = −$3: Therefore, stockholders of *A* lose $3.
$40 − $37 = $3: Therefore, bondholders of *A* gain $3.

When firm *A* merges with firm *B,* the combined firm *AB* will have a market value of $100. There is no synergy from this merger, and consequently the value of firm *AB* is the sum of the values of firm *A* and firm *B*. Stockholders of *B* receive stock with a value of $40, and therefore stockholders of *A* have a value of $100 − $40 = $60. Thus, stockholders of *A* and *B* are indifferent to the proposed merger.

One Firm Has Debt

Alternatively, imagine firm *A* has some debt and some equity outstanding before the merger.[16] Firm *B* is an all-equity firm. Firm *A* will default on its debt in state 3 because the net present value of firm *A* in this state is $25, and the value of the debt claim is $40. As a consequence, the full value of the debt claim cannot be paid by firm *A*. The creditors take this into account, and the value of the debt is $37 ($40 × 0.5 + $40 × 0.3 + $25 × 0.2).

Though default occurs without a merger, no default occurs with a merger. To see this, notice that, when the two firms are separate, firm *B* does not guarantee firm *A*'s debt. That is, if firm *A* defaults on its debt, firm *B* does not help the bondholders of firm *A*. However, after the merger the bondholders can draw on the cash flows from both *A* and *B*. When one of the divisions of the combined firm fails, creditors can be paid from the profits of the other division. This mutual guarantee, which is called the *coinsurance effect,* makes the debt less risky and more valuable than before.

---

[16]This example was provided by David Babbel.

The bonds are worth $40 after the merger. Thus, the bondholders of *AB* gain $3 ($40 − $37) from the merger.

The stockholders of firm *A* lose $3 ($20 − $23) from the merger. That is, firm *A*'s stock is worth $23 prior to the merger. The stock is worth $60 after the merger. However, stockholders in firm *B* receive $40 of stock in firm *A*. Hence, those individuals who were stockholders in firm *A* prior to the merger have stock worth only $20 ($60 − $40) after the merger.

There is no net benefit to the firm as a whole. The bondholders gain the coinsurance effect, and the stockholders lose the coinsurance effect. Some general conclusions emerge from the preceding analysis.

1. Bondholders in the aggregate will usually be helped by mergers and acquisitions. The size of the gain to bondholders depends on the reduction of bankruptcy states after the combination. That is, the less risky the combined firm is, the greater are the gains to bondholders.

2. Stockholders of the acquiring firm will be hurt by the amount that bondholders gain.

3. The conclusions apply to mergers and acquisitions where no synergy is present. In the case of synergistic combinations, much depends on the size of the synergy.

How Can Shareholders Reduce Their Losses from the Coinsurance Effect?

The coinsurance effect allows some mergers to increase bondholder values by reducing shareholder values. However, there are at least two ways that shareholders can reduce or eliminate the coinsurance effect. First, the shareholders in firm *A* could retire its debt *before* the merger announcement date and reissue an equal amount of debt after the merger. Because debt is retired at the low, pre-merger price, this type of refinancing transaction can neutralize the coinsurance effect to the bondholders.

Also, note that the debt capacity of the combined firm is likely to increase because the acquisition reduces the probability of financial distress. Thus, the shareholders' second alternative is simply to issue more debt after the merger. An increase in debt following the merger will have two effects, even without the prior action of debt retirement. The interest deduction from new corporate debt raises firm value. In addition, an increase in debt after the merger raises the probability of financial distress, thereby reducing or eliminating the bondholders' gain from the coinsurance effect.

30.8 Two "Bad" Reasons for Mergers

Earnings Growth

An acquisition can create the appearance of earnings growth, which may fool investors into thinking that the firm is worth more than it really is. Suppose Global Resources, Ltd., acquires Regional Enterprises. The financial positions of Global and Regional before the acquisition are shown in Table 30.7. Regional has had very poor earnings growth and sells at a price-earnings ratio much lower than that of Global. The merger creates no additional value. If the market is smart, it will realize that the combined firm is worth the sum of the values of the separate firms. In this case, the market value of the combined firm will be $3,500, which is equal to the sum of the values of the separate firms before the merger.

■ TABLE 30.7   **Financial Positions of Global Resources, Ltd.,
and Regional Enterprises**

	Global Resources before Merger	Regional Enterprises before Merger	Global Resources after Merger	
			The Market Is "Smart"	The Market Is "Fooled"
Earnings per share	$ 1.00	$ 1.00	$ 1.43	$ 1.43
Price per share	$ 25.00	$ 10.00	$ 25.00	$ 35.71
Price-earnings ratio	25	10	17.5	25
Number of shares	100	100	140	140
Total earnings	$ 100	$ 100	$ 200	$ 200
Total value	$2,500	$1,000	$3,500	$5,000

Exchange ratio: 1 share in Global for 2.5 shares in Regional.

At these values, Global will acquire Regional by exchanging 40 of its shares for 100 Regional shares,[17] so that Global will have 140 shares outstanding after the merger. Because the stock price of Global after the merger is the same as before the merger, the price-earnings ratio must fall. This is true because the market is smart and recognizes that the total market has not been altered by the merger. This scenario is represented by the third column of Table 30.7.

Let us now consider the possibility that the market is fooled. One can see from Table 30.7 that the acquisition enables Global to increase its earnings per share from $1 to $1.43. If the market is fooled, it might mistake the 43-percent increase in earnings per share for true growth. In this case, the price-earnings ratio of Global may not fall after the merger. Suppose the price-earnings ratio of Global remains equal to 25. The total value of the combined firm will increase to $5,000 (25 × $200), and the stock price per share of Global will increase to $35.71 ($5,000/140). This is reflected in the last column of Table 30.7.

This is earnings-growth magic. Like all good magic, it is an illusion and the shareholders of Global and Regional will receive something for nothing. This may work for a while, but in the long run the efficient market will work its wonders and the value will decline.

Diversification

Diversification often is mentioned as a benefit of one firm acquiring another. Earlier in this chapter, we noted that U.S. Steel included diversification as a benefit in its acquisition of Marathon Oil. In 1982 U.S. Steel was a cash-rich company (over 20 percent of its assets were in the form of cash and marketable securities). It is not uncommon to see firms with surplus cash articulating a need for diversification.

However, we argue that diversification, by itself, cannot produce increases in value. To see this, recall that a business's variability of return can be separated into two parts: (1) what is specific to the business and called *unsystematic,* and (2) what is *systematic* because it is common to all businesses.

---

[17]This ratio implies a fair exchange because a share of Regional is selling for 40 percent ($10/$25) of the price of a share of Global.

Systematic variability cannot be eliminated by diversification, so mergers will not eliminate this risk at all. By contrast, unsystematic risk can be diversified away through mergers. However, the investor does not need widely diversified companies such as General Electric to eliminate unsystematic risk. Shareholders can diversify more easily than corporations by simply purchasing common stock in different corporations. For example, the shareholders of U.S. Steel could have purchased shares in Marathon if they believed there would be diversification gains in doing so. Thus, diversification through conglomerate merger may not benefit shareholders.[18]

Diversification can produce gains to the acquiring firm only if two things are true:

1. Diversification decreases the unsystematic variability at lower costs than by investors via adjustments to personal portfolios. This seems very unlikely.

2. Diversification reduces risk and thereby increases debt capacity. This possibility was mentioned earlier in the chapter.

QUESTION CONCEPT ?

• Why can a merger create the appearance of earnings growth?

30.9 THE NPV OF A MERGER

Firms typically use NPV analysis when making acquisitions.[19] The analysis is relatively straightforward when the consideration is cash. The analysis becomes more complex when the consideration is stock.

Cash

Suppose firm *A* and firm *B* have values as separate entities of $500 and $100, respectively. They are both all-equity firms. If firm *A* acquires firm *B,* the merged firm *AB* will have a combined value of $700 due to synergies of $100. The board of firm *B* has indicated that it will sell firm *B* if it is offered $150 in cash.

---

[18]Recent evidence suggests that diversification can actually hurt shareholders. Randall Mork, Andrei Shleifer, and Robert W. Vishney ["Do Managerial Objectives Drive Bad Acquisitions," *Journal of Finance* 45 (1990), pp. 31–48] show that shareholders did poorly in firms that diversified by acquisition in the 1980s. There is also evidence that diversified firms trade at a discount relative to a portfolio of single-segment firms, most recently from Karl Lins and Henri Servaes, "The International Evidence on the Value of Corporate Diversification," *Journal of Finance* 54 (1999). On the other hand, Matsusaka and Hubbard and Palia find some benefits to diversification in internal capital allocation. See John Matsusaka, "Takeover Motives During the Conglomerate Merge Wave," *Rand Journal of Economics* 24 (1993).

See also R. Glenn Hubbard and Darius Palia, "A Reexamination of the Conglomerate Merger Wave in the 1960s: An Internal Capital Markets View," *Journal of Finance* (June 1999).

One interesting recent study reports a positive relationship between focus and value for diversified firms. See P. G. Berger and E. Ofek, "Diversification's Effect on Firm Value," *Journal of Financial Economics,* 37 (1995). Also see P. G. Berger and E. Ofek, "Causes and Effects of Corporate Refocusing Program," *Review of Financial Studies* 12 (1999).

[19]The NPV framework for evaluating mergers can be found in S. C. Myers, "A Framework for Evaluating Mergers," in *Modern Developments in Financial Management,* ed. by S. C. Myers (New York: Praeger, 1976).

■ TABLE 30.8   Cost of Acquisition: Cash versus Common Stock

	Before Acquisition		After Acquisition: Firm A		
	(1)	(2)	(3)	(4) Common Stock† Exchange Ratio (0.75:1)	(5) Common Stock† Exchange Ratio (0.6819:1)
	Firm A	Firm B	Cash*		
Market value (V_A, V_B)	$500	$100	$550	$700	$700
Number of shares	25	10	25	32.5	31.819
Price per share	$ 20	$ 10	$ 22	$ 21.54	$ 22

*Value of firm *A* after acquisition: cash

$$V_A = V_{AB} - \text{Cash}$$
$$\$550 = \$700 - \$150$$

†Value of firm *A* after acquisition: common stock

$$V_A = V_{AB}$$
$$\$700 = \$700$$

Should firm *A* acquire firm *B?* Assuming that firm *A* finances the acquisition out of its own retained earnings, its value after the acquisition is[20]

$$\begin{aligned}
\text{Value of firm } A \\
\text{after the acquisition} &= \text{Value of combined firm} - \text{Cash paid} \\
&= \$700 - \$150 \\
&= \$550
\end{aligned}$$

Because firm *A* was worth $500 prior to the acquisition, the NPV to firm *A*'s stockholders is

$$\$50 = \$550 - \$500 \tag{30.1}$$

Assuming that there are 25 shares in firm *A,* each share of the firm is worth $20 ($500/25) prior to the merger and $22 ($550/25) after the merger. These calculations are displayed in the first and third columns of Table 30.8. Looking at the rise in stock price, we conclude that firm *A* should make the acquisition.

We spoke earlier of both the synergy and the premium of a merger. We can also value the NPV of a merger to the acquirer as

$$\text{NPV of a merger to acquirer} = \text{Synergy} - \text{Premium}$$

Because the value of the combined firm is $700 and the premerger values of *A* and *B* were $500 and $100, respectively, the synergy is $100 [$700 − ($500 + $100)]. The premium is $50 ($150 − $100). Thus, the NPV of the merger to the acquirer is

$$\text{NPV of merger to firm } A = \$100 - \$50 = \$50$$

One caveat is in order. This textbook has consistently argued that the market value of a firm is the best estimate of its true value. However, we must adjust our analysis when discussing mergers. If the true price of firm *A without the merger* is $500, the market value of firm *A*

---

[20]The analysis will be essentially the same if new stock is issued. However, the analysis will differ if new debt is issued to fund the acquisition because of the tax shield to debt. An adjusted present value (APV) approach would be necessary here.

may actually be above $500 when merger negotiations take place. This occurs because the market price reflects the possibility that the merger will occur. For example, if the probability is 60 percent that the merger will take place, the market price of firm A will be

	Market value of firm A	×	Probability of merger	+	Market value of firm A without merger	×	Probability of no merger
	with merger						
$530 =	$550	×	0.60	+	$500	×	0.40

The managers would underestimate the NPV from merger in equation (30.1) if the market price of firm A is used. Thus, managers are faced with the difficult task of valuing their own firm without the acquisition.

Common Stock

Of course, firm A could purchase firm B with common stock instead of cash. Unfortunately, the analysis is not as straightforward here. In order to handle this scenario, we need to know how many shares are outstanding in firm B. We assume that there are 10 shares outstanding, as indicated in column 2 of Table 30.8.

Suppose firm A exchanges 7.5 of its shares for the entire 10 shares of firm B. We call this an exchange ratio of 0.75:1. The value of each share of firm A's stock before the acquisition is $20. Because $7.5 \times \$20 = \$150$, this exchange *appears* to be the equivalent of purchasing firm B in cash for $150.

This is incorrect: The true cost is greater than $150. To see this, note that firm A has 32.5 (25 + 7.5) shares outstanding after the merger. Firm B shareholders own 23 percent (7.5/32.5) of the combined firm. Their holdings are valued at $161 (23% × $700). Because these stockholders receive stock in firm A worth $161, the cost of the merger to firm A's stockholders must be $161, not $150.

This result is shown in column 4 of Table 30.8. The value of each share of firm A's stock after a stock-for-stock transaction is only $21.54 ($700/32.5). We found out earlier that the value of each share is $22 after a cash-for-stock transaction. The difference is that the cost of the stock-for-stock transaction to firm A is higher.

This nonintuitive result occurs because the exchange ratio of 7.5 shares of firm A for 10 shares of firm B was based on the *premerger* prices of the two firms. However, since the stock of firm A rises after the merger, firm B stockholders receive more than $150 in firm A stock.

What should the exchange ratio be so that firm B stockholders receive only $150 of firm A's stock? We begin by defining α, the proportion of the shares in the combined firm that firm B's stockholders own. Because the combined firm's value is $700, the value of firm B stockholders after the merger is

Value of Firm B Stockholders after Merger:

$$\alpha \times \$700$$

Setting $\alpha \times \$700 = \$150$, we find that $\alpha = 21.43\%$. In other words, firm B's stockholders will receive stock worth $150 if they receive 21.43 percent of the firm after merger.

Now we determine the number of shares issued to firm B's shareholders. The proportion, α, that firm B's shareholders have in the combined firm can be expressed as

$$\alpha = \frac{\text{New shares issued}}{\text{Old shares + New shares issued}} = \frac{\text{New shares issued}}{25 + \text{New shares issued}}$$

Plugging our value of α into the equation yields

$$0.2143 = \frac{\text{New shares issued}}{25 + \text{New shares issued}}$$

Solving for the unknown, we have

$$\text{New shares} = 6.819 \text{ shares}$$

Total shares outstanding after the merger are 31.819 (25 + 6.819). Because 6.819 shares of firm *A* are exchanged for 10 shares of firm *B,* the exchange ratio is 0.6819:1.

Results at the exchange ratio of 0.6819:1 are displayed in column 5 of Table 30.8. Each share of common stock is worth $22, exactly what it is worth in the stock-for-cash transaction. Thus, given that the board of firm *B* will sell its firm for $150, this is the fair exchange ratio, not the ratio of 0.75:1 mentioned earlier.

Cash versus Common Stock

Whether to finance an acquisition by cash or by shares of stock is an important decision. The choice depends on several factors, as follows:

1. *Overvaluation.* If in the opinion of management the acquiring firm's stock is overvalued, using shares of stock can be less costly than using cash.
2. *Taxes.* Acquisition by cash usually results in a taxable transaction. Acquisition by exchanging stock is tax free.
3. *Sharing Gains.* If cash is used to finance an acquisition, the selling firm's shareholders receive a fixed price. In the event of a hugely successful merger, they will not participate in any additional gains. Of course, if the acquisition is not a success, the losses will not be shared and shareholders of the acquiring firm will be worse off than if stock were used.

CONCEPT QUESTION

• In an efficient market with no tax effects, should an acquiring firm use cash or stock?

30.10 DEFENSIVE TACTICS

Target-firm managers frequently resist takeover attempts. Resistance usually starts with press releases and mailings to shareholders that present management's viewpoint. It can eventually lead to legal action and solicitation of competing bids. Managerial action to defeat a takeover attempt may make target shareholders better off if it elicits a higher offer premium from the bidding firm or another firm. Of course, management resistance may simply reflect pursuit of self-interest at the expense of shareholders. That is, the target managers may resist a takeover in order to preserve their jobs. It is also possible that the target-firm management will take corrective action to increase stock price in order to reduce the takeover benefits. In this section we describe various defensive tactics that have been used by target-firm managements to resist unfriendly takeover attempts.

Divestitures

Target-firm managers considering the prospect of a takeover may decide a narrowing of strategic focus can increase stock price, thereby making a takeover too expensive. If so, they will consider the pros and cons of three kinds of divestitures: a sale of assets, a spin-off, and the issuance of a tracking stock. The basic idea of all three types of divestitures is to reduce the potential diversification discount associated with commingled operations and to increase corporate focus. The sale of a business segment is usually for cash. With a spin-off, the parent company distributes shares of a subsidiary to its shareholders. As a consequence, the shareholders end up with a stake in the parent as well as the subsidiary. Typically, the stock in the subsidiary is distributed pro rata to the parent-company shareholders. No actual asset sale is involved, and the subsidiary becomes a completely separate company (with its own board of directors, etc.). A variant of the spin-off is called an *equity curveout,* where the stock of the subsidiary is sold to the public in an IPO. Sometimes a spin-off and an equity curveout are combined. A tracking stock is a class of common stock whose value is connected to the performance of a particular segment (division or subsidiary) of the parent company's business. The intent of a tracking stock is quite similar to an asset sale or spin-off, which is to give shareholders a pure play on a particular part of the firm. The issue of tracking stock shares can be some form of combination between a pro rata distribution and an IPO. The first tracker was when General Motors issued stock that tracked Electronic Data Systems (EDS). Recently General Motors, AT&T, and Sprint PCS have issued trackers. Tracking stock does not involve a separate, formal entity, as in the case of a spin-off or equity curveout.[21]

The Corporate Charter

The corporate charter refers to the articles of incorporation and corporate bylaws that govern the firm. The corporate charter establishes the conditions that allow a takeover. Firms frequently amend corporate charters to make acquisitions more difficult. For example, usually two-thirds of the shareholders of record must approve a merger. Firms can make it more difficult to be acquired by requiring 80-percent approval by the shareholders. This is called a *supermajority amendment.* Another device is to *stagger* the election of the board members, which increases the difficulty of electing a new board of directors quickly. DeAngelo and Rice, and Linn and McConnell examine the adoption of antitakeover amendments related to the corporate charter on stock prices of the adopting firms and find no adverse effect.[22]

Repurchase Standstill Agreements

Managers may arrange a *targeted repurchase* to forestall a takeover attempt. In a targeted repurchase, a firm buys back its own stock from a potential bidder, usually at a substantial premium. These premiums can be thought of as payments to potential bidders to delay or stop unfriendly takeover attempts. Critics of such payments label them *greenmail.*

In addition, managers of target firms may simultaneously negotiate standstill agreements. *Standstill agreements* are contracts where the bidding firm agrees to limit its holdings

---

[21]There have been several studies of tracking stocks that seem to suggest returns of about three percent upon the announcement of a tracking stock issue. For example: M. T. Billet and D. C. Mauer, "Diversification and the Value of Internal Capital Market, The Case of Tracking Stock," *Journal of Banking and Finance* (Forthcoming); D. Sousa J. and J. Jacob, "Why Firms Issue Tracking Stock," *Journal of Financial Economics,* (Forthcoming); D. E. Logue, J. K. Seward, and J. P. Walsh, "Rearranging Residual Claim: A Case for Targeted Stock," *Financial Management* 25, (1996).

On the other hand, Mathew T. Billet and Anand M. Vijh, "Long-Term Returns from Tracking Stocks," University of Iowa, unpublished paper, report negative long-term returns from tracking stocks.

Several recent articles report stock-price gains from asset sales spin-offs and equity curveouts that increase a firm's focus. See, for example: J. Desai and P. Jain, "Firm Performance and Focus: Long Run Stock Market Performance Following Spin-offs," *Journal of Financial Economics* 54 (1999); K. John and E. Ofek, "Asset Sales and Increase in Focus," *Journal of Financial Economics* 37 (1999); and A. Vijh, "Long Term Returns from Equity Curveouts," *Journal of Financial Economics* 51 (1999).

[22]H. DeAngelo and E. M. Rice, "Antitakeover Charter Amendments and Stockholder Wealth," *Journal of Financial Economics* 11 (April 1983); and S. G. Linn and J. J. McConnell, "An Empirical Investigation of the Impact of Antitakeover Amendments on Common Stock Prices," *Journal of Financial Economics* 11 (April 1983).

of another firm. These agreements usually lead to cessation of takeover attempts, and announcement of such agreements has had a negative effect on stock prices.

EXAMPLE

On April 2, 1986, Ashland Oil, Inc., the nation's largest independent oil refiner, had 28 million shares outstanding. The company's stock price closed the day before at $49¾ per share on the New York Stock Exchange. On April 2, Ashland's board of directors made two decisions:

1. The board approved management's agreement with the Belzberg family of Canada to buy, for $51 a share, the Belzbergs' 2.6 million shares in Ashland. This was part of a standstill agreement that ended a takeover skirmish in which the Belzberg family offered $60 per share for all of the common stock of Ashland.
2. The board authorized the company to repurchase 7.5 million shares (27 percent of the outstanding shares) of its stock. The board simultaneously approved a proposal to establish an employee stock-ownership plan to be funded with 5.3 million shares of Ashland stock.

The result of these two actions was to make Ashland invulnerable to unfriendly takeover attempts. In effect, the company was selling about 20 percent of its stock to the employee stock-ownership plan. Earlier Ashland had put in place a provision that said 80 percent of the stockholders have to approve a takeover. Ashland's stock price fell by $0.25 over the next two days. Because this move can probably be explained by random error, there is no evidence that Ashland's actions reduced shareholder value.

Exclusionary Self-Tenders

An *exclusionary self-tender* is the opposite of a targeted repurchase. Here, the firm makes a tender offer for a given amount of its own stock while excluding targeted stockholders.

In one of the most celebrated cases in financial history, Unocal, a large integrated oil firm, made a tender offer for 29 percent of its shares while excluding its largest shareholder, Mesa Partners II (led by T. Boone Pickens). Unocal's self-tender was for $72 per share, which was $16 over the prevailing market price. It was designed to defeat Mesa's attempted takeover of Unocal by transferring wealth, in effect, from Mesa to Unocal's other stockholders.

Going Private and Leveraged Buyouts

Going private refers to what happens when the publicly owned stock in a firm is purchased by a private group, usually composed of existing management. As a consequence, the firm's stock is taken off the market (if it is an exchange-traded stock, it is delisted) and is no longer traded. Thus, in going-private transactions, shareholders of publicly held firms are forced to accept cash for their shares.

Going-private transactions are frequently *leveraged buyouts* (LBOs). In a leveraged buyout, the cash-offer price is financed with large amounts of debt. LBOs have recently become quite popular because the arrangement calls for little equity capital. This equity capital is generally supplied by a small group of investors, some of whom are likely to be managers of the firm being purchased.

The selling stockholders are invariably paid a premium above market price in an LBO, just as they are in a merger.[23] As with a merger, the acquirer profits only if the synergy

---

[23]H. DeAngelo, L. DeAngelo, and E. M. Rice, "Going Private: Minority Freezeouts and Shareholder Wealth," *Journal of Law and Economics* 27 (1984). They show that the premiums paid to existing shareholders in LBOs and other going-private transactions are about the same as in interfirm acquisitions.

created is greater than the premium. Synergy is quite plausible in a merger of *two* firms, and we delineated a number of types of synergy earlier in the chapter. However, it is much more difficult to explain synergy in an LBO, because only *one* firm is involved.

There are generally two reasons given for the ability of an LBO to create value. First, the extra debt provides a tax deduction, which, as earlier chapters suggested, leads to an increase in firm value. Most LBOs are on firms with stable earnings and with low to moderate debt. The LBO may simply increase the firm's debt to its optimum level. In fact, Congress has recently taken a skeptical look at LBOs, partly because the increase in debt reduces the U.S. Treasury's tax revenues.

Second, the LBO usually turns the previous managers into owners, thereby increasing their incentive to work hard. The increase in debt is a further incentive because the managers must earn more than the debt service to obtain any profit for themselves.

Though it is easy to value the additional tax shields from an LBO, it is quite difficult to value the gains from increased efficiency. Nevertheless, this increased efficiency is considered to be at least as important as the tax shield in explaining the LBO phenomenon.[24]

Of course, one cannot be entirely sure that LBOs create value at all, because the stock price cannot be observed once the company has been taken private. Though one frequently hears of LBO investors achieving great wealth, this is only casual empirical evidence. There may be an equal number of LBO investors who are left with little value after purchasing a company at a premium. The full story on LBOs has certainly not been told at this point.

Other Devices and Jargon of Corporate Takeovers

As corporate takeovers have become more common, a new lexicon has developed. The terms are colorful, and some are listed here:

1. **Golden parachutes.** Some target firms provide compensation to top-level management if a takeover occurs. For example, when the Scoville board endorsed a $523 million tender offer by First City Properties, it arranged for 13 top executives to receive termination payments of about $5 million. This can be viewed as a payment to management to make it less concerned for its own welfare and more interested in stockholders when considering a takeover bid. Alternatively, the payment can be seen as an attempt to enrich management at the stockholders' expense.

2. **Crown jewels.** Firms often sell major assets—crown jewels—when faced with a takeover threat. This is sometimes referred to as the *scorched earth strategy.*

3. **Poison pill.** Poison pill is a term taken from the world of espionage. Agents are supposed to bite a pill of cyanide rather than permit capture. Presumably this prevents enemy interrogators from learning important secrets. In finance, poison pills are used to make a stock repellent to others. A poison pill is generally a right to buy shares in the merged firm at a bargain price. The right is granted to the target firm's shareholders, contingent on another firm acquiring control.[25] The right dilutes the stock so much that the bidding firm loses money on its shares. Thus, wealth is transferred from the bidder to the target.

---

[24]For the academic community's view of LBOs, see "A Discussion of Corporate Restructuring," *Midland Corporate Finance Journal* (Summer 1984), which features a roundtable discussion by a number of prominent university professors.

[25]P. H. Malatesta and R. A. Walkling, "Poison Pill Securities: Stockholder Wealth, Profitability and Ownership Structure," *Journal of Financial Economics* (January/March 1988). The authors conclude that the poison pill reduces stockholder wealth. Also see R. A. Walkling and M. Long, "Agency Theory, Managerial Welfare and Takeover Bid Resistance," *Rand Journal of Economics* (Spring 1984).

• What can a firm do to make a takeover less likely?

30.11 SOME EVIDENCE ON ACQUISITIONS

One of the most controversial issues surrounding our subject is whether mergers and acquisitions benefit shareholders.

Do Acquisitions Benefit Shareholders?

Much research has attempted to estimate the effect of mergers and takeovers on stock prices of the bidding and target firms. These studies are called *event studies* because they estimate abnormal stock-price changes on and around the offer-announcement date—the event. Abnormal returns are usually defined as the difference between actual stock returns and a market index or a control group of stocks, to take account of the influence of marketwide effects on the returns of individual securities.

The Short Run

An overview of the short run evidence is reported in Jensen and Ruback. Tables 30.9 and 30.10 summarize the results of numerous studies that look at the effects of mergers and tender offers on stock prices from the announcement date to the completion date. Table 30.9 shows that the shareholders of target companies in successful takeovers achieve large abnormal returns. When the takeover is done by merger the gains are 20 percent, and when the takeover is done by tender offer the gains are 30 percent.

The shareholders of bidding firms do not fare nearly as well. According to the studies summarized in Table 30.9, bidders experience abnormal returns of 4 percent in tender offers, and in mergers the percentage is zero. These numbers are sufficiently small to leave doubt about the effect on bidders. Table 30.10 shows that the shareholders of firms involved in unsuccessful takeover attempts experience small negative returns in both mergers and tender offers. What conclusions can be drawn from Tables 30.9 and 30.10?

■ TABLE 30.9   **Abnormal Stock-Price Changes Associated with Successful Corporate Takeover Bids**

Takeover Technique	Target	Bidders
Tender offer	30%	4%
Merger	20%	0
Proxy contest	8%	n.a.

n.a. = Not applicable.
Modified from Michael C. Jensen and Richard S. Ruback, "The Market for Corporate Control: The Scientific Evidence," *Journal of Financial Economics* 11 (April 1983), pp. 7, 8. © Elsevier Science Publishers B. V. (North-Holland).

■ TABLE 30.10 **Abnormal Stock-Price Changes Associated with Unsuccessful Corporate Takeover Bids**

Takeover Technique	Target	Bidders
Tender offer	−3%	−1%
Merger	−3%	−5%
Proxy contest	8%	n.a.

n.a. = Not applicable.
Modified from Michael C. Jensen and Richard S. Ruback, "The Market for Corporate Control: The Scientific Evidence," *Journal of Financial Economics* 11 (April 1983), pp. 7, 8. © Elsevier Science Publishers B. V. (North-Holland).

1. The results of all event studies suggest that the shareholders of target firms achieve substantial short-term gains as a result of successful takeovers.[26] The gains appear to be larger in tender offers than in mergers. This may reflect the fact that takeovers sometimes start with a friendly merger proposal from the bidder to the management of the target firm. If management rejects the offer, the bidding firm may take the offer directly to the shareholders with an unfriendly tender offer. The target management may actively oppose the offer with defensive tactics. This often has the result of raising the tender offer from the bidding firm, and, thus, on the average, friendly mergers are arranged at a lower premium than unfriendly tender offers.

2. The shareholders of bidding firms earn comparatively little from takeovers. They earn an average of only 4 percent from tender offers and do not appear to earn anything from mergers. In fact, in a study by Asquith the shareholders of acquiring firms in successful mergers experienced significantly abnormal losses after the announcement of the merger.[27] These findings are a puzzle.

   a. One possible explanation is that anticipated merger gains were not completely achieved, and thus shareholders experienced losses. Managers of bidding firms may have hubris and tend to overestimate the gains from acquisition.[28]

   b. The bidding firms are usually much larger than the target firms. Thus, the dollar gains to the bidder may be approximately the same as the dollar gains to the shareholders of the target firm at the same time that the *percentage* returns are much lower for the bidding firms.

   c. Management may not be acting in the interests of shareholders when it attempts to acquire other firms. Perhaps it is attempting to increase the size of its firm, even if this reduces its value.

   d. Several studies indicate that the returns of bidding firms cannot be measured very easily. Malatesta, and Schipper and Thompson show that many of the gains to the shareholders of bidding firms come when acquisition programs commence. The incremental effect of each acquisition on stock price may be very small, because the stock price at commencement reflects the anticipated gains from future acquisitions.[29]

---

[26]This has been a consistent finding in all merger studies. G. Mandelker, "Risk and Return: The Case of the Merging Firm," *Journal of Financial Economics* (1974), was one of the first to document the premiums to acquired firms.

[27]P. Asquith, "Merger Bids, Uncertainty and Stockholder Returns," *Journal of Financial Economics* 11 (April 1983).

[28]R. Roll, "The Hubris Hypothesis of Corporate Takeover," *Journal of Business* (April 1986).

[29]P. H. Malatesta, "The Wealth Effect of Merger Activity and the Objective Function of Merging Firms," *Journal of Financial Economics* 11 (April 1983); and K. Schipper and R. Thompson, "Evidence on the Capitalized Value of Merger Activity for Acquiring Firms," *Journal of Financial Economics* 11 (April 1983).

■ TABLE 30.11   **Abnormal Five-Year Stock Returns of Acquiring Firms from 1970 to 1989**

Acquirers using unfriendly cash tender offers	61.7%
Acquirers who pay cash (both friendly and unfriendly)	18.5%
All acquirers	−6.5%
Acquirers using stock	−24.2%

Source: T. Loughran and A. Vijh, "Do Long-Term Shareholders Benefit from Corporate Acquisitions," *Journal of Finance* (December, 1997), Table II. The abnormal returns are measured over a five-year period beginning at the date of the acquisition. For example, the overall sample of 947 acquisitions experienced an average five-year return of 88.2 percent compared to 94.7 percent for a sample of matching firms. The difference equals −6.5 percent (see above).

3. The return to the shareholders of targets of unsuccessful merger, measured from the offer date to the cancellation date, is negative. Thus, all the initial gains are lost over the time period during which the merger failure becomes known. The overall average return to shareholders of unsuccessful tender offers is about the same as for unsuccessful merger attempts. However, the story is more complicated. Bradley, Desai, and Kim report that how well shareholders of target firms do in unsuccessful tender offers depends on whether or not future takeover offers are forthcoming. They find that target-firm shareholders realize additional positive gains when a new offer is made but lose everything previously gained if no other offer occurs.[30]

The Long Run

The evidence on long run stock returns following acquisition is provided by Loughran and Vijh. Table 30.11 summarizes the results of their study of nearly 1,000 acquiring (bidding) firms from 1970 to 1989. They compute the average abnormal return to shareholders from the date of the acquisition over a subsequent five-year period. Table 30.11 shows that shareholders of acquiring firms earn negative average abnormal returns. Previously we reported that shareholders of acquiring firms did not fare particularly well in the short run. Now we see that five years after the date of the acquisition, shareholders of acquiring firms continue to do poorly, earning an abnormal average return of −6.5 percent.

Table 30.11 also shows that the method of payment in acquisitions is important in the distribution of long run returns. When the acquirer pays cash for the target, shareholders gain an abnormal average return of 18.5 percent. However, when the acquirer pays with its own stock, shareholders experience a negative abnormal average return of −24.2 percent. Several conclusions can be drawn from Table 30.11.

1. In the long run, the shareholders of acquiring firms experience below average returns. If significant, this finding raises questions about the efficient market hypothesis, since any negative information implicit in an acquisition should be reflected in stock returns by the date of the acquisition.

2. Cash-financed mergers are different than stock-financed mergers. When an acquisition is financed by stock, it is useful to think of the acquisition as a combination of two events: an issue of stock and an acquisition. It is known from Loughran and Ritter (Chap-

---

[30]M. Bradley, A. Desai, and E. H. Kim, "The Rationale behind Interfirm Tender Offers: Information or Synergy," *Journal of Financial Economics* 11 (April 1983).

ter 18) that the long-term abnormal returns following new equity issues are negative. The poor long run performance of stock-financed mergers could be the result of new stock issues that take place with these mergers.

3. Acquirers can also be divided into friendly and unfriendly cash acquirers. The shares of unfriendly cash acquirers have significantly outperformed those of friendly cash acquirers. One possible interpretation of this is that unfriendly cash bidders are more likely to replace poor management. If so, the removal of poor managers may contribute to the above average long run performance.

Real Productivity

There are many potential synergies from mergers and acquisitions. Unfortunately, it is very hard to precisely measure synergy. In the previous section, we focused on stock-market gains or losses to the shareholders of the acquiring and acquired firms. In very general terms, we found that target-firm shareholders experience stock-market gains and acquiring-firm shareholders experience stock-market losses. There appear to be net gains to stockholders. This would suggest that mergers can increase real productivity. In fact, several recent studies suggest that mergers can increase real productivity. Healey, Palepu, and Ruback report that merged companies' after-tax returns increased substantially after the mergers. They trace this gain to an increase in selling activity (turnover). They find no evidence that merged firms cut back on positive NPV capital expenditures.[31]

CONCEPT QUESTION

? • What does the evidence say about the benefits of mergers and acquisitions?

30.12 THE JAPANESE KEIRETSU

In Japan it has been unusual for firms to grow by large-scale mergers and acquisitions. However, in the late 1980s several Japanese firms acquired large U.S. firms.[32] Most notably, Sony acquired CBS Records in November 1987 and Columbia Pictures in September 1989. Sony's acquisition of Columbia Pictures for $3.45 billion is the largest Japanese acquisition of a U.S. firm. The second largest was Bridgestone Corporation's acquisition of Firestone Tire and Rubber for $2.6 billion in March 1988.

The most interesting Japanese business combinations involve reciprocal shareholding and trading agreements. These networks are called **keiretsu** and involve a group of firms affiliated around a large bank, industrial firm, or trading firm. The Mitsubishi and the Mitsui keiretsu groups are shown in Figure 30.3.

Participation in the Mitsubishi or Mitsui keiretsu implies significant reciprocal ownership of common stock. It is widely understood that firms within the keiretsu are not to sell these cross-held shares.

---

[31]P. Healey, K. Palepu, and R. Ruback, "Does Corporate Performance Improve After Mergers," *Journal of Financial Economics* 31 (1997).

[32]W. Carl Kester, *Japanese Takeovers, the Global Contest for Corporate Control*, Cambridge, Mass.: 1991 (Harvard Business School Press). Chapter 5 describes the acquisition experience of several Japanese firms.

■ FIGURE 30.3 **Japanese Keiretsu**

	Mitsubishi	Mitsui
Financial Services	Mitsubishi Bank	Mitsui Taiyo Kobe Bank
	Mitsubishi Trust & Banking	Mitsui Trust & Banking
	Meiji Mutual Life	Mitsui Mutual Life
	Tokio Marine & Fire	Taisho Marine & Fire
Computers, Electronics, and Electrical Equipment	Mitsubishi Electric	Toshiba
Cars	Mitsubishi Motors	Toyota Motor*
Trading and Retailing	Mitsubishi	Mitsui
		Mitsukoshi
Food and Beverage	Kirin Brewery	Nippon Flour Mills
Construction	Mitsubishi Construction	Mitsui Construction
		Sanki Engineering
Metals	Mitsubishi Steel Mfg.	Japan Steel Works
	Mitsubishi Materials	Mitsui Mining & Smelting
	Mitsubishi Aluminum	
	Mitsubishi Cable Industries	
Real Estate	Mitsubishi Estate	Mitsui Real Estate Development
Oil and Coal	Mitsubishi Oil	
Rubber and Glass	Asahi Glass	
Chemicals	Mitsubishi Kasei	Mitsui Toatsu Chemicals
	Mitsubishi Petrochemical	Mitsui Petrochemical Industries
	Mitsubishi Gas Chemical	
	Mitsubishi Plastics Industries	
	Mitsubishi Kasei Polytec	
Fibers and Textiles	Mitsubishi Rayon	Tory Industries
Pulp and Paper	Mitsubishi Paper Mills	Oji Paper
Mining and Forestry		Mitsui Mining
		Hokkaido Colliery & Steamship
Industrial Equipment	Mitsubishi Heavy Industries	Mitsui Engineering & Shipbuilding
	Mitsubishi Kakoki	
Cameras and Optics	Nikon	
Cement		Onoda Cement
Shipping and Transportation	Nippon Yusen	Mitsui OSK Lines
	Mitsubishi Warehouse & Transportation	Mitsui Warehouse

This table describes the network of firms in the Mitsubishi and Mitsui keiretsu.
*Companies affiliated with more than one group.
Source: *Fortune* (July 15, 1991), p. 81.

Nobody knows for sure what the main benefit of the keiretsu is. However, one of the most important features of the keiretsu is the relationship between the industrial firms and the financial institutions. For example, Mitsubishi Motors may have an extensive relationship with Mitsubishi Trust and Banking, Meiji Mutual Life, and Tokio Marine and Fire. This connection between industrial firms and financial institutions within the group may benefit the group by reducing the costs of financial distress that come from getting creditors to agree to a restructuring if one of the keiretsu members gets into financial trouble.[33] Reaching an agreement between Mitsubishi Bank and Mitsubishi Motors will be easier if Mitsubishi Motors gets into trouble because both are in the Mitsubishi keiretsu.

30.13 SUMMARY AND CONCLUSIONS

1. One firm can acquire another in several different ways. The three legal forms of acquisition are merger and consolidation, acquisition of stock, and acquisition of assets. Mergers and consolidations are the least costly to arrange from a legal standpoint, but they require a vote of approval by the shareholders. Acquisition by stock does not require a shareholder vote and is usually done via a tender offer. However, it is difficult to obtain 100-percent control with a tender offer. Acquisition of assets is comparatively costly because it requires more difficult transfer of asset ownership.

2. Mergers and acquisitions require an understanding of complicated tax and accounting rules. Mergers and acquisitions can be taxable or tax-free transactions. In a taxable transaction, each selling shareholder must pay taxes on the stock's capital appreciation. Should the acquiring firm elect to write up the assets, additional tax implications arise. However, acquiring firms do not generally elect to write up the assets for tax purposes. The selling stockholders do not pay taxes at the time of a tax-free acquisition.

   Accounting for mergers and acquisitions involves a choice of the purchase method or the pooling-of-interests method. The choice between these two methods does not affect after-tax cash flows of the combined firm. However, most financial managers prefer the pooling-of-interests method, because net income of the combined firm under this method is higher than it is under the purchase method.

3. The synergy from an acquisition is defined as the value of the combined firm (V_{AB}) less the value of the two firms as separate entities (V_A and V_B), or

$$\text{Synergy} = V_{AB} - (V_A + V_B)$$

   The shareholders of the acquiring firm will gain if the synergy from the merger is greater than the premium.

4. The possible benefits of an acquisition come from the following:
   a. Revenue enhancement
   b. Cost reduction
   c. Lower taxes
   d. Lower cost of capital
      In addition, the reduction in risk from a merger may actually help bondholders and hurt stockholders.

5. Some of the most colorful language of finance stems from defensive tactics in acquisition battles. *Poison pills, golden parachutes, crown jewels,* and *greenmail* are terms that describe various antitakeover tactics. These tactics are discussed in this chapter.

---

[33]This is the argument of Takeo Hoshi, Anil K. Kashyup, and David Scharfstein, "The Role of Banks in Reducing Financial Distress in Japan." A paper in the Finance and Economic Discussion Series, No. 134, Federal Reserve Board, Washington, D. C. (October 1990). See also, W. Carl Kester, "Japanese Corporate Governance and the Conservation of Value in Financial Distress," *Journal of Applied Corporate Finance* (Summer 1991).

6. The empirical research on mergers and acquisitions is extensive. Its basic conclusions are that, on average, the shareholders of acquired firms fare very well, while the shareholders of acquiring firms do not gain much.

7. The keiretsu is a Japanese form of business network. It involves reciprocal shareholding and agreements among member firms.

KEY TERMS

Bidder   818
Consolidation   817
Crown jewels   841
Golden parachutes   841
Goodwill   821
Keiretsu   845

Merger   817
Poison pill   841
Pooling of interests   822
Purchase   821
Tender offer   817

SUGGESTED READINGS

Several fun-to-read trade books on mergers and acquisitions have recently been published, including:

Wasserstein, Bruce. *Big Deal: 2000 and Beyond.* Warner Books, 2000. Pitaro, Regina M. *Deals, Deals and More Deals.* Gabelli University Press, 1998.

QUESTIONS AND PROBLEMS

The Basic Forms of Acquisitions

30.1 The Lager Brewing Corporation has acquired the Philadelphia Pretzel Company in a vertical merger. Lager Brewing has issued $300,000 in new long-term debt to pay for its purchase. ($300,000 is the purchase price.) Construct the balance sheet for the new corporation if the merger is treated as a purchase for accounting purposes. The balance sheets shown here represent the assets of both firms at their true market values. Assume these market values are also the book values.

LAGER BREWING CORPORATION
Balance Sheet
(in $ thousands)

Current assets	$ 400	Current liabilities	$ 200
Other assets	100	Long-term debt	100
Net fixed assets	500	Equity	700
Total	$1,000	Total	$1,000

PHILADELPHIA PRETZEL COMPANY
Balance Sheet
(in $ thousands)

Current assets	$ 80	Current liabilities	$ 80
Other assets	40	Equity	120
Net fixed assets	80		
Total	$200	Total	$200

30.2 Suppose the balance sheet for Philadelphia Pretzel in problem 30.1 shows the assets at their book value and not their market value of $240,000. Construct the balance sheet for the new corporation. Again, treat the transaction as a purchase.

30.3 Keep the assumptions of 30.2. Construct the balance sheet for the new corporation. Use the pooling-of-interests method to treat the transaction.

Source of Synergy from Acquisitions

30.4 Indicate whether you think the following claims regarding takeovers are true or false. In each case provide a brief explanation for your answer.

a. By merging competitors, takeovers have created monopolies that will raise product prices, reduce production, and harm consumers.

b. Managers act in their own interests at times and, in reality, may not be answerable to shareholders. Takeovers may reflect runaway management.

c. In an efficient market, takeovers would not occur because market price would reflect the true value of corporations. Thus, bidding firms would not be justified in paying premiums above market prices for target firms.

d. Traders and institutional investors, having extremely short time horizons, are influenced by their perceptions of what other market traders will be thinking of stock prospects and do not value takeovers based on fundamental factors. Thus, they will sell shares in target firms despite the true value of the firms.

e. Mergers are a way of avoiding taxes because they allow the acquiring firm to write up the value of the assets of the acquired firm.

f. Acquisitions analysis frequently focuses on the total value of the firms involved. An acquisition, however, will usually affect relative values of stocks and bonds, as well as their total value.

Calculating the Value of the Firm after an Acquisition

30.5 The following table shows the projected cash flows and their respective discount rates after the acquisition of Small Fry Co. by Whale Co. Fill in the blanks and calculate the stock price of the new firm if it has $100 million of debt and 5 million shares of stock outstanding.

	Net Cash Flow per Year (Perpetual) (in $ millions)	Discount Rate (%)	Value (in $ millions)
Small Fry Co.	$ 8.	16%	?
Whale Co.	20	10	?
Benefits from acquisition	5	?	42.5
Revenue enhancement	2.5	?	12.5
Cost reduction	2	10	?
Tax shelters	0.5	5	?
Whale-Co.	33	?	?

A Cost to Stockholders from Reduction in Risk

30.6 The Chocolate Ice Cream Company and the Vanilla Ice Cream Company have agreed to merge and form Fudge Swirl Consolidated. Both companies are exactly alike except that they are located in different towns. The end-of-period value of each firm is determined by the weather, as shown.

State	Probability	Value
Rainy	0.1	$100,000
Warm	0.4	200,000
Hot	0.5	400,000

The weather conditions in each town are independent of those in the other. Furthermore, each company has an outstanding debt claim of $200,000. Assume that no premiums are paid in the merger.

a. What is the distribution of joint values?

b. What is the distribution of end-of-period debt values and stock values after the merger?

c. Show that the value of the combined firm is the sum of the individual values.

d. Show that the bondholders are better off and the stockholders are worse off in the combined firm than they would have been if the firms remained separate.

30.7 Cholern Electric Company (CEC) is a public utility that provides electricity to the central Colorado area. Recent events at its Mile-High Nuclear Station have been discouraging. Several shareholders have expressed concern over last year's financial statements.

Income Statement Last Year (in $ millions)		Balance Sheet End of Year (in $ millions)	
Revenue	$110	Assets	$400
Fuel	50	Debt	300
Other expenses	30	Equity	100
Interest	30		
Net income	$ 0		

Recently, a wealthy group of individuals has offered to purchase one-half of CEC's assets at fair market price. Management recommends that this offer be accepted because, "We believe our expertise in the energy industry can be better exploited by CEC if we sell our electricity generating and transmission assets and enter the telecommunications business. Although telecommunications is a riskier business than providing electricity as a public utility, it is also potentially very profitable."

Should the management approve this transaction? Why or why not?

Two "Bad" Reasons for Mergers

30.8 Refer to the Global Resources example in section 30.8 of the text. Suppose that instead of 40 shares, Global exchanges 100 of its shares for the 100 shares of Regional. The new Global Resources will now have 200 shares outstanding and earnings of $200. Assume the market is smart.

a. Calculate Global's value after the merger.

b. Calculate Global's earnings per share.

c. Calculate Global's price per share.

d. Redo your answers to (a), (b), and (c) if the market is fooled.

30.9 Coldran Aviation has voted in favor of being bought out by Arcadia Financial Corporation. Information about each company is presented below.

	Arcadia Financial	Coldran Aviation
Price-earnings ratio	16	10.8
Number of shares	100,000	50,000
Earnings	$225,000	$100,000

Stockholders in Coldran Aviation will receive six-tenths of a share of Arcadia for each share they hold.

a. How will the earnings per share (EPS) for these stockholders be changed?

b. What will be the effect on the original Arcadia stockholders of changes in the EPS?

The NPV of a Merger

30.10 Fly-By-Night Couriers is analyzing the possible acquisition of Flash-in-the-Pan Restaurants. Neither firm has debt. The forecasts of Fly-By-Night show that the purchase would increase its annual after-tax cash flow by $600,000 indefinitely. The current market value of Flash-in-the-Pan is $20 million. The current market value of Fly-By-Night is $35 million. The appropriate discount rate for the incremental cash flows is 8 percent.

a. What is the synergy from the merger?

b. What is the value of Flash-in-the-Pan to Fly-By-Night?

Fly-By-Night is trying to decide whether it should offer 25 percent of its stock or $15 million in cash to Flash-in-the-Pan.

c. What is the cost to Fly-By-Night of each alternative?

d. What is the NPV to Fly-By-Night of each alternative?

e. Which alternative should Fly-By-Night use?

30.11 Freeport Manufacturing is considering making an offer to purchase Portland Industries. The treasurer of Freeport has collected the following information:

	Freeport	Portland
Price-earnings ratio	15	12
Number of shares	1,000,000	250,000
Earnings	$1,000,000	$750,000

The treasurer also knows that securities analysts expect the earnings and dividends (currently $1.80 per share) of Portland to grow at a constant rate of 5 percent each year. Her research indicates, however, that the acquisition would provide Portland with some economies of scale that would improve this growth rate to 7 percent per year.

a. What is the value of Portland to Freeport?

b. If Freeport offers $40 in cash for each outstanding share of Portland, what would the NPV of the acquisition be?

c. If instead Freeport were to offer 600,000 of its shares in exchange for the outstanding stock of Portland, what would the NPV of the acquisition be?

d. Should the acquisition be attempted, and if so, should it be a cash or stock offer?

e. Freeport's management thinks that 7-percent growth is too optimistic and that 6 percent is more realistic. How does this change your previous answers?

30.12 Harrods PLC has a market value of £600 million and 30 million shares outstanding. Selfridge Department Store has a market value of £200 million and 20 million shares outstanding. Harrods is contemplating acquiring Selfridge Department Store. Harrods' CFO concludes that the combined firm with synergy will be worth £1 billion and Selfridge can be acquired at a premium of £100 million.

a. If Harrods offers 15 million shares to exchange for the 20 million shares of Selfridge, what will the after-acquisition stock price of Harrods be?

b. To make the value of a stock offer equivalent to a cash offer of £300 million, what would be the proper exchange ratio of the two stocks?

30.13 Company *A* is contemplating acquiring company *B*. Company *B*'s projected revenues, cost, and required investment appear in the table that follows. The table also shows sources for financing company *B*'s investments if *B* is acquired by *A*. The table incorporates the following information:

Company *B* will immediately increase its leverage with a $110 million loan, which would be followed by a $150 million dividend to company *A*. (This operation will increase the debt-to-equity ratio of company *B* from 1/3 to 1/1.)

Company *A* will use $50 million of tax-loss carryforwards available from the firm's other operations.

The terminal, total value of company *B* is estimated to be $900 million in five years, and the projected level of debt then is $300 million.

The risk-free rate and the expected rate of return on the market portfolio are 6 percent and 14 percent, respectively. Company *A* analysts estimate the weighted average cost of capital for their company to be 10 percent. The borrowing rate for both companies is 8 percent. The beta coefficient for the stock of company *B* (at its current capital structure) is estimated to be 1.25.

The board of directors of company *A* is presented with an offer for $68.75 per share of company *B,* or a total of $550 million for the 8 million shares outstanding. Evaluate this proposal. The table produced below may help you.

Projections for Company *B*
if Acquired by Company *A*
(in $ millions)

	Year 1	Year 2	Year 3	Year 4	Year 5
Sales	$800	$900	$1,000	$1,125	$1,250
Production costs	562	630	700	790	875
Depreciation	75	80	82	83	83
Other expenses	80	90	100	113	125
EBIT	83	100	118	139	167
Interest	19	22	24	25	27
EBT	64	78	94	114	140
Taxes	32	39	47	57	70
Net income	32	39	47	57	70
Investments:					
Net working capital	20	25	25	30	30
Net fixed assets	15	25	18	12	7
Total	35	50	43	42	37
Sources of financing:					
Net debt financing	35	16	16	15	12
Profit retention	0	34	27	27	25
Total	$ 35	$ 50	$ 43	$ 42	$ 37

Cash Flows—Company *A*

	Year 0	Year 1	Year 2	Year 3	Year 4	Year 5
Acquisition of *B*	—					
Dividends from *B*	150	—	—	—	—	—
Tax-loss carryforwards			25	25		—
Terminal value	—	—	—	—	—	—
Total	—	—	—	—	—	—

Defensive Tactics

30.14 List the defensive tactics commonly used by target-firm managers to resist unfriendly takeover attempts.

MINICASE: U.S. STEEL'S ACQUISITION OF MARATHON OIL

In the summer of 1981, Marathon Oil Company commissioned the First Boston Corporation to prepare an analysis of the underlying asset value of Marathon based solely on publicly available information. Before First Boston could complete the study, Mobil Corporation announced a tender offer for Marathon's common equity, thus launching one of the most eventful takeover stories in American corporate history.

On October 30, 1981, Mobil bid $85 per share for up to 40 million shares of Marathon's common equity. Before the announcement, Marathon stock traded for about $64 per share on the New York Stock Exchange. Before trading on the new information commenced, Marathon management rejected Mobil's offer as grossly inadequate and began seeking a white knight merger candidate. When trading began on Monday, November 2, 1981, Marathon's shares shot up immediately to the $90-per-share range for a one-day abnormal excess return of more than 30 percent. The market reacted to Mobil's offer by bidding Mobil's common stock down to $25⅝ for a one-day abnormal return of −4.26 percent. (November 2, 1981, was also the ex-dividend date for a $0.50 per share dividend declared earlier. The share price, however, fell $⅝.) These data suggest that the market viewed the possible acquisition of Marathon by Mobil at $85 per share as a near-zero net-present-value transaction for Mobil. The dramatic response of Marathon's share price was very likely caused by anticipation of more bidding. These traders were not to be disappointed.

On November 9, the management of U.S. Steel Corporation expressed an interest in acquiring Marathon. The possible takeover price was rumored to be $100 per share in cash and notes. Presumably because the market actually valued this offer as less than Mobil's offer, Marathon's common stock showed an abnormal return for the day of −2.91 percent. The effect of the rumors on U.S. Steel's share price was insignificant, so it may be concluded that the market felt that the transaction at this price would be a zero net-present-value transaction for U.S. Steel as well.

During subsequent negotiations, U.S. Steel raised its price and actually tendered $125 per share for up to 30 million shares of Marathon stock on November 18. On the next trading day Marathon showed a one-day abnormal excess return on its share price of almost 35 percent; again the market roared its approval for the reevaluation of Marathon. U.S. Steel's common, however, showed significantly negative abnormal returns in response to this news. This indicates that the market believed U.S. Steel overbid for Marathon. Mobil's share price showed no significant abnormal return on November 18 and 19.

However, on November 25, Mobil raised its bid to $126 per share, and the market responded by lowering the value of both Mobil and U.S. Steel by significant amounts. Apparently the market believed that at this price the merger was unattractive for both Mobil and U.S. Steel. Marathon's stock fell in price by a significant amount in response to Mobil's offer, perhaps because Mobil's offer and U.S. Steel's offer were valued nearly equally by the market, and this signaled the end of the bidding and the end of speculating in Marathon.

Suppose that a U.S. Steel tender offer is structured in the following way. U.S. Steel will pay $125 (in cash) for 30 million shares of Marathon giving it 50.1 percent of the Marathon shares. After gaining voting control, U.S. Steel intends to merge with Marathon and will pay the remaining shareholders with seven-year notes worth about $85 per share. Further, suppose you own 10 shares of Marathon stock. Should you tender your shares?

CHAPTER 31

Financial Distress

EXECUTIVE SUMMARY

This chapter discusses financial distress, private workouts, and bankruptcy. A firm that does not generate enough cash flow to make a contractually required payment, such as an interest payment, will experience financial distress. A firm that defaults on a required payment may be forced to liquidate its assets. More often, a defaulting firm will reorganize its financial structure. Financial restructuring involves replacing old financial claims with new ones and takes place with private workouts or legal bankruptcy. Private workouts are voluntary arrangements to restructure a company's debt, such as postponing a payment or reducing the size of the payment. Sometimes a private workout is not possible and formal bankruptcy is required. The largest formal bankruptcy in U.S. financial history occurred in April 1987 when Texaco filed Chapter 11 bankruptcy. (See Table 31.1 for information on the largest U.S. bankruptcies.)

31.1 WHAT IS FINANCIAL DISTRESS?

Financial distress is surprisingly hard to define precisely. This is true partly because of the variety of events befalling firms under financial distress. The list of events is almost endless but here are some examples:

Dividend reductions
Plant closings
Losses
Layoffs
CEO resignations
Plummeting stock prices

Financial distress is a situation where a firm's operating cash flows are not sufficient to satisfy current obligations (such as trade credits or interest expenses) and the firm is forced to take corrective action.[1] Financial distress may lead a firm to default on a contract, and it may involve financial restructuring between the firm, its creditors, and its equity investors. Usually the firm is forced to take actions that it would not have taken if it had sufficient cash flow.

Our definition of financial distress can be expanded somewhat by linking it to insolvency. Insolvency is defined in *Black's Law Dictionary* as[2]

---

[1]This definition is close to the one used by Karen Wruck, "Financial Distress: Reorganization and Organization Efficiency," *Journal of Financial Economics* 27 (1990), p. 425.

[2]Taken from *Black's Law Dictionary*, 5th ed. (St. Paul, Minn.: West Publishing Company), p. 716.

■ TABLE 31.1 The Largest U.S. Bankruptcies

Firm	Liabilities (in $ millions)	Bankruptcy Date
Texaco (including subsidiaries)	$21,603	April 1987
Executive Life Insurance	14,577	April 1991
Mutual Benefit Life	13,500	July 1991
Campeau (Allied & Federated)	9,947	January 1990
First Capital Holdings	9,291	May 1991
Baldwin United	9,000	September 1983
Continental Airlines (II)	6,200	December 1990
Lomas Financial	6,127	September 1989
Macy's	5,300	January 1992
Columbia Gas	4,998	July 1991
LTV (including LTV International NV)	4,700	July 1986
Maxwell Communication	4,100	December 1991
TWA	3,470	January 1992
Southland	3,380	October 1990
Penn Central Transportation	3,300	June 1970
Eastern Airlines	3,196	March 1989
Drexel Burnham Lambert	3,000	February 1990
Pan Am World Airlines	3,000	January 1991
Interco	2,213	May 1990
Laventhol & Horwath	2,000	November 1990
Wickes	2,000	April 1982
Global Marine	1,800	January 1986
ITEL	1,700	January 1981
Public Service, New Hampshire	1,700	January 1988
Continental Information Systems	1,669	January 1989
Integrated Resources	1,600	February 1990
Revco	1,500	July 1988

Source: Supplied by Edward I. Altman.

> Inability to pay one's debts; lack of means of paying one's debts. Such a condition of a woman's (or man's) assets and liability that the former made immediately available would be insufficient to discharge the latter.

This definition has two general themes, stocks and flows.[3] These two ways of thinking about insolvency are depicted in Figure 31.1. The stock-based insolvency occurs when a firm has negative net worth, and so the value of assets is less than the value of its debts. Flow-based insolvency occurs when operating cash flow is insufficient to meet current obligations. Flow-based insolvency refers to the inability to pay one's debts.

CONCEPT QUESTIONS
- Can you describe financial distress?
- What are stock-based insolvency and flow-based insolvency?

---

[3]Edward Altman was one of the first to distinguish between stock-based insolvency and flow-based insolvency. See Edward Altman, *Corporate Financial Distress: A Complete Guide to Predicting, Avoiding and Dealing with Bankruptcy* (New York: John Wiley & Sons, 1983).

■ FIGURE 31.1 **Insolvency**

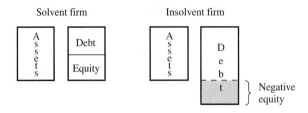

A. Stock-based insolvency

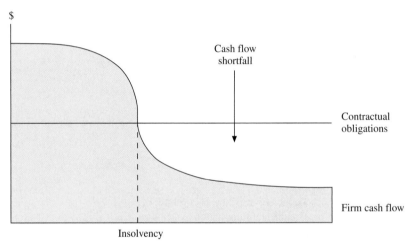

B. Flow-based insolvency

Stock-based insolvency occurs when the value of the assets of a firm is less than the value of the debts. This implies negative equity. Flow-based insolvency occurs when firm cash flows are insufficient to cover contractually required payments.

31.2 WHAT HAPPENS IN FINANCIAL DISTRESS?

In the early 1990s Trans World Airline, Inc. (TWA) experienced financial distress. It lost money in 1989, 1990, and 1991 and steadily lost its market share to rivals United, American, and Delta. Having seen Eastern and Pan Am disappear, airline travelers had good reason to be nervous about buying tickets from TWA.

In the summer of 1991, TWA General Counsel Mark A. Buckstein bet Carl Icahn, TWA owner and CEO, $1,000 that the airline would be forced to involuntary bankruptcy by September 1991.[4] Icahn argued that he could arrange a private restructuring and avoid formal bankruptcy. Icahn won the bet, but TWA eventually filed for bankruptcy on January 31, 1992. Icahn was quoted as saying the bankruptcy reorganization would give TWA the time it needed to turn the firm around. The odds favored Icahn because financial distress does not usually result in a firm's death. TWA was reorganized in 1993. Icahn resigned as CEO

---

[4]The bet was reported in "Carl has 9 lives but he is betting up to 8½," *Business Week,* February 24, 1992.

and gave up all ownership claims. However, TWA continued to struggle and for the second time, on July 3, 1995, filed for bankruptcy. Several months later, it emerged from bankruptcy after exchanging $500 million of debt for equity. Remarkably, on January 9, 2001, the board of TWA again approved a plan to file for bankruptcy. The plan included the purchase of TWA by American Airlines for $500 million.

Firms deal with financial distress in several ways, such as

1. Selling major assets.
2. Merging with another firm.
3. Reducing capital spending and research and development.
4. Issuing new securities.
5. Negotiating with banks and other creditors.
6. Exchanging debt for equity.
7. Filing for bankruptcy.

Items (1), (2), and (3) concern the firm's assets. Items (4), (5), (6), and (7) involve the right-hand side of the firm's balance sheet and are examples of financial restructuring. Financial distress may involve both asset restructuring and financial restructuring (i.e., changes on both sides of the balance sheet).

Some firms may actually benefit from financial distress by restructuring their assets. In an earlier chapter we showed that, in 1986, Goodyear Tire and Rubber's levered recapitalization changed the firm's behavior and forced the firm to dispose of unrelated businesses. Goodyear's cash flow was not sufficient to cover required payments, and it was forced to sell its noncore businesses. For some firms financial distress may bring about new organizational forms and new operating strategies. However, in this chapter we focus on financial restructuring.

Financial restructuring may occur in a private workout or a bankruptcy reorganization under Chapter 11 of the U.S. Bankruptcy Code. Figure 31.2 shows how large public firms move through financial distress. Approximately one-half of the financial restructurings have been done via private workouts. As was true for TWA, most large public firms (83 percent) that file for Chapter 11 bankruptcy are able to reorganize and continue to do business.[5]

Financial distress can serve as a firm's "early warning" system for trouble. Firms with more debt will experience financial distress earlier than firms with less debt. However, firms that experience financial distress earlier will have more time for private workouts and reorganization. Firms with low leverage will experience financial distress later and, in many instances, be forced to liquidate.

CONCEPT QUESTIONS

- Why doesn't financial distress always cause firms to die?
- What is a benefit of financial distress?

31.3 BANKRUPTCY LIQUIDATION AND REORGANIZATION

Firms that cannot or choose not to make contractually required payments to creditors have two basic options: liquidation or reorganization. This section discusses bankruptcy liquidation and reorganization.

---

[5]However, only about 15 percent of all firms (public or private) going through a Chapter 11 bankruptcy are successfully reorganized.

■ FIGURE 31.2 **What Happens in Financial Distress**

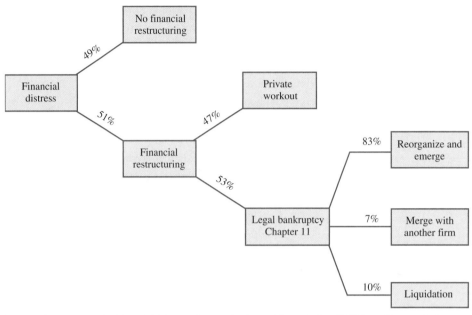

Source: Karen H. Wruck, "Financial Distress: Reorganization and Organizational Efficiency," *Journal of Financial Economics* 27 (1990), Figure 2. See also Stuart C. Gilson; Kose John; and Larry N. P. Lang, "Troubled Debt Restructurings: An Empirical Study of Private Reorganization of Firms in Defaults," *Journal of Financial Economics* 27 (1990); and Lawrence A. Weiss, "Bankruptcy Resolution: Direct Costs and Violation of Priority of Claims," *Journal of Financial Economics* 27 (1990).

Liquidation means termination of the firm as a going concern; it involves selling the assets of the firm for salvage value. The proceeds, net of transactions costs, are distributed to creditors in order of established priority.

Reorganization is the option of keeping the firm a going concern; it sometimes involves issuing new securities to replace old securities.

Liquidation and formal reorganization may be done by bankruptcy. *Bankruptcy* is a legal proceeding and can be done voluntarily with the corporation filing the petition or involuntarily with the creditors filing the petition.

Bankruptcy Liquidation

Chapter 7 of the Bankruptcy Reform Act of 1978 deals with "straight" liquidation. The following sequence of events is typical:

1. A petition is filed in a federal court. Corporations may file a voluntary petition, or involuntary petitions may be filed against the corporation.

2. A trustee-in-bankruptcy is elected by the creditors to take over the assets of the debtor corporation. The trustees will attempt to liquidate the assets.

3. When the assets are liquidated, after payment of the costs of administration, assets are distributed among the creditors.

4. If any assets remain, after expenses and payments to creditors, they are distributed to the shareholders.

Conditions Leading to Involuntary Bankruptcy   An involuntary bankruptcy petition may be filed by creditors if both the following conditions are met:

1. The corporation is not paying debts as they become due.
2. If there are more than 12 creditors, at least three with claims totaling $5,000 or more must join in the filing. If there are fewer than 12 creditors, then only one with a claim of $5,000 is required to file.

Priority of Claims   Once a corporation is determined to be bankrupt, liquidation takes place. The distribution of the proceeds of the liquidation occurs according to the following priority:

1. *Administration expenses,* associated with liquidating the bankrupt's assets.
2. Unsecured claims arising after the filing of an involuntary bankruptcy petition.
3. Wages, salaries, and commissions, not to exceed $2,000 per claimant, earned within 90 days before the filing date.
4. Contributions to employee benefit plans arising within 180 days before the filing date.
5. Consumer claims, not exceeding $900.
6. Tax claims.
7. Secured and unsecured creditors' claims.
8. Preferred stockholders' claims.
9. Common stockholders' claims.

The priority rule in liquidation is the **absolute priority rule** (APR).

One qualification to this list concerns secured creditors. Liens on property are outside APR ordering. However, if the secured property is liquidated and provides cash insufficient to cover the amount owed them, the secured creditors join with unsecured creditors in dividing the remaining liquidating value. In contrast, if the secured property is liquidated for proceeds greater than the secured claim, the net proceeds are used to pay unsecured creditors and others.

EXAMPLE

The B. O. Drug Company is to be liquidated. Its liquidating value is $2.7 million. Bonds worth $1.5 million are secured by a mortgage on the B. O. Drug Company corporate headquarters building, which is sold for $1 million; $200,000 is used to cover administrative costs and other claims (including unpaid wages, pension benefits, consumer claims, and taxes). After paying $200,000 to the administrative priority claims, the amount available to pay secured and unsecured creditors is $2.5 million. This is less than the amount of unpaid debt of $4 million.

Under APR all creditors must be paid before shareholders, and the mortgage bondholders have first claim on the $1 million obtained from the sale of the headquarters building.

The trustee has proposed the following distribution:

Type of Claim	Prior Claim	Cash Received under Liquidation
Bonds (secured by mortgage)	$ 1,500,000	$1,500,000
Subordinated debentures	2,500,000	1,000,000
Common stockholders	10,000,000	0
Total	$14,000,000	$2,500,000

Calculation of the Distribution

Cash received from sale of assets available for distribution	$2,500,000
Cash paid to secured bondholders on sale of mortgaged property	1,000,000
Available to bond- and debenture-holders	$1,500,000
Total claims remaining ($4,000,000 less payment of $1,000,000 on secured bonds)	$3,000,000
Distribution of remaining $1,500,000 to cover total remaining claims of $3,000,000	

Type of Claim Remaining	Claim on Liquidation Proceeds	Cash Received
Bonds	$ 500,000	$ 500,000
Debentures	2,500,000	1,000,000
Total	$3,000,000	$1,500,000

IN THEIR OWN WORDS

Edward I. Altman* on Corporate Financial Distress and Bankruptcy

Financial distress of private and public entities throughout the world is a frequent occurrence with important implications to their many stakeholders. While the role of corporate bankruptcy laws is clear—either to provide a legal procedure that permits firms, which have temporary liquidity problems, to restructure and successfully emerge as continuing entities or to provide an orderly process to liquidate assets for the benefit of creditors before asset values are dissipated—bankruptcy laws differ markedly from country to country. It is generally agreed that the U.S. Chapter 11 provisions under the Bankruptcy Reform Act of 1978 provide the most protection for bankrupt firms' assets and result in a greater likelihood of successful reorganization than is found in other countries where liquidation and sale of the assets for the benefit of creditors is more likely the result. But, the U.S. Code's process is usually lengthy (averaging close to two years, except where a sufficient number of creditors agree in advance via a prepackaged Chapter 11) and expensive and the reorganized entity is not always successful in avoiding subsequent distress. If the reorganization is not successful, then liquidation under Chapter 7 will usually ensue.

Bankruptcy processes in the industrialized world outside the United States strongly favor senior creditors who obtain control of the firm and seek to enforce greater adherence to debt contracts. The U.K. process, for example, is speedy and less costly but the reduced costs can result in undesirable liquidations, unemployment and underinvestment. The new bankruptcy code in

(continued)

Germany attempts to reduce the considerable power of secured creditors but it is still closer to the U.K. system. In the United States, creditors and owners can negotiate "violations" to the "absolute priority rule"—this "rule" holds that more senior creditors must be paid in full, prior to any payments to more junior creditors or to owners. (However, the so-called "violations" to absolute priority have empirically been shown to be relatively small, e.g., under 10 percent of firm value.) Finally, the U.S. system gives the court the right to sanction post-petition debt financing, usually with super-priority status over existing claims, thereby facilitating the continuing operation of the firm. Recently, France has had similar successful experience.

A measure of performance of the U.S. bankruptcy system is the proportion of firms which emerge successfully. The results in the United States of late are somewhat mixed, with close to 70 percent of large firms emerging but probably less than 20 percent of smaller entities. And, a not insignificant number of firms suffer subsequent distress and may file again (Chapter 22).

Regardless of the location, one of the objectives of bankruptcy and other distressed workout arrangements is that creditors and other suppliers of capital clearly know their rights and expected recoveries in the event of a distressed situation. When these are not transparent and/or are based on outdated processes with arbitrary and possibly corrupt outcomes, then the entire economic system suffers and growth is inhibited. Such is the case in several emerging market countries. Revision of these outdated systems should be a priority.

In addition to the comparative benefits of different national restructuring systems, a number of intriguing theoretical and empirical issues are related to the distressed firm. Among these are corporate debt capacity, manager-creditor-owner incentives, ability to predict distress, data and computations for default rate estimation, investment in securities of distressed firms and post-reorganization performance assessment.

Corporate distress has a major impact on creditor/debtor relationships and, combined with business risk and tax considerations, affects the capital structure of companies. One key question is how costly are the *expected* distress costs compared to the *expected* tax benefits of using leverage—the so-called

trade-off theory. Most analysts agree that the sum of direct (e.g., legal fees) and indirect costs is in the range of 10–20 percent of firm value.

Whether the taking of excess risk and over-investment are examples of agency conflicts between managers and creditors rests upon one's view as to who are the true residual owners of a distressed firm—the existing equity-holders or creditors who will more than likely be the new owners of a reorganized entity. Existing management has the exclusive right to file the first plan of reorganization within 120 days of filing, with exclusivity extensions possible. Their incentives and influence can be biased, however, and not always in accord with other stake-holders, primarily creditors. Limiting this exclusivity would appear to be desirable to speed up the process and restrict managerial abuse.

Distress prediction models have intrigued researchers and practitioners for more than 50 years. Models have evolved from univariate financial statement ratios to multivariate statistical classification models, to contingent claim and market value based approaches and finally to using artificial intelligence techniques. Most large financial institutions have one or more of the above types of models in place as more sophisticated credit-risk management frameworks are being introduced, sometimes combined with aggressive credit asset portfolio strategies. Increasingly, private credit assets are being treated as securities with estimates of default and recovery given default the critical inputs to their valuation.

Perhaps the most intriguing by-product of corporate distress is the development of a relatively new class of investors known as "vultures." These money managers specialize in securities of distressed and defaulted companies. Defaulted bonds have had a small following ever since the great depression of the 1930s but this has grown to 50–60 institutional "vulture" specialists, actively managing over $25 billion in 1998. Distressed debt investors have target annual rates of return of 20–25 percent. Although these annual rates are sometimes earned, the overall annual rate of return from 1978–1997 has been about 12 percent—similar to high yield bonds but much below returns in the stock market.

*Max L. Heine Professor of Finance, NYU Stern School of Business.

Bankruptcy Reorganization

Corporate reorganization takes place under Chapter 11 of the Federal Bankruptcy Reform Act of 1978. The general objective of a proceeding under Chapter 11 is to plan to restructure the corporation with some provision for repayment of creditors. A typical sequence of events follows:

1. A voluntary petition can be filed by the corporation, or an involuntary petition can be filed by three or more creditors (or one creditor if the total creditors are fewer than 12— see the previous section). The involuntary petition must allege that the corporation is not paying its debts.

2. A federal judge either approves or denies the petition. If the petition is approved, a time for filing proofs of claims of creditors and of shareholders is set.

3. In most cases, the corporation (the "debtor in possession") continues to run the business.

4. The corporation is given 120 days to submit a reorganization plan.

5. Creditors and shareholders are divided into classes. A class of creditors accepts the plan if two-thirds of the class (in dollar amount) and one-half of the class (in number) have indicated approval.[6]

6. After acceptance by creditors, the plan is confirmed by the court.

7. Payments in cash, property, and securities are made to creditors and shareholders. The plan may provide for the issuance of new securities.

EXAMPLE

Suppose B. O. Drug Co. decides to reorganize under Chapter 11. Generally, senior claims are honored in full before various other claims receive anything. Assume that the "going concern" value of B. O. Drug Co. is $3 million and that its balance sheet is as shown:

Assets	$3,000,000
Liabilities	
Mortgage bonds	1,500,000
Subordinated debentures	2,500,000
Stockholders' equity	−1,000,000

The firm has proposed the following reorganization plan:

Old Security	Old Claim	New Claim with Reorganization Plan
Mortgage bonds	$1,500,000	$1,500,000
Subordinated debentures	2,500,000	1,000,000

and a distribution of new securities under a new claim with a reorganization plan:

---

[6]We are describing the standard events in a bankruptcy reorganization. The general rule is that a reorganization plan will be accepted by the court if all of the creditor class accept it and it will be rejected if all of the creditor class reject it. However, if one or more (but not all) of the classes accept it, the plan may be eligible for a "cram down" procedure. A cram down takes place if the bankruptcy court finds a plan fair and equitable and accepts the plan for all creditors.

ABSOLUTE PRIORITY RULE

The absolute priority rule states that senior claims are fully satisfied before junior claims receive anything.

Deviation from Rule

Equityholders	Expectation: No payout
	Reality: Payout in 81 percent of cases
Unsecured creditors	Expectation: Full payout after secured creditors
	Reality: Violation in 78 percent of cases
Secured creditors	Expectation: Full payout
	Reality: Full payout in 92 percent of cases

Reasons for Violations

Creditors want to avoid the expense of litigation. Debtors are given a 120-day opportunity to cause delay and harm value.

Managers often own equity and demand to be compensated.

Bankruptcy judges like consensual plans and pressure parties to compromise.

Source: Lawrence A. Weiss, "Bankruptcy Resolution: Direct Costs and Violation of Priority of Claims," *Journal of Financial Economics* 27 (1990).

Old Security	Received under Proposed Reorganization Plan
Mortgage bonds	$1,000,000 in 9% senior debentures
	$500,000 in 11% subordinated debentures
Debentures	$1,000,000 in 8% preferred stock
	$500,000 in common stock

However, it will be very difficult for the firm to convince secured creditors (mortgage bonds) to consent to accepting unsecured debentures of equal face value. In addition, the corporation may wish to allow the old stockholders to retain some participation in the firm. Needless to say, this would be a violation of the absolute priority rule and the holders of the debentures would not be happy.

QUESTIONS
CONCEPT
?

- What is bankruptcy?
- What is the difference between liquidation and reorganization?

31.4 PRIVATE WORKOUT OR BANKRUPTCY: WHICH IS BEST?

A firm that defaults on its debt payments will need to restructure its financial claims. The firm will have two choices: formal bankruptcy or **private workout.** The previous section described two types of formal bankruptcies: bankruptcy liquidation and bankruptcy reorganization. This section compares private workouts with bankruptcy reorganizations. Both types of financial restructuring involve exchanging new financial claims for old financial claims. Usually senior debt is replaced with junior debt and debt is replaced with equity. Much recent academic research has described what happens in private workouts and formal bankruptcies.[7]

- Historically, one-half of financial restructurings have been private but, recently, formal bankruptcy has dominated.
- Firms that emerge from private workouts experience stock-price increases that are much greater than those for firms emerging from formal bankruptcies.
- The direct costs of private workouts are much less than the costs of formal bankruptcies.
- Top management usually loses pay and sometimes jobs in both private workouts and formal bankruptcies.

These facts, when taken together, seem to suggest that a private workout is much better than a formal bankruptcy. We then ask the question: Why do firms ever use formal bankruptcies to restructure?

The Marginal Firm

For the average firm a formal bankruptcy is more costly than a private workout, but for other firms formal bankruptcy is better. Formal bankruptcy allows firms to issue debt that is senior to all previously incurred debt. This new debt is "debtor in possession" (DIP) debt. For firms that need a temporary injection of cash, DIP debt makes bankruptcy reorganization an attractive alternative to a private workout. There are some tax advantages to bankruptcy. Firms do not lose tax carryforwards in bankruptcy, and the tax treatment of the cancellation of indebtness is better in bankruptcy. Also, interest on prebankruptcy unsecured debt stops accruing in formal bankruptcy.

Holdouts

Bankruptcy is usually better for the equity investors than it is for the creditors. Using DIP debt and stopping prebankruptcy interest on unsecured debt helps the stockholders and hurts the creditors. As a consequence, equity investors can usually hold out for a better deal in bankruptcy. The absolute priority rule, which favors creditors over equity investors, is usually violated in formal bankruptcies. One recent study found that in 81 percent of recent bankruptcies the equity investor obtained some compensation.[8] Under Chapter 11 the creditors are often forced to give up some of their seniority rights to get management and the equity investors to agree to a deal.

---

[7]For example, see Stuart Gilson, "Managing Default: Some Evidence on How Firms Choose between Workouts and Bankruptcy," *Journal of Applied Corporate Finance* (Summer 1991); and Stuart C. Gilson, Kose John, and Larry N. P. Lang, "Troubled Debt Restructuring: An Empirical Study of Private Reorganization of Firms in Defaults," *Journal of Financial Economics* 27 (1990).

[8]Lawrence A. Weiss, "Bankruptcy Dissolution: Direct Costs and Violation of Priority and Claims," *Journal of Financial Economics* 23 (1990). However, W. Beranek, R. Boehmer, and B. Smith, in "Much Ado about Nothing: Absolute Priority Deviations in Chapter 11," *Financial Management* (Autumn 1996), find 33.8 percent of bankruptcy reorganizations leave the stockholders with nothing. They also point out deviations from the absolute priority rule are to be expected because the bankruptcy code allows creditors to waive their rights if they perceive a waiver to be in their best interests. A rejoinder can be found in Allan C. Eberhart and Lawrence A. Weiss, "The Importance of Deviations from the Absolute Priority Rule in Chapter 11 Bankruptcy Proceedings," *Financial Management* 27 (1998).

Complexity

A firm with a complicated capital structure will have more trouble putting together a private workout. Firms with secured creditors and trade creditors such as Macy's and Carter Hale will usually use formal bankruptcy because it is too hard to reach an agreement with many different types of creditors.

Lack of Information

There is an inherent conflict of interest between equity investors and creditors, and the conflict is accentuated when both have incomplete information about the circumstances of financial distress. When a firm initially experiences a cash flow shortfall, it may not know whether the shortfall is permanent or temporary. If the shortfall is permanent, creditors will push for a formal reorganization or liquidation. However, if the cash flow shortfall is temporary, formal reorganization or liquidation may not be necessary. Equity investors will push for this viewpoint. This conflict of interest cannot easily be resolved.

These last two points are especially important. They suggest that financial distress will be more expensive (cheaper) if complexity is high (low) and information is incomplete (complete). Complexity and lack of information make cheap workouts less likely.

CONCEPT QUESTIONS

- What are two ways a firm can restructure its finances?
- Why do firms use formal bankruptcy?

31.5 PREPACKAGED BANKRUPTCY[9]

On October 1, 1986, the Crystal Oil Company filed for protection from its creditors under Chapter 11 of the U.S. Bankruptcy Code. Given the firm's heavy indebtedness, perhaps the outcome was not very surprising. However, less than three months later Crystal Oil came out of bankruptcy with a different capital structure. This surprised many people because, traditionally, bankruptcy has been very costly and often takes many years to emerge from. Crystal Oil avoided a lengthy bankruptcy by negotiating a reorganization plan with its creditors several months before the bankruptcy filing date.

This new reorganization arrangement has been called **prepackaged bankruptcy.** Table 31.2 lists several recent prepackaged bankruptcies of large firms. Prepackaged bankruptcy is a combination of private workout and legal bankruptcy. In prepackaged bankruptcy the firm and most of its creditors agree to private reorganization outside formal bankruptcy. After the private reorganization is put together (i.e., prepackaged), the firm files a formal bankruptcy under Chapter 11.

Prepackaged bankruptcy arrangements require that most creditors reach agreement privately. Prepackaged bankruptcy doesn't seem to work when there are thousands of reluctant trade creditors, such as in the case of a retail trading firm like Macy's and Revco D. S.[10]

---

[9]John McConnell and Henri Servaes "The Economics of Pre-packaged Bankruptcy," *Journal of Applied Corporate Finance* (Summer 1991), describe prepackaged bankruptcy and the Crystal Oil Company.

[10]S. Chattergee, U. S. Dhillon, and G. G. Ramirez, in "Prepackaged Bankruptcies and Workouts," *Financial Management* (Spring 1996), find that firms using prepackaged bankruptcy arrangements are smaller, in better financial shape, and have greater short-term liquidity problems than firms using private workouts or Chapter 11.

■ TABLE 31.2 **Recent Prepackaged Bankruptcies of Large U.S. Firms**

Firm	Business	Filing Dates	Approved Date
TWA	Air transport	July 3, 1995	August 23, 1995
Memorex Telex	Computer equipment	January 6, 1992	February 7, 1992
Taj Mahal	Casino	August 8, 1991	October 4, 1991
JPS Textiles	Textiles	February 7, 1991	March 21, 1991
Southland	7-11 convenience stores	October 24, 1990	March 5, 1991

The main benefit of prepackaged bankruptcy is that it forces holdouts to accept a bankruptcy reorganization. If a large fraction of a firm's creditors can agree privately to a reorganization plan, the holdout problem may be avoided. It makes a reorganization plan in formal bankruptcy easier to put together.[11]

A recent study by McConnell, Lease, and Tashjian reports that prepackaged bankruptcies offer many of the advantages of a formal bankruptcy, but they are also more efficient. Their results suggest that the time spent and the direct costs of resolving financial distress are less in a prepackaged bankruptcy than in a formal bankruptcy.[12]

CONCEPT QUESTIONS

• What is prepackaged bankruptcy?
• What is the main benefit of prepackaged bankruptcy?

CASE STUDY: *The Decision to File for Bankruptcy: The Case of Revco*[13]

■ ■ ■ ■ ■ Revco D. S. has a special place in the history of finance. It was both one of the largest leveraged buyouts and one of the largest bankruptcies in U.S. financial history.

In July 1988, Revco filed for bankruptcy under Chapter 11 of the U.S. Bankruptcy Code. At the time of its bankruptcy it was one of the largest retail drugstore chains in the United States. Revco's bankruptcy came at the end of four very turbulent years.

Up to 1984 the shareholders of Revco had reason to be pleased with its operating results. By 1984 Revco was operating approximately 2,000 stores in 30 states. Its gross profit margins averaged close to 7 percent. From 1971 to 1984 Revco had grown in sales and profits in excess of 20 percent per annum. In January 1984, its stock traded at an all-time high of $37.50. Revco's financial difficulty began in the spring of 1984.[14]

I. In April 1984, E-Ferol, a vitamin product manufactured by a Revco subsidiary, was allegedly linked to 38 infant deaths and was recalled.

---

[11]The original reorganization plan of Crystal Oil was accepted by the public creditors, but it was not accepted by the secured creditors. During bankruptcy a slightly revised plan was "crammed down" on the secured creditors. A bankruptcy court can force creditors to participate in a reorganization if it can be shown that the plan is "fair and equitable."

[12]John J. McConnell, Ronald Lease, and Elizabeth Tashjian, "Prepacks as a Mechanism for Resolving Financial Distress: The Evidence," *Journal of Applied Corporate Finance* 8 (1996).

[13]See Karen H. Wruck, "What Really Went Wrong at Revco," *Journal of Applied Corporate Finance* (Summer 1991), pp. 71–92. This article contains an excellent description of the troubles of Revco.

[14]Stephen Phillips, "Revco, Anatomy of an LBO That Failed," *Business Week* (October 3, 1988), describes the troubles of Revco.

2. In May 1984, Revco acquired Odd Lot Trading, Inc., for over $100 million of Revco common stock. The acquisition gave Barnard Marden and Isaac Perlmutter, owners of Odd Lot Trading, 12 percent ownership in Revco. However, Perlmutter and Marden were not passive investors, and they had many new ideas for "improving" Revco. Eventually, hostility broke out between Perlmutter and Marden and Stanley Dworkin, the CEO of Revco.

3. In 1985 Revco's competitors, Rite-Aid and Eckerd, adopted aggressive pricing tactics in an attempt to gain market share.

4. In July 1985, Revco bought out Marden's and Perlmutter's stakes in Revco for $98 million.

5. On December 29, 1986, Revco announced a leveraged buyout (LBO) with a private investor group. Because of the LBO, Revco's long-term debt increased from $44.7 million in 1985 to over $700 million after the LBO in 1986. Eventually, its total debt rose to $1.3 billion, and, in April 1988, Revco announced that it could not make the interest payment on its subordinated notes.

6. In March 1987, Revco decided to change its strategic orientation. Instead of "everyday low prices" on a narrow product line, Revco expanded its product line to include TVs, furniture, and appliances, and used selective promotions.

7. The new strategic orientation did not work, and Revco generated large losses in 1987.

8. In July 1988, Revco filed for bankruptcy under Chapter 11 of the Bankruptcy Code.

9. Four years later, Revco emerged from bankruptcy.

10. On June 2, 1997, Revco was merged into CVS in a $2.9 billion stock swap, making CVS the second largest drugstore chain in the United States. It was reported that CVS would close Revco's headquarters in Twinsburg, Ohio, and reduce costs by eliminating redundant corporate offices and outlets.

Why did Revco file for formal bankruptcy instead of private restructuring? What were the costs of the Revco bankruptcy? There are no easy answers to these questions.

1. *The Direct Costs of Bankruptcy.* Formal bankruptcy can be expensive and time-consuming. Revco was in Chapter 11 bankruptcy for almost four years and paid out over $40.5 million in direct bankruptcy costs (2.7 percent of the buyout price).[15] Below are some of the direct bankruptcy fees (in millions).

Law firms	
Baker & Hostetler	$ 7.5
Fried Frank	3.2
Accounting firms	
Arthur Andersen	7.4
Ernst & Young	4.2
Investment bankers	
Lazard Freres	3.5
Other	14.3
	$40.5

2. *The Indirect Costs of Financial Distress.* There are many indirect costs of financial distress, including management distractions, loss of customers, and loss of reputation. The indirect costs of financial distress may occur whether or not formal bankruptcy is declared. In the case of Revco, financial distress caused a costly change in management and strategic direction.

3. *The Costs of a Complicated Financial Structure.* Firms such as Revco that have bank loans, senior subordinated debt, and junior subordinated debt will have a very hard time getting all claimholders to agree to an out-of-court settlement. For a retailer like Revco private agreements are especially difficult because of the large number of trade creditors. It is axiomatic that the more complicated a firm's financial structure, the more difficult it will be to work out private arrangements to avoid bankruptcy. Conflicts between managers, shareholders, and creditors make reaching a private agreement difficult. There is a natural tendency for each group to try to gain value at the expense of the others. ▪ ▪ ▪ ▪ ▪

---

[15]George Anders, "Revco Saga: On How the Buy Out Bonanza Became a Frenzy of Fees in Chapter 11," *The Wall Street Journal* (May 16, 1991).

- Why did it take Revco D. S. so long to emerge from bankruptcy?
- What are some of the costs of the Revco D. S. bankruptcy?

31.6 SUMMARY AND CONCLUSIONS

This chapter examines what happens when firms experience financial distress.

1. Financial distress is a situation where a firm's operating cash flow is not sufficient to cover contractual obligations. Financially distressed firms are often forced to take corrective action and undergo financial restructuring. Financial restructuring involves exchanging new financial claims for old ones.

2. Financial restructuring can be accomplished with a private workout or formal bankruptcy. Financial restructuring can involve liquidation or reorganization. However, liquidation is not common.

3. Corporate bankruptcy involves Chapter 7 liquidation or Chapter 11 reorganization. An essential feature of the U.S. Bankruptcy Code is the absolute priority rule. The absolute priority rule states that senior creditors are paid in full before junior creditors receive anything. However, in practice the absolute priority rule is often violated.

4. A new form of financial restructuring is prepackaged bankruptcy. It is a hybrid of a private workout and formal bankruptcy.

5. One of the most well-known bankruptcies involved Revco D. S. Revco's bankruptcy was long and costly. The main reason was Revco's complicated financial structure, which made agreement among creditors very difficult.

KEY TERMS

Absolute priority rule   859
Financial distress   854
Liquidation   858

Prepackaged bankruptcy   865
Private workout   863
Reorganization   858

SUGGESTED READINGS

An excellent book on financial distress by one of the leading authorities is

Altman, Edward I. *Corporate Financial Distress: A Complete Guide to Predicting, Avoiding and Dealing with Bankruptcy* (New York: John Wiley & Sons, 1983).

Many recent academic articles on financial distress can be found in

Jenson, Michael, and Richard Rubeck, eds. "Symposium on the Structure and Governance of Enterprise Part II." *Journal of Financial Economics* 27 (1990). Articles by Lawrence Weiss, Stuart G. Gilson, Kose John, Larry N. P. Lang, Steven Kaplan, David Reishus, Frank Easterbrook, and Karen H. Wruck appear.

Senbet, L., and James Seward. "Financial Distress, Bankruptcy and Reorganization." Chapter 28 in *Handbooks in OR and MS,* Vol. 9, R. A. Jarrow, V. Maksimovic, and W. T. Ziembe, eds. (1995).

QUESTIONS AND PROBLEMS

Financial Distress?

31.1 Define financial distress using the stock-based and flow-based approaches.

31.2 What are some benefits of financial distress?

Bankruptcy Liquidation and Reorganization

31.3 When the Beacon Computer Company (BCC) filed for bankruptcy under Chapter 7 of the U.S. Bankruptcy Code, it had the following balance sheet:

Liquidating Value		Claims	
Net realizable assets	$5,000	Trade credit	$1,000
		Secured notes (by a mortgage)	1,000
		Senior debenture	3,000
		Junior debenture	1,000
		Equity	(−1,000)

As trustee, what distribution of liquidating value do you propose?

31.4 When the Master Printing Company filed for bankruptcy, it filed under Chapter 11 of the U.S. Bankruptcy Code. Its balance sheet is shown below:

Assets		Claims	
Going concern value	$15,000	Mortgage bonds	$10,000
		Senior debenture	6,000
		Junior debenture	4,000
		Equity	(−5,000)

As trustee, what reorganization plan would you accept?

Private Workout or Bankruptcy: Which Is Best?

31.5 Explain the following two terms.
a. APR
b. DIP

31.6 Why do so many firms file for legal bankruptcy when private workouts are so much less expensive?

Appendix 31A PREDICTING CORPORATE BANKRUPTCY: THE Z-SCORE MODEL[16]

Many potential lenders use credit scoring models to assess the creditworthiness of prospective borrowers. The general idea is to find factors that enable the lenders to discriminate between good and bad credit risks. To put it more precisely, lenders want to identify attributes of the borrower that can be used to predict default or bankruptcy.

---

[16]Edward I. Altman, *Corporate Financial Distress and Bankruptcy,* John Wiley & Sons, N.Y. (1993), Chapter 3.

Edward Altman has developed a model using financial statement ratios and multiple discriminant analyses to predict bankruptcy for publicly traded manufacturing firms. The resultant model is of the form:

$$Z = 3.3 \frac{\text{EBIT}}{\text{Total assets}} + 1.2 \frac{\text{Net working capital}}{\text{Total assets}}$$
$$+ 1.0 \frac{\text{Sales}}{\text{Total assets}} + .6 \frac{\text{Market value of equity}}{\text{Book value of debt}}$$
$$+ 1.4 \frac{\text{Accumulated retained earnings}}{\text{Total assets}}$$

where Z is an index of bankruptcy.

A score of Z less than 2.675 indicates that a firm has a 95 percent chance of becoming bankrupt within one year. However, Altman's results show that in practice the area between 1.81 and 2.99 should be thought of as a gray area. In actual use, bankruptcy would be predicted if $Z \leq 1.81$ and nonbankruptcy if $Z \geq 2.99$. Altman shows that bankrupt firms and nonbankrupt firms have very different financial profiles one year before bankruptcy. These different financial profits are the key intuition behind the Z-score model and are depicted in Table 31A.1.

Altman's original Z-score model requires a firm to have publicly traded equity and be a manufacturer. He uses a revised model to make it applicable for private firms and nonmanufacturers. The resulting model is

$$Z = 6.56 \frac{\text{Net working capital}}{\text{Total assets}} + 3.26 \frac{\text{Accumulated retained earnings}}{\text{Total assets}}$$
$$+ 1.05 \frac{\text{EBIT}}{\text{Total assets}} + 6.72 \frac{\text{Book value of equity}}{\text{Total liabilities}}$$

where $Z < 1.23$ indicates a bankruptcy prediction,
$1.23 \geq Z \leq 2.90$ indicates a gray area,
and $Z > 2.90$ indicates no bankruptcy.

EXAMPLE

The U.S. Composite Corporation is attempting to increase its line of credit with the First National State Bank. The director of credit management of First National State Bank uses the Z-score model to determine creditworthiness. The U.S. Composite Corporation is not a publicly traded firm so that the revised Z-score model must be used.

The balance sheet and income statement of the U.S. Composite Corporation are in Tables 2.1 and 2.2 (Chapter 2).

The first step is to determine the value of each of the financial statement variables and in the revised Z-score model.

$$\text{(in millions)}$$

$$\frac{\text{Net working capital}}{\text{Total assets}} = \frac{275}{1,879} = 0.146$$

$$\frac{\text{Accumulated retained earnings}}{\text{Total assets}} = \frac{390}{1,879} = 0.208$$

$$\frac{\text{EBIT}}{\text{Total assets}} = \frac{219}{1,879} = 0.117$$

$$\frac{\text{Book value of equity}}{\text{Total liabilities}} = \frac{805}{588} = 1.369$$

■ TABLE 31A.1   **Financial Statement Ratios One Year before**
                Bankruptcy: Manufacturing Firms

	Average Ratios One Year before Bankruptcy of	
	Bankrupt Firms	Nonbankrupt Firms
$\dfrac{\text{Net working capital}}{\text{Total assets}}$	−6.1%	41.4%
$\dfrac{\text{Accumulated retained earnings}}{\text{Total assets}}$	−62.6%	35.5%
$\dfrac{\text{EBIT}}{\text{Total assets}}$	−31.8%	15.4%
$\dfrac{\text{Market value of equity}}{\text{Total liabilities}}$	40.1%	247.7%
$\dfrac{\text{Sales}}{\text{Assets}}$	150%	190%

Source: Edward I. Altman, *Corporate Financial Distress and Bankruptcy,* John Wiley & Sons (1993), Table 3.1, p. 109.

The next step to calculate the revised Z-score is

$$Z = 6.56 \times 0.146 + 3.26 \times 0.208$$
$$+1.05 \times 0.117 + 6.72 \times 1.369$$
$$= 10.96$$

Finally, we determine that the Z-score is above 2.9, and we conclude that U.S. Composite is a good credit risk.

CHAPTER 32

International Corporate Finance

EXECUTIVE SUMMARY

Corporations that have significant foreign operations are often referred to as *international corporations* or *multinationals*. Table 32.1 lists the largest international corporations using several different measures. There are many familiar names on this list. International corporations must consider many financial factors that do not directly affect purely domestic firms. These include foreign exchange rates, different interest rates from country to country, complex accounting methods for foreign operations, foreign tax rates, and foreign government intervention.

The basic principles of corporate finance still apply to international corporations; like domestic companies, they seek to invest in projects that create more value for the shareholders than they cost and to arrange financing that raises cash at the lowest possible cost. That is, the net present value principle holds for both foreign and domestic operations. However, it is usually more complicated to apply the NPV principle to foreign operations.

Perhaps the most important complication of international finance is foreign exchange. The foreign exchange markets provide information and opportunities for an international corporation when it undertakes capital-budgeting and financing decisions. The relationship among foreign exchange, interest rates, and inflation is defined by the basic theories of exchange rates: purchasing-power parity, interest-rate parity, and the expectations theory.

Typically, international financing decisions involve a choice of three basic approaches:

1. Export domestic cash to the foreign operations.
2. Borrow in the country where the investment is located.
3. Borrow in a third country.

We discuss the merits of each approach.

32.1 TERMINOLOGY

A common buzzword for the student of finance is **globalization.** The first step in learning about the globalization of financial markets is to conquer the new vocabulary. Here are some of the most common terms used in international finance and in this chapter:

1. An **American Depository Receipt (ADR)** is a security issued in the United States to represent shares of a foreign stock, allowing that stock to be traded in the United States. Foreign companies use ADRs, which are issued in U.S. dollars, to expand the pool of potential U.S. investors. ADRs are available in two forms for about 690 foreign companies:

■ TABLE 32.1   The Top International Corporations

Company	Industry	Foreign Assets as % of Total	Foreign Sales as % of Total	Foreign Employment as % of Total
Royal Dutch/Shell	Energy	67.8	73.3	77.9
Ford	Automotive	29.0	30.6	29.8
General Electric	Electronics	30.4	24.4	32.4
Exxon	Energy	73.1	79.6	53.7
General Motors	Automotive	24.9	29.2	33.9
Volkswagen	Automotive	84.8	60.8	44.4
IBM	Computers	51.9	62.7	50.1
Toyota	Automotive	30.5	45.1	23.0
Nestlé	Food	86.9	98.2	97.0
Bayer	Chemicals	89.8	63.3	54.6
ABB	Electrical equipment	84.7	87.2	93.9
Nissan	Automotive	42.7	44.2	43.5
Elf Aquitaine	Energy	54.5	65.4	47.5
Mobil	Energy	61.8	65.9	52.2
Daimler-Benz	Automotive	39.2	63.2	22.2

Source: *The Economist,* November 22, 1997, p. 92.

company-sponsored, which are listed on an exchange, and unsponsored, which are usually held by the investment bank that makes a market in the ADR. Both forms are available to individual investors, but only company-sponsored issues are quoted daily in newspapers.

2. The **cross rate** is the exchange rate between two foreign currencies, generally neither of which is the U.S. dollar. The dollar, however, is used as an interim step in determining the cross rate. For example, if an investor wants to sell Japanese yen and buy Swiss francs, he would sell yen against dollars and then buy francs with those dollars. So, although the transaction is designed to be yen for francs, the dollar's exchange rate serves as a benchmark.

3. A **European Currency Unit (ECU)** is a basket of 10 European currencies devised in 1979 and intended to serve as a monetary unit for the *European Monetary System* (EMS). By charter, EMS members reevaluate the composition of the ECU every five years or when there has been a shift of 25 percent or more in the weight of any currency. The German deutschemark is the most heavily weighted currency in the basket, with the French franc, the British pound, and the Dutch guilder each comprising more than 10 percent of the currency. The smallest weights are the Greek drachma, the Luxembourg franc, and the Irish punt.

4. **Eurobonds** are bonds denominated in a particular currency and issued simultaneously in the bond markets of several European countries. For many international companies and governments, they have become an important way to raise capital. Eurobonds are issued outside the restrictions that apply to domestic offerings and are typically syndicated in London. Trading can and does take place anywhere a buyer and a seller are.

5. **Eurocurrency** is money deposited in a financial center outside of the country whose currency is involved. For instance, Eurodollars—the most widely used Eurocurrency— are U.S. dollars deposited in banks outside the United States.

6. **Foreign bonds,** unlike Eurobonds, are issued by foreign borrowers in another nation's capital market and traditionally denominated in that nation's currency. Yankee bonds, for example, are issued in the United States by a foreign country, bank, or company; in recent years, however, some Yankee offerings have been denominated in currencies other than the U.S. dollar. Often the country in which these bonds are issued will draw distinctions between them and bonds issued by domestic issuers, including different tax laws, restrictions on the amount of issues, or tougher disclosure rules.

   Foreign bonds often are nicknamed for the country of issuance: Yankee bonds (United States), Samurai bonds (Japan), Rembrandt bonds (the Netherlands), and Bulldog bonds (Britain). Partly because of tougher regulations and disclosure requirements, the foreign-bond market hasn't grown in the past several years with the vigor of the Eurobond market. Nearly half of all foreign bonds are issued in Switzerland.

7. **Gilts,** technically, are British and Irish government securities, although the term also includes issues of local British authorities and some overseas public-sector offerings.

8. The **London Interbank Offered Rate (LIBOR)** is the rate that most international banks charge one another for loans of Eurodollars overnight in the London market. LIBOR is a cornerstone in the pricing of money-market issues and other short-term debt issues by both governments and corporate borrowers. Less creditworthy issuers will often borrow at a rate of more than one point over LIBOR.

9. There are two basic kinds of **swaps:** interest rate and currency. An interest-rate swap occurs when two parties exchange debt with a floating-rate payment for debt with a fixed-rate payment, or vice versa. Currency swaps are agreements to deliver one currency against another currency. Often both types of swaps are used in the same transaction when debt denominated in different currencies is swapped.

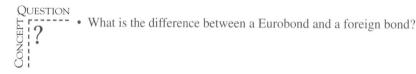

CONCEPT QUESTION
? • What is the difference between a Eurobond and a foreign bond?

32.2 FOREIGN EXCHANGE MARKETS AND EXCHANGE RATES

The **foreign exchange market** is undoubtedly the world's largest financial market. It is the market where one country's currency is traded for another's. Most of the trading takes place in a few currencies: the U.S. dollar ($), German deutschemark (DM), British pound sterling (£), Japanese yen (¥), Swiss franc (SF), and French franc (FF).

The foreign exchange market is an over-the-counter market. There is no single location where traders get together. Instead, traders are located in the major commercial and investment banks around the world. They communicate using computer terminals, telephones, and other telecommunication devices. One element in the communications network for foreign transactions is the *Society for Worldwide Interbank Financial Telecommunications* (SWIFT). It is a Belgian not-for-profit cooperative. A bank in New York can send messages to a bank in London via SWIFT's regional processing centers. The connections are through data-transmission lines.

The many different types of participants in the foreign exchange market include the following:

1. Importers who convert their domestic currency to foreign currency to pay for goods from foreign countries.

2. Exporters who receive foreign currency and may want to convert to the domestic currency.
3. Portfolio managers who buy and sell foreign stocks and bonds.
4. Foreign exchange brokers who match buy and sell orders.
5. Traders who make the market in foreign exchange.

Exchange Rates

An **exchange rate** is the price of one country's currency for another's. In practice, almost all trading of currencies takes place in terms of the U.S. dollar. For example, both the German deutschemark and the British pound will be traded with their price quoted in U.S. dollars. If the quoted price is the price in dollars of a unit of foreign exchange, the quotation is said to be in *direct* (or American) terms. For example, $1.50 = £1 and $0.40 = DM1 are in direct terms. The financial press frequently quotes the foreign currency price of a U.S. dollar. If the quoted price is the foreign currency price of a U.S. dollar, the quotation is *indirect* (or European). For example, £0.67 = $1 and DM2.5 = $1.

EXAMPLE

In 1984, Japan's economic growth and low inflation began to increase the demand for the yen compared to the dollar. Large U.S. trade deficits in the 1980s and 1990s contributed to this tendency. Figure 32.1 plots the Japanese yen value of a U.S. dollar from 1980 to 1998. The strong U.S. economy in the mid–1990s caused a dollar rebound.

■ FIGURE 32.1   **Japanese Yen Price of a U.S. Dollar from 1980 to 2000**

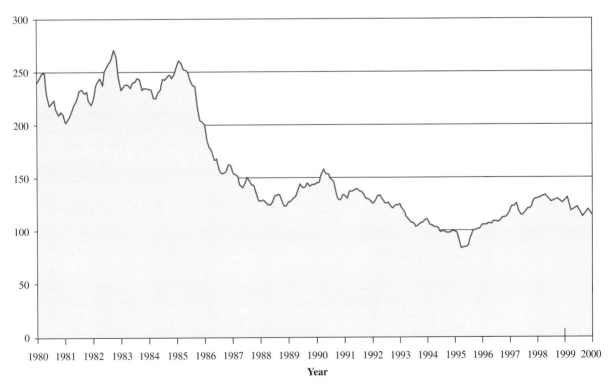

Source: Various issues of the *Los Angeles Times* and *The Wall Street Journal*.

■ FIGURE 32.2   **Triangular Arbitrage**

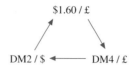

There are two reasons for quoting all foreign currencies in terms of the U.S. dollar. First, it reduces the number of possible cross-currency quotes. For example, with five major currencies, there would potentially be 10 exchange rates. Second, it makes **triangular arbitrage** more difficult. If all currencies were traded against each other, it would make inconsistencies more likely. That is, the exchange rate of the French franc against the deutschemark would be compared to the exchange rate between the U.S. dollar and the deutschemark. This implies a particular rate between the French franc and the U.S. dollar to prevent triangular arbitrage.

EXAMPLE

> What if the pound traded for DM4 in Frankfurt and $1.60 in London? If the dollar traded for DM2 in Frankfurt, the trader would have a triangular opportunity. Starting with $1.60, a trader could purchase £1 in London. This pound could then be used to buy DM4 in Frankfurt. With the dollar trading at DM2, the DM4 could then be traded for $2 in Frankfurt as illustrated in Figure 32.2. The net gain from going around this "triangle" would be $2.00 − $1.60 = $0.40. Imagine what the return would be on an initial $1 billion purchase.

Types of Transactions

Three types of trades take place in the foreign exchange market: spot, forward, and swap. **Spot trades** involve an agreement on the exchange rate today for settlement in two days. The rate is called the **spot-exchange rate. Forward trades** involve an agreement on exchange rates today for settlement in the future. The rate is called the **forward-exchange rate.** The maturities for forward trades are usually 1 to 52 weeks. A swap is the sale (purchase) of a foreign currency with a simultaneous agreement to repurchase (resell) it sometime in the future. The difference between the sale price and the repurchase price is called the **swap rate.**

EXAMPLE

> On October 11, bank *A* pays dollars to bank *B*'s account at a New York bank and *A* receives pounds sterling in its account at a bank in London. On November 11, as agreed to on October 11, the transaction is reversed. *A* pays the sterling back to *B,* while *B* pays back the dollars to *A*. This is a swap. In effect, *A* has borrowed pounds sterling while giving up the use of dollars to *B*.

32.3 THE LAW OF ONE PRICE AND PURCHASING-POWER PARITY

What determines the level of the spot-exchange rate? One answer is the **law of one price (LOP).** The law of one price says that a commodity will cost the same regardless of the country in which it is purchased. More formally, let $S_£(t)$ be the spot-exchange rate, that is, the number of dollars needed to purchase a British pound at time t.[1] Let $P^{US}(t)$ and $P^{UK}(t)$ be the current U.S. and British prices of a particular commodity, say, apples. The law of one price says that

$$P^{US}(t) = S_£(t)\, P^{UK}(t)$$

for apples.

The rationale behind LOP is similar to that of triangular arbitrage. If LOP did not hold, arbitrage would be possible by moving apples from one country to another. For example, suppose that apples in New York are selling for $4 per bushel, while in London the price is £2.50 per bushel. Then the law of one price implies that

$$\$4 = S_£(t) \times £2.50$$

and

$$S_£(t) = \$1.60/£$$

That is, the LOP implied spot-exchange rate is $1.60 per pound.

Suppose instead that the actual exchange rate is $2.00 per pound. Starting with $4, a trader could buy a bushel of apples in New York, ship it to London, and sell it there for £2.50. The pounds sterling could then be converted into dollars at the exchange rate, $2/£, yielding a total of $5 for $1 ($5 − $4) gain.

The rationale of the LOP is that if the exchange rate is not $1.60/£ but is instead, say, $2/£, then forces would be set in motion to change the rate and/or the price of apples. In our example, there would be a whole lot of apples flying from New York to London. Thus, demand for apples in New York would raise the dollar price for apples there, and the supply in London would lower the pound-sterling price. The apple traders converting pounds sterling into dollars, that is, supplying pounds sterling and demanding dollars, would also put pressure on the exchange rate to fall from $2/£.

As you can see, for the LOP to be strictly true, three assumptions are needed:

1. The transactions cost of trading apples—shipping, insurance, wastage, and so on—must be zero.
2. No barriers to trading apples, such as tariffs or taxes, can exist.
3. Finally, an apple in New York must be identical to an apple in London. It won't do for you to send red apples to London if the English eat only green apples.

Given the fact that the transaction costs are not zero and that the other conditions are rarely exactly met, the LOP is really applicable only to traded goods, and then only to very uniform ones. The LOP does not imply that a Mercedes costs the same as a Ford or that a nuclear power plant in France costs the same as one in New York. In the case of the cars, they are not identical. In the case of the power plants, even if they were identical, they are expensive and very difficult to ship.

---

[1]Throughout this chapter, we quote foreign exchange in direct or American terms.

Because consumers purchase many goods, economists speak of **purchasing-power parity (PPP),** the idea that the exchange rate adjusts so that a *market basket* of goods costs the same, regardless of the country in which it is purchased. In addition, a relative version of purchasing-power parity has evolved. **Relative purchasing-power parity (RPPP)** says that the rate of change in the price level of commodities in one country relative to the rate of change in the price level in another determines the rate of change of the exchange rate between the two countries. Formally,

$$\frac{P^{US}(t+1)}{P^{US}(t)} = \frac{S_£(t+1)}{S_£(t)} \times \frac{P^{UK}(t+1)}{P^{UK}(t)}$$

$$\begin{array}{ccc} 1 + \text{U.S.} & = & 1 + \text{Change in} & \times & 1 + \text{British} \\ \text{inflation rate} & & \text{foreign exchange rate} & & \text{inflation rate} \end{array}$$

This states that the rate of inflation in the United States relative to that in Great Britain determines the rate of change in the value of the dollar relative to that of the pound during the interval t to $t+1$. It is common to write Π_{US} as the rate of inflation in the United States. $1 + \Pi_{US}$ is equal to $P^{US}(t+1)/P^{US}(t)$. Similarly, Π_{UK} is the rate of inflation in Great Britain. $1 + \Pi_{UK}$ is equal to $P^{UK}(t+1)/P^{UK}(t)$.

Using Π to represent the rate of inflation, the preceding equation can be rearranged as

$$\frac{1 + \Pi_{US}}{1 + \Pi_{UK}} = \frac{S_£(t+1)}{S_£(t)} \tag{32.1}$$

We can rewrite this in an appropriate form as

$$\Pi_{US} \cong \Pi_{UK} + \frac{\dot{S}_£}{S_£}$$

where $\dot{S}_£/S_£$ now stands for the rate of change in the dollars-per-pound exchange rate.

As an example, suppose that inflation in France during the year is equal to 4 percent and inflation in the United States is equal to 10 percent. Then, according to the RPPP, the price of the French franc in terms of the U.S. dollar should rise; that is, the U.S. dollar declines in value in terms of the French franc. Using our approximation, the dollars-per-franc exchange rate should rise by

$$\frac{\dot{S}_{FF}}{S_{FF}} \approx \Pi_{US} - \Pi_F$$
$$= 10\% - 4\%$$
$$= 6\%$$

where $\dot{S}_{FF}/S_{FF}$ stands for the rate of change in the dollars-per-franc exchange rate. That is, if the French franc is worth \$0.20 at the beginning of the period, it should be worth approximately \$0.212 (\$0.20 $\times$ 1.06) at the end of the period.

The RPPP says that the change in the ratio of domestic commodity prices of two countries must be matched in the exchange rate. This version of the law of one price suggests that to estimate changes in the spot rate of exchange, it is necessary to estimate the difference in relative inflation rates. In other words, we can express our formula in expectational terms as

$$E\left(\frac{\dot{S}_{FF}}{S_{FF}}\right) = E(\Pi_{US}) - E(\Pi_F)$$

If we expect the U.S. inflation rate to exceed the French inflation rate, we should expect the dollar price of French francs to rise, which is the same as saying that the dollar is expected to fall against the franc.

The more exact relationship of equation (32.1) can be expressed in expectational terms as

$$\frac{E(1 + \Pi_{US})}{E(1 + \Pi_{UK})} = \frac{E[S_{\pounds}(t + 1)]}{S_{\pounds}(t)} \tag{32.2}$$

CONCEPT QUESTIONS

?
- What is the law of one price? What is purchasing-power parity?
- What is the relationship between inflation and exchange-rate movements?

32.4 INTEREST RATES AND EXCHANGE RATES: INTEREST-RATE PARITY

The forward-exchange rate and the spot-exchange rate are tied together by the same sort of arbitrage that underlies the law of one price. First, here is some useful terminology. If forward-exchange rates are greater than the spot-exchange rate in a particular currency, the forward foreign currency is said to be at a *premium* (this implies the domestic currency is at a discount). If the values of forward-exchange rates are less than the spot-exchange rate, the forward rate of foreign currency is at a discount.

Suppose we observe that the spot DM rate is DM2.50 = $1.00 and the one-month forward DM is DM2.40 = $1.00. Because fewer marks are needed to buy a dollar at the forward rate than are needed to buy a dollar at the spot rate, the mark is more valuable in the forward market than in the spot market. This means that the one-month forward DM is at a premium. Of course, whatever we say for the mark must be the opposite of what we say for the dollar. In this example, the dollar is at a discount because the forward value is less than the spot value. Forward exchange is quoted in terms of the premium or discount that is to be added onto the spot rate.

Whether forward rates are at a premium or a discount when compared to a domestic currency depends on the relative interest rates in the foreign and domestic currency markets. The **interest-rate–parity theorem** implies that, if interest rates are higher domestically than in a particular foreign country, the foreign country's currency will be selling at a premium in the forward market; and if interest rates are lower domestically, the foreign currency will be selling at a discount in the forward market.

We need some notation to develop the interest-rate–parity theorem. Let $S(0)$ be the current domestic-currency price of spot foreign exchange (current time is denoted by 0). If the domestic currency is the dollar and the foreign exchange is the deutschemark, we might observe $S(0) = \$0.40/DM$. $S(0)$ is in direct or U.S. terms. Let $F(0,1)$ be the current domestic-currency price of forward exchange for a contract that matures in one month. Thus, the contract is for forward exchange one month hence. Let i and i^* be the yearly rates of interest paid on Eurocurrency deposits denominated in the domestic (i) and foreign (i^*) currencies, respectively. Of course, the maturity of the deposits can be chosen to coincide with the maturity of the forward contract. Now consider a trader who has access to the interbank market in foreign exchange and Eurocurrency deposits. Suppose the trader has some dollars to invest for one month. The trader can make a dollar loan or a deutschemark loan. The annual interest rate is 10 percent in deutschemarks and 6 percent in dollars. Which is better?

The Dollar Investment

Given an annual interest rate of 6 percent, the one-month rate of interest is 0.5 percent, ignoring compounding. If the trader invests $1 million now, the trader will get $1 million × 1.005 = $1.005 million at the end of the month. Following is an illustration:

Time 0	Time 1
Lend 1 unit of dollars $1,000,000	Obtain $1 + i \times (1/12)$ units of domestic currency $1,000,000 \times (1 + 0.005) = \$1,005,000$

The Deutschemark Investment

The current spot rate is $0.40/DM. This means the trader can currently obtain $1 million/0.40 = DM2.5 million. The rate of interest on one-year DM loans is 10 percent. For one month, the interest rate is $0.10/12 = 0.0083$. Thus, at the end of one month the trader will obtain DM2.5 million $\times 1.0083 =$ DM2,520,750. Of course, if the trader wants dollars at the end of the month, the trader must convert the deutschemarks back into dollars. The trader can fix the exchange rate for one-month conversion. Suppose the one-month forward is $0.39869/DM. Then the trader can sell deutschemarks forward. This will ensure that the trader gets DM2,520,750 $\times 0.39869 = \$1.005$ million at the end of the month. The general relationships are set forth here:

Time 0	Time 1
Purchase 1 unit $[1/S(0)]$ of foreign exchange	Deposit matures and pays $[1/S(0)] \times [1 + i \times (1/12)]$ units of foreign exchange
DM2,500,000	DM2,500,000 $\times 1.0083 =$ DM2,520,750
Sell forward $[1/S(0)] \times [1 + i^* \times (1/12)]$ units of forward exchange at the forward rate $F(0,1)$	Deliver foreign exchange in fulfillment of forward contract, receiving $[1/S(0)] \times [1 + i^* \times (1/12)] \times [F(0,1)]$ DM2,500,000 $\times 1.0083 \times 0.39869 = \$1,005,000$

In our example, the investments earned exactly the same rate of return and $1 + [i \times (1/12)] = [1/S(0)] \times [1 + i^* \times (1/12)] \times [F(0,1)]$. In competitive financial markets, this must be true for risk-free investments. When the trader makes the deutschemark loan, he or she gets a higher interest rate. But the return is the same because the deutschemark must be sold forward at a lower price than it can be exchanged for initially. If the domestic interest rate were different from the covered foreign interest rate, the trader would have arbitrage opportunities.

To summarize, to prevent arbitrage possibilities from existing, we must have equality of the U.S. interest rate and covered foreign interest rates:

$$1 + i = \frac{1}{S(0)} \times (1 + i^*) \times F(0,1)$$

or

$$\frac{1 + i}{1 + i^*} = \frac{F(0,1)}{S(0)} \tag{32.3}$$

The last equation is the famous interest-rate–parity theorem. It relates the forward-exchange rate and the spot-exchange rate to interest-rate differentials. Notice that, if $i > i^*$, the spot rate (expressed as dollars per unit of foreign currency) will be less than the forward rate.

EXAMPLE

Let the spot rate $S(0) = \$0.40/DM$ and the one-year forward rate $F(0,1) = \$0.42/DM$. Let the one-year rates on Eurodollar deposits and Euro-DM deposits be, respectively, $i = 11.3\%$ and $i^* = 6\%$. Then, comparing the return on domestic borrowing with the return on covered foreign lending,

$$\$(1 + i) = \$(1 + 0.113) = \$1.113$$
$$\$[1/S(0)] \times (1 + i^*) \times F(0,1) = \$(1/0.40) \times (1 + 0.06) \times \$0.42 = \$1.113$$

For each dollar borrowed domestically, a trader must repay $\$1.113$. The return from using the $\$1.00$ to buy spot foreign exchange, placing the deposit at the foreign rate of interest, and selling the total return forward would be $\$1.113$. These two amounts are equal, so it would not be worth anyone's time to try to exploit the difference. In this case, interest parity can be said to hold.

The Forward-Discount and Expected Spot Rates

A close connection exists between forward-exchange rates and expected spot rates. A trader's buy and sell decisions in today's forward market are based on the trader's market expectation of the future spot rate. In fact, if traders were completely indifferent to risk, the forward rate of exchange would depend solely on expectations about the future spot rate. For example, suppose the one-year forward rate of deutschemarks is $\$0.40/DM$ [that is, $F(0,1) = \$0.40/DM$]. This must mean that traders expect the spot rate to be $\$0.40/DM$ in one year [$E(S(1)) = \$0.40/DM$]. If they thought it would be higher, it would create an arbitrage opportunity. Traders would buy deutschemarks forward at the low price and sell deutschemarks one year later at the expected higher price. This implies that the forward rate of exchange is equal to the expected spot, or (in general terms)

$$F(0,1) = E[S(1)]$$

and

$$\frac{F(0,1)}{S(0)} = \frac{E[S(1)]}{S(0)} \tag{32.4}$$

An equilibrium is achieved only when the forward discount (or premium) equals the expected change in the spot-exchange rate.

Exchange-Rate Risk

Exchange-rate risk is the natural consequence of international operations in a world where foreign currency values move up and down. International firms usually enter into some contracts that require payments in different currencies. For example, suppose that the treasurer of an international firm knows that one month from today the firm must pay £2 million for goods it will receive in England. The current exchange rate is $\$1.50/£$, and if that rate prevails in one month, the dollar cost of the goods to the firm will be $\$1.50/£ \times £2$ million $= \$3$ million. The treasurer in this case is obligated to pay pounds in one month. (Alternately, we say that he is *short* in pounds.) A net short or long position of this type can be very risky. If the pound rises in the month to $\$2/£$, the treasurer must pay $\$2/£ \times £2$ million $= \$4$ million, an extra $\$1$ million.

IN THEIR OWN WORDS

Richard M. Levich on Forward Exchange Rates

What is the relationship between today's three-month forward exchange rate, which can be observed in the market, and the spot exchange rate of three months from today, which cannot be observed until the future? One popular answer is that there is no relationship. As every bank trader knows, the possibility of covered interest arbitrage between domestic and foreign securities establishes a close link between the forward premium and the interest rate differential. At any moment, a trader can check his screen and observe that the forward premium and the interest rate differentials are nearly identical, especially when Eurocurrency interest rates are used. Thus the trader might say, "The forward rate reflects today's interest differential. It has nothing to do with expectations."

To check the second popular belief, that the forward rate reflects exchange rate expectations, takes a bit more work. Take today's three-month forward rate as of January 15 and compare it to the spot exchange rate that actually exists three months later on April 15. This produces one observation on the forward rate as a forecaster—not enough to accept or reject a theory. The idea that the forward rate might be an unbiased predictor of the future spot rate suggests that, on average and looking at many observations, the prediction error is small. So collect more data using the forward rate of April 15 and match it with the spot rate of July 15, and then the

forward rate of July 15 matched to the spot rate of October 15, and so on. Look at the data for 8–10 years to have a large sample of observations.

The data suggest that in the early 1980s when the dollar was very strong, the forward rate significantly *under*estimated the strength of the dollar, and the forward rate was a biased predictor. But from 1985–1987 when the dollar depreciated sharply, the forward rate tended to *over*estimate the strength of the dollar, and the forward rate was again a biased predictor, but with the opposite sign as the earlier period. Looking at all of the 1980s— you guessed it—the forward rate was on average very close to the future spot exchange rate.

There are two messages here. First, even if there were "no relationship" between the forward rate and the future spot rate, the treasurer of General Motors would want to know exactly what that "nonrelationship" was. Because if the forward rate were *consistently* 3 percent higher than, or *consistently* 5 percent lower than, the future spot rate, the treasurer would be facing a tantalizing profit opportunity. A watch that is three minutes fast or five minutes slow is a very useful watch, as long as the bias is known and consistent.

Richard M. Levich is Professor of Finance and International Business at New York University. He has written extensively on exchange rates and other issues in international economics and finance.

This is the essence of foreign exchange risk. The treasurer may want to hedge his position. When forward markets exist, the most convenient means of hedging is the purchase or sale of forward contracts. In this example, the treasurer may want to consider buying 2 million pounds sterling one month forward. If the one-month forward rate quoted today is also $1.50/£, the treasurer will fulfill the contract by exchanging $3 million for £2 million in one month. The £2 million he receives from the contract can then be used to pay for the goods. By hedging today, he fixes the outflow one month from now to exactly $3 million.

Should the treasurer hedge or speculate? There are usually two reasons why the treasurer should hedge:

1. In an efficient foreign exchange-rate market, speculation is a zero NPV activity. Unless the treasurer has special information, nothing will be gained from foreign exchange speculation.

2. The costs of hedging are not large. The treasurer can use forward contracts to hedge, and if the forward rate is equal to the expected spot, the costs of hedging are negligible. Of course, there are ways to hedge foreign exchange risk other than to use forward con-

tracts. For example, the treasurer can borrow dollars and buy pounds sterling in the spot market today and lend them for one month in London. By the interest-rate–parity theorem, this will be the same as buying the pounds sterling forward.

Which Firms Hedge Exchange-Rate Risk?

Not all firms with exchange-rate risk exposure hedge. Géczy, Minton, and Schrand report about 41 percent of Fortune 500 firms with foreign currency risk actually attempt to hedge these risks.[2] They find that larger firms with greater growth opportunities are more likely to use currency derivatives to hedge exchange-rate risk than smaller firms with fewer investment opportunities. This suggests that some firms hedge to make sure that they have enough cash on hand to finance their growth. In addition, firms with greater growth opportunities will tend to have higher indirect bankruptcy costs. For these firms, hedging exchange-rate risk will reduce these costs and increase the probability that they will not default on their debt obligations.

   The fact that larger firms are more likely to use hedging techniques suggests that the costs of hedging are not insignificant. There may be fixed costs of establishing a hedging operation, in which case, economies of scale may explain why smaller firms hedge less than larger firms.

CONCEPT QUESTIONS

- What is the interest-rate-parity theorem?
- Why is the forward rate related to the expected future spot rate?
- How can one offset foreign exchange risk through a transaction in the forward markets?

32.5 INTERNATIONAL CAPITAL BUDGETING

Kihlstrom Equipment, a U.S.-based international company, is evaluating an investment in France. Kihlstrom's exports of drill bits have increased to such a degree that the company is considering operating a plant in France. The project will cost FF20 million, and it is expected to produce cash flows of FF8 million a year for the next three years. The current spot-exchange rate for French francs is $S(0) = \$0.20/FF$. How should Kihlstrom calculate the net present value of the projects in U.S. dollars?

   Nothing about the fact that the investment is made abroad alters Kihlstrom's NPV criterion. Kihlstrom must identify incremental cash flows and discount them at the appropriate cost of capital. After making the required discounted cash flow calculations, Kihlstrom should undertake projects with a positive NPV. However, two major factors that complicate such international NPV calculations are foreign exchange conversion and repatriation of funds.

Foreign Exchange Conversion

The simplest way for Kihlstrom to calculate the NPV of the investment is to convert all French-franc cash flows to U.S. dollars. This involves a three-step process:

   Step 1. Estimate future cash flows in French francs.
   Step 2. Convert to U.S. dollars at the predicted exchange rate.
   Step 3. Calculate NPV using the cost of capital in U.S. dollars.

---

[2]C. Géczy, B. Minton, and C. Schrand, "Why Firms Use Currency Derivatives," *Journal of Finance* (September 1997). See also D. R. Nance, C. Smith, Jr., and C. W. Smithson, "On the Determinants of Corporate Hedging," *Journal of Finance,* 1993.

■ TABLE 32.2   **Net Present Value of Foreign Cash Flows: Kihlstrom Equipment**

	End of Year			
	0	1	2	3
Incremental cash flows (CF_{FF}) (FF millions)	−20	8	8	8
Foreign exchange rate ($/FF)	0.15	0.145	0.14	0.135
Foreign exchange-rate conversion	-20×0.15	8×0.145	8×0.14	8×0.135
Incremental cash flows ($ millions)	−3	1.16	1.12	1.08

NPV at 15% = −$0.43 million.

In Table 32.2 we show the application of these three steps to Kihlstrom's French investment. Notice in Table 32.2 that Kihlstrom's French-franc cash flows were converted to dollars by multiplying the foreign cash flows by the predicted foreign exchange rate.

How might Kihlstrom predict future exchange rates? Using the theory of efficient markets, Kihlstrom could calculate NPV using the foreign exchange market's implicit predictions. To figure these out, Kihlstrom can use the basic foreign exchange relationships described in earlier sections of this chapter.

Kihlstrom begins by obtaining publicly available information on exchange rates and interest rates. It finds:

Exchange rate: $S_{FF}(0) = \$0.15/FF$, i.e., 1 French franc can be purchased for $0.15.

Interest rate in United States: $i_{US} = 8\%$
Interest rate in France: $i_F = 12\%$

Using equations (32.2), (32.3), and (32.4), Kihlstrom can calculate the following set of relationships:

$$\frac{E(1 + \Pi_{US})}{E(1 + \Pi_F)} = \frac{E(S_{FF}(1))}{S_{FF}(0)} = \frac{F_{FF}(0,1)}{S_{FF}(0)} = \frac{1 + i_{US}}{1 + i_F} \quad (32.5)$$

Relative purchasing-power parity   Forward rate related to expected spot rate   Interest-rate parity

(32.2)   (32.4)   (32.3)

From the left, the first equality follows from relative purchasing-power parity. The expected inflation rates in the two countries determine the expected movement in the spot rate, expressed earlier in equation (32.2). The equality between the second and third terms is a consequence of our discussion on forward rates and expected spot rates, expressed earlier in equation (32.4). The last equality is interest-rate parity and appeared earlier in equation (32.3).

We now compare the left-hand term to the right-hand term. We have

$$\frac{1 + i_{US}}{1 + i_F} = \frac{E(1 + \Pi_{US})}{E(1 + \Pi_F)}$$

$$\frac{1.08}{1.12} = \frac{E(1 + \Pi_{US})}{E(1 + \Pi_F)}$$

If the expected inflation rate in the United States is 8 percent, it follows that the expected inflation rate in France is 12 percent:

$$\frac{1.08}{1.12} = \frac{1.08}{E(1 + \Pi_F)}$$

$$E(\Pi_F) = 12\%$$

Using relative purchasing-power parity, Kihlstrom can compute the expected spot-exchange rate in one year:

$$\frac{E(1 + \Pi_{US})}{E(1 + \Pi_F)} = \frac{E[S_{FF}(1)]}{S_{FF}(0)}$$

$$\frac{1.08}{1.12} = \frac{E[S_{FF}(1)]}{0.15}$$

which implies $E[S_{FF}(1)] = 0.145$. The exchange rate expected at the end of year 2 is obtained from

$$0.15 \times \left(\frac{1.08}{1.12}\right)^2 = 0.14$$

For year 3, the expected exchange rate is obtained from

$$0.15 \times \left(\frac{1.08}{1.12}\right)^3 = 0.135$$

Finally, the NPV of the project is computed:

$$\text{NPV} = \sum_{t=0}^{3} \frac{\text{CF}_{FF}(t) \times E[S_{FF}(t)]}{(1 + r^*)^t}$$

where $\text{CF}_{FF}(t)$ refers to the French francs forecasted to be received in each of the next three years. The discount rate we use is Kihlstrom's U.S. cost of capital. We do not use the U.S. risk-free rate of 8 percent because Kihlstrom's project is risky; a risk-adjusted discount rate must be used. Because the NPV at 15 percent is −$430,000, Kihlstrom should not invest in a subsidiary in France.

In this example we used the foreign exchange market's implicit forecast of future exchange rates. Why not use management's own forecast of foreign exchange rates in the calculations? Suppose that the financial management of Kihlstrom feels optimistic about the French franc. If its forecasts are sufficiently optimistic and they are used, Kihlstrom's investment in a French subsidiary will generate a positive NPV. But, in general, it is a good idea to separate the economic prospects of an investment and the foreign exchange prospects, and it is unwise to use the latter projections in the NPV calculation. If Kihlstrom wishes to speculate on an increase in the French franc relative to the U.S. dollar, the best way to do this is to buy French francs in the forward foreign exchange market. By using the forward-exchange rates implicit in the domestic and foreign interest rates, the firm is using the actual dollar flows that it could, in principle, lock in today by borrowing in the foreign currency. This makes the foreign cash flows equivalent to domestic cash flows.

Unremitted Cash Flows

The previous example assumed that all after-tax cash flows from the foreign investment were remitted to the parent firm. The remittance decision is similar to the dividend for a purely domestic firm. Substantial differences can exist between the cash flows of a project and the amount that is actually remitted to the parent firm. Of course, the net present value of a project will not be changed by deferred remittance if the unremitted cash flows are reinvested at a rate of return equal (as adjusted for exchange rates) to the domestic cost of capital.

A foreign subsidiary can remit funds to a parent in many ways, including the following:

1. Dividends.
2. Management fees for central services.
3. Royalties on the use of trade names and patents.

International firms must pay special attention to remittance for two reasons. First, there may be present and future exchange controls. Many governments are sensitive to the charge of being exploited by foreign firms. Therefore, governments are tempted to limit the ability of international firms to remit cash flows. Another reason is taxes. It is always necessary to determine what taxes must be paid on profits generated in a foreign country. International firms must usually pay foreign taxes on their foreign profits. The total taxes paid by an international firm may be a function of the time of remittance. For example, Kihlstrom's French subsidiary would need to pay taxes in France on the profits it earns in France. Kihlstrom will also pay taxes on dividends it remits to the United States. In most cases Kihlstrom can offset the payment of foreign taxes against the U.S. tax liability. Thus, if the French corporate income tax is 34 percent, Kihlstrom will not be liable for additional U.S. taxes.

The Cost of Capital for International Firms

An important question for firms with international investments is whether the required return for international projects should be different from that of similar domestic projects.

Lower Cost of Capital from International Firm Diversification   In the previous chapter, we expressed some skepticism concerning the benefits of diversification. We can make a stronger case for diversification in international firms than for purely domestic firms. Suppose barriers prevented shareholders in the United States from holding foreign securities; the financial markets of different countries would be segmented. Further suppose that firms in the United States were not subject to the same barriers. In such a case, a firm engaging in international investing could provide indirect diversification for U.S. shareholders that they could not achieve by investing within the United States. This could lead to the lowering of the risk premium on international projects. In general, if the costs of investing abroad are lower for a firm than for its shareholders, there is an advantage to international diversification by firms, and this advantage will be reflected in a lower risk-adjusted discount rate.

Alternatively, if there were no barriers to international investing for shareholders, shareholders could obtain the benefit of international diversification for themselves by buying foreign securities. In this case the project cost of capital for a firm in the United States would not depend on whether the project was in the United States or in a foreign country. In practice, holding foreign securities involves substantial expenses. These expenses include taxes, the costs of obtaining information, and trading costs. This implies that although U.S. investors are free to hold foreign securities, they will not be perfectly internationally diversified.

Lower Cost of Capital from International Shareholder Diversification   Recall our discussion of the CAPM and the market portfolio. Consider the U.S. stock market and a U.S. investor who is not internationally diversified but, instead, is invested only in U.S. stocks. From our previous discussion of diversification, we know this investor would be bearing more risk than if she were able to diversify in the stocks of different countries. Now imagine she can invest in many foreign stocks by diversifying internationally. She should be able to reduce the variance (or standard deviation) of her portfolio significantly.

For this investor, the market-risk premium will be lower than for investors who cannot diversify internationally. In internationally integrated markets, investors with internationally diversified portfolios will measure the risk of an individual stock in terms of a world-market portfolio and global betas. Therefore, the cost of capital of a particular firm will be in terms of a global CAPM, such as

$$E(R_I) = r_F + B_G \left[E(R_G) - r_F \right]$$

where R_I is the required return on a stock when markets are global, r_F is the risk free rate, B_G is the global beta, and R_G is the return on the world-market portfolio. A firm with internationally diversified investors will have a cost of capital with a lower market-risk premium [i.e., $E(R_G - r_F)$] and a global beta when compared to a firm with investors that cannot diversify internationally.

Solnik has presented evidence that suggests that international diversification significantly reduces risk for shareholders.[3] He shows that the variance of an internationally diversified portfolio of common stocks is about 33 percent of the variance of individual securities. A diversified portfolio of U.S. stocks will reduce variance by only 50 percent. Table 32.3 shows that a world portfolio has lower risk than a portfolio of stocks within a single country. For example, a citizen of Hong Kong can reduce risk from 12.8 percent to 4.2 percent by investing in a world portfolio. This evidence is consistent with a lower global market-risk premium than is a purely domestic-risk premium. Global betas will be different than purely domestic betas. Stulz has argued that the preceding claim for why internationalization reduces the cost of capital doesn't capture the complete picture. He agrees that the global market-risk premium is likely to be substantially lower than the risk premium for an isolated country. In addition, he argues that global investing is likely to improve corporate governance and reduce agency costs. The argument goes something like this: Firms in countries with less-developed financial markets will need to improve their governance so that they can raise capital in well-developed capital markets such as the U.S. Foreign firms raising capital in the U.S. must appeal to more sophisticated investors and better market architectures with superior monitoring abilities.[4] Table 32.3 also shows that the systematic risk of foreign stock investment can be very low, as is the case of Austria, or very high, as is the case of Hong Kong.

Foreign Political Risks   Firms may determine that international investments inherently involve more political risk than domestic investments. This extra risk may offset the gains from international diversification. Firms may increase the discount rate to allow for the risk of expropriation and foreign exchange remittance controls.

---

[3]B. H. Solnik, "Why Not Diversify Internationally Rather than Domestically?" *Financial Analysts Journal* (July–August 1974). A recent estimate of the benefits of international diversification can be found in Georgio DeSantis and Bruno Gerard, "International Asset Pricing and Portfolio Diversification with Time-Varying Risk, *Journal of Finance* 52 (1997). They estimate that an internationally diversified portfolio will reduce standard deviation by 20 percent when compared to investing in U.S. stocks only.

[4]René M. Stulz, "Globalization, Corporate Finance, and the Cost of Capital," *Journal of Applied Corporate Finance* 12 (1999). See also Ronald M. Schramm and Henry N. Wang, "Measuring the Cost of Capital in an International CAPM Framework," *Journal of Corporate Finance* 12 (1999) and Thomas I. O'Brian, "The Global CAPM and a Firm's Cost of Capital in Different Currencies," *Journal of Corporate Finance* 12 (1999).

■ TABLE 32.3   **Risk Measures for Foreign Market Portfolios**

	Beta	Monthly Standard Deviation (%)
Hong Kong	2.08	12.8%
Japan	1.42	6.1
Sweden	.73	6.2
Norway	.57	5.3
Belgium	1.06	6.0
Netherlands	1.01	5.6
United Kingdom	1.38	7.9
Denmark	.49	5.5
France	.69	7.4
Austria	.19	5.4
Germany	.70	6.0
Switzerland	.83	5.7
Australia	1.39	8.2
Canada	1.04	5.9
United States	.97	4.7
World	1.00	4.2

Source: Campbell R. Harvey, "The World Price of Covariance Risk," *Journal of Finance* (March 1991) from Table I, p. 122 and Table VI, p. 140.

QUESTION
CONCEPT
?
• What problems do international projects pose for the use of net-present-value techniques?

32.6 INTERNATIONAL FINANCIAL DECISIONS

An international firm can finance foreign projects in three basic ways:

1. It can raise cash in the home country and export it to finance the foreign project.
2. It can raise cash by borrowing in the foreign country where the project is located.
3. It can borrow in a third country where the cost of debt is lowest.

If a U.S. firm raises cash for its foreign projects by borrowing in the United States, it has an exchange-rate risk. If the foreign currency depreciates, the U.S. parent firm may experience an exchange-rate loss when the foreign cash flow is remitted to the United States. Of course, the U.S. firm may sell foreign exchange forward to hedge this risk. However, it is difficult to sell forward contracts beyond one year.

Firms in the United States may borrow in the country where the foreign project is located. This is the usual way of hedging long-term foreign exchange risk. Thus, if Kihlstrom Equipment wishes to invest FF20 million in France, it may attempt to raise much of the cash in France. Kihlstrom should know that long-term hedging of foreign exchange risk by borrowing in the foreign country is effective only up to the amount borrowed. Any residual (equity) would not be hedged.

Another alternative is to find a country where interest rates are low. However, foreign interest rates may be lower because of lower expected foreign inflation. Thus, financial managers must be careful to look beyond nominal interest rates to real interest rates.

Short-Term and Medium-Term Financing

In raising short-term and medium-term cash, U.S. international firms often have a choice between borrowing from a U.S. bank at the U.S. interest rate or borrowing Eurodollars in the Eurocurrency market.

A **Eurodollar** is a dollar deposited in a bank outside the United States. For example, dollar deposits in Paris, France, are Eurodollars. The Eurocurrency markets are the banks (**Eurobanks**) that make loans and accept deposits in foreign currencies. Most Eurocurrency trading involves the borrowing and lending of time deposits at Eurobanks. For example, a Eurobank receives a Eurodollar deposit from a domestic U.S. bank. Afterward, the Eurobank will make a dollar-denominated loan to a borrowing party. This is the Eurocurrency market. It is not a retail bank market. The customers are corporations and governments.

One important characteristic of the Eurocurrency market is that loans are made on a floating-rate basis. The interest rates are set at a fixed margin above the London Interbank Offered Rate for the given period and currency involved. For example, if the margin is 0.5 percent for dollar loans and the current LIBOR is 8 percent for dollar loans, the dollar borrower will pay an interest rate of 8.5 percent. This rate is usually changed every six months. The dollar loans will have maturities ranging from 3 to 10 years.

It is obvious that in a perfectly competitive financial market the interest rate on a Eurodollar loan in a Eurocurrency market must be the same as the interest rate in the U.S. loan market. If the interest rate on a Eurodollar loan were higher than that on a domestic-dollar loan, arbitrageurs would borrow in the domestic-dollar market and lend in the Eurodollar market. This type of arbitrage trading would force interest rates to be the same in both dollar markets. However, from time to time there are differences between the Eurodollar loan rate and the domestic loan rate. Risk, government regulations, and taxes explain most of the differences.

International Bond Markets

The worldwide public bond market is made up of $21.5 trillion in bonds issued in many currencies. Table 32.4 shows that bonds denominated in dollars make up 44.6 percent of the total. The total worldwide bond market can be divided into domestic bonds and international bonds. Domestic bonds are those issued by a firm in its home country. International bonds are those issued by firms in another currency than the currency of the home country.

Trading in international bonds is over the counter and takes place in loosely connected individual markets. These individual markets are closely tied to the corresponding domestic bond markets. International bonds can be divided into two main types: foreign bonds and Eurobonds.

Foreign Bonds   Foreign bonds are bonds that are issued by foreign borrowers in a particular country's domestic bond market. They are often nicknamed for the country of issuance. They are denominated in the country's domestic currency. For example, suppose a Swiss watch company issues U.S. dollar-denominated bonds in the United States.

These foreign bonds would be called **Yankee bonds.** Like all foreign bonds issued in the United States, Yankee bonds must be registered under the Securities Act of 1933. Yankee bonds are usually rated by a bond-rating agency such as Standard & Poor's Corporation. Many Yankee bonds are listed on the New York Stock Exchange.

■ TABLE 32.4 **The Top 10 Bond Markets**

Bond Market	Total Publicly Issued (in $ billions)	Percentage of Total
U.S. dollar	$ 9,683	44.6%
Japanese yen	3,666	17.1
German mark	2,303	10.7
Italian lira	1,274	5.9
French franc	1,044	4.9
British pound	662	3.1
Canadian dollar	446	2.1
Dutch guilder	401	1.9
Belgian franc	387	1.8
Danish krone	288	1.3
Rest of the world	1,446	6.7
Total world bonds	$21,500	100.00%

Source: *Fortune,* November 10, 1997. See also *The Economist,* May 25, 1996.

Many foreign bonds, such as Yankee bonds, are registered. This makes them less attractive to investors having a disdain for tax authorities. For obvious reasons, these traders like the Eurobond market better than the foreign-bond market. Registered bonds have an ownership name assigned to the bond's serial number. The transfer of ownership of a registered bond can take place only via legal transfer of the registered name. Transfer agents (for example, commercial banks) are required.

Eurobonds   Eurobonds are denominated in a particular currency and are issued simultaneously in the bond markets of several countries. The prefix *Euro* means that the bonds are issued outside the countries in whose currencies they are denominated.

Most Eurobonds are bearer bonds. The ownership of the bonds is established by possession of the bond. In contrast, many foreign bonds are registered.

Most issues of Eurobonds are arranged by underwriting. However, some Eurobonds are privately placed.[5] A public issue with underwriting is similar to the public debt sold in domestic bond markets. The borrower sells its bonds to a group of management banks. Managing banks, in turn, sell the bonds to other banks. The other banks are divided into two groups: underwriters and sellers. The underwriters and sellers sell the bonds to dealers and fund investors. The managing banks also serve as underwriters and sellers. Underwriters usually sell Eurobonds on a firm commitment basis. That is, they are committed to buy the bonds at a prenegotiated price and attempt to sell them at a higher price in the market. Eurobonds appear as straight bonds, floating-rate notes, convertible bonds, zero-coupon bonds, mortgage-backed bonds, and dual-currency bonds.[6]

---

[5]In general, the issue costs are lower in private placements, as compared to public issues, and the yields are higher.

[6]There is a small but growing international equity market. International equities are stock issues underwritten and distributed to a mix of investors without regard to national borders. Our definition of international equity encompasses two basic types: those issues that have been internationally syndicated and distributed outside all national exchanges (termed *Euroequities*) and those that are issued by underwriters in domestic markets other than their own.

EXAMPLE

> A French automobile firm issues 50,000 bonds with a face value of $1,000 each. When the bonds are issued, they are managed by London merchant bankers and listed on the London Stock Exchange. These are Eurobonds. Each bond has a fixed coupon rate of 6 percent paid annually on August 15.

EXAMPLE

> An American firm makes an offering of $500 million of floating-rate notes. The notes are offered in London. The notes mature in 2020 and have semiannual interest of 0.5 percent above the six-month London Interbank Offered Rate. When the bonds are issued, the six-month LIBOR is 10 percent. Thus, in the first six months the American firm will pay interest (at the annual rate) of $10\% + 0.5\% = 10.5\%$.

32.7 REPORTING FOREIGN OPERATIONS

When a U.S. company prepares consolidated financial statements, the firm translates the local-currency accounts of foreign subsidiaries into the currency that is used for reporting purposes, usually the currency of the home country (that is, dollars). If exchange rates change during the accounting period, accounting gains or losses can occur.

Suppose a U.S. firm acquired a British company in 1982. At that time the exchange rate was £1 = $2. The British firm performed very well during the next few years (according to sterling measurements). During the same period, the value of the pound fell to $1.25. Did the corresponding increase in the value of the dollar make the U.S. company better off? Should the increase be reflected in the measurement of income?

These questions have been among the most controversial accounting questions in recent years. Two issues seem to arise:

1. What is the appropriate exchange rate to use for translating each balance-sheet account?
2. How should unrealized accounting gains and losses from foreign-currency translation be handled?

Currency is currently translated under complicated rules set out in Financial Accounting Standards Boards (FASB) Statement Number 52, which was issued in December 1981. For the most part, FASB Number 52 requires that all assets and liabilities be translated from the subsidiary's currency into the parent's, using the exchange rate that currently prevails. Gains and losses are accumulated in a special account within the shareholders' equity section of the balance sheet. Thus, the impact of translation gains and losses will not be recognized explicitly in net income until the underlying assets and liabilities are sold or liquidated.

CONCEPT QUESTION
? • What issues arise when reporting foreign operations?

32.8 SUMMARY AND CONCLUSIONS

The international firm has a more complicated life than the purely domestic firm. Management must understand the connection between interest rates, foreign-currency exchange rates, and inflation, and it must become aware of a large number of different financial market regulations and tax systems.

1. This chapter describes some fundamental theories of international finance:
   - The purchasing-power–parity theorem (law of one price).
   - The expectations theory of exchange rates.
   - The interest-rate–parity theorem.
2. The purchasing-power–parity theorem states that $1 should have the same purchasing power in each country. This means that an apple costs the same whether you buy it in New York or in Tokyo. One version of the purchasing-power–parity theorem states that the change in exchange rates between the currencies of two countries is connected to the inflation rates in the countries' commodity prices.
3. The expectations theory of exchange rates states that the forward rate of exchange is equal to the expected spot rate.
4. The interest-rate–parity theorem states that the interest-rate differential between two countries will be equal to the difference between the forward-exchange rate and the spot-exchange rate. This equality must prevail to prevent arbitrageurs from devising get-rich-quick strategies. The equality requires the rate of return on risk-free investments in the United States to be the same as that in other countries.

   Of course, in practice the purchasing-power–parity theorem and the interest-rate-parity theorem cannot work perfectly. Government regulations and taxes prevent this. However, there is much empirical work and intuition that suggests that these theories describe international financial markets in an approximate way.
5. The chapter also describes some of the problems of international capital budgeting. The net-present-value rule is still the appropriate way to choose projects, but the main problem is to choose the correct cost of capital. We argue that it should be equal to the rate that shareholders can expect to earn on a portfolio of domestic and foreign securities. This rate should be about the same as is true for a portfolio of domestic securities. However, two adjustments may be necessary:
   a. The cost of capital of an international firm may be *lower* than that of a domestic counterpart because of the benefits of international diversification.
   b. The cost of capital of an international firm may be *higher* because of the extra foreign political risks.
6. We briefly describe international financial markets. International firms may want to consider borrowing cash in the local financial market or in Eurocurrency and Eurobond markets. The interest rates are likely to appear different in these markets. Thus, international firms must be careful to consider differences in taxes and government regulations.

KEY TERMS

American Depository Receipt (ADR)   872

Cross rate   873

Eurobanks   889

Eurobonds   873

Eurocurrency   873

Eurodollar   889

European Currency Unit (ECU)   873

Exchange rate   875

Foreign bonds   874

Foreign exchange market   874

Forward-exchange rate   876

Forward trades   876

Gilts   874

Globalization   872

Interest-rate–parity theorem   879

Law of one price (LOP)   877

London Interbank Offered Rate (LIBOR)   874

Purchasing-power parity (PPP)   878

Relative purchasing-power parity (RPPP)   878

Spot-exchange rate   876

Spot trades   876

Swap rate   876

Swaps   874

Triangular arbitrage   876

Yankee bonds   889

SUGGESTED READINGS

Some of the latest academic research in international finance appears in the *Journal of Applied Corporate Finance:* "Global Finance" (Fall 1999); "Emerging Markets and the Asian Crisis" (Fall 1998); "Global Finance and Risk Management" (Fall 1997).

QUESTIONS AND PROBLEMS

Some Basics

32.1 Use Table 32.5 to answer the following questions:

a. What is the quote in direct terms for the British pound sterling and the U.S. dollar on spot exchange? What is it in European terms for the West German mark and the U.S. dollar?

b. Is the Japanese yen at a premium or a discount to the U.S. dollar in the forward markets?

c. To which type of foreign exchange participants would the forward prices of the Japanese yen be important? Why? What types of transactions might these participants use to cover their exposed risk in the foreign exchange markets?

d. Suppose you are a Swiss exporter of watches. If you are to be paid in U.S. dollars three months from now for a shipment made to the United States worth $100,000, how many Swiss francs would you receive if you locked in the price today with a forward contract? Would you buy or sell the dollar forward?

e. Calculate the U.K. pound–West German deutschemark cross rate for spot exchange in terms of the U.S. dollar. Do the same for the yen–Swiss franc cross rate.

f. In the text a swap transaction is described. Why might both banks profit from the use of such a mutual agreement?

32.2 Determine whether arbitrage opportunities exist given the following foreign exchange rates.

a. $1.8/L   DM2/$ DM4/L

b. ¥100/$ DM2/$ ¥50/DM

c. HKD7.8/$ ¥100/$ ¥14/HKD

The Law of One Price and Purchasing-Power Parity

32.3 Are the following statements true or false? Explain.

a. If the general price index in Japan rises faster than that in the United States (assuming that there are zero transaction costs, that no barriers to trade exist, and that products are identical in both countries), we would expect the yen to appreciate with respect to the dollar.

■ TABLE 32.5   Foreign Exchange, Week Ended Thursday, April 16, 200X

	Foreign Currency in Dollars	Dollar in Foreign Currency
f-Argent (Austral)	0.6515	1.5350
Australia (Dollar)	0.7160	1.3966
Austria (Schilling)	0.0784	12.76
c-Belgium (Franc)	0.0267	37.52
f-Belgium (Franc)	0.0264	37.82
Brazil (Cruzado)	0.0419	23.88
Britain (Pound)	1.6317	0.6129
30-day fut	1.6277	0.6144
60-day fut	1.6238	0.6158
90-day fut	1.6204	0.6171
Canada (Dollar)	0.7593	1.3170
30-day fut	0.7591	1.3173
60-day fut	0.7588	1.3179
90-day fut	0.7584	1.3185
y-Chile (Peso)	0.0047	211.34
Colombia (Peso)	0.0043	230.50
Denmark (Krone)	0.1466	6.8220
c-Egypt (Pound)	0.7353	1.3600
f-Ecuador (Sucre)	0.006325	158.10
Finland (Mark)	0.2270	4.4050
France (Franc)	0.1661	6.0220
Greece (Drachma)	0.0075	132.75
Hong Kong (Dollar)	0.1282	7.8015
y-India (Rupee)	0.0779	12.8400
Indonesia (Rupiah)	0.000611	1635.75
Ireland (Punt)	1.4710	0.6798
Israel (Shekel)	0.6246	1.6010
Italy (Lira)	0.000775	1290.50
Japan (Yen)	0.006993	143.00
30-day fut	0.007009	142.66
60-day fut	0.007027	142.30
90-day fut	0.007042	142.01
Jordan (Dinar)	3.0211	0.33100
Kuwait (Dinar)	3.6740	0.27218
Lebanon (Pound)	0.00813	123.00
z-Mexico (Peso)	0.000860	1163.00
Netherlands (Guilder)	0.4900	2.0410
New Zealand (Dollar)	0.5800	1.7241
Norway (Krone)	0.1477	6.7700
Pakistan (Rupee)	0.0578	17.30
y-Peru (Inti)	0.0673	14.85
z-Philippines (Peso)	0.0494	20.2500
Portugal (Escudo)	0.007153	139.80
Saudi Arabia (Rijal)	0.2666	3.7505
Singapore (Dollar)	0.4690	2.1320
S. Korea (Won)	0.001183	845.50
S. Africa (Rand)	0.4975	2.01010
Spain (Peseta)	0.007890	126.75
Sweden (Krona)	0.1586	6.3070

■ TABLE 32.5 *(concluded)*

	Foreign Currency in Dollars	Dollar in Foreign Currency
Switzerland (Franc)	0.6691	1.4945
30-day fut	0.6710	1.4904
60-day fut	0.6730	1.4858
90-day fut	0.6743	1.4830
Taiwan (NT $)	0.0294	33.97
Turkey (Lira)	0.001273	785.85
U.A.E. (Dirham)	0.2723	3.6723
z-Uruguay (Peso)	0.0050	201.4
z-Venezuela (Bolivar)	0.0422	23.7000
W. Germany (Mark)	0.5522	1.8110
30-day fut	0.5534	1.8070
60-day fut	0.5548	1.8023
90-day fut	0.5562	1.7978
Yugoslavia (Dinar)	0.001774	563.71

The Federal Reserve Board's index measuring the value of the dollar against 10 other currencies weighted on the basis of trade was 96.92 Thursday, up 18 points or 0.18 percent from Wednesday's 96.74. A year ago the index was 115.10.

Late prices as of 3:30 P.M. Eastern time as gathered by First American Bank of New York. c, commercial rate; f, financial rate; y, official rate; z, floating rate; r, revised.

Reprinted by permission of *The Wall Street Journal.* © Dow Jones & Company, Inc. All rights reserved.

  b. Suppose you are a French wine exporter who receives all payments in foreign currency. The French government begins to undertake an expansionary monetary policy. If it is certain that the result will be higher inflation in France than in other countries, you would be wise to use forward markets to protect yourself against future losses resulting from the deterioration of the value of the French franc.

  c. If you could accurately estimate differences in relative inflation between two countries over a long period of time (and other participants in the market were unable to do so), you could successfully speculate in spot currency markets.

32.4 The inflation rates for Empire White and Empire Black are 5 percent and 10 percent, respectively. At the beginning of the year, the spot rate between the two currencies is 2.5 black dollars per white dollar. What is the approximate spot rate at year-end?

Interest Rates and Exchange Rates: Interest-Rate Parity

32.5 A U.S. corporation, Forever Young, Inc., intends to import $1,000,000 worth of cosmetics from France and will make payment in FF three months from now. The foreign exchange spot rate of French franc to the U.S. dollar is FF6/$. Annual interest rates for U.S. dollar and French franc are 5 percent and 8 percent, respectively.

  a. What is the three-month forward rate for French franc if interest-rate parity holds?

  b. How can Forever Young, Inc., use currency trading to hedge against the foreign exchange risk associated with the purchase?

International Capital Budgeting

32.6 *a.* The treasurer of a major U.S. firm has $5 million to invest for three months. The annual interest rate in the United States is 12 percent. The interest rate in the United Kingdom is 9 percent. The spot rate of exchange is $2/£ and the three-month forward rate is $2.015/£. Ignoring transaction costs, in which country would the treasurer want to invest the company's capital if he can fix the exchange rate three months hence through a forward contract?

    b. The spot rate of foreign exchange between the United States and the United Kingdom at time *t* is \$1.50/£. If the interest rate in the United States is 13 percent and 8 percent in the United Kingdom, what would you expect the one-year forward rate to be if no immediate arbitrage opportunities existed?

    c. If you are an exporter who must make payments in foreign currency three months after receiving each shipment and you predict that the domestic currency will appreciate in value over this period, is there any value in hedging your currency exposure?

32.7 *a.* Suppose it is your task to evaluate two different investments in new subsidiaries for your company, one in your own country and the other in a foreign country. You calculate the cash flows of both projects to be identical after exchange-rate differences. Under what circumstances might you choose to invest in the foreign subsidiary? Give an example of a country where certain factors might influence you to alter this decision and invest at home.

    b. Suppose Strom Equipment comes across another investment in Germany. The project costs DM10 million and is expected to produce cash flows of DM4 million in year 1 and DM3 million in each of years 2 and 3. The current spot-exchange rate is \$0.5/DM1 and the current risk-free rate in the United States is 11.3 percent, compared to that in Germany of 6 percent. The appropriate discount rate for the project is estimated to be 15 percent, the U.S. cost of capital for the company. In addition, the subsidiary can be sold at the end of three years for an estimated DM2.1 million. What is the NPV of the project?

    c. An investment in a foreign subsidiary is estimated to have a positive NPV, after the discount rate used in the calculations is adjusted for political risk and any advantages from diversification. Does this mean the project is acceptable? Why or why not?

    d. If a U.S. firm raises funds for a foreign subsidiary, what are the disadvantages to borrowing in the United States? How would you overcome them?

International Financial Decisions

32.8 *a.* What is a Euroyen?

    b. If financial markets are perfectly competitive and the Eurodollar rate is above that offered in the U.S. loan market, you would immediately want to borrow money in the United States and invest it in Eurodollars. True or false? Explain.

    c. What distinguishes a Eurobond from a foreign bond? Which particular feature makes the Eurobond more popular than the foreign bond?

    d. How would you describe a bond issued by a Canadian firm in the United States with payments denominated in U.S. dollars?

APPENDIX A

Mathematical Tables

■ TABLE A.1   **Present Value of \$1 to Be Received after *T* Periods = $1/(1 + r)^T$**

Period	\multicolumn{9}{c}{Interest Rate}								
	1%	2%	3%	4%	5%	6%	7%	8%	9%
1	0.9901	0.9804	0.9709	0.9615	0.9524	0.9434	0.9346	0.9259	0.9174
2	0.9803	0.9612	0.9426	0.9246	0.9070	0.8900	0.8734	0.8573	0.8417
3	0.9706	0.9423	0.9151	0.8890	0.8638	0.8396	0.8163	0.7938	0.7722
4	0.9610	0.9238	0.8885	0.8548	0.8227	0.7921	0.7629	0.7350	0.7084
5	0.9515	0.9057	0.8626	0.8219	0.7835	0.7473	0.7130	0.6806	0.6499
6	0.9420	0.8880	0.8375	0.7903	0.7462	0.7050	0.6663	0.6302	0.5963
7	0.9327	0.8706	0.8131	0.7599	0.7107	0.6651	0.6227	0.5835	0.5470
8	0.9235	0.8535	0.7894	0.7307	0.6768	0.6274	0.5820	0.5403	0.5019
9	0.9143	0.8368	0.7664	0.7026	0.6446	0.5919	0.5439	0.5002	0.4604
10	0.9053	0.8203	0.7441	0.6756	0.6139	0.5584	0.5083	0.4632	0.4224
11	0.8963	0.8043	0.7224	0.6496	0.5847	0.5268	0.4751	0.4289	0.3875
12	0.8874	0.7885	0.7014	0.6246	0.5568	0.4970	0.4440	0.3971	0.3555
13	0.8787	0.7730	0.6810	0.6006	0.5303	0.4688	0.4150	0.3677	0.3262
14	0.8700	0.7579	0.6611	0.5775	0.5051	0.4423	0.3878	0.3405	0.2992
15	0.8613	0.7430	0.6419	0.5553	0.4810	0.4173	0.3624	0.3152	0.2745
16	0.8528	0.7284	0.6232	0.5339	0.4581	0.3936	0.3387	0.2919	0.2519
17	0.8444	0.7142	0.6050	0.5134	0.4363	0.3714	0.3166	0.2703	0.2311
18	0.8360	0.7002	0.5874	0.4936	0.4155	0.3503	0.2959	0.2502	0.2120
19	0.8277	0.6864	0.5703	0.4746	0.3957	0.3305	0.2765	0.2317	0.1945
20	0.8195	0.6730	0.5537	0.4564	0.3769	0.3118	0.2584	0.2145	0.1784
21	0.8114	0.6598	0.5375	0.4388	0.3589	0.2942	0.2415	0.1987	0.1637
22	0.8034	0.6468	0.5219	0.4220	0.3418	0.2775	0.2257	0.1839	0.1502
23	0.7954	0.6342	0.5067	0.4057	0.3256	0.2618	0.2109	0.1703	0.1378
24	0.7876	0.6217	0.4919	0.3901	0.3101	0.2470	0.1971	0.1577	0.1264
25	0.7798	0.6095	0.4776	0.3751	0.2953	0.2330	0.1842	0.1460	0.1160
30	0.7419	0.5521	0.4120	0.3083	0.2314	0.1741	0.1314	0.0994	0.0754
40	0.6717	0.4529	0.3066	0.2083	0.1420	0.0972	0.0668	0.0460	0.0318
50	0.6080	0.3715	0.2281	0.1407	0.0872	0.0543	0.0339	0.0213	0.0134

*The factor is zero to four decimal places.

■ TABLE A.1 *(concluded)*

Interest Rate										
10%	12%	14%	15%	16%	18%	20%	24%	28%	32%	36%
0.9091	0.8929	0.8772	0.8696	0.8621	0.8475	0.8333	0.8065	0.7813	0.7576	0.7353
0.8264	0.7972	0.7695	0.7561	0.7432	0.7182	0.6944	0.6504	0.6104	0.5739	0.5407
0.7513	0.7118	0.6750	0.6575	0.6407	0.6086	0.5787	0.5245	0.4768	0.4348	0.3975
0.6830	0.6355	0.5921	0.5718	0.5523	0.5158	0.4823	0.4230	0.3725	0.3294	0.2923
0.6209	0.5674	0.5194	0.4972	0.4761	0.4371	0.4019	0.3411	0.2910	0.2495	0.2149
0.5645	0.5066	0.4556	0.4323	0.4104	0.3704	0.3349	0.2751	0.2274	0.1890	0.1580
0.5132	0.4523	0.3996	0.3759	0.3538	0.3139	0.2791	0.2218	0.1776	0.1432	0.1162
0.4665	0.4039	0.3506	0.3269	0.3050	0.2660	0.2326	0.1789	0.1388	0.1085	0.0854
0.4241	0.3606	0.3075	0.2843	0.2630	0.2255	0.1938	0.1443	0.1084	0.0822	0.0628
0.3855	0.3220	0.2697	0.2472	0.2267	0.1911	0.1615	0.1164	0.0847	0.0623	0.0462
0.3505	0.2875	0.2366	0.2149	0.1954	0.1619	0.1346	0.0938	0.0662	0.0472	0.0340
0.3186	0.2567	0.2076	0.1869	0.1685	0.1372	0.1122	0.0757	0.0517	0.0357	0.0250
0.2897	0.2292	0.1821	0.1625	0.1452	0.1163	0.0935	0.0610	0.0404	0.0271	0.0184
0.2633	0.2046	0.1597	0.1413	0.1252	0.0985	0.0779	0.0492	0.0316	0.0205	0.0135
0.2394	0.1827	0.1401	0.1229	0.1079	0.0835	0.0649	0.0397	0.0247	0.0155	0.0099
0.2176	0.1631	0.1229	0.1069	0.0930	0.0708	0.0541	0.0320	0.0193	0.0118	0.0073
0.1978	0.1456	0.1078	0.0929	0.0802	0.0600	0.0451	0.0258	0.0150	0.0089	0.0054
0.1799	0.1300	0.0946	0.0808	0.0691	0.0508	0.0376	0.0208	0.0118	0.0068	0.0039
0.1635	0.1161	0.0829	0.0703	0.0596	0.0431	0.0313	0.0168	0.0092	0.0051	0.0029
0.1486	0.1037	0.0728	0.0611	0.0514	0.0365	0.0261	0.0135	0.0072	0.0039	0.0021
0.1351	0.0926	0.0638	0.0531	0.0443	0.0309	0.0217	0.0109	0.0056	0.0029	0.0016
0.1228	0.0826	0.0560	0.0462	0.0382	0.0262	0.0181	0.0088	0.0044	0.0022	0.0012
0.1117	0.0738	0.0491	0.0402	0.0329	0.0222	0.0151	0.0071	0.0034	0.0017	0.0008
0.1015	0.0659	0.0431	0.0349	0.0284	0.0188	0.0126	0.0057	0.0027	0.0013	0.0006
0.0923	0.0588	0.0378	0.0304	0.0245	0.0160	0.0105	0.0046	0.0021	0.0010	0.0005
0.0573	0.0334	0.0196	0.0151	0.0116	0.0070	0.0042	0.0016	0.0006	0.0002	0.0001
0.0221	0.0107	0.0053	0.0037	0.0026	0.0013	0.0007	0.0002	0.0001	*	*
0.0085	0.0035	0.0014	0.0009	0.0006	0.0003	0.0001	*	*	*	*

■ TABLE A.2   **Present Value of an Annuity of $1 per Period for T Periods $= [1 - 1/(1 + r)^T]/r$**

Number of Periods	Interest Rate								
	1%	2%	3%	4%	5%	6%	7%	8%	9%
1	0.9901	0.9804	0.9709	0.9615	0.9524	0.9434	0.9346	0.9259	0.9174
2	1.9704	1.9416	1.9135	1.8861	1.8594	1.8334	1.8080	1.7833	1.7591
3	2.9410	2.8839	2.8286	2.7751	2.7232	2.6730	2.6243	2.5771	2.5313
4	3.9020	3.8077	3.7171	3.6299	3.5460	3.4651	3.3872	3.3121	3.2397
5	4.8534	4.7135	4.5797	4.4518	4.3295	4.2124	4.1002	3.9927	3.8897
6	5.7955	5.6014	5.4172	5.2421	5.0757	4.9173	4.7665	4.6229	4.4859
7	6.7282	6.4720	6.2303	6.0021	5.7864	5.5824	5.3893	5.2064	5.0330
8	7.6517	7.3255	7.0197	6.7327	6.4632	6.2098	5.9713	5.7466	5.5348
9	8.5660	8.1622	7.7861	7.4353	7.1078	6.8017	6.5152	6.2469	5.9952
10	9.4713	8.9826	8.5302	8.1109	7.7217	7.3601	7.0236	6.7101	6.4177
11	10.3676	9.7868	9.2526	8.7605	8.3064	7.8869	7.4987	7.1390	6.8052
12	11.2551	10.5753	9.9540	9.3851	8.8633	8.3838	7.9427	7.5361	7.1607
13	12.1337	11.3484	10.6350	9.9856	9.3936	8.8527	8.3577	7.9038	7.4869
14	13.0037	12.1062	11.2961	10.5631	9.8986	9.2950	8.7455	8.2442	7.7862
15	13.8651	12.8493	11.9379	11.1184	10.3797	9.7122	9.1079	8.5595	8.0607
16	14.7179	13.5777	12.5611	11.6523	10.8378	10.1059	9.4466	8.8514	8.3126
17	15.5623	14.2919	13.1661	12.1657	11.2741	10.4773	9.7632	9.1216	8.5436
18	16.3983	14.9920	13.7535	12.6593	11.6896	10.8276	10.0591	9.3719	8.7556
19	17.2260	15.6785	14.3238	13.1339	12.0853	11.1581	10.3356	9.6036	8.9501
20	18.0456	16.3514	14.8775	13.5903	12.4622	11.4699	10.5940	9.8181	9.1285
21	18.8570	17.0112	15.4150	14.0292	12.8212	11.7641	10.8355	10.0168	9.2922
22	19.6604	17.6580	15.9369	14.4511	13.1630	12.0416	11.0612	10.2007	9.4424
23	20.4558	18.2922	16.4436	14.8568	13.4886	12.3034	11.2722	10.3741	9.5802
24	21.2434	18.9139	16.9355	15.2470	13.7986	12.5504	11.4693	10.5288	9.7066
25	22.0232	19.5235	17.4131	15.6221	14.0939	12.7834	11.6536	10.6748	9.8226
30	25.8077	22.3965	19.6004	17.2920	15.3725	13.7648	12.4090	11.2578	10.2737
40	32.8347	27.3555	23.1148	19.7928	17.1591	15.0463	13.3317	11.9246	10.7574
50	39.1961	31.4236	25.7298	21.4822	18.2559	15.7619	13.8007	12.2335	10.9617

■ TABLE A.2   *(concluded)*

			Interest	Rate					
10%	12%	14%	15%	16%	18%	20%	24%	28%	32%
0.9091	0.8929	0.8772	0.8696	0.8621	0.8475	0.8333	0.8065	0.7813	0.7576
1.7355	1.6901	1.6467	1.6257	1.6052	1.5656	1.5278	1.4568	1.3916	1.3315
2.4869	2.4018	2.3216	2.2832	2.2459	2.1743	2.1065	1.9813	1.8684	1.7663
3.1699	3.0373	2.9137	2.8550	2.7982	2.6901	2.5887	2.4043	2.2410	2.0957
3.7908	3.6048	3.4331	3.3522	3.2743	3.1272	2.9906	2.7454	2.5320	2.3452
4.3553	4.1114	3.8887	3.7845	3.6847	3.4976	3.3255	3.0205	2.7594	2.5342
4.8684	4.5638	4.2883	4.1604	4.0386	3.8115	3.6046	3.2423	2.9370	2.6775
5.3349	4.9676	4.6389	4.4873	4.3436	4.0776	3.8372	3.4212	3.0758	2.7860
5.7590	5.3282	4.9464	4.7716	4.6065	4.3030	4.0310	3.5655	3.1842	2.8681
6.1446	5.6502	5.2161	5.0188	4.8332	4.4941	4.1925	3.6819	3.2689	2.9304
6.4951	5.9377	5.4527	5.2337	5.0286	4.6560	4.3271	3.7757	3.3351	2.9776
6.8137	6.1944	5.6603	5.4206	5.1971	4.7932	4.4392	3.8514	3.3868	3.0133
7.1034	6.4235	5.8424	5.5831	5.3423	4.9095	4.5327	3.9124	3.4272	3.0404
7.3667	6.6282	6.0021	5.7245	5.4675	5.0081	4.6106	3.9616	3.4587	3.0609
7.6061	6.8109	6.1422	5.8474	5.5755	5.0916	4.6755	4.0013	3.4834	3.0764
7.8237	6.9740	6.2651	5.9542	5.6685	5.1624	4.7296	4.0333	3.5026	3.0882
8.0216	7.1196	6.3729	6.0472	5.7487	5.2223	4.7746	4.0591	3.5177	3.0971
8.2014	7.2497	6.4674	6.1280	5.8178	5.2732	4.8122	4.0799	3.5294	3.1039
8.3649	7.3658	6.5504	6.1982	5.8775	5.3162	4.8435	4.0967	3.5386	3.1090
8.5136	7.4694	6.6231	6.2593	5.9288	5.3527	4.8696	4.1103	3.5458	3.1129
8.6487	7.5620	6.6870	6.3125	5.9731	5.3837	4.8913	4.1212	3.5514	3.1158
8.7715	7.6446	6.7429	6.3587	6.0113	5.4099	4.9094	4.1300	3.5558	3.1180
8.8832	7.7184	6.7921	6.3988	6.0442	5.4321	4.9245	4.1371	3.5592	3.1197
8.9847	7.7843	6.8351	6.4338	6.0726	5.4509	4.9371	4.1428	3.5619	3.1210
9.0770	7.8431	6.8729	6.4641	6.0971	5.4669	4.9476	4.1474	3.5640	3.1220
9.4269	8.0552	7.0027	6.5660	6.1772	5.5168	4.9789	4.1601	3.5693	3.1242
9.7791	8.2438	7.1050	6.6418	6.2335	5.5482	4.9966	4.1659	3.5712	3.1250
9.9148	8.3045	7.1327	6.6605	6.2463	5.5541	4.9995	4.1666	3.5714	3.1250

■ TABLE A.3   Future Value of $1 at the End of T Periods $= (1 + r)^T$

Period	Interest Rate								
	1%	2%	3%	4%	5%	6%	7%	8%	9%
1	1.0100	1.0200	1.0300	1.0400	1.0500	1.0600	1.0700	1.0800	1.0900
2	1.0201	1.0404	1.0609	1.0816	1.1025	1.1236	1.1449	1.1664	1.1881
3	1.0303	1.0612	1.0927	1.1249	1.1576	1.1910	1.2250	1.2597	1.2950
4	1.0406	1.0824	1.1255	1.1699	1.2155	1.2625	1.3108	1.3605	1.4116
5	1.0510	1.1041	1.1593	1.2167	1.2763	1.3382	1.4026	1.4693	1.5386
6	1.0615	1.1262	1.1941	1.2653	1.3401	1.4185	1.5007	1.5869	1.6771
7	1.0721	1.1487	1.2299	1.3159	1.4071	1.5036	1.6058	1.7138	1.8280
8	1.0829	1.1717	1.2668	1.3686	1.4775	1.5938	1.7182	1.8509	1.9926
9	1.0937	1.1951	1.3048	1.4233	1.5513	1.6895	1.8385	1.9990	2.1719
10	1.1046	1.2190	1.3439	1.4802	1.6289	1.7908	1.9672	2.1589	2.3674
11	1.1157	1.2434	1.3842	1.5395	1.7103	1.8983	2.1049	2.3316	2.5804
12	1.1268	1.2682	1.4258	1.6010	1.7959	2.0122	2.2522	2.5182	2.8127
13	1.1381	1.2936	1.4685	1.6651	1.8856	2.1329	2.4098	2.7196	3.0658
14	1.1495	1.3195	1.5126	1.7317	1.9799	2.2609	2.5785	2.9372	3.3417
15	1.1610	1.3459	1.5580	1.8009	2.0789	2.3966	2.7590	3.1722	3.6425
16	1.1726	1.3728	1.6047	1.8730	2.1829	2.5404	2.9522	3.4259	3.9703
17	1.1843	1.4002	1.6528	1.9479	2.2920	2.6928	3.1588	3.7000	4.3276
18	1.1961	1.4282	1.7024	2.0258	2.4066	2.8543	3.3799	3.9960	4.7171
19	1.2081	1.4568	1.7535	2.1068	2.5270	3.0256	3.6165	4.3157	5.1417
20	1.2202	1.4859	1.8061	2.1911	2.6533	3.2071	3.8697	4.6610	5.6044
21	1.2324	1.5157	1.8603	2.2788	2.7860	3.3996	4.1406	5.0338	6.1088
22	1.2447	1.5460	1.9161	2.3699	2.9253	3.6035	4.4304	5.4365	6.6586
23	1.2572	1.5769	1.9736	2.4647	3.0715	3.8197	4.7405	5.8715	7.2579
24	1.2697	1.6084	2.0328	2.5633	3.2251	4.0489	5.0724	6.3412	7.9111
25	1.2824	1.6406	2.0938	2.6658	3.3864	4.2919	5.4274	6.8485	8.6231
30	1.3478	1.8114	2.4273	3.2434	4.3219	5.7435	7.6123	10.063	13.268
40	1.4889	2.2080	3.2620	4.8010	7.0400	10.286	14.974	21.725	31.409
50	1.6446	2.6916	4.3839	7.1067	11.467	18.420	29.457	46.902	74.358
60	1.8167	3.2810	5.8916	10.520	18.679	32.988	57.946	101.26	176.03

*FVIV > 99,999.

■ TABLE A.3   *(concluded)*

					Interest Rate					
10%	12%	14%	15%	16%	18%	20%	24%	28%	32%	36%
1.1000	1.1200	1.1400	1.1500	1.1600	1.1800	1.2000	1.2400	1.2800	1.3200	1.3600
1.2100	1.2544	1.2996	1.3225	1.3456	1.3924	1.4400	1.5376	1.6384	1.7424	1.8496
1.3310	1.4049	1.4815	1.5209	1.5609	1.6430	1.7280	1.9066	2.0972	2.3000	2.5155
1.4641	1.5735	1.6890	1.7490	1.8106	1.9388	2.0736	2.3642	2.6844	3.0360	3.4210
1.6105	1.7623	1.9254	2.0114	2.1003	2.2878	2.4883	2.9316	3.4360	4.0075	4.6526
1.7716	1.9738	2.1950	2.3131	2.4364	2.6996	2.9860	3.6352	4.3980	5.2899	6.3275
1.9487	2.2107	2.5023	2.6600	2.8262	3.1855	3.5832	4.5077	5.6295	6.9826	8.6054
2.1436	2.4760	2.8526	3.0590	3.2784	3.7589	4.2998	5.5895	7.2058	9.2170	11.703
2.3579	2.7731	3.2519	3.5179	3.8030	4.4355	5.1598	6.9310	9.2234	12.166	15.917
2.5937	3.1058	3.7072	4.0456	4.4114	5.2338	6.1917	8.5944	11.806	16.060	21.647
2.8531	3.4785	4.2262	4.6524	5.1173	6.1759	7.4301	10.657	15.112	21.199	29.439
3.1384	3.8960	4.8179	5.3503	5.9360	7.2876	8.9161	13.215	19.343	27.983	40.037
3.4523	4.3635	5.4924	6.1528	6.8858	8.5994	10.699	16.386	24.759	36.937	54.451
3.7975	4.8871	6.2613	7.0757	7.9875	10.147	12.839	20.319	31.691	48.757	74.053
4.1772	5.4736	7.1379	8.1371	9.2655	11.974	15.407	25.196	40.565	64.359	100.71
4.5950	6.1304	8.1372	9.3576	10.748	14.129	18.488	31.243	51.923	84.954	136.97
5.0545	6.8660	9.2765	10.761	12.468	16.672	22.186	38.741	66.461	112.14	186.28
5.5599	7.6900	10.575	12.375	14.463	19.673	26.623	48.039	86.071	148.02	253.34
6.1159	8.6128	12.056	14.232	16.777	23.214	31.948	59.568	108.89	195.39	344.54
6.7275	9.6463	13.743	16.367	19.461	27.393	38.338	73.864	139.38	257.92	468.57
7.4002	10.804	15.668	18.822	22.574	32.324	46.005	91.592	178.41	340.45	637.26
8.1403	12.100	17.861	21.645	26.186	38.142	55.206	113.57	228.36	449.39	866.67
8.9543	13.552	20.362	24.891	30.376	45.008	66.247	140.83	292.30	593.20	1178.7
9.8497	15.179	23.212	28.625	35.236	53.109	79.497	174.63	374.14	783.02	1603.0
10.835	17.000	26.462	32.919	40.874	62.669	95.396	216.54	478.90	1033.6	2180.1
17.449	29.960	50.950	66.212	85.850	143.37	237.38	634.82	1645.5	4142.1	10143.
45.259	93.051	188.88	267.86	378.72	750.38	1469.8	5455.9	19427.	66521.	*
117.39	289.00	700.23	1083.7	1670.7	3927.4	9100.4	46890.	*	*	*
304.48	897.60	2595.9	4384.0	7370.2	20555.	56348.	*	*	*	*

■ TABLE A.4   Sum of Annuity of \$1 per Period for *T* Periods = $[(1 + r)^T - 1]/r$

Number of Periods	Interest Rate								
	1%	2%	3%	4%	5%	6%	7%	8%	9%
1	1.0000	1.0000	1.0000	1.0000	1.0000	1.0000	1.0000	1.0000	1.0000
2	2.0100	2.0200	2.0300	2.0400	2.0500	2.0600	2.0700	2.0800	2.0900
3	3.0301	3.0604	3.0909	3.1216	3.1525	3.1836	3.2149	3.2464	3.2781
4	4.0604	4.1216	4.1836	4.2465	4.3101	4.3746	4.4399	4.5061	4.5731
5	5.1010	5.2040	5.3091	5.4163	5.5256	5.6371	5.7507	5.8666	5.9847
6	6.1520	6.3081	6.4684	6.6330	6.8019	6.9753	7.1533	7.3359	7.5233
7	7.2135	7.4343	7.6625	7.8983	8.1420	8.3938	8.6540	8.9228	9.2004
8	8.2857	8.5830	8.8932	9.2142	9.5491	9.8975	10.260	10.637	11.028
9	9.3685	9.7546	10.159	10.583	11.027	11.491	11.978	12.488	13.021
10	10.462	10.950	11.464	12.006	12.578	13.181	13.816	14.487	15.193
11	11.567	12.169	12.808	13.486	14.207	14.972	15.784	16.645	17.560
12	12.683	13.412	14.192	15.026	15.917	16.870	17.888	18.977	20.141
13	13.809	14.680	15.618	16.627	17.713	18.882	20.141	21.495	22.953
14	14.947	15.974	17.086	18.292	19.599	21.015	22.550	24.215	26.019
15	16.097	17.293	18.599	20.024	21.579	23.276	25.129	27.152	29.361
16	17.258	18.639	20.157	21.825	23.657	25.673	27.888	30.324	33.003
17	18.430	20.012	21.762	23.698	25.840	28.213	30.840	33.750	36.974
18	19.615	21.412	23.414	25.645	28.132	30.906	33.999	37.450	41.301
19	20.811	22.841	25.117	27.671	30.539	33.760	37.379	41.446	46.018
20	22.019	24.297	26.870	29.778	33.066	36.786	40.995	45.762	51.160
21	23.239	25.783	28.676	31.969	35.719	39.993	44.865	50.423	56.765
22	24.472	27.299	30.537	34.248	38.505	43.392	49.006	55.457	62.873
23	25.716	28.845	32.453	36.618	41.430	46.996	53.436	60.893	69.532
24	26.973	30.422	34.426	39.083	44.502	50.816	58.177	66.765	76.790
25	28.243	32.030	36.459	41.646	47.727	54.865	63.249	73.106	84.701
30	34.785	40.568	47.575	56.085	66.439	79.058	94.461	113.28	136.31
40	48.886	60.402	75.401	95.026	120.80	154.76	199.64	259.06	337.88
50	64.463	84.579	112.80	152.67	209.35	290.34	406.53	573.77	815.08
60	81.670	114.05	163.05	237.99	353.58	533.13	813.52	1253.2	1944.8

*FVIFA > 99,999.

■ TABLE A.4   (concluded)

					Interest Rate					
10%	12%	14%	15%	16%	18%	20%	24%	28%	32%	36%
1.0000	1.0000	1.0000	1.0000	1.0000	1.0000	1.0000	1.0000	1.0000	1.0000	1.0000
2.1000	2.1200	2.1400	2.1500	2.1600	2.1800	2.2000	2.2400	2.2800	2.3200	2.3600
3.3100	3.3744	3.4396	3.4725	3.5056	3.5724	3.6400	3.7776	3.9184	4.0624	4.2096
4.6410	4.7793	4.9211	4.9934	5.0665	5.2154	5.3680	5.6842	6.0156	6.3624	6.7251
6.1051	6.3528	6.6101	6.7424	6.8771	7.1542	7.4416	8.0484	8.6999	9.3983	10.146
7.7156	8.1152	8.5355	8.7537	8.9775	9.4420	9.9299	10.980	12.136	13.406	14.799
9.4872	10.089	10.730	11.067	11.414	12.142	12.916	14.615	16.534	18.696	21.126
11.436	12.300	13.233	13.727	14.240	15.327	16.499	19.123	22.163	25.678	29.732
13.579	14.776	16.085	16.786	17.519	19.086	20.799	24.712	29.369	34.895	41.435
15.937	17.549	19.337	20.304	21.321	23.521	25.959	31.643	38.593	47.062	57.352
18.531	20.655	23.045	24.349	25.733	28.755	32.150	40.238	50.398	63.122	78.998
21.384	24.133	27.271	29.002	30.850	34.931	39.581	50.895	65.510	84.320	108.44
24.523	28.029	32.089	34.352	36.786	42.219	48.497	64.110	84.853	112.30	148.47
27.975	32.393	37.581	40.505	43.672	50.818	59.196	80.496	109.61	149.24	202.93
31.772	37.280	43.842	47.580	51.660	60.965	72.035	100.82	141.30	198.00	276.98
35.950	42.753	50.980	55.717	60.925	72.939	87.442	126.01	181.87	262.36	377.69
40.545	48.884	59.118	65.075	71.673	87.068	105.93	157.25	233.79	347.31	514.66
45.599	55.750	68.394	75.836	84.141	103.74	128.12	195.99	300.25	459.45	700.94
51.159	64.440	78.969	88.212	98.603	123.41	154.74	244.03	385.32	607.47	954.28
57.275	72.052	91.025	102.44	115.38	146.63	186.69	303.60	494.21	802.86	1298.8
64.002	81.699	104.77	118.81	134.84	174.02	225.03	377.46	633.59	1060.8	1767.4
71.403	92.503	120.44	137.63	157.41	206.34	271.03	469.06	812.00	1401.2	2404.7
79.543	104.60	138.30	159.28	183.60	244.49	326.24	582.63	1040.4	1850.6	3271.3
88.497	118.16	158.66	184.17	213.98	289.49	392.48	723.46	1332.7	2443.8	4450.0
98.347	133.33	181.87	212.79	249.21	342.60	471.98	898.09	1706.8	3226.8	6053.0
164.49	241.33	356.79	434.75	530.31	790.95	1181.9	2640.9	5873.2	12941.	28172.3
442.59	767.09	1342.0	1779.1	2360.8	4163.2	7343.9	22729.	69377.	*	*
1163.9	2400.0	4994.5	7217.7	10436.	21813.	45497.	*	*	*	*
3034.8	7471.6	18535.	29220.	46058.	*	*	*	*	*	*

■ TABLE A.5   **Future Value of $1 with a Continuously Compounded Rate *r* for *T* Periods: Values of e^{rT}**

Period (T)	Continuously Compounded Rate (r)									
	1%	2%	3%	4%	5%	6%	7%	8%	9%	10%
1	1.0101	1.0202	1.0305	1.0408	1.0513	1.0618	1.0725	1.0833	1.0942	1.1052
2	1.0202	1.0408	1.0618	1.0833	1.1052	1.1275	1.1503	1.1735	1.1972	1.2214
3	1.0305	1.0618	1.0942	1.1275	1.1618	1.1972	1.2337	1.2712	1.3100	1.3499
4	1.0408	1.0833	1.1275	1.1735	1.2214	1.2712	1.3231	1.3771	1.4333	1.4918
5	1.0513	1.1052	1.1618	1.2214	1.2840	1.3499	1.4191	1.4918	1.5683	1.6487
6	1.0618	1.1275	1.1972	1.2712	1.3499	1.4333	1.5220	1.6161	1.7160	1.8221
7	1.0725	1.1503	1.2337	1.3231	1.4191	1.5220	1.6323	1.7507	1.8776	2.0138
8	1.0833	1.1735	1.2712	1.3771	1.4918	1.6161	1.7507	1.8965	2.0544	2.2255
9	1.0942	1.1972	1.3100	1.4333	1.5683	1.7160	1.8776	2.0544	2.2479	2.4596
10	1.1052	1.2214	1.3499	1.4918	1.6487	1.8221	2.0138	2.2255	2.4596	2.7183
11	1.1163	1.2461	1.3910	1.5527	1.7333	1.9348	2.1598	2.4109	2.6912	3.0042
12	1.1275	1.2712	1.4333	1.6161	1.8221	2.0544	2.3164	2.6117	2.9447	3.3201
13	1.1388	1.2969	1.4770	1.6820	1.9155	2.1815	2.4843	2.8292	3.2220	3.6693
14	1.1503	1.3231	1.5220	1.7507	2.0138	2.3164	2.6645	3.0649	3.5254	4.0552
15	1.1618	1.3499	1.5683	1.8221	2.1170	2.4596	2.8577	3.3201	3.8574	4.4817
16	1.1735	1.3771	1.6161	1.8965	2.2255	2.6117	3.0649	3.5966	4.2207	4.9530
17	1.1853	1.4049	1.6653	1.9739	2.3396	2.7732	3.2871	3.8962	4.6182	5.4739
18	1.1972	1.4333	1.7160	2.0544	2.4596	2.9447	3.5254	4.2207	5.0531	6.0496
19	1.2092	1.4623	1.7683	2.1383	2.5857	3.1268	3.7810	4.5722	5.5290	6.6859
20	1.2214	1.4918	1.8221	2.2255	2.7183	3.3201	4.0552	4.9530	6.0496	7.3891
21	1.2337	1.5220	1.8776	2.3164	2.8577	3.5254	4.3492	5.3656	6.6194	8.1662
22	1.2461	1.5527	1.9348	2.4109	3.0042	3.7434	4.6646	5.8124	7.2427	9.0250
23	1.2586	1.5841	1.9937	2.5093	3.1582	3.9749	5.0028	6.2965	7.9248	9.9742
24	1.2712	1.6161	2.0544	2.6117	3.3201	4.2207	5.3656	6.8210	8.6711	11.0232
25	1.2840	1.6487	2.1170	2.7183	3.4903	4.4817	5.7546	7.3891	9.4877	12.1825
30	1.3499	1.8221	2.4596	3.3204	4.4817	6.0496	8.1662	11.0232	14.8797	20.0855
35	1.4191	2.0138	2.8577	4.0552	5.7546	8.1662	11.5883	16.4446	23.3361	33.1155
40	1.4918	2.2255	3.3201	4.9530	7.3891	11.0232	16.4446	24.5235	36.5982	54.5982
45	1.5683	2.4596	3.8574	6.0496	9.4877	14.8797	23.3361	36.5982	57.3975	90.0171
50	1.6487	2.7183	4.4817	7.3891	12.1825	20.0855	33.1155	54.5982	90.0171	148.4132
55	1.7333	3.0042	5.2070	9.0250	15.6426	27.1126	46.9931	81.4509	141.1750	244.6919
60	1.8221	3.3201	6.0496	11.0232	20.0855	36.5982	66.6863	121.5104	221.4064	403.4288

■ TABLE A.5   (*continued*)

			Continuously Compounded Rate (*r*)							
11%	12%	13%	14%	15%	16%	17%	18%	19%	20%	21%
1.1163	1.1275	1.1388	1.1503	1.1618	1.1735	1.1853	1.1972	1.2092	1.2214	1.2337
1.2461	1.2712	1.2969	1.3231	1.3499	1.3771	1.4049	1.4333	1.4623	1.4918	1.5220
1.3910	1.4333	1.4770	1.5220	1.5683	1.6161	1.6653	1.7160	1.7683	1.8221	1.8776
1.5527	1.6161	1.6820	1.7507	1.8221	1.8965	1.9739	2.0544	2.1383	2.2255	2.3164
1.7333	1.8221	1.9155	2.0138	2.1170	2.2255	2.3396	2.4596	2.5857	2.7183	2.8577
1.9348	2.0544	2.1815	2.3164	2.4596	2.6117	2.7732	2.9447	3.1268	3.3201	3.5254
2.1598	2.3164	2.4843	2.6645	2.8577	3.0649	3.2871	3.5254	3.7810	4.0552	4.3492
2.4109	2.6117	2.8292	3.0649	3.3201	3.5966	3.8962	4.2207	4.5722	4.9530	5.3656
2.6912	2.9447	3.2220	3.5254	3.8574	4.2207	4.6182	5.0531	5.5290	6.0496	6.6194
3.0042	3.3201	3.6693	4.0552	4.4817	4.9530	5.4739	6.0496	6.6859	7.3891	8.1662
3.3535	3.7434	4.1787	4.6646	5.2070	5.8124	6.4883	7.2427	8.0849	9.0250	10.0744
3.7434	4.2207	4.7588	5.3656	6.0496	6.8210	7.6906	8.6711	9.7767	11.0232	12.4286
4.1787	4.7588	5.4195	6.1719	7.0287	8.0045	9.1157	10.3812	11.8224	13.4637	15.3329
4.6646	5.3656	6.1719	7.0993	8.1662	9.3933	10.8049	12.4286	14.2963	16.4446	18.9158
5.2070	6.0496	7.0287	8.1662	9.4877	11.0232	12.0871	14.8797	17.2878	20.0855	23.3361
5.8124	6.8210	8.0045	9.3933	11.0232	12.9358	15.1803	17.8143	20.9052	24.5325	28.7892
6.4883	7.6906	9.1157	10.8049	12.8071	15.1803	17.9933	21.3276	25.2797	29.9641	35.5166
7.2427	8.6711	10.3812	12.4286	14.8797	17.8143	21.3276	25.5337	30.5694	36.5982	43.8160
8.0849	9.7767	11.8224	14.2963	17.2878	20.9052	25.2797	30.5694	36.9661	44.7012	54.0549
9.0250	11.0232	13.4637	16.4446	20.0855	24.5325	29.9641	36.5982	44.7012	54.5982	66.6863
10.0744	12.4286	15.3329	18.9158	23.3361	28.7892	35.5166	43.8160	54.0549	66.6863	82.2695
11.2459	14.0132	17.4615	21.7584	27.1126	33.7844	42.0980	52.4573	65.3659	81.4509	101.4940
12.5535	15.7998	19.8857	25.0281	31.5004	39.6464	49.8990	62.8028	79.0436	99.4843	125.2110
14.0132	17.8143	22.6464	28.7892	36.5982	46.5255	59.1455	75.1886	95.5835	121.5104	154.4700
15.6426	20.0855	25.7903	33.1155	42.5211	54.5982	70.1054	90.0171	115.5843	148.4132	190.5663
27.1126	36.5982	49.4024	66.6863	90.0171	121.5104	164.0219	221.4064	298.8674	403.4288	544.5719
46.9931	66.6863	94.6324	134.2898	190.5663	270.4264	383.7533	544.5719	772.7843	1096.633	1556.197
81.4509	121.5104	181.2722	270.4264	403.4288	601.8450	897.8473	1339.431	1998.196	2980.958	4447.067
141.1750	221.4064	347.2344	544.5719	854.0588	1339.431	2100.646	3294.468	5166.754	8103.084	12708.17
244.6919	403.4288	665.1416	1096.633	1808.042	2980.958	4914.769	8103.084	13359.73	22026.47	36315.50
424.1130	735.0952	1274.106	2208.348	3827.626	6634.244	11498.82	19930.37	34544.37	59874.14	103777.0
735.0952	1339.431	2440.602	4447.067	8103.084	14764.78	26903.19	49020.80	89321.72	162754.8	296558.6

■ TABLE A.5   *(concluded)*

Period (T)	Continuously Compounded Rate (r)						
	22%	23%	24%	25%	26%	27%	28%
1	1.2461	1.2586	1.2712	1.2840	1.2969	1.3100	1.3231
2	1.5527	1.5841	1.6161	1.6487	1.6820	1.7160	1.7507
3	1.9348	1.9937	2.0544	2.1170	2.1815	2.2479	2.3164
4	2.4109	2.5093	2.6117	2.7183	2.8292	2.9447	3.0649
5	3.0042	3.1582	3.3201	3.4903	3.6693	3.8574	4.0552
6	3.7434	3.9749	4.2207	4.4817	4.7588	5.0351	5.3656
7	4.6646	5.0028	5.3656	5.7546	6.1719	6.6194	7.0993
8	5.8124	6.2965	6.8210	7.3891	8.0045	8.6711	9.3933
9	7.2427	7.9248	8.6711	9.4877	10.3812	11.3589	12.4286
10	9.0250	9.9742	11.0232	12.1825	13.4637	14.8797	16.4446
11	11.2459	12.5535	14.0132	15.6426	17.4615	19.4919	21.7584
12	14.0132	15.7998	17.8143	20.0855	22.6464	25.5337	28.7892
13	17.4615	19.8857	22.6464	25.7903	29.3708	33.4483	38.0918
14	21.7584	25.0281	28.7892	33.1155	38.0918	43.8160	50.4004
15	27.1126	31.5004	36.5982	42.5211	49.4024	57.3975	66.6863
16	33.7844	39.6464	46.5255	54.5982	64.0715	75.1886	88.2347
17	42.0980	49.8990	59.1455	70.1054	83.0963	98.4944	116.7459
18	52.4573	62.8028	75.1886	90.0171	107.7701	129.0242	154.4700
19	65.3659	79.0436	95.5835	115.5843	139.7702	169.0171	204.3839
20	81.4509	99.4843	121.5104	148.4132	181.2722	221.4064	270.4264
21	101.4940	125.2110	154.4700	190.5663	235.0974	290.0345	357.8092
22	126.4694	157.5905	196.3699	244.6919	304.9049	379.9349	473.4281
23	157.5905	198.3434	249.6350	314.1907	395.4404	497.7013	626.4068
24	196.3699	249.6350	317.3483	403.4288	512.8585	651.9709	828.8175
25	244.6919	314.1907	403.4288	518.0128	665.1416	854.0588	1096.633
30	735.0952	992.2747	1339.431	1808.042	2440.602	3294.468	4447.067
35	2208.348	3133.795	4447.067	6310.688	8955.293	12708.17	18033.74
40	6634.244	9897.129	14764.78	22026.47	32859.63	49020.80	73130.44
45	19930.37	31257.04	49020.80	76879.92	120571.7	189094.1	296558.6
50	59874.14	98715.77	162754.8	268337.3	442413.4	729416.4	1202604
55	179871.9	311763.4	540364.9	936589.2	1623346	2813669	4876801
60	540364.9	984609.1	1794075	3269017	5956538	10853520	19776403

■ TABLE A.6   **Present Value of $1 with a Continuous Discount Rate *r* for *T* Periods: Values of e^{-rT}**

Period (T)	Continuous Discount Rate (r)						
	1%	2%	3%	4%	5%	6%	7%
1	0.9900	0.9802	0.9704	0.9608	0.9512	0.9418	0.9324
2	0.9802	0.9608	0.9418	0.9231	0.9048	0.8869	0.8694
3	0.9704	0.9418	0.9139	0.8869	0.8607	0.8353	0.8106
4	0.9608	0.9231	0.8869	0.8521	0.8187	0.7866	0.7558
5	0.9512	0.9048	0.8607	0.8187	0.7788	0.7408	0.7047
6	0.9418	0.8869	0.8353	0.7866	0.7408	0.6977	0.6570
7	0.9324	0.8694	0.8106	0.7558	0.7047	0.6570	0.6126
8	0.9231	0.8521	0.7866	0.7261	0.6703	0.6188	0.5712
9	0.9139	0.8353	0.7634	0.6977	0.6376	0.5827	0.5326
10	0.9048	0.8187	0.7408	0.6703	0.6065	0.5488	0.4966
11	0.8958	0.8025	0.7189	0.6440	0.5769	0.5169	0.4630
12	0.8869	0.7866	0.6977	0.6188	0.5488	0.4868	0.4317
13	0.8781	0.7711	0.6771	0.5945	0.5220	0.4584	0.4025
14	0.8694	0.7558	0.6570	0.5712	0.4966	0.4317	0.3753
15	0.8607	0.7408	0.6376	0.5488	0.4724	0.4066	0.3499
16	0.8521	0.7261	0.6188	0.5273	0.4493	0.3829	0.3263
17	0.8437	0.7118	0.6005	0.5066	0.4274	0.3606	0.3042
18	0.8353	0.6977	0.5827	0.4868	0.4066	0.3396	0.2837
19	0.8270	0.6839	0.5655	0.4677	0.3867	0.3198	0.2645
20	0.8187	0.6703	0.5488	0.4493	0.3679	0.3012	0.2466
21	0.8106	0.6570	0.5326	0.4317	0.3499	0.2837	0.2299
22	0.8025	0.6440	0.5169	0.4148	0.3329	0.2671	0.2144
23	0.7945	0.6313	0.5016	0.3985	0.3166	0.2516	0.1999
24	0.7866	0.6188	0.4868	0.3829	0.3012	0.2369	0.1864
25	0.7788	0.6065	0.4724	0.3679	0.2865	0.2231	0.1738
30	0.7408	0.5488	0.4066	0.3012	0.2231	0.1653	0.1225
35	0.7047	0.4966	0.3499	0.2466	0.1738	0.1225	0.0863
40	0.6703	0.4493	0.3012	0.2019	0.1353	0.0907	0.0608
45	0.6376	0.4066	0.2592	0.1653	0.1054	0.0672	0.0429
50	0.6065	0.3679	0.2231	0.1353	0.0821	0.0498	0.0302
55	0.5769	0.3329	0.1920	0.1108	0.0639	0.0369	0.0213
60	0.5488	0.3012	0.1653	0.0907	0.0498	0.0273	0.0150

■ TABLE A.6   (*continued*)

Period (T)	Continuous Discount Rate (r)									
	8%	9%	10%	11%	12%	13%	14%	15%	16%	17%
1	0.9231	0.9139	0.9048	0.8958	0.8869	0.8781	0.8694	0.8607	0.8521	0.8437
2	0.8521	0.8353	0.8187	0.8025	0.7866	0.7711	0.7558	0.7408	0.7261	0.7118
3	0.7866	0.7634	0.7408	0.7189	0.6977	0.6771	0.6570	0.6376	0.6188	0.6005
4	0.7261	0.6977	0.6703	0.6440	0.6188	0.5945	0.5712	0.5488	0.5273	0.5066
5	0.6703	0.6376	0.6065	0.5769	0.5488	0.5220	0.4966	0.4724	0.4493	0.4274
6	0.6188	0.5827	0.5488	0.5169	.04868	0.4584	0.4317	0.4066	0.3829	0.3606
7	0.5712	0.5326	0.4966	0.4630	0.4317	0.4025	0.3753	0.3499	0.3263	0.3042
8	0.5273	0.4868	0.4493	0.4148	0.3829	0.3535	0.3263	0.3012	0.2780	0.2576
9	0.4868	0.4449	0.4066	0.3716	0.3396	0.3104	0.2837	0.2592	0.2369	0.2165
10	0.4493	0.4066	0.3679	0.3329	0.3012	0.2725	0.2466	0.2231	0.2019	0.1827
11	0.4148	0.3716	0.3329	0.2982	0.2671	0.2393	0.2144	0.1920	0.1720	0.1541
12	0.3829	0.3396	0.3012	0.2671	0.2369	0.2101	0.1864	0.1653	0.1466	0.1300
13	0.3535	0.3104	0.2725	0.2393	0.2101	0.1845	0.1620	0.1423	0.1249	0.1097
14	0.3263	0.2837	0.2466	0.2144	0.1864	0.1620	0.1409	0.1225	0.1065	0.0926
15	0.3012	0.2592	0.2231	0.1920	0.1653	0.1423	0.1225	0.1054	0.0907	0.0781
16	0.2780	0.2369	0.2019	0.1720	0.1466	0.1249	0.1065	0.0907	0.0773	0.0659
17	0.2567	0.2165	0.1827	0.1541	0.1300	0.1097	0.0926	0.0781	0.0659	0.0556
18	0.2369	0.1979	0.1653	0.1381	0.1153	0.0963	0.0805	0.0672	0.0561	0.0469
19	0.2187	0.1809	0.1496	0.1237	0.1023	0.0846	0.0699	0.0578	0.0478	0.0396
20	0.2019	0.1653	0.1353	0.1108	0.0907	0.0743	0.0608	0.0498	0.0408	0.0334
21	0.1864	0.1511	0.1225	0.0993	0.0805	0.0652	0.0529	0.0429	0.0347	0.0282
22	0.1720	0.1381	0.1108	0.0889	0.0714	0.0573	0.0460	0.0369	0.0296	0.0238
23	0.1588	0.1262	0.1003	0.0797	0.0633	0.0503	0.0400	0.0317	0.0252	0.0200
24	0.1466	0.1153	0.0907	0.0714	0.0561	0.0442	0.0347	0.0273	0.0215	0.0169
25	0.1353	0.1054	0.0821	0.0639	0.0498	0.0388	0.0302	0.0235	0.0183	0.0143
30	0.0907	0.0672	0.0498	0.0369	0.0273	0.0202	0.0150	0.0111	0.0082	0.0061
35	0.0608	0.0429	0.0302	0.0213	0.0150	0.0106	0.0074	0.0052	0.0037	0.0026
40	0.0408	0.0273	0.0183	0.0123	0.0082	0.0055	0.0037	0.0025	0.0017	0.0011
45	0.0273	0.0174	0.0111	0.0071	0.0045	0.0029	0.0018	0.0012	0.0007	0.0005
50	0.0183	0.0111	0.0067	0.0041	0.0025	0.0015	0.0009	0.0006	0.0003	0.0002
55	0.0123	0.0071	0.0041	0.0024	0.0014	0.0008	0.0005	0.0003	0.0002	0.0001
60	0.0082	0.0045	0.0025	0.0014	0.0007	0.0004	0.0002	0.0001	0.0001	0.0000

■ TABLE A.6   *(continued)*

					Continuous Discount Rate (*r*)					
18%	19%	20%	21%	22%	23%	24%	25%	26%	27%	28%
0.8353	0.8270	0.8187	0.8106	0.8025	0.7945	0.7866	0.7788	0.7711	0.7634	0.7558
0.6977	0.6839	0.6703	0.6570	0.6440	0.6313	0.6188	0.6065	0.5945	0.5827	0.5712
0.5827	0.5655	0.5488	0.5326	0.5169	0.5016	0.4868	0.4724	0.4584	0.4449	0.4317
0.4868	0.4677	0.4493	0.4317	0.4148	0.3985	0.3829	0.3679	0.3535	0.3396	0.3263
0.4066	0.3867	0.3679	0.3499	0.3329	0.3166	0.3012	0.2865	0.2725	0.2592	0.2466
0.3396	0.3198	0.3012	0.2837	0.2671	0.2516	0.2369	0.2231	0.2101	0.1979	0.1864
0.2837	0.2645	0.2466	0.2299	0.2144	0.1999	0.1864	0.1738	0.1620	0.1511	0.1409
0.2369	0.2187	0.2019	0.1864	0.1720	0.1588	0.1466	0.1353	0.1249	0.1153	0.1065
0.1979	0.1809	0.1653	0.1511	0.1381	0.1262	0.1153	0.1054	0.0963	0.0880	0.0805
0.1653	0.1496	0.1353	0.1225	0.1108	0.1003	0.0907	0.0821	0.0743	0.0672	0.0608
0.1381	0.1237	0.1108	0.0993	0.0889	0.0797	0.0714	0.0639	0.0573	0.0513	0.0460
0.1154	0.1023	0.0907	0.0805	0.0714	0.0633	0.0561	0.0498	0.0442	0.0392	0.0347
0.0963	0.0846	0.0743	0.0652	0.0573	0.0503	0.0442	0.0388	0.0340	0.0299	0.0263
0.0805	0.0699	0.0608	0.0529	0.0460	0.0400	0.0347	0.0302	0.0263	0.0228	0.0198
0.0672	0.0578	0.0498	0.0429	0.0369	0.0317	0.0273	0.0235	0.0202	0.0174	0.0150
0.0561	0.0478	0.0408	0.0347	0.0296	0.0252	0.0215	0.0183	0.0156	0.0133	0.0113
0.0469	0.0396	0.0334	0.0282	0.0238	0.0200	0.0169	0.0143	0.0120	0.0102	0.0086
0.0392	0.0327	0.0273	0.0228	0.0191	0.0159	0.0133	0.0111	0.0093	0.0078	0.0065
0.0327	0.0271	0.0224	0.0185	0.0153	0.0127	0.0105	0.0087	0.0072	0.0059	0.0049
0.0273	0.0224	0.0183	0.0150	0.0123	0.0101	0.0082	0.0067	0.0055	0.0045	0.0037
0.0228	0.0185	0.0150	0.0122	0.0099	0.0080	0.0065	0.0052	0.0043	0.0034	0.0028
0.0191	0.0153	0.0123	0.0099	0.0079	0.0063	0.0051	0.0041	0.0033	0.0026	0.0021
0.0159	0.0127	0.0101	0.0080	0.0063	0.0050	0.0040	0.0032	0.0025	0.0020	0.0016
0.0133	0.0105	0.0082	0.0065	0.0051	0.0040	0.0032	0.0025	0.0019	0.0015	0.0012
0.0111	0.0087	0.0067	0.0052	0.0041	0.0032	0.0025	0.0019	0.0015	0.0012	0.0009
0.0045	0.0033	0.0025	0.0018	0.0014	0.0010	0.0007	0.0006	0.0004	0.0003	0.0002
0.0018	0.0013	0.0009	0.0006	0.0005	0.0003	0.0002	0.0002	0.0001	0.0001	0.0001
0.0007	0.0005	0.0003	0.0002	0.0002	0.0001	0.0001	0.0000	0.0000	0.0000	0.0000
0.0003	0.0002	0.0001	0.0001	0.0001	0.0000	0.0000	0.0000	0.0000	0.0000	0.0000
0.0001	0.0001	0.0000	0.0000	0.0000	0.0000	0.0000	0.0000	0.0000	0.0000	0.0000
0.0001	0.0000	0.0000	0.0000	0.0000	0.0000	0.0000	0.0000	0.0000	0.0000	0.0000
0.0000	0.0000	0.0000	0.0000	0.0000	0.0000	0.0000	0.0000	0.0000	0.0000	0.0000

■ TABLE A.6   *(concluded)*

Period (T)	Continuous Discount Rate (r)						
	29%	30%	31%	32%	33%	34%	35%
1	0.7483	0.7408	0.7334	0.7261	0.7189	0.7118	0.7047
2	0.5599	0.5488	0.5379	0.5273	0.5169	0.5066	0.4966
3	0.4190	0.4066	0.3946	0.3829	0.3716	0.3606	0.3499
4	0.3135	0.3012	0.2894	0.2780	0.2671	0.2567	0.2466
5	0.2346	0.2231	0.2122	0.2019	0.1920	0.1827	0.1738
6	0.1755	0.1653	0.1557	0.1466	0.1381	0.1300	0.1225
7	0.1313	0.1225	0.1142	0.1065	0.0993	0.0926	0.0863
8	0.0983	0.0907	0.0837	0.0773	0.0714	0.0659	0.0608
9	0.0735	0.0672	0.0614	0.0561	0.0513	0.0469	0.0429
10	0.0550	0.0498	0.0450	0.0408	0.0369	0.0334	0.0302
11	0.0412	0.0369	0.0330	0.0296	0.0265	0.0238	0.0213
12	0.0308	0.0273	0.0242	0.0215	0.0191	0.0169	0.0150
13	0.0231	0.0202	0.0178	0.0156	0.0137	0.0120	0.0106
14	0.0172	0.0150	0.0130	0.0113	0.0099	0.0086	0.0074
15	0.0129	0.0111	0.0096	0.0082	0.0071	0.0061	0.0052
16	0.0097	0.0082	0.0070	0.0060	0.0051	0.0043	0.0037
17	0.0072	0.0061	0.0051	0.0043	0.0037	0.0031	0.0026
18	0.0054	0.0045	0.0038	0.0032	0.0026	0.0022	0.0018
19	0.0040	0.0033	0.0028	0.0023	0.0019	0.0016	0.0013
20	0.0030	0.0025	0.0020	0.0017	0.0014	0.0011	0.0009
21	0.0023	0.0018	0.0015	0.0012	0.0010	0.0008	0.0006
22	0.0017	0.0014	0.0011	0.0009	0.0007	0.0006	0.0005
23	0.0013	0.0010	0.0008	0.0006	0.0005	0.0004	0.0003
24	0.0009	0.0007	0.0006	0.0005	0.0004	0.0003	0.0002
25	0.0007	0.0006	0.0004	0.0003	0.0003	0.0002	0.0002
30	0.0002	0.0001	0.0001	0.0001	0.0001	0.0000	0.0000
35	0.0000	0.0000	0.0000	0.0000	0.0000	0.0000	0.0000
40	0.0000	0.0000	0.0000	0.0000	0.0000	0.0000	0.0000
45	0.0000	0.0000	0.0000	0.0000	0.0000	0.0000	0.0000
50	0.0000	0.0000	0.0000	0.0000	0.0000	0.0000	0.0000
55	0.0000	0.0000	0.0000	0.0000	0.0000	0.0000	0.0000
60	0.0000	0.0000	0.0000	0.0000	0.0000	0.0000	0.0000

Solutions to Selected End-of-Chapter Problems

Chapter 2

2.1 Total assets = $128,000
Common stock = $ 88,000

2.2 Common stock = $110,000,000
RE = $ 22,000,000

2.7 Total cash flow to investors = ($5,000)

2.8 *a.* $25
b. − $25

Chapter 3

3.1 $65,000

3.2 $73,600

3.8 *a.* $11 million
b. ii. $11 million − ($5 million × 1.1) = $5.5 million

Chapter 4

4.1 *a.* $1,628.89
b. $1,967.15
c. $2,653.30
d. $628.89

4.4 $92.30

4.5 $187,780.23

4.6 *a.* PV_1 = $10,000 PV_2 = $20,000
b. PV_1 = $ 9,090.91 PV_2 = $12,418.43
c. PV_1 = $ 8,333.33 PV_2 = $ 8,037.55
d.   r = 18.921%

4.9 $6,714.61

4.10 $1,609,866.18

4.15 *a.* $1,259.71
b. $1,265.32
c. $1,270.24
d. $1,271.25

4.19 P = $800

4.22 *a.* $10,000
b. $ 4,545.45
c. $20,000

4.28 NPV = $201.88

4.29 $16,834.88

4.31 9.0648%

4.32 *a.* $4,347.26
b. $17,824.65

4.36 Option 1 value = $1,201,178.88
Option 2 value = $1,131,897.47

4.38 18.921%

4.39 PV of both children's education (today) = $14,880.44
Required payment = $14,880.44/$A^{15}_{15\%}$ = $2,544.80

4.42 $457,611.46

4.43 NPV = $282.87, purchase the machine

Chapter 5

5.2 *a.* $1,000.00
b. $828.41
c. $1,231.15

5.6 *a.* 12.36%
b. $748.48
c. $906.15

5.16 2,754 Shares

5.19 $26.95

5.21 P = $23.75

Chapter 6

6.1 *a.* Project A
b. Project B

6.3 *a.* 56.25%

6.5 a.

6.7 For Project A: IRR_1 = 0%;
IRR_2 = 100%
For Project B: IRR = 36.1944%

6.9 *a.* IRR (Project A) = 25.69%
IRR (Project B) = 19.43%
e. 19.09%
g. NPV_A = $689.98
NPV_B = $5,671.08
Choose Project B

6.16 *a.* Project A
 b. AAR (Sunday) = 22.22%
  AAR (Saturday) = 19.05%

Chapter 7

7.4 E(Salary) = $295,000
 PV = $1,594,825.68
7.6 EPS = $4
 NPVGO = $3
  Price = $36.33
7.8 NPV = −$7,722.52, No
7.13 NPV_A = $1,446.76
 NPV_B = $119.17
 Choose Project A
7.15 $705,882.35
7.23 $150,100
7.31 Bang EAC = $47,456
 IOU EAC = $49,592

Chapter 8

8.5 350 units
8.6 *a.* 265,625 abalones
 b. $28,600

Chapter 9

9.1 *a.* $1 per share
 b. $1,500
 c. 8.11%
9.4 15.865%
9.6 $E(R)$ = 14.7%
9.11 *b.* 8.49%
9.12 *a.* 0.088
 b. 0.03311
9.13 *a.* $E(R)$ = 0.056
 b. Standard deviation = 3.137%
9.14 *a.* $\overline{R}_M$ = 15.3%
 b. $\overline{R}_T$ = 6.28%

Chapter 10

10.1 *a.* $\overline{R}$ = 10.57%
 b. σ = 7.20%
10.4 Weight of Atlas stock = $\frac{2}{3}$
 Weight of Babcock stock = $\frac{1}{3}$
10.5 $\overline{R}_p$ = 16.2%
 σ_p = 18.23%
10.14 *b.* 13.5%

10.19 *a.* 5.9375%
 b. $x_A = \frac{2}{3}$
  $x_B = \frac{1}{3}$
 c. σ_p^2 = 0. This is a riskless portfolio.
10.27 β = 1.4

Chapter 11

11.4 *a.* R_A = 10.5 + 1.2 × $(R_M - 14.2) + \epsilon_A$
  R_B = 13.0 + 0.98 × $(R_M - 14.2) + \epsilon_B$
  R_C = 15.7 + 1.37 × $(R_M - 14.2) + \epsilon_C$
 b. R_p = 12.925 + 1.1435 × $(R_M - 14.2) + 0.30\epsilon_A$
  $+ 0.45\epsilon_B + 0.25\epsilon_C$
 c. R_p = 13.8398%
11.6 *a.* $\text{Var}(R_{1p})$ = .0225
  $\text{Var}(R_{2p})$ = .00225
  A risk-averse investor will prefer to invest in the second market.
 b. $\text{Var}(R_{1p})$ = .0585
  $\text{Var}(R_{2p})$ = .0025
  A risk-averse investor will prefer to invest in the second market.
 c. $\text{Var}(R_{1p})$ = .0225
  $\text{Var}(R_{2p})$ = .0225
  Indifferent between investing in the two markets.
 d. Indifference implies that the variances of the portfolios in the two markets are equal.
  Corr $(\epsilon_{2i}, \epsilon_{2j})$ = Corr $(\epsilon_{1i}, \epsilon_{1j})$ + .5

Chapter 12

12.5 *a.* $\overline{R}_T$ = 0.01633; β_T = 1.0032
12.6 *b.* *i.* $\overline{R}_M$ = 0.18
  iii. σ_M = 0.01265
 d. *i.* $\overline{R}_j$ = 0.2
  ii. σ_j^2 = 0.00048
 e. Corr (R_m, R_i) = 0.635
 f. β_j = 1.1

Chapter 14

14.1 *a.* 67,715 shares
 b. Average price = $5 per share
 c. Book value = $40 per share
14.2 *a.* Common stock = $500
  Total = $150,500

Chapter 15

15.3 0.125
15.7 *a.* 18%
 b. r_s = 20%
15.9 *a.* Value = $300 million
 b. Value = $300 million
 c. r_s = 10.14%

15.15 *a.* $V_U = \$1,530,000$

b. $273,000

15.16 $2,800,000

Chapter 16

16.11 *a.* Total cash flow to stakeholders:
Equity plan = $1,260,000
Debt plan = $1,638,000
b. Taxes (Debt) = $1,362,000
Taxes (Equity) = $1,740,000
c. $V_U = \$\ 6,300,000$
$V_L = \$11,700,000$
d. Total cash flow to stakeholders:
Equity plan = $1,440,000
Debt plan = $1,399,500

16.14 *a.* Value = $15,000
b. *i.* $V = \$15,000$
ii. $B = \$7,500$
iii. $S = \$7,500$
c. *i.* $r_s = 30\%$
ii. $r_o = .20 = 20\%$
d. *i.* $V_L = \$12,000$
e. *i.* $9,000   Debt no longer adds value to the firm.
ii. $6,500   Debt lowers the value of the firm.

Chapter 17

17.1 *a.* $I = \$350,625.29$
b. B/C NPV = $18,285.17
APV = $40,005.51
c. $I = \$403,222.85$

17.6 *a.* $r_s = 17.576\%$
b. $r_B = 10\%$, pre-tax
After-tax cost of debt = 6.6%
c. 13.917%

17.7 *a.* *i.* WACC = 0.1047
ii. WACC = 0.1173
iii. WACC = 0.1047

17.8 $\beta_S = 1.21$; $r_S = 17.293\%$
$V = \$84,000,000$; WACC = 14.426%
NPV = $3.084 million

Chapter 18

18.5 *a.* $P = \$15$
b. Each year you receive $4,613.38

18.6 *a.* Value = $1,412,000
b. Ex-dividend price = $138
c. *ii.* $P = \$136.95$
Number of shares sold = 76.67

18.13 *a.* $P_0 = \$19.17$
b. $P_0 = \$20.00$

18.15 *a.* 0.0891
b. 11%
c.

	Preferred Stock	Debt
i.	8.91%	11.00%
ii.	8.00%	7.26%
iii.	6.42%	7.92%

Chapter 19

19.6 At $40, $P = \$40.00$
At $20, $P = \$33.33$
At $10, $P = \$30.00$

19.10 *a.* 800,000 shares
b. 3
c. $15 and three rights

19.11 *a.* Ex-rights price = $24.55
b. Value of a right = $0.45
c. Value = $2,700,500

19.13 *a.* $36.25
b. $ 8.75

Chapter 20

20.6 *a.* $P = \$1,266.41$

20.8 *a.* $V_{NC} = \$1,164.61$
b. $C = \$77.63$
c. $130.12

20.10 NPV = $17,857,143

Chapter 21

21.7 *a.* Lease vs. buy NPV = $3,177.78
c. $18,177.78

Chapter 22

22.6 *a.* $5
b. $0

22.7 *a.* $0
b. $5

22.10 $42.36

22.16 $0.5974

22.19 $C = \$1.61$

22.21 *a.* $C = \$5.89$
b. $P = \$11.28$

Chapter 23

23.3 NPV (Fixed Plant) = $12,382,644.67
NPV (Flexible Plant) = $8,759,346.74
Choose Fixed Plant

23.4 The value of the option is worth $229,400.
Mr. Lusk should reject the $500 offer

Chapter 24

24.4 *a.* $1,750
    b. $514.29
    c. *i.* $3,640
       iii. $5,440/3 = $1,813.33
       iv. Gain = $13.33
    d. $20

24.5 *a.* Lower limit = $0
      Upper limit = $2
    b. Lower limit = $.5
      Upper limit = $3

24.14 *a.* *i.* 28
      ii. $35.71
      iii. 14.27%
    b. *i.* 28
      ii. The conversion price is only meaningful if the bond is selling at par.
    c. $875
    d. Method One = $931
      Method Two = $931

24.16 $333.33

Chapter 25

25.3 *a.* *i.* $5.10
      ii. $5.00
    b. *i.* $4.98
      ii. $5.00

25.11 *a.* C = $35,237.89

25.13 *a.* A = $900.90; B = $593.45; C = $352.18
    b. A = $877.19; B = $519.37; C = $269.74
    c. A = -2.63%; B = -12.48%; C = -23.41%

25.17 3.5315 years

25.20 *a.* 2.943 years
    b. 2.752 years

25.21 *a.* 3.327 years
    b. 2.434 years

Chapter 26

26.3 *a.* 5.26%

26.5 *a.* 7.14%
    b. Increase dividend payout ratio to $d = 1$.

Chapter 27

27.3 Total sources = $82,325

27.4 Total sources = $646,000

27.12 *a.* S = $42,857
    b. January = $44,143
      February = $66,000
      March = $76,000

Chapter 28

28.3 $2,631.62

28.4 *a.* Retain $243,193 in cash.
    b. 17 times

28.6 Z^* = $34,536
    H^* = $63,608

28.8 Reduction in float = $6,750,000
    Cost of lockbox = $107,375

28.9 N = 33.43

28.12 $5,793.12 in present value terms

Chapter 29

29.1 PV(Old) = $26,948.12
    T = 50 days (for customers not taking the discount)

29.2 $1,232,876.71

29.3 PV(New) = $29,110,225.07

29.4 *a.* NPV(Credit) = $3,029.13
    b. 99.57%

29.10 Accounts receivable = $384,247

Chapter 30

30.6 *b.* Prob (Joint value = $200,000) = 0.01
      Prob (Joint value = $600,000) = 0.40
      Prob (Debt value = $300,000) = 0.08
      Prob (Debt value = $400,000) = 0.91
      Prob (Stock value = $0) = 0.25
    c. Value of each company = $290,000
    d. Total debt value before merger = $380,000
      Total debt value after merger = $390,000

30.10 *a.* $7,500,000
    b. V = $27,500,000
    c. Cash: $15,000,000
      Stock: $15,625,000

30.11 *a.* $14,815,385

30.13 NPV = $-$21.2

Chapter 32

32.1 *a.* In direct terms, $1.6317/£
      In European terms, DM 1.8110/£
    e. £ 0.3384/DM
      ¥ 95.6813/SF

32.7 *b.* $E[\$/DM(1)]$ = $0.525/DM
      $E[\$/DM(3)]$ = $0.5788/DM
      NPV = $17,582

Glossary

AAR Average accounting return.

ACRS Accelerated cost recovery system.

APT Arbitrage pricing theory.

Absolute priority rule (APR) Establishes priority of claims under liquidation.

Accelerated cost recovery system (ACRS) A system used to depreciate assets for tax purposes. The current system, enacted by the 1986 Tax Reform Act, is very similar to the ACRS established in 1981. The current system specifies the depreciable lives (recovery periods) and rates for each of several classes of property.

Accounting insolvency Total liabilities exceed total assets. A firm with negative net worth is insolvent on the books.

Accounting liquidity The ease and quickness with which assets can be converted to cash.

Accounts payable Money the firm owes to suppliers.

Accounts receivable Money owed to the firm by customers.

Accounts receivable financing A secured short-term loan that involves either the assigning of receivables or the factoring of receivables. Under assignment, the lender has a lien on the receivables and recourse to the borrower. Factoring involves the sale of accounts receivable. Then the purchaser, called the factor, must collect on the receivables.

Accounts receivable turnover Credit sales divided by average accounts receivable.

Additions to net working capital Component of cash flow of firm, along with operating cash flow and capital spending.

Advance commitment A promise to sell an asset before the seller has lined up purchase of the asset. This seller can offset risk by purchasing a futures contract to fix the sales price.

Agency costs Costs of conflicts of interest among stockholders, bondholders, and managers. Agency costs are the costs of resolving these conflicts. They include the costs of providing managers with an incentive to maximize shareholder wealth and then monitoring their behavior, and the cost of protecting bondholders from shareholders. Agency costs are borne by stockholders.

Agency theory The theory of the relationship between principals and agents. It involves the nature of the costs of resolving conflicts of interest between principals and agents.

Aggregation Process in corporate financial planning whereby the smaller investment proposals of each of the firm's operational units are added up and in effect treated as a big picture.

Aging schedule A compilation of accounts receivable by the age of account.

American Depository Receipt (ADR) A security issued in the United States to represent shares of a foreign stock, enabling that stock to be traded in the United States.

American option An option contract that may be exercised anytime up to the expiration date. A European option may be exercised only on the expiration date.

Amortization Repayment of a loan in installments.

Angels Individuals providing venture capital.

Annualized holding-period return The annual rate of return that when compounded T times, would have given the same T-period holding return as actually occurred from period 1 to period T.

Annuity A level stream of equal dollar payments that lasts for a fixed time. An example of an annuity is the coupon part of a bond with level annual payments.

Annuity factor The term used to calculate the present value of the stream of level payments for a fixed period.

Annuity in advance An annuity with an immediate initial payment.

Annuity in arrears An annuity with a first payment one full period hence, rather than immediately. That is, the first payment occurs on date 1 rather than on date 0.

Appraisal rights Rights of shareholders of an acquired firm that allow them to demand that their shares be purchased at a fair value by the acquiring firm.

Arbitrage Buying an asset in one market at a lower price and simultaneously selling an identical asset in another market at a higher price. This is done with no cost or risk.

Arbitrage pricing theory (APT) An equilibrium asset pricing theory that is derived from a factor model by using diversification and arbitrage. It shows that the expected return on any risky asset is a linear combination of various factors.

Arithmetic average The sum of the values observed divided by the total number of observations—sometimes referred to as the mean.

Assets Anything that the firm owns.

Assets requirements A common element of a financial plan that describes projected capital spending and the proposed uses of net working capital.

Auction market A market where all traders in a certain good meet at one place to buy or sell an asset. The NYSE is an example.

Autocorrelation The correlation of a variable with itself over successive time intervals.

Availability float Refers to the time required to clear a check through the banking system.

Average accounting return (AAR) The average project earnings after taxes and depreciation divided by the average book value of the investment during its life.

Average collection period Average amount of time required to collect an account receivable. Also referred to as days sales outstanding.

Average cost of capital A firm's required payout to the bondholders and the stockholders expressed as a percentage of capital contributed to the firm. Average cost of capital is computed by dividing the total required cost of capital by the total amount of contributed capital.

Average daily sales Annual sales divided by 365 days.

Balance sheet A statement showing a firm's accounting value on a particular date. It reflects the equation, Assets = Liabilities + Stockholders' equity.

Balloon payment Large final payment, as when a loan is repaid in installments.

Banker's acceptance Agreement by a bank to pay a given sum of money at a future date.

Bankruptcy State of being unable to pay debts. Thus the ownership of the firm's assets is transferred from the stockholders to the bondholders.

Bankruptcy costs See **Financial distress costs.**

Bargain-purchase-price option Gives lessee the option to purchase the asset at a price below fair market value when the lease expires.

Basic IRR rule Accept the project if IRR is greater than the discount rate; reject the project if IRR is less than the discount rate.

Bearer bond A bond issued without record of the owner's name. Whoever holds the bond (the bearer) is the owner.

Best-efforts underwriting An offering in which an underwriter agrees to distribute as much of the offering as possible and to return any unsold shares to the issuer.

Beta coefficient A measure of the sensitivity of a security's return to movements in an underlying factor. It is a measured systematic risk.

Bidder A firm or person that has made an offer to take over another firm.

Black-Scholes call pricing equation An exact formula for the price of a call option. The formula requires five variables: the risk-free interest rate, the variance of the underlying stock, the exercise price, the price of the underlying stock, and the time to expiration.

Blanket inventory lien A secured loan that gives the lender a lien against all the borrower's inventories.

Bond A long-term debt of a firm. In common usage, the term *bond* often refers to both secured and unsecured debt.

Book cash A firm's cash balance as reported in its financial statements. Also called ledger cash.

Book value per share Per-share accounting equity value of a firm. Total accounting equity divided by the number of outstanding shares.

Borrow To obtain or receive money on loan with the promise or understanding of returning it or its equivalent.

Break-even analysis Analysis of the level of sales at which a project would make zero profit.

Bubble theory (of speculative markets) Security prices sometimes move wildly above their true values.

Business failure The risk that the firm's stockholders bear if the firm is financed only with equity.

Buying the index Purchasing the stocks in the Standard & Poor's 500 in the same proportion as the index to achieve the same return.

CAPM Capital asset pricing model.

CAR Cumulative abnormal return.

Call option The right—but not the obligation—to buy a fixed number of shares of stock at a stated price within a specified time.

Call premium The price of a call option on common stock.

Call price of a bond Amount at which a firm has the right to repurchase its bonds or debentures before the stated maturity date. The call price is always set at equal to or more than the par value.

Call protected Describes a bond that is not allowed to be called, usually for a certain early period in the life of the bond.

Call provision A written agreement between an issuing corporation and its bondholders that gives the corporation the option to redeem the bond at a specified price before the maturity date.

Callable Refers to a bond that is subject to be repurchased at a stated call price before maturity.

Capital asset pricing model (CAPM) An equilibrium asset pricing theory that shows that equilibrium rates of expected return on all risky assets are a function of their covariance with the market portfolio.

Capital budgeting Planning and managing expenditures for long-lived assets.

Capital gains The positive change in the value of an asset. A negative capital gain is a capital loss.

Capital market line The efficient set of all assets, both risky and riskless, which provides the investor with the best possible opportunities.

Capital markets Financial markets for long-term debt and for equity shares.

Capital rationing The case where funds are limited to a fixed dollar amount and must be allocated among competing projects.

Capital structure The mix of the various debt and equity capital maintained by a firm. Also called financial structure. The composition of a corporation's securities used to finance its investment activities; the relative proportions of short-term debt, long-term debt, and owners' equity.

Capital surplus Amounts of directly contributed equity capital in excess of the par value.

Carrying costs Costs that increase with increases in the level of investment in current assets.

Carrying value Book value.

Cash budget A forecast of cash receipts and disbursements expected by a firm in the coming year. It is a short-term financial planning tool.

Cash cow A company that pays out all earnings per share to stockholders as dividends.

Cash cycle In general, the time between cash disbursement and cash collection. In net working capital management, it can be thought of as the operating cycle less the accounts payable payment period.

Cash discount A discount given for a cash purchase. One reason a cash discount may be offered is to speed up the collection of receivables.

Cash flow Cash generated by the firm and paid to creditors and shareholders. It can be classified as (1) cash flow from operations, (2) cash flow from changes in fixed assets, and (3) cash flow from changes in net working capital.

Cash flow after interest and taxes Net income plus depreciation.

Cash-flow time line Line depicting the operating activities and cash flows for a firm over a particular period.

Cash offer A public equity issue that is sold to all interested investors.

Cash transaction A transaction where exchange is immediate, as contrasted to a forward contract, which calls for future delivery of an asset at an agreed-upon price.

Cashout Refers to situation where a firm runs out of cash and cannot readily sell marketable securities.

Certificates of deposit Short-term loans to commercial banks.

Change in net working capital Difference between net working capital from one period to another.

Changes in fixed assets Component of cash flow that equals sales of fixed assets minus the acquisition of fixed assets.

Characteristic line The line relating the expected return on a security to different returns on the market.

Clearing The exchanging of checks and balancing of accounts between banks.

Clientele effect Argument that stocks attract clienteles based on dividend yield or taxes. For example, a tax clientele effect is induced by the difference in tax treatment of dividend income and capital gains income; high tax-bracket individuals tend to prefer low-dividend yields.

Coinsurance effect Refers to the fact that the merger of two firms decreases the probability of default on either's debt.

Collateral Assets that are pledged as security for payment of debt.

Collateral trust bond A bond secured by a pledge of common stock held by the corporation.

Collection float An increase in book cash with no immediate change in bank cash, generated by checks deposited by the firm that have not cleared.

Collection policy Procedures followed by a firm in attempting to collect accounts receivable.

Commercial draft Demand for payment.

Commercial paper Short-term, unsecured promissory notes issued by corporations with a high credit standing. Their maturity ranges up to 270 days.

Common equity Book value.

Common stock Equity claims held by the "residual owners" of the firm, who are the last to receive any distribution of earnings or assets.

Compensating balance Deposit that the firm keeps with the bank in a low-interest or non-interest-bearing account to compensate banks for bank loans or services.

Competitive offer Method of selecting an investment banker for a new issue by offering the securities to the underwriter bidding highest.

Composition Voluntary arrangement to restructure a firm's debt, under which payment is reduced.

Compound interest Interest that is earned both on the initial principal and on interest earned on the initial principal in previous periods. The interest earned in one period becomes in effect part of the principal in a following period.

Compound value Value of a sum after investing it over one or more periods. Also called future value.

Compounding Process of reinvesting each interest payment to earn more interest. Compounding is based on the idea that interest itself becomes principal and therefore also earns interest in subsequent periods.

Concentration banking The use of geographically dispersed collection centers to speed up the collection of accounts receivable.

Conditional sales contract An arrangement whereby the firm retains legal ownership of the goods until the customer has completed payment.

Conflict between bondholders and stockholders These two groups may have interests in the corporation that conflict. Sources of conflict include dividends, dilution, distortion of investment, and underinvestment. Protective covenants work to resolve these conflicts.

Conglomerate acquisition Acquisition in which the acquired firm and the acquiring firm are not related, unlike a horizontal or a vertical acquisition.

Consol A bond that carries a promise to pay a coupon forever; it has no final maturity date and therefore never matures.

Consolidation A merger in which an entirely new firm is created.

Consumer credit Credit granted to consumers. Trade credit is credit granted to other firms.

Contingent claim Claim whose value is directly dependent on, or is contingent on, the value of its underlying assets. For example, the debt and equity securities issued by a firm derive their value from the total value of the firm.

Contingent pension liability Under ERISA, the firm is liable to the plan participants for up to 30 percent of the net worth of the firm.

Continuous compounding Interest compounded continuously, every instant, rather than at fixed intervals.

Contribution margin Amount that each additional product, such as a jet engine, contributes to after-tax profit of the whole project: (Sales price − Variable cost) × $(1 - T_c)$, where T_c is the corporate tax rate.

Conversion premium Difference between the conversion price and the current stock price divided by the current stock price.

Conversion price The amount of par value exchangeable for one share of common stock. This term really refers to the stock price and means the dollar amount of the bond's par value that is exchangeable for one share of stock.

Conversion ratio The number of shares per $1,000 bond (or debenture) that a bondholder would receive if the bond were converted into shares of stock.

Conversion value What a convertible bond would be worth if it were immediately converted into the common stock at the current price.

Convertible bond A bond that may be converted into another form of security, typically common stock, at the option of the holder at a specified price for a specified period of time.

Corporation Form of business organization that is created as a distinct "legal person" composed of one or more actual individuals or legal entities. Primary advantages of a corporation include limited liability, ease of ownership, transfer, and perpetual succession.

Correlation A standardized statistical measure of the dependence of two random variables. It is defined as the covariance divided by the standard deviations of two variables.

Cost of equity capital The required return on the company's common stock in capital markets. It is also called the equity holders' required rate of return because it is what equity holders can expect to obtain in the capital market. It is a cost from the firm's perspective.

Coupon The stated interest on a debt instrument.

Covariance A statistical measure of the degree to which random variables move together.

Credit analysis The process of determining whether a credit applicant meets the firm's standards and what amount of credit the applicant should receive.

Credit instrument Device by which a firm offers credit, such as an invoice, a promissory note, or a conditional sales contract.

Credit period Time allowed a credit purchaser to remit the full payment for credit purchases.

Credit scoring Determining the probability of default when granting customers credit.

Creditor Person or institution that holds the debt issued by a firm or individual.

Cross rate The exchange rate between two foreign currencies, neither of which is generally the U.S. dollar.

Crown jewels An antitakeover tactic in which major assets—the crown jewels—are sold by a firm when faced with a takeover threat.

Cum dividend With dividend.

Cumulative abnormal return (CAR) Sum of differences between the expected return on a stock and the actual return that comes from the release of news to the market.

Cumulative dividend Dividend on preferred stock that takes priority over dividend payments on common stock. Dividends may not be paid on the common stock until all past dividends on the preferred stock have been paid.

Cumulative probability The probability that a drawing from the standardized normal distribution will be below a particular value.

Cumulative voting A procedure whereby a shareholder may cast all of his or her votes for one member of the board of directors.

Current asset Asset that is in the form of cash or that is expected to be converted into cash in the next 12 months, such as inventory.

Current liabilities Obligations that are expected to require cash payment within one year or the operating period.

Current ratio Total current assets divided by total current liabilities. Used to measure short-term solvency of a firm.

Date of payment Date that dividend checks are mailed.

Date of record Date on which holders of record in a firm's stock ledger are designated as the recipients of either dividends or stock rights.

Dates convention Treating cash flows as being received on exact dates—date 0, date 1, and so forth—as opposed to the end-of-year convention.

Days in receivables Average collection period.

Days sales outstanding Average collection period.

De facto Existing in actual fact although not by official recognition.

Dealer market   A market where traders specializing in particular commodities buy and sell assets for their own account. The OTC market is an example.

Debenture   An unsecured bond, usually with maturity of 15 years or more. A debt obligation backed by the general credit of the issuing corporation.

Debt   Loan agreement that is a liability of the firm. An obligation to repay a specified amount at a particular time.

Debt capacity   Ability to borrow. The amount a firm can borrow up to the point where the firm value no longer increases.

Debt displacement   The amount of borrowing that leasing displaces. Firms that do a lot of leasing will be forced to cut back on borrowing.

Debt ratio   Total debt divided by total assets.

Debt service   Interest payments plus repayments of principal to creditors, that is, retirement of debt.

Decision trees   A graphical representation of alternative sequential decisions and the possible outcomes of those decisions.

Declaration date   Date on which the board of directors passes a resolution to pay a dividend of a specified amount to all qualified holders of record on a specified date.

Dedicated capital   Total par value (number of shares issued multiplied by the par value of each share). Also called dedicated value.

Deed of trust   Indenture.

Deep-discount bond   A bond issued with a very low coupon or no coupon and selling at a price far below par value. When the bond has no coupon, it is also called a pure-discount or original-issue-discount bond.

Default risk   The chance that interest or principal will not be paid on the due date and in the promised amount.

Defeasance   A debt-restructuring tool that enables a firm to remove debt from its balance sheet by establishing an irrevocable trust that will generate future cash flows sufficient to service the decreased debt.

Deferred call   A provision that prohibits the company from calling the bond before a certain date. During this period the bond is said to be call protected.

Deferred nominal life annuity   A monthly fixed-dollar payment beginning at retirement age. It is nominal because the payment is fixed in dollar amount at any particular time, up to and including retirement.

Deferred taxes   Noncash expense.

Deficit   The amount by which a sum of money is less than the required amount; an excess of liabilities over assets, of losses over profits, or of expenditure over income.

Deliverable instrument   The asset in a forward contract that will be delivered in the future at an agreed-upon price.

Denomination   Face value or principal of a bond.

Depreciation   A noncash expense, such as the cost of plant or equipment, charged against earnings to write off the cost of an asset during its estimated useful life.

Depreciation tax shield   Portion of an investment that can be deducted from taxable income.

Dilution   Loss in existing shareholders' value. There are several kinds of dilution: (1) dilution of ownership, (2) dilution of market value, and (3) dilution of book value and earnings, as with warrants and convertible issues. Firms with significant amounts of warrants or convertible issues outstanding are required to report earnings on a "fully diluted" basis.

Direct lease   A lease under which a lessor buys equipment from a manufacturer and leases it to a lessee.

Disbursement float   A decrease in book cash but no immediate change in bank cash, generated by checks written by the firm.

Discount   If a bond is selling below its face value, it is said to sell at a discount.

Discount rate   Rate used to calculate the present value of future cash flows.

Discounted payback period rule   An investment decision rule in which the cash flows are discounted at an interest rate and the payback rule is applied on these discounted cash flows.

Discounting   Calculating the present value of a future amount. The process is the opposite of compounding.

Distribution   A type of dividend paid by a firm to its owners from sources other than current or accumulated retained earnings.

Diversifiable risk   A risk that specifically affects a single asset or a small group of assets. Also called unique or unsystematic risk.

Dividend   Payment made by a firm to its owners, either in cash or in stock. Also called the "income component" of the return on an investment in stock.

Dividend growth model   A model wherein dividends are assumed to be at a constant rate in perpetuity.

Dividend payout   Amount of cash paid to shareholders expressed as a percentage of earnings per share.

Dividend yield   Dividends per share of common stock divided by market price per share.

Dividends per share   Amount of cash paid to shareholders expressed as dollars per share.

Double-declining balance depreciation   Method of accelerated depreciation.

DuPont system of financial control   Highlights the fact that return on assets (ROA) can be expressed in terms of the profit margin and asset turnover.

Duration   The weighted average time of an asset's cash flows. The weights are determined by present value factors.

EAC   Equivalent annual cost.

EBIT   Earnings before interest and taxes.

EMH   Efficient market hypothesis.

ERISA   Employee Retirement Income Security Act of 1974.

Economic assumptions   Economic environment in which the firm expects to reside over the life of the financial plan.

Effective annual interest rate   The interest rate as if it were compounded once per time period rather than several times per period.

Efficient market hypothesis (EMH)   The prices of securities fully reflect available information. Investors buying bonds and stocks in an efficient market should expect to obtain an equilibrium rate of return. Firms should expect to receive the "fair" value (present value) for the securities they sell.

Efficient set   Graph representing a set of portfolios that maximize expected return at each level of portfolio risk.

End-of-year convention   Treating cash flows as if they occur at the end of a year (or, alternatively, at the end of a period), as opposed to the date convention. Under the end-of-year convention, the end of year 0 is the present, end of year 1 occurs one period hence, and so on.

Equilibrium rate of interest   The interest rate that clears the market. Also called market-clearing interest rate.

Equity   Ownership interest of common and preferred stockholders in a corporation. Also, total assets minus total liabilities, or net worth.

Equity kicker   Used to refer to warrants because they usually are issued in combination with privately placed bonds.

Equity share   Ownership interest.

Equivalent annual cost (EAC)   The net present value of cost divided by an annuity factor that has the same life as the investment.

Equivalent loan   The amount of the loan that makes leasing equivalent to buying with debt financing in terms of debt capacity reduction.

Erosion   Cash-flow amount transferred to a new project from customers and sales of other products of the firm.

Eurobanks   Banks that make loans and accept deposits in foreign currencies.

Eurobond   An international bond sold primarily in countries other than the country in whose currency the issue is denominated.

Eurocurrency   Money deposited in a financial center outside of the country whose currency is involved.

Eurodollar   A dollar deposited in a bank outside the United States.

Eurodollar CD   Deposit of dollars with foreign banks.

European Currency Unit (ECU)   An index of foreign exchange consisting of about 10 European currencies, originally devised in 1979.

European option   An option contract that may be exercised only on the expiration date. An American option may be exercised any time up to the expiration date.

Event study   A statistical study that examines how the release of information affects prices at a particular time.

Ex rights or ex dividend   Phrases used to indicate that a stock is selling without a recently declared right or dividend. The ex-rights or ex-dividend date is generally four business days before the date of record.

Exchange rate   Price of one country's currency for another's.

Exclusionary self-tender   The firm makes a tender offer for a given amount of its own stock while excluding targeted stockholders.

Ex-dividend date   Date four business days before the date of record for a security. An individual purchasing stock before its ex-dividend date will receive the current dividend.

Exercise price   Price at which the holder of an option can buy (in the case of a call option) or sell (in the case of a put option) the underlying stock. Also called the striking price.

Exercising the option   The act of buying or selling the underlying asset via the option contract.

Expectations hypothesis (of interest rates)   Theory that forward interest rates are unbiased estimates of expected future interest rates.

Expected return   Average of possible returns weighted by their probability.

Expiration date   Maturity date of an option.

Extension   Voluntary arrangements to restructure a firm's debt, under which the payment date is postponed.

Extinguish   Retire or pay off debt.

Face value   The value of a bond that appears on its face. Also referred to as par value or principal.

Factor   A financial institution that buys a firm's accounts receivables and collects the debt.

Factor model   A model in which each stock's return is generated by common factors, called the systematic sources of risk.

Factoring   Sale of a firm's accounts receivable to a financial institution known as a factor.

Fair market value   Amount at which common stock would change hands between a willing buyer and a willing seller, both having knowledge of the relevant facts. Also called market price.

Feasible set   Opportunity set.

Federal agency securities   Securities issued by corporations and agencies created by the U.S. government, such as the Federal Home Loan Bank Board and Government National Mortgage Association (Ginnie Mae).

Field warehouse financing   A form of inventory loan in which a public warehouse company acts as a control agent to supervise the inventory for the lender.

Financial Accounting Standards Board (FASB) The governing body in accounting.

Financial distress Events preceding and including bankruptcy, such as violation of loan contracts.

Financial distress costs Legal and administrative costs of liquidation or reorganization (direct costs); an impaired ability to do business and an incentive toward selfish strategies such as taking large risks, underinvesting, and milking the property (indirect costs).

Financial intermediaries Institutions that provide the market function of matching borrowers and lenders or traders. Financial institutions may be categorized as depository, contractual savings, and investment-type.

Financial lease A long-term noncancelable lease, generally requiring the lessee to pay all maintenance fees.

Financial leverage Extent to which a firm relies on debt. Financial leverage is measured by the ratio of long-term debt to long-term debt plus equity.

Financial markets Markets that deal with cash flows over time, where the savings of lenders are allocated to the financing needs of borrowers.

Financial requirements In the financial plan, financing arrangements that are necessary to meet the overall corporate objective.

Financial risk The additional risk that the firm's stockholders bear when the firm is financed with debt as well as equity.

Firm commitment underwriting An underwriting in which an investment banking firm commits to buy the entire issue and assumes all financial responsibility for any unsold shares.

Firm's net value of debt Total firm value minus value of debt.

First principle of investment decision making An investment project is worth undertaking only if it increases the range of choices in the financial markets. To do this, it must be at least as desirable as what is available to shareholders in the financial markets.

Fixed asset Long-lived property owned by a firm that is used by a firm in the production of its income. Tangible fixed assets include real estate, plant, and equipment. Intangible fixed assets include patents, trademarks, and customer recognition.

Fixed cost A cost that is fixed in total for a given period of time and for given volume levels. It is not dependent on the amount of goods or services produced during the period.

Fixed-dollar obligations Conventional bonds for which the coupon rate is set as a fixed percentage of the par value.

Flat benefit formula Method used to determine a participant's benefits in a defined benefit plan by multiplying months of service by a flat monthly benefit.

Float The difference between bank cash and book cash. Float represents the net effect of checks in the process of col-

lection, or clearing. *Positive float* means the firm's bank cash is greater than its book cash until the check's presentation. Checks written by the firm generate *disbursement float,* causing an immediate decrease in book cash but no change in bank cash. In *neutral float position,* bank cash equals book cash. Checks written by the firm represent *collection float,* which increases book cash immediately but does not immediately change bank cash. The sum of disbursement float and collection float is *net float.*

Floater Floating-rate bond.

Floating-rate bond A debt obligation with an adjustable coupon payment.

Forced conversion If the conversion value of a convertible is greater than the call price, the call can be used to force conversion.

Foreign bonds An international bond issued by foreign borrowers in another nation's capital market and traditionally denominated in that nation's currency.

Foreign exchange market Market in which arrangements are made today for future exchange of major currencies; used to hedge against major swings in foreign exchange rates.

Forward contract An arrangement calling for future delivery of an asset at an agreed-upon price.

Forward exchange rate A future day's exchange rate between two major currencies.

Forward trade An agreement to buy or sell based on exchange rates established today for settlement in the future.

Frequency distribution The organization of data to show how often certain values or ranges of values occur.

Fully diluted See **Dilution.**

Funded debt Long-term debt.

Future value Value of a sum after investing it over one or more periods. Also called compound value.

Futures contract Obliges traders to purchase or sell an asset at an agreed-upon price on a specified future date. The long position is held by the trader who commits to purchase. The short position is held by the trader who commits to sell. Futures differ from forward contracts in their standardization, exchange trading, margin requirements, and daily settling (market to market).

GAAP Generally Accepted Accounting Principles.

General cash offer A public issue of a security that is sold to all interested investors, rather than only to existing shareholders.

General partnership Form of business organization in which all partners agree to provide some portion of the work and cash and to share profits and losses. Each partner is liable for the debts of the partnership.

Generally Accepted Accounting Principles (GAAP) A common set of accounting concepts, standards, and procedures by which financial statements are prepared.

Geometric mean   Annualized holding-period return.

Gilts   British and Irish government securities.

Going-private transactions   Publicly owned stock in a firm is replaced with complete equity ownership by a private group. The shares are delisted from stock exchanges and can no longer be purchased in the open market.

Golden parachute   Compensation paid to top-level management by a target firm if a takeover occurs.

Goodwill   The excess of the purchase price over the sum of the fair market values of the individual assets acquired.

Greenmail   Payments to potential bidders to cease unfriendly takeover attempts.

Green-shoe provision   A contract provision that gives the underwriter the option to purchase additional shares at the offering price to cover overallotments.

Growing perpetuity   A constant stream of cash flows without end that is expected to rise indefinitely. For example, cash flows to the landlord of an apartment building might be expected to rise a certain percentage each year.

Growth opportunity   Opportunity to invest in profitable projects.

Hedging   Taking a position in two or more securities that are negatively correlated (taking opposite trading positions) to reduce risk.

High-yield bond   Junk bond.

Holder-of-record date   The date on which holders of record in a firm's stock ledger are designated as the recipients of either dividends or stock rights. Also called date of record.

Holding period   Length of time that an individual holds a security.

Holding-period return   The rate of return over a given period.

Homemade dividends   An individual investor can undo corporate dividend policy by reinvesting excess dividends or selling off shares of stock to receive a desired cash flow.

Homemade leverage   Idea that as long as individuals borrow (and lend) on the same terms as the firm, they can duplicate the effects of corporate leverage on their own. Thus, if levered firms are priced too high, rational investors will simply borrow on personal accounts to buy shares in unlevered firms.

Homogeneous expectations   Idea that all individuals have the same beliefs concerning future investments, profits, and dividends.

Horizontal acquisition   Merger between two companies producing similar goods or services.

IPO   Initial public offering.

IRR   Internal rate of return.

Idiosyncratic risk   An unsystematic risk.

Immunized   Immune to interest-rate risk.

In the money   Describes an option whose exercise would produce profits. Out of the money describes an option whose exercise would not be profitable.

Income bond   A bond on which the payment of income is contingent on sufficient earnings. Income bonds are commonly used during the reorganization of a failed or failing business.

Income statement   Financial report that summarizes a firm's performance over a specified time period.

Incremental cash flows   Difference between the firm's cash flows with and without a project.

Incremental IRR   IRR on the incremental investment from choosing a large project instead of a smaller project.

Indenture   Written agreement between the corporate debt issuer and the lender, setting forth maturity date, interest rate, and other terms.

Independent project   A project whose acceptance or rejection is independent of the acceptance or rejection of other projects.

Inflation   An increase in the amount of money in circulation, resulting in a fall in its value and rise in prices.

Inflation-escalator clause   A clause in a contract providing for increases or decreases in inflation based on fluctuations in the cost of living, production costs, and so forth.

Information-content effect   The rise in the stock price following the dividend signal.

In-house processing float   Refers to the time it takes the receiver of a check to process the payment and deposit it in a bank for collection.

Initial public offering (IPO)   The original sale of a company's securities to the public. Also called an unseasoned new issue.

Inside information   Nonpublic knowledge about a corporation possessed by people in special positions inside a firm.

Instruments   Financial securities, such as money market instruments or capital market instruments.

Interest coverage ratio   Earnings before interest and taxes divided by interest expense. Used to measure a firm's ability to pay interest.

Interest on interest   Interest earned on reinvestment of each interest payment on money invested.

Interest rate   The price paid for borrowing money. It is the rate of exchange of present consumption for future consumption, or the price of current dollars in terms of future dollars.

Interest rate on debt   The firm's cost of debt capital. Also called return on the debt.

Interest-rate-parity theorem   The interest rate differential between two countries will be equal to the difference between the forward-exchange rate and the spot-exchange rate.

Interest-rate risk   The chance that a change in the interest rate will result in a change in the value of a security.

Interest subsidy   A firm's deduction of the interest payments on its debt from its earnings before it calculates its tax bill under current tax law.

Internal financing Net income plus depreciation minus dividends. Internal financing comes from internally generated cash flow.

Internal rate of return (IRR) A discount rate at which the net present value of an investment is zero. The IRR is a method of evaluating capital expenditure proposals.

Inventory A current asset, composed of raw materials to be used in production, work in process, and finished goods.

Inventory loan A secured short-term loan to purchase inventory. The three basic forms are a blanket inventory lien, a trust receipt, and field warehouse financing.

Inventory turnover ratio Ratio of annual sales to average inventory that measures how quickly inventory is produced and sold.

Investment bankers Financial intermediaries who perform a variety of services, including aiding in the sale of securities, facilitating mergers and other corporate reorganizations, acting as brokers to both individual and institutional clients, and trading for their own accounts.

Investment grade bond Debt that is rated BBB and above by Standard & Poor's or Baa and above by Moody's.

Invoice Bill written by a seller of goods or services and submitted to the purchaser.

Irrelevance result The MM theorem that a firm's capital structure is irrelevant to the firm's value.

Junk bond A speculative grade bond, rated Ba or lower by Moody's, or BB or lower by Standard & Poor's, or an unrated bond. Also called a high-yield or low-grade bond.

LBO Leveraged buyout.

LIBOR London interbank offered rate.

Law of one price (LOP) A commodity will cost the same regardless of what currency is used to purchase it.

Lease A contractual arrangement to grant the use of specific fixed assets for a specified time in exchange for payment, usually in the form of rent. An operating lease is generally a short-term cancelable arrangement, whereas a financial, or capital, lease is a long-term noncancelable agreement.

Ledger cash A firm's cash balance as reported in its financial statements. Also called book cash.

Legal bankruptcy A legal proceeding for liquidating or reorganizing a business.

Lend To provide money temporarily on the condition that it or its equivalent will be returned, often with an interest fee.

Lessee One that receives the use of assets under a lease.

Lessor One that conveys the use of assets under a lease.

Letter of comment A communication to the firm from the Securities and Exchange Commission that suggests changes to a registration statement.

Level-coupon bond Bond with a stream of coupon payments that are the same throughout the life of the bond.

Leveraged buyout Takeover of a company by using borrowed funds, usually by a group including some member of existing management.

Leveraged equity Stock in a firm that relies on financial leverage. Holders of leveraged equity face the benefits and costs of using debt.

Leveraged lease Tax-oriented leasing arrangement that involves one or more third-party lenders.

Liabilities Debts of the firm in the form of financial claims on a firm's assets.

Limited partnership Form of business organization that permits the liability of some partners to be limited by the amount of cash contributed to the partnership.

Limited-liability instrument A security, such as a call option, in which all the holder can lose is the initial amount put into it.

Line of credit A *noncommitted* line of credit is an informal agreement that allows firms to borrow up to a previously specified limit without going through the normal paperwork. A *committed* line of credit is a formal legal arrangement and usually involves a commitment fee paid by the firm to the bank.

Lintner's observations John Lintner's work (1956) suggested that dividend policy is related to a target level of dividends and the speed of adjustment of change in dividends.

Liquidating dividend Payment by a firm to its owners from capital rather than from earnings.

Liquidation Termination of the firm as a going concern. Liquidation involves selling the assets of the firm for salvage value. The proceeds, net of transaction costs, are distributed to creditors in order of established priority.

Liquidity Refers to the ease and quickness of converting assets to cash. Also called marketability.

Liquidity-preference hypothesis Theory that the forward rate exceeds expected future interest rates.

Lockbox Post office box set up to intercept accounts receivable payments. Lockboxes are the most widely used device to speed up collection of cash.

London Interbank Offered Rate (LIBOR) Rate the most creditworthy banks charge one another for large loans of Eurodollars overnight in the London market.

Long hedge Protecting the future cost of a purchase by purchasing a futures contract to protect against changes in the price of an asset.

Long run A period of time in which all costs are variable.

Long-term debt An obligation having a maturity of more than one year from the date it was issued. Also called funded debt.

Low-grade bond Junk bond.

MM Proposition I A proposition of Modigliani and Miller (MM) which states that a firm cannot change the total value of its outstanding securities by changing its capital structure proportions. Also called an irrelevance result.

MM Proposition II   A proposition by Modigliani and Miller (MM) which states that the cost of equity is a linear function of the firm's debt-equity ratio.

Mail float   Refers to the part of the collection and disbursement process where checks are trapped in the postal system.

Make a market   The obligation of a specialist to offer to buy and sell shares of assigned stocks. It is assumed that this makes the market liquid because the specialist assumes the role of a buyer for investors if they wish to sell and a seller if they wish to buy.

Making delivery   Refers to the seller's actually turning over to the buyer the asset agreed upon in a forward contract.

Marked to market   Describes the daily settlement of obligations on futures positions.

Market capitalization   Price per share of stock multiplied by the number of shares outstanding.

Market clearing   Total demand for loans by borrowers equals total supply of loans from lenders. The market clears at the equilibrium rate of interest.

Market model   A one-factor model for returns where the index that is used for the factor is an index of the returns on the whole market.

Market portfolio   In concept, a value-weighted index of all securities. In practice, it is an index, such as the S&P 500, that describes the return of the entire value of the stock market, or at least the stocks that make up the index. A market portfolio represents the average investor's return.

Market price   The current amount at which a security is trading in a market.

Market risk   Systematic risk. This term emphasizes the fact that systematic risk influences to some extent all assets in the market.

Market value   The price at which willing buyers and sellers trade a firm's assets.

Marketability   Refers to the ease and quickness of converting an asset to cash. Also called liquidity.

Marketed claims   Claims that can be bought and sold in financial markets, such as those of stockholders and bondholders.

Market-to-book (M/B) ratio   Market price per share of common stock divided by book value per share.

Maturity date   The date on which the last payment on a bond is due.

Merger   Combination of two or more companies.

Minimum variance portfolio   The portfolio of risky assets with the lowest possible variance. By definition, this portfolio must also have the lowest possible standard deviation.

Money markets   Financial markets for debt securities that pay off in the short term (usually less than one year).

Money purchase plan   A defined benefit contribution plan in which the participant contributes some part and the firm contributes at the same or a different rate. Also called an individual account plan.

Mortgage securities   A debt obligation secured by a mortgage on the real property of the borrower.

Multiple rates of return   More than one rate of return from the same project that make the net present value of the project equal to zero. This situation arises when the IRR method is used for a project in which negative cash flows follow positive ones.

Multiples   Another name for price/earnings ratios.

Mutually exclusive investment decisions   Investment decisions in which the acceptance of a project precludes the acceptance of one or more alternative projects.

NPV   Net present value.

NPVGO model   A model valuing the firm in which net present value of new investment opportunities is explicitly examined. NPVGO stands for net present value of growth opportunities.

Negative covenant   Part of the indenture or loan agreement that limits or prohibits actions that the company may take.

Negotiated offer   The issuing firm negotiates a deal with one underwriter to offer a new issue rather than taking competitive bidding.

Net cash balance   Beginning cash balance plus cash receipts minus cash disbursements.

Net float   Sum of disbursement float and collection float.

Net investment   Gross, or total, investment minus depreciation.

Net operating losses (NOL)   Losses that a firm can take advantage of to reduce taxes.

Net present value (NPV)   The present value of future cash returns, discounted at the appropriate market interest rate, minus the present value of the cost of the investment.

Net present value rule   An investment is worth making if it has a positive NPV. If an investment's NPV is negative, it should be rejected.

Net working capital   Current assets minus current liabilities.

Netting out   To get or bring in as a net; to clear as profit.

Neutral flat position   See **Float.**

Nominal cash flow   A cash flow expressed in nominal terms if the actual dollars to be received (or paid out) are given.

Nominal interest rate   Interest rate unadjusted for inflation.

Noncash item   Expense against revenue that does not directly affect cash flow, such as depreciation and deferred taxes.

Nonmarketed claims   Claims that cannot be easily bought and sold in the financial markets, such as those of the government and litigants in lawsuits.

Normal annuity form   The manner in which retirement benefits are paid out.

Normal distribution   Symmetric bell-shaped frequency distribution that can be defined by its mean and standard deviation.

Note   Unsecured debt, usually with maturity of less than 15 years.

Odd lot Stock trading unit of less than 100 shares.

Off balance sheet financing Financing that is not shown as a liability on a company's balance sheet.

One-factor APT A special case of the arbitrage pricing theory that is derived from the one-factor model by using diversification and arbitrage. It shows the expected return on any risky asset is a linear function of a single factor. The CAPM can be expressed as one-factor APT in which a single factor is the market portfolio.

Open account A credit account for which the only formal instrument of credit is the invoice.

Operating activities Sequence of events and decisions that create the firm's cash inflows and cash outflows. These activities include buying and paying for raw materials, manufacturing and selling a product, and collecting cash.

Operating cash flow Earnings before interest and depreciation minus taxes. It measures the cash generated from operations, not counting capital spending or working capital requirements.

Operating cycle The time interval between the arrival of inventory stock and the date when cash is collected from receivables.

Operating lease Type of lease in which the period of contract is less than the life of the equipment and the lessor pays all maintenance and servicing costs.

Operating leverage The degree to which a company's costs of operation are fixed as opposed to variable. A firm with high operating costs compared to a firm with a low operating leverage, and hence relatively larger changes in EBIT with respect to a change in the sales revenue.

Opportunity cost Most valuable alternative that is given up. The rate of return used in NPV computation is an opportunity interest rate.

Opportunity set The possible expected return—standard deviation pairs of all portfolios that can be constructed from a set of assets. Also called a feasible set.

Option A right—but not an obligation—to buy or sell underlying assets at a fixed price during a specified time period.

Original-issue-discount bond A bond issued with a discount from par value. Also called a deep-discount or pure-discount bond.

Out of the money Describes an option whose exercise would not be profitable. In the money describes an option whose exercise would produce profits.

Oversubscribed issue Investors are not able to buy all the shares they want, so underwriters must allocate the shares among investors. This occurs when a new issue is underpriced.

Oversubscription privilege Allows shareholders to purchase unsubscribed shares in a rights offering at the subscription price.

Over-the-counter (OTC) market An informal network of brokers and dealers who negotiate sales of securities (not a formal exchange).

Par value The nominal or face value of stocks or bonds. For stock, it is a relatively unimportant value except for bookkeeping purposes.

Partnership Form of business organization in which two or more co-owners form a business. In a general partnership each partner is liable for the debts of the partnership. Limited partnership permits some partners to have limited liability.

Payback period rule An investment decision rule which states that all investment projects that have payback periods equal to or less than a particular cutoff period are accepted, and all of those that pay off in more than the particular cutoff period are rejected. The payback period is the number of years required for a firm to recover its initial investment required by a project from the cash flow it generates.

Payments pattern Describes the lagged collection pattern of receivables, for instance the probability that a 72-day-old account will still be unpaid when it is 73 days old.

Payout ratio Proportion of net income paid out in cash dividends.

Pecking order in long-term financing Hierarchy of long-term financing strategies, in which using internally generated cash is at the top and issuing new equity is at the bottom.

Perfect markets Perfectly competitive financial markets.

Perfectly competitive financial markets Markets in which no trader has power to change the price of goods or services. Perfect markets are characterized by the following conditions: (1) Trading is costless, and access to the financial markets is free. (2) Information about borrowing and lending opportunities is freely available. (3) There are many traders, and no single trader can have a significant impact on market prices.

Performance shares Shares of stock given to managers on the basis of performance as measured by earnings per share and similar criteria—a control device used by shareholders to tie management to the self-interest of shareholders.

Perpetuity A constant stream of cash flows without end. A British consol is an example.

Perquisites Management amenities such as a big office, a company car, or expense-account meals. "Perks" are agency costs of equity, because managers of the firm are agents of the stockholders.

Pie model of capital structure A model of the debt-equity ratio of the firms, graphically depicted in slices of a pie that represents the value of the firm in the capital markets.

Plug A variable that handles financial slack in the financial plan.

Poison pill Strategy by a takeover target company to make a stock less appealing to a company that wishes to acquire it.

Pooling of interests Accounting method of reporting acquisitions under which the balance sheets of the two companies are simply added together item by item.

Portfolio Combined holding of more than one stock, bond, real estate asset, or other asset by an investor.

Portfolio variance   Weighted sum of the covariances and variances of the assets in a portfolio.

Positive covenant   Part of the indenture or loan agreement that specifies an action that the company must abide by.

Positive float   See **Float.**

Post   Particular place on the floor of an exchange where transactions in stocks listed on the exchange occur.

Preemptive right   The right to share proportionally in any new stock sold.

Preferred stock   A type of stock whose holders are given certain priority over common stockholders in the payment of dividends. Usually the dividend rate is fixed at the time of issue. Preferred stockholders normally do not receive voting rights.

Premium   If a bond is selling above its face value, it is said to sell at a premium.

Present value   The value of a future cash stream discounted at the appropriate market interest rate.

Present value factor   Factor used to calculate an estimate of the present value of an amount to be received in a future period.

Price takers   Individuals who respond to rates and prices by acting as though they have no influence on them.

Priced out   Means the market has already incorporated information, such as a low dividend, into the price of a stock.

Price-to-earnings (P/E) ratio   Current market price of common stock divided by current annual earnings per share.

Primary market   Where new issues of securities are offered to the public.

Principal   The value of a bond that must be repaid at maturity. Also called the face value or par value.

Principle of diversification   Highly diversified portfolios will have negligible unsystematic risk. In other words, unsystematic risks disappear in portfolios, and only systematic risks survive.

Private placement   The sale of a bond or other security directly to a limited number of investors.

Pro forma statements   Projected income statements, balance sheets, and sources and uses statements for future years.

Profit margin   Profits divided by total operating revenue. The net profit margin (net income divided by total operating revenue) and the gross profit margin (earnings before interest and taxes divided by the total operating revenue) reflect the firm's ability to produce a good or service at a high or low cost.

Profitability index   A method used to evaluate projects. It is the ratio of the present value of the future expected cash flows after initial investment divided by the amount of the initial investment.

Promissory note   Written promise to pay.

Prospectus   The legal document that must be given to every investor who contemplates purchasing registered securities in an offering. It describes the details of the company and the particular offering.

Protective covenant   A part of the indenture or loan agreement that limits certain actions a company takes during the term of the loan to protect the lender's interest.

Proxy   A grant of authority by the shareholder to transfer his or her voting rights to someone else.

Proxy contest   Attempt to gain control of a firm by soliciting a sufficient number of stockholder votes to replace the existing management.

Public issue   Sales of securities to the public.

Purchase accounting   Method of reporting acquisitions requiring that the assets of the acquired firm be reported at their fair market value on the books of the acquiring firm.

Purchasing power parity (PPP)   Idea that the exchange rate adjusts to keep purchasing power constant among currencies.

Pure discount bond   Bonds that pay no coupons and only pay back face value at maturity. Also referred to as "bullets" and "zeros."

Put option   The right to sell a specified number of shares of stock at a stated price on or before a specified time.

Put provision   Gives holder of a floating-rate bond the right to redeem his or her note at par on the coupon payment date.

Put-call parity   The value of a call equals the value of buying the stock plus buying the put plus borrowing at the risk-free rate.

Q ratio or Tobin's Q ratio   Market value of firm's assets divided by replacement value of firm's assets.

Quick assets   Current assets minus inventories.

Quick ratio   Quick assets (current assets minus inventories) divided by total current liabilities. Used to measure short-term solvency of a firm.

R squared (R^2)   Square of the correlation coefficient proportion of the variability explained by the linear model.

Random walk   Theory that stock price changes from day to day are at random; the changes are independent of each other and have the same probability distribution.

Real cash flow   A cash flow is expressed in real terms if the current, or date 0, purchasing power of the cash flow is given.

Real interest rate   Interest rate expressed in terms of real goods; that is, the nominal interest rate minus the expected inflation rate.

Receivables turnover ratio   Total operating revenues divided by average receivables. Used to measure how effectively a firm is managing its accounts receivable.

Red herring   First document released by an underwriter of a new issue to prospective investors.

Refunding   The process of replacing outstanding bonds, typically to issue new securities at a lower interest rate than those replaced.

Registration statement   The registration that discloses all the pertinent information concerning the corporation that wants to make the offering. The statement is filed with the Securities and Exchange Commission.

Regular cash dividend   Cash payment by firm to its shareholders, usually four times a year.

Regulation A   The securities regulation that exempts small public offerings (those valued at less than $1.5 million) from most registration requirements.

Relative purchasing power parity (RPPP)   Idea that the rate of change in the price level of commodities in one country relative to the price level in another determines the rate of the exchange rate between the two countries' currencies.

Reorganization   Financial restructuring of a failed firm. Both the firm's asset structure and its financial structure are changed to reflect their true value, and claims are settled.

Replacement value   Current cost of replacing the firm's assets.

Replacement-chain problem   Idea that future replacement decisions must be taken into account in selecting among projects.

Repurchase agreement (repos)   Short-term, often overnight, sales of government securities with an agreement to repurchase the securities at a slightly higher price.

Repurchase of stock   Device to pay cash to firm's shareholders that provides more preferable tax treatment for shareholders than dividends. Treasury stock is the name given to previously issued stock that has been repurchased by the firm.

Residual dividend approach   An approach that suggests that a firm pay dividends if and only if acceptable investment opportunities for those funds are currently unavailable.

Residual losses   Lost wealth of the shareholders due to divergent behavior of the managers.

Residual value   Usually refers to the value of a lessor's property at the time the lease expires.

Restrictive covenants   Provisions that place constraints on the operations of borrowers, such as restrictions on working capital, fixed assets, future borrowing, and payment of dividend.

Retained earnings   Earnings not paid out as dividends.

Retention ratio   Retained earnings divided by net income.

Return   Profit on capital investment or securities.

Return on assets (ROA)   Income divided by average total assets.

Return on equity (ROE)   Net income after interest and taxes divided by average common stockholders' equity.

Reverse split   The procedure whereby the number of outstanding stock shares is reduced; for example, two outstanding shares are combined to create only one.

Rights offer   An offer that gives a current shareholder the opportunity to maintain a proportionate interest in the company before the shares are offered to the public.

Risk averse   A risk-averse investor will consider risky portfolios only if they provide compensation for risk via a risk premium.

Risk class   A partition of the universal set of risk measure so that projects that are in the same risk class can be comparable.

Risk premium   The excess return on the risky asset that is the difference between expected return on risky assets and the return on risk-free assets.

Round lot   Common stock trading unit of 100 shares or multiples of 100 shares.

S&P 500   Standard & Poor's Composite Index.

SEC   Securities and Exchange Commission.

SML   Security market line.

SMP   Security market plane.

Safe harbor lease   A lease to transfer tax benefits of ownership (depreciation and debt tax shield) from the lessee, if the lessee could not use them, to a lessor that could.

Sale and lease-back   An arrangement whereby a firm sells its existing assets to a financial company which then leases them back to the firm. This is often done to generate cash.

Sales forecast   A key input to the firm's financial planning process. External sales forecasts are based on historical experience, statistical analysis, and consideration of various macroeconomic factors; internal sales forecasts are obtained from internal sources.

Sales-type lease   An arrangement whereby a firm leases its own equipment, such as IBM leasing its own computers, thereby competing with an independent leasing company.

Scale enhancing   Describes a project that is in the same risk class as the whole firm.

Scenario analysis   Analysis of the effect on the project of different scenarios, each scenario involving a confluence of factors.

Seasoned new issue   A new issue of stock after the company's securities have previously been issued. A seasoned new issue of common stock can be made by using a cash offer or a rights offer.

Secondary markets   Already-existing securities are bought and sold on the exchanges or in the over-the-counter market.

Security market line (SML)   A straight line that shows the equilibrium relationship between systematic risk and expected rates of return for individual securities. According to the SML, the excess return on a risky asset is equal to the excess return on the market portfolio multiplied by the beta coefficient.

Security market plane (SMP)   A plane that shows the equilibrium relationship between expected return and the beta coefficient of more than one factor.

Semistrong-form efficiency   Theory that the market is efficient with respect to all publicly available information.

Seniority   The order of repayment. In the event of bankruptcy, senior debt must be repaid before subordinated debt receives any payment.

Sensitivity analysis   Analysis of the effect on the project when there is some change in critical variables such as sales and costs.

Separation principle The principle that portfolio choice can be separated into two independent tasks: (1) determination of the optimal risky portfolio, which is a purely technical problem, and (2) the personal choice of the best mix of the risky portfolio and the risk-free asset.

Separation theorem The value of an investment to an individual is not dependent on consumption preferences. All investors will want to accept or reject the same investment projects by using the NPV rule, regardless of personal preference.

Serial covariance The covariance between a variable and the lagged value of the variable; the same as autocovariance.

Set of contracts perspective View of corporation as a set of contracting relationships among individuals who have conflicting objectives, such as shareholders or managers. The corporation is a legal contrivance that serves as the nexus for the contracting relationships.

Shareholder Holder of equity shares. The terms *shareholders* and *stockholders* usually refer to owners of common stock in a corporation.

Shelf life Number of days it takes to get goods purchased and sold, or days in inventory.

Shelf registration An SEC procedure that allows a firm to file a master registration statement summarizing planned financing for a two-year period, and then file short statements when the firm wishes to sell any of the approved master statement securities during that period.

Shirking The tendency to do less work when the return is smaller. Owners may have more incentive to shirk if they issue equity as opposed to debt, because they retain less ownership interest in the company and therefore may receive a smaller return. Thus, shirking is considered an agency cost of equity.

Short hedge Protecting the value of an asset held by selling a futures contract.

Short run That period of time in which certain equipment, resources, and commitments of them are fixed.

Short sale Sale of a security that an investor doesn't own but has instead borrowed.

Shortage costs Costs that fall with increases in the level of investment in current assets.

Short-run operating activities Events and decisions concerning the short-term finance of a firm, such as how much inventory to order and whether to offer cash terms or credit terms to customers.

Short-term debt An obligation having a maturity of one year or less from the date it was issued. Also called unfunded debt.

Short-term tax exempts Short-term securities issued by states, municipalities, local housing agencies, and urban renewal agencies.

Side effects Effects of a proposed project on other parts of the firm.

Sight draft A commercial draft demanding immediate payment.

Signaling approach Approach to the determination of optimal capital structure asserting that insiders in a firm have information that the market does not; therefore the choice of capital structure by insiders can signal information to outsiders and change the value of the firm. This theory is also called the asymmetric information approach.

Simple interest Interest calculated by considering only the original principal amount.

Sinking fund An account managed by the bond trustee for the purpose of repaying the bonds.

Small issues exemption Securities issues that involve less than $1.5 million are not required to file a registration statement with the Securities and Exchange Commission. Instead they are governed by Regulation A, for which only a brief offering statement is needed.

Sole proprietorship A business owned by a single individual. The sole proprietorship pays no corporate income tax but has unlimited liability for business debts and obligations.

Spot-exchange rate Exchange rate between two currencies for immediate delivery.

Spot-interest rate Interest rate fixed today on a loan that is made today.

Spot trade An agreement on the exchange rate today for settlement in two days.

Spread underwriting Difference between the underwriter's buying price and the offering price. The spread is a fee for the service of the underwriting syndicate.

Spreadsheet A computer program that organizes numerical data into rows and columns on a terminal screen, for calculating and making adjustments based on new data.

Stakeholders Both stockholders and bondholders.

Stand-alone principle Investment principle that states a firm should accept or reject a project by comparing it with securities in the same risk class.

Standard deviation The positive square root of the variance. This is the standard statistical measure of the spread of a sample.

Standardized normal distribution A normal distribution with an expected value of 0 and a standard deviation of 1.

Standby fee Amount paid to an underwriter who agrees to purchase any stock that is not subscribed to the public investor in a rights offering.

Standby underwriting An agreement whereby an underwriter agrees to purchase any stock that is not purchased by the public investor.

Standstill agreements Contracts where the bidding firm in a takeover attempt agrees to limit its holdings of another firm.

Stated annual interest rate The interest rate expressed as a percentage per annum, by which interest payment is determined.

Static theory of capital structure Theory that the firm's capital structure is determined by a trade-off of the value of tax shields against the costs of bankruptcy.

Stock dividend Payment of a dividend in the form of stock rather than cash. A stock dividend comes from treasury stock, increasing the number of shares outstanding, and reduces the value of each share.

Stock split The increase in the number of outstanding shares of stock while making no change in shareholders' equity.

Stockholder Holder of equity shares in a firm. The terms *stockholder* and *shareholders* usually refer to owners of common stock.

Stockholders' books Set of books kept by firm management for its annual report that follows Financial Accounting Standards Board rules. The tax books follow the IRS rules.

Stockholders' equity The residual claims that stockholders have against a firm's assets, calculated by subtracting total liabilities from total assets; also net worth.

Stockout Running out of inventory.

Straight voting A shareholder may cast all of his or her votes for each candidate for the board of directors.

Straight-line depreciation A method of depreciation whereby each year the firm depreciates a constant proportion of the initial investment less salvage value.

Striking price Price at which the put option or call option can be exercised. Also called the exercise price.

Strong-form efficiency Theory that the market is efficient with respect to all available information, public or private.

Subordinate debt Debt whose holders have a claim on the firm's assets only after senior debtholders' claims have been satisfied.

Subscription price Price that existing shareholders are allowed to pay for a share of stock in a rights offering.

Sum-of-the-year's-digits depreciation Method of accelerated depreciation.

Sunk cost A cost that has already occurred and cannot be removed. Because sunk costs are in the past, such costs should be ignored when deciding whether to accept or reject a project.

Super-majority amendment A defensive tactic that requires 80 percent of shareholders to approve a merger.

Surplus funds Cash flow available after payment of taxes in the project.

Sustainable growth rate The only growth rate possible with preset values for four variables: profit margin, payout ratio, debt-equity ratio, and asset utilization ratio, if the firm issues no new equity.

Swap Exchange between two securities or currencies. One type of swap involves the sale (or purchase) of a foreign currency with a simultaneous agreement to repurchase (or sell) it.

Swap rate The difference between the sale (purchase) price and the price to repurchase (resell) it in a swap.

Sweep account Account in which the bank takes all excess available funds at the close of each business day and invests them for the firm.

Syndicate A group of investment banking companies that agree to cooperate in a joint venture to underwrite an offering of securities for resale to the public.

Systematic Common to all businesses.

Systematic risk Any risk that affects a large number of assets, each to a greater or lesser degree. Also called market risk or common risk.

Systematic risk principle Only the systematic portion of risk matters in large, well-diversified portfolios. Thus, the expected returns must be related only to systematic risk.

T-bill Treasury bill.

T-period holding-period return The percentage return over the T-year period an investment lasts.

Takeover General term referring to transfer of control of a firm from one group of shareholders to another.

Taking delivery Refers to the buyer's actually assuming possession from the seller of the asset agreed upon in a forward contract.

Target cash balance Optimal amount of cash for a firm to hold, considering the trade-off between the opportunity costs of holding too much cash and the trading costs of holding too little.

Target firm A firm that is the object of a takeover by another firm.

Target payout ratio A firm's long-run dividend-to-earnings ratio. The firm's policy is to attempt to pay out a certain percentage of earnings, but it pays a stated dollar dividend and adjusts it to the target as increases in earnings occur.

Targeted repurchase The firm buys back its own stock from a potential bidder, usually at a substantial premium, to forestall a takeover attempt.

Tax books Set of books kept by firm management for the IRS that follows IRS rules. The stockholders' books follow Financial Accounting Standards Board rules.

Taxable acquisition An acquisition in which shareholders of the acquired firm will realize capital gains or losses that will be taxed.

Taxable income Gross income less a set of deductions.

Tax-free acquisition An acquisition in which the selling shareholders are considered to have exchanged their old shares for new ones of equal value, and in which they have experienced no capital gains or losses.

Technical analysis Research to identify mispriced securities that focuses on recurrent and predictable stock price patterns.

Technical insolvency Default on a legal obligation of the firm. For example, technical inventory occurs when a firm doesn't pay a bill.

Tender offer   Public offer to buy shares of a target firm.

Term structure   Relationship between spot-interest rates and maturities.

Terms of sale   Conditions on which firm proposes to sell its goods and services for cash or credit.

Time value of money   Price or value put on time. Time value of money reflects the opportunity cost of investing at a risk-free rate. The certainty of having a given sum of money today is worth more than the certainty of having an equal sum at a later date because money can be put to profitable use during the intervening time.

Tobin's Q   Market value of assets divided by replacement value of assets. A Tobin's Q ratio greater than 1 indicates the firm has done well with its investment decisions.

Tombstone   An advertisement that announces a public offering of securities. It identifies the issuer, the type of security, the underwriters, and where additional information is available.

Total asset-turnover ratio   Total operating revenue divided by average total assets. Used to measure how effectively a firm is managing its assets.

Total cash flow of the firm   Total cash inflow minus total cash outflow.

Trade acceptance   Written demand that has been accepted by a firm to pay a given sum of money at a future date.

Trade credit   Credit granted to other firms.

Trading costs   Costs of selling marketable securities and borrowing.

Trading range   Price range between highest and lowest prices at which a security is traded.

Transactions motive   A reason for holding cash that arises from normal disbursement and collection activities of the firm.

Treasury bill   Short-term discount debt maturing in less than one year. T-bills are issued weekly by the federal government and are virtually risk free.

Treasury bond or note   Debt obligations of the federal government that make semiannual coupon payments and are sold at or near par value in denominations of $1,000 or more. They have original maturities of more than one year.

Treasury stock   Shares of stock that have been issued and then repurchased by a firm.

Triangular arbitrage   Striking offsetting deals among three markets simultaneously to obtain an arbitrage profit.

Trust receipt   A device by which the borrower holds the inventory in "trust" for the lender.

Underpricing   Issuing of securities below the fair market value.

Underwriter   An investment firm that buys an issue of security from the firm and resells it to the investors.

Unfunded debt   Short-term debt.

Unit benefit formula   Method used to determine a participant's benefits in a defined benefit plan by multiplying years of service by the percentage of salary.

Unseasoned new issue   Initial public offering (IPO).

Unsystematic   What is specific to a firm.

Unsystematic risk   See **Diversifiable risk.**

VA principle   Value additivity principle.

Value additivity (VA) principle   In an efficient market the value of the sum of two cash flows is the sum of the values of the individual cash flows.

Variable cost   A cost that varies directly with volume and is zero when production is zero.

Variance of the probability distribution   The expected value of squared deviation from the expected return.

Venture capital   Early-stage financing of young companies seeking to grow rapidly.

Vertical acquisition   Acquisition in which the acquired firm and the acquiring firm are at different steps in the production process.

WACC   Weighted average cost of capital.

Waiting period   Time during which the Securities and Exchange Commission studies a firm's registration statement. During this time the firm may distribute a preliminary prospectus.

Warrant   A security that gives the holder the right—but not the obligation—to buy shares of common stock directly from a company at a fixed price for a given time period.

Wash   Gains equal losses.

Weak-form efficiency   Theory that the market is efficient with respect to historical price information.

Weighted average cost of capital (WACC)   The average cost of capital on the firm's existing projects and activities. The weighted average cost of capital for the firm is calculated by weighting the cost of each source of funds by its proportion of the total market value of the firm. It is calculated on a before- and after-tax basis.

Weighted average maturity   A measure of the level of interest-rate risk calculated by weighting cash flows by the time to receipt and multiplying by the fraction of total present value represented by the cash flow at that time.

Winner's curse   The average investor wins—that is, gets the desired allocation of a new issue—because those who knew better avoided the issue.

Wire transfer   An electronic transfer of funds from one bank to another that eliminates the mailing and check-clearing times associated with other cash-transfer methods.

Yankee bonds   Foreign bonds issued in the United States by foreign banks and corporations.

Yield to maturity   The discount rate that equates the present value of interest payments and redemption value with the present price of the bond.

Zero-balance account (ZBA)   A checking account in which a zero balance is maintained by transfer of funds from a master account in an amount only large enough to cover checks presented.

Name Index

Subject Index

Some Useful Formulas

1 **Present Value** (Chapters 3 and 4)
The discounted value of T future cash flows

$$PV = \frac{C_1}{1+r} + \frac{C_2}{(1+r)^2} + \ldots + \frac{C_T}{(1+r)^T} = \sum_{t=1}^{T} \frac{C_t}{(1+r)^t}$$

2 **Net Present Value** (Chapters 3 and 4)
Present value minus initial costs

NPV = PV − Cost

$C_O = -$ Cost

$$\text{NPV} = C_O + \sum_{t=1}^{T} \frac{C_t}{(1+r)^t}$$

3 **Perpetuity** (Chapter 4)
The value of C received each year, forever

$$PV = \frac{C}{r}$$

4 **Annuity** (Chapter 4)
The value of C received each year for T years

$$PV = \frac{C}{r}[1 - 1/(1+r)^t]$$

5 **Growing Perpetuity** (Chapter 4)
The value of a perpetuity that grows at rate g, where the first payment is C

$$PV = \frac{C}{r-g}$$

6 **Growing Annuity** (Chapter 4)
The value of a T-period annuity that grows at the rate g, where the first payment is C

$$PV = C\left[\frac{1}{r-g} - \frac{1}{r-g} \times \left(\frac{1+g}{1+r}\right)^T\right]$$

7 **Measures of Risk for Individual Assets** (Chapter 10)

$$\text{Var}(R_A) = \sigma_A^2 = \text{Expected value of } (R_A - \overline{R}_A)^2$$

$$\text{SD}(R_A) = \sigma_A = \sqrt{\text{Var}(R_A)}$$

$$\text{Cov}(R_A, R_B) = \sigma_{AB} = \text{Expected value of } [(R_A - \overline{R}_A)(R_B - \overline{R}_B)]$$

$$\text{Corr}(R_A, R_B) = \rho_{AB} = \text{Cov}(R_A R_B)/\sigma_A \sigma_B$$

8 **Expected Return on a Portfolio of Two Assets** (Chapter 10)

$$\overline{R}_p = X_A \overline{R}_A + X_B \overline{R}_B$$

9 **Variance of a Portfolio of Two Assets** (Chapter 10)

$$\sigma_p^2 = X_A^2 \times \sigma_A^2 + 2X_A X_B \times \sigma_{AB} + X_B^2 \times \sigma_B^2$$